**VIDEO 10.4**
*Separation Anxiety*

**VIDEO 11.1**
*Self Awareness*

**VIDEO 11.2**
*Identity/Role Development*

**VIDEO 11.3**
*Imaginary Audience*

**VIDEO 11.4**
*Invincibility Fable*

**VIDEO 12.1**
*Moral Development*

**VIDEO 12.2**
*Bullying*

**VIDEO 12.3**
*Reactive Aggression*

**VIDEO 12.4**
*Relational Aggression*

**VIDEO 13.1**
*Gender Consistency*

**VIDEO 15.1**
*Parten's Play Categories*

**VIDEO 15.2**
*Sociodramatic Play (social pretend play)*

**VIDEO 15.3**
*Rough and Tumble Play*

**VIDEO 15.4**
*Neglected Child*

# Children
## and Their
# Development

**Fourth Edition**

## Robert V. Kail

Purdue University

Upper Saddle River, NJ 07458

**Library of Congress Cataloging-in-Publication Data**

Kail, Robert V.
  Children and their development / Robert V. Kail.—4th ed.
    p. cm.
  Includes bibliographical references and index.
  ISBN 0-13-194911-X
    1. Child development.   I. Title.
HQ767.9.K345   2006
305.231—dc22                           2005037473

*VP, Editor-in-Chief:* Leah Jewell
*Executive Editor:* Jennifer Gilliland
*Editorial Assistant:* Lisa Longo
*Editor-in-Chief, Development:* Rochelle Diogenes
*Developmental Editor:* Susan Moss
*Senior Media Editor:* David Clevinger
*Director of Marketing:* Brandy Dawson
*Senior Marketing Manager:* Jeanette Moyer
*Marketing Assistant:* Alexandra Trum
*VP, Director Production and Manufacturing:* Barbara Kittle
*Managing Editor, Production:* Joanne Riker
*Assistant Managing Editor:* Maureen Richardson
*Production Liaison:* Kathy Sleys
*Production Editor:* Caterina Melara, Prepare Inc.
*Manufacturing Manager:* Nick Sklitsis
*Manufacturing Buyer:* Sherry Lewis

*Creative Design Director:* Leslie Osher
*Art Directors:* Nancy Wells; Kathryn Foot
*Interior and Cover Design:* John Christiana
*Illustrators (Interior):* Prepare, Inc.
*Director, Image Resource Center:* Melinda Reo
*Manager, Rights and Permissions:* Zina Arabia
*Interior Image Specialist:* Beth Brenzel
*Cover Image Specialist:* Karen Sanatar
*Image Permission Coordinator:* Frances Toepfer
*Photo Researcher:* Toni Michaels/Photo Find
*Project Management/Composition:* This book was set in 10.5/11.6 Minion by Prepare Inc.
*Printer/Binder:* This book was printed and bound by R. R. Donnelley and Sons, Inc. The cover was printed by Lehigh Press

Credits and acknowledgments borrowed from other sources and reproduced, with permission, in this textbook appear on appropriate page within text (or on pages 525-526).

Pearson Education Ltd.
Pearson Education Australia PTY, Ltd.
Pearson Education Singapore, Pte, Ltd.
Pearson Education North Asia Ltd.

Pearson Education, Canada, Ltd.
Pearson Educación de Mexico, S.A. de C.V.
Pearson Education-Japan
Pearson Education Malaysia, Pte, Ltd.

10 9 8 7 6 5 4 3 2 1
ISBN 0-13-194911-X

*To Laura, Matt, and Ben*

# BRIEF CONTENTS

Preface   xvii

1   The Science of Child Development   2

2   Genetic Bases of Child Development   38

3   Prenatal Development, Birth, and the Newborn   60

4   Growth and Health   100

5   Perceptual and Motor Development   132

6   Theories of Cognitive Development   162

7   Cognitive Processes and Academic Skills   198

8   Intelligence and Individual Differences in Cognition   236

9   Language and Communication   266

10   Emotional Development   300

11   Understanding Self and Others   330

12   Moral Understanding and Behavior   362

13   Gender and Development   396

14   Family Relationships   426

15   Influences Beyond the Family   458

# CONTENTS

Preface   *xvii*

## The Science of Child Development   2

**1.1   Setting the Stage   4**
Historical Views of Children and Childhood   4
Origins of a New Science   5

**1.2   Foundational Theories of Child Development   8**
The Biological Perspective   9
The Psychodynamic Perspective   10
The Learning Perspective   11
The Cognitive-Developmental Perspective   13
The Contextual Perspective   14

**1.3   Themes in Child-Development Research   17**
Early Development Is Related to Later Development but Not Perfectly   17
Development Is Always Jointly Influenced by Heredity and Environment   18
Children Influence Their Own Development   18
Development in Different Domains Is Connected   19

**1.4   Doing Child-Development Research   20**
Measurement in Child-Development Research   21
General Designs for Research   25
Designs for Studying Age-Related Change   28
Ethical Responsibilities   33
Communicating Research Results   34

*See for Yourself, Resources, Key Terms   36*
*SUMMARY   37*

## Genetic Bases of Child Development   38

**2.1   Mechanisms of Heredity   40**
The Biology of Heredity   40
Single Gene Inheritance   42
Genetic Disorders   44

**2.2   Heredity, Environment, and Development   48**
Behavioral Genetics   48
Paths From Genes to Behavior   54

*See for Yourself, Resources, Key Terms   58*
*SUMMARY   59*

# Prenatal Development, Birth, and the Newborn 60

## 3

### 3.1 From Conception to Birth 62
Period of the Zygote (Weeks 1–2) 62
Period of the Embryo (Weeks 3–8) 63
Period of the Fetus (Weeks 9–38) 65

### 3.2 Influences on Prenatal Development 68
General Risk Factors 69
Teratogens: Diseases, Drugs, and Environmental Hazards 73
How Teratogens Influence Prenatal Development 77
Prenatal Diagnosis and Treatment 79

### 3.3 Happy Birthday! 82
Labor and Delivery 83
Approaches to Childbirth 84
Adjusting to Parenthood 86
Birth Complications 87

### 3.4 The Newborn 91
Assessing the Newborn 91
The Newborn's Reflexes 93
Newborn States 94
Perception and Learning in the Newborn 96

*See for Yourself, Resources, Key Terms 97*
*SUMMARY 99*

# Growth and Health 100

## 4

### 4.1 Physical Growth 102
Features of Human Growth 102
Mechanisms of Physical Growth 105
The Adolescent Growth Spurt and Puberty 109

### 4.2 Challenges to Healthy Growth 117
Malnutrition 117
Eating Disorders: Anorexia and Bulimia 118
Obesity 119
Disease 120
Accidents 121

### 4.3 The Developing Nervous System 123
Organization of the Mature Brain 123
The Developing Brain 124

*See for Yourself, Resources, Key Terms 129*
*SUMMARY 131*

# Perceptual and Motor Development 132

## 5

### 5.1 Basic Sensory and Perceptual Processes 134
Smell, Taste, and Touch 135
Hearing 136
Seeing 137
Integrating Sensory Information 138

**5.2**   **Complex Perceptual and Attentional Processes**   **141**
Perceiving Objects   141
Attention   147
Attention Deficit Hyperactivity Disorder   148

**5.3**   **Motor Development**   **151**
Locomotion   152
Fine-Motor Skills   155
Physical Fitness   157

*See for Yourself, Resources, Key Terms*   *160*
*SUMMARY*   *161*


# Theories of Cognitive Development   162

6

**6.1**   **Setting the Stage: Piaget's Theory**   **164**
Basic Principles of Piaget's Theory   164
Stages of Cognitive Development   166
Piaget's Contributions to Child Development   171

**6.2**   **Modern Theories of Cognitive Development**   **174**
The Sociocultural Perspective: Vygotsky's Theory   174
Information Processing   178
Core-Knowledge Theories   183

**6.3**   **Understanding in Core Domains**   **185**
Understanding Objects and Their Properties   186
Understanding Living Things   188
Understanding People   190

*See for Yourself, Resources, Key Terms*   *196*
*SUMMARY*   *197*


# Cognitive Processes and Academic Skills   198

7

**7.1**   **Memory**   **200**
Origins of Memory   200
Strategies for Remembering   201
Knowledge and Memory   203

**7.2**   **Problem Solving**   **212**
Developmental Trends in Solving Problems   212
Features of Children's and Adolescents' Problem Solving   214
Scientific Problem Solving   218

**7.3**   **Academic Skills**   **219**
Reading   220
Writing   225
Knowing and Using Numbers   227

*See for Yourself, Resources, Key Terms*   *234*
*SUMMARY*   *235*

# Intelligence and Individual Differences in Cognition   236

**8.1**   **What Is Intelligence?**   **238**
Psychometric Theories   238
Gardner's Theory of Multiple Intelligences   239
Sternberg's Theory of Successful Intelligence   242

**8.2**   **Measuring Intelligence**   **245**
Binet and the Development of Intelligence Testing   246
Do Tests Work?   248
Hereditary and Environmental Factors   251
Impact of Ethnicity and Socioeconomic Status   254

**8.3**   **Special Children, Special Needs**   **256**
Gifted and Creative Children   257
Children With Mental Retardation   259
Children With Learning Disabilities   260

*See for Yourself, Resources, Key Terms*   263
*SUMMARY*   265

# Language and Communication   266

**9.1**   **The Road to Speech**   **268**
Elements of Language   268
Perceiving Speech   269
First Steps to Speech   272

**9.2**   **Learning the Meanings of Words**   **274**
Understanding Words as Symbols   274
Fast Mapping Meanings to Words   275
Individual Differences in Word Learning   279
Encouraging Word Learning   280
Beyond Words: Other Symbols   283

**9.3**   **Speaking in Sentences**   **284**
From Two-Word Speech to Complex Sentences   285
How Do Children Acquire Grammar?   287

**9.4**   **Using Language to Communicate**   **291**
Taking Turns   292
Speaking Effectively   293
Listening Well   296

*See for Yourself, Resources, Key Terms*   298
*SUMMARY*   299

# Emotional Development   300

**10.1**   **Emerging Emotions**   **302**
The Function of Emotions   302
Experiencing and Expressing Emotions   303
Recognizing and Using Others' Emotions   307
Regulating Emotions   309

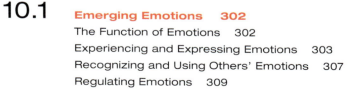

**10.2 Temperament 311**

What Is Temperament? 311

Hereditary and Environmental Contributions to Temperament 313

Stability of Temperament 314

Temperament and Other Aspects of Development 315

**10.3 Attachment 318**

The Growth of Attachment 319

The Quality of Attachment 321

*See for Yourself, Resources, Key Terms 327*
*SUMMARY 329*


## Understanding Self and Others 330

**11**

**11.1 Who Am I? Self-Concept 332**

Origins of Self-Recognition 332

The Evolving Self-Concept 334

The Search for Identity 335

**11.2 Self-Esteem 342**

Measuring Self-Esteem 342

Developmental Change in Self-Esteem 345

Sources of Self-Esteem 348

Low Self-Esteem: Cause or Consequence? 350

**11.3 Understanding Others 351**

Describing Others 352

Understanding What Others Think 353

Prejudice 355

*See for Yourself, Resources, Key Terms 359*
*SUMMARY 361*


## Moral Understanding and Behavior 362

**12**

**12.1 Self-Control 364**

Beginnings of Self-Control 364

Influences on Self-Control 367

Improving Children's Self-Control 368

**12.2 Reasoning About Moral Issues 369**

Piaget's Views 370

Kohlberg's Theory 371

Beyond Kohlberg's Theory 375

Promoting Moral Reasoning 378

**12.3 Helping Others 380**

Development of Prosocial Behavior 380

Skills Underlying Prosocial Behavior 381

Situational Influences 382

Socializing Prosocial Behavior 383

**12.4**    **Aggression**    **385**

Change and Stability    385

Roots of Aggressive Behavior    387

Victims of Aggression    391

*See for Yourself, Resources, Key Terms    394*
*SUMMARY    395*

## Gender and Development    396

**13**

**13.1**    **Gender Stereotypes    398**

How Do We View Men and Women?    398

Learning Gender Stereotypes    399

**13.2**    **Differences Related to Gender    402**

Differences in Physical Development and Behavior    403

Differences in Intellectual Abilities and Achievement    404

Differences in Personality and Social Behavior    407

Frank Talk about Gender Differences    409

**13.3**    **Gender Identity    411**

The Socializing Influences of People and the Media    412

Cognitive Theories of Gender Identity    417

Biological Influences    419

**13.4**    **Gender Roles in Transition    420**

Emerging Gender Roles    420

Beyond Traditional Gender Roles    421

*See for Yourself, Resources, Key Terms    424*
*SUMMARY    425*

## Family Relationships    426

**14**

**14.1**    **Parenting    428**

The Family as a System    428

Styles of Parenting    430

Parental Behavior    432

Influences of the Marital System    435

Children's Contributions    436

**14.2**    **The Changing Family    437**

Impact of Divorce on Children    438

Blended Families    440

The Role of Grandparents    441

Children of Gay and Lesbian Parents    443

**14.3**    **Brothers and Sisters    444**

Firstborn, Laterborn, and Only Children    445

Qualities of Sibling Relationships    447

**14.4**    **Maltreatment: Parent–Child Relationships Gone Awry    449**

Consequences of Maltreatment    450

Causes of Maltreatment    451

Preventing Maltreatment    453

*See for Yourself, Resources, Key Terms    455*
*SUMMARY    457*

## Influences Beyond the Family    458

**15**

**15.1    Peers    460**
Development of Peer Interactions    460
Friendship    464
Romantic Relationships    468
Groups    471
Popularity and Rejection    472

**15.2    Electronic Media    475**
Television    475
Computers    479

**15.3    Institutional Influences    480**
Day Care    480
Part-Time Employment    483
Neighborhoods    485
School    489

*See for Yourself, Resources, Key Terms    492*
*SUMMARY    493*

*Glossary*    494
*References*    501
*Acknowledgments*    525
*Name Index*    527
*Subject Index*    537

## Focus on Research

2   Hereditary and Environmental Bases of Cognitive Development   53

3   Impact of Prenatal Exposure to PCBs on Cognitive Functioning   75

4   Right-Hemisphere Specialization for Face Processing   126

5   Specialized Face Processing During Infancy   146

6   Interpreting Actions as Goal Directed   190

7   Do Stereotypes and Suggestions Influence Preschoolers' Reports?   208

8   Improving Reading Skill in Children with Reading Disability   261

9   When Listeners Don't Understand, Preschoolers Try Again   294

10   Temperament Influences Helping Others   316

11   Developmental Change in Self-Esteem in Different Domains   347

12   Growth of Effortful Control in Toddlers and Preschoolers   365

13   How Mothers Talk to Children About Gender   412

15   Influence of Best Friends on Sexual Activity   467

## Cultural Influences

2   Why Do African Americans Inherit Sickle-Cell Disease?   44

3   Infant Mortality   90

4   How the Apache Celebrate Menarche   112

5   Cultural Practices That Promote Motor Development   154

6   How Do Parents in Different Cultures Scaffold Their Children's Learning?   176

7   Fifth Grade in Taiwan   231

8   How Culture Defines What Is Intelligent   244

9   Growing Up Bilingual   282

10   Why Is Yoshimi's Son So Tough?   314

11   Dea's Ethnic Identity   338

12   Moral Reasoning in India   374

13   Around the World With Four Gender Stereotypes   398

14   Grandmothers in African American Families   442

15   Keys to Popularity   473

## Improving Children's Lives

2   Genetic Counseling   46

3   Five Steps Toward a Healthy Baby   68

4   What's the Best Food for Babies?   106

5   Hearing Impairment in Infancy   137

6   Teaching Practices That Foster Cognitive Growth—Educational Applications of Piaget's Theory   172

7   Rhyme Is Sublime Because Sounds Abounds   221

8   Fostering Creativity   258

9   Promoting Language Development   291

10   "But I Don't Want to Go to School!"   306

11   Self-Esteem in Gifted Classes   349

13   Encouraging Valuable Traits, Not Gender Traits   422

14   Helping Children Adjust After Divorce   440

15   Get the Kids Off the Couch!   478

## Spotlight on Theories

3   A Theory of the Risks Associated with Teenage Motherhood   71

4   A Paternal Investment Theory of Girls' Pubertal Timing   114

5   The Theory of Intersensory Redundancy   139

6   Speech About Mental States and Children's Theory of Mind   194

7   Fuzzy Trace Theory   205

8   The Theory of Successful Intelligence   242

9   A Shape-Bias Theory of Word Learning   278

10   A Theory of the Structure of Temperament in Infancy   312

12   Social Information Processing Theory and Children's Aggressive Behavior   389

13   Gender Schema Theory   417

15   The Family Economic Stress Model   487

## Child Development and Family Policy

2   Screening for PKU    55

3   Back to Sleep!    96

4   Preventing Osteoporosis    110

5   What's the Best Treatment for ADHD?    149

7   Interviewing Children Effectively    211

8   Providing Children with a Head Start for School    252

9   Are Cochlear Implants Effective for Young Children?    271

10  Determining Guidelines for Child Care for Infants
    and Toddlers    326

11  Ending Segregated Schools    357

12  Promoting More Advanced Moral Reasoning    379

14  Assessing the Consequences of China's One-Child
    Policy    446

# PREFACE

Like many professors turned textbook authors, I began this book because none of the texts available met the aims of the child-development classes that I taught at Purdue. What were those aims? I wanted a book that would:

- provide a solid, research-oriented overview of child-development science but would also use effective pedagogy to enhance students' learning;

- use fundamental developmental issues as a foundation for integrating the many discoveries that make child-development science a dynamic and exciting field;

- explain the many different methods used by researchers, then illustrate them repeatedly to drive home the lesson that science progresses when complementary methods converge; *and*

- demonstrate that the results of child-development research can be used to enhance the lives of children and their families.

*Children and Their Development*, first published in 1998, is my effort to meet these goals. In the next few pages, I want to explain how the book is designed to achieve the goals I just described.

**Goal 1: Use effective pedagogy to promote students' learning.** The focus on a student-friendly book begins with the structure of the chapters, which is designed to promote students' learning. Each chapter consists of three or four modules that provide a clear and well-defined organization to the chapter. Each module begins with a set of learning objectives and a vignette that introduces the topic to be covered. Within each module, all figures, tables, and photos are fully integrated with the exposition, eliminating the need for students to search for a graphic. Similarly, special topics that are set off in other textbooks as feature boxes are, by contrast, fully integrated with the main text and identified by a distinctive icon. Each module ends with several questions intended to help students check their understanding of the major ideas in the module.

The end of each chapter includes several additional study aids. "Unifying Themes" links the ideas in the chapter to a major developmental theme (more about this in a minute. . . .). "See for Yourself" suggests activities that allow students to observe topics in child development firsthand. "Resources" includes books and Web-sites where students can learn more about child development. "Key Terms" is a list of all of the important boldface terms appearing in the chapter. The "Summary" is organized by module and the primary headings within each module; it reviews the entire chapter.

These different pedagogical elements *do* work; students using previous editions frequently comment that the book is easy to read and presents complex topics in an understandable way.

**Goal 2: Use fundamental developmental issues as a foundation for students' learning of research and theory in child development.** The child-development course sometimes overwhelms students because of the sheer number of topics and studies that don't "hang together"—students see only the trees and never the forest. Of course, today's child-development science is really propelled by a concern with a handful of fundamental developmental issues, such as the continuity of development and the roles of nature and nurture in development. In *Children and Their Development,* four of these foundational issues are introduced in Chapter 1, then reappear in subsequent chapters to scaffold students' understanding. As I mentioned already, the end of the chapter includes "Unifying Themes" in which the ideas from the chapter are used to illustrate one of the foundational themes. By occurring repeatedly throughout the text, the themes remind students that all child-development science ultimately addresses a set of core issues.

**Goal 3: Teach students that child-development science draws on many complementary research methods, each of which contributes uniquely to scientific progress.** In Module 1.4, I portray child-development research as a dynamic process in which scientists make a series of decisions as they plan their work. In the process, they create a study that has both strengths and weaknesses. Each of the remaining chapters of the book contains a "Focus on Research" feature that illustrates this process by showing—in an easy-to-read question-and-answer format—the different decisions that investigators made in designing a particular study. I trace each of the steps and explain the decisions that were made. Then the results are shown, usually with an annotated figure, so that students can learn how to interpret graphs. The investigators' conclusions are described, and I then end each "Focus on Research" by mentioning the kind of converging evidence that would strengthen the author's conclusions. Thus, the research methods introduced in Chapter 1 reappear in every chapter, depicting research as a collaborative enterprise that depends on the contributions of many scientists using different methods.

**Goal 4: Show students how the findings from child-development research can improve children's lives.** Child-development scientists and students alike want to know how the findings of research can be used to promote children's development. In Chapter 1 of *Children and Their Development,* I describe the different means by which researchers can use their work to improve children's lives. In the chapters that follow, these ideas come alive in two special features. "Improving Children's Lives" provides research-based solutions to common problems in children's lives. "Child Development and Family Policy" demonstrates how research has inspired change in social policies that affect children and families. From these features, students see that child-development research really matters—parents, teachers, and policy makers can use research to foster children's development.

## New to the Fourth Edition

The fourth edition of *Children and Their Development* has several improvements designed to make the book more useful to students and instructors.

- **Reorganized Coverage of Cognitive Development** In previous editions, one chapter was devoted to Piaget's theory and a second chapter was devoted to information-processing approaches to cognitive development. In this fourth edition, one chapter covers theories of cognitive development, using Piaget's theory to set the stage, then moving to contemporary theories. A second chapter then covers the development of cognitive processes and academic skills. This reorganization reflects contemporary views of Piaget's work as groundbreaking but no longer a driving force behind "everyday" science.

- **New Pedagogical Features** A new feature, "Spotlight on Theories" is designed to show students the key role that theories play in modern child-development research. The fill-in-the-blank "Check Your Learning" questions have been eliminated and replaced with different forms of open-ended questions: *Recall* questions test students' understanding of material, *Interpret* questions assess their ability to think critically about material, and *Apply* questions encourage students to use material they've read. The "Real Children" feature of previous editions has been replaced by brief descriptions of children in real-world settings; ending with a question, these descriptions encourage students to think about what they've read.

- **Enhanced Illustration Program** More than one third of the photos in this edition are new. In addition, a number of new figures have been added, updated, or otherwise revised.

- **Updated Research Coverage** In updating the coverage of research, I have added hundreds of new citations to research published since 2000.

- **Substantive Content Additions** I have also added significant new content to every chapter. Of particular note:

  **Chapter 1** has expanded coverage of the history of child development and information about physiological measures.

  **Chapter 2** has been reorganized so that Module 2.1 focuses on basics of genetic action and Module 2.2 focuses on genetics in child development. In addition, the material on "Heredity is not destiny" has been reorganized around four important principles of gene–environment interaction in a developmental context.

  **Chapter 3** provides expanded coverage of postpartum depression.

  **Chapter 4** has expanded coverage on sleep in adolescence and on eating disorders, a revamped section on the psychological consequences of pubertal timing, and a new "Focus on Research" feature.

  **Chapter 5** has a comprehensively updated section on depth perception, new material on infants' perception of music, and additional material on face perception, including a new "Focus on Research" feature.

  **Chapter 6** is mostly new and includes a description of Piaget's theory, coverage of three other theoretical views, and material on children's knowledge in core domains.

  **Chapter 7** includes material on memory and academic skills from previous editions along with a completely new module on problem solving.

  **Chapter 8** has a revamped presentation of Sternberg's work on intelligence.

  **Chapter 9** contains expanded and reorganized coverage of word learning.

  **Chapter 10** has information covering new material on cultural differences in expression of anger and on the later developing emotions of regret and relief.

  **Chapter 11** has much reorganized coverage of children's self-esteem.

**Chapter 12** has condensed and updated coverage about influences on children's self-control as well as a revised Module 12.4 with new material on biological and community contributions to aggressive behavior.

**Chapter 13** presents new material on toddlers' and preschoolers' knowledge of stereotypes, along with a substantially revised module on gender identity that includes a new "Focus on Research" feature along with new ideas about evolutionary bases for boys' and girls' play styles.

**Chapter 14** includes new material on socioeconomic status–related differences in parenting style, a new section on the impact of the marital system on children, and expanded coverage of blended families. In addition, material on divorce from prior editions is now contained in a module on the changing family.

**Chapter 15** has reorganized and expanded coverage of parental influence on peer interactions, the section on friends has a revised account of developmental change and expanded coverage of friends' influence, including a new "Focus on Research" feature, coverage of after-school care has been elaborated, and I provide new material on the impact of neighborhoods on children's development.

## Support Materials

*Children and Their Development* is accompanied by a superb set of ancillary materials. They include the following:

### Print and Media Supplements for the Instructor

**NEW OneKey** for *Children and Their Development, Fourth Edition* New to this edition is Prentice Hall's all-inclusive online resource that offers instructors and students all of their resources—all in one place, available 24/7—all organized to accompany this text. With OneKey, you will enliven your lectures with more presentation material than you ever imagined. Your students will study smarter with the ebook and diagnostic test that creates a customized study plan designed to help students prepare for—and perform better on—exams. OneKey is available for instructors by going to **www.prenhall.com/onekey** and following the instructions on the page. Students get OneKey with an access code that is available with the purchase of a new text for college adoptions. OneKey is available in *WebCT, BlackBoard,* or *Course Compass* formats. See your Prentice Hall representative for further information.

**NEW Virtual Child Simulation** Created by Frank Manis, University of Southern California and Michael Radford. Available in OneKey or as a separate online activity, this simulation allows students to raise a child from conception to adolescence. At each age range, students will hear about various milestones their child has attained, specific problems or experiences that occur in the family or in the school or community environment, and students will use this information to make decisions about how to raise their child. Students will be given feedback about their child, based on the students prior "parenting" decisions, which will allow students to make more informed parenting decisions in future scenarios. Through this simulation, students will be able to integrate their course work with their practical experiences in raising a child.

**NEW Instructor's Resource Binder** This binder includes an exhaustive collection of teaching resources for both new and experienced instructors alike. Organized by chapter, this binder includes the *Instructor's Resource Manual*, The Test-Item File, Prentice Hall's Developmental Psychology Overhead Transparencies, the Instructor's Resource CD-ROM, and the TestGen computerized testing software. All of these resources are described below.

**Instructor's Resource Manual** Each chapter in the manual includes the following resources: Chapter Learning Objectives; Lecture Suggestions and Discussion Topics; Classroom Activities, Demonstrations, and Exercises; Out-of-Class Assignments and Projects; Overhead Transparency Slide Previews and Lecture Notes; Multimedia Resources; Video Resources; and Handouts. Designed to make your lectures more effective and to save you preparation time, this extensive resource gathers together the most effective activities and strategies for teaching your developmental psychology course.

**Test-Item File** This test bank contains over 2,500 multiple choice, true/false, and short-answer essay questions, and *many enhancements*. The NEW Total Assessment Guide *test planner chapter overview* makes creating tests easier by listing all of the test items in an easy-to-reference grid. The Total Assessment Guide organizes all test items by text section, question type, and level of difficulty. The Test-Item File now includes questions for key student supplements, too: the APS reader *Current Directions in Developmental Psychology* available to be packaged with this text for college adoptions; the Observation Videos packaged with this text; and the Lecture Launcher Videos for Developmental Psychology. Finally, each chapter includes two ready-made quizzes with answer keys for immediate use in class.

**Prentice Hall's TestGen** Available on one dual-platform CD-ROM, this test generator program provides instructors "best in class" features in an easy-to-use program. Create tests using the TestGen Wizard and easily select questions with drag-and-drop or point-and-click functionality. Add or modify test questions using the built-in Question Editor. TestGen also offers algorithmic functionality, which allows for the creation of unlimited versions of a single test. The Quiz Master feature allows for online test delivery. Comes complete with an instructor gradebook and full technical support.

**Instructor's Resource Center on CD-ROM** Included in the Instructor's Resource Binder, and as a stand-alone item, this valuable, time-saving resource provides you with electronic versions of a variety of teaching resources all in one place allowing you to customize your lecture notes, PowerPoint slides, and media presentations. This CD-ROM includes PowerPoint slides customized for *Children and Their Development,* Fourth Edition, electronic versions of the artwork from the text, the Overhead Transparencies, the *Instructor's Resource Manual*, and the Test-Item File.

**PowerPoint Slides for *Children and Their Development*** Each chapter's PowerPoint presentation highlights the key points covered in the text. Provided in two versions—one with the chapter graphics and one without—to give you flexibility in preparing your lectures. Available on the Instructor's Resource Center CD-ROM or online at **www.prenhall.com**.

**Prentice Hall's Developmental Psychology Overhead Transparencies** This set of over 100 full-color transparencies is designed to be used in large lecture settings and includes illustrations from the text as well as images from a variety of other sources. Available in acetate form, on the Instructor's Resource Center CD-ROM or online at **www.prenhall.com**.

**Classroom Response Systems** Pearson Education is pleased to offer the benefits of our partnerships with two of the leading classroom response systems on the market. Customers using a Classroom Response System with their text are entitled to student and department savings exclusively from Pearson Education.

Whether you are considering a system for the first time or are interested in expanding a program department wide, we can help you select the best system for your needs. For more information about Classroom Response Systems and our partnerships, please visit our Websites at **http://www.prenhall.com/crs**

Prentice Hall also offers content for use with a classroom response system in PowerPoint format to accompany *Children and Their Development,* Fourth Edition. Contact your local Prentice Hall representative for more information.

## Video Resources for Instructors

Prentice Hall is proud to present you with the following video packages, available exclusively to qualified adopters of *Children and Their Development,* Fourth Edition.

**NEW Prentice Hall Lecture Launcher Video for Developmental Psychology** Adopters can receive this new video that includes short clips covering all major topics in developmental psychology. The videos have been carefully selected from the *Films for the Humanities and Sciences* library and edited to provide brief and compelling video content for enhancing your lectures. Contact your local representative for a full list of the video clips on this tape.

**ABCNEWS** **NEW ABC News/Prentice Hall Video Library for Life Span Development** This video library consists of brief segments from award-winning news programs such as *Good Morning America, Nightline, 20/20,* and *World News Tonight.* These videos discuss current issues and are a great way to launch your lectures and demonstrate the applicability of what students are learning in class to everyday situations.

**Films for the Humanities and Sciences Video Library** Qualified adopters can select videos on various topics in psychology from the extensive library of *Films for the Humanities and Sciences.* Contact your local sales representative for a list of videos.

## Print and Media Supplements for the Student

**NEW SafariX WebBooks** This new **Pearson Choice** offers students an online subscription to *Children and Their Development* online at a 50% savings. With the SafariX WebBook, students can search the text, make notes online, print out reading assignments, and bookmark important passages. Ask your Prentice Hall representative for details, or visit **www.safarix.com**.

**Prentice Hall's Observations in Developmental Psychology** Packaged with every new text, this CD-ROM brings to life more than 30 key concepts discussed in the narrative of the text. Students get to view each video twice: once with an introduction tothe concept being illustrated and again with commentary describing what is taking place at crucial points in the video. Whether your course has an observation component or not, this CD-ROM provides your students the opportunity to see children in action.

**Study Guide** This student study guide helps students master the core concepts presented in each chapter. Each chapter includes learning objectives, a brief chapter summary, and practice tests to help them master the content in each chapter.

**Companion Website at www.prenhall.com/kail** This online study guide allows students to review each chapter's material, take practice tests, research topics for course projects and more! The *Children and Their Development* Companion Website includes many study resources for each chapter: Chapter Objectives, Interactive Lectures, many types of quizzing that provide immediate, text-specific feedback and coaching comments, including WebEssays, WebDestinations, NetSearch, and FlashCards. Access to the Website is unrestricted to all students.

**OneSearch Guide with ResearchNavigator™** This guide gives students a quick introduction to conducting research on the Web and introduces Research Navigator™. Research Navigator helps students find, cite, and conduct research with three exclusive databases: EBSCO's ContentSelect Academic Journal Database; The *New York Times* Search by Subject Archive; and Best of the Web Link Library. Available with a new text, ask your Prentice Hall representative for ordering information.

## Supplementary Texts

Contact your Prentice Hall representative to package any of these supplementary texts with *Children and Their Development,* Fourth Edition.

*Current Directions in Developmental Psychology: Readings from the Association for Psychological Science* This new and exciting reader includes over 20 articles that have been carefully selected for the undergraduate audience, and taken from from the very accessible *Current Directions in Psychological Science* journal. These timely, cutting-edge articles allow instructors to bring their students real-world perspective about today's most current and pressing issues in psychology. Available with a new text, ask your Prentice Hall representative for ordering information.

*Twenty Studies That Revolutionized Child Psychology, by Wallace E. Dixon, Jr.* Presenting the seminal research studies that have shaped modern developmental psychology, this brief text provides an overview of the environment that gave rise to each study, its experimental design, its findings, and its impact on current thinking in the discipline.

*Human Development in Multicultural Context: A Book of Readings,* by Michele A. Paludi. This compilation of readings highlights cultural influences in developmental psychology.

*The Psychology Major: Careers and Strategies for Success,* by Eric Landrum (Idaho State University) and Stephen F. Davis (Texas Wesleyan University). This 208-page paperback provides valuable information on career options available to psychology majors, tips for improving academic performance, and a guide to the APA style of research reporting.

# Acknowledgments

Textbook authors do not produce books on their own. I want to thank the many reviewers who generously gave their time and effort to help sharpen my thinking about child development and shape the development of this text. I am especially grateful to the following people who reviewed various aspects of the manuscript:

Renate Brenneke, *Kellogg Community College*

Gary E. Krolikowski, *SUNY Geneseo*

Grace E. Cho, *University of Illinois at Urbana-Champaign*

Andrew L. Carrano, *Southern Connecticut State University*

Glenn I. Roisman, *University of Illinois at Urbana-Champaign*

Sandra Crosser, *Ohio Northern University*

Ty W. Boyer, *University of Maryland*

Linda Dunlap, *Marist College*

Tanya Boone, *California State University, Bakersfield*

Michael S. McGee, *Radford University*

Beth Hentges, *University of Houston-Clear Lake*

Ric Wynn, *County College of Morris*

Suzanne Koprowski, *Waukesha County Technical College*

Barbara Zimmerman, *Dana College*

George Hollich, *Purdue University*

Carol S. Huntsinger, *College of Lake County*

Arlene Rider, *Marist College*

Jessica Carpenter, *Elgin Community College*

Everett Waters, *SUNY Stony Brook*

R. M. J. Bennett, *University of Dundee*

E. Mark Cummings, *University of Notre Dame*

Lonna M. Murphy, *Iowa State University*

Thanks, as well, to those who reviewed the previous editions of this book: William Holt, UMASS Dartmouth; Dennis A. Lichty, Wayne State College; Monica L. McCoy, Converse College; Robert Pasnak, George Mason University; Christopher Radi, University of New Mexico; Lesa Rae Vartanian, Indiana University–Purdue University Fort Wayne; John Bates, Indiana University; Lisabeth DiLalla, Southern University School of Medicine; Marta Laupa, University of Nevada; Jane E. Clark, University of Maryland; Maureen Callanan, University of California–Santa Cruz; Malinda Colwell, Texas Tech University; Erika Hoff, Florida Atlantic University; Susan McClure, Westmoreland County Community College; Rebecca Bigler, University of Texas–Austin; Kathleen Fox, Salisbury State University; Rick Medlin, Stetson University; Joan Cook, County College of Morris; Elizabeth Lemerise, Western Kentucky University; Jim Dannemiller, University of Wisconsin–Madison; Mark B. Alcorn, University of Northern Colorado; Vernon C. Hall, Syracuse University; May X. Wang, Metropolitan State College of Denver; Jack Meacham, University of Buffalo; Lesa Rae Vartanian, Indiana University–Purdue

University Fort Wayne; Adam Winsler, George Mason University; Tony Simon, Furman University; K. Robert Bridges, Pennsylvania State University; Frank Manis, University of Southern California; Marianne Taylor, University of Puget Sound; Karen Rudolph, University of Illinois; Cynthia Stifter, Pennsylvania State University; James Black, University of Illinois; Laura Hess, Purdue University; Lisa Oakes, University of Iowa; Jacquelyn Mice, Auburn University; Amy Weiss, University of Iowa; Brad Pillow, Northern Illinois University; Janet DiPietro, Johns Hopkins University; Lee Ann Thompson, Case Western Reserve University; Gary Ladd, University of Illinois. Without their thoughtful comments, this book would be less complete, less accurate, and less interesting.

I also owe a debt of thanks to many people who helped take this project from a first draft to a bound book. John Christiana designed a book that is both beautiful and functional. Kathy Sleys and Caterina Melara skillfully orchestrated the many activities that were involved in actually producing the book. Toni Michaels found many of the marvelous photographs that appear throughout the book. Will Bankston helped to compile the many new references that were added to this edition.

I am particularly grateful to three people whose contributions to *Children and Their Development* are especially noteworthy. Jennifer Gilliland has long supported this book enthusiastically and served as a savvy guide to its revision. On the first and second editions, Harriett Prentiss labored long to make my writing clear and inviting. This task fell to Susan Moss on the third and fourth editions and she did a superb job of making sure that topics were covered thoroughly and clearly. To all these individuals, many, many thanks.

*—Robert V. Kail*

## To the Student

In this book, we'll trace children's development from conception through adolescence. Given this goal, you may expect to find chapters devoted to early childhood, middle childhood, and the like. Instead, if you look at the table of contents, you'll see that this book is organized differently—around topics. Chapters 2 through 5 are devoted to the genetic and biological bases of human development, and the growth of perceptual and motor skills. Chapters 6 through 9 cover intellectual development—how children learn, think, reason, and solve problems. Chapters 10 through 15 concern social and emotional development—how children acquire the customs of their society and learn to play the social roles expected of them.

This organization reflects the fact that when scientists conduct research on children's development, they usually study how some specific aspect of a child develops. For example, a researcher might study how memory changes as children grow or how friendship in childhood differs from that in adolescence. Thus, the organization of this book reflects the way researchers actually study child development.

Each of the chapters follows the same format, one that is designed to help you understand the material within the chapter. This format is explained in the next section.

## Organization of Chapters

Each of the 15 chapters in the book includes two to four modules that are listed at the beginning of each chapter. As you can see in the inset page below, each module begins with a set of learning objectives phrased as questions.

---

**2.2**    HEREDITY, ENVIRONMENT, AND DEVELOPMENT

Behavioral Genetics

Paths From Genes to Behavior

**LEARNING OBJECTIVES**

- What methods do scientists use to study the impact of heredity and environment on children's development?
- How do heredity and environment work together to influence child development?

*Sadie and Molly are fraternal twins. As babies, Sadie was calm and easily comforted, but Molly was fussy and hard to soothe. When they entered school, Sadie relished contact with other people and preferred play that involved others. Meanwhile, Molly was more withdrawn and was quite happy to play alone. Their grandparents wonder why these twins seem so different.*

---

Next is a brief vignette that introduces the topic to be covered in the module by describing an issue or problem like the kind faced by real people. In the margin is a mini outline listing the major subheadings of the module—a kind of road map for reading. The learning objectives, vignette, and mini outline tell you what to expect in the module.

Each module typically examines three to four major topics that are listed in the mini outline. In addition, each module in Chapters 2 through 15 includes at least one special feature that expands or highlights a topic. There are four different kinds of features; you can recognize each one by its distinctive icon:

 *Focus on Research* provides details on the design and methods used in a particular research study. Closely examining specific studies demystifies research and shows that scientific work is a series of logical steps conducted by real people.

 *Cultural Influences* shows how culture influences children and illustrates that developmental journeys are diverse. All children share the biological aspects of development, but their cultural contexts differ. This feature celebrates the developmental experiences of children from different backgrounds.

 *Improving Children's Lives* shows how research and theory can be applied to improve children's development. These practical solutions to everyday problems show the relevance of research and theory to real life.

 *Child Development and Family Policy* shows how results from research are used to create social policy that is designed to improve the lives of children and their families.

 *Spotlight on Theories* examines an influential theory of development and shows how it has been tested in research.

The inset below shows another important element of each module: All illustrations and tables are integrated with the text.

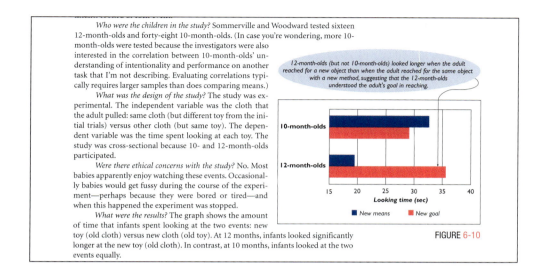

*Who were the children in the study?* Sommerville and Woodward tested sixteen 12-month-olds and forty-eight 10-month-olds. (In case you're wondering, more 10-month-olds were tested because the investigators were also interested in the correlation between 10-month-olds' understanding of intentionality and performance on another task that I'm not describing. Evaluating correlations typically requires larger samples than does comparing means.)

*What was the design of the study?* The study was experimental. The independent variable was the cloth that the adult pulled: same cloth (but different toy from the initial trials) versus other cloth (but same toy). The dependent variable was the time spent looking at each toy. The study was cross-sectional because 10- and 12-month-olds participated.

*Were there ethical concerns with the study?* No. Most babies apparently enjoy watching these events. Occasionally babies would get fussy during the course of the experiment—perhaps because they were bored or tired—and when this happened the experiment was stopped.

*What were the results?* The graph shows the amount of time that infants spent looking at the two events: new toy (old cloth) versus new cloth (old toy). At 12 months, infants looked significantly longer at the new toy (old cloth). In contrast, at 10 months, infants looked at the two events equally.

FIGURE 6-10

You won't need to turn pages searching for a picture or table that is described in the text; instead, pictures, tables, and words are linked to tell a unified story.

Three other elements are designed to help you focus on the main points of the text. First, whenever a key term is introduced in the text, it appears in *red bold italic* like this and the definition appears in **black boldface type.** This format should make key terms easier for you to find and learn. Second, about half the pages in the book include a sentence in large type that extends into the margin. This sentence summarizes a key point that is made in the surrounding text. When you see one of these sentences, take a moment to think about it—it captures an important idea; and reviewing these sentences later will help you prepare for exams. Third, summary tables throughout the book review key ideas and provide a capsule account of each. For example, the following Summary Table shows the many study aids that I've included in the book.

## SUMMARY TABLE

### STUDY AIDS USED IN *CHILDREN AND THEIR DEVELOPMENT*

| Study Aid | Key Features |
|---|---|
| Module-opening material | Learning objectives, vignette, mini outline |
| Special features | Focus on Research, Improving Children's Lives, Cultural Influences, Spotlight on Theories, Child Development and Family Policy |
| Design elements that promote learning | Integrated art and text, boldface key terms defined in text, key concepts in margin, summary tables (like this one) |
| Check Your Learning | Recall, interpret, and apply questions |
| End-of-chapter material | Unifying Themes, See for Yourself, Resources, Key Terms, Summary |

Each module concludes with "Check Your Learning" questions to help you review the major ideas in that module. As you can see in the inset, there are three kinds of questions: recall, interpret, and apply.

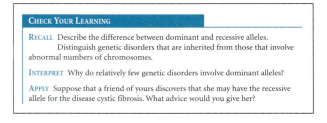

**CHECK YOUR LEARNING**

RECALL  Describe the difference between dominant and recessive alleles.
Distinguish genetic disorders that are inherited from those that involve abnormal numbers of chromosomes.

INTERPRET  Why do relatively few genetic disorders involve dominant alleles?

APPLY  Suppose that a friend of yours discovers that she may have the recessive allele for the disease cystic fibrosis. What advice would you give her?

If you can answer the questions in "Check Your Learning" correctly, you are on your way to mastering the material in the module. However, do not rely exclusively on "Check Your Learning" as you study for exams. The questions are designed to give you a quick check of your understanding, not a comprehensive assessment of your knowledge of the entire module.

At the very end of each chapter are several additional study aids. "Unifying Themes" links the contents of the chapter to the developmental themes that I introduce in Module 1.3. "See for Yourself" suggests some simple activities for exploring issues in child development on your own. "Resources" includes books and Websites where you can learn more about children and their development. "Key Terms" is a list of all the important terms that appear in the chapter, along with the page where each term is defined. Finally, drawing the chapter to a close is a "Summary"—a review of the entire chapter, organized by module and the primary headings within the module.

## How to Use This Book

I strongly encourage you to take advantage of these learning and study aids as you read the book. In the next few paragraphs, I'm going to suggest how you could do this. Obviously, I can't know exactly how your course is organized, but my suggestions should work well with most courses, sometimes with a few changes.

Your instructor will probably assign about one chapter per week. Don't try to read an entire chapter in one sitting. Instead, on the first day, preview the chapter. Read the introduction and notice how the chapter fits into the scheme of the whole book. Then page through the chapter, reading the learning objectives, vignettes, mini outlines, and major headings to see the general framework of the material. Also read the sentences in the margins and the boldface sentences. Your goal is to get a general overview of the entire chapter—a sense of what it's all about.

Now you're ready to begin reading. Return to the first module and preview it again, reminding yourself of the topics covered. Then start to read. As you do, think about what you're reading. Make predictions about what will come next; make mental images that depict what you've read. Every few paragraphs, stop briefly. Try to summarize the main ideas in your own words; ask yourself if the ideas remind you of something in your own childhood or that of others whom you know; tell a roommate about something interesting in the material. In other words, *read actively*—get involved in what you're reading. Don't just stare glassy-eyed at the page!

Continue this process—reading, summarizing, relating, and reviewing—until you finish the module. Then answer the questions in "Check Your Learning" to determine how well you've learned what you've read. If you've followed the read-summarize-think cycle as you worked your way through the module, you should be able to answer most of the questions. If you can't answer the questions, then skim the module again until you can find the correct answer.

The next time you sit down to read—preferably the next day—start by previewing the second module and then tackle it with the read-summarize-think cycle. Repeat this procedure for all the modules.

After you've finished the last module, wait a day or two and then review each module, paying careful attention to the sentences in the margins, the boldface terms, and the "Check Your Learning" questions. Reread confusing or complex passages. Also, use the study aids at the end of the chapter to help you integrate the ideas in the chapter.

With this approach, you should need several 30- to 45-minute study sessions to complete each chapter. Don't be tempted to blast through an entire chapter in a single session. Research consistently shows that you learn more effectively by having daily (or nearly daily) study sessions devoted to both reviewing familiar material *and* taking on a relatively small amount of new material.

Finally, *Children and Their Development* has its own Website (**www.prenhall.com/kail/**) that includes much additional material that should be useful to you. In particular, as you begin to prepare for exams, the Website has questions that you can use to see how well you've mastered the material in the book.

## Terminology

Every field has its own terminology, and child development is no exception. I will be using several terms to refer to different periods of infancy, childhood, and adolescence. Although these terms are familiar, I will use each to refer to a specific range of ages:

| | |
|---|---|
| Newborn | Birth to 1 month |
| Infant | 1 month to 1 year |
| Toddler | 1 to 2 years |
| Preschooler | 2 to 6 years |
| School-age child | 6 to 12 years |
| Adolescent | 12 to 18 years |
| Adult | 18 years and older |

Sometimes for the sake of variety I will use other terms that are less tied to specific ages, such as *babies*, *youngsters*, and *elementary-school children*. When I do, you will be able to tell from the context what groups are being described.

I will also use very specific terminology in describing research findings from different cultural and ethnic groups. The appropriate terms to describe different cultural, racial, and ethnic groups change over time. For example, the terms *colored people*, *Negroes*, *Black Americans*, and *African Americans* have all been used to describe Americans who trace their ancestry to the individuals who emigrated from Africa. In this book, I will use the term *African American* because it emphasizes the unique cultural heritage of this group of people. Following this same line of reasoning, I will use the terms *European American* (instead of *Caucasian* or *White*), *Native American* (instead of *Indian* or *American Indian*), *Asian American*, and *Hispanic American*.

These labels are not perfect. Sometimes, they blur distinctions within ethnic groups. For example, the term *Hispanic American* ignores differences between individuals who came to the United States from Puerto Rico, Mexico, and Guatemala; the term *Asian American* blurs variations among people whose heritage is Japanese, Chinese, or Korean. Whenever researchers identified the subgroups in their research sample, I will use the more specific terms in describing results. When you see the more general terms, remember that conclusions may not apply to all subgroups within the group.

## A Final Word

I wrote this book to make child development come alive for my students at Purdue. Although I can't teach you directly, I hope this book sparks your interest in children and their development. Please let me know what you like and dislike about the book so that I can improve it in later editions. You can send email to me at **rkail@cla.purdue.edu**—I'd love to hear from you.

# ABOUT THE AUTHOR

**Robert V. Kail** is Professor of Psychological Sciences at Purdue University. His undergraduate degree is from Ohio Wesleyan University and his Ph.D. is from the University of Michigan. Kail is editor of the *Journal of Experimental Child Psychology* and of *Advances in Child Development and Behavior*. He received the McCandless Young Scientist Award from the American Psychological Association, was named the Distinguished Sesquicentennial Alumnus in Psychology by Ohio Wesleyan University, and is a fellow of the Association for Psychological Science. His research focuses on cognitive development during childhood and adolescence. Away from the office, he enjoys photography and working out.

**Beginning as a microscopic cell, every person takes a fascinating journey designed to lead to adulthood.** This trip is filled with remarkably interesting and challenging events. In this book, we'll trace this journey as we learn about the science of child development, a multidisciplinary study of all aspects of growth from conception to young adulthood. As an adult, you've already lived the years that are the heart of this book. I hope you enjoy reviewing your own developmental path from the perspective of child-development research and that this perspective leads you to new insights into the developmental forces that have made you the person you are today.

Chapter 1 sets the stage for our study of child development. We begin, in Module 1.1, by looking at philosophical foundations for child development and the events that led to the creation of child development as a new science. In Module 1.2, we examine theories that are central to the science of child development. In Module 1.3, we explore themes that guide much research in child development. Finally, in Module 1.4, we learn about the methods scientists use to study children and their development.

1.1  Setting the Stage

1.2  Foundational Theories of Child Development

1.3  Themes in Child-Development Research

1.4  Doing Child-Development Research

# The Science of Child Development

1

2   Genetic Bases of Child Development

3   Prenatal Development, Birth, and the Newborn

4   Growth and Health

5   Perceptual and Motor Development

6   Theories of Cognitive Development

7   Cognitive Processes and Academic Skills

8   Intelligence and Individual Differences in Cognition

9   Language and Communication

10  Emotional Development

11  Understanding Self and Others

12  Moral Understanding and Behavior

13  Gender and Development

14  Family Relationships

15  Influences Beyond the Family

# 1.1    SETTING THE STAGE

**Historical Views of Children and Childhood**

**Origins of a New Science**

## LEARNING OBJECTIVES

- What ideas did philosophers have about children and childhood?

- How did the modern science of child development emerge?

- How do child-development scientists use research findings to improve children's lives?

*Kendra loves her 12-month-old son Joshua, but she is eager to return to her job as a loan officer at a local bank. Kendra knows a woman in her neighborhood who has cared for some of her friends' children and they all think she is wonderful. But down deep Kendra wishes she knew more about whether this type of care is really best for Joshua. She also wishes that her neighbor's day-care center had a "stamp of approval" from someone who knows how to evaluate these facilities.*

Kendra is worried about the best way to care for her infant son. This is certainly not the first question she's raised concerning her son because Kendra dearly loves him and wants what's best for his development. When Joshua was just a few months old, Kendra wondered if he could recognize her face and her voice. And as her son grows she'll continue to have questions: Why is he so shy at preschool? Should he take classes for gifted children or would he be better off in regular classes? What can she do to be sure that he doesn't use drugs?

These questions—and hundreds more like them—touch issues and concerns that parents such as Kendra confront regularly as they do their best to rear their children. And parents aren't the only ones asking these questions. Many professionals who deal with children—teachers, health-care providers, and social workers, for example—often wonder what's best for children's development. Does children's self-esteem affect their success in school? Should we believe young children when they claim they have been abused? And ultimately, government officials must decide what programs and laws provide the greatest benefit for children and their families. How does welfare reform affect families? Are teenagers less likely to have sex when they participate in abstinence-only programs?

So many questions—all of them important! Fortunately, the field of child development, which traces physical, mental, social, and emotional development from conception to maturity, provides answers to many of them. To begin, let's look at the origins of child development as a science.

## Historical Views of Children and Childhood

*Philosophers have long asked questions about child development but only since the 19th century have scientists studied child development.*

For thousands of years, philosophers have speculated on the fundamental nature of childhood and the conditions that foster children's well-being. The famous Greek philosophers, Plato (428–347 B.C.) and Aristotle (384–322 B.C.), wrote about ideal forms of government and believed that schools and parents had the responsibility for teaching children the self-control that would make them effective citizens. But both philosophers, particularly Aristotle, also worried that too much self-discipline would stifle children's initiative and individuality, making them unfit as leaders.

Given their interest in education, it's not surprising that Plato and Aristotle also had ideas about knowledge and how it was acquired. Plato believed that experience could not be the source of knowledge because human senses are too fallible. He argued, instead, that children are born with innate knowledge of many concrete objects, such as animals and people, as well as with knowledge of abstractions such as courage, love, and goodness. In Plato's view, children's sensory experiences simply trigger knowledge that they've had since birth. The first time that a child sees a dog, her innate knowledge allows her to recognize it as such; no learning is necessary. In contrast, Aristotle denied the existence of innate knowledge; instead, knowledge is rooted in perceptual experience. Children acquire knowledge piece by piece, based on the information provided by their senses. Aristotle likened a child's mind to a tablet that is blank, ready for experience to do the writing.

These contrasting views resurfaced during the Age of Enlightenment. The English philosopher John Locke (1632–1704), asserting that the human infant is a *tabula rasa* or "blank slate," claimed that experience molds the infant, child, adolescent, and adult into a unique individual. According to Locke, parents should instruct, reward, and discipline young children, gradually relaxing their authority as children grow. In our opening vignette, Locke would advise Kendra that child-care experiences will surely affect Joshua's development (though Locke would not specify how).

During the following century, Locke's view was challenged by the French philosopher Jean Jacques Rousseau (1712–1778), who believed that newborns are endowed with an innate sense of justice and morality that unfolds naturally as children grow. In this unfolding, children move through the developmental stages that we recognize today—infancy, childhood, and adolescence. And instead of emphasizing parental discipline, Rousseau argued that parents should be responsive and encouraged them to be receptive to their children's needs. Rousseau would downplay the impact of child-care experiences per se on Joshua's development, insisting instead that the key is having caregivers who are responsive to the child's needs.

Rousseau shared Plato's view that children begin their developmental journeys well prepared with a stockpile of knowledge. Locke, like Aristotle 2,000 years before him, believed that children begin these journeys very lightly packed but pick up necessary knowledge along the way, through experience. These philosophical debates might have continued for millennia except for a landmark event: the emergence of child development as a science.

**Q&A Question**

Morgan is an 18-month-old and her father believes it's important that she have a very structured day, one that includes some physical activity, time spent reading and doing puzzles, and, finally, lots of reassuring hugs and kisses. Is Morgan's dad a believer in the Rousseau or Locke view of childhood? | **1.1**

## Origins of a New Science

The push toward child development as a science came from two unexpected sources: making cotton and a cruise. Let's start with cotton. For much of recorded history, as soon as children no longer needed constant care from adults—by about 5 to 7 years of age—they were considered grown up and entered the world of work. Many children worked at home, in the fields, or were apprenticed to learn a trade. Life for child workers changed radically—for the worse—with the Industrial Revolution. Beginning in the mid-1700s, England was transformed from a largely rural nation relying on agriculture to an urban-oriented society organized around factories, including textile mills that produced cotton cloth. Children moved with their families to cities and worked long hours in factories under horrendous conditions and for little pay. Accidents were common and many children were maimed or killed. In the textile mills, for example, the youngest children often had the job of picking up loose cotton from beneath huge power looms while the machines were in operation.

Reformers, appalled at these conditions, worked hard to enact legislation that would limit child labor and put more children in schools. These were prominent political debates throughout much of the 1800s; after all, the factory owners were among the most powerful people in Britain and they adamantly opposed efforts to limit their access to plentiful, cheap labor. But the reformers ultimately carried the day and in the process made the well-being of children a national concern.

As for the aforementioned cruise, this was no week-long voyage through tropical islands; it was a five-year journey around the world and the traveler was Charles Darwin. Throughout his trip, Darwin made meticulous notes of the plants and animals that he observed. Upon his return to London, Darwin worked many years to construct a theory that would account for his observations. He argued that individuals within a species differ; some individuals are better adapted to an environment, making them more likely to survive and to pass along their characteristics to future generations.

The outcome—his well-known theory of evolution—took the scientific world by storm; its impact throughout the 19th century was every bit as great as the impact of Einstein's theory of relativity on science in the 20th century. Although a theory of evolution may seem far removed from a science of child development, there are two important links. First, Darwin's focus on the origin of species (the title of the book outlining his theory) started interest in the origins of human behavior in children. Second, some scientists of the day noted similarities between Darwin's description of evolutionary change in species and age-related changes in human behavior. **This prompted many scientists—including Darwin himself—to write what became known as *baby biographies*, detailed, systematic observations of individual children.** The observations in the biographies were often subjective and conclusions were sometimes reached on the basis of minimal evidence. Nevertheless, the systematic and extensive records in baby biographies paved the way for objective, analytic research.

> Reformers' concern for children's well being and scientists' enthusiasm for Darwin's theory of evolution paved the way for a new science of child development.

Taking the lead in the new science at the dawn of the 20th century was G. Stanley Hall (1844–1924), who generated theories of child development based on evolutionary theory and conducted many studies to determine age trends in children's beliefs and feelings about a range of topics. More importantly, Hall founded the first scientific journal in English where scientists could publish findings from child-development research. Hall also founded a child-study institute at Clark University and was the first president of the American Psychological Association.

Meanwhile, in France Alfred Binet (1857–1911) had begun to devise the first mental tests, which we'll examine in Module 8.2. In Austria, Sigmund Freud (1856–1939) had startled the world with his suggestion that the experiences of early childhood seemed to account for patterns of behavior in adulthood; and American John B. Watson (1878–1958), the founder of behaviorism, had begun to write and lecture on the importance of reward and punishment for child-rearing practices. (You'll learn more about Freud's and Watson's contributions in the next module.)

In 1933, these emerging scientific forces came together in a new interdisciplinary organization, the Society for Research in Child Development (SRCD). Among its members were psychologists, physicians, educators, anthropologists, and biologists, all of whom were linked by a common interest in discovering the conditions that would promote children's welfare and foster their development (Parke, 2004). In the ensuing years, SRCD has grown to a membership of more than 5,000 scientists and is now the main professional organization for child-development researchers. It continues to promote multidisciplinary research and to encourage application of research findings to improve children's lives.

Progress in the field was halted by World War II, when most child-development scientists in America abandoned their research to assist the war effort (Sears, 1975). But by the 1950s and 1960s the field was thriving, marking the beginning of the modern era of child-development research. Most of the research described in this book has its origins in work done during these years.

Child-development researchers have learned much during these 50 years. Because of this success, a new branch of child-development research has emerged. *Applied developmental science* **uses developmental research to promote healthy development, particularly for vulnerable children and families** (Fisher & Lerner, 2005). Scientists with this research interest contribute to sound family policy through a number of distinct pathways (White, 1996). Some ensure that the general consideration of policy issues and options is based on factual knowledge derived from child-development research: When government officials need to address problems affecting children, child-development experts can provide useful information about children and their development (Fasig, 2002). Others contribute by serving as advocates for children. Working with a child-advocacy group, child-development researchers can alert policymakers to children's needs and can argue for family policy that addresses those needs. Still other child-development experts evaluate the impact of government policies (e.g., the No Child Left Behind Act) on children and families. Finally, one of the best ways to sway policymakers is to create an actual program that works. When researchers create a program that effectively combats problems affecting children or adolescents (e.g., sudden infant death syndrome or teenage pregnancy), this can become powerful ammunition for influencing policy.

Thus, from its origins more than 100 years ago, modern child-development science has become a mature discipline. It has generated a vast catalog of knowledge of children from which exciting discoveries continue to emanate. Scientists actively use this knowledge to improve children's lives, as we'll see in the "Child Development and Family Policy" features that appear in many chapters throughout the book.

This research effort is rooted in a set of foundational theories, which are the focus of the next module.

## CHECK YOUR LEARNING

**RECALL**  What were the two major forces that led to the creation of child-development science?

Who were the leaders of the newly found field of child development before the formation of the Society for Research in Child Development?

**INTERPRET**  Explain the similarities between Rousseau's and Plato's views of child development; how did their views differ from those shared by Locke and Aristotle?

**APPLY**  Suppose a child-development researcher was an expert on the impact of nutrition on children's physical and emotional development. Describe several different ways in which the researcher might help to inform public policy concerning children's nutrition.

His emphasis on structure suggests that he believes in the importance of children's experiences, which is a basic concept in Locke's view of childhood.   **1.1**

# 1.2　FOUNDATIONAL THEORIES OF CHILD DEVELOPMENT

The Biological Perspective

The Psychodynamic Perspective

The Learning Perspective

The Cognitive-Developmental Perspective

The Contextual Perspective

## LEARNING OBJECTIVES

- What are the major tenets of the biological perspective?
- How do psychodynamic theories account for development?
- What is the focus of learning theories?
- How do cognitive-developmental theories explain changes in children's thinking?
- What are the main points of the contextual approach?

*Will has just graduated from high school, first in his class. For his proud mother, Betty, this is a time to reflect on Will's past and ponder his future. Will has always been a happy, easygoing child—a joy to rear. And he's always been interested in learning. Betty wonders why he is so perpetually good-natured and so curious. If she knew the secret, she laughed, she could write a best-selling book and be a guest on Oprah!*

Before you read on, stop for a moment and think about Betty's question. How would you explain Will's interest in learning, his good nature, and his curiosity? Perhaps Betty has been a fantastic mother, doing all the right things at just the right time? Perhaps year after year his teachers quickly recognized Will's curiosity and encouraged it? Or was it simply Will's destiny to be this way? Each of these explanations is a very simple theory: Each tries to explain Will's curiosity and good nature. In child-development research, theories are much more complicated, but the purpose is the same—to explain behavior and development. **In child development, a *theory* is an organized set of ideas that is designed to explain and make predictions about development.**

A theory leads to hypotheses that we can test in research; in the process, each hypothesis is confirmed or rejected. Think about the different explanations for Will's behavior. Each one leads to unique hypotheses. If, for example, teachers' encouragement has caused Will to be curious, we hypothesize that he should no longer be curious if teachers stop encouraging that curiosity. When the outcomes of research are as hypothesized, the theory gains support. When results run counter to the hypothesis, the theory is incorrect and is revised.

Perhaps now you see why theories are essential for child-development research: They are the source of hypotheses for research, which often lead to changes in the theories. These revised theories then provide the basis for new hypotheses, which lead to new research, and the cycle continues. With each step along the way, the theory comes closer to becoming a complete account. Throughout the book, in "Spotlight on Theories" features we'll look at specific theories, the hypotheses derived from them, and the outcomes of research testing those hypotheses.

Over the 100-year history of child development as a science, many theories have guided research and thinking about children's development. The earliest developmental theories were useful in generating research, but findings from that research led child-development scientists to newer, improved theories. In this module, I describe the earlier theories that provide the scientific foundation

*Five major theoretical perspectives have guided most research on children and their development.*

for modern ones, because newer theories are best understood in terms of their historical roots.

Some theories share assumptions and ideas about children and development; grouped together they form five major theoretical perspectives in child-development research: the biological, psychodynamic, learning, cognitive-developmental, and contextual perspectives. As you read about each perspective in the next few pages, think about how it differs from the others in its view of development.

## The Biological Perspective

According to the biological perspective, intellectual and personality development, as well as physical and motor development, proceed according to a biological plan. One of the first biological theories, maturational theory, was proposed by Arnold Gesell (1880–1961). **According to *maturational theory*, child development reflects a specific and prearranged scheme or plan within the body.** In Gesell's view, development is simply a natural unfolding of a biological plan; experience matters little. Like Jean Jacques Rousseau 200 years before him, Gesell encouraged parents to let their children develop naturally. Without interference from adults, Gesell claimed, such behaviors as speech, play, and reasoning would emerge spontaneously according to a predetermined developmental timetable.

Maturational theory was discarded because it had little to say about the impact of the environment on children's development. However, other biological theories give greater weight to experience. *Ethological theory* views development from an evolutionary perspective. In this theory, many behaviors are adaptive—they have survival value. For example, clinging, grasping, and crying are adaptive for infants because they elicit caregiving from adults. Ethological theorists assume that people inherit many of these adaptive behaviors.

So far, ethological theory seems like maturational theory, with a dash of evolution for taste. How does experience fit in? Ethologists believe that all animals are biologically programmed so that some kinds of learning occur only at certain ages. **A *critical period* is the time in development when a specific type of learning can take place; before or after the critical period, the same learning is difficult or even impossible.**

One of the best-known examples of a critical period comes from the work of Konrad Lorenz (1903–1989), a Nobel Prize–winning Austrian zoologist. Lorenz noticed that newly hatched chicks follow their mother about. He theorized that chicks are biologically programmed to follow the first moving object that they see after hatching. **Usually this was the mother, so following her was the first step in *imprinting*, creating an emotional bond with the mother.** Lorenz tested his theory by showing that if he removed the mother immediately after the chicks hatched and replaced it with another moving object, the chicks would follow that object and treat it as "Mother." As the photo shows, this included Lorenz himself!

Lorenz also discovered that the chick had to see the moving object within about a day of hatching. Otherwise, the chick would not imprint on the moving object. In other words, the critical period for imprinting lasts about a day; when chicks experience the moving object outside of the critical period, imprinting does not take place. Even though the underlying mechanism is biological, experience is essential for triggering programmed, adaptive behaviors.

### Q&A Question

Keunho and Young-shin | 1.2
are sisters who moved to Toronto from Korea when they were 15 and 10 years old, respectively. Although both of them have spoken English almost exclusively since their arrival in Canada, Keunho still speaks with a bit of an accent and occasionally makes grammatical errors; Young-shin's English is flawless—she speaks like a native. How could you explain Young-shin's greater skill in terms of a critical period?

Newly hatched chicks follow the first moving object that they see, treating it as "Mother" even when it's a human.

Ethological theory and maturational theory both highlight the biological bases of child development. Biological theorists remind us that children's genes, which are the product of a long evolutionary history, influence virtually every aspect of children's development. Consequently, a biological theorist would tell Betty that Will's good nature and his outstanding academic record are both largely products of heredity.

## The Psychodynamic Perspective

The psychodynamic perspective is the oldest scientific perspective on child development, tracing its roots to the work of Sigmund Freud (1856–1939) in the late 19th and early 20th centuries. Freud was a physician who specialized in diseases of the nervous system. Many of his patients were adults who suffered from ailments that seemed to have no obvious biological causes. As Freud listened to his patients describe their problems and their lives, he became convinced that early experiences establish patterns that endure throughout a person's life. **Using his patients' case histories, Freud created the first *psychodynamic theory*, which holds that development is largely determined by how well people resolve conflicts they face at different ages.**

As part of his theory, Freud argued that personality includes three primary components that emerge at distinct ages. **The *id* is a reservoir of primitive instincts and drives.** Present at birth, the id presses for immediate gratification of bodily needs and wants. A hungry baby crying illustrates the id in action. **The *ego* is the practical, rational component of personality.** The ego begins to emerge during the first year of life, as infants learn that they cannot always have what they want. The ego tries to resolve conflicts that occur when the instinctive desires of the id encounter the obstacles of the real world. The ego often tries to channel the id's impulsive demands into socially more acceptable channels. For example, the child in the photo without the toy is obviously envious of the child who has the toy. According to Freud, the id would urge the child to grab the toy, but the ego would encourage the child to play with the peer and, in the process, the attractive toy.

**The third component of personality, the *superego*, is the "moral agent" in the child's personality.** It emerges during the preschool years as children begin to internalize adult standards of right and wrong. If the peer in the previous example left the attractive toy unattended, the id might tell the child to grab the toy and run; the superego would remind the child that taking another's toy would be wrong.

According to Freud's theory, the id would encourage the child on the left to grab the toy away from the child but the superego would remind him that this would be wrong.

Subsequently, scientists criticized many aspects of Freud's work. They argued that his views of development were based on adults recalling the past, not from observing children directly. Although these and other shortcomings have undermined much of Freud's theory, two of his insights have had lasting impact on child-development research and theory. First, he noted that early experiences can have enduring effects on children's development. Second, he suggested that children often experience conflict between what they want to do and what they know they should do.

**ERIKSON'S PSYCHOSOCIAL THEORY.** Erik Erikson (1902–1994), Freud's student, embraced Freud's idea of conflict, but he emphasized the psychological and social aspects of conflict rather than the biological and physical aspects. **In Erikson's *psychosocial theory*, development consists of a sequence of stages, each defined by a unique crisis or challenge.** The complete theory includes the eight stages shown in the table below. The name of each stage reflects the challenge that individuals face at a particular age. For example, the challenge for young adults is to become involved in a loving relationship. Adults who establish this relationship experience intimacy; those who don't, experience isolation.

**TABLE 1-1**

### ERIKSON'S EIGHT STAGES OF PSYCHOSOCIAL DEVELOPMENT

| Psychosocial Stage | Age | Challenge |
|---|---|---|
| Basic trust versus mistrust | Birth to 1 year | To develop a sense that the world is safe, a "good place" |
| Autonomy versus shame and doubt | 1 to 3 years | To realize that one is an independent person who can make decisions |
| Initiative versus guilt | 3 to 6 years | To develop a willingness to try new things and to handle failure |
| Industry versus inferiority | 6 years to adolescence | To learn basic skills and to work with others |
| Identity versus identity confusion | Adolescence | To develop a lasting, integrated sense of self |
| Intimacy versus isolation | Young adulthood | To commit to another in a loving relationship |
| Generativity versus stagnation | Middle adulthood | To contribute to younger people, through child rearing, child care, or other productive work |
| Integrity versus despair | Late life | To view one's life as satisfactory and worth living |

Erikson also argued that the earlier stages of psychosocial development provide the foundation for the later stages. For example, adolescents who do not meet the challenge of developing an identity will not establish truly intimate relationships. Instead, they will become overly dependent on their partners as a source of identity.

Whether we call them conflicts, challenges, or crises, the psychodynamic perspective emphasizes that the trek to adulthood is difficult because the path is strewn with obstacles. Outcomes of development reflect the manner and ease with which children surmount life's barriers. When children overcome early obstacles easily, they are better able to handle the later ones. Returning to this module's opening vignette, a psychodynamic theorist would tell Betty that Will's cheerful disposition and his academic record suggest that he handled life's early obstacles well, which is a good sign for his future development.

*Psychodynamic theories emphasize that development is a product of the child's responses to life's challenges.*

## The Learning Perspective

Learning theorists endorse John Locke's view that the infant's mind is a blank slate on which experience writes. John Watson (1878–1958) was the first theorist to apply this approach to child development. Watson argued that learning determines what children will be. He assumed that with the correct techniques anything could be learned by almost anyone. In other words, in Watson's view, experience was just about all that mattered in determining the course of development.

**EARLY LEARNING THEORIES.**  Watson did little research to support his claims, but B. F. Skinner (1904–1990) filled this gap. **Skinner studied** *operant conditioning*, **in which the consequences of a behavior determine whether a behavior is**

**repeated in the future.** Skinner showed that two kinds of consequences were especially influential. **A *reinforcement* is a consequence that increases the future likelihood of the behavior that it follows.** Positive reinforcement consists of giving a reward—such as chocolate, gold stars, or paychecks—to increase the likelihood of repeating a previous behavior. When a child is reluctant to clear her room, her parents could use positive reinforcement to encourage her. Every time she cleaned her room, they could reinforce her with praise, food, or money. Negative reinforcement consists of rewarding people by taking away unpleasant things. The same parents could use negative reinforcement by saying that whenever she cleaned her room, she wouldn't have to wash the dishes or fold laundry.

**A *punishment* is a consequence that decreases the future likelihood of the behavior that it follows.** Punishment suppresses a behavior by either adding something aversive or by withholding a pleasant event. When the child failed to clean her room, the parents could punish her by making her do extra chores (adding something aversive) or by not allowing her to watch television (withholding a pleasant event).

Skinner's research was done primarily with animals, but child-development researchers soon showed that the principles of operant conditioning could be extended readily to children's behavior (Baer & Wolf, 1968). Applied properly, reinforcement and punishment are indeed powerful influences on children. However, researchers discovered that children sometimes learn without reinforcement or punishment. **Children learn much simply by watching those around them, which is known as *imitation* or *observational learning*.** For example, imitation occurs when one toddler throws a toy after seeing a peer do so or when a school-age child offers to help an older adult carry groceries because she's seen her parents do the same, or, as in the photo, when a son tries to shave like his father.

**SOCIAL COGNITIVE THEORY.** Perhaps imitation makes you think of "monkey-see, monkey-do," or simple mimicking. Early investigators had this view, too, but research quickly showed that this was wrong. Children do not always imitate what they see around them. Children are more likely to imitate if the person they see is popular, smart, or talented. They're also more likely to imitate when the behavior they see is rewarded than when it is punished. Findings like these imply that imitation is more complex than sheer mimicry. Children do not mechanically copy what they see and hear; instead, they look to others for information about appropriate behavior. When popular, smart peers are reinforced for behaving in a particular way, it makes sense to imitate them.

**Albert Bandura (1925–) based his *social cognitive theory* on this more complex view of reward, punishment, and imitation.** Bandura calls his theory "cognitive" because he believes that children are actively trying to understand what goes on in their world; the theory is "social" because, along with reinforcement and punishment, what other people do is an important source of information about the world (Bandura, 2000).

Throughout development, children learn much from imitating the actions of others.

The learning perspective emphasizes the role of experience in children's development.

**Bandura also argues that experience gives children a sense of *self-efficacy*, beliefs about their own abilities and talents.** Self-efficacy beliefs help determine when children will imitate others. A child who sees himself as athletically untalented, for example, will not try to imitate Tiger Woods driving a golf ball, despite the fact that he is obviously talented and popular. But the youngster in the photo on page 13 is likely to imitate Tiger, because he believes he's talented and thus it makes sense to try to imitate him. Thus, whether children imitate others depends on who the other person is, whether that person's behavior is rewarded, and the children's beliefs about their own talents.

Bandura's social cognitive theory is a far cry from Skinner's operant conditioning. The social cognitive child, who actively interprets events, has replaced the operant conditioning child, who responds mechanically to reinforcement and punishment. Nevertheless, Skinner, Bandura, and all learning theorists share the view that experience propels children along their developmental journeys. Returning to this module's opening scenario, they would tell Betty that she can thank experience for making Will both happy and successful academically.

## The Cognitive-Developmental Perspective

**The *cognitive-developmental perspective* focuses on how children think and on how their thinking changes over time.** Jean Piaget (1896–1980) proposed the best known of these theories. He believed that children naturally try to make sense of their world. Throughout infancy, childhood, and adolescence, youngsters want to understand the workings of both the physical and the social world. For example, infants want to know about objects: "What happens when I push this toy off the table?" And babies want to know about people: "Who is this person who feeds and cares for me?"

Piaget argued that in their efforts to comprehend their world, children act like scientists in creating theories about the physical and social worlds. They try to weave all that they know about objects and people into a complete theory. Children's theories are tested daily by experience because their theories lead them to expect certain things to happen. As with real scientific theories, when the predicted events do occur, a child's belief in her theory grows stronger. When the predicted events do not occur, the child must revise her theory. For example, think about the baby in the photo and her theory of objects like the rattle she's holding. Her theory of objects might include the idea that "If I let go, the rattle will fall to the floor." If the infant drops some other object—a plate or an article of clothing—she will find that it, too, falls to the floor and can make the theory more general: Objects that are dropped fall to the floor.

Piaget also believed that at a few critical points in development, children realize their theories have basic flaws. When this happens, they revise their theories radically. These changes are so fundamental that the revised theory is, in many respects, a brand-new theory. Piaget claimed that radical revisions occur three times in development: once at about age 2, a second time at about age 7, and a third time just before adolescence. These radical changes mean children go through four distinct stages in cognitive development. Each stage represents a fundamental change in how children understand and organize their environment, and each stage is characterized by more sophisticated types of reasoning. For example, the sensorimotor stage begins at birth and lasts until about age 2. As the name implies, sensorimotor thinking is closely linked to the infant's sensory and motor skills. This stage and the three later stages are shown in the table on the top of page 14.

When someone is as talented as Tiger Woods, it makes sense for others to try to imitate him—and young children often do just that (for Tiger and other talented people).

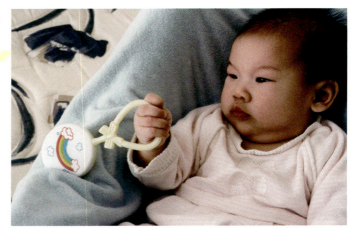

In Piaget's theory, even infants have rudimentary theories about objects and their properties.

**TABLE 1-2**

## PIAGET'S FOUR STAGES OF COGNITIVE DEVELOPMENT

| Stage | Approximate Age | Characteristics |
|-------|-----------------|-----------------|
| Sensorimotor | Birth to 2 years | Infant's knowledge of the world is based on senses and motor skills. By the end of the period, infant uses mental representations. |
| Preoperational | 2 to 6 years | Child learns how to use symbols such as words and numbers to represent aspects of the world, but relates to the world only through his or her perspective. |
| Concrete operational | 7 to 11 years | Child understands and applies logical operations to experiences, provided they are focused on the here and now. |
| Formal operational | Adolescence and beyond | Adolescent or adult thinks abstractly, speculates on hypothetical situations, and reasons deductively about what may be possible. |

According to Piaget, children's thinking becomes more sophisticated as they develop, reflecting the more sophisticated theories that children create. Returning to our opening scenario, Piaget would have little to say about Will's good nature. As for his academic success, Piaget would explain that all children naturally want to understand their worlds; Will is simply unusually skilled in this regard. In Module 6.1, we will further explore Piaget's contribution to our understanding of cognitive development, as well as more modern theories.

### The Contextual Perspective

Most developmentalists agree that the environment is an important force in development. Traditionally, however, most theories of child development have emphasized environmental forces that affect children directly. Examples of direct environmental influences would be a parent praising a child, an older sibling teasing a younger one, and a nursery-school teacher discouraging girls from playing with trucks. These direct influences are important in children's lives, but in the contextual perspective they are simply one part of a much larger system, where each element of the system influences all other elements. This larger system includes one's parents and siblings as well as important individuals outside of the family, such as extended family, friends, and teachers. The system also includes institutions that influence development, such as schools, television, the workplace, and a church, temple, or mosque.

**All these people and institutions fit together to form a person's *culture*—the knowledge, attitudes, and behavior associated with a group of people.** Culture can refer to a particular country or people (e.g., French culture), to a specific point in time (e.g., popular culture of the 1990s), or to groups of individuals who maintain specific, identifiable cultural traditions, such as African American families that celebrate Kwanzaa. A culture provides the context in which a child develops and thus is a source of many important influences on development throughout childhood and adolescence.

> The contextual approach emphasizes the many different elements of culture that affect children's development.

One of the first theorists to emphasize cultural context in children's development was Lev Vygotsky (1896–1934). A Russian psychologist, Vygotsky focused on ways that adults convey to children the beliefs, customs, and skills of their culture. Vygotsky believed that because a fundamental aim of all societies is to enable children to acquire essential cultural values and skills, every aspect of a child's development must be considered against this backdrop. For example, most parents in the United States want their children to work hard in school and to be admitted to college, because earning a degree is one of the keys to getting a good job. In the same way, parents in Efe (a developing nation in Africa) want their children to learn to gather food, build houses, and, as you can see in the photo, to hunt; these skills are fundamental to the Efe for they are critical for survival in their environment. Vygotsky viewed development as an apprenticeship in which children develop when they work with skilled adults, including teachers and parents. In Module 6.2, we'll learn more about Vygotsky's distinctive contributions to our understanding of cognitive development.

Returning to our opening vignette, Vygotsky would agree with learning theorists in telling Betty that the environment has been pivotal in her son's amiable disposition and his academic achievements. However, the contextual theorist would insist that "environment" means much more than the reinforcements, punishments, and observations that are central to learning theory. The contextual theorist would emphasize the manner in which Betty had conveyed the value of curiosity and academic success to her son; also contributing to Will's development was Betty's membership in a cultural group that values doing well in school.

**THE BIG PICTURE.**   Comparing the basics of five major perspectives in 5 pages is like trying to see all the major sights of a large city in a day: It can be done, but it's demanding and, after a while, everything blurs together. Relax. The Summary Table gives a capsule account of all five perspectives and their important theories.

According to the contextual view, parents help children master the essential values and skills of their culture, such as learning how to hunt.

## SUMMARY TABLE

### CHARACTERISTICS OF DEVELOPMENTAL PERSPECTIVES

| Perspective | Key Assumptions | Illustrative Theories |
| --- | --- | --- |
| Biological | Development is determined primarily by biological forces. | *Maturational theory:* emphasizes development as a natural unfolding of a biological plan<br>*Ethological theory:* emphasizes that children's and parents' behavior has adapted to meet specific environmental challenges |
| Psychodynamic | Development is determined primarily by how a child resolves conflicts at different ages. | *Freud's theory:* emphasizes the conflict between primitive biological forces and societal standards for right and wrong<br>*Erikson's theory:* emphasizes the challenges posed by the formation of trust, autonomy, initiative, industry, and identity |
| Learning | Development is determined primarily by a child's environment. | *Skinner's operant conditioning:* emphasizes the role of reinforcement and punishment<br>*Bandura's social cognitive theory:* emphasizes children's efforts to understand their world, using reinforcement, punishment, and others' behavior |
| Cognitive-Developmental | Development reflects children's efforts to understand the world. | *Piaget's theory:* emphasizes the different stages of thinking that result from children's changing theories of the world |
| Contextual | Development is influenced by immediate and more distant environments, which typically influence each other. | *Vygotsky's theory:* emphasizes the role of parents (and other adults) in conveying culture to the next generation |

These perspectives are the basis for contemporary theories that I introduce throughout this book. For example, Piaget's theory is the forerunner of modern explanations of infants' understanding of objects and of preschoolers' theory of mind (both described in Module 6.3). Similarly, Erikson's theory has contributed to work on mother–infant attachment (see Module 10.3) and formation of identity during adolescence (see Module 11.1).

The modern theories described throughout the book are derived from all five perspectives listed in the Summary Table on page 15. Why? Because no single perspective provides a truly complete explanation of all aspects of children's development. Theories from the cognitive-developmental perspective are useful for understanding how children's thinking changes as they grow older. By contrast, theories from the contextual and learning perspectives are particularly valuable in explaining how environmental forces such as parents, peers, schools, and culture influence children's development. By drawing on all the perspectives, we'll be better able to understand the different forces that contribute to children's development. Just as you can better appreciate a beautiful painting by examining it from different vantage points, child-development researchers often rely on multiple perspectives to understand why children develop as they do.

Another way to understand the forces that shape development is to consider several themes of development—themes that cut across different theoretical perspectives and specific research topics. We'll look at these themes in Module 1.3.

| 1.2 | Perhaps there is a critical period for |
|---|---|

language learning that ends at the beginning of adolescence. That is, children learn to speak a language like a native if exposed to that language extensively in childhood but not if most of their exposure takes place later, in adolescence and young adulthood. (We'll learn more about such a critical period in Chapter 9.)

### CHECK YOUR LEARNING

**RECALL** Describe different theories that typify the biological perspective on child development.

What are the main features of the contextual perspective on child development?

**INTERPRET** Explain the similarities and the differences in Erikson's and Piaget's stage theories of children's development.

**APPLY** Imagine that a friend complains that his 1-year-old seems to cry a lot compared to other 1-year-olds. How would theorists from each of the five perspectives listed in the table on page 15 explain his son's excessive crying?

# THEMES IN CHILD-DEVELOPMENT RESEARCH

## 1.3

**LEARNING OBJECTIVES**

- How well can developmental outcomes be predicted from early life?

- How do heredity and environment influence development?

- What role do children have in their own development?

- Is development in different domains connected?

Early Development Is Related to Later Development but Not Perfectly

Development Is Always Jointly Influenced by Heredity and Environment

Children Influence Their Own Development

Development in Different Domains Is Connected

*Javier Suarez smiled broadly as he held his newborn grandson for the first time. So many thoughts rushed into his mind—What would Ricardo experience growing up? Would the poor neighborhood they live in prevent him from reaching his potential? Would the family genes for good health be passed on? How would Ricardo's life growing up as a Chicano in the United States differ from Javier's own experiences growing up in Mexico?*

Like many grandparents, Javier wonders what the future holds for his grandson. And his questions actually reflect several fundamental themes in development that are the focus of this module. These four themes will provide you with a foundation to understand and organize the many specific facts about child development that fill the rest of this book. To help you do this, at the end of Chapters 2 through 15, "Unifying Themes" links the contents of the chapter to one of the themes.

Following are the four unifying themes.

## Early Development Is Related to Later Development but Not Perfectly

This theme concerns the predictability of development. Do you believe that happy, cheerful 5-year-olds remain outgoing and friendly throughout their lives? If you do, this shows that you believe development is a continuous process: According to this view, once a child begins down a particular developmental path, he or she stays on that path throughout life. In other words, if Ricardo is friendly and smart as a 5-year-old, he should be friendly and smart as a 15- and 25-year-old. The other view, that development is not continuous, is shown in the cartoon on page 18. Sweet, cooperative Trixie has become a demanding, assertive child. According to this view, Ricardo might be friendly and smart as a 5-year-old but obnoxious and foolish at 15 and quiet but wise at 25! **Thus, the *continuity-versus-discontinuity* issue is really about the "relatedness" of development: Are early aspects of development consistently related to later aspects?**

In reality, neither of these views is accurate. Development is not perfectly predictable. A friendly, smart 5-year-old does not guarantee a friendly, smart

*Development is not perfectly predictable; early development sets the stage for later development but does not fix it.*

Trixie's transition from a cooperative child to a demanding one illustrates discontinuity in development.

**1.3** As a child, Heather was painfully shy and withdrawn, but as an adult she was very outgoing, the life of many a party. What does Heather's life tell us about the continuity or discontinuity of shyness?

15- or 25-year-old, but the chances of a friendly, smart adult are greater than if the child were obnoxious and foolish. There are many ways to become a friendly and smart 15-year-old; being a friendly and smart 5-year-old is not a required step, but it is probably the most direct route!

## Development Is Always Jointly Influenced by Heredity and Environment

I want to introduce this theme with a story about my sons. Ben, my first son, was a delightful baby and toddler. He awoke each morning with a smile on his face, eager to start another fun-filled day. When Ben was upset, which occurred infrequently, he was quickly consoled by being held or rocked. I presumed that his cheerful disposition must reflect fabulous parenting. Consequently, I was stunned when my second son, Matt, spent much of the first year of his life being fussy and cranky. He was easily irritated and hard to soothe. Why wasn't the all-star parenting that had been so effective with Ben working with Matt? The answer, of course, is that Ben's parenting wasn't the sole cause of his happiness. I thought environmental influences accounted for his amiable disposition, but in fact, biological influences also played an important role.

This anecdote illustrates the *nature–nurture* issue: **What roles do biology (nature) and environment (nurture) play in child development?** If Ricardo is outgoing and friendly, is it due to his heredity or his experiences? Scientists once hoped to answer questions like this by identifying either heredity or environment as *the* cause. Their goal was to be able to say, for example, that intelligence was due to heredity or that personality was due to experience. Today, we know that virtually no aspects of child development are due exclusively to either heredity or environment. Instead, development is always shaped by both—nature and nurture interact. In fact, a major goal of child-development research is to understand how heredity and environment jointly determine children's development. Biology will be more influential in some areas and environment will prevail in others.

> *Virtually all aspects of development are determined by the combined forces of heredity and environment.*

## Children Influence Their Own Development

Whenever I teach child development, I ask students their plans for when they have children. How will they rear them? What do they want them to grow up to be? It's interesting to hear students' responses. Many have big plans for their future children. It's just as interesting, though, to watch students who already have children roll their eyes in a "You don't have a clue" way at what the others say. The parent-students in class admit that they, too, once had grand designs about child rearing. What they quickly learned, however, was that their children shaped the way in which they parented.

**These two points of view illustrate the *active–passive child* issue: Are children simply at the mercy of the environment (passive child) or do children actively influence their own development through their own unique individual characteristics (active child)?** The passive view corresponds to Locke's description of the child as a blank slate on which experience writes; whereas the active view corresponds to Rousseau's view of development as a natural unfolding that takes place within the child. Today, we know that experiences are indeed crucial but not always in the way Locke envisioned. Often, it's a child's interpretation of experiences that shapes his or her development. From birth, children like Ricardo are trying to make sense of their world; and in the process, they help shape their own destinies.

Also, a child's unique characteristics may cause him or her to have some experiences but not others. Think about the child in the photo, who loves having parents read picture books. Her excitement is contagious and makes her parents eager to read to her night after night. In contrast, if a child squirms or seems bored during reading, parents may be less likely to take the time to read to the child. In both cases, children's behavior during reading influences whether parents read to them in the future.

This youngster's obvious enjoyment makes it more likely that her parents will read to her more in the future, showing that children can influence their own development.

## Development in Different Domains Is Connected

Child-development researchers usually examine different domains or areas of development, such as physical growth, cognition, language, personality, and social relationships. One researcher might study how children learn to speak grammatically; another might explore children's reasoning about moral issues. Of course, you should *not* think of each aspect of development as an independent entity, one that is completely separate from the others. To the contrary, development in different domains is always intertwined. Cognitive and social development, for example, are not independent; advances in one area affect advances in the other. Ricardo's cognitive growth (e.g., he becomes an excellent student) will influence his social development (e.g., he becomes friends with peers who share his zeal for school).

Having introduced the themes, let's see them together once before we move on.

- *Continuity:* Early development is related to later development but not perfectly.
- *Nature and nurture:* Development is always jointly influenced by heredity and environment.
- *Active children:* Children influence their own development.
- *Connections:* Development in different domains is connected.

Most child-development scientists would agree that these are important general themes in children's development. However, just as lumber, bricks, pipe, and wiring can be used to assemble an incredible assortment of houses, these themes show up in different ways in the major theories of child development. Think, for example, about the nature–nurture issue. Of the five perspectives, the biological perspective is at one extreme in emphasizing the impact of nature; at the other extreme are the learning and contextual perspectives, which emphasize nurture.

The perspectives also see different degrees of connectedness across different domains of development. Piaget's cognitive-developmental theory takes the hardest line: Because children strive to have a single integrated theory to explain the world, cognitive and social growth are closely interconnected. That is, because children interpret all aspects of their lives with the same unified view of the world, everything is linked. The learning perspective, in contrast, holds that the degree of connectedness depends entirely on the nature of environmental influences. Similar environmental influences in different domains of children's lives produce many connections; dissimilar environmental influences would produce few connections.

---

### CHECK YOUR LEARNING

**RECALL**  Describe the difference between continuous development and discontinuous development.

Cite examples showing that development in different domains is connected.

**INTERPRET**  Explain the difference between nature and nurture and how these forces are thought to affect children's development.

**APPLY**  How might parents respond differently to a very active child compared to a very quiet child?

| **1.3** | In Heather's life, shyness was definitely discontinuous. Even though Heather was shy early in life, she was not shy later. |

## 1.4

# DOING CHILD-DEVELOPMENT RESEARCH

**Measurement in Child-Development Research**

**General Designs for Research**

**Designs for Studying Age-Related Change**

**Ethical Responsibilities**

**Communicating Research Results**

### LEARNING OBJECTIVES

- How do scientists measure topics of interest in children's development?

- What general research designs are used in child-development research? What designs are unique to the study of age-related change?

- What ethical procedures must researchers follow?

- How do researchers communicate results to other scientists?

> *Leah and Joan are both mothers of 10-year-old boys. Their sons have many friends, but the basis for the friendships is not obvious to the mothers. Leah believes that opposites attract—children form friendships with peers who have complementary interests and abilities. Joan doubts this; her son seems to seek out other boys who are near clones of himself in their interests and abilities.*

Suppose Leah and Joan know you're taking a course in child development, so they ask you to settle their argument. You know, from Module 1.2, that Leah and Joan each have simple theories about children's friendships. Leah's theory is that complementary children are more often friends, whereas Joan's theory is that similar children are more often friends. And you know that these theories should be tested with research. But how? In fact, like all scientists, child-development researchers follow the scientific method, which involves several steps:

- Identify a question to be answered or a phenomenon to be understood.
- Form a hypothesis that is a tentative answer to the question or a tentative explanation of the phenomenon.
- Select a method for collecting data that can be used to evaluate the hypothesis.

In our vignette, Leah and Joan have already taken the first two steps: They want to know why children become friends and each has a simple theory of this phenomenon, a theory that can be used to generate hypotheses. What remains is to find a method for collecting data, which is our focus for the rest of this module. How do child-development scientists select methods that provide evidence that's useful for testing hypotheses about child development?

In fact, in devising methods, child-development scientists must make several important decisions. They need to decide how to measure the topic; they must design their study; they must be sure their proposed research respects the rights of the individuals participating; and, once the study is complete, they must communicate their results to other researchers.

Child-development researchers do not always stick to this sequence of steps. For example, researchers usually consider the rights of research participants as they make each of the other decisions, perhaps rejecting a procedure because it violates those rights. Nevertheless, for simplicity, I will use this sequence to describe the steps in doing developmental research.

> Child-development researchers use the scientific method in which they formulate hypotheses, then collect data to evaluate those hypotheses.

## Measurement in Child-Development Research

Research usually begins by deciding how to measure the topic or behavior of interest. For example, the first step toward answering Leah and Joan's question about friendships would be to decide how to measure friendships. Child-development researchers typically use one of four approaches: observing systematically, using tasks to sample behavior, asking children for self reports, and measuring physiological changes.

**SYSTEMATIC OBSERVATION.  As the name implies, *systematic observation* involves watching children and carefully recording what they do or say.** Two forms of systematic observation are common. **In *naturalistic observation*, children are observed as they behave spontaneously in some real-life situation.** Of course, researchers can't keep track of everything that a child does. **Beforehand they must decide which *variables*—factors subject to change—to record.** Researchers studying friendship, for example, might decide to observe children in a school lunchroom like the one in the photo. They would record where each child sits and who talks to whom. They might also decide to observe children at the start of the first year in a middle school, because many children make new friends at this time.

Naturalistic observation is illustrated in research by Pepler, Craig, and Roberts (1998), who studied 6- to 12-year-olds' responses to their peers' prosocial and aggressive behavior. They used video cameras that overlooked a school playground; for 20 minutes, the experimenter video-taped one child before moving on to the next child on the list. This procedure was repeated another day, providing researchers with a 40-minute record of each child's behavior on the playground. From these video-tapes, the experimenter first measured instances of prosocial behavior (e.g., laughing with peers, friendly pats on the back) and antisocial behavior (e.g., hitting, kicking, verbal aggression), then looked at what children did when they were the focus of prosocial or antisocial behavior.

In naturalistic observation, researchers record children's spontaneous behavior in natural environments, such as this school cafeteria.

Structured observation involves creating a situation—asking children to play a game—that is likely to lead to behaviors of interest, such as competition.

**In** *structured observation*, **the researcher creates a setting likely to elicit the behavior of interest.** Structured observations are particularly useful for studying behaviors that are difficult to observe naturally. Some phenomena occur rarely, such as emergencies. An investigator using natural observations to study children's responses to emergencies wouldn't make much progress because, by definition, emergencies don't occur at predetermined times and locations. However, using structured observation, an investigator might stage an emergency, perhaps by having a nearby adult cry for help and then observing children's responses.

Other behaviors are difficult for researchers to observe because they occur in private settings, not public ones. For example, much interaction between friends takes place at home, where it would be difficult for investigators to observe unobtrusively. However, children who are friends could be asked to come to the researcher's laboratory, which might be furnished with comfortable chairs and tables. They would be asked to perform some activity typical of friends, such as playing a game or deciding what movie to see. By observing friends' interactions in a setting like the one in the photo (perhaps through a one-way mirror), researchers could learn more about how friends interact.

A good example of structured observation comes from a study by Belsky et al. (2005) of parenting strategies. These researchers had mothers and their 3-year-olds sit in a room that included many attractive toys. The child was given one toy, then mothers were asked to complete a questionnaire and simultaneously make sure that her child did not play with any of the other toys in the room. The 10-minute session was videotaped and later the researchers used the tapes to measure parental behavior, including, for example, the extent to which mothers overcontrolled their children (e.g., repeatedly saying, "Don't touch! Don't touch!" when the child wasn't interested in the toys). By creating a situation that would be challenging for mothers, Belsky et al. hoped to gain insights into parental behavior.

Although structured observations allow researchers to observe behaviors that would otherwise be difficult to study, investigators must be careful that the settings they create do not disturb the behavior of interest. For instance, observing friends as they play a game in a mock family room has many artificial aspects to it: The friends are not in their own homes, they were told (in general terms) what to do, and they know they're being observed. Any or all of these factors may cause children to behave differently than they would in the real world. Researchers must be careful that their method does not distort the behavior they are observing.

**SAMPLING BEHAVIOR WITH TASKS.**    When investigators can't observe a behavior directly, an alternative is to create tasks that are thought to sample the behavior of interest. For example, to measure memory, investigators sometimes use a digit span task: Children listen as a sequence of numbers is presented aloud. After the last digit is presented, children try to repeat the digits in the exact order in which they heard them. To measure children's ability to recognize different emotions, investigators sometimes use the task shown in the diagram. The child has been asked to look at the facial expressions and point to the person who is happy.

Sampling behavior with tasks is popular with child-development researchers because it is so convenient. A major problem with this approach, however, is whether the task really samples the behavior of interest. For example, asking children to judge emotions from photographs may not be valid, because it underestimates what children do in real life.

**FIGURE 1-1**

Can you think of reasons why this might be the case? I mention several reasons on page 35, just before "Check Your Learning."

**SELF REPORTS.** The third approach to measurement, using self reports, is actually a special case of using tasks to measure children's behavior. *Self reports* **are simply children's answers to questions about the topic of interest.** When questions are posed in written form, the report is a questionnaire; when questions are posed orally, the report is an interview. In either format, questions are created that probe different aspects of the topic of interest. For example, if you believe that children more often become friends when they have interests in common, then research participants might be told the following:

> Jacob and Dave just met each other at school. Jacob likes to read, plays the clarinet in the school orchestra, and is not interested in sports; Dave likes to watch videos on MTV, plays video games, and is a star on the soccer team. Do you think Jacob and Dave will become friends?

Child participants would decide, perhaps using a rating scale, if the boys are likely to become friends.

A typical questionnaire comes from a study by Rudolph, Caldwell, and Conley (2005), who were interested in measuring the extent to which children's views of themselves depended on their peers' approval. They created an 8-item questionnaire that included statements such as "When other kids like me, I feel happier about myself" and "I feel like I'm a bad person when other kids don't like me." Children indicated whether each statement was true of them, using a 5-point scale that ranged from "not at all" to "very much."

Self reports are useful because they can lead directly to information on the topic of interest. They are also relatively convenient, particularly when they can be administered to groups of children or adolescents. However, self reports are not always valid measures of children's behavior, because children's answers are sometimes inaccurate. Why? When asked about past events, children may not remember them accurately. For example, an adolescent asked about childhood friends may not remember those friendships well. **Also, children sometimes answer incorrectly due to** *response bias*—**some responses may be more socially acceptable than others, and children are more likely to select those than socially unacceptable answers.** For example, some children in the Rudolph et al. (2005) study may have been reluctant to admit that their self-perception was strongly influenced by peer approval. But, as long as investigators keep these weaknesses in mind, self reports are a valuable tool for child-development research.

**PHYSIOLOGICAL MEASURES.** A final approach is less common but can be very powerful—measuring children's physiological responses. Heart rate, for example, often slows down when children are paying close attention to something interesting. Consequently, researchers often measure heart rate to determine a child's degree of attention. As another example, the hormone cortisol is often secreted in response to stress. By measuring cortisol levels in children's saliva, scientists can determine when children are experiencing stress (Kertes & Gunnar, 2004).

As both of these examples suggest, physiological measures are usually specialized—they focus on a particular aspect of a child's behavior (attention and stress in the two examples). What's more, they're often used alongside other behaviorally oriented methods. A researcher studying stress might observe children, looking for overt signs of stress, ask parents to rate their children's stress, and also measure cortisol in children's saliva. If all three measures lead to the same conclusions about stress, then the researcher can be much more confident about those conclusions.

*Child-development researchers study children's development with systematic observation, sampling behavior with tasks, self reports, and physiological measures.*

Another important group of physiological measures includes those used to study brain activity. For centuries, philosophers and scientists could only guess about the role of the brain in thinking and feeling. But techniques developed during the past 25 years allow modern scientists to record many facets of brain functioning in real time—as children are performing specific tasks. I describe these methods in Module 4.3. For now, the important point is that child-development scientists are making great strides in identifying the brain regions associated with reasoning, memory, emotions, and other psychological functions.

The four approaches to measurement are presented in the Summary Table.

## SUMMARY TABLE

### WAYS OF MEASURING BEHAVIOR IN CHILD-DEVELOPMENT RESEARCH

| Method | Strength | Weakness |
|---|---|---|
| **Systematic observation** | | |
| Naturalistic observation | Captures children's behavior in its natural setting | Difficult to use with behaviors that are rare or that typically occur in private settings |
| Structured observation | Can be used to study behaviors that are rare or that typically occur in private settings | May be invalid if the structured setting distorts the behavior |
| Sampling behavior with tasks | Convenient—can be used to study most behaviors | May be invalid if the task does not sample behavior as it occurs naturally |
| Self reports (questionnaires and interviews) | Convenient—can be used to study most behaviors | May be invalid because children answer incorrectly due to forgetting or response bias |
| Physiological measures | Can provide independent, converging evidence that can confirm behavioral measures | Are often specific to particular types of behaviors and, consequently, may not be available for all topics |

If arguments like this one are more common among boys than girls, then that difference should be evident in observations of children's behavior as well as in other measures, such as self reports.

**EVALUATING MEASURES.**    After researchers choose a method of measurement, they must show that it is both reliable and valid. **A measure is *reliable* if the results are consistent over time.** A measure of friendship, for example, would be reliable if it yields the same results about friendship each time it is administered. All measures used in child-development research must be shown to be reliable, or they cannot be used. **A measure is *valid* if it really measures what researchers think it measures.** For example, a measure of friendship is only valid if it can be shown to actually measure friendship (and not, for example, popularity). Validity is often established by showing that the measure in question is closely related to another measure known to be valid. We could show the validity of a questionnaire that claims to measure friendship by showing that scores on the questionnaire are related to peers' and parents' measures of friendship.

Throughout this book, you'll come across many studies using these different methods. You'll also see that studies of the same topic or behavior often use different methods. This is very desirable: Because the approaches to measurement have different strengths and weaknesses, finding the same results regardless of the approach leads to particularly strong conclusions. Suppose, for example, that a researcher using self reports claims that arguments, like the one shown in the photo, are more common in boys' friendships than in girls' friendships. It would be reassuring that other investigators have found the same result from systematic observation and from sampling behavior with tasks.

**REPRESENTATIVE SAMPLING.**    Valid measures depend not only on the method of measurement, but also on the children who are tested. **Researchers are usually interested in broad groups of children called *populations.*** Examples of populations would be all American 7-year-olds or all African American adolescents. However, it would be extremely difficult for researchers to study every member of such large groups. **Virtually all studies include only a *sample* of children, a subset of the population.** Researchers must take care that their sample really represents the population of interest. An unrepresentative sample can lead to invalid research. For example, what would you think of a study of children's friendship if you learned that the sample consisted entirely of 8-year-olds whose friends were primarily preschool children? You would decide quite correctly that this sample is not representative of the population of 8-year-olds, and you would hesitate to generalize the results from this sample back to the population at large.

Much research is based on samples of children living in developed countries in North America and other parts of the world; those results may not generalize to children living in developing nations.

As you read on, you'll discover that much of the research I describe was conducted with samples of middle-class European American youngsters. Are these samples representative of all children in the United States? Of children like those in the photo who grow up in developing countries? Sometimes, but not always. Be careful not to assume that findings from this group necessarily apply to people in other groups.

## General Designs for Research

**Having formulated a hypothesis, identified variables, and selected a method to collect data on the topic or behavior of interest, researchers must then choose and implement an overall conceptual approach called a *research design.*** Child-development researchers usually use one of two designs: correlational or experimental studies.

**CORRELATIONAL STUDIES.**    **In a *correlational study*, investigators look at relations between variables as they exist naturally in the world.** In the simplest possible correlational study, a researcher measures two variables, then sees how they are related. Imagine a researcher who wants to test the idea that smarter children have more friends. To test this claim, the researcher would measure two variables for each child in the sample: the number of friends the child has and the child's intelligence.

**The results of a correlational study are usually expressed as a *correlation coefficient*, abbreviated *r*, which stands for the direction and strength of a relation between two variables.** Correlations can range from −1.0 to +1.0:

- *When* r *equals 0, two variables are completely unrelated:* Children's intelligence is unrelated to the number of friends they have.

- *When* r *is greater than 0, scores are related positively:* Children who are smart tend to have more friends than children who are not as smart. That is, more intelligence is associated with having more friends.

- *When* r *is less than 0, scores are related, but inversely:* Children who are smart tend to have fewer friends than children who are not as smart. That is, more intelligence is associated with having fewer friends.

> Correlational studies allow scientists to examine relations between variables that occur naturally.

In interpreting a correlation coefficient, you need to consider both the sign *and* the size of the correlation. The sign indicates the *direction* of the relation between variables. **A *positive correlation* means that larger values on one variable are associated with larger values on the second variable; a *negative correlation* means that larger values on one variable are associated with smaller values on a second variable.** For example, in a study by Kail and Hall (1999) the correlation between children's age and the number of errors they made solving arithmetic word problems was −.37: in general, as children got older, they made fewer errors.

The *strength* of a relation is measured by how much the correlation differs from 0, either positively or negatively. If the correlation between intelligence and number of friends were .9, the relation between these variables would be very strong: Knowing a child's intelligence, you could accurately predict how many friends the child has. If, instead, the correlation were .3, the link between intelligence and number of friends would be relatively weak: Although more intelligent children would have more friends on the average, there would be many exceptions to this rule. Similarly, a correlation of −.9 would indicate a strong negative relation between intelligence and number of friends, but a correlation of −.3 would indicate a weak negative relation.

The results of a correlational study tell whether variables are related, but this design doesn't address the question of cause and effect between the variables. In other words, finding a correlation between variables does not necessarily imply a causal relation between them. Suppose a researcher finds that the correlation between intelligence and number of friends is .7. This means that children who are smarter have more friends than children who are not as smart. How would you interpret this correlation? The diagram shows that three interpretations are possible. Maybe being smart causes children to have more friends. Another interpretation is that having more friends causes children to be smarter. A third interpretation is that neither variable causes the other; instead, intelligence and number of friends are caused by a third variable that was not measured in the study. Perhaps parents who are warm and supportive tend to have children who are smart and who also have many friends. Any of these interpretations could be true. Cause and effect cannot be distinguished in a correlational study. When investigators want to track down causes, they must use a different design, an experimental study.

FIGURE 1-2

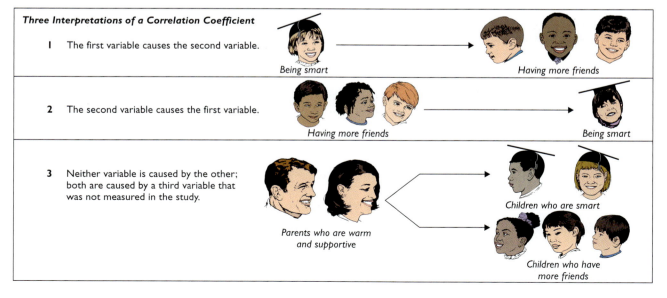

**Three Interpretations of a Correlation Coefficient**

1  The first variable causes the second variable.

*Being smart* → *Having more friends*

2  The second variable causes the first variable.

*Having more friends* → *Being smart*

3  Neither variable is caused by the other; both are caused by a third variable that was not measured in the study.

*Parents who are warm and supportive* → *Children who are smart* / *Children who have more friends*

**EXPERIMENTAL STUDIES.**   In an *experiment* an investigator systematically varies the factors thought to cause a particular behavior. The factor that is varied is called the *independent variable*; the behavior that is measured is called the *dependent variable*. In an experiment, the investigator begins with one or more treatments, circumstances, or events (independent variables) that are thought to affect a particular behavior. Children are then assigned randomly to different groups. Next, the dependent variable is measured in all groups. Because each child has an equal chance of being assigned to any group (due to random assignment), the groups should be the same except in the treatment they receive. Any differences between the groups can then be attributed to the differential treatment the children received in the experiment, rather than to other factors.

Suppose, for example, that an investigator hypothesizes that children share more with friends than with children they do not know. The diagram shows how the investigator might test this hypothesis. Based on random assignment, some fifth-grade children would be asked to come to the investigator's laboratory with a good friend. Other fifth graders would come to the laboratory site without a friend and would be paired with a child they don't know. The laboratory itself would be decorated to look like a family room in a house. The investigator creates a task in which one child is given an interesting object to play with—perhaps an Xbox—but the other child receives nothing. The experimenter explains the task to the children and then claims that she needs to leave the room briefly. Actually, the experimenter goes to a room with a one-way mirror and observes whether the child with the Xbox offers to let the other child play with it.

This same scenario would be used with all pairs of children: The room and toy would be the same and the experimenter would always be away for the same amount of time. The circumstances would be held as constant as possible for all children, except that some children participate with friends but others do not. If children who participated with friends gave the toy more quickly or more readily to the other child, the investigator could say with confidence that children are more likely to share with their friends than with children they don't know. Conclusions about cause and effect are possible because there was a direct manipulation of an independent variable (participating with a friend or with an unknown child) under controlled conditions.

You can see the use of an experiment in research by Roebers and Schneider (2005), who wanted to know the impact of incentives on children's memory. They had 6- to 8-year-olds watch a brief video about children on vacation. Three weeks later, children were asked questions about the video. Some of the children were randomly assigned to a condition in which they were simply encouraged to answer as accurately as possible. The remaining children received the same instructions and were told that they would get a coin for every correct answer. Then the experimenter asked them 22 questions.

In this experiment, the presence or absence of incentives was the independent variable and the percentage of questions answered correctly was the dependent variable. In fact, children responded more

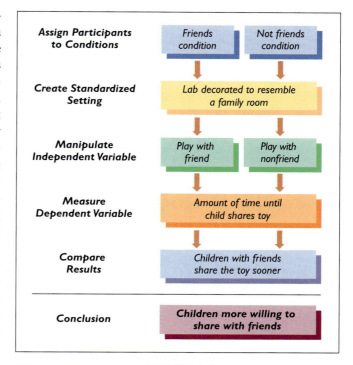

FIGURE 1-3

Experimental studies allow scientists to make conclusions about cause and effect.

accurately with incentives than without them (44% versus 33%). Because children were randomly assigned to conditions and because the conditions were alike in every respect except the presence of incentives, Roebers and Schneider (2005) could conclude that giving incentives to children *caused* them to remember more accurately.

Child-development researchers usually conduct experiments such as this one in laboratory-like settings to control all the variables that might influence the outcome of the research. A shortcoming of laboratory work is that the behavior of interest is not studied in its natural setting. Consequently, the results may be invalid because they are artificial—specific to the laboratory setting and not representative of the behavior in the natural environment.

To avoid this limit, researchers sometimes rely on a special type of experiment. **In a *field experiment*, the researcher manipulates independent variables in a natural setting so that the results are more likely to be representative of behavior in real-world settings.** To illustrate a field experiment, let's return to the hypothesis that children share more with friends. We might conduct the research in a classroom where students must complete a group assignment. In collaboration with teachers, we place the children in groups of three—in some groups, all three children are good friends; in others, the three children are acquaintances but not friends. When the assignment is complete, the teacher gives each group leader many stickers and tells the leader to distribute them to group members based on how much each child contributed. We predict that leaders will share more (i.e., distribute the stickers more evenly) when group members are friends than when they are not.

> Field experiments allow strong conclusions about cause and effect because they are conducted in natural settings.

Field experiments allow investigators to draw strong conclusions about cause and effect because they embed manipulation of an independent variable in a natural setting. However, field experiments are often impractical because of logistical problems. In most natural settings, children are supervised by adults (e.g., parents and teachers) who must be willing to become allies in the proposed research. Adults may not want to change their routines to fit a researcher's needs. In addition, researchers usually sacrifice some control in field experiments. In the example of distributing stickers to group members, some children, no doubt, actually worked harder than others, which means children's sharing will not be based simply on whether the other children are friends.

Both research designs used by developmentalists—correlational and experimental—have strengths and weaknesses. No method is perfect. Consequently, no single investigation can definitely answer a question, and researchers rarely rely on one study or even one method to reach conclusions. Instead, they prefer to find converging evidence from as many different kinds of studies as possible. Suppose, for example, our hypothetical laboratory and field experiments showed that children did, indeed, share more readily with their friends. One way to be more confident of this conclusion would be to do correlational research, perhaps by observing children during lunch and measuring how often they share food with different people.

## Designs for Studying Age-Related Change

Sometimes child-development research is directed at a single age group, such as fifth-grade children in the experiment on sharing between friends and nonfriends, memory in preschool-age children, or mother–infant relationships in 1-year-olds. When this is the case, after deciding how to measure the behavior of interest and whether the study will be correlational or experimental, the investigator could skip directly to the last step and determine whether the study is ethical.

However, much research in child development concerns changes that occur as children develop. Consequently, in conjunction with the chosen general research design, investigators must also decide which strategy will be most appropriate for assessing age-related change. Three strategies are used to incorporate different age groups into experimental and correlational research: the longitudinal approach, the cross-sectional approach, and the longitudinal-sequential approach.

**LONGITUDINAL DESIGN.    In a *longitudinal design*, the same individuals are observed or tested repeatedly at different points in their lives.** As the name implies, the longitudinal approach takes a lengthwise view of development and is the most direct way to watch growth occur. As the diagram shows, in a longitudinal study, children might be tested first at age 6 and then again at ages 9 and 12. The longitudinal approach is well suited to studying almost any aspect of development. More important, it is the only way to answer questions about the continuity or discontinuity of behavior: Will characteristics such as aggression, dependency, or mistrust observed in infancy or early childhood persist into adulthood? Will a traumatic event, such as being abandoned by one's parents, influence later social and intellectual development? Such questions can be explored only by testing children early in development and then retesting them later. For example, the study by Belsky et al. (2005) of parenting (described on page 22) was part of an ongoing longitudinal study of more than 1,000 children born in New Zealand in the early 1970s, in which children were tested repeatedly during childhood, adolescence, and young adulthood. Consequently, investigators can see how children's experiences during the preschool years affect them as adolescents and young adults.

FIGURE 1-4

Usually the repeated testing of longitudinal studies extends over years, but not always. **In a *microgenetic study*, a special type of longitudinal design, children are tested repeatedly over a span of days or weeks, typically with the aim of observing change directly as it occurs.** For example, researchers might test children every week, starting when they are 12 months old and continuing until 18 months. Microgenetic studies are particularly useful when investigators have hypotheses about a specific period when developmental change should occur. In this case, researchers arrange to test children frequently before, during, and after this period, hoping to see change as it happens (e.g., Opfer & Siegler, 2004).

The longitudinal approach, however, has disadvantages that frequently offset its strengths. An obvious one is cost: The expense of merely keeping up with a large sample of people can be staggering. Other problems are not so obvious:

- *Practice effects:* When children are given the same test many times, they may become "test-wise." Improvement over time that is attributed to development may actually stem from practice with a particular test. Changing the test from one session to the next solves the practice problem but makes it difficult to compare responses to different tests.

- *Selective attrition:* Another problem is the constancy of the sample over the course of research. Some children may drop out because they move away. Others may simply lose interest and choose not to continue. These dropouts are often significantly different from their more research-minded peers, which alone may distort the outcome. For example, a study might find that memory improves between 8 and 11 years. What has actually happened, however, is that 8-year-olds who found the testing too difficult quit the study, thereby raising the group average for the 11-year-olds.

- *Cohort effects:* **When children in a longitudinal study are observed over a period of several years, the developmental change may be specific to a specific generation of people known as a** *cohort*. For example, the longitudinal study being conducted in New Zealand includes babies born in 1972 and 1973. The results of this study may be general (i.e., apply to infants born in 1950 as well as infants born in 2000), but they may reflect experiences that were unique to infants born in the early 1970s.

> *Cross-sectional designs are convenient but only longitudinal designs can answer questions about the continuity of development.*

Because of these and other problems with the longitudinal method, child-development researchers often use cross-sectional studies instead.

**CROSS-SECTIONAL DESIGN.** In a *cross-sectional design*, **developmental changes are identified by testing children of different ages at one point in their development.** In other words, as shown in the diagram at the top of page 31, a researcher might chart the differences in some attribute between, say, 6-, 9-, and 12-year-olds. For example, when Lynda Hall and I (1999) studied age-related change in performance on arithmetic word-problems, we tested 8-, 9-, 10-, 11-, and 12-year-olds (24 children at each age) during the 1996–1997 school year. This was much faster than waiting the four years for the 8-year-olds to become 12-year-olds, and avoided many of the problems associated with longitudinal studies, including practice effects and selective attrition. But cohort effects are still a problem: The results may apply to children who are 6, 9, and 12 years old at the time of testing (in the example, 2006) and not generalize to previous or future generations. And cross-sectional studies have a unique shortcoming: Because children are tested at only one point in their development, we learn nothing about the continuity of development. Consequently, we cannot tell whether an aggressive 6-year-old remains aggressive at age 9 and 12, because an individual child would be tested at age 6, 9, or 12, but not at all three ages.

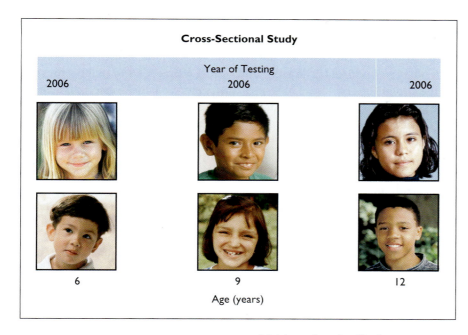

FIGURE 1-5

**LONGITUDINAL-SEQUENTIAL STUDIES.** Neither longitudinal nor cross-sectional studies are foolproof; each has weaknesses. Consequently, sometimes investigators use a design that is a hybrid of the traditional designs. A longitudinal-sequential study includes sequences of samples, each studied longitudinally. For example, researchers might start with 6- and 9-year-olds. As shown in the diagram below, each group is tested twice—at the beginning of the study and again, 3 years later. As in a pure longitudinal study, the longitudinal-sequential design provides some information about continuity of development: Researchers can determine whether aggressive 6-year-olds become aggressive 9-year-olds and whether aggressive 9-year-olds become aggressive 12-year-olds. Of course, to determine whether aggressive 6-year-olds become aggressive 12-year-olds would require a full-blown longitudinal study.

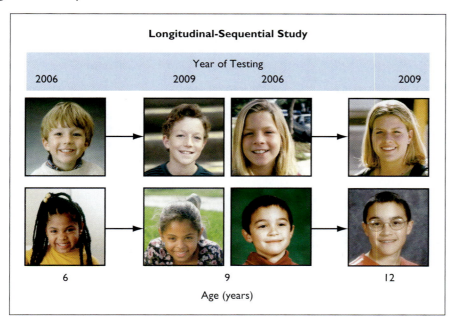

FIGURE 1-6

Another advantage of the longitudinal-sequential study is that researchers can determine whether their study is plagued by practice effects or cohort effects: The key is to compare the results for the age common to both sequences (in the example in the figure, 9-year-olds). Practice and cohort effects tend to make scores different for the two groups of 9-year-olds, so if scores are the same, a researcher can be confident that practice and cohort effects are not a problem in the study.

Each of the three designs for studying development (longitudinal, cross-sectional, longitudinal-sequential) can be combined with the two general research designs (observational, experimental), resulting in six prototypic designs. To illustrate the different possibilities, think back to our hypothetical laboratory experiment on children's sharing with friends and nonfriends (described on page 27). If we tested 7- and 11-year-olds with either friends or nonfriends, this would be a cross-sectional experimental study. If instead we observed 7-year-olds' spontaneous sharing at lunch, then observed the same children 4 years later, this would be a longitudinal correlational study.

The different designs are summarized in the following table. In this book, you'll read about studies using these various designs, although the two cross-sectional designs will show up more frequently than the other designs. Why? For most developmentalists, the ease of cross-sectional studies compared to longitudinal studies more than compensates for the limitations of cross-sectional studies.

## SUMMARY TABLE

### DESIGNS USED IN CHILD-DEVELOPMENT RESEARCH

| Type of Design | Definition | Strengths | Weaknesses |
|---|---|---|---|
| **General Designs** | | | |
| Correlational | Observe variables as they exist in the world and determine their relations | Behavior is measured as it occurs naturally | Cannot determine cause and effect |
| Experimental | Manipulate independent and dependent variables | Control of variables allows conclusions about cause and effect | Work is often laboratory based, which can be artificial |
| **Developmental Designs** | | | |
| Longitudinal | One group of children is tested repeatedly as they develop | Only way to chart an individual's development and look at the continuity of behavior over time | Expensive, participants drop out, and repeated testing can distort performance |
| Cross-sectional | Children of different ages are tested at the same time | Convenient—solves most problems associated with longitudinal studies | Cannot study continuity of behavior; cohort effects complicate interpretation of differences between groups |
| Longitudinal-sequential | Different sequences of children are tested longitudinally | Provides information about continuity; researchers can determine the presence of practice and cohort effects | Provides less information about continuity than a full longitudinal study and is more time consuming than a cross-sectional study |

**INTEGRATING FINDINGS FROM DIFFERENT STUDIES.** Several times in this module, I've emphasized the value of conducting multiple studies on a topic using different methods. The advantage of this approach, of course, is that conclusions are most convincing when the results are the same regardless of method.

In reality, though, findings are often inconsistent. Suppose, for example, many researchers find that children often share with friends, some researchers find that children share occasionally with friends, and a few researchers find that children never share with friends. What results should we believe? What should we conclude? *Meta-analysis* **is a tool that allows researchers to synthesize the results of many studies to estimate relations between variables** (Rosenthal, Rosnow, & Rubin, 2000). In conducting a meta-analysis, investigators find all studies published on a topic over a substantial period of time (e.g., 10 to 20 years), then record and analyze the results and important methodological variables.

The usefulness of meta-analysis is illustrated in a study by McClure (2000), who asked whether boys and girls differ in their ability to recognize emotions in facial expressions. She found 60 studies, published between 1931 and 1999, that included nearly 10,000 children and adults. In each of the 60 studies, participants were administered some sort of task like the one shown on page 22, in which the aim is to select a face expressing a particular emotion. Analyzing across the results of all 60 studies, McClure found that overall, girls recognized emotions in facial expressions more accurately than boys. The sex difference was constant from 4 to 16 years of age and was the same when the faces were shown as photos and as drawings. However, the sex difference was larger when participants judged emotions in children's faces than when they judged emotions in adults' faces.

Thus, meta-analysis is a particularly powerful tool because it allows scientists to determine whether a finding generalizes across many studies that used different methods. In addition, meta-analysis can reveal the impact of those different methods on results.

> Meta-analysis allows researchers to integrate the findings of many similar studies, making it possible to determine the generality and consistency of research results.

## Ethical Responsibilities

Having selected a way of measuring the behavior of interest and having chosen appropriate general and developmental designs, researchers must confront one very important remaining step: They must determine whether their research is ethical, that it does not violate the rights of the children who participate in it. Of course, scientists must always consider the ethics of research with humans, but especially for children who are vulnerable and sensitive. Professional organizations and government agencies have codes of conduct that specify the rights of research participants and procedures to protect those participants. The following guidelines are included in all those codes:

- *Minimize risks to research participants:* Use methods that have the least potential for harm or stress for research participants. During the research, monitor the procedures to be sure to avoid any unforeseen stress or harm.
- *Describe the research to potential participants so they can determine whether they wish to participate:* **Prospective research participants should be told all details of the research so they can make an educated decision about participating, which is known as obtaining** *informed consent*. Children are minors and are not legally capable of giving consent; consequently, as shown in the photograph, researchers must describe the study to parents and ask them for permission for their children to participate.

Before children can participate in research, a parent or legal guardian must provide written consent.

**1.4** Ethan, a 10-year-old, was at school when a researcher asked if he wanted to earn $10 doing an experiment. The money sounded good to Ethan so he participated. Despite the pay, Ethan left the experiment upset because he overheard the experimenter telling his teacher how poorly Ethan had done. What are three ethical problems with this research?

- *Avoid deception; if participants must be deceived, provide a thorough explana- tion of the true nature of the research as soon as possible:* Providing complete information about a study in advance can sometimes bias or distort partici- pants' responses. Consequently, investigators sometimes provide only partial information or even mislead participants about the true purpose of the study. As soon as it is feasible—typically just after the experiment—any false infor- mation must be corrected and the reasons for the deception must be provided.
- *Keep results anonymous or confidential:* Research results should be anony- mous, which means that participants' data cannot be linked to their name. When anonymity is not possible, research results should be confidential, which means that only the investigator conducting the study knows the identities of the individuals.

Before researchers can conduct a study, they must convince review boards con- sisting of scientists from many disciplines that they have carefully addressed each of these ethical points. If the review board objects to some aspects of the proposed study, the researcher must revise those aspects and present them anew for the review board's approval.

Much child-development research does not raise ethical red flags because the methods are harmless and avoid deception. Some methods, however, involve risk or deception; in these cases, review boards must balance the rights of children against the value of the research for contributing to knowledge and thereby improving children's lives. For example, in Module 10.3 we'll see that one tool for studying mother–infant relationships involves separating mothers and infants briefly, then watching infants' responses. Many infants are upset when the mother leaves and some are difficult to console when she returns. Obviously, this method is not pleas- ant for infants. But scientists have determined that it produces no lasting harm and therefore is suitable as long as parents receive a thorough description of the study be- forehand and they consent to participate.

## Communicating Research Results

When the study is complete and the data have been analyzed, researchers write a re- port of their work. This report uses a standard format that usually includes four main sections: an introduction that describes the topic or question that was studied and the authors' hypotheses; a method section that describes the research design and the procedures used; a results section that presents the study's findings, verified with statistical analyses, and a discussion section in which the authors explain the links between their results and their hypotheses.

Reseachers submit the report to one of several scientific journals that specialize in child-development research. Some of these are *Child Development*, *Developmental Psychology*, and the *Journal of Experimental Child Psychology*. The editor of the jour- nal asks other scientists to evaluate the report, to decide whether the work was well done and the findings represent a substantial advance in scientific understanding of a topic. If the scientists recommend that the report be published, it will appear in the journal, where other child-development researchers can learn of the results.

These reports of research are the basis for virtually all the information I pre- sent in this book. As you read, you'll see names in parentheses, followed by a date, like this:

(Levine & Waite, 2000).

This indicates the person who did the research and the year it was published. By looking in the References, which begin on page 503 and are organized alphabetically, you can find the title of the article and the journal in which it was published.

Maybe all these different steps in research seem tedious and involved to you. For a child-development researcher, however, much of the fun of doing research is planning a novel study that will provide useful information to other specialists. This is one of the most creative and challenging parts of child-development research.

The "Focus on Research" features that appear in the remaining chapters of this book are designed to convey both the creativity and the challenge of doing child-development research. Each feature focuses on a specific study. Some are studies that have just recently been published; others are classics that defined a new area of investigation or provided definitive results in some area. In each "Focus" feature, I trace the decisions that researchers made as they planned their study. In the process, you'll see the ingenuity of researchers as they pursue questions of child development. You'll also see that any individual study has limitations. Only when converging evidence from many studies—each using a unique combination of measurement methods and designs—points to the same conclusion can we feel confident about research results.

*Responses to question on page 23 about using photographs to measure children's understanding of emotions:* Children's understanding of emotions depicted in photographs may be less accurate than in real life because (1) in real life, facial features are usually moving—not still, as in the photographs—and movement may be one of the clues that children naturally use to judge emotions; (2) in real life, facial expressions are often accompanied by sounds, and children may use both sight and sound to understand emotion; and (3) in real life, children most often judge facial expressions of people they know (parents, siblings, peers, teachers), and knowing the "usual" appearance of a face may help children determine emotions accurately.

## Check Your Learning

**RECALL** List the ethical responsibilities of scientists who do research with children.

What steps are involved in reporting the results of research to the scientific community?

**INTERPRET** Compare the strengths and weaknesses of different approaches to measurement in child-development research.

**APPLY** Suppose you wanted to determine the impact of divorce on children's academic achievement. What would be the merits of correlational versus experimental research on this topic? How would a longitudinal study differ from a cross-sectional study?

First, the experimenter apparently did not describe the study in detail to Ethan, only mentioning the pay. Second, children can participate only with the written consent of a parent or legal guardian. Third, results are anonymous and not to be shared with others.

**1.4**

## SEE FOR YOURSELF

One good way to see how children influence their own development is to interview parents who have more than one child. Ask them if they used the same child-rearing methods with each child or if they used different techniques with each. If they used different techniques, find out why. You should see that, although parents try to be consistent in a general philosophy for rearing their children, many of the specific parenting techniques will vary from one child to the next, reflecting the children's influence on the parents. See for yourself!

## RESOURCES

For more information about . . .

**the different theories described in Module 1.2,** I recommend Patricia H. Miller's *Theories of Developmental Psychology* (Worth, 2001) for its comprehensive account of each of the theoretical perspectives.

**research in child development,** visit the Society for Research in Child Development (SRCD) Web site: **www.srcd.org**

## KEY TERMS

active–passive child issue  19
applied developmental science  7
baby biographies  6
cognitive-developmental perspective  13
cohort  30
continuity–discontinuity issue  17
correlation coefficient  25
correlational study  25
critical period  9
cross-sectional study  30
culture  14
dependent variable  27
ego  10
ethological theory  9
experiment  27
field experiment  28
id  10
imitation (observational learning)  12
imprinting  9
independent variable  27
informed consent  33
longitudinal study  29
maturational theory  9
meta-analysis  33

microgenetic study  29
naturalistic observation  21
nature–nurture issue  18
negative correlation  26
operant conditioning  11
population  25
positive correlation  26
psychodynamic theory  10
psychosocial theory  10
punishment  12
reinforcement  12
reliability  24
research design  25
response bias  23
sample  25
self-efficacy  12
self reports  23
social cognitive theory  12
structured observation  22
superego  10
systematic observation  21
theory  8
validity  24
variable  21

# SUMMARY

## 1.1 SETTING THE STAGE

### Historical Views of Children and Childhood

Plato and Aristotle provided the first philosophical views of childhood. Their ideas were picked up in the 17th century. Locke emphasized the role of experience in children's lives, but Rousseau viewed development as a natural unfolding.

### Origins of a New Science

Child development emerged as a science in the 19th century, reflecting reformers' concern for children's well being and scientists' enthusiasm for Darwin's theory of evolution. Leaders in the new field were G. Stanley Hall (theories of child development), Binet (mental tests), Freud (role of early experience), and Watson (behaviorism). Child-development researchers help shape family policy by providing knowledge about children so that policies can be based on accurate information. They also contribute by serving as advocates for children, by evaluating the impact of social programs, and by developing effective programs that can be implemented elsewhere.

## 1.2 THEORIES OF CHILD DEVELOPMENT

Theories provide explanations for development and hypotheses for research. Traditionally, five broad perspectives have guided researchers.

### The Biological Perspective

According to this perspective, biological factors are critical for development. In maturational theory, child development reflects a natural unfolding of a prearranged biological plan. Ethological theory states that children's and parents' behavior is often adaptive.

### The Psychodynamic Perspective

Freud emphasized the roles of early experience and conflict in children's development. Erikson proposed that psychosocial development consisting of eight universal stages, each characterized by a particular struggle.

### The Learning Perspective

Operant conditioning is based on reinforcement, punishment, and environmental control of behavior. Social learning theory proposes that people learn by observing others. Social cognitive theory emphasizes that children actively interpret what they see.

### The Cognitive-Developmental Perspective

The cognitive-developmental perspective focuses on thought processes. Piaget proposed that children's thinking progresses through four stages.

### The Contextual Perspective

Vygotsky emphasized the role of culture in children's development. He argued that, with the help of skillful adults, children acquire the beliefs, customs, and skills of their culture.

## 1.3 THEMES IN CHILD-DEVELOPMENT RESEARCH

Four themes help unify the findings from child-development research that are presented throughout this book.

### Early Development is Related to Later Development but Not Perfectly

Development is not perfectly predictable; early development sets the stage for later development but does not fix it.

### Development Is Always Jointly Influenced by Heredity and Environment

Heredity and environment are interactive forces that work together to chart the course of development.

### Children Influence Their Own Development

Children constantly interpret their experiences and, by their individual characteristics, often influence the experiences they have.

### Development in Different Domains Is Connected

Development in different domains of children's lives is always connected. Cognitive development affects social development and vice versa.

## 1.4 DOING CHILD-DEVELOPMENT RESEARCH

### Measurement in Child-Development Research

Research typically begins by determining how to measure the topic of interest. Systematic observation involves recording children's behavior as it takes place, either in a natural environment or in a structured setting. Researchers sometimes create tasks to obtain samples of children's behavior. In self reports, children answer questions posed by the experimenter. Sometimes researchers also measure physiological responses (e.g., heart rate). Researchers must also obtain a sample that is representative of some larger population.

### General Designs for Research

In correlational studies, investigators examine relations between variables as they occur naturally. In experimental studies, they manipulate an independent variable to determine the impact on a dependent variable. Field studies involve manipulation of independent variables in a natural setting. The best approach is to use both experimental and correlational studies to provide converging evidence.

### Designs for Studying Age-related Change

To study developmental change, some researchers use a longitudinal design in which the same children are observed repeatedly as they grow. A cross-sectional design involves testing children in different age groups. Meta-analysis is used to synthesize the results of different studies on the same topic.

### Ethical Responsibilities

Planning research also involves selecting methods that preserve the rights of research participants. Experimenters must minimize the risks to potential research participants, describe the research so that potential participants can decide whether they want to participate, avoid deception, and keep results anonymous or confidential.

### Communicating Research Results

Once research data are analyzed, investigators publish the results in scientific journals where they form the foundation of scientific knowledge about child development.

**I wish I had a dollar for every time my parents or in-laws said about one of my children, "He (or she) comes by that naturally."** The usual prompt for their comment is that the child has just done something exactly as I or my wife did at that same age. By their remarks, grandparents are reminding us that many behavioral characteristics are inherited from parents just as physical characteristics like height and hair color are inherited.

In this chapter, we'll see how heredity influences children and their development. We'll start, in Module 2.1, by examining the basic mechanisms of heredity. Then, in Module 2.2, we'll see how heredity and environment work together to shape children's development.

**2.1** Mechanisms of Heredity

**2.2** Heredity, Environment, and Development

1    The Science of Child Development

# Genetic Bases
# of Child Development

**2**

3    Prenatal Development, Birth, and the Newborn

4    Growth and Health

5    Perceptual and Motor Development

6    Theories of Cognitive Development

7    Cognitive Processes and Academic Skills

8    Intelligence and Individual Differences in Cognition

9    Language and Communication

10   Emotional Development

11   Understanding Self and Others

12   Moral Understanding and Behavior

13   Gender and Development

14   Family Relationships

15   Influences Beyond the Family

# 2.1                    MECHANISMS OF HEREDITY

The Biology of Heredity

Single Gene Inheritance

Genetic Disorders

## LEARNING OBJECTIVES

- What are chromosomes and genes?

- What are dominant and recessive traits? How are they inherited?

- What disorders are inherited? Which are caused by too many or too few chrosomomes?

*Leslie and Glenn have decided to try to have a baby. They are thrilled at the thought of starting their own family but also worried because Leslie's grandfather had sickle-cell disease and died when he was just 20 years old. Leslie is terrified that their baby could inherit the disease that killed her grandfather. Leslie and Glenn wish someone could reassure them that their baby will be okay.*

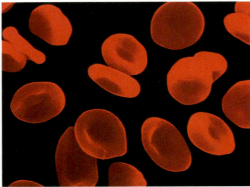

Red blood cells carry oxygen throughout the body.

How could we reassure Leslie and Glenn? For starters, we need to know more about sickle-cell disease. Red blood cells like the ones in the top photo carry oxygen and carbon dioxide to and from the body. When a person has sickle-cell disease, the red blood cells look like those in the bottom photo—long and curved like a sickle: These stiff, misshapen cells can't pass through small capillaries, so oxygen can't reach all parts of the body. The trapped sickle cells also block the way of white blood cells that are the body's natural defense against bacteria. As a result, people with sickle-cell disease—including Leslie's grandfather and many other African Americans, who are more prone to this painful disease than other groups—often die from infections before age 20.

Sickle-cell disease is inherited. Because Leslie's grandfather had the disorder, it apparently runs in her family. Would Leslie's baby inherit the disease? To answer this question, we need to examine the mechanisms of heredity.

## The Biology of Heredity

The teaspoon of semen released into the vagina during an ejaculation contains from 200 million to 500 million sperm. Only a few hundred of these actually complete the 6- or 7-inch journey to the fallopian tubes. If an egg is present, many sperm simultaneously begin to burrow their way through the cluster of nurturing cells that surround the egg.

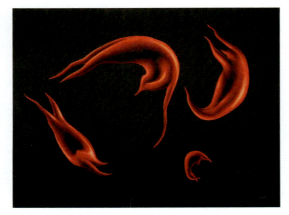

Sickle-shaped blood cells associated with sickle-cell disease cannot pass through the body's smallest blood vessels.

When a sperm like the one in the photo at the top of page 41 penetrates the cellular wall of the egg, chemical changes that occur immediately block out all other sperm. **Each egg and sperm cell contains 23 *chromosomes*, tiny structures in the nucleus that contain genetic material.** When a sperm penetrates an egg, their chromosomes combine to produce 23 pairs of chromosomes. The development of a new human being is under way.

For most of history, the merging of sperm and egg took place only after sexual intercourse. No longer. In 1978, Louise Brown captured the world's attention as the first test-tube baby conceived in a laboratory dish instead of in her mother's body. Today, assisted reproductive technology is no longer experimental; it is used more than 100,000 times annually with American women, producing nearly 50,000 babies (U.S. Department of Health and Human Services, 2004). Many new techniques are available to couples who cannot conceive a child through sexual inter-course. **The best known,** *in vitro fertilization*, **involves mixing sperm and egg together in a laboratory dish and then placing several fertilized eggs in the mother's uterus.** The photo at the bottom of the page shows this lab-oratory version of conception, with the sperm in the dropper being placed in the dish containing the eggs. If the eggs are fertilized, in about 24 hours they are placed in the mother's uterus, with the hope that they will become implanted in the wall of her uterus.

Fertilization takes place when a sperm pene-trates an egg cell.

The sperm and egg usually come from the prospective parents, but sometimes they are provided by donors. Occasionally the fertilized egg is placed in the uterus of a surrogate mother who carries the baby through-out pregnancy. Thus, a baby could have as many as five "parents": the man and woman who provide the sperm and egg, the surrogate mother who carries the baby, and the couple who rears the child.

New reproductive techniques offer hope for couples who have long wanted a child, and studies of the first generation of children conceived via these techniques indicates that their social and emotional development is perfectly normal (Golom-bok, MacCallum, & Goodman, 2001; Golombok et al., 2004). But there are difficulties as well. Only about one-third of the attempts at in vitro fertilization succeed. What's more, when a woman becomes pregnant, she is more likely to have twins or triplets because multiple eggs are transferred to increase the odds that at least one fertilized egg will implant in the mother's uterus. She is also at greater risk for giving birth to a baby with low birth weight or birth defects. Finally, the procedure is expensive—the average cost in the United States of a single cycle of treatment is about $10,000—and typically is not covered by health insurance (Katz, Nachtigall, & Showstack, 2002). These problems emphasize that, although technology has increased the alternatives for infertile couples, pregnancy on demand is still in the realm of science fiction.

Whatever the source of the egg and sperm, and wherever they meet, their merger is a momentous event: The resulting 23 pairs of chromosomes define a child's heredity—what he or she "will do naturally." For Leslie and Glenn, this mo-ment also determines whether their child inherits sickle-cell disease.

To understand how heredity influences child development, let's begin by tak-ing a closer look at chromosomes. The photo at the top of page 42 shows all 46 chro-mosomes, organized in pairs ranging from the largest to the smallest. **The first 22 pairs of chromosomes are called** *autosomes*; **the chromosomes in each pair are about the same size.** In the 23rd pair, however, the chro-mosome labeled X is much larger than the chromosome labeled Y. **The 23rd pair determines the sex of the child; hence, these two are known as the** *sex chromosomes.* An egg always contains an X 23rd chromosome, but a sperm contains either an X or a Y. When an X-carrying sperm fertilizes the egg, the 23rd pair is XX and the re-sult is a girl. When a Y-carrying sperm fertilizes the egg, the 23rd pair is XY and the result is a boy.

A dropper is being used to place sperm in the dish that contains egg cells.

**Each chromosome actually consists of one mole-cule of** *deoxyribonucleic acid—DNA* **for short.** The DNA molecule resembles a spiral staircase. As you can see in the diagram on page 42, the rungs of the staircase carry the ge-netic code, which consists of pairs of nucleotide bases: Adenine is paired with thymine, and guanine is paired

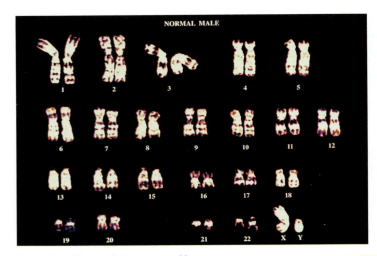

Humans have 23 pairs of chromosomes, 22 pairs of autosomes, and one pair of sex chromosomes.

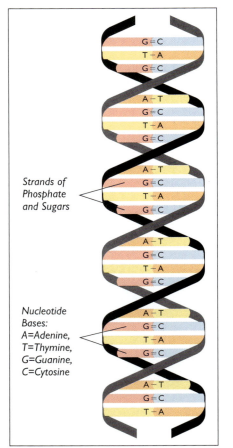

Strands of Phosphate and Sugars

Nucleotide Bases:
A=Adenine,
T=Thymine,
G=Guanine,
C=Cytosine

FIGURE 2-1

with cytosine. The order of the nucleotide pairs is the code that causes the cell to create specific amino acids, proteins, and enzymes—important biological building blocks. **Each group of nucleotide bases that provides a specific set of biochemical instructions is a *gene*.** For example, three consecutive thymine nucleotides is the instruction to create the amino acid phenylalanine.

The diagram on page 43 summarizes these links between chromosomes, genes, and DNA. The diagram shows that each cell contains chromosomes that carry genes made up of DNA.

Altogether, a child's 46 chromosomes include roughly 25,000 genes (Pennisi, 2005). Through biochemical instructions that are coded in DNA, genes regulate the development of all human characteristics and abilities. **The complete set of genes makes up a person's heredity and is known as the person's *genotype*. Genetic instructions, in conjunction with environmental influences, produce a *phenotype*, an individual's physical, behavioral, and psychological features.**

In the rest of this module, we'll see the different ways that instructions contained in genes produce different phenotypes.

## Single Gene Inheritance

How do genetic instructions produce the misshapen red blood cells of sickle-cell disease? **Genes come in different forms that are known as *alleles*.** In the case of red blood cells, for example, one of two alleles can be present on chromosome 11. One allele has instructions for normal red blood cells; the other allele has instructions for sickle-shaped red blood cells. **The alleles in the pair of chromosomes are sometimes the same, which makes them *homozygous*. The alleles sometimes differ, which makes them *heterozygous*.** In Leslie's case, her baby could be homozygous, in which case it would have two alleles for normal cells or two alleles for sickle-shaped cells. Leslie's baby might also be heterozygous, which means that it would have one allele for normal cells and one for sickle-shaped cells.

How does a genotype produce a phenotype? The answer is simple if a person is homozygous. When both alleles are the same and therefore have chemical instructions for the same phenotype, that phenotype results. If Leslie's baby had alleles for normal red blood cells on both of the chromosomes in its 11th pair, the baby would be almost guaranteed to have normal cells. If, instead, the baby had two alleles for sickle-shaped cells, her baby would almost certainly suffer from the disease.

When a person is heterozygous, the process is more complex. **Often one allele is *dominant*, which means that its chemical instructions are followed whereas instructions of the other, the *recessive* allele, are ignored.** In the case of sickle-cell disease, the allele for normal cells is dominant and the allele for sickle-shaped cells is recessive. This is good news for Leslie: As long as either she or Glenn contribute the allele for normal red blood cells, her baby will not develop sickle-cell disease.

Figure 2-3 on page 43 summarizes what we've learned about sickle-cell disease. The letter *A* denotes the allele for normal blood cells, and *a* denotes the allele for sickle-shaped cells. In the diagram, Glenn's genotype is homozygous dominant because he's positive that no one in his family has had sickle-cell disease. From

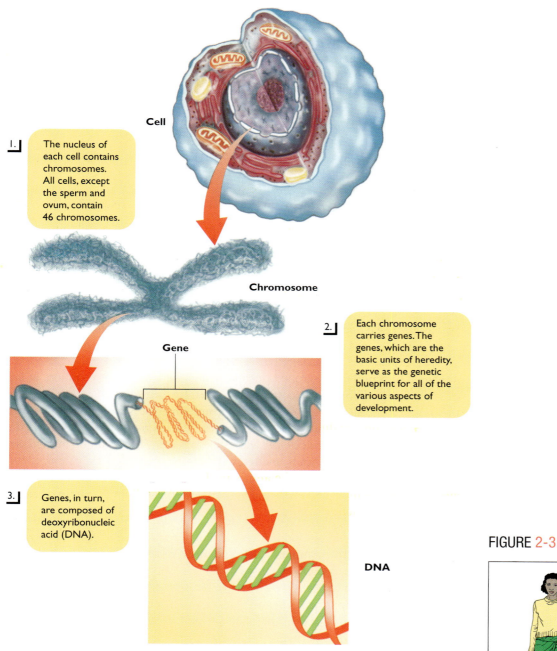

Cell

1. The nucleus of each cell contains chromosomes. All cells, except the sperm and ovum, contain 46 chromosomes.

Chromosome

2. Each chromosome carries genes. The genes, which are the basic units of heredity, serve as the genetic blueprint for all of the various aspects of development.

Gene

3. Genes, in turn, are composed of deoxyribonucleic acid (DNA).

DNA

**FIGURE** 2-2

Leslie's family history, she could be homozygous dominant or heterozygous; in the diagram, I've assumed the latter. You can see that Leslie and Glenn cannot have a baby with sickle-cell disease. However, their baby might be affected in another way. **Sometimes one allele does not dominate another completely, a situation known as** *incomplete dominance.* In incomplete dominance, the phenotype that results often falls between the phenotype associated with either allele. This is the case for the genes that control red blood cells. **Individuals with one dominant and one recessive allele have** *sickle-cell trait*: **In most situations they have no**

**FIGURE** 2-3

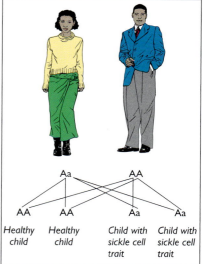

Aa       AA

AA    AA    Aa    Aa

Healthy child   Healthy child   Child with sickle cell trait   Child with sickle cell trait

**2.1**   If Glenn learned that he was heterozygous dominant for sickle-cell disease instead of homozygous dominant, how would this affect the chance that he and Leslie would have a child with sickle-cell disease?

problems, but when they are seriously short of oxygen they suffer a temporary, relatively mild form of the disease. Thus, sickle-cell trait is likely to appear when the person exercises vigorously or is at high altitudes (Sullivan, 1987). Leslie and Glenn's baby would have sickle-cell trait if it inherited a recessive gene from Leslie and a dominant gene from Glenn.

One aspect of sickle-cell disease that we haven't considered so far is why this disorder primarily affects African American children. The "Cultural Influences" feature addresses this point and, in the process, tells more about how heredity operates.

## Cultural Influences

### Why Do African Americans Inherit Sickle-Cell Disease?

Sickle-cell disease affects about 1 in 400 African American children. In contrast, virtually no European American children have the disorder. Why? Surprisingly, because the sickle-cell allele has a benefit: Individuals with this allele are more resistant to malaria, an infectious disease that is one of the leading causes of childhood death worldwide. Malaria is transmitted by mosquitos, so it is most common in warm climates, including many parts of Africa. Compared to Africans who have alleles for normal blood cells, Africans with the sickle-cell allele are less likely to die from malaria, which means that the sickle-cell allele is passed along to the next generation.

This explanation of sickle-cell disease has two implications. First, sickle-cell disease should be found in any group of people living where malaria is common. In fact, sickle-cell disease affects Hispanic Americans who trace their roots to malaria-prone regions of the Caribbean, Central America, and South America. Second, malaria is rare in the United States, which means that the sickle-cell allele has no survival value to African Americans. Accordingly, the sickle-cell allele should become less common in successive generations of African Americans, and research indicates that this is happening.

There is an important general lesson here. The impact of heredity depends on the environment: An allele may have survival value in one environment but not in others. ∎

The simple genetic mechanism responsible for sickle-cell disease, involving a single gene pair with one dominant allele and one recessive allele, is also responsible for many other common traits, as shown in Table 2-1 on page 45. In each case, individuals with the recessive phenotype have two recessive alleles, one from each parent. Individuals with the dominant phenotype have at least one dominant allele.

Most of the traits listed in the table are biological and medical phenotypes. These same patterns of inheritance can cause serious disorders, as we'll see in the next section.

## Genetic Disorders

Genetics can derail development in two ways. First, some disorders are inherited. Sickle-cell disease is an example of an inherited disorder. Second, sometimes eggs or sperm have more or fewer than the usual 23 chromosomes. In the next few pages, we'll see how inherited disorders and abnormal numbers of chromosomes can alter a child's development.

**INHERITED DISORDERS.**   Sickle-cell disease is one of many disorders that are homozygous recessive—triggered when a child inherits recessive alleles from both parents. Table 2-2 lists four more disorders that are commonly inherited in this manner.

Relatively few serious disorders are caused by dominant alleles. Why? If the allele for the disorder is dominant, every person with at least one of these alleles will have the disorder. But individuals affected with these disorders typically do not live long enough to reproduce, so dominant alleles that produce fatal disorders soon vanish from the species. **An exception is *Huntington's disease*, a fatal disease characterized by progressive degeneration of the nervous system.** Huntington's disease is caused by a dominant allele found on chromosome 4. Individuals who inherit this disorder develop normally through childhood, adolescence, and young adulthood. However, during middle age, nerve cells begin to deteriorate, causing muscle spasms, depression, and significant changes in personality. By the time symptoms of Huntington's disease appear, adults who are affected may already have produced children, many of whom go on to develop the disease themselves.

Fortunately, most inherited disorders are rare. PKU, for example, occurs once in every 10,000 births, and Huntington's disease occurs even less frequently. Nevertheless, adults who believe that these disorders run in their family often want to know whether their children are likely to inherit the disorder. The "Improving Children's Lives" feature shows how these couples can get help in deciding whether to have children.

## TABLE 2-1

### SOME COMMON PHENOTYPES ASSOCIATED WITH SINGLE PAIRS OF GENES

| Dominant Phenotype | Recessive Phenotype |
| --- | --- |
| Curly hair | Straight hair |
| Normal hair | Pattern baldness (men) |
| Dark hair | Blond hair |
| Thick lips | Thin lips |
| Cheek dimples | No dimples |
| Normal hearing | Some types of deafness |
| Normal vision | Nearsightedness |
| Farsightedness | Normal vision |
| Normal color vision | Red-green color blindness |
| Type A blood | Type O blood |
| Type B blood | Type O blood |
| Rh-positive blood | Rh-negative blood |

Source: McKusick, 1995.

## TABLE 2-2

### COMMON DISORDERS ASSOCIATED WITH RECESSIVE ALLELES

| Disorder | Frequency | Characteristics |
| --- | --- | --- |
| Albinism | 1 in 10,000 to 1 in 20,000 births | Skin lacks melanin, which causes visual problems and extreme sensitivity to light. |
| Cystic fibrosis | 1 in 2,500 births among European Americans; less common in African and Asian Americans | Excess mucus clogs digestive and respiratory tracts. Lung infections common. |
| Phenylketonuria (PKU) | 1 in 10,000 births | Phenylalanine, an amino acid, accumulates in the body and damages the nervous system, causing mental retardation. |
| Tay–Sachs disease | 1 in 3,000 births among Jews of European descent | The nervous system degenerates in infancy, causing deafness, blindness, mental retardation, and, during the preschool years, death. |

Source: Based on Committee on Genetics, 1998; McKusick, 1995.

### *Improving Children's Lives*

### Genetic Counseling

Family planning is not easy for couples who fear that children they have may inherit serious or even fatal diseases. The best advice is to seek the help of a genetic counselor before the woman becomes pregnant. With the couple's help, a genetic counselor constructs a detailed family history that can be used to decide whether it's likely that either the man or the woman has the allele for the disorder that concerns them.

A family tree for Leslie and Glenn, the couple from the opening vignette, would confirm that Leslie is likely to carry the recessive allele for sickle-cell disease. The genetic counselor would then take the next step, obtaining a sample of Leslie's cells (probably from a blood test). The cells would be analyzed to determine whether the 11th chromosome carries the recessive allele for sickle-cell disease. If Leslie learns she is homozygous—has two dominant alleles for healthy blood cells—then she and Glenn can be assured their children will not have sickle-cell disease. If Leslie learns that she has one recessive allele, then she and Glenn will know they have a 50% risk of having a baby with sickle-cell trait. Tests can also be administered after a woman is pregnant to determine whether the child she is carrying has an inherited disorder. We'll learn about these tests in Chapter 3. ■

More common than inherited diseases are disorders caused by the wrong number of chromosomes, as we'll see next.

**ABNORMAL NUMBER OF CHROMOSOMES.** Sometimes individuals do not receive the normal complement of 46 chromosomes. If they are born with extra, missing, or damaged chromosomes, development is always disturbed. **The best example is *Down syndrome*, a genetic disorder that is caused by an extra 21st chromosome and that results in mental retardation.**\* Like the child in the photo on page 47, persons with Down syndrome have almond-shaped eyes and a fold over the eyelid. The head, neck, and nose of a child with this disorder are usually smaller than normal. During the first several months, babies with Down syndrome seem to develop normally. Thereafter, though, their mental and behavioral development begins to lag behind the average child's. For example, a child with Down syndrome might not sit up without help until about 1 year, not walk until 2, or not talk until 3—months or even years behind children without Down syndrome. By childhood, mental retardation is apparent.

> Extra or missing autosomes always affect development because autosomes contain so much genetic material.

Rearing a child with Down syndrome presents special challenges. During the preschool years, children with Down syndrome need special programs to prepare them for school. Educational achievements of children with Down syndrome are likely to be limited and their life expectancy ranges from 25 to 60 years (Yang, Rasmussen, & Friedman, 2002). Nevertheless, as we'll see in Chapter 8, many persons with Down syndrome lead fulfilling lives.

What causes Down syndrome? Individuals with Down syndrome typically have an extra 21st chromosome that is usually provided by the egg (Antonarakis & the Down Syndrome Collaborative Group, 1991). Why the mother provides two 21st chromosomes is unknown. However, the odds that a woman will bear a child with

---

\*The scientific name is Trisomy 21, reflecting the fact that a person with the disorder has a trio of 21st chromosomes instead of a pair. But most people refer to the disorder as Down syndrome, reflecting the name of the English physician, John Langdon Down, who identified the disorder in the 1860s.

Down syndrome increase markedly as she gets older. For a woman in her late 20s, the risk of giving birth to a baby with Down syndrome is about 1 in 1,000; for a woman in her early 40s, the risk is about 1 in 50. The increased risk may be because a woman's eggs have been in her ovaries since her own prenatal development. Eggs may deteriorate over time as part of aging, or eggs may become damaged because an older woman has a longer history of exposure to hazards in the environment, such as X rays.

An extra autosome (as in Down syndrome), a missing autosome, or a damaged autosome always has far-reaching consequences for development because the autosomes contain huge amounts of genetic material. In fact, nearly half of all fertilized eggs abort spontaneously within 2 weeks, primarily because of abnormal autosomes. Thus, most eggs that could not develop normally are removed naturally (Moore & Persaud, 1993).

Abnormal sex chromosomes can also disrupt development. Table 2-3 lists four of the more frequent disorders associated with atypical numbers of X and Y chromosomes. Keep in mind that *frequent* is a relative term; although these disorders occur more frequently than PKU or Huntington's disease, the table shows that most are rare. Notice that no disorders consist solely of Y chromosomes. The presence of an X chromosome appears to be necessary for life. These genetic disorders demonstrate the remarkable power of heredity. Nevertheless, to fully understand how heredity influences development, we need to consider the environment, which we'll do in Module 2.2.

Children with Down syndrome typically have upward slanting eyes with a fold over the eyelid, a flattened facial profile, as well as a smaller-than-average nose and mouth.

## TABLE 2-3

| COMMON DISORDERS ASSOCIATED WITH THE SEX CHROMOSOMES | | | |
|---|---|---|---|
| Disorder | Sex Chromosomes | Frequency | Characteristics |
| Klinefelter's syndrome | XXY | 1 in 500 male births | Tall, small testicles, sterile, below-normal intelligence, passive |
| XYY complement | XYY | 1 in 1,000 male births | Tall, some cases apparently have below-normal intelligence |
| Turner's syndrome | X | 1 in 2,500 to 5,000 female births | Short, limited development of secondary sex characteristics, problems perceiving spatial relations |
| XXX syndrome | XXX | 1 in 500 to 1,200 female births | Normal stature but delayed motor and language development |

Source: Based on Bancroft et al., 1982; Downey et al., 1991; Linden et al., 1988; Plomin et al., 1990.

**2.1**   Glenn and Leslie would have a 25% chance of having a child with sickle-cell disease, a 50% chance of a child with sickle-cell trait, and a 25% chance of having a child with neither sickle-cell disease nor sickle-cell trait.

## CHECK YOUR LEARNING

**RECALL**   Describe the difference between dominant and recessive alleles.
Distinguish genetic disorders that are inherited from those that involve abnormal numbers of chromosomes.

**INTERPRET**   Why do relatively few genetic disorders involve dominant alleles?

**APPLY**   Suppose that a friend of yours discovers that she may have the recessive allele for the disease cystic fibrosis. What advice would you give her?

# 2.2

# HEREDITY, ENVIRONMENT, AND DEVELOPMENT

Behavioral Genetics

Paths From Genes to Behavior

## LEARNING OBJECTIVES

- What methods do scientists use to study the impact of heredity and environment on children's development?

- How do heredity and environment work together to influence child development?

  *Sadie and Molly are fraternal twins. As babies, Sadie was calm and easily comforted, but Molly was fussy and hard to soothe. When they entered school, Sadie relished contact with other people and preferred play that involved others. Meanwhile, Molly was more withdrawn and was quite happy to play alone. Their grandparents wonder why these twins seem so different.*

Why are Sadie and Molly so different despite having similar genes? To answer this question, we'll first look at the methods that child-development scientists use to study hereditary and environmental influences on children's development. Then we'll examine some basic principles that govern hereditary and environmental influences.

## Behavioral Genetics

*Behavioral genetics* **is the branch of genetics that deals with inheritance of behavioral and psychological traits.** Behavioral genetics is complex, in part because behavioral and psychological phenotypes are complex. The traits controlled by single genes—like those shown in Table 2-1 on page 45—usually represent "either–or" phenotypes. That is, the genotypes are usually associated with two (or sometimes three) well-defined phenotypes. For example, a person either has normal color vision or has red-green color blindness; a person has blood that clots normally, has sickle-cell trait, or has sickle-cell disease.

Most important behavioral and psychological characteristics are not either–or cases but represent an entire range of different outcomes. Take extroversion as an example. You probably know a few extremely outgoing individuals and a few intensely shy persons, but most of your friends and acquaintances are somewhere in between. Classifying your friends would produce a distribution of individuals across a continuum, from extreme extroversion at one end to extreme introversion at the other.

Many behavioral and psychological characteristics are distributed in this fashion, including intelligence and many aspects of personality. **When phenotypes reflect the combined activity of many separate genes, the pattern is known as** *polygenic inheritance.* Because so many genes are involved in polygenic inheritance, we usually cannot trace the effects of each gene. But we can use a hypothetical example to show how many genes work together to produce a behavioral phenotype that spans a continuum. Let's suppose that four pairs of genes contribute to extroversion, that the allele for extroversion is dominant, and that the total amount of extroversion is simply the sum of the dominant alleles. If we continue to use uppercase letters to represent dominant alleles and lowercase letters to represent the recessive allele, the four gene pairs would be *Aa, Bb, Cc,* and *Dd.*

These four pairs of genes produce 81 different genotypes and 9 distinct phenotypes. For example, a person with the genotype *AABBCCDD* has 8 alleles for extroversion (a party animal). A person with the genotype *aabbccdd* has no alleles for extroversion (a wallflower). All other genotypes involve some combinations of dominant and recessive alleles, so these are associated with phenotypes representing intermediate levels of extroversion. In fact, the diagram shows that the most common outcome is for people to inherit exactly 4 dominant and 4 recessive alleles: 19 of the 81 genotypes produce this pattern (e.g., *AABbccDd, AaBbcCDd*). A few extreme cases (very outgoing or very shy), when coupled with many intermediate cases, produce the familiar bell-shaped distribution that characterizes many behavioral and psychological traits.

Remember, this example is completely hypothetical. Extroversion is *not* based on the combined influence of eight pairs of genes. But this example shows how several genes working together could produce a continuum of phenotypes. Something

> Behavioral characteristics often reflect polygenic inheritance in which a phenotype depends on the combined actions of many genes.

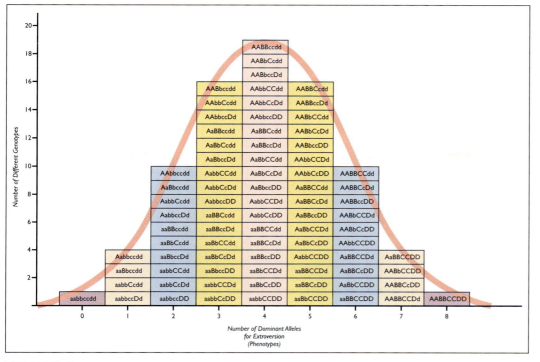

FIGURE 2-4

Identical twins are called monozygotic twins because they came from a single fertilized egg that split in two and, consequently, they have identical genes.

like our example is probably involved in the inheritance of numerous human behavioral traits, except that many more pairs of genes are involved and the environment also influences the phenotype (Plomin et al., 2001).

**METHODS OF BEHAVIORAL GENETICS.** If many behavioral phenotypes involve countless genes, how can we hope to unravel the influence of heredity? Traditionally, behavior geneticists have relied on statistical methods in which they compare groups of people known to differ in their genetic similarity. Twins, for example, provide important clues about the influence of heredity. **Identical twins are called** *monozygotic twins* **because they come from a single fertilized egg that splits in two.** Because identical twins come from the same fertilized egg, they have the same genes that control body structure, height, and facial features, which explains why identical twins like those in the photo look alike. **In contrast, fraternal or** *dizygotic twins* **come from two separate eggs fertilized by two separate sperm.** Genetically, fraternal twins are just like any other siblings; on average, about half their genes are the same. In twin studies, scientists compare identical and fraternal twins to measure the influence of heredity. If identical twins are more alike than fraternal twins, this implicates heredity.

An example will help illustrate the logic underlying comparisons of identical and fraternal twins. Suppose we want to determine whether extroversion is inherited. We would first measure extroversion in a large number of identical and fraternal twins. We might use a questionnaire with scores ranging from 0 to 100 (100 indicating maximal extroversion). Some of the hypothetical results are shown in the table.

Look first at the results for the fraternal twins. Most have similar scores: The Aikman twins both have high scores but the Herrod twins have low scores. Looking at the identical twins, their scores are even more alike, typically differing by no more than five points. This greater similarity among identical twins than among fraternal twins would be evidence that extroversion is inherited, just as the fact that identical twins look more alike than fraternal twins is evidence that facial appearance is inherited.

**TABLE 2-4**

| TWINS' HYPOTHETICAL SCORES ON A MEASURE OF EXTROVERSION | | | | | | | |
|---|---|---|---|---|---|---|---|
| **Fraternal Twins** | | | | **Identical Twins** | | | |
| Family | One Twin | Other Twin | Difference Between Twins | Family | One Twin | Other Twin | Difference Between Twins |
| Aikman | 80 | 95 | 15 | Bettis | 100 | 95 | 5 |
| Fernandez | 70 | 50 | 20 | Harbaugh | 32 | 30 | 2 |
| Herrod | 10 | 35 | 25 | Park | 18 | 15 | 3 |
| Stewart | 25 | 5 | 20 | Ramirez | 55 | 60 | 5 |
| Tomczak | 40 | 65 | 25 | Robinson | 70 | 62 | 8 |

Adopted children are another important source of information about heredity. In this case, adopted children are compared with their biological parents and their adoptive parents. The idea is that biological parents provide the child's genes but adoptive parents provide the child's environment. Consequently, if a behavior has genetic roots, then adopted children's behavior should resemble their biological parents even though they have never met them. But if the adopted children resemble their adoptive parents, we know that family environment affects behavior.

If we wanted to use an adoption study to determine whether extroversion is inherited, we would measure extroversion in a large sample of adopted children, their biological mothers, and their adoptive mothers. (Why just mothers? Obtaining data from biological fathers of adopted children is often difficult.) The results of this hypothetical study are shown in the table.

**TABLE 2-5**

**HYPOTHETICAL SCORES FROM AN ADOPTION STUDY ON A MEASURE OF EXTROVERSION**

| Child's Name | Child's Score | Biological Mother's Score | Adoptive Mother's Score |
|---|---|---|---|
| Anila | 60 | 70 | 35 |
| Jerome | 45 | 50 | 25 |
| Kerri | 40 | 30 | 80 |
| Michael | 90 | 80 | 50 |
| Troy | 25 | 5 | 55 |

First, compare children's scores with their biological mothers' scores. Overall, they are related: Extroverted children like Michael tend to have extroverted biological mothers. Introverted children like Troy tend to have introverted biological mothers. In contrast, children's scores don't show any clear relation to their adoptive mothers' scores. For example, although Michael has the highest score and Troy has the lowest, their adoptive mothers have very similar scores. Children's greater similarity to biological than to adoptive parents would be evidence that extroversion is inherited.

Twin studies and adoption studies, which are described in the Summary Table on page 52, are powerful tools. They are not foolproof, however. Maybe you thought of a potential flaw in twin studies: Parents and other people may treat identical twins more similarly than they treat fraternal twins. This would make identical twins more similar than fraternal twins in their experiences as well as in their genes. Adoption studies have their own Achilles' heel. Adoption agencies sometimes try to place youngsters in homes like those of their biological parents. For example, if an agency believes that the biological parents are bright, the agency may try harder to have the child adopted by parents that the agency believes are bright. This can bias adoption studies because biological and adoptive parents end up being similar.

Heredity is implicated when identical twins are more alike than fraternal twins and when adopted children resemble their biological parents more than their adoptive parents.

## SUMMARY TABLE

### PRIMARY RESEARCH METHODS FOR BEHAVIORAL GENETICS

| Method | Defined | Evidence for Heredity | Main Weakness |
|---|---|---|---|
| Twin study | Compare monozygotic and dizygotic twins | Monozygotic twins more alike than dizygotic twins | Others may treat monozygotic twins more similarly than they treat dizygotic twins |
| Adoption study | Compare children with their biological and adoptive parents | Children more like biological parents than adoptive parents | Selective placement: Children's adoptive parents may resemble their biological parents |

The problems associated with twin and adoption studies are not insurmountable. Because twin and adoption studies have different faults, if the two kinds of studies produce similar results on the influence of heredity, we can be confident of those results. In addition, behavioral geneticists are moving beyond traditional methods such as twin and adoption studies to connect behavior to molecular genetics (Dick & Rose, 2002; Plomin & Crabbe, 2000). Today, researchers are able to isolate particular segments of DNA in human chromosomes. These segments then serve as markers for identifying specific alleles. The procedure is complicated, but the basic approach often begins by identifying people who differ in the behavior or psychological trait of interest. For example, researchers might identify children who are outgoing and children who are shy. Or they might identify children who read well and children who read poorly. The children rub the inside of their mouth with a cotton swab, which yields cheek cells that contain DNA. The cells are analyzed in a lab, and the DNA markers for the two groups are compared. If the markers differ consistently, then the alleles near the marker probably contribute to the differences between the groups.

Techniques like these have the potential to identify the many different genes that contribute to complex behavioral and psychological traits. Of course, these new methods have limits. Some require very large samples of children, which can be hard to obtain when studying rare disorders. Also, some require that an investigator have an idea, before even beginning the study, about which chromosomes to search and where. These can be major hurdles. But, when used with traditional methods of behavioral genetics (e.g., adoption studies), the new methods promise much greater understanding of how genes influence behavior and development (Plomin & Crabbe, 2000).

### WHICH PSYCHOLOGICAL CHARACTERISTICS ARE AFFECTED BY HEREDITY?

Research reveals consistent genetic influence in many psychological areas, including personality, mental ability, psychological disorders, and attitudes and interests. One expert summarized this work by saying, "Nearly every . . . psychological phenotype (normal and abnormal) is significantly influenced by genetic factors" (Bouchard, 2004, p. 151). **To illustrate, let's consider** *depression*, **a disorder in which individuals have pervasive feelings of sadness, are irritable, and have low self-esteem.** In twin studies, identical twins show remarkable similarity for depression: If one identical twin is depressed, the other twin has roughly a 50% chance of being depressed. For fraternal twins, the odds are much lower—approximately 25% (Plomin & Crabbe, 2000).

*Personality, mental ability, psychological disorders, and attitudes are all strongly influenced by heredity.*

We can see the influence of heredity in another domain—cognitive development—in the "Focus on Research" feature.

## Focus On Research

### Hereditary and Environmental Bases of Cognitive Development

*Who were the investigators, and what was the aim of the study?* Children and adolescents differ in their cognitive skills. Some are quite skilled cognitively—they remember accurately and solve problems easily. Other children and adolescents are less skilled in remembering and solving problems. Robert Plomin and his colleagues (1997) measured cognitive skills in children, their biological parents, and their adoptive parents to understand the influence of heredity on the development of cognitive skill.

*How did the investigators measure the topic of interest?* The parents completed a comprehensive battery of standardized tests that assessed a broad range of cognitive skills. Biological mothers were tested in the last few months of pregnancy. Adoptive parents were tested in the first year after the adoption. Every few years, the children took an intelligence test. (The test varied depending on the child's age.)

*Who were the children in the study?* The sample included 245 children whose mothers relinquished them at birth. The children were approximately 1 month old when they were adopted.

*What was the design of the study?* This study was correlational because Plomin and his colleagues examined how children's cognitive skill was related to their biological parents' cognitive skill and their adoptive parents' cognitive skill. The study was longitudinal because children were tested repeatedly, every year or two.

*Were there ethical concerns with the study?* No. The tests were ones used commonly by psychologists. Biological and adoptive parents provided written consent for their own and their children's participation.

*What were the results?* The primary results, correlations between children's skills and their parents' skills, are shown in the graph. At every age, the correlation between children's skill and their biological parents' skill (shown by the blue line) is greater than the correlation between children's skill and their adoptive parents' skill (shown by the red line). In fact, children's scores are essentially unrelated to their adoptive parents' scores. Notice, too, that the relation between children's scores and their biological parents' scores actually gets stronger as children get older. In other words, as adopted children grow, their test scores increasingly resemble their biological parents' scores despite the fact that these adopted children have had no contact with their biological parents for 16 years.

*What did the investigators conclude?* Children's cognitive skill reflects heredity and the impact of heredity actually is stronger in adolescence than in childhood. However, the correlations between children's scores and their biological parents' scores are not very large, which says that heredity is not the sole influence on cognitive growth; the environment must contribute, too.

The correlations are always larger for biological parents and the gap widens as children get older.

FIGURE 2-5

*What converging evidence would strengthen these conclusions?* As I described on page 51, selective placement can weaken adoption studies. But this was not a problem in the study by Plomin and his colleagues: Biological parents' cognitive scores were unrelated to adoptive parents' scores. However, there is another problem: The adoptive parents were not representative of all parents—they tended to be somewhat older, smarter, and more affluent than the national average. Of course, this is often true of adoptive parents (they tend to be older and financially more secure), so it would be difficult to redo the study with adoptive parents who are more representative of average parents. A different approach would be to conduct a longitudinal study of twins, with the expectation that identical twins' cognitive skills would be more alike as they grew. ◼

We will look at cognitive development in greater detail later in this book. For now, keep in mind two conclusions from twin studies and adoption studies like the one described in the "Focus on Research" feature. On the one hand, the impact of heredity on behavioral development is substantial and widespread. Heredity has a sizable influence on such different aspects of development as intelligence and personality. In understanding children and their development, we must always think about how heredity may contribute. On the other hand, heredity is never the sole determinant of behavioral development. For example, roughly 50% of the differences among children's scores on intelligence tests is due to heredity. But the remaining 50% is due to environment. How do nature and nurture work together? We'll answer that question throughout the rest of the book, but we can identify some general principles in the remainder of this module.

## Paths From Genes to Behavior

How do genes work together to make, for example, some children brighter than others and some children more outgoing than others? That is, how does the information in strands of DNA influence a child's behavioral and psychological development? The specific paths from genes to behavior are largely uncharted, but in the next few pages we'll discover some of their general properties.

**1. The behavioral consequences of genetic instructions depend on the environment in which those instructions develop.** In other words, a genotype can lead to many different phenotypes, depending on the specific environment in which the genotype is expressed (Gottesman & Hanson, 2005). *Reaction range* refers to the fact that the same genotype can produce a range of phenotypes, in reaction to the environment where development takes place. For example, imagine two children with the same genotype for "average intelligence." The children's phenotypic intelligence would depend on the environments in which they develop. If one child is brought up in an impoverished, unstimulating environment, his or her phenotypic intelligence may be below average. In contrast, if the second child is brought up in an enriched environment filled with stimulation, this child's phenotypic intelligence may be above average. Thus the same genotype for intelligence can lead to a range of phenotypes, depending on the quality of the rearing environment. Of course, what makes a "good" or "rich" environment is not the same for all facets of behavioral or psychological development. Throughout this book, you will see how specific kinds of environments influence very particular aspects of development (Wachs, 1983).

> The influence of genes on behavior always depends on the environment in which genetic instructions are carried out.

This principle is responsible for the following warning that you'll find in the fine print on a can of diet soda (and some other food products):

"Phenylketonurics: contains phenylalanine."

Why? Children with phenylketonuria (PKU) are missing an enzyme that breaks down phenylalanine. When phenylalanine accumulates, it damages the nervous system and leads to mental retardation. Today, most American hospitals check for PKU at birth—with a blood or urine test. Newborns who have the disease are immediately placed on a diet that limits intake of phenylalanine, and mental retardation is avoided. Thus, an individual who has the genotype for PKU but is not exposed to phenylalanine has normal intelligence. PKU illustrates that development depends on heredity and a child's dietary environment. And, as you'll see in the "Child Development and Family Policy" feature, PKU represents an exciting example of how research has influenced family policy.

## Child Development and Family Policy
### Screening for PKU

PKU was first discovered in 1934 when a Norwegian mother asked a physician, Dr. Asbjørn Fjølling, to help her two children, both of whom suffered from mental retardation. Dr. Fjølling discovered that the children had large amounts of phenylpyruvic acid in their urine and phenylalanine in their blood. By the 1950s, other scientists had determined that the buildup of phenylalanine damaged the nervous system and had shown that a low-protein diet would leave the nervous system unharmed. The missing link was an effective way to diagnose PKU in newborns, before phenylalanine had a chance to accumulate and cause damage. In 1959, Dr. Robert Guthrie devised a quick and inexpensive way to determine levels of phenylalanine in a newborn's blood. Studies soon proved that the test was effective. Armed with this information and aided by a complimentary story in *Life* magazine, Dr. Guthrie and the National Association for Retarded Children lobbied vigorously for laws that required newborns to be screened for PKU. In 1965, New York became the first state to require mandatory screening; by the end of the 1960s, most U.S. states required screening. Today, all states require PKU screening and require health insurance providers to cover the cost of low-protein formula for infants with PKU. Thus, research revealed the mechanisms of PKU and led to a simple screening test; public policy that required mandatory screening and low-protein diets means that hundreds of children who are born each year with PKU can lead healthy, normal lives.

2. **Heredity and environment interact dynamically throughout development.** A simple-minded view of heredity and environment is that heredity provides the clay of life and experience does the sculpting. In fact, genes and environments constantly influence each other throughout a child's life (Gottesman & Hanson, 2005). This principle actually has two parts. First, genes are expressed—"turned on"—throughout a child's development. For example, genes initiate the onset of menstruation in the early teens and the graying of hair in midlife. Second, the environment can trigger genetic expression: Children's experiences can help to determine how and when genes are activated (Gottlieb, 2000). For instance, teenage girls begin to menstruate at a younger age if they've had a stressful childhood. The exact pathway of influence is unknown (though it probably involves the hormones that are triggered by stress and those that initiate ovulation) but this is a clear case in which the environment advances the developmental clock (Ellis, 2004).

Children who are outgoing often like to be with other people and they deliberately seek them out, a phenomenon known as niche-picking.

Returning to the analogy of sculpting clay, a more realistic view is that new clay is constantly being added to the sculpture, leading to resculpting, which causes more clay to be added, and the cycle continues. Hereditary clay and environmental sculpting are continuously interweaving and influencing each other.

**3. Genes can influence the kind of environment to which a child is exposed.** In other words, "nature" can help to determine the kind of "nurturing" that a child receives (Scarr, 1992; Scarr & McCartney, 1983). A child's genotype can lead people to respond to the child in a specific way. For example, imagine a child who is bright and outgoing (both due, in part, to the child's genes). That child may receive plenty of attention and encouragement from teachers. In contrast, a child who is not as bright and more withdrawn (again, due in part to heredity) may be easily overlooked by teachers. In addition, as children grow and are more independent, they actively seek environments related to their genetic makeup. Children who are bright (due in part to heredity) may actively seek peers, adults, and activities that strengthen their intellectual development. Similarly, children like the one in the photo, who are outgoing (due in part to heredity), seek the company of other people, particularly extroverts like themselves. **This process of deliberately seeking environments that fit one's heredity is called *niche-picking*.** Niche-picking is first seen in childhood and becomes more common as children get older and can control their environments.

Niche-picking illustrates that genes and environment rarely influence development alone. Instead, nature and nurture interact. Experiences determine which phenotypes emerge, and genotypes influence the nature of children's experiences. The story of Sadie and Molly also makes it clear that, to understand how genes influence development, we need to look carefully at how environments work, our next topic.

**4. Environmental influences typically make children within a family different.** One of the fruits of behavioral genetic research is greater understanding of the manner in which environments influence children. Traditionally, scientists considered some environments beneficial for children and others detrimental. This view has been especially strong in regard to family environments. Some parenting practices are thought to be more effective than others, and parents who use these effective practices are believed to have children who are, on average, better off than children of parents who don't use these practices. This view leads to a simple prediction: Children within a family should be similar because they all receive the same type of effective (or ineffective) parenting. However, dozens of behavioral genetic studies show that, in reality, siblings are not very much alike in their cognitive and social development (Plomin & Spinah, 2004).

Does this mean that family environment is not important? No. **These findings point to the importance of *nonshared environmental influences*, the environmental forces that make siblings different from one another.** Although environmental forces are important, they usually affect each child in a unique way, which makes siblings differ. For example, parents may be more affectionate with one child than another, they may use more physical punishment with one child than another, or they may have higher expectations for school achievement for one child than another. One teenager may have friends who like to drink but a sibling has friends who discourage drinking. All

Genes help to determine the kinds of experiences that children have.

**2.2**   Erik, 19, and Jason, 16, are brothers. Erik excels in school—he gets straight A's, is president of the math club, and enjoys tutoring younger children. Jason hates school and his grades show it. How can nonshared environmental influences explain these differences?

these contrasting environmental influences tend to make siblings different, not alike (Tyrkheimer & Waldron, 2000). Environments are important, but, as I describe their influence throughout this book, you should remember that each child in a family experiences a unique environment.

Much of what I have said about genes, environment, and development is summarized in the diagram. Parents are the source of children's genes and, at least for young children, the primary source of children's experiences. Children's genes also influence the experiences they have and the impact of those experiences on them. However, to capture the idea of nonshared environmental influences, we would need a separate diagram for each child, reflecting the fact that parents provide unique genes and a unique family environment for each of their offspring. And to capture the idea that genes are expressed across a child's lifetime, we would need to repeat the diagram for each child many times, emphasizing that heredity–environment influences at any given point are affected by prior heredity–environment exchanges.

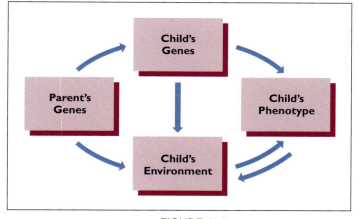

FIGURE 2-6

Using this framework, we can speculate about why Sadie and Molly, the fraternal twins from this module's opening vignette, are so different. Perhaps their parents passed along more genes for sociability to Sadie than to Molly. During infancy, their parents included both girls in play groups with other babies. Sadie found this exciting but Molly found it annoying and a bit stressful. Over time, their parents unwittingly worked hard to foster Sadie's relationships with her peers. But they worried less about Molly's peer relationships because she seemed to be perfectly content to look at books, to color, or to play alone with puzzles. Apparently heredity gave Sadie a slighter larger dose of sociability but experience ended up accentuating the difference between the sisters.

In a similar manner, throughout the rest of this book we'll examine links between nature, nurture, and development. One of the best places to see the interaction of nature and nurture is during prenatal development, which is the topic of Chapter 3.

## CHECK YOUR LEARNING

RECALL  What is polygenic inheritance and how does it explain behavioral phenotypes?

Describe the basic features, logic, and weaknesses of twin and adoption studies.

INTERPRET  Explain how reaction range and niche-picking show the interaction between heredity and environment.

APPLY  Leslie and Glenn, the couple from Module 2.1 who were concerned that their baby could have sickle-cell disease, are already charting their baby's life course. Leslie, who has always loved to sing, is confident that her baby will be a fantastic musician and easily imagines a regular routine of music lessons, rehearsals, and concerts. Glenn, a pilot, is just as confident that his child will share his love of flying; he is already planning trips the two of them can take together. Are Leslie's and Glenn's ideas more consistent with the active or passive views of children? What advice might you give to Leslie and Glenn about factors they are ignoring?

Here are three examples of nonshared environmental influences. First, as the older child, Erik's parents may have had higher academic standards for him and insisted that he do well in school; perhaps they relaxed their standards for Jason. Second, perhaps Erik found a circle of friends who enjoyed school and encouraged one another to do well in school; Jason may have found a group of friends who enjoyed hanging out at the mall instead of studying. Third, by the luck of the draw, Erik may have had a string of outstanding teachers who made school exciting; Jason may have had an equal number of not-so-talented teachers who made school boring.

## ☘ UNIFYING THEMES: Nature and Nurture

This entire chapter is devoted to a single theme: *Development is always jointly influenced by heredity and environment.* We have seen, again and again, how heredity and environment are essential ingredients in all developmental recipes, though not always in equal parts. In sickle-cell disease, an allele has survival value in malaria-prone environments but not in environments where malaria has been eradicated. In PKU, persons who inherit the disorder experience retarded development when their dietary environment includes foods with phenylalanine but not when they avoid phenylalanine. And children with genes for normal intelligence develop below-average, average, or above-average intelligence, depending on the environment in which they grow. Nature and nurture . . . development always depends on both.

## SEE FOR YOURSELF

The Human Genome Project, launched in the late 1980s by U.S. scientists, aims to identify the exact location of all 25,000 human genes. It is a vast undertaking that first requires determining the sequence of roughly 3 billion pairs of nucleotides like those shown in the diagram on page 42. The project has produced maps of each chromosome showing the location of known genes. You can see these maps at a Web site maintained by the Human Genome Project. The address is: **http://www.ornl.gov/hgmis/posters/chromosome/**

At this site, you can select a "favorite" chromosome and see which genes have been located on it. See for yourself!

## RESOURCES

For more information about . . .

🖎 **human heredity,** try Matt Ridley's *Genome: The Autobiography of a Species in 23 Chapters* (HarperCollins, 2000), which describes progress in genetics research by telling fascinating stories about the impact of chromosomes on intelligence, language, cancer, and sex, to name just a few.

↗ **children with Down syndrome,** visit the Down syndrome Web site: **http://www.nas.com/downsyn**

## KEY TERMS

alleles  42
autosomes  41
behavioral genetics  48
chromosomes  40
deoxyribonucleic acid (DNA)  41
depression  52
dizygotic (fraternal) twins  50
dominant  42
Down syndrome  46
gene  42
genotype  42
heterozygous  42
homozygous  42

Huntington's disease  45
in vitro fertilization  41
incomplete dominance  43
monozygotic (identical) twins  50
niche-picking  56
nonshared environmental influences  56
phenotype  42
polygenic inheritance  49
reaction range  54
recessive  42
sex chromosomes  41
sickle-cell trait  43

## 2.1 MECHANISMS OF HEREDITY

### The Biology of Heredity

At conception, the 23 chromosomes in the sperm merge with the 23 chromosomes in the egg. The 46 chromosomes that result include 22 pairs of autosomes plus 2 sex chromosomes. Each chromosome is one molecule of DNA, which consists of nucleotides organized in a structure that resembles a spiral staircase. A section of DNA that provides specific biochemical instructions is called a gene. All of a person's genes make up a genotype; phenotype refers to the physical, behavioral, and psychological characteristics that develop when the genotype is exposed to a specific environment.

### Single Gene Inheritance

Different forms of the same gene are called alleles. A person who inherits the same allele on a pair of chromosomes is homozygous; in this case, the biochemical instructions on the allele are followed. A person who inherits different alleles is heterozygous; in this case, the instructions of the dominant allele are followed whereas those of the recessive allele are ignored. In incomplete dominance, the person is heterozygous but the phenotype is midway between the dominant and recessive phenotypes.

### Genetic Disorders

Most inherited disorders are carried by recessive alleles. Examples include sickle-cell disease, albinism, cystic fibrosis, phenylketonuria, and Tay–Sachs disease. Inherited disorders are rarely carried by dominant alleles because individuals with such a disorder usually don't live long enough to have children. An exception is Huntington's disease, which doesn't become symptomatic until middle age.

Most fertilized eggs that do not have 46 chromosomes are aborted spontaneously soon after conception. One exception is Down syndrome, caused by an extra 21st chromosome. Down-syndrome individuals have a distinctive appearance and are mentally retarded. Disorders of the sex chromosomes, such as Klinefelter's syndrome, are more common because these chromosomes contain less genetic material.

## 2.2 HEREDITY, ENVIRONMENT, AND DEVELOPMENT

### Behavioral Genetics

Behavioral and psychological phenotypes that reflect an underlying continuum (such as intelligence) often involve polygenic inheritance. In polygenic inheritance, the phenotype reflects the combined activity of many distinct genes. Polygenic inheritance has been examined traditionally by studying twins and adopted children, and more recently, by identifying DNA markers. These studies indicate substantial influence of heredity in many areas, including intelligence, psychological disorders, and personality.

### Paths From Genes to Behavior

The impact of heredity on a child's development depends on the environment in which the genetic instructions are carried out; these heredity–environment interactions occur throughout a child's life. A child's genotype can affect the kinds of experiences he has; children and adolescents often actively seek environments related to their genetic makeup. Environments affect siblings differently (nonshared environmental influence): Each child in a family experiences a unique environment.

If you ask parents to name some of the
most memorable experiences of their
lives, many mention events associated
with pregnancy and childbirth. From the
exciting news that a woman is pregnant through
birth 9 months later, the entire experience evokes
awe and wonder. The events of pregnancy and birth
provide the foundation on which all child development is built. In Module 3.1, we'll trace the events of
prenatal development that transform sperm and
egg into a living, breathing human being. In Module
3.2, we'll learn about some developmental prob-
lems that can occur before birth. In Module 3.3, we'll turn to birth.
We'll see what happens during labor and delivery, and we'll consider
some problems that can arise. In Module 3.4, we'll discover what
newborn babies are like.

**3.1**    From Conception to Birth

**3.2**    Influences on Prenatal
Development

**3.3**    Happy Birthday!

**3.4**    The Newborn

1   The Science of Child Development

2   Genetic Bases of Child Development

# Prenatal Development, Birth, and the Newborn

**3**

4   Growth and Health

5   Perceptual and Motor Development

6   Theories of Cognitive Development

7   Cognitive Processes and Academic Skills

8   Intelligence and Individual Differences in Cognition

9   Language and Communication

10  Emotional Development

11  Understanding Self and Others

12  Moral Understanding and Behavior

13  Gender and Development

14  Family Relationships

15  Influences Beyond the Family

# 3.1

# FROM CONCEPTION TO BIRTH

**Period of the Zygote (Weeks 1–2)**

**Period of the Embryo (Weeks 3–8)**

**Period of the Fetus (Weeks 9–38)**

### LEARNING OBJECTIVES

- What happens to a fertilized egg in the first 2 weeks after conception?
- When do body structures and internal organs emerge in prenatal development?
- When do body systems begin to function well enough to support life?

*Eun Jung has just learned that she is pregnant with her first child. Like many other parents-to-be, she and her husband, Kinam, are ecstatic. But they also soon realize how little they know about "what happens when" during pregnancy. Eun Jung is eager to visit her obstetrician to learn more about the normal timetable of events during pregnancy.*

**The changes that transform a fertilized egg into a newborn human make up** *prenatal development.* Prenatal development takes an average of 38 weeks, which are divided into three stages: the period of the zygote, the period of the embryo, and the period of the fetus. Each period gets its name from the term used to describe the baby-to-be at that point in prenatal development.

In this module, we'll trace the major developments during each period. As we go, you'll learn the answer to the "what happens when" question that intrigues Eun Jung.

## Period of the Zygote (Weeks 1–2)

VIDEO 3.1

Prenatal Development

The diagram traces the major events of the first period of prenatal development, which begins with fertilization and lasts about 2 weeks. **It ends when the fertilized**

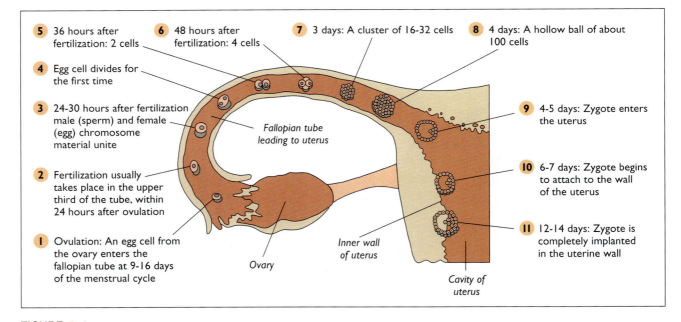

**5** 36 hours after fertilization: 2 cells

**6** 48 hours after fertilization: 4 cells

**7** 3 days: A cluster of 16-32 cells

**8** 4 days: A hollow ball of about 100 cells

**4** Egg cell divides for the first time

**3** 24-30 hours after fertilization male (sperm) and female (egg) chromosome material unite

**2** Fertilization usually takes place in the upper third of the tube, within 24 hours after ovulation

**1** Ovulation: An egg cell from the ovary enters the fallopian tube at 9-16 days of the menstrual cycle

*Fallopian tube leading to uterus*

*Ovary*

*Inner wall of uterus*

*Cavity of uterus*

**9** 4-5 days: Zygote enters the uterus

**10** 6-7 days: Zygote begins to attach to the wall of the uterus

**11** 12-14 days: Zygote is completely implanted in the uterine wall

FIGURE 3-1

egg, called a *zygote*, **implants itself in the wall of the uterus.** During these 2 weeks, the zygote grows rapidly through cell division and travels down the fallopian tube toward the uterus. Within hours, the zygote divides for the first time; then division occurs every 12 hours. Occasionally, the zygote separates into two clusters that develop into identical twins. Fraternal twins, which are more common, are created when two eggs are released and each is fertilized by a different sperm cell. **After about 4 days, the zygote consists of about 100 cells, resembles a hollow ball, and is called a** *blastocyst.*

By the end of the first week, the zygote reaches the uterus. **The next step is** *implantation***: The blastocyst burrows into the uterine wall and establishes connections with the mother's blood vessels.** Implantation takes about a week to complete and triggers hormonal changes that prevent menstruation, letting the woman know she has conceived.

The implanted blastocyst, shown in the photograph, is less than a millimeter in diameter. Yet its cells have already begun to differentiate. In the diagram, which shows a cross section of the blastocyst and the wall of the uterus, you can see different layers of cells. **A small cluster of cells near the center of the blastocyst, the** *germ disc,* **eventually develops into the baby.** The other cells are destined to become structures that support, nourish, and protect the developing organism. **The layer of cells closest to the uterus becomes the** *placenta***, a structure for exchanging nutrients and wastes between the mother and the developing organism.**

Implantation and differentiation of cells mark the end of the period of the zygote. Comfortably sheltered in the uterus, the blastocyst is well prepared for the remaining 36 weeks of the marvelous journey to birth.

By the end of the period of the zygote, the fertilized egg has been implanted in the wall of the uterus and has begun to make connections with the mother's blood vessels.

## Period of the Embryo (Weeks 3–8)

**Once the blastocyst is completely embedded in the uterine wall, it is called an** *embryo.* This new period typically begins the 3rd week after conception and lasts until the end of the 8th week. During the period of the embryo, body structures and internal organs develop. At the beginning of the period, three layers form in the embryo. **The outer layer or** *ectoderm* **will become hair, the outer layer of skin, and the nervous system; the middle layer or** *mesoderm* **will form muscles, bones, and the circulatory system; the inner layer or** *endoderm* **will form the digestive system and the lungs.**

One dramatic way to see the changes that occur during the embryonic period is to compare a 3-week-old embryo with an 8-week-old embryo. The 3-week-old embryo shown in the left photo at the top of page 64 is about 2 millimeters long. Cell specialization is under way, but the organism looks more like a salamander than a human being. But growth and specialization proceed so rapidly that the 8-week-old embryo shown in the photo on the right on page 64 looks very different:

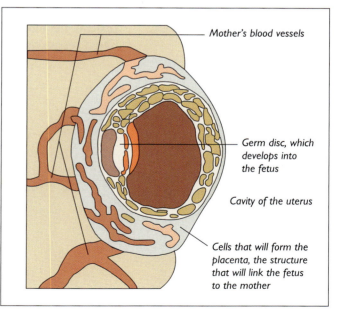

Mother's blood vessels

Germ disc, which develops into the fetus

Cavity of the uterus

Cells that will form the placenta, the structure that will link the fetus to the mother

FIGURE 3-2

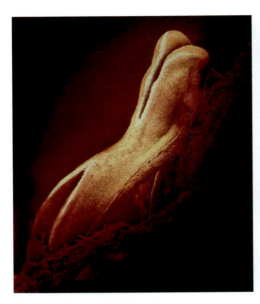

At 3 weeks after conception, the fertilized egg is about 2 millimeters long and resembles a salamander.

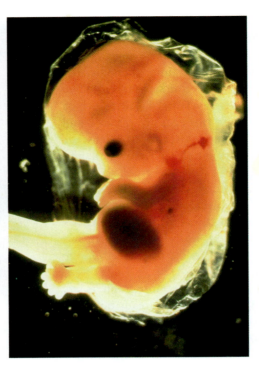

At 8 weeks after conception, near the end of the period of the embryo, the fertilized egg is obviously recognizable as a baby-to-be.

You can see an eye, the jaw, an arm, and a leg. The brain and the nervous system are also developing rapidly, and the heart has been beating for nearly a month. Most of the organs found in a mature human are in place, in some form. (The sex organs are a notable exception.) Yet, being only an inch long and weighing a fraction of an ounce, the embryo is much too small for the mother to feel its presence.

The embryo's environment is shown in the diagram. **The embryo rests in an *amniotic sac*, which is filled with *amniotic fluid* that cushions the embryo and maintains a constant temperature.** The embryo is linked to the mother by two structures. **The *umbilical cord* houses blood vessels that join the embryo to the placenta.** In the placenta, the blood vessels from the umbilical cord run close to the mother's blood vessels but aren't actually connected to them. **Instead, the blood flows through *villi*, finger-like projections from the umbilical blood vessels that are shown in the diagram.** As you can see, villi lie in close prox-

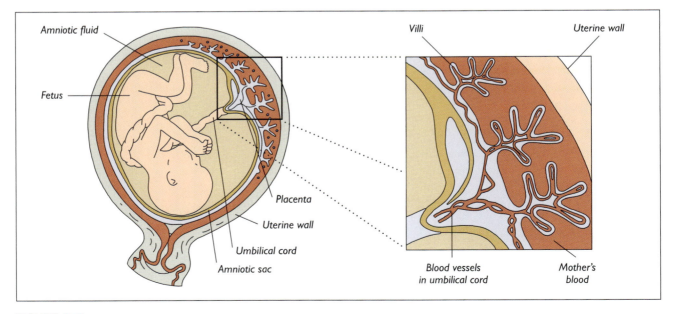

FIGURE 3-3

imity to the mother's blood vessels and thus allow nutrients, oxygen, vitamins, and waste products to be exchanged between mother and embryo.

With body structures and internal organs in place, another major milestone passes in prenatal development. What's left is for these structures and organs to begin working properly. This is accomplished in the final period of prenatal development, as we'll see in the next section.

> Body parts and systems are formed in the period of the embryo and begin to work effectively in the period of the fetus.

## Period of the Fetus (Weeks 9–38)

**The final and longest phase of prenatal development, the *period of the fetus*, extends from the 9th week after conception until birth.** During this period, the baby-to-be becomes much larger and its bodily systems begin to work. The increase in size is remarkable. At the beginning of this period, the fetus weighs less than an ounce. At about 4 months, the fetus weighs roughly 4 to 8 ounces, enough for the mother to feel it move: Pregnant women often describe these fluttering movements as feeling like popcorn popping or a goldfish swimming inside them! During the last 5 months of pregnancy, the fetus gains an average of an additional 7 or 8 pounds before birth. The chart, which depicts the fetus at one eighth of its actual size, shows these incredible increases in size.

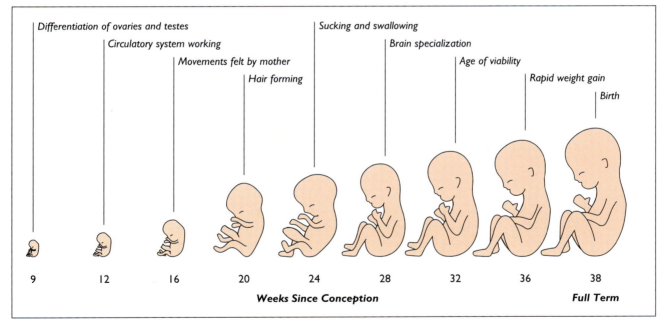

Differentiation of ovaries and testes
Circulatory system working
Movements felt by mother
Hair forming
Sucking and swallowing
Brain specialization
Age of viability
Rapid weight gain
Birth

9      12      16      20      24      28      32      36      38

**Weeks Since Conception**                                    **Full Term**

FIGURE 3-4

During the fetal period, the finishing touches are put on the body systems that are essential to human life, such as the nervous, respiratory, and digestive systems. Some highlights of this period include the following:

- At 4 weeks after conception, a flat set of cells curls to form a tube. One end of the tube swells to form the brain; the rest forms the spinal cord. By the start of the fetal period, the brain has distinct structures and has begun to regulate body functions. **During the period of the fetus, all regions of the brain grow, particularly the *cerebral cortex*, the wrinkled surface of the brain that regulates many important human behaviors.**

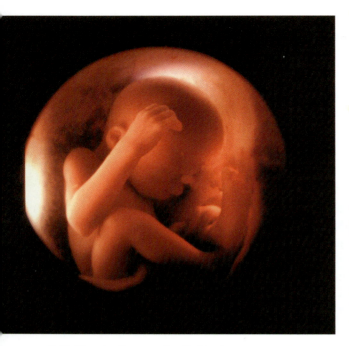

At 22–28 weeks after conception, the fetus has achieved the age of viability, meaning that it has a chance of surviving if born prematurely.

- Near the end of the embryonic period, male embryos develop testes and female embryos develop ovaries. In the 3rd month, the testes in a male fetus secrete a hormone that causes a set of cells to become a penis and scrotum; in a female fetus, this hormone is absent, so the same cells become a vagina and labia.

- During the 5th and 6th months after conception, eyebrows, eyelashes, and scalp hair emerge. **The skin thickens and is covered with a thick greasy substance,** *vernix*, **that protects the fetus during its long bath in amniotic fluid.**

**With these and other rapid changes, by 22 to 28 weeks most systems function well enough that a fetus born at this time has a chance to survive, which is why this age range is called the** *age of viability.* By this age, the fetus has a distinctly baby-like look, as you can see in the photo. However, babies born this early have trouble breathing because their lungs are not yet mature. Also, they cannot regulate their body temperature very well because they lack the insulating layer of fat that appears in the 8th month after conception. With modern neonatal intensive care, infants born this early can survive, but they face other challenges, as I'll describe in Module 3.3.

**FETAL BEHAVIOR.**    During the fetal period, the fetus actually starts to behave (Joseph, 2000). The delicate movements that were barely noticeable at 4 months are now obvious. In fact, the fetus is a budding gymnast and kick-boxer rolled into one. It will punch or kick and turn somersaults. When active the fetus will move about once a minute (DiPietro et al., 2004). But these bursts of activity are followed by times when the fetus is still, as regular activity cycles emerge. Although movement is common in a healthy pregnancy, some fetuses are more active than others, and these differences predict infants' behavior: An active fetus is more likely than an inactive fetus to be an unhappy, difficult baby (DiPietro et al., 1996).

Another sign of growing behavioral maturity is that the senses work. There's not much to see in the uterus (imagine being in a cave with a flashlight that has a weak battery) but there are sounds galore. The fetus can hear the mother's heart beating and can hear her food digesting. More importantly, the fetus can hear her speak and hear others speak to her (Lecanuet, Granier-Deferre, & Busnel, 1995). And there are tastes: As the fetus swallows amniotic fluid, it responds to different flavors in amniotic fluid.

Not only can the fetus detect sounds and flavors, sensory experiences from pregnancy can have lasting effects. In one study (Menella, Jagnow, & Beauchamp, 2001), women drank carrot juice several days a week during the last month of pregnancy. When their infants were 5 and 6 months old, they preferred cereal flavored with carrot juice. In another study, pregnant women read aloud *The Cat in the Hat* daily for the last several weeks of pregnancy (DeCasper & Spence, 1986). After birth, the newborns were allowed to suck on a special pacifier that controlled a tape recorder. The newborns would suck to hear a tape of their mother reading *The Cat in the Hat* but not to hear her reading other stories. Evidently, newborns recognized the familiar, rhythmic quality of *The Cat in the Hat* from their prenatal story times. The ability of the fetuses in these studies to learn from experience shows that prenatal development leaves babies well prepared for life outside the uterus.

**3.1**  Julia is 8 months pregnant and spends hours each day talking to her baby-to-be. Julia's husband considers this a waste of time but Julia's convinced that her baby-to-be must benefit. What do you think?

These and other important prenatal changes are summarized in the table. The milestones listed in the table make it clear that prenatal development does a remarkable job of preparing the fetus for independent living as a newborn baby. But these astonishing prenatal changes can only take place when a woman provides a healthy environment for her baby-to-be. The "Improving Children's Lives" feature describes what pregnant women should do to provide the best foundation for prenatal development.

**SUMMARY TABLE**

## CHANGES DURING PRENATAL DEVELOPMENT

| Trimester | Period | Weeks | Size | Highlights |
|---|---|---|---|---|
| First | Zygote | 1–2 | | Fertilized egg becomes a blastocyst that is implanted in the uterine wall |
| | Embryo | 3–4 | 1/4 inch | Period of rapid growth; most body parts including nervous system (brain and spinal cord), heart, and limbs are formed |
| | Embryo | 5–8 | 1 inch, fraction of an ounce | |
| | Fetus | 9–12 | 3 inches, about an ounce | Rapid growth continues, most body systems begin to function |
| Second | Fetus | 13–24 | 12–15 inches, about 2 pounds | Continued growth; fetus is now large enough for a woman to feel its movements, fetus is covered with vernix |
| Third | Fetus | 25–38 | 20 inches, 7–8 pounds | Continued growth; body systems become mature in preparation for birth, layer of fat is acquired, reaches the age of viability |

## *Improving Children's Lives*

**Five Steps Toward a Healthy Baby**

1. Visit a health-care provider for regular prenatal checkups. You should have monthly visits until you get close to your due date, when you will have a check-up every other week or maybe even weekly.

2. Eat healthy foods. Be sure your diet includes foods from each of the five major food groups (cereals, fruits, vegetables, dairy products, and meats and beans). Your health-care provider may recommend that you supplement your diet with vitamins, minerals, and iron to be sure you are providing your baby with all the nutrients it needs.

3. Stop drinking alcohol and caffeinated beverages. Stop smoking. Consult your health-care provider before taking any over-the-counter medications or prescription drugs.

4. Exercise throughout pregnancy. If you are physically fit, your body is better equipped to handle the needs of the baby.

5. Get enough rest, especially during the last 2 months of pregnancy. Also, attend childbirth education classes so that you'll be prepared for labor, delivery, and your new baby. ▪

As critically important as these steps are, they unfortunately do not guarantee a healthy baby. In Module 3.2, we'll see how prenatal development can sometimes go awry.

**3.1**  The fetus can hear Julia speaking and these one-sided conversations probably help the fetus to become familiar with Julia's voice. There aren't other obvious benefits, however, because the fetus can't understand *what* she's saying.

### CHECK YOUR LEARNING

**RECALL**  Describe the three stages of prenatal development. What are the highlights of each?

What findings show that the fetus behaves?

**INTERPRET**  Compare the events of prenatal development that precede the age of viability with those that follow it.

**APPLY**  In the last few months before birth, the fetus has some basic perceptual and motor skills; a fetus can hear, see, taste, and move. What are the advantages of having these skills in place months before they're really needed?

## 3.2

# INFLUENCES ON PRENATAL DEVELOPMENT

General Risk Factors

Teratogens: Diseases, Drugs, and Environmental Hazards

How Teratogens Influence Prenatal Development

Prenatal Diagnosis and Treatment

### LEARNING OBJECTIVES

- How is prenatal development influenced by a pregnant woman's nutrition, the stress she experiences while pregnant, and her age?

- What is a teratogen, and what specific diseases, drugs, and environmental hazards can be teratogens?

- How do teratogens affect prenatal development?

- How can prenatal development be monitored? Can abnormal prenatal development be corrected?

*Chloe was barely 2 months pregnant at her first prenatal checkup. As she wait-ed for her appointment, she looked at the list of questions that she wanted to ask her obstetrician. "I spend much of my workday at a computer. Is radiation from the monitor harmful to my baby?" "When my husband and I get home from work, we'll have a glass of wine to help unwind from the stress of the day. Is moderate drinking like this okay?" "I'm 38. I know older women more often give birth to mentally retarded babies. Is there any way I can know if my baby will be mentally retarded?"*

All of Chloe's questions concern potential harm to her baby-to-be. She worries about the safety of her computer monitor, about her nightly glass of wine, and about her age. Chloe's concerns are well-founded. Beginning with conception, environmental factors influence the course of prenatal development, and they are the focus of this module. If you're sure you can answer all of Chloe's questions, skip this module and go directly to Module 3.3 on page 82. Otherwise, read on to learn about problems that sometimes arise in pregnancy.

## General Risk Factors

As the name implies, general risk factors can have widespread effects on prenatal development. Scientists have identified three general risk factors: nutrition, stress, and a mother's age.

**NUTRITION.** The mother is the developing child's sole source of nutrition, so a balanced diet that includes foods from each of the five major food groups is vital. Most pregnant women need to increase their intake of calories by about 10 to 20% to meet the needs of prenatal development. A woman should expect to gain between 25 and 35 pounds during pregnancy, assuming that her weight was normal before pregnancy. A woman who was underweight before becoming pregnant may gain as much as 40 pounds; a woman who was overweight should gain at least 15 pounds (Institute of Medicine, 1990). Of this gain, about one-third reflects the weight of the baby, the placenta, and the fluid in the amniotic sac; another third comes from increases in a woman's fat stores; yet another third comes from the increased volume of blood and increases in the size of her breasts and uterus (Whitney & Hamilton, 1987).

Adequate nutrition—in terms of calories as well as proteins, vitamins, and minerals—is essential for healthy prenatal development.

Sheer amount of food is only part of the equation for a healthy pregnancy. *What* a pregnant woman eats is also very important. Proteins, vitamins, and minerals are essential for normal prenatal development. For example, folic acid, one of the B vitamins, is important for the nervous system to develop properly (Shaw et al., 1995). **When mothers do not consume adequate amounts of folic acid, their babies are at risk for *spina bifida*, a disorder in which the embryo's neural tube does not close properly during the 1st month of pregnancy.** Since the neural tube develops into the brain and spinal cord, when it does not close properly, the result is permanent damage to the spinal cord and the nervous system. Many children with spina bifida need crutches, braces, or wheelchairs. Other prenatal problems have also been traced to inadequate proteins, vitamins, or minerals, so health-care providers typically recommend that pregnant women supplement their diet with additional proteins, vitamins, and minerals.

When a pregnant woman does not provide adequate nourishment, the infant is likely to be born prematurely and to be underweight. Inadequate nourishment during the last few months of pregnancy can particularly affect the nervous system, because this is a time of rapid brain growth. Finally, babies who do not receive adequate nourishment are vulnerable to illness (Guttmacher & Kaiser, 1986).

When pregnant women experience chronic stress, they're more likely to give birth early or have smaller babies, but this may be because women who are stressed are more likely to smoke or drink and less likely to rest, exercise, and eat properly.

**STRESS.** Does a pregnant woman's mood affect the zygote, embryo, or fetus in her uterus? Is a woman who is happy during pregnancy more likely to give birth to a happy baby? Is a pregnant woman like the harried office worker in the photo more likely to give birth to an irritable baby? **These questions address the impact on prenatal development of chronic *stress*, which refers to a person's physical and psychological responses to threatening or challenging situations.** We can answer these questions with some certainty for nonhumans. When pregnant female animals experience constant stress such as repeated electric shock or intense overcrowding, their offspring are often smaller than average and prone to other physical and behavioral problems (DiPietro, 2004).

Determining the impact of stress on human pregnancy is more difficult because we must rely solely on correlational studies. (It would be unethical to do an experiment that assigned some pregnant women to a condition of extreme stress.) Studies typically show that women who report greater anxiety during pregnancy more often give birth early or have babies who weigh less than average (Copper et al., 1996; Paarlberg et al., 1995). What's more, when women are anxious throughout pregnancy, their children are less able to pay attention as infants and more prone to behavioral problems as preschoolers (Huizink et al., 2002; O'Conner et al., 2002).

Increased stress can harm prenatal development in several ways. First, when a pregnant woman experiences stress, her body secretes hormones that reduce the flow of oxygen to the fetus while increasing its heart rate and activity level (Monk et al., 2000). Second, stress can weaken a pregnant woman's immune system, making her more susceptible to illness (Cohen & Williamson, 1991), which can, in turn, damage fetal development. Third, pregnant women under stress are more likely to smoke or drink alcohol and less likely to rest, exercise, and eat properly (DiPietro et al., 2004). All these behaviors endanger prenatal development.

> Problems during pregnancy are more common when a woman experiences chronic stress and when she is 35 or older.

I want to emphasize that the results described here apply to women who experience prolonged, extreme stress. Virtually all women sometimes become anxious or upset while pregnant. But occasional, relatively mild anxiety is not thought to have any harmful consequences for prenatal development.

**MOTHER'S AGE.** Traditionally, the 20s were thought to be the prime childbearing years. Teenage women as well as women who were 30 or older were considered less fit for the rigors of pregnancy. Is being a 20-something really important for a successful pregnancy? Let's answer this question separately for teenage and older women. Compared to women in their 20s, teenage women are more likely to have problems during pregnancy, labor, and delivery. This is largely because pregnant teenagers are more likely to be economically disadvantaged and do not get good prenatal care, because they are unaware of the need and wouldn't be able to afford it if they did. For example, in one study (Turley, 2003), children of teenage moms were compared with their cousins, whose mothers were the older sisters of the teenage moms but had given birth when they were in their 20s. The two groups of children were very similar in academic skills and behavioral problems, indicating that it's the typical family background of teenage moms that is the obstacle, not their age. Similarly, research done on African American adolescents indicates that when differences in prenatal care are taken into account, teenagers are just as likely as women in their 20s to have problem-free pregnancies and give birth to healthy babies (Goldenberg & Klerman, 1995).

Nevertheless, even when a teenager receives adequate prenatal care and gives birth to a healthy baby, all is not rosy. Children of teenage mothers generally do less well in school and more often have behavioral problems (Fergusson & Woodward, 2000). The problems of teenage motherhood—incomplete education, poverty, and marital difficulties—affect the child's later development (Moore & Brooks-Gunn, 2002). In the "Spotlight on Theories" feature, we'll see one way that child-development researchers have explained why these problems occur.

## *Spotlight on Theories*

### A Theory of the Risks Associated with Teenage Motherhood

#### *BACKGROUND*

Children born to teenage mothers typically don't fare very well. During childhood and adolescence, these children usually have lower scores on mental-ability tests, they get lower grades in school, and they more often have behavioral problems (e.g., they're too aggressive). However, why teen motherhood leads to these outcomes remains poorly understood.

#### *THE THEORY*

Sarah Jaffee and her colleagues (2001) believe that teenage motherhood leads to harmful consequences through two distinct mechanisms. **One mechanism, called** *social influence*, **refers to events set in motion when a teenage girl gives birth, events that make it harder for her to provide an environment that's positive for her child's development.** For example, she may drop out of school, limiting her employment opportunities. Or she may try to finish school but becomes a neglectful parent because she spends so much time studying.

**According to the second mechanism, called** *social selection*, **some teenage girls are more likely than others to become pregnant and those same factors that cause girls to become pregnant may put their children at risk.** Take conduct disorder as an example. Teenage girls with conduct disorder—they often lie, break rules, and are aggressive physically and verbally—are more likely to get pregnant than girls who don't have conduct disorder. The behaviors that define conduct disorder don't bode well for effective parenting. In addition, conduct disorder has a genetic component, which teenage mothers could pass along to their children.

According to social selection, the mother's age at birth is not really critical—these girls would have difficulty parenting even if they delayed motherhood into their 20s and 30s. Instead, the factors that put girls at risk for becoming pregnant as teenagers also put children from those pregnancies at risk.

HYPOTHESIS: According to the social influence mechanism, measures of the child-rearing environment should predict outcomes for children born to teenage moms. For example, if teenage motherhood results in less education and less income, then these variables should predict children's outcomes. According to the social selection mechanism, the same characteristics of a teenage girl that are associated with her becoming pregnant should predict outcomes for her children. For example, if teenage girls are more likely to get pregnant when they're not as bright and have conduct disorder, then these same variables should predict outcomes for the children of teenage moms.

**TEST:** Jaffee et al. (2001) evaluated both hypotheses in a 20-year longitudinal study conducted in New Zealand in which about 20% of the mothers had given birth while teenagers. The investigators measured mothers' antisocial behavior as well as their education and income. They also assessed children's outcomes; for simplicity, we'll consider just one—whether the children had, as adolescents or young adults, committed any criminal offenses.

Jaffee et al. found that, compared to children born to older mothers, children born to teenage mothers were nearly three times more likely to have committed a criminal offense. This was due to both social influence and social selection mechanisms. Consistent with the social influence mechanism, teenage moms were less educated and had lower incomes, and these variables predicted their children's criminal activity. Consistent with the social selection mechanism, teenage moms were more likely to have a history of antisocial behavior and this history predicted their children's criminal activity.

**CONCLUSION:** The adverse outcomes associated with teenage motherhood don't have a single explanation. Some of the adversity can be traced to cascading events brought on by giving birth as a teenager: Early motherhood limits education and income, hindering a mother's efforts to provide an environment that's conducive to a child's development. But some of the adversity does not reflect early motherhood per se; instead, girls who become pregnant teenagers often have characteristics that lead to adverse outcomes regardless of the age when they gave birth.

**APPLICATION:** Policy makers have created many social programs designed to encourage teenagers to delay childbearing. Jaffee et al.'s work suggests two additional needs. First, policies are needed to limit the cascading harmful effects of childbearing for those teens who do get pregnant (e.g., programs to allow them to complete their education without neglecting their children). Second, many of the problems associated with teenage pregnancy are only coincidentally related to the fact that the mother is a teenager; programs are needed to help these girls learn effective parenting methods. ■

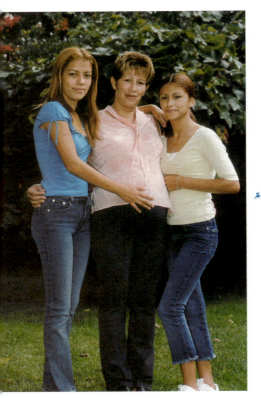

Older women have more difficulty getting pregnant and are more likely to have miscarriages.

Of course, not all teenage mothers and their infants follow this dismal life course. Some teenage mothers finish school, find good jobs, and have happy marriages; their children do well in school, academically and socially. These successes are more likely when teenage moms live with a relative—typically the child's grandmother (Gordon, Chase-Lansdale, & Brooks-Gunn, 2004). However, teenage pregnancies with "happy endings" are definitely the exception; for many teenage mothers and their children, life is a struggle. Educating teenagers about the true consequences of teen pregnancy is crucial.

Are older women better suited for pregnancy? This is an important question because present-day American women typically are waiting longer than ever to become pregnant. Completing an education and beginning a career often delay childbearing. In fact, the birthrate in the early 2000s among 30- to 44-year-olds was nearly double what it was 1980 (Martin et al., 2002).

Today we know that older women like the one in the photo have more difficulty getting pregnant and are less likely to have successful pregnancies. Women in their 20s are twice as fertile as women in their 30s (Dunson et al., 2002). And, past 35 years of age, the risks of miscarriage and stillbirth increase rapidly. Among 40- to 45-year-olds, for example, nearly half of all pregnancies result in miscarriage (Andersen et al., 2000).

What's more, women in their 40s are more liable to give birth to babies with Down syndrome.

In general, then, prenatal development is most likely to proceed normally when women are between the ages of 20 and 35, are healthy and eat right, get good health care, and lead lives that are free of chronic stress. But even in these optimal cases, prenatal development can be disrupted, as we'll see in the next section.

## Teratogens: Diseases, Drugs, and Environmental Hazards

In the late 1950s, many pregnant women in Germany took thalidomide, a drug to help them sleep. Soon, however, came reports that many of these women were giving birth to babies with deformed arms, legs, hands, or fingers. **Thalidomide was a powerful *teratogen*, an agent that causes abnormal prenatal development.** Ultimately, more than 10,000 babies worldwide were harmed before thalidomide was withdrawn from the market (Kolberg, 1999).

Prompted by the thalidomide disaster, scientists began to study teratogens extensively. Today, we know a great deal about the three primary types of teratogens: diseases, drugs, and environmental hazards. Let's look at each.

**DISEASES.**    Sometimes women become ill while pregnant. Most diseases, such as colds and many strains of flu, do not affect the developing organism. However, several bacterial and viral infections can be very harmful and, in some cases, fatal to the embryo or fetus; five of the most common of these are listed in the table.

**TABLE 3-1**

| TERATOGENIC DISEASES AND THEIR CONSEQUENCES | |
| --- | --- |
| **Disease** | **Potential Consequences** |
| AIDS | Frequent infections, neurological disorders, death |
| Cytomegalovirus | Deafness, blindness, abnormally small head, mental retardation |
| Genital herpes | Encephalitis, enlarged spleen, improper blood clotting |
| Rubella (German measles) | Mental retardation; damage to eyes, ears, and heart |
| Syphilis | Damage to the central nervous system, teeth, and bones |

Some of these diseases pass from the mother through the placenta to attack the embryo or fetus directly. They include cytomegalovirus (a type of herpes), rubella, and syphilis. Other diseases attack at birth: The virus is present in the lining of the birth canal, and the baby is infected as it passes through to be born. Genital herpes is transmitted this way. AIDS is transmitted both ways—through the placenta and during passage through the birth canal.

**Many bacterial and viral infections are very harmful to the fetus.**

The only way to guarantee that these diseases do not harm prenatal development is for a woman to not contract the disease before or during her pregnancy. Medication may help the woman, but does not prevent the disease from damaging the developing baby.

**DRUGS.** Thalidomide illustrates the harm that drugs can cause during prenatal development. The table lists other drugs that are known teratogens.

**TABLE 3-2**

## TERATOGENIC DRUGS AND THEIR CONSEQUENCES

| Drug | Potential Consequences |
|------|------------------------|
| Alcohol | Fetal alcohol syndrome, cognitive deficits, heart damage, retarded growth |
| Aspirin | Deficits in intelligence, attention, and motor skills |
| Caffeine | Lower birth weight, decreased muscle tone |
| Cocaine and heroin | Retarded growth, irritability in newborns |
| Marijuana | Lower birth weight, less motor control |
| Nicotine | Retarded growth, possible cognitive impairments |

Notice that most of the drugs in the list are substances that you may use routinely—alcohol, aspirin, caffeine, and nicotine. Nevertheless, when consumed by pregnant women, they present special dangers (Behnke & Eyler, 1993).

Cigarette smoking is typical of the potential harm from teratogenic drugs (Cornelius et al., 1995; Fried, O'Connell, & Watkinson, 1992). The nicotine in cigarette smoke constricts blood vessels and thus reduces the oxygen and nutrients that can reach the fetus through the placenta. Therefore, pregnant women who smoke are more likely to miscarry (abort the fetus spontaneously) and to bear children who are smaller than average at birth (Cnattingius, 2004; Ernst et al., 2000). And, as children develop, they are more likely to show signs of impaired attention, language, and cognitive skills, along with behavioral problems (Brennan et al., 2002). Finally, even secondhand smoke harms the fetus: When pregnant women don't smoke but fathers do, babies tend to be smaller at birth (Friedman & Polifka, 1996). The message is clear and simple: Pregnant women shouldn't smoke and they should avoid others who do.

> Whenever possible, pregnant women should take no drugs.

Alcohol also carries serious risk. **Pregnant women who consume large quantities of alcoholic beverages often give birth to babies with *fetal alcohol syndrome (FAS).*** Children with FAS usually grow more slowly than normal and have heart problems and misshapen faces. Like the child in the photo, youngsters with FAS often have a small head, a thin upper lip, a short nose, and widely spaced eyes. FAS is the leading cause of mental retardation in the United States, and children with FAS have serious attentional, cognitive, and behavioral problems. FAS is most common among pregnant women who are heavy recreational drinkers—that is, women who drink 5 or more ounces of alcohol a few times each week (Jacobson & Jacobson, 2000; Lee, Mattson, & Riley, 2004).

Does this mean that moderate drinking is safe? No. When women drink moderately throughout pregnancy, their children are often afflicted with alcohol-related neurodevelopmental disorder (ARND). Children with ARND are normal in appearance but have deficits in attention, memory, and intelligence (Jacobson et al., 1998).

Is there any amount of drinking that's safe during pregnancy? Maybe, but that amount is yet to be determined. Gathering definitive data is complicated by two factors: First, researchers usually determine the amount a woman drinks by her own responses to interviews or questionnaires. If for some reason she does not accurately

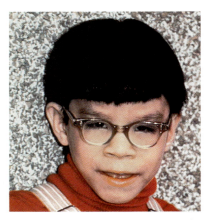

When pregnant women drink large amounts of alcohol their children often have fetal alcohol syndrome. Children with fetal alcohol syndrome tend to have a small head and a thin upper lip as well as retarded mental development.

report her consumption, it is impossible to accurately estimate the amount of harm associated with drinking. Second, any safe level of consumption is probably not the same for all women. Based on their health and heredity, some women may be able to consume more alcohol more safely than others.

These factors make it impossible to guarantee safe levels of alcohol or any of the other drugs listed in the table at the top of page 74. The best policy, therefore, is for a pregnant woman to avoid drugs if at all possible (including over-the-counter, prescription, and illegal drugs) and to consult a health-care professional before using essential drugs.

**ENVIRONMENTAL HAZARDS.**   As a by-product of life in an industrialized world, people are often exposed to toxins in food they eat, fluids they drink, and air they breathe. Chemicals associated with industrial waste are the most common environmental teratogens, and the quantities involved are usually minute. However, as is true for drugs, amounts that go unnoticed by an adult can cause serious damage to a developing fetus. Several environmental hazards that are known teratogens are listed in the table.

Sarah is 22 and pregnant for the first time. She smokes half a pack of cigarettes each day and has one bottle of light beer with dinner. Sarah can't believe that relatively small amounts of smoking and drinking could hurt the baby she's carrying. What would you say?

**3.2**

## TABLE 3-3

### ENVIRONMENTAL TERATOGENS AND THEIR CONSEQUENCES

| Hazard | Potential Consequences |
|--------|------------------------|
| Lead | Mental retardation |
| Mercury | Retarded growth, mental retardation, cerebral palsy |
| PCBs | Impaired memory and verbal skill |
| X rays | Retarded growth, leukemia, mental retardation |

You'll notice that although X rays are included in this table, radiation associated with computer monitors and video display terminals (VDTs) is not. Several major studies have examined the impact of exposure to the electromagnetic fields that are generated by VDTs, and they have found no negative results. For example, Schnorr and her colleagues (1991) compared the pregnancies in telephone operators who worked at VDTs at least 25 hours weekly with operators who never used VDTs. For both groups of women, about 15% of the pregnancies ended in miscarriage. Other investigators have found no relation between exposure to VDTs and birth defects (Parazzini et al., 1993; Shaw, 2001). Evidently, VDTs can be used safely by pregnant women.

In the "Focus on Research" feature, we look at one of the environmental teratogens in detail.

## *Focus on Research*

### Impact of Prenatal Exposure to PCBs on Cognitive Functioning

*Who were the investigators, and what was the aim of the study?* For many years, polychlorinated biphenyls (PCBs) were used in electrical transformers and paints, but the U.S. government banned them in the 1970s. Like many industrial by-products, they seeped into the waterways, where they contaminated fish and wildlife. The amount of PCBs in a typical contaminated fish does not affect adults, but Joseph Jacobson and Sandra Jacobson wanted to determine if this level of exposure was harmful to prenatal development. In particular, they knew from earlier work that substantial prenatal exposure to PCBs affected cognitive skills in infants and preschoolers; they hoped to determine if prenatal exposure similarly affected cognitive skills in school-age children.

*How did the investigators measure the topic of interest?* Jacobson and Jacobson needed to measure prenatal exposure to PCBs and cognitive skill. To measure prenatal exposure, they measured concentrations of PCBs in (a) blood obtained from the umbilical cord and (b) breast milk of mothers who were breast-feeding. To measure cognitive skill, they used a standardized test of intelligence (the WISC, described on page 247) and a standardized test of reading comprehension.

*Who were the children in the study?* The sample included 212 children who were born in western Michigan in 1980–1981. This region was chosen because, at the time, Lake Michigan contained many contaminated salmon and lake trout.

*What was the design of the study?* The study was correlational because the investigators were interested in the relation that existed naturally between two variables: exposure to PCBs and cognitive skill. The study was longitudinal because children were tested several times: Their exposure to PCBs was measured immediately after birth, and their cognitive skill was measured at three ages: 7 months, 4 years, and 11 years.

*Were there ethical concerns with the study?* No. The children had been exposed to PCBs naturally, prior to the start of the study. (Obviously, it would not have been ethical for researchers to do an experiment that involved asking pregnant women to eat contaminated fish.) The investigators obtained permission from the parents for the children to participate.

*What were the results?* PCB exposure affects intelligence and reading comprehension. However, as you can see in the graphs, lower levels of exposure to PCBs apparently had little effect on intelligence and reading comprehension. Only children with high levels of exposure to PCBs were affected.

*What did the investigators conclude?* Prenatal exposure to PCBs affects children's cognitive skills. Though children's scores were in the normal range, their reduced cognitive skills may create special hurdles in school.

*What converging evidence would strengthen these conclusions?* The results show that PCBs affect children's scores on standardized tests. More convincing would be longitudinal results showing that children exposed to PCBs were more likely to be diagnosed with a learning disability or language impairment, more likely to repeat a grade, or less likely to graduate from high school. ■

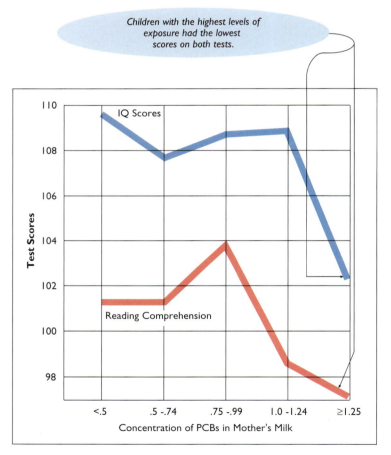

Children with the highest levels of exposure had the lowest scores on both tests.

**FIGURE 3-5**

Environmental teratogens are treacherous because people are unaware of their presence in the environment. The women in the Jacobson and Jacobson (1996) study, for example, did not realize they were eating PCB-laden fish. This invisibility makes it more difficult for a pregnant woman to protect herself from environmental teratogens. Pregnant women need to be particularly careful of the foods they eat and the air they breathe. Be sure all foods are cleaned thoroughly to rid them of insecticides. Avoid convenience foods, which often contain many chemical additives. Stay away from air that's been contaminated by household products such as cleansers, paint strippers, and fertilizers. Women in jobs that require contact with potential teratogens (e.g., housecleaners, hairdressers) should switch to less potent chemicals. For example, they should use baking soda instead of more chemically laden cleansers. And they should wear protective gloves, aprons, and masks to reduce their contact with potential teratogens. Finally, because environmental teratogens continue to increase, check with a health-care provider to learn if other materials should be avoided.

> Environmental teratogens are particularly dangerous because a pregnant woman may not know they are present in the environment.

## How Teratogens Influence Prenatal Development

By assembling all the evidence of harm caused by diseases, drugs, and environmental hazards, scientists have identified five important general principles about how teratogens usually work (Hogge, 1990; Jacobson & Jacobson, 2000; Vorhees & Mollnow, 1987).

1. **The impact of a teratogen depends on the genotype of the organism.** A substance may be harmful to one species but not to another. To determine thalidomide's safety, researchers had tested thalidomide in pregnant rats and rabbits, whose offspring had had normal limbs. Yet, when pregnant women took the same drug in comparable doses, many produced children with deformed limbs. Thalidomide was harmless to rats and rabbits but not to people. Moreover, some women who took thalidomide gave birth to babies with normal limbs, yet others who took comparable doses at the same time in their pregnancies gave birth to babies with deformities. Apparently, heredity makes some individuals more susceptible than others to a teratogen.

2. **The impact of teratogens changes over the course of prenatal development.** The timing of exposure to a teratogen is critical. The chart on page 78 shows how the consequences of teratogens differ for the periods of the zygote, embryo, and fetus. During the period of the zygote, exposure to teratogens usually results in spontaneous abortion of the fertilized egg. During the embryonic period, exposure produces major defects in body structure. For example, women who took thalidomide during the embryonic period had babies with ill-formed or missing limbs. Women who contract rubella during the embryonic period have babies with heart defects. During the fetal period, exposure to teratogens either produces minor defects in body structure or causes body systems to function improperly. For example, when women drink large quantities of alcohol during the fetal period, the fetus develops fewer brain cells.

   Even within the different periods of prenatal development, developing body parts and systems are more vulnerable at certain times. The blue shading in the chart indicates a time of maximum vulnerability; orange shading indicates a time when the developing organism is less vulnerable. The heart, for example, is most sensitive to teratogens during the first two thirds of the embryonic period. Exposure to teratogens before this time rarely produces heart damage; exposure after this time results in milder damage.

3. **Each teratogen affects a specific aspect (or aspects) of prenatal development.** Said another way, teratogens do not harm all body systems; instead, damage is

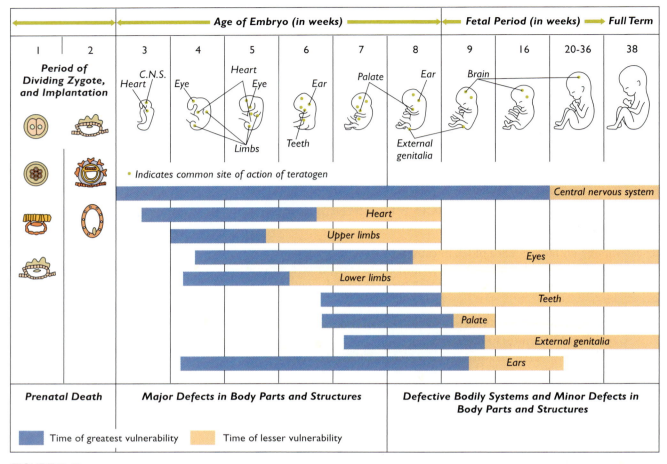

FIGURE 3-6

selective. If a pregnant woman contracts rubella, her baby may have problems with eyes, ears, and heart, but limbs will be normal. If a pregnant woman consumes PCB-contaminated fish, her baby typically has normal body parts and normal motor skills but below-average cognitive skills.

4. **The impact of teratogens depends on the dose.** Just as a single drop of oil won't pollute a lake, small doses of teratogens may not harm the fetus. In research on PCBs, for example, cognitive skills were affected only among children who had the greatest prenatal exposure to these by-products. In general, the greater the exposure, the greater the risk for damage (Adams, 1999).

> The impact of teratogens depends on the genotype of the organism and the timing and amount of exposure to the teratogen.

An implication of this principle is that researchers should be able to determine safe levels for a teratogen. In reality, this is very difficult because sensitivity to teratogens will not be the same for all people (and it's not practical to establish separate safe amounts for each person). Hence, the safest rule is zero exposure to teratogens.

5. **Damage from teratogens is not always evident at birth but may appear later in life.** In the case of malformed infant limbs or babies born addicted to cocaine, the effects of a teratogen are obvious immediately. A cocaine baby goes through withdrawal shaking, crying, and being unable to sleep. Sometimes, however, the damage from a teratogen becomes evident only as the child develops. For

example, between 1947 and 1971 many pregnant women in North America and Europe took the drug diethylstilbestrol (DES) to prevent miscarriages. The babies appeared normal at birth, but, as adults, they are more likely to have a rare cancer of the vagina and to have difficulty becoming pregnant themselves (Friedman & Polifka, 1996). Sons of women who took DES may be less fertile and at risk for cancer of the testes (Sharpe & Skakkebaek, 1993). This is a case in which the impact of the teratogen is not evident until decades after birth.

**THE REAL WORLD OF PRENATAL RISK.**    I have discussed risk factors individually, as if each were the only potential threat to prenatal development. In reality, many infants are exposed to multiple general risks and multiple teratogens. Pregnant women who drink alcohol often smoke and drink coffee (Haslam & Lawrence, 2004). Pregnant women who are under stress often drink alcohol, and may self-medicate with aspirin or other over-the-counter drugs. Many of these same women live in poverty, which means they may have inadequate nutrition and receive minimal medical care during pregnancy. When all the risks are combined, prenatal development is rarely optimal.

This pattern explains why it's often challenging for child-development researchers to determine the harm associated with individual teratogens. Cocaine is a perfect example. You may remember stories in newspapers and magazines about "crack babies" and their developmental problems. In fact, the jury is still out on the issue of cocaine as a teratogen. Some investigators (e.g., Singer et al., 2002) find the harmful effects that made headlines in the 1990s, whereas others (e.g., Brown et al., 2004; Frank et al., 2001) argue that most of the effects attributed to cocaine actually stem from concurrent smoking and drinking and to the inadequate parenting that these children receive.

From what I've said so far in this module, you may think that developing children have little chance of escaping harm. But most babies are born in good health. Of course, a good policy for pregnant women is to avoid diseases, drugs, and environmental hazards that are known teratogens. This, coupled with thorough prenatal medical care and adequate nutrition, is the best recipe for normal prenatal development.

## Prenatal Diagnosis and Treatment

"I really don't care whether I have a boy or girl, just as long as my baby's healthy." Legions of parents worldwide have felt this way, but until recently all they could do was hope for the best. Today, however, advances in technology give parents a much better idea whether their baby is developing normally.

Even before a woman becomes pregnant, a couple may go for genetic counseling, which I described in Module 2.1. A counselor constructs a family tree for each prospective parent to check for heritable disorders. If it turns out that one (or both) carries a disorder, further tests can determine the person's genotype. With this more detailed information, a genetic counselor can discuss choices with the prospective parents. They may choose to go ahead and conceive "naturally," taking their chances that the child will be healthy. Or they could decide to use sperm or eggs from other people. Yet another choice would be to adopt a child.

After a woman is pregnant, how can we know if prenatal development is progressing normally? Traditionally, obstetricians gauged development by feeling the size and position of the fetus through a woman's abdomen. This technique was not very precise and, of course, couldn't be done at all until the fetus was large enough to feel.

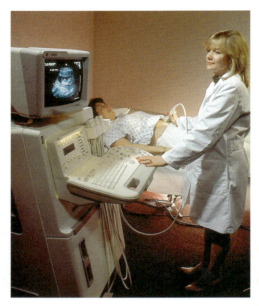

Today, however, new techniques have revolutionized our ability to monitor prenatal growth and development. **A standard part of prenatal care in North America is *ultrasound*, a procedure using sound waves to generate a picture of the fetus.** As the top photo shows, an instrument about the size of a hair dryer is rubbed over the woman's abdomen; the image is shown on a nearby TV monitor. The pictures that are generated are hardly portrait quality; they are grainy and it takes an expert's eye to distinguish what's what. Nevertheless, the procedure is painless and parents are thrilled to be able to see their babies and watch them move.

Ultrasound can be used as early as 4 or 5 weeks after conception; before this time the fetus is not large enough to generate an interpretable image. Ultrasound pictures are useful for determining the date of conception, which enables the physician to predict the due date more accurately. Ultrasound pictures are also valuable in showing the position of the fetus and placenta in the uterus, and they can be used to identify gross physical deformities, such as abnormal growth of the head. As shown in the bottom photo, ultrasound can also help in detecting twins or other multiple pregnancies. Finally, beginning at about 20 weeks after conception, ultrasound images can reveal the child's sex.

A standard part of prenatal care is ultrasound, in which sound waves are used to generate an image of the fetus that can be used to determine the position of the fetus in the uterus.

When a genetic disorder is suspected, two other techniques are particularly valuable because they provide a sample of fetal cells that can be analyzed. **In *amniocentesis*, a needle is inserted through the mother's abdomen to obtain a sample of the amniotic fluid that surrounds the fetus.** Amniocentesis is typically performed at approximately 16 weeks after conception. As you can see in the left diagram, ultrasound is used to guide the needle into the uterus. The fluid contains skin cells that can be grown in a laboratory dish and then analyzed to determine the genotype of the fetus.

**In *chorionic villus sampling (CVS)*, a sample of tissue is obtained from the chorion (a part of the placenta) and analyzed.** The right diagram shows that a small tube, inserted through the vagina and into the uterus, is used to collect a small plug of cells from the placenta. CVS is often preferred over amniocentesis because it can be done about 10 to 12 weeks after conception, nearly 4 to 6 weeks earlier than amniocentesis. (Amniocentesis can't be performed until the amniotic sac is large enough to provide easy access to amniotic fluid.) In both procedures, results are returned from the lab within several days.

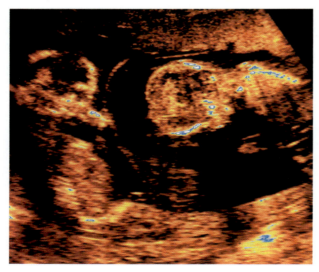

Ultrasound images can reveal the position of the fetus in the uterus and reveal the presence of multiple pregnancies.

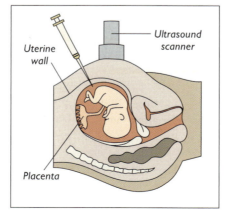

FIGURE 3-7

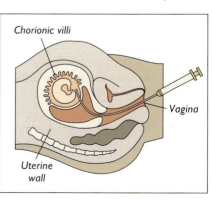

FIGURE 3-8

With samples obtained from either amniocentesis or CVS, about 200 different genetic disorders can be detected. For example, for pregnant women in their late 30s or 40s, either amniocentesis or CVS will often be used to determine if the fetus has Down syndrome. These procedures are virtually error-free, but they have a price: Miscarriages are slightly more likely after amniocentesis or CVS (Wilson, 2000). A woman must decide if the beneficial information gained from amniocentesis or CVS justifies the slight risk of a miscarriage. These procedures are summarized in the table.

## SUMMARY TABLE

### METHODS OF PRENATAL DIAGNOSIS

| Procedure | Description | Primary Uses |
|---|---|---|
| Ultrasound | Sound waves used to generate an image of the fetus | Determine due date and position of fetus in uterus; check for physical deformities, multiple births, and child's sex |
| Amniocentesis | Sample of fetal cells are obtained from amniotic fluid | Screen for genetic disorders |
| Chorionic villus sampling (CVS) | Sample of tissue obtained from the chorion (part of the placenta) | Screen for genetic disorders |

Ultrasound, amniocentesis, and chorionic villus sampling have made it much easier to determine if prenatal development is progressing normally. But what happens when it is not? Until recently a woman's options were limited: She could continue the pregnancy or end it. But options are expanding. **A whole new field called** *fetal medicine* **is concerned with treating prenatal problems before birth.** Many tools are now available to solve problems that are detected during pregnancy (Evans, Platt, & De La Cruz, 2001). One approach is to treat disorders medically, by administering drugs or hormones to the fetus. For example, in fetal hypothyroidism, the fetal thyroid gland does not produce enough hormones, leading to retarded physical and mental development. This disorder can be treated by injecting the necessary hormones directly into the amniotic cavity, resulting in normal growth. Another example is congenital adrenal hyperplasia, an inherited disorder in which the fetal adrenal glands produce too much androgen, causing early maturation of boys or masculinization of girls. In this case, treatment consists of injecting hormones into the mother that reduce the amount of androgen secreted by the fetal adrenal glands (Evans et al., 2001).

Another way to correct prenatal problems is fetal surgery. For example, more than 200 cases of spina bifida have been corrected with fetal surgery in the 7th or 8th month of pregnancy. Surgeons cut through the mother's abdominal wall to expose the fetus, then cut through the fetal abdominal wall; the spinal cord is repaired, and the fetus is returned to the uterus (Okie, 2000).

Fetal surgery has also been used to treat a disorder affecting identical twins in which one twin—the "donor"—pumps blood through its own and the other twin's circulatory system. The donor twin usually fails to grow; surgery corrects the problem by sealing off the unnecessary blood vessels between the twins (McCormick, 2000). Fetal surgery holds great promise, but it is still highly experimental and therefore considered as a last resort.

*The emerging field of fetal medicine treats prenatal problems medically, with surgery, and with genetic engineering.*

Yet another approach to treating prenatal problems is *genetic engineering—replacing defective genes with synthetic normal genes.* Take PKU as an example. Remember, from Module 2.1, that if a baby inherits the recessive allele for PKU from both parents, toxins accumulate that cause mental retardation. In theory, it should be possible to take a sample of cells from the fetus, remove the recessive genes from the 12th pair of chromosomes, and replace them with the dominant genes. These "repaired" cells could then be injected into the fetus, where they would multiply and cause enough enzyme to be produced to break down phenylalanine, thereby avoiding PKU (Verma, 1990). As with fetal surgery, however, translating idea into practice has been difficult, and there are many problems yet to be solved (Cooke, 2005). Nevertheless, gene therapy has been successful in a few cases.

Fetal medicine may sound like science fiction, but these techniques have been used with humans. Granted, they are highly experimental and failures occur, but prenatal treatment should progress rapidly in the 21st century.

*Answers to Chloe's questions:* Return to Chloe's questions in the module-opening vignette (page 68–69) and answer them for her. If you're not certain, I'll help by giving you the pages in this module where the answers appear:

- **Question about her computer monitor—page 75**
- **Question about her nightly glass of wine—page 74**
- **Question about giving birth to a baby with mental retardation—page 73**

**3.2** She's probably wrong. There are no known "safe" amounts of cigarette smoking and drinking. For example, her drinking might be enough to cause alcohol-related neurodevelopmental disorder.

## CHECK YOUR LEARNING

RECALL What are the important general factors that pose risks for prenatal development?

Describe the main techniques for prenatal diagnosis that are available today.

INTERPRET Explain how the impact of a teratogen changes over the course of prenatal development.

APPLY What would you say to a 45-year-old woman who is eager to become pregnant but is unsure about the possible risks associated with pregnancy at this age?

# 3.3 HAPPY BIRTHDAY!

Labor and Delivery

Approaches to Childbirth

Adjusting to Parenthood

Birth Complications

## LEARNING OBJECTIVES

- What are the stages in labor and delivery?
- What are "natural" ways of coping with the pain of childbirth? Is childbirth at home safe?
- What are the effects of postpartum depression?
- What are some complications that can occur during birth?

*Marlena is about to begin classes to prepare for her baby's birth. She is relieved that the classes are finally starting because this means the end of pregnancy is in sight. But all the talk she has heard about "breathing exercises" and "coaching" sounds pretty silly to her. Marlena would prefer to get knocked out for the delivery and wake up when everything is over.*

As women near the end of pregnancy, they find that sleeping and breathing become more difficult, they tire more rapidly, they become constipated, and their legs and feet swell. Women look forward to birth, both to relieve their discomfort and, of course, to see their baby. In this module, we'll see the different stages involved in birth, review various approaches to childbirth, and look at problems that can arise. We'll also look at childbirth classes like the one Marlena is taking.

## Labor and Delivery

In a typical pregnancy, a woman goes into labor about 38 weeks after conception. The timing of labor depends on the flow of hormonal signals between the placenta and the brain and adrenal glands of the fetus. When estrogen and other hormones reach critical levels, the muscles in the uterus begin to contract, the first sign of labor (Smith, 1999).

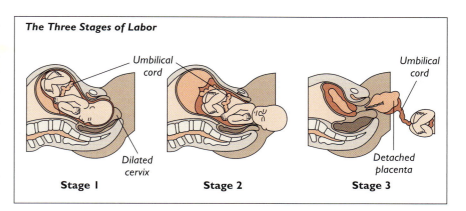

**The Three Stages of Labor**

Umbilical cord

Dilated cervix

**Stage 1**

**Stage 2**

Umbilical cord

Detached placenta

**Stage 3**

FIGURE 3-9

*Labor* is named appropriately, for it is the most intense, prolonged physical effort that humans experience. Labor is usually divided into the three stages shown in the diagram. The first stage begins when the muscles of the uterus start to contract. These contractions force amniotic fluid up against the cervix, the opening at the bottom of the uterus that is the entry-way to the birth canal. The wavelike motion of the amniotic fluid with each contraction causes the cervix to enlarge gradually.

In the early phase of Stage 1, the contractions are weak and spaced irregularly. By the end of the early phase, the cervix is about 5 centimeters (2 inches) in diameter. In the late phase of Stage 1, contractions are stronger and occur at regular intervals. By the end of the late phase, the cervix is about 7 to 8 centimeters (3 inches) in diameter. In the transition phase of Stage 1, contractions are intense and sometimes occur without interruption. Women report that the transition phase is the most painful part of labor. At the end of transition, the cervix is about 10 centimeters (4 inches) in diameter.

Stage 1 lasts from 12 to 24 hours for the birth of a first child, and most of the time is spent in the relative tranquility of the early phase. Stage 1 is usually shorter for subsequent births, with 3 to 8 hours being common. However, as the wide ranges suggest, these times are only rough approximations; the actual times vary greatly among women and are virtually impossible to predict.

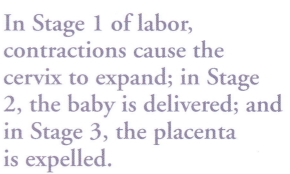

In Stage 1 of labor, contractions cause the cervix to expand; in Stage 2, the baby is delivered; and in Stage 3, the placenta is expelled.

When the cervix is fully enlarged, the second stage of labor begins. Most women feel a strong urge to push the baby out, using their abdominal muscles. This pushing, along with uterine contractions, propels the baby down the birth canal. **Soon the top of the baby's head appears, an event known as** *crowning*. In about an hour for first births and less for later births, the baby passes through the birth canal and emerges from the mother's body. **Most babies arrive head first, but a small percentage come out feet or bottom first, which is known as a** *breech presentation*. (I was one of these rare bottom-first babies and have been the butt of bad jokes ever since.) The baby's birth marks the end of the second stage of labor.

With the baby born, you might think that labor is over, but it's not. There is a third stage, in which the placenta (also called, appropriately, the *afterbirth*) is expelled from the uterus. The placenta becomes detached from the wall of the uterus and contractions force it out through the birth canal. This stage is quite brief, typically lasting 10 to 15 minutes.

You can see the growing intensity of labor in this typical account. For Jerrica, a 27-year-old pregnant for the first time, the early phase of Stage 1 labor lasted 8 hours. For the first 4 hours, Jerrica averaged one 30-second contraction every 20 minutes. Then the contractions became longer—lasting 45 seconds. They came about every 15 minutes for 3 hours, and then every 8 to 10 minutes for another 11 hours. At this point, Jerrica's cervix was 5 centimeters in diameter—the early phase was over.

The late phase of Stage 1 lasted 3 hours. For 2 hours Jerrica had one 60-second contraction every 5 minutes. Then for 1 hour she had a 75-second contraction every 3 minutes. At this point, her cervix was 8 centimeters in diameter and she entered the transition phase. For the next 30 minutes she had a 90-second contraction every 2 minutes. Finally, her cervix was a full 10 centimeters and she could push. Thirty minutes later, her baby was born.

The stages of labor are summarized in the table.

## SUMMARY TABLE

### STAGES OF LABOR

| Stage | Duration | Primary Milestone |
|-------|----------|-------------------|
| 1 | 12–24 hours | Cervix enlarges to 10 cm |
| 2 | 1 hour | Baby moves down the birth canal |
| 3 | 10–15 minutes | Placenta is expelled |

## Approaches to Childbirth

When my mother went into labor (with me), she was admitted to a nearby hospital, where she soon was administered a general anesthetic. My father went to a waiting room, where he and other fathers-to-be anxiously awaited news of their babies. Some time later my mother recovered from anesthesia and learned that she had given birth to a healthy baby boy. My father, who had grown tired of waiting, had gone back to work, so he got the good news in a phone call.

These were standard hospital procedures in 1950, and virtually all American babies were born this way. No longer. In the middle of the 20th century, two European physicians—Grantly Dick-Read (1959) and Ferdinand Lamaze (1958)—criticized the traditional view in which labor and delivery had come to involve elaborate medical procedures that were often unnecessary and that often left women afraid of giving birth. Their fear led them to be tense, thereby increasing the pain they experienced during labor. These physicians argued for a more "natural" or prepared approach to childbirth, viewing labor and delivery as life events to be celebrated, rather than medical procedures to be endured.

*Prepared childbirth emphasizes education, relaxation, and the presence of a supportive coach.*

Today many varieties of prepared childbirth are available to pregnant women. However, most share some fundamental beliefs. One is that birth is more likely to be problem free and rewarding when mothers and fathers understand what's happening during pregnancy, labor, and delivery. Consequently, prepared childbirth means going to classes to learn basic facts about pregnancy and childbirth (like the material presented in this chapter).

A second common element is that natural methods of dealing with pain are emphasized over medication. Why? When a woman is anesthetized either with general anesthesia or regional anesthesia (in which only the lower body is numbed), she can't use her abdominal muscles to help push the baby through the birth canal. Without this pushing, the obstetrician may have to use mechanical devices to pull the baby through the birth canal, which involves some risk (Johanson et al., 1993). Also, drugs that reduce the pain of childbirth cross the placenta and can affect the baby. Consequently, when a woman receives large doses of pain-relieving medication, her baby is often withdrawn or irritable for days or even weeks (Brazelton, Nugent, & Lester, 1987; Ransjoe-Arvidson et al., 2001). These effects are temporary, but they may give the new mother the impression that she has a difficult baby. It is best, therefore, to minimize the use of pain-relieving drugs during birth.

Relaxation is the key to reducing birth pain without drugs. Because pain often feels greater when a person is tense, pregnant women learn to relax during labor, through deep breathing or by visualizing a reassuring, pleasant scene or experience. Whenever they begin to experience pain during labor, they use these methods to relax.

A third common element of prepared childbirth is to involve a supportive "coach." The father-to-be, a relative, or close friend attends childbirth classes with the mother-to-be. The coach learns the techniques for coping with pain and, like the man in the photo, practices them with the pregnant woman. During labor and delivery, the coach is present to help the woman use the techniques she has learned and to offer support and encouragement. **Sometimes the coach is accompanied by a *doula*, a person familiar with childbirth who is not part of the medical staff but instead provides emotional and physical support throughout labor and delivery.**

Although Marlena, the pregnant woman in our opening vignette, may have her doubts about prepared childbirth classes, they are beneficial. For example, prepared childbirth reduces the amount of drugs used to cope with the pain of labor. And mothers and fathers who attend childbirth classes feel more positive about labor and birth compared to mothers and fathers who do not attend classes (Hetherington, 1990).

Another basic premise of the trend toward natural childbirth is that birth need not always take place in a hospital. Nearly all babies in the United States are born in hospitals; only 1% are born at home (Curtain & Park, 1999). However, home birth is a common practice in some European countries. In the Netherlands, for example, about one third of all births take place at home (Wiegers, Zee, & Keirse, 1998). Advocates note that home delivery is less expensive and that most women are more relaxed during labor in their homes. Many women also enjoy the greater control they have over labor and birth in a home delivery. A health-care professional is present for home labor and delivery. Sometimes this is a doctor, but more often it is a trained nurse–midwife like the one in the photo.

For Americans accustomed to hospital delivery, home delivery can seem like a risky proposition. Is it safe? Yes, but with a very important catch. Birth problems are

During childbirth preparation classes, pregnant women learn exercises that help them to relax and reduce the pain associated with childbirth.

In many countries around the world and, to a lesser extent in the United States, a nurse–midwife is present to deliver the baby.

no more common in babies delivered at home than in babies delivered in a hospital if the woman is healthy, her pregnancy has been problem free, the labor and delivery are expected to be problem free, and a trained health-care professional is there to assist (Olsen, 1997). If there is any reason to believe that problems requiring medical assistance might occur, labor and delivery should take place in the hospital, rather than at home.

Another alternative to home or hospital birth is the freestanding birth center. Birthing centers are typically small, independent clinics. A woman, her coach, and other family members and friends are assigned a birthing room that is often decorated to look homelike rather than institutional. A doctor or nurse–midwife assists in labor and delivery, which takes place entirely in the birthing room, where it can be observed by all. Like home deliveries, birthing centers are best for deliveries that are expected to be trouble-free.

## Adjusting to Parenthood

For parents, the time immediately after a trouble-free birth is full of excitement, pride, and joy—the much anticipated baby is finally here! But it is also a time of adjustments for parents. (And for siblings, as we'll see in Module 14.3). A woman experiences many physical changes after birth. Her breasts begin to produce milk and her uterus gradually becomes smaller, returning to its normal size in 5 or 6 weeks. And levels of female hormones (e.g., estrogen) drop.

Parents must also adjust psychologically. They reorganize old routines, particularly for first-born children, to fit the young baby's sleep–wake cycle (which is described in Module 3.4). In the process, fathers sometimes feel left out when mothers devote most of their attention to the baby.

> Mothers must adjust physically and psychologically to their newborn; some mothers experience postpartum depression in which they are constantly irritable and apathetic.

Researchers once believed that an important part of parents' adjustment involved forming an emotional bond to the infant. That is, the first few days of life were thought to be a critical period for close physical contact between parents and babies; without such contact, parents and babies would find it difficult to bond emotionally (Klaus & Kennell, 1976). Today, however, we know that such contact in the first few days after birth—although beneficial for babies and pleasurable for babies and parents alike—is not essential for normal development (Eyer, 1992). In Module 10.3, we'll learn what steps are essential to forge these emotional bonds and when they typically take place.

Becoming a parent can be a huge adjustment, so it's not surprising that roughly half of all new mothers find that their initial excitement gives way to irritation, resentment, and crying spells. These feelings usually last a week or two and probably reflect both the stress of caring for a new baby and the physiological changes that take place as a woman's body returns to a nonpregnant state (Brockington, 1996).

**For 10 to 15% of new mothers, however, irritability continues for months and is often accompanied by feelings of low self-worth, disturbed sleep, poor appetite, and apathy—a condition known as *postpartum depression*.** Postpartum depression does not strike randomly. Biology contributes: Particularly high levels of hormones during the later phases of pregnancy place women at risk for postpartum depression (Harris et al., 1994). Experience also contributes: Women are more likely to experience postpartum depression when they were depressed before pregnancy, are coping with other life stresses (e.g., death of a loved one or moving to a new residence), did not plan to become pregnant, and lack other adults (e.g., the father) to support their adjustment to motherhood (Brockington, 1996; Campbell et al., 1992).

Women who are lethargic and emotionless do not mother warmly and enthusiastically. They don't touch and cuddle their new babies much or talk to them. If the depression lasts only a few weeks, babies are unaffected. However, if postpartum depression lasts for months and months, children of depressed mothers are more likely to become depressed themselves and are also at risk for other behavior problems (e.g., Dawson et al., 2003). For example, in one study (Hay et al., 2003), when mothers had postpartum depression, as 11-year-olds their children were more likely to be involved in aggressive behavior with peers (e.g., bullying them). One explanation of this finding emphasizes the role of early interactions with a mother in helping babies learn to regulate their emotions: When hungry, tired, uncomfortable, or frightened, infants with nondepressed moms soon learn that Mom usually responds quickly and makes them feel better; over time, these infants become less upset when hungry or tired because they know that their discomfort will be brief. In contrast, when moms are depressed they often fail to respond promptly to their infant's needs, which causes infants to be frustrated and angry with their lingering discomfort.

Thus, postpartum depression is a serious condition that can harm moms and babies alike: If a mother's depression doesn't lift after a few weeks, she should seek help. Home visits by trained health-care professionals can be valuable. During these visits, these visitors show moms better ways to cope with the many changes that accompany her new baby; they also provide emotional support by being a caring, sensitive listener; and, if necessary, they can refer the mother to other needed resources in the community. Finally, it's worth mentioning one simple way to reduce the risk of postpartum depression—breast-feeding. Moms who breast-feed are less likely to become depressed, perhaps because breast-feeding releases hormones that are antidepressants (Gagliardi, 2005).

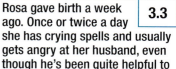

Rosa gave birth a week ago. Once or twice a day she has crying spells and usually gets angry at her husband, even though he's been quite helpful to her and the baby. Do you think Rosa has postpartum depression? | 3.3

## Birth Complications

Women who are healthy when they become pregnant usually have a normal pregnancy, labor, and delivery. When women are not healthy or don't receive adequate prenatal care, problems can surface during labor and delivery. (Of course, even healthy women can have problems, but not as often.) The more common birth complications are listed in the table.

**TABLE 3-4**

| COMMON BIRTH COMPLICATIONS | |
|---|---|
| **Complication** | **Features** |
| Cephalopelvic disproportion | The infant's head is larger than the pelvis, making it impossible for the baby to pass through the birth canal. |
| Irregular position | In shoulder presentation, the baby is lying crosswise in the uterus and the shoulder appears first; in breech presentation, the buttocks appear first. |
| Preeclampsia | A pregnant woman has high blood pressure, protein in her urine, and swelling in her extremities (due to fluid retention). |
| Prolapsed umbilical cord | The umbilical cord precedes the baby through the birth canal and is squeezed shut, cutting off oxygen to the baby. |

Some of these complications, such as a prolapsed umbilical cord, are dangerous because they can disrupt the flow of blood through the umbilical cord. **If this flow of blood is disrupted, infants do not receive adequate oxygen, a condition known as** *hypoxia***.** Hypoxia sometimes occurs during labor and delivery because the umbilical cord is pinched or squeezed shut, cutting off the flow of blood. Hypoxia is very serious because it can lead to mental retardation or death (Petrie, 1991).

To guard against hypoxia, fetal heart rate is monitored during labor, either by ultrasound or with a tiny electrode that is passed through the vagina and attached to the scalp of the fetus. An abrupt change in heart rate can be a sign that the fetus is not receiving enough oxygen. If the heart rate does change suddenly, a health-care professional will try to determine whether the fetus is in distress, perhaps by measuring fetal heart rate with a stethoscope on the mother's abdomen.

When a fetus is in distress or when the fetus is in an irregular position or is too large to pass through the birth canal, a physician may decide to remove it from the mother's uterus surgically (Guillemin, 1993). **In a** *cesarean section (or C-section)* **an incision is made in the abdomen to remove the baby from the uterus.** A C-section is riskier for mothers than a vaginal delivery because of increased bleeding and greater danger of infection. A C-section poses little risk for babies, although they are often briefly depressed from the anesthesia that the mother receives before the operation. And mother–infant interactions are much the same for babies delivered vaginally or by planned or unplanned C-sections (Durik, Hyde, & Clark, 2000).

Birth complications not only are hazardous for a newborn's health, but also have long-term effects. When babies experience many birth complications, they are at risk for becoming aggressive or violent and for developing schizophrenia (e.g., Cannon et al., 2000; Kandel & Mednick, 1991). This is particularly true for newborns with birth complications who later experience family adversity, such as living in poverty. In one study (Arseneault et al., 2002), boys who had life-threatening birth complications such as umbilical cord prolapse or preeclampsia were more aggressive as 6-year-olds and more violent as 17-year-olds (e.g., they participated in gang fights or carried weapons). But this was only true when boys had also experienced family adversity, such as limited income or the absence of a parent. This outcome underscores the importance of receiving excellent health care through pregnancy and labor and the need for a supportive environment throughout childhood.

**PREMATURITY AND LOW BIRTH WEIGHT.** Normally, gestation takes 38 weeks from conception to birth. *Premature infants* **are born less than 38 weeks after conception.** *Small-for-date infants* **are substantially smaller than would be expected based on the length of time since conception.** Sometimes these two complications coincide, but not necessarily. Some, but not all, small-for-date infants are premature. And some, but not all, premature infants are small-for-date. In other words, an infant can go the full 9-month term and be under the average 7- to 8-pound birth weight of newborns; the child is therefore small-for-date but not premature. Similarly, an infant born at 7 months that weighs 3 pounds (the average weight of a 7-month fetus) is only premature. But if the baby born after 7 months weighs less than the average, it is both premature and small-for-date.

Of the two complications, prematurity is the less serious. In the first year or so, premature infants often lag behind full-term infants in many facets of development, but by age 2 or 3 years, differences vanish and most premature infants develop normally thereafter (Greenberg & Crnic, 1988).

Prospects are usually not so optimistic for small-for-date babies such as the one shown in the photo. These infants are most often born to women who smoke or drink alcohol frequently during pregnancy or who do not eat enough nutritious food (Chomitz, Cheung, & Lieberman, 1995). Babies that weigh less than 1,500 grams (3.3 pounds) at birth often do not survive; when they do, they are usually delayed in their cognitive and motor development. For example, in one study (Taylor et al., 2000), low-birth-weight babies as 11-year-olds were more likely to have low IQ, to be receiving special education, to have repeated a grade in school, and to have behavioral problems.

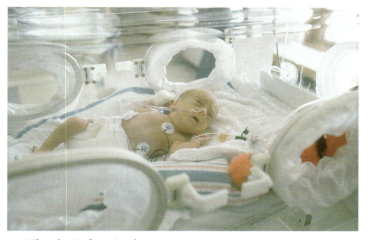

Small-for-date babies often survive but their cognitive and motor development typically is delayed.

Small-for-date babies who weigh more than 1,500 grams have better prospects if they receive appropriate care. Like the infant in the photo, small-for-date babies are placed in special, sealed beds where temperature and air quality are regulated carefully. These beds effectively isolate infants, depriving them from environmental stimulation. Consequently, they often receive auditory stimulation, such as a tape recording of soothing music or their mother's voice, or visual stimulation provided from a mobile placed over the bed. Infants also receive tactile stimulation—they are "massaged" several times daily. These forms of stimulation foster physical and cognitive development in small-for-date babies (Field, Hernandez-Reif, & Freedman, 2004; Teti, 2005).

This special care should continue when infants leave the hospital for home. Consequently, intervention programs for small-for-date babies typically include training programs designed for parents of infants and young children. In these programs, parents learn how to respond appropriately to their child's behaviors. For example, they are taught the signs that a baby is in distress, overstimulated, or ready to interact. Parents also learn games and activities to use to foster their child's development. In addition, children are enrolled in high-quality child-care centers where the curriculum is coordinated with the parent training. This sensitive care promotes development in low-birth-weight babies; for example, sometimes they catch up to full-term infants in terms of cognitive development (Hill, Brooks-Gunn, & Waldfogel, 2003).

Long-term positive outcomes for these infants depends critically on providing a supportive and stimulating home environment. Unfortunately, not all at-risk babies have these optimal experiences. Many experience stress or disorder in their family life. In these cases, development is usually delayed. The importance of a supportive environment for at-risk babies was demonstrated dramatically in a longitudinal study of all children born in 1955 on the Hawaiian island of Kauai (Werner, 1995). At-risk newborns who grew up in stable homes were indistinguishable from children born without birth complications. ("Stable family environment" was defined as two supportive, mentally healthy parents present throughout childhood.) When at-risk newborns had an unstable family environment because of divorce, parental alcoholism, or mental illness, for example, they lagged behind their peers in intellectual and social development.

**Premature babies often develop normally, but small-for-date babies usually do not.**

The Hawaiian study underscores a point I have made several times in this chapter: Development is best when pregnant women receive good prenatal care and children live in a supportive environment. The "Cultural Influences" feature makes the same point in a different way, by looking at infant mortality around the world.

## *Cultural Influences*

### Infant Mortality

In many respects, medical facilities in the United States are the finest in the world. Why, then, do American babies fare so poorly compared to infants from other countries? *Infant mortality* **is the number of infants out of 1,000 births who die before their first birthday.** In the United States, about 7 babies out of 1,000—slightly less than 1%—live less than a year. As you can see in the graph, the United States is near the bottom of the industrialized countries of the world (UNICEF, 2004).

One reason so many American babies die is low birth weight. The United States has more babies with low birth weight than virtually all other industrialized countries, and we've already seen that low birth weight places an infant at risk. Low birth weight can usually be prevented when a pregnant woman gets regular prenatal care, but many pregnant women in the United States receive inadequate or no prenatal care. Virtually all the countries that rank ahead of the United States provide complete prenatal care at little or no cost. Many of these countries also provide for paid leaves of absence for pregnant women (Kamerman, 1993).

Prenatal development is the foundation of all development, and only with regular prenatal checkups can we know if this foundation is being laid properly. Pregnant women and the children they carry need this care, and countries need to be sure that they receive it. ■

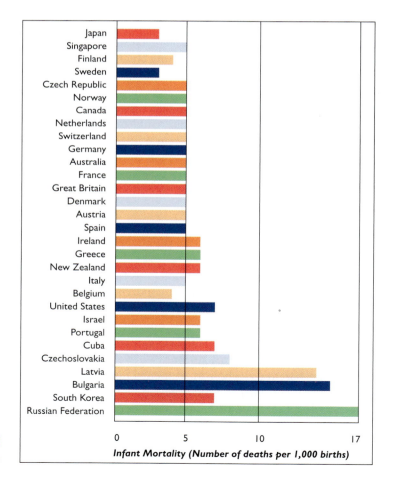

FIGURE 3-10

Source: Unicef 2003

**RECALL**  What are the three stages of labor? What are the highlights of each? Describe the main features of prepared approaches to childbirth.

**INTERPRET**  Explain why some at-risk newborns develop normally but others do not.

**APPLY**  Lynn is pregnant with her first child and would like to give birth at home. Her husband is totally against the idea and claims that it's much too risky. What advice would you give them?

At this point, probably not. It's normal for women to feel sad and angry soon after giving birth. But if Rosa's feelings persist for a few more weeks, then they're likely to be symptoms of postpartum depression.

**3.3**

# THE NEWBORN

**3.4**

## LEARNING OBJECTIVES

- How do we determine if a baby is healthy and adjusting to life outside the uterus?

- How do reflexes help newborns interact with the world?

- What behavioral states are observable in newborns?

- How well do newborns experience the world? Can they learn from experience?

Assessing the Newborn

The Newborn's Reflexes

Newborn States

Perception and Learning in the Newborn

*Lisa and Steve, the proud but exhausted parents, were astonished at how their lives revolved around 10-day-old Dan's eating and sleeping. Lisa felt as if she were feeding Dan around the clock. When Dan napped, Lisa would think of many things she should do but usually napped herself because she was so tired. Steve wondered when Dan would start sleeping through the night so that he and Lisa could get a good night's sleep themselves.*

The newborn baby that thrills parents like Lisa and Steve is actually rather homely, as this photo of my son Ben shows. I took it when he was 20 seconds old. Like other newborns, Ben is covered with blood and vernix, the white-colored "grease" that protects the fetus's skin during the many months of prenatal development. His head is temporarily distorted from coming through the birth canal, he has a beer belly, and he is bow-legged. Still, to us he was beautiful, and we were glad he'd finally arrived.

What can newborns like Dan and Ben do? We'll answer that question in this module and, as we do, learn when Lisa and Steve can expect to resume a full night's sleep.

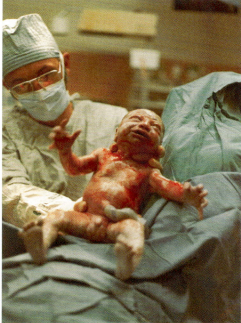

This newborn baby is covered with vernix, is bow-legged, and his head is distorted from the journey down the birth canal.

## Assessing the Newborn

Imagine that a mother has just asked you if her newborn baby is healthy. How would you decide? **The *Apgar score*, a measure devised by Virginia Apgar, is used to evaluate the newborn baby's condition.** Health professionals look for five vital signs including breathing, heartbeat, muscle tone, presence of reflexes (e.g., coughing), and skin tone. As you can see in the table, each of the five vital signs receives a score of 0, 1, or 2, with 2 being optimal.

**TABLE 3-5**

| FIVE SIGNS EVALUATED IN THE APGAR SCORE | | | | | |
| --- | --- | --- | --- | --- | --- |
| Points | Activity | Pulse | Grimace (response to irritating stimulus) | Appearance (skin color) | Respiration |
| 2 | Baby moves limbs actively | 100 beats per minute or more | Baby cries intensely | Normal color all over | Strong breathing and crying |
| 1 | Baby moves limbs slightly | Fewer than 100 beats per minute | Baby grimaces or cries | Normal color except for extremities | Slow, irregular breathing |
| 0 | No movement; muscles flaccid | Not detectable | Baby does not respond | Baby is blue-gray, pale all over | No breathing |

The five scores are added together, with a score of 7 or more indicating a baby in good physical condition. A score of 4 to 6 means the newborn will need special attention and care. A score of 3 or less signals a life-threatening situation that requires emergency medical care (Apgar, 1953).

The Apgar score provides a quick, approximate assessment of the newborn's status by focusing on the body systems needed to sustain life. For a comprehensive evaluation of the newborn's well-being, pediatricians and child-development specialists use the Neonatal Behavioral Assessment Scale, or NBAS (Brazelton & Nugent, 1995). The NBAS is used with newborns to 2-month-olds to provide a detailed portrait of the baby's behavioral repertoire. The scale includes 28 behavioral items along with 18 items that test reflexes. The baby's performance is used to evaluate functioning of four systems:

*The Apgar score provides a quick assessment of the newborn's physical health.*

- *Autonomic*. The newborn's ability to control body functions such as breathing and temperature regulation
- *Motor*. The newborn's ability to control body movements and activity level
- *State*. The newborn's ability to maintain a state (e.g., staying alert or staying asleep)
- *Social*. The newborn's ability to interact with people

The NBAS is based on the view that newborns are remarkably competent individuals who are well prepared to interact with the environment. Reflecting this view, examiners go to great lengths to bring out a baby's best performance. They do everything possible to make a baby feel comfortable and secure during testing. And if the infant does not first succeed on an item, the examiner provides some assistance (Alberts, 2005).

Not only is the NBAS useful to clinicians in evaluating the well-being of individual babies, researchers have found it a valuable tool. Sometimes performance on the NBAS is used as a dependent variable. For example, harm associated with teratogens has been shown with lower scores on the NBAS (e.g., Stewart et al.,

2000). Researchers also use scores on the NBAS to predict later development (e.g., Crockenberg & Smith, 2002).

## The Newborn's Reflexes

As we've just seen, the NBAS was based on a view—shared widely by child-development researchers that newborns are well prepared to begin interacting with their world. **An important part of this preparation is a rich set of *reflexes*, unlearned responses that are triggered by a specific form of stimulation.** The table lists the many reflexes commonly found in newborn babies.

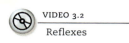 VIDEO 3.2
Reflexes

**TABLE 3-6**

### SOME MAJOR REFLEXES FOUND IN NEWBORNS

| Name | Response | Significance |
|------|----------|--------------|
| Babinski | A baby's toes fan out when the sole of the foot is stroked from heel to toe. | Unknown |
| Blink | A baby's eyes close in response to bright light or loud noise. | Protects the eyes |
| Moro | A baby throws its arms out and then inward (as if embracing) in response to a loud noise or when its head falls. | May help a baby cling to its mother |
| Palmar | A baby grasps an object placed in the palm of its hand. | Precursor to voluntary walking |
| Rooting | When a baby's cheek is stroked, it turns its head toward the stroking and opens its mouth. | Helps a baby find the nipple |
| Stepping | A baby who is held upright by an adult and is then moved forward begins to step rhythmically. | Precursor to voluntary walking |
| Sucking | A baby sucks when an object is placed in its mouth. | Permits feeding |
| Withdrawal | A baby withdraws its foot when the sole is pricked with a pin. | Protects a baby from unpleasant stimulation |

Some reflexes pave the way for newborns to get the nutrients they need to grow: Rooting and sucking ensure that the newborn is well prepared to begin a new diet of life-sustaining milk. Other reflexes protect the newborn from danger in the environment. The blink and withdrawal reflexes, for example, help newborns avoid unpleasant stimulation.

Yet other reflexes serve as the foundation for larger, voluntary patterns of motor activity. For example, the stepping reflex looks like a precursor to walking. In fact, we'll see in Module 5.3 that babies who practice the stepping reflex learn to walk earlier.

Reflexes indicate whether the newborn's nervous system is working properly. For example, infants with damage to their sciatic nerve, which is found in the spinal cord, do not show the withdrawal reflex; and infants who have problems with the lower part of the spine do not show the Babinski reflex. If these or other reflexes are weak or missing altogether, a thorough physical and behavioral assessment is called for (Falk & Bornstein, 2005).

A baby's cry can take many forms—a basic, mad, or pain cry—and thus represents a baby's way to communicate with others.

## Newborn States

Newborns spend most of their day alternating among four states (St James-Roberts & Plewis, 1996; Wolff, 1987):

- *Alert inactivity.*   The baby is calm with eyes open and attentive; the baby looks as if he is deliberately inspecting his environment.
- *Waking activity.*   The baby's eyes are open, but they seem unfocused; the baby moves her arms or legs in bursts of uncoordinated motion.
- *Crying.*   The baby cries vigorously, usually accompanying this with agitated but uncoordinated motion.
- *Sleeping.*   The baby's eyes are closed and the baby drifts back and forth from periods of regular breathing and stillness to periods of irregular breathing and gentle arm and leg motion.

Researchers have been particularly interested in crying—because parents want to know why babies cry and how to calm them—and sleeping—because babies spend so much time asleep!

**CRYING.**   Newborns spend 2 to 3 hours each day crying or on the verge of crying. If you've not spent much time around newborns, you might think that all crying is pretty much alike. But it's not. Babies cry for different reasons and cry differently for each one. In fact, scientists and parents can identify three distinctive types of cries (Snow, 1998). **A *basic cry* starts softly, then gradually becomes more intense and usually occurs when a baby is hungry or tired; a *mad cry* is a more intense version of a basic cry; and *a pain cry* begins with a sudden, long burst of crying, followed by a long pause and gasping.**

Parents are naturally concerned when their baby cries, and if they can't quiet a crying baby, their concern mounts and can easily give way to frustration and annoyance. It's no surprise, then, that parents develop little tricks for soothing their babies. Many Western parents will lift a baby to the shoulder and walk or gently rock the baby. Sometimes they will also sing lullabies, pat the baby's back, or give the baby a pacifier. Yet another method is to put a newborn into a car seat and go for a drive; I remember doing this, as a last resort, at 2 A.M. with my son Ben when he was 10 days old. After about the 12th time around the block, he finally stopped crying and fell asleep! Finally, in some countries around the world, swaddling is used to soothe a crying baby. The infant is wrapped tightly in a blanket (Delaney, 2000). All these techniques work and they probably calm babies by providing moderate stimulation.

Parents are sometimes reluctant to respond to their crying infant for fear of producing a baby who cries constantly. Yet they hear their baby's cry as a call for help that they shouldn't ignore. What to do? Should parents respond? "Yes, usually" is probably the best answer (Hubbard & van IJzendoorn, 1991). If parents respond *immediately, everytime* their infant cries, the result may well be a fussy, whiny baby. Instead, parents need to consider why their infant is crying and the intensity of the crying. On the one hand, when a baby wakes during the night and cries quietly, a parent might wait before responding, giving the baby a chance to calm herself. On the other hand, when parents hear a loud noise from an infant's bedroom followed by a mad cry, they should respond immediately. Parents need to remember that crying is actually the newborn's first attempt to communicate with others. They need to decide what the infant is trying to tell them and whether that warrants a quick response or whether they should let the baby soothe herself.

**3.4** When Mary's 4-month-old son cries, she rushes to him immediately and does everything possible to console him. Is this a good idea?

**SLEEPING.** Crying may get parents' attention, but sleep is what newborns do more than anything else. They sleep 16 to 18 hours daily. The problem for tired parents—like the mom in the photo and Lisa and Steve from the vignette—is that newborns sleep in naps taken round the clock. Newborns typically go through a cycle of wakefulness and sleep about every 4 hours. That is, they will be awake for about an hour, sleep for 3 hours, then start the cycle anew. During the hour when newborns are awake, they regularly move between the different waking states several times. Cycles of alert inactivity, waking activity, and crying are common.

As babies grow older, the sleep–wake cycle gradually begins to correspond to the day–night cycle (St James-Roberts & Plewis, 1996). Most babies begin sleeping through the night at about 3 or 4 months, a major milestone for bleary-eyed parents like Lisa and Steve.

**Roughly half of newborns' sleep is irregular or *rapid-eye-movement (REM) sleep*, a time when the body is quite active.** During REM sleep, newborns move their arms and legs, they may grimace, and their eyes may dart beneath their eyelids. Brain waves register fast activity, the heart beats more rapidly, and breathing is more rapid. **In regular or *non-REM sleep*, breathing, heart rate, and brain activity are steady and newborns lie quietly without the twitching associated with REM sleep.** REM sleep becomes less frequent as infants grow. By 4 months, only 40% of sleep is REM sleep. By the first birthday, REM sleep drops to 25%, not far from the adult average of 20% (Halpern, MacLean, & Baumeister, 1995).

Mothers (and fathers) of newborns are often tired because their babies take naps 24/7 instead of sleeping through the night.

The function of REM sleep is still debated. Older children and adults dream during REM sleep, and brain waves during REM sleep resemble those of an alert, awake person. Consequently, many scientists believe that REM sleep stimulates the brain in some way that helps foster growth in the nervous system (Halpern et al., 1995; Roffwarg, Muzio, & Dement, 1966).

**SUDDEN INFANT DEATH SYNDROME.** For many parents of young babies, sleep is sometimes a cause of concern. **In *sudden infant death syndrome (SIDS)*, a healthy baby dies suddenly, for no apparent reason.** Approximately 1 to 3 of every 1,000 American babies dies from SIDS. Most of them are between 2 and 4 months old.

Scientists don't know the exact causes of SIDS, but they do know several contributing factors. Babies are more vulnerable to SIDS if they were born prematurely or with low birth weight. They are also more vulnerable if their parents smoke. SIDS is more likely when a baby sleeps on its stomach (face down) than when it sleeps on its back (face up). Finally, SIDS is more likely during winter, when babies sometimes become overheated from too many blankets and too heavy sleepwear (Carroll & Loughlin, 1994). Evidently, SIDS infants, many of whom were born prematurely or with low birth weight, are less able to withstand physiological stresses and imbalances that are brought on by cigarette smoke, breathing that is temporarily interrupted, or overheating (Simpson, 2001).

As evidence about causes of SIDS accumulated, child advocates called for action. The result is described in the "Child Development and Family Policy" feature.

> Infants are at greater risk for SIDS when they are born prematurely or with low birth weight and then are exposed to physiological stresses such as overheating.

### Child Development and Family Policy
**Back to Sleep!**

In 1992, based on mounting evidence that SIDS more often occurred when infants slept on their stomachs, the American Academy of Pediatrics (AAP) began advising parents to put babies to sleep on their backs or sides. In 1994, the AAP joined forces with the U.S. Public Health Service to launch a national program to educate parents about the dangers of SIDS and the importance of putting babies to sleep on their backs. The "Back to Sleep" campaign was widely publicized through brochures, posters like the one shown here, and videos. Since the "Back to Sleep" campaign began, research shows that far more infants are now sleeping on their backs and that the incidence of SIDS has dropped (National Institutes of Health, 2000). However, it became clear that African American infants were still twice as likely as to die from SIDS, apparently because they were much more likely to be placed on their stomachs to sleep. Consequently, in the 21st century the National Institutes of Health has partnered with groups such as the Women in the NAACP and the National Council of 100 Black Women to train thousands of people to convey the "Back to Sleep" message in a culturally appropriate manner to African American communities (NICHD, 2004). The goal is for African American infants to benefit from the life-saving benefits of the "Back to Sleep" program. The message for all parents—particularly if their babies were premature or small-for-date—is to keep their babies away from smoke, to put them on their backs to sleep, and don't overdress them or wrap them too tightly in blankets (Willinger, 1995). ■

FIGURE 3-11

## Perception and Learning in the Newborn

Do you believe it is important to talk to newborns and give them fuzzy little toys? Should their rooms be bright and colorful? If you do, you really believe two things about newborns. First, you believe that newborns can perceive experiences—they can see, smell, hear, taste, and feel. Second, you believe that sensory experiences are somehow registered in the newborn through learning and memory, because unless experiences are registered, they can't influence later behavior. You'll be happy to know that research confirms your beliefs. All the basic perceptual systems are operating at some level at birth. The world outside the uterus can be seen, smelled, heard, tasted, and felt (Aslin, 1987). Moreover, newborns show the capacity to learn and remember. They change their behavior based on their experiences (Rovee-Collier, 2000).

*Perceptual systems functions at birth, allowing the baby to experience the world.*

We'll discuss these perceptual changes in more detail in Chapter 5, and we'll discuss learning and memory in Chapter 7. For now, the important point is that newborns are remarkably prepared to interact with the world. Adaptive reflexes coupled with perceptual and learning skills provide a solid foundation for the rest of child development.

RECALL   What are the different functions of reflexes?
          Describe the four primary states of infant behavior.

INTERPRET   Compare the Apgar and the NBAS as measures of a newborn baby's well-being.

APPLY   What would you recommend to parents of a 2-month-old who are very worried about SIDS?

Probably not. Mary needs to relax a bit. If her son is in danger, she'll recognize a pain cry or a mad cry. Otherwise, Mary should wait a moment before going to her son, to try to decide why he's crying and to give him a chance to calm himself. | 3.4

## ≈ UNIFYING THEMES: Continuity

This chapter is a good opportunity to highlight the theme that *early development is related to later development but not perfectly*. Remember the Hawaiian study? This study showed that outcomes for at-risk infants are not uniform. When at-risk infants grow up in a stable, supportive environment, they become quite normal children. But when they grow up in stressful environments, they lag intellectually and socially. Similarly, SIDS is more likely to affect babies born prematurely and with low birth weight, yet not all of these babies die of SIDS. When premature and low-birth-weight babies sleep on their backs, are not overheated, and do not inhale smoke, they're unlikely to die from SIDS. Traumatic events early in development, such as being born early or underweight, do not predetermine the rest of a child's life, but they do make some developmental paths easier to follow than others.

## SEE FOR YOURSELF

Words can hardly capture the miracle of a newborn baby. If you have never seen a newborn, you need to see one, or even better, a roomful. Arrange to visit the maternity ward of a local hospital, which will include a nursery for newborns. Through a large viewing window, you will be able to observe a few or as many as 15 to 20 newborns. These babies will no longer be covered with blood or vernix, but you will be able to see how the newborn's head is often distorted by its journey from the birth canal. As you watch the babies, look for reflexive behavior and changes in states. Watch while a baby sucks its fingers. Find a baby who seems to be awake and alert, then note how long the baby stays this way. When alertness wanes, watch for the behaviors that replace it. Finally, observe how different the newborns look and act from each other. The wonderful variety and diversity found among human beings is already evident in those who are hours or days old. See for yourself!

## RESOURCES

For more information about

babies, try T. Berry Brazelton's *Infants and Mothers: Differences in Development* (Delacorte, 1994). This classic book, written by the famous pediatrician and scientist, traces the early development of three very different babies. In the process, it shows the wide range of normal patterns of development.

prenatal development, visit the Web site of the Multi-Dimensional Human Embryo, which has images and animations depicting the fetus at various stages of prenatal development: **http://embryo.soad.umich.edu/**

## KEY TERMS

age of viability  66

amniocentesis  80

amniotic fluid  64

amniotic sac  64

Apgar score  91

basic cry  94

blastocyst  63

breech presentation  83

cerebral cortex  65

cesarean section (C-section)  88

chorionic villus sampling (CVS)  80

crowning  83

doula  85

ectoderm  63

embryo  63

endoderm  63

fetal alcohol syndrome (FAS)  74

fetal medicine  81

genetic engineering  82

germ disc  63

hypoxia  88

implantation  63

infant mortality  90

mad cry  94

mesoderm  63

non-REM (regular) sleep  95

pain cry  94

period of the fetus  65

placenta  63

postpartum depression  86

premature infants  88

prenatal development  62

rapid-eye-movement (REM) sleep (irregular sleep)  95

reflexes  93

small-for-date infants  88

social influence  71

social selection  71

spina bifida  69

stress  70

sudden infant death syndrome (SIDS)  95

teratogen  73

ultrasound  80

umbilical cord  64

vernix  66

villi  64

zygote  63

# 3.1 FROM CONCEPTION TO BIRTH

### Period of the Zygote (Weeks 1–2)

The first period of prenatal development lasts 2 weeks. It begins when the egg is fertilized by the sperm and ends when the fertilized egg has implanted in the wall of the uterus.

### Period of the Embryo (Weeks 3–8)

The second period of prenatal development begins 2 weeks after conception and ends 8 weeks after. This is a period when most major body structures are formed.

### Period of the Fetus (Weeks 9–38)

The third period of prenatal development begins 9 weeks after conception and lasts until birth. In this period, the fetus becomes much larger and body systems begin to function.

# 3.2 INFLUENCES ON PRENATAL DEVELOPMENT

### General Risk Factors

Prenatal development can be harmed if a pregnant woman does not provide adequate nutrition for the developing organism or experiences considerable stress. Teenagers often have problem pregnancies because they rarely receive adequate prenatal care. After age 35, women are less fertile and more likely to have problem pregnancies.

### Teratogens: Diseases, Drugs, and Environmental Hazards

Teratogens are agents that can cause abnormal prenatal development. Several diseases are teratogens. Only by avoiding these diseases entirely can a pregnant woman escape their harmful consequences. Many drugs that adults take are teratogens. Environmental teratogens are particularly dangerous because a pregnant woman may not know when these substances are present.

### How Teratogens Influence Prenatal Development

The effect of teratogens depends on the genotype of the organism, when during prenatal development the organism is exposed to the teratogen, and the amount of exposure. The impact of a teratogen may not be evident until later in life.

### Prenatal Diagnosis and Treatment

Ultrasound uses sound waves to generate a picture of the fetus that reveals the position of the fetus, its sex, and any gross physical deformities. When genetic disorders are suspected, amniocentesis or chorionic villus sampling is used to determine the genotype of the fetus. Fetal medicine corrects problems of prenatal development medically, surgically, or through genetic engineering.

# 3.3 HAPPY BIRTHDAY!

### Labor and Delivery

Labor consists of three stages. In Stage 1, the muscles of the uterus contract. The contractions, which are weak at first and gradually become stronger, cause the cervix to enlarge. In Stage 2, the baby moves through the birth canal. In Stage 3, the placenta is delivered.

### Approaches to Childbirth

Prepared childbirth assumes that parents should understand what takes place during pregnancy and birth. In prepared childbirth, women learn to cope with pain through relaxation and the help of a supportive coach.

Although most American babies are born in hospitals, home birth is safe when the mother is healthy, the delivery is expected to be trouble free, and a health-care professional is present.

### Adjusting to Parenthood

Following the birth of a child, a woman's body undergoes several changes: her breasts become filled with milk, her uterus becomes smaller, and hormone levels drop. Both parents also adjust psychologically and sometimes fathers feel left out. After giving birth, some women experience postpartum depression: They are irritable, have poor appetite and disturbed sleep, and are apathetic.

### Birth Complications

During labor and delivery, the flow of blood to the fetus can be disrupted, causing hypoxia, a lack of oxygen to the fetus. If the fetus is endangered, the doctor may do a cesarean section, removing it from the uterus surgically. Babies with many birth complications are at risk for becoming aggressive and developing schizophrenia.

Premature babies develop more slowly at first but catch up in a few years. Small-for-date babies who weigh less than 1,500 grams often do not develop normally; larger small-for-date babies fare well when their environment is stimulating and stress-free.

Infant mortality is relatively high in the United States, primarily because of low birth weight and inadequate prenatal care.

# 3.4 THE NEWBORN

### Assessing the Newborn

The Apgar score measures five vital signs to determine a newborn's physical well-being. The Neonatal Behavioral Assessment Scale provides a comprehensive evaluation of a baby's behavioral and physical status.

### The Newborn's Reflexes

Some reflexes help infants to adjust to life outside the uterus, some protect them, and some are the basis for later motor behavior.

### Newborn States

Newborns spend their day in one of four states: alert inactivity, waking activity, crying, and sleeping. A newborn's crying includes a basic cry, a mad cry, and a pain cry.

Newborns spend approximately two thirds of every day asleep and go through a complete sleep–wake cycle once every 4 hours. Newborns spend about half their time in REM sleep, characterized by active brain waves and frequent movements of the eyes and limbs. REM sleep may stimulate nervous system growth.

Some healthy babies die from sudden infant death syndrome (SIDS). Babies are vulnerable to SIDS when they are premature, have low birth weight, sleep on their stomachs, are overheated, and are exposed to cigarette smoke. Encouraging parents to have babies sleep on their backs has reduced the number of SIDS cases.

### Perception and Learning in the Newborn

Newborns' perceptual and learning skills function reasonably well, which allows them to experience the world.

**Humans take longer to become physically mature than any other animal.**
We spend about 20% of our lives—all of childhood and adolescence—growing physically. This slow journey to physical maturity is an interesting story in itself. But physical growth is just as important for its impact on other aspects of children's development, including cognition, social behavior, and personality. As children grow physically, they become less dependent on others for care, they're treated differently by adults, and they come to view themselves as older and more mature. By knowing more about children's physical growth, you'll be better prepared to understand other aspects of development that we'll study in the rest of this book.

In this chapter, we'll learn how children grow physically. In Module 4.1, we'll look at different facets of physical growth and some of the reasons why people differ in their physical growth and stature. Then, in Module 4.2, we'll explore problems that can disrupt physical growth. In Module 4.3, we'll look at physical growth that's not so obvious—the development of the brain.

**4.1**   Physical Growth

**4.2**   Challenges to Healthy Growth

**4.3**   The Developing Nervous System

1  The Science of Child Development

2  Genetic Bases of Child Development

3  Prenatal Development, Birth, and the Newborn

4

# Growth and Health

5   Perceptual and Motor Development

6   Theories of Cognitive Development

7   Cognitive Processes and Academic Skills

8   Intelligence and Individual Differences in Cognition

9   Language and Communication

10  Emotional Development

11  Understanding Self and Others

12  Moral Understanding and Behavior

13  Gender and Development

14  Family Relationships

15  Influences Beyond the Family

# 4.1    PHYSICAL GROWTH

Features of Human Growth

Mechanisms of Physical Growth

The Adolescent Growth Spurt
and Puberty

## LEARNING OBJECTIVES

- What are the important features of physical growth during childhood? How do they vary from child to child?

- How do sleep and nutrition contribute to healthy growth?

- What are the physical changes associated with puberty, and what are their consequences?

*Pete has just had his 15th birthday, but, as far as he is concerned, there is no reason to celebrate. Although most of his friends have grown about 6 inches in the past year or so, have a much larger penis and larger testicles, and have mounds of pubic hair, Pete looks just as he did when he was 10 years old. He is embarrassed by his appearance, particularly in the locker room, where he looks like a little boy among men. "Won't I ever change?" he wonders.*

For parents and children alike, physical growth is a topic of great interest. Parents marvel at how quickly babies add pounds and inches; 2-year-olds proudly proclaim, "I bigger now!" Many adolescents take great satisfaction in finally becoming taller than a parent; others, like Pete, suffer through their teenage years as they wait for the physical signs of maturity.

In this module, we'll examine some of the basic features of physical growth and variations in growth patterns. We'll also consider the mechanisms responsible for growth. Finally, we'll end the module with puberty—a phase of physical growth that is so special it needs to be considered separately.

VIDEO4.1
Physical Growth

## Features of Human Growth

**DESCRIBING GROWTH.**    Probably the most obvious way to measure physical growth is in terms of sheer size—height and weight. The growth charts at the top of page 103 show the average changes in height and weight that take place as children grow from birth to age 20. Between birth and 2 years, for example, average height increases from 19 to 32 inches; average weight increases from 7 to 22 pounds. (An interesting rule of thumb is that boys achieve half their adult height by 2 years, and girls by 18 months.)

What is not so obvious in growth charts is that increases in height and weight are not steady. Looking at the average increase in weight and height annually—as opposed to the average total weight and height for each year—gives quite a different picture of the pattern of physical growth. The graphs at the bottom of page 103 show that growth is extraordinarily rapid during the first year, when the average baby gains about 10 inches and 15 pounds. Growth is fairly steady through the preschool and elementary-school years, about 3 inches and 7 to 8 pounds each year. In early adolescence, growth is rapid again. During this growth spurt, which corresponds to the peaks in the middle of the charts, teenagers typically grow 4 inches and gain 16 to 17 pounds each year. After this spurt, which begins 1 to 2 years earlier in girls, growth again slows as children reach adulthood.

*Growth is particularly rapid in infancy and adolescence.*

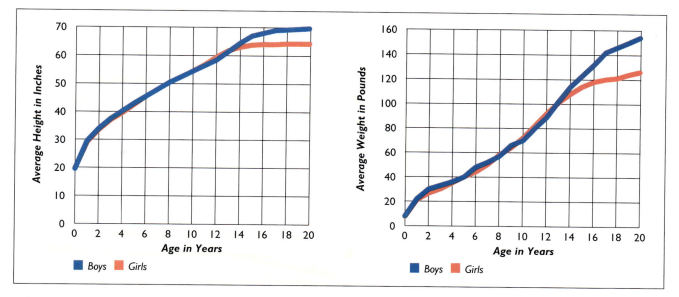

FIGURE 4-1

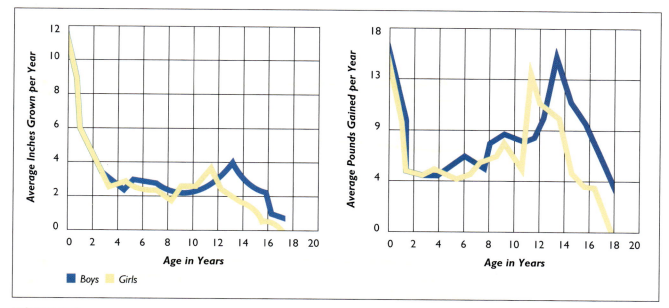

FIGURE 4-2

As children grow, their body parts develop at different rates, which means that infants and young children are not simply scaled-down versions of adults. The head and trunk grow faster than the legs. As you can see in the diagram on page 104, infants and toddlers have disproportionately large heads and trunks, making them look top-heavy compared to older children and adolescents. As growth of the hips,

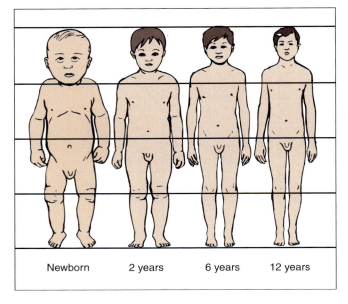

Newborn    2 years    6 years    12 years

FIGURE 4-3

legs, and feet catches up later in childhood, bodies take on proportions that are more adultlike.

**MUSCLE, FAT, AND BONES.**    Other important features of physical growth take place inside the body, with the development of muscle, fat, and bones. Virtually all of the body's muscle fibers are present at birth. During childhood, muscles become longer and thicker as individual fibers fuse together. This process accelerates during adolescence, particularly for boys.

A layer of fat appears under the skin near the end of the fetal period of prenatal development; its purpose is to help the fetus and infant regulate body temperature (just as insulation in walls stabilizes the temperature inside a house). Fat continues to accumulate rapidly during the first year after birth, producing the familiar look we call *baby fat*. During the preschool years, children actually become leaner, but in the early elementary-school years they begin to acquire more fat again. This happens gradually at first, then more rapidly during adolescence. The increase in fat in adolescence is more pronounced in girls than in boys.

Bone begins to form during prenatal development. What will become bone starts as *cartilage*, a soft, flexible tissue. During the embryonic period, the center of the tissue turns to bone. **Then, shortly before birth, the ends of the cartilage structures, known as *epiphyses*, turn to bone.** Now the structure is hard at each end and in the center. Working from the center, cartilage turns to bone until finally the enlarging center section reaches the epiphyses, ending skeletal growth.

If you combine the changes in muscle, fat, and bone with changes in body size and shape, you have a fairly complete picture of physical growth during childhood. What's missing? The central nervous system, which we cover separately in Module 4.3.

**VARIATIONS ON THE AVERAGE PROFILE.**    Of course, the picture of children's physical growth that I have described so far is a typical profile; there are important variations on this prototype. For example, when the University of Oregon Ducks won the first NCAA men's basketball tournament in 1939, the average height of their starting lineup was 6 feet, 2 inches. When the University of North Carolina Tar Heels won the tournament in 2005, the average height of their starting lineup was 6 feet, 6 inches, a difference of 4 inches. Of course, the changing heights of basketball players simply correspond to changes in the U.S. population at large. Today, adults and children are taller and heavier than previous generations, due largely to improved health and nutrition. **Changes in physical development from one generation to the next are known as *secular growth trends*.** Secular trends have been quite large. A medieval knight's armor would fit today's 10- to 12-year-old boy; the average height of American sailors in the War of 1812 was 5 feet 2 inches!

"Average" physical growth varies not only from one generation to the next, but also from one country to another. The graph at the top of page 105 shows the average height of 8-year-old boys and girls in several countries around the world. Youngsters from the United States, western European countries, Japan, and China are about the same height, approximately 49 inches. Children in Africa and India are shorter, averaging just under 46 inches. And 8-year-olds in Polynesia are shorter still, averaging 43 inches.

We also need to remember that "average" and "normal" are not the same. Many children are much taller or shorter than average and perfectly normal, of course. For example, among American 8-year-old boys, normal weights range from approximately 44 pounds to 76 pounds. In other words, an extremely light but normal 8-year-old boy would weigh only slightly more than half as much as his extremely heavy but normal peer. What is normal can vary greatly, and this applies not only to height and other aspects of physical growth, but also to all aspects of development. Whenever a "typical" or average age is given for a developmental milestone, you should remember that the normal range for passing the milestone is much wider. Some children pass the milestone sooner than the stated age and some later, but all are normal.

We've seen that children's heights vary within a culture, across time, and between cultures. What accounts for these differences? To answer this question, we need to look at the mechanisms responsible for human growth.

## Mechanisms of Physical Growth

Physical growth is easily taken for granted. Compared to other milestones of child development, such as learning to read, physical growth seems to come so easily. Children, like weeds, seem to sprout without any effort at all. In reality, of course, physical growth is complicated. Of course, heredity is involved: As a general rule, two tall parents will have tall children; two short parents will have short children; and one tall parent and one short parent will have average-height offspring.

How are genetic instructions translated into actual growth? Sleep and nutrition are both involved.

**SLEEP.**    In Module 3.4, we saw that infants spend more time asleep than awake. The amount of time that children spend asleep drops gradually, from roughly 12 hours at age 3 to 10 hours at age 7 and 8 hours at age 12 (Sadeh, Raviv, & Gruber, 2000). **Sleep is essential for normal growth because about 80% of the hormone that stimulates growth—named, appropriately,** *growth hormone*—**is secreted while children and adolescents sleep** (Smock, 1998). Growth hormone is secreted during sleep by the pituitary gland in the brain; from the brain, growth hormone travels to the liver, where it triggers the release of another hormone, somatomedin, which causes muscles and bones to grow (Tanner, 1990).

Sleep also affects children's development in a less direct but no less important manner. Children's sleep affects their cognitive processes and their adjustment to school. When children do not sleep well—they wake frequently during the night or they do not sleep a consistent amount each night—they often are unable to pay attention in school (Sadeh, Gruber, & Raviv, 2002). And they're more likely to disregard teachers' requests, and they're often aggressive (Bates et al., 2002).

The key to avoiding sleep-related problems is a bedtime routine that helps children to wind down from busy daytime activities. This routine should start at about the same time every night ("It's time to get ready for bed") and end at about the same time (when the parent leaves the child and the child tries to fall asleep). By following the routine consistently, children will find it easier to fall asleep and are more likely to get a restful night's sleep.

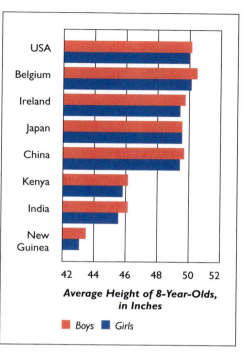

**Average Height of 8-Year-Olds, in Inches**

■ *Boys*  ■ *Girls*

FIGURE 4-4

*[handwritten notes:]* sleep essential to growth 80% of hormones that stimulate growth are secreted during sleep.

sleep affects the cognitive powers

*[printed marginal note:]* Sleep is essential because most growth hormone is secreted when children are asleep and because children do poorly in school when they don't sleep well.

Sleep loss can be a particular problem for adolescents. On the one hand, adolescents often stay up later at night finishing ever larger amounts of homework, spending time with friends, or working at a part-time job. On the other hand, adolescents often start school earlier than younger elementary-school students. The result is often a sleepy adolescent who struggles to stay awake during the school day (Carskadon, 2002). Over time, being "sleepless in school" is clearly harmful. In one longitudinal study (Fredriksen et al., 2004), children who gradually slept less between sixth and eighth grade had the most symptoms of depression and the largest drop in self-esteem. Thus, for adolescents and children, a good night's sleep is an important part of healthy academic and personal development.

**NUTRITION.**   The fuel for growth comes from the foods children eat and the liquids they drink. Nutrition is particularly important during infancy, when physical growth is so rapid. In a 2-month-old, roughly 40% of the body's energy is devoted to growth. Most of the remaining energy fuels basic bodily functions, such as digestion and respiration.

Because growth requires so much high energy, young babies must consume an enormous number of calories in relation to their body weight. An adult needs to consume only 15 to 20 calories per pound, depending on level of activity but a 12-pound 3-month-old should eat about 50 calories per pound of body weight, or 600 calories. What's the best way for babies to receive the calories they need? The "Improving Children's Lives" feature has some answers.

## *Improving Children's Lives*
### What's the Best Food for Babies?

Breast-feeding is the best way to ensure that babies get the nourishment they need. Human milk contains the proper amounts of carbohydrates, fats, protein, vitamins, and minerals for babies. Breast-feeding also has several other advantages compared to bottle-feeding (Dewey, 2001). First, breast-fed babies are ill less often because a mother's breast milk contains antibodies that kill bacteria and viruses. Second, breast-fed babies are less prone to diarrhea and constipation. Third, breast-fed babies typically make the transition to solid foods more easily, apparently because they are accustomed to changes in the taste of breast milk that reflect a mother's diet. Fourth, breast milk cannot be contaminated (as long as a nursing mother avoids certain drugs, such as cocaine); in contrast, contamination is often a significant problem when formula is used in developing countries to bottle-feed babies.

The many benefits of breast-feeding do not mean that bottle-feeding is harmful. Formula, when prepared in sanitary conditions, provides generally the same nutrients as human milk, but infants are more prone to develop allergies from formula, and formula does not protect infants from disease. However, bottle-feeding does have advantages. A mother who cannot readily breast-feed can still enjoy the intimacy of feeding her baby, and other family members can participate in feeding. In fact, long-term longitudinal studies typically find that breast- and bottle-fed babies are similar in physical and psychological development (Fergusson, Horwood, & Shannon, 1987), so women in industrialized countries can choose either method and know that their babies' dietary needs will be met.

In the United States and Canada, newborns and very young babies are often breast-fed exclusively. Beginning at about 4 to 6 months, breast-feeding is supplemented by cereal and strained fruits and vegetables. Strained meats are introduced at 7 to 9 months and finely chopped table foods are introduced at 10 to 12 months (IFICF, 2000).

**Q&A**
**Question**

**4.1**   Tameka is pregnant with her first child and wonders whether breast-feeding is really worthwhile. What advantages of breast-feeding would you mention to her?

A good rule is to introduce only one new food at a time. For instance, a 7-month-old having cheese for the first time should have no other new foods for a few days. In this way, allergies that may develop—manifested as skin rash or diarrhea—can be linked to a particular food, making it easier to prevent recurrences. ■

Preschoolers grow more slowly than infants and toddlers, so they need to eat less per pound than before. One rule of thumb is that preschoolers should consume about 40 calories per pound of body weight, which works out to be roughly 1,500 to 1,700 calories daily for many children in this age group.

More important than the sheer number of calories, however, is a balanced diet that includes all five major food groups. The table shows a healthy diet that provides adequate calories and nutrients for preschool children. The servings listed in the table are definitely not a complete a list of the foods good for young children; they simply are examples of healthy choices (and quantities) for children. Many other foods could have been listed. A healthy diet doesn't mean that children must eat the same foods over and over again.

> When babies are breast-fed, they get proper nourishment, are ill less often, and adjust more rapidly to solid food.

## TABLE 4-1

### EATING TO MEET PRESCHOOLERS' NUTRITIONAL NEEDS

| Group | Number of Servings | What Counts as a Serving? |
|---|---|---|
| Grains | 6 | 1 slice of bread, 1 cup of cereal |
| Vegetables | 3 | 1 cup of raw leafy vegetables, 3/4 cup of vegetable juice |
| Fruits | 2 | 1 medium apple, 1/2 cup of canned fruit |
| Milk | 2 | 1 cup of milk, 1 1/2 ounces of natural cheese |
| Meat and beans | 2 (5 ounces total) | 2 to 3 ounces of cooked lean meat, 2 tablespoons of peanut butter |

Source: USDA, 2000.

Many American children eat far too many fast-food meals, which are notoriously high in calories.

A healthy diet not only draws on all five food groups, but also avoids too much sugar and, especially, too much fat. For preschool children, no more than approximately 30% of the daily caloric intake should come from fat, which works out to be roughly 500 calories from fat. Unfortunately, too many preschool children like the ones in the photo become hooked on fast-food meals, which are notoriously high in fat. A Whopper®, fries, and shake have nearly 600 calories from fat, 100 more than children should consume all day! Excessive fat intake is the first step toward obesity (which I'll discuss later in this chapter), so parents need to limit their preschool children's fat intake (Whitaker et al., 1997).

Beginning at about 2 years of age, many young-sters become very picky eaters; they reject food that they once ate willingly.

Encouraging preschool children to eat healthy foods is tough for parents because some preschoolers become notoriously picky eaters. Like the little girl in the photo, toddlers and preschool children find foods that they once ate willingly "yucky." As a toddler, my daughter loved green beans. When she reached 2, she decided that green beans were awful and refused to eat them. Though such finickiness can be annoying, it may actually be adaptive for increasingly independent preschoolers. Because preschoolers don't know what is safe to eat and what isn't, eating only familiar foods protects them from potential harm (Birch & Fisher, 1995).

Parents should not be overly concerned about this finicky period. Although some children do eat less than before (in terms of calories per pound), virtually all picky eaters get adequate food for growth. Nevertheless, picky-eating children can make mealtime miserable for all. What's a parent to do? Experts (Leach, 1991; American Academy of Pediatrics, 1992) recommend several guidelines for encouraging children to be more open-minded about foods and for dealing with them when they aren't:

- When possible, allow children to pick among different healthy foods (e.g., milk versus yogurt).
- Allow children to eat foods in any order they want.
- Offer children new foods one at a time and in small amounts; encourage but don't force children to eat new foods.
- Don't force children to "clean their plates."
- Don't spend mealtimes talking about what the child is or is not eating; instead, talk about other topics that interest the child.
- Never use food to reward or punish children.

By following these guidelines, mealtimes can be pleasant and children can receive the nutrition they need to grow.

**Children and adolescents need a well-balanced diet that represents each of the five primary food groups.**

As children enter elementary school, they need to eat more to support growth and to provide energy for their active lives. Although preschool children need only consume about 1,500 to 1,700 calories per day, the average 7- to 10-year-old needs about 2,400 calories each day. During adolescence, a typical girl should consume about 2,200 calories per day; a typical boy should consume about 2,700 calories. Of course, the exact levels depend on a number of factors, including body composition, growth rate, and activity level.

School-age children and adolescents also need a well-balanced diet. They should eat regularly from each of the five food groups shown in the table on page 107, but with larger servings. Teenagers also need calcium for growth and iron to make extra hemoglobin, the matter in red blood cells that carries oxygen. Boys need additional hemoglobin because of their increased muscle mass; girls need hemoglobin to replace that lost during menstruation. Unfortunately, children and adolescents too often consume calories from sweet foods and beverages, which are "empty"—they have very little nutritional value; this can lead to obesity, as we'll see in Module 4.2.

## The Adolescent Growth Spurt and Puberty

**For many child-development researchers, adolescence begins officially with *puberty*, which refers to the adolescent growth spurt and sexual maturation.** The adolescent growth spurt is easy to see in the graphs on page 103. Physical growth is slow during the elementary-school years: In an average year, a 6- to 10-year-old girl or boy gains about 5 to 7 pounds and grows 2 to 3 inches. But during the peak of the adolescent growth spurt, a girl may gain as many as 20 pounds in a year and a boy, 25 (Tanner, 1970). This growth spurt lasts a few years.

The figure on page 103 also shows that girls typically begin their growth spurt about 2 years before boys do. That is, girls typically start the growth spurt at about age 11, reach their peak rate of growth at about 12, and achieve their mature stature at about age 15. In contrast, boys start the growth spurt at 13, hit peak growth at 14, and reach mature stature at 17. This 2-year difference in the growth spurt can lead to awkward social interactions between 11- and 12-year-old boys and girls because during those years, as the photo shows, girls are often taller and much more mature looking than boys.

During the growth spurt, girls are often much taller than boys of the same age.

During the growth spurt, bones become longer (which, of course, is why adolescents grow taller) and become more dense. Bone growth is accompanied by several other changes that differ for boys and girls. Muscle fibers become thicker and denser during adolescence, producing substantial increases in strength. However, muscle growth is much more pronounced in boys than in girls (Smoll & Schutz, 1990). Body fat also increases during adolescence, but much more rapidly in girls than boys. Finally, heart and lung capacities increase more in adolescent boys than in adolescent girls. Together, these changes help to explain why the typical adolescent boy has more strength, is quicker, and has greater endurance than the typical adolescent girl.

In the "Child Development and Family Policy" feature, you'll see how healthy bone growth in adolescence is also an essential defense against a disease that strikes during middle age.

## *Child Development and Family Policy*
### Preventing Osteoporosis

*Osteoporosis* **is a disease in which a person's bones become thin and brittle, and, as a consequence, sometimes break.** Although osteoporosis can strike at any age, people over 50 are at greatest risk because bone tissue starts to break down more rapidly than new bone can be formed. About 10 million Americans have osteoporosis. Approximately 80% are women because after menopause the ovaries no longer produce as much estrogen, which guards against bone deterioration.

Osteoporosis often has its roots in childhood and adolescence, for this is when bones acquire nearly all their mass. For bones to develop properly, children and adolescents need to consume approximately 1,300 milligrams of calcium daily. This is the equivalent of about 3 cups of milk, half an ounce of cheese, and a cup of spinach. In addition, children and adolescents should engage in weight-bearing exercise for 30 minutes daily, for at least 5 days a week. Weight-bearing exercises cause bones to carry the body weight, strengthening them. Walking briskly, running, playing tennis, climbing stairs, aerobic dancing, and cross-country skiing are all good forms of weight-bearing exercise. Swimming, cycling, and rowing do not require the bones to support body weight, so they are not good weight-bearing exercises (although, of course, they do benefit the heart, lungs, and muscles).

Unfortunately, many adolescents do not get enough calcium or exercise for healthy bone growth. Consequently, the U.S. Centers for Disease Control and Prevention, the U.S. Department of Health and Human Services' Office of Women's Health, and the National Osteoporosis Foundation have collaborated to create the National Bone Health Campaign (NBHC). This multiyear program is designed to encourage 9- to 12-year-olds (girls, especially) to consume more calcium and to exercise more often. Launched in 2001, the NBHC uses several media to communicate with adolescents. Ads appearing in magazines and newspapers and on radio and TV emphasize the importance of healthy bone growth. The Web site shown in the figure—Powerful Girls. Powerful Bones.™—includes information about bone health along with games that allow adolescents to learn more about how diet and exercise contribute to healthy growth.

Working with partners in the public and private sectors, the NBHC establishes links with local

**FIGURE** 4-5

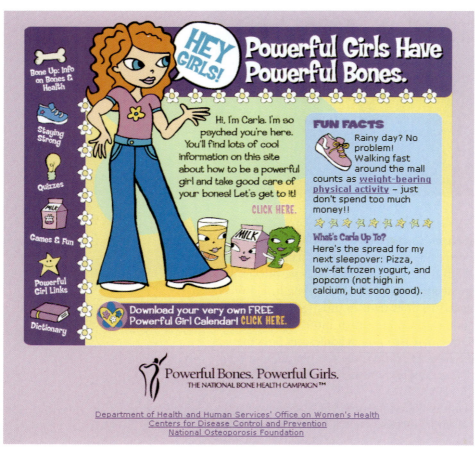

communities, such as providing lesson plans on bone health for science and health teachers.

The NBHC is too new for us to know its effectiveness. (After all, the real test won't come for another 35 to 40 years when the girls in the target audience reach the age when they'll be at risk for osteoporosis.) However, the hope is that by communicating effectively with adolescents and their parents (emphasizing that healthy bones are an essential part of overall healthy, positive growth), adolescents will get more calcium and become more active physically, thereby forging the strong bones that are the best defense against osteoporosis. ▪

Adolescents not only become taller and heavier, but also become mature sexually. **Sexual maturation includes change in *primary sex characteristics*, which refer to organs that are directly involved in reproduction.** These include the ovaries, uterus, and vagina in girls and the scrotum, testes, and penis in boys. **Sexual maturation also includes change in *secondary sex characteristics*, which are physical signs of maturity that are not linked directly to the reproductive organs.** These include the growth of breasts and the widening of the pelvis in girls, the appearance of facial hair and the broadening of shoulders in boys, and the appearance of body hair and changes in voice and skin in both boys and girls.

Changes in primary and secondary sexual characteristics occur in a predictable sequence for boys and for girls. The chart shows these changes and the ages when they typically occur for boys and girls. For girls, puberty begins with growth of the breasts and the growth spurt, followed by the appearance of pubic hair. *Menarche*, **the onset of menstruation, typically occurs at about age 13.** Early menstrual cycles are usually irregular and without ovulation.

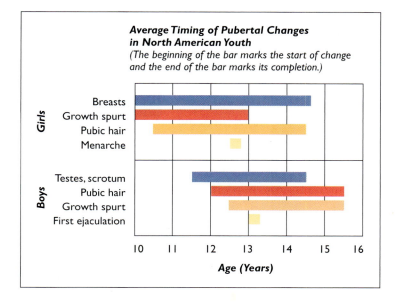

FIGURE 4-6

For boys, puberty usually commences with the growth of the testes and scrotum, followed by the appearance of pubic hair, the start of the growth spurt, and growth of the penis. **At about age 13, most boys reach *spermarche*, the first spontaneous ejaculation of sperm-laden fluid.** Initial ejaculations often contain relatively few sperm; only months or sometimes years later are there sufficient sperm to fertilize an egg (Chilman, 1983).

The onset of sexual maturity is one of the first signs that an adolescent is on the threshold of adulthood. This achievement is celebrated in many societies, including the Native American culture described in the "Cultural Influences" feature.

## Cultural Influences
### How the Apache Celebrate Menarche

The Western Apache, who live in the southwest portion of the United States, traditionally have a spectacular ceremony to celebrate a girl's menarche (Basso, 1970). After a girl's first menstrual period, a group of older adults decide when the ceremony will be held and select a sponsor—a woman of good character and wealth (she helps to pay for the ceremony) who is unrelated to the initiate. On the day before the ceremony, the sponsor serves a large feast for the girl and her family; at the end of the ceremony, the family reciprocates, symbolizing that the sponsor is now a member of their family.

The Apache celebrate menarche with a special ceremony in which a girl is said to become a legendary hero.

The ceremony itself begins at sunrise and lasts a few hours. As shown in the photo, the initiate dresses in ceremonial attire. The ceremony includes eight distinct phases in which the initiate dances or chants, sometimes accompanied by her sponsor or a medicine man. The intent of these actions is to transform the girl into "Changing Woman," a heroic figure in Apache myth. With this transformation comes longevity and perpetual strength.

The ceremony is a signal to all in the community that the initiate is now an adult. And it tells the initiate herself that her community now has adultlike expectations for her. ■

**MECHANISMS OF MATURATION.** What causes the many physical changes that occur during puberty? The pituitary gland in the brain is the key player. As I mentioned on page 105, the pituitary helps to regulate physical development by releasing growth hormone. In addition, the pituitary regulates pubertal changes by signaling other glands to secrete hormones. During the early elementary-school years—long before there are any outward signs of puberty—the pituitary signals the adrenal glands to release androgens, initiating the biochemical changes that will produce body hair. A few years later, in girls the pituitary signals the ovaries to release estrogen, which causes the breasts to enlarge, the female genitals to mature, and fat to accumulate. In boys the pituitary signals the testes to release the andro-gen testosterone, which causes the male genitals to mature and muscle mass to increase.

The timing of pubertal events is regulated, in part, by genetics. This is shown by the closer synchrony of pubertal events in identical twins than in fraternal twins: If one identical twin has body hair, the odds are that the other twin will, too (Mus-tanski et al., 2004). Genetic influence is also shown by the fact that a mother's age at menarche is related to her daughter's age at menarche (Weichold & Silbereisen, 2005). However, these genetic forces are strongly influenced by the environment, particularly an adolescent's nutrition and health. In general, puberty occurs earlier in adolescents who are well nourished and healthy than in adolescents who are not. For example, puberty occurs earlier in girls who are heavier and taller but later in girls who are afflicted with chronic illnesses or who receive inadequate nutrition (St. George et al., 1994).

Two other findings underscore the importance of nutrition and health in the onset of puberty. Cross-cultural comparisons reveal that menarche occurs earlier in areas of the world where nutrition and health care are adequate. For example, menar-che occurs an average of 2 to 3 years earlier in western European and North American countries than in African countries. And, within regions, socioeco-nomic status matters: Girls from affluent homes are more likely to re-ceive adequate nutrition and health care and, consequently, they reach menarche earlier (Steinberg, 1999).

Historical data point to the same conclusion concerning the importance of nutrition and health care. In many industrialized countries around the world, the average age of menarche has declined steadily over the past 150 years. For example, in Europe the average age of menarche was 17 in 1840, compared to about 13 years today. This drop reflects improvements and better health care over this period. In these countries, age of menarche is no longer dropping, which suggests that with adequate nutrition the biological lower limit for menarche is, on average, about 13 years.

> The timing of menarche is determined by genetics, nutrition, health, and social environment.

What may surprise you is that the social environment also influences the onset of puberty, at least for girls. Menarche occurs at younger ages in girls who experience chronic stress or who are depressed (Belsky, Steinberg, & Draper, 1991; Moffit et al., 1992). For example, Ellis and Garber (2000) found that girls entered puberty at a younger age when their mothers' romantic relationships were stressful and when their mothers had remarried or had a boyfriend. Other research shows that girls begin pu-berty at a younger age when their father is no longer living at home (Hoier, 2003).

The exact nature of these links is not known, but many explanations focus on the circumstances that would trigger the release of hormones that regulate menarche menstruation. One proposal is that when young girls experience chronic socio-emotional stress—their family life is harsh and they lack warm, supportive parents—the hormones elicited by this stress may help to activate the hormones that trigger menarche. This mechanism would even have an evolutionary advantage: If events of a girl's life suggest that her future reproductive success is uncertain—as indicated by chronic socioemotional stress—then it may be adaptive to reproduce as soon as pos-sible instead of waiting until later when she would be more mature and better able to care for her offspring. That is, the evolutionary gamble in this case might favor "lower quality" offspring early over "higher quality" offspring later (Ellis, 2004).

A different account, one that emphasizes the role of fathers, is described in the "Spotlight on Theories" feature.

## *Spotlight on Theories*
## A Paternal Investment Theory of Girls' Pubertal Timing

### BACKGROUND

Environmental factors can cause adolescent girls to enter puberty earlier. Some scientists believe that stress is the main factor in an adolescent girl's life that may cause her to mature early, but other scientists have continued to look for other factors that influence the onset of puberty in girls.

### THE THEORY

Bruce J. Ellis (Ellis & Garber, 2000; Ellis et al., 2003) has proposed a parental investment theory that emphasizes the role of fathers in determining timing of puberty. This theory is rooted in an evolutionary perspective that links timing of puberty—and, in the process, timing of reproduction—to the resources (defined broadly) in the child's environment. When an environment is predictable and rich in resources, it is adaptive to delay reproduction because this allows an adolescent girl to complete her own physical, cognitive, and social–emotional development, with the end result that she is a better parent. In contrast, when an environment is unstable and has few resources, it may be adaptive to mature and reproduce early rather than risk the possibility that reproduction may be impossible later.

According to Ellis, when a girl's childhood experiences indicate that paternal investment is common and of high quality, this may delay timing of maturation. But when those experiences indicate that paternal investment is uncommon and often of low quality, this may trigger early maturation. Delaying puberty is adaptive when high-quality fathers are plentiful, because it allows the girl to mature herself; but accelerating puberty is adaptive when high-quality fathers are rare, because it allows a girl to be mature sexually should a high-quality father become available and because it means that her mother is likely to be available to help with child care.*

**HYPOTHESIS:** If a girl's childhood experiences with paternal investment influence timing of maturation, then the quantity and quality of a girl's experiences with her own father should predict the age when she enters puberty. Girls who have infrequent or negative interactions with their fathers should enter puberty earlier than girls who have frequent or positive interactions with their fathers because infrequent or negative experiences would indicate that the environment has few high-quality fathers.

**TEST:** Ellis et al. (1999) conducted a longitudinal study in which they measured how much fathers were involved in caring for their daughters up to 5 years of age. They also observed fathers interacting with their daughters at age 5. Finally, they determined the extent of each girl's pubertal development in grade 7.

Two main findings both support the theory. First, the amount of time that fathers spent caring for their daughters was negatively correlated with their pubertal development in grade 7. When fathers spent much time caring for their daughters as infants and preschoolers, those daughters tended to have slower pubertal development. Second, the amount of affectionate and positive interactions at age 5 was negatively correlated with pubertal development. When fathers enjoyed interacting with their daughters and expressed affection toward them, their daughter's pubertal development was slower.

---

*These are not conscious mechanisms: 9-year-old girls are not thinking to themselves "The men around here are losers; I need to be ready in case a good one comes along." Instead, neural pathways that are sensitive to the presence of caring men may act to suppress the paths that trigger puberty.

**CONCLUSION:** As predicted, pubertal timing was influenced by the quantity and quality of father–daughter interactions. Puberty was earlier when father–daughter interactions were uncommon or negative, which, according to Ellis, indicates that the environment contains relatively few high-quality fathers.

**APPLICATION:** We saw in Module 3.2 that teenage moms and their children usually travel a rocky road; it's always best if adolescent girls delay childbearing until they're older. Paternal investment theory suggests that one way to reduce teen pregnancy is to encourage fathers to have more and more positive interactions with their daughters. This will help delay the onset of puberty, reducing the odds that she'll become pregnant as a teenager and helping in other ways as well, as we'll see on pages 320–321. Of course, a father's investment in his daughters (as well as his sons) has benefits that extend far beyond physical maturation, as we'll see throughout the book. ■

These and other theories are being actively studied today. Where scientists agree, however, is that onset of menarche is *not* just under genetic and biological control; social and emotional factors also contribute.

**PSYCHOLOGICAL IMPACT OF PUBERTY.**   Of course, teenagers are well aware of the changes taking places in their bodies. Not surprisingly, some of these changes affect adolescents' psychological development. For example, compared to children and adults, adolescents are much more concerned about their overall appearance. Like the girl in the photo, many teenagers look in the mirror regularly, checking for signs of additional physical change. Generally, girls worry more than boys about

As teenagers enter puberty, they become very concerned with their appearance.

appearance and are more likely to be dissatisfied with their appearance (Vander Wal & Thelen, 2000). Girls are particularly likely to be unhappy with their appearance when appearance is a frequent topic of conversation with friends, leading girls to spend more time comparing their own appearance with that of their peers. Peers have relatively little influence on boys' satisfaction with their appearance; instead, boys are unhappy with their appearance when they expect to have an idealized strong, muscular body but don't (Jones, 2004).

Because children enter puberty at different ages, early-maturing children often tower over their late-maturing agemates.

In addition, adolescents are affected by the timing of maturation: Many children begin puberty years before or after these norms. An early-maturing boy might begin puberty at age 11, whereas a late-maturing boy might start at 15 or 16. An early-maturing girl might start puberty at 9, a late-maturing girl, at 14 or 15. For example, the girls shown in the photo are the same age, but only one has reached puberty.

Maturing early or late has psychological consequences that differ for boys and girls. Several longitudinal studies show that early maturation can be harmful for girls. Girls who mature early often lack self-confidence, are less popular, are more likely to be depressed and have behavior problems, and are more likely to smoke and drink (Dick et al., 2000; Ge, Conger, & Elder, 2001; Stice, Presnell, & Bearman, 2001). Early maturation may hamper girls' development by leading them to associate with older adolescents who apparently encourage them to engage in age-inappropriate activities, such as drinking, smoking, and sex, for which they are ill-prepared. And early maturation can have life-changing effects on early-maturing girls who are pressured into sex and become mothers while still teenagers (Weichold & Silbereisen, 2005). The good news here is that the harmful effects of early maturation can be offset by other factors: When early-maturing girls have warm, supportive parents, for example, they are less likely to suffer the consequences of early maturation (Ge et al., 2002).

The findings for boys are much more confusing. Some early studies suggested that early maturation benefits boys. For example, in an extensive longitudinal study of adolescents growing up in Milwaukee during the 1970s (Simmons & Blyth, 1987) the early-maturing boys dated more often and had more positive feelings about their physical development and their athletic abilities. But other studies have supported the "off-time hypothesis" for boys. In this view, being early *or* late is stressful for boys, who strongly prefer to be "on time" in their physical development. Yet another view is that puberty per se is stressful for boys; but the timing is not (Ge et al., 2003).

Scientists cannot yet explain this bewildering pattern of results. But it's clear that the transition to puberty seems to have few long-lasting effects for boys. In contrast to what happens with girls, by young adulthood, the effects associated with puberty and its timing vanish. When Pete, the late-maturing boy in the opening vignette, finally matures, others will treat him like an adult and the few extra years of being treated like a child will not be harmful (Weichold & Silbereisen, 2005).

**4.1** You could tell her that breast-fed babies tend to be healthier, get diarrhea less often, and make the transition to solid foods more easily. You could also mention that it's impossible to contaminate breast milk.

## CHECK YOUR LEARNING

**RECALL** Summarize the nutritional needs of infants, preschool children, and school-age children.

What is puberty and how does it differ for boys and girls?

**INTERPRET** Why is sleep important for healthy growth and development?

**APPLY** At first blush, the onset of puberty would seem to be due entirely to biology. In fact, the child's environment influences the onset of puberty. Summarize the ways in which biology and experience interact to trigger the onset of puberty.

# CHALLENGES TO HEALTHY GROWTH

## 4.2

**LEARNING OBJECTIVES**

- What is malnutrition? What are its consequences? What is the solution to malnutrition?

- How do nature and nurture lead some adolescent girls to diet excessively?

- Why do some children become obese? How can they lose weight permanently?

- How do diseases and accidents threaten children's development?

Malnutrition

Eating Disorders: Anorexia and Bulimia

Obesity

Disease

Accidents

*Ricardo, 12, has been overweight for most of his life. He dislikes the playground games that entertain most of his classmates during recess, preferring to stay indoors. He has relatively few friends and is not particularly happy with his lot in life. Many times Ricardo has lost weight from dieting, but he's always regained it quickly. His parents know that being overweight is a health hazard, and they wonder if there is anything that will help their son.*

Compared to many childhood tasks, physical growth seems easy. To paraphrase a famous line from the movie *Field of Dreams*, "If you feed them, they will grow." Of course, it's not this simple, in part because many children face obstacles on the path of healthy physical growth. Some obstacles concern nutrition. Growth requires enormous reserves of energy, and many children do not eat enough food to provide this energy. Other children and adolescents eat too much. Other problems are diseases and accidents, which affect millions of children worldwide. We'll look at these problems in this module, and as we do, we'll understand some of the reasons why Ricardo is overweight and what he can do about it.

## Malnutrition

An adequate diet is only a dream to many of the world's children. **Worldwide, about one in three children under age 5 suffers from *malnutrition*, as indicated by being small for their age** (Grantham-McGregor, Ani, & Fernald, 2001). Many, like the children in the photo, are from third-world countries. But malnutrition is regrettably common in industrialized countries, too. Many American children growing up homeless and in poverty are malnourished. Approximately 20% of American children receive inadequate amounts of iron, and 10% go to bed hungry (Children's Defense Fund, 1996; Pollitt, 1994).

Malnourishment is especially damaging during infancy because growth is so rapid during these years. A longitudinal study conducted in Barbados in the West Indies (Galler & Ramsey, 1989; Galler, Ramsey, & Forde, 1986) followed a group of children who were severely malnourished as infants and a group from similar family environments who had adequate nutrition as infants. As older children, the two groups were indistinguishable physically: Children who were malnourished as infants were just as tall and weighed just as much as their peers. However, the children with a history of

Malnutrition is acute in third-world countries, where one child in three is malnourished.

infant malnutrition had much lower scores on intelligence tests. They also had difficulty maintaining attention in school; they were easily distracted. Malnutrition during rapid periods of growth apparently damages the brain, affecting a child's intelligence and ability to pay attention (Morgane et al., 1993).

Malnutrition would seem to have a simple cure—an adequate diet. But the solution is more complex than that. Malnourished children are frequently listless and inactive, behaviors that are useful because they conserve energy. At the same time, when children are routinely unresponsive and lethargic, parents may provide fewer and fewer experiences that foster their children's development. For example, parents who start out reading to their children at night may stop because their malnourished children seem uninterested and inattentive. The result is a self-perpetuating cycle in which malnourished children are forsaken by parents, who feel that nothing they do gets a response, so they quit trying. A biological influence—lethargy stemming from insufficient nourishment—causes a profound change in the experiences—parental teaching—that shape a child's development (Worobey, 2005).

> Treating malnutrition requires improving children's diet and teaching parents to stimulate their children's development.

To break the vicious cycle, children need more than an improved diet. Their parents must also be taught how to foster their children's development. Programs that combine dietary supplements with parent training offer promise in treating malnutrition (Grantham-McGregor et al., 2001). Children in these programs often catch up with their peers in physical and intellectual growth, showing that the best way to treat malnutrition is by addressing both biological and sociocultural factors (Super, Herrera, & Mora, 1990).

**SHORT-TERM HUNGER.**    Breakfast should provide about one fourth of a child's daily calories. Yet, many children—in developed and developing countries—do not eat breakfast (Grantham-McGregor et al., 2001). When children don't eat breakfast, they often have difficulty paying attention or remembering in school (Pollitt, 1995).

One strategy to attack this problem is to provide free and reduced-price meals for children at school. Lunch programs are the most common, but breakfast and dinner are sometimes available, too. These programs have a tremendous positive impact on children. Because they are better fed, they are absent from school less often and their achievement scores improve (Grantham-McGregor et al., 2001).

Adolescent girls with anorexia nervosa believe that they are overweight and refuse to eat.

## Eating Disorders: Anorexia and Bulimia

Just days after turning 18, Mary-Kate Olsen, a TV and movie star and successful businesswoman, entered a rehabilitation clinic. She was rail thin and was being treated for an eating disorder. *Anorexia nervosa* **is a disorder marked by a persistent refusal to eat and an irrational fear of being overweight.** Individuals with anorexia nervosa have a grossly distorted image of their own body. Like the girl in the photo, they claim to be overweight despite being painfully thin (Wilson, Heffernan, & Black, 1996). Anorexia is a very serious disorder, often leading to heart damage. Without treatment, as many as 15% of adolescents with anorexia die (Wang & Brownell, 2005). A related eating disorder is bulimia nervosa. **Individuals with** *bulimia nervosa* **alternate between binge eating periods when they eat uncontrollably and purging through self-induced vomiting or with laxatives.** The frequency of binge eating varies remarkably among people with bulimia nervosa, from a few times a week to more than 30 times. What's common to all is the feeling that they cannot stop eating (Mizes et al., 1995).

Anorexia and bulimia are alike in many respects. Both disorders primarily affect females and emerge in adolescence (Wang & Brownell, 2005). What's more, many of the same factors put teenage girls at risk for both eating disorders. Corinna Jacobi and her colleagues (2004) conducted a meta-analysis of more than 300 longitudinal and cross-sectional studies of individuals with eating disorders. They concluded that heredity puts some girls at risk and that psychosocial factors amplify that risk:

- During childhood: A history of eating problems, such as being a picky eater or being diagnosed with pica, which refers to eating nonfood objects such as chalk, paper, or dirt.
- During adolescence: Negative self-esteem, a mood or anxiety disorder, and, most strongly of all, being overly concerned about one's body and weight and having a history of dieting.

The meta-analysis also identified some risk factors that are unique to anorexia and bulimia. For example, overprotective parenting is associated with anorexia but not bulimia. In contrast, obesity in childhood is associated with bulimia but not anorexia.

Although eating disorders are more common in girls, boys make up about 10% of diagnosed cases of eating disorders. Because boys with eating disorders are far less common, researchers have conducted much less research with males. However, some of the known risk factors are childhood obesity, low self-esteem, pressure from parents and peers to lose weight, and participating in sports that emphasize being lean (Ricciardelli & McCabe, 2004).

Fortunately, there are programs that can help protect teens from eating disorders (Stice & Shaw, 2004). The most effective programs are designed for at-risk youth; for example, for those who already say they are unhappy with their body. The best programs are interactive—they encourage youth to become involved and to learn new skills, such as ways to resist social pressure to be thin. And they work to change critical attitudes (e.g., ideals regarding thinness) and critical behaviors (e.g., dieting and overeating). At-risk adolescents who participate in these programs are helped; they are more satisfied with their appearance and less likely to diet or overeat. And for those teens affected by eating disorders, treatment is available: Like prevention programs, treatment typically focuses on modifying key attitudes and behaviors (Puhl & Brownell, 2005).

Childhood obesity has reached epidemic proportions in the United States.

## Obesity

Ricardo, the boy in this module's opening vignette, is overweight; he is very heavy for his height. **The technical definition for overweight is based on the *body mass index (BMI)*, which is an adjusted ratio of weight to height.** Children and adolescents who are in the upper 5% (very heavy for their height) are defined as being overweight. Using these standards, in 2001 the U.S. Surgeon General announced that childhood obesity had reached epidemic proportions. In the past 25 to 30 years, the number of overweight children has doubled and the number of overweight adolescents has tripled, so that today roughly one child or adolescent out of seven is overweight (U.S. Department of Health and Human Services, 2001).

Like the boy in the photo, overweight youngsters are often unpopular and have low self-esteem (Braet, Mervielde, & Vandereycken, 1997). Furthermore, throughout life they are at risk for many medical problems, including high blood pressure and diabetes, because the vast majority of overweight children and adolescents become overweight adults (Serdula et al., 1993).

Heredity plays an important role in juvenile obesity. In adoption studies, children and adolescents' weight is related to the weight of their biological parents, rather than the weight of their adoptive parents (Stunkard et al., 1986). Genes may influence obesity by influencing a person's activity level. In other words, being genetically more prone to inactivity makes it more difficult to burn off calories and easier to gain weight. **Heredity may also help set *basal metabolic rate*, the speed at which the body consumes calories.** Children and adolescents with a slower basal metabolic rate burn off calories less rapidly, making it easier for them to gain weight (Epstein & Cluss, 1986).

The environment is also influential. Television advertising, for example, encourages youth to eat tasty but fattening foods. Parents play a role, too. They may inadvertently encourage obesity by emphasizing external rather than internal eating signals. Infants eat primarily because of internal signals: They eat when they experience hunger and stop eating when they feel full. During the preschool years, this internal control of eating is often gradually replaced by external signals. Parents who urge their children to "clean their plates" even when they are no longer hungry are teaching their children to ignore internal cues to eating. Thus, obese children and adolescents may overeat because they rely on external cues and disregard internal cues to stop (Birch, 1991).

> In programs designed to treat obesity, children and parents set goals for eating and exercise, then monitor children's progress toward those goals.

Obese youth can lose weight. The most effective weight-loss programs have several features in common (Epstein et al., 1995; Foreyt & Goodrick, 1995; Israel et al., 1994):

- The focus of the program is to change obese children's eating habits, encourage them to become more active, and discourage sedentary behavior.

- As part of the treatment, children learn to monitor their eating, exercise, and sedentary behavior. Goals are established in each area, and rewards are earned when the goals are met.

- Parents are trained to help children set realistic goals and to use behavioral principles to help children meet these goals. Parents also monitor their own lifestyles to be sure they aren't accidentally fostering their child's obesity.

When programs incorporate these features, obese children do lose weight. However, even after losing weight, many of these children remain overweight. Consequently, it is best to avoid overweight and obesity in the first place; the *Surgeon General's Call for Action* emphasizes the role of increased physical activity and good eating habits in warding off overweight and obesity (U.S. Department of Health and Human Services, 2001).

**4.2** | Joshua is a 10-year-old who is 25 pounds overweight. What can he and his parents do to help him lose weight?

## Disease

Around the world an estimated 11 million children aged 4 years and younger die every year. These are staggering numbers—roughly the equivalent of *all U.S.* 1-, 2-, and 3-year-olds dying in a single year. The leading killers of young children worldwide are infectious diseases—acute respiratory infections (including pneumonia and influenza) and diarrheal diseases each kill 2 million children annually (World Health Organization, 1999). The majority of these deaths can be prevented with proven, cost-effective treatments. For example, measles kills nearly 1 million children annually but can be prevented with vaccinations. Similarly, diarrhea kills by dehydrating youngsters, yet children can avert death by promptly drinking water that contains salt and potassium.

As part of a vigorous effort to prevent childhood illness, for the past 2 decades, the World Health Organization (WHO) has worked to vaccinate children worldwide. Due to these efforts, vaccination rates have skyrocketed in many developing countries. More recently, WHO has joined with the United Nations Children's Fund (UNICEF) to create Integrated Management of Childhood Illness (IMCI), a program to combat the five conditions that account for the vast majority of childhood deaths: pneumonia, diarrhea, measles, malaria, and malnutrition (World Health Organization, 1997). Because many children who are ill have symptoms related to two or more of these five conditions, IMCI takes an integrated strategy that focuses on the overall health of the child. One component of IMCI is training health-care professionals to become more skilled in dealing with childhood illnesses. A second component is improving health-care systems so that they are better able to respond to childhood illness (e.g., ensuring that required medicines are available). A third component involves changing family and community practices to make them more conducive to healthy growth. For example, to protect children from mosquitoes that carry malaria, children are encouraged to sleep in netting, as the baby in the photo is doing. IMCI has been adopted in more than 60 countries and is playing a pivotal role in improving children's health worldwide.

One way to protect young children from disease is to adapt practices that foster healthy growth, such as having them sleep in netting that protects them from mosquitoes that carry malaria.

## Accidents

In the United States, most infant deaths are due to medical conditions associated with birth defects or low birth weight. From age 1 on, however, children are more likely to die from accidents than from any other single cause (Centers for Disease Control and Prevention, 2000). Motor vehicle accidents are the most common cause of accidental death in children. Regrettably, many of these deaths could have been prevented had children and adolescents been wearing seat belts, or had infants been restrained properly in an approved infant car seat like the one shown in the photo. Without such restraint, children and adolescents typically suffer massive head injuries when thrown through the windshield or onto the road.

One simple way to protect infants, toddlers, and young children is to insist that they be restrained in an approved seat when riding in a car.

Many infants and toddlers also drown, die from burns, or suffocate. Often these deaths result because young children are supervised inadequately. All too common, for example, are reports of young children who wander away, jump or fall into an unfenced swimming pool, then drown. Parents need to remember

Children sometimes have accidents because parents overestimate their children's abilities, such as allowing them to ride bikes on unsafe streets.

that children are often eager to explore their environs yet they are unable to recognize many hazards. Parents must constantly keep a protective eye on their young children. And, with older children, parents must be careful that they don't overestimate their children's skills. Some accidents happen because parents have too much confidence in their children's cognitive and motor skills. They may allow a child like the boy in the photo to ride to school in a bike lane adjacent to a street filled with commuters, even though many children may not consistently pay attention while biking or may be unable to maneuver their bike around unexpected hazards, such as a pothole.*

For adolescents, motor vehicle accidents remain the leading cause of death. The difference, of course, is that adolescents are no longer passengers but are driving. And, sadly, far too many adolescents are killed because they drive too fast, drive while drunk, and drive without wearing a seatbelt (U.S. Department of Health and Human Services, 1997). Among teenage boys, firearms represent a leading cause of death. In fact, firearms kill more 15- to 19-year-old African American boys and Hispanic American boys than any other single cause (Federal Interagency Forum on Child and Family Statistics, 2000).

Although the term *accident* implies that the event happened by chance and no one was to blame, in reality most accidents involving children and adolescents can be foreseen and either prevented or steps taken to reduce injury. In the case of automobile accidents, for example, the simple step of wearing a seat belt enhances safety immensely. Accidents involving firearms can be reduced by making guns less accessible to children and adolescents (e.g., locking away guns and ammunition separately). School-based safety programs can also help to reduce childhood accidents. Children can learn safe ways of walking or riding their bikes to school, then be allowed to practice these skills, supervised by an adult. With programs like these, children readily learn behaviors that foster safety (Zins et al., 1994).

**4.2** Joshua and his parents need to work together to create a healthier lifestyle, one that changes his eating habits and encourages him to be more active. They need to agree upon realistic goals (e.g., losing 6 pounds in a month, 20 minutes of outdoor play each day) and use rewards to help Joshua achieve those goals. Also, Joshua needs to learn how to record what and how much he eats, along with recording his exercise.

## CHECK YOUR LEARNING

RECALL Summarize the factors that put adolescent girls at risk for anorexia nervosa and for bulimia nervosa.

What are the leading causes of death for toddlers and preschool children? For adolescents?

INTERPRET Distinguish the biological factors that contribute to obesity from the environmental factors.

APPLY How does malnutrition show the impact that children can have on their own development?

---

*As a 10-year-old, my son Matt crashed his new bike right into the back of a parked car because he was too busy watching the gears shift. Fortunately, he escaped with just a few scrapes, but this illustrates how easily a childhood lapse in concentration can lead to a cycling accident.

# THE DEVELOPING NERVOUS SYSTEM

## 4.3

**LEARNING OBJECTIVES**

- What are the parts of a nerve cell? How is the brain organized?

- When is the brain formed in prenatal development? When do different regions of the brain begin to function?

Organization of the Mature Brain

The Developing Brain

> *While crossing the street, 10-year-old Martin was struck by a passing car. He was in a coma for a week, but then gradually became more alert, and now he seems to be aware of his surroundings. Needless to say, Martin's mother is grateful that he survived the accident, but she wonders what the future holds for her son.*

The physical changes that we see as children grow are impressive, but even more awe-inspiring are the changes we cannot see, those involving the brain and the nervous system. An infant's feelings of hunger, a child's laugh, and an adolescent's efforts to learn algebra all reflect the functioning brain and the rest of the nervous system. All the information that children learn, including language and other cognitive skills, is stored in the brain.

How does the brain accomplish these many tasks? How is the brain affected by an injury like the one that Martin suffered? To begin to answer these questions, let's look at how the brain is organized in adults.

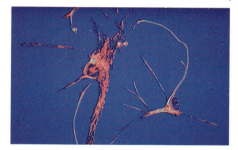

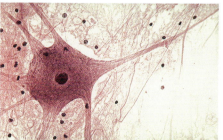

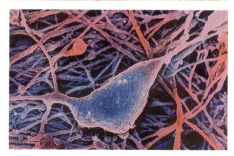

Neurons come in many shapes but they all have the same function of transmitting information.

## Organization of the Mature Brain

**The basic unit of the brain and the rest of the nervous system is the *neuron*, a cell that specializes in receiving and transmitting information.** Neurons come in many different shapes, as you can see in the different photos. The diagram makes it easier to understand the basic parts found in all neurons. **The *cell body* at the center of the neuron contains the basic biological machinery that keeps the neuron alive. The receiving end of the neuron, the *dendrite*, looks like a tree with many branches.** The highly branched dendrite allows one neuron to receive input from many thousands of other neurons (Morgan & Gibson, 1991). **The tubelike structure at the other end of the cell body is the *axon*, which sends information to other neurons. The axon is wrapped in *myelin*, a fatty sheath that allows it to transmit information more rapidly.** The boost in neural speed from myelin is like the difference between driving and flying: from about 6 feet per second to 50 feet per second. **At the end of the axon are small knobs called *terminal buttons*, which release *neurotransmitters*, chemicals that carry information to nearby neurons.** Finally, you'll see that the terminal buttons of one axon don't actually touch the dendrites of other neurons. **The gap between one neuron and the next is a *synapse*.** Neurotransmitters cross synapses to carry information between neurons.

Take 50 to 100 billion neurons like these and you have the beginnings of a human brain. An adult's brain weighs a little less than 3 pounds, and it easily fits into your hands.

**FIGURE 4-7**

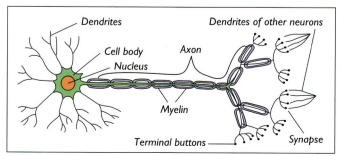

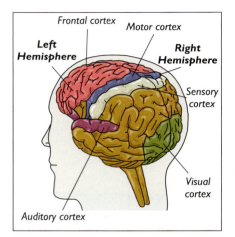

**FIGURE** 4-8

The wrinkled surface of the brain is the *cerebral cortex*; made up of about 10 billion neurons, the cortex regulates many of the functions that we think of as distinctly human. The cortex consists of left and right halves, called *hemispheres*, that are linked by millions of axons in a thick bundle called the *corpus callosum*. The characteristics that you value most—your engaging personality, your "way with words," your uncanny knack for reading others—are all controlled by specific regions of the cortex, many of which are shown in the diagram.

Personality and your ability to make and carry out plans are largely functions of an area at the front of the cortex that is called, appropriately, the *frontal cortex*. For most people, the ability to produce and understand language, to reason, and to compute is largely due to neurons in the cortex of the left hemisphere. Also for most people, artistic and musical abilities, perception of spatial relations, and the ability to recognize faces and emotions come from neurons in the right hemisphere.

Now that we know a bit of the organization of the mature brain, let's look at how the brain develops and begins to function.

## The Developing Brain

Scientists who study the brain's development are guided by several key questions: How and when do brain structures develop? When do different brain regions begin to function? Why do brain regions take on different functions? In this section, we'll see how research has answered each question.

**EMERGING BRAIN STRUCTURES.** We know from Module 3.1 that the beginnings of the brain can be traced to the period of the zygote. **At roughly 3 weeks after conception, a group of cells form a flat structure known as the *neural plate*.** At 4 weeks, the neural plate folds to form a tube that ultimately becomes the brain and spinal cord. When the ends of the tube fuse shut, neurons are produced in one small region of the neural tube. Production of neurons begins about 10 weeks after conception, and by 28 weeks the developing brain has virtually all the neurons it will ever have. During these weeks, neurons form at the incredible rate of more than 4,000 per second (Kolb, 1989).

From the neuron-manufacturing site in the neural tube, neurons migrate to their final positions in the brain. The brain is built in stages, beginning with the innermost layers. Neurons in the deepest layer are positioned first, followed by neurons in the second layer, and so on. This layering process continues until all six layers of the mature brain are in place, which occurs about 7 months after conception (Rakic, 1995). As you can see in the diagram, the nerve cells move to the top by wrapping themselves around supporting cells, just as a snake might climb a pole.

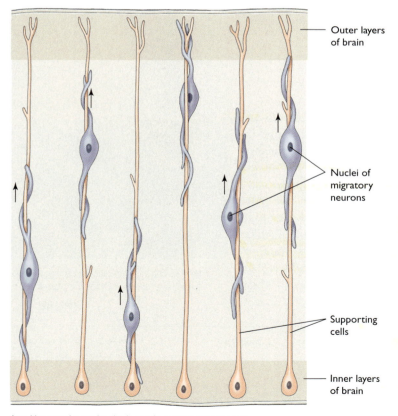

Just like a snake might climb a pole, neurons migrate to their final location in the brain by wrapping themselves around supporting cells.

**FIGURE** 4-9

In the 4th month of prenatal development, axons begin to acquire myelin—the fatty wrap that speeds neural transmission. This process continues through infancy and into childhood and adolescence (Casaer, 1993). Neurons that carry sensory information are the first to acquire myelin; neurons in the cortex are among the last. You can see the effect of more myelin in improved coordination and reaction times. The older the infant and, later, the child, the more rapid and coordinated are his or her reactions. (We'll talk more about this phenomenon when we discuss fine-motor skills in Module 5.3.)

VIDEO4.2

Synaptic Development

In the months after birth, the brain grows rapidly. Axons and dendrites grow longer, and, like a maturing tree, dendrites quickly sprout new limbs. As the number of dendrites increases, so does the number of synapses, reaching a peak at about the first birthday. This rapid neural growth is shown in the diagram. **Soon after, synapses begin to disappear gradually, a phenomenon known as** *synaptic pruning*. Thus, beginning in infancy and continuing into early adolescence, the brain goes through its own version of "downsizing," weeding out unnecessary connections between neurons. This pruning depends on the activity of the neural circuits—synapses that are active are preserved but those that aren't active are eliminated (Webb, Monk, & Nelson, 2001). Pruning is completed first for brain regions associated with sensory and motor functions. Regions associated with basic language and spatial skills are completed next, followed by regions associated with attention and planning (Casey et al., 2005).

> During infancy and childhood, some synapses are pruned and axons become wrapped in myelin.

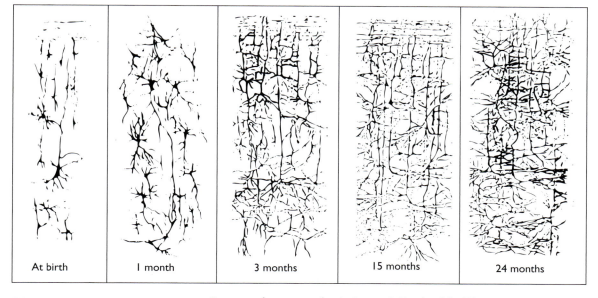

| At birth | 1 month | 3 months | 15 months | 24 months |

**FIGURE 4-10**

**STRUCTURE AND FUNCTION.**   Because the mature brain is specialized, with different psychological functions localized in particular regions, a natural question for developmental researchers is, "How early in development does brain functioning become localized?" To answer this question, scientists have used many different methods to map functions onto particular brain regions.

- *Studies of children with brain damage:*  Children who suffer brain injuries provide valuable insights into brain structure and function. If a region of the brain regulates a particular function (e.g., understanding speech), then damage to that region should impair the function.

One way to study brain functioning is to record the brain's electrical activity using electrodes placed on a child's scalp.

- *Studies of electrical activity:* **Metal electrodes placed on an infant's scalp, as shown in the top photo, produce an *electroencephalogram (EEG)*, a pattern of brain waves.** If a region of the brain regulates a function, then the region should show distinctive EEG patterns while a child is using that function.
- *Studies using imaging techniques:* **Functional magnetic resonance imaging *(f-MRI)* uses magnetic fields to track the flow of blood in the brain.** With this method, shown in the bottom photo, the research participant's brain is literally wrapped in an incredibly powerful magnet that can track blood flow as participants perform different cognitive tasks (Casey et al., 2005).

None of these methods is perfect; each has drawbacks. In cases of brain injury, for example, multiple areas of the brain may be damaged, making it hard to link impaired functioning to a particular brain region. fMRI is used sparingly because it's very expensive and participants must lie still for several minutes at a time.

Despite these limitations, the combined outcome of research using these different approaches indicates that many areas of the cortex begin to function in infancy. Early specialization of the frontal cortex is shown by the finding that damage to this region in infancy results in impaired decision making and abnormal emotional responses (Anderson et al., 2001). Similarly, EEG studies show that a newborn infant's left hemisphere generates more electrical activity in response to speech than the right hemisphere (Molfese & Burger-Judisch, 1991). Thus, by birth, the cortex of the left hemisphere is already specialized for language processing. As we'll see in Chapter 9, this specialization allows language to develop rapidly during infancy. Finally, studies of children with prenatal brain damage indicate that by infancy the right hemisphere is specialized for understanding certain kinds of spatial relations (Stiles et al., 2005).

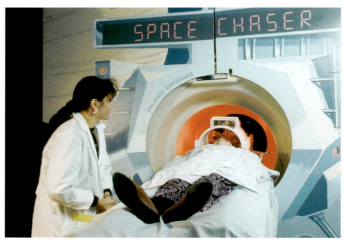

In functional magnetic resonance imaging (fMRI) a powerful magnet tracks the flow of blood to different brain regions, which shows parts of the brain that are active as children perform different tasks.

Of course, this early specialization does not mean that the brain is functionally mature. During the remainder of childhood and into adulthood, these and other regions of the brain continue to become more specialized. That is, with development the brain regions active during cognitive processing become more focused and less diffuse; an analogy would be to a thunderstorm that covers a huge region versus one that packs the same power in a much smaller region.

You can see this specialization in the "Focus on Research" feature.

## Focus On Research
### Right-Hemisphere Specialization for Face Processing

*Who were the investigators, and what was the aim of the study?* Regions of the brain's right hemisphere are critical in allowing us to recognize and distinguish faces. For example, when people experience damage to the right hemisphere of the brain, they sometimes suffer prosopagnosia—they can't recognize familiar faces: Alessandra Passarotti and her colleagues—Brianni Paul, Joseph Bussiere, Richard Buxton, Eric Wong, and Joan Stiles—wanted to know whether the brain regions involved in recognizing faces were the same in adults and in 10- to 12-year-olds.

*How did the investigators measure the topic of interest?* Passarotti and her colleagues showed pairs of faces very rapidly: one face was shown for a half second, followed by another face that was also presented for a half second. Participants pressed one button if the faces were the same and another button if the faces differed. They made these judgments while lying in an fMRI scanner like the one shown on page 126.

*Who were the participants in the study?* The researchers tested fifteen 10- to 12-year-olds as well as sixteen adults (19- to 28-year-olds).

*What was the design of the study?* This study was correlational because Passarotti and her colleagues were interested in the natural relation between two variables: age and brain activity. The study was cross-sectional because it included one group of children and a separate group of adults.

*Were there ethical concerns with the study?* No. The behavioral task was harmless—deciding whether faces were the same. Generally fMRI is very safe. However, researchers routinely check to see whether prospective participants might have metal in their body (e.g., a pacemaker or hearing aid or an object from an accident, such as a bullet), which is a hazard because of the powerful magnets that are built into scanners.

*What were the results?* The graph shows the speed and accuracy of children's and adults' responses. Adults were slightly faster and slightly more accurate, but these differences were not significant. Thus, in terms of their performance on the task, children and adults were very similar. Nevertheless, there were developmental differences in patterns of brain activation. The diagram shows a top view of the brain, with areas active in face processing shown in yellow. Children and adults are alike in having greater activation in the right hemisphere than in the left hemisphere. However, activation is more widespread in children and much more focused in adults.

*What did the investigators conclude?* By middle childhood face processing is well established in the right hemisphere. Nevertheless, between middle childhood and adulthood, a smaller area of the right hemisphere becomes active during face processing: The brain continues to "fine tune" its face-processing systems during adolescence.

*What converging evidence would strengthen these conclusions?* This work could be extended naturally in two directions. First, by testing younger children and adolescents, the investigators could provide a more precise account of the developmental course of brain specialization for face processing. Second, face processing is one example of nonverbal processing that is associated with the right hemisphere. It would be revealing to determine whether other forms of nonverbal processing show a similar pattern of brain specialization during childhood and adolescence. ■

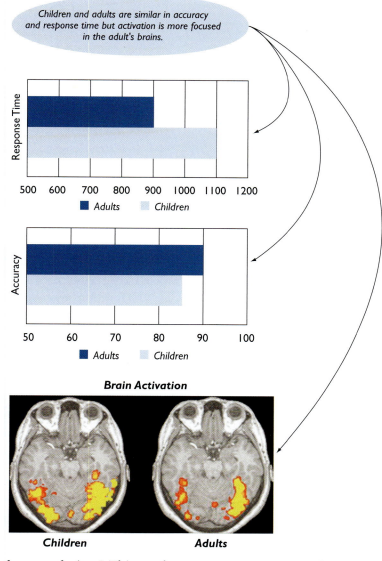

FIGURE 4-11

After the brain specializes, can those functions be transferred to other regions? If a child or adolescent suffers brain damage, are the processes associated with the damaged region shifted to other, intact regions? The next section will address these questions.

**BRAIN PLASTICITY AND THE ROLE OF ENVIRONMENTAL INPUT.** *Plasticity* **refers to the extent to which brain organization is flexible.** How plastic is the human brain? Answers to this question reflect the familiar views on the nature–nurture issue (Nelson, 1999; Stiles, 2001). Some theorists believe that organization of brain function is predetermined genetically; it's simply in most children's biological makeup that, for example, the left hemisphere will specialize in language processing. According to this view, the brain is like a house—a structure that's specialized from the very beginning, with some rooms designed for cooking, others for sleeping, and others for bathing. In contrast, other theorists believe that few functions are rigidly assigned to specific brain sites at conception. Instead, experience helps determine the functional organization of the brain. According to this view, the brain is more like an office building—an all-purpose structure with rooms designed to be used flexibly to meet the different business needs of the companies with offices in the building.

Research designed to test these views shows that the brain has some plasticity. Remember Martin, the child in the vignette whose brain was damaged when he was struck by a car? His language skills were impaired after the accident. This was not surprising, because the left hemisphere of Martin's brain had absorbed most of the force of the collision. But within several months, Martin had completely recovered his language skills. Apparently other neurons took over language-related processing from the damaged neurons. This recovery of function is not uncommon—particularly for young children—and shows that the brain is plastic. In other words, young children often recover more skills after brain injury than older children and adults, apparently because functions are more easily reassigned in the young brain (Stiles et al., 2005).

However, the brain is not completely plastic—brains have a similar structure and similar mapping of functions on those structures. The visual cortex, for example, is always near the back of the brain. The sensory cortex and motor cortex always run across the middle of the brain. But if a neuron's function is not specified at conception, how do different neurons take on different functions and in much the same pattern for most people? Researchers are trying to answer this question and many details still need to be worked out. The answer probably lies in complex biochemical processes (Barinaga, 1997; Kunzig, 1998). You can get an idea of what's involved by imagining people arriving for a football game at a stadium where there are no reserved seats. As fans enter the stadium, they see others wearing their own school colors and move in that direction. Of course, not everyone does this. Some fans sit with friends from the other team. Some pick seats based on other factors (e.g., to avoid looking into the sun, to be close to the concession stand). In general, though, by game time, most fans have taken seats on their respective sides of the field.

In much the same way, as neurons are created and begin migrating through the layers of cortex, cellular biochemistry makes some paths more attractive than others. Yet, just as each fan can potentially sit anywhere because there are no reserved seats, an individual neuron can end up in many different locations because genetic instructions do not assign specific brain regions. Thus, the human brain *is* plastic—its organization and function can be affected by experience—but its development follows some general biochemical instructions that ensure most people end up with brains organized along similar lines.

**Q & A Question**

**4.3** Ashley was distraught when her 2-year-old daughter fell down a full flight of steps and hit her head against a concrete wall, which led to a trip to the emergency room. What could you say to reassure Ashley about her daughter's prognosis?

When children suffer brain damage, cognitive processes are usually impaired; these processes often improve gradually, showing the brain's plasticity.

Finally, it's important to emphasize the role of environmental stimulation in normal brain development. To return to the analogy of the brain as a building, the newborn's brain is perhaps best conceived as a partially finished, partially furnished house: A general organizational framework is there, with preliminary neural pathways designed to perform certain functions. The left hemisphere no doubt has some language pathways and the frontal cortex has some emotion-related pathways. However, completing the typical organization of the mature brain requires input from the environment that stimulates other "general purpose" neurons to specialize. When infants hear speech, these experiences may stimulate other neurons in the brain to specialize in language processing. In this manner, experience is the catalyst that converts the partially furnished, partially finished newborn brain into a mature, specialized brain (Johnson, 2000; Webb et al., 2001).

## CHECK YOUR LEARNING

RECALL  List the major parts of a nerve cell and the major regions of the cerebral cortex.

Describe evidence that shows the brain's plasticity.

INTERPRET  Compare growth of the brain before birth with growth of the brain after birth.

APPLY  How does the development of the brain, as described in this module, compare to the general pattern of physical growth described in Module 4.1?

You could explain that young children recover from brain injury more often than older children and adults do. So, unless her daughter has suffered extensive damage to the brain, she should be okay.

4.3

## UNIFYING THEMES: Connections

This chapter is an excellent opportunity to highlight the theme that *development in different domains is connected.* Consider the impact of the timing of puberty. Whether a child matures early or late affects social development (early-maturing girls are often less popular), and academic performance (early-maturing girls often do poorly in school). Or consider the impact of malnutrition. Malnourished youngsters are often listless, which affects how their parents interact with them (they're less likely to provide stimulating experiences). Less stimulation, in turn, slows the children's intellectual development. Physical, cognitive, social, and personality development are linked: Change in one area generally leads to change of some kind in the others.

## SEE FOR YOURSELF

Children love playgrounds. Unfortunately, hundreds of thousands of American children are injured on playgrounds annually. Some of these accidents could have been prevented had parents (or other adults) been present, or, if present, had they been paying closer attention to the children at play.

Go to a local playground and watch children as they play. Notice how many children unknowingly put themselves at risk as they play. Also notice how well the children's play is monitored by adults. See for yourself!

# RESOURCES

For more information about . . .

✏️ **ways to help children and adolescents stay physically fit,** try Kenneth H. Cooper's *Fit Kids* (Broadman & Holman, 1999), which describes a program of diet and exercise developed by the originator of the concept of aerobic fitness.

🏹 **children's nutrition,** visit the Web site of Children's Nutrition Research Center at Baylor College of Medicine: **http://www.bcm.tmc.edu/cnrc/**

# KEY TERMS

**anorexia nervosa** 118
**axon** 123
**basal metabolic rate** 120
**body mass index** 119
**bulimia nervosa** 118
**cell body** 123
**cerebral cortex** 124
**corpus callosum** 124
**dendrite** 123
**electroencephalogram (EEG)** 126
**epiphyses** 104
**frontal cortex** 124
**functional magnetic resonance imaging (fMRI)** 126
**growth hormone** 105
**hemispheres** 124
**malnutrition** 117

**menarche** 111
**myelin** 123
**neural plate** 124
**neuron** 123
**neurotransmitters** 123
**osteoporosis** 110
**plasticity** 128
**primary sex characteristics** 111
**puberty** 109
**secular growth trends** 104
**secondary sex characteristics** 111
**spermarche** 111
**synapse** 123
**synaptic pruning** 125
**terminal buttons** 123

## 4.1 PHYSICAL GROWTH

### Features of Human Growth

Physical growth is particularly rapid during infancy, slows during the elementary-school years, and then accelerates again during adolescence. Physical growth refers not only to height and weight but also to development of muscle, fat, and bones.

Children are taller today than in previous generations. Average heights vary around the world and within any culture there is considerable variation in the normal range of height.

### Mechanisms of Physical Growth

Physical growth depends on sleep, in part because most growth hormone is secreted while children sleep. Nutrition is also important, particularly during periods of rapid growth, such as infancy and adolescence. Breast-feeding provides babies with all the nutrients they need and has other advantages. Many children and adolescents do not get adequate nutrients because of poor diets.

### The Adolescent Growth Spurt and Puberty

Puberty includes the adolescent growth spurt as well as sexual maturation. Girls typically begin the growth spurt earlier than boys, who acquire more muscle, less fat, and greater heart and lung capacities. Sexual maturation, which includes primary and secondary sex characteristics, occurs in predictable sequences for boys and girls.

Pubertal changes occur when the pituitary gland signals the adrenal gland, ovaries, and testes to secrete hormones that initiate physical changes. The timing of puberty is influenced strongly by health, nutrition, and social environment.

Pubertal change affects adolescents' psychological functioning. Teens become concerned about their appearance. Early maturation tends to be harmful for girls because it may cause them to engage in age-inappropriate behavior. Timing of maturation seems to be less of an issue for boys.

## 4.2 CHALLENGES TO HEALTHY GROWTH

### Malnutrition

Malnutrition is a global problem—including in the United States—that is particularly harmful during infancy, when growth is so rapid. Malnutrition can cause brain damage, affecting children's intelligence and ability to pay attention. Treating malnutrition requires improving children's diet and training their parents to provide stimulating environments.

### Eating Disorders: Anorexia and Bulimia

Anorexia and bulimia are eating disorders that typically affect adolescent girls. They are characterized by an irrational fear of being overweight. Several factors contribute to these disorders, including heredity, a childhood history of eating problems, and, during adolescence, negative self-esteem and a preoccupation with one's body and weight. Eating disorders are far less common in boys; risk factors include childhood obesity, low self-esteem, social pressure to lose weight, and participation in some sports. Treatment and prevention programs emphasize changing adolescents' views toward thinness and their eating-related behaviors.

### Obesity

Many obese children and adolescents are unpopular, have low self-esteem, and are at risk for medical disorders. Obesity reflects both heredity and acquired eating habits. In the most effective programs for treating obesity in youth, both children and their parents set eating and exercise goals and monitor their daily progress.

### Disease

Millions of children around the world die annually from infectious diseases. Integrated Management of Childhood Illness is a new, integrated approach designed to promote children's health.

### Accidents

In the United States, children and adolescents are more likely to die from accidents than any other single cause. Many of these fatalities involve motor vehicles and could be prevented if passengers were restrained properly. Older children and adolescents are sometimes involved in accidents because parents overestimate their abilities.

## 4.3 THE DEVELOPING NERVOUS SYSTEM

### Organization of the Mature Brain

Nerve cells, called *neurons*, are composed of a cell body, a dendrite, and an axon. The mature brain consists of billions of neurons organized into nearly identical left and right hemispheres connected by the corpus callosum. The frontal cortex is associated with personality and goal-directed behavior; the cortex in the left hemisphere, with language; and the cortex in the right hemisphere, with nonverbal processes.

### The Developing Brain

Brain structure begins in prenatal development, when neurons form at an incredible rate. After birth, neurons in the central nervous system become wrapped in myelin, allowing them to transmit information more rapidly. Throughout childhood, unused synapses disappear gradually through a process of pruning.

Methods used to investigate brain functioning in children include (a) studying children with brain damage, (b) recording electrical activity (the electroencephalogram or EEG), and (c) using imaging techniques. Research with these methods reveals that many regions of an infant's brain specialize early in life: The frontal cortex specializes in decision making, the left hemisphere in language, and the right hemisphere in processing spatial information. The infant's brain is moderately flexible: It has a preliminary organization that tends to be followed as long as infants receive typical stimulation from the environment.

When my son, Ben, was a preschooler, he loved to watch *CHiPs* with Erik Estrada zooming around L.A. on his Kawasaki. Ben was totally absorbed by the show and oblivious to everything else around him. His behavior illustrates perception in action: Our senses are assaulted with stimulation, but much of it is ignored. *Sensory and perceptual processes* are the means by which people receive, select, modify, and organize stimulation from the world. Sensory and perceptual processes are the first step in the complex process that eventually results in "knowing." We'll begin studying perceptual development, in Module 5.1, by looking at the origins of sensory processes in infancy. In Module 5.2 we'll see how more complex perceptual and attentional processes develop in childhood.

Perceptual processes are closely linked to *motor skills*—coordinated movements of the muscles and limbs. Perception often guides a child's movement: A child uses vision to avoid obstacles. In turn, a child's movement in the environment provides enormous variety in perceptual stimulation. In Module 5.3, we'll see how improvements in motor skill enhance children's ability to explore, understand, and enjoy the world.

**5.1**    **Basic Sensory and Perceptual Processes**

**5.2**    **Complex Perceptual and Attentional Processes**

**5.3**    **Motor Development**

1 The Science of Child Development

2 Genetic Bases of Child Development

3 Prenatal Development, Birth, and the Newborn

4 Growth and Health

5

# Perceptual and Motor Development

6 Theories of Cognitive Development

7 Cognitive Processes and Academic Skills

8 Intelligence and Individual Differences in Cognition

9 Language and Communication

10 Emotional Development

11 Understanding Self and Others

12 Moral Understanding and Behavior

13 Gender and Development

14 Family Relationships

15 Influences Beyond the Family

# 5.1

# BASIC SENSORY AND PERCEPTUAL PROCESSES

Smell, Taste, and Touch

Hearing

Seeing

Integrating Sensory Information

**LEARNING OBJECTIVES**

- Are newborn babies able to smell and taste? Do they respond to touch and experience pain?

- How well do infants hear? How do they use sounds to understand their world?

- How accurate is infants' vision? Do infants perceive color?

- How do infants integrate information from different senses?

> *Darla adores her 3-day-old daughter, Olivia. She loves holding her, talking to her, and simply watching her. Darla is certain that Olivia is already getting to know her, coming to recognize her face and the sound of her voice. Darla's husband, Steve, thinks she is crazy. He tells her, "Everyone knows that babies are born blind. And they probably can't hear much either." Darla doubts that Steve is right, but she wishes someone would tell her about babies' vision and hearing.*

Darla's questions are really about her newborn daughter's sensory and perceptual skills. To help her understand, we need to remember that humans have different kinds of sense organs, each receptive to a unique kind of physical energy. The retina at the back of the eye, for example, is sensitive to some types of electromagnetic energy, and sight is the result. The eardrum detects changes in air pressure, and hearing is the result. Cells at the top of the nasal passage detect airborne molecules, and smell is the result. In each case, the sense organ translates the physical stimulation into nerve impulses that are sent to the brain.

The senses begin to function early in life, which is why this module is devoted entirely to infancy. How can we know what an infant senses? Because infants can't tell us what they smell, hear, or see, researchers have had to devise other ways to find out. In many studies, an investigator presents two stimuli to a baby, such as a high-pitched tone and a low-pitched tone or a sweet-tasting substance and a sour-tasting substance. Then the investigator records the baby's responses, such as heart rate, facial expression, or head movement. If the baby consistently responds differently to the two stimuli (e.g., she looks in the direction of one tone, but not the other), the baby must be distinguishing between them.

> *Infants' perception is studied by presenting several distinct stimuli, then determining whether infants respond the same or differently to the stimuli.*

Another approach is based on the fact that infants usually prefer novel stimuli over familiar stimuli. **When a novel stimulus is presented, babies pay much attention, but they pay less attention as it becomes more familiar, a phenomenon known as *habituation*.** Researchers use habituation to study perception by repeatedly presenting a stimulus such as a low-pitched tone until an infant barely responds. Then they present a second stimulus, such as a high-pitched tone. If the infant responds strongly, then he can distinguish the two stimuli.

In this module, you'll learn what researchers using these techniques have discovered about infants' perception. We begin with smell, taste, and touch because these senses are particularly mature at birth.

## Smell, Taste, and Touch

Newborns have a keen sense of smell; they respond positively to pleasant smells and negatively to unpleasant smells (Mennella & Beauchamp, 1997). They have a relaxed, contented-looking facial expression when they smell honey or chocolate, but they frown, grimace, or turn away when they smell rotten eggs or ammonia. Young babies can also recognize familiar odors. Newborns will look in the direction of a pad that is saturated with their own amniotic fluid. They will also turn toward a pad saturated with the odor of their mother's breast milk or her perfume (Porter & Winburg, 1999; Schaal, Soussignan & Marlier, 2002).

Newborns also have a highly developed sense of taste. They readily differentiate salty, sour, bitter, and sweet tastes (Rostenstein & Oster, 1997). Most infants seem to have a "sweet tooth." They react to sweet substances by smiling, sucking, and licking their lips (e.g., Steiner et al., 2001). In contrast, you can probably guess what the infant in the photo has tasted! This grimace is typical when infants are fed bitter- or sour-tasting substances (Kaijura, Cowart, & Beauchamp, 1992). Infants are also sensitive to changes in the taste of breast milk that reflect a mother's diet. Infants will nurse more after their mother has consumed a sweet-tasting substance such as vanilla (Mennella & Beauchamp, 1996).

Infants and toddlers do *not* like bitter and sour tastes!

Newborns are sensitive to touch. As I described in Module 3.4, many areas of the newborn's body respond reflexively when touched. Touching an infant's cheek, mouth, hand, or foot produces reflexive movements, documenting that infants perceive touch.

If babies react to touch, does this mean they experience pain? This is difficult to answer because pain has such a subjective element to it. The same pain-eliciting stimulus that leads some adults to complain of mild discomfort causes others to report that they are in agony. Because infants cannot express their pain to us directly, we must use indirect evidence.

The infant's nervous system definitely is capable of transmitting pain: Receptors for pain in the skin are just as plentiful in infants as they are in adults (Anand & Hickey, 1987). What's more, babies' behavior in response to apparent pain-provoking stimuli also suggests that they experience pain (Buchholz et al., 1998). Look, for example, at the baby in the photo who is receiving an inoculation. She's opened her mouth to cry and, although we can't hear her, the sound of her cry is probably the unique pattern associated with pain. The pain cry begins suddenly, is high-pitched, and is not easily soothed. This baby is also agitated, her heart rate has jumped, and she's moving her hands, arms, and legs (Craig et al., 1993; Goubet et al., 2001). All together, these signs strongly suggest that babies experience pain.

Perceptual skills are extraordinarily useful to newborns and young babies. Smell and touch help them recognize their mothers and make it much easier for them to learn to eat. Early development of smell, taste, and touch prepares newborns and young babies to learn about the world.

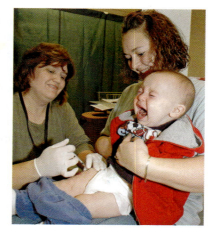

An infant's response to an inoculation—a distinctive facial expression coupled with a distinctive cry—clearly suggests that the baby feels pain.

## Hearing

We know, from Module 3.1, that a fetus can hear at 7 or 8 months. As you would expect from these results, newborns typically respond to sounds in their surroundings. If a parent is quiet but then coughs, an infant may startle, blink his eyes, and move his arms or legs. These responses may seem natural, but they do indeed indicate that infants are sensitive to sound.

Not surprisingly, infants do not hear as well as adults. *Auditory threshold* **refers to the quietest sound that a person can hear.** An adult's auditory threshold is fairly easy to measure: A tone is presented, and the adult simply tells when he or she hears it. To test auditory thresholds in infants, who obviously cannot report what they hear, researchers have devised a number of clever techniques (Aslin, Jusczyk, & Pisoni, 1998). For example, in one simple method, the infant is seated on a parent's lap. Both parent and baby wear headphones, as does an observer seated in another room who watches the baby through an observation window. When the observer believes the baby is attentive, he signals the experimenter, who sometimes presents a tone over the baby's headphones and at other times does nothing. Neither the observer nor the parent knows when tones are going to be presented, and they can't hear the tones through their headphones. On each trial, the observer simply judges if the baby responds in any fashion, such as by turning her head or changing her facial expression or activity level. Afterwards, the experimenter determines how well the observer's judgments match the trials: If a baby can hear the tone, the observer should have noted a response only when a tone was presented.

> Infants can distinguish different sounds and they use sound to judge the distance and location of objects.

This type of testing reveals that, overall, adults can hear better than infants; adults can hear some very quiet sounds that infants can't (Aslin et al., 1998). More importantly, this testing shows that infants hear sounds best that have pitches in the range of human speech—neither very high- nor very low-pitched. Infants can differentiate vowels from consonant sounds, and by $4\frac{1}{2}$ months they can recognize their own names (Jusczyk, 1995; Mandel, Jusczyk, & Pisoni, 1995). In Module 9.1, we'll learn more about infants' remarkable skill at hearing language sounds.

Infants also can distinguish different musical sounds. They can distinguish different melodies and prefer melodies that are pleasant sounding over those that are unpleasant sounding or dissonant (Trainor & Heinmiller, 1998). And infants are sensitive to the rhythmic structure of music. After infants have heard a simple sequence of notes, they can tell the difference between a new sequence that fits the original versus one that doesn't (Hannon & Trehub, 2005). This early sensitivity to music is remarkable but perhaps not so surprising when you consider that music is (and has been) central in all cultures.

Infants also use sound to locate objects, determining whether they are to the left or to the right, and nearby or far away. In one study (Clifton, Perris, & Bullinger, 1991), experimenters showed a rattle to 7-month-old infants. Then the experimenters darkened the room and shook the rattle, either 6 inches away from the infant or about 2 feet away. Infants often reached for the rattle in the dark when it was 6 inches away but seldom did so when it was 2 feet away. These 7-month-olds were quite capable of using sound to estimate distance—in this case, distinguishing a toy they could reach from one they could not.

Thus, by the middle of the 1st year, most infants respond to much of the information provided by sound. However, not all infants are able to do so, which is the topic of the "Improving Children's Lives" feature.

**5.1** Tiffany is worried that her 12-month-old daughter may be hearing impaired. What symptoms would suggest that she has cause for concern? If these symptoms are present, what should she do?

## Improving Children's Lives

### Hearing Impairment in Infancy

Some infants are born with limited hearing. Others are born deaf. (Exact figures are hard to determine, because infants' hearing is rarely tested precisely.) African, Asian, European, and Hispanic American babies are equally susceptible. Heredity is the leading cause of hearing impairment in newborns. After birth, the leading cause is meningitis, an inflammation of the membranes surrounding the brain and spinal cord.

What are signs of hearing impairment that a parent should watch for? Obviously, parents should be concerned if a young baby never responds to sudden, loud sounds. They should also be concerned if their baby has repeated ear infections, if he does not turn his head in the direction of sounds by 4 or 5 months, does not respond to his own name by 8 or 9 months, and does not begin to imitate speech sounds and simple words by 12 months.

If parents see these problems, their baby should be examined by a physician, who will check for ear problems, and an audiologist, who will measure the infant's hearing. Parents should never delay checking for possible hearing impairment. The earlier the problem is detected, the more the baby can be helped (Smith et al., 1998).

If testing reveals that a baby has impaired hearing, several treatments are possible, depending on the degree of hearing loss. Some children with partial hearing benefit from mechanical devices. Hearing aids help some children, but others—like the child in the photo—benefit from a cochlear implant, in which an electronic device placed in the ear converts speech into electric signals that stimulate nerve cells in the inner ear. Training in lipreading helps others. Children with profound hearing loss can learn to communicate with sign language. By mastering language (either oral language or sign language) and communicating effectively, a child's cognitive and social development will be normal. The key is to recognize impairment promptly. ■

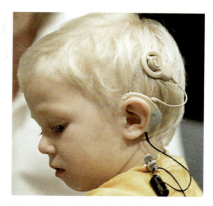

Many children with hearing impairments benefit from a cochlear implant, a device that converts speech signals into electrical impulses that can stimulate nerve cells.

## Seeing

If you've watched infants, you've probably noticed that, while awake, they spend a lot of time looking around. Sometimes they seem to be scanning their environment broadly, and sometimes they seem to be focusing on nearby objects. But what do they actually see? Is their visual world a sea of gray blobs? Or do they see the world essentially as adults do? Actually, neither is the case, but, as you'll see, the second is closer to the truth.

From birth, babies respond to light and can track moving objects with their eyes. But what is the clarity of their vision, and how can we measure it? *Visual acuity* **is defined as the smallest pattern that can be distinguished dependably.** You've undoubtedly had your visual acuity measured by trying to read rows of progressively smaller letters or numbers from a chart. The same basic logic is used in tests of infants' acuity, which are based on two premises. First, most infants will look at patterned stimuli instead of plain, nonpatterned stimuli. For example, if we were to show the two stimuli in the diagram to infants, most would look longer at the striped pattern than at the gray pattern. Second, as we make the lines narrower (along with the spaces between them), there comes a point at which the black and

FIGURE 5-1

FIGURE 5-2

white stripes become so fine that they simply blend together and appear gray, just like the all-gray pattern.

To estimate an infant's acuity, then, we pair the gray square with squares that differ in the width of their stripes, like those in the diagram: When infants look at the two stimuli equally, it indicates that they are no longer able to distinguish the stripes of the patterned stimulus. By measuring the width of the stripes and their distance from an infant's eye, we can estimate acuity (detecting thinner stripes indicates better acuity). Measurements of this sort indicate that newborns and 1-month-olds see at 20 feet what normal adults see at 200 to 400 feet. Infants' acuity improves rapidly and, by the first birthday, is essentially the same as that of a normal adult (Kellman & Banks, 1998).

Infants begin to see the world not only with greater acuity during the 1st year, but also in color! How do we perceive color? The wavelength of light is the source of color perception. The diagram shows that lights we see as red have a relatively long wavelength, whereas violet, at the other end of the color spectrum, has a much short-

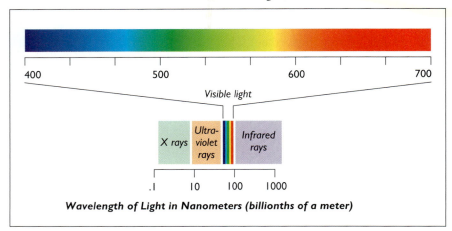

Visible light

Wavelength of Light in Nanometers (billionths of a meter)

FIGURE 5-3

er wavelength. **We detect wavelength— and therefore color—with specialized neurons called *cones* that are in the retina of the eye.** Some cones are particularly sensitive to short-wavelength light (blues and violets), others are sensitive to medium-wavelength light (greens and yellows), and still others are sensitive to long-wavelength light (reds and oranges). These different kinds of cones are linked in complex circuits of neurons in the eye and in the brain, and this neural circuitry allows us to see the world in color.

These circuits gradually begin to function in the first few months after birth. Newborns and young babies can perceive few colors, but by 3 months the three kinds of cones and their associated circuits are working and infants are able to see the full range of colors (Kellman & Banks, 1998). In fact, by 3 to 4 months, infants' color perception seems similar to that of adults (Adams & Courage, 1995; Franklin, Pilling, & Davies, 2005). In particular, infants, like adults, tend to see categories of color. For example, if a yellow light's wavelength is gradually increased, the infant will suddenly perceive it as a shade of red rather than a shade of yellow (Dannemiller, 1998).

The ability to perceive color, along with rapidly improving visual acuity, gives infants great skill in making sense out of their visual experiences. What makes this growing visual skill even more powerful is that, as we'll see in the next section, infants are also starting to connect information obtained from different senses.

## Integrating Sensory Information

So far, we have discussed infants' sensory systems separately. In reality, of course, most infant experiences are better described as "multimedia events." A nursing mother like the one in the photo at the top of page 139 provides visual and taste cues to her baby. A rattle stimulates vision, hearing, and touch. In fact, much stimulation is not specific to one sense but spans multiple senses. Temporal information, such as duration or tempo, can be conveyed by sight or sound. For example, you can detect the rhythm of a person clapping by seeing the hands meet or by hearing the sound of hands striking. Similarly, the texture of a surface—whether it's rough or smooth, for example—can be detected by sight or by feel.

Infants readily perceive many of these relations. For example, infants can recognize visually an object that they have only touched previously. Similarly, they can detect relations between information presented visually and auditorily. They know, for example, that an object moving into the distance looks smaller and is harder to hear (Bahrick & Lickliter, 2002). And they can link the temporal properties of visual and auditory stimulation, such as duration and rhythm (Lewkowicz, 2000). Finally, they even link their own body movement to their perceptions of musical rhythm, giving new meaning to the phrase "feel the beat, baby!" (Phillips-Silver & Trainor, 2005).

Traditionally, coordinating information from different senses (e.g., vision with hearing, vision with touch) was thought to be a demanding task for infants. However, recent thinking challenges this view, as we'll see in the "Spotlight on Theories" feature.

A mother who breast-feeds provides her baby with a multimedia event: The baby sees, smells, hears, feels, and tastes her!

## Spotlight on Theories
### The Theory of Intersensory Redundancy

#### BACKGROUND
Traditionally, coordinating information from different senses (e.g., vision with hearing, vision with touch) has been perceived as a challenging task for infants and, consequently, one that should emerge relatively late. The idea was that infants must first master perceptual processes in each sense separately before coordinating and integrating information across the senses. With this view, a baby might perceive a favorite teddy bear's appearance, feel, and smell but would only gradually integrate these perceptions.

#### THE THEORY
Recently, however, Lorraine Bahrick and Robert Lickliter (2002, 2004) have proposed a different view. **They note that certain information, such as duration, rate, and intensity is *amodal* in that it can be presented in different senses.** For example, when a mother claps her hands in time to music, the sounds of the claps as well as the appearance of the hands coming together and moving apart provide clues to the tempo of the music.

In Bahrick and Lickliter's *intersensory redundancy theory*, **the infant's perceptual system is particularly attuned to amodal information that is presented to multiple sensory modes.** That is, perception is best when information is presented redundantly to multiple senses. When an infant sees and hears the mother clapping (visual, auditory information), he focuses on the information conveyed to both senses and pays less attention to information that's only available in one sense, such as the color of the mother's nail polish or the sounds of her humming along with the tune. Or the infant can learn that the mom's lips are chapped from seeing the flaking skin and by feeling the roughness as the mother kisses him. According to intersensory redundancy theory, it's as if infants follow the rule "Any information that's presented in multiple senses must be important, so pay attention to it!"

Infants readily integrate information that is presented redundantly to different senses.

**HYPOTHESIS:** If infants are particularly attentive to information presented redundantly to multiple senses, then they should notice changes in amodal information *more often* when the information is presented to multiple senses than when it's presented to a single sense. In other words, if the mom claps slowly at first but then quickly, infants should detect this change more readily if they see and hear the clapping than if they only see her or only hear her.

**TEST:** Bahrick and Lickliter (2000) studied 5-month-olds' ability to detect a change in the rhythm with which a hammer struck a wooden surface. Some infants watched a videotape that showed hammering and had an accompanying sound track. Other infants watched a video with the sound turned off. Still other infants heard the sound track of the video while looking at a still photograph of the hammer. After infants were familiar with the initial rhythm, it was changed. Only the infants who had information about hammering presented in both visual and auditory modes detected the change.

**CONCLUSION:** This result supports the hypothesis. Infants detected a change only when it was presented visually and auditorily, as predicted by the theory that infants best perceive amodal information when it is presented in multiple sensory modes.

**APPLICATION:** The theory of intersensory redundancy says that infants learn best when information is simultaneously presented to multiple senses. Parents can use this principle to help babies learn. Language learning is a good example. Of course, talking to babies is beneficial (a topic we explore in depth in Chapter 9). But talking face-to-face with babies is best because then they see the visual cues that distinguish language sounds. When Mom says, "oooh" her lips form a tight circle; when she says, "ahhhh" her mouth is open wide. By talking face-to-face, Mom is presenting information about sounds redundantly—auditorily and visually—making it easier for her infants to distinguish these sounds (Burnham & Dodd, 2004). ■

Integrating information from different senses is yet another variation on the theme that has dominated this module: Infants' sensory and perceptual skills are impressive. Darla's newborn daughter, from the opening vignette, can definitely smell, taste, and feel pain. She can distinguish sounds, and at about 7 months she will use sound to locate objects. Her vision is a little blurry now but will improve rapidly, and in a few months she'll see the full range of colors. Within only a month, she'll be making connections between sights and sounds and between other senses. In short, Darla's daughter, like most infants, is well prepared to make sense out of her environment.

**5.1** By 12 months, Tiffany's daughter should be looking in the direction of sounds (and should have been doing so for several months), should respond to her name, and make some speech-like sounds of her own. If she doesn't do these things, Tiffany should take her daughter to see a pediatrician and to an audiologist, right away!

## CHECK YOUR LEARNING

**RECALL** Summarize what is known about infants' ability to smell, taste, and touch. Describe the important developmental milestones in vision during infancy.

**INTERPRET** Compare the impact of nature and nurture on the development of infants' sensory and perceptual skills.

**APPLY** Perceptual skills are quite refined at birth and become mature very rapidly. What evolutionary purposes are served by this rapid development?

# COMPLEX PERCEPTUAL AND ATTENTIONAL PROCESSES

## 5.2

**LEARNING OBJECTIVES**

- How do infants perceive objects?

- How does attention improve as children grow older?

- What is attention deficit hyperactivity disorder?

Perceiving Objects

Attention

Attention Deficit Hyperactivity Disorder

> *Linda was only 36 hours old when John and Jean brought her home from the hospital. They quickly noticed that loud noises startled Linda, which worried them because their apartment was near a freeway entrance ramp. Trucks accelerating to enter the freeway made an incredible amount of noise that caused Linda to "jump" and sometimes cry. John and Jean wondered if Linda would get enough sleep. However, within days, the trucks no longer disturbed Linda; she slept blissfully. Why was a noise that had been so troubling no longer a problem?*

Where we draw the dividing line between "basic" and "complex" perceptual processes is quite arbitrary. As you'll see, Module 5.2 is a logical extension of the information presented in Module 5.1. We'll begin by looking at how we perceive objects. We'll also look at the processes of attention and some children who have attentional problems. By the end of the module, you'll know why Linda is no longer bothered by noises that once disturbed her.

Perceptual processes allow us to interpret this pattern of lines, textures, and colors as an eyeball.

## Perceiving Objects

When you look at the pattern in the top photo, what do you see? You probably recognize it as part of a human eyeball, even though all that's physically present in the photograph are many different colored dots. In this case, perception actually creates an object from sensory stimulation. That is, our perceptual processes determine that certain features go together to form objects. This is particularly challenging because we often see only parts of objects—nearby objects often obscure parts of more distant objects. Nevertheless, in the bottom photo we recognize that the orange is one object even though it is partially hidden by the apple.

Many cues tell us that these are two objects, not one unusually shaped object: The two objects differ in color, the apple has a slightly different texture than the orange, and the apples in the foreground partially block the oranges in the background.

Perception of objects is limited in newborns but develops rapidly in the first few months after birth (Johnson, 2001). By 4 months, infants use a number of cues to determine which elements go together to form objects. One important cue is motion: Elements that move together are usually part of the same object (Kellman & Banks, 1998). For example, at the left of the diagram at the top of page 142, a pencil appears to be moving back and forth behind a colored square. If the square were removed, you would be surprised to see a pair of pencil stubs, as shown on the right side of the diagram. The common movement of the pencil's eraser and point lead us to believe that they're part of the same pencil.

Young infants, too, are surprised by demonstrations like this. If they see a display like the moving pencils, they will then look very briefly at a whole pencil, apparently because they expected it. In contrast, if after seeing the moving pencil they're shown the two pencil stubs, they look much longer, as if trying to figure out what happened (Eizenman & Bertenthal, 1998; Johnson & Aslin, 1995). Evidently, even very young babies use common motion to create objects from different parts.

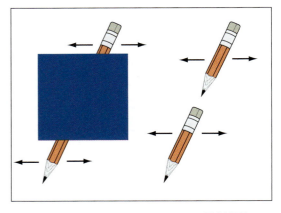

FIGURE 5-4

Motion is one clue to object unity, but infants use others, too, including, color, texture, and aligned edges. As you can see in the bottom diagram, infants more often group features together (i.e., believe they're part of the same object), when they're the same color, have the same texture, and when their edges are aligned (Johnson, 2001).

**PERCEPTUAL CONSTANCIES.** An important part of perceiving objects is that the same object can look very different. For example, when a mother moves away from her baby, the image that she casts on the retinas of her baby's eyes gets smaller. Do babies have a nightmare that their mother's head is shrinking as she moves away? No. **Early on, infants master *size constancy*, the realization that an object's actual size remains the same despite changes in the size of its retinal image.**

How do we know that infants have a rudimentary sense of size constancy? Suppose we let an infant look at an unfamiliar teddy bear. Then we show the infant the same bear, at a different distance, paired with a larger replica of the bear. If infants lack size constancy, the two bears will be equally novel and babies should respond to each similarly. If, instead, babies have size constancy, they will recognize the first bear as familiar, the larger bear as novel, and be more likely to respond to the novel bear. In fact, by 4 or 5 months, babies treat the bear that they've seen twice at different distances—and, therefore, with different retinal images—as familiar (Granrud, 1986). This outcome is possible only if infants have size constancy. Thus, infants do not believe that mothers (and other people or objects) constantly change size as they move closer or farther away.

Size is just one of several perceptual constancies. Others are brightness and color constancy as well as shape constancy, shown in the diagram on page 143. All these constancies are achieved, at least in rudimentary form, by 4 months (Aslin, 1987; Dannemiller, 1998). Consequently, even young infants are not confused, thinking that the world is filled with many very similar-looking but different objects. Instead, they can tell that an object is the same, even though it may look different. Mom is still Mom, whether she's nearby or far away and whether she's clearly visible outdoors or barely visible in a dimly lit room.

**5.2** When 6-month-old Sebastian watches his mother type on a keyboard, how does he know that her fingers and the keyboard are not simply one big unusual object?

FIGURE 5-5

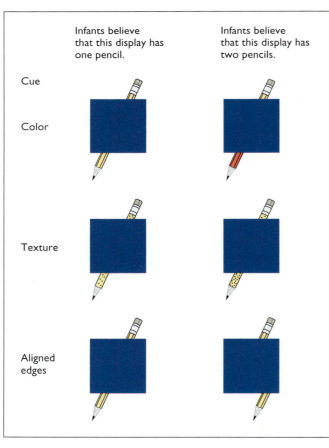

| Cue | Infants believe that this display has one pencil. | Infants believe that this display has two pencils. |
| --- | --- | --- |
| Color | | |
| Texture | | |
| Aligned edges | | |

**DEPTH.** In addition to knowing *what* an object is, babies need to know *where* it is. Knowing that a rattle resting on a book are two separate objects, it's also useful for infants to know the location of the rattle and toy. Determining left and right as well as up and down is relatively easy because these dimensions (horizontal, vertical) can be represented directly on the retina's flat surface. Distance or depth is more complicated because this dimension is not represented directly on the retina. Instead, many different cues are used to estimate distance or depth.

At what age can infants perceive depth? Eleanor Gibson and Richard Walk (1960) addressed this question in a classic experiment that used a specially designed apparatus. **The *visual cliff* is a glass-covered platform; on one side a pattern appears directly under the glass, but on the other it appears several feet below the glass.** Consequently, one side looks shallow but the other appears to have a steep drop-off, like a cliff. As you can see in the photo, in the experiment the baby is placed on the platform and the mother coaxes her infant to come to her. Most babies willingly crawl to their mothers when she stands on the shallow side. But virtually all babies refuse to cross the deep side, even when the mother calls the infant by name and tries to lure him or her with an attractive toy. Clearly, infants can perceive depth by the time they are old enough to crawl.

What about babies who cannot yet crawl? When babies as young as $1\frac{1}{2}$ months are simply placed on the deep side of the platform, their heartbeat slows down. Heart rate often decelerates when people notice something interesting, so this would suggest that $1\frac{1}{2}$-month-olds notice that the deep side is different. At 7 months, infants' heart rate accelerates, a sign of fear. Thus, although young babies can detect a difference between the shallow and deep sides of the visual cliff, only older, crawling babies are actually afraid of the deep side (Campos et al., 1978).

How do infants infer depth, on the visual cliff or anywhere? They use several kinds of cues. **Among the first are *kinetic cues*, in which motion is used to estimate depth. *Visual expansion* refers to the fact that as an object moves closer, it fills an ever-greater proportion of the retina.** Visual expansion is why we flinch when someone unexpectedly tosses a soda can toward us and it's what allows a batter to estimate when a baseball will arrive over the plate. **Another cue, *motion parallax*, refers to the fact that nearby moving objects move across our visual field faster than those at a distance.** Motion parallax is in action when you look out the side window in a moving car: Trees next to the road move rapidly across the visual field but mountains in the distance move much more slowly. Babies use these cues in the first weeks after birth; for example, 1-month-olds blink if a moving object looks as if it's going to hit them in the face (Nánez & Yonas, 1994).

Another cue becomes important at about 4 months. *Retinal disparity* **is based on the fact that the left and right eyes often see slightly different versions of the same scene.** When objects are distant, the images appear in very similar positions on the

*Shape Constancy: Even though the door appears to change shape as it opens, we know that it really remains a rectangle.*

**FIGURE 5-6**

Infants avoid the "deep side" of the visual cliff, indicating that they perceive depth.

Infants use multiple cues to perceive depth.

retina; when objects are near, the images appear in much different positions. Thus, greater disparity in positions of the image on the retina signals that an object is close. At about 4 months, infants use retinal disparity as a depth cue, correctly inferring that objects are nearby when disparity is great (Kellman & Banks, 1998; Yonas & Owsley, 1987).

By 7 months, infants use several cues for depth that depend on the arrangement of objects in the environment. **These are sometimes called *pictorial cues* because they're the same cues that artists use to convey depth in drawings and paintings.** They are illustrated below.

*Texture gradient*: **The texture of objects changes from coarse but distinct for nearby objects to finer and less distinct for distant objects.** In the photo, we judge the distinct flowers to be close and the blurred ones, distant.

*Linear perspective*: **Parallel lines come together at a single point in the distance.** Thus, we use the space between the lines as a cue to distance and, consequently, decide the train in the photo is far away because the parallel tracks grow close together.

*Interposition*: **Nearby objects partially obscure more distant objects.** The glasses obscure the bottle, so we decide the glasses are closer (and use this same cue to decide the grapes are closer than the left glass).

*Relative size*: **Nearby objects look substantially larger than objects in the distance.** Knowing that the runners are really about the same size, we judge the ones that look smaller to be farther away.

So far in this module, we've seen that young babies use simple relations between stimuli to infer an object, recognize that objects are the same despite changes in appearance, and use many cues to infer depth. We can understand infants' perceptual skills from a different perspective by looking at their perception of faces.

**PERCEIVING FACES.**     The human face is a particularly important object to infants. Young babies readily look at faces. From the diagram, which shows a pattern of eye fixations, you can see that 1-month-olds look mostly at the outer edges of the face. Three-month-olds, however, focus almost entirely on the interior of the face, particularly the eyes and lips.

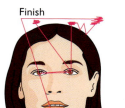
1-Month-Olds

3-Month-Olds

FIGURE 5-7

Some theorists argue that babies are innately attracted to stimuli that are face-like. The claim here is that some aspect of the face—perhaps two eyes and a mouth in the correct arrangement—constitutes a distinctive stimulus that is readily recognized, even by newborns. For example, newborns turn their eyes to follow a moving face more than they turn their eyes for nonface stimuli (Mondloch et al., 1999; Morton & Johnson, 1991). This preference for faces over face-like stimuli supports the view that infants are innately attracted to faces. However, preference for tracking a moving face changes abruptly at about 4 weeks of age—infants now track all moving stimuli. One idea is that newborns' face-tracking is a reflex, based on primitive circuits in the brain, that is designed to enhance attention to face-like stimuli. Starting at about 4 weeks, circuits in the brain's cortex begin to control infants' looking at faces and other stimuli (Morton & Johnson, 1991).

A built-in face processing mechanism could explain another amazing fact: Infants prefer to look at attractive faces rather than unattractive faces. This is true even when children have had little experiences with the faces! Newborns look longer at a face that adults find attractive than at a face that adults find unattractive (Slater et al., 2000). What's more, older infants look longer at faces of attractive people from other races, even when they've had little or no exposure to individuals from those races (Langlois et al., 1991). It's as if infants not only have a built-in sense of faces in general, but they appreciate a pretty face, too!

Other scientists, however, are skeptical. They believe that general principles of perception explain how infants perceive faces (Turati, 2004). They argue that infants are attracted to faces because faces have stimuli that move (the eyes and mouth) and stimuli with dark and light contrast (the eyes, lips, and teeth). Research by Easterbrooks and her colleagues (1999) supports this view. They found that when face and nonface stimuli are matched for a number of important variables, newborns turn their head and eyes equally for face and nonface stimuli. These results go along with the idea that infants look at faces because of general perceptual principles (for example, babies prefer contrasting stimuli), not because faces are intrinsically attractive to infants. In much the same vein, infants may look at attractive faces simply because those faces contain features that draw attention to any stimulus (not just faces) such as symmetry (Gangestad & Thornhill, 1997).

More research is needed to decide whether face perception follows general perceptual principles or represents a special case. What is clear, though, is that by 3 or 4 months babies have the perceptual skills that allow them to begin to distinguish individual faces (Carey, 1992). And, they gradually use more information to recognize faces: Three-month-olds rely mostly on the overall configuration of a face but 5- and 6-month-olds also rely on more fine-grained spatial relations, such as the distances between the eyes and between the nose and lips (Bhatt et al., 2005). And, as we'll see in the "Focus on Research" feature, by 9 months, these skills have become specific to human faces.

> Infants readily look at faces, a preference that may reflect innate attraction to faces or the fact that faces have many properties that attract infants' attention.

## *Focus On Research*

### Specialized Face Processing During Infancy

*Who were the investigators, and what was the aim of the study?* Over the 1st year, infants rapidly become more skilled at recognizing faces, presumably as they are exposed to an ever-larger number of faces and are able to fine tune their face-recognition processes. If this argument is correct, infants might also *lose* the ability to recognize some face-like stimuli. For example, a monkey's face has many of the same basic features of a human face—eyes, nose, and mouth in the familiar configuration. A young infant's broadly tuned face-recognition processes might work well for monkey faces but an older infant's more finely tuned processes might not. Testing this hypothesis was the aim of a study by Olivier Pascalis, Michelle de Haan, and Charles A. Nelson (2002).

*How did the investigators measure the topic of interest?* Pascalis and colleagues wanted to determine whether 6-month-olds, 9-month-olds, and adults could recognize human faces and monkey faces. Consequently, they had infants and adults view a photo of a monkey face or a human face. Then that face was paired with a novel face of the same species, as shown in the photo. Experimenters recorded participants' looking at the two faces—the expectation was that, if the participants recognized the familiar stimulus, they would look longer at the novel stimulus.

*Who were the participants in the study?* The study included thirty 6-month-olds, thirty 9-month-olds, and 11 adults. Half the infants at each age saw human faces; the others saw monkey faces. Adults saw both human and monkey faces.

Pascalis and colleagues had participants in their study view one of the human faces or one of the monkey faces. Then that face was shown with the other face of the same type (e.g., both human faces if the participant had seen the human face first). If participants remember the first face, they should look longer at the novel face.

**FIGURE** 5-8

*What was the design of the study?* This study was experimental. The independent variables included the type of face (human, monkey) and the familiarity of the face on the test trial (novel, familiar). The dependent variable was the participants' looking at the two faces on the test trials. The study was cross-sectional because it included 6-month-olds, 9-month-olds, and adults, each tested once.

*Were there ethical concerns with the study?* No. There was no obvious harm associated with looking at pictures of faces.

*What were the results?* If participants recognized the familiar face, they should look more at the novel face; if they did not recognize the familiar face, they should look equally at the novel and familiar faces. The graphs show the percentage of time that participants looked at the novel face. When human faces were shown, all three age groups looked longer at the novel face (more than 50% preference for the novel face). In contrast, when monkey faces were shown, 6-month-olds looked longer at the novel face, but 9-month-olds and adults looked at novel and familiar faces equally. Remarkably, 6-month-olds showed greater skill than older infants and adults.

*What did the investigators conclude?* Pascalis and colleagues (2002) concluded that their findings ". . . support the hypothesis that the perceptual window narrows with

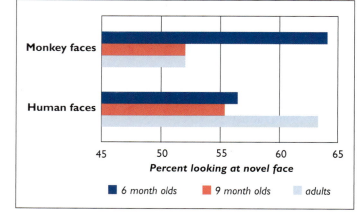

age and that during the first year of life the face processing system is tuned to a human template" (p. 1322). That is, from experience infants finely tune their face-processing systems to include only human faces.

*What converging evidence would strengthen these conclusions?* These findings show that 6-month-olds' face processing systems work equally well on human and monkey faces. The investigators could determine how broadly the system is tuned by studying young infants' recognition of other species that have faces in a human-like configuration. In addition, it would be beneficial to use brain mapping methods (described on page 126) to determine if the brain regions associated with face recognition change as face-processing systems become more finely tuned between 6 and 9 months. ■

These rapid changes in face-recognition skill are adaptive, for they provide the basis for social relationships that infants form during the rest of the 1st year, which we'll examine in Module 10.3. And there's a practical benefit as well: If you see a giant ape in New York City and wonder whether it's really King Kong or an imposter, ask a 6-month-old.

## Attention

Have you ever been in a class where you knew you should be listening and taking notes, but the lecture was just so boring that you started noticing other things—the construction going on outside or an attractive person seated nearby? After a while, maybe you reminded yourself to "pay attention!" We get distracted because our perceptual systems are marvelously powerful. They provide us with far more information at any time than we could possible interpret. **Attention is the process by which we select information that will be processed further.** In a class, for example, where the task is to direct your attention to the lecture, it is easy to ignore other stimuli if the lecture is interesting. But if the lecture is not interesting, other stimuli intrude and capture your attention.

The roots of attention can be seen in infancy. Remember Linda, the newborn in the vignette who jumped when trucks accelerated past her home? Her response was normal not only for infants but also for children and adults. **When presented with a strong or unfamiliar stimulus, an *orienting response* usually occurs: A person startles, fixes the eyes on the stimulus, and shows changes in heart rate and brain-wave patterns.** Collectively, these responses indicate that the infant is attending to this stimulus. Remember, too, that Linda soon began to ignore the sounds of trucks. After repeated presentations of a stimulus, people become accustomed to it, so their orienting response diminishes and eventually disappears, signs of habituation, which we discussed on page 134. Habituation indicates that attention is selective: A stimulus that once garnered attention no longer does.

> Infants typically respond to an unfamiliar stimulus but pay less attention as it becomes more familiar.

The orienting response and habituation can both be demonstrated easily in the laboratory. For example, in one study (Zelazo et al., 1989) speech was played through one of two loudspeakers placed on either side of an infant. At first, most newborns turned their heads toward the source of the speech, but after several trials they no longer responded. Thus, newborns oriented to the novel sound but then gradually habituated to the sound as it became more familiar.

The orienting response and habituation are both useful to infants. On the one hand, orienting makes the infant aware of potentially important or dangerous events in the environment. On the other hand, constantly responding to insignificant stimuli is wasteful, so habituation keeps infants like the one in the photo from

Attentional processes allow infants (and older children) to ignore stimuli that aren't important.

wasting too much energy on biologically nonsignificant stimuli (Rovee-Collier, 1987). Given the biological significance of being able to habituate, it's not too surprising that infants who habituate more rapidly tend to grow up to be more intelligent children (Rose et al., 1997).

During the preschool years, children gradually become better able to regulate their attention. You can see these changes in the way that youngsters play with novel toys. When $3\frac{1}{2}$-year-old Michael got a new truck, he looked at it carefully, bringing it close to his face for careful inspection. Then he spent minutes rolling it back and forth on the floor, making "Rrr-rrr" sounds. When Michael plays like this, he often ignores nearby distractions such as the start of a TV show. In contrast, when 1-year-old Michele got a new "busy box" she looked at it and played, but without the intensity and focus that marked Michael's play with the truck. And she was easily distracted, readily turning her head when her sister entered the room (Ruff & Capozzoli, 2003). Similar age differences are evident when children watch TV: Older children stay engaged longer and are less easily distracted (Richards & Anderson, 2004). Maintaining focused attention is a demanding skill, one that emerges gradually during the preschool years and beyond (Enns, 1990).

In the meantime, we can help young children pay attention better. One approach is to make relevant information more salient than irrelevant information. For example, closing a classroom door may not eliminate competing sounds and smells entirely, but it will make them less salient. Or, when preschoolers are working at a table or desk, we can remove all objects that are not necessary for the task. And periodically reminding children to pay attention helps them to stay focused.

Techniques like these improve some but not all children's attention, as we'll see in the next section.

### Attention Deficit Hyperactivity Disorder

Children with attention deficit hyperactivity disorder—ADHD for short—have special problems when it comes to paying attention. Roughly 3 to 5% of all school-age children are diagnosed with ADHD; boys outnumber girls by a 3:1 ratio (Wicks-Nelson & Israel, 2006). Stephen, a fourth grader, is typical. Soon after Stephen entered kindergarten, his teacher remarked that he sometimes seemed out of control. He was easily distracted, often moving aimlessly from one activity to another. He also seemed to be impulsive, and compared to other youngsters his age, he had much more difficulty waiting his turn. At first, Stephen's parents just attributed his behavior to boyish energy. But when Stephen progressed to first and second grade, his pattern of behavior continued. He began to fall behind in reading and arithmetic. His classmates were annoyed by his behavior and began to avoid him. This just made Stephen mad, so he often got into fights with his classmates. Finally, Stephen's parents took him to a psychologist, who determined that Stephen had attention deficit hyperactivity disorder.

> Children with ADHD are overactive, inattentive, and impulsive; they often do poorly in school and are disliked by peers.

Stephen exhibits three symptoms at the heart of ADHD (American Psychiatric Association, 1994):

- *Inattention:* Youngsters with ADHD skip from one task to another. They do not pay attention in class and seem unable to concentrate on schoolwork.

- *Hyperactivity:* Children with ADHD are unusually energetic, fidgety, and unable to keep still, especially in situations like school classrooms where they need to limit their activity.

- *Impulsivity:* Children with ADHD often act before thinking; they may run into a street before looking for traffic or interrupt others who are speaking.

Hyperactivity is one of three main symptoms of ADHD; the others are inattention and impulsivity.

Not all children with ADHD show all these symptoms to the same degree. Some, like the boy in the photograph, may be primarily hyperactive and impulsive. Others may be primarily inattentive and show fewer signs of hyperactivity and impulsivity; their disorder is often described simply as attention-deficit disorder (Barkley, 1990). Children with ADHD often have problems with conduct and academic performance. Like Stephen, many hyperactive children are aggressive and therefore are not liked by their peers (Barkley, 1990; McGee, Williams, & Feehan, 1992). Although youngsters with ADHD usually have normal intelligence, their scores on reading, spelling, and arithmetic achievement tests are often below average (Pennington, Groisser, & Welsh, 1993).

Many myths surround ADHD. Some concern causes. At one time or another, TV, food allergies, sugar, and poor home life have all been proposed as causes of ADHD, but research does not consistently support any of these (e.g., Wolraich et al., 1994). Instead, heredity is an important factor. Twin studies show that identical twins are often both diagnosed with ADHD but this is uncommon for fraternal twins (Pennington, Willcutt, & Rhee, 2005). Similarly, adoption studies show that children are more prone to ADHD when a biological parent has been diagnosed with ADHD than when an adoptive parent has (Sherman, Iacono, & McGue, 1997). In addition, prenatal exposure to alcohol and other drugs can place children at risk for ADHD (Milberger et al., 1997).

Another myth is that most children "grow out of" ADHD in adolescence or young adulthood. More than half the children who are diagnosed with ADHD will have problems related to overactivity, inattention, and impulsivity as adolescents and young adults. Few of these young adults complete college, and some will have work- and family-related problems (Fischer et al., 1993; Rapport, 1995). One final myth is that many healthy children are wrongly diagnosed with ADHD. The number of children diagnosed with ADHD *has* increased substantially over the past 10 to 15 years but not because children are being routinely misdiagnosed; the increased numbers reflect growing awareness of ADHD and more frequent diagnoses of ADHD in girls and adolescents (Goldman et al., 1998).

Because ADHD affects academic and social success throughout childhood and adolescence, researchers have worked hard to find effective treatments. The "Child Development and Family Policy" feature describes these efforts.

## *Child Development and Family Policy*
### What's the Best Treatment for ADHD?

By the mid-1980s, it was clear that ADHD could be treated. For example, children with ADHD often respond well to stimulant drugs such as Ritalin. It may seem odd that stimulants are given to children who are already overactive, but these drugs stimulate the parts of the brain that normally inhibit hyperactive and impulsive behavior. Thus, stimulants actually have a calming influence for many youngsters with ADHD, allowing them to focus their attention (Aman, Roberts, & Pennington, 1998).

Drug therapy was not the only approach: Psychosocial treatments also worked and were designed to improve children's cognitive and social skills and often included home-based intervention and intensive summer programs (Richters et al., 1995). For example, children can be taught to remind themselves to read instructions before starting assignments. And they can be reinforced by others for inhibiting impulsive and hyperactive behavior (Barkley, 1994).

These treatments were well known by the late 1980s, yet many researchers were troubled by large gaps in our understanding. One gap concerned the long-term success of treatment. Most studies had measured the impact of weeks or months of treatment; virtually nothing was known about the effectiveness of treatment over longer periods. Another gap concerned the most effective combination of treatments and whether this was the same for all children. That is, is medication plus psychosocial treatment the best for all children and for all facets of children's development (i.e., academic and social)?

Prompted by these concerns, scientific advisory groups met in the late 1980s and early 1990s to identify the gaps in understanding and the research needed to fill the gaps. In 1992, the National Institute of Mental Health used reports of these groups to request proposals for research. After intensive review, the top six applications were selected and synthesized to create the Multimodal Treatment Study of Children with ADHD—the MTA for short (Richters et al., 1995). The MTA involves 18 scientists who are experts on ADHD and nearly 600 elementary-school children with ADHD. The children were assigned to different treatment modes and the impact of treatment is measured in several different domains of children's development.

The MTA is ongoing but initial results show that medical treatment alone is the best way to treat hyperactivity per se. However, for a variety of other measures, including academic and social skills as well as parent–child relations, medication plus psychosocial treatment is somewhat more effective than medication alone. The MTA also makes it clear that medication treatment is effective only when dosage is monitored carefully with regular follow-up visits to a health-care professional, and there is regular communication with schools regarding children's functioning (Arnold et al., 2004; Jensen et al., 2001).

Thus, the MTA demonstrates one way in which research can influence practices for children, in this case, the treatment of children with ADHD. Scientists identify gaps in understanding of an important childhood disorder, research is proposed and conducted to eliminate the gaps, and evidence indicates the best practices for children, their parents, teachers, and health-care professionals. ■

---

**5.2** Her hands and fingers move together, independently of the keyboard, and her hands and fingers have a common color and texture that differs from the keyboard's.

## CHECK YOUR LEARNING

**RECALL** Describe the cues that babies use to infer depth.
What are the main symptoms of ADHD?

**INTERPRET** Compare the view that face perception is based on a built-in mechanism that's designed just to perceive faces with the view that face perception is based solely on general perceptual processes.

**APPLY** What happens to children with ADHD when they become adolescents and young adults? How does this address the issue of continuity of development?

# MOTOR DEVELOPMENT                5.3

## LEARNING OBJECTIVES

Locomotion

Fine-Motor Skills

Physical Fitness

- What are the component skills involved in learning to walk, and at what age do infants typically master them?

- How do infants learn to coordinate the use of their hands? When and why do most children begin to prefer to use one hand?

- Are children physically fit? Do they benefit from participating in sports?

*Nancy is 14 months old and a world-class crawler. Using hands and knees, she gets nearly anywhere she wants to go. Nancy does not walk and seems to have no interest in learning how. Her dad wonders whether he should be doing something to help Nancy progress beyond crawling. And down deep, he worries that perhaps he should have provided more exercise or training for Nancy when she was younger.*

The photos on this page have a common theme. Each depicts an activity involving motor skills—coordinated movements of the muscles and limbs. In each activity, success demands that each movement be done in a precise way and in a specific sequence. For example, to use a stick shift properly, you need to move the clutch pedal, gas pedal, and the stick shift in specific ways and in exactly the right sequence. If you don't give the car enough gas as you let out the clutch, you'll kill the engine. If you give it too much gas, the engine races and the car lurches forward.

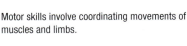
Motor skills involve coordinating movements of muscles and limbs.

If new activities are demanding for adults, think about the challenges infants face. **Infants must learn** *locomotion*, **that is, to move about in the world.** Newborns are relatively immobile, but infants soon learn to crawl, stand, and walk. Learning to move through the environment upright leaves the arms and hands free. Taking full advantage of this arrangement, the human hand has fully independent fingers (instead of a paw), with the thumb opposing the remaining four fingers. An opposable thumb makes it possible for humans to grasp and manipulate objects. **Infants must learn the** *fine-motor skills* **associated with grasping, holding, and manipulating objects.** In the case of feeding, for example, infants progress from being fed by others to holding a bottle, to feeding themselves with their fingers, to eating with a spoon. Each new skill requires incredibly complex physical movements.

Although demanding, locomotion and fine-motor skills are well worth mastering because of their benefits. Being able to locomote and to grasp gives children access to an enormous amount of information about their environment. They can explore objects that look interesting, and they can keep themselves close to parents. Improved motor skills promote children's cognitive and social development, not to mention make a child's life more interesting!

In this module, we'll see how children acquire locomotor and fine-motor skills. As we do, we'll find out if Nancy's dad should be worrying about her lack of interest in walking.

## Locomotion

In little more than a year, advances in posture and locomotion change the newborn from an almost motionless being into an upright, standing individual who walks through the environment. The chart shows some of the important milestones in

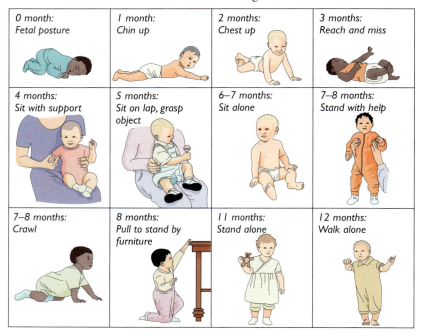

| 0 month: Fetal posture | 1 month: Chin up | 2 months: Chest up | 3 months: Reach and miss |
| 4 months: Sit with support | 5 months: Sit on lap, grasp object | 6–7 months: Sit alone | 7–8 months: Stand with help |
| 7–8 months: Crawl | 8 months: Pull to stand by furniture | 11 months: Stand alone | 12 months: Walk alone |

FIGURE 5-9

motor development and the age by which most infants achieve them. By about 4 months, most babies can sit upright with support. By 6 or 7 months, they can sit without support, and by 7 or 8 months, can stand if they hold on to an object for support. A typical 11-month-old can stand alone briefly and walk with assistance. **Youngsters at this age are called** *toddlers*, **after the toddling manner of early walking.** Of course, not all children walk at exactly the same age. Some walk before their first birthday; others, like Nancy, the world-class crawler in the module-opening vignette, take their first steps as late as 17 or 18 months of age. By 24 months, most children can climb steps, walk backwards, and kick a ball.

Researchers once thought these developmental milestones reflected maturation (e.g., McGraw, 1935). Walking, for example, was thought to emerge naturally when the necessary muscles and neural circuits matured. Today, however, locomotion—and, in fact, all motor development—is viewed from a new perspective. **According to** *dynamic systems theory*, **motor development involves many distinct skills that are organized and reorganized over time to meet the demands of specific tasks.** For example, walking includes maintaining balance, moving limbs, perceiving the environment, and having a reason to move. Only by understanding each of these skills and how they are combined to allow movement in a specific situation can we understand walking (Thelen & Smith, 1998).

In the remainder of this section, we'll see how learning to walk reflects the maturity and coalescence of many component skills.

**POSTURE AND BALANCE.** The ability to maintain an upright posture is fundamental to walking. But upright posture is virtually impossible for young infants because the shape of their body makes them top-heavy. Consequently, as soon as a young infant starts to lose her balance, she tumbles over. Only with growth of the legs and muscles can infants maintain an upright posture (Thelen, Ulrich, & Jensen, 1989).

Once infants can stand upright, they must continuously adjust their posture to avoid falling down. By a few months after birth, infants begin to use visual cues and an inner-ear mechanism to adjust their posture. To show the use of visual cues for balance, researchers had babies sit in a room with striped walls that moved. When adults sit in such a room, they perceive themselves as moving (not the walls) and adjust their posture accordingly; so do infants, which shows that they use vision to maintain upright posture (Bertenthal & Clifton, 1998). In addition, when 4-month-olds who are propped in a sitting position lose their balance, they try to keep their head upright. They do this even when blindfolded, which means they are using cues from their inner ear to maintain balance (Woollacott, Shumway-Cook, & Williams, 1989).

Balance is not, however, something that infants master just once. Instead, infants must relearn balancing for sitting, crawling, walking, and other postures. Why? The body rotates around different points in each posture (e.g., the wrists for crawling versus the ankles for walking) and different muscle groups are used to generate compensating motions when infants begin to lose their balance. Consequently, it's hardly surprising that infants who easily maintain their balance while sitting topple over time after time when crawling. Infants must recalibrate the balance system as they take on each new posture, just as basketball players recalibrate their muscle movements when they move from dunking to shooting a three pointer (Adolph, 2000, 2002).

> To walk, infants must learn to stand upright, to maintain their balance, to step alternately, and to use perceptual information to evaluate surfaces.

**STEPPING.**   Another essential element of walking is moving the legs alternately, repeatedly transferring the weight of the body from one foot to the other. Children don't step spontaneously until approximately 10 months because they must be able to stand upright to step.

Can younger children step if they are held upright? Thelen and Ulrich (1991) devised a clever procedure to answer this question. Infants were placed on a treadmill and held upright by an adult. When the belt on the treadmill started to move, infants could respond in one of several ways. They might simply let both legs be dragged rearward by the belt. Or they might let their legs be dragged briefly, then move them forward together in a hopping motion. Many 6- and 7-month-olds demonstrated the mature pattern of alternating steps on each leg that is shown in the photo. Even more amazing is that when the treadmill was equipped with separate belts for each leg that moved at different speeds, babies adjusted, stepping more rapidly on the faster belt. Apparently, the alternate stepping motion that is essential for walking is evident long before infants walk independently. Walking unassisted is not possible, though, until other component skills are mastered.

**PERCEPTUAL FACTORS.**   Many infants learn to walk in the relative security of flat, uncluttered floors at home. But they soon discover that the environment offers a variety of surfaces, some more conducive to walking than others. Infants use perceptual information to judge whether a surface is suitable for walking. When placed on a surface that gives way underfoot (e.g., a waterbed), they quickly judge it unsuitable for walking and resort to crawling (Gibson et al., 1987). And when toddlers encounter a surface that slopes down steeply, few try to walk down (which would result in a fall). Instead, they slide or scoot backwards (Adolph, Eppler, & Gibson, 1993; Adolph, 1997). Results like these show that infants use perceptual cues to decide whether a surface is safe for walking.

**COORDINATING SKILLS.**   Dynamic systems theory emphasizes that learning to walk demands orchestration of many individual skills. Each component skill must first be mastered alone and then integrated with the other skills (Werner, 1948). **That is, mastery of intricate motions requires both *differentiation*—mastery of component skills—and their *integration*—combining them in proper sequence into a coherent, working whole.** In the case of walking, not until 9 to 15 months of age has the child mastered the component skills so that they can be coordinated to allow independent, unsupported walking.

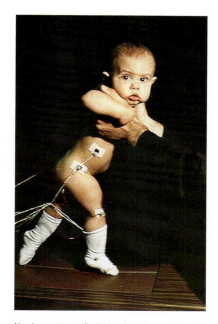

Newborns step reflexively when they are held upright and moved forward.

Mastering individual skills and coordinating them well does not happen overnight. Instead, each takes time and repeated practice. For example, when parents give their infants daily practice in sitting, their infants master sitting at a younger age. However, such practice has no effect on stepping, because different muscles and movements are involved (Zelazo et al., 1993). Similarly, when infants practice crawling on their bellies, this helps them crawl on hands and feet because many of the motions are the same (Adolph, Vereijken, & Denny, 1998). But when infants practice crawling on steep slopes, there is no transfer to walking on steep slopes, because the motions differ (Adolph, 1997). Thus, experience can improve the rate of motor development, but the improvement is limited to the movements that were trained. In other words, just as daily practice kicking a soccer ball won't improve your golf game, infants who receive much practice in one motor skill don't usually improve in others.

These findings from laboratory research are not the only evidence that practice promotes motor development. As you'll see in the "Cultural Influences" feature, cross-cultural research points to the same conclusion.

## Cultural Influences
### Cultural Practices That Promote Motor Development

Compared to infants growing up in Europe and North America, many infants from traditional African cultures reach the motor milestones shown on page 152 at an early age. For example, traditional African infants sit and walk at younger ages. Careful observations of these infants reveal two factors responsible for this early advantage in motor development. First, many common child-care practices in traditional African societies have the unanticipated benefit of improving motor skill. For example, infants are commonly carried by their parents in the "piggyback" style shown in the photo, which helps develop muscles in the infants' trunk and legs. Second, mothers in traditional African cultures believe that practice is essential for motor skills to develop normally and so they (or siblings) provide daily training sessions. For example, they may help children to learn to sit by having them sit while propped up (Super, 1981). The combined effect of this unintentional and deliberate training is to provide additional opportunities for children to learn the elements of different motor skills. Not surprisingly, African infants with these opportunities learn to sit and walk earlier. ■

In many African cultures, infants are routinely carried piggyback style, which strengthens the infant's legs, allowing them to walk at a younger age.

**BEYOND WALKING.**    If you can recall the feeling of freedom that accompanied your first driver's license, you can imagine how the world expands for infants and toddlers as they learn to move independently. The first tentative steps soon are followed by others that are more skilled. With more experience, infants take longer, straighter steps. And, like adults, they begin to swing their arms, rotating the left arm forward as the right leg moves, then repeating with the right arm and left leg (Ledebt, 2000; Ledebt, van Wieringen, & Savelsbergh, 2004). Children's growing skill is evident in their running and hopping. Most 2-year-olds have a hurried walk instead of a true run; they move their legs stiffly (rather than bending them at the knees) and are not airborne as is the case when running. By 5 or 6 years, children run easily, quickly changing directions or speed. Similarly, an average 2- or 3-year-old will hop a few times on one foot, typically keeping the upper body very stiff; by age 5 or 6, children can hop long distances on one foot or alternate hopping first on one foot a few times, then on the other.

## Fine-Motor Skills

A major accomplishment in infancy is skilled use of the hands (Bertenthal & Clifton, 1998). Newborns have little apparent control of their hands, but 1-year-olds are extraordinarily talented.

**REACHING AND GRASPING.**    At about 4 months, infants can successfully reach for objects (Bertenthal & Clifton, 1998). These early reaches often look clumsy, and for a good reason. When infants reach, their arms and hands don't move directly and smoothly to the desired object (as is true for older children and adults). Instead, the infant's hand moves like a ship under the direction of an unskilled navigator. It moves a short distance, slows, then moves again in a slightly different direction, a process that's repeated until the hand finally contacts the object (McCarty & Ashmead, 1999). As infants grow, their reaches have fewer movements, though they are still not as continuous and smooth as older children's and adults' reaches (Berthier, 1996).

A typical 4-month-old grasps an object with fingers alone.

Reaching requires that an infant move the hand to the location of a desired object. Grasping poses a different challenge: Now the infant must coordinate movements of individual fingers in order to grab an object. Grasping, too, becomes more efficient during infancy. Most 4-month-olds just use their fingers to hold objects. Like the baby in the photo, they wrap an object tightly with their fingers alone. Not until 7 or 8 months do most infants use their thumbs to hold objects (Siddiqui, 1995). At about this age, infants begin to position their hands to make it easier to grasp an object. In trying to grasp a long, thin rod, for example, infants place their fingers perpendicular to the rod, which is the best position for grasping (Wentworth et al., 2000). Infants need not see their hand to position it correctly: They position the hand just as accurately in reaching for a lighted object in a darkened room as when reaching in a lighted room (McCarty et al., 2000).

Infants' growing control of each hand is accompanied by greater coordination of the two hands. Although 4-month-olds use both hands, their motions are not coordinated; rather, each hand seems to have a mind of its own. Infants may hold a toy motionless in one hand while shaking a rattle in the other. At roughly 5 to 6 months of age, infants can coordinate the motions of their hands so that each hand performs different actions that serve a common goal. So a child might, for example, hold a toy animal in one hand and pet it with the other (Karniol, 1989). These skills continue to improve after children's first birthday: 1-year-olds reach for most objects with one hand; by 2 years, they reach with one or two hands, as appropriate, depending on the size of the object (van Hof, van der Kamp, & Savelsbergh, 2002).

> Infants gradually gain control over each hand, then learn to coordinate the actions of both hands.

These many changes in reaching and grasping are well illustrated as infants learn to feed themselves. At about 6 months, they are often given "finger foods" such as sliced bananas and green beans. Infants can easily pick up such foods, but getting them into their mouths is another story. The hand grasping the food may be raised to the cheek, then moved to the edge of the lips, and finally shoved into the mouth.

At about their first birthday, many babies start to feed themselves with a spoon. Or try to, at least.

Mission accomplished, but only with many detours along the way! Eye–hand coordination improves rapidly, so before long foods that vary in size, shape, and texture reach the mouth directly.

At about the first birthday, youngsters are usually ready to try eating with a spoon. At first, they simply play with the spoon, dipping it in and out of a dish filled with food or sucking on an empty spoon. With a little help, they learn to fill the spoon with food and place it in their mouth, though the motion is awkward because they don't rotate their wrist. Instead, most 1-year-olds fill a spoon by placing it directly over a dish, and lowering it until the bowl of the spoon is full. Then, like the child in the photo, they raise the spoon to the mouth—all the while keeping the wrist rigid. In contrast, 2-year-olds rotate the hand at the wrist while scooping food from a dish and placing the spoon in the mouth—the same motion that adults use.

After infancy, fine-motor skills progress rapidly. Preschool children become much more dexterous, able to make many precise and delicate movements with their hands and fingers. Greater fine-motor skill means that preschool children can begin to care for themselves. No longer must they rely primarily on parents to feed and clothe them; instead, they become increasingly skilled at feeding and dressing themselves. A 2- or 3-year-old, for example, can put on some simple clothing and use zippers but not buttons; by 3 or 4 years, children can fasten buttons and take off their clothes when going to the bathroom; like the child in the photo, most 5-year-olds can dress and undress themselves, except for tying shoes, which children typically master at about age 6.

By age 5, fine-motor skills are developed to the point that most youngsters can dress themselves.

In each of these actions, the same principles of dynamic systems theory apply as seen in our earlier discussion about locomotion. Complex acts involve many component movements. Each must be performed correctly and in the proper sequence. Development involves first mastering the separate elements and then assembling them to form a smoothly functioning whole. Eating finger food, for example, requires grasping food, moving the hand to the mouth, then releasing the food.

As the demands of tasks change and as children develop, the same skills are often reassembled to form a different sequence of movements.

**HANDEDNESS.** When young babies reach for objects, they don't seem to prefer one hand over the other; they use their left and right hands interchangeably. They may shake a rattle with their left hand and moments later pick up blocks with their right. In one study, infants and toddlers were videotaped as they played with toys that could be manipulated with two hands, such as a pinwheel (Cornwell, Harris, & Fitzgerald, 1991). The 9-month-olds used their left and right hands equally, but by 13 months most grasped the toy with their right hand. Then, like the toddler in the photo, they used their left hand to steady the toy while the right hand manipulated the object. This early preference for one hand becomes stronger and more consistent during the preschool years. By the time children are ready to enter kindergarten, handedness is well established and very difficult to reverse (McManus et al., 1988).

What determines whether children become left- or right-handed? Some scientists believe that a gene biases children toward right-handedness (Annett, 2002). Consistent with this idea, identical twins are more likely than fraternal twins to have the same handedness—both are right-handed or both are left-handed (Sicotte, Woods, & Mazziotta, 1999). But experience also contributes to handedness. Modern industrial cultures favor right-handedness. School desks, scissors, and can openers, for example, are designed for right-handed people and can be used by left-handers only with difficulty. In the United States, elementary-school teachers used to urge left-handed children to use their right hands. As this practice has diminished in the last 50 years, the percentage of left-handed children has risen steadily (Levy, 1976). Thus, handedness seems to have both hereditary and environmental influences.

## Physical Fitness

Using one's motor skills—that is, being active physically—has many benefits for children. It promotes growth of muscles and bone, promotes cardiovascular health (National High Blood Pressure Education Program Working Group, 1996), and can help to establish a lifelong pattern of exercise. And, individuals who exercise regularly—30 minutes, at least three times a week—reduce their risk for obesity, cancer, heart disease, diabetes, and psychological disorders including depression and anxiety. Running, vigorous walking, swimming, aerobic dancing, biking, and cross-country skiing are all examples of activities that can provide this level of intensity.

How fit are U.S. children and adolescents? According to their own reports, youth are quite active—they report spending more than 2 hours each day in moderate to vigorous activity (Simons-Morton et al., 1997). However, when children are tested against objective criteria, the picture is different. In studies that include a full battery of fitness tests, such as the mile run, pull-ups, and sit-ups, fewer than half the children usually meet standards for fitness on all tasks (Corbin & Pangrazi, 1992; Looney & Plowman, 1990). And, you'll remember, from Module 4.2, the U.S. Surgeon General pronounced that obesity has reached epidemic proportions among American children and adolescents (U.S. Department of Health and Human Services, 2001).

Many factors contribute to low levels of fitness. In most schools, physical education classes meet only once or twice a week. And, even when students are in these classes, they spend a surprisingly large proportion of time—nearly half—standing around instead of exercising (Lowry et al., 2001; Parcel et al., 1987). Television and other sedentary leisure-time activities may contribute, too. Children who watch TV often tend to be less fit physically, but the nature of this relation remains poorly understood: Children who watch TV a lot may have fewer opportunities to exercise, but it may be that children who are in poor physical condition would rather watch TV than exercise.

Most toddlers use their left hand to hold an object steady and the right hand is used to explore the object.

Jenny and Ian are both left-handed and they fully expected their son, Tyler, to prefer his left hand, too. But he's 8 months old already and seems to use both hands to grasp toys and other objects. Should Jenny and Ian give up their dream of being the three left-handed musketeers?

**5.3**

Most youth claim to be active physically but in reality they are neither active nor physically fit.

Activities like biking represent one good way for all family members to stay physically fit.

Participating in sports can enhance children's physical, motor, cognitive, and social development.

Many experts believe that U.S. schools should offer physical education more frequently each week. And many suggest that physical education classes should offer a range of activities in which all children can participate and that can be the foundation for a lifelong program of fitness. Thus, instead of emphasizing team sports such as touch football, physical education classes should emphasize activities like running, walking, racquet sports, and swimming; these can be done throughout adolescence and adulthood—either alone or with another person (American Academy of Pediatrics Committee on Sports Medicine and Committee on School Health, 1989). Families can encourage fitness, too. Instead of spending an afternoon watching TV and eating popcorn, they can, like the family in the photo, go biking together.

**PARTICIPATING IN SPORTS.** Many children and adolescents get exercise by participating in many team sports, including baseball, softball, basketball, and soccer. Obviously, when children such as the girls in the photo play sports, they get exercise and improve their motor skills. But there are other benefits. Sports can enhance participants' self-esteem and can help them to learn initiative (Larson, 2000; Whitehead & Corbin, 1997). Sports can also provide children a chance to learn important social skills, such as how to work effectively as part of a group, often in complementary roles. Finally, playing sports allows children to use their emerging cognitive skills as they devise new playing strategies or modify the rules of a game.

In days gone by, children gathered together informally—at a playground, a vacant lot, or someone's backyard—to play these sports. However, today the setting is often an official league, organized and run by adults. This turns out to be a mixed blessing. Adults' involvement in children's sports has several advantages: Children learn how to improve their skills and get knowledgeable feedback, and they can enjoy spending time with a positive role model. But there are disadvantages as well. Adults sometimes overemphasize competition instead of skill development; they can be so controlling that children have little opportunity to learn leadership skills; and they may so emphasize drills, strategy, and performance that the activity becomes more like work instead of play.

When adult coaches encourage their players and emphasize skill development, children usually enjoy playing, often improve their skills, and increase their self-esteem (Smith & Smoll, 1997; Smoll et al., 1993). In contrast, when coaches—like the man in the photo at the top of page 159—emphasize winning over skill development and criticize or punish players for bad plays, children lose interest and stop playing (Bailey & Rasmussen, 1996; Smith & Stoll, 1996). Many youth sports organizations provide guidelines for players, coaches, and parents, so that children will enjoy participating. For example, the American Youth Soccer Organization has a code for coaches that includes the following principles:

- Coach positively: Praise children, don't criticize them.
- Be sure that children have fun!
- Have realistic expectations for children and use these to form reasonable demands.
- Develop children's respect for their opponents, opposing coaches, referees, and the game itself.
- Be a good role model for children.

When adult coaches emphasize winning or frequently criticize players, many children lose interest and quit.

When coaches (and parents) follow these guidelines, it's a good bet that their players will have fun and continue to play the sport. And everyone involved needs to remember that this is the whole point: Children (and adults) play games for recreation, which means to have fun!

## CHECK YOUR LEARNING

**RECALL** Describe the skills that infants must master to be able to walk. How do fine-motor skills improve with age?

**INTERPRET** What are the pros and cons of children and adolescents participating in organized sports?

**APPLY** Describe how participation in sports illustrates connections between motor, cognitive, and social development.

No. At 8 months it's too early for Tyler to show a consistent preference for one hand. They need to wait; by 13 to 15 months of age they should have a much better idea whether Tyler will be left-handed.

5.3

## UNIFYING THEMES: Active Children

Each module in this chapter touched on the theme that *children influence their own development*. That is, repeatedly we saw that infants are extremely well equipped to interpret and explore their environments. In Module 5.1, we saw that most sensory systems function quite well in the 1st year, providing infants with accurate raw data to interpret. In Module 5.2, we learned that attentional skills originate in infancy—through habituation, infants ignore some stimuli and attend to others. Finally, in Module 5.3, we discovered that locomotor and fine-motor skills improve rapidly in infancy; by the first birthday, infants can move independently and handle objects skillfully. Collectively, these accomplishments make the infants extraordinarily well prepared to explore their world and make sense of it.

## SEE FOR YOURSELF

To see the origins of attention, you need a baby and a small bell. A 1- to 5-month-old is probably best because babies at this age can't locomote, so they won't wander away. While the infant is awake, place it on its back. Then move behind the baby's head (out of sight) and ring the bell a few times. You don't need to ring the bell loudly—an "average" volume will do. You should see the orienting response described on page 147: The baby will open its eyes wide and perhaps try to turn in the direction of the sound. Every 2 or 3 minutes, ring the bell again. You should see the baby respond less intensely each time until, finally, it ignores the bell completely. Attention in action! See for yourself!

## RESOURCES

For more information about . . .

infant development in general, including perceptual development, try Charles W. Snow and Cindy G. McGaha's *Infant Development* (3rd edition) (Prentice Hall, 2003)

ADHD, visit this Web site, maintained by the U.S. National Institute of Mental Health:
**http://www.nimh.nih.gov/healthinformation/adhdmenu.cfm**

## KEY TERMS

**amodal information**  139
**attention**  147
**auditory threshold**  136
**cones**  138
**differentiation**  153
**dynamic systems theory**  152
**fine-motor skills**  151
**habituation**  134
**integration**  153
**interposition**  144
**intersensory redundancy theory**  139
**kinetic cues**  143
**linear perspective**  144
**locomotion**  151

**motion parallax**  143
**motor skills**  132
**orienting response**  147
**pictorial cues**  144
**relative size**  144
**retinal disparity**  143
**sensory and perceptual processes**  132
**size constancy**  142
**texture gradient**  144
**toddler**  152
**visual acuity**  137
**visual cliff**  143
**visual expansion**  143

**SUMMARY**

# 5.1 BASIC SENSORY AND PERCEPTUAL PROCESSES

### Smell, Taste, and Touch

Newborns are able to smell and can recognize their mother's odor; they also taste, preferring sweet substances and responding negatively to bitter and sour tastes. Infants respond to touch. Judging from their responses to painful stimuli, which are similar to older children's, we can say they experience pain.

### Hearing

Babies can hear, although they are less sensitive to high- and low-pitched sounds than are adults. Babies can distinguish different sounds (both from language and music) and use sound to locate objects in space.

### Seeing

A newborn's visual acuity is relatively poor, but 1-year-olds can see as well as adults with normal vision. Color vision develops as different sets of cones begin to function; by 3 or 4 months, children can see color as well as adults.

### Integrating Sensory Information

Infants begin to integrate information from different senses (e.g., sight and sound, sight and touch). Infants are often particularly attentive to information presented redundantly to multiple senses.

# 5.2 COMPLEX PERCEPTUAL AND ATTENTIONAL PROCESSES

### Perceiving Objects

Infants use motion, color, texture, and edges to distinguish objects. By about 4 months, infants have begun to master size, brightness, shape, and color constancy. Infants first perceive depth by means of kinetic cues, including visual expansion and motion parallax. Later, they use retinal disparity and pictorial cues (linear perspective, texture gradient, relative size, interposition) to judge depth. Infants perceive faces early in the 1st year. However, it is not clear whether perception of faces involves specific perceptual mechanisms or whether it is based on the same processes used to perceive other objects.

### Attention

Attention helps select information for further processing. Infants orient to a novel stimulus, but as it becomes more familiar, they habituate, meaning that they respond less. Compared to older children, preschoolers are less able to pay attention to a task. Younger children's attention can be improved by getting rid of irrelevant stimuli.

### Attention Deficit Hyperactivity Disorder

Children with ADHD are typically inattentive, hyperactive, and impulsive. They sometimes have conduct problems and do poorly in school. According to the Multimodal Treatment Study of Children with ADHD, the most effective approach to ADHD combines medication with psychosocial treatment.

# 5.3 MOTOR DEVELOPMENT

### Locomotion

Infants progress through a sequence of motor milestones during the 1st year, culminating in walking a few months after the first birthday. Like most motor skills, learning to walk involves differentiation of individual skills, such as maintaining balance and stepping on alternate legs, and then integrating these skills into a coherent whole. This differentiation and integration of skills is central to the dynamic systems theory of motor development. Experience can accelerate specific motor skills.

### Fine-Motor Skills

Infants first use only one hand at a time, then both hands independently, then both hands in common actions, and, finally, both hands in different actions with a common purpose.

Most people are right-handed, a preference that emerges after the first birthday and that becomes well established during the preschool years. Handedness is determined by heredity but can be influenced by experience and cultural values.

### Physical Fitness

Although children report spending much time being physically active, in fact, fewer than half of American school children meet all standards for physical fitness. Part of the explanation for the lack of fitness is inadequate physical education in school. Television may also contribute. Physical education in the schools needs to be more frequent and more oriented toward developing patterns of lifetime exercise. Families can become more active, thereby encouraging children's fitness.

Participating in sports can promote motor, cognitive, and social development. Adult coaches often can help children to improve their skills but they sometimes overemphasize competition, being so controlling that children have little opportunity to experience leadership; they often overemphasize drills, strategy, and performance, which turns play into work.

On the TV show *Family Guy*, Stewie is a 1-year-old who can't stand his mother (Stewie: "Hey, mother, I come bearing a gift. I'll give you a hint. It's in my diaper and it's not a toaster.") and hopes to dominate the world. Much of the humor, of course, turns on the idea that babies are capable of sophisticated thinking—they just can't express it. But when asked, few TV viewers, if any, would attribute such advanced language skills to a baby. What thoughts, then, *do* lurk in the mind of an infant who is not yet speaking? And how do an infant's fledgling thoughts blossom into the powerful reasoning skills that older children, adolescents, and adults use daily? In other words, how does thinking change as children develop; and why do these changes take place?

For many years, the best answers to these questions came from the theory proposed by Jean Piaget that was mentioned in Module 1.2. We'll look at this theory in more detail in Module 6.1. In Module 6.2, we'll examine some of the modern theories that guide today's research on children's thinking. Finally, in Module 6.3, we'll see how children acquire knowledge of objects, living things, and people.

**6.1**  Setting the Stage: Piaget's Theory

**6.2**  Modern Theories of Cognitive Development

**6.3**  Understanding in Core Domains

1   The Science of Child Development

2   Genetic Bases of Child Development

3   Prenatal Development, Birth, and the Newborn

4   Growth and Health

5   Perceptual and Motor Development

# Theories of Cognitive Development

7   Cognitive Processes and Academic Skills

8   Intelligence and Individual Differences in Cognition

9   Language and Communication

10  Emotional Development

11  Understanding Self and Others

12  Moral Understanding and Behavior

13  Gender and Development

14  Family Relationships

15  Influences Beyond the Family

## 6.1

## SETTING THE STAGE: PIAGET'S THEORY

Basic Principles of Piaget's Theory

Stages of Cognitive Development

Piaget's Contributions to Child Development

### LEARNING OBJECTIVES

- What are the basic principles of Piaget's theory of cognitive development?

- How does thinking change as children move through Piaget's four stages of development?

- What are the lasting contributions of Piaget's theory? What are some of its shortcomings?

*When Ethan, an energetic $2\frac{1}{2}$-year-old, saw a monarch butterfly for the first time, his mother, Kat, told him, "Butterfly, butterfly; that's a butterfly, Ethan." A few minutes later, a zebra swallowtail landed on a nearby bush and Ethan shouted in excitement, "Butterfly, Mama, butterfly!" A bit later, a moth flew out of another bush; with even greater excitement in his voice, Ethan shouted, "Butterfly, Mama, more butterfly!" As Kat was telling Ethan, "No, honey, that's a moth, not a butterfly," she marveled at how rapidly Ethan seemed to grasp new concepts with so little direction from her. How was this possible?*

For many years, our best answer to Kat's question came from Jean Piaget, who began work on his theory of mental development in the 1920s. Piaget was trained as a biologist, but he developed a keen interest in the branch of philosophy dealing with the nature and origins of knowledge. He decided to investigate the origins of knowledge not as philosophers had—that is, through discussion and debate—but by doing experiments with children.

Because Piaget's theory led the way to all modern theories of cognitive development, it's a good introduction to the study of children's thinking. We'll first consider some basic principles of the theory, where we will discover why Ethan understands as quickly as he does. Then we'll look at Piaget's stages of development and, finally, end the module by examining the enduring contributions of Piaget's work to child-development science.

### Basic Principles of Piaget's Theory

Piaget believed that children are naturally curious. They constantly want to make sense out of their experience and, in the process, construct their understanding of the world. For Piaget, children at all ages are like scientists in that they create theories about how the world works. Of course, children's theories are often incomplete. Nevertheless, their theories are valuable because they make the world seem more predictable.

In using their theories to make sense of what's going on around them, children often have new experiences that are readily understood within the context of these theories. **According to Piaget, *assimilation* occurs when new experiences are readily incorporated into a child's existing theories.** Imagine an infant like the one in the photo on page 165 who knows that the family dog barks and often licks her in the face. When she has the same experience at a relative's house, this makes sense because it fits her simple theory of dogs. Thus, understanding the novel dog's behavior represents assimilation. But sometimes theories are incomplete or incorrect, causing children to have unexpected experiences. **For Piaget,** *accommodation* **occurs when a child's theories are modified based on experience.** The baby with a theory of dogs is surprised the first time she encounters a cat—it resembles a dog but meows instead of barks and rubs up against her instead of licking. Revising her theory to include this new kind of animal illustrates accommodation.

This infant's "theory of dogs" includes the facts that dogs are friendly and like licking people's faces.

Assimilation and accommodation are illustrated in the vignette at the beginning of the module. Piaget would say that when Kat named the monarch butterfly for Ethan, he formed a simple theory something like "butterflies are bugs with big wings." The second butterfly differed in color but was still a bug with big wings, so it was readily assimilated into Ethan's new theory of butterflies. However, when Ethan referred to the moth as a butterfly, Kat corrected him. Presumably, Ethan was then forced to accommodate to this new experience. The result was that he changed his theory of butterflies to make it more precise; the new theory might be something like "butterflies are bugs with thin bodies and big, colorful wings." He also created a new theory, something like "a moth is a bug with a bigger body and plain wings."

Assimilation and accommodation are usually in balance, or equilibrium. That is, children find they can readily assimilate most experiences into their existing theories, but occasionally they need to accommodate their theories to adjust to new experiences. This balance between assimilation and accommodation is illustrated both by the baby's theories of small animals and by Ethan's understanding of butterflies.

Periodically, however, the balance is upset and a state of disequilibrium results. Children discover that their current theories are not adequate because they are spending much more time accommodating than assimilating. **When disequilibrium occurs, children reorganize their theories to return to a state of equilibrium, a process that Piaget called** *equilibration.* To restore the balance, current but now-outmoded ways of thinking are replaced by a qualitatively different, more advanced theory.

Returning to the metaphor of the child as a scientist, sometimes scientists find that a theory contains critical flaws. When this occurs, they can't simply revise; they must create a new theory that draws upon the older theory but is fundamentally different. For example, when the astronomer Copernicus realized that the Earth-centered theory of the solar system was wrong, he retained the concept of a central object but proposed that it was the Sun, a fundamental change in the theory. In much the same way, children periodically reach a point when their current theories seem to be wrong much of the time, so they abandon these theories in favor of more advanced ways of thinking about their physical and social worlds.

> All children were said to pass through all four of Piaget's stages, but some were said to do so more rapidly than others.

According to Piaget, these revolutionary changes in thought occur three times over the life span, at approximately 2, 7, and 11 years of age. This divides cognitive development into four stages: the *sensorimotor stage* (birth to age 2, encompassing infancy); the *preoperational stage* (ages 2 to 6, encompassing preschool and early elementary school); the *concrete operational stage* (ages 7 to 11, encompassing middle and late elementary school); and the *formal operational stage* (ages 11 and up, encompassing adolescence and adulthood).

Piaget held that all children go through these four stages and in exactly this sequence. For example, he contended that sensorimotor thinking always gives rise to preoperational thinking; a child cannot "skip" preoperational thinking and move directly from sensorimotor to concrete operational thought. However, the ages listed are only approximate: Some youngsters were thought to move through the stages more rapidly than others, depending on their ability and their experience. In the next section, we'll look more closely at each stage.

## Stages of Cognitive Development

Just as you can recognize a McDonald's restaurant by the golden arches and Nike products by the swoosh, each of Piaget's stages is marked by a distinctive way of thinking about and understanding the world. In the next few pages, we'll learn about these unique trademarks of Piaget's stages.

*Sensorimotor thinking involves adapting to the environment, understanding objects, and becoming able to use symbols.*

**THE SENSORIMOTOR STAGE.** We know from Chapter 5 that infants' perceptual and motor skills improve quickly during the 1st year. Piaget proposed that these rapidly changing perceptual and motor skills in the first 2 years of life form a distinct phase in human development: **The *sensorimotor stage* spans birth to 2 years, a period during which the infant progresses from simple reflex actions to symbolic processing.** In the 24 months of this stage, infants' thinking progresses remarkably along three important fronts.

***Adapting to and Exploring the Environment.*** Newborns respond reflexively to many stimuli but between 1 and 4 months, reflexes are first modified by experience. An infant may inadvertently touch his lips with his thumb, thereby initiating sucking and the pleasing sensations associated with sucking. Later, the infant tries to recreate these sensations by guiding his thumb to his mouth. Sucking no longer occurs only reflexively when a mother places a nipple at the infant's mouth; instead, the infant has found a way to initiate sucking himself.

Between 4 and 8 months, infants eagerly explore new objects.

Between 4 and 8 months, the infant shows greater interest in the world, paying far more attention to objects. For example, the infant shown in the photo accidentally shook a new rattle. Hearing the interesting noise, the infant grasped the rattle again, tried to shake it, and expressed great pleasure at the sound that resulted. This sequence was repeated several times.

At about 8 months, infants reach a watershed: The onset of deliberate, intentional behavior. For the first time, the "means" and "end" of activities are distinct. If, for example, a father places his hand in front of a toy, an infant will move his hand to be able to play with the toy. "Moving the hand" is the means to achieve the goal of "grasping the toy." Using one action as a means to achieve another end is the first indication of purposeful, goal-directed behavior during infancy.

Beginning at about 12 months, infants become active experimenters. An infant may deliberately shake a number of different objects trying to discover which produce sounds and which do not. Or an infant may decide to drop different objects to see what happens. An infant will discover that stuffed animals land quietly whereas bigger toys often make a more satisfying "clunk" when they hit the ground. These actions represent a significant extension of intentional behavior: Now babies repeat actions with different objects solely for the purpose of seeing what will happen.

*Understanding Objects.* Objects fill the world. Some, including dogs, spiders, and college students, are animate; others, including cheeseburgers, socks, and this textbook, are inanimate. But they all share a fundamental property—they exist independently of our actions and thoughts toward them. Much as we may dislike spiders, they still exist when we close our eyes or wish they would go away. **Piaget's term for this understanding that objects exist independently was *object permanence*.** And Piaget made the astonishing claim that infants lacked this understanding for much of the 1st year. That is, he proposed that an infant's understanding of objects could be summarized as "out of sight, out of mind." For infants, objects are ephemeral, existing when in sight and no longer existing when out of sight.

VIDEO6.1

Object
Permanence

The photo illustrates the sort of research that led Piaget to conclude that infants have little understanding of objects. If a tempting object such as an attractive toy is placed in front of a 4- to 8-month-old, the infant will probably reach and grasp the object. If, however, the object is then hidden by a barrier, or, as in the photo, covered with a cloth, the infant will neither reach nor search. Instead, like the baby in the photo, the infant seems to have lost all interest in the object, as if the now-hidden object no longer exists. Paraphrasing the familiar phrase, "out of sight, out of existence!"

Beginning at about 8 months, infants search for an object that an experimenter has covered with a cloth. In fact, many 8- to 12-month-olds love to play this game—an adult covers the object and the infant sweeps away the cover, laughing and smiling all the while! But, despite this accomplishment, their understanding of object permanence remains incomplete according to Piaget. If 8- to 10-month-olds see an object hidden under one container several times, then see it hidden under a second container, they usually look for the toy under the first container. Piaget claimed that this behavior shows only a fragmentary understanding of objects because infants do not distinguish the object from the actions they use to locate it, such as lifting a particular container. In fact, according to Piaget, infants do not have full understanding of object permanence until about 18 months of age.

According to Piaget, 8-month-olds have limited understanding of objects: They believe that when objects are out of sight, they no longer exist.

By 18 months of age, most toddlers will use simple gestures, which is evidence of their emerging ability to use symbols.

*Using Symbols.* By 18 months, most infants have begun to talk and gesture, evidence of the emerging capacity to use symbols. Words and gestures are symbols that stand for something else. When the baby in the photo waves, it is just as effective and symbolic as saying "goodbye" to bid farewell. Children also begin to engage in pretend play, another use of symbols. A 20-month-old may move her hand back and forth in front of her mouth, pretending to brush her teeth.

Once infants can use symbols, they can begin to anticipate the consequences of actions mentally instead of having to perform them. Imagine that an infant and parent construct a tower of blocks next to an open door. Leaving the room, a 12- to 18-month-old might close the door, knocking over the tower, because he cannot foresee the outcome of closing the door. But an 18- to 24-month-old can anticipate the consequence of closing the door and move the tower beforehand.

In just 2 years, the infant progresses from reflexive responding to actively exploring the world, understanding objects, and using symbols. These achievements are remarkable and set the stage for preoperational thinking, which we'll examine next.

**THE PREOPERATIONAL STAGE.** With the magic power of symbols, the child crosses the hurdle into preoperational thinking. **The *preoperational***

*stage*, **which spans ages 2 to 7, is marked by the child's use of symbols to represent objects and events.** Throughout this period, preschool children gradually become proficient at using common symbols, such as words, gestures, graphs, maps, and models. Although preschool children's ability to use symbols represents a huge advance over sensorimotor thinking, their thinking remains quite limited compared to that of school-age children. Why? To answer this question, we need to look at some important characteristics of thought during the preoperational stage.

Preoperational children typically believe that others see the world—both literally and figuratively—exactly as they do. *Egocentrism* **refers to young children's difficulty in seeing the world from another's viewpoint.** When youngsters stubbornly cling to their own way, they are not simply being contrary. Instead, preoperational children do not comprehend that other people have different ideas and feelings.

Suppose, for example, you ask the preschooler in Figure 6-1 to select the image that shows how the objects on the table look to you. Most will select the drawing on the far left, which shows how the objects look to the child, rather than the drawing on the far right—correct choice. Preoperational youngsters evidently suppose that the mountains are seen the same way by all; they presume that theirs is the only view, rather than one of many conceivable views (Piaget & Inhelder, 1956).

Children in the preoperational stage also have the psychological equivalent of tunnel vision: They often concentrate on one aspect of a problem but totally ignore other equally relevant aspects. *Centration* **is Piaget's term for this narrowly focused thought that characterizes preoperational youngsters.** Piaget demonstrated centration in his experiments involving conservation. In the conservation experiments, Piaget wanted to determine when children realize that important characteristics of objects (or sets of objects) stay the same despite changes in their physical appearance.

A typical conservation problem, involving conservation of liquid quantity, is shown in the photos below. Children are shown identical beakers filled with the same amount of juice. After children agree that the two beakers have the same amount, juice is poured from one beaker into a taller, thinner beaker. The juice looks different in the tall, thin beaker—it rises higher—but of course the amount is unchanged. Nevertheless, preoperational children claim that the tall, thin beaker has more juice than the original beaker. (And, if the juice is poured into a wider beaker, they believe it has less.)

**FIGURE 6-1**

In the conservation task, preoperational children believe that the tall, thin beaker has more water, an error that reflects centered thought that is common in children at this stage.

What is happening here? According to Piaget, preoperational children center on the level of the juice in the beaker. If the juice is higher after it is poured, preoperational children believe that there must be more juice now than before. Because preoperational thinking is centered, these youngsters ignore the fact that the change in the level of the juice is always accompanied by a change in the diameter of the beaker.

Centration and egocentrism are major limits to preoperational children's thinking but these are overcome in the next stage, the concrete operational stage.

**THE CONCRETE OPERATIONAL STAGE.**   During the early elementary-school years, children enter a new stage of cognitive development that is distinctly more adultlike and much less childlike. **In the *concrete operational stage*, which spans ages 7 to 11, children first use mental operations to solve problems and to reason.** What are the mental operations that are so essential to concrete operational thinking? *Mental operations* **are strategies and rules that make thinking more systematic and more powerful.** Some mental operations apply to numbers. For example, addition, subtraction, multiplication, and division are familiar arithmetic operations that concrete operational children use. Other mental operations apply to categories of objects. For example, classes can be added (mothers + fathers = parents) and subtracted (parents − mothers = fathers). Still other mental operations apply to spatial relations among objects. For example, if point A is near points B and C, then points B and C must be close to each other.

Another important property of mental operations is that they can be reversed. Each operation has an inverse that can "undo" or reverse the effect of an operation. If you start with 5 and add 3, you get 8; by subtracting 3 from 8, you reverse your steps and return to 5. For Piaget, reversibility of this sort applied to all mental operations. Concrete operational children are able to reverse their thinking in a way that preoperational youngsters cannot. In fact, reversible mental operations are part of why concrete operational children pass the conservation tasks described on page 168: Concrete operational thinkers understand that if the transformation were reversed (for example, the juice was poured back into the original container), the objects would be identical.

Concrete operational thinking is much more powerful than preoperational thinking. Remember that preoperational children are egocentric (believing that others see the world as they do) and centered in their thinking; neither of these limitations applies to children in the concrete operational stage.

Concrete operational thinking is a major cognitive advance, but it has its own limits. As the name implies, concrete operational thinking is limited to the tangible and real, to the here and now. The concrete operational youngster takes "an earthbound, concrete, practical-minded sort of problem-solving approach, one that persistently fixates on the perceptible and inferable reality right there in front of him" (Flavell, 1985, p. 98). That is, thinking abstractly and hypothetically is beyond the ability of concrete operational thinkers.

**THE FORMAL OPERATIONAL STAGE.**   In the *formal operational stage*, **which extends from roughly age 11 into adulthood, children and adolescents apply mental operations to abstract entities; they think hypothetically and reason deductively.** Freed from the concrete and the real, adolescents explore the possible—what might be and what could be.

Unlike reality-oriented concrete operational children, formal operational thinkers understand that reality is not the only possibility. They can envision alternative realities and examine their consequences. For example, ask a concrete

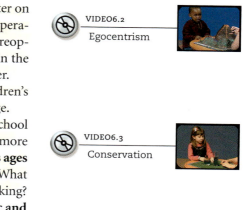

VIDEO6.2
Egocentrism

VIDEO6.3
Conservation

Concrete operational thinking is based on mental operations that yield consistent results and that can be reversed.

Question

When 3-year-old Jamila talks on the phone, she often replies to questions by nodding her head. Jamila's dad has explained that her listeners can't hear her—that she needs to say "yes" or "no." But Jamila invariably returns to head nodding. How would Jean Piaget explain this behavior to Jamila's dad?   **6.1**

operational child, "What would happen if gravity meant that objects floated up?" or "What would happen if men gave birth?" and you're likely to get a confused or even irritated look and comments like "It doesn't—they fall" or "They don't—women have babies." Reality is the foundation of concrete operational thinking. In contrast, formal operational adolescents use hypothetical reasoning to probe the implications of fundamental change in physical or biological laws.

Formal operations also allow adolescents to take a different, more sophisticated approach to problem solving. Formal operational thinkers can solve problems by creating hypotheses (sets of possibilities) and testing them. Piaget (Inhelder & Piaget, 1958) showed this aspect of adolescent thinking by presenting children and adolescents with several flasks, each containing what appeared to be the same clear liquid. They were told that one combination of the clear liquids would produce a blue liquid and were asked to determine the necessary combination.

A typical concrete operational youngster, like the ones in the photo, plunges right in, mixing liquids from different flasks haphazardly. In contrast, formal operational adolescents understand that the key is setting up the problem in abstract, hypothetical terms. The problem is not really about pouring liquids but about systematically forming hypotheses about different combinations of liquids and testing them systematically. A teenager might mix liquid from the first flask with liquids from each of the other flasks. If none of these combinations produces a blue liquid, he or she would mix the liquid in the second flask with each of the remaining liquids. A formal operational thinker would continue in this manner until he or she found the critical pair that produced the blue liquid.

Children in the concrete-operational stage often solve problems by "plunging right in" instead of thinking hypothetically to come up with a well-defined set of solutions to a problem.

Because adolescents' thinking is not concerned solely with reality, they are also better able to reason logically from premises and draw appropriate conclusions. **The ability to draw appropriate conclusions from facts is known as *deductive reasoning*.** Suppose we tell a person the following two facts:

1. If you hit a glass with a hammer, the glass will break.

2. Don hit a glass with a hammer.

The correct conclusion is that "the glass broke," a conclusion that formal operational adolescents will reach. Concrete operational youngsters, too, will sometimes reach this conclusion, but based on their experience and not because the conclusion is logically necessary. To see the difference, imagine that the two facts are now:

1. If you hit a glass with a feather, the glass will break.

2. Don hit a glass with a feather.

The conclusion "the glass broke" follows from these two statements just as logically as it did from the first pair. In this instance, however, the conclusion is counterfactual—it goes against what experience tells us is really true. Concrete operational 10-year-olds resist reaching conclusions that are counter to known facts; they reach conclusions based on their knowledge of the world. In contrast, formal operational 15-year-olds often reach counterfactual conclusions (Markovits & Vachon, 1989). They understand that these problems are about abstract entities that need not correspond to real-world relations.

VIDEO6.4

Deductive
Reasoning

Hypothetical reasoning and deductive reasoning are powerful tools for formal operational thinkers. In fact, we can characterize this power by paraphrasing the quotation about concrete operational thinking that appears on page 169: "Formal operational youth take an abstract, hypothetical approach to problem solving; they are not constrained by the reality that is staring them in the face but are open to different possibilities and alternatives." The ability to ponder different alternatives makes possible the experimentation with lifestyles and values that occurs in adolescence, topics we'll encounter on several occasions later in this book.

> Formal operational adolescents can think hypothetically and can reason deductively.

With the achievement of formal operations, cognitive development is over in Piaget's theory. Adolescents and adults acquire more knowledge as they grow older, but their fundamental way of thinking remains unchanged, in Piaget's view. The table summarizes Piaget's description of cognitive changes between birth and adulthood.

**TABLE 6-1**

### PIAGET'S FOUR STAGES OF COGNITIVE DEVELOPMENT

| Stage | Approximate Age | Characteristics |
|---|---|---|
| Sensorimotor | Birth to 2 years | Infant's knowledge of the world is based on senses and motor skills. By the end of the period, infant uses mental representations. |
| Preoperational | 2 to 6 years | Child learns how to use symbols such as words and numbers to represent aspects of the world, but relates to the world only through his or her own perspective. |
| Concrete operational | 7 to 11 years | Child understands and applies logical operations to experiences, provided they are focused on the here and now. |
| Formal operational | Adolescence and beyond | Adolescent or adult thinks abstractly, speculates on hypothetical situations, and reasons deductively about what may be possible. |

## Piaget's Contributions to Child Development

Ask a child-development researcher to name the person who dominated the field for much of the 20th century and most will say Piaget; his impact on every aspect of child-development research was and is profound. As one writer phrased it, "many of Piaget's contributions have become so much a part of the way we view cognitive development nowadays that they are virtually invisible" (Flavell, 1996, p. 202). I want to emphasize three of these enduring, now nearly invisible contributions (Brainerd, 1996; Siegler & Ellis, 1996):

- *The study of cognitive development itself.* Before Piaget, cognition simply was not part of the research agenda for child-development scientists. Piaget showed why cognitive processes are central to development and offered some methods that could be used to study them.

- *A new view of children.* **Piaget emphasized *constructivism*, the view that children are active participants in their own development who systematically construct ever more sophisticated understandings of their worlds.** This view now pervades thinking about children (so much so that it's one of the themes in this book), but it began with Piaget.

- *Fascinating, often counterintuitive discoveries.* One reason why Piaget's work attracted so much attention is that many of the findings were completely unexpected and became puzzles that child-development researchers couldn't resist trying to solve. In the words of one commentator, "Piaget had the greenest thumb ever for unearthing fascinating and significant developmental progressions" (Flavell, 1996, p. 202).

Piaget's contributions extended beyond child-development research per se. Many teachers and parents also have found Piaget's theory a rich source of ideas for fostering children's development. Some of these ideas are described in the "Improving Children's Lives" feature.

## *Improving Children's Lives*
**Teaching Practices That Foster Cognitive Growth—Educational Applications of Piaget's Theory**

Piaget's view of cognitive development has some straightforward implications for teaching practices that promote cognitive growth:

- *Facilitate rather than direct children's learning.* Cognitive growth occurs as children construct their own understanding of the world, so the teacher's role is to create environments where children can discover for themselves how the world works. A teacher shouldn't simply try to tell children how addition and subtraction are complementary but instead should provide children with materials that allow them to discover the complementarity themselves.

- *Be sensitive to children's readiness to learn.* Children profit from experience only when they can interpret this experience with their current cognitive structures. It follows, then, that *the best teaching experiences are slightly ahead of children's current level of thinking.* As a youngster begins to master basic addition, don't jump right to subtraction but first go to slightly more difficult addition problems.

- *Emphasize exploration and interaction.* Cognitive growth can be particularly rapid when children discover inconsistencies and errors in their own thinking. *Teachers should therefore encourage children to look at the consistency of their thinking but then let children take the lead in sorting out the inconsistencies.* If a child is making mistakes in borrowing on subtraction problems, a teacher shouldn't correct the error directly but should encourage the child to look at a large number of these errors to discover what he or she is doing wrong. ■

**WEAKNESSES OF PIAGET'S THEORY.**     Although Piaget's contributions to child development are legendary, some elements of his theory have held up better than others (Siegler & Alibali, 2005).

- *Piaget's theory underestimates cognitive competence in infants and young children and overestimates cognitive competence in adolescents.* In Piaget's theory, cognitive development is steady in early childhood but not particularly rapid. In contrast, a main theme of modern child-development science is that of the extraordinarily competent infant and toddler. By using more sensitive tasks than Piaget's, modern investigators have shown that infants and toddlers are vastly more capable than expected based on Piaget's theory. For example, we'll see in Module 6.3 that infants have much greater understanding of objects than Piaget believed. Paradoxically, however, Piaget *overestimated* cognitive skill in adolescents, who often fail to reason according to formal operational principles and revert to less sophisticated reasoning. For example, we'll see in Module 7.2 that adolescents often let their beliefs bias their reasoning.

- *Piaget's theory is vague with respect to processes and mechanisms of change.* One important shortcoming is that many of the key components of the theory, such as accommodation and assimilation, turned out to be too vague to test scientifically. Consequently, scientists abandoned them in favor of other cognitive processes that could be evaluated more readily and provide more convincing accounts of children's thinking.

- *Piaget's stage model does not account for variability in children's performance.* An even more important criticism is that cognitive development is nowhere near as stage-like as Piaget believed. In Piaget's view, each stage of intellectual development has unique characteristics that leave their mark on everything a child does. Preoperational thinking is defined by egocentrism and centration; formal operational thinking is defined by abstract and hypothetical reasoning. Consequently, children's performance on different tasks should be very consistent. On the conservation and the three-mountains tasks, for instance, according to Piaget a 4-year-old should always respond in a preoperational way: He should say the water is not the same after pouring, and that another person sees the mountains the same way he does. In fact, children's thinking falls far short of this consistency. A child's thinking may be sophisticated in some domains but naïve in others (Siegler, 1981). This inconsistency does not support Piaget's view that children's thinking should always reflect the distinctive imprint of their current stage of cognitive development.

- *Piaget's theory undervalues the influence of the sociocultural environment on cognitive development.* Returning to the metaphor of the child as scientist, Piaget describes the child as a lone scientist, constantly trying to figure out by herself how her theory coordinates with data. In reality, a child's effort to understand her world is a far more social enterprise than Piaget described. Her growing understanding of the world is profoundly influenced by interactions with family members, peers, and teachers and takes place against the backdrop of cultural values. Piaget's theory did not neglect these social and cultural forces entirely, but they are not prominent in the theory.

Because of the criticisms of Piaget's theory, many researchers have taken several different paths in studying cognitive development. In the next module, we'll look at three different approaches that are linked to Piaget's work.

> Piaget's theory was criticized for underestimating infants' competence and for overestimating adolescents' competence.

**RECALL**  What are the stages of cognitive development in Piaget's theory? What are the defining characteristics of each?

Summarize the main shortcomings of Piaget's account of cognitive development.

**INTERPRET**  Piaget championed the view that children participate actively in their own development. How do the sensorimotor child's contributions differ from the formal-operational child's contributions?

**APPLY**  Based on what you know about Piaget's theory, what would his position have been on the continuity–discontinuity issue discussed in Module 1.3?

**6.1**  Piaget would reassure Jamila's dad that her behavior is perfectly normal. Preschoolers usually believe that others see the world as they do, a phenomenon that Piaget called egocentrism. In this case, since Jamila knows that she's nodding her head, she believes that others must know it, too.

## 6.2

# MODERN THEORIES OF COGNITIVE DEVELOPMENT

The Sociocultural Perspective: Vygotsky's Theory

Information Processing

Core-Knowledge Theories

**LEARNING OBJECTIVES**

- In Vygotsky's sociocultural theory, how do adults and other people contribute to children's cognitive development?

- According to information-processing psychologists, how does thinking change with development?

- What naïve theories do children hold about physics, psychology, and biology?

*Victoria, a 4-year-old, loves solving jigsaw puzzles with her dad. She does the easy ones by herself. But she often has trouble with the harder ones, so her dad helps—he orients pieces correctly and reminds Victoria to look for edge pieces. Victoria may do 10 to 12 puzzles before she loses interest, then delights in telling her mom, in great detail, about all the puzzles she solved. After these marathon puzzle sessions, Victoria's dad is often surprised that a child who is sophisticated in her language skills struggles on the harder puzzles.*

Many theories have built on the foundation of Piaget's pioneering work. In this module, we'll look at three different theoretical approaches, each designed to take research in cognitive development beyond Piaget's theory. As we do, you'll learn more about Victoria's cognitive and language skills.

## The Sociocultural Perspective: Vygotsky's Theory

Child-development scientists often refer to child development as a journey that can proceed along many different paths. As we've seen, in Piaget's theory, children make the journey alone as they interact with the physical world. Other people (and culture in general) certainly influence the direction that children take, but the child is seen as a solitary adventurer–explorer boldly forging ahead.

In contrast, according to the *sociocultural perspective*, children are products of their culture: Children's cognitive development is not only brought about by social interaction; it is inseparable from the cultural contexts in which children live. To illustrate, Gauvain (1998) argues that cultural contexts organize cognitive development in several ways. First, culture often defines which cognitive activities are valued: American youngsters are expected to learn to read but not to navigate using the stars. Second, culture provides tools that shape the way children think. The cognitive skills that children use to solve arithmetic problems, for example, depend on whether their culture provides an abacus like the one in the photograph, or paper and pencil, or a handheld calculator. Third, higher level cultural practices help children to organize their knowledge and communicate it to others. For instance, in most American schools, students are expected to think and work alone rather than collaborate (Matusov, Bell, & Rogoff, 2002). Thus, as Gauvain (1998) emphasizes, "Culture penetrates human intellectual functioning and its development at many levels, and it does so through many organized individual and social practices" (p. 189).

Sociocultural theories emphasize that cultures influence cognitive development by the tools that are available to support children's thinking, such as an abacus.

One of the original—and still quite influential—sociocultural theories was proposed by Lev Vygotsky (1896–1934), the Russian psychologist described in Chapter 1. Vygotsky saw development as an apprenticeship in which children advance when they collaborate with others who are more skilled. That is, according to Vygotsky (1978), child development is never a solitary journey. Instead, children always travel with others and usually progress most rapidly when they walk hand in hand with an expert partner. **For Vygotsky and other sociocultural theorists, the social nature of cognitive development is captured in the concept of** *intersubjectivity*, **which refers to mutual, shared understanding among participants in an activity.** When Victoria and her father solve puzzles together, they share an understanding of the goals of their activity and of their roles in solving the puzzles. Such shared understanding allows Victoria and her dad to work together in complementary fashion on the puzzles. **Such interactions typify** *guided participation*, **in which cognitive growth results from children's involvement in structured activities with others who are more skilled than they.** Through guided participation, children learn from others how to connect new experiences and new skills with what they already know (Rogoff, 2003). Guided participation is shown when a child learns a new video game from a peer or an adolescent learns a new karate move from a partner.

Vygotsky died of tuberculosis when he was only 37 years old, so he never had the opportunity to formulate a complete theory of cognitive development like that of Piaget. Nevertheless, his ideas are influential because they fill some gaps in Piaget's account of cognitive development. Three of Vygotsky's most important contributions are the concepts of zone of proximal development, scaffolding, and private speech.

> Vygotsky viewed development as an apprenticeship in which children progress by collaborating with skilled partners.

**THE ZONE OF PROXIMAL DEVELOPMENT.**    Angela likes helping her 11-year-old son with his math homework, particularly when it includes word problems. Her son does most of the work but Angela often gives him hints. For example, she might help him decide what arithmetic operations are required. When Angela's son tries to solve these problems by himself, he rarely succeeds. **The difference between what Angela's son can do with assistance and what he can do alone defines the** *zone of proximal development*. That is, the zone refers to the difference between the level of performance a child can achieve when working independently and the higher level of

VIDEO6.5
Zone of Proximal
Development

performance that is possible when working under the guidance of more skilled adults or peers (Wertsch & Tulviste, 1992).

Think, for example, about a preschooler who is asked to clean her bedroom. She doesn't know where to begin. By structuring the task for the child—"start by putting away your books, then your toys, then your dirty clothes"—an adult can help the child accomplish what she cannot do by herself. Similarly, the zone of proximal development explains why Victoria, in the module-opening vignette, solves difficult jigsaw puzzles with a bit of help from her dad. Just as training wheels help children learn to ride a bike by allowing them to concentrate on other aspects of bicycling, collaborators help children perform effectively by providing structure, hints, and reminders.

Experienced teachers often provide much direct instruction as children first encounter a task, then provide less instruction as children "catch on."

The idea of a zone of proximal development follows naturally from Vygotsky's basic premise that cognition develops first in a social setting and only gradually comes under the child's independent control. Understanding how the shift from social to individual learning occurs brings us to the second of Vygotsky's key contributions.

**SCAFFOLDING.**    Have you ever had the good fortune to work with a master teacher, one who seemed to know exactly when to say the right thing to help you over an obstacle but otherwise let you work uninterrupted? *Scaffolding* **refers to a teaching style that matches the amount of assistance to the learner's needs.** Early in learning a new task, when a child knows little, teachers such as the one in the photo provide a lot of direct instruction. But, as the child begins to catch on to the task, the teacher provides less instruction and only occasional reminders (Gauvain, 2001).

We saw earlier how a parent helping a preschooler clean her room must provide detailed structure. As the child does the task more often, the parent needs to provide less structure. Similarly, when high-school students first try to do proofs in geometry, the teacher must lead them through each step; as the students begin to understand how proofs are done and can do more on their own, the teacher gradually provides less help.

Do parents worldwide scaffold their children's learning? If so, do they use similar methods? The "Cultural Influences" feature answers these questions.

VIDEO6.6

Scaffolding

### Cultural Influences

**How Do Parents in Different Cultures Scaffold Their Children's Learning?**

Cross-cultural research by Barbara Rogoff and her colleagues (1993) suggests that parents and other adults in many cultures scaffold learning, but they do it in different ways. These researchers studied parents and 1- to 2-year-olds in four different settings: a medium-sized U.S. city, a small tribal village in India, a large city in Turkey, and a town in the highlands of Guatemala. In one part of the study, parents tried to get their toddlers to operate a novel toy (for example, a wooden doll that danced when a string was pulled). No ground rules or guidelines concerning teaching were given; parents were free to be as direct or uninvolved as they cared.

What did parents do? In all four cultural settings, the vast majority attempted to scaffold their children's learning, either by dividing a difficult task into easier sub-tasks or by doing parts of the task themselves, particularly the more complicated parts. However, as the graphs show, parents in different cultures scaffold in different ways. Turkish parents give the most verbal instruction and use some gestures (point-ing, nodding, and shrugging). U.S. parents also use these methods but to slightly

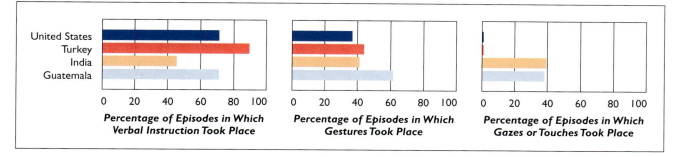

| | United States | Turkey | India | Guatemala |

*Percentage of Episodes in Which Verbal Instruction Took Place*

*Percentage of Episodes in Which Gestures Took Place*

*Percentage of Episodes in Which Gazes or Touches Took Place*

FIGURE 6-2

lesser degrees. Turkish and U.S. parents almost never touch (such as nudging a child's elbow) or gaze (use eye contact, such as winking or staring). Indian parents seem to use roughly equal amounts of speech, gesture, and touch or gaze to scaffold. Guatemalan parents also use all three techniques, and, overall, Guatemalan parents give the most scaffolding of the four cultures. Evidently, parents worldwide try to simplify learning tasks for their children, but the methods that they use to scaffold learning vary across cultures. ■

The defining characteristic of scaffolding—giving help but not more than is needed—clearly promotes learning (Cole, 2006). Youngsters do not learn read-ily when they are constantly told what to do or when they are simply left to struggle through a problem unaided. However, when teachers collaborate with them—allowing children to take on more and more of a task as they master its different elements—they learn more effectively (Murphy & Messer, 2000). Scaf-folding is an important technique for transferring skills from others to the child, both in formal settings like schools and in informal settings like the home or playground.

**PRIVATE SPEECH**     The little boy in the photo is talking to himself as he is playing. **This behavior demonstrates** *private speech*, **comments not directed to others but intended to help children regulate their own behavior.** Vygotsky (1896–1934) viewed private speech as an intermediate step toward self-regulation of cognitive skills. At first, children's behavior is regulated by speech from other people that is di-rected toward them. When youngsters first try to control their own behavior and thoughts without others present, they instruct themselves by speaking aloud. **Finally, as children gain ever greater skill, private speech becomes** *inner speech*, **Vygotsky's term for thought.**

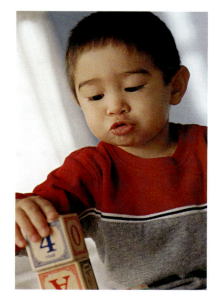

Young children often talk to themselves as they're performing difficult tasks; this helps them control their own behavior.

If children use private speech to help control their behavior, then we should see children using it more often on difficult tasks than on easy tasks, and more often after a mistake than after a correct response. These predictions are generally sup-ported in research (Berk, 1992), which documents the power of language in helping children learn to control their own behavior and thinking.

Vygotsky's view of cognitive development as an apprenticeship, a collaboration between expert and novice, complements the Piagetian view of cognitive development described in Module 6.1. Next we will consider another perspective, information processing, which goes beyond Piaget's theory in a different direction.

## Information Processing

In Module 6.1, we saw that a criticism of Piaget's theory is that the mechanisms of change—accommodation, assimilation, and equilibration—were vague and difficult to study scientifically. Consequently, identifying mechanisms of growth has been a priority of child-development scientists and in the 1960s researchers first began to use computer systems to explain how thinking develops. **Just as computers consist of both hardware (disk drives, random-access memory, and a central-processing unit) and software (the programs that the computer runs),** *information-processing theory* **proposes that human cognition consists of mental hardware and mental software.**

Mental software includes organized sets of cognitive processes that allow children to complete specific tasks, such as reading a sentence, playing a video game, or hitting a baseball. For example, suppose a mother asks her son to make his bed, brush his teeth, and take out the trash. A bit later, the mother wonders if she asked her son about the trash, so she says, "Did I ask you to take out the trash?" Almost immediately, he says, "Yes." Despite the speed of the boy's reply, information-processing theorists believe that his mental software has gone through four general steps to answer the question, as shown in the diagram. First, the mental software must understand the mother's question. That is, the software must decode the sounds of the mother's speech and give them meaning. Next, the software searches memory for the mother's earlier requests. When that information is located and retrieved, the software compares "take out the trash" with each of the mother's requests. Finding a match, the software selects "yes" as the appropriate answer to the question.

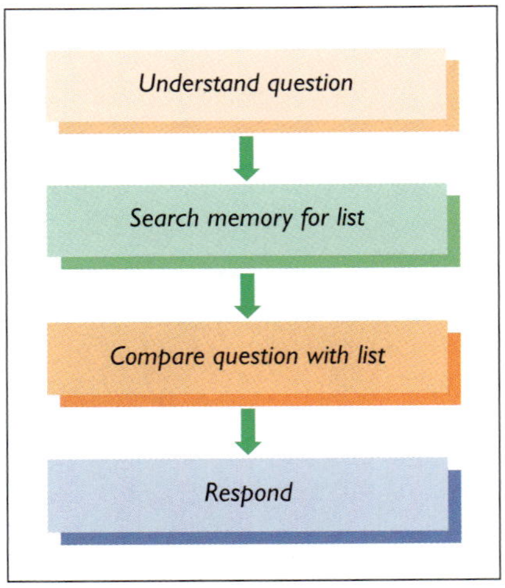

Thus, the processes of understanding, searching, comparing, and responding create a mental program that allows the boy to answer his mother. The mental software for solving a calculus problem or writing a poem is more elaborate—involving more processes and more steps—but the basic idea of breaking down a task into many simpler components is the same. As children get older and more knowledgeable, their mental software becomes more sophisticated and more powerful, just as the current version of PowerPoint is vastly more capable than PowerPoint 1.0 (which ran only in black and white when it was released in 1987!).

**MENTAL HARDWARE** Mental hardware refers to mental and neural structures that are built in and that allow the mind to operate. If the hardware in a personal computer refers to random-access memory, the central processor, and the like, what does mental hardware refer to? Information-processing theorists generally agree that mental hardware has three components: sensory memory, working memory, and long-term memory. The diagram shows how they are related.

**Understand question**

**Search memory for list**

**Compare question with list**

**Respond**

FIGURE 6-3

FIGURE 6-4

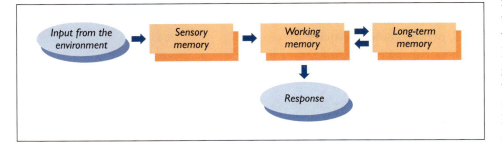

Input from the environment → Sensory memory → Working memory ⇄ Long-term memory

↓

Response

*Sensory memory* **is where information is held in raw, unanalyzed form very briefly (no longer than a few seconds).** For example, look at your hand as you clench your fist, rapidly open your hand (to extend your fingers), and then rapidly reclench your fist. If you watch carefully, you'll see an image of your fingers that lasts momentarily after you reclench your hand. What you're seeing is an image stored in sensory memory.

*Working memory* **is the site of ongoing cognitive activity.** In a personal computer, RAM (random-access memory) holds the software that we're using and stores data used by the software. In much the same way, working memory includes both ongoing cognitive processes and the information that they require (Baddeley, 1996). For example, as you read these sentences, part of working memory is allocated to the cognitive processes responsible for determining the meanings of individual words; working memory also stores the results of these analyses briefly while they are used by other cognitive processes to give meaning to sequences of words.

*Long-term memory* **is a limitless, permanent storehouse of knowledge of the world.** Long-term memory is like a computer's hard drive, a fairly permanent storehouse of programs and data. It includes facts (e.g., Charles Lindbergh flew the Atlantic in the *Spirit of St. Louis*), personal events (e.g., "I moved to Maryland in July 1999"), and skills (e.g., how to play the cello).

Information rarely is forgotten from long-term memory, though it is sometimes hard to access. For example, do you remember the name of the African American agricultural chemist who pioneered crop rotation methods and invented peanut butter? If his name doesn't come to mind, look at this list:

Marconi    Carver    Fulton    Luther

Now do you know the answer? (If not, it appears before "Check Your Learning," on page 185.) Just as books are sometimes misplaced in a library, you sometimes cannot find a fact in long-term memory. Given a list of names, though, you can go directly to the location in long-term memory associated with each name and determine which is the famed chemist.

**HOW INFORMATION PROCESSING CHANGES WITH DEVELOPMENT**   A fundamental question for child-development researchers is "Why do cognitive processes become steadily more powerful during childhood and adolescence?" That is, what is the "push" behind cognitive development? What are the forces underlying the steady age-related march to ever-more sophisticated thinking? Information-processing psychologists draw upon the basic ideas of mental hardware and mental software to describe several mechanisms that drive cognitive development (Kail, 2004; Siegler & Alibali, 2005). Let's look at some of them.

*Better Strategies.* Older children usually use better strategies to solve problems (Bjorklund, 2005). That is, as children develop they use strategies that are faster, more accurate, and easier. For example, trying to find a parent in a crowded auditorium, a younger child might search each row, looking carefully at every person; an older child might remember that the parent is wearing an orange T-shirt and only look at people in orange. Both children will probably find the parent, but the older child's approach is more efficient.

How do children learn more effective strategies? Of course, parents and teachers often help youngsters learn new strategies. By structuring children's actions and

> In the information-processing approach, mental hardware includes sensory, working, and long-term memories.

providing hints, adults demonstrate new strategies and how best to use them. However, youngsters also learn new strategies by watching and working with more-skilled children (Tudge, Winterhoff, & Hogan, 1996). For example, children and adolescents at an arcade watch others play in order to learn good game strategies. Children also discover new strategies on their own (Siegler, 2000). For example, when my daughter was 5, I watched her match words with their antonyms in a language workbook. The pages always had an equal number of words and antonyms, so she quickly learned to connect the last word with the one remaining antonym, without thinking about the meaning of either.

***Increased Capacity of Working Memory.*** Modern personal computers can run more complex software than ever before, in part because they have much more

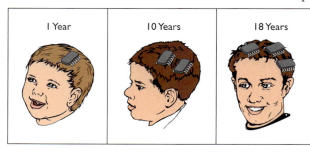

FIGURE 6-5

RAM than their counterparts from the 1980s and 1990s. If you use this technological change as a metaphor for children's development, the implication is clear. The diagram shows that, compared to younger children, it's as if older children have more working memory "chips" to allocate to mental software and to information storage (Case, 1992; Kail, 2004). Consequently, older children usually outperform younger children on tasks where working memory is important for performance, such as reading or solving complicated problems.

***More Effective Inhibitory Processes and Executive Functioning.*** Yesterday I was listening to the radio and heard that classic oldie "The Lion Sleeps Tonight." Unfortunately, I spent the rest of the afternoon hearing "aweem away, aweem away" over and over in my mind. Undoubtedly, you, too, have had this experience—a thought gets into your head and you can't get rid of it.

Fortunately, most of the time, irrelevant and unwanted ideas do not intrude on our thinking. Why not? *Inhibitory processes* **prevent task-irrelevant information from entering working memory.** These processes, which rely on the attentional processes described in Module 5.2, improve steadily during childhood (Dempster, 1995). Consequently, thinking in older children and adolescents is more sophisticated because better inhibition means fewer disruptions from irrelevant stimulation and, therefore, more efficient working memory. When an older child is deciding the best way to a new friend's house, the sound of popcorn popping or thoughts of an upcoming swim meet are less likely to intrude on working memory and disrupt his planning (Kail, 2003).

**Inhibitory processes, along with planning and cognitive flexibility, define** *executive functioning.* In many ways, executive functioning is synonymous with skilled problem solving, which helps to explain the presence of each of the elements in the definition. That is, good problem solving usually involves a plan and often requires flexibility (the ability to respond differently when the old response no longer works) and the ability to inhibit irrelevant responses (Wright et al., 2003). Each of the elements of executive functioning has been linked to the frontal cortex, a brain region known to develop throughout infancy and childhood (Davis et al., 2003). Thus, with age children are better able to inhibit irrelevant responses, to formulate effective plans, and to adjust those plans as needed.

***Increased Automatic Processing.*** Think back to when you were learning a new skill, like how to type. At first, you had to think about every single step in the process. If you were asked to type "child," you probably started, like the child in the photograph on page 181, by trying to remember the location of "c" on the keyboard and then deciding which finger to use to reach that key. You had to repeat this process for each of the remaining four letters. But as your skill grew, each step became easier until you could type "child" without even thinking about it; your fingers seem to move automatically to the right keys, in the right sequence. **Cognitive activities that require virtually no effort are known as *automatic processes*.**

To understand how automatic processes affect developmental change, we need to return to working memory. In the early phases of learning a skill, each individual step (such as finding a "c" on the keyboard) must be stored in working memory. Because there are so many

As children and adolescents acquire greater skill at new tasks such as typing, some aspects of the task are performed automatically, which means they require no effort.

steps, an unmastered skill can easily occupy much of the capacity of working memory. In contrast, when a skill has been mastered, individual steps are no longer stored in working memory, which means that more capacity is available for other activities.

Compared to adolescents and adults, children have limited experience in most tasks, so they perform few processes automatically. Instead, their processing requires substantial working memory capacity. As children gain experience, however, some processes become automatic, freeing working memory capacity for other processes (Rubinstein et al., 2002). Thus, when faced with complex tasks involving many processes, older children are more likely to succeed because they can perform some of the processes automatically. In contrast, younger children must think about all or most of the processes, taxing or even exceeding the capacity of their working memory.

***Increased Speed of Processing.*** As children develop, they complete most mental processes at an ever-faster rate (Cerella & Hale, 1994). Improved speed is obvious when we measure how fast children of different ages respond on tasks. Across a wide range of cognitive tasks such as deciding which of two numbers is greater, naming a pictured object, and searching memory, 4- and 5-year-olds are generally one-third as fast as adults, whereas 8- and 9-year-olds are one-half as fast as adults (Kail, 2005).

Age differences in processing speed are critical when a specified number of actions must be completed in a fixed period of time. For example, perhaps you've had the unfortunate experience of trying to understand a professor who lectures at warp speed. The instructor's speech was so rapid that your cognitive processes couldn't keep up, which meant that you didn't get much out of the lecture. The problem is even more serious for children, who process information much more slowly than adults.

The five types of developmental change in the information-processing approach, summarized in the table on page 182, occur throughout infancy, childhood, adolescence, and adulthood. What's more, sometimes the different types of change interact with each other. To understand this interaction, think back to the concepts of mental hardware and mental software. Just as installing additional RAM makes it possible to run more complex software, increases in working memory allow children to use more complex mental software.

### Question

Fifteen-year-old Quinn has just completed driver's ed and he loves to get behind the wheel. For the most part, his parents are okay while he's driving but they absolutely refuse to let him listen to the radio. Quinn thinks this is a stupid rule. Do you?

**6.2**

Older children have better inhibitory processes, more automatic processes, and more rapid processing.

**SUMMARY TABLE**

### TYPES OF DEVELOPMENTAL CHANGE IN INFORMATION PROCESSING

| Type of Developmental Change | Defined | Example |
|---|---|---|
| Better strategies | Older children use faster, more accurate, and easier strategies. | Younger children may "sound out" a word's spelling but older children simply retrieve it. |
| Increased capacity of working memory | Older children have a larger mental workspace for cognitive processes. | An older child could simultaneously watch TV and converse with a friend but a young child could do one but not both. |
| Greater inhibitory control and executive functioning | Older children are less prone to interference from irrelevant stimulation and are more flexible in their thinking. | Asked by a teacher to format assignments in a new way (e.g., place a name in a different location, provide the day but not the date), older children are more successful in adapting to the new format. |
| Increased automatic processing | Older children execute more processes automatically (without using working memory). | Asked to get ready for bed, an older child goes through all the tasks (e.g., brush teeth, put on pajamas) thinking about other things, but a younger child focuses on each task as well as what to do next. |
| Increased speed of processing | Older children can execute mental processes more rapidly than younger children. | Shown a picture of a dog, older children can retrieve the name "dog" from memory more rapidly. |

With the five types of change interacting in this fashion (and functioning independently), information processing provides a set of powerful mechanisms to drive cognitive development during childhood and adolescence. The combined result of these mechanisms is a steady age-related increase in cognitive skill. In contrast to Piaget's theory, there are no abrupt or qualitative changes that create distinct cognitive stages.

Finally, what would information-processing researchers say about Victoria, from the module-opening vignette? They would probably want to explain why she finds some puzzles harder than others. Using the list of developmental mechanisms that we've examined in the past few pages, they would note that complex puzzles may require more sophisticated strategies that are too demanding for her limited working-memory capacity. However, as she does more and more puzzles with her dad, some parts of these complex strategies may become automated, making it easier for Victoria to use the strategy.

## Core-Knowledge Theories

Imagine a 10-year-old (a) trying to program a new MP3 player, (b) wondering why her dad is grouchy today, and (c) taking her pet dog for a walk. According to Piaget and most information-processing theories, in each case the same basic mechanisms of thinking are at work, even though the contents of the child's thinking ranges from objects to people to pets. In this view, different types of knowledge are like different kinds of cars—they come in countless numbers of makes, models, and colors, but down deep they are alike in consisting of an engine, four wheels, doors, windows, and so on.

**In contrast to this view,** *core-knowledge theories* **propose distinctive domains of knowledge, some of which are acquired very early in life.** In this view, knowledge is more like the broader class of vehicles: Much knowledge is general, represented by the large number of cars. But there are also distinct, specialized forms of knowledge, represented by buses, trucks, and motorcycles. And returning to our hypothetical 10-year-old, core-knowledge theorists would claim that her thinking about objects, people, and pets may reflect fundamentally different ways of thinking.

Core-knowledge theories were created, in part, to account for the fact that most children acquire some kinds of knowledge relatively easily and early in life. For example, think about learning language (a native language, not a second language) versus learning calculus. Most children learn to talk—in fact, the inability to talk is a sign of atypical development—and they do so with little apparent effort. (When was the last time you saw a 3-year-old complaining that learning to talk was just *too* hard?) Calculus, in comparison, is mastered by relatively few, usually only after hours of hard work solving problem after problem.

> According to core-knowledge theories, infants are endowed with knowledge in specialized domains that were historically significant for human survival, such as language.

According to core-knowledge theorists, some forms of knowledge are so important for human survival that specialized systems have evolved that simplify learning of those forms of knowledge. In the case of language, for example, spoken communication has been so essential throughout human history that mental structures evolved that simplified language learning. Other evolutionarily important domains of knowledge include knowledge of objects and simple understanding of people.

The nature of these mental structures, or modules, is very much a matter of debate. Some core-knowledge theorists believe they're like the math or graphics co-processor on a computer: They're prewired to analyze one kind of data very efficiently (numbers and images, respectively, for the computer) but nothing else. The language module, for example, would be very sensitive to speech sounds and would be prewired to derive grammatical rules from sequences of words. Another view of these specialized mental structures borrows from Piaget's metaphor of the child as a scientist who creates informal theories of the world. However, core-knowledge theorists believe that children's theories are focused on core domains, rather than being all-encompassing as Piaget proposed. And, in creating their theories, children don't start from scratch; instead, a few innate principles provide the starting point. For example, infants' early theories of objects seem to be rooted in a few key principles such as the principle of cohesion, the idea that objects move as connected wholes (Spelke, 1994). Both of these ideas of mental structures may be right—some forms of knowledge may be better described as modular but others are more consistent with the child-as-scientist view.

What are the domains of knowledge that have these specialized mental structures? Language was the first core domain identified by scientists; there is so much to learn about children's mastery of language that I've devoted an entire chapter to it (Chapter 9). In addition, many child-development researchers agree that young children rapidly acquire knowledge of objects, people, and living things. That is, they create informal or naïve theories of physics, psychology, and biology. Like language, acquiring knowledge in each of these domains has been central to human existence: Naïve physics allows children to predict where and how objects will move in the environment; naïve psychology makes for more successful interactions with others; and naïve biology is important in avoiding predators and in maintaining health.

Finally, if core-knowledge theorists were asked to comment on Victoria (from the module-opening vignette), they would emphasize the contrast between her sophisticated language skill and her relatively undeveloped puzzle-solving skill. Language represents an evolutionarily important domain, so Victoria's precocity here is not surprising; doing jigsaw puzzles is not a specialized domain with evolutionary significance, which explains her relative lack of skill.

We'll see how knowledge in several fundamental domains changes with development in Module 6.3. For now, the Summary Table reviews the defining features of the three theories that we've explored in Module 6.2.

## SUMMARY TABLE

### CHARACTERISTICS OF MODERN THEORIES OF COGNITIVE DEVELOPMENT

| Approach | Characteristics |
|---|---|
| Vygotsky's sociocultural theory | Views cognitive development as a sociocultural enterprise; experts use scaffolding to help a novice acquire knowledge; children use private speech to regulate their own thinking. |
| Information processing | Based on the computer metaphor, views cognitive change in terms of better strategies, increased capacity of working memory, more effective inhibitory and executive processing, more automatic processing, and faster processing speed. |
| Core knowledge | Views cognitive development as an innate capability to easily acquire knowledge in such specialized domains of evolutionary importance as language, knowledge of objects, and understanding people. |

As you think about the three theoretical perspectives listed in the Summary Table, keep in mind that each goes beyond Piaget's theory in a unique direction. The sociocultural approach expands the focus of cognitive development research from a solitary child to one who is surrounded by people and the culture they represent; the information-process perspective expands the focus of developmental mechanisms from accommodation and assimilation to working memory, processing speed, and other mechanisms derived from mental hardware and mental software; core-knowledge theories expand the focus to recognize distinct domains of evolutionarily significant knowledge. Thus, these three perspectives provide complementary, not competing, accounts of cognitive development.

*Response to question on page 179:* The agricultural chemist who pioneered crop rotation while on the faculty of Tuskegee Institute of Technology is George Washington Caver.

**Though Quinn may not like the rule, it's probably a good one. Beginning drivers like Quinn are told to keep the music turned off because listening would consume working-memory capacity that is needed for driving. However, with more experience behind the wheel, many driving skills will become automatic, freeing capacity that can be used to listen to the radio. Patience, Quinn, your time will come!**    `6.2`

## CHECK YOUR LEARNING

**RECALL** What three concepts are fundamental to Vygotsky's sociocultural theory? What specialized domains of knowledge have been identified by core-knowledge theorists?

**INTERPRET** Do the five developmental mechanisms in the information-processing perspective emphasize nature, nurture, or both? How?

**APPLY** How might an information-processing theorist explain sociocultural influences on cognitive development (e.g., scaffolding)?

# UNDERSTANDING IN CORE DOMAINS    6.3

## LEARNING OBJECTIVES

- What do infants understand about the nature of objects?

- When and how do young children distinguish between living and nonliving things?

- How do young children acquire a theory of mind?

**Understanding Objects and Their Properties**

**Understanding Living Things**

**Understanding People**

*Amy, a reporter for a magazine that featured reviews of products, was assigned to a story on different kinds of "sippy cups"—plastic cups with a lid and spout that are spill-proof and so are perfect for babies who are learning to use a cup. Amy brought home the sippy cups—12 different models in all—and used each one for a day with her 10-month-old son. She discovered that some definitely worked better than others but what amazed her was that after the first day her son always knew what to do with the cup. Despite differences in color, size, and the shape of the spout, he apparently recognized each one as a sippy cup because he immediately lifted each new style to his mouth and started drinking. Amy wondered how he could do this.*

The world is filled with endless varieties of "stuff," including sippy cups, cats, and basketball players. Recognizing different instances of the same kind of thing—that is, being able to categorize—is an essential skill for young children. By knowing that an object belongs to a category, we learn some of its properties, including what it can do, and where we're likely to find it. Amy's son, for example, quickly learned the essentials of a sippy cup; later he recognized each different cup as being a member of the general category of sippy cups and knew exactly what to do with them. If he couldn't categorize, every experience would be novel—upon seeing yet another slightly different sippy cup, he'd need to figure out what to do with it as if it were a uniquely new object.

How do infants form categories? Important clues come from perceptual features and their organization. A sippy cup, for example, consists of a cylinder with a spout at one end. After infants have learned these features and how they're related, they can recognize sippy cups regardless of their color or size (Quinn, 2004). And they can learn the features that distingish, for example, dogs from cats, or plants from chairs. One popular view is that infants' first categories are very broad (e.g., animals, furniture), then become more specific as infants learn the cues that distinguish subcategories. Infants' category of animals, which is based on common perceptual features of overall body shape and motion, is divided into the subcategories of dogs, cats, horses, fish, and the like (Rakison & Hahn, 2004). These are further subdivided as infants' recognize the features that distinguish beagles from Saint Bernards.

In the remainder of this module, we'll see how infants and older children use these categorization skills to carve the world into domains and create theories within those domains. We'll consider infants' knowledge of objects, living things, and people.

## Understanding Objects and Their Properties

As adults, we know much about objects and their properties. For example, we know that if we place a coffee cup on a table, it will remain there unless moved by another person; it will not move by itself or simply disappear. And we don't release a coffee cup in midair because we know that an unsupported object will fall. Child-development researchers have long been interested in young children's understanding of objects, in part because Piaget claimed that understanding of objects develops slowly, taking many months to become complete. However, by devising some clever procedures, other investigators have shown that babies understand objects much earlier than Piaget claimed. Renée Baillargeon (1987, 1994), for example, assessed *object permanence* using a procedure in which infants first saw a silver screen that appeared to be rotating back and forth. When they were familiar with this display, one of two new displays was shown. In the realistic event, a red box appeared in a position behind the screen, making it impossible for the screen to rotate as far back as it had previously. Instead, the screen rotated until it made contact with the box, then rotated forward.

> *Contrary to Piaget's claims, infants know much about the properties of objects.*

with the box, then rotated forward. In the unrealistic event, shown in Figure 6-6 on page 187, the red box appeared but the screen continued to rotate as before. The screen rotated back until it was flat, then rotated forward, again revealing the red box. The illusion was possible because the box was mounted on a movable platform that allowed it to drop out of the way of the moving screen. However, from the infant's perspective, it appeared as if the box vanished behind the screen, only to reappear.

The disappearance and reappearance of the box violates the idea that objects exist permanently. Consequently, an infant who understands the permanence of objects should find the unrealistic event a truly novel stimulus and look at it longer than the realistic event. Baillargeon found that $4\frac{1}{2}$-month-olds consistently looked longer at the unrealistic event than the realistic event. Infants apparently thought that the unrealistic event was novel, just as we are surprised when an object vanishes from a magician's scarf. Evidently, then, infants have some understanding of object permanence early in the 1st year of life.

Of course, understanding that objects exist independently is just a start; objects have numerous other important properties and infants know many of them. Infants know, for instance, that objects move along connected, continuous paths and that

1. The silver screen is lying flat on the table and the red box is fully visible.

2. The silver screen has begun to rotate, but the red box is largely visible.

3. The silver screen is now vertical, blocking the red box.

4. The silver screen continues to rotate, blocking the red box, which has started to drop through the trap door.

5. The silver screen is completely flat, apparently having "rotated through" the red box, which is actually now under the table.

6. The silver screen is rotating back toward the infant but still blocks the red box.

7. The silver screen is again flat and the box fully visible to the infant.

**FIGURE 6-6**

objects cannot move "through" other objects (Hespos & Baillargeon, 2001; Spelke, 1994). Infants look longer at objects that violate these properties than at objects that are consistent with them. For example, imagine one ball that rolls through a hole in a wall and a second ball that rolls directly through a hole-less wall. By 5 months, infants look much longer at the second ball, apparently because they are surprised when objects move in ways not predicted by their naïve theory of physics. By the middle of the 1st year, babies also understand that one object striking a second object will cause the latter to move (Kotovsky & Baillargeon, 1998; Spelke, 1994).

Later in the 1st year, if infants are shown the two situations shown in Figure 6-7, they will look intently at the object that appears unsupported, apparently because it violates their expectations about what happens to unsupported objects (Baillargeon, 1998). And infants are surprised when a tall object is completely hidden when placed behind a shorter

**FIGURE 6-7**

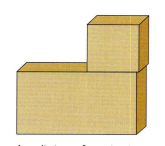

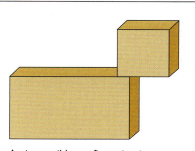

A realistic configuration in which the small box rests on the larger one

An impossible configuration in which the small box has no apparent means of support

object, apparently because it violates their expectations about concealment (Aguiar & Baillargeon, 2002; Wang & Baillargeon, 2005).

These amazing demonstrations attest to the fact that the infant is indeed an accomplished naïve physicist (Baillargeon, 2004). Of course, the infant's theories are far from complete; physical properties can be understood at many different levels (Hood, Carey, & Prosada, 2000). Using gravity as an example, infants can expect that unsupported objects will fall, elementary-school children know that such objects fall due to gravity, and physics students know that the force of gravity equals the mass of an object times the acceleration caused by gravity. Obviously, infants do not understand objects at the level of physics students. However, the important point is that infants rapidly create a reasonably accurate theory of some basic properties of objects, a theory that helps them to expect that objects such as toys will act in predictable ways.

## Understanding Living Things

Fundamental to adults' naïve theories is the distinction between living and nonliving things. Adults know that living things, for example, are made of cells, inherit properties from parents, and move spontaneously. Adults' theories of living things begin in infancy, when babies first distinguish animate objects (e.g., people, insects, other animals) from inanimate objects (e.g., rocks, plants, furniture, tools). Motion is critical in early understanding of the difference between animate and inanimate objects: That is, infants and toddlers use motion to identify animate objects; by 12 to 15 months children have determined that animate objects are self-propelled, can move in irregular paths, and act to achieve goals (Rakison & Hahn, 2004; Rakison & Poulin-Dubois, 2001).

By the preschool years, children's naïve theories of biology have come to include many of the specific properties associated with living things (Wellman & Gelman, 1998). Many 4-year-olds' theories of biology include the following elements:

- *Movement:* Children understand that animals can move themselves but inanimate objects can only be moved by other objects or by people. Shown the events in the diagram on page 189—an animal and a toy car hopping across a table in exactly the same manner—preschoolers claim that only the animal can really move itself (Gelman & Gottfried, 1996).

- *Growth:* Children understand that, from their first appearance, animals get bigger and physically more complex but that inanimate objects do not change in this way. They believe, for example, that sea otters and termites become larger as time goes by but that tea kettles and teddy bears do not (Rosengren et al., 1991).

- *Internal parts:* Children know that the insides of animate objects contain different materials than the insides of inanimate objects. Preschool children judge that blood and bones are more likely to be inside an animate object but that cotton and metal are more likely to be inside an inanimate object (Simons & Keil, 1995).

- *Inheritance:* Children realize that only living things have offspring that resemble their parents. Asked to explain why a dog is pink, preschoolers believe that some biological characteristic of the parents probably made the dog pink; asked to explain why a phone is pink, preschoolers rely on mechanical causes (e.g., a worker used a machine), not biological ones (Springer & Keil, 1991;

**6.3** | One afternoon, 15-month-old Brandon and 6-month-old Justin saw a dragonfly for the first time as it flew around in the backyard, hunting mosquitoes. Would either Brandon or Justin be likely to conclude that a dragonfly is a living thing?

*Preschool children know many properties of living things, including movement, growth, and that they heal when injured.*

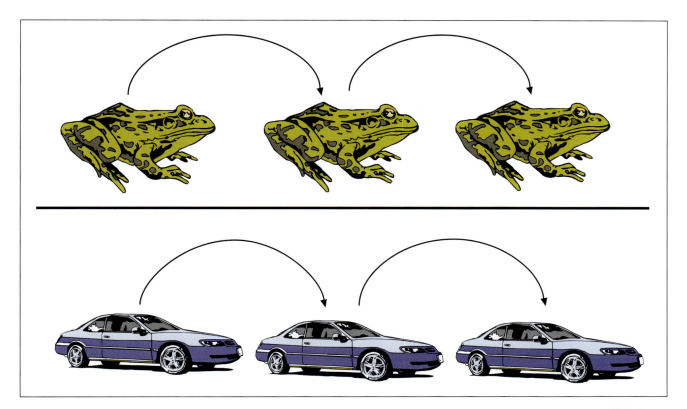

FIGURE 6-8

Weissman & Kalish, 1999). And both U.S. and Brazilian children believe that a baby pig that is adopted by a cow would grow up to look and behave like a pig (Sousa, Altran, & Medin, 2002).

- *Illness:* Preschoolers believe that permanent illnesses such as color blindness or food allergies are more likely to be inherited from parents but that temporary illnesses such as a sore throat or a runny nose are more likely to be transmitted through contact with other people (Raman & Gelman, 2005).

- *Healing:* Children understand that, when injured, animate things heal by regrowth whereas inanimate things must be fixed by humans. Preschoolers know that hair will grow back when cut from a child's head but must be repaired by a person when cut from a doll's head (Backscheider, Shatz, & Gelman, 1993).

Where do children get this knowledge of living things? Some of it comes just by watching animals, which children love to do. But parents also contribute: When reading books about animals to preschoolers, they frequently mention the properties that distinguish animals, including self-initiated motion (e.g., "the seal is jumping in the water") and psychological properties (e.g., "the bear is really mad!"). Such talk helps to highlight important characteristics of animals for youngsters (Gelman et al., 1998).

Of course, although preschoolers' naïve theories of biology are complex, their theories aren't complete. Preschoolers don't know, for instance, that genes are the biological basis for inheritance (Springer & Keil, 1991); and preschoolers' theories include some misconceptions. They believe that body parts have intentions—that the heart "wants" to pump blood and bones "want" to grow (Morris, Taplin, & Gelman, 2000). In addition, although preschoolers know that plants grow and heal, they nevertheless don't consider plants to be living things. It's not until 7 or 8 years that children routinely decide that plants are alive. Preschoolers' reluctance to call plants living things may stem from their belief in goal-directed motion as a key property of living things: This is not easy to see in plants, but when 5-year-olds are told that plants move in goal-directed ways—for example, tree roots turn toward a source of water or a venus flytrap closes its leaves to trap an insect—they decide that plants are alive after all (Opfer & Siegler, 2004).

Despite these limits, children's naïve theories of biology, when joined with their naïve theory of physics, provide powerful tools for making sense of their world and for understanding new experiences.

## Understanding People

**The last of the three fundamental theories concerns *naïve psychology*, which refers to our informal beliefs about other people and their behavior.** Think back to the last time you wanted to figure out why someone—a friend, lover, coworker, sibling, or parent—acted as he or she did. Why did your friend go to a movie with someone else instead of going to a concert with you? Why did your brother say nothing about your brand-new coat? In common situations like this, adults are often naïve psychologists—we try to explain why people act as they do and usually our explanations emphasize that desires or goals cause people's behavior. Your friend went to the movie because she was mad at you for not loaning her your car; your brother didn't comment on your coat because he was preoccupied with something else. Just as naïve physics allows us to predict how objects act and naïve biology allows us to understand living things, naïve psychology allows us to predict how people act (Lillard, 1999).

> *Even infants seem to interpret other people's actions in terms of the intent of those actions.*

Amazingly, even infants understand some important psychological phenomena—they understand that people's behavior is often intentional—designed to achieve a goal. Imagine a father who says, "Where are the crackers?" in front of his 1-year-old daughter, then begins opening kitchen cabinets, moving some objects to look behind them. Finding the box of crackers, he says, "There they are!" An infant who understands intentionality would realize how her father's actions—searching, moving objects—was related to the goal of finding the crackers.

Many clever experiments have revealed that 1-year-olds do indeed have this understanding of intentionality. One of them is described in the "Focus on Research" feature.

## *Focus on Research*

### Interpreting Actions as Goal Directed

*Who were the investigators, and what was the aim of the study?* Jessica Sommerville and Amanda Woodward (2005) wanted to determine whether 1-year-olds interpret sequences of actions in terms of the intentions of the person performing the actions.

*How did the investigators measure the topic of interest?* Infants viewed a table that had two distinctive toys placed on it: a fish on a blue cloth and a frog on a yellow cloth. As you can see in Figure 6-9 on page 191, during several trials an adult pulled on the blue cloth to bring the fish within reach, then grasped the fish. On

**Initial trials**　　**Test trial:**
**New goal (same means)**　　**Test trial:**
**Same goal (new means)**

FIGURE 6-9

test trials, the toys were switched so that each was placed on the other cloth. On some test trials, the adult again reached for the fish, which was now on the yellow cloth. On other test trials, the adult reached for the frog, which was located on the blue cloth (where the fish had been before). If infants interpret these events in terms of the adult's intentions, they should interpret reaching for the frog to be novel (a new goal) and look longer at it (even though the experimenter is still reaching for the blue cloth). If, instead, infants focus on the actions per se (i.e., grasping a blue cloth) rather than the goals of the action, they should interpret reaching to the yellow cloth to be novel and look longer at it (even though the experimenter is reaching for the same toy). Infants were videotaped throughout the experiment; research assistants later watched the videotapes and coded how long infants looked at each event.

*Who were the children in the study?* Sommerville and Woodward tested sixteen 12-month-olds and forty-eight 10-month-olds. (In case you're wondering, more 10-month-olds were tested because the investigators were also interested in the correlation between 10-month-olds' understanding of intentionality and performance on another task that I'm not describing. Evaluating correlations typically requires larger samples than does comparing means.)

*What was the design of the study?* The study was experimental. The independent variable was the cloth that the adult pulled: same cloth (but different toy from the initial trials) versus other cloth (but same toy). The dependent variable was the time spent looking at each toy. The study was cross-sectional because 10- and 12-month-olds participated.

*Were there ethical concerns with the study?* No. Most babies apparently enjoy watching these events. Occasionally babies would get fussy during the course of the experiment—perhaps because they were bored or tired—and when this happened the experiment was stopped.

*What were the results?* The graph shows the amount of time that infants spent looking at the two events: new toy (old cloth) versus new cloth (old toy). At 12 months, infants looked significantly longer at the new toy (old cloth). In contrast, at 10 months, infants looked at the two events equally.

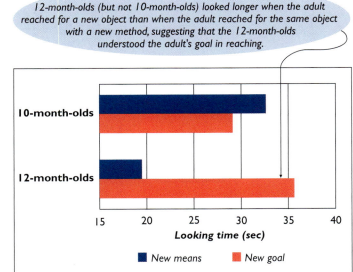

*12-month-olds (but not 10-month-olds) looked longer when the adult reached for a new object than when the adult reached for the same object with a new method, suggesting that the 12-month-olds understood the adult's goal in reaching.*

FIGURE 6-10

*What did the investigators conclude?* When 12-month-olds looked at a simple sequence of events—pull a cloth, then play with a toy—they seem to interpret it as goal-directed action: The adult is pulling the cloth so she can play with the toy. Sommerville and Woodward reached this conclusion because infants looked relatively infrequently when the adult had to pull a different cloth to reach the same toy. It was as if the infants thought, "Even though she's pulling a yellow cloth instead of a blue one, the aim is the same, to play with the fish. I've seen enough of that already!" In contrast, 10-month-olds looked equally at the two events, suggesting that infants at this age do not routinely interpret a sequence of events in terms of an adult's intentions.

*What converging evidence would strengthen these conclusions?* The task that Sommerville and Woodward used was effective because infants enjoy it and, consequently, are willing to watch the many trials that are required. An important next step would be to determine infants' understanding of intentionality in other action sequences, such as those that have more intermediate steps or those that have different goals. In addition, it would be useful to know the experiences that contribute to infants' understanding of intentions. ■

Other kinds of experiments also show infants' understanding of intentions. Meltzoff (1995) had 18-month-olds watch an experimenter perform an action but fail to achieve an apparent goal. The experimenter might, for example, look as if she wanted to drop a bead necklace in a jar but instead it falls onto the table. Or an experimenter looks as if she wants to use a stick to push a button, but she misses. When 18-month-olds were given the same objects, they typically imitated the experimenter's intended action—placing the necklace in the jar or pushing the button—not what she really did. Infants' interpretations emphasized what the actions were to accomplish, not the actions per se.

From this early understanding of intentionality, young children's naïve psychology expands rapidly. **Between ages 2 and 5, children develop a *theory of mind*, a naïve understanding of the relations between mind and behavior.** One of the leading researchers on theory of mind, Henry Wellman (1992; 1993; 2002), believes that children's theory of mind moves through three phases during the preschool years. In the earliest phase, common in 2-year-olds, children are aware of desires, and they often speak of their wants and likes, as in "Lemme see" or "I wanna sit." Also, they often link their desires to their behavior, as in "I happy there's more cookies" (Wellman, 1990). Thus, by age 2, children understand that they and other people have desires and that desires can cause behavior.

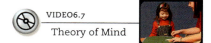

VIDEO6.7
Theory of Mind

By about age 3, an important change takes place. Now children clearly distinguish the mental world from the physical world. For example, if told about one girl who has a cookie and another girl who is thinking about a cookie, 3-year-olds know that only the first girl's cookie can be seen, touched, and eaten (Harris et al., 1991). And, most 3-year-olds use "mental verbs" like *think*, *believe*, *remember*, and *forget*, which suggests that they have a beginning understanding of different mental states (Bartsch & Wellman, 1995). Although 3-year-olds talk about thoughts and beliefs, they nevertheless emphasize desires when trying to explain why people act as they do.

Not until age 4 do mental states really take center stage in children's understanding of their own and other people's actions. That is, by 4 years, children understand that their own and other people's behavior is based on their beliefs about events and situations, even when those beliefs are wrong.

This developmental transformation is particularly evident when children are tested on false-belief tasks like the one shown in the diagram. In all false-belief tasks, a situation is set up so that the child being tested has accurate information, but someone else does not. For example, in the story in the figure, the child being tested knows that the marble is really in the box, but Sally, the girl in the story, believes that the marble is still in the basket. Remarkably, although 4-year-olds correctly say that Sally will look for the marble in the basket (acting on her false belief), most 3-year-olds say she will look in the box. The 4-year-olds understand that Sally's behavior is based on her beliefs, despite the fact that her beliefs are incorrect (Frye, 1993).

This basic developmental progression is remarkably robust. Wellman, Cross, and Watson (2001) conducted a meta-analysis of approximately 175 studies in which more than 4,000 young children were tested on false-belief tasks. Before $3\frac{1}{2}$ years, children typically make the false-belief error: Attributing their own knowledge of the marble's location to Sally, they say she will search in the correct location. Yet 6 short months later, children now understand that Sally's false belief will cause her to look for the marble in the basket. This rapid developmental transition from incorrect to correct performance is unaffected by many procedural variables (e.g., whether Sally is a doll, a picture, a person in a videotape, or a real person) and is much the same whether the children are from Europe, North America, Africa, or Asia.

Thus, at about 4 years of age there is a fundamental change in children's understanding of the centrality of beliefs in a person's thinking about the world. Children now "realize that people not only have thoughts and beliefs, but also that thoughts and beliefs are crucial to explaining why people do things; that is, actors' pursuits of their desires are inevitably shaped by their beliefs about the world" (Bartsch & Wellman, 1995, p. 144).

The early stages of children's theory of mind seem clear. How this happens is very much a matter of debate, however. According to one view, theory of mind is based on an innate, specialized module that automatically recognizes behaviors associated with different mental states such as wanting, pretending, and believing. Another view is that growth of theory of mind reflects change in basic psychological processes such as language and executive functioning (e.g., Harris, de Rosnay, & Pons, 2005). For example, theory of mind emerges as children's improved executive functioning allows them to inhibit salient events in their environment in order to think about their own mental states and those of others (Carlson, Mandell, & Williams (2004). Yet another approach is the focus of the "Spotlight on Theories" feature.

FIGURE 6-11

Preschool children acquire a theory of mind—a naive understanding of the links between thoughts, beliefs, and behavior.

### *Spotlight on Theories*
**Speech About Mental States and Children's Theory of Mind**

*BACKGROUND*

Theory of mind develops rapidly during the preschool years: 2-year-olds understand that people have desires and that desires can cause behavior, 3-year-olds distinguish the mental world from the physical world, but only 4-year-olds understand that their behavior is based on beliefs, even when beliefs are wrong.

However, scientists disagree on the factors that are responsible for this rapid acquisition of a theory of mind.

*THE THEORY*

Beginning with the work of Dunn (1996, 2002), many child-development scientists (e.g., Peterson & Slaughter, 2003; Ruffman, Perner, & Parkin, 1999) have contributed to a theory in which a child's theory of mind emerges from interactions with other people, interactions that provide children with insights into different mental states. Through conversations with parents and older siblings that focus on other people's mental states, children learn facts of mental life and this helps children to see that others often have different perspectives than they do. In other words, when children frequently participate in conversations that focus on other people's moods, their feelings, and their intentions, this helps them to learn that people's behavior is based on their beliefs, regardless of the accuracy of those beliefs.

**HYPOTHESIS:** Children have a more advanced theory of mind when conversations with their mothers focus on mental states. That is, when mother–child conversations focus on other people's desires (e.g., "She wants some ice cream"), their emotions (e.g., "She's really angry now") or their knowledge (e.g., "She knows the toy is broken"), children should perform more accurately on theory-of-mind tasks.

**TEST:** Ruffman, Slade, and Crowe (2002) tested 3- and 4-year-olds on several theory-of-mind tasks, including one like that illustrated on page 193. In addition, they recorded mother–child conversations as mothers read picture books to their children. From these recordings, Ruffman et al. determined how often mothers referred to mental states concerning desires, emotions, and knowledge. Some mothers mentioned mental states rarely; others did so repeatedly. More importantly, the correlation between the frequency with which mothers mentioned mental states and children's performance on the theory-of-mind tasks was .60. That is, children had higher scores on the theory-of-mind tasks when their mothers routinely talked about a story character wanting, feeling, thinking, or knowing.

**CONCLUSION:** As predicted, theory of mind was more advanced in children whose mothers emphasized mental states in their conversations. This finding supports the general view that theory of mind emerges from conversations that focus on what other people are feeling or thinking.

**APPLICATION:** Child-development scientists always encourage parents of preschool children to talk with their children; the more, the better! But the research that we've just discussed points to the specific advantages of focusing a conversation on other people's mental states. By talking about how others feel or think, parents can help their children more quickly grasp the idea that behavior is driven by thoughts and beliefs. ■

> Conversations with parents and siblings about mental states help preschoolers to understand that behavior is driven by a person's thoughts and beliefs.

After the preschool years, children's naïve psychology moves beyond theory of mind and embraces an ever-expanding range of psychological phenomena. For example, at about age 7, children understand that the same event can trigger different thoughts in different people: They understand that seeing a fish may make one child happy because it reminds her of her pet goldfish, but the same fish may make another child sad because her goldfish died recently (Eisbach, 2004). At about age 10, children know that such psychological states as being nervous or frustrated can produce physical states such as vomiting or having a headache (Notaro, Gelman, & Zimmerman, 2001). Furthermore, as children develop they understand the links among emotions, thoughts, and behavior. For example, although 8-year-olds understand that mental states—thoughts and feelings—can cause a person's mood, most 5-year-olds attribute such mood changes to external, observable causes (Flavell, Flavell, & Green, 2001). We'll look at these links more carefully in Module 10.1. Finally, as children develop, their descriptions of other people become more abstract and more psychological, a phenomenon that we'll consider in more detail in Module 11.3.

For now, the important point is that children's naïve psychology flourishes in the preschool years. Armed with this theory, children see that other people's behavior is not unpredictable but follows regular patterns. When joined with their theories of naïve biology and naïve physics, very young children have extensive knowledge of the physical and social world, knowledge that they can use to function successfully in those worlds.

## CHECK YOUR LEARNING

**RECALL**  Summarize the evidence indicating that Piaget underestimated infants' understanding of object permanence.

What properties of living things are featured in young children's theories of biology?

**INTERPRET**  A typical 1-year-old's understanding of objects exceeds her understanding of people. Why might this be the case?

**APPLY**  A meta-analysis of children's performance on false-belief tasks (Wellman et al., 2001) showed that the pattern of age-related change in growth of theory of mind was much the same worldwide. What do you think would happen if you conducted a similar meta-analysis on studies of infants' understanding of objects? Would the pattern of age-related change in understanding objects be much the same around the world?

By 12 to 15 months, toddlers know that living things are self-propelled, move along irregular paths, and act to achieve goals. They saw evidence of these last two (movement along an irregular path to achieve a goal) so it's likely that Brandon—but not Justin—was old enough to decide the dragonfly was alive. **6.3**

## UNIFYING THEMES: Active Children

This chapter emphasizes that *children influence their own development*. This idea is the cornerstone of Piaget's theory and to the core-knowledge account of development. Beginning in infancy and continuing through childhood and adolescence, children are constantly trying to make sense out of what goes on around them. Experiences provide intellectual food for children to digest. Parents, teachers, and peers are important in cognitive development, not so much for what they teach directly as for the guidance and challenges they provide. Thus, throughout the developmental journey, the child is a busy navigator, trying to understand the routes available and trying to decide among them.

## SEE FOR YOURSELF

The best way to see some of the developmental changes that Piaget described is to test some children with the same tasks that Piaget used. The conservation task shown on page 168 is good because it's simple to set up and children usually enjoy it. Get yourself some glasses and colored liquids, then ask a 3- or 4-year-old and a 7- or 8-year-old to confirm that the two quantities are the same. Then pour one liquid as shown on page 168 and ask children if the quantities are still the same. Ask them to explain their answers. The differences between 3- and 7-year-olds' answers are truly remarkable. See for yourself!

## RESOURCES

For more information about . . .

**activities for babies that promote cognitive development,** read L. Acredolo and S. Goodwyn's *Baby Minds: Brain-Building Games Your Baby Will Love* (Bantam, 2000), in which the authors, child psychologists, use modern research on child development as the basis for techniques and activities that foster infants' cognitive development.

**Piaget's life, his theory, and his research (as well as related research on cognitive development),** visit the Web site of the Jean Piaget Society: **http://www.piaget.org**

## KEY TERMS

accommodation   165
assimilation   164
automatic processes   181
centration   168
concrete operational stage   169
constructivism   172
core-knowledge theories   183
deductive reasoning   170
egocentrism   168
equilibration   165
executive functioning   180
formal operational stage   169
guided participation   175
information-processing theory   178
inhibitory processes   180

inner speech   177
intersubjectivity   175
long-term memory   179
mental operations   169
naïve psychology   190
object permanence   167
preoperational stage   167
private speech   177
scaffolding   176
sensorimotor stage   166
sensory memory   179
sociocultural perspective   175
theory of mind   192
working memory   179
zone of proximal development   175

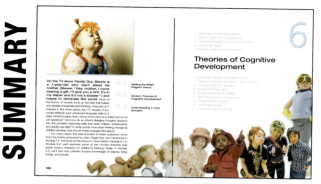

# 6.1 SETTING THE STAGE: PIAGET'S THEORY

### Basic Principles of Piaget's Theory

In Piaget's view, children construct theories that reflect their understanding of the world. Children's theories are constantly changing, based on their experiences. In assimilation, experiences are readily incorporated into existing theories. In accommodation, experiences cause theories to be modified to encompass new information.

When accommodation becomes much more frequent than assimilation, it is a sign that children's theories are inadequate, so children reorganize them. This reorganization produces four different stages of mental development from infancy through adulthood. All individuals go through all four phases, but not necessarily at the same rate.

### Stages of Cognitive Development

The first 2 years of life constitute Piaget's sensorimotor stage. Over these 2 years, infants adapt to and explore their environment, understand objects, and begin to use symbols.

From ages 2 to 7 years, children are in Piaget's preoperational stage. Although now capable of using symbols, their thinking is limited by egocentrism, the inability to see the world from another's point of view. Preoperational children also are centered in their thinking, focusing narrowly on particular parts of a problem.

Between ages 7 and 11 children begin to use and can reverse mental operations to solve perspective-taking and conservation problems. The main limit to thinking at this stage is that it is focused on the concrete and real.

With the onset of formal operational thinking, adolescents can think hypothetically and reason abstractly. In deductive reasoning, they understand that conclusions are based on logic, not experience.

### Piaget's Contributions to Child Development

Among Piaget's enduring contributions are emphasizing the importance of cognitive processes in development, viewing children as active participants in their own development, and discovering many counterintuitive developmental phenomena. The theory's weaknesses include poorly defined mechanisms of change and an inability to account for variability in children's performance.

# 6.2 MODERN THEORIES OF COGNITIVE DEVELOPMENT

### The Sociocultural Perspective: Vygotsky's Theory

Vygotsky believed that cognition develops first in a social setting and only gradually comes under the child's independent control. The difference between what children can do with assistance and what they can do alone defines the zone of proximal development.

Control of cognitive skills is most readily transferred from others to the child through scaffolding, a teaching style that allows children to take on more and more of a task as they master its different components.

### Information Processing

According to the information-processing approach, cognitive development involves changes in mental hardware and mental software. Mental hardware refers to mental processes that are built-in and allow the mind to function, including sensory, working, and long-term memories. Mental software refers to mental programs that allow people to perform specific tasks.

Information-processing psychologists believe that cognitive development reflects more effective strategies, increased capacity of working memory, more effective inhibitory processes, increased automatic processing, and increased speed of processing.

### Core-Knowledge Theories

According to core-knowledge theories, there are distinctive domains of knowledge (e.g., language, understanding objects), some of which are acquired by infants, toddlers, and preschoolers. These domains have typically evolved because they were essential for human survival. Some theorists believe these domains of knowledge are rooted in prewired systems; others use Piaget's metaphor of child-as-scientist and describe them as specialized theories.

# 6.3 UNDERSTANDING IN CORE DOMAINS

### Understanding Objects and Their Properties

Infants understand that objects exist independently. They also know that objects move along continuous paths and do not move through other objects.

### Understanding Living Things

Infants and toddlers use motion to distinguish animate from inanimate objects. By the preschool years, children know that living things move themselves, grow bigger and physically more complex, have different internal parts than objects, resemble their parents, inherit some diseases from parents but contract other diseases from contact with people, and heal when injured. Preschoolers' understanding is limited, however. They believe that body parts can have intentions and do not consider plants to be living things.

### Understanding People

By age 1, infants recognize that people perform many acts intentionally, with a goal in mind. At about age 2, children understand that people have desires and that desires can cause behavior. Beginning at 3 years of age, children distinguish the mental world from the physical world but still emphasize desires when explaining behavior. By 4 years of age, children understand that people's behavior is based on beliefs about events and situations, even when those beliefs are wrong. Contributing to children's acquisition of a theory of mind are a specialized cognitive module, basic psychological processes such as executive functioning, and social interactions that allow children to experience different mental states.

**A few weeks ago I spent a morning in a first-grade classroom watching 6- and 7-year-olds learn to read, to spell simple words, and to do simple addition problems.** I then spent the afternoon in a fifth-grade classroom. Like the younger students, these 10- and 11-year-olds devoted much of their time to the traditional three Rs. but with much more complicated material. They were reading books with hundreds of pages, writing two-page essays, and solving story problems that involved multiplication and division.

This remarkable transformation over the course of just a few years became possible, in part, because of profound changes in children's thinking. We'll examine these changes in Module 7.1, where we'll see how memory expands as children grow, and also in Module 7.2, where we'll consider children's and adolescents' problem-solving skills. Finally, in Module 7.3 we'll take a closer look at academic skills, tracing children's evolving mastery of reading, writing, and mathematics.

**7.1**  Memory

**7.2**  Problem Solving

**7.3**  Academic Skills

1 The Science of Child Development

2 Genetic Bases of Child Development

3 Prenatal Development, Birth, and the Newborn

4 Growth and Health

5 Perceptual and Motor Development

6 Theories of Cognitive Development

7

# Cognitive Processes and Academic Skills

8 Intelligence and Individual Differences in Cognition

9 Language and Communication

10 Emotional Development

11 Understanding Self and Others

12 Moral Understanding and Behavior

13 Gender and Development

14 Family Relationships

15 Influences Beyond the Family

# 7.1   MEMORY

Origins of Memory

Strategies for Remembering

Knowledge and Memory

## LEARNING OBJECTIVES

- How well do infants remember?

- How do strategies help children to remember?

- How does children's knowledge influence what they remember?

> One afternoon 4-year-old Cheryl came home sobbing and reported that Mr. Johnson, a neighbor and longtime family friend, had taken down her pants and touched her "private parts." Her mother was shocked. Mr. Johnson had always seemed an honest, decent man, which made her wonder if Cheryl's imagination had simply run wild. Yet, at times, he did seem a bit peculiar, so her daughter's claim had a ring of truth.

Regrettably, episodes like this are all too common in America today. When child abuse is suspected and the child is the sole eyewitness, the child often testifies to prosecute the alleged abuser. But can preschool children like Cheryl be trusted to recall events accurately on the witness stand? To answer this question, we need to understand more about how memory develops. We'll start by examining the origins of memory in infancy, then see what factors contribute to its development in childhood and adolescence.

## Origins of Memory

Roots of memory are laid down in the first few months after birth. Young babies remember events for days or even weeks at a time. Among the studies that opened our eyes to the infant's ability to remember were those conducted by Carolyn Rovee-Collier (1997, 1999). The method used in her studies is shown in the photo. A ribbon from a mobile is attached to a 2- or 3-month-old's leg; in each case, within a few minutes, the babies learn to kick to make the mobile move. When Rovee-Collier brought the mobile to the infants' homes several days or a few weeks later, babies would still kick to make the mobile move. If Rovee-Collier waited several weeks to return, most babies forgot that kicking moved the mobile. When that happened, she gave them a reminder—she moved the mobile herself without attaching the ribbon to their foot. Then she would return the next day, hook up the apparatus, and the babies would kick to move the mobile.

Rovee-Collier's experiments show that three important features of memory exist as early as 2 and 3 months of age: (1) an event from the past is remembered, (2) over time, the event can no longer be recalled, and (3) a cue can serve to dredge up a forgotten memory.

From these humble origins, memory improves rapidly in older infants and toddlers. Youngsters can recall more of what they experience and remember it longer (Courage & Howe, 2004; Pelphrey et al., 2004). When shown novel actions with toys and later asked to imitate what they saw, toddlers can remember more than infants and remember the actions for longer periods (Bauer, Burch, & Kleinknecht, 2002). For example, if shown how to make a rattle by first placing a wooden block inside a container, then putting a lid on

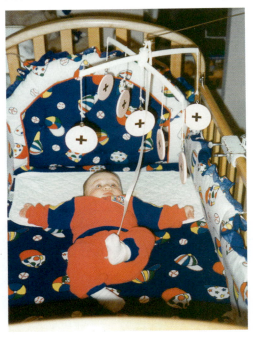

Infants rapidly learn that kicking moves the mobile; days later, babies will kick immediately, showing that they remember the connection between their action and the mobile's movement.

the container, toddlers are more likely than infants to remember the necessary sequence of steps. Similarly, when infants and toddlers learn to push a lever to move a toy train, older children remember the lever–train link longer (Rovee-Collier, 1999). Combining the results for this task with those of the mobile task used with infants reveals steady growth in memory over the first 18 months. Figure 7-1 shows remarkable change in the length of time that children can remember the connection between actions (kicking, pushing) and consequences (movements of mobile or train): From a week or less in young babies to more than 3 months for $1\frac{1}{2}$-year-olds.

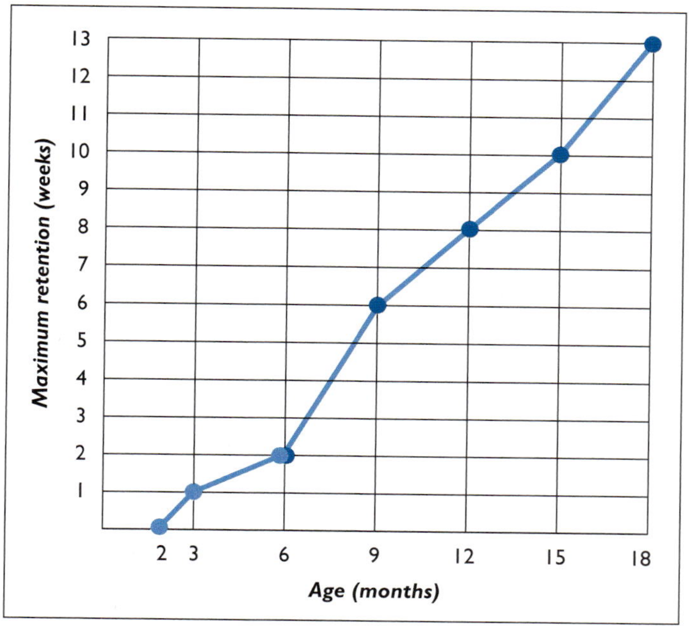

**BRAIN DEVELOPMENT AND MEMORY.** These improvements in memory can be traced, in part, to growth in the brain regions that support memory (Bauer, 2004). On the one hand, the brain structures primarily responsible for the initial storage of information, including the hippocampus and amygdala, seem to develop very early—by age 6 months. On the other hand, the structure responsible for retrieving these stored memories, the frontal cortex, for example, develops much later—into the 2nd year. Development of memory during the first 2 years reflects growth in these two different brain regions.

FIGURE 7-1

Once youngsters begin to talk, we can study their memory skills using most of the same methods we use with older children and adults. Research using these methods has linked age-related improvement in memory to two factors (Kail, 1990; Schneider & Bjorklund, 1998). First, as children grow, they use more effective strategies for remembering. Second, children's growing factual knowledge of the world allows them to organize information more completely and, therefore, to remember better. We'll look at each of these factors in the next few pages.

## Strategies for Remembering

Last week, after I wrote four pages for this book at a pace that would have made popular novelist Tom Clancy green with envy, the unthinkable happened—a power failure knocked out my computer and all those wonderful words were lost. If I had only saved the text to the hard drive . . . but I hadn't.

This tale of woe sets the stage for understanding how strategies aid memory. Recall that working memory is used for briefly storing a small amount of information, such as the words in these sentences. However, as you read additional sentences, they displace words read earlier from working memory. If you want to learn all of this information, it must be transferred to and retained in long-term memory. Anything not transferred from working memory to long-term memory will be lost, just as my unsaved words vanished from the computer's memory with the power failure.

*Memory strategies* **are techniques or activities that improve remembering.** There are many of these. Some strategies help maintain information in working memory, whereas others help transfer information to long-term memory. Still others help retrieve information from long-term memory.

Children begin to use memory strategies early. Preschool children look at or touch objects that they've been told to remember

As children develop, they begin to use different strategies to improve memory.

(DeLoache, 1984). Looking and touching aren't very effective, but they tell us that preschoolers understand that they should be doing *something* to try to remember; remembering doesn't happen automatically!

During the elementary-school years, children begin to use more powerful strategies. **For example, 7- and 8-year-olds use *rehearsal*, a strategy of repetitively naming information that is to be remembered.** A child wanting to call a new friend will rehearse the phone number from the time she finds the number in the phone book until she places the call.

As children get older, they learn other memory strategies. **One is *organization*: structuring material to be remembered so that related information is placed together.** For example, a seventh grader trying to remember major battles of the American Civil War could organize them geographically (e.g., Shiloh and Fort Donelson in Tennessee, Antietam and Monocacy in Maryland) or chronologically (e.g., Fort Sumter and First Manassas in 1861, Gettysburg and Vicksburg in 1863). **Another strategy is *elaboration*—embellishing information to be remembered to make it more memorable.** To see elaboration in action, imagine a child who can never remember if the second syllable of *rehearsal* is spelled *her* (as it sounds) or *hear*. The child could remember the correct spelling by reminding herself that *rehearsal* is like *re-hear-ing*. Thus, imaging herself "re-hearing" a sound would make it easier to remember the spelling of *rehearsal*. Finally, as children grow they're also more likely to use external aids to memory: They are more likely to make notes and to write down information on calendars so that, like the girl in the photo, they won't forget future events (Eskitt & Lee, 2002).

**METACOGNITION.** Just as there's not much value to a filled toolbox if you don't know how to use the tools, memory strategies aren't much good unless children know when to use them. For example, rehearsal is a great strategy for remembering phone numbers but a lousy one for remembering amendments to the U.S. Constitution or the plot of *Hamlet*. During the elementary-school years and adolescence, children gradually learn to identify different kinds of memory problems and the memory strategies most appropriate to each. For example, when reading a textbook or watching a television newscast, outlining or writing a summary are good strategies because they identify the main points and organize them. Children gradually become more skilled at selecting appropriate strategies, but even high-school students do not always use effective learning strategies when they should (Kuhn, 2000; Pierce & Lange, 2000).

School-age children often use external aids to help them remember, such as writing down events on a calendar.

> Metamemory includes the ability to diagnose problems accurately and to monitor the effectiveness of a memory strategy.

After children choose a memory strategy, they need to monitor its effectiveness. That is, they need to decide if the strategy is working. For example, by self-testing—asking themselves questions about the material—children can determine if the strategy is helping them learn. If it's not, they need to begin anew, reanalyzing the memory task to select a better approach. If the strategy is working, they should determine the portion of the material they have not yet mastered and concentrate their efforts there. Monitoring improves gradually with age. For example, elementary-school children can accurately identify which material they have not yet learned, but they do not consistently focus their study efforts on this material (Bjorklund, 2005).

**Diagnosing memory problems accurately and monitoring the effectiveness of memory strategies are two important elements of *metamemory*, which refers to a child's informal understanding of memory.** That is, as children develop, they learn more about how memory operates and devise intuitive theories of memory that represent an extension of the theory of mind described in Module 6.3. For example, children learn that memory is fallible (i.e., they sometimes forget!) and that some types of memory tasks are easier than others (e.g., remembering the main idea of the Gettysburg address is simpler than remembering it word for word). This growing knowledge of memory helps children to use memory strategies more effectively, just as an experienced carpenter's accumulated knowledge of wood tells her when to use nails, screws, or glue to join two boards.

Of course, children's growing understanding of memory is paralleled by growing understanding of all cognitive processes. **Such knowledge and awareness of cognitive processes is called *metacognitive knowledge*.** Metacognitive knowledge grows rapidly during the elementary-school years: Children come to know much about perception, attention, intentions, knowledge, and thinking (Flavell, 1999, 2000). For example, school-age children know that sometimes they deliberately direct their attention—as in searching for a parent's face in a crowd. But they also know that sometimes events capture attention—as with an unexpected clap of thunder (Parault & Schwanenflugel, 2000).

One of the most important features of children's metacognitive knowledge is their understanding of the connections among goals, strategies, monitoring, and outcomes. That is, as shown in the diagram, children come to realize that on a broad spectrum of tasks—ranging from learning words in a spelling list to learning to spike a volleyball to learning to get along with an overly talkative classmate seated nearby—they need to regulate their learning by understanding the goal and selecting a means to achieve that goal. Then they determine whether the chosen method is working. **Effective *cognitive self-regulation*—that is, skill at identifying goals, selecting effective strategies, and monitoring accurately—is a characteristic of successful students** (McCormick & Pressley, 1997; Zimmerman, 2001). A student may decide that writing each spelling word twice before the test is a good way to get all the words right. When the student gets only 70 percent correct on the first test, he switches to a new strategy (e.g., writing each word four times, plus writing its definition), showing the adaptive nature of cognitive processes in self-regulated learners.

Strategies, metamemory, and metacognition are essential for effective remembering, but as you'll see in the next few pages, knowledge is also an aid to memory.

## Knowledge and Memory

To see how knowledge influences memory, let's look at a study in which 10-year-olds and adults tried to remember sequences of numbers (Chi, 1978). As shown in the graph, adults remembered more numbers than children. Next participants tried to remember the positions of objects in a matrix. This time, 10-year-olds' recall was much better than that of adults.

What was responsible for this unusual reversal of the expected age difference? Actually, the objects were chess pieces on a chessboard; and the

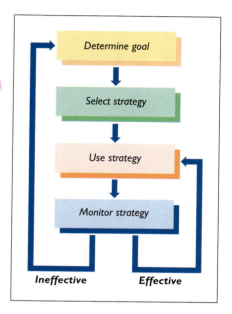

FIGURE 7-2

FIGURE 7-3

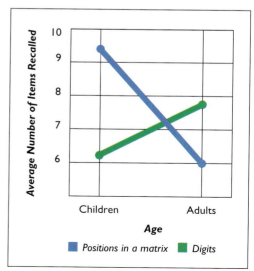

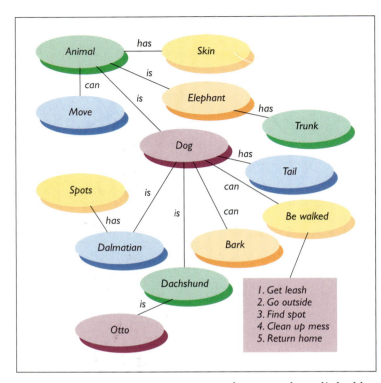

**FIGURE 7-4**

Highly familiar activities, such as baking cookies, are often stored in memory as scripts, which denote the events in the activity and the sequence in which they occur.

children were skilled chess players but the adults were novices. The positions of the pieces were taken from actual games, so the configurations were familiar to the child chess players. For the adults, who lacked knowledge of chess, the patterns seemed arbitrary. The children, in contrast, had prior knowledge to organize and give meaning to the patterns, and thus could recognize and then recall the whole configuration instead of many isolated pieces. It was as if the adults were seeing this meaningless pattern:

nnccbasbccbn

whereas the children were seeing this:

nbc cbs abc cnn.

Usually, of course, the knowledge that allows a child to organize information and give it meaning increases gradually with age (Schneider & Bjorklund, 1998). Researchers often depict knowledge as a network like the one in the diagram, which shows part of a 13-year-old's knowledge of animals. The entries in the network are linked by different types of associations. Some of the links denote membership in categories (dalmatian is a dog), and others denote properties (elephant has a trunk). **Still others denote a *script*, a memory structure used to describe the sequence in which events occur.** The list of events in walking the dog is a script.

A network diagram like this for a younger child would have fewer entries and fewer and weaker connecting links. Consequently, the youngster cannot organize information as extensively, which makes remembering more difficult than for an older child.

Nevertheless, the knowledge that young children have is organized; and this turns out to be a powerful asset. In the case of events that fit scripts, for example, they needn't try to remember each individual activity; instead, they simply remember the script. When the preschooler in the photo wants to tell his dad about baking cookies, he can simply retrieve the "baking cookies" script and use it to organize his recall of the different events. Knowledge can also distort memory. If a specific experience does not match a child's knowledge (e.g., it differs from a script), the experience is sometimes forgotten or distorted so that it conforms to the existing knowledge (Farrar & Boyer-Pennington, 1999; Levy & Boston, 1994). For example, told a story about a female helicopter pilot, many youngsters will remember the pilot as a man because their knowledge network specifies that pilots are men.

Because older children often have more knowledge than younger children, they are sometimes more prone to memory distortions than younger children. In the "Spotlight on Theories" feature, we'll see one theory that accounts for this surprising finding.

## Spotlight on Theories
**Fuzzy Trace Theory**

### BACKGROUND

Children's knowledge of the world usually helps them remember, but sometimes it leads to inaccurate or distorted memory. Such memory errors, although common for children and adolescents, are still poorly understood.

### THE THEORY

According to *fuzzy trace theory*, developed by Charles J. Brainerd and Valerie Reyna (2004, 2005), most experiences can be stored in memory exactly (verbatim) or in terms of their basic meaning (gist). A 10-year-old who reads an invitation to a birthday party may store the information in memory as "the party starts at 7:30 P.M." (verbatim) or as "the party is after dinner" (gist). A 14-year-old who gets a grade on a science test may store it as "I got 75% correct" (verbatim) or "I got an average grade" (gist).

Throughout development, children store information in memory in both verbatim and gist formats, but young children are biased toward verbatim memory traces; during childhood and adolescence, a bias toward gist traces emerges. That is, older children and adolescents typically represent experiences and information in terms of gist, instead of verbatim. (The theory gets its name from its emphasis on gist memory traces that are vague or fuzzy.)

**HYPOTHESIS:** Some memory errors depend on gist processing. If older children and adolescents are biased to gist processing, they should be more prone to those errors than are younger children. For example, a common error occurs when people are asked to remember related words such as *rest, awake, bed, snooze, blanket, snore,* and *dream.* Typically, about three fourths of adults will claim to have seen *sleep* even though it was not presented. Because older children and adolescents extract the gist of the meanings of these words ("they're about sleep"), they should be more susceptible to the illusion than younger children, who more often store the words verbatim.

> According to fuzzy trace theory, younger children more often remember verbatim but older children and adolescents typically remember the gist.

**TEST:** Brainerd, Reyna, and Forrest (2002) presented lists of 15 words to 5-year-olds, 11-year-olds, and adults. As in the previous example, the words in each list were highly associated with a critical word, which was not presented. Later, participants were asked to recall the word lists. Not surprisingly, word recall increased substantially with age: adults recalled 60 percent of the words, compared to 39 percent for 11-year-olds and 19 percent for 5-year-olds. More interesting is how frequently children and adults "remembered" the critical word that had not actually been presented: Adults did so 53 percent of the time, compared to 27 percent for 11-year-olds and 10 percent for 5-year-olds.

**CONCLUSION:** False memories—in this case "remembering" a word that was never presented—were rare in young children but more common in older children and much more frequent in adults. This result is consistent with fuzzy trace theory, in which these memory errors are a consequence of the greater tendency for older children and adults to remember the gist of what they've experienced.

**APPLICATION:** Siblings sometimes argue about past events—who did (or said) something in the past. For example:

OLDER CHILD:   "I took the trash out last night just like I always do."

YOUNGER CHILD:   "Nuh-uh. You were too busy. So I did it."

Listening to these arguments, it's tempting for parents to side with the older child, assuming that older children usually remember past events more accurately. That's not a bad assumption but the paradox is that the same processes that enhance older children's remembering also make them more prone to certain kinds of memory errors. Consequently, parents need to be cautious and be certain that the situation is not one in which an older child's memory is likely to be inaccurate, an illusion caused by the older child's greater reliance on gist processing. In the example here, the older child's memory of what happened may actually be based on his well-established script of what he *usually* does in the evening. ■

Thus, although children's growing knowledge usually helps them to remember, sometimes it can interfere with accurate memory. In the next section, we'll look at another link between knowledge and memory—children's memory of their own lives.

**AUTOBIOGRAPHICAL MEMORY.**   Start by answering these questions:

Who was your teacher in fourth grade?

Where (and with whom) was your first kiss?

Was your high-school graduation indoors or outdoors?

In answering these questions, you searched memory, just as you would search memory to answer questions such as "What is the capital of Canada?" and "Who invented the sewing machine?" However, answers to questions about Canada and sewing machines are based on general knowledge that you have not experienced personally; answers to questions about your fourth-grade teacher, your first kiss, and your high-school graduation are based on knowledge unique to your own life. *Autobiographical memory* **refers to people's memory of the significant events and experiences of their own lives.** Autobiographical memory is important because it helps people construct a personal life history. In addition, autobiographical memory allows people to relate their experiences to others, creating socially shared memories (Bauer, 2006).

Autobiographical memory originates in the preschool years. According to one influential theory (Nelson & Fivush, 2004), autobiographic memory emerges gradually, as children acquire the component skills. Infants and toddlers have the basic memory skills that allow them to remember past events. Layered on top of these memory skills during the preschool years are language skills and a child's sense of self. Language allows children to become conversational partners. After infants begin to talk, parents often converse with them about past and future events—particularly about personal experiences in the child's past and future. Parents may talk about what the child did today at day care or remind the child about what she will be doing this weekend. In conversations like these, parents teach their children the important features of events and how events are organized. Children's autobiographical memories are richer when parents talk about past events in detail and encourage their children to participate in these conversations. In contrast, when parents' talk is limited to direct questions that can be answered "yes" or "no," children's autobiographical memories are less extensive.

> Infantile amnesia, in which people can't recall events from early in life, may be due to limits in toddlers' language and their sense of self.

How does an emergent sense of self contribute to autobiographical memory? I describe sense of self in detail in Module 11.1, but the key idea is that 1- and 2-year-olds rapidly acquire a sense that they exist independently, in space and time. An emerging sense of self thus provides coherence and continuity to children's experience. Children realize that the self who went to the park a few days ago is the same self who is now at a birthday party and is the same self who will read a book with Dad before bedtime. The self provides a personal timeline that anchors a child's recall of the past (and anticipation of the future). Thus, a sense of self, language skills that allow children to converse with parents about past and future, and basic memory skills all contribute to the emergence of autobiographical memory in preschool children.

Older children, adolescents, and adults remember few events from their lives that took place before autobiographical memory is in place (Kail, 1990). *Infantile amnesia* refers to the inability to remember events from one's early life. Adults recall nothing from infancy, but they remember an ever-increasing number of events from about age 3 or 4 years (Eacott, 1999; Schneider & Bjorklund, 1998). For example, when the 2-year-old in the photo is older, he won't remember his brother's birth (Peterson & Rideout, 1998; Quas et al., 1999).* But there's a good chance the older boy will remember his brother's second—or certainly his third—birthday.

Many of the same factors that forge an autobiographical memory contribute to infantile amnesia. For example, once children learn to talk (at about age 2 years), they tend to rely on language to represent their past (Nelson, 1993). Consequently, their earlier, prelingual experiences may be difficult to retrieve from memory, just as after you reorganize your bedroom you may have trouble finding things (Simcock & Hayne, 2002). And some theorists would argue that, because infants and toddlers have no sense of self, they lack the autobiographical timeline that's used to organize experiences later in life (Howe & Courage, 1997).

Thus, personal experiences from our earliest years usually can't be recalled because of inadequate language or inadequate sense of self (Harley & Reese, 1999). Beginning in the preschool years, however, autobiographical memory provides a cohesive framework for remembering life's significant events. Unfortunately, some children's autobiographical memories include memories of abuse. Can these memories be trusted? We'll see in the next section.

**EYEWITNESS TESTIMONY.**   Remember Cheryl, the 4-year-old in the module-opening vignette who claimed that a neighbor had touched her "private parts"? If Cheryl's comments lead to a police investigation, Cheryl's testimony will be critical. But can her recall of events be trusted? This question is difficult to answer. In legal proceedings, children are often interviewed repeatedly, sometimes as many as 10 to 15 times. Over the course of repeated questioning, they may confuse what actually happened with what others suggest may have happened. When, as in the

Infantile amnesia is the inability to remember events from early in one's life, such as the birth of a younger sibling.

When Courtney was 12 months old she fell on the sidewalk and went to the emergency room for stitches in her chin. Now she's a mother and enjoys telling her children how brave she was at the hospital. What aspect of this story doesn't ring true?

7.1

*Perhaps you're not convinced because you vividly recall significant events that occurred when you were 2, such as the birth of a sibling, a move to a different home, or the death of a close friend or relative. In reality, you are probably not remembering the actual event. Instead, I can almost guarantee that you're remembering others' retelling of these events and your role in them, not the events themselves. Events like these are often socially shared memories and that's the basis for your memory.

When trying to remember past events, young children sometimes "remember" what others suggest might have happened in the past, particularly when the suggestion comes from a person in authority.

situation in the photo, the questioner is an adult in a position of authority, children often believe that what is suggested by the adult actually happened (Lampinen & Smith, 1995). As you'll see in the "Focus on Research" feature, preschoolers are particularly prone to confusion of this sort (Ceci & Bruck, 1995, 1998).

## Focus on Research

### Do Stereotypes and Suggestions Influence Preschoolers' Reports?

*Who were the investigators, and what was the aim of the study?* During legal proceedings, children are often interviewed repeatedly. In the process, interviewers sometimes suggest that certain events took place. Cheryl might be asked, "When Mr. Johnson touched your private parts, was anyone else around?" a question implying that Mr. Johnson definitely touched Cheryl. Furthermore, interviewers may suggest to children that the accused is a bad person, which may make suggestions of abuse more plausible to children. Michelle D. Leichtman and Stephen J. Ceci (1995) wanted to know if repeated questioning and hints about an adult's nature would influence preschool children's recall of events.

*How did the investigators measure the topic of interest?* Leichtman and Ceci had a man named Sam Stone briefly visit classes of 3- and 4-year-olds and 5- and 6-year-olds at a day-care center. During his visit, Sam greeted the teacher, who introduced him to the class. Sam mentioned that the story being read by the teacher was one of his favorites; then he waved goodbye and left the room.

Leichtman and Ceci created four different conditions, shown in the diagram, that differed in what children were told before and after Sam's visit. Children in the control condition were interviewed after the visit, every week for 4 weeks. In these interviews, youngsters were simply asked to describe Sam's visit.

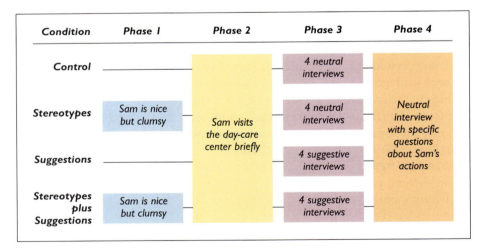

| Condition | Phase 1 | Phase 2 | Phase 3 | Phase 4 |
|---|---|---|---|---|
| **Control** | | | 4 neutral interviews | |
| **Stereotypes** | Sam is nice but clumsy | Sam visits the day-care center briefly | 4 neutral interviews | Neutral interview with specific questions about Sam's actions |
| **Suggestions** | | | 4 suggestive interviews | |
| **Stereotypes plus Suggestions** | Sam is nice but clumsy | | 4 suggestive interviews | |

FIGURE 7-5

The *stereotype* condition differed from the control condition in one way: Three times prior to Sam's visit, teachers described Sam as a nice but clumsy man, thereby implying that children should expect Sam to be clumsy. The *suggestions* condition also differed from the control condition: During each of the 4 weekly interviews that followed Sam's visit, the interviewer made misleading suggestions that Sam had ripped a book and soiled a teddy bear, such as "Remember when Sam Stone ripped the book? Did he rip it on purpose or by accident?" (p. 577). Of course, he had done neither. In the fourth condition, *stereotypes plus suggestions*, teachers told children about Sam's clumsiness before the visit and interviewers made misleading suggestions afterward.

Finally, 10 weeks after Sam had visited the classroom, a different interviewer, one not present during Sam's visit or the previous interviews, asked children several questions about what had happened when Sam visited, including whether Sam had ripped a book or soiled a teddy bear.

*Who were the children in the study?* A total of 176 preschool children participated. Half were 3- and 4-year-olds and half were 5- and 6-year-olds.

*What was the design of the study?* This study was experimental. There were three independent variables: (a) the age of the child, (b) whether the child was told before Sam's visit that he was clumsy, and (c) whether the child received misleading suggestions after Sam's visit. The dependent variable was the child's answer to the interviewers' misleading questions. That is, Leichtman and Ceci counted the percentage of time that children said they had actually seen Sam rip a book or soil the teddy bear, events that never happened. The study was also cross-sectional because it included a group of younger children (3- and 4-year-olds) and a group of older children (5- and 6-year-olds).

*Were there ethical concerns with the study?* No. Sam's visit, the teachers' comments about Sam beforehand, and the interviews afterward posed no special risks to children.

*What were the results?* Children's answers to the misleading questions are shown in the graph. For simplicity, I've shown only the data for 3- and 4-year-olds. The data for 5- and 6-year-olds were similar but the effects were smaller. (That is, the older children were less suggestible than the younger children.) Almost no children in the control condition claimed to have seen Sam rip a book or soil a bear. However, some children in the stereotyped condition claimed to have seen Sam rip a book or soil a bear, and more than one third of the children in the suggestions condition claimed he did one or the other. When stereotypes and suggestions were combined, almost half the children said they had seen events that never took place. Although the 5- and 6-year-olds described events much more accurately, even 15 percent of these youngsters claimed to have seen Sam rip a book or soil a bear.

*What did the investigators conclude?* Leichtman and Ceci believe that whether preschoolers are suggestible depends entirely on how their memory for events is probed. The results from their control condition suggest that, without stereotypes and suggestions, preschoolers are unlikely to report events that never happened. However, when adults suggest that a person is likely to behave in a particular way and later imply that some events actually did happen, many preschoolers will go along. From their results, since Cheryl's report was spontaneous, not elicited by repeated questions, it is probably trustworthy.

*What converging evidence would strengthen these conclusions?* Falsely claiming that a visitor ripped a book is a far cry from testifying falsely in a case of child abuse. You can think of many ways in which the target events differ: Abuse involves the child

Unless misled by others, preschoolers rarely "recall" events that didn't happen.

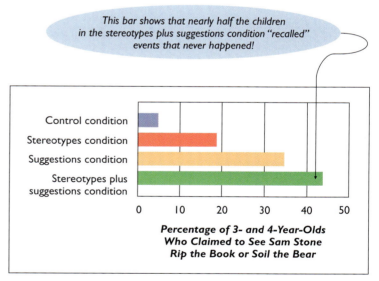

This bar shows that nearly half the children in the stereotypes plus suggestions condition "recalled" events that never happened!

Percentage of 3- and 4-Year-Olds Who Claimed to See Sam Stone Rip the Book or Soil the Bear

FIGURE 7-6

directly, is very embarrassing to the child, and is extraordinarily stressful; observing the torn book is none of these. Consequently, it would be valuable to determine whether young children are equally suggestible when remembering incidents of abuse. Of course, designing an experiment of this sort would be unethical; we can't expose children directly to abuse nor can we suggest to them that others have been abused. A compromise is to study children's memory for the events of a physical exam by a health care professional. These exams involve the child's body and are often mildly embarrassing and mildly stressful. Research such as this can demonstrate whether young children are suggestible in settings that more closely resemble actual child abuse, yet it still preserves the rights of children as research participants. ■

Perhaps you're skeptical of findings like these. Surely it must be possible to tell when a young child is describing events that never happened. In fact, although law enforcement officials and child protection workers believe they can usually tell whether children are telling the truth, professionals often cannot distinguish true and false reports (Gordon, Baker-Ward, & Ornstein, 2001). And maybe you doubt that interviewers routinely ask the leading or suggestive questions that are the seeds of false memories. But analyses of videotapes of actual interviews reveal that trained investigators often ask children leading questions and make suggestive comments (Lamb, Steinberg, & Esplin, 2000). For example, in one famous case in which a preschool teacher named Kelly was accused of sexually abusing children in her class, the children were asked the following leading questions (among many, many others):

Do you think that Kelly was not good when she was hurting you all?

When did Kelly say these words? Piss, shit, sugar?

When Kelly kissed you, did she ever put her tongue in your mouth?
(Bruck & Ceci, 1995)

Each of the questions is misleading by implying that something happened when actually it might not have.

Adults aren't the only ones who taint children's memories; peers can, too! When, for example, some children in a class experience an event (e.g., a class field trip or a special class visitor), they often talk about the event with classmates who weren't there; later, these absent classmates readily describe what happened and often insist they were actually there (Principe & Ceci, 2002).

Preschool children are particularly suggestible. Why? One idea is that they are more suggestible due to limited source-monitoring skills (Poole & Lindsay, 1995). Older children, adolescents, and adults often know the source of information that they remember. For example a father recalling his daughter's piano recitals will know the source of many of his memories: Some are from personal experience (he attended the recital), some he saw on video tape, and some are based on his daughter's descriptions. Preschool children are not particularly skilled at such source monitoring. When recalling past events, preschoolers are often confused about who did or said what and, when confused in this manner, they frequently assume that they must have experienced something personally. Consequently, when preschool children are asked leading questions (e.g., "When the man touched you, did it hurt?'), this information is also stored in memory, but without the source. Because preschool children are not skilled at monitoring sources, they have trouble distinguishing what they actually experienced from what interviewers imply that they experienced.

Although preschoolers are easily mislead, they can provide reliable testimony. Here are guidelines derived from research for improving the reliability of child witnesses (Ceci & Bruck, 1995, 1998; Gordon et al., 2001):

- Warn children that interviewers may sometimes try to trick them or suggest things that didn't happen.
- Ensure that interviewers' questions evaluate alternative explanations of what happened and who was involved.
- Do not question children repeatedly on a single issue.

Following these guidelines will foster the conditions under which preschoolers (and older children, too) are likely to recall the past more accurately and thereby be better witnesses. The "Child Development and Family Policy" feature shows one way in which research findings have changed the methods used to interview children.

> Preschoolers' testimony is more accurate when children are warned that interviewers may try to trick them, when interviewers test alternate hypotheses, and when children aren't questioned repeatedly.

## Child Development and Family Policy
### Interviewing Children Effectively

Toward the end of the 20th century, the number of instances of child abuse had skyrocketed, followed soon by reports that some adults were wrongly convicted based on children's false memories. Consequently, many state and federal agencies created task forces to determine the best way to respond to the challenges of evaluating allegations of child abuse. In Michigan, for example, the Governor's Task Force on Children's Justice was created in 1992 and quickly identified the need for a standard protocol for interviewing children in child-abuse cases, a protocol that would avoid contaminating children's testimony by using, for example, misleading questions like those listed on page 210. Debra Poole, a psychologist at Central Michigan University and a leading expert on children's eyewitness testimony, was hired to develop the protocol. Poole was an obvious choice because she had recently written a book with Michael E. Lamb (1998), *Investigative Interviews of Children: A Guide for Helping Professionals*, which was published by the American Psychological Association. Working with agencies in nine Michigan counties, Poole devised a preliminary interview protocol that was tested in those counties. The revised protocol was then published by the Governor's Task Force (1998) and the procedures were implemented statewide. The new procedures, derived largely from research such as I described earlier in this module, is designed to meet the needs of all parties involved: The procedures "will reduce trauma to children, make the information gained more credible in the court process, and protect the rights of the accused" (Governor's Task Force, 1998, p. v). And the new procedures document that research findings can be the stable foundation for public policy. ▪

### CHECK YOUR LEARNING

RECALL  Describe how children use strategies to help them remember.
Summarize the processes that give rise to autobiographical memory in toddlers.

INTERPRET  Distinguish the situations in which gist processing of experience is advantageous (i.e., it leads to better memory) from those in which it is not.

APPLY  Describe how research on children's eyewitness testimony illustrates connections among emotional, cognitive, and social development.

Due to infantile amnesia, it's not very likely that Courtney is remembering her actual experience at the emergency room. Instead, her recall of these events is based on what she remembers others saying about what happened that day. She's heard these stories so many times, she can easily imagine seeing herself in the emergency room as a 12-month-old.

**7.1**

# 7.2 PROBLEM SOLVING

**Developmental Trends in Solving Problems**

**Features of Children's and Adolescents' Problem Solving**

**Scientific Problem Solving**

## LEARNING OBJECTIVES

- Do older children and adolescents typically solve problems better than younger children?

- What factors contribute to children's and adolescents' success in solving problems?

- Can children and adolescents reason scientifically?

*Brad, age 12, wanted to go to a hobby shop on New Year's Day. His mother, Terri, doubted that the store was open on a holiday, so she asked Brad to call first. Moments later Brad returned and said, "Let's go!" When they arrived at the hobby shop, it was closed. Annoyed, Terri snapped, "I thought you called!" Brad answered, "I did. They didn't answer, so I figured they were too busy to come to the phone." Later that day, Brad's 3-year-old sister grabbed an opened can of soda from the kitchen counter, looked at Terri and said, "This isn't yours 'cause there's no lipstick." Terri thought her daughter's inference was sophisticated, particularly when compared to her son's illogical reasoning earlier in the day.*

According to Piaget's theory, reasoning and problem solving become progressively more sophisticated as children develop. Piaget believed that young children's reasoning (reflected in the name "preoperational thought") was particularly limited and that adolescents' reasoning (reflected in the name "formal operational thought") was quite powerful. But research has since shown that this account was wrong in two ways: It underestimated young children, who, like Brad's sister, often astonish us with the inferences they draw. And it overestimated adolescents who, like Brad, frequently frustrate us with their flawed logic.

In this module, we'll trace the growth of problem-solving skills in childhood and adolescence. We'll see that young children do indeed solve problems with far greater skill than predicted by Piaget but that, throughout development, many factors limit the success with which children, adolescents, and adults solve problems.

## Developmental Trends in Solving Problems

Solving problems is as much a part of children's daily lives as eating and sleeping. Think about some of the following common examples:

- After dinner a child tries to figure out how to finish homework and watch his favorite TV program.

- A child wants to get her bike out of the garage, where it's trapped behind the car and the lawn mower.

- At school, a first grader tries to decide the surest way to be at the head of the line for lunch.

- A teenager wants to come up with a way to avoid raking the leaves.

In each case, there's a well-defined goal (e.g., riding the bike, being at the head of the line) and the child is deciding how to achieve it.

As a general rule, of course, as children get older they solve problems like these more often and solve them more effectively. This general developmental trend is evident in a classic study by Siegler (1976) in which children were asked to solve problems involving a balance scale. They saw a scale like the one in Figure 7-7, in

FIGURE 7-7

which identical weights had been placed at various positions on either side. Children were asked which side would go down if the supporting blocks were removed. Across problems, the number of weights varied, as did their positions. The 5- and 6-year-olds solved slightly fewer than half of the problems correctly, but 16- and 17-year-olds solved two thirds of them correctly.

The younger children in Siegler's (1976) study failed more often than they succeeded, but this doesn't mean that younger children are always inept at solving problems. In fact, research has produced many instances in which young children solve problems successfully. For example, when asked what they could do if they went to the grocery store but didn't have enough money or if they went to the beach but forgot to bring lunch, most 4- and 5-year-olds suggest plausible, effective solutions. For example, they suggest borrowing money from someone they know and buying lunch at the concession building (Hudson, Shapiro, & Sosa, 1995). What's more, even infants can solve simple problems. If an attractive toy is placed on a cloth, so that the cloth but not the toy is within the infant's reach, 7-month-olds quite regularly grab the cloth, then pull it to get the toy—a simple but wonderfully effective method of achieving the goal of playing with an interesting toy (Willatts, 1999).

Even infants can solve some problems effectively, for example, by pulling on the string to bring the toy within reach.

And adolescents don't always solve problems as readily as they solved the balance-scale problems in Siegler's (1976) study. Here, too, it's not hard to find counter examples—instances in which adolescents' problem solving is inefficient, haphazard, or just plain wrong. For example, consider everyday problems like the following, in which statistical evidence suggests one solution but personal experience suggests another:

> Erica wants to go to a baseball game to try to catch a fly ball. She calls the main office and learns that almost all fly balls have been caught in section 43. Just before she chooses her seats, she learns that her friend Jimmy caught 2 fly balls last week sitting in section 10. Which section is most likely to give Erica the best chance to catch a fly ball? (Kokis et al., 2002, p. 34).

Teenagers rely upon the friend's personal experience nearly half the time, ignoring the much stronger statistical evidence (Kokis et al., 2002).

Or think about the following problem:

> Imagine that you want to enter one of two raffles. The first one advertises, "50 tickets, 5 winners, so you have a 10 percent chance of winning!" The second advertises, "500 tickets, 40 winners, so you have an 8 percent chance of winning!" Which raffle would you enter?

Many adolescents choose to enter the second raffle—even though they've just read that the odds of winning are less (8 percent versus 10 percent)—apparently because they see that there are 40 winning tickets, not just 5 (Kokis et al., 2002). In the

*Children typically solve problems more readily as they get older, but young children sometimes solve problems well and older children are sometimes quite error prone.*

process, of course, they ignore the fact that the second raffle has 460 losing tickets compared to only 45 in the first raffle!

Thus, research confirms what we saw in the vignette with Brad and his sister: Although children tend to become more effective problem solvers as they get older, even young children sometimes show remarkable problem-solving skill and adolescents often are error prone. In the next section, we'll look at some of the elements that govern children's success in solving problems.

## Features of Children's and Adolescents' Problem Solving

Because problem solving is such an important skill, child-development scientists have been eager to reveal the circumstances that promote children's problem solving. The results of this work are described in the next few pages, organized around important themes that characterize children's problem solving.

**YOUNG CHILDREN SOMETIMES FAIL TO SOLVE PROBLEMS BECAUSE THEY DON'T ENCODE ALL THE IMPORTANT INFORMATION IN A PROBLEM.** When solving a problem, people construct a mental representation that includes the important features of a problem. *Encoding processes* **transform the information in a problem into a mental representation.** In the balance-scale problems, for example, encoding must translate the instructions and each problem into a representation that includes the goal (decide whether the scale will balance) as well as the number of weights and their positions on the scale.

Quite often children's representations of problems are incorrect or incomplete. They fail to encode problem features (or encode them incorrectly), making it unlikely that they will solve problems. On balance-scale problems, for example, young children's representations often include the goal and number of weights, but not their positions (Siegler, 1976). And on conservation of liquid problems like the one shown on page 168, young children's representations often include the heights of the containers but not their diameters. A more subtle form of flawed encoding emerges in transitive inference problems, in which children might be told, "Jon is older than Dave. Dave is older than Rob. Who's older, Jon or Rob?" Young children often encode these statements in absolute terms, not relative ones, like this:

Jon = OLD; Dave = NOT OLD

Dave = OLD; Rob = NOT OLD

Encoding in this way leaves children with the conflicting information that Dave is both OLD and NOT OLD, and no way to determine the relative ages of Jon and Rob (Halford, 1993).

When young children's representations lack these key features, it's not surprising that they fail to solve problems. As children grow, their encodings are more likely to be complete, perhaps due to increases in the capacity of working memory and because of greater knowledge of the world (as we'll see in the next section). But even adults' representations are often incomplete. To illustrate, what appears on the head of a U.S. penny? Lincoln's bust (but facing left or right?), a date (but where?), and some words (but what are they?). Your representation of the penny is far from complete, because you've only encoded the features that are essential for using a penny in solving real problems involving cash (i.e., it's copper colored with Lincoln's face). You can see all the features of a penny in the photo.

Our memory representations of familiar objects, such as a penny, are often incomplete, in part because much of the information is not particularly useful (e.g., we don't need to know whether Lincoln is facing left or right).

**YOUNG CHILDREN SOMETIMES FAIL TO SOLVE PROBLEMS BECAUSE THEY DON'T PLAN AHEAD.**    Solving problems, particularly complex ones, often requires planning ahead. For example, the goal "get ready for school" requires planning because it involves coordinating a number of goals—get dressed, eat breakfast, brush teeth, find backpack—which must be completed under time pressure. Faced with problems like this one, young children rarely come up with effective plans. Why? Several factors contribute (Ellis & Siegler, 1997):

- Young children often believe—unrealistically—that they can solve a problem by boldly forging ahead, without an explicit plan. Like many people who hate to read directions that come with new toys or games, young children often find it difficult to inhibit the urge to "let's get moving" in favor of "let's figure this out."
- Planning is hard work and if young children find that their plans often fail, they may see little point in investing the effort.
- Young children may expect parents and other adults to solve complex problems for them.

These factors don't mean that young children never plan or can't plan. For example, when 4-year-olds are asked to solve mazes and are urged to avoid "dead ends" in the maze, they typically pause before drawing and look ahead to find a solution. Often they trace it with their finger first, then draw it (Gardner & Rogoff, 1990). Thus, young children can plan, if they're asked to and the problem is not too complex. But many problems make it difficult or pointless for young children to plan.

**SUCCESSFUL PROBLEM SOLVING TYPICALLY DEPENDS UPON KNOWLEDGE SPECIFIC TO THE PROBLEM AS WELL AS GENERAL PROCESSES.**    Solving a problem often requires that children know some critical facts. For example, in the balance-scale problem described earlier, problem solving depends on knowing the number of weights and their distances; it turns out that 5- and 6-year-olds know that the number of weights matters but don't know that their distance does, which is one reason why they solve fewer problems than older children (Siegler, 1976). Similarly, during the elementary-school years, children become much more adept at solving arithmetic word problems such as this one: "Joe has two candy bars, then Jessica gives him four more. How many candy bars does Joe have in all?" This improvement comes about as children master their basic arithmetic facts and as they learn how to map different types of word problems onto arithmetic problems (Kail & Hall, 1999).

> Young children sometimes fail to solve problems because they don't encode the necessary information from the problem, they don't plan ahead, and they lack the necessary knowledge.

More often than not, of course, older children have more of the knowledge relevant to solving a problem and so they will be more successful. But effective problem solving depends on more than problem-specific knowledge. **Children often rely on** *heuristics***, rules of thumb that do not guarantee a solution but are often useful in solving a range of problems. One simple but effective strategy is** *means-ends analysis***, in which a person determines the difference between the current and desired situations, then does something to reduce the difference.** If no single action leads directly to the goal, then a person establishes a subgoal, one that moves them closer to the goal. To illustrate, think of a 9-year-old who has pangs of hunger while reading in her bedroom—her goal is getting something to eat. There's no food in her bedroom, so "go to the kitchen" becomes a subgoal and, once there, she can achieve her goal. And the baby on page 213 used means-ends analysis in pulling the cloth toward herself to achieve the main goal of grabbing the toy.

Even preschool children use means-ends analyses to solve problems. This is evident in their efforts to solve the dog-cat-mouse problem shown in the diagram. Three animals and their favorite foods are placed on corners and the child is asked to move the animals along the paths, one at a time, until each animal is paired with its favorite food. In the problem in the figure, moving the cat to the opposite corner would achieve part of that goal and that's what most children do. In contrast, they rarely move an animal away from its favorite food (even though that's often required temporarily) because that is a "bad move" according to means-end analyses (Klahr, 1985). Even though young children often use means-end analyses, they're usually successful only on relatively simple problems in which the difference between the current and desired situations can be achieved in a few moves. They struggle with more complex problems that require generating many subgoals and keeping track of them while en route to the overall goal (DeLoache, Miller, & Pierroutsakos, 1998).

**7.2** Ten-year-old Kayla woke to see the season's first snowfall. She could hardly wait to get outside but then remembered that her sled is hanging on a hook in the garage, beyond her reach. Use means-ends analysis to show how she could achieve her goal of sledding.

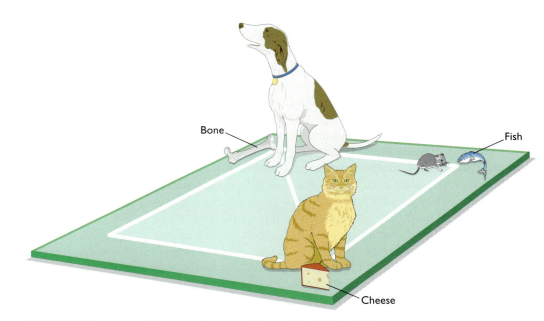

Bone

Fish

Cheese

FIGURE 7-8 Source: With permission from Blackwell Publishing, Ltd.

**CHILDREN AND ADOLESCENTS USE A VARIETY OF STRATEGIES TO SOLVE PROBLEMS.** In Piaget's view, children and adolescents solve problems in fundamentally different ways: 8-year-olds, for example, consistently do so using concrete operational logic; but 13-year-olds do so using formal operational logic. The modern view, introduced in Module 6.2, differs: Children and adolescents call upon several different strategies to solve problems. For example, while playing board games in which a roll of the dice determines how many spaces to move, young children use many strategies to determine the number of moves from the dice (Bjorklund & Rosenblum, 2002). If the dice show 5 and 2, sometimes a child counts aloud "1, 2, 3, 4, 5, 6, 7" and then moves seven spaces; sometimes the child simply counts "5. . .6, 7" and moves; and other times the child glances briefly at the dice, then moves, as if she recalled the sum from memory.

Much the same thing happens, of course, when older children or adolescents learn a new game or a new skill. Initially, they try many different ways to solve a problem. Given enough experience solving a problem, they learn the easiest, most effective strategy and use it as often as possible (Siegler, 2000).

This general approach is captured in Siegler's (1996) overlapping waves model. According to Siegler (1996), children use multiple strategies to solve problems and, over time they tend to use strategies that are faster, more accurate, and take less effort. The model is illustrated in Figure 7-9, which shows how often different hypothetical strategies are used, based on a person's age. Strategy A, for example, is very common among young children but becomes less common with age; Strategy E shows just the opposite profile, becoming more common with age. The vertical lines make it easy to see how often various strategies are used at different ages. Among 7-year-olds, Strategy A is most common, followed by B and D; in contrast, among 14-year-olds, Strategy D is most common, followed by C and E. Thus, children and adolescents are alike in drawing upon a well-stocked kit of tools from which to choose to solve problems; they differ in adolescents typically having a more sophisticated set of tools.

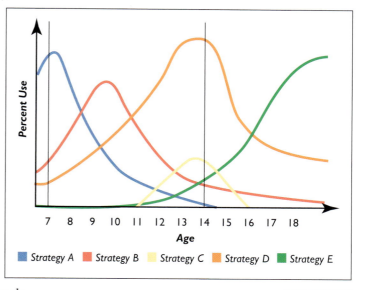

FIGURE 7-9

**COLLABORATION OFTEN ENHANCES CHILDREN'S PROBLEM SOLVING.** In research, children typically solve problems by themselves but in everyday life they often collaborate with parents, siblings, and peers. This collaboration is usually beneficial when the partner is a parent, older child, or more knowledgeable peer. As we saw in Module 6.2, parents and older children often scaffold children's efforts to solve problems, providing structure and direction that allow younger children to accomplish more than they could alone. In laboratory studies, for example, parents often tailor help to the child's needs, watching quietly when children are making headway but giving words of encouragement and hints when their children are stumped (Rogoff, 1998).

Collaboration with peers is sometimes but not always productive and the set-tings that are conducive to effective peer collaboration remain something of a mystery (Siegler & Alibali, 2004). On the one hand, collaboration involving young children like the ones shown in the photo often fails, simply because preschool children lack many of the social and linguistic skills needed to work as part of a team. And peer collaboration is often unproductive when problems are so difficult that neither child has a clue about how to proceed. On the other hand, peer collaboration works when both children are invested in solving the problem and when they share responsibility for doing so.

Collaborative problem solving is often ineffective with young children because they lack the cognitive and social skills needed to work together.

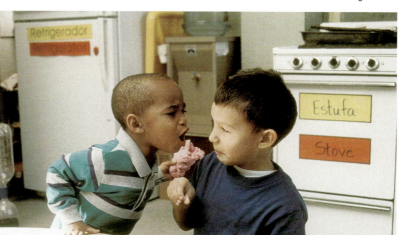

## Scientific Problem Solving

In Chapter 6, we saw that many child-development researchers rely on the child-as-scientist metaphor, in which experiences provide the "data" from which children construct theories that capture their understanding of the material and social world. These theories are usually described as informal because they lack the rigor of real scientific theories and because children and adolescents rarely conduct true experiments designed to test their theories. However, when it comes to the skills associated with real scientific reasoning, children and even adolescents typically have some conspicuous faults:

- **Children and adolescents often devise experiments in which variables are *confounded*—they are combined instead of evaluated independently—so that the results are ambiguous.** For example, if asked to determine how the size of a car's engine, wheels, and tail fins affect its speed, children often manipulate more than one variable at a time. They compare a car with a large engine, large wheels, and large tail fins against a car with a small engine, small wheels, and small tail fins. Not until adulthood do individuals commonly devise experiments in which one variable is manipulated (e.g., size of the wheels) and the rest are held constant, which allows clear conclusions regarding cause and effect (Schauble, 1996).

> Despite the popularity of the "child-as-scientist" metaphor, children and adolescents have limited skill in designing and evaluating real experiments.

- *Children and adolescents often reach conclusions prematurely, basing them on too little evidence.* That is, instead of conducting all of the experiments necessary to isolate the impact of variables, children and adolescents typically conduct a subset of the experiments, and then reach conclusions prematurely. In the previous example about determining a car's speed, children rarely do enough experimentation to provide conclusive evidence about each variable. They might perform experiments showing that a car runs fast with a large engine and slower with large tail fins but also assume that wheel size has no effect without actually doing the critical experiments (Kuhn, Garcia-Mila, Zohar, & Andersen, 1995).

- *Children and adolescents often have difficulty integrating theory and data.* For example, if the results of an experiment are consistent with adolescents' own beliefs, they tend to discount the value of the study (Klaczynski, 2004): if Baptist adolescents read about a flawed experiment, they tend to overlook the flaws if the results show that Baptists make better parents but not when the results show that Baptists make worse parents. (And the same is true of adolescents of other faiths.) In these cases, adolescents use less rigorous standards to evaluate experiments when the evidence supports what they believe (Jacobs & Klaczynski, 2002; Klaczynski, 2000).

These findings suggest that children and adolescents have limited scientific skills. Other findings, however, indicate that young children have some rudimentary scientific skill. For example, children can sometimes tell the kind of evidence that would support a hypothesis. If trying to determine whether an animal has a good sense of smell, 6- to 8-year-olds know that it's better to conduct an experiment that uses a weak-smelling food than a strong-smelling food. And if trying to decide whether a mouse that's loose in a house is large or small, they know that it's better to place a piece of food in a box that has a small opening instead of one with a large opening (Sodian, Zaitchik, & Carey, 1991). In these studies, young children are not designing complete experiments on their own; instead, they are simply evaluating part of an experiment that someone else has planned, which may explain their improved skill (DeLoache et al., 1998).

And it's also clear that even young children can be trained to think more scientifically. For example, 9- and 10-year-olds can be trained in the need to avoid confounded experiments by manipulating one variable at a time. Such training is straightforward—by showing both confounded and unconfounded experiments, then illustrating the difficulty in drawing clear conclusions from confounded experiments—and results in long-lasting improvements in children's understanding of well-designed experiments (Chen & Klahr, 1999).

Thus, the general developmental trend for scientific reasoning resembles the one we saw previously for general problem solving: Overall, children's skill improves steadily as they grow but young children are sometimes amazingly skilled while older children and adolescents are sometimes surprisingly inept. In the next module, we'll see whether children's academic skills (reading, writing, arithmetic) develop in a similar manner.

## Check Your Learning

**Recall** Describe findings that counter the general trend in which children are more successful at solving problems as they get older.

Summarize the reasons why young children often fail to solve problems.

**Interpret** Compare the widely held metaphor of "children as scientists" with the outcomes from research on actual scientific reasoning by children and adolescents.

**Apply** Based on what you know about children's success at solving problems collaboratively, would you recommend that children and adolescents work together on homework?

**Q&Answer**

| | 7.2 |
|---|---|
| Top goal: go sledding | |

Subgoal 1: Get sled

Fact: Sled is on hook in garage, out of reach

Subgoal 2: Get parent to reach sled

Fact: Mom left for work, Dad is asleep

Subgoal 3: Wake Dad

# ACADEMIC SKILLS

# 7.3

## LEARNING OBJECTIVES

- What are the components of skilled reading?

- As children develop, how does their writing improve?

- When do children understand and use quantitative skills?

Reading

Writing

Knowing and Using Numbers

*When Jasmine, a bubbly 3-year-old, is asked how old she'll be on her next birthday, she proudly says, "Four!" while holding up five fingers. Asked to count four objects, whether they're candies, toys, or socks, Jasmine almost always says, "1, 2, 6, 7. . .SEVEN!" Jasmine's older brothers find all this very funny, but her mother thinks that, the obvious mistakes notwithstanding, Jasmine's behavior shows that she knows a lot about numbers and counting. But what, exactly, does Jasmine understand? That question has her mother stumped!*

Children and adolescents use their cognitive skills to accomplish many tasks in a variety of settings. Among the most important of these, however, are the school-related tasks of learning to read, write, and do math. Child-development researchers have studied these domains extensively, as you'll see in this module, which examines the traditional three Rs. We'll start with reading, then examine writing, and end with numbers, where you'll learn why Jasmine counts as she does.

## Reading

Try reading the following sentence:

> Андрей достал билеты на концерт.

Unless you know Russian, you probably didn't make much headway, did you? Now try this one:

> Snore secretary green plastic sleep trucks.

These are English words and you probably read them quite easily, but did you get anything more out of this sentence than the one in Russian? These examples show two important processes involved in skilled reading. **Word recognition is the process of identifying a unique pattern of letters.** Without knowing Russian, your word recognition was not successful in the first sentence. You did not know that *билеты* means "tickets" or that концерт means "concert." What's more, because you could not recognize individual words, you had no idea of the meaning of this sentence. **Comprehension is the process of extracting meaning from a sequence of words.** In the second sentence, your word recognition was perfect, but comprehension was still impossible because the words were presented in a random sequence. These examples remind us just how difficult learning to read can be.

> **Prereading skills involve knowing the letters of the alphabet and the sounds they make.**

In the next few pages, we'll look at how children read. We'll start with the skills that children must have if they are to learn to read, then move to word recognition and comprehension.

**FOUNDATIONS OF READING SKILL.** Reading involves extracting meaning from print and children have much to learn to do this successfully. Children need to know that reading is done with words made of letters, not with pictures or scribbles; that words on a page are separated by spaces; and that in English words are read from left to right. And, of course, they need to know the names of individual letters. These skills improve gradually over the preschool years; for example, U.S. and Canadian 4-year-olds know the names for about half of the letters (Levy et al., 2006; Treiman & Kessler, 2003).

Children learn more about letters and word forms when they're frequently involved in literacy-related activities such as reading with an adult, playing with magnetic letters, or trying to print simple words. And, not surprisingly, children who know more about letters and word forms learn to read more easily than their peers who know less (Levy et al., 2006; Treiman & Kessler, 2003).

A second essential skill is sensitivity to language sounds. **The ability to hear the distinctive sounds of letters is a skill known as *phonological awareness*.** One way to measure phonological awareness is to present several words—*fun, pin, bun, gun*—and then ask the child to pick the word that didn't rhyme with the others. Another way is to ask children to say the first, last, or middle sound of a word: "What's the first sound in *cat*?" These measures have been used in dozens of studies and the outcome is always the same: Phonological awareness is strongly related to success in learning to read (Muter, Hulme, Snowling, & Stevenson, 2004). That is, children who can readily distinguish language sounds learn to read more readily than children who do not. And, as we'll see in Module 8.3, an insensitivity to language sounds is one of the core features of reading disability.

If phonological skill is so essential for learning to read, how can we help children master language sounds? The "Improving Children's Lives" feature describes one easy way.

## *Improving Children's Lives*

### Rhyme Is Sublime Because Sounds Abounds

*The Cat in the Hat* and *Green Eggs and Ham* are two books in the famous Dr. Seuss series. You probably know these stories for their zany plots and extensive use of rhyme. When parents frequently read rhymes—not just Dr. Seuss, but also Mother Goose and other nursery rhymes—their children become more aware of word sounds. Passages like the following one draw children's attention to the different sounds that make up words:

> I do not like them in a house. I do not like them with a mouse. I do not like them here or there. I do not like them anywhere. I do not like green eggs and ham. I do not like them, Sam-I-Am (Geisel, 1960, p. 20).

The more parents read rhymes to their children, the greater their children's phonological awareness, which makes learning to read much easier (Bradley & Bryant, 1983; Erhi et al., 2001).

So the message is clear. Read to children—the more, the better. As the photo shows, children love it when adults read to them, and learning more about word sounds is icing on the cake! ■

Picture-book reading is mutually enjoyable for parent and child and often fosters a child's pre-reading skills.

Storybook reading like that described in this feature is an informal way that parents can foster prereading skills. Sometimes, however, parents go beyond simply reading and take on the role of teacher. They may talk about the names of letters and the sounds they make: "This is a *u*. Sometimes it goes *oo-oo-oo* and sometimes it goes *uh*." Both activities—reading for fun and teaching letter names and sounds while reading—promote phonological awareness and early reading skill (Sénéchal & LeFevre, 2002). And the benefits are not limited to the first steps in learning to read but persist into the middle elementary-school years: Third graders read better when they spent much time as preschoolers reading with their parents (de Jong & Leseman, 2001; Sénéchal & LeFevre, 2002).

**RECOGNIZING WORDS.**    The first step in actual reading is *decoding*, identifying individual words. One way to do this is to say the sounds associated with each letter and then blend the sounds to produce a recognizable word. Such "sounding out" is a common technique among beginning readers. Older children sometimes sound out words, but only when they are unfamiliar, which points to another common way of recognizing words (Coltheart et al., 1993). Words are recognized through direct retrieval from long-term memory: As the individual letters in a word are identified, long-term memory is searched to see if there is a matching sequence of letters. After the child knows that the letters are, in sequence, *c-a-t*, long-term memory is searched for a match and the child recognizes the word as *cat* (Rayner et al., 2001).

So far, word recognition may seem like a one-way street where readers first recognize letters and then recognize words. In reality, we know that information flows both ways: Readers constantly use context to help them recognize letters and words (Rayner et al., 2001). For example, readers typically recognize *t* faster in *cast* than in *asct*. That is, readers recognize letters faster when they appear in words than in nonwords. How do the nearby letters in *cast* help readers to recognize the *t*? As children recognize the first letters in the word as *c*, *a*, and *s*, the possibilities for the last letter become more limited. Because English only includes 4 four-letter words that start with *cas* (well, 5 if you include *Cass*), the last letter can only be *e*, *h*, *k*, or *t*. In contrast, there are no four-letter words (in English) that begin with *acs*, so all 26 letters must be checked, which takes more time than just checking four letters. In this way, a reader's knowledge of words simplifies the task of recognizing letters, which in turn makes it easier to recognize words.

> ## Even beginning readers use context to help recognize letters and words.

Readers also use the sentence context to speed word recognition. Read these two sentences:

The last word in this sentence is cat.

The little girl's pet dog chased the cat.

Most readers recognize cat more rapidly in the second sentence. The reason is that the first seven words put severe limits on the last word: It must be something "chaseable," and because the "chaser" is a dog, cat is a very likely candidate. In contrast, the first seven words in the first sentence put no limits on the last word; virtually any word could end the sentence. Readers use sentence context like this to help them recognize words, particularly difficult ones (Archer & Bryant, 2001; Kim & Goetz, 1994).

Beginning readers rely heavily on "sounding out" to recognize words, but even beginning readers retrieve some words from memory.

As you can imagine, most beginning readers, like the child in the photo, rely more heavily on "sounding out" because they know fewer words. As they gain more reading experience, they are more likely to be able to retrieve a word directly from long-term memory. You might be tempted to summarize this as "Beginning readers sound out and more advanced readers retrieve directly." Don't! From their very first efforts to read, most children use direct retrieval for a few words. From that point on, the general strategy is to try retrieval first and, if that fails, to sound out the word or ask a more skilled reader for help (Siegler, 1986). For example, when my daughter Laura was just beginning to read, she knew *the*, *Laura*, and several one-syllable words that ended in *at*, such as *bat*, *cat*, and *fat*. Shown a sentence like

Laura saw the fat cat run.

she would say, "Laura s-s-s . . . ah-h . . . wuh . . . saw the fat cat er-r-r . . . uh-h-h . . . n-n-n . . . run." Familiar words were retrieved rapidly, but the unfamiliar ones were slowly sounded out.

With more experience, children sound out fewer words and retrieve more (Siegler, 1986). That is, by sounding out novel words, children store information about words in long-term memory that is required for direct retrieval (Cunningham et al., 2002; Share, 1999). Of course, all readers sometimes fall back on sounding out when they confront unfamiliar words. Try reading

The rock star rode to the concert in a palanquin.

You may well need to do some sounding out, then consult a dictionary (or look at the answers just before "Check Your Learning") for the correct meaning.

**EDUCATIONAL IMPLICATIONS FOR TEACHING READING.**  Teaching young children to read is probably the most important instructional goal for most American elementary schools. Historically, teachers have used one of three methods to teach reading (Rayner et al., 2001, 2002). The oldest is teaching phonics; for hundreds of years, American children have learned to read by first focusing on letter names, then their typical sounds, and then moving on to syllables and words. Young children might be taught that *b* sounds like "buh" and that *e* sounds like "eeee," so that putting them together makes "buh-eee . . . be."

Learning all the letters and their associated sounds can be tedious, perhaps discouraging children from their efforts to learn to read. Consequently, teachers have looked to other methods. In the whole-word method, children are taught to recognize whole words on sight. This usually begins with a small number (50 to 100) of very familiar words, which are repeated over and over to help children learn their appearance (e.g., "Run, Spot, run!"). In the whole-language method, which has been quite popular in the United States for 20 years, learning to read is thought to occur naturally as a by-product of immersing the child in language-related activities, such as following print as a teacher reads aloud or writing their own stories, inventing their own spellings as necessary (e.g., "Hr nak wz sor."). Teaching phonics is discouraged.

Each of these three methods has some strengths, but research clearly shows that phonics instruction is essential (Rayner et al., 2001, 2002). Children are far more likely to become successful readers when they're taught letter–sound correspondences, and this is particularly true for children at risk for reading failure. That is, the mapping of sounds onto letters, which is the basis of all alphabet-based languages such as English and German, is not something that most children master naturally and incidentally; most children need to be taught letter–sound relations explicitly.

Of course, mindless drilling of letter–sound combinations can be deathly boring. But flash cards and drills aren't the only way to master this knowledge; children can acquire it in the context of language games and activities that they enjoy. And, teaching children to read some words visually is a good practice, as is embedding reading instruction in other activities that encourage language literacy. However, these practices should be designed to complement phonics instruction, not replace it (Rayner et al., 2001, 2002).

**COMPREHENSION.**   As children become more skilled at decoding words, reading begins to have a lot in common with understanding speech. That is, the means by which people understand a sequence of words is much the same whether the source of words is printed text or speech or, for that matter, Braille or sign language (Oakhill & Cain, 2002). **In all these cases, children derive meaning by combining words to form *propositions* or ideas and then combining propositions.** For example, as you read

The tall boy rode his bike.

you spontaneously derive a number of propositions, including "There is a boy," "The boy is tall," and "The boy was riding." If this sentence were part of a larger body of text, you would derive propositions for each sentence, then link the propositions together to derive meaning for the passage as a whole (Perfetti & Curtis, 1986).

As children gain more reading experience, they better comprehend what they read. Several factors contribute to this improved comprehension (Siegler & Alibali, 2005):

- *Children become more skilled at recognizing words, allowing more working capacity to be devoted to comprehension* (Zinar, 2000): When children struggle to recognize individual words, they often cannot link them to derive the meaning of a passage. In contrast, when children recognize words effortlessly, they can focus their efforts on deriving meaning from the whole sentence.

- *Working memory capacity increases, which means that older and better readers can store more of a sentence in memory as they try to identify the propositions it contains* (De Beni & Palladino, 2000; Nation et al., 1999): This extra capacity is handy when readers move from sentences like "Kevin hit the ball" to "In the bottom of the ninth, with the bases loaded and the Cardinals down 7 to 4, Kevin put a line drive into the left-field bleachers, his fourth home run of the series."

- *Children acquire more general knowledge of their physical, social, and psychological worlds, which allows them to understand more of what they read* (Ferreol-Barbey, 2000; Graesser, Singer, & Trabasso, 1994): For example, even if a 6-year-old could recognize all of the words in the longer sentence about Kevin's home run, the child would not fully comprehend the meaning of the passage because he or she lacks the necessary knowledge of baseball.

- *With experience, children better monitor their comprehension:* When readers don't grasp the meaning of a passage because it is difficult or confusing, they read it again (Baker, 1994). Try this sentence (adapted from Carpenter & Daneman, 1981): "The Midwest State Fishing Contest would draw fishermen from all around the region, including some of the best bass guitarists in Michigan." When you first encountered "bass guitarists" you probably interpreted "bass" as a fish. This didn't make much sense, so you reread the phrase to determine that "bass" refers to a type of guitar. Older readers are better able to realize that their understanding is not complete and take corrective action.

- *With experience, children use more appropriate reading strategies:* The goal of reading and the nature of the text dictate how you read. When reading a popular or romance novel, for example, do you often skip sentences (or perhaps paragraphs or entire pages) to get to the "good parts"? This approach makes sense for casual reading but not for reading textbooks, recipes, or how-to manuals. Reading a textbook requires attention to both the overall organization and the relationship of details to that organization. Older, more experienced readers are better able to select a reading strategy that suits the material being read; in contrast, younger, less-skilled readers less often adjust their reading to fit the material (Brown et al., 1996; Cain, 1999).

Greater word recognition skill, greater working memory capacity, greater world knowledge, greater monitoring skill, and use of more appropriate reading strategies are all part of the information-processing explanation of how older and more experienced readers get more meaning from what they read. In the next part of this module, you'll see how child-development researchers use similar ideas to explain children's developing ability to write.

> Older children comprehend more because they recognize words easier, have more working memory, know more of the world, monitor their reading, and use appropriate reading strategies.

## Writing

Though few of us end up being a Maya Angelou, a Sandra Cisneros, or a John Grisham, most adults do write, both at home and at work. Learning to write begins early but takes years. Before children enter school, they know some of the essentials of writing. For example, 4- and 5-year-olds often know that writing involves placing letters on a page to communicate an idea (McGee & Richgels, 2004). But skilled writing develops very gradually because it's a complex activity that requires coordinating cognitive and language skills to produce coherent text.

Developmental improvements in children's writing can be traced to a number of factors (Adams, Treiman, & Pressley, 1998; Siegler & Alibali, 2005).

**GREATER KNOWLEDGE AND ACCESS TO KNOWLEDGE ABOUT TOPICS.** Writing is about telling "something" to others. With age, children have more to tell as they gain more knowledge about the world and incorporate this knowledge into their writing (Benton et al., 1995). For example, asked to write about a mayoral election, children are apt to describe it as much like a popularity contest; adolescents, on the other hand, more often describe it in terms of political issues that are both subtle and complex. Of course, students are sometimes asked to write about topics quite unfamiliar to them. In this case, older children's and adolescents' writing is usually better because they are more adept at finding useful reference material and incorporating it into their writing.

**GREATER UNDERSTANDING OF HOW TO ORGANIZE WRITING.**   One difficult aspect of writing is organization, arranging all the necessary information in a manner that readers find clear and interesting. In fact, children and young adolescents organize their writing differently than older adolescents and adults (Bereiter & Scardamalia, 1987). **Young writers often use a *knowledge-telling strategy*, writing down information on the topic as they retrieve it from memory.** For example, asked to write about the day's events at school, a second grader wrote:

> *It is a rainy day. We hope the sun will shine. We got new spelling books. We had our pictures taken. We sang "Happy Birthday" to Barbara.* (Waters, 1980, p. 155)

The story has no obvious structure. The first two sentences are about the weather, but the last three deal with completely independent topics. Apparently, the writer simply described each event as it came to mind.

**During adolescence, writers begin to use a *knowledge-transforming strategy*, deciding what information to include and how best to organize it for the point they wish to convey to their reader.** This approach involves considering the purpose of writing (e.g., to inform, to persuade, to entertain) and the information needed to achieve this purpose. It also involves considering the needs, interests, and knowledge of the anticipated audience.

Asked to describe the day's events, most older adolescents can select from among genres in creating a piece of writing, depending on their purpose for writing and the intended audience. An essay written to entertain peers about humorous events at school, for example, would differ from a persuasive one written to convince parents about problems with the required course load. And both of these essays would differ from one written to inform an exchange student about a typical day in a U.S. high school. In other words, although children's knowledge-telling strategy gets words on paper, the more mature knowledge-transforming strategy produces a more cohesive text for the reader.

**GREATER EASE IN DEALING WITH THE MECHANICAL REQUIREMENTS OF WRITING.**    Soon after I earned my pilot's license, I took my son Matt for a flight. A few days later, he wrote the following story for his second-grade weekly writing assignment:

*This weekend I got to ride in a one propellered plane. But this time my dad was alone. He has his license now. It was a long ride. But I fell asleep after five minutes. But when we landed I woke up. My dad said, "You missed a good ride." My dad said, "You even missed the jets!" But I had fun.*

Matt spent more than an hour writing this story, and the original (hanging in my office) is filled with erasures where he corrected misspelled words, ill-formed letters, and incorrect punctuation. Had Matt simply described our flight aloud (instead of writing it), his task would have been much easier. In oral language, he could ignore capitalization, punctuation, spelling, and printing of individual letters. These many mechanical aspects of writing can be a burden for all writers, but particularly for young writers.

In fact, research shows that when youngsters such as the one in the photo are absorbed by the task of printing letters correctly, the quality of their writing usually suffers; as children master printed and cursive letters, they can pay more attention to other aspects of writing (Graham, Harris, & Fink, 2000; Jones & Christensen, 1999). Similarly, correct spelling and good sentence structure are particularly hard for younger writers; as they learn to spell and to generate clear sentences, they write more easily and more effectively (Graham et al., 1997; McCutchen et al., 1994).

Young children often find writing difficult because of the difficulty they experience in printing letters properly, spelling words accurately, and using correct punctuation.

**GREATER SKILL IN REVISING.**    Few authors get it down right the first time. Instead, they revise and revise, then revise some more. In the words of one expert, "Experienced writers get something down on paper as fast as they can, just so they can revise it into something clearer" (Williams, 1997, p. 11).

Unfortunately, young writers often don't revise at all—the first draft is usually the final draft. To make matters worse, when young writers revise, the changes do not necessarily improve their writing (Fitzgerald, 1987). Effective revising requires being able to detect problems and knowing how to correct them (Baker & Brown, 1984; Beal, 1996). As children develop, they're better able to find problems with their writing and to know how to correct them. Children and adolescents are more likely to find flaws in others' writing than in their own (Cameron et al., 1997). And they are more likely to revise successfully when the topic is familiar to them and when more time passes between initial writing and revising (Chanquoy, 2001; McCutchen, Francis, & Kerr, 1997).

If you look over these past few paragraphs, it's quite clear why good writing is so gradual in developing. Many different skills are involved and each is complicated in its own right. Word processing software makes writing easier by handling some of these skills (e.g., checking spelling, simplifying revising) and research indicates that writing improves when people use word processors

*Older children write better because they know how to organize their writing, have mastered the mechanical aspects of writing, and revise more effectively.*

(Bangert-Downs, 1993; Clements, 1995). Nevertheless, mastering the full set of writing skills is a huge challenge, one that spans all of childhood, adolescence, and adulthood. Much the same could be said for mastering quantitative skills, as we'll see in the next section.

## Knowing and Using Numbers

Basic number skills originate in infancy, long before babies learn names of numbers. Many babies experience daily variation in quantity. They play with two blocks and see that another baby has three; they watch as a father sorts laundry and finds two black socks but only one blue sock, and they eat one hot dog for lunch while an older brother eats three.

From these experiences, babies apparently come to appreciate that quantity or amount is one of the ways in which objects in the world can differ. This conclusion is based on research in which babies are tested with sequences of pictures like those shown in the diagram. The actual objects in the pictures differ, as do their size, color, and position in the picture. Notice, however, that the first three pictures each show two things: two flowers, two cats, two butterflies.

FIGURE 7-10

When the first of these pictures is shown, infants look at it for several seconds. But, as more pictures of two things are presented, infants habituate (see Module 5.1): They glance at the picture briefly, then look away, as if saying, "Enough of these pictures of two things; let's move on to something else." And, in fact, if a picture of a single object or, like the last drawing in the diagram, a picture of three objects is then shown, infants again look for several seconds, their interest apparently renewed. Because the only systematic change is the number of objects depicted in the picture, we know that babies can distinguish stimuli on the basis of number. Typically, 5-month-olds can distinguish two objects from three and, less often, three objects from four (Canfield & Smith, 1996; Wynn, 1996).

How do infants distinguish differences in quantity? Older children might count, but, of course, infants have not yet learned names of numbers. Instead, the process is probably more perceptual in nature. As we saw in Module 5.1, the infant's perceptual system is sensitive to characteristics such as shape and color (Bornstein, 1981). Quantity may well be another characteristic of stimuli to which infants are sensitive. That is, just as colors (reds, blues) and shapes (triangles, squares) are basic perceptual properties, small quantities ("twoness" and "threeness") may be perceptually obvious (Strauss & Curtis, 1984).

What's more, young babies can do simple addition and subtraction—*very* simple. In experiments using the method shown in Figure 7-11, infants view a stage with one mouse. A screen hides the mouse and then a hand appears with a second mouse, which is placed behind the screen. When the screen is removed and reveals one mouse, 5-month-olds look longer than when two mice appear. Apparently, 5-month-olds expect that one mouse plus another mouse should equal two mice and they look longer when this expectancy is violated (Wynn, 1992). And when the stage first has two mice, one of which is removed, infants are surprised when the screen is removed and two mice are still on the stage. These experiments only work with very small numbers, indicating that the means by which infants add and subtract are very simple and probably unlike the processes that older children use (Mix, Huttenlocher, & Levine, 2002).

**Sequence of events 1+1=1 or 2**

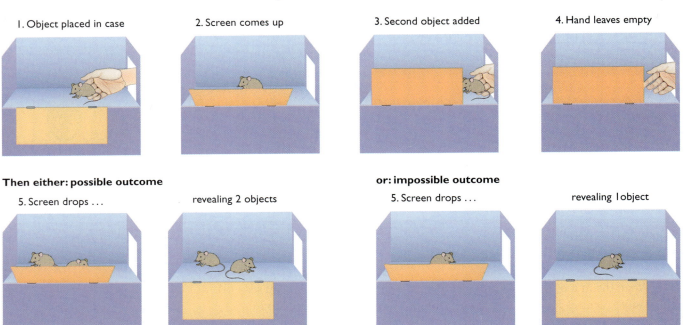

1. Object placed in case
2. Screen comes up
3. Second object added
4. Hand leaves empty

**Then either: possible outcome**

5. Screen drops . . .    revealing 2 objects

**or: impossible outcome**

5. Screen drops . . .    revealing 1 object

**FIGURE 7-11**

Source: Adapted by permission from Macmillan Publishers Ltd: Karen Wynn, Addition and subtraction by human infants. Nature, Vol.358, Issue 6389, pp.749-750 © 1992.

Finally, somewhat older infants are aware of "more than" and "less than" relations. ***Ordinality* refers to the fact that numbers can differ in magnitude; some values are greater than others.** Near the first birthday, infants can identify the larger set. If 10-month-olds watch an adult place two crackers in one container but three crackers in a second container, the infants usually reach for the container with more crackers (Feigenson, Carey, & Hauser, 2002), showing early sensitivity to the ordinal properties of sets.

**LEARNING TO COUNT.** Names of numbers are not among most babies' first words, but by 2 years, youngsters know some number words and have begun to count. Usually, their counting is full of mistakes. In Jasmine's counting sequence that was described in the vignette—"1, 2, 6, 7"—she skips 3, 4, and 5. But research has shown that if we ignore her mistakes momentarily, the counting sequence reveals that she does understand a great deal. Gelman and Meck (1986) simply placed several objects in front of a child and asked, "How many?" By analyzing children's answers to many of these questions, they discovered that by age 3 most children have mastered three basic principles of counting, at least when it comes to counting up to five objects.

- *One-to-one principle:* **There must be one and only one number name for each object that is counted.** A child who counts three objects as "1, 2, a" understands this principle because the number of number words matches the number of objects to be counted.
- *Stable-order principle:* **Number names must be counted in the same order.** A child who counts in the same sequence—for example, consistently counting four objects as "1, 2, 4, 5"—shows understanding of this principle.
- *Cardinality principle:* **The last number name differs from the previous ones in a counting sequence by denoting the number of objects.** Typically, 3-year-olds reveal their understanding of this principle by repeating the last number name, often with emphasis: "1, 2, 4, 8 . . . EIGHT!"

During the preschool years, children master these basic principles and apply them to ever larger sets of objects. By age 5, most youngsters apply these counting principles to as many as nine objects. Of course, children's understanding of these principles does not mean that they always count accurately. To the contrary, children can apply all these principles consistently while counting incorrectly. They must master the conventional sequence of the number names and the counting principles to learn to count accurately. (To see if you understand the counting principles, go back to Jasmine's counting in the vignette and decide which principles she has mastered; my answer is given before "Check Your Learning" on page 233.)

Learning the number names beyond 9 is easier because the counting words can be generated based on rules for combining decade number names (20, 30, 40) with unit names (1, 2, 3, 4). Later, similar rules are used for hundreds, thousands, and so on. By age 4, most youngsters know the numbers to 20, and some can count to 99. Usually, they stop counting at a number ending in 9 (29, 59), apparently because they don't know the next decade name (Siegler & Robinson, 1982).

Learning to count beyond 10 is more complicated in English than in other languages. For example, *eleven* and *twelve* are completely irregular names, following no rules. Also, the remaining "teen" number names differ from the 20s, 30s, and the rest in that the decade number name comes after the unit (thir-*teen*, four-*teen*) rather than before (*twenty*-three, *thirty*-four). Also, some decade names only loosely correspond to the unit names on which they are based: *twenty, thirty,* and *fifty* resemble *two, three,* and *five* but are not the same.

In contrast, the Chinese, Japanese, and Korean number systems are almost perfectly regular. *Eleven* and *twelve* are expressed as *ten-one* and *ten-two*. There are no special names for the decades: *Two-ten* and *two-ten-one* are names for 20 and 21. These simplified number names help explain why youngsters growing up in Asian countries count more accurately than U.S. preschool children of the same age (Miller et al., 1995). What's more, the direct correspondence between the number names and the base-ten system makes it easier for Asian youngsters to learn some mathematical concepts. For example, if a child has 10 blocks, then gets 6 more, an American 5-year-old will carefully count the additional blocks to determine that he now has 16. In contrast, a Chinese 5-year-old will not count but quickly say "16" because she understands that in the base-ten system, 10 + 6 = 16 (Ho & Fuson, 1998).

> Preschool children know many of the principles underlying counting even though they often count inaccurately.

Young children use many strategies to solve simple arithmetic problems, including counting on their fingers.

**7.3** Barb enjoys asking her 6-year-old, Erin, to solve simple arithmetic problems, such as 4 + 2 and 3 + 1. Erin likes solving these problems but Barb finds it puzzling that Erin may solve a problem by counting on her fingers one day and simply saying the answer aloud on the next day. Is Erin's behavior unusual?

**ADDING AND SUBTRACTING.** By 4 or 5 years, most children have encountered arithmetic problems that involve simple addition or subtraction. A 4-year-old might put one green bean on her plate, then watch in dismay as her dad gives her three more. Now she wonders, "Now how many do I have to eat?" Like the child in the photo, many youngsters solve this sort of problem by counting. They first count out four fingers on one hand, then count out two more on the other. Finally, they count all six fingers on both hands. To subtract, they do the same procedure in reverse (Siegler & Jenkins, 1989; Siegler & Shrager, 1984).

Youngsters soon abandon this approach for a slightly more efficient method. Instead of counting the fingers on the first hand, they simultaneously extend the number of fingers on the first hand corresponding to the larger of the two numbers to be added. Next, they count out the smaller number with fingers on the second hand. Finally, they count all of the fingers to determine the sum (Groen & Resnick, 1977).

After children begin to receive formal arithmetic instruction in first grade, addition problems are solved less frequently by counting aloud or by counting fingers. Instead, children add and subtract by counting mentally. That is, children act as if they are counting silently, beginning with the larger number, and adding on. By age 8 or 9, children have learned the addition tables so well that sums of the single-digit integers (from 0 to 9) are facts that are simply retrieved from memory (Ashcraft, 1982).

These counting strategies do *not* occur in a rigid developmental sequence. Instead, as I mentioned in describing Siegler's (1996) overlapping waves model (see page 217), individual children use many different strategies for addition, depending on the problem. Children usually begin by trying to retrieve an answer from memory. If they are not reasonably confident that the retrieved answer is correct, then they resort to counting aloud or on fingers (Siegler, 1996). Retrieval is most likely for problems with small addends (e.g., 1 + 2, 2 + 4) because these problems are presented frequently in textbooks and by teachers. Consequently, the sum is highly associated with the problem, which makes the child confident that the retrieved answer is correct. In contrast, problems with larger addends, such as 9 + 8, are presented less often. The result is a weaker link between the addends and the sum and, consequently, a greater chance that children need to determine an answer by resorting to a backup strategy such as counting.

Of course, arithmetic skills continue to improve as children move through elementary school. They become more proficient in addition and subtraction, learn multiplication and division, and in high school and college move on to the more sophisticated mathematical concepts involved in algebra, geometry, trigonometry, and calculus.

**COMPARING U.S. STUDENTS WITH STUDENTS IN OTHER COUNTRIES.** Let's return to the issue of cultural differences in mathematical competence. When compared to students worldwide in terms of math skills, U.S. students don't fare well. For example, the graph on page 231 shows the math results from a major international comparison involving students in 25 countries (Gonzalez et al., 2004). U.S. eighth graders have substantially lower scores than eighth graders in many leading nations. Phrased another way, the very best U.S. students only perform at the level of average students in Asian countries like Singapore and Korea. What's more, the cultural differences in math achievement hold for both math operations and math problem solving (Stevenson & Lee, 1990).

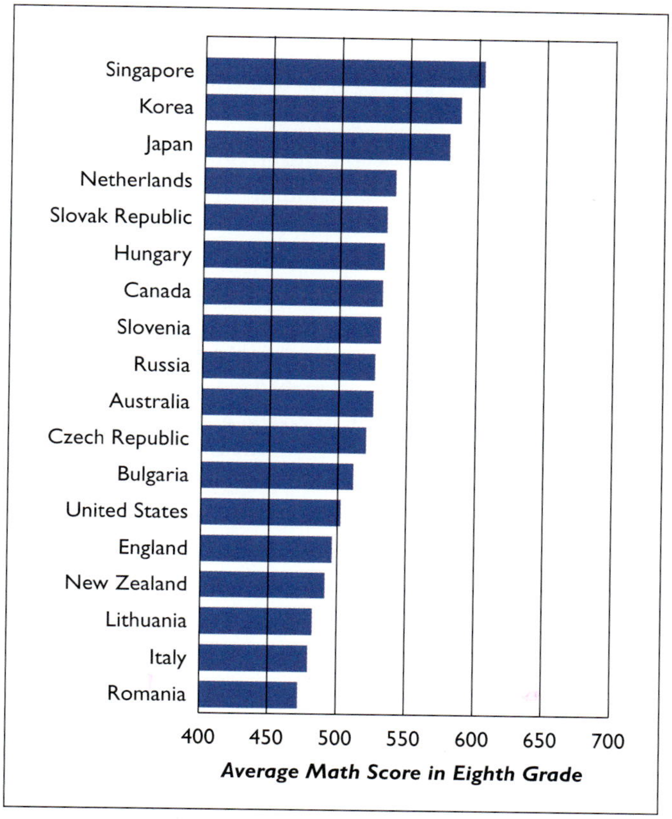

Singapore
Korea
Japan
Netherlands
Slovak Republic
Hungary
Canada
Slovenia
Russia
Australia
Czech Republic
Bulgaria
United States
England
New Zealand
Lithuania
Italy
Romania

400    450    500    550    600    650    700

*Average Math Score in Eighth Grade*

FIGURE 7-12

Why do American students rate so poorly? The "Cultural Influences" feature gives some answers.

## *Cultural Influences*
### Fifth Grade in Taiwan

Shin-ying is an 11-year-old attending school in Taipei, the largest city in Taiwan. Like most fifth graders, Shin-ying is in school from 8 A.M. until 4 P.M. daily. Most evenings, she spends 2 to 3 hours doing homework. This academic routine is grueling by U.S. standards, where fifth graders typically spend 6 to 7 hours in school each day and less than an hour doing homework. I asked Shin-ying what she thought of school and schoolwork. Her answers surprised me.

RK:    Why do you go to school?

SHIN-YING:    I like what we study.

RK:    Any other reasons?

SHIN-YING    The things that I learn in school are useful.

RK: What about homework? Why do you do it?

SHIN-YING: My teacher and my parents think it's important. And I like doing it.

RK: Do you think that you would do nearly as well in school if you didn't work so hard?

SHIN-YING: Oh no. The best students are always the ones who work the hardest.

Schoolwork is the focal point of Shin-ying's life. Although many American schoolchildren are unhappy when schoolwork intrudes on time for play and television, Shin-ying is enthusiastic about school and school-related activities.

Shin-ying is not unusual among Chinese elementary-school students. Many of her comments illustrate findings that emerge from detailed analyses of classrooms, teachers, students, and parents in studies comparing students in Japan, Taiwan, and the United States (Perry, 2000; Stevenson & Lee, 1990; Stigler, Gallimore, & Hiebert, 2000):

> **Students in Asia spend more time on school tasks and their parents set high standards for academic achievement.**

- *Time in school and how it is used.* By fifth grade, students in Japan and Taiwan spend 50 percent more time than American students in school, more of this time is devoted to academic activities than in the United States, and instruction in Asian schools is often better organized and more challenging.

- *Time spent in homework and attitudes toward it.* Students in Taiwan and Japan spend more time on homework and value homework more than American students.

- *Parents' attitudes.* American parents are more often satisfied with their children's performance in school; in contrast, Japanese and Taiwanese parents set much higher standards for their children.

- *Parents' beliefs about effort and ability.* Japanese and Taiwanese parents believe more strongly than American parents that effort, not native ability, is the key factor in school success.

Thus, students in Japan and Taiwan excel because they spend more time both in and out of school on academic tasks. Furthermore, their parents (and teachers) set loftier scholastic goals and believe that students can attain these goals with hard work. Japanese classrooms even post a motto describing ideal students—*gambaru kodomo*—those who strive the hardest.

Parents underscore the importance of schoolwork in many ways to their children. For example, even though homes and apartments in Japan and China are very small by U.S. standards, Asian youngsters, like the child in the photo, typically have a desk in a quiet area where they can study undisturbed (Stevenson & Lee, 1990). For Japanese and Taiwanese teachers and parents, academic excellence is paramount, and it shows in their children's success. ■

Many Asian school children have a quiet area at home where they can study undisturbed.

**EDUCATIONAL IMPLICATIONS OF CROSS-CULTURAL FINDINGS ON ACADEMIC ACHIEVEMENT.** What can Americans learn from Japanese and Taiwanese educational systems? From their experiences with Asian students, teachers, and schools, Stevenson and Stigler (1992) suggest several ways American schools could be improved:

- Give teachers more free time to prepare lessons and correct students' work.

- Improve teachers' training by allowing them to work closely with older, more experienced teachers.

- Organize instruction around sound principles of learning such as providing multiple examples of concepts and giving students adequate opportunities to practice newly acquired skills.

- Set higher standards for children, who need to spend more time and effort in school-related activities in order to achieve those standards.

Changing teaching practices and attitudes toward achievement would begin to reduce the gap between American students and students in other industrialized countries, particularly Asian countries. Ignoring the problem will mean an increasingly undereducated workforce and citizenry in a more complex world—an alarming prospect.

*Definition on page 223:* A palanquin is a covered couch resting on two horizontal poles that are carried by four people, one at the end of each pole.

*Response to question about Jasmine's counting on page 229:* Since Jasmine uses four number names to count four objects ("1, 2, 6, 7 . . . SEVEN!"), she understands the one-to-one principle. The four number names are always used in the same order, so she grasps the stable-order principle. And, finally, she repeats the last number name with emphasis, so she understands the cardinality principle.

## CHECK YOUR LEARNING

**RECALL** What are some of the prerequisite skills that children must master to learn to read?

Summarize the differences between education in China and education in the United States.

**INTERPRET** Understanding what one reads and writing text that's understandable seem to be similar tasks. Compare the factors associated with developmental improvements in reading comprehension and in writing.

**APPLY** In this module, most of the research on reading focused on children learning to read English. How might outcomes of research differ if they were based on children learning to read languages like Dutch or Italian, where letter–sound correspondences are much more consistent than they are in English or languages like Japanese, where each graphic unit corresponds to an entire syllable?

No. In many domains, including simple arithmetic, children use multiple strategies. They will solve a problem one way (e.g., counting on their fingers) and when asked the problem again, solve it a different way (e.g., retrieving the answer from memory).    **7.3**

## UNIFYING THEMES: Active Children

This chapter highlights the theme that *children influence their own development*: Japanese and Chinese elementary-school children typically enjoy studying (an attitude fostered by their parents), and this makes them quite willing to do homework for 2 or 3 hours nightly. This, in turn, contributes to their high levels of scholastic achievement. American schoolchildren usually detest homework and do as little of it as possible, which contributes to their relatively lower level of scholastic achievement. Thus, children's attitudes help to determine how they behave, which determines how much they will achieve over the course of childhood and adolescence.

## SEE FOR YOURSELF

Create several small sets of objects that vary in number. You might have two pennies, three candies, four buttons, five pencils, six erasers, seven paper clips, and so on. Place each set of objects on a paper plate. Then find some preschool children; 4- and 5-year-olds would be ideal. Put a plate in front of each child and ask, "How many?" Then watch to see what the child does. If possible, tape-record the children's counting so that you can analyze it later. If this is impossible, try to write down exactly what each child says as he or she counts. Later, go back through your notes and determine whether the children follow the counting principles described on page 229. You should see that children, particularly younger ones, more often follow the principles while counting small sets of objects than larger sets. See for yourself!

## RESOURCES

For more information about . . .

cultural differences in scholastic achievement, try Harold W. Stevenson and James W. Stigler's *The Learning Gap* (Summit Books, 1992), which describes research comparing schooling in the United States and in Asia.

tips and exercises to help develop better study skills for college, visit the Web site of the University Counseling Center of the Virginia Polytechnic Institute and State University, **http://www.ucc.vt.edu/stdysk/stdyhlp.html**

## KEY TERMS

**autobiographical memory**  206
**cardinality principle**  229
**cognitive self-regulation**  203
**comprehension**  220
**confounded**  218
**decoding**  221
**elaboration**  202
**encoding processes**  214
**fuzzy trace theory**  205
**heuristics**  215
**infantile amnesia**  207
**knowledge-telling strategy**  225
**knowledge-transforming strategy**  225

**means-end analysis**  215
**memory strategies**  201
**metacognitive knowledge**  203
**metamemory**  203
**one-to-one principle**  229
**ordinality**  228
**organization**  202
**phonological awareness**  220
**propositions**  223
**rehearsal**  202
**script**  204
**stable-order principle**  229
**word recognition**  220

## 7.1 MEMORY

### Origins of Memory

Rovee-Collier's studies of kicking show that infants can remember, forget, and be reminded of events that occurred in the past.

### Strategies for Remembering

Beginning in the preschool years, children use strategies to help them remember. With age, children use more powerful strategies, such as rehearsal and outlining. Using memory strategies successfully depends, first, on analyzing the goal of a memory task and, second, on monitoring the effectiveness of the chosen strategy. Analyzing goals and monitoring are two important elements of metamemory, which is a child's informal understanding of how memory operates.

### Knowledge and Memory

A child's knowledge of the world can be used to organize information that is to be remembered. When several events occur in a specific order, they are remembered as a single script. Knowledge improves memory for children and adolescents, although older individuals often reap more benefit because they have more knowledge. Knowledge can also distort memory by causing children and adolescents to forget information that does not conform to their knowledge or to remember events that are part of their knowledge but that did not actually take place.

Autobiographical memory refers to a person's memory about his or her own life. Autobiographical memory emerges in the early preschool years, often prompted by parents' asking children about past events. Infantile amnesia, children's and adults' inability to remember events from early in life, may reflect the absence of language or a sense of self.

Young children's memory in court cases is often inaccurate because children are questioned repeatedly, which makes it hard for them to distinguish what actually occurred from what adults suggest may have occurred. Children's testimony would be more reliable if interviewers tested alternate hypotheses during their questioning, avoided repeated questioning, and warned children that they may try to trick them.

## 7.2 PROBLEM SOLVING

### Developmental Trends in Solving Problems

As a general rule, as children develop they solve problems more often and solve them more effectively. However, exceptions to the rule are not uncommon: Young children sometimes solve problems successfully while adolescents sometimes fail.

### Features of Children's and Adolescents' Problem Solving

Young children sometimes fail to solve problems because they don't plan ahead and because they don't encode all of the necessary information in a problem. Successful problem solving typically depends upon knowledge specific to the problem along with general processes, involves the use of a variety of strategies, and is enhanced by collaborating with an adult or older child.

### Scientific Problem Solving

Although the "child-as-scientist" metaphor is popular, in fact, children and adolescents lack many of the skills associated with real scientific reasoning: They tend to design confounded experiments; they reach conclusions prematurely, based on inadequate evidence; and they have difficulty integrating theory and data.

## 7.3 ACADEMIC SKILLS

### Reading

Reading encompasses a number of component skills. Prereading skills include knowing letters and the sounds associated with them. Word recognition is the process of identifying a word. Beginning readers more often accomplish this by sounding-out words; advanced readers more often retrieve a word from long-term memory. Comprehension, the act of extracting meaning from text, improves with age because of several factors: working memory capacity increases, readers gain more world knowledge, and readers are better able to monitor what they read and to match their reading strategies to the goals of the reading task.

### Writing

As children develop, their writing improves, reflecting several factors: They know more about the world and so they have more to say; they use more effective ways of organizing their writing; they master the mechanics (e.g., handwriting, spelling) of writing; and they become more skilled at revising their writing.

### Knowing and Using Numbers

Infants can distinguish quantities, probably by means of basic perceptual processes. Children begin to count by about age 2, and by 3 years most children have mastered the one-to-one, stable-order, and cardinality principles, at least when counting small sets of objects. Counting is how children first add, but it is replaced by more effective strategies such as retrieving sums directly from memory.

In mathematics, American students lag behind students in most other industrialized nations, chiefly because of cultural differences in the time spent on schoolwork and homework and in parents' attitudes toward school, effort, and ability.

Have you ever stopped to think how many standardized tests you've taken in your student career? You probably took either the SAT or the ACT to enter college. Before that, you took countless achievement and aptitude tests during elementary school and high school. Psychological testing began in schools early in the 20th century and continues to be an integral part of American education in the 21st century.

Of all standardized tests, none attracts more attention and generates more controversy than tests designed to measure intelligence. Intelligence tests have been hailed by some as one of psychology's greatest contributions to society and cursed by others. Intelligence tests and what they measure are the focus of Chapter 8. We'll start, in Module 8.1, by looking at different definitions of intelligence. In Module 8.2, we'll see how intelligence tests work and examine some factors that influence test scores. Finally, in Module 8.3, we'll look at special children—youngsters whose intelligence sets them apart from their peers.

**8.1**  What Is Intelligence?

**8.2**  Measuring Intelligence

**8.3**  Special Children, Special Needs

1  The Science of Child Development

2  Genetic Bases of Child Development

3  Prenatal Development, Birth, and the Newborn

4  Growth and Health

5  Perceptual and Motor Development

6  Theories of Cognitive Development

7  Cognitive Processes and Academic Skills

# Intelligence and Individual Differences in Cognition

9  Language and Communication

10  Emotional Development

11  Understanding Self and Others

12  Moral Understanding and Behavior

13  Gender and Development

14  Family Relationships

15  Influences Beyond the Family

## 8.1 WHAT IS INTELLIGENCE?

Psychometric Theories

Gardner's Theory of Multiple Intelligences

Sternberg's Theory of Successful Intelligence

### LEARNING OBJECTIVES

- What is the psychometric view of the nature of intelligence?
- How does Gardner's theory of multiple intelligences differ from the psychometric approach?
- What are the components of Sternberg's theory of successful intelligence?

*Max is 22 years old and is moderately mentally retarded. That is, he performs most tasks at the level of a normally developing 5- or 6-year-old. For example, he can't do many of Piaget's conservation tasks and he reads very slowly and with much effort. Nevertheless, if Max hears a song on the radio, he can immediately sit down at the piano and play the melody flawlessly, despite having had no musical training. Everyone who sees Max do this is astonished. How can a person who is otherwise so limited intellectually perform such an amazing feat?*

Before you read further, how would you define intelligence? If you're typical of most Americans, your definition probably includes the ability to reason logically, connect ideas, and solve real problems. You might mention verbal ability, meaning the ability to speak clearly and articulately. You might also mention social competence, referring, for example, to an interest in the world at large and an ability to admit when you make a mistake (Sternberg & Kaufman, 1998).

As you'll see in this module, many of these ideas about intelligence are included in psychological theories of intelligence. We'll begin by considering the oldest theories of intelligence, those associated with the psychometric tradition. Then we'll look at two newer approaches and, along the way, get some insights into Max's uncanny musical skill.

### Psychometric Theories

*Psychometricians* are psychologists who specialize in measuring psychological characteristics such as intelligence and personality. When psychometricians want to research a particular question, they usually begin by administering a large number of tests to many individuals. Then they look for patterns in performance across the different tests. The basic logic underlying this technique is similar to the logic a jungle hunter uses to decide whether some dark blobs in a river are three separate rotting logs or a single alligator (Cattell, 1965). If the blobs move together, the hunter decides they are part of the same structure, an alligator. If they do not move together, they are three different structures—three logs. Similarly, if changes in performance on one psychological test are accompanied by changes in performance on a second test—that is, if the scores move together—one assumes the tests are measuring the same attribute or factor.

> **Using patterns of test scores, psychometricians have found evidence for general intelligence as well as for specific abilities.**

Suppose, for example, that you believe there is such a thing as general intelligence. In other words, you believe that some people are smart regardless of the situation, task, or problem, whereas others are not so smart. According to this view, children's performance should be very consistent across tasks. Smart children should always receive high scores and less smart youngsters should always get lower scores.

In fact, more than 100 years ago, Charles Spearman (1904) reported findings supporting the idea that a general factor for intelligence, or *g*, is responsible for performance on all mental tests.

Other researchers, however, have found that intelligence consists of distinct abilities. For example, Thurstone and Thurstone (1941) analyzed performance on a wide range of tasks and identified seven distinct patterns, each reflecting a unique ability: perceptual speed, word comprehension, word fluency, space, number, memory, and induction. Thurstone and Thurstone also acknowledged a general factor that operated in all tasks, but they emphasized that the specific factors were more useful in assessing and understanding intellectual ability.

These conflicting findings have led many psychometric theorists to propose hierarchical theories of intelligence that include both general and specific components. John Carroll (1993, 1996), for example, proposed the hierarchical theory with three levels that's shown in the diagram. At the top of the hierarchy is *g*, general intelligence. In the middle level are eight broad categories of intellectual skill. **For example, *fluid intelligence* refers to the ability to perceive relations among stimuli.** Each of the abilities in the second level is further divided into the skills listed in the bottom and most specific level. ***Crystallized intelligence*, for example, comprises a person's culturally influenced accumulated knowledge and skills, including understanding printed language, comprehending language, and knowing vocabulary.**

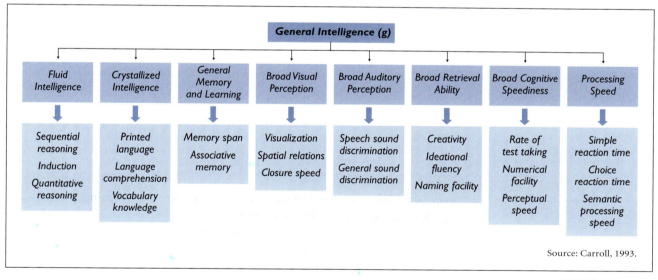

Source: Carroll, 1993.

FIGURE 8-1

Carroll's hierarchical theory is, in essence, a compromise between the two views of intelligence—general versus distinct abilities. But some critics still find it unsatisfactory because it ignores the research and theory on cognitive development described in Chapters 6 and 7. They believe we need to look beyond the psychometric approach to understand intelligence. In the remainder of this module, then, we'll look at two newer theories that have gained a following.

## Gardner's Theory of Multiple Intelligences

Only recently have child-development researchers viewed intelligence from the perspective of modern theories of cognition and cognitive development. These new theories present a much broader theory of intelligence and how it develops. Among the most ambitious is Howard Gardner's (1983, 1999, 2002) theory of multiple intelligences. Rather than using test scores as the basis for his theory, Gardner drew on research in child development, studies of brain-damaged persons, and studies of exceptionally talented people. Using these resources, Gardner identified seven distinct intelligences when he first proposed the theory in 1983. In subsequent work, Gardner (1999, 2002) has identified two additional intelligences; the complete list is shown in the table.

**TABLE 8-1**

### NINE INTELLIGENCES IN GARDNER'S THEORY OF MULTIPLE INTELLIGENCES

| Type of Intelligence | Definition |
|---|---|
| Linguistic | Knowing the meanings of words, having the ability to use words to understand new ideas, and using language to convey ideas to others |
| Logical-mathematical | Understanding relations that exist among objects, actions, and ideas, as well as the logical or mathematical operations that can be performed on them |
| Spatial | Perceiving objects accurately and imagining in the "mind's eye" the appearance of an object before and after it has been transformed |
| Musical | Comprehending and producing sounds varying in pitch, rhythm, and emotional tone |
| Bodily-kinesthetic | Using one's body in highly differentiated ways, as dancers, craftspeople, and athletes do |
| Interpersonal | Identifying different feelings, moods, motivations, and intentions in others |
| Intrapersonal | Understanding one's emotions and knowing one's strengths and weaknesses |
| Naturalistic | Recognizing and distinguishing among members of a group (species) and describing relations between such groups |
| Existential | Considering "ultimate" issues, such as the purpose of life and the nature of death |

Source: Gardner, 1983, 1999, 2002

The first three intelligences in this list—linguistic intelligence, logical-mathematical intelligence, and spatial intelligence—are included in psychometric theories of intelligence. The last six intelligences are not: Musical, bodily-kinesthetic, interpersonal, intrapersonal, naturalistic, and existential intelligences are unique to Gardner's theory. According to Gardner, Yo-Yo Ma's wizardry on the cello, the Williams sisters' remarkable shots on the tennis court, and Oprah Winfrey's grace and charm in dealing with people are all features of intelligence that are totally ignored in traditional theories.

How did Gardner arrive at these nine distinct intelligences? First, each has a unique developmental history. Linguistic intelligence, for example, develops much earlier than the other eight. Second, each intelligence is regulated by distinct regions of the brain, as shown in studies of brain-damaged persons. Spatial intelligence, for example, is regulated by particular regions in the brain's right hemisphere. Third, each has special cases of talented individuals. **Musical intelligence is often shown by** *savants*, **individuals with mental retardation who are extremely talented in one domain.** Max, the 22-year-old in the module-opening vignette, is a savant whose special talent is music. Like Max, Eddie B., the 10-year-old savant in the photo, can play a tune correctly after a single hearing and without ever having had formal musical training (Shuter-Dyson, 1982).

Prompted by Gardner's theory, researchers have begun to look at other nontraditional aspects of intelligence. **Probably the best known is** *emotional intelligence*,

Savants are individuals with mental retardation who show extraordinary talent in one domain, such as music.

**which is the ability to use one's own and others' emotions effectively for solving problems and living happily.** Emotional intelligence made headlines in 1995 due to a best-selling book, *Emotional Intelligence*, in which the author, Daniel Goleman (1995), argued that "emotions [are] at the center of aptitudes for living" (p. xiii). In fact, research shows that emotional intelligence has a number of different components, including perceiving emotions accurately (in others and in oneself) and regulating one's emotions. People who are emotionally intelligent tend to have high scores on traditional IQ tests, have higher self-esteem, and are more sociable (Mayer, Caruso, & Salovey, 1999; Mayer, Salovey, & Caruso, 2000).

Most of the research on emotional intelligence has been done with adults, in large part because Goleman (1998; Goleman, Bayatzis, & McKee, 2002) has argued that emotional intelligence can be the key to a successful career. Child-development researchers have studied emotion, but usually from a developmental angle—they've wanted to know how emotions change with age. We'll look at their research in Module 10.1.

**IMPLICATIONS FOR EDUCATION.** The theory of multiple intelligence has important implications for education. Gardner (1993, 1995) believes that schools should foster all intelligences, rather than just the traditional linguistic and logical-mathematical intelligences. Teachers should capitalize on the strongest intelligences of individual children. Some students may best understand unfamiliar cultures, for example, by studying their dance, whereas other students may understand these cultures by studying their music.

These guidelines do not mean that teachers should gear instruction solely to a child's strongest intelligence, pigeonholing youngsters as numerical learners or spatial learners. Instead, whether the topic is the signing of the Declaration of Independence or Shakespeare's *Hamlet*, instruction should try to engage as many different

From research in child development, studies of people with brain damage, and studies of talented people, Gardner proposed nine distinct intelligences.

intelligences as possible (Gardner, 1999, 2002). The typical result is a much richer understanding of the topic by all students.

Some American schools have enthusiastically embraced Gardner's ideas (Gardner, 1993). Are these schools better than those that have not? Educators in schools using the theory think so; they claim that their students have higher test scores and better discipline and that their parents are more involved (Project Zero, 1999). Although these opinions are encouraging, they need to be supported by research that evaluates children's learning and achievement. In the meantime, there is no doubt that Gardner's work has helped liberate researchers from narrow psychometric-based views of intelligence.

A comparably broad but different view of intelligence comes from another new theory that we'll look at in the next section.

## Sternberg's Theory of Successful Intelligence

Robert Sternberg has studied intelligence for more than 30 years. He began by asking how adults solve problems on intelligence tests. Over the years, this work led to a comprehensive theory of intelligence, one that is the focus of the "Spotlight on Theories" feature.

### *Spotlight on Theories*
**The Theory of Successful Intelligence**

*BACKGROUND*
Traditional theories of intelligence have been rooted in test scores. Today, however, many scientists believe that these classic theories are too narrow; they argue that we need to look to modern theories of thinking and development for broader, more comprehensive views of intelligence.

*THE THEORY*
Robert Sternberg (1999) defines successful intelligence as using one's abilities skillfully to achieve one's personal goals. Goals can be short term—getting an A on a test, making a snack in the microwave, or winning the 100 meter hurdles—or longer term—having a successful career and a happy family life. Achieving these goals by using one's skills defines successful intelligence.

In achieving personal goals, people use three different kinds of abilities. *Analytic ability* involves analyzing problems and generating different solutions. Suppose a teenager wants to download songs to her MP3 player but something isn't working. Analytic intelligence is shown in considering different causes of the problem—maybe the MP3 player is broken or maybe the software to download songs wasn't installed correctly. Analytic intelligence also involves thinking of different solutions: She could surf the Internet for clues about what's wrong or ask a sibling for help.

*Creative ability* involves dealing adaptively with novel situations and problems. Returning to our teenager, suppose that she discovers her MP3 player is broken just as she's ready to leave on a day-long car trip. Lacking the time (and money) to buy a new player, creative intelligence is shown in dealing successfully with a novel goal: finding something enjoyable to do to pass the time on a long drive.

**Finally,** *practical ability* **involves knowing what solution or plan will actually work.** That is, often problems can be solved in different ways in principle but in reality only one solution is practical. Our teenager may realize that surfing the net for a way to fix the player is the only real choice because her parents wouldn't approve of many of the songs and she doesn't want a sibling to know that she's downloading them anyway.

**HYPOTHESIS:** If successful intelligence consists of three distinct abilities—analytic, creative, and practical—then this leads to an important hypothesis: Scores from tests that measure different abilities should be unrelated. Creative ability scores should be unrelated to practical ability scores; and both should be unrelated to analytic ability scores.

**TEST:** Sternberg and his colleagues (2001) had adolescents in three countries—Finland, Spain, and the United States—complete 12 tasks, 4 for each ability. For example, on one test of creative ability, students were taught a novel arithmetic operation, then had to use that operation to solve problems. In another test of creative ability, students were given a false statement (e.g., "Money grows on trees") before being asked to solve reasoning problems as if the statement were true. Finally, one measure of practical ability described common problems facing teenagers and students selected the best solution.

The critical finding concerns correlations between test scores. If analytic, creative, and practical abilities are completely distinct, then test scores should be unrelated: The correlations between analytic test scores and creative test scores, for example, should be 0. At the other extreme, if analytic, creative, and practical abilities are really all the same "thing"—such as general intelligence, *g*—then the correlation between test scores should be 1. In reality, the pattern was midway between these two alternatives: Scores were related but not perfectly as they would be if all tests were simply measuring general intelligence.

**CONCLUSION:** The results are not perfectly consistent with the hypothesis, but do provide some support for it: Intelligence includes analytic, creative, and practical abilities, but these may not be completely independent as Sternberg had proposed initially.

**APPLICATION:** If people differ in the analytic, creative, and practical abilities, then they may learn best when instruction is geared to their strength. A child with strong analytic ability, for example, may find algebra simpler when the course emphasizes analyses and evaluation; a child with strong practical ability may be at his best when the material is organized around practical applications. Thus, the theory of successful intelligence shows how instruction can be matched to students' strongest abilities, enhancing students' prospects for mastering the material (Grigorenko, Jarvin, & Sternberg, 2002). ■

Sternberg emphasizes that successful intelligence is revealed in people's pursuit of goals. Of course, these goals vary from one person to the next and, just as importantly, often vary even more in different cultural, ethnic, or racial groups. This makes it tricky—at best—to compare intelligence and intelligence-test scores for individuals from different groups, as we'll see in the "Cultural Influences" feature.

> According to Robert Sternberg, intelligence involves using analytic, creative, and practical abilities to achieve personal goals.

Kathryn is convinced that her daughter is really smart because she has a huge vocabulary for her age. Would a psychometrician, Howard Gardner, and Robert Sternberg agree with Kathryn's opinion?

8.1

## *Cultural Influences*
### How Culture Defines What Is Intelligent

In Brazil, many elementary-school-age boys like the two in the photo sell candy and fruit to bus passengers and pedestrians. These children often cannot identify the numbers on paper money, yet they know how to purchase their goods from wholesale stores, make change for customers, and keep track of their sales (Saxe, 1988).

In Brazil, many school-age boys sell candy and fruit on the streets, yet they often cannot identify the numbers on money.

Adolescents living on islands in the Pacific Ocean near New Guinea navigate small boats across hundreds of miles of open water, yet they have no formal training in mathematics.

Adolescents who live on Pacific Ocean islands near New Guinea learn to sail boats, like the one in the photo, hundreds of miles across open seas to get from one small island to the next. They have no formal training in mathematics, yet they can use a complex navigational system based on the positions of stars and estimates of the boat's speed (Hutchins, 1983).

If either the Brazilian vendors or the island navigators were given the tests that measure intelligence in U.S. students, they would fare poorly. And they probably couldn't repair a broken MP3 player. Does this mean they are less intelligent than U.S. children? Of course not. The specific skills and goals that are important to American conceptions of successful intelligence and that are assessed on many intelligence tests are less valued in these other cultures and so are not cultivated in the young. And, by the same token, most bright U.S. children would be lost trying to navigate a boat in the open sea. Each culture defines what it means to be intelligent, and the specialized computing skills of vendors and navigators are just as intelligent in their cultural settings as verbal skills are in American culture (Sternberg & Kaufman, 1998). ■

As with Gardner's theory, researchers are still evaluating Sternberg's theory. And, as you can see in the table on page 245 that summarizes the different approaches, theorists are still debating the question of what intelligence is. But, however it is defined, the fact is that individuals differ substantially in intellectual ability, and numerous tests have been devised to measure these differences. The construction, properties, and limit of these tests are the focus of the next module.

## SUMMARY TABLE

### FEATURES OF MAJOR APPROACHES TO INTELLIGENCE

| Approach | Distinguishing Features |
|---|---|
| Psychometric | Intelligence is a hierarchy of general and specific skills |
| Gardner's theory of multiple intelligences | Nine distinct intelligences exist—linguistic, logical-mathematical, spatial, musical, bodily-kinesthetic, interpersonal, intrapersonal, naturalistic, and existential |
| Sternberg's theory of successful intelligence | Successful intelligence is defined as the use of analytic, creative, and practical abilities to pursue personal goals |

### CHECK YOUR LEARNING

RECALL  Describe the psychometric perspective on intelligence.
Summarize the main features of Sternberg's theory of successful intelligence.

INTERPRET  Compare and contrast the major approaches to intelligence in terms of the extent to which they make connections between different aspects of development. That is, to what extent does each perspective emphasize cognitive processes versus integrating physical, cognitive, social, and emotional processes?

APPLY  Suppose that you're a fifth-grade teacher who wants to spend a week covering the American Civil War. How might you use Gardner's theory of multiple intelligences to create lessons that would engage many of your students?

Each of them would
agree that verbal ability
is one part of intelligence. A
psychometrician and Howard
Gardner would both tell her that
intelligence includes other skills
(although they wouldn't mention
the same ones); Sternberg would
emphasize that it's the application
of verbal skill in the context of
analytic, creative, and practical
abilities that really matters.

**8.1**

# MEASURING INTELLIGENCE    8.2

## LEARNING OBJECTIVES

- Why were intelligence tests devised initially? What are modern tests like?

- How well do modern intelligence tests work?

- What are the roles of heredity and environment in determining intelligence?

- How do ethnicity and socioeconomic status influence intelligence test scores?

  Binet and the Development of Intelligence Testing

  Do Tests Work?

  Hereditary and Environmental Factors

  Impact of Ethnicity and Socioeconomic Status

  *Charlene, an African American third grader, received a score of 75 on an intelligence test administered by a school psychologist. Based on the test score, the psychologist believes that Charlene is mildly mentally retarded and should receive special education. Charlene's parents are indignant; they believe that the tests are biased against African Americans and that the score is meaningless.*

American schools faced a crisis at the beginning of the 20th century. Between 1890 and 1915, school enrollment nearly doubled nationally as great numbers of immigrants arrived and as reforms restricted child labor and emphasized education (Chapman, 1988). Increased enrollment meant that teachers now had larger numbers of students who did not learn as readily as the "select few" who had populated their classes previously. How to deal with these less capable children was one of the pressing issues of the day. In this module, you'll see how intelligence tests were devised initially to address a changed school population. Then we'll look at a simple question: "How well do modern tests work?" Finally, we'll examine how race, ethnicity, social class, environment, and heredity influence intelligence, and we'll learn how to interpret Charlene's test score.

## Binet and the Development of Intelligence Testing

*Binet and Simon created the first intelligence test by using simple tasks to distinguish children who would do well in school from those who wouldn't.*

The problems facing educators at the beginning of the 20th century were not unique to the United States. In 1904, the minister of public instruction in France asked two noted psychologists, Alfred Binet and Theophile Simon, to formulate a way to identify children who were likely to succeed in school. Binet and Simon's approach was to select simple tasks that French children of different ages ought to be able to do, such as naming colors, counting backwards, and remembering numbers in order. Based on preliminary testing, Binet and Simon determined problems that normal 3-year-olds could solve, that normal 4-year-olds could solve, and so on. **Children's *mental age* or *MA* referred to the difficulty of the problems that they could solve correctly.** A child who solved problems that the average 7-year-old could pass would have an MA of 7.

Binet and Simon used mental age to distinguish "bright" from "dull" children. A bright child would have the MA of an older child; for example, a 6-year-old with an MA of 9 was considered bright. A dull child would have the MA of a younger child, for example, a 6-year-old with an MA of 4. Binet and Simon confirmed that bright children did better in school than dull children. Voilá—the first standardized test of intelligence!

**THE STANFORD-BINET.**    Lewis Terman, of Stanford University, revised Binet and Simon's test and published a version known as the Stanford-Binet in 1916. **Terman described performance as an *intelligence quotient*, or *IQ*, which was simply the ratio of mental age to chronological age, multiplied by 100:**

$$IQ = MA/CA \times 100$$

At any age, children who are perfectly average will have an IQ of 100 because their mental age equals their chronological age. The figure shows the typical distribution of test scores in the population. Roughly two thirds of children taking a test will have IQ scores between 85 and 115 and 95% will have scores between 70 and 130.

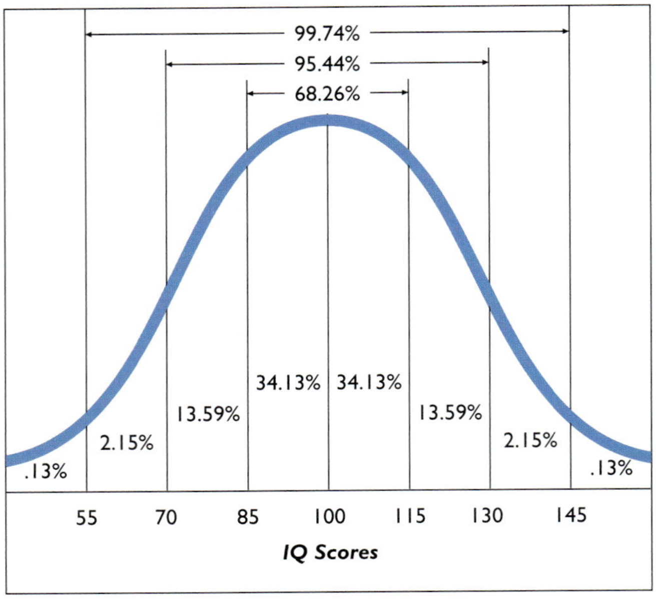

The IQ score can also be used to compare intelligence in children of different ages. A 4-year-old with an MA of 5 has an IQ of 125 (5/4 × 100) the same as an 8-year-old with an MA of 10 (10/8 × 100).

IQ scores are no longer computed in this manner. Instead, children's IQ scores are determined by comparing their test performance to that of others their age. When children perform at the average for their age, their IQ is 100. Children who perform above the average have IQs greater than 100; children who perform below the average have IQs less than 100. Nevertheless, the concept of IQ as the ratio of MA to CA helped popularize the Stanford-Binet test.

By the 1920s, the Stanford-Binet had been joined by many other intelligence tests. Educators enthusiastically embraced the tests as an efficient and objective way to assess a student's chances of succeeding in school (Chapman, 1988).

**FIGURE** 8-2

Distribution curve showing:
99.74%
95.44%
68.26%
.13%  2.15%  13.59%  34.13% | 34.13%  13.59%  2.15%  .13%
55   70   85   100   115   130   145
*IQ Scores*

Today, more than 80 years later, the Stanford-Binet remains a popular test; the latest version was revised in 2003. Like the earlier versions, the modern Stanford-Binet consists of various cognitive and motor tasks, ranging from the extremely easy to the extremely difficult. The test may be administered to individuals ranging in age from approximately 2 years to adulthood, but the test items depend on the child's age. For example, preschool children may be asked to name pictures of familiar objects, string beads, answer questions about everyday life, or fold paper into shapes. Older individuals may be asked to define vocabulary words, solve an abstract problem, or decipher an unfamiliar code. The examiner determines, according to specific guidelines, the appropriate starting place on the test and administers progressively more difficult questions until the child fails all the questions at a particular level. An IQ score is assigned on the basis of how many questions the child passed compared with the average number passed by children of the same age.

Another test used frequently with children is the Wechsler Intelligence Scale for Children-III, or WISC-III for short. Unlike the Stanford-Binet, the WISC-III includes subtests for verbal and performance skills, some of which are shown in the figure. Based on their performance, children receive three scores: verbal IQ, performance IQ, and a combination of the two, the full-scale IQ.

---

**Items Like Those Appearing on Different Subtests of the WISC-III**

| Verbal Scale | *Information: The child is asked questions that tap his or her factual knowledge of the world.* |
| | 1. *How many wings does a bird have?* |
| | 2. *What is steam made of?* |
| | *Comprehension: The child is asked questions that measure his or her judgment and common sense.* |
| | 1. *What should you do if you see someone forgot his book when he leaves a restaurant?* |
| | 2. *What is the advantage of keeping money in a bank?* |
| | *Similarities: The child is asked to describe how words are related.* |
| | 1. *In what way are a lion and a tiger alike?* |
| | 2. *In what way are a saw and a hammer alike?* |
| Performance Scale | *Picture arrangement: Pictures are shown and the child is asked to place them in order to tell a story.* 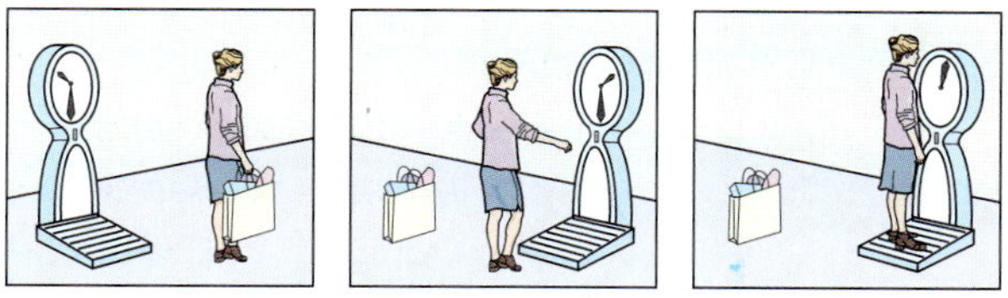 |
| | |
| | *Picture completion: The child is asked to identify the part that is missing from the picture.*  |
| | |

FIGURE 8-3

Source: Simulated items similar to those in the Wechsler Intelligence Scales for Adults and Children. Copyright 1949, 1955, 1974, 1981, and 1990 by the Psychological Corporation. Reproduced by permission. All rights reserved.

An advantage of an individual intelligence test is that the examiner can be sure that the child is attentive and not anxious during testing.

The Stanford-Binet and the WISC-III are alike in that they are administered to one person at a time. Other tests can be administered to groups of individuals, with the advantage of providing information about many individuals quickly and inexpensively, typically without the need of trained psychologists. But individual testing like that shown in the photo optimizes the motivation and attention of the child and provides an opportunity for a sensitive examiner to assess factors that may influence test performance. The examiner may notice that the child is relaxed and that test performance is therefore a reasonable sample of the individual's talents. Or the examiner may observe that child is so anxious that she cannot do her best. Such determinations are not possible with group tests. Consequently, most psychologists prefer individualized tests of intelligence over group tests.

**INFANT TESTS.** The Stanford-Binet and the WISC-III cannot be used to test intelligence in infants. For this purpose, many psychologists use the Bayley Scales of Infant Development (Bayley, 1970, 1993, 2005). Designed for 1- to 42-month-olds, the Bayley Scales consist of five scales: cognitive, language, motor, social-emotional, and adaptive behavior. To illustrate, the motor scale assesses an infant's control of its body, its coordination, and its ability to manipulate objects. For example, 6-month-olds should turn their head toward an object that the examiner drops on the floor, 12-month-olds should imitate the examiner's actions, and 16-month-olds should build a tower from three blocks.

## Do Tests Work?

To determine whether intelligence tests work, we need to consider two separate issues, reliability and validity.

**RELIABILITY.** As I described in Module 1.4, a test is reliable if it yields scores that are consistent. Reliability is often measured by administering similar forms of a test on two occasions. If the test is reliable, a child will have similar scores both times. Today's intelligence tests are very reliable. If a child takes an intelligence test and then retakes it days or a few weeks later, the two scores are usually quite similar (Wechsler, 1991).

Reliability over the long term is more complex. In general, scores from infant intelligence tests are not related to IQ scores obtained later in childhood, adolescence, or adulthood (McCall, 1989). Apparently, children must be at least 18 to 24 months old before their Bayley scores, or scores from similar scales, can predict later IQ scores on the Wechsler or Stanford-Binet scales (Kopp & McCall, 1982).

Why don't scores on infant intelligence tests predict childhood or adult IQ more accurately? One reason is that infant tests measure different abilities than tests administered to children and adolescents: Infant tests place more emphasis on sensorimotor skills and less on tasks involving cognitive processes such as language, thinking, and problem solving.

According to this reasoning, a measure of infant cognitive processing might yield more accurate predictions of later IQ. In fact, habituation, a measure of information processing described in Module 6.1, does predict later IQ more effectively than do scores from the Bayley. The average correlation between habituation and later IQ is approximately .5 (Bornstein, 1997). That is, 1- to 6-month-olds who habituate to visual stimuli more rapidly tend to have higher IQs as children.

**8.2** Amanda's 12-month-old son completed an intelligence test and received a slightly below-average score. Amanda is distraught because she's afraid her son's score means that he'll struggle in school. What advice would you give Amanda?

Infants' performance on habituation tasks predicts their intelligence as an adult more accurately than their performance on infant intelligence tests.

Apparently, infants who rapidly make sense of their world—in this case, thinking "I've seen this picture before, so let's see something new!"—are smarter during the elementary-school years.

If scores on the Bayley Scales do not predict later IQs, why are these tests used at all? The answer is that they are important diagnostic tools: Researchers and health-care professionals use scores from the Bayley Scales to determine whether development is progressing normally.

Although infant test scores don't reliably predict IQ later in life, scores obtained in childhood do. The graph shows the results from several longitudinal studies that correlated IQ scores obtained at different points in childhood or adolescence and at maturity. Each line in the graph represents a different study. You can see that the correlation between IQ at 5 years and maturity is approximately .5 and that the correlations get steadily larger as children get older.

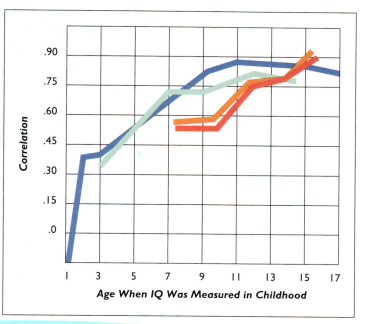

FIGURE 8-4

These correlations appear to support the idea that intelligence is relatively stable from early childhood on. However, when individual performance over time is examined, stability is not a hard-and-fast rule. McCall, Appelbaum, and Hogarty (1973) conducted a longitudinal study in which 80 individuals had their intelligence tested roughly 14 times between ages 2 and 17. They discovered several different developmental patterns. The most common pattern—found in nearly 50% of the participants—was for little change in IQ from 2 to 17 years of age. However, for about 15% of the participants, IQ scores first increased, then decreased with age. For another 15%, the pattern was just the opposite: IQ scores first decreased, then increased with age.

McCall and his colleagues (1973) also found that children were most likely to have increasing IQ scores when their parents deliberately trained their intellectual and motor skills. When parents did not train their youngsters' intellectual and motor development (or, in some cases, actually discouraged it), IQ scores were likely to decline as children got older. Thus, although IQ is often relatively stable throughout childhood and adolescence, this is definitely not the only pattern. For many children, IQ will change both up and down as they develop.

**VALIDITY.**   Reliability of tests, whether short- or long-term, is not the only criterion for evaluating a test. What do test scores mean? Are they really measuring intelligence? These questions raise the issue of *validity*, which refers to the extent that a test really measures what it claims to measure. Validity is usually measured by determining the relation between test scores and other independent measures of what the test is thought to measure. For example, to measure the validity of a test of extroversion, we would have children take the test, then observe them in a social setting, such as a school recess, and record who is outgoing and who is shy. The test would be valid if scores correlated highly with our independent observations of extroverted behavior.

How would we extend this approach to intelligence tests? Ideally, we would administer the intelligence tests and then correlate the scores with other independent estimates of intelligence. But this approach has a fundamental flaw: There are no other independent ways to estimate intelligence; the only way to measure intelligence is with tests. Consequently, many researchers follow Binet's lead and obtain measures of performance in school, such as grades or teachers' ratings of their students. Correlations between these measures and scores on intelligence tests typically fall somewhere between .4 and .6 (Neisser et al., 1996). For example, the correlation between scores on the WISC-III and grade point average is .47 (Wechsler, 1991). This correlation is positive but far from a correlation of 1. Obviously, some youngsters with high test scores do not excel in school, whereas others with low test scores manage to get good grades. In general, however, tests do a reasonable job of predicting school success.

Intelligence tests are reasonable predictors of performance not only in school, but also in the workplace, particularly for more complex jobs (Gottfredson, 1997; Schmidt & Hunter, 1998). Workers with higher IQ scores tend to be more successful in their on-the-job training and, after training, more successful in their actual work performance. If, for example, two teenagers have summer jobs running tests in a biology lab, the smarter of the two will probably learn the procedures more rapidly and, once learned, conduct them more accurately.

> Most test developers argue that their tests are valid measures of intelligence by showing that test scores are related to children's grades in school.

**INCREASING VALIDITY WITH DYNAMIC TESTING.** Traditional tests of intelligence such as the Stanford-Binet and the WISC-III measure knowledge and skills that a child has accumulated up to the time of testing. These tests do not directly measure a child's potential for future learning; instead, the usual assumption is that children who have learned more in the past will probably learn more in the future. Critics argue that tests would be more valid if they directly assessed a child's potential for future learning.

*Dynamic testing* **measures a child's learning potential by having the child learn something new in the presence of the examiner and with the examiner's help.** Thus, dynamic testing is interactive and measures new achievement rather than past achievement. It is based on Vygotsky's ideas of the zone of proximal development and scaffolding (see pages 174-178). Learning potential can be estimated by the amount of material the child learns during interaction with the examiner and from the amount of help the child needs to learn the new material (Grigorenko & Sternberg, 1998; Sternberg & Grigorenko, 2002).

To understand the difference between traditional, static methods of intelligence testing and new, dynamic approaches, imagine a group of children attending a week-long basketball camp. On the first day, all children are tested on a range of basketball skills and receive a score that indicates their overall level of basketball skill. If this score were shown to predict later success in basketball, such as number of points scored in a season, this would be a valid static measure of basketball skill. To make this a dynamic measure of basketball skill, children would spend all week at camp being instructed in new skills. At the end of the week, the test of basketball skills would be readministered. The amount of the child's improvement over the week would measure learning potential, with greater improvement indicating greater learning potential.

Dynamic testing is a recent innovation that is still being evaluated. Preliminary research does indicate, however, that static and dynamic testing both provide useful and independent information. If the aim is to predict future levels of a child's skill, it is valuable to know a child's current level of skill (static testing) as well as the child's potential to acquire greater skill (dynamic testing). By combining both forms of testing, we achieve a more comprehensive view of a child's talents than by relying on either method alone (Day et al., 1997).

## Hereditary and Environmental Factors

Joanna, a 5-year-old girl, took the WISC-III and obtained a score of 112. Ted, a 5-year-old boy, took the same test and received a score of 92. What accounts for the 20-point difference in these youngsters' scores? Heredity and experience both matter.

Some of the evidence for hereditary factors is shown in the graph. If genes influence intelligence, then siblings' test scores should become more alike as siblings become more similar genetically (Plomin & Petrill, 1997). In other words, since identical twins are identical genetically, they typically have virtually identical test scores, which would be a correlation of 1. Fraternal twins have about 50% of their genes in common, just like nontwin siblings of the same biological parents. Consequently, we could predict that their test scores should be (a) less similar than scores for identical twins, (b) similar to scores of other siblings who have the same biological parents, and (c) more similar than scores of children and their adopted siblings. You can see in the graph that each of these predictions is supported.

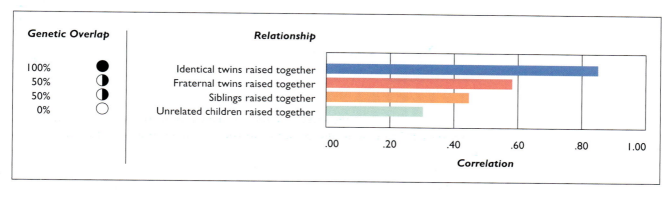

FIGURE 8-5

Heredity also influences developmental profiles for IQ scores (Wilson, 1983). Developmental profiles for IQ are more alike for identical twins than for fraternal twins. If one identical twin gets higher IQ scores with age, the other twin almost certainly will, too. In contrast, if one fraternal twin gets higher scores with age, the other twin may not necessarily show the same pattern. Thus, identical twins are not only more alike in overall IQ, but in developmental change in IQ as well.

Studies of adopted children also suggest the impact of heredity on IQ: If heredity helps determine IQ, then children's IQs should be more like those of their biological parents than of their adoptive parents. In fact, as we saw in the "Focus on Research" feature in Module 2.1, throughout childhood and adolescence, the correlation between children's IQ and their biological parents' IQ is greater than the correlation between children's IQ and their adoptive parents' IQ. What's more, as adopted children get older, their test scores increasingly resemble those of their biological parents. These results are evidence for the greater impact of heredity on IQ as a child grows.

Do these results mean that heredity is the sole determiner of intelligence? No. Three areas of research show the importance of environment on intelligence. The first is research on characteristics of families and homes. If intelligence were solely due to heredity, environment should have little or no impact on children's

Children who achieve high scores on intelligence tests often come from homes that are well organized and include many age-appropriate books and toys that can stimulate a child's intellectual growth.

intelligence. But we know that many characteristics of parents' behavior and home environments are related to children's intelligence. For example, children with high test scores tend to come from homes that are well organized and, like the one in the photo, have plenty of appropriate play materials (Bradley et al., 1989).

The impact of the environment on intelligence is also implicated by research on historical change in IQ scores. During most of the 20th century, IQ test scores rose dramatically (Flynn, 1998; Sundet, Barlaug, & Torjussen, 2004). For example, scores on the WISC increased by nearly 10 points over a 25-year period (Flynn, 1999). Heredity cannot account for such a rapid increase over a few decades (a mere fraction of a second in genetic time). Consequently, the rise must reflect the impact of some aspect of the environment. The change might reflect smaller, better educated families with more leisure time (Daley et al., 2003; Dickens & Flynn, 2001). Or it might be due to movies, television, and, more recently, the computer and the Internet, providing children with an incredible wealth of virtual experience (Greenfield, 1998). Although the exact cause remains a mystery, the increase per se shows the impact of changing environmental conditions on intelligence.

The importance of a stimulating environment for intelligence is also demonstrated by intervention programs that prepare economically disadvantaged children for school. Without preschool, children from low-income families often enter kindergarten or first grade lacking key readiness skills for academic success, which means they rapidly fall behind their peers who have these skills. Consequently, providing preschool experiences for children from poor families has long been a part of federal policies to eliminate poverty. The "Child Development and Family Policy" feature traces the beginnings of these programs.

## *Child Development and Family Policy*
### Providing Children with a Head Start for School

For more than 40 years, Head Start has been helping to foster the development of preschool children from low-income families. This program's origins can be traced to two forces. First, in the early 1960s, child-development researchers argued that environmental influences on children's development were much stronger than had been estimated previously. The year 1961 marked the appearance of *Intelligence and Experience* by psychologist Joseph McVicker Hunt. Hunt reviewed the scientific evidence concerning the impact of experience on intelligence and concluded that children's intellectual development could reach unprecedented heights once child-development scientists identified optimal environmental influences. In addition, a novel program in Tennessee directed by Susan Gray (Gray & Klaus, 1965) gave credibility to the argument by showing that a summer program coupled with weekly home visits throughout the school year could raise intelligence and language in preschool children living in poverty. Gray's findings suggested that Hunt's claims were not simply pipe dreams.

The second force was a political twist of fate. When President Lyndon Johnson launched the War on Poverty in 1964, the Office of Economic Opportunity (OEO) was the command center. Sargent Shriver, OEO's first director, found himself with a huge budget surplus. Most of the War on Poverty programs targeted adults; and because many of these programs were politically unpopular, Shriver was reluctant to spend more money on them. Shriver realized that no programs were aimed specifically at children and that such programs would be much less controversial politically. (After all, critics may try to argue that poor adults "deserve their fate" because they're lazy or irresponsible financially, but such arguments are not very convincing when applied to young children.) What's more, he was personally familiar with the potential impact of programs targeted at young children through his experience as the president of the Chicago School Board and his wife's work on the President's Panel on Mental Retardation (Zigler & Muenchow, 1992).

Shriver envisioned a program that would better prepare poor children for first grade. In December 1964, he convened a 14-member planning committee that included professionals from medicine, social work, education, and psychology. Over a 6-week period, the planning committee devised a comprehensive program that would, by involving professionals and parents, meet the health and educational needs of young children. In May 1965, President Johnson announced the opening of Head Start and by that summer, a half-million American youngsters were enrolled. The program continues today and has now served the needs of millions of American children living in poverty. ■

> The impact of well-organized home environments, historical change, and intervention programs on IQ scores document the role of the environment in the development of intelligence.

How effectively do these programs meet the needs of preschool youngsters? This turns out to be a question that's hard to answer because of the very nature of Head Start. Since the beginnings in the 1960s, Head Start has been tailored to cope with the needs of individual communities; no two Head Start programs are exactly alike. Because Head Start takes on different forms in different communities, this makes it difficult to make blanket statements about the overall effectiveness of the program. However, high-quality Head Start programs *are* effective overall. When children such as those in the photo attend good Head Start programs, they are healthier and do better in school (Lazar & Darlington, 1982; Zigler & Styfco, 1994). For example, Head Start graduates are less likely to repeat a grade level or to be placed in special education classes. And they are more likely to graduate from high school.

High-quality Head Start programs are effective: Graduates of such programs are less likely to repeat a grade in school and are more likely to graduate from high school.

One of the success stories is the Carolina Abecedarian Project designed by Frances Campbell and Craig Ramey (1994; Campbell et al., 2001; Ramey & Campbell, 1991). This project included 111 children; most were born to African American mothers who had less than a high-school education, an average IQ score of 85, and typically no income. About half the children were assigned to a control group in which they received no special attention. The others attended a special day-care facility daily from age 4 months until 5 years. The curriculum emphasized mental, linguistic, and social development for infants, and prereading skills for preschoolers.

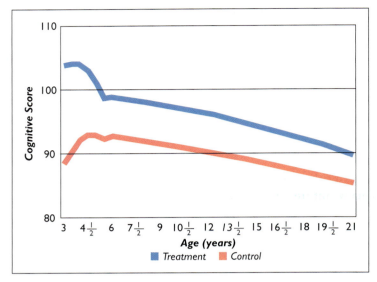

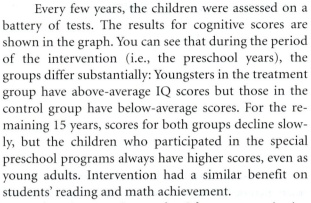

FIGURE 8-6

Every few years, the children were assessed on a battery of tests. The results for cognitive scores are shown in the graph. You can see that during the period of the intervention (i.e., the preschool years), the groups differ substantially: Youngsters in the treatment group have above-average IQ scores but those in the control group have below-average scores. For the remaining 15 years, scores for both groups decline slowly, but the children who participated in the special preschool programs always have higher scores, even as young adults. Intervention had a similar benefit on students' reading and math achievement.

Thus, intervention works. Of course, massive intervention over many years is expensive. But so are the economic consequences of poverty, unemployment, and their by-products. Programs like the Abecedarian Project show that the repetitive cycle of school failure and education can be broken. In the process, they show that intelligence is fostered by a stimulating and responsive environment.

## Impact of Ethnicity and Socioeconomic Status

On many intelligence tests, ethnic groups differ in their average scores: Asian Americans tend to have the highest scores, followed by European Americans, Hispanic Americans, and African Americans (Loehlin, 2000). To a certain extent, these differences in test scores reflect group differences in socioeconomic status. Children from economically advantaged homes tend to have higher test scores than children from economically disadvantaged homes; and European American and Asian American families are more likely to be economically advantaged, whereas Hispanic American and African American families are more likely to be economically disadvantaged. Nevertheless, when children of comparable socioeconomic status are compared, group differences in IQ test scores are reduced but not eliminated (Brooks-Gunn, Klebanov, & Duncan, 1996). Let's look at four explanations for this difference.

**A ROLE FOR GENETICS?**   On page 251, you learned that heredity helps determine a child's intelligence: Smart parents tend to beget smart children. Does this also mean that group differences in IQ scores reflect genetic differences? No. Most researchers agree that there is no evidence that some ethnic groups have more "smart genes" than others. Instead, they believe that the environment is largely responsible for these differences (Bronfenbrenner & Morris, 1998; Neisser et al., 1996).

A popular analogy (Lewontin, 1976) demonstrates the thinking here. Imagine two kinds of corn: Each kind produces both short and tall plants; and height is known to be due to heredity. If one kind of corn grows in a good soil—with plenty of water and nutrients—the mature plants will reach their genetically determined heights; some short, some tall. If the other kind of corn grows in poor soil, few of the plants will reach their full height and overall the plants of this kind will be much shorter. Thus, even though height is quite heritable for each type of corn, the difference in height between the two groups is due solely to the quality of the environment.

**EXPERIENCE WITH TEST CONTENTS.** Some critics contend that differences in test scores reflect bias in the tests themselves. They argue that test items reflect the cultural heritage of the test creators, most of whom are economically advantaged European Americans, and so tests are biased against economically disadvantaged children from other groups. They point to test items like this one:

> A conductor is to an orchestra as a teacher is to what?
>
> book school class eraser

Children whose background includes exposure to orchestras are more likely to answer this question correctly than children who lack this exposure.

**The problem of bias led to the development of *culture-fair intelligence tests*, which include test items based on experiences common to many cultures.** An example is Raven's Progressive Matrices, which consist solely of items like the one shown here. Examinees are asked to select the piece that would complete the design correctly (6, in this case). Although items like this are thought to reduce the impact of specific experience, ethnic group differences remain in performance on so-called culture-fair intelligence tests (Anastasi, 1988; Herrnstein & Murray, 1994). Apparently, familiarity with test-related items per se is not the key factor responsible for group differences in performance.

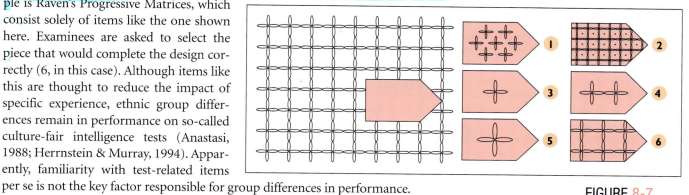

FIGURE 8-7

**STEREOTYPE THREAT.** When people know that they belong to a group that is said to lack skill in a domain, this makes them anxious when performing in that domain for fear of confirming the stereotype, and they often do poorly as a result. **This self-fulfilling prophecy, in which knowledge of stereotypes leads to anxiety and reduced performance consistent with the original stereotype, is called *stereotype threat*.** Applied to intelligence, the argument is that African American children experience stereotype threat when they take intelligence tests and this contributes to their lower scores (Steele, 1997; Steele & Aronson, 1995). For example, imagine two 10-year-olds taking an intelligence test for admission to a special program for gifted children. The European American child worries that if he fails the test, he won't be admitted to the program. The African American child has the same fears but also worries that if he does poorly it will confirm the stereotype that African American children don't get good scores on IQ tests (Suzuki & Aronson, 2005).

**TEST-TAKING SKILLS.** The impact of experience and cultural values can extend beyond particular items to a child's familiarity with the entire testing situation. Tests underestimate a child's intelligence if, for example, the child's culture encourages children to solve problems in collaboration with others and discourages them from excelling as individuals. What's more, because they are wary of questions posed by unfamiliar adults, many economically disadvantaged children often answer test questions by saying, "I don't know." Obviously, this strategy guarantees an artificially low test score. When these children are given extra time to feel at ease with the examiner, they respond less often with "I don't know" and their test scores improve considerably (Zigler & Finn-Stevenson, 1992).

> Children from minority groups often get low scores on intelligence tests because they worry about stereotypes and are wary in testing situations.

**CONCLUSION: INTERPRETING TEST SCORES.** If all tests reflect cultural influences, at least to some degree, how should we interpret test scores? Remember that tests assess successful adaptation to a particular cultural context. Most intelligence tests predict success in a school environment, which usually espouses middle-class values. Regardless of ethnic group—African American, Hispanic American, or European American—a child with a high test score has the intellectual skills needed for academic work based on middle-class values. A child with a low test score, like Charlene in the module-opening vignette, apparently lacks those skills. Does a low score mean Charlene is destined to fail in school? No. It simply means that, based on her current skills, she's unlikely to do well. Improving Charlene's skills will improve her school performance.

I want to end this module by emphasizing a crucial point: By focusing on groups of people, it's easy to overlook the fact that the average difference in IQ scores between various ethnic groups is relatively small compared to the entire range of scores for these groups (Sternberg, Grigorenko, & Kidd, 2005). You can easily find youngsters with high IQ scores from all ethnic groups, just as you can find youngsters with low IQ scores from all groups. And, in the next module, we'll look at children at these extremes of ability.

**8.2** Tell her to relax. Scores on intelligence tests for infants are not related to scores taken on tests in childhood or adolescence, so the lower-than-average score has virtually no predictive value.

## CHECK YOUR LEARNING

**RECALL** What are modern intelligence tests like? How well do they work?
Describe the reasons why ethnic groups differ in their average scores on intelligence tests.

**INTERPRET** Explain the evidence that shows the roles of heredity and environment on intelligence.

**APPLY** Suppose that a local government official proposes to end all funding for preschool programs for disadvantaged children. Write a letter to this official in which you describe the value of these programs.

**8.3**

# SPECIAL CHILDREN, SPECIAL NEEDS

Gifted and Creative Children

Children with Mental Retardation

Children with Learning Disabilities

**LEARNING OBJECTIVES**

- What are the characteristics of gifted and creative children?

- What are the different forms of mental retardation?

- What are learning disabilities?

*Sanjit, a second grader, has taken two separate intelligence tests, and both times he had above-average scores. Nevertheless, Sanjit absolutely cannot read. Letters and words are as mysterious to him as Metallica's music would be to Mozart. His parents took him to an ophthalmologist, who determined that Sanjit's vision was 20-20; nothing is wrong with his eyes. What is wrong?*

Throughout history, societies have recognized children with limited mental abilities as well as those with extraordinary talents. Today, we know much about the extremes of human talents. We'll begin this module with a look at gifted and creative children. Then we'll look at children with mental retardation and learning disabilities and discover why Sanjit can't read.

## Gifted and Creative Children

In many respects the boy in the photo, Bernie, is an ordinary middle-class 12-year-old: He is the goalie on his soccer team, takes piano lessons on Saturday mornings, sings in his church youth choir, and likes to go roller blading. However, when it comes to intelligence and academic prowess, Bernie leaves the ranks of the ordinary. He received a score of 175 on an intelligence test and is taking a college calculus course. **Bernie is *gifted*, which traditionally has referred to individuals with scores of 130 or greater on intelligence tests** (Horowitz & O'Brien, 1986).

Because giftedness was traditionally defined in terms of IQ scores, exceptional ability is often associated primarily with academic skill. But modern definitions of giftedness are broader and include exceptional talent in an assortment of areas, including art, music, creative writing, and dance (Robinson & Clinkenbeard, 1998; Winner, 2000).

Whether the field is music or math, though, exceptional talent seems to have several prerequisites (Rathunde & Csikszentmihalyi, 1993):

- The child loves the subject and has an almost overwhelming desire to master it.
- Instruction to develop the child's special talent usually begins at an early age with inspiring and talented teachers.
- Parents are committed to promoting their child's talent.

Traditional definitions of giftedness emphasized test scores; modern definitions emphasize exceptional talent in a variety of areas, beginning with academic areas but also including the arts.

The message here is that exceptional talent must be nurtured. Without encouragement and support from parents and stimulating and challenging mentors, a youngster's talents will wither. Talented children need a curriculum that is challenging and complex; they need teachers who know how to foster talent; and they need like-minded peers who stimulate their interests (Feldhusen, 1996).

The stereotype is that gifted children are often thought to be emotionally troubled and unable to get along with their peers. In reality, gifted youngsters tend to be more mature than their peers and have fewer emotional problems (Luthar, Zigler, & Goldstein, 1992).

**CREATIVITY.**   Mozart and Salieri were rival composers in Europe during the 18th century. Both were talented, ambitious musicians. Yet, more than 200 years later, Mozart is revered and Salieri is all but forgotten. Why? Then and now, Mozart was considered creative but Salieri was not. What is creativity, and how does it differ from intelligence?

**Intelligence is associated with *convergent thinking*, using information that is provided to determine a standard, correct answer. In contrast, creativity is associated with *divergent thinking*, where the aim is not a single correct answer (often there isn't one) but novel and unusual lines of thought** (Callahan, 2000).

Divergent thinking is often measured by asking children to produce many ideas in response to some specific stimulus (Kogan, 1983). For example, children might be asked to name different uses for a common object, such as a coat hanger. Or they might be shown a page filled with circles and asked to draw as many different pictures as they can, as shown in the figure. Both the number of responses and the originality of the responses are used to measure creativity.

FIGURE 8-8

Creativity, like giftedness, must be cultivated. The "Improving Children's Lives" feature gives some guidelines for fostering children's creativity.

## *Improving Childrens's Lives*

### Fostering Creativity

Here are some guidelines for helping children be more creative.

1. Encourage children to take risks. Not all novel ideas bear fruit; some won't work and some are silly. But only by repeatedly thinking in novel and unusual ways are children likely to produce something truly original.

2. Encourage children to think of alternatives to conventional wisdom. Have them think what would happen if accepted practices were changed. For example, "What would life be like without cars?" or "Why not eat breakfast in the evening and dinner in the morning?"

3. Praise children for working hard. As the saying goes, creativity is one part inspiration and nine parts perspiration. The raw creative insight must be polished to achieve the luster of a finished product.

4. Help children get over the "I'm not creative" hurdle. Too often they believe that only others are creative. Assure children that anyone who follows these guidelines will become more creative. ■

Gifted and creative children represent one extreme of human ability. At the other extreme are youngsters with mental retardation, the topic of the next section.

## Children with Mental Retardation

"Little David," so named because his father was also named David, was the oldest of four children. He learned to sit only days before his first birthday, he began to walk at 2, and he said his first words as a 3-year-old. By age 5, David was far behind his age mates developmentally. David had Down syndrome, described in Module 2.2. An extra 21st chromosome caused David's retarded mental development.

*Mental retardation* **refers to substantially below-average intelligence and problems adapting to an environment that emerge before the age of 18.** Below-average intelligence is defined as a score of 70 or less on an intelligence test such as the Stanford-Binet. Adaptive behavior is usually evaluated from interviews with a parent or other caregiver and refers to the daily living skills needed to live, work, and play in the community—skills for caring for oneself and social skills. Only individuals who are under 18, have problems in these areas, and IQ scores of 70 or less are considered mentally retarded (Detterman, Gabriel, & Ruthsatz, 2002).

**TYPES OF MENTAL RETARDATION**    Your image of a mentally retarded child may be someone with Down syndrome, like the child shown on page 47. In reality, mentally retarded individuals are just as varied as nonretarded people. How, then, can we describe this variety? One approach is to distinguish the causes of mental retardation. **Some cases of mental retardation—no more than 25%—can be traced to a specific biological or physical problem and are known as** *organic mental retardation.* Down syndrome is the most common organic form of mental retardation. Other types of mental retardation apparently do not involve biological damage. *Familial mental retardation* **simply represents the lower end of the normal distribution of intelligence.**

> Mental retardation is defined by below-average scores on intelligence tests and problems adapting to the environment.

Organic mental retardation is usually substantial, and familial mental retardation is usually less pronounced. The American Association on Mental Retardation (AAMR) identifies four levels of retardation. The levels, along with the range of IQ scores associated with each level, are shown in the chart. Also shown are the three levels of retardation typically used by educators in the United States (Cipani, 1991).

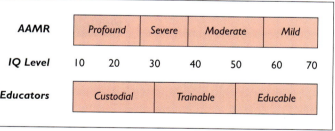

FIGURE 8-9

Fortunately, the most severe forms of mental retardation are relatively uncommon. Profound, severe, and moderate retardation together make up only 10% of all cases. Individuals who are profoundly and severely retarded usually have so few skills that they must be supervised constantly. Consequently, they usually live in institutions for persons with mental retardation, where they can sometimes be taught self-help skills such as dressing, feeding, and toileting (Reid, Wilson, & Faw, 1991).

Persons who are moderately retarded may develop the intellectual skills of a nonretarded 7- or 8-year-old. With this level of functioning, they can sometimes support themselves, typically at a sheltered workshop, where they perform simple tasks under close supervision. For example, beginning as a teenager and continuing

Individuals with mild mental retardation are often employed and they sometimes marry.

into adulthood, "Little David" took a city bus from home to a sheltered workshop. He worked 6 hours daily at tasks such as making bows for packages and stuffing envelopes. He saved his earnings to buy what became his prized possessions—a camera, a color TV, and a VCR.

The remaining 90% of individuals with mental retardation are classified as mildly or educably mentally retarded. These individuals go to school and can master many academic skills, but at an older age than a nonretarded child. Individuals with mild mental retardation can lead independent lives. Like the man in the photograph, many people who are mildly retarded work. Some marry. Comprehensive training programs that focus on vocational and social skills help individuals with mild mental retardation be productive citizens and satisfied human beings (Ellis & Rusch, 1991).

From these descriptions, it's clear that *mental retardation* is a catch-all term. Some individuals with mental retardation have substantial disability but others have a much smaller disability. What they have in common, though, is that with support from family, health-care professionals, and the community, many individuals with mental retardation can become contributing members of society.

## Children with Learning Disabilities

**8.3** Ryan's 8-year-old daughter has been diagnosed with a reading disability. Ryan is concerned that this is just a politically correct way of saying that his daughter is stupid. Is he right?

Youngsters with reading disability often struggle to distinguish different letter sounds.

For some children with normal intelligence, learning is a struggle. **These youngsters have a *learning disability*: they (a) have difficulty mastering an academic subject, (b) have normal intelligence, and (c) are not suffering from other conditions that could explain poor performance, such as sensory impairment or inadequate instruction** (Hammill, 1990).

In the United States, about 5% of school-age children are classified as learning disabled, which translates into nearly 3 million youngsters. The number of distinct disabilities and the degree of overlap among them are still debated (Torgesen, 2004). However, one common classification scheme distinguishes disability in language (including listening, speaking, and writing), in reading, and in arithmetic (Dockrell & McShane, 1993).

The variety of learning disabilities complicates the task for teachers and researchers because it suggests that each type of learning disability may have its own cause and treatment (Lyon, 1996). For example, reading is the most common area of learning disability. Many children with a reading disability have problems in phonological awareness (described in Module 7.3), which refers to understanding and using the sounds in written and oral language. For a reading-disabled child like Sanjit (in the vignette that opened this module) or the boy in the photograph, all vowels sound alike. Thus *pin* sounds like *pen*, which sounds like *pan*. These youngsters benefit from explicit, extensive instruction on the connections between letters and their sounds (Lyon, 1996).

The "Focus on Research" feature looks at one such successful training program.

## Focus on Research

**Improving Reading Skill in Children with Reading Disability**

*Who were the investigators, and what was the aim of the study?* Most reading experts agree that, compared to children who read normally, children with reading disability have difficulty translating print into sound. Experts also agree that the aim of treatment should be to improve such translation skills. Where experts disagree is in the best way to achieve this aim. Some emphasize exercises in which children manipulate sounds and letters in syllables (e.g., "Which one is 'ook'?" "Which is 'koo'?"). Other experts emphasize articulatory awareness in which children learn the positions of their mouth and tongue as they make different vowel and consonant sounds. Barbara Wise, Jerry Ring, and Richard Olson (1999) wanted to compare the effects of these two approaches in improving reading in children with reading disability.

*How did the investigators measure the topic of interest?* Children in the study were assigned to one of four conditions. Some were in a control group that received no special treatment. Others were in a sound-manipulation condition, an articulatory-awareness condition, or a condition that included both sound-manipulation and articulatory-awareness. The training included exercises like those that I just mentioned and lasted 6 months. All children took many reading-related tests before and after training. For simplicity, I'm going to focus on just one outcome measure: children's ability to read individual words accurately.

*Who were the children in the study?* Wise and her colleagues tested 122 children with reading disability from grades 2 through 5. About one fourth of the children were assigned to each of the four conditions.

*What was the design of the study?* The study was experimental. The independent variable was the condition to which the child was assigned; the dependent variable was the number of words that children read accurately. The study was also longitudinal: Students were tested in October and again in May of the same school year.

*Were there ethical concerns with the study?* No. Parental permission was obtained for all children who participated. You may question the ethics of denying treatment to one fourth of the children (those in the control group). However, all these children were promised treatment in the following school year and this was deemed an acceptable risk by the review panel at the University of Colorado, where the study was conducted.

*What were the results?* As I mentioned, the children were given a large battery of tasks. On some of the tasks, the training groups differed. For example, children who had sound-manipulation training were more accurate on phoneme deletion tasks (e.g., "Say 'pran' without the *r*?"). But the most important result is shown in the graph on page 262: In actual reading, the various training methods were equally effective. That is, in terms of the increase in reading skill from before training to after training, all three experimental groups improved 12 to 15%, compared to 4% for the control group.

*What did the investigators conclude?* Children with reading disability must learn about language sounds, but apparently there is no single best method. Consequently, teachers can be successful with either method and can alter their approach based on their own background and their students' strengths.

Children with reading disability have problems understanding and using language sounds.

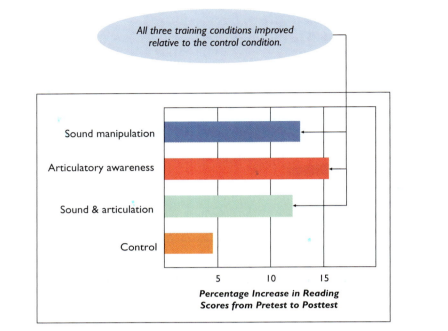

FIGURE 8-10

*What converging evidence would strengthen these conclusions?* Two types of findings would complement the results of this study. First, it would be useful to include a group of children who read normally as another way to assess the effectiveness of training. By comparing the performance of this group to the groups of children who received training, we could determine whether training improved children's reading to normal or near-normal levels. Second, it would be important to test these children in subsequent years to determine whether the training has long-lasting benefits. ■

The findings in the "Focus on Research" feature are good news for children with learning disabilities, such as reading disability. The key to helping these children is to move beyond the generic label *learning disability* to pinpoint specific cognitive and academic deficits that hamper an individual child's performance in school (e.g., for children with reading disability, processing language sounds). Then instruction can be specifically tailored to improve the child's skills (Moats & Lyon, 1993).

Planning effective instruction for children with learning disabilities is much easier said than done, however, because diagnosing learning disability is very difficult. Some children have both reading and language disabilities; other children have reading and arithmetic disabilities. Despite these difficulties, with ingenuity, hard work, and care, children with learning disabilities—and all exceptional children, for that matter—can develop their full intellectual potential.

## CHECK YOUR LEARNING

**RECALL**   Summarize the different forms of mental retardation.
How is learning disability defined? What are the different types of learning disability?

**INTERPRET**   Compare and contrast traditional and modern definitions of giftedness.

**APPLY**   How might Jean Piaget, Howard Gardner, and Robert Sternberg define mental retardation?

No. Part of the definition of learning disability is normal intelligence; children with learning disability have a specific, well-defined disability in conjunction with normal intelligence.

8.3

## UNIFYING THEMES: Nature and Nurture

In this chapter, I want to underscore the theme that *development is always jointly influenced by heredity and environment.* In no other area of child development is this theme as important, because the implications for social policy are so profound. If intelligence were completely determined by heredity, for example, intervention programs would be a waste of time and tax dollars because no amount of experience would change nature's prescription for intelligence. But we've seen several times in this chapter that neither heredity nor environment is all powerful when it comes to intelligence. Studies of twins, for example, remind us that heredity clearly has substantial impact on IQ scores. Identical twins' IQs are consistently more alike than are fraternal twins' IQs, a result that documents heredity's influence on intelligence. Yet, at the same time, intervention studies such as Head Start and the Carolina Abecedarian Project show that intelligence is malleable. Children's intelligence can be enhanced by intensely stimulating environments.

Thus, heredity imposes some limits on how a child's intelligence will develop, but the limits are fairly modest. We can nurture all children's intelligence considerably if we are willing to invest the time and effort.

## SEE FOR YOURSELF

We've seen that the definition of intelligence differs across cultural settings. See how parents define intelligence by asking them to rate the importance of four common aspects of intelligence:

- Problem-solving skill (thinking before acting, seeing different sides to a problem)
- Verbal skill (speaking clearly, having a large vocabulary)
- Creative skill (asking many questions, trying new things)

- Social skill (playing and working well with other people, respecting and caring for others)

Ask parents to rate the importance of each element on a 6-point scale, where 1 means extremely unimportant to intelligence and 6 means extremely important. Try to ask parents from different ethnic groups; then compare your results with other students' results to see if parents' views of intelligence are similar or different and if cultural background affects parents' definitions. See for yourself!

## RESOURCES

For more information about . . .

the **lives of brilliant and creative people,** read Howard Gardner's *Creating Minds* (Basic Books, 1993), which illustrates each different intelligence in Gardner's theory by tracing its development in the life of an extraordinary person, including Albert Einstein, Martha Graham, and Pablo Picasso.

**learning disabilities,** visit the Web site of the National Center for Learning Disabilities **www.ncld.org**

## KEY TERMS

**analytic ability**  242
**convergent thinking**  257
**creative ability**  242
**crystallized intelligence**  239
**culture-fair intelligence tests**  255
**divergent thinking**  257
**dynamic testing**  250
**emotional intelligence**  241
**familial mental retardation**  259
**fluid intelligence**  239

**gifted**  257
**intelligence quotient (IQ)**  246
**learning disability**  260
**mental age (MA)**  246
**mental retardation**  259
**organic mental retardation**  259
**practical ability**  243
**psychometricians**  238
**savants**  240
**stereotype threat**  255

# SUMMARY

## 8.1 WHAT IS INTELLIGENCE?

### Psychometric Theories

Psychometric approaches to intelligence include theories that describe intelligence as a general factor as well as theories that include specific factors. Hierarchical theories include both general intelligence as well as various specific skills, such as verbal and spatial ability.

### Gardner's Theory of Multiple Intelligences

Gardner's theory of multiple intelligences proposes nine distinct intelligences. Three are found in psychometric theories (linguistic, logical-mathematical, and spatial intelligence), but six are new (musical, bodily-kinesthetic, interpersonal, intrapersonal, naturalistic, and existential intelligence). Gardner's theory has stimulated research on nontraditional forms of intelligence, such as emotional intelligence. The theory also has implications for education, suggesting, for example, that schools should adjust teaching to each child's unique intellectual strengths.

### Sternberg's Theory of Successful Intelligence

According to Robert Sternberg, intelligence is defined as using abilities to achieve short- and long-term goals and depends upon three abilities: analytic ability to analyze problem and generate solution, creative ability to deal adaptively with novel situations, and practical ability to know what solutions will work.

## 8.2 MEASURING INTELLIGENCE

### Binet and the Development of Intelligence Testing

Binet created the first intelligence test to identify students who would have difficulty in school. Using this work, Terman created the Stanford-Binet, which introduced the concept of the intelligence quotient (IQ). Another widely used test, the WISC-III, provides IQs based on verbal and performance subtests. Infant tests, such as the Bayley Scales, typically assess mental and motor development.

### Do Tests Work?

In the short term, intelligence tests are reliable, which means that people usually get consistent scores on the tests. In the longer term, scores on infant intelligence tests do not predict adult IQ scores, but infant habituation predicts childhood IQs, and preschool IQ scores predict adult IQs. Intelligence tests are reasonably valid measures of achievement in school. They also predict people's performance in the workplace. Dynamic tests are designed to improve validity by measuring children's potential for future learning.

### Hereditary and Environmental Factors

Evidence for the impact of heredity on IQ comes from the findings that (a) siblings' IQ scores become more alike as siblings become more similar genetically, and (b) adopted children's IQ scores are more like their biological parents' test scores than their adoptive parents' scores. Evidence for the impact of the environment comes from the finding that children who live in responsive, well-organized home environments tend to have higher IQ scores, as do children who participate in intervention programs.

### Impact of Ethnicity and Socioeconomic Status

Ethnic groups differ in their average scores on IQ tests. This difference is not due to genetics or to familiarity with specific test items but is due to children's familiarity and comfort with the testing situation. Nevertheless, IQ scores remain valid predictors of school success because middle-class experience is often a prerequisite for school success.

## 8.3 SPECIAL CHILDREN, SPECIAL NEEDS

### Gifted and Creative Children

Traditionally, gifted children have been those with high scores on IQ tests. Modern definitions of giftedness are broader and include exceptional talent in, for example, the arts. Gifted children are socially mature and emotionally stable.

Creativity is associated with divergent thinking, thinking in novel and unusual directions. Tests of divergent thinking can predict which children are most likely to be creative when they are older. Creativity can be fostered by experiences that encourage children to think flexibly and explore alternatives.

### Children with Mental Retardation

Individuals with mental retardation have IQ scores of 70 or lower and problems in adaptive behavior. Organic mental retardation is due to specific biological or physical causes; familial mental retardation reflects the lower end of the normal distribution of intelligence. Most retarded persons are classified as mildly or educably retarded; they attend school, work, and have families.

### Children with Learning Disabilities

Children with a learning disability have normal intelligence but have difficulty mastering specific academic subjects. The most common is reading disability, which often can be traced to inadequate understanding and use of language sounds. When such language-related skills are taught, children's reading improves.

Toni Morrison, a contemporary African American writer who won the Nobel Prize in literature in 1993, said, "We die. That may be the meaning of life. But we do language. That may be the measure of our lives." Language is indeed a remarkable human tool. Language allows us to express thoughts and feelings to others and to preserve our ideas and learn from the past.

What's truly amazing, given the complexities of language, is that most children master it rapidly and easily. We'll study this mastery in Chapter 9, focusing on four different facets of language. We begin, in Module 9.1, by looking at the first steps in acquiring language—learning about speech sounds. Module 9.2 concerns how children learn to speak and how they learn new words thereafter. In Module 9.3, we'll examine children's early sentences and the rules that children follow in creating them. Finally, in Module 9.4, we'll learn how children use language to communicate with others.

**9.1** The Road to Speech

**9.2** Learning the Meanings of Words

**9.3** Speaking in Sentences

**9.4** Using Language to Communicate

1   The Science of Child Development
2   Genetic Bases of Child Development
3   Prenatal Development, Birth, and the Newborn
4   Growth and Health
5   Perceptual and Motor Development
6   Theories of Cognitive Development
7   Cognitive Processes and Academic Skills
8   Intelligence and Individual Differences in Cognition

# Language and Communication

10  Emotional Development
11  Understanding Self and Others
12  Moral Understanding and Behavior
13  Gender and Development
14  Family Relationships
15  Influences Beyond the Family

# 9.1 THE ROAD TO SPEECH

Elements of Language

Perceiving Speech

First Steps to Speech

## LEARNING OBJECTIVES

- What are the basic sounds of speech, and how well can infants distinguish them?
- How does infant-directed speech help children learn about language?
- What is babbling, and how does it become more complex in older infants?

*As a 7-month-old, Chelsea began to make her first word-like sounds, saying "dah" and "nuh." Several weeks later, she began to repeat these syllables, saying "dah-dah" and "nuh-nuh." By 11 months her speech resembled sentences with stressed words: "dah-NUH-bah-BAH!" Chelsea's parents were astonished that her sentences could sound so much like real speech yet still be absolutely meaningless!*

From birth, infants make sounds—they laugh, cry, and, like Chelsea, produce sounds that resemble speech. Yet, for most of their 1st year, infants do not talk. This contrast raises two important questions about infants as nonspeaking creatures. First, can babies who are unable to speak understand any of the speech that is directed to them? Second, how do infants like Chelsea progress from crying to more effective methods of oral communication, such as speech? We'll answer both questions in this module, but let's begin by considering exactly what we mean by *language*.

## Elements of Language

When you think of language, what comes to mind? English, perhaps? Or maybe German, Spanish, Korean, or Zulu? What about American Sign Language? **Defined broadly,** *language* **is a system that relates sounds (or gestures) to meaning.** Languages are expressed in many forms—through speech, writing, and gesture. Furthermore, languages consist of different subsystems. Spoken languages usually involve four distinct but interrelated elements:

*The elements of language include phonology, semantics, grammar, and pragmatics.*

- *Phonology* **refers to the sounds of a language.** For example, all the different words in English are constructed from about 45 different sounds.
- *Semantics* **is the study of words and their meaning.** *Webster's Third New International Dictionary* includes roughly a half-million words, and a typical college-educated English speaker has a vocabulary of about 150,000 words.
- *Grammar* **refers to the rules used to describe the structure of a language. The most important element of grammar is** *syntax***, rules that specify how words are combined to form sentences.**
- *Pragmatics* **is the study of how people use language to communicate effectively.** Our communication must be appropriate, suited to the audience and occasion. We wouldn't, for example, use fancy vocabulary and long sentences with a 5-year-old.

Learning language involves mastering each of these elements. Children must learn to hear the differences in speech sounds and how to produce them; they must learn the meaning of words and rules for combining them in sentences; and they must learn appropriate and effective ways to talk with others. In the remainder of this module (and the other three in this chapter), we'll see how children come to understand language and speak it themselves.

## Perceiving Speech

We learned in Module 5.1 that even newborn infants hear remarkably well. But can babies distinguish speech sounds? To answer this question, we first need to know more about the elements of speech. **The basic building blocks of language are _phonemes_, unique sounds that can be joined to create words.** Phonemes include consonant sounds such as the sound of *t* in *toe* and *tap* along with vowel sounds such as the sound of *e* in *get* and *bed*. Infants can distinguish most of these sounds, many of them by as early as 1 month after birth (Aslin, Jusczyk, & Pisoni, 1998).

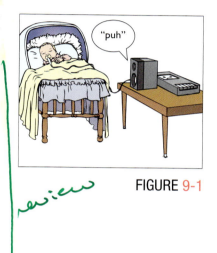

FIGURE 9-1

How do we know that infants can distinguish different vowels and consonants? Researchers have devised a number of clever techniques to determine if babies respond differently to distinct sounds. One approach is illustrated in the diagram. A rubber nipple is connected to a tape recorder so that sucking turns on the tape and sound comes out of a loudspeaker. In just a few minutes, 1-month-olds learn the relation between their sucking and the sound: They suck rapidly to hear a tape that consists of nothing more than the sound of *p* as in *pin, pet,* and *pat* (pronounced "puh").

After a few more minutes, infants seemingly tire of this repetitive sound and suck less often, which represents the habituation phenomenon described in Module 5.1. But, if the tape is changed to a different sound, such as the sound of *b* in *bed, bat,* or *bird* (pronounced "buh") babies begin sucking rapidly again. Evidently, they recognize that the sound of *b* is different from *p* because they suck more often to hear the new sound (Jusczyk, 1995).

Of course, the language environment for young infants is not solely auditory; much exposure to language comes in face-to-face interaction with adults. These interactions provide many visual cues about sounds and infants use these cues: Shown a video of an adult saying "ba," infants notice when the adult looks to be saying "sha" even though the audio still presents "ba" (Patterson & Werker, 2003).

**THE IMPACT OF LANGUAGE EXPOSURE.** Not all languages use the same set of phonemes; a distinction that is important in one language may be ignored in another. For example, unlike English, French and Polish differentiate between nasal and nonnasal vowels. To hear the difference, say the word *rod*. Now repeat it, but holding your nose. The subtle difference between the two sounds illustrates a non-nasal vowel (the first version of *rod*) and a nasal one (the second).

Because an infant might be exposed to any of the world's languages, it would be adaptive for young infants to be able to perceive a wide range of phonemes. In fact, research shows that infants can distinguish phonemes that are not used in their native language. For example, Japanese does not distinguish the consonant sound of *r* in *rip* from the sound of *l* in *lip* and Japanese adults trying to learn English have great difficulty distinguishing these sounds. At about 6 months, infants in both Japanese- and English-speaking environments can distinguish them, but by 11 or 12 months, only infants in English-speaking environments can (Werker & Tees, 1999).

Newborns apparently are biologically capable of hearing the entire range of phonemes in all languages worldwide. But as babies grow and are more exposed to a particular language, they only notice the linguistic distinctions that are meaningful in their own language. Thus specializing in one language apparently comes at the cost of making it more difficult to hear sounds in other languages (Best, 1995).

**IDENTIFYING WORDS.** Of course, hearing individual phonemes is only the first step in perceiving speech. One of the biggest challenges for infants is identifying recurring patterns of sounds—words. Imagine, for example, an infant overhearing this conversation between a parent and an older sibling:

SIBLING: Jerry got a new *bike.*

PARENT: Was his old *bike* broken?

SIBLING: No. He'd saved his allowance to buy a new mountain *bike.*

An infant listening to this conversation hears *bike* three times. Can the infant learn from this experience? Yes. When 7- to 8-month-olds hear a word repeatedly in different sentences, they later pay more attention to this word than to words they haven't heard previously. Evidently, 7- and 8-month-olds can listen to sentences and recognize the sound patterns that they hear repeatedly (Houston & Juscyzk, 2003; Saffran, Aslin, & Newport, 1996). And, by 6 months, infants pay more attention to content words (e.g., nouns, verbs) than to function words (e.g., articles, prepositions) and they look at the correct parent when they hear "mommy" or "daddy" (Shi & Werker, 2001; Tincoff & Jusczyk, 1999).

In normal conversation, there are no silent gaps between words, so how do infants pick out words? Stress is one important clue. English contains many one-syllable words that are stressed and many two-syllable words that have a stressed syllable followed by an unstressed syllable (e.g., dough´ -nut, tooth´ -paste, bas´ -ket). Infants pay more attention to stressed syllables than unstressed syllables, which is a good strategy for identifying the beginnings of words (Thiessen & Saffran, 2003; Mattys et al., 1999).

> Infants use stress and the co-occurence of sounds to identify words in speech.

Of course, stress is not a foolproof sign. Many two-syllable words have stress on the second syllable (e.g., gui-tar´, sur-prise´), so infants need other methods to identify words in speech. One method is statistical. Infants notice syllables that go together frequently (Jusczyk, 2002). For example, in a study by Aslin, Saffran, and Newport (1998), 8-month-olds heard the following sounds, which consisted of 4 three-syllable artificial words, said over and over in a random order.

<u>pa bi ku</u> <u>go la tu</u> <u>da ro pi</u> <u>ti bu do</u> <u>da ro pi</u> <u>go la tu</u> <u>pa bi ku</u> <u>da ro pi</u>

I've underlined the words and inserted gaps between them so that you can see them more easily, but in the study there were no breaks at all—just a steady flow of syllables for 3 minutes. Later, infants listened to these words less than to new words that were novel combinations of the same syllables. They had detected *pa bi ku, go la tu, da ro pi,* and *ti bu do* as familiar patterns and listened to them less than to words like *tu da ro,* a new word made up from syllables they'd already heard.

Yet another way that infants identify words is through their emerging knowledge of how sounds are used in their native language. For example, think about these two pairs of sounds: *s* followed by *t* and *s* followed by *d.* Both pairs of sounds are quite common at the end of one word and the beginning of the next: bu*s t*akes, ki*ss t*ook; thi*s d*og, pa*ss d*irectly. However, *s* and *t* occur frequently within a word (*st*op, li*st,* pe*st, st*ink) but *s* and *d* do not. Consequently, when *d* follows an *s,* it probably starts a new word. In fact, 9-month-olds follow rules like this one because when they hear novel words embedded in continuous speech, they're more likely to identify the novel word when the final sound in the preceding word occurs infrequently with the first sound of the novel word (Mattys & Jusczyk, 2001).

Thus, infants use many powerful tools to identify words in speech. Of course, they don't yet understand the meanings of these words; at this point, they simply recognize a word as a distinct configuration of sounds. Nevertheless, these early perceptual skills are important because infants who are more skilled at detecting speech sounds know more words as toddlers (Tsao, Liu, & Kuhl, 2004).

Parents (and other adults) often help infants master language sounds by talking in a distinctive style. **In *infant-directed* *speech*, adults speak slowly and with exaggerated changes in pitch and loudness.** If you could hear the mother in the photo talking to her baby, you would notice that she alternates between speaking softly and loudly and between high and low pitches and that her speech seems very expressive emotionally (Trainor, Austin, & Desjardins, 2000). (Infant-directed speech is also known as *motherese*, because this form of speaking was first noted in mothers, although it's now known that most caregivers talk this way to infants.)

Infant-directed speech may attract infants' attention more than adult-directed speech (Kaplan et al., 1995; Lewkowicz, 2000a) because its slower pace and accentuated changes provide infants with increasingly more salient language clues. Infant-directed speech includes especially good examples of vowels (Kuhl et al., 1997), which may help infants learn to distinguish these sounds. And when talking to infants, speaking clearly is a good idea. In one study (Liu, Kuhl, & Tsao, 2003), infants who could best distinguish speech sounds had the mothers who spoke most clearly.

Infant-directed speech, then, helps infants perceive the sounds that are fundamental to their language. Unfortunately, some babies cannot hear speech sounds because they are deaf. How can these infants best learn language? The "Child Development and Family Policy" feature addresses this question.

When parents talk to babies, they often use "infant-directed speech," which is slower and more varied in pitch and volume than adult-directed speech.

**Q&A** uestion

Kristin spends hours talking to her infant son. **9.1** Her husband enjoys spending time with his wife and son but wishes Kristin would stop using "baby talk" with their son and just talk in her regular voice. The sing-song pattern drives him crazy and he can't believe that it's of any good for her son. Is he right?

### *Child Development and Family Policy*
### Are Cochlear Implants Effective for Young Children?

About 2 infants and toddlers out of 1,000 are born deaf or have profound hearing loss before they master language. Of these youngsters, about 10% are born to deaf parents. In these cases, the child's deafness is usually detected early and parents communicate with their children using sign language. Deaf infants and toddlers seem to master sign language in much the same way and at about the same pace that hearing children master spoken language. For example, deaf 10-month-olds often babble in signs: They produce sequences of signs that are meaningless but resemble the tempo and duration of real signs.

The remaining 90% of deaf infants and toddlers have parents with normal hearing. For these children, communicating with signs is not really an option because their parents don't know sign language. Consequently, the usual recommendation for deaf children of hearing parents is to master spoken language, sometimes through methods that emphasize lip reading and speech therapy and sometimes with these methods along with signs and gestures. Unfortunately, with any of these methods, deaf children and parents rarely master spoken language. Their ability to produce and comprehend spoken language falls years behind their peers with normal language (Hoff, 2005).

Since the mid-1990s, however, deaf children have had a new option. As I described on page 137, the cochlear implant is a device that picks up speech sounds and converts them to electrical impulses that stimulate nerve cells in the ear. Cochlear implants are a tremendous benefit for people who lose their hearing after they master language. Adults with cochlear implants can converse readily with hearing speakers and some can converse on the phone (which is difficult otherwise because they can't lip read and because telephone lines sometimes distort speech sounds).

The potential benefit of cochlear implants for young children is a more controversial issue. Some critics (e.g., Lane, 1992; Lane & Bahan, 1998) argue that although cochlear implants benefit adults who have already learned language, there is no evidence that they can help young children to learn language. That is, the critics doubt that the quality of sensory information provided by cochlear implants is sufficient to guide language acquisition.

To determine whether cochlear implants should be recommended for deaf infants and toddlers, researchers would need to compare language development in deaf children who have cochlear implants with that in deaf children who do not. Mario Svirsky and his colleagues (2000) provided such data in a study of 70 children who had become profoundly deaf before age 3 and had received cochlear implants at an average age of $4\frac{1}{2}$ years. Their results were clear: Language development was enhanced in children with cochlear implants. That is, language skills improved more rapidly in children who had cochlear implants than in children who did not. In fact, after children had received cochlear implants, their language acquisition progressed at the same rate as language in children with normal hearing.

But this good news comes with several cautions. First, because most children did not receive their cochlear implants until 4 or 5 years of age, their language skills are still substantially behind that of hearing children. Second, a cochlear implant does not replace other forms of therapy for deaf children; a cochlear implant is used with these other forms to make them more effective. Third, the benefits of a cochlear implant are not the same for all children: Improvements in language are astonishing for some children but modest for others.

These findings, along with similar outcomes from other studies (e.g., Blamey et al., 2001; Connor & Zwola, 2004) have clear implications for policies that concern young deaf children. A cochlear implant is an effective tool that can enhance children's language; it should be made available to deaf children. At the same time, research is needed to determine, first, the value of cochlear implants for younger infants and, second, why cochlear implants are so beneficial for some children but not others. ■

## First Steps to Speech

As any new parent can testify, newborns and young babies make many sounds—they cry, burp, and sneeze. However, language-based sounds don't appear immediately. **At 2 months, infants begin to produce vowel-like sounds, such as "ooooooo" or "ahh-hhhh," a phenomenon known as** *cooing*. Sometimes infants become quite excited as they coo, perhaps reflecting the joy of simply playing with sounds.

**After cooing comes** *babbling*, **speech-like sound that has no meaning.** A typical 6-month-old might say "dah" or "bah," utterances that sound like a single syllable consisting of a consonant and a vowel. Over the next few months, babbling becomes more elaborate as babies apparently experiment with more complex speech sounds. Older infants sometimes repeat a sound as in "bahbahbah" and begin to combine different sounds, "dahmahbah" (Hoff, 2005).

Babbling is not just mindless playing with sounds; instead, it's a precursor to real speech. We know this, in part, from video records of people's mouths while speaking. When adults speak, their mouth is open somewhat wider on the right side than on the left side, reflecting the left hemisphere's control of language and muscle movements on the body's right side (Graves & Landis, 1990). Infants do the same when they babble, but not when making other nonbabbling sounds, which suggests that babbling is fundamentally linguistic (Holowka & Petitto, 2002).

Other evidence for the linguistic nature of babbling comes from studies of developmental change in babbling: At roughly 8 to 11 months, infants' babbling sounds more like real speech because infants, such as Chelsea (in the vignette), stress some syllables and they vary the pitch of their speech (Davis et al., 2000). In English declarative sentences, for example, pitch first rises, then falls toward the end of the sentence. In questions, however, the pitch is level, then rises toward the end of the question. **This pattern of rising or falling pitch is known as *intonation*.** Older babies' babbling reflects these patterns: Babies who are brought up by English-speaking parents have both the declarative and question patterns of intonation in their babbling. Babies exposed to a language with different patterns of intonation, such as Japanese or French, reflect their language's intonation in their babbling (Levitt & Utman, 1992).

The appearance of intonation in babbling indicates a strong link between perception and production of speech: Infants' babbling is influenced by the characteristics of the speech that they hear. Beginning in the middle of the 1st year, infants try to reproduce the sounds of language that others use in trying to communicate with them (or, in the case of deaf infants with deaf parents, the signs that others use). Hearing *dog*, an infant may first say "dod," then "gog" before finally saying "dog" correctly. In the same way that beginning typists gradually link movements of their fingers with particular keys, through babbling infants learn to use their lips, tongue, and teeth to produce specific sounds, gradually making sounds that approximate real words (Poulson et al., 1991). Fortunately, learning to produce language sounds is easier for most babies than the cartoon suggests!

> Babbling appears at 5 or 6 months with a single consonant and vowel, then combines different speech sounds and, later, adds intonation.

The ability to produce sound, coupled with the 1-year-old's advanced ability to perceive speech sounds, sets the stage for the infant's first true words. In Module 9.2, we'll see how this happens.

**9.1** No, he's wrong. Infant-directed speech helps babies to learn language, in part because changes in pitch attract an infant's attention and because the slower pace and accentuated changes help infants to detect differences in speech sounds. But I'll agree with Kristin's husband that infant-directed speech can become grating after a while!

## 9.2

# LEARNING THE MEANINGS OF WORDS

**Understanding Words as Symbols**

**Fast Mapping Meanings to Words**

**Individual Differences in Word Learning**

**Encouraging Word Learning**

**Beyond Words: Other Symbols**

### LEARNING OBJECTIVES

- How do children make the transition from babbling to talking?
- What different styles of language learning do young children use?
- What rules do children follow to learn new words?
- What conditions foster children's learning of new words?

*Sebastien is 20 months old and loves to talk. What amazes his parents is how quickly he adds words to his vocabulary. For example, the day his parents brought home a computer, Sebastien watched as they set it up. The next day, he spontaneously pointed to the computer and said, "puter." This happens all the time—Sebastien hears a word once or twice, then uses it correctly himself. Sebastien's parents wonder how he does this, particularly because learning vocabulary in a foreign language is so difficult for them!*

At about their first birthday, most youngsters say their first words. Typically, these words are an extension of advanced babbling, consisting of a consonant–vowel pair that may be repeated. *Mama* and *dada* are probably the most common first words that stem from advanced babbling. Other early vocabulary words include animals, food, body parts, and clothing (Nelson, 1973). Also common are words that denote actions (for example, *go*). By age 2, most youngsters have a vocabulary of a few hundred words, and by age 6, a typical child's vocabulary includes over 10,000 words (Anglin, 1993).

Like Sebastien, most children learn new words with extraordinary ease and speed. How do they do it? We'll answer that question in this module.

## Understanding Words as Symbols

When my daughter, Laura, was 9 months old, she sometimes babbled "bay-bay." A few months later, she still said "bay-bay" but with an important difference. As a 9-month-old, "bay-bay" was simply an interesting set of sounds that she made for no reason (at least, none that was obvious to us). As a 13-month-old, "bay-bay" was her way of saying "baby." What had happened between 9 and 13 months? Laura had begun to understand that speech is more than just entertaining sound. She realized that sounds form words that refer to objects, actions, and properties. Put another way, Laura recognized that words are symbols, entities that stand for other entities. She already had formed concepts such as "round, bouncy things" and "furry things that bark" and "little humans that adults carry" based on her own experiences. With the insight that speech sounds can denote these concepts, she began to match sound patterns (words) and concepts (Reich, 1986).

If this argument is correct, we should find that children use symbols in other areas, not just in language. They do. Gestures are symbols, and like the baby in the photo, infants begin to gesture shortly before their first birthday (Goodwyn & Acredolo, 1993). Young children may smack their lips to indicate hunger or wave "bye-bye" when leaving. In these cases, gestures and words convey a message equally well.

What's more, gesture sometimes paves the way for language. Before knowing an object's name, infants often point to it or pick it up for a listener, as if saying, "I want this!" or "What's this?" In one study, 50% of all objects were first referred to by gesture and, about 3 months later, by word (Iverson & Goldin-Meadow, 2005). After children know that objects have names, a gesture is a convenient substitute for pronouns like "it" or "that" and often cause an adult to say the object's name.

Babies begin to gesture at about the same time that they say their first words; both accomplishments show that infants are mastering symbols.

## Fast Mapping Meanings to Words

Once children have the insight that a word can symbolize an object or action, their vocabularies grow slowly at first. A typical 15-month-old, for example, may learn two to three new words each week. **However, at about 18 months, many children experience a *naming explosion* during which they learn new words—particularly names of objects—much more rapidly than before.** Children now learn 10 or more new words each week (Fenson et al., 1994).

When a parent points to an object and says a word, babies conceivably could link the name to the object, to a property of the object (e.g., color), or to the act of pointing. In fact, babies consistently interpret the word as the object's name, an assumption that allows them to learn words rapidly.

This rapid rate of word learning is astonishing when we realize that most words have many plausible but incorrect referents. To illustrate, imagine what's going through the mind of the child in the photo. The mother has just pointed to the flowers, saying, "Flowers. These are flowers. See the flowers." To the mother (and you), this all seems crystal clear and incredibly straightforward. But what might a child learn from this episode? Perhaps the correct referent for "flowers." But a youngster could, just as reasonably, conclude that "flowers" refers to the petals, to the color of the flowers, or to the mother's actions in pointing to the flowers.

Surprisingly, though, most youngsters learn the proper meanings of simple words in just a few presentations. **Children's ability to connect new words to their meanings so rapidly that they cannot be considering all possible meanings for the new word is termed** *fast mapping*. How can young children learn new words so rapidly? Researchers believe that many distinct factors contribute to young children's rapid word learning (Hollich et al., 2000).

**JOINT ATTENTION.** Parents encourage word learning by carefully watching what interests their children. When toddlers touch or look at an object, parents often label it for them. When a youngster points to a banana, a parent may say, "Banana, that's a banana." And parents do their best to simplify the task for children by using one label consistently for an object (Callanan & Sabbagh, 2004).

Of course, to take advantage of this help, infants must be able to tell when parents are labeling instead of just conversing. In fact, when adults label an unfamiliar object, 18- to 20-month-olds assume that the label is the object's name *only* when adults show signs that they are referring to the object. For example, toddlers are more likely to learn the name of an object or action when adults look at the object or action while saying its name than when adults look elsewhere while labeling (Diesenbruck et al., 2004; Poulin-Dubois & Forbes, 2002). Thus, beginning in the toddler years, parents and children work together to create conditions that foster word learning: Parents label objects and youngsters rely on adults' behavior to interpret the words they hear.

Although joint attention helps children to learn words, it is not required: Children learn new words when they are used in ongoing conversation and when they overhear others use novel words (Akhtar, Jipson, & Callanan, 2001). And when speakers appear unfamiliar with a novel person or object, 4- and 5-year-olds are less likely to learn new words, as if they doubt that speakers know what they're talking about (Birch & Bloom, 2002; Jaswal, 2004).

**CONSTRAINTS ON WORD NAMES.** Joint attention simplifies word learning for children, but the problem still remains: How does a toddler know that *banana* refers to the object that she's touching, as opposed to her activity (touching) or to the object's color? Many researchers believe that young children follow several simple rules that limit their conclusions about what labels mean.

> Young children use several simple rules to learn word names, such as the rule that a name applies to an entire object.

A study by Au and Glusman (1990) shows how researchers have identified some of the rules that young children use. These investigators presented preschoolers with a stuffed animal with pink horns that otherwise resembled a monkey and called it a *mido*. *Mido* was then repeated several times, always referring to the monkey-like stuffed animal with pink horns. Later, these youngsters were asked to find a *theri* in a set of stuffed animals that included several *mido*. Never having heard of a *theri*, what did the children do? They never picked a *mido*; instead, they selected other stuffed animals. Knowing that *mido* referred to monkey-like animals with pink horns, evidently they decided that *theri* had to refer to one of the other stuffed animals.

Apparently children were following this simple but effective rule for learning new words:

- If an unfamiliar word is heard in the presence of objects that already have names and objects that don't, the word refers to one of the objects that doesn't have a name.

Researchers have discovered several other simple rules that help children match words with the correct referent (Hoff, 2005; Woodward & Markman, 1998):

- A name refers to a whole object, not its parts or its relation to other objects, and refers not just to this particular object but to all objects of the same type. For example, when a grandparent points to a stuffed animal on a shelf and says "dinosaur," children conclude that *dinosaur* refers to the entire dinosaur, not just its ears or nose, not to the fact that the dinosaur is on a shelf, and not to this specific dinosaur but to all dinosaur-like objects.

- If an object already has a name and another name is presented, the new name denotes a subcategory of the original name. If the child who knows the meaning of *dinosaur* sees a brother point to another dinosaur and hears the brother say "T-rex," the child will conclude that *T-rex* is a special type of dinosaur.

- Given many similar category members, a word applied consistently to only one of them is a proper noun. If a child who knows *dinosaur* sees that one of a group of dinosaurs is always called "Dino," the child will conclude that *Dino* is the name of that dinosaur.

Rules like these make it possible for children such as Sebastien, the child in the vignette, to learn words rapidly because they reduce the number of possible referents. The child in the photo on page 275 follows these rules to decide that *flower* refers to the entire object, not its parts or the action of pointing to it.

**SENTENCE CUES.**   Children hear many unfamiliar words embedded in sentences containing words they already know. The other words and the overall sentence structure can be helpful clues to a word's meaning.

For example, when a parent describes an event using familiar words but an unfamiliar verb, children often infer that the verb refers to the action performed by the subject of the sentence (Fisher, 1996; Woodward & Markman, 1998). When the youngsters in the photo hear, "The man is juggling," they will infer that *juggling* refers to the man's actions with the bats, because they already know *man* and because *-ing* refers to ongoing actions.

Preschool children know that *-ing* is added to a verb to indicate an ongoing action; consequently, when they hear an unfamiliar verb (e.g., "juggle") with *-ing* they infer that the unfamiliar verb must refer to the current action.

As another example of how sentence context aids word learning, look at the blocks in the diagram and point to "the boz block." I imagine you pointed to the middle block. Why? In English, adjectives usually precede the nouns they modify, so you inferred that *boz* is an adjective describing *block*. Since *the* before *boz* implies that only one block is *boz*, you picked the middle one, having decided that *boz* means "winged." Toddlers, too, use sentence cues like these to judge word meanings. Hearing "This is a Zav," 2-year-olds will interpret *Zav* as a category name but hearing "This is Zav" (without the *a*), they interpret *Zav* as a proper name (Hall, Lee, & Belanger, 2001).

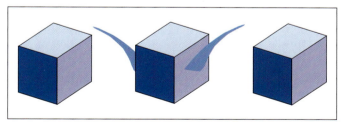

FIGURE 9-2

**COGNITIVE FACTORS.**   The naming explosion coincides with a time of rapid cognitive growth, and children's increased cognitive skill helps them to learn new words. As children's thinking becomes more sophisticated and, in particular, as they start to have goals and intentions, language becomes a means to express those goals and to achieve them. Thus, intention provides children with an important motive to learn language—to help achieve their goals (Bloom & Tinker, 2001). In addition, young children's improving attentional and perceptual skills also promote word learning. In the "Spotlight on Theories" feature, we'll see how children's attention to shape (e.g., balls are round, pencils are slender rods) helps them learn new words.

### *Spotlight on Theories*
## A Shape-Bias Theory of Word Learning

*BACKGROUND:*
Many developmental scientists believe that young children could master a complex task like word learning only by using built-in, language-specific mechanisms (e.g., fast-mapping rules such as "unfamiliar words refer to objects that don't have names"). However, not all scientists agree that specialized processes are required; they argue that word learning can be accomplished by applying basic processes of attention and learning.

*THE THEORY:*
Linda B. Smith (2000) argues that shape plays a central role in learning words. Infants and young children spontaneously pay attention to an object's shape and they use this bias to learn new words. In Smith's theory, children first associate names with a single object: "ball" is associated with a specific tennis ball and "cup" is associated with a favorite sippy cup. As children encounter new balls and new cups, however, they hear the same words applied to similarly shaped objects and reach the conclusion that balls are round and cups are cylinders with handles. With further experience, children derive an even more general rule: Objects that have the same shape have the same name. From this, children realize that paying attention to shape is an easy way to learn names.

**HYPOTHESIS:** If bias to attend to shape helps children learn words names, then the age at which children first show the shape bias should coincide with a jump in the number of names that children learn. In other words, as soon as children realize that similarly shaped objects have the same name, they should start learning names much more rapidly.

**TEST:** Gershkoff-Stowe and Smith (2004) conducted a longitudinal study in which parents kept detailed records of their toddlers' word learning for several months. In addition, toddlers were tested every 3 weeks. They were shown a multicolored U-shaped wooden object and told it was a "dax." Then they were shown several objects, some of which were also U-shaped but differed in color and material (e.g., a blue U-shaped sponge). Other objects were the same color (i.e., multicolored) or the same material (i.e., wood) but not U-shaped. Children were asked to give all the "dax" to the experimenter.

> ## Young children use an object's shape to help them learn its name.

The crucial findings concern the age at which shape bias emerges and the age of the beginning of the naming explosion. Gershkoff-Stowe and Smith defined the onset of shape bias as the first session in which toddlers gave both U-shaped objects—but no others—to the experimenter. The onset of the naming explosion was defined as the 1st week in which toddlers learned 10 or more new words. These two ages were highly correlated—$r = .85$—indicating a tight link between onset of shape bias and the naming explosion.

**CONCLUSION:** As predicted, once toddlers showed a shape bias—that is, they realized that a name applies to objects that have the same shape but not to objects of the same color or made of the material—they used this knowledge to learn new words faster. This result supports Smith's theory and the general idea that word learning may not require specialized mechanisms.

**APPLICATION:** If shape bias helps children learn words, can we teach this bias and foster word learning? Yes. Smith and colleagues (2002) had toddlers and an experimenter play with four pairs of novel objects; each pair of objects had the same name and the same shape but differed in color and material. A "dax" was still a U-shaped object; a "zup" referred to an elliptical-shaped object with a slot in one end. During play, the experimenter named each object 10 times. When children played with objects in this way, they learned the names of real words rapidly. From playing with "dax" and "zup" toddlers apparently learned that paying attention to shape is a good way to learn object names. Likewise, by systematically showing toddlers that the same name applies to many similarly shaped objects (e.g., book, crayon, comb, spoon), parents can teach youngsters the value of paying attention to shape to learn word names. ■

**NAMING ERRORS.**    Of course, these many ways of learning new words are not perfect; initial mappings of words onto meanings are often only partially correct (Hoff & Naigles, 2002). **A common mistake is *underextension*, defining a word too narrowly.** Using *car* to refer only to the family car and *ball* to a favorite toy ball are examples of underextension. **Between 1 and 3 years, children sometimes make the opposite error, *overextension*, defining a word too broadly.** Children may use *car* to also refer to buses and trucks or use *doggie* to refer to all four-legged animals.

The overextension error occurs more frequently when children are producing words than when they are comprehending words. Two-year-old Jason may say "doggie" to refer to a goat but nevertheless correctly point to a picture of a goat when asked. Because overextension is more common in word production, it may actually reflect another fast-mapping rule that children follow: "If you can't remember the name for an object, say the name of a related object" (Naigles & Gelman, 1995).

Both underextension and overextension disappear gradually as youngsters refine meanings for words with more exposure to language.

## Individual Differences in Word Learning

The naming explosion typically occurs at about 18 months, but like many developmental milestones, the timing of this event varies widely for individual children. Some youngsters have a naming explosion as early as 14 months but for others it may be as late as 22 months (Goldfield & Reznick, 1990). Another way to make this point is to look at variation in the size of children's vocabulary at a specific age. At 18 months, for example, an average child's vocabulary would have about 75 words, but a child in the 90th percentile would know nearly 250 words and a child in the 10th percentile fewer than 25 words (Fenson et al., 1994).

The range in vocabulary size for normal 18-month-olds is huge—from 25 to 250 words! What can account for this difference? Heredity contributes: Twin studies find that vocabulary size is more similar in identical twins than in fraternal twins (Dionne et al., 2003). But the difference is fairly small, indicating a relatively minor role for genetics.

More important are two other factors. **One is *phonological memory*, the ability to remember speech sounds briefly.** This is often measured by saying a nonsense word to children—"ballop" or "glistering"—and asking them to repeat it immediately. Children's skill in recalling such words is strongly related to the size of their vocabulary (Gathercole et al., 1992). Children who have difficulty remembering speech sounds accurately find word learning particularly challenging, which is not surprising since word learning involves associating meaning with an unfamiliar sequence of speech sounds.

**9.2**  Gavin and Mitch are both 16-month-olds. Gavin's vocabulary includes about 14 words but Mitch's has about 150 words, more than 10 times as many as Gavin. What factors contribute to this difference?

However, the single most important factor in growth of vocabulary is the child's language environment. Children have larger vocabularies when they are exposed to much high-quality language. The more words that children hear, the better. Specifically, children learn more words when their parents' speech is rich in different words and is grammatically sophisticated (Hoff, 2003; Hoff & Naigles, 2002), and when parents respond promptly and appropriately to their children's talk (Tamis-Lemonda & Bornstein, 2002).

**WORD LEARNING STYLES.**   Size of vocabulary is not the only way in which young children differ in their word learning. As youngsters expand their vocabulary, they often adopt a distinctive style of learning language (Bates, Bretherton, & Snyder, 1988). **Some children have a *referential style*; their vocabularies mainly consist of words that name objects, persons, or actions. Other children have an *expressive style*; their vocabularies include some names but also many social phrases that are used like a single word, such as "go away," "what'd you want?" and "I want it."**

Katherine Nelson (1973) was the investigator who discovered these two basic styles of learning language. She studied 18 children for about a year, starting at approximately their first birthdays, a period during which the children's vocabularies increased from fewer than 10 words to nearly 200. She visited each child monthly for about an hour to tape-record samples of spontaneous speech and to test language development.

By the time children had 50-word vocabularies—typically at about $1\frac{1}{2}$ years—two distinct groups had emerged. Children in the referential group had vocabularies dominated by names of objects, persons, or actions, such as *milk*, *Jo-Jo*, and *up*. Other children, the expressive group, learned some names but knew a much higher percentage of words that were used in social interactions (*go away*, *I want it*, *lemme see*) and question words (*what*, *where*). For example, Rachel, a referential child, had 41 name words in her 50-word vocabulary but only 2 words for social interaction or questions. Elizabeth, an expressive child, had a more balanced vocabulary: 24 name words and 14 for social interactions and questions.

> Language is primarily an intellectual tool for referential children and primarily a social tool for expressive children.

We know now that referential and expressive styles represent end points on a continuum; most children are somewhere in between. For children with referential emphasis, language is primarily an intellectual tool—a means of learning and talking about objects (Masur, 1995). In contrast, for children with expressive emphasis, language is more of a social tool—a way of enhancing interactions with others. Of course, both of these functions—intellectual and social—are important functions of language, which explains why most children blend the referential and expressive styles of learning language.

## Encouraging Word Learning

How can parents and other adults help children learn words? For children to expand their vocabularies, they need to hear others speak. Not surprisingly, then, children learn words more rapidly if their parents speak to them frequently (Huttenlocher et al., 1991; Roberts, Burchinal, & Durham, 1999). Of course, sheer quantity of parental speech is not all that matters. Parents can foster word learning by naming objects that are the focus of a child's attention (Dunham, Dunham, & Curwin, 1993). Parents can name different products on store shelves as they point to them. During a walk, parents can label the objects—birds, plants, vehicles—that the child sees.

Parents can also help children learn words by reading books with them. Reading together is fun for parents and children alike, and it provides opportunities for children to learn new words. However, the way that parents read makes a difference. When parents carefully describe pictures as they read, preschoolers' vocabularies increase (Reese & Cox, 1999). Asking children questions also helps. In a study of 4-year-olds (Sénéchal, Thomas, & Monker, 1995), some parents simply read the story and children listened. Other parents read the story but stopped periodically to ask a "what" or "where" question that the child could answer with the target word. Later, the researchers tested children's abilities to recognize the target words and produce them. The graph shows that children who answered questions comprehended more target words than children who only listened. Children who answered questions were also much more likely to produce the target words.

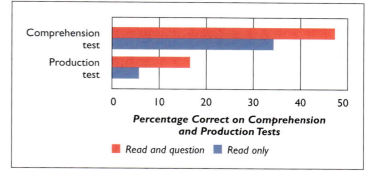

Percentage Correct on Comprehension and Production Tests

FIGURE 9-3

Why is questioning effective? When an adult reads a sentence (e.g., "Arthur is *angling*"), then asks a question (e.g., "What is Arthur doing?"), a child must match the new word (*angling*) with the pictured activity (fishing) and say the word aloud. When parents read without questioning, children can ignore words they don't understand. Questioning forces children to identify meanings of new words and practice saying them.

Viewing television can also help word learning under some circumstances. For example, preschool children who regularly watch *Sesame Street* usually have larger vocabularies by the time they enter kindergarten than preschoolers who watch *Sesame Street* only occasionally (Rice et al., 1990). Other television programs, notably cartoons, do not have this positive influence. What accounts for the difference? *Sesame Street* involves children in language activities that help them learn words (in the photo, words with *E*). Cartoons, however, require no interaction at all.

For school-age children, parents remain an important influence on vocabulary development: Children learn words when exposed to a parent's advanced vocabulary, particularly in the context of instructive and helpful interactions (Weizman & Snow, 2001). Reading is another great way to learn new words. Written material—books, magazines, newspapers, textbooks—almost always contains more unfamiliar words than conversational language, so reading is rich in opportunities to expand vocabulary (Hayes, 1988). Not surprisingly, children who read frequently tend to have larger vocabularies than children who read less often (Allen, Cipielewski, & Stanovich, 1992).

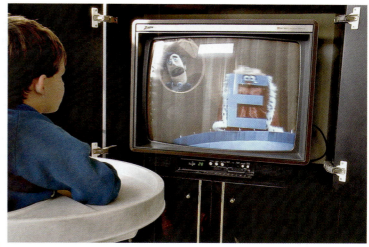

Children can learn language from *Sesame Street* because the programs encourage children to participate in language activities.

Research on reading, along with research on television and parents' influence, points to a simple but powerful conclusion: Children are most likely to learn new words when they participate in activities that force them to understand the meanings of new words and use those new words. Is learning new words (and other aspects of language) more difficult for children learning two languages? The "Cultural Influences" feature has the answer.

## *Cultural Influences*
### Growing Up Bilingual

About 6 million American schoolchildren come from homes where English is not the primary language. In some states, 25% or more of the children are bilingual, and the percentages are even higher in some urban areas (U.S. Bureau of the Census, 1995). These youngsters usually speak English and another language, such as Spanish or, like the children in the photo, Chinese.

Is learning two languages easier or harder than learning just one language? For much of the 20th century, the general view was that bilingualism harmed children's development. One child psychology text published in 1952 surveyed the research and concluded, "There can be no doubt that the child reared in a bilingual environment is handicapped in his language growth" (Thompson, 1952, p. 367). Today, we know this conclusion is wrong because it was based on studies of poor, immigrant children's scores on intelligence tests. In retrospect, immigrant children's test scores had more to do with their poverty and unfamiliarity with a new culture than with their bilingualism.

In fact, modern studies lead to a different picture. When 1- and 2-year-olds learn two languages simultaneously, they often progress somewhat slowly at first because they mix words from the two languages. By age 3 or 4, however, children separate the languages; and by the time they begin elementary school, they are proficient in both languages (Baker, 1993; Lanza, 1992). When each language is considered separately, bilingual children often have somewhat smaller vocabularies than monolingual children (Umbel et al., 1992). However, since bilingual youngsters often know words in one language but not the other, their total vocabulary (i.e., words known in both languages + words known in either language but not both) is greater than that of monolingual children.

What's more, bilingual children surpass monolingual children in other language skills. Bilingual preschoolers are more likely to understand that the printed form of a word is unrelated to the meaning of the word (Bialystok, 1997; Bialystok, Shenfield, & Codd, 2000). For example, bilingual preschoolers are less likely to believe that words denoting large objects (e.g., *bus*) are longer than words denoting small objects (e.g., *bug*). Bilingual children also better understand that words are simply arbitrary symbols. Bilingual youngsters, for instance, are more likely than monolingual children to understand that, as long as all English speakers agreed, *dog* could refer to cats and *cat* could refer to dogs (Bialystok, 1988; Campbell & Sais, 1995).

Of course, many children in America can't speak English at the time when they should begin school. How to teach these children has prompted much national debate. One view is that all Americans should speak English and so all teaching should be in English. Another view is that children learn more effectively in their native tongue and so all teaching should be done in that language.

Much of the debate over the proper language of instruction is political, reflecting people's desire for a society with a universal cultural heritage and language rather than a society with pluralistic heritages and languages. Ignoring the political aspects, research shows that the best method uses the child's native language *and* English (Padilla et al., 1991; Wong-Fillmore et al., 1985). Initially, children receive basic English-language teaching while they are taught other subjects in their native language. Gradually, more instruction is in English, in step with children's growing proficiency in the second language. When instruction is in children's native language and English, they are most likely to master academic content and English, outcomes that are less likely when instruction is solely in the native language or in English. ■

Bilingual children learn language at about the same rate as monolingual children and often have more sophisticated understanding of the underlying symbolic nature of language.

> Compared to monolingual children, bilingual children better understand the symbolic nature of words.

## Beyond Words: Other Symbols

To end this module, let's return to the topic that began the module—symbols. Words are indeed powerful and immensely useful symbols. However, as children grow they learn other symbol systems. Pictures, for example, are symbols that represent something else. The link between a picture and what it represents is often very clear. Wallet photos, for example, are easily recognized as representations of familiar people (at least to the wallet's owner!). But the seemingly transparent connection between photographs and the object photographed actually poses a problem for young children—photos are not the actual object but simply a representation of it. Young children must learn that shaking a picture of a rattle will not make a noise and inverting a picture of a glass of juice will not cause it to spill. In fact, if shown realistic photos of familiar toys, 9-month-olds often try to grasp the toy in the photo, much as they would grasp the real object. By 18 months, toddlers rarely do this, indicating that toddlers understand that photos are representations of objects, not the objects themselves (Troseth, Pierroutsakos, & DeLoache, 2004).

A scale model is another kind of symbolic representation. A scale model of the solar system helps students to understand the relative distances of planets from the Sun; a scale model of a college campus shows the location of campus landmarks to new students; and a scale model of an airplane allows aeronautical engineers to measure how air flows over a wing. Scale models are useful because they are realistic-looking—simply smaller versions of the real thing. Nevertheless, young children do not understand the relation between scale models and the objects they represent: The ability to use scale models develops early in the preschool years. To illustrate, if young children watch an adult hide a toy in a full-size room, then try to find the toy in a scale model of the room that contains all the principal features of the full-scale room (e.g., carpet, window, furniture), 3-year-olds find the hidden toy readily but $2\frac{1}{2}$-year-olds do not (DeLoache, 1995).

Why is this task so easy for 3-year-olds and so difficult for $2\frac{1}{2}$-year-olds? Do the younger children simply forget the location of the toy by the time they look at the scale model of the room? No. If returned to the full-size room, they easily find the hidden toy. Judy DeLoache and her colleagues believe that $2\frac{1}{2}$-year-olds' "attention to a scale model as an interesting and attractive object makes it difficult for them to simultaneously think about its relation to something else" (DeLoache, Miller, & Rosengren, 1997, p. 308). In other words, young children are drawn to the model as a real object and therefore find it hard to think about the model as a symbol of the full-size room.

If this argument is correct, $2\frac{1}{2}$-year-olds should be more successful using the model if they don't have to think of it as a symbol for the full-size room. DeLoache and her colleagues tested this hypothesis in what is my favorite study of all time, for reasons that will soon be obvious. To test this argument, they created a condition designed to eliminate the need for children to think of the model as an object and as a symbol. Children saw the oscilloscope shown in the photograph, which was described as a shrinking machine. They saw a toy doll—"Terry the Troll"—placed in front of the oscilloscope; then the experimenter and child left the room briefly while a tape recorder played sounds that were described as sounds "the machine makes when it's shrinking something." When experimenter and child returned, Terry had shrunk from 8 inches to 2 inches. Next, Terry was hidden in the full-size room, the experimenter aimed the "shrinking machine" at the

In a study that examined children's understanding of scale models as symbols, Judy DeLoache and her colleagues convinced $2\frac{1}{2}$-year-olds that this oscilloscope could shrink the doll and other objects.

full-size room, then experimenter and child left the room. While the tape recorder played shrinking sounds, research assistants quickly removed everything from the full-size room and substituted the model. Experimenter and child returned and the child was asked to find Terry. This procedure was repeated so that children searched for Terry on four separate trials.

Children rarely found the toy when tested with the usual instructions, but they usually did in the "shrinking machine" condition. Apparently, $2\frac{1}{2}$-year-olds find it very difficult to think of the model as an object and as a symbol, and, consequently, cannot find the hidden toy, even though the model is an exact replica of the full-size room. In contrast, when children can think of the model as the room, but much smaller, they readily find the toy.

Of course, after children have mastered scale models, a host of other symbolic forms awaits them, including maps, graphs, and musical notation, to name a few. But children take their first steps toward lifelong access to symbols as infants, when they master words and gestures.

**9.2** The two main factors are phonological memory and the boys' language environments. It's likely that Mitch has a better phonological memory—he can remember speech sounds more accurately and longer—and he gets exposed to more speech and more sophisticated speech.

## CHECK YOUR LEARNING

**RECALL** What factors help children learn new words so rapidly?

Summarize some of the ways in which children's vocabularies differ quantitatively and qualitatively.

**INTERPRET** Explain why a child's first words are best viewed as a breakthrough in children's understanding of symbols.

**APPLY** Suppose you've been asked to write a brochure for first-time parents about ways they can foster word learning in their toddlers. What would you say?

# 9.3 SPEAKING IN SENTENCES

From Two-Word Speech to Complex Sentences

How Do Children Acquire Grammar?

## LEARNING OBJECTIVES

- How do children progress from speaking single words to complicated sentences?
- How do children acquire the grammar of their native language?

*Jaime's daughter, Luisa, is a curious $2\frac{1}{2}$-year-old who bombards her father with questions. Jaime enjoys Luisa's questioning, but he is bothered by the way she phrases her questions. Luisa will say, "What you are doing?" and "Why not she sleep?" Obviously, Jaime doesn't talk this way, so he wonders where Luisa learned to ask questions like this. Is it normal, or is it a symptom of some type of language disorder?*

Not long after children begin to talk, they start combining words to form simple sentences. These simple sentences are the first step in a new area of language learning, mastering *syntax*—a language's rules for combining words to create sentences.

We'll begin this module by tracing the stages in children's acquisition of syntax and, along the way, see that Luisa's way of asking questions is quite normal for youngsters learning English. Then we'll examine different factors that influence children's mastery of syntax.

## From Two-Word Speech to Complex Sentences

At about $1\frac{1}{2}$ years, children begin to combine individual words to create two-word sentences, like *more juice, gimme cookie, truck go, my truck, Mommy go, Daddy bike*. **Researchers call this kind of talk *telegraphic speech* because, like telegrams of days gone by, it consists of only words directly relevant to meaning.** Before cell phones and e-mail, people sent urgent messages by telegraph, and the cost was based on the number of words. Consequently, telegrams were brief and to the point, containing only the important nouns, verbs, adjectives, and adverbs, much like children's two-word speech.

In their two-word speech, children follow rules to express different meanings. For example, the sentences *truck go* and *Daddy eat* are both about agents—people or objects that do something and the actions they perform. Here the rule is "agent + action." In contrast, *my truck* is about a possessor and a possession; the rule for creating these sentences is "possessor + possession."

When children are in the two-word stage, they use several basic rules to express meaning (Brown, 1973). These are listed in the table.

> Children use a common set of rules to create two-word sentences that describe people, actions, and properties.

**TABLE 9-1**

| RULES USED TO EXPRESS MEANING DURING THE TWO-WORD STAGE | |
|---|---|
| **Rule** | **Example** |
| Agent + action | Daddy eat |
| possessor + possession | my truck |
| action + object | gimme cookie |
| agent + object | boy car (meaning the boy is pushing the car) |
| action + location | put chair (meaning put the object on the chair) |
| entity + location | truck chair (meaning the truck is on the chair) |
| attribute + entity | big car |
| demonstrative + entity | that cup |

Source: Based on Brown, 1973.

Of course, not all children use all eight rules, but most do. And this is true of children around the world (Tager-Flusberg, 1993). Regardless of the language they learn, children's two-word sentences follow a common set of rules that are very useful in describing ideas concerning people and objects, their actions, and their properties.

**BEYOND TELEGRAPHIC SPEECH.** Beginning at about the second birthday, children move to three-word and even longer sentences. For example, at $1\frac{1}{2}$ years, my daughter Laura would say, "gimme juice" or "bye-bye Mom." As a $2\frac{1}{2}$-year-old, she had progressed to "When I finish my ice cream, I'll take a shower, okay?" and "Don't turn the light out—I can't see better!" **Children's longer sentences are filled with *grammatical morphemes*, words or endings of words (such as *-ing*, *-ed*, or *-s*) that make a sentence grammatical.** To illustrate, a $1\frac{1}{2}$-year-old might say, "kick ball," but a 3-year-old would be more likely to say, "I am kicking the ball." Compared to the $1\frac{1}{2}$-year-old's telegraphic speech, the 3-year-old has added several elements, including a pronoun, *I*, to serve as the subject of the sentence, the auxiliary verb *am, -ing* to the erb *kick*, and an article, *the*, before *ball*. Each of these grammatical morphemes makes the older child's sentence slightly more meaningful and much more grammatical.

How do children learn all of these subtle nuances of grammar? Conceivably, a child might learn that *kicking* describes kicking that is ongoing and that *kicked* describes kicking that occurred in the past. Later, the child might learn that *raining* describes current weather and *rained* describes past weather. But learning different tenses for individual verbs—one by one—would be remarkably slow going. More effective would be to learn the general rules that "verb + *-ing*" denotes an ongoing activity and "verb + *-ed*" denotes a past activity. In fact, this is what children do: They learn general rules about grammatical morphemes.

Jean Berko (1958) conducted one of the first studies showing that children's use of grammatical morphemes is based on their growing knowledge of grammatical rules, rather than merely their memory for individual words. She showed preschoolers pictures of nonsense objects like the one in the diagram. The experimenter labeled it, saying, "This is a wug." Then youngsters were shown pictures of two of the objects while the experimenter said, "Now there is another one. There are two of them. There are two . . ." Most children spontaneously said, "Wugs." Because *wug* is a novel word, children could answer correctly only by applying the rule of adding *-s* to indicate plural.

Sometimes, of course, applying the general rule can lead to very creative communication. As a 3-year-old, my daughter would say, "unvelcro it," meaning detach the Velcro. She had never heard *unvelcro*, but she created this word from the rule that "*un-* + verb" means to reverse or stop the action of a verb. Creating such novel words is, in fact, evidence that children learn grammar by applying rules, not learning individual words.

**Additional evidence that children master grammar by learning rules comes from preschoolers' *overregularization*, applying rules to words that are exceptions to the rule.** Youngsters learning English may incorrectly add an *-s* instead of using an irregular plural—*two mans* instead of *two men* or *two foots* instead of *two feet*. With the past tense, children may add *-ed* instead of using an irregular past tense—*I goed* instead of *I went* or *she runned* instead of *she ran* (Marcus et al., 1992). Children apparently know the general rule but not all the words that are exceptions.

The rules governing grammatical morphemes range from fairly simple to very complex. The rule for plurals—add *-s*—is simple to apply, and, as you might expect, it's one of the first grammatical morphemes that children master. Adding *-ing* to denote ongoing action is also simple, and it too is mastered early. More complex forms, such as the various forms of the verb *to be*, are mastered later; but, remarkably, by the

This is a wug.

Now there is another one. There are two of them. There are two_____ .

**FIGURE 9-4**

**9.3** Describing a vacation, 3-year-old Kelly said, "I sleeped in a tent!" What feature of grammatical development does her comment illustrate?

end of the preschool years, children typically have mastered most of the rules that govern grammatical morphemes.

At the same time that preschoolers are mastering grammatical morphemes, they extend their speech beyond the subject-verb-object construction that is basic in English. You can see these changes in the way children ask questions. Children's questions during two-word speech are marked by intonation alone. Soon after a child can declare, "My ball," he can also ask "My ball?" Children quickly discover *wh* words (*who, what, when, where, why*), but they don't use them correctly. Like Luisa, the $2\frac{1}{2}$-year-old in the module-opening vignette, many youngsters merely attach the *wh* word to the beginning of a sentence without changing the rest of the sentence: *What he eating? What we see?* But by 3 or $3\frac{1}{2}$ years, youngsters insert the required auxiliary verb before the subject, creating *What is he eating?* or *What will we see?* (deVilliers & deVilliers, 1985).

Between ages 3 and 6, children also learn to use negation ("That isn't a butterfly") and embedded sentences ("Jennifer thinks that Bill took the book"). They begin to comprehend passive voice ("The ball was kicked by the girl") as opposed to the active voice ("The girl kicked the ball"), although full understanding of this form continues into the elementary-school years (Hoff, 2005). In short, by the time most children enter kindergarten, they use most of the grammatical forms of their native language with great skill.

> As children move beyond two-word speech, they begin to master questions, negation, and other more complex sentences.

## How Do Children Acquire Grammar?

Ponder young children's grammatical accomplishments for a moment, particularly in light of their other cognitive skills. Most youngsters can neither read nor do arithmetic, and some don't know the letters of the alphabet, but virtually all have mastered the fundamentals of grammar of their native tongue. How do they do it? Theorists have proposed several different answers to this question.

**THE BEHAVIORIST ANSWER.**    If you were asked to explain how children master grammar, where would you begin? You might propose that children learn to speak grammatically by listening to and then copying adult sentences. Children might simply imitate the grammatical forms they hear. In fact, B. F. Skinner (1957) and other learning theorists once claimed that all aspects of language—sounds, words, grammar, and communication—are learned through imitation and reinforcement (Whitehurst & Vasta, 1975).

Critics were quick to point to some flaws in the learning explanation of grammar, however. One problem is that children produce many sentences they've never ever heard. In fact, most of children's sentences are novel, which is difficult to explain in terms of simple imitation of adults' speech. For example, when young children create questions by inserting a *wh* word at the beginning of a sentence ("What she doing?"), who are they imitating?

Also troublesome for the learning view is that, even when children imitate adult sentences, they do not imitate adult grammar. In simply trying to repeat "I am drawing a picture," young children will say "I draw picture." Furthermore, linguists, particularly Noam Chomsky (1957, 1995), have argued that grammatical rules are far too complex for toddlers and preschoolers to infer them solely on the basis of speech that they hear.

**THE LINGUISTIC ANSWER.** Beginning with Chomsky (1957), linguists proposed children are born with mechanisms that simplify the task of learning grammar (Slobin, 1985). According to this view, children are born with neural circuits in the brain that allow them to infer the grammar of the language that they hear. That is, grammar itself is not built into the child's nervous system, but processes that guide the learning of grammar are. **For example, according to *semantic bootstrapping theory*, children are born knowing that nouns usually refer to people or objects and that verbs are actions; they use this knowledge to infer grammatical rules.*** Hearing sentences such as "Billy drinks," "Susan sleeps," and "Jen reads," children infer that Noun + Verb makes a grammatical sentence in English (Pinker, 1989).

This proposal that inborn mechanisms help children learn grammar might not be as intuitively appealing as imitation, but many findings indirectly support this view:

1. **Specific regions of the brain are known to be involved in language processing.** If children are born with a "grammar-learning processor," it should be possible to locate a specific region or regions of the brain that are involved in learning grammar. In fact, you may remember from Module 4.3 that for most people the left hemisphere of the brain plays a critical role in understanding language. Some functions of language have been located even more precisely. For example, the area in blue in the diagram is Broca's area—a region in the left frontal cortex that is necessary for combining words into meaningful sentences. The fact that specific areas in the brain, such as Broca's area, have well-defined functions for language makes it plausible that children have specialized neural circuits that help them learn grammar.

2. **Only humans learn grammar readily.** If grammar is learned solely through imitation and reinforcement, then it should be possible to teach rudimentary grammar to nonhumans. If, instead, learning grammar depends on specialized neural mechanisms that are unique to humans, then efforts to teach grammar to nonhumans should fail. This prediction has been tested many times by trying to teach grammar to chimpanzees, the species closest to humans on the evolutionary ladder. For example, the chimpanzee in the photo, Nim Chimpsky, was taught to communicate using gestures taken from sign language. Other chimps have been taught using plastic chips to stand for words. The result? Chimps master a handful of grammatical rules governing two-word speech, but only with massive effort that is completely unlike the preschool child's learning of grammar (Savage-Rumbaugh et al., 1993; Seyfarth & Cheney, 1996). And the resulting language is unlike children's grammar in many ways (Kako, 1999). For example, Nim gradually used longer sentences but because he repeated himself (e.g., "eat Nim eat Nim"), not because he expressed more complicated ideas. Because numerous efforts to teach grammar to chimps have failed, this suggests that children rely on some type of mechanism specific to humans to master grammar.

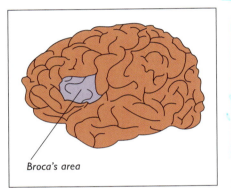

Broca's area

**FIGURE 9-5**

Chimps can be taught very simple grammatical rules, but only after massive training that is unlike what toddlers and preschoolers experience.

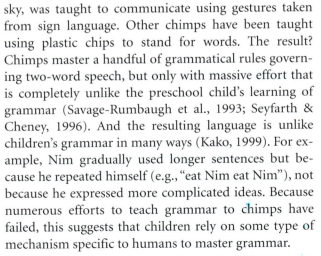

*The name for this theory comes from the phrase "pull yourself up by your bootstraps" which means improving your situation by your own efforts. The phrase is from an 18th century fantasy tale about a baron who falls in a deep hole and escapes by pulling up on his bootstraps.

3.  **There is a critical period for learning language.** The period from birth to about 12 years is a critical period for acquiring language generally and mastering grammar particularly. If children do not acquire language in this period, they will never truly master language later. Evidence of a critical period for language comes from studies of isolated children. In one tragic instance, a baby girl named Genie was restrained by a harness during the day and a straightjacket-like device at night. No one was permitted to talk to Genie, and she was beaten when she made any noise. When Genie was discovered, at age 13, she did not speak at all. After several years of language training, her mastery of grammar remained limited, resembling the telegraphic speech of a 2-year-old (Curtiss, 1989; Rymer, 1993).

Further evidence for a critical period for language comes from studies of individuals learning second languages. Individuals master the grammar of a foreign language at the level of a native speaker only if they are exposed to the language prior to adolescence (Newport, 1991). Why can one period of time be so much more influential for language than others? Why can't missed language experiences be made up after age 12? A critical period for language answers these questions. That is, just as females ovulate for only a limited portion of the life span, the neural mechanisms involved in learning grammar may function only during infancy and childhood.

Although these findings are consistent with the idea that children have innate grammar-learning mechanisms, they do *not* prove the existence of such mechanisms. Consequently, scientists have continued to look for other explanations.

**THE COGNITIVE ANSWER.**   Not all researchers believe that children must have specialized mechanisms to learn grammar. Some theorists (e.g., Braine, 1992) believe that children learn grammar through powerful cognitive skills that help them rapidly detect regularities in their environments, including patterns in the speech they hear. According to this approach, it's as if children establish a huge Excel spreadsheet that has the speech they've heard in one column and the context in which they heard it in a second column; periodically infants scan the columns looking for recurring patterns (Maratsos, 1998). For example, children might be confused the first time they hear -*s* added to the end of a familiar noun. However, as the database expands to include many instances of familiar nouns with an added -*s*, children discover that -*s* is always added to a noun when there are multiple instances of the object. Thus, they create the rule: noun + -*s* = plural. With this view, children learn language by searching for regularities across many examples that are stored in memory, not through an inborn grammar-learning device.

Scientists who subscribe to this view argue that infants' impressive ability to extract regularities in the speech sounds that they hear (described on page 270) would work just as effectively to extract regularities in sentence structure (Gerken, 2005). They also emphasize close connections between language development and cognitive development: Young children typically achieve cognitive and language milestones at about the same age, which suggests that common mechanisms are at work in cognitive and linguistic development (Bates, 1994).

**THE SOCIAL-INTERACTION ANSWER.**   This approach is eclectic, drawing on each of the views we've considered so far. From the behaviorist approach, it takes an emphasis on the environment; from the linguistic approach, that language learning is distinct; and, from the cognitive view, that children have powerful cognitive skills they can use to master language. The unique contribution of

> Children learn grammar by relying on some language-specific mechanisms, by noting regularities in the speech they hear, and by participating in linguistically rich interactions.

this perspective is emphasizing that children master language generally and grammar specifically in the context of social interactions (Bloom & Tinker, 2001). That is, much language learning takes place in the context of interactions between children and adults, with both parties eager for better communication. Children have an ever-expanding repertoire of ideas and intentions that they wish to convey to others and caring adults want to understand their children, so both parties work to improve language skills as a means toward better communication. Thus, improved communication provides an incentive for children to master language and for adults to help them.

According to the social-interaction account of language learning, children are eager to master grammar because it allows them to communicate their wishes and needs more effectively.

You can see the nature of these interactions in the following example, in which a child wants a cookie (after Hulit & Howard, 2002, pp. 37–38). Like the child in the photo, a 9-month-old who wants a cookie might point to it while looking at the mother. In turn, the mother gives the cookie, saying, "Here's the cookie." By age 2, a child might say, "Gimme cookie, please?" with the mother responding, "Yes, I'll give you the cookie." At 9 months and 2 years, the child's desire to have the cookie motivates communication (pointing at 9 months, spoken language at 2 years) and gives the mother opportunities to demonstrate more advanced forms of language.

None of these accounts, summarized in the table, provides a comprehensive account of how grammar is mastered. But many scientists believe the final explanation will include contributions from the linguistic, cognitive, and social-interaction accounts. That is, children's learning of grammar will be explained in terms of some mechanisms specific to learning grammar, children actively seeking to identify regularities in their environment, and linguistically rich interactions between children and adults (MacWhinney, 1998).

## SUMMARY TABLE

### DIFFERENT APPROACHES TO EXPLAINING CHILDREN'S ACQUISITION OF GRAMMAR

| Approach | Children are thought to master grammar . . . |
|---|---|
| Behaviorist | by imitating speech they hear. |
| Linguistic | with inborn mechanisms that allow children to infer the grammatical rules of their native language. |
| Cognitive | using powerful cognitive mechanisms that allow children to find recurring patterns in the speech they hear. |
| Social Interaction | in the context of social interactions with adults in which both parties want improved communication. |

Of course, many parents don't care much about theories of language, but they do want to know how they can help their children master grammar and other aspects of language. The "Improving Children's Lives" feature provides some guidelines.

## *Improving Children's Lives*

### Promoting Language Development

Adults eager to promote children's language development can follow a few guidelines:

1. Talk with children frequently and treat them as partners in conversation. That is, try talking with children interactively, not directively.

2. Use a child's speech to show new language forms. Expand a child's remark to introduce new vocabulary or new grammatical forms. Rephrase a child's ungrammatical remark to show the correct grammar.

3. Encourage children to go beyond minimal use of language. Have them answer questions in phrases and sentences, not single words. Have them replace vague words such as *stuff* or *somebody* with more descriptive ones.

4. Listen. This guideline has two parts. First, because children often talk slowly, it's tempting for adults to complete their sentences for them. Don't. Let children express themselves. Second, pay attention to what children are saying and respond appropriately. Let children learn that language works.

5. Make language fun. Use books, rhymes, songs, jokes, and foreign words to increase a child's interest in learning language.

Of course, as children's language improves during the preschool years, others can understand it more readily, which means that children become better at communicating. The emergence and growth of communication skills is the topic of the next module.

---

### CHECK YOUR LEARNING

**RECALL** Describe the major milestones that mark children's progress from two-word speech to complex sentences.

What are the main accounts of how children master grammar?

**INTERPRET** How do the various explanations of grammatical development differ in their view of the child's role in mastering grammar?

**APPLY** How might the cognitive processes described in Chapter 7 help children learn grammar?

Saying "sleeped" instead of "slept" shows that Kelly knows the rule about adding -*ed* to a verb to make it past tense. It also illustrates that children overgeneralize these rules—using them with verbs to which they don't apply. **9.3**

---

# USING LANGUAGE TO COMMUNICATE

# 9.4

## LEARNING OBJECTIVES

- When and how do children learn to take turns in conversation?

- What are the skills required to be an effective speaker?

- What is involved in becoming a good listener?

Taking Turns

Speaking Effectively

Listening Well

*Marla and Kitty, both 7-year-olds, usually are good friends, but right now they're boiling mad at each other. Marla was going to the store with her dad to buy some new markers. Kitty found out and gave Marla money to buy some markers for her, too. Marla returned with the markers, but they weren't the kind that Kitty liked, so she was angry. Marla was angry because she didn't think Kitty should be mad; after all, it was Kitty's fault for not telling her what kind to buy. Meanwhile, Marla's dad hopes they come to some understanding soon and cut out all the shouting.*

Imagining these girls arguing is an excellent way to learn what is needed for effective communication. Both talk at the same time, their remarks are rambling and incoherent, and neither bothers to listen to the other. In short, for effective oral communication, don't do what they do. These girls need to follow a few simple guidelines for effective communication:

- People should take turns, alternating as speaker and listener.
- A speaker's remarks should relate to the topic and be understandable to the listener.
- A listener should pay attention and let the speaker know if his or her remarks don't make sense.

Complete mastery of these guidelines is a lifelong pursuit; after all, even adults often miscommunicate with one another because they don't observe one or more of these rules. However, in this module, we'll trace the development of effective communication skills and, along the way, discover why young children like Marla and Kitty sometimes fail to communicate.

## Taking Turns

Many parents begin to encourage turn taking long before infants say their first words. Parents often structure a "conversation" around a baby's early sounds, even when those sounds lack any obvious communicative intent (Field & Widmayer, 1982):

| | |
|---|---|
| PARENT: | Can you see the bird? |
| INFANT (COOING): | ooooh |
| PARENT: | It is a pretty bird. |
| INFANT: | ooooh |
| PARENT: | You're right, it's a cardinal. |

When parents speak with young babies, they often alternate roles of speaker and listener, showing conversational turn taking.

Soon after 1-year-olds begin to speak, parents such as the mother in the photo encourage their youngsters to participate in conversational turn taking. To help children along, parents often carry both sides of a conversation to demonstrate how the roles of speaker and listener alternate (Shatz, 1983):

| | |
|---|---|
| PARENT (TO INFANT): | What's Amy eating? |
| PARENT (ILLUSTRATING REPLY): | She's eating a cookie. |

Parents and other caregivers seem to do whatever is necessary to allow infants and toddlers to "fit in" to a conversation. That is, caregivers scaffold youngsters' attempts to converse, making it more likely that children will succeed.

Such early "conversations" between caregivers and infants are not universal. In some non-Western cultures, preverbal infants are not considered appropriate conversational partners, so adults don't talk to them. Only after infants are older do others begin to converse with them (Ochs, 1988).

By age 2, spontaneous turn taking is common in conversations between youngsters and adults (Barton & Tomasello, 1991). And by age 3, children have progressed to the point that if a listener fails to reply promptly, the child repeats his or her remark in order to elicit a response (Garvey & Berninger, 1981). A 3-year-old might say, "Hi, Paul" to an older sibling who's busy reading. If Paul doesn't answer in a few seconds, the 3-year-old might say, "Hi, Paul" again. When Paul remains unresponsive, the 3-year-old is likely to shout, "PAUL!"—showing that by this age children understand the rule that a comment deserves a response. Preschool children seem to interpret the lack of a response as, "I guess you didn't hear me, so I'll say it again, louder!"

## Speaking Effectively

When do children first try to initiate communication with others? In fact, what appear to be the first deliberate attempts to communicate typically emerge at 10 months (Bates et al., 1979; Golinkoff, 1993). Infants at this age may touch or point to an object while simultaneously looking at another person. They continue this behavior until the person acknowledges them. It's as if the child is saying, "This is a neat toy! I want you to see it, too."

Beginning at 10 months, an infant may point, touch, or make noises to get an adult to do something. An infant in a playpen like the one in the photo who wants a toy that is out of reach may make noises while pointing to the toy. The noises capture an adult's attention, and the pointing indicates what the baby wants (Blake, O'Rourke, & Borzellino, 1994). The communication may be a bit primitive by adult standards, but it works for babies!

After the first birthday, children begin to use speech to communicate and often initiate conversations with adults (Bloom et al., 1996). Toddlers' first conversations are about themselves, but their conversational scope expands rapidly to include objects in the environment (e.g., toys, food). Later, conversations begin to include more abstract notions, such as hypothetical objects and past or future events (Foster, 1986).

Of course, young children are not always skilled conversational partners. At times their communications are confusing, leaving a listener to wonder, "What was that all about?" Every message—whether an informal conversation or a formal lecture—should have a clear meaning. But saying something clearly is often difficult because clarity can only be judged by considering the listener's age, experience, and knowledge of the topic, along with the context of the conversation. For example, think about the simple request, "Please hand me the Phillips-head screwdriver." This message may be clear to older listeners familiar with different types of screwdrivers, but it won't mean much to younger listeners who think all screwdrivers are alike. And, if the toolbox is filled with Phillips-head screwdrivers of assorted sizes, the message won't be clear even to a knowledgeable listener.

Constructing clear messages is a fine art, but, amazingly, by the preschool years, youngsters begin to adjust their messages to match the listener and the context. In a classic study, Marilyn Shatz and Rochel Gelman (1973) asked 4-year-olds to explain how a toy worked, once to a 2-year-old and once to an adult. Shatz and Gelman found that 4-year-olds talked more overall to adults than to 2-year-olds and used longer sentences with adult listeners than with 2-year-old listeners. Also, children used simpler grammar and more attention-getting words, such as *see*, *look*, *watch*, and *hey*, when speaking with 2-year-olds. Here, for example, is how one

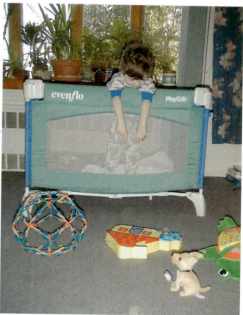

Even before children can speak, they make gestures to communicate with others.

**Question**

**9.4** Shauna's older brother asked, "Where's your locker this year?" Shauna replied, "Next to Mrs. Rathert's room". When Shauna's grandmother, who lived in another city, asked the same question, Shauna's reply was much longer: "After you go in the front door, you turn left and go down a long hall until you get to some stairs. Then . . ." What feature of effective communication is shown in Shauna's two answers to the same question?

4-year-old child explained the toy to her two different listeners (the toy is a garage with drivers and trucks that carry marbles to a dumping station):

> Adult listener: You're supposed to put one of these persons in, see? Then one goes with the other little girl. And then the little boy. He's the little boy and he drives. And then they back up . . . . And then the little girl falls out and then it goes backwards.

> 2-year-old listener: Watch, Perry. Watch this. He's back in here. Now he drives up. Look, Perry. Look here, Perry. Those are marbles, Perry. Put the men in here. Now I'll do it. (Shatz & Gelman, 1973, p. 13)

Shatz and Gelman's findings show that preschoolers are already sensitive to characteristics of the listener in formulating a clear message. More recent findings also show that children consider the listener and setting in devising clear messages:

- Preschool children give more elaborate messages to listeners who lack critical information than to listeners who have the information (Nadig & Sedivy, 2002; O'Neill, 1996). For example, a child describing where to find a toy will give more detailed directions to a listener whose eyes were covered when the toy was hidden.

- School-age children speak differently to adults and peers. They are more likely to speak politely with adults and be more demanding with peers (Warren-Leubecker & Bohannon, 1989). A child might ask a parent, "May I have one of your cookies?" but say to a peer, "Give me one of your cookies."

- Some African Americans speak **African American English**, **a variant of standard English that has slightly different grammatical rules.** For example, "He be tired" in African American English is synonymous with "He usually is tired" in standard English. Many African American children learn both African American English and standard English, and they switch back and forth, depending on the situation (Warren & McCloskey, 1993). They use standard English more often in school and when talking with European Americans but use African American English more often at home and when talking with African American peers.

**Young children adjust their messages based on a listener's age and knowledge.**

All these findings show that school-age children (and sometimes preschoolers) are well on their way to understanding the factors that must be considered in creating clear messages. Even so, sometimes messages are not clear to listeners. Speakers need to pay attention to listeners; if they don't seem to understand the message, they need to try again. The "Focus on Research" feature shows that even young children have mastered this basic step toward effective communication.

### Focus on Research

**When Listeners Don't Understand, Preschoolers Try Again**

*Who were the investigators, and what was the aim of the study?* A good general rule for effective communication is that speakers should monitor their listeners' comprehension. When listeners get puzzled expressions on their faces, this is usually a sign that the message was not crystal clear and the speaker should clarify. Do preschool children know this important communicative rule? Do they pay attention to a listener's comprehension? These were the questions that Helen Shwe and Ellen Markman (1997) wanted to answer.

*How did the investigators measure the topic of interest?* Shwe and Markman showed two objects (e.g., a toy car and a sock) to $2\frac{1}{2}$-year-olds and asked which one they'd like to see. After the child had chosen, the experimenter said, "You asked for the _____. I think you want the _____. I'm going to give you the _____. Here's the _____." In one condition, the experimenter mentioned the chosen toy and actually gave the child the chosen toy. In three other conditions, the experimenter sometimes mentioned the wrong toy or gave the wrong toy or both. Then the experimenter recorded what the child did.

*Who were the children in the study?* Shwe and Markman tested 22 preschoolers with an average age of 31 months.

*What was the design of the study?* This study was experimental: There were two independent variables. One was whether the experimenter mentioned the correct toy in replying to the child's choice; the other was whether the experimenter gave the child the chosen toy. The dependent variable was the frequency with which children repeated their preference for the original toy, either by vocalizing, pointing, or gazing. The study was not developmental (only $2\frac{1}{2}$-year-olds participated and they were tested just once), so it was neither cross-sectional nor longitudinal.

*Were there ethical concerns with the study?* No. The task asking children to choose a toy posed no danger to the children. Mothers were present during testing.

*What were the results?* The top of the graph shows what children did when they received the wrong toy. Not surprisingly, they were much more likely to repeat their preference spontaneously when they received the wrong toy than when they received the right one. (After all, when the child received the expected object, there was no reason to repeat the request.) More interesting are the results in the bottom of the graph, which show what children did when the experimenter described the wrong toy. Children were much more likely to restate their preference when the experimenter described it incorrectly than when the experimenter described it correctly.

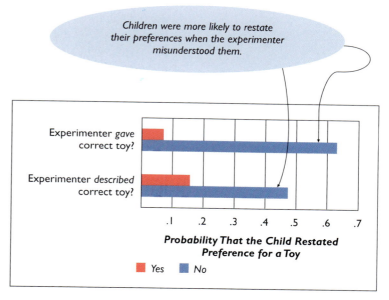

Children were more likely to restate their preferences when the experimenter misunderstood them.

FIGURE 9-6

*What did the investigators conclude?* Even very young children seem to understand that, when listeners misunderstand, speakers need to do something. In the grander scheme of things, repeating what you've just said is not a very good strategy. But in this simple experimental setting, it was adequate to convey to the adult, "You think I wanted the sock but, no, I wanted the car." As Shwe and Markman (1997) phrased it, "Young children monitor their communicative partner's knowledge state and care about their listener's comprehension . . ." (p. 636).

*What converging evidence would strengthen these conclusions?* One interesting extension of this study would involve naturalistic observation of young children's communications. Observing young children communicating with peers might be particularly fruitful because young listeners often do not understand what speakers mean. Doing this research as part of a longitudinal study would be useful in revealing developmental change in effective communication during the preschool years. ■

Thus, from a surprisingly young age, children express themselves to others and adjust their conversations to fit listeners. Are young children equally adept at listening? We'll find out in the next section.

## Listening Well

Listening well may seem easy, but it's not. A skilled listener must continuously decide whether a speaker's remarks make sense. If they do, then a listener needs to make an appropriate reply, typically by extending the conversation with another remark that's on the topic.

Few toddlers master this fundamental conversation skill. Their replies are more likely to be unrelated to the topic than related to it (Bloom, Rocissano, & Hood, 1976). Asked "Where's the sock?" a $1\frac{1}{2}$-year-old may say something like "I'm hungry!" By 3 years, children are more adept at continuing conversations by making remarks that relate to the topic being discussed.

If a message is vague or confusing, the listener should ask the speaker to clarify the message. This seems obvious enough, but young children do not always realize when a message is ambiguous. Told to find "the red toy," they may promptly select the red ball from a pile that includes a red toy car, a red block, and a red toy hammer. Instead of asking the speaker which *specific* red toy, young listeners often assume that they know which toy the speaker had in mind (Beal & Belgrad, 1990). Only when messages almost defy comprehension—when they are too quiet to be heard or when they impart obviously ambiguous or even conflicting information—do youngsters detect a problem.

**Young children often ignore ambiguities in messages.**

Because young children's remarks often contain ambiguities and because, as listeners, they often do not detect ambiguities, young children often miscommunicate, just like Marla and Kitty in the opening vignette. Kitty probably didn't communicate exactly what kind of markers she wanted, and Marla didn't understand that the directions were unclear. Throughout the elementary-school years, youngsters gradually master the many skills involved in determining whether a message is consistent and clear (Ackerman, 1993).

Sometimes messages are confusing because they conflict with what a listener thinks is true. For example, suppose a child is told that the family cat, which always stays indoors, has run away. Even preschoolers are more likely to believe such a message when told by a parent than by a classmate because they know the parent is better informed about this particular topic (Robinson, Champion, & Mitchell, 1999). And by 7 or 8 years, children can be skeptical listeners—taking what a speaker says with a grain of salt—because, for example, a speaker has a vested interest in a topic. When a child announces to an entire class that her birthday party is going to be the "best one all year," school-age children believe her less than if they heard the information from an independent, third party (Mills & Keil, 2005).

Sometimes listeners must go beyond the words to understand the real meaning of a message. Metaphor is one example. When parents tell their teenagers, "Your bedroom is a junk yard," you (and they) know that this remark is not to be taken literally. Instead, the metaphor highlights the fact that the bedroom is a mess and filled with things that could be thrown away.

As you might expect, understanding nonliteral meanings of messages develops slowly (e.g., Dews et al., 1996). In the case of metaphor, young children easily understand simple metaphors in which the nonliteral meaning is based on references to concrete objects and their properties. For example, a parent might say to a 5-year-old, "You're a fish," referring to how well the child swims and enjoys the water, and the child will likely understand.

More complex metaphors require that children make connections based on abstract relations. For example, in Shakespeare's *Romeo and Juliet*, Romeo proclaims that "Juliet is the Sun." You might interpret this line to mean that Juliet is the center of Romeo's universe or that without Juliet Romeo will die. The first interpretation depends on your knowledge of astronomy; the second, on your knowledge of biology. Younger children lack this sort of knowledge to comprehend metaphors, so they try to interpret them literally. Only when children gain the necessary content knowledge do they understand metaphors based on abstract relations (Franquart-Declercq & Gineste, 2001).

Sarcasm is another form of communication that is not to be interpreted literally. When a soccer player misses the ball entirely and a teammate says, "Nice kick," the literal meaning of the remark is the opposite of the intended meaning. Like understanding of metaphor, understanding of sarcasm develops gradually (Creusere, 1999). When people emphasize their sarcasm by speaking in mocking or overly enthusiastic tones, school-age children can detect their meaning. However, if sarcasm must be detected solely from the context—by realizing that the comment is the opposite of what would be expected—only adolescents and adults are likely to understand the real meaning of the remark (Capelli, Nakagawa, & Madden, 1990).

This discussion of listening skills completes our catalog of the important accomplishments that take place in communication during childhood. As children enter kindergarten, they have mastered many of the fundamental rules of communication, and as they grow older, they acquire even greater proficiency.

## CHECK YOUR LEARNING

**RECALL**  What findings illustrate that preschool children are sometimes effective speakers?

Summarize children's understanding of messages that are not meant to be taken literally.

**INTERPRET**  What are the strengths and weaknesses of infants as communicators?

**APPLY**  In Chapter 6, we saw that Piaget characterized preschool children as egocentric. Are the findings described in this module consistent with Piaget's view?

Shauna has changed her description to reflect her listener's knowledge. Her description is more elaborate for her grandmother (who's unfamiliar with, her school than for her brother). | **9.4**

## UNIFYING THEMES: Connections

This chapter is an appropriate occasion to stress the theme that *development in different domains is connected:* Language has important connections to biological, cognitive, and social development. A link to biological development would be children's mastery of grammar: In ways that we don't yet fully understand, children seem to be endowed with a mechanism that smooths the path to mastering grammar. A link to cognitive development would be children's first words: Speaking words reflects the cognitive insight that speech sounds are symbols. A link to social development would be the communication skills that enable children to interact with peers and adults.

## SEE FOR YOURSELF

Berko's (1958) "wugs" task is fun to try with preschool children. Photocopy the drawing on page 286 and show it to a preschooler, repeating the instructions that appear on that page. You should find that the child quite predictably says, "two wugs." Create some pictures of your own to examine other grammatical morphemes, such as adding -*ing* to denote ongoing activity or adding -*ed* to indicate past tense. See for yourself!

## RESOURCES

For more information about . . .

how children master language in the first 3 years of life, read Roberta M. Golinkoff and Kathy Hirsch-Pasek's *How Babies Talk: The Magic and Mystery of Language in the First Three Years of Life* (Dutton/Penguin, 1999).

**American Sign Language (ASL),** visit the American Sign Language Browser, **http://commtechlab.msu.edu/sites/aslweb/browser.htm**

## KEY TERMS

**African American English**  294
**babbling**  272
**cooing**  272
**expressive style**  280
**fast mapping**  276
**grammar**  268
**grammatical morphemes**  286
**infant-directed speech**  271
**intonation**  273
**language**  268
**naming explosion**  275
**overextension**  279
**overregularization**  286
**phonemes**  269
**phonological memory**  279
**phonology**  268
**pragmatics**  268
**referential style**  280
**semantic bootstrapping theory**  288
**semantics**  268
**syntax**  268
**telegraphic speech**  285
**underextension**  279

SUMMARY

# 9.1 THE ROAD TO SPEECH

### Elements of Language

Language includes four distinct elements: phonology (sounds), semantics (word meaning), grammar (rules for language structure), and pragmatics (rules for communication). Syntax, which is part of grammar, describes how words are ordered in sentences.

### Perceiving Speech

Phonemes are the basic units of sound that make up words. Infants can hear phonemes soon after birth. They can even hear phonemes that are not used in their native language, but this ability is lost by the first birthday. Before they speak, infants can recognize words, apparently by noticing stress and syllables that go together. Infants prefer infant-directed speech—adults' speech to infants that is slower and has greater variation in pitch—because it provides them additional language clues.

### First Steps to Speech

Newborns are limited to crying, but at about 3 months, babies coo. Babbling soon follows, consisting of a single syllable; over several months, infants' babbling includes longer syllables and intonation.

# 9.2 LEARNING THE MEANINGS OF WORDS

### Understanding Words as Symbols

Children's first words represent a cognitive accomplishment that is not specific to language. Instead, the onset of language is due to a child's ability to interpret and use symbols. Consistent with this view, there are parallel developments in the use of gestures.

### Fast Mapping Meanings to Words

Most children learn the meanings of words too rapidly for them to consider all plausible meanings systematically. Instead, children use a number of fast-mapping rules to determine probable meanings of new words. Joint attention, constraints, sentence cues, and cognitive skills all help children learn words. The rules do not always lead to the correct meaning. An underextension denotes a child's meaning that is narrower than an adult's meaning; an overextension denotes a child's meaning that is broader.

### Individual Differences in Word Learning

Individual children differ in vocabulary size, differences attributable to phonological memory and the quality of the child's language environment. Some youngsters use a referential word-learning style that emphasizes words as names and that views language as an intellectual tool. Other children use an expressive style that emphasizes phrases and views language as a social tool.

### Encouraging Word Learning

Children's word learning is fostered by experience, including being read to, watching television, and, for school-age children, reading to themselves. The key ingredient is making children think about the meanings of new words.

### Beyond Words: Other Symbols

As children learn language, they also learn about other symbol systems. By 18 months, toddlers understand that photos are representations of other objects; by 3 years, children understand that a scale model is a representation of an identical but larger object.

# 9.3 SPEAKING IN SENTENCES

### From Two-Word Speech to Complex Sentences

Not long after their first birthday, children produce two-word sentences that are based on simple rules for expressing ideas or needs. These sentences are sometimes called telegraphic because they use the fewest possible words to convey meaning. Moving from two-word to more complex sentences involves adding grammatical morphemes. Children first master grammatical morphemes that express simple relations, then those that denote complex relations.

As children acquire grammatical morphemes, they also extend their speech to other sentence forms, such as questions, and later to more complex constructions, such as passive sentences.

### How Do Children Acquire Grammar?

Behaviorists proposed that children acquire grammar through imitation, but that explanation is incorrect. Today's explanations come from three perspectives: The linguistic emphasizes inborn mechanisms that allow children to infer the grammatical rules of their native language, the cognitive perspective emphasizes cognitive processes that allow children to find recurring patterns in the speech they hear, and the social-interaction perspective emphasizes social interactions with adults in which both parties want improved communication.

# 9.4 USING LANGUAGE TO COMMUNICATE

### Taking Turns

Parents encourage turn taking even before infants talk and later demonstrate both the speaker and listener roles for their children. By age 3, children spontaneously take turns and prompt one another to speak.

### Speaking Effectively

Before they can speak, infants use gestures and noises to communicate. During the preschool years, children gradually become more skilled at constructing clear messages, in part by adjusting their speech to fit their listeners' needs. They also begin to monitor their listeners' comprehension, repeating messages if necessary.

### Listening Well

Toddlers are not good conversationalists because their remarks don't relate to the topic. Preschoolers are unlikely to identify ambiguities in another's speech. Also, they sometimes have difficulty understanding messages that are not to be taken literally, such as metaphor and sarcasm.

**If you're a fan of _Star Trek_, you know that Mr. Spock feels little emotion because he's half Vulcan and people from the planet Vulcan don't have emotions.** Would you like to live an emotionless life like Mr. Spock? Probably not. For most of us, feelings enrich our lives. As partial testimony to their importance, the English language has more than 500 words that refer to emotions (Averill, 1980). Joy, happiness, satisfaction, and yes, anger, guilt, and humiliation are just a few of the feelings that give life meaning.

In this chapter, we'll see how emotions emerge and how they affect development. In Module 10.1, we'll discuss when children first express different emotions and recognize emotions in others. Next, in Module 10.2, we'll see that children have different behavioral styles and that these styles are rooted, in part, in emotions. Finally, in Module 10.3, we'll examine the infant's first emotional relationship, the one that develops with the primary caregiver.

10.1    **Emerging Emotions**

10.2    **Temperament**

10.3    **Attachment**

1  The Science of Child Development

2  Genetic Bases of Child Development

3  Prenatal Development, Birth, and the Newborn

4  Growth and Health

5  Perceptual and Motor Development

6  Theories of Cognitive Development

7  Cognitive Processes and Academic Skills

8  Intelligence and Individual Differences in Cognition

9  Language and Communication

# Emotional Development

11  Understanding Self and Others

12  Moral Understanding and Behavior

13  Gender and Development

14  Family Relationships

15  Influences Beyond the Family

**10**

# 10.1   EMERGING EMOTIONS

The Function of Emotions

Experiencing and Expressing Emotions

Recognizing and Using Others' Emotions

Regulating Emotions

## LEARNING OBJECTIVES

- Why do people "feel"? Why do they have emotions?

- At what ages do children begin to experience and express different emotions?

- When do children begin to understand other people's emotions? How do they use this information to guide their own behavior?

- When do children show evidence of regulating emotion, and why is this an important skill?

> Nicole was ecstatic that she was finally going to see her 7-month-old nephew, Claude. She rushed into the house and, seeing Claude playing on the floor with blocks, swept him up in a big hug. After a brief, puzzled look, Claude burst into angry tears and began thrashing around, as if saying to Nicole, "Who are you? What do you want? Put me down! Now!" Nicole quickly handed Claude to his mother, who was surprised by her baby's outburst and even more surprised that he continued to sob while she rocked him.

This vignette illustrates three common emotions. Nicole's initial joy, Claude's anger, and his mother's surprise are familiar to all of us. In this module, we begin by discussing *why* people have feelings at all. Then we look at when children first express emotions, how children come to understand emotions in others, and, finally, how children regulate their emotions. As we do, we'll learn why Claude reacted to Nicole as he did and how Nicole could have prevented Claude's outburst.

## The Function of Emotions

Why do people feel emotions? Wouldn't life be simpler if people were emotionless like computers or residents of Mr. Spock's Vulcan? Probably not. Think, for example, about activities that most adults find pleasurable: a good meal, sex, holding one's children, and accomplishing a difficult but important task. These activities were and remain essential to the continuity of humans as a species, so it's not surprising that we find them pleasant (Gaoulin & McBurney, 2001).

*Basic emotions such as happiness and fear include a subjective feeling, a physiological response, and an overt behavior.*

Modern theories emphasize the functional value of emotion. That is, according to the functional approach, emotions are useful because they help people adapt to their environment (Izard & Ackerman, 2000). Take fear as an example. Most of us would rather not be afraid but there are instances in which feeling fearful is very adaptive. Imagine you are walking alone, late at night, in a poorly lighted section of campus. You become frightened and, as a consequence, are particularly attentive to sounds that might signal the presence of threat, and you probably walk quickly to a safer location. Thus, fear is adaptive because it organizes your behavior around an important goal—avoiding danger (Cosmides & Tooby, 2000).

Similarly, other emotions are adaptive. Happiness, for example, is adaptive in contributing to stronger interpersonal relationships: When people are happy with another person, they smile, and this often causes the other person to feel happy too, strengthening their relationship (Izard & Ackerman, 2000). Disgust is adaptive in keeping people away from substances that might make them ill: As we discover that the milk in a glass is sour, we experience disgust and push the glass away. Thus, in the functional approach, most emotions developed over the course of human history to meet unique life challenges and help humans to survive.

## Experiencing and Expressing Emotions

The three emotions from the vignette—joy, anger, and surprise—are considered "basic emotions," as are interest, disgust, distress, sadness, and fear (Dragh-Lorenz, Reddy, & Costall, 2001). *Basic emotions* **are experienced by people worldwide, and each consists of three elements: a subjective feeling, a physiological change, and an overt behavior** (Izard, 1991). For example, suppose you wake to the sound of a thunderstorm and then discover your roommate has left for class with your umbrella. Subjectively, you might feel ready to explode with anger; physiologically, your heart would beat faster; and behaviorally, you would probably be scowling.

**MEASURING EMOTIONS.**    How can we determine when infants first experience basic emotions? Overt behaviors such as facial expressions provide important clues. To see for yourself, look at the photos of young babies. Which one is angry? Which are the sad and happy babies? The facial expressions are so revealing that I'm sure you guessed that the babies are, in order, sad, happy, and angry. But do these distinctive facial expressions mean that the infants are actually experiencing these emotions? Not necessarily. Facial expressions are only one component of emotion—the behavioral manifestation. Emotion also involves physiological responses and subjective feelings. Of course, infants can't express their feelings to us verbally, so we don't know much about their subjective experiences. But at least some of the physiological responses that accompany facial expressions are the same in infants and adults. For example, when infants and adults smile—which suggests they're happy—the left frontal cortex of the brain tends to have more electrical activity than the right frontal cortex (Fox, Kimmerly, & Schafer, 1991).

Facial expressions often reveal the emotions that infants are experiencing.

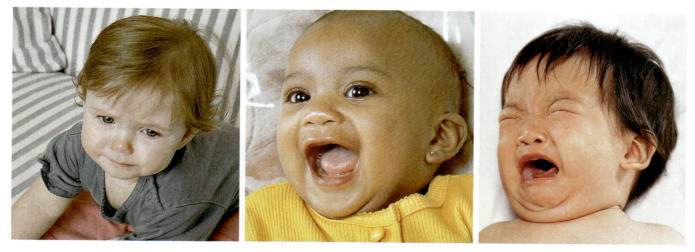

Research has revealed several other reasons to believe that facial expressions are an accurate barometer of an infant's emotional state:

- Infants (and adults) worldwide express basic emotions in much the same way (Izard, 1991). For example, the boy in the photo on page 304 shows the universal signs of fear. His eyes are open wide, his eyebrows are raised, and his

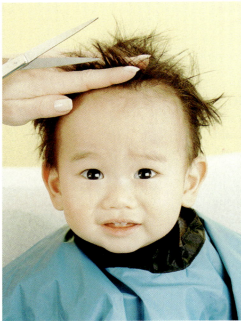

The universal signs of fear include wide-open eyes, raised eyebrows, and an open mouth.

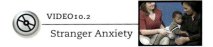

**VIDEO 10.2**

Stranger Anxiety

By 6 months, infants are wary of strangers and often become upset when they encounter people they don't know, particularly when strangers rush to greet or hold them.

mouth is relaxed but slightly open. The universality of emotional expression suggests that humans are biologically programmed to express basic emotions in a specific way.

- By 5 to 6 months, infants' facial expressions change predictably and meaningfully in response to events. When a happy mother greets her baby, the baby usually smiles in return; when a tired, distracted mother picks up her baby roughly, the baby usually frowns at her (Izard et al., 1995; Weinberg & Tronick, 1994).

- When adults are really happy or amused, they smile differently than when they smile to greet an acquaintance or to hide hurt feelings. In "joyful" smiles, the muscles around the eyes contract, which lifts the cheeks. Similarly, infants smile both at moms and interesting objects, but are more likely to raise their cheeks during smiling when looking at Mom (Messinger, 2002). The close parallel between the details of infants' and adults' smiles suggests that smiling has the same meaning, emotionally, for infants and adults.

Collectively, these findings make it reasonable to assume that facial expressions reflect an infant's underlying emotional state.

**DEVELOPMENT OF BASIC EMOTIONS.** Using facial expressions and other overt behaviors, scientists have traced the growth of basic emotions in infants. According to one influential theory (Lewis, 2000), newborns experience only two general emotions: pleasure and distress. Rapidly, though, more discrete emotions emerge, and by 8 or 9 months of age, infants are thought to experience all basic emotions. For example, joy emerges at about 2 or 3 months. **At this age, *social smiles* first appear: Infants smile when they see another human face.** Sometimes social smiling is accompanied by cooing, the early form of vocalization described in Module 9.1 (Sroufe & Waters, 1976). Smiling and cooing seem to be the infant's way of expressing pleasure at seeing another person. Sadness is also observed at about this age: Infants look sad, for example, when their mothers stop playing with them (Lewis, 2000).

Anger typically emerges between 4 and 6 months. Infants will become angry, for example, if a favorite food or toy is taken away (Sternberg & Campos, 1990). Reflecting their growing understanding of goal-directed behavior (see Module 6.1), infants also become angry when their attempts to achieve a goal are frustrated. For example, if a parent restrains an infant trying to pick up a toy, the guaranteed result is a very angry baby.

Like anger, fear emerges later in the 1st year. **At about 6 months, infants become wary in the presence of an unfamiliar adult, a reaction known as *stranger wariness*.** When a stranger approaches, a 6-month-old typically looks away and begins to fuss (Mangelsdorf, Shapiro, & Marzolf, 1995). The baby in the photo is showing the signs of stranger wariness. The grandmother has picked him up without giving him a chance to warm up to her, and the outcome is as predictable as it was with Claude, the baby in the vignette who was frightened by his aunt: He cries, looks frightened, and reaches with arms outstretched in the direction of someone familiar.

How wary an infant feels around strangers depends on a number of factors (Thompson & Limber, 1991). First, infants tend to be less fearful of strangers when the environment is familiar and more fearful when it is not. Many parents know this firsthand from traveling with their infants: Enter a friend's house for the first time and the baby clings tightly to its mother. Second, the amount of anxiety depends on the stranger's behavior. Instead of rushing to greet or pick up the baby, as Nicole did in the vignette, a stranger should talk with other adults and, in a while, perhaps offer the baby a toy (Mangelsdorf, 1992). Handled this way, many infants will soon be curious about the stranger instead of afraid.

Wariness of strangers is adaptive because it emerges at the same time that children begin to master creeping and crawling (described in Module 5.3). Like Curious George, the monkey in a famous series of children's books, babies are inquisitive and want to use their new locomotor skills to explore their worlds. Being wary of strangers provides a natural restraint against the tendency to wander away from familiar caregivers. However, as youngsters learn to interpret facial expressions and recognize when a person is friendly, their wariness of strangers declines.

**EMERGENCE OF COMPLEX EMOTIONS.**   In addition to basic emotions such as joy and anger, people feel complex emotions such as pride, guilt, and embarrassment. **Sometimes known as the** *self-conscious emotions*, **they involve feelings of success when one's standards or expectations are met and feelings of failure when they aren't.** Most scientists (e.g., Lewis, 2000) believe that complex emotions don't surface until 18 to 24 months of age, because they depend on the child having some understanding of the self, which typically occurs between 15 and 18 months. Children feel guilty or embarrassed, for example, when they've done something they know they shouldn't have done (Kochanska et al., 2002). For example, a child who breaks a toy is thinking, "You told me to be careful. But I wasn't!" Similarly, children feel pride when they accomplish a challenging task for the first time. The toddler in the photo is probably thinking something like, "I've never done this before, but this time I did it—all by myself!" Thus, children's growing understanding of themselves (which I discuss in detail in Module 11.1), allows them to experience complex emotions like pride and guilt (Lewis, 2000).

The features of basic and complex emotions are summarized in the table.

By 18 to 24 months, children start to experience complex emotions, including pride in accomplishing a difficult task.

## SUMMARY TABLE

### INFANTS' EXPRESSION OF EMOTIONS

| Type | Defined | Emerge | Examples |
|---|---|---|---|
| Basic | Experienced by people worldwide and include a subjective feeling, a physiological response, and an overt behavior | Birth to 9 months | Joy, anger, fear |
| Complex (self-conscious) | Responses to meeting or failing to meet expectations or standards | 18 to 24 months | Pride, guilt, embarrassment |

Katrina often expresses her joy, anger, and fear but has yet to show pride, guilt, or embarrassment. Based on this profile, how old do you think Katrina is?   **10.1**

**LATER DEVELOPMENTS.**   As children grow, their catalog of emotions continues to expand. For example, think about regret and relief, emotions that adults experience when they compare their actions with alternatives. Imagine, for example, that you're cramming for a test and decide that you have time to review your lecture notes but not re-read the text. If the test questions turned out to be based largely on the lectures, you'll feel a sense of relief because your decision led to a positive outcome compared to "what might have been." If, instead, test questions cover only the text, you'll feel regret because your decision led to a terrible outcome; "If only I had re-read the text!" In fact, by 7 years of age children experience feelings of regret, but they're less likely to experience feelings of relief (Guttentag & Ferrell, 2004).

In addition to adding emotions to their repertoire, older children experience basic and complex emotions in response to different situations or events. In the case of complex emotions, cognitive growth means that elementary-school children experience shame and guilt in situations where they would not have when they were younger (Reimer, 1996). For example, unlike preschool children, many school-age children would be ashamed if they neglected to defend a classmate who had been wrongly accused of a theft.

Fear is another emotion that can be elicited in different ways, depending on a child's age. Many preschool children are afraid of the dark and of imaginary creatures. These fears typically diminish during the elementary-school years as children grow cognitively and better understand the difference between appearance and reality. Replacing these fears are concerns about school, health, and personal harm (Silverman, La Greca, & Wasserstein, 1995). Such worries are common and not cause for concern in most children. In some youngsters, however, they become so extreme they overwhelm the child (Chorpita & Barlow, 1998). For example, a 7-year-old's worries about school would not be unusual unless her concern grew to the point that she refused to go to school. In the "Improving Children's Lives" feature, we'll look at this form of excessive fear and how it can be treated.

## *Improving Children's Lives*
### "But I Don't Want to Go to School!"

Many youngsters plead, argue, and fight with their parents daily over going to school. **An overwhelming fear of going to school and active resistance to attending school constitutes** *school phobia.* For example, every school day, 9-year-old Keegan would cling to his mother and start to sob as soon as he finished his breakfast. When it was time to leave the house to catch the bus, he would drop to the floor and start kicking.

Children may develop school phobia because they are overanxious generally and school is full of situations that can cause anxiety, such as reading aloud, taking tests, or learning new activities with competitive classmates. **School-phobic children can be helped with** *systematic desensitization,* **a technique that associates deep relaxation with progressively more anxiety-provoking situations.** First the therapist asks the child to generate a list of school-related situations, from pleasant ("I got the highest grade on my math test") to neutral ("We say the pledge of allegiance every morning") to very anxiety provoking ("I got home and realized that I'd left my assignments in my locker"). Setting the list aside, the therapist then teaches the child how to reduce tension by relaxing different muscle groups. When the child masters the relaxation techniques, the therapist asks the child to relax and imagine the pleasant school-related situations. Over several sessions, the child imagines progressively more anxiety-provoking situations while relaxed, so that the anxiety the child used to feel is replaced by feelings of calm relaxation. Children taught this technique report feeling much less anxious, and their school attendance improves (Kearney & Silverman, 1995). ∎

**CULTURAL DIFFERENCES IN EMOTIONAL EXPRESSION.** Children worldwide express many of the same basic and complex emotions. However, cultures differ in the extent to which emotional expression is encouraged (Hess & Kirouac, 2000). In many Asian countries, for example, outward displays of emotion are discouraged in favor of emotional restraint. Consistent with these differences, in one study (Camras et al., 1998), European American 11-month-olds cried and smiled more often than Chinese 11-month-olds. In another study (Zahn-Waxler et al., 1996), U.S. preschoolers were more likely than Japanese preschoolers to express anger in interpersonal conflicts.

Cultures also differ in the events that trigger emotions, particularly complex emotions. Situations that evoke pride in one culture may evoke embarrassment or shame in another. For example, American elementary-school children often show pride at personal achievement, such as getting the highest grade on a test or, as shown in the photo, being chosen student of the month. In contrast, Asian elementary-school children are embarrassed by a public display of individual achievement but show great pride when their entire class is honored for an achievement (Stevenson & Stigler, 1992).

Expression of anger also varies around the world. For example, think about the following two events: (a) a friend grabs and eats a piece of candy just as you were about to eat it yourself, and (b) you fall down while running and your friend laughs at you. By 10 or 11 years of age, most American children respond to these and similar events with anger. In contrast, children growing up in east Asian countries that practice Buddhism (e.g., Mongolia, Thailand, Nepal) rarely respond with anger because this goes against the Buddhist tenet to extend loving kindness to all people, even those whose actions hurt others (Cole, Bruschi, & Tamang, 2002).

Thus, culture can influence when and how much children express emotion. Of course, expressing emotion is only part of the developmental story. Children must also learn to recognize others' emotions, which is our next topic.

Children living in the United States, Canada, and Europe often express great pride at personal achievement.

> Cultures differ in the extent to which they encourage children to express emotions and in the circumstances that lead to emotions.

## Recognizing and Using Others' Emotions

Imagine you are broke and plan to borrow $20 from your roommate when she returns from class. Shortly, she storms into your apartment, slams the door, and throws her backpack on the floor. Immediately, you change your plans, realizing that now is hardly a good time to ask for a loan. This example reminds us that, just as it is adaptive to be able to express emotions, it is adaptive to be able to recognize others' emotions and sometimes change our behavior as a consequence.

When can infants first identify emotions in others? Perhaps as early as 4 months and definitely by 6 months, infants begin to distinguish facial expressions associated with different emotions. They can, for example, distinguish a happy, smiling face from a sad, frowning face (Bornstein & Arterberry, 2003; Montague & Walker-Andrews, 2001). Of course, infants might be able to distinguish an angry face from a happy one but not know the emotional significance of the two faces. How can we tell whether infants understand the emotions expressed in a face? The best evidence is that infants often match their own emotions to other people's emotions. When happy mothers smile and talk in a pleasant voice, infants express happiness themselves. If mothers are angry or sad, infants become distressed, too (Haviland & Lelwica, 1987; Montague & Walker-Andrews, 2001).

Also like adults, infants use others' emotions to direct their behavior. **Infants in an unfamiliar or ambiguous environment often look at their mother or father, as if searching for cues to help them interpret the situation, a phenomenon known as** *social referencing.* If a parent looks afraid when shown a novel object, 12-month-olds are less likely to play with the toy than if a parent looks happy (Repacholi, 1998). Furthermore, an infant can use parents' facial expressions or their vocal expressions alone to decide whether they want to explore an unfamiliar object (Mumme, Fernald, & Herrera, 1996). And infants' use of parents' cues is precise. If two unfamiliar toys are shown to a parent, who expresses disgust at one toy but not the other, 12-month-olds will avoid the toy that elicited the disgust but not the other toy (Moses et al., 2001). And by 14 months, infants remember this information: They avoid a toy that elicited disgust an hour earlier (Hertenstein & Campos, 2004). Thus, social referencing shows that infants are remarkably skilled in using their parents' emotions to help them direct their own behavior.

As their cognitive skills grow, children begin to understand why people feel as they do. By kindergarten, for example, children know that undesirable or unpleasant events often make a person feel angry or sad (Levine, 1995). Children even know that they more often feel sad when they think about the undesirable event itself (e.g., a broken toy or a friend who moves away) but feel angry when they think about the person who caused the undesirable event (e.g., the person who broke the toy or the friend's parents who wanted to live in another city). Kindergarten children also understand that remembering past sad events can make a person unhappy again (Lagattuta, Wellman, & Flavell, 1997).

During the elementary-school years, children begin to comprehend that people sometimes experience "mixed feelings." For example, Wintre and Vallance (1994) read sentences describing emotionally evocative situations to 4- through 8-year-olds and asked them how happy, angry, sad, scared, or loving they would feel in each situation. A sentence describing a fear-provoking situation was "You are home all alone," and one describing a sad situation was "Your best friend moves away." Not until 8 years of age did children realize how people can feel good and bad at the same time. The increased ability to see multiple, differing emotions coincides with the freedom from centered thinking that characterizes the concrete operational stage (Module 6.1).

**As children develop, they also begin to learn** *display rules,* **culturally specific standards for appropriate expressions of emotion in a particular setting or with a particular person or persons.** Adults know, for example, that expressing sadness is appropriate at funerals but expressing joy is not. Similarly, expressing sadness is appropriate with relatives and close friends but less so with strangers. Preschool children's understanding of display rules is shown by the fact that they control their anger more when provoked by peers they like than when provoked by peers they don't like (Fabes et al., 1996). Also, school-age children and adolescents are more willing to express anger than sadness and, like the child in the photo on page 309, more willing to express both anger and sadness to parents than to peers (Zeman & Garber, 1996; Zeman & Shipman, 1997).

What experiences contribute to children's understanding of emotions? Parents and children frequently talk about past emotions and why people felt as they did; this is particularly true for negative emotions such as fear and anger (Lagattuta & Wellman, 2002). Not surprisingly, children learn about emotions by hearing parents talk about feelings, explaining how they differ and the situations that elicit them (Brown & Dunn, 1996; Cervantes & Callanan, 1998). Also, a positive, rewarding

VIDEO 10.3
Social
Referencing

By the first birthday, infants can recognize others' emotions and use these emotions to direct their own behavior.

As children develop, they learn their culture's rules for expressing emotions; for example, many children living in North America might cry in private or with parents but they would avoid crying in public, particularly when with their peers.

relationship with parents and siblings is related to children's understanding of emotions (Brown & Dunn, 1996; Thompson, Laible, & Ontai, 2003). The nature of this connection is still a mystery. One possibility is that within positive parent–child and sibling relationships, people express a fuller range of emotions (and do so more often) and are more willing to talk about why they feel as they do, providing children more opportunities to learn about emotions.

Children's growing understanding of emotions in others contributes in turn to a growing ability to help others. They are more likely to recognize the emotions that signal a person's need. Better understanding of emotions in others also contributes to children's growing ability to play easily with peers because they can see the impact of their behavior on others. We'll cover empathy and social interaction in detail later in the book; for now, the important point is that recognizing emotions in others is an important prerequisite for successful, satisfying interactions. Another element of successful interactions is regulating emotions, our next topic.

## Regulating Emotions

Think back to a time when you were *really* angry at a good friend. Did you shout at the friend? Did you try to discuss matters calmly? Or did you simply ignore the situation altogether? Shouting is a direct expression of anger, but calm conversation and overlooking a situation are deliberate attempts to regulate emotion. People often regulate emotions; for example, we routinely try to suppress fear (because we know there's no real need to be afraid of the dark), anger (because we don't want to let a friend know just how upset we are), and joy (because we don't want to seem like we're gloating over our good fortune).

Child-development researchers have studied two aspects of emotion regulation: its origins and its links to social competence. Emotion regulation clearly begins in infancy. By 4 to 6 months, infants use simple strategies to regulate their emotions (Buss & Goldsmith, 1998; Rothbart & Rueda, 2005). When something frightens or confuses an infant—for example, a stranger or a mother who suddenly stops responding—he or she often looks away (just as older children and even adults often turn away or close their eyes to block out disturbing stimuli). Frightened infants also move closer to a parent, another effective way of helping to control their fear (Parritz, 1996). And by 24 months, a distressed toddler's face typically expresses sadness instead of fear or anger; apparently by this age toddlers have learned that a sad facial expression is the best way to get a mother's attention and support (Buss & Kiel, 2004).

Older children and adolescents encounter a wider range of emotional situations, so it's fortunate they develop a number of related new ways to regulate emotion (Eisenberg & Morris, 2002):

- Children begin to regulate their own emotions and rely less on others to do this for them. A fearful child no longer runs to a parent but instead devises her own methods for dealing with fear. For example, she might reassure herself by saying, "I know the thunderstorm won't last long and I'm safe inside the house."
- Children more often rely on mental strategies to regulate emotions. For example, a child might reduce his disappointment at not receiving a much-expected gift by telling himself that he didn't really want the gift in the first place.
- Children more accurately match the strategies for regulating emotion with the particular setting. For example, when faced with emotional situations that are unavoidable, such as going to the dentist to have a cavity filled, children adjust to the situation (for instance, by thinking of the positive consequences of treating the tooth) instead of trying to avoid the situation.

Collectively, these age-related trends give older children and adolescents plenty of tools for regulating emotions. Nevertheless, not all children regulate their emotions well and those who don't tend to have problems interacting with peers and have adjustment problems (Eisenberg & Morris, 2002; Eisenberg et al., 2005). When children can't control their anger, worry, or sadness, they often have difficulty resolving the conflicts that inevitably surface in peer relationships (Fabes et al., 1999). For example, when children argue over which game to play or which movie to watch, their unregulated anger can interfere with finding a mutually satisfying solution. Thus, ineffective regulation of emotions leads to more frequent conflicts with peers, and, consequently, less satisfying peer relationships and less adaptive adjustment to school (Eisenberg et al., 2001; Olson et al., 2005).

In this module, we've seen how children express, recognize, and regulate emotions; in the next module, we'll discover that emotion is an important feature of children's temperament.

> *Even infants can regulate their emotions and school-age children have mastered several techniques for regulating emotions.*

**10.1** Because Katrina expresses joy, anger, and fear, she's at least 6 months old. Because she hasn't expressed any of the complex emotions (pride, guilt, embarrassment), she's not yet 18 months old. Thus, she's probably between 6 and 15 months old.

## CHECK YOUR LEARNING

**RECALL** Describe biological and cultural contributions to children's expression of emotion.

How do infants and children regulate their emotions? What are the consequences when children can't regulate their emotions well?

**INTERPRET** Distinguish basic emotions from complex (self conscious) emotions.

**APPLY** Cite similarities between developmental change in infants' expression and regulation of emotion and developmental change in infants' comprehension and expression of speech (described in Module 9.1).

# TEMPERAMENT

## 10.2

### LEARNING OBJECTIVES

- What are the different features of temperament?

- How do heredity and environment influence temperament?

- How stable is a child's temperament across childhood?

- What are the consequences of different temperaments?

*Soon after Yoshimi arrived in the United States from Japan to begin graduate studies, she enrolled her 5-month-old son in day care. She was struck by the fact that, compared to her son, the European American babies in the day-care center were "wimps" (slang she had learned from American television). The other babies cried often and with minimal provocation. Yoshimi wondered whether her son was unusually "tough" or whether he was just a typical Japanese baby.*

What Is Temperament?

Hereditary and Environmental Contributions to Temperament

Stability of Temperament

Temperament and Other Aspects of Development

When you've observed young babies—perhaps as part of "See for Yourself" in Chapter 3—were some babies like Yoshimi's, quiet most of the time, while others cried often and impatiently? Maybe you saw some infants who responded warmly to strangers and others who seemed very shy. **Such behavioral styles, which are fairly stable across situations and are biologically based, make up an infant's *temperament*.** For example, all babies become upset occasionally and cry. However, some, like Yoshimi's son, recover quickly and others are very hard to console. These differences in emotion and style of behavior are evident in the first few weeks after birth and are important throughout life.

We'll begin this module by looking at different ways that scientists define temperament.

## What Is Temperament?

Alexander Thomas and Stella Chess (Thomas, Chess, & Birch, 1968; Thomas & Chess, 1977) pioneered the study of temperament with the New York Longitudinal Study, in which they traced the lives of 141 individuals from infancy through adulthood. Thomas and Chess gathered their initial data by interviewing the babies' parents and asking individuals unfamiliar with the children to observe them at home. Based on these interviews and observations, Thomas and Chess suggested that infants' behavior varied along nine temperamental dimensions. One dimension was activity, which referred to an infant's typical level of motor activity. A second was persistence, which referred to the amount of time that an infant devoted to an activity, particularly when obstacles were present.

Using these and other dimensions, Thomas and Chess identified three patterns of temperament. Most common were "easy" babies, who were usually happy and cheerful, tended to adjust well to new situations, and had regular routines for eating, sleeping, and toileting. A second, less common group were "difficult" babies, who tended to be unhappy, were irregular in their eating and sleeping, and often responded intensely to unfamiliar situations. Another less common group were "slow to warm up" babies. Like difficult babies, slow-to-warm-up babies were often unhappy; but unlike difficult babies, slow-to-warm-up were not upset by unfamiliar situations.

VIDEO 10.1
Temperament

Ten-month-old Nina is usually cheerful, enjoys going on outings with her dad, and sleeps soundly every night. How would Thomas and Chess describe Nina's temperament?

**10.2**

The New York Longitudinal Study launched research on infant temperament, but today's researchers no longer emphasize creating different categories of infants, such as "easy" or "slow to warm up." Instead, researchers want to determine the different dimensions that underlie temperament. One modern approach to temperament is described in the "Spotlight on Theories" feature.

### *Spotlight on Theories*
### **A Theory of the Structure of Temperament in Infancy**

#### *BACKGROUND*

Most scientists agree that *temperament* refers to biologically based differences in infants' and children's emotional reactivity and emotional self-regulation. However, scientists disagree on the number and nature of the dimensions that make up temperament.

#### *THE THEORY*

Mary K. Rothbart (2004; Rothbart & Hwang, 2005) has devised a theory of temperament that includes three different dimensions:

- *Surgency/extraversion* refers to the extent to which a child is generally happy, active, vocal, and regularly seeks interesting stimulation.
- *Negative affect* refers to the extent to which a child is angry, fearful, frustrated, shy, and not easily soothed.
- *Effortful control* refers to the extent to which a child can focus attention, is not readily distracted, and can inhibit responses.

Rothbart claims that these dimensions of temperament are evident in infancy, continue into childhood, and are related to dimensions of personality that are found in adolescence and adulthood. However, the dimensions are not independent: Specifically, infants who are high on effortful control tend to be high on surgency/extraversion and low on negative affect. In other words, babies who can control their attention and inhibit responses tend to be happy and active but not angry or fearful.

**HYPOTHESIS:** If temperament is biologically based and includes the three dimensions of Rothbart's theory, then those dimensions of temperament should be observed in children around the world. That is, cross-cultural studies of temperament should consistently reveal the dimensions of surgency/extraversion, negative affect, and effortful control.

*According to Mary Rothbart's theory, temperament includes three primary dimensions: surgency/extraversion, negative affect, and effortful control.*

**TEST:** Garstein, Knyazev, and Slobodskaya (2005) conducted a cross-cultural study in which they examined the structure of temperament in infants growing up in the United States and in Russia. The sample in the United States included approximately 600 parents of 3- to 12-month-olds; the sample in Russia included about 200 parents of 3- to 12-month-olds. Both samples included roughly the same number male and female babies and most were Caucasian. Parents in both countries completed the revised version of the Infant Behavior Questionnaire (IBQ-R) which consists of 184 items assessing different dimensions of Rothbart's theory of temperament. For example, the items "When given a new toy, how often did the baby get very excited about getting it?" and "When put into the bath water, how often did the baby splash or kick?" both measure the surgency/extraversion dimension; "When frustrated with something, how often did the baby calm down within 5 minutes?" measures the negative affect dimension. For each item, parents rated how often the behavior had been observed in the past 7 days, using a scale that ranged from "never" to "always."

Gartstein et al. used factor analysis (described on page 238 in Module 8.1) to examine relations between parents' responses to different questionnaire items. This method looks for patterns in parents' responses. To illustrate, the surgency/extraversion dimension would be supported if parents who judged that their infants were always excited about a new toy also said that their babies always splashed or kicked during a bath (because both items are thought to measure surgency/extraversion). In fact, factor analyses revealed that three temperamental dimensions—surgency/extraversion, negative affect, and effortful control—were evident in the pattern of parents' responses to the 184 items on the IBQ-R. That is, the basic dimensions of temperament are evident in U.S. infants and Russian infants, at least based on parents' ratings.

**CONCLUSION:** As predicted, the structure of temperament was the same in two cultures. This supports Rothbart's claim that the dimensions of her theory of temperament are biologically rooted and, consequently, should be evident regardless of the specific environment or culture in which a child develops.

**APPLICATION:** An important theme of temperament research—one that began with Thomas and Chess (1977) and has been picked up by other temperament researchers—is that children's development proceeds best when there is a good fit between their temperament and the environment in which they grow up. That is, because temperament is rooted in biological factors, parents should accept their baby's unique temperamental characteristics and adjust their parenting accordingly. For example, babies who are quiet and shy clearly benefit when parents actively stimulate them (e.g., by describing and explaining). But these same activities are actually counterproductive with active, outoing babies who would rather explore the world on their own (Miceli et al., 1998). Thus, Rothbart's theory, and other research on temperament, reminds us that parent–child interactions represent a two-way street in which interactions are most successful when both parties—child and parent—adjust to the needs of the other. ■

The hereditary contribution to temperament is shown by the fact that twins are typically similar in their level of activity.

## Hereditary and Environmental Contributions to Temperament

Most theories agree that temperament reflects both heredity and experience (Caspi et al., 2005). The influence of heredity is shown in twin studies: Identical twins are more alike in most aspects of temperament than fraternal twins. For example, Goldsmith, Buss, and Lemery (1997) found that the correlation for identical twins' activity level was .72, but the correlation for fraternal twins was only .38. In other words, like the youngsters in the photo, if one identical twin is temperamentally active, the other usually is, too. However, the impact of heredity also depends on the temperamental dimension and the child's age. For example, negative affect is more influenced by heredity than the other dimensions; and temperament in childhood is more influenced by heredity than is temperament in infancy (Wachs & Bates, 2001).

The environment also contributes to children's temperament. Positive emotionality—laughing often, being generally happy, and often expressing pleasure—seems to reflect environmental influences (Goldsmith et al., 1997). Conversely, infants more often develop intense, difficult temperaments when mothers are abrupt in dealing with them and lack confidence (Belsky, Fish, & Isabella, 1991).

Heredity and experience may also explain why Yoshimi, the Japanese mother in the vignette, has such a hardy son. The "Cultural Influences" feature tells the story.

## *Cultural Influences*
### Why Is Yoshimi's Son So Tough?

If you've ever watched an infant getting an injection, you know the inevitable response. After the syringe is removed, the infant's eyes open wide and then the baby begins to cry, as if saying, "Wow, that hurt!" Infants differ in how intensely they cry and in how readily they are soothed, reflecting differences in the emotionality dimension of temperament, but virtually all European American babies cry. It's easy to suppose that crying is a universal response to the pain from the inoculation, but it's not.

In such stressful situations, Japanese and Chinese infants are less likely to become upset (Kagan et al., 1994). Lewis, Ramsay, and Kawakami (1993) found that most European American 4-month-olds cried loudly within 5 seconds of an injection, but only half the Japanese babies in their study cried. What's more, when Japanese and Chinese babies become upset, they are soothed more readily than European American babies. Lewis and his colleagues found that about three fourths of the Japanese babies were no longer crying 90 seconds after the injection, compared to fewer than half the European American babies. The conclusion seems clear: Yoshimi's son appears to be a typical Japanese baby in crying less often and less intensely than the European American babies at his day-care center.

Why are Asian infants less emotional than their European American counterparts? Heredity may be involved. Perhaps the genes that contribute to emotionality are less common among Asians than among European Americans. But we can't overlook experience. Compared to European American mothers, Japanese mothers spend more time in close physical contact with their babies, constantly and gently soothing them; this may reduce the tendency to respond emotionally.

There's no question that heredity and experience cause babies' temperaments to differ, but how stable is temperament across childhood and adolescence? We'll find out in the next section.

## Stability of Temperament

Do calm, easygoing babies grow up to be calm, easygoing children, adolescents, and adults? Are difficult, irritable infants destined to grow up to be cranky, whiny children? The first answers to these questions came from the Fels longitudinal project, a study of many aspects of physical and psychological development from infancy. Although not a study of temperament per se, Jerome Kagan and his collaborators (Kagan, 1989; Kagan & Moss, 1962) found that fearful preschoolers in the Fels project tended to be inhibited as older children and adolescents.

**Temperament is moderately stable throughout infancy, childhood, and adolescence.**

Spurred by findings like this one, later investigators attempted to learn more about the stability of temperament. This research shows that temperament is moderately stable throughout infancy, childhood, and adolescence (Wachs & Bates, 2001). For example, newborns who cry under moderate stress tend, as 5-month-olds, to cry when they are placed in stressful situations like the one in the photo, in which the mother is not allowing her baby to move its body (Stifter & Fox, 1990). In addition, when inhibited toddlers are adults, they respond more strongly to unfamiliar stimuli. Schwartz et al. (2003) had adults who were either inhibited or uninhibited as toddlers view novel and familiar faces. Records of brain activity showed that when adults who had been inhibited as toddlers viewed novel faces, they had significantly more activity in the amygdala, a brain region that regulates perception of fearful stimuli. Thus, the same individuals who avoided strangers as 2-year-olds had, as adults, the strongest response to novel faces.

Temperament is moderately stable throughout infancy; for example, babies who as newborns cry when they experience stress tend, as 5-month-olds, to cry when they experience stress when being restrained.

The finding of modest stability in temperament means that Sam, an inhibited 1-year-old, is more likely to be shy as a 12-year-old than Dave, an outgoing 1-year-old. However, it's not a "sure thing" that Sam will still be shy as a 12-year-old. Instead, think of temperament as a predisposition. Some infants are naturally predisposed to be sociable, emotional, or active; others *can* act in these ways, too, but only if the behaviors are nurtured by parents and others.

In many respects, temperament resembles personality, so it's not surprising that many child-development researchers have speculated about potential connections between the two. In fact, personality in adulthood includes many of the same dimensions observed for temperament in infancy and childhood (Caspi et al., 2005; Costa & McCrae, 2001). For example, extroversion is a dimension of personality that refers to a person's warmth, gregariousness, and activity level. Extroverted individuals tend to be affectionate, prefer the company of others, and like being active; introverted people tend to be more reserved, enjoy solitude, and prefer a more sedate pace (Costa & McCrae, 2001).

Extroversion looks like a blend of the temperamental dimensions of positive affect and activity level; and longitudinal studies find that inhibited children are more likely as adults to be introverted than extroverted (Caspi et al., 2005). However, research of this sort also reveals many instances in which temperament is poorly related to personality in adulthood (Wachs & Bates, 2001). This may seem surprising, but remember that temperament changes as children develop, depending on their experiences. An inhibited child who finds herself in a school group with children with similar interests may "open up" and become much more outgoing over time; her early inhibited temperament is not related to her later outgoing personality. Thus, we should not expect children's temperament to be consistently related to their personality as adults.

In the next section, we'll see some of the connections between temperament and other aspects of development.

## Temperament and Other Aspects of Development

One of the goals of Thomas and Chess's New York Longitudinal Study was to discover temperamental features of infants that would predict later psychological adjustment. In fact, Thomas and Chess discovered that about two thirds of the preschoolers with difficult temperaments had developed behavioral problems by the time they entered school. In contrast, fewer than one fifth of the children with easy temperaments had behavioral problems (Thomas et al., 1968).

Other scientists have followed the lead of the New York Longitudinal Study in looking for links between temperament and outcomes of development, and they've found that temperament is an important influence on development. Consider these examples:

*Temperament is linked to school success, good peer relations, compliance to parents' requests, and to depression.*

- Persistent children are likely to succeed in school, whereas active and distractible children are less likely to succeed (Martin, Olejnik, & Gaddis, 1994).

- Shy, inhibited children often have difficulty interacting with their peers and often do not cope effectively with problems (Eisenberg et al., 1998; Kochanska & Radke-Yarrow, 1992).

- Anxious, fearful children are more likely to comply with a parent's rules and requests, even when the parent is not present (Kochanska, 1995).

- Children who are frequently angry or fearful are more prone to depression (Lengua, West, & Sandler, 1998).

The "Focus on Research" feature shows that temperament is also related to children's tendency to help people in distress.

## Focus on Research

### Temperament Influences Helping Others

*Who were the investigators, and what was the aim of the study?* When people are in obvious distress, some children readily step forward to help but others seem reluctant to help. Why are some children so helpful whereas others aren't? Shari Young, Nathan Fox, and Carolyn Zahn-Waxler (1999) argued that temperament may be part of the answer. Specifically, inhibited, shy youngsters may find it difficult to overcome their reticence to help another, particularly when they do not know the person and when the other person does not specifically request help. Young and her colleagues examined this hypothesis by studying inhibition and helping in 2-year-olds.

*How did the investigators measure the topic of interest?* The researchers videotaped children as they interacted with their mother and a stranger during free play. At some point during the session, the experimenter feigned injury (e.g., she pretended that she had caught her fingers in the clipboard). Later in the session, the mother also feigned injury (e.g., she pretended to bump into a chair). While feigning injury, the experimenter and the mother did not solicit the child's help in any way, either directly (e.g., by saying, "Help me, help me") or indirectly (e.g., by calling the child's name). Later, observers scored children's behaviors on several dimensions, including:

- *Inhibition:* The extent to which children avoided the experimenter, even when he began playing with a novel, attractive toy.

- *Concerned expression:* The extent to which children displayed obvious concern for the injured experimenter or mother, as shown by, for example, expressions of sadness.

- *Helpful behavior:* The extent to which children acted in ways apparently aimed at reducing distress, such as sharing a toy or stroking the injured body part.

*Who were the children in the study?* The study involved fifty 2-year-olds. Children were tested within 2 weeks of their second birthday.

*What was the design of the study?* This study was correlational because Young and her colleagues were interested in the relation that existed naturally between inhibition and helping. The study was actually longitudinal (children were also tested at 4 months), but I'm only describing the results from the second testing session, which took place at age 2 years.

*Were there ethical concerns with the study?* No. The children enjoyed most of the free-play session. The experimenters and mothers "recovered" quickly from their feigned injuries—in approximately 1 minute—and no children were visibly upset by the injury.

*What were the results?* The graph shows some correlations between inhibition and (a) expressing concern, and (b) helping behavior, separately for helping the mother and helping the experimenter. Let's begin with the correlations for mothers. Neither correlation is significant, which indicates that when interacting with their moms, shy and outgoing children were equally likely to express concern and to provide help. The results differ for helping the experimenter. The correlation between inhibition and expressing concern is again small, indicating that shy and outgoing youngsters were equally likely to express concern when the experimenter feigned injury. However, the correlation between inhibition and helping is negative: shy, inhibited 2-year-olds were less likely than outgoing 2-year-olds to help an experimenter who appeared to be hurt.

*What did the investigators conclude?* A young child's temperament helps determine whether that child will help. When mothers and experimenters feigned injury, both shy and outgoing children noticed and were disturbed by their distress. Outgoing children typically translated this concern into action, helping both mothers and experimenters. In contrast, shy youngsters helped mothers but could not overcome their reticence to help an unfamiliar adult who did not specifically ask for help. Even though shy children see that a person is suffering, their apprehensiveness in unfamiliar social settings often prevents them from helping.

*What converging evidence would strengthen these conclusions?* One way to test the generality of these results would be to repeat the experiment, replacing the mother and adult experimenter with an older sibling and unfamiliar child who is the same age as the older sibling. The prediction is that shy and outgoing children would help the familiar older sibling, but only outgoing children would help the unfamiliar older child. ■

Although these findings underscore that temperament is an important force in children's development, temperament rarely is the sole determining factor. Instead, the influence of temperament often depends on the environment in which children develop. To illustrate, let's consider the link between temperament and behavior problems. Infants and toddlers who temperamentally resist control—those who are difficult to manage, who are often unresponsive, and who are sometimes impulsive—tend to be prone to behavior problems, particularly aggression, when they are older. However, more careful analysis shows that resistant temperament leads to behavior problems primarily when mothers do not exert much control over their children. Among mothers who do exert control—those who prohibit, warn, and scold their children when necessary—resistant temperament is not linked to behavior problems (Bates et al., 1998).

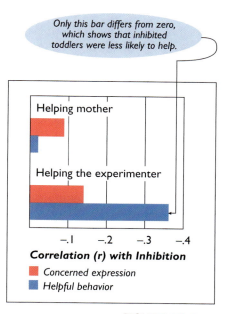

Only this bar differs from zero, which shows that inhibited toddlers were less likely to help.

FIGURE 10-1

Similarly, young adolescents are more likely to drink, smoke, and use drugs when they experience many life stressors (e.g., when someone in the family has a serious accident or illness, when a parent loses a job, or when parents and the child are frequently in conflict) and their parents themselves smoke and drink. But this is less true for young adolescents with temperaments marked by positive affect (Wills et al., 2001). That is, young adolescents who are temperamentally cheerful apparently are less affected by life stressors and consequently are less likely to drink, smoke, or use drugs.

This research reminds us that emotion is a fundamental element of temperament. In the next module, we'll look at emotion from yet another perspective, that of the emotional relationship formed between an infant and its primary caregiver.

**10.2** Thomas and Chess would say that she's a prototypic "easy" baby: she's happy, she adjusts well to new situations (shown by how much she enjoys going to new places with her dad), and she has a regular routine for sleeping.

## CHECK YOUR LEARNING

**RECALL**  How is temperament influenced by heredity and environment?
Summarize the influence of temperament on other aspects of development.

**INTERPRET**  Compare and contrast the Thomas and Chess approach to temperament with Rothbart's theory of temperament.

**APPLY**  Based on what you know about the stability of temperament, what would you say to a parent who's worried that her 15-month-old seems shy and inhibited?

# 10.3    ATTACHMENT

The Growth of Attachment

The Quality of Attachment

## LEARNING OBJECTIVES

- How does an attachment relationship develop between an infant and primary caregiver?

- What different types of attachment relationships are there? What are the consequences of different types of relationships?

*Ever since Samantha was a newborn, Karen and Dick looked forward to going to their favorite restaurant on Friday night. Karen enjoyed the break from child-care responsibilities and Dick liked being able to talk to Karen without interruptions. But recently they've had a problem. When they leave her with a sitter, 8-month-old "Sam" gets a frightened look on her face and usually begins to cry hysterically. Karen and Dick wonder if Sam's behavior is normal and if their Friday night dinners are coming to an end.*

The social-emotional relationship that develops between an infant and a parent (usually, but not necessarily, the mother) is special. This is a baby's first social-emotional relationship, so scientists and parents alike believe it should be satisfying and trouble-free to set the stage for later relationships. In this module, we'll look at the steps involved in creating the baby's first emotional relationship.

Along the way, we'll see why 8-month-old Sam has begun to cry when Karen and Dick leave her with a sitter.

## The Growth of Attachment

Today's parents are encouraged to shower their babies with hugs and kisses; the more affection young children receive, the better! This advice may seem obvious but actually it's a relatively recent recommendation, dating from the middle of the 20th century. It emerged, in part, from observations of European children whose parents were killed during World War II. Despite being well fed and receiving necessary health care, the children's development was far from normal: their mental development was slow and they often seemed withdrawn and listless (Bowlby, 1953; Spitz, 1965). Some scientists claimed that these problems came about because the children lived in institutions (e.g., orphanages and refugee camps) where they could not form a close social-emotional bond with adults.

Soon after, studies of monkeys that were reared in isolation confirmed this idea. Although the monkeys received excellent physical care, they stayed huddled in a corner of their cages, clutching themselves, and rocking constantly; when placed with other monkeys, they avoided them as much as they could (Harlow & Harlow, 1965). Clearly, in the absence of regular social interactions with caring adults, normal development is thrown way off course.

In explaining the essential ingredients of these early social relationships, most modern accounts take an evolutionary perspective. **According to** *evolutionary psychology,* **many human behaviors represent successful adaptation to the environment.** That is, over human history, some behaviors have made it more likely that people will reproduce and pass on their genes to following generations. For example, we take it for granted that most people enjoy being with other people. But evolutionary psychologists argue that our "social nature" is a product of evolution: For early humans, being in a group offered protection from predators and made it easier to locate food. Thus, early humans who were social were more likely than their asocial peers to live long enough to reproduce, passing on their social orientation to their offspring (Gaulin & McBurney, 2001). Over many, many generations, "being social" had such a survival advantage that nearly all people are socially oriented (though in varying amounts, as we know from research on temperament in Module 10.2).

Applied to child development, evolutionary psychology highlights the adaptive value of children's behavior at different points in development (Bjorklund & Pellegrini, 2000). For example, think about the time and energy that parents invest in child rearing. Without such effort, infants and young children would die before they were sexually mature, which means that a parent's genes could not be passed along to grandchildren (Geary, 2002). Here, too, parenting just seems "natural" but really represents an adaptation to the problem of guaranteeing that one's helpless offspring can survive until they're sexually mature.

An evolutionary perspective of early human relationships comes from John Bowlby (1969, 1991). **According to Bowlby, children who form an** *attachment* **to an adult—that is, an enduring social-emotional relationship—are more likely to survive.** This person is usually the mother but need not be; the key is a strong emotional relationship with a responsive, caring person. Attachments can form with fathers, grandparents, or someone else. Bowlby described four phases in the growth of attachment:

## According to Bowlby, mother-infant attachment progresses through four stages in infancy.

- *Preattachment* (birth to 6–8 weeks). Evolution has endowed infants with many behaviors that elicit caregiving from an adult. When babies cry, smile, or gaze intently at a parent's face, parents usually smile back or hold the baby. The infant's behaviors and the responses they evoke in adults create an interactive system that is the first step in the formation of attachment relationships.

- *Attachment in the making* (6–8 weeks to 6–8 months). During these months, babies begin to behave differently in the presence of familiar caregivers and unfamiliar adults. Babies now smile and laugh more often with the primary caregiver. And when babies are upset, they're more easily consoled by the primary caregiver. Babies are gradually identifying the primary caregiver as the person they can depend on when they're anxious or distressed.

- *True attachment* (6–8 months to 18 months). By approximately 7 or 8 months, most infants have singled out the attachment figure—usually the mother—as a special individual. The attachment figure is now the infant's stable social-

According to evolutionary psychology, parents invest time and energy in child rearing because this increases the odds that one's genes are passed along to the next generation.

emotional base. For example, a 7-month-old like the one in the photo will explore a novel environment but periodically look toward his mother, as if seeking reassurance that all is well. The behavior suggests the infant trusts his mother and indicates the attachment relationship has been established. In addition, this behavior reflects important cognitive growth: It means that the infant has a mental representation of the mother, an understanding that she will be there to meet the infant's needs (Lewis et al., 1997). And infants like 8-month-old Sam are distressed when they're separated from the attachment figure because they've lost their secure base.

- *Reciprocal relationships* (18 months on). Infants' growing cognitive and language skills and their accumulated experience with their primary caregiver makes infants better able to act as true partners in the attachment relationship. They often take the initiative in interactions and negotiate with parents ("Please read me another story!"). They begin to understand parents' feelings and goals and sometimes use this knowledge to guide their own behavior (e.g., social referencing, described on page 308). And they cope with separation more effectively because they can anticipate that parents will return.

**THE ROLE OF FATHERS.**   Attachment typically first develops between infants and their mothers because mothers are usually the primary caregivers of American infants. Babies soon become attached to fathers, too, despite some consistent differences in the ways that American mothers and fathers interact with infants. In a typical two-parent family, fathers spend far less time than mothers with infants and are far less likely than mothers to be responsible for child-care tasks. For example, in a nationally representative sample of mothers and fathers of infants and toddlers, fathers spent an average of 32 minutes each day in caregiving tasks (e.g., feeding, bathing) compared to

70 minutes for mothers (Yeung et al., 2001). Over the past 40 years, child care has shifted some from being "women's work" to a responsibility that can be shared equally by mothers and fathers. But women are still far more likely to be involved in direct care of infants and toddlers, despite no evidence that they provide better care than fathers do (Parke, 2002).

Another difference between mothers and fathers is *how* they interact with young children. Fathers typically spend much more time playing with their babies than taking care of them. And even their style of play differs. Physical play like that shown in the photo is the norm for fathers, whereas mothers spend more time reading and talking to babies, showing them toys, and playing games like patty-cake (Parke, 2002). Given the opportunity to play with mothers or fathers, infants more often choose their fathers. However, when infants are distressed, mothers are preferred (Field, 1990). Thus, although most infants become attached to both parents, mothers and fathers typically have distinctive roles in their children's early social development.

Fathers spend much of their time with babies playing with them (instead of taking care of them) and tend to play with them more vigorously and physically than mothers do.

## The Quality of Attachment

Attachment between infant and mother usually occurs by 8 or 9 months of age, but the attachment can take on different forms. Mary Ainsworth (1978, 1993) pioneered the study of attachment relationships using a procedure that has come to be known as the Strange Situation. You can see in the diagram that the Strange Situation involves a series of episodes, each about 3 minutes long. The mother and infant enter an unfamiliar room filled with interesting toys. The mother leaves briefly, then mother and baby are reunited. Meanwhile, the experimenter observes the baby, recording its response to both events.

FIGURE 10-2

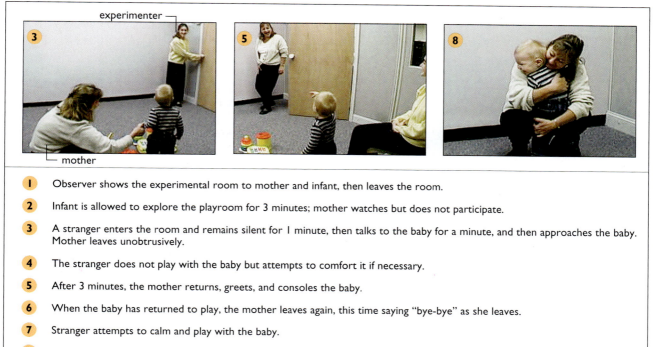

1  Observer shows the experimental room to mother and infant, then leaves the room.

2  Infant is allowed to explore the playroom for 3 minutes; mother watches but does not participate.

3  A stranger enters the room and remains silent for 1 minute, then talks to the baby for a minute, and then approaches the baby. Mother leaves unobtrusively.

4  The stranger does not play with the baby but attempts to comfort it if necessary.

5  After 3 minutes, the mother returns, greets, and consoles the baby.

6  When the baby has returned to play, the mother leaves again, this time saying "bye-bye" as she leaves.

7  Stranger attempts to calm and play with the baby.

8  After 3 minutes, the mother returns and the stranger leaves.

VIDEO 10.4
Separation
Anxiety

Based on how the infant reacts to separation from the mother and then reunion, Ainsworth (1993) and other researchers (Main & Cassidy, 1988) have identified four primary types of attachment relationships. One is a secure attachment and three are insecure attachments (avoidant, resistant, disorganized):

- *Secure attachment:* **The baby may or may not cry when the mother leaves, but when she returns, the baby wants to be with her and if the baby is crying, it stops.** Babies in this group seem to be saying, "I missed you terribly, but now that you're back, I'm okay." Approximately 60 to 65% of American babies have secure attachment relationships.

- *Avoidant attachment:* **The baby is not visibly upset when the mother leaves and, when she returns, may ignore her by looking or turning away.** Infants with an avoidant attachment look as if they're saying, "You left me again. I always have to take care of myself!" About 20% of American infants have avoidant attachment relationships, which is one of the three forms of insecure attachment.

- *Resistant attachment:* **The baby is upset when the mother leaves and remains upset or even angry when she returns, and is difficult to console.** Like the baby in the photo, these babies seem to be telling the mother, "Why do you do this? I need you desperately and yet you just leave me without warning. I get so angry when you're like this." About 10 to 15% of American babies have this resistant attachment relationship, which is another form of insecure attachment.

- *Disorganized (disoriented) attachment:* **The baby seems confused when the mother leaves and, when she returns, seems as if it doesn't really understand what's happening.** The baby often has a dazed look on its face as if wondering, "What's going on here? I want you to be here, but you left and now you're back. I don't know whether to laugh or cry!" About 5 to 10% of American babies have this disorganized attachment relationship, the last of the three kinds of insecure attachment.

Infants with a resistant attachment are upset or angry with Mom when reunited following a separation from her.

More than 30 years later, the Strange Situation remains an important tool for studying attachment. But some scientists have criticized its emphasis on separation and reunion as the primary means for assessing quality of attachment; they suggest that what is considered an appropriate response to separation may not be the same in all cultures (Rothbaum et al., 2000). Consequently, investigators now use other methods to complement the Strange Situation. One of them, the Attachment Q-Set, can be used with young children as well as infants and toddlers. In this method, trained observers watch mothers and children interact at home; then the observer rates the interaction on many attachment-related behaviors (e.g., "Child greets mother with a big smile when she enters the room"). The ratings are totaled to provide a measure of the security of the child's attachment. Scores obtained with the Q-set converge with assessments derived from the Strange Situation (van IJzeendorn et al., 2004).

**STABILITY OF ATTACHMENT.** The quality of attachment during infancy predicts parent–child relations during childhood, adolescence, and young adulthood. Infants with secure attachment relationships tend to report, as adolescents and young adults, that they depend on their parents for care and support. In contrast, infants with insecure attachment relationships often report, as adolescents and young adults, being angry with their parents or deny being close to them. However, consistency is far from perfect. Stressful life events—death of a parent, divorce, life-threatening illness, poverty—help to determine stability and change in attachment. Stressful life events are associated with insecure attachments during adolescence and young adulthood. Consequently, when infants with insecure attachments experience stressful life events, their attachment tends to remain insecure; when infants with secure attachment experience these same events, their attachment often becomes insecure, perhaps because stress makes parents less available and less responsive to their children (Hamilton, 2000; Waters et al., 2000).

**CONSEQUENCES OF QUALITY OF ATTACHMENT.** Erikson, Bowlby, and other theorists (Waters & Cummings, 2000) believe that attachment, as the first social relationship, provides the basis for all of an infant's later social relationships. In this view, infants who experience the trust and compassion of a secure attachment should develop into preschool children who interact confidently and successfully with their peers. In contrast, infants who do not experience a successful, satisfying first relationship should be more prone to problems in their social interactions as preschoolers.

> Infants with a secure attachment relationship tend to interact successfully with peers.

Many findings are consistent with these predictions. For example, children with secure attachment relationships have higher quality friendships and fewer conflicts in their friendships than children with insecure attachment relationships (Lieberman, Doyle, & Markiewicz, 1999). And, school-age children are less likely to have behavior problems if they have secure attachment relationships and more likely if they have insecure attachment relationships (Carlson, 1998; Moss et al., 1998).

However, the most compelling evidence comes from a meta-analysis of 63 studies that examined possible links between parent–child attachment and children's peer relations (Schneider, Atkinson, & Tardif, 2001). As predicted, children with secure attachments tended to have better relations with their peers and, in particular, had higher quality friendships. And, although some theorists (Thompson, 1998) have argued that an insecure attachment is particularly detrimental to peer relations in children who are exposed to other risk factors (e.g., if they have a history of maltreatment or if one of their parents has a psychiatric disorder), the positive relation between attachment and peer relations was evident in children from high- and low-risk groups.

The conclusion seems inescapable: As infants who have secure attachment relationships develop, their social interactions tend to be more satisfying. Why? Secure attachment evidently promotes trust and confidence in other humans, which leads to more skilled social interactions later in childhood. Of course, attachment is only one step along the long road of social development. Infants with insecure attachments are not doomed, but this initial misstep can interfere with their social development.

**FACTORS DETERMINING QUALITY OF ATTACHMENT.** Because secure attachment is so important to a child's later development, researchers have tried to identify the factors involved. Undoubtedly the most important is the interaction between parents and their babies (De Wolff & van IJzendoorn, 1997). A secure attachment is most likely when parents respond to infants predictably and appropriately. For example, the mother in the photo has promptly responded to her baby's crying and is trying to reassure the baby. The mother's behavior evidently conveys that social interactions are predictable and satisfying, and apparently this behavior instills in infants the trust and confidence that are the hallmark of secure attachment.

A key ingredient in creating a secure mother—infant attachment is for the mother to respond appropriately and predictably to her infant's needs.

*A secure attachment relationship is most likely to develop when parents respond to their infant's needs reliably and sensitively.*

Why does predictable and responsive parenting promote secure attachment relationships? To answer this question, think about your own friendships and romantic relationships. These relationships are usually most satisfying when we believe we can trust the other people and depend on them in times of need. The same formula seems to hold for infants. **Infants develop an *internal working model*, a set of expectations about parents' availability and responsiveness, generally and in times of stress.** When parents are dependable and caring, babies come to trust them, knowing they can be relied upon for comfort. That is, babies develop an internal working model in which they believe their parents are concerned about their needs and will try to meet them (Huth-Bocks et al., 2004; Thompson, 2000).

Many research findings attest to the importance of a caregiver's sensitivity for developing secure attachment:

- In a longitudinal study, infants were more likely to have a secure attachment relationship at 12 months when their parents were sensitive and responded quickly and appropriately to their infant at 3 months (Cox et al., 1992).

- In a study conducted in Israel, infants were less likely to develop secure attachment when they slept in dormitories with other children, where they received inconsistent (if any) attention when they became upset overnight (Sagi et al., 1994).

- In a study conducted in the Netherlands, infants were more likely to form a secure attachment when their mother had 3 months of training that emphasized monitoring an infant's signals and responding appropriately and promptly (van den Boom, 1994, 1995).

Thus, secure attachment is most likely when parents are sensitive and responsive. Of course, not all caregivers react to babies in a reliable and reassuring manner. Some respond intermittently or only after the infant has cried long and hard. And when these caregivers finally respond, they are sometimes annoyed by the infant's demands and may misinterpret the infant's intent. Over time, these babies tend to see social relationships as inconsistent and often frustrating, conditions that do little to foster trust and confidence.

Why are some parents more responsive (and thus more likely to foster secure attachment) than others? According to modern attachment theory (e.g., Cassidy, 1994), parents have internal working models of the attachment relationship with their own parents, and these working models guide interactions with their own infants. When questioned about attachment relationships with the Adult Attachment Interview (George, Kaplan, & Main, 1985), adults can be classified into one of three groups, one corresponding to the secure attachment of childhood and the other two corresponding to insecure attachments:

- *Secure adults* describe childhood experiences objectively and value the impact of their parent–child relationship on their development.

- *Dismissive adults* sometimes deny the value of childhood experiences and sometimes are unable to recall those experiences precisely, yet they often idealize their parents.

- *Preoccupied adults* describe childhood experiences emotionally and often express anger or confusion regarding relationships with their parents.

According to attachment theory, only parents with autonomous attachment representations are likely to provide the sensitive caregiving that promotes secure attachment relationships. In fact, many studies show that parents' secure attachment representations are associated with sensitive caregiving, and, in turn, with secure attachment in their infants (van IJzendoorn, 1995; Pederson et al., 1998). Furthermore, as I mentioned earlier, infants with secure attachment relations often become young adults with secure attachment representations, completing the circle.

The sensitive and responsive caregiving that is essential for secure attachments is often taxing, particularly for babies with difficult temperaments. That is, babies who fuss often and are difficult to console are more prone to insecure attachment (Goldsmith & Harman, 1994; Seifer et al., 1996). Insecure attachment may also be more likely when a difficult, emotional infant has a mother whose personality is rigid and traditional than when the mother is accepting and flexible (Mangelsdorf et al., 1990). Rigid mothers do not adjust well to the often erratic demands of their difficult babies; instead, they want the baby to adjust to them. This means that rigid mothers less often provide the responsive, sensitive care that leads to secure attachment.

Fortunately, even brief training for mothers of newborns can help them respond to their babies more effectively (Bakermans-Kranenburg, van IJzendoorn, & Juffer, 2003). Mothers can be taught how to interact more sensitively, affectionately, and responsively, paving the way for secure attachment and the lifelong benefits associated with a positive internal working model of interpersonal relationships.

**When infants receive high-quality parenting, they're likely to form a secure attachment relationship regardless of the amount of time spent in child care.**

**WORK, ATTACHMENT, AND CHILD CARE.** Since the 1970s, more women in the workforce and more single-parent households have made child care a fact of life for many American families. I describe child care in detail in Module 15.3, but here I want to focus on one specific aspect: What happens to mother–infant attachment when other people care for the infant much of the time? Parents and policymakers alike have been concerned about the impact of such care. Is there, for example, a maximum amount of time per week that infants should spend in care outside the home? Is there a minimum age below which infants should not be placed in care outside the home? The "Child Development and Family Policy" feature describes work that has attempted to answer these and other questions about the impact of early child care on children's development.

## Child Development and Family Policy
### Determining Guidelines for Child Care for Infants and Toddlers

Because so many American families need child care for their infants and toddlers, a comprehensive study of early child care was required to provide parents and policymakers with appropriate guidelines. The task fell to the U.S. National Institute of Child Health and Human Development, which began the Early Child Care study in 1991. Researchers recruited 1,364 mothers and their newborns from 12 U.S. cities. Both mothers and children have been tested repeatedly (and the testing continues, because the study is ongoing).

From the outset, one of the concerns was the impact of early child care on mother–infant attachment. In fact, the results so far show no overall effects of child-care experience on mother–infant attachment, for either 15- or 36-month-olds (NICHD Early Child Care Research Network, 1997, 2001). In other words, a secure mother–infant attachment was just as likely, regardless of the quality of child care, the amount of time the child spent in care, the age when the child began care, how frequently the parents changed child-care arrangements, and the type of child care (e.g., at a child-care center or in the home with a nonrelative).

However, when the effects of child care were considered along with characteristics of mothers, an important pattern was detected: At 15 and 36 months, insecure attachments were more common when less sensitive mothering was combined with low quality or large amounts of child care (NICHD Early Child Care Research Network, 1997, 2001). As the investigators put it "poor quality, unstable, or more than minimal amounts of child care apparently added to the risks already inherent in poor mothering, so that the combined effects were worse than those of low maternal sensitivity and responsiveness alone" (1997, p. 877). These conclusions are particularly convincing because the same pattern of results was found in Israel in a large-scale study of child care and attachment that was modeled after the NICHD Early Child Care study (Sagi et al., 2002).

These results provide clear guidelines for parents. The essential ingredient for secure attachment is high-quality parenting. With such parenting, a secure attachment is likely regardless of a child's experience in child care. Of course, parents should still look for high-quality child care; and we'll explore this topic in detail in Module 15.3. ■

**10.3** Malak is the mother of a 3-month-old. She's eager to return to her job as civil engineer but she worries that she may harm her baby by going back to work so soon. What could you say to reassure her?

## CHECK YOUR LEARNING

**RECALL**  Describe the evolutionary perspective on mother–infant attachment. What are the different forms of mother–infant attachment? What are the consequences of these different forms?

**INTERPRET**  Compare the infant's contributions to the formation of mother–infant attachment with the mother's contributions.

**APPLY**  Based on what you know about the normal developmental timetable for the formation of mother–infant attachment, what would seem to be the optimal age range for children to be adopted?

**10.3**

Tell her that the findings of the NICHD Early Child Care Study make it clear that as long as Malak provides high-quality parenting—she responds appropriately and predictably to her baby's needs—she and her baby should have a secure attachment even if the baby is in day-care full time.

## UNIFYING THEMES: Active Children

Temperament is one of the best examples in this book of the theme that *children influence their own development*. Temperament helps determine how parents, peers, and other adults respond to children. Parents and peers, for example, usually respond positively to temperamentally easy children. Parents find it more straightforward to establish a secure attachment with an easy child than with a difficult child. Peers get along better with easy children than with shy, inhibited children. Children's temperament does not alone dictate the direction of their development, but it makes some directions much easier to follow than others.

## SEE FOR YOURSELF

Arrange to visit a local day-care center where you can unobtrusively observe preschoolers for several days. As you watch the children, see if you can detect the temperamental differences that are described in Module 10.2. Can you identify an emotional child, an active child, and a social child? Also, notice how adults respond to the children. Notice if the same behaviors lead to different responses from adults, depending on the child's temperament. See for yourself!

## RESOURCES

For more information about

the **development of emotion,** read Carolyn Saarni's *The Development of Emotional Competence* (Guilford, 1999) which focuses on the growth of eight key emotional skills.

**attachment,** visit the Web site of a group of prominent attachment researchers:
**http://www.johnbowlby.com**

# KEY TERMS

attachment  319

avoidant attachment  322

basic emotions  303

dismissive adults (attachment representation)  325

disorganized (disoriented) attachment  322

display rules  308

effortful control  312

evolutionary psychology  319

internal working model  324

negative affect  312

preoccupied adults (attachment representation)  325

resistant attachment  322

school phobia  306

secure adults (attachment representation)  325

secure attachment  322

self-conscious emotions  305

social referencing  308

social smiles  304

stranger wariness  304

surgency/extraversion  312

systematic desensitization  306

temperament  311

SUMMARY

## 10.1 EMERGING EMOTIONS

### The Function of Emotions

Modern theories emphasize the functional value of emotion. Emotions such as fear, happiness, and disgust are valuable because they help people adapt: keeping them away from danger and strengthening social relationships.

### Experiencing and Expressing Emotions

Scientists often use infants' facial expressions to judge when different emotional states emerge in development. Basic emotions, which include joy, anger, and fear, emerge in the first year. Fear first appears in infancy as stranger wariness. Complex emotions have an evaluative component and include guilt, embarrassment, and pride. They appear between 18 and 24 months and require more sophisticated cognitive skills than basic emotions like happiness and fear. Cultures differ in the rules for expressing emotions and the situations that elicit particular emotions.

### Recognizing and Using Others' Emotions

By 6 months, infants have begun to recognize the emotions associated with different facial expressions. They use this information to help them evaluate unfamiliar situations. Beyond infancy, children understand the causes and consequences of different emotions, that people can feel multiple emotions simultaneously, and the rules for displaying emotions appropriately.

### Regulating Emotions

Infants use simple strategies to regulate emotions such as fear. As children grow, they become better skilled at regulating their emotions. Children who do not regulate emotions well tend to have problems interacting with others.

## 10.2 TEMPERAMENT

### What Is Temperament?

Temperament refers to biologically based, stable patterns of behavior that are evident soon after birth. The New York Longitudinal Study suggested three main categories of temperament, but most modern theories focus on dimensions of temperament. According to Rothbart's theory, temperament includes three main dimensions: surgency/extraversion, negative affect, and effortful control.

### Hereditary and Environmental Contributions to Temperament

The major theories agree that both heredity and environment contribute to temperament. For many dimensions of temperament, identical twins are more alike than fraternal twins. Positive emotionality reflects environmental influences, and difficult temperament is linked to abrupt parenting.

### Stability of Temperament

Temperament is moderately stable in infancy, childhood, and adolescence. Temperament in childhood is somewhat related to personality in adulthood. The relations are not very strong because temperament itself is changing as children develop.

### Temperament and Other Aspects of Development

Many investigators have shown that temperament is related to other aspects of development. Difficult babies are more likely to have behavioral problems by the time they are old enough to attend school. Persistent children are more successful in school, shy children sometimes have problems with peers, anxious children are more compliant with parents, and angry or fearful children are prone to depression. However, the impact of temperament always depends on the environment in which children develop.

## 10.3 ATTACHMENT

### The Growth of Attachment

Attachment is an enduring social-emotional relationship between infant and parent. Bowlby's theory of attachment is rooted in evolutionary psychology and describes four stages in the development of attachment: preattachment, attachment in the making, true attachment, and reciprocal relationships.

### The Quality of Attachment

Research with the Strange Situation, in which infant and mother are separated briefly, reveals four primary forms of attachment. Most common is a secure attachment, in which infants have complete trust in the mother. Less common are three types of insecure attachment relationships that lack this trust. In avoidant relationships, infants deal with the lack of trust by ignoring the mother; in resistant relationships, infants often seem angry with her; in disorganized (disoriented) relationships, infants seem to not understand the mother's absence.

Children who have had secure attachment relationships during infancy often interact with their peers more readily and more skillfully. Secure attachment is most likely to occur when mothers respond sensitively and consistently to their infants' needs. Adults who value their relationship with their own parents are most likely to use the sensitive caregiving that promotes secure attachments with their own infants.

A century ago, G. Stanley Hall, an influential American developmental psychologist, wrote that adolescence was "strewn with wreckage of mind, body and morals" (1904, p. xiv). Judging by today's movies and media, Hall's portrayal persists: When teens aren't presented as runaways, drug addicts, and shoplifters, they're moody and withdrawn or manic. But how accurate is this picture? What does current research show about adolescence and the process of developing independence and identity?

In Module 11.1, we'll look at the mechanisms that give rise to a person's identity, and we'll see if adolescent "storm and stress" is a necessary step in achieving an identity. Of course, people are often happier with some aspects of themselves than with others. These evaluative aspects of identity are the focus of Module 11.2. Finally, in Module 11.3, we'll look at how we develop an understanding of others, because as we learn more about ourselves, we learn more about other people too.

**11.1**    Who Am I? Self-Concept

**11.2**    Self-Esteem

**11.3**    Understanding Others

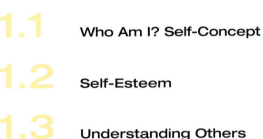

1 The Science of Child Development

2 Genetic Bases of Child Development

3 Prenatal Development, Birth, and the Newborn

4 Growth and Health

5 Perceptual and Motor Development

6 Theories of Cognitive Development

7 Cognitive Processes and Academic Skills

8 Intelligence and Individual Differences in Cognition

9 Language and Communication

10 Emotional Development

# Understanding Self and Others

12 Moral Understanding and Behavior

13 Gender and Development

14 Family Relationships

15 Influences Beyond the Family

**11**

# 11.1     WHO AM I? SELF-CONCEPT

Origins of Self-Recognition

The Evolving Self-Concept

The Search for Identity

## LEARNING OBJECTIVES

- When do infants first acquire a sense of self?
- How does self-concept become more elaborate as children grow?
- How do adolescents achieve an identity?

> *Dea was born in Seoul of Korean parents but was adopted by a Dutch couple in Michigan when she was 3 months old. Growing up, she considered herself a red-blooded American. In high school, however, Dea realized that others saw her as an Asian American, an identity about which she had never given much thought. She began to wonder, who am I really? American? Dutch American? Asian American?*

Like Dea, do you sometimes wonder who you are? **Answers to "Who am I?" reflect a person's *self-concept*, which refers to the attitudes, behaviors, and values that a person believes make him or her a unique individual.** One answer to "Who am I?"—from a teenage girl—shows just how complex a person's self-concept can be.

> I'm sensitive, friendly, outgoing, popular, and tolerant, though I can also be shy, self-conscious, and even obnoxious! I'd like to be friendly and tolerant all of the time. That's the kind of person I want to be, and I'm disappointed when I'm not. I'm responsible, even studious now and then, but on the other hand, I'm a goof-off, too, because if you're too studious, you won't be popular (Harter, 1990, p. 352).

As an adult, your answer is probably even more complex because, after all, most people are complex creatures. But how did you acquire this complex self-concept? We'll answer that question in this module, beginning with the origins of an infant's sense of self. Later, we'll see how identity becomes elaborated after infancy and see how individuals like Dea develop an ethnic identity.

VIDEO 11.1
Self Awareness

Although even very young babies enjoy looking at that "thing" in the mirror, not until about 15 months of age do babies realize that *they* are the thing in the mirror; this is one of the first signs of an emerging sense of self.

## Origins of Self-Recognition

What is the starting point for self-concept? Following the lead of the 19th-century philosopher and psychologist William James, modern researchers believe that the foundation of self-concept is the child's awareness that he or she exists. At some point early in life, children must realize that they exist independently of other people and objects in the environment and that their existence continues over time.

Measuring the onset of this awareness is not easy. Obviously, we can't simply ask a 3-year-old, "So, tell me, when did you first realize that you existed and weren't simply part of the furniture?" A less direct approach is needed, and the photo shows one route that many investigators have taken. Like many babies his age, the 9-month-old in the photo is looking at the face he sees in the mirror. Babies at this age sometimes touch the face in the mirror or wave at it, but none of their behaviors indicates that they recognize themselves in the mirror. Instead, babies act as if the face in the mirror is simply a very interesting stimulus.

How would we know that infants recognize themselves in a mirror? One clever approach is to have the mother place a red mark on her infant's nose; she does this surreptitiously, while wiping the baby's face. Then the infant is returned to the mirror. Many 1-year-olds touch the red mark on the mirror, showing that they notice the mark on the face in the mirror. At about 15 months, however, an important change occurs: Many babies see the red mark in the mirror, then reach up and touch *their own* noses. By age 2, most children do this (Bullock & Lütkenhaus, 1990; Lewis, 1997). When these older toddlers notice the red mark in the mirror, they understand that the funny-looking nose in the mirror is their own.

Do you doubt that the mirror task shows an infant's emerging sense of self? Perhaps you think it tells more about an infant's growing understanding of mirrors than the baby's self-awareness. One way to examine this possibility would be to test infants who have never seen mirrors previously. Priel and deSchonen (1986) took this approach, testing infants from Israeli desert communities. These babies had never seen mirrors or, for that matter, virtually any reflective surfaces. Nevertheless, the same developmental trend appeared in the desert infants as in a comparison group of infants living in a nearby city. No 6- to 12-month-olds in either group touched their noses after they saw the mark, a few 13- to 19-month-olds did, and nearly all the 20- to 26-month-olds did.

We don't need to rely solely on the mirror task to know that self-awareness emerges between 18 and 24 months. During this same period, toddlers look more at photographs of themselves than at photos of other children. They also refer to themselves by name or with a personal pronoun, such as *I* or *me*, and sometimes they know their age and their gender. These changes, which often occur together, suggest that self-awareness is well established in most children by age 2 (Lewis & Ramsay, 2004; Pinquart, 2005).

> By 2 years of age, most children recognize themselves and refer to themselves by name or with I and me.

The self-awareness that's evident in toddlers clearly has its roots in infancy (Rochat, 2001). Some of the roots are social. From regular, predictable interactions with caregivers, infants learn that those interactions involve different roles—one for the infant and one for the caregiver. Such differentiation of roles into the "my" and "other" roles is an important early step toward self-awareness. Other roots of self-awareness involve infants' understanding of their own bodies. As adults, we know that when we raise our hand to scratch our nose, the hand we see "doing the scratching" is our hand; it's part of our physical self. From experience watching their bodies move, infants learn this aspect of self-awareness—"that's not any old hand, that's my hand"—by 3 to 5 months of age. And play with objects also contributes to self-recognition (Keller et al., 2004), perhaps because it provides many opportunities for infants to explore how their arm and hand movements relate to the physical world.

Soon after children are self-aware, autobiographical memory (described in Module 7.1) begins to emerge (Harley & Reese, 1999). That is, children begin to recognize continuity in the self over time; the "I" in the present is linked to the "I" in the past (Nelson, 2001). Awareness of a self that is extended in time is fostered by conversations with parents about the past and the future. Through such conversations, a 3-year-old celebrating a birthday understands that she's an older version of the same person who had a birthday a year previously.

Children's growing awareness of a self extended in time is also revealed by children's understanding of ownership (Fasig, 2000). When a toddler sees his favorite toy and says "mine," this implies awareness of continuity of the self over time: "In the

Young children often use their toys as a way to tell others who they are; "Mine!" means "That's part of me!" not "That belongs to me—hands off!"

past, I played with that." And when toddlers like the girl in the photo say "Mine!" they are often not being aggressive or selfish; instead "mine" is a way of indicating ownership and in the process defining themselves. Thus, the girl in the photo is not trying to deny the doll to the other girl; she is simply saying that playing with dolls is part of who she is (Levine, 1983).

Finally, once self-awareness is established, children begin to acquire a self-concept. That is, once children fully understand that they exist and that they have a unique mental life, they begin to wonder who they are. They want to define themselves. In the next section, we'll see how this self-concept becomes more complex as children develop.

## The Evolving Self-Concept

Before you go any further, return to the quotation on page 332 from the teenager. In describing herself, this girl relies heavily on psychological traits. The first sentence alone includes eight adjectives referring to these traits: *sensitive, friendly, outgoing, popular, tolerant, shy, self-conscious,* and *obnoxious.* How do children develop such a complex view of themselves? For toddlers and preschoolers, self-concept is *much* simpler. Asked to describe themselves, preschoolers are likely to mention physical characteristics ("I have blue eyes"), their preferences ("I like cookies"), their possessions ("I have trucks"), and their competencies ("I can count to 50"). What these features have in common is a focus on a child's characteristics that are observable and concrete (Damon & Hart, 1988).

> A preschooler's self-concept is linked to the concrete and real but an adolescent's self-concept is more abstract and psychological.

At about 6 to 8 years of age, children's self-descriptions begin to change (Harter, 1994, 2005). Children are more likely to mention emotions ("Sometimes I get angry"). They are also more likely to mention the social groups to which they belong ("I'm on the lacrosse team"). Finally, in contrast to preschool children, who simply mention their competencies, elementary-school children describe their level of skill in relation to their peers ("I'm the best speller in my whole class").

Self-concepts change again as children enter adolescence (Harter & Monsour, 1992). They now include attitudes ("I love algebra") and personality traits ("I'm usually a very happy person"). Adolescents also begin to make religious and political beliefs part of their self-concept ("I'm a Catholic" or "I'm a conservative Republican"). Another change is that adolescents' self-concepts often vary with the setting. A teenager might say, "I'm really shy around people that I don't know, but I let loose when I'm with my friends and family."

Yet another change is that adolescents' self-concepts are often future oriented: Adolescents often describe themselves in terms of what they will be when they reach adulthood (Harter, 1990, 2005). These descriptions may include occupational goals ("I'm going to be an English teacher"), educational plans ("I plan to go to a community college to learn about computers"), or social roles ("I want to get married as soon as I finish high school").

The gradual elaboration of self-concept from the preschool years to adolescence is summarized in the table. Two general changes are evident: First, self-concept becomes richer as children grow; adolescents simply know much more about themselves than preschoolers. Second, the type of knowledge that children have of themselves changes. Preschoolers' understanding is linked to the concrete, the real, and the here and now. Adolescents' understanding, in contrast, is more abstract and more psychological, and sees the self as evolving over time. The change in children's knowledge of themselves should not surprise you because it's exactly the type of change that Piaget described. Concrete operational children's focus on the real and tangible extends to their thoughts about themselves, just as formal operational adolescents' focus on the abstract and hypothetical applies to their thoughts about themselves.

## SUMMARY TABLE

### DEVELOPMENTAL CHANGE IN SELF-CONCEPT

| Preschoolers | School-Age Children | Adolescents |
| --- | --- | --- |
| Possessions | Emotions | Attitudes |
| Physical characteristics | Social groups | Personality traits |
| Preferences | Comparisons with peers | Beliefs vary with the setting |
| Competencies | | Future oriented |
| *I like cars and trucks.* | *I'm the best goalie in my class.* | *I'm quiet and shy at school.* |

Adolescence is also a time of increasing self-reflection. Adolescents look for an identity to integrate the many different and sometimes conflicting elements of the self (Marcia, 1991). We'll look at this search for identity in detail in the next section.

## The Search for Identity

Erik Erikson (1968) believed that adolescents struggle to achieve an identity that will allow them to participate in the adult world. How exactly do they accomplish this? To learn more about possible identities, adolescents use the hypothetical reasoning skills of the formal operational stage to experiment with different selves (Nurmi, Poole, & Kalakoski, 1996). Adolescents' advanced cognitive skills allow them to imagine themselves in different roles.

VIDEO11.2
Identity/role develompent

As part of their search for an identity, adolescents often try on different roles, such as trying to imagine what life might be like as a rock star.

Much of the testing and experimentation is career oriented. Some adolescents, like the ones shown in the photo, may envision themselves as rock stars; others may imagine being a professional athlete, a Peace Corps worker, or a best-selling novelist. Other testing is romantically oriented. Teens may fall in love and imagine living with the loved one. Still other exploration involves religious and political beliefs (King, Elder, & Whitbeck, 1997; Yates & Youniss, 1996). Teens give different identities a trial run just as you might test drive different cars before selecting one. By fantasizing about their future, adolescents begin to discover who they will be.

The self-absorption that marks the teenage search for identity is referred to as *adolescent egocentrism* (Elkind, 1978). Unlike preschoolers, adolescents know that others have different perspectives on the world. At the same time, many adolescents believe, wrongly, that they are the focus of others' thinking. A teen like the one in the photo

Adolescents often believe that others are constantly watching them, a phenomenon known as imaginary audience; consequently, they're often upset or embarrassed when they make obvious mistakes or blunders, such as spilling food or drink.

who spills food on herself may imagine that all her friends are thinking only about the stain on her blouse and how sloppy she is. **Many adolescents feel that they are, in effect, actors whose performance is being watched constantly by their peers, a phenomenon known as the *imaginary audience.***

**Adolescent self-absorption is also demonstrated by the *personal fable*, teenagers' tendency to believe that their experiences and feelings are unique, that no one has ever felt or thought as they do.** Whether the excitement of first love, the despair of a broken relationship, or the confusion of planning for the future, adolescents often believe they are the first to experience these feelings and that no one else could possibly understand the power of their emotions (Elkind & Bowen, 1979). **Adolescents' belief in their uniqueness also contributes to an *illusion of invulnerability*—the belief that misfortune only happens to others.** They think they can have sex without becoming pregnant or drive recklessly without being in an auto accident. Those misfortunes, according to them, only happen to others.

Adolescent egocentrism, imaginary audiences, personal fables, and the illusion of invulnerability become less common as adolescents make progress toward achieving an identity. What exactly is involved in achieving an identity? Most adolescents

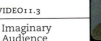

VIDEO11.3
Imaginary
Audience

VIDEO11.4
Invincibility
Fable

progress through different phases or *statuses*, though not necessarily in this order (Marcia, 1980, 1991):

- *Diffusion*: **Individuals in this status are confused or overwhelmed by the task of achieving an identity and are doing little to achieve one.**

- *Foreclosure*: **Individuals in this status have an identity determined largely by adults, rather than from personal exploration of alternatives.**

- *Moratorium*: **Individuals in this status are still examining different alternatives and have yet to find a satisfactory identity.**

- *Achievement*: **Individuals in this status have explored alternatives and have deliberately chosen a specific identity.**

Unlike Piaget's stages, these four phases do not necessarily occur in sequence. Most young adolescents are in a state of diffusion or foreclosure. The common element in these phases is that teens are not exploring alternative identities. They are avoiding the crisis altogether or have resolved it by taking on an identity suggested by parents or other adults. However, as individuals move beyond adolescence and into young adulthood and have more opportunity to explore alternative identities, diffusion and foreclosure become less common, and, achievement and moratorium become more common (Kroger, 2005).

Typically, young people do not reach the achievement status for all aspects of identity at the same time (Dellas & Jernigan, 1990; Kroger & Green, 1996). Some adolescents may reach the achievement status for occupations before achieving it for religion and politics. Others reach the achievement status for religion before other domains. Evidently, few youth achieve a sense of identity all at once; instead, the crisis of identity is first resolved in some areas and then in others.

**CHOOSING A CAREER.**　One element of identity that has been examined in some detail is career development. According to a theory proposed by Donald Super (1976, 1990), identity is a primary force in an adolescent's choice of a career. **At about age 13 or 14, adolescents use their emerging identities as a source of ideas about careers, a process called** *crystallization.* Teenagers use their ideas about their own talents and interests to limit potential career prospects. A teenager who is extroverted and sociable may decide that working with people would be the career for him. Another who excels in math and science may decide she'd like to teach math. Decisions are provisional, and adolescents experiment with hypothetical careers, trying to envision what each might be like. Rarely, however, are careers as hypothetical as the one imagined by the teenager in the cartoon!

At about age 18, adolescents extend the activities associated with crystallization and enter a new phase. **During** *specification*, **individuals further limit their career possibilities by learning more about specific lines of work and starting to obtain the training required for a specific job.** Our extroverted teenager who wants to work with people may decide that a career in sales would be a good match for his abilities and interests. The teen who likes math may have learned more about careers

**Q&A Question　11.1**

Jenny thinks she might like to be an engineer, but she also enjoys dance. To help decide what path would be best for her, Jenny has taken a battery of interest inventories and is exploring different majors at her university. Which of the four statuses best describes Jenny, at least as far as her occupation is concerned?

"Your son has made a career choice, Mildred. He's going to win the lottery and travel a lot."

In the specification stage of career development, adolescents try to learn more about different careers, sometimes by serving an apprenticeship.

and decided she'd like to be an accountant. Some teens, like the young man in the photo, may begin an apprenticeship as a way to learn a trade.

The end of the teenage years or the early 20s marks the beginning of the third phase. **During *implementation*, individuals enter the workforce and learn firsthand about jobs.** This is a time of learning about responsibility and productivity, of learning to get along with coworkers, and of altering one's lifestyle to accommodate work. This period is often unstable; individuals may change jobs frequently as they adjust to the reality of life in the workplace.

In each of Super's three phases of career development, there is continuous give and take between an individual's identity and career choice. A person's self-concept makes some careers more attractive than others; occupational experiences, in turn, refine and shape a person's identity.

What circumstances help adolescents decide on a career and achieve identity? Parents are influential (Marcia, 1980). When parents encourage discussion and recognize their children's autonomy, their children are more likely to reach the achievement status. Apparently these youth feel encouraged to undertake the personal experimentation that leads to identity. In contrast, when parents set rules with little justification and enforce them without explanation, children are more likely to remain in the foreclosure status. These teens are discouraged from experimenting personally; instead, their parents simply tell them what identity to adopt. Overall, adolescents are most likely to establish a well-defined identity in a family atmosphere where parents encourage children to explore alternatives on their own but do not pressure or provide explicit direction (Harter, 1990, 1999).

**ETHNIC IDENTITY.** For many adolescents growing up in North America today, achieving an identity is even more challenging because they are members of ethnic minority groups. The "Cultural Influences" feature describes one example.

## Cultural Influences

### Dea's Ethnic Identity

Dea, the adolescent in the opening vignette, belongs to the one third of adolescents and young adults living in the United States who are members of ethnic minority groups. They include African Americans, Asian Americans, Hispanic Americans, and Native Americans. **These individuals typically develop an *ethnic identity*: They feel a part of their ethnic group and learn the special customs and traditions of their group's culture and heritage** (Phinney, 2005).

An ethnic identity seems to be achieved in three phases. Initially, adolescents have not examined their ethnic roots. A teenage African American girl in this phase remarked, "Why do I need to learn about who was the first Black woman to do this or that? I'm just not too interested" (Phinney, 1989, p. 44). For this girl, ethnic identity is not yet an important personal issue.

In the second phase, adolescents begin to explore the personal impact of their ethnic heritage. The curiosity and questioning that are characteristic of this stage are captured in the comments of a teenage Mexican American girl who said, "I want to know what we do and how our culture is different from others. Going to festivals and cultural events helps me to learn more about my own culture and about myself" (Phinney, 1989, p. 44). Part of this phase involves learning cultural traditions; for example, like the girl in the photo, many adolescents learn to prepare ethnic food.

In the third phase, individuals achieve a distinct ethnic self-concept. One Asian American adolescent explained his ethnic identification like this: "I have been born Filipino and am born to be Filipino. I'm here in America, and people of many different cultures are here, too. So I don't consider myself only Filipino, but also American" (Phinney, 1989, p. 44).

To see if you understand the differences between these stages of ethnic identity, reread the vignette on page 332 about Dea and decide which stage applies to her. The answer appears on page 341, just before "Check Your Learning." ■

Part of the search for an ethnic identity involves learning cultural traditions, such as learning how to prepare foods associated with one's ethnic group.

Older adolescents are more likely than younger ones to have achieved an ethnic identity because they are more likely to have had opportunities to explore their cultural heritage (Phinney & Chavira, 1992). Also, as with overall identity, adolescents are most likely to achieve an ethnic self-concept when their parents encourage them to explore alternatives instead of pressuring them to adopt a particular ethnic identity (Rosenthal & Feldman, 1992).

Ethnic identity poses a special challenge for immigrant adolescents. Unlike native-born ethnic children, who have exposure to mainstream and ethnic culture from a young age, from the time immigrant adolescents enter a new country, they face the task of negotiating a culture largely unfamiliar to them. And many immigrant adolescents have already established a strong identity with their native land. Consequently, it's not surprising that immigrant adolescents do not immediately identify with their new culture. For example, in one study (Birman & Trickett, 2001), Jewish adolescents who had fled the former Soviet Union reported that, although they acted like most American teenagers (e.g., they ate American food, spent time with native-born American teens), they still "felt Russian" despite having lived in the United States for nearly 10 years.

> Adolescents with an ethnic identity have higher self-esteem, find interactions with others more satisfying, and do better in school.

Do adolescents benefit from a strong ethnic identity? Yes. Adolescents who have achieved an ethnic identity tend to have higher self-esteem and find their interactions with family and friends more satisfying (R. E. Roberts et al., 1999). In addition, many investigators have found that adolescents with a strong ethnic identity do better in school than adolescents whose ethnic identities are weaker. For example, Chavous et al. (2003) found that African American adolescents were most likely to stay in high school and go on to college when they had a strong African American identity coupled with awareness of racism in American society.

Some individuals achieve a well-defined ethnic self-concept and, at the same time, identify strongly with the mainstream culture. In the United States, for example, many Chinese Americans embrace both Chinese and American culture; in England, many Indians identify with both Indian and British cultures. For other individuals, the cost of strong ethnic identification is a weakened tie to mainstream culture. Some investigators report that, for Hispanic Americans, strong identification with American culture is associated with a weaker ethnic self-concept (Phinney, 1990).

We shouldn't be too surprised that identifying with mainstream culture weakens ethnic identity in some groups but not others. Racial and ethnic groups living in the United States are diverse. African American, Asian American, Hispanic American, and Native American cultures and heritages differ; and so we should expect that the nature and consequences of a strong ethnic self-concept will differ across these and other ethnic groups (Phinney, 2005).

Even within any particular group, the nature and consequences of ethnic identity may change over successive generations (Cuellar et al., 1997). As successive generations become more assimilated into mainstream culture, they may identify less strongly with ethnic culture. Thus, parents may maintain strong feelings of ethnic identity that their children don't share (Phinney, Ong, & Madden, 2000).

Finally, let's think about adolescents for whom an ethnic identity is a particular challenge—those whose parents come from different racial or ethnic groups. As recently as 1970, only 1% of U.S. children were multiracial; now 5% are multiracial (Jones & Smith, 2001). When children have one European American parent and the other is African American, Asian American, or Hispanic, children tend to adopt the ethnic minority identity. A child with an Asian mother and a European American father will probably consider herself Asian (Herman, 2004).

**STORM AND STRESS.**   According to American novelists and filmmakers, the search for identity that I've described in the past few pages is inherently a struggle, a time of storm and stress for adolescents. Although this view may make for best-selling novels and hit movies, in reality the rebellious teen is largely a myth. Think about the following conclusions derived from research findings (Steinberg, 1990). Most adolescents

FIGURE 11-1

Percentage of Adolescents Agreeing That "Most of the Time, I Am Happy"

Percentage of Adolescents Agreeing That "I Try to Stay Away from Home Most of the Time"

Source: Offer et al., 1988.

- admire and love their parents,
- rely upon their parents for advice,
- embrace many of their parents' values, and
- feel loved by their parents.

Not exactly the image of the rebel, is it? Cross-cultural research provides further evidence that for most teens adolescence is not a time of turmoil and conflict. Offer and his colleagues (1988) interviewed adolescents from 10 different countries: the United States, Australia, Germany, Italy, Israel, Hungary, Turkey, Japan, Taiwan, and Bangladesh. These investigators found most adolescents moving confidently and happily toward adulthood. As the graphs show, most adolescents around the world reported that they were usually happy, and few avoided their homes.

Of course, parent–child relations do change during adolescence. As teens become more independent, their relationships with their parents become more egalitarian. Parents must adjust to their children's growing sense of autonomy by treating them more like equals (Laursen & Collins, 1994). This growing independence means that teens spend less time with their parents, are less affectionate toward them, and argue more often with them about matters of style, taste, and freedom. Teenagers are also more moody and more likely to enjoy spending some time alone (Larson, 1997; Wolfson & Carskadon, 1998). But these changes are natural by-products of an evolving parent–child relationship in which the "child" is nearly a fully independent young adult (Steinberg, 1990).

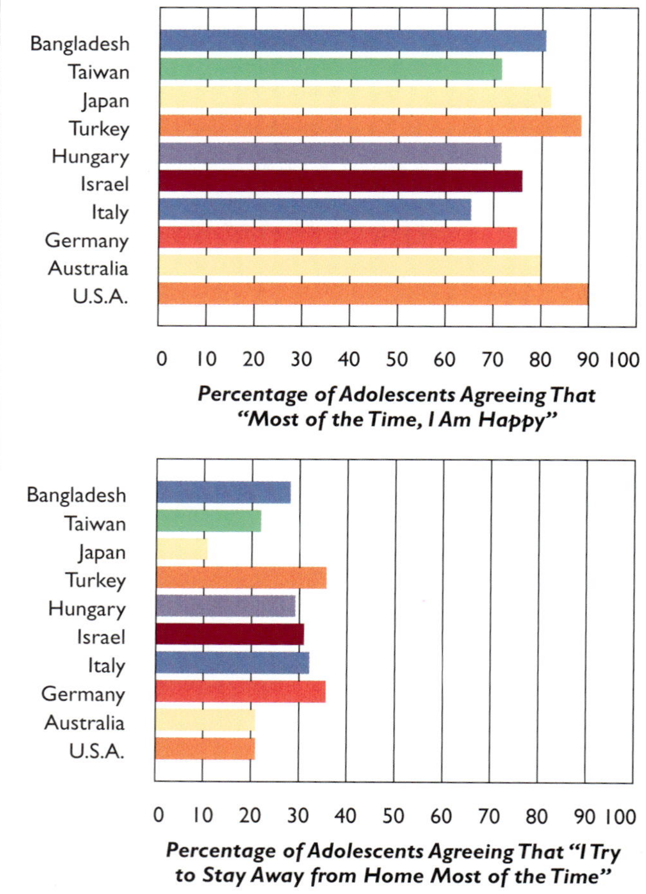

**DEPRESSION.**    The challenges of adolescence can lead some youth to become depressed (Fried, 2005). As we saw in Chapter 3, depressed individuals have pervasive feelings of sadness, are irritable, have low self-esteem, sleep poorly, and are unable to concentrate. About 3 to 8% of adolescents are depressed; adolescent girls are more often affected than boys, probably because social challenges in adolescence are often greater for girls than boys (Avenevoli & Steinberg, 2001; Nolen-Hoeksema & Girgus, 1994).

Depression is often triggered when adolescents experience a serious loss (e.g., the death of a loved one), disappointment (e.g., a much anticipated date is a fiasco), or failures (e.g., a defender falls down, allowing the opponent to score a game-winning goal). Of course, many adolescents and adults experience negative events like these, but most don't become depressed. Why? **One view emphasizes adolescents' *attributions*, their personal explanations of success and failure** (Nevid, Rathus, & Greene, 2003). Depression-prone adolescents are, for example, more likely to blame themselves for failure. Thus, after the disappointing date, a depression-prone teen is like to think, "I acted like a fool" instead of placing blame elsewhere by thinking "Gee. What a jerk!" And depression-prone teens more often believe that such personal "flaws" are stable and wide ranging (e.g., "I just don't get along well with other people!") instead of thinking of them as temporary (e.g., "I was just getting over the flu, so it's not surprising that the date went poorly") or specific (e.g., "I think softball is boring, so going to a game on a first date was really stupid").

Although attributions can lead to depression, biology also contributes, apparently through neurotransmitters. **Some depressed adolescents have reduced levels of *norepinephrine* and *serotonin*, neurotransmitters that help regulate brain centers that allow people to experience pleasure.** Some adolescents may feel depressed because lower levels of neurotransmitters make it difficult for them to experience happiness, joy, and other pleasurable emotions (Peterson, 1996).

To treat depression, some adolescents take antidepressant drugs designed to correct the imbalance in neurotransmitters. The well-known drug, Prozac, for example, is designed to reduce depression by increasing levels of serotonin (Peterson, 1996). However, drug treatment has no lasting effects—it only works while people are taking the drugs. More long-lasting effects are observed with psychotherapy. The most effective forms emphasize cognitive and social skills—adolescents learn how to have rewarding social interactions and to interpret them appropriately (Hollon, Haman, & Brown, 2002). These treatments *are* effective and depressed adolescents do need help; left untreated, depression can interfere with performance in school and social relationships, and may also lead to recurring depression in adulthood (Nevid et al., 2003).

> Depression is often triggered when adolescents blame themselves for a negative event.

*Response to question on page 339 about Dea's ethnic identity:* Dea, the Dutch Asian American high-school student, doesn't know how to integrate the Korean heritage of her biological parents with the Dutch American culture in which she was reared. This would put her in the second phase of acquiring an ethnic identity. On the one hand, she is examining her ethnic roots, which means she's progressed beyond the initial stage. On the other hand, she has not yet integrated her Asian and European roots, and so has not reached the third and final phase.

**11.1** Jenny looks to be in the moratorium status because she is actively exploring different alternatives.

## CHECK YOUR LEARNING

**RECALL** What evidence indicates that sense of self emerges during the 2nd year of life? What contributes to the emergence of a sense of self?

Describe research that undermines the view of adolescence as a period of "storm and stress."

**INTERPRET** Compare and contrast the three stages of career development with the three stages in the achievement of an ethnic identity.

**APPLY** The Tran family has just immigrated to the United States from Vietnam. The mother and father want their two children to grow up appreciating their Vietnamese heritage but worry that a strong ethnic identity may not be good for their kids. What advice would you give Mr. and Mrs. Tran about the impact of ethnic identity on children's development?

## 11.2 SELF-ESTEEM

**Measuring Self-Esteem**

**Developmental Change in Self-Esteem**

**Sources of Self-Esteem**

**Low Self-Esteem: Cause or Consequence?**

### LEARNING OBJECTIVES

- What is self-esteem? How is it measured?

- How does self-esteem change as children develop?

- What factors influence the development of self-esteem?

- Is children's development affected by low self-esteem?

*Darnel, age 10, loves school and for good reason: Every year, he is always one of the best students in his class. Darnel's mother, Karen, wants to enroll him in a program for gifted children, where she believes the pace will be more appropriate for her talented son. Darnel's dad, Jon, doesn't think this is such a great idea. He's afraid that if Darnel doesn't do well against all those other bright kids, his son will begin to doubt his academic ability.*

**Jon is concerned about Darnel's *self-esteem*, which refers to a person's judgment and feelings about his or her own worth.** Children with high self-esteem judge themselves favorably and feel positive about themselves. In contrast, children with low self-esteem judge themselves negatively, are unhappy with themselves, and often would rather be someone else. In this module, we'll see how self-esteem is measured, how it changes as children develop, and what forces shape it.

### Measuring Self-Esteem

Think about your own self-esteem. Do you think you have high self-esteem or low self-esteem? To help you answer this question, read each of these sentences and decide how well each applies to you:

I'm very good at schoolwork.

I find it very easy to make friends.

I do very well at all kinds of different sports.

I'm happy with the way I look.

If you agreed strongly with each of these statements, you definitely have high self-esteem. Usually, however, people agree with some of these statements more strongly than others. This tells us that, in addition to an overall sense of self-worth, people evaluate themselves in different areas.

How can we measure different aspects of self-esteem? The method depends on the age of the child. With 4- to 7-year-olds, one popular approach devised by Harter and Pike (1984) uses pairs of pictures. The sample pictures show a girl either solving a puzzle easily or having difficulty. During testing, children are first asked to point to the pictured child who is most like them. Then they point to the larger circle if they believe that they are "a lot" like the child in that picture or the smaller one if they believe they are "a little" like the child in that picture. Harter and Pike used 24 pairs of pictures like these to measure children's self-worth in four areas: cognitive competence, physical competence, acceptance by peers, and acceptance by mother.

FIGURE 11-2

Another productive approach with young children uses puppets (Ablow & Measelle, 1993; Measelle et al., 1998). One puppet describes itself to the child: "I like pizza." A second puppet then describes itself in opposite terms—"I don't like pizza"—and then motions to the child, "How about you?" Children can respond verbally ("I like pizza, too!"), by nodding their heads in agreement or disagreement, or by pointing to one of the puppets. Children are presented pairs of statements measuring academic competence ("I learn/don't learn things well"), achievement motivation ("I try/don't try my best at school"), social competence ("It's hard/not hard for me to make new friends"), and peer acceptance ("Kids are/are not nice to me").

Self-esteem in older children and adolescents can be measured with a questionnaire. The child reads statements like the ones at the beginning of this section. The most widely used self-esteem questionnaire of this sort is the *Self-Perception Profile for Children* (SPPC) devised by Susan Harter (1985, 1988). The SPPC is designed to evaluate self-worth in children age 8 and older in five domains (Harter, 1988, p. 62):

*Young children's self-esteem is measured by describing more and less competent people, then asking preschool children which person is more like them.*

- *Scholastic competence:* How competent or smart the child feels in doing schoolwork

- *Athletic competence:* How competent the child feels at sports and games requiring physical skill or athletic ability

- *Social acceptance:*   How popular or accepted the child feels in social interactions with peers
- *Behavioral conduct:*   How adequate the child feels about behaving the way one is supposed to
- *Physical appearance:*   How good-looking the child feels and how much the child likes his or her physical characteristics, such as height, weight, face, and hair

The SPPC includes six statements for each domain. For example, the figure lists two of the statements used to evaluate scholastic competence, shown as they actually appear on the SPPC. In both statements, the child has checked the response that indicates the highest level of self-esteem. A child's answers to all six statements are used to create an average level of self-esteem in that domain. The averages for each of the five domains are then used to generate a self-perception profile for each child. Two profiles are illustrated in the figure. Allison's self-esteem is high across all five domains; Colleen's self-esteem is much more varied. She feels positive about her social acceptance and physical appearance and, to a lesser extent, about her conduct. However, she feels negative about her scholastic and athletic competence.

FIGURE 11-3

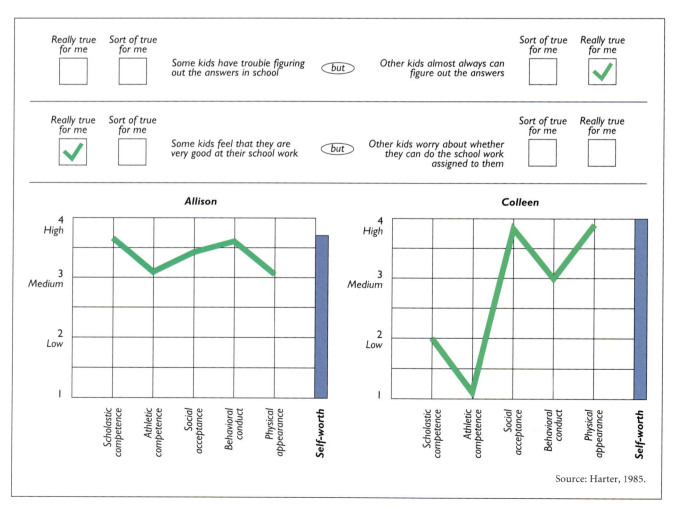

Source: Harter, 1985.

Notice that each profile ends with a bar graph depicting the child's overall self-worth. Overall self-worth is measured on the SPPC with six more items, such as "Some kids like the way they are leading their life" and "Some kids like the kind of person they are." Children's responses to these statements are then averaged to create a measure of overall self-worth.

The SPPC is intended for use with children and young adolescents. For assessing self-esteem in older adolescents and young adults, Harter (1990) created a more extensive scale. This scale includes the five domains in the SPPC, along with job competence, close friendships, and romantic appeal.

*The Self-Perception Profile for Children measures children's overall self-worth and esteem in five specific areas.*

## Developmental Change in Self-Esteem

When children and adolescents complete the measures we've just reviewed, their responses reveal two important developmental changes in self-esteem: change in the structure of self-esteem and change in overall levels of self-esteem.

**STRUCTURE OF SELF-ESTEEM.** By 4 or 5 years, which is the earliest we can measure self-esteem, children have a differentiated view of themselves. They can distinguish overall self-esteem as well as self-esteem in specific domains (Marsh, Ellis, & Craven, 2002). This structure should seem familiar because it's like intelligence: In Module 8.1, we saw that hierarchical theories of intelligence begin with a general intelligence that is divided into more specific abilities, such as verbal ability and spatial ability.

Children's overall self-worth is not simply the average of their self-worth in specific domains. Overall feelings of self-worth are related to but distinct from feelings of self-worth in specific domains. You can see this in the profiles for Allison and Colleen on page 344. Both girls feel very positive about themselves overall. This isn't surprising for Allison based on her ratings in the individual domains. But it is hardly what we would expect for Colleen if overall self-worth were simply the sum of self-worth in specific domains. She feels positive overall despite having low feelings of self-worth for her scholastic and athletic competence.

As children develop, they evaluate themselves in more domains, and their evaluations in each domain are increasingly independent. That is, younger children's ratings of self-esteem are often like Allison's (on page 344): The ratings are consistent across the different dimensions. In contrast, older children's and adolescents' ratings more often resemble Colleen's, with self-esteem varying from one domain to another.

During the school years, children's academic self-concepts become particularly well defined (Byrne & Gavin, 1996; Marsh & Yeung, 1997). As children accumulate successes and failures in school, they form beliefs about their ability in different content areas (e.g., English, math, science), and these beliefs contribute to their overall academic self-concept. A child who believes that she is skilled at English and math but not so skilled in science will probably have a positive academic self-concept overall. But a child who believes he is untalented in most academic areas will have a negative academic self-concept.

During adolescence, the social component of self-esteem becomes particularly well differentiated. Adolescents distinguish self-worth in many different social relationships. A teenager may, for example, feel very positive about her relationships with her parents but believe that she's a loser in romantic relationships. Another teen may feel loved and valued by his parents but think that coworkers at his part-time job can't stand him (Harter, Waters, & Whitesell, 1998).

Thus, between the late preschool years and adolescence, self-esteem becomes more complex, as older children and adolescents identify distinct domains of self-worth. This growing complexity is not surprising—it reflects the older child's and adolescent's greater cognitive skill and the more extensive social world of older children and adolescents.

**CHANGES IN LEVEL OF SELF-ESTEEM.** At what age is self-esteem greatest? The answer may surprise you—it's during the preschool years. Most preschool children have very positive views of themselves across many different domains. For example, when Harter and Pike (1984) used the pictures shown on page 343 to estimate kindergarten children's cognitive competence, the average score was 3.6 out of a possible 4. In other words, virtually all the children said they were either a little or a lot like the competent child.

As children progress through the elementary-school years, self-esteem usually drops somewhat. Why? In reality, of course, all children are *not* above average. During the elementary-school years, children begin to compare themselves with peers (Ruble et al., 1980). When they do, they discover that they are not necessarily the best readers or the fastest runners. They may realize, instead, that they are only average readers. Or, like the girl in the background of the photo, they come to understand that they are among the slowest runners in the class. This realization means that children's self-esteem usually drops somewhat at the beginning of elementary school.

Children's self-esteem is often influenced by comparisons with peers; a child who discovers that she's not a very fast runner may lose athletic self-esteem.

By the end of the elementary-school years, children's self-esteem has usually stabilized (Harter, Whitesell, & Kowalski, 1992) as children learn their place in the "pecking order" of different domains and adjust their self-esteem accordingly. However, self-esteem sometimes drops when children move from elementary school to middle school or junior high (Twenge & Campbell, 2001). Apparently, when students from different elementary schools enter the same middle school or junior high, they know where they stand compared to their old elementary-school classmates but not compared to students from other elementary schools. Thus, peer comparisons begin anew, and self-esteem often suffers temporarily. But, as a new school becomes familiar and students gradually adjust to the new pecking order, self-esteem again increases.

There is more to developmental change in self-esteem, however. The pattern of change also depends on the specific domain and the child's sex, as we'll see in the "Focus on Research" feature.

## *Focus on Research*

### Developmental Change in Self-Esteem in Different Domains

*Who were the investigators, and what was the aim of the study?* The developmental change that we see in global self-esteem need not hold for all domains. Specific domains (e.g., academic, behavior) might change in different ways as children develop. In addition, developmental change in self-esteem in specific domains might differ for boys and girls. To study these issues, David Cole and his colleagues (2001) examined developmental change in five domains of self-esteem between grades 3 and 11.

*How did the investigators measure the topic of interest?* The investigators assessed self-perception in five domains—academic, sports, social, appearance, and behavior—using Harter's SPPC. Examples of items included: "very good at schoolwork" (academic), "popular with others" (social), "better than others at sports" (sports), "happy with the way they look" (appearance), and "act as supposed to" (behavior). Each domain was assessed with five different items.

*Who were the children in the study?* The study began in the fall of 1993 with 435 third graders and 420 sixth graders attending public schools in a medium-sized city in the midwestern United States. The sample included approximately equal numbers of boys and girls; roughly half of the participants were European American and one-third were African American. The children completed the SPPC every fall and spring for a 5-year period. Thus, the younger participants were eighth graders when the study ended and the older participants were eleventh graders.

*What was the design of the study?* This study was correlational because Cole and his colleagues were interested in the relations that existed naturally between children's self-perception and their age and sex. The study was longitudinal-sequential because children in the two groups (those in grades 3 and 6 at the start of the study) were tested repeatedly over a 5-year period.

*Were there ethical concerns with the study?* No. The investigators obtained permission from the parents for the children to participate.

*What were the results?* Average levels of self-esteem are shown in the graphs. For

FIGURE 11-4

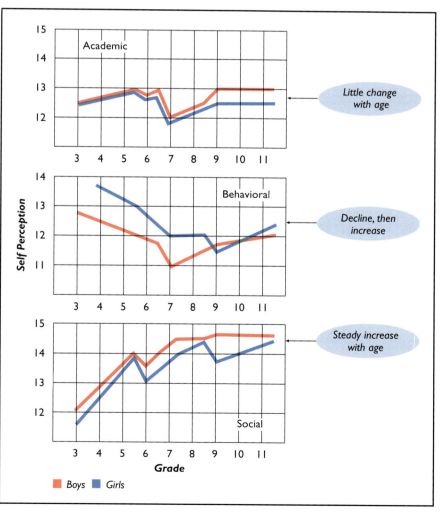

**11.2** During the summer, Karina moved with her family to a new city, where she will begin middle school. What will probably happen to Karina's self-esteem as she enters her new school?

simplicity, I've only shown the results for three domains: academic, behavioral, and social. Let's look at three aspects of these findings. First, compare the outcomes for boys and girls. Their self-perceptions were similar for the academic and social domains, but in the behavioral domain, girls have greater self-esteem than boys in the elementary-school years but not during middle school and high school. Next, let's examine developmental change in different domains: Academic self-perception changes little with age, social self-perception increases substantially, and behavioral self-perception declines during the elementary-school years but increases somewhat in middle school and high school. Finally, let's consider the impact of school transitions on children's self-perceptions: These students entered middle school in grade 7 and high school in grade 9. You can see that the middle-school transition affects children's self-perceptions in the academic domain more than in the social and behavioral domains.

*What did the investigators conclude?* Each of the three results leads to a straightforward conclusion. Let's review them in order. First, boys' and girls' self-perceptions are similar in some domains but not others. Second, the nature of developmental change in self-perception depends on the domain. Third, school transitions do affect self-perceptions—more so in some domains than in others.

*What converging evidence would strengthen these conclusions?* One limitation of the study concerns the sample. The results may be specific to children and adolescents growing up in the midwestern United States. Testing samples from other populations would strengthen the authors' conclusions. Another limit concerns the assessment of self-perception. Although the SPPC is the gold standard for measuring children's self-esteem, it is always a good idea to confirm that the same results are obtained when self-esteem is assessed with other measures. ■

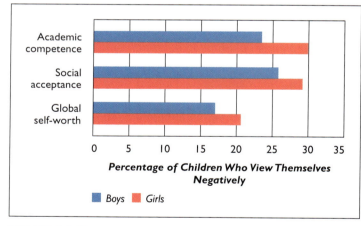

FIGURE 11-5

Sadly, at any age and in any domain, it's easy to find children who do not view themselves very positively. Some children are ambivalent about who they are; others actually feel negative about themselves. The graph shows that roughly 25% of 9- and 10-year-olds in one study (Cole, 1991) had negative self-esteem on three scales of the SPPC. Why do these children have so little self-worth compared to their peers? We'll answer this question in the next section.

## Sources of Self-Esteem

Think back to Allison and Colleen, the two girls whose self-perceptions are graphed on page 344. Both girls evaluated their overall self-worth very positively. In general, they were happy with themselves and with their lives. Why do these girls feel so positive while some children feel so negative about themselves? Research indicates two important sources of children's self-esteem. One is based on children's actual competence in domains that are important to them: Children's self-worth is greater when they are skilled in areas that matter. Think about two students who are struggling in math. This performance will probably create feelings of low self-worth in a student who believes that she's really smart and expects to get straight As. But the same performance wouldn't faze a student who couldn't care less about math because her life revolves around boys and hanging at the mall.

Phrased more positively, for children to feel good about themselves overall, they don't need to be superstars in everything. Doing well in something that matters—getting good grades, being popular, excelling in athletics—is enough for children and adolescents to have positive feelings of self-worth (Harter, 2005).

This explanation of self-esteem has implications for academically talented youngsters, like Darnel in the opening vignette, who might be placed in classes for gifted children. We'll look at these implications in the "Improving Children's Lives" feature.

> Children's self-esteem is determined by their actual competence and by how they are viewed by people who are important to them.

## *Improving Children's Lives*

### Self-Esteem in Gifted Classes

In a traditional classroom of students with a wide range of ability, talented youngsters compare themselves with other students, see that they're doing very well in class, and their academic self-esteem flourishes. But in classes for gifted students, many talented youngsters do only "average" work and some are "below average." Consequently, they sometimes lose sight of the bigger picture, believing themselves to be incompetent in a domain that's important to them, causing their academic self-esteem to drop (Marsh et al., 1995).

There is a clear lesson here for parents and teachers: When parents like Karen and Jon (from the module-opening vignette) think about enrolling their child in classes for gifted children, they should understand that accelerated academic progress often comes at a price: Children's academic self-esteem often declines somewhat, even though their actual skills are improving.

What can parents do? First, they should look honestly at their child and decide whether he or she values learning per se versus being at the top of the class. Students who value being at the top of the class will be more affected by social comparisons in a gifted class than students who are more intent on mastering challenging academic material. Second, parents should find out whether common assignments and comparative evaluations are made, as in typical classrooms, or whether the gifted class emphasizes individualized work. The latter is more conducive to self-esteem. Carefully considering these factors can help parents decide if a gifted program is likely to lower their child's self-esteem, a very unwelcome side effect. ■

Children's and adolescents' self-worth is also affected by how others view them, particularly other people who are important to them. Parents matter, of course, even to adolescents. Children are more likely to view themselves positively when their parents are affectionate toward them and involved with them (Lord, Eccles, & Mc-Carthy, 1994). Around the world, children have higher self-esteem when families live in harmony and parents nurture their children (Scott, Scott, & McCabe, 1991). A father who routinely hugs his daughter and gladly takes her to piano lessons is saying to her, "You are important to me." When children hear this regularly from parents, they evidently internalize the message and come to see themselves positively.

Parents' discipline also is related to self-esteem. Children with high self-esteem generally have parents who aren't afraid to set rules but are also willing to discuss rules and discipline with their children (Coopersmith, 1967). Parents who fail to set rules are, in effect, telling their children that they don't care—they don't value them enough to go to the trouble of creating rules and enforcing them. In much the same way, parents who refuse to discuss discipline with their children are saying, "Your opinions don't matter to me." Not surprisingly, when children internalize these messages, the result is lower overall self-worth.

Peers' views are important, too. Children's and particularly adolescents' self-worth is greater when they believe that their peers think highly of them (Harter, 2005). Lauren's self-worth increases, for example, when she hears that Pedro, Matt, and Michael think she's the hottest girl in the eighth grade.

Thus, children's and adolescents' self-worth depends on their being competent at something they value and in being valued by people who are important to them. By encouraging children to find their special talents and by being genuinely interested in their progress, parents and teachers can enhance the self-esteem of all students.

## Low Self-Esteem: Cause or Consequence?

Having low self-esteem is associated with many developmental problems (Baumeister et al., 2003). Children with low self-esteem are

- more likely to have problems with peers (Parker et al., 2005; Verschueren, Buyck, & Marcoen, 2001),
- more prone to psychological disorders such as depression (Garber, Robinson, & Valentiner, 1997; McDonald et al., 2005),
- more likely to be involved in bullying and aggressive behavior (Donnellan et al., 2005; O'Moore & Kirkham, 2001), and
- more likely to do poorly in school (Marsh & Yeung, 1997).

These outcomes provide an excellent opportunity to remember the difficulty in identifying causal forces from correlational studies. Does low self-esteem cause children to have few friends, because peers want to avoid them? Or do poor peer relations cause children to have low self-esteem? Either claim is plausible and what often happens is that low self-esteem contributes to the outcome but is itself also caused by the outcome. For example, the claim that "low self-esteem leads to poor peer relations" is supported by findings that over the course of a school year, children with low social self-esteem often withdraw from peer interactions, and by year's end, are more likely to be left out of social activities and to have few or no friends. But the claim that "poor peer relations reduces social self-worth" is also supported, this time by findings that children who have few friends at the beginning of a school year (but adequate social self-worth) tend to withdraw socially and by year's end, their self-worth has dropped (Caldwell et al., 2004). Thus, poor peer relations reduces self-esteem in the peer context and disrupting future peer interactions, causing social self-worth to drop even more, making children even less likely to have good peer relations—the cycle goes on and on.

*Children with low self-esteem typically have poor peer relations, are at risk for psychological disorders, are involved in antisocial activities, and do poorly in school.*

A similar vicious circle applies to the link between low academic self-esteem and poor performance in school: Over time, children who are unskilled academically do not keep up in school, which causes a drop in their academic self-esteem, making them less confident and probably less successful in future school learning, causing their academic self-esteem to continue to fall (Marsh & Yeung, 1997). Thus, low self-esteem is a cause of future harmful outcomes *and* a consequence of past harmful outcomes. Of course, the same kind of circle can increase children's self-worth: success in academics, athletics, or social relationships can breed positive self-worth, which breeds more success.

Understanding this complex cause-effect-cause pattern is important in deciding how to help children with low self-esteem. Some children benefit directly from therapy that increases their low self-esteem. Others, however, who need to change their own behavior, also benefit from learning how to improve their social skills (a topic that I discuss again in Modules 12.4 and 15.1). And, we need to remember that all children have some talents that can be nurtured. Taking the time to recognize each child creates the feelings of "being special" that promote self-esteem.

Thus far in this chapter, we've focused on children's growing understanding of themselves. In the next module, we'll look at parallel changes that occur in children's understanding of other people.

---

## CHECK YOUR LEARNING

**RECALL**  How is children's self-esteem measured?

Summarize the ways in which self-esteem changes during childhood and adolescence.

**INTERPRET**  Explain the forces that lead some children to have high self-esteem but others to have low self-esteem.

**APPLY**  Suppose you attended a presentation for parents of middle-school students in which a counselor emphasized the importance of children having high self-esteem. The counselor asserts that when children have low self-esteem, they do poorly in school and don't get along well with their peers. Would you agree or disagree with the counselor's claims? Why?

Karina's self-esteem is likely to drop, at least temporarily, because she won't know "where she stands" in comparison to her new classmates (e.g., whether she still is one of the smartest kids, one of the best basketball players). After she's discovered where she fits in, her self-esteem will increase.    **11.2**

---

# UNDERSTANDING OTHERS    11.3

## LEARNING OBJECTIVES

- As children develop, how do they describe others differently?

- How does understanding of others' thinking change as children develop?

- When do children develop prejudice toward others?

**Describing Others**

**Understanding What Others Think**

**Prejudice**

> When 12-year-old Ian agreed to baby-sit for his 5-year-old brother, Kyle, his mother reminded him to keep Kyle out of the basement because Kyle's birthday presents were there, unwrapped. But as soon as their mother left, Kyle wanted to go to the basement to ride his tricycle. When Ian told him no, Kyle burst into angry tears and shouted, "I'm gonna tell Mom you were mean to me!" Ian wished he could explain to Kyle, but he knew that would just cause more trouble!

We know from Modules 11.1 and 11.2 that Ian, as a young adolescent, has a growing understanding of himself. This vignette suggests that his understanding of other people is also growing. He understands why Kyle is angry, and he also knows that if he gives in to Kyle, his mother will be angry when she returns. Children's growing understanding of others is the focus of this module. We'll begin by looking at how children describe others, then examine their understanding of how others think. We'll also see how children's recognition of different social groups can lead to prejudices.

## Describing Others

As children develop, their self-descriptions become richer, more abstract, and more psychological. These same changes occur in children's descriptions of others. Children begin by describing other people in terms of concrete features, such as behavior and appearance, and progress to describing them in terms of abstract traits (Barenboim, 1981; Livesley & Bromley, 1973). For instance, when asked to describe a girl that she liked a lot, 7-year-old Tamsen said,

> Vanessa is short. She has black hair and brown eyes. She uses a wheelchair because she can't walk. She's in my class. She has dolls just like mine. She likes to sing and read.

Tamsen's description of Vanessa is probably not too different from the way she would have described herself: The emphasis is on concrete characteristics, such as Vanessa's appearance, possessions, and preferences. Contrast this with the following description, which Tamsen gave as a 10-year-old:

*Children's descriptions of others first focus on concrete features, then focus on psychological traits, then on integrating different characteristics.*

> Kate lives in my apartment building. She is a very good reader and is also good at math and science. She's nice to everyone in our class. And she's very funny. Sometimes her jokes make me laugh so-o-o hard! She takes piano lessons and likes to play soccer.

Tamsen's account still includes concrete features, such as where Kate lives and what she likes to do. However, psychological traits are also evident: Tamsen describes Kate as nice and funny. By age 10, children move beyond the purely concrete and observable in describing others. During adolescence, descriptions become even more complex, as you can see in the following, from Tamsen as a 16-year-old:

> Jeannie is very understanding. Whenever someone is upset, she's there to give a helping hand. Yet, in private, Jeannie can be so sarcastic. She can say some really nasty things about people. But I know she'd never say that stuff if she thought people would hear it because she wouldn't want to hurt their feelings.

This description is more abstract: Tamsen now focuses on psychological traits like understanding and concern for others' feelings. It's also more integrated: Tamsen tries to explain how Jeannie can be both understanding and sarcastic. Although she began, as a 7-year-old, by emphasizing concrete characteristics, as a 16-year-old she tries to integrate traits to form a cohesive picture.

The progression in how children perceive others was illustrated vividly in a classic study by Livesley and Bromley (1973). They interviewed 320 7- to 15-year-olds attending school in Merseyside, England (near Liverpool, home of the Beatles).

All participants were asked to describe eight people that they knew: two boys, two girls, two men, and two women. The examiner told the participants, "I want you to describe what sort of person they are. I want you to tell me what you think about them and what they are like" (p. 97).

The participants at different ages typically produced descriptions much like Tamsen's at different ages. Livesley and Bromley then categorized the contents of the descriptions. Some of their results appear in the graph. Descriptions referring to appearances or possessions become less common as children grow older, as do descriptions giving general information, such as the person's age, sex, religion, or school. In contrast, descriptions of personality traits (for example, "friendly" or "conceited") increase between ages 8 and 14 years. This pattern of changes in children's descriptions of others resembles children's changing understanding of the self, which I explained on pages 334–335.

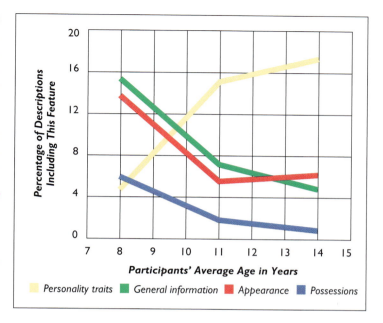

FIGURE 11-6

By age 5, children use the information in their descriptions to predict others' future behavior (Heyman & Gelman, 1999; Yuill & Pearson, 1998). To illustrate, suppose kindergarten children are told that Alissa did something nice (e.g., helped another child finish a difficult puzzle), but Celeste did something mean (e.g., scribbled in another child's favorite book). Kindergarten children will judge that, in the future, Alissa is more likely than Celeste to help a child who is hurt, to give money to a needy child, and to hope that an elaborate art project turns out well for the child who created it. Thus, descriptions of others are useful, even for young children, because they allow children to predict how others will behave in the future.

## Understanding What Others Think

One trademark of the preschool child's thinking is difficulty in seeing the world from another's point of view. Piaget's term for this was *egocentrism*, and it was a defining characteristic of his preoperational stage of development (see Module 6.1). In much the same way, preschool children's communication is often ineffective because they don't consider the listener's perspective when they talk (see Module 9.4). As children move beyond the preschool years, though, they realize that others see the world differently, both literally and figuratively. For example, in the module-opening vignette, 12-year-old Ian knows why his little brother, Kyle, is angry: Kyle thinks that Ian is being bossy and mean. Ian understands that Kyle doesn't know there is a good reason why he can't go to the basement.

Sophisticated understanding of how others think is achieved gradually throughout childhood and adolescence. Robert Selman (1980, 1981) has proposed a theory of how understanding others' thinking—or *perspective taking*—occurs. Selman's theory is based on two of Piaget's key assumptions, namely, that understanding of others occurs in stages and that movement from one stage to the next is based on cognitive development. The table on page 354 shows Selman's five stages of perspective taking.

**TABLE 11-1**

| SELMAN'S STAGES OF PERSPECTIVE TAKING | | |
|---|---|---|
| **Stage** | **Approximate Ages** | **Description** |
| Undifferentiated | 3–6 years | Children know that self and others can have different thoughts and feelings, but often confuse the two. |
| Social-informational | 4–9 years | Children know that perspectives differ because people have access to different information. |
| Self-reflective | 7–12 years | Children can step into another's shoes and view themselves as others do; they know that others can do the same. |
| Third-person | 10–15 years | Children and adolescents can step outside the immediate situation to see how they and another person are viewed by a third person. |
| Societal | 14 years to adult | Adolescents realize that a third person's perspective is influenced by broader personal, social, and cultural contexts. |

A good way to appreciate the progression from stage to stage is to look at one of the social dilemmas that Selman used to explore children's perspective taking.

> Holly is an 8-year-old girl who likes to climb trees. She is the best tree climber in the neighborhood. One day while climbing down from a tall tree she falls off the bottom branch but does not hurt herself. Her father sees her fall. He is upset and asks her to promise not to climb trees anymore. Holly promises.
>
> Later that day, Holly and her friends meet Sean. Sean's kitten is caught up in a tree and cannot get down. Something has to be done right away or the kitten may fall. Holly is the only one who climbs well enough to reach the kitten and get it down, but she remembers her promise to her father (Selman & Byrne, 1974, p. 805).

This dilemma is typical in that it includes people who don't share the same knowledge about the events taking place. After hearing the story, children are asked questions to investigate their ability to take on each character's view and predict what Holly does.

As children grow, their answers reflect ever more sophisticated understanding of who is thinking what and why in these dilemmas (Selman, 1980, 1981; Selman & Byrne, 1974). The youngest children, those in the undifferentiated stage, might reply, "Holly's father will be happy if she gets the kitten because he likes kittens." This answer confuses the child's own feelings with the father's and ignores Holly's promise. Children in the social-informational stage might say, "If Holly's father knew why she climbed the tree, he probably wouldn't be angry." This answer indicates that the child thinks the father's response depends on whether he knows the reason for Holly's behavior.

In the self-reflective stage, a child might say, "Holly's father would understand that she thought saving the kitten's life was really important, so he wouldn't be mad. He'd probably be proud." This comment shows Holly's father stepping into Holly's shoes, the defining characteristic of the self-reflective stage.

At the next level, the third-person stage, a child might respond, "Holly remembers the promise, but she doesn't think her father will be angry when she explains

**11.3** | Gracie can hardly wait for her cousin Andrew to arrive for a week-long visit. Gracie knows Andrew will want to go swimming right away because Gracie loves to swim. Based on this example, what stage of perspective-taking is Gracie in? About how old is she?

that she wouldn't have climbed the tree except to save the kitten's life. Her father might wish that Holly had asked an adult for help, but he'd also understand why it was important to Holly to save the kitten." This child simultaneously considers both Holly's and her father's perspectives on the dilemma. In answering, the child has stepped outside the immediate situation to take the perspective of a neutral third party who can look at both Holly's and her father's views.

At the most advanced level, the societal stage, an adolescent might reply, "Holly and her father both know that she almost always obeys him. So, they'd both know that if she disobeyed him to climb the tree, there would have to be an awfully good reason. So, they'd talk about it." This child's answer, like the previous one, considers Holly's and her father's perspectives simultaneously. The difference is that this comment puts the issue in the broader context of the history of their father–daughter relationship.

As predicted by Selman's theory, research shows that, as children develop, their reasoning moves through each stage, in sequence. In addition, regardless of age, children at more advanced cognitive levels tend to be at more advanced stages in perspective taking (Gurucharri & Selman, 1982; Krebs & Gillmore, 1982).

Additional support for Selman's theory comes from studies on perspective taking and social behavior. In the photo, the children with the soccer ball apparently recognize that the girl on the sideline wants to play, so they're inviting her to join the game. Children who can anticipate what others are thinking should get along better with their peers, and research indicates that they do. For example, children with good perspective-taking skills are typically well liked by their peers (LeMare & Rubin, 1987). Of course, mere understanding does not guarantee good social behavior; sometimes children who understand what another child is thinking take advantage of that child. But, in general, greater understanding of others seems to promote positive interactions, a topic that we'll discuss further in Chapter 12 on moral understanding and behavior.

> In Selman's theory, young children confuse their own and others' views, but adolescents can see their own and another's views from a third person's perspective.

Children get along better with their peers when they can anticipate what their peers think: The girl in the purple shirt understands that the girl on the sidelines wants to join them and consequently she invites her to play.

## Prejudice

As children learn more about others, they discover that people belong to different social groups, based on variables such as sex, ethnicity, and social class. By the preschool years, most children can distinguish males from females and can identify people from different ethnic groups (Aboud, 1993). **Once children learn their membership in a specific group, they typically show *prejudice*, a negative view of others based on their membership in a specific group.** Actually, in young children prejudice is not so much a negative view of others as it is an enhanced view of one's own group. That is, preschool and kindergarten children attribute many positive traits such as being friendly and smart to their own group and few negative traits such as being mean (Bigler, Jones, & Lobliner, 1997; Black-Gutman & Hickson, 1996).

Negative views of other groups form more slowly. In young children, negative views typically don't involve overt hostility, it's simply that other groups "come up short" when compared to one's own group (Aboud, 2003). However, when children believe that children from other groups dislike them or think they're better, then children's views of other groups become more negative (Nesdale et al., 2005).

As children move into the elementary-school years, prejudice usually declines somewhat (Powlishta et al., 1994). Cognitive development explains the decline. Preschool and kindergarten children usually view people in social groups as much more homogeneous than they really are. People from other groups are seen as all alike and, typically, not as good as people from the child's own group. As children grow, they begin to understand that people in social groups are heterogeneous—they know that individual European Americans, girls, and obese children, for example, are not all alike. And they have learned that people from different groups may be more alike than people from the same group. Gary, an African American whose passion is computers, finds that he enjoys being with Vic, an Italian American who shares his love of computers, but not Curtis, another African American whose passion is music. As children realize that social groups consist of all kinds of different people, prejudice lessens.

At the same time, children's knowledge of racial stereotypes and prejudices increases steadily. In one study (McKown & Weinstein, 2003), relatively few 7-year-olds were aware of broadly held racial stereotypes, but most 10- and 11-year-olds were. What's more, children from groups that are often victims of discrimination (e.g., Latino, African American) were aware of racial stereotypes at a younger age than children from other groups.

> **Prejudice is reduced with friendly and constructive contacts between children from different groups.**

As children learn more about stereotypes, they also learn norms that discourage openly favoring their own group over others. For example, Rutland and colleagues (2005) videotaped some children and adolescents as they completed questionnaires dealing with racial attitudes and told the participants that adults might watch the videotapes later; other children were not videotaped and were led to believe that their responses were completely anonymous. When children and adolescents believed that their responses might be made public, they were less enthusiastic about their own group and less negative about other groups.

During early adolescence, prejudice often increases again. This resurgence apparently reflects two different processes (Black-Gutman & Hickson, 1996; Teichman, 2001). One is experiential: Exposed to prejudices of those around them, children and adolescents internalize some of these views. A second process concerns adolescents' identity. In the search for identity (described on pages 335–340), adolescents' preferences for their own groups often intensifies. Thus, greater prejudice in older children and adolescents reflects both a more positive view of their own group as well as a more negative view of other groups. Bob, a 14-year-old European American growing up in Arizona, becomes more prejudiced because he views his own European American heritage more positively and acquires prejudicial attitudes toward Native Americans from his parents and peers.

Identifying *how* children form actual prejudices is challenging because ethical concerns limit us to correlational studies. (Obviously, we could not do an experiment in which some children are deliberately exposed to biased information about actual groups of children.) Consequently, to study the processes underlying prejudice, researchers sometimes conduct experiments in which children are temporarily assigned to different groups.

To illustrate this approach, many theorists believe that social status contributes to prejudice: Children are more likely to develop strong preferences for their group when it has high status. In experimentation designed to test this prediction (Bigler,

Brown, & Markell, 2001; Brown & Bigler, 2002), children attending a summer-school program were assigned to wear either a blue or yellow T-shirt. To increase the status of children wearing yellow shirts, children were told that in the previous summer, students wearing yellow shirts were smarter, better leaders, and better athletes. Throughout the 4-week program, teachers mentioned T-shirt color frequently (e.g., had children sit with others wearing the same color of shirt), but did *not* favor one group over the other. Nevertheless, at the end of the program, children wearing yellow shirts viewed themselves much more positively than they viewed children wearing blue shirts; in contrast, children wearing blue shirts (low status) had no biases. Thus, high status breeds a preference for one's own group (Nesdale & Flesser, 2001).

What can parents, teachers, and other adults do to rid children of prejudice? One way is to encourage contacts between children from different groups. However, contact alone usually accomplishes little. Instead, intergroup contact reduces prejudice when the participating groups of children are equal in status, when the contact between groups involves pursuing common goals (instead of competing), and, finally when parents and teachers support the goal of reducing prejudice (Killen & McGlothlin, 2005). To illustrate, adults might have children from different groups work together on a class project, as shown in the photo. In sports, it might be mastering a new skill. By working together, Gary starts to realize that Vic acts, thinks, and feels as he does simply because he's Vic, not because he's an Italian American.

One way to reduce children's prejudice is to have children from different groups work together toward a common goal, such as completing a school assignment.

Another useful approach is to ask children to play different roles (Davidson & Davidson, 1994). They can be asked to imagine that, because of their race, ethnic background, or sex, they have been insulted verbally or not allowed to participate in special activities. A child might be asked to imagine that she can't go to a private swimming club because she's African American or that she wasn't invited to a party because she's Hispanic. Afterwards, children reflect on how they felt when prejudice and discrimination were directed at them. And they're asked to think about what would be fair—what should be done in situations like these?

From such experiences, children and adolescents discover for themselves that a person's membership in a social group tells us very little about that person. They learn, instead, that all children are different, each a unique mix of experiences, skills, and values.

Increasing interaction between children of different racial groups was one of the consequences of the U.S. Supreme Court's decision in *Brown v. Board of Education*, a case that shows how child-development research influenced social policy.

## Child Development and Family Policy
### Ending Segregated Schools

In 1950, African American and white children in most states attended separate schools. Segregated schooling had been the law of the land for more than 100 years, bolstered by several famous Supreme Court decisions. In the fall of 1950, the chapter of the National Association for the Advancement of Colored People (NAACP) in Topeka, Kansas, decided to test the constitutionality of the law. Thirteen African American parents, including Oliver Brown, attempted to enroll their children in white-only schools; when they were turned away, the NAACP sued the Topeka Board of Education.

A key element in the NAACP's case was that separate schools were inherently harmful to African American children because such schools apparently legitimized their second-class status. To support this claim, the NAACP legal team relied on testimony from Dr. Kenneth B. Clark. In previous work, Clark (1945; Clark & Clark, 1940) had shown that African American children typically thought that white dolls were "nice" but that brown dolls were "bad." He found the same results in African American children attending segregated Topeka schools, leading him to testify that,

Dr. Kenneth B. Clark's research on prejudice was influential in the Supreme Court's ruling that segregated schools are unconstitutional.

> these children . . . like other human beings who are subjected to an obviously inferior status in the society in which they live, have been definitely harmed in the development of their personalities . . .

In May 1954, the Supreme Court rendered the landmark decision that segregated schools were unconstitutional. The impact of Clark's research and testimony was evident in the decision in *Brown v. Board of Education*, delivered by Chief Justice Earl Warren:

> Segregation of white and colored children in public schools has a detrimental effect upon the colored children. The impact is greater when it has the sanction of the law, for the policy of separating the races is usually interpreted as denoting the inferiority of the negro group. A sense of inferiority affects the motivation of a child to learn. Segregation with the sanction of law, therefore, has a tendency to [retard] the educational and mental development of negro children and to deprive them of . . . benefits they would receive in a racial[ly] integrated school system.

After the *Brown* decision, Clark continued his work on civil rights and worked on behalf of African American youth. For his lifelong effort to inform public policy on African American children and their families, in 1987 he received the Gold Medal for Life Achievement in Psychology in the Public Interest from the American Psychological Foundation; he died in 2005. ■

Clark's work is a compelling demonstration of the manner in which child-development research can have far-reaching implications for policy—in this case, helping to eliminate racially segregated schools in America. And the integrated schools that resulted have helped to reduce prejudice by providing children with opportunities to learn about peers from other ethnic and racial groups.

## CHECK YOUR LEARNING

**RECALL**  Describe the different stages in Selman's theory of perspective-taking. Summarize developmental change in prejudice.

**INTERPRET**  Compare developmental change in children's descriptions of others with developmental change in children's self-concept (described in Module 11.1).

**APPLY**  Based on what you've learned in this module, what can parents and teachers do to discourage prejudice in children?

Gracie is confusing what she wants to do ("I love to swim and can't wait to go!") with what Andrew wants to do (which she doesn't know). This would put her in Selman's undifferentiated stage because she is confusing her thoughts with his. And this means she's probably between 3 and 6 years old. **11.3**

## UNIFYING THEMES: Nature and Nurture

This chapter is a good occasion to feature the theme that *development is always jointly influenced by heredity and environment*. The emergence of self-awareness between 15 and 24 months is primarily due to biological forces. Regardless of circumstances, children become self-aware between ages 1 and 2. However, elaborating self-awareness into a specific self-concept depends largely on a child's experiences at home and in school. The specific direction that children take in establishing an identity is strongly influenced by those around them, particularly their parents and teachers.

## SEE FOR YOURSELF

The mirror recognition task, described on pages 332–333, is great fun to do, and you'll be astonished by the rapid change in children's responses between 1 and 2 years. For this task, you simply need a mirror, some tissue, blush, and a few cooperative parents of 12- to 18-month-olds. Have the parents play with their toddler near the mirror and, in the process, wipe the toddler's nose with a tissue that has blush on it.

Then see how the toddler responds to the now red nose. Some 12-month-olds will do nothing; others will touch the red nose in the mirror. When the 15- or 18-month-olds see themselves, though, they should stop, get a curious expression on their faces, and then reach up to touch their nose. See for yourself!

## RESOURCES

For more information about . . .

**adolescent search for identity,** read Erik Erikson's *Gandhi* (Norton, 1969), a Pulitzer Prize–winning book in which Erikson shows how the adolescent search for identity influenced the development of this great leader of India.

**deciding on a career or finding a job that's right for you,** visit a Web site maintained by the *Wall Street Journal:* http://www.collegejournal.com/careersqa/findcareerpath/

## KEY TERMS

achievement status  337

adolescent egocentrism  336

attributions  341

crystallization  337

diffusion status  337

ethnic identity  338

foreclosure status  337

illusion of invulnerability  336

imaginary audience  336

implementation  338

moratorium status  337

norepinephrine  341

personal fable  336

prejudice  355

self-concept  332

self-esteem  342

serotonin  341

specification  337

# SUMMARY

## 11.1 WHO AM I? SELF-CONCEPT

### Origins of Self-Recognition

At about 15 months, infants begin to recognize themselves in the mirror, one of the first signs of self-recognition. They also begin to prefer to look at pictures of themselves, to refer to themselves by name and with personal pronouns, and sometimes to know their age and gender. Evidently, by 2 years, most children have the rudiments of self-awareness.

### The Evolving Self-Concept

Preschoolers often define themselves in terms of observable characteristics, such as possessions, physical characteristics, preferences, and competencies. During the elementary-school years, self-concept begins to include emotions, a child's membership in social groups, and comparisons with peers. During adolescence, self-concept includes attitudes, personality traits, beliefs, and future plans. In general, adolescents' self-concepts are more abstract, more psychological, and more future oriented than self-concepts in younger children.

### The Search for Identity

The search for identity typically involves four statuses. Diffusion and foreclosure are more common in early adolescence; moratorium and achievement are more common in late adolescence and young adulthood. Adolescents are most likely to achieve an identity when parents encourage discussion and recognize their autonomy; they are least likely to achieve an identity when parents set rules and enforce them without explanation.

According to Super's theory, an adolescent's developing identity is a primary influence on his or her career aspirations. Super proposes three phases of vocational development during adolescence and young adulthood: crystallization, when basic ideas about careers are identified, based on the person's identity; specification, when lines of work associated with interests are identified; and implementation, which marks entry into the workforce.

Adolescents from ethnic groups often progress through three phases in acquiring an ethnic identity: initial disinterest, exploration, and identity achievement. Achieving an ethnic identity usually results in higher self-esteem but is not consistently related to the strength of one's identification with mainstream culture.

Contrary to myth, adolescence is not usually a period of storm and stress. Most adolescents love their parents, feel loved by them, rely on them for advice, and adopt their values. The parent–child relationship becomes more egalitarian during the adolescent years, reflecting adolescents' growing independence. A small number of adolescents become depressed, often because their explanations of their own behavior is flawed.

## 11.2 SELF-ESTEEM

### Measuring Self-Esteem

Most tasks assess self-esteem in different areas. One of the most common measures is Harter's *Self-Perception Profile for Children* (SPPC), which is designed for children as young as 8 years. It assesses self-esteem in five areas: scholastic competence, athletic competence, social acceptance, behavioral conduct, and physical appearance. It also measures overall self-worth. For measuring self-esteem in older adolescents, job competence, close friendships, and romantic appeal are added.

### Developmental Change in Self-Esteem

Global self-esteem is very high during the preschool years but declines in the elementary-school years as children compare themselves to peers. Self-esteem also declines, temporarily, when children make school transitions. Some specific domains of self-esteem increase steadily with age but others decline. Self-esteem becomes more differentiated in older children and adolescents as they evaluate themselves on more aspects of self-esteem, including different types of academic skills.

### Sources of Self-Esteem

Children's self-esteem is greater when parents are affectionate and involved with them and when parents set rules and discuss disciplinary action. Self-esteem also depends on peer comparisons. Self-esteem is usually greater when children know that others view them positively.

### Low Self-Esteem: Cause or Consequence?

When children have low self-esteem, they are more likely to have poor peer relations, suffer psychological disorders such as depression, be involved in antisocial activities, and do poorly in school. Therapy and improved social skills can enhance children's self-esteem.

## 11.3 UNDERSTANDING OTHERS

### Describing Others

Children's descriptions of others change in much the same way that their descriptions of themselves change. During the early elementary-school years, descriptions emphasize concrete characteristics. In the late elementary-school years, they emphasize personality traits. In adolescence, they emphasize an integrated picture of a person. Children use their descriptions to predict others' behaviors.

### Understanding What Others Think

According to Selman's perspective-taking theory, children's understanding of how others think progresses through five stages. In the first, the undifferentiated stage, children often confuse their own and another's view. In the last, the societal stage, adolescents take a third person's perspective and understand that this perspective is influenced by context.

### Prejudice

Prejudice emerges in the preschool years, soon after children recognize different social groups. Prejudice declines during childhood, as children's cognitive growth helps them understand that social groups are heterogeneous, not homogeneous, but often increases in older children and adolescents. The best way to reduce prejudice is with additional exposure to individuals from other social groups and through role play that allows children to experience prejudice and discrimination.

**Consider the following hypothetical situation. You enter a nursery filled with 2-day-olds. The babies look like babies in any nursery—some are asleep, some are crying, others are simply lying quietly.** However, the nurse tells you that the newborns include Mother Teresa, Adolf Hitler, Mohandas Gandhi, and Martin Luther King Jr. Although seemingly identical now, three of the newborns will rank among the 20th century's greatest figures and one will be guilty of unspeakable horrors.

Why? What determines whether children act morally or immorally? Whether they care about others or take from others? Whether they become samaritans or follow a path of evil? The four modules in this chapter provide some answers to these questions. In Module 12.1, we'll see how children learn to control their behavior. In Module 12.2, we'll look at how children and adolescents reason about moral issues, and in Module 12.3, we'll look at factors that encourage children to be kind to others. Finally, in Module 12.4, we'll see why children act aggressively toward others.

**12.1**   Self-Control

**12.2**   Reasoning About Moral Issues

**12.3**   Helping Others

**12.4**   Aggression

12

1 The Science of Child Development

2 Genetic Bases of Child Development

3 Prenatal Development, Birth, and the Newborn

4 Growth and Health

5 Perceptual and Motor Development

6 Theories of Cognitive Development

7 Cognitive Processes and Academic Skills

8 Intelligence and Individual Differences in Cognition

9 Language and Communication

10 Emotional Development

11 Understanding Self and Others

# Moral Understanding and Behavior

13 Gender and Development

14 Family Relationships

15 Influences Beyond the Family

# 12.1 SELF-CONTROL

Beginnings of Self-Control

Influences on Self-Control

Improving Children's Self-Control

## LEARNING OBJECTIVES

- When does self-control begin, and how does it change as children develop?
- What factors influence children's ability to maintain self-control?
- What strategies can children use to improve their self-control?

*Shirley returned from a long day at work tired but eager to celebrate her son Ryan's fourth birthday. Her excitement quickly turned to dismay when she discovered that Ryan had taken a huge bite of icing from the birthday cake while the baby-sitter fixed lunch. Before she had left for work that morning, Shirley had explicitly told Ryan not to touch the cake. Why couldn't Ryan wait? Why did he give in to temptation? What could she do to help Ryan control himself better in the future?*

In this vignette, Shirley wishes that Ryan had greater *self-control*, **the ability to control one's behavior and to inhibit impulsive responding to temptations.** A child who saves her allowance to buy a much-desired object instead of spending it immediately on candy is showing self-control, as is an adolescent who studies for an exam instead of going to the mall with his friends, knowing that tomorrow he can enjoy the mall and a good grade on his exam.

Self-control is one of the first steps toward moral behavior because children must learn that they cannot constantly do whatever tempts them at the moment. Instead, society has rules for behavior in certain situations, and children must learn to restrain themselves.

In this module, we'll first see how self-control emerges during the preschool years. Then we'll learn some of the factors that determine how well children control themselves. Finally, we'll look at strategies that children use to improve their self-control.

## Beginnings of Self-Control

In this cartoon, Calvin shows little self-control. Is he typical for his age? Thankfully, no. Self-control emerges in infancy and gradually improves during the preschool years (Kopp, 1997; Kopp & Neufeld, 2003). A rough chronology looks like this:

# Calvin and Hobbes                                    by Bill Watterson

- At approximately the first birthday, infants become aware that people impose demands on them and they must react accordingly. Infants learn that they are not entirely free to behave as they wish; instead, others set limits on what they can do. These limits reflect both concern for their safety ("Don't touch! It's hot") as well as early socialization efforts ("Don't grab Ravisha's toy").

- At about 2 years, toddlers have internalized some of the controls imposed by others and are capable of some self-control in parents' absence. For example, although the boy on the left in the photo certainly looks as if he wants to play with the toy that the other toddler has, so far he has inhibited his desire to grab the toy, perhaps because he remembers that his parents have told him not to take things from others.

- At about 3 years, children become capable of self-regulation, which "involves flexible and adaptive control processes that can meet quickly changing situational demands" (Kopp, 1987, p. 38). Children can devise ways to regulate their own behavior. To return to the example of a playmate's interesting toy, children might tell themselves that they really don't want to play with it, or they might turn to another activity that removes the temptation to grab it.

These gradual improvements in self-control are revealed in the study profiled in the "Focus on Research" feature.

By 2 years of age, many children have enough self-control that they can resist the temptation to take an interesting toy away from another child.

Two-year-old Amanda spilled a cup filled with juice, just after she'd been asked to leave it on the counter. Amanda's dad thinks she should be disciplined for disobeying a direct instruction; her mom thinks Amanda is too young to control herself. How would you advise Amanda's parents?

**12.1**

## Focus on Research

### Growth of Effortful Control in Toddlers and Preschoolers

*Who were the investigators, and what was the aim of the study?* Grazyna Kochanska and her colleagues Kathleen Murray and Elena Harlan (2000) wanted to examine improvements in self-control between 2 and 3 years of age. In addition, they wanted to determine if self-control in situations where children must comply with prohibitions ("Don't look!") was related to their ability to regulate their own emotions.

*How did the investigators measure the topic of interest?* Kochanska and her colleagues tested children on many measures of control; for simplicity, I'm only going to describe four. In one measure of self-control, children were asked to sit with their backs turned away from an adult as she wrapped a gift; the experimenter recorded how quickly children peeked at the gift. In a second measure of self-control, an adult placed a nicely wrapped gift on a table and told children not to touch the gift while she went to get a bow; the experimenter recorded how quickly children touched the gift. To measure regulation of joy, an adult presented a funny puppet show to children that ended with the puppets tickling the child; the experimenter recorded how much children smiled and laughed during this episode. Finally, to measure regulation of anger, mothers strapped the child tightly in a car seat; the experimenter recorded how quickly and intensely the child became angry.

*Who were the children in the study?* Kochanska and her colleagues tested one hundred six 2-year-olds and retested 103 of them approximately 1 year later. Most of the children were European American.

By age 3, children are capable of self-regulation, because they can make simple plans to deal with the demands of different situations.

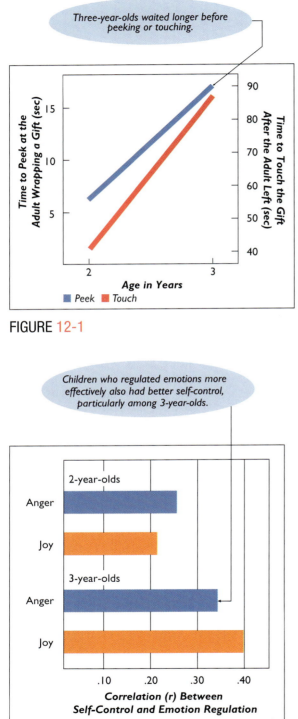

**FIGURE 12-1**

**FIGURE 12-2**

*What was the design of the study?* This study was correlational because Kochanska was interested in relations that existed naturally between age and children's self-control and between children's self-control and their regulation of emotion (anger, joy). The study was longitudinal because children were tested twice, at approximately 2 and 3 years of age.

*Were there ethical concerns with the study?* No. The tasks involved minimal risk and weren't much different from experiences that children would encounter in daily life.

*What were the results?* Let's begin by looking at age differences in self-control. The top graph shows that 3-year-olds waited longer than 2-year-olds to peek at the gift being wrapped and to touch the gift after the adult left. Of course, these improvements should not obscure the fact almost no children in either group are truly showing self-control. All children eventually turn to look at the gift being wrapped or touch the wrapped gift on the table.

The bottom graph shows correlations between children's performance on the self-control and emotional self-regulation tasks. You can see that the correlations were positive: Children who showed good self-control (by waiting longer to peek or touch) tended to regulate their emotions better (e.g., they were less angry when strapped in the car seat).

*What did the investigators conclude?* Self-control improves considerably between 2 and 3 years (but is still far from perfect). And the ability to control one's behavior in the face of temptation is related to the ability to control one's emotions.

*What converging evidence would strengthen these conclusions?* Kochanska and her colleagues measured children's self-control with specially designed tasks. Consequently, a useful next step would be to complement the results from those tasks with observations of self-control as it occurs naturally in children's homes. Also, since the 3-year-olds have hardly mastered self-control, another logical extension would be to continue the longitudinal study, testing children annually as they get older.

As we've seen, preschoolers have much to learn about regulating impulsive behavior, and control is achieved only gradually throughout the elementary-school years. For example, in a study by Rotenberg and Mayer (1990), after children had completed a task, they were offered the choice of a relatively small reward immediately or a much larger reward if they waited 1 day. About one third of the 6- to 8-year-olds opted to wait for the larger reward. In contrast, half of the 9- to 11-year-olds and nearly all of the 12- to 15-year-olds waited a day to obtain the larger reward. Thus, although self-control may be evident in toddlers, mastery occurs gradually throughout childhood.

Perhaps you wonder about the validity of these tasks. That is, are these tasks measuring important aspects of self-control in children's natural environments? Mothers' reports of their youngsters' self-control represent one source of evidence for the validity of these tasks. Children who are less likely to touch prohibited toys are, according to their mothers' reports, more likely to spontaneously confess to misdeeds at home and more likely to do as asked at home, without parental supervision (Kochanska et al., 1994).

Even more remarkable are the results from longitudinal studies on the long-term consistency of self-control. Shoda, Mischel, and Peake (1990) tracked down nearly two hundred 15- to 18-year-olds who had participated in self-control experiments as 4-year-olds. In the original experiments, 4-year-olds were told that if they waited alone in a room until the experimenter returned, they would receive a big prize. If they rang a bell to signal the experimenter to return, they would re-ceive a much smaller prize. Then the researchers simply recorded the length of time children waited until the experimenter returned. Amaz-ingly, how long 4-year-olds waited was related to a host of characteris-tics some 11 to 14 years later. In general, 4-year-olds who waited the longest before calling the experimenter were still, as 15- to 18-year-olds, better able to exert self-control and more attentive and able to plan, and they had higher SAT scores. For example, the correlation be-tween the amount of time that children waited at age 4 and their SAT-verbal score was .42. And, when these individuals were tested in their late 20s, the 4-year-olds who waited the longest were better educated and had higher self-esteem (Ayduk et al., 2000).

Obviously, individuals differ in their ability to resist temptation, and this char-acteristic is remarkably stable over time. But why are some children and adults better able than others to exert self-control? As you'll see in the next section of this module, parents and children's temperament both contribute to children's self-control.

> Preschool children who are better able to resist temptation often grow up to be adolescents who have better self-control, are more planful, and have higher SAT scores.

## Influences on Self-Control

Parents like Shirley are disappointed and upset when their children lack self-control. What can parents do? Research consistently links greater self-control with a discipli-nary style in which parents are warm and loving but establish well-defined limits on what behavior is acceptable (Feldman & Klein, 2003). And parent–child interactions about discipline are *dialogues* filled with suggestions and negotiations, not mono-logues in which parents simply assert their power (e.g., "You'll do it because I say so"). When Shirley disciplines Ryan, she should remind him of the clear behavioral standard (not touching the cake), explain her disappointment ("Now nobody else will see how pretty your cake was!"), and suggest ways that he could resist similar temptations in the future.

Research also shows that children's self-control is usually *lower* when parents are very strict with them (Donovan, Leavitt, & Walsh, 2000; Feldman & Wentzel, 1990). By constantly directing them to do one thing but not another, parents do not give their children either the opportunity or the incentive to internalize control (Kochanska, Coy, & Murray, 2001).

But parents aren't the only important influence on children's self-control; re-member, from Module 10.2 that temperament also matters. Emotional toddlers and preschoolers are less able to control themselves (Stifter, Spinrad, & Braungart-Riek-er, 1999). That is, youngsters who have difficulty regulating their emotions usually have difficulty regulating their behavior.

Temperament also influences how children respond to parents' efforts to teach self-control. In children the aspect of temperament that's most important for self-control is anxiety and fearfulness (Kochanska, 1991, 1993). Some anxious and fearful children become nervous at the prospect of potential wrongdoing. When told not to eat a cookie until after dinner, fearful children may leave the room because they're afraid that otherwise they might give in to temptation. With these children, a simple parental reminder usually guarantees compliance because they are so anxious about not following instructions, getting caught, or having to confess to a misdeed.

For children who are not naturally fearful at the thought of misdeeds, other approaches are necessary. More effective with these children are positive appeals to the child to cooperate, appeals that build on the strong attachment relationship between parent and child. Fearless children comply with parental requests out of positive feelings for a loved one, not out of distress caused by fear of misdeeds (Kochanska, 1997a).

Of course, regardless of their temperament, children are not perfectly consistent in their self-control. Children who are able to resist temptation on one occasion may give in the next time. Why do children show self-control on some tasks but not on others? As we'll see in the next section, the answer lies in children's plans for resisting temptation.

## Improving Children's Self-Control

Imagine it's one of the first nice days of spring. You have two major exams that you should study for, but it's so-o-o-o tempting to spend the entire day with your friends, sitting in the sun. What do you do to resist this temptation and stick to studying? You might remind yourself that these exams are very important. You might also move to a windowless room to keep your mind off the tempting weather. Stated more generally, effective ways to resist temptation include (a) reminding yourself of the importance of long-term goals over short-term temptations and (b) reducing the attraction of the tempting event.

During the preschool years, some youngsters begin to use both of these methods spontaneously. In an experiment by Mischel and Ebbesen (1970), 3- to 5-year-olds were asked to sit alone in a room for 15 minutes. If they waited the entire time, they would receive a desirable reward. Children could call the experimenter back to the room at any time by a prearranged signal; in this case, they would receive a much less desirable reward.

Some children, of course, were better able than others to wait the full 15 minutes. How did they do it? Some children talked to themselves: "I've gotta wait to get the best prize!" As Vygotsky described (Module 6.2), these youngsters were using private speech to control their own behavior. Others, like the child in the photograph, sang. Still others invented games. All were effective techniques for enduring 15 boring minutes to receive a desired prize.

One way to resist the temptation of desirable objects is to think about something else or do something else, such as singing.

Later studies show that children who have a concrete way of handling such a situation are far better able to resist temptation (Mischel, Cantor, & Feldman, 1996; Peake, Hebl, & Mischel, 2002). Effective plans include (a) reminders to avoid looking at the tempting object, (b) reminders of rules against touching a tempting object, and (c) activities designed to divert attention from the tempting object, such as playing with other objects. For example, in the vignette, Shirley could have helped Ryan make a plan to resist temptation. She might have told him, "When you feel like you want to eat some cake, tell yourself, 'No cake until Mom gets home' and go play in your bedroom."

Overall, then, how children think about tempting objects or outcomes makes all the difference. Even preschoolers can achieve self-control by making plans that include appropriate self-instruction. As children learn to regulate their own behavior, they also begin to learn about moral rules—cultural rights and wrongs—which are described in the next module.

## CHECK YOUR LEARNING

**RECALL**  Describe the three phases in the emergence of self-control during infancy and the preschool years.

How does temperament influence a child's self-control?

**INTERPRET**  What does longitudinal research on preschool children's ability to delay gratification tell us about the continuity of development?

**APPLY**  What if Shirley described the birthday cake episode to her own mother, who replied, "It's simple, my dear. You're the parent. He's the kid. You're the boss. Tell him what to do." What would you say to Shirley's mom?

All other things being equal, I'd side with Amanda's dad. A typical 2-year-old should be able to control himself or herself when the standard is clear and reasonable, which it seems to be in this case. | **12.1**

# REASONING ABOUT MORAL ISSUES    12.2

## LEARNING OBJECTIVES

- How does reasoning about moral issues change during childhood and adolescence?

- How do concern for justice and caring for other people contribute to moral reasoning?

- What factors help promote more sophisticated reasoning about moral issues?

Piaget's Views

Kohlberg's Theory

Beyond Kohlberg's Theory

Promoting Moral Reasoning

*Howard, the least popular boy in the eighth grade, had been wrongly accused of stealing a sixth grader's portable CD player. Min-shen, another eighth grader, knew that Howard was innocent but said nothing to the school principal for fear of what his friends would say about siding with Howard. A few days later, when Min-shen's father heard about the incident, he was upset that his son apparently had so little "moral fiber." Why hadn't Min-shen acted in the face of an injustice?*

On one of the days when I was writing this module, my local paper had two articles about youth from the area. One article was about a 14-year-girl who was badly burned while saving her younger brothers from a fire in their apartment. Her mother said she wasn't surprised by her daughter's actions because she had always been an extraordinarily caring person. The other article was about two 17-year-old boys who had beaten an elderly man to death. They had only planned to steal his wallet, but when he insulted them and tried to punch them, they became enraged.

Reading articles like these, you can't help but question why some people act in ways that earn our deepest respect and admiration, whereas others earn our utter contempt as well as our pity. And, at a more mundane level, we wonder why Min-shen didn't tell the truth about the theft to the lunchroom supervisor. In this module, we'll begin our exploration of moral understanding and behavior by looking at children's thinking about moral issues: How do children judge what is "good" and what is "bad"? Let's start by looking at Jean Piaget's ideas about the development of moral reasoning.

## Piaget's Views

I remember playing Chutes and Ladders® with my son Matt when he was about 6. This is a board game in which you can advance rapidly when you land on a space that has a ladder but must go backward if you land on a chute. To speed up the game, I suggested to Matt that we be allowed to advance if we landed on a chute as well as a ladder. I reminded him that he liked to climb up slides at playgrounds, so my suggestion had some logic to it. Matt would have none of this. He told me, "It's a rule that you have to go backward when you land on a chute. You can't go forward. The people who made Chutes and Ladders® say so. Just read the instructions, Daddy." I tried again to persuade him (because, in my humble opinion, Chutes and Ladders® gives new meaning to "bored" games), but he was adamant.

Matt's inflexibility, which is typical of 6-year-olds, can be explained by Piaget's stage theory of moral development. Based on children's play and their responses to stories about children who misbehave, Piaget proposed one of the first theories of moral development. In the first stage of moral development, which lasts from age 2 years to about 4, children have no well-defined ideas about morality. **But, beginning at about 5 years and continuing through age 7, children are in a stage of *moral realism*; they believe that rules are created by wise adults and therefore must be followed and cannot be changed. Another characteristic of the stage of moral realism is that children believe in *immanent justice*, the idea that breaking a rule always leads to punishment.** Suppose I had forced Matt to use my new rules for Chutes and Ladders® and that, the next day, he had tripped on his way to school, scraping his knee. Believing in immanent justice, he would have seen the scraped knee as the inevitable consequence of breaking the rule the previous day.

> In Piaget's view, 5- to 7-year-olds believe that rules are absolute; by age 8, children understand that rules are created by people to help them get along.

**At about age 8, children progress to the stage of *moral relativism*, the understanding that rules are created by people to help them get along.** Children progress to this more advanced level of moral reasoning in part because advances in cognitive development allow them to understand the reasons for rules. Furthermore, from interactions with their peers, children come to understand the need for rules and how they are created. For example, as the boys in the photograph decide where to ride their skateboards, they might follow a rule that everybody can suggest some place and then they'll vote. The boys understand that this rule isn't absolute; they follow it because it's reasonably fair and, by using this rule, they spend more time skating and less time arguing.

Children in the stage of moral relativism also understand that because people agree to set rules in the first place, they can also change them if they see the need. If the skateboarding boys decided another rule would be fairer and would help them get along better, they could adopt the new rule.

Some of Piaget's ideas about moral reasoning have stood the test of time better than others. For example, later

By 8 years of age, children understand that people create rules to get along; for example, these boys may follow the rule that they'll vote to decide where to ride their skateboards.

research has showed that children's early moral reasoning does not consider adult authority final and absolute. Instead, preschool children believe adults' authority is limited. Preschoolers believe that pushing a child or damaging another child's possession is wrong even when an adult says that it's okay (Tisak, 1993). A lasting contribution of Piaget's work, however, is the idea that moral reasoning progresses through a sequence of stages, driven by cognitive development and interactions with peers. One important theory that builds on Piaget's stage approach comes from Lawrence Kohlberg; it's the focus of the next section.

## Kohlberg's Theory

To begin, I'd like to tell you a story about Heidi, a star player on a soccer team that I coached several years ago. Heidi was terribly upset because our team was undefeated and scheduled to play in a weekend tournament to determine the league champion. But on Sunday of this same weekend, a Habitat-for-Humanity house was to be dedicated to her grandfather, who had died a few months previously. If Heidi skipped the tournament game, her friends on the team would be upset; if she skipped the dedication, her family would be disappointed. Heidi couldn't do both and didn't know what to do.

VIDEO 12.1

Moral Development

    Kohlberg created stories like this one to study how people reason about moral dilemmas. He made it very difficult to reach a decision in his stories because every alternative involved some undesirable consequences. In fact, there is no "correct" answer—that's why the stories are referred to as moral "dilemmas." For Heidi, pleasing her friends means disappointing her family; pleasing her family means letting down her teammates. Kohlberg was more interested in the reasoning used to justify a decision—Why should Heidi go to the tournament? Why should she go to the dedication?—not in the decision itself.*

    Kohlberg's best-known moral dilemma is about Heinz, whose wife is dying:

> In Europe, a woman was near death from cancer. One drug might save her, a form of radium that a druggist in the same town had recently discovered. The druggist was charging $2,000, ten times what the drug cost him to make. The sick woman's husband, Heinz, went to everyone he knew to borrow the money, but he could only get together about half of what it cost. He told the druggist that his wife was dying and asked him to sell it cheaper or let him pay later. But the druggist said, "No." The husband got desperate and broke into the man's store to steal the drug for his wife (Kohlberg, 1969, p. 379).

Although more hangs in the balance for Heinz than for Heidi, both are moral dilemmas in that the alternative courses of action have desirable and undesirable features.

    Kohlberg analyzed children's, adolescents', and adults' responses to a large number of dilemmas and identified three levels of moral reasoning, each divided into two stages. Across the six stages, the basis for moral reasoning shifts. In the earliest stages, moral reasoning is based on external forces, such as the promise of reward or the threat of punishment. At the most advanced levels, moral reasoning is based on a personal, internal moral code and is unaffected by others' views or society's expectations. You can clearly see this gradual shift in the three levels:

---

*As it turned out, Heidi didn't have to resolve the dilemma. We lost our tournament game on Saturday, so she went to the dedication on Sunday.

- *Preconventional level*: **For most children, many adolescents, and some adults, moral reasoning is controlled almost solely by obedience to authority and by rewards and punishments.**

  *Stage 1: Obedience orientation.* People believe that adults know what is right and wrong. Consequently, a person should do what adults say is right to avoid being punished. A person at this stage might argue that Heinz should not steal the drug because it is against the law (which was set by adults).

  *Stage 2: Instrumental orientation.* People look out for their own needs. They often are nice to others because they expect the favor to be returned in the future. A person at this stage might say it was all right for Heinz to steal the drug because his wife might do something nice for him in return (that is, she might reward him).

- *Conventional level*: **For most adolescents and most adults, moral decision making is based on social norms—what is expected by others.**

  *Stage 3: Interpersonal norms.* Adolescents and adults believe that they should act according to others' expectations. The aim is to win the approval of others by behaving like "good boys" and "good girls." An adolescent or adult at this stage might argue that Heinz should not steal the drug because then others would see him as an honest citizen who obeys the law.

  *Stage 4: Social system morality.* Adolescents and adults believe that social roles, expectations, and laws exist to maintain order within society and to promote the good of all people. An adolescent or adult in this stage might reason that Heinz should steal the drug because a husband is obligated to do all that he possibly can to save his wife's life. Or a person in this stage might reason that Heinz should not steal the drug because stealing is against the law and society must prohibit theft.

> In Kohlberg's theory, moral reasoning is first based on reward and punishment but ultimately is based on a personal moral code.

- *Postconventional level*: **For some adults, typically those older than 25, moral decisions are based on personal, moral principles.**

  *Stage 5: Social contract orientation.* Adults agree that members of cultural groups adhere to a "social contract" because a common set of expectations and laws benefits all group members. However, if these expectations and laws no longer promote the welfare of individuals, they become invalid. Consequently, an adult in this stage might reason that Heinz should steal the drug because social rules about property rights are no longer benefiting individuals' welfare.

  *Stage 6: Universal ethical principles.* Abstract principles like justice, compassion, and equality form the basis of a personal moral code that may sometimes conflict with society's expectations and laws. An adult at this stage might argue that Heinz should steal the drug because life is paramount and preserving life takes precedence over all other rights.

The table on page 373 puts all the stages together, providing a quick summary of Kohlberg's theory.

## SUMMARY TABLE

### STAGES IN KOHLBERG'S THEORY OF MORAL DEVELOPMENT

**Preconventional Level: Punishment and Reward**

Stage 1: Obedience to authority

Stage 2: Nice behavior in exchange for future favors

**Conventional Level: Social Norms**

Stage 3: Live up to others' expectations

Stage 4: Follow rules to maintain social order

**Postconventional Level: Moral Codes**

Stage 5: Adhere to a social contract when it is valid

Stage 6: Personal morality based on abstract principles

**SUPPORT FOR KOHLBERG'S THEORY.**   Kohlberg proposed that his stages form an invariant sequence. That is, individuals move through the six stages in the order listed and in only that order. If his stage theory is right, then level of moral reasoning should be strongly associated with age and level of cognitive development: Older and more advanced thinkers, on the average, should be more advanced in their moral development, and indeed they usually are (Stewart & Pascual-Leone, 1992).

For example, the graph shows developmental change in the percentage of individuals who reason at Kohlberg's different stages. Stages 1 and 2 are common among children and young adolescents but not older adolescents and adults. Stages 3 and 4 are common among older adolescents and adults. The graph also shows that most individuals do not progress to the final stages. Most adults' moral reasoning is at Stages 3 and 4.

FIGURE 12-3

Support for Kohlberg's invariant sequence of stages also comes from longitudinal studies measuring individuals' level of reasoning over several years. Individuals do progress through each stage in sequence, and virtually no individuals skip any stages (Colby et al., 1983). Longitudinal studies also show that, over time, individuals become more advanced in their level of moral reasoning or remain at the same level. They do not regress to a lower level (Walker & Taylor, 1991).

Additional support for Kohlberg's theory comes from research on the link between moral reasoning and moral behavior. In general, level of moral reasoning should be linked to moral behavior. Remember that less advanced moral reasoning reflects the influence of external forces such as rewards and social norms, whereas more advanced reasoning is based on a personal moral code. Therefore, individuals at the preconventional and conventional levels would act morally when external forces demand, but otherwise they might not. In contrast, individuals at the postconventional level, where reasoning is based on personal principles, should be compelled to moral action even when external forces may not favor it.

Let's return to the example in the vignette. Suppose you knew that one of the least popular students has been wrongly accused of stealing a CD player; you know that some friends in your group are actually responsible. What would you do? Speaking out on behalf of the unpopular student is unlikely to lead to reward. Furthermore, there are strong social norms against "squealing" on friends. So if you are in the preconventional or conventional level of moral reasoning like Min-shen, the boy in the vignette, you would probably let the unpopular student be punished unfairly. But if you are at the postconventional level and see the situation in terms of principles of justice and fairness, you would be more likely to identify the real perpetrators, despite the price to be paid in rejection by the group.

Many researchers report findings that support the hypothesized link between moral reasoning and moral action. In one study (Gibbs et al., 1986), high-school teachers were asked to judge whether their students would defend their principles in difficult situations or if they would act morally only when it was fashionable or handy. High-school students who were judged by their teachers to have greater moral courage tended to be more advanced in Kohlberg's stages than students who were judged less courageous. That is, students like those in the photograph who protest social conditions tend to have higher moral reasoning scores. The converse is also true: Delinquent adolescents, whose actions are more likely to be morally offensive, tend to have lower moral reasoning scores than nondelinquent adolescents (Chandler & Moran, 1990). That is, delinquent adolescents are more likely to emphasize punishment and reward in their moral reasoning, rather than social norms and personal moral codes.

On another point of Kohlberg's theory, support is mixed. Kohlberg claimed that his sequence of stages is universal: All people in all cultures should progress through the six-stage sequence. Some research shows that children and adolescents in cultures worldwide reason about moral dilemmas at Stages 2 or 3, just like North American children and adolescents. But, as we'll see in the "Cultural Influences" feature, beyond the earliest stages, moral reasoning in other cultures is often not described well by Kohlberg's theory (Turiel & Neff, 2000).

Students who show moral courage by participating in protest movements typically have more advanced moral reasoning.

## Cultural Influences

### Moral Reasoning in India

Many critics note that Kohlberg's emphasis on individual rights and justice reflects traditional American culture and Judeo-Christian theology. Not all cultures and religions share this emphasis; consequently, moral reasoning might be based on different values in other cultures (Carlo et al., 1996; Keller et al., 1998).

The Hindu religion, for example, emphasizes duty and responsibility to others, not individual rights and justice (Simpson, 1974). Accordingly, children and adults reared with traditional Hindu beliefs might emphasize caring for others in their moral reasoning more than individuals brought up in the Judeo-Christian tradition.

Miller and Bersoff (1992) tested the hypothesis that cultural differences affect moral reasoning by constructing dilemmas with both justice- and care-based solutions. For example:

> Ben planned to travel to San Francisco in order to attend the wedding of his best friend. He needed to catch the very next train if he was to be on time for the ceremony, as he had to deliver the wedding rings. However, Ben's wallet was stolen in the train station. He lost all of his money as well as his ticket to San Francisco.
>
> Ben approached several officials as well as passengers . . . and asked them to loan him money to buy a new ticket. But, because he was a stranger, no one was willing to lend him the money he needed.
>
> While Ben . . . was trying to decide what to do next, a well-dressed man sitting next to him walked away. . . . Ben noticed that the man had left his coat unattended. Sticking out of the man's coat pocket was a train ticket to San Francisco. . . . He also saw that the man had more than enough money in his coat pocket to buy another train ticket (p. 545).

**Moral reasoning is influenced by culture; in India, for example, moral judgments emphasize caring for others.**

One solution emphasized individual rights and justice:

> Ben should not take the ticket from the man's coat pocket even though it means not getting to San Francisco in time to deliver the wedding rings to his best friend (p. 545).

The other solution placed a priority on caring for others:

> Ben should go to San Francisco to deliver the wedding rings to his best friend even if it means taking the train ticket from the other man's coat pocket (p. 545).

When children and adults living in the United States responded to dilemmas like this one about Ben, a slight majority selected the justice-based alternative. In contrast, when Hindu children and adults living in India responded to the same dilemmas, the overwhelming majority selected the care-based alternative.

Clearly, moral reasoning reflects the culture in which a person is reared. Consistent with Kohlberg's theory, judgments by American children and adults reflect their culture's emphasis on individual rights and justice. But judgments by Indian children and adults reflect their culture's emphasis on caring for other people. The bases of moral reasoning are not universal as Kohlberg claimed; instead, they reflect cultural values. ◼

## Beyond Kohlberg's Theory

Kohlberg's theory obviously is not the final word on moral development. Much about his theory seems valid, but investigators have addressed its shortcomings. In the next few pages I describe some work that helps complete our picture of the development of moral thinking.

**GILLIGAN'S ETHIC OF CARING.**　Findings like those described in the "Cultural Influences" feature indicate that Kohlberg's theory is not universal but applies primarily to cultures with Western philosophical and religious traditions. But researcher Carol Gilligan (1982; Gilligan & Attanucci, 1988) questioned how applicable Kohlberg's theory is even within the Western tradition. Gilligan argued that Kohlberg's emphasis on justice applies more to men than to women, whose reasoning about moral issues is often rooted in concern for others. Gilligan wrote, "The moral imperative that emerges repeatedly in interviews with women is an injunction to care, a responsibility to discern and alleviate the real and recognizable trouble of this world" (1982, p. 100).

In Gilligan's theory the most advanced level of moral reasoning is based on the understanding that caring is the cornerstone of all human relationships, ranging from parent–child relationships to the relationship that exists between a homeless person and a volunteer at a shelter.

Gilligan proposed a developmental progression in which individuals gain greater understanding of caring and responsibility. In the first stage, children are preoccupied with their own needs. In the second stage, people care for others, particularly those who are less able to care for themselves, like infants and the aged. The third stage unites caring for others and for oneself by emphasizing caring in all human relationships and by denouncing exploitation and violence between people. For example, consider the teen in the photo, who is helping at a homeless shelter. She does so not because she believes the homeless are needy but because she believes, first, that all humans should care for each other, and second, that many people are in the shelter because they've been exploited in the past.

Like Kohlberg, Gilligan also believes that moral reasoning becomes qualitatively more sophisticated as individuals develop, progressing through a number of distinct stages. However, Gilligan emphasizes care (helping people in need) instead of justice (treating people fairly).

What does research tell us about the importance of justice and care in moral reasoning? Do females and males differ in the bases of their moral reasoning? The best answer to these questions comes from a comprehensive meta-analysis conducted by Jaffee and Hyde (2000) that included 113 studies with more than 12,000 participants. Overall, boys and men tended to get slightly higher scores on problems that emphasized justice, whereas girls and women tended to get slightly higher scores on problems that emphasized caring. But the differences are small and do not indicate that moral reasoning by females is predominated by a concern with care and moral reasoning by males is predominated by a concern with justice. Instead, girls and boys as well as men and women reason about moral issues similarly; both often think about moral issues in terms of care and interpersonal relationships (Turiel, 2006).

**EISENBERG'S LEVELS OF PROSOCIAL REASONING.** Nancy Eisenberg (1982; Eisenberg et al., 1995) argues that Kohlberg's theory is flawed because the dilemmas are unrealistic. They involve breaking a law or disobeying a person in authority. In real life, says Eisenberg, most children's moral dilemmas involve choosing between self-interest and helping others. For example, in one of Eisenberg's moral dilemmas, a child walking to a party comes upon a child injured from a fall. The first child must decide whether to continue to the party or help the second child and miss the party.

> According to Eisenberg, children's prosocial reasoning shifts from self-interest to concern for others based on empathy.

Like Kohlberg, Eisenberg focuses on how children explain their choices. **Most preschool and many elementary-school children have a *hedonistic orientation*: They pursue their own pleasure.** These children do not help the injured child because they would miss the party. Or they might help because they expect that the injured child would return the favor in the future. In either case, self-interest is the basis of their decision.

**Some preschool and many elementary-school children have a *needs-oriented orientation*: They are concerned about others' needs and want to help.** Children at this stage have learned a simple rule, to help others. They often explain their desire to help as a straightforward, "He needs my help." Their desire to help is not based on imagining how the injured child feels or on a personal moral code.

**Many elementary-school children and adolescents have a *stereotyped, approval-focused orientation*, behaving as they think society expects "good people" to behave.** The helpful teen in the photo would explain her behavior by saying that the person she's helping will like her more because she's helping.

**Finally, some children and many adolescents develop an *empathic orientation*; they consider the injured child's perspective and how their own actions will make them feel.** An adolescent with this orientation might say, "He'd be in pain, so I'd feel bad if I didn't help."

The same kinds of evidence that support Kohlberg's theory support Eisenberg's. For example, longitudinal studies indicate that children in many countries move through Eisenberg's different orientations in sequence (Eisenberg, 1986; Eisenberg et al., 1995). What's more, children who reason at more advanced levels are more likely to actually help others than children who reason at less advanced levels (Miller et al., 1996).

Elementary-school children and younger adolescents often help other people because they think that's how they're supposed to behave, not necessarily because they want to or because they're very concerned about the people that they're helping.

Eisenberg's theory is like Kohlberg's in emphasizing that moral development involves a developmental shift away from self-centered thinking to social norms and moral principles. Her theory is like Gilligan's in emphasizing that caring for others is an important element in everyday moral reasoning.

**DEVELOPMENT OF DOMAINS OF SOCIAL JUDGMENT.**    The research I've described so far tells us that there is more to moral reasoning than justice; concern for others is important, too. Elliot Turiel (1997, 1998) has taken these ideas a step further and argued that moral judgments (whether based on justice or care) represent one of several important domains that make up social judgments. To illustrate the domains, think about the following preschool children:

- Brian, who often kicks or pushes his younger brother when their mom isn't looking.
- Kathryn, who never puts her toys away when she's done playing with them.
- Brad, who likes to wear his underpants inside out.

Although each child's behavior is in some sense "wrong," only the first child's behavior—kicking and pushing—represents a moral transgression because Brian's actions can harm another person. **In contrast, *social conventions* are arbitrary standards of behavior agreed to by a cultural group to facilitate interactions within the group.** Thus social convention says that we can eat French fries but not green beans with our fingers and that, in the case of Kathryn, children should clean up after themselves. **Finally, the *personal domain* pertains to choices concerning one's body (e.g., what to eat and wear) and choices of friends or activities.** Decisions here are not right or wrong but instead are seen as personal preferences left up to the individual (Smetana, 2002). Thus, Brad's decision to wear his underpants inside out is unusual but not wrong.

During the preschool years, children begin to differentiate these domains (Turiel, 1998). For example, they believe that breaking a moral rule is more serious and should be punished more severely than breaking a social convention. Furthermore, preschool children believe that adults have authority over social conventions

**Question**

Fourteen-year-old Paige was getting settled to watch the latest episode of *7th Heaven,* her favorite show, when the phone rang. Jasna was completely stumped by the algebra homework and wanted Paige to talk her through it. Paige didn't want to help but she did anyway because she knew that if she didn't, Jasna would tell everyone in the class that Paige had been mean to her. Which of Eisenberg's stages best describes Paige's thinking?

**12.2**

but not moral rules (which stem from higher authority) or the personal domain (which is up to the individual). For example, preschool children believe that teachers could decide it is okay for students to talk during storytime, but could not decide it is okay for students to hit each other; and teachers should not tell students what clothes to wear to school (Nucci & Weber, 1995; Yau & Smetana, 2003).

Children's early understanding of these different domains of social judgment is rooted in their experiences and parents' responses to different kinds of transgressions (Turiel, 1998). When a child breaks a moral rule, adults talk about the impact of the act on the victim and how that person could be hurt. In contrast, when a child violates a social convention, adults more often talk about the need to follow rules and to obey parents, teachers, and other people in authority. Finally, conversations in the personal domain are different: Here adults typically do not specify a "right" or "wrong" choice but instead encourage children to make their own choices (Nucci & Weber, 1995). Thus, in Turiel's view (1998, Turiel & Neff, 2000), moral reasoning is part of a much larger developmental accomplishment: Children understand that there are different domains of social decision making, each with unique rules of authority and sanctions for misbehavior. And, by the preschool years, children have made remarkable progress in understanding the distinction between the moral, social-conventional, and personal domains.

> *Preschool children distinguish moral decisions and social conventions from the personal domain.*

The net result of Gilligan's work, Eisenberg's research, and Turiel's study of domains of social judgment is a much broader view of moral reasoning. As Kohlberg claimed, moral reasoning becomes progressively more sophisticated as children develop. However, contrary to Kohlberg's original claims, moral reasoning is not always based on justice and rights. Concern for others is sometimes the basis. And moral reasoning is simply one important part of children's understanding of domains of social judgment.

## Promoting Moral Reasoning

Whether it is based on justice or care, most cultures and most parents want to encourage adolescents to think carefully about moral issues. What can be done to help adolescents develop more mature forms of moral reasoning? Sometimes simply being exposed to more advanced moral reasoning is sufficient to promote developmental change (Walker, 1980). Adolescents may notice, for example, that older friends do not wait to be rewarded to help others. Or a teenager may notice that respected peers take courageous positions regardless of the social consequences. Such experiences apparently cause adolescents to reevaluate their reasoning on moral issues and propel them toward more sophisticated thinking.

Discussion can be particularly effective in revealing shortcomings in moral reasoning. When people, such as the adolescents in the photo, reason about moral issues with others whose reasoning is at a higher level, the usual result is that individuals reasoning at lower levels improve (Berkowitz & Gibbs, 1985). This is particularly true when the conversational partner with the more sophisticated reasoning makes an effort to understand the other's view, by requesting

When adolescents discuss moral issues with people whose reasoning is at a more advanced level, their reasoning often becomes more mature.

clarification or paraphrasing what the other child is saying (Walker, Hennig, & Krettenauer, 2000).

The "Child Development and Family Policy" feature shows how Kohlberg used research results like these to foster moral thinking.

## *Child Development and Family Policy*
### Promoting More Advanced Moral Reasoning

Kohlberg wasn't content to simply chart how moral reasoning changed with age. He also wanted to devise ways to foster sophisticated moral reasoning. **To foster discussion and expose students to more advanced moral thinking, Kohlberg and his colleagues set up** *"Just Communities,"* **special groups of students and teachers within public high schools** (Higgins, 1991; Power, Higgins, & Kohlberg, 1989). Teachers and students met weekly to plan school activities and discuss school policies. Decisions were reached democratically, with teachers and students alike each having one vote. However, during discussions, teachers acted as facilitators, encouraging students to consider the moral consequences of different courses of action. Students who participated in Just Communities tended to be more advanced in their moral thinking (Higgins, 1991; Power, Higgins, & Kohlberg, 1989).

Research findings such as these send an important message to parents: Discussion is probably the best way for parents to help their children think about moral issues in more mature terms (Walker & Taylor, 1991). Research consistently shows that mature moral reasoning comes about when adolescents are free to express their opinions on moral issues to their parents, who are, in turn, expressing their own opinions and, consequently, exposing their adolescent children to more mature moral reasoning (Hoffman, 1988, 1994). ■

In this module, we've seen how moral reasoning changes as children develop. To see how these changes lead to changes in moral action, we'll look at children's prosocial behavior in the next module.

### CHECK YOUR LEARNING

**RECALL** Summarize research that supports and refutes Kohlberg's theory of moral reasoning.

Describe ways to foster children's moral reasoning.

**INTERPRET** How do Piaget's stages of moral realism and moral relativism fit with Kohlberg's six stages?

**APPLY** Based on what you know about domains of social judgment, which domains would you expect to vary the most across cultures? Which would you expect to be similar across cultures?

Paige's thinking conforms to Eisenberg's stereotyped, approval-focused orientation. She knows that "good people" are expected to help and she doesn't want Jasna telling her classmates that Paige wasn't a "good person" because she refused to help.

12.2

# 12.3 HELPING OTHERS

Development of Prosocial Behavior

Skills Underlying Prosocial Behavior

Situational Influences

Socializing Prosocial Behavior

## LEARNING OBJECTIVES

- At what age do children begin to act prosocially? How does prosocial behavior change with age?

- What skills do children need to behave prosocially?

- What situations influence children's prosocial behavior?

- How can parents foster prosocial behavior in their children?

*Six-year-old Juan got his finger trapped in the VCR when he tried to remove a tape. While he cried and cried, his 3-year-old brother, Antonio, and his 2-year-old sister, Carla, watched but did not help. Later, when their mother had soothed Juan and saw that his finger was not injured, she worried about her younger children's reactions. In the face of their brother's obvious distress, why had Antonio and Carla done nothing?*

Most parents, most teachers, and most religions try to teach children to act in cooperative, helping, giving ways—at least most of the time and in most situations. **Actions that benefit others are known as *prosocial behavior*.** Of course, cooperation often "works" because individuals gain more than they would by not cooperating. ***Altruism* is prosocial behavior that helps another with no direct benefit to the individual.** Altruism is driven by feelings of responsibility for other people. Two youngsters pooling their funds to buy a candy bar to share demonstrates cooperative behavior. One youngster giving half her lunch to a friend who forgot his own lunch demonstrates altruism.

Many scientists believe that humans are biologically predisposed to be helpful, to share, to cooperate, and to be concerned for others (Hoffman, 2000; Wilson, 1975). Why has prosocial behavior evolved over time? The best explanation has nothing to do with lofty moral principles; instead, it's much more pragmatic: People who frequently help others are more likely to receive help themselves and this increases the chance that they'll pass along their genes to future generations.

But, as the story of Juan and his siblings shows, children (and adults, for that matter) are not always helpful or cooperative. In this module, you'll learn how prosocial behavior changes with age and discover some factors that promote prosocial behavior.

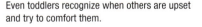
Even toddlers recognize when others are upset and try to comfort them.

## Development of Prosocial Behavior

Simple acts of altruism can be seen by 18 months of age. When toddlers and preschoolers see other people who are obviously hurt or upset, they appear concerned, like the child in the photo. They try to comfort the person by hugging him or patting him (Zahn-Waxler et al., 1992). Apparently, at this early age, children recognize signs of distress.

During the toddler and preschool years, children gradually begin to understand others' needs and learn more appropriate altruistic responses (van der Mark, van IJzendorn, & Bakermans-Kranenburg, 2002). When 3-year-old Alexis sees that her infant brother is crying because he's dropped his favorite bear, she retrieves it for him; when 4-year-old Darren sees his mom crying while watching a TV show, he may turn off the TV. These early attempts at altruistic behavior are limited because young children's knowledge of what they can do to help is modest. As youngsters acquire more strategies to help others, their preferred strategies become more adultlike (Eisenberg, Fabes, & Spinrad, 2006).

Thus, as a general rule, intentions to act prosocially increase with age, as do children's strategies for helping. Of course, not all children respond to the needs of others, either in toddlerhood or at later ages. Some children attach greater priority to looking out for their own interests. What makes some children more likely than others to help? We'll answer this question in the next section.

## Skills Underlying Prosocial Behavior

Think back to an occasion when you helped someone. How did you know that the person needed help? Why did you decide to help? Although you didn't realize it at the time, your decision to help was probably based on several skills:

- *Perspective taking.* In Module 6.1, you learned about Piaget's concept of egocentrism, the preoperational youngster's inability to see things from another's point of view. Egocentrism limits children's ability to share or help because they simply do not realize the need for prosocial behavior. They have only one perspective—their own. For example, young children might not help someone carrying many packages because they cannot envision that carrying lots of bulky things is a burden. Older children, however, can take the perspective of others, so they recognize the burden and are more inclined to help. In general, the better children understand the thoughts and feelings of other people, the more willing they are to share and help others (Strayer & Roberts, 2004).

> Skills that foster prosocial behavior include perspective taking, empathy, and advanced moral reasoning.

- *Empathy.* **The ability to experience another person's emotions is** *empathy.* Children who deeply feel another person's fear, disappointment, sorrow, or loneliness are more inclined to help that person than are children who do not feel these emotions (Eisenberg et al., 2006). In other words, youngsters like the one in the photo, who is obviously distressed by what she is seeing, are most likely to help others.

- *Moral reasoning.* In Module 12.2, you learned that reward and punishment influence young children's moral reasoning, whereas a concern for moral principles characterizes adolescents' and adults' moral decision making. Therefore, as you would expect, prosocial behavior in young children is usually determined by the chance of reward or punishment. It also follows that, as children mature and begin to make moral decisions on the basis of fairness and justice, they become more prosocial. Consistent with this idea, Eisenberg, Zhou, and Koller (2001) found that Brazilian 13- to 16-year-olds were more likely to act prosocially when their moral reasoning was more advanced (e.g., based on internalized moral standards).

In sum, children and adolescents who help others tend to be better able to take another's view, to feel another's emotions, and to act on the basis of principles, rather than rewards, punishments, or social norms. For example, a

Children who are empathic—they understand how others feel—are more likely to help others in need.

15-year-old who spontaneously loans his favorite video game to a friend does so because he sees that the friend would like to play the game, he feels the friend's disappointment at not owning the game, and he believes that friends should share with each other.

Of course, perspective taking, empathy, and moral reasoning skills do not guarantee that children always act altruistically. Even though children have the skills needed to act altruistically, they may not because of the particular situation, as we'll see in the next section.

## Situational Influences

Kind children occasionally disappoint us by being cruel, and children who are usually stingy sometimes surprise us by their generosity. Why? The setting helps determine whether children act altruistically or not.

> *Children are most likely to help when they feel responsible, have the needed skills, are happy, and believe they will lose little by helping.*

- *Feelings of responsibility.* Children act altruistically when they feel responsible to the person in need. They are more likely to help siblings and friends than strangers, simply because they feel a direct responsibility to people that they know well (Costin & Jones, 1992).

- *Feelings of competence.* Children act altruistically when they feel that they have the skills necessary to help the person in need. Suppose, for example, that a preschooler is growing more and more upset because she can't figure out how to work a computer game. A classmate who knows little about computer games is not likely to help because he doesn't know what to do to help. By helping, he could end up looking foolish (Peterson, 1983).

- *Mood.* Children act altruistically when they are happy or feeling successful but not when they are sad or feeling as if they have failed. In other words, a preschooler who has just spent an exciting morning as the "leader" in nursery school is more inclined to share treats with siblings than is a preschooler who was punished by the teacher (Eisenberg, 2000).

- *Cost of altruism.* Children act altruistically when it entails few or modest sacrifices. A preschooler who has received a snack that she doesn't particularly like is more inclined to share it than is a child who has received her very favorite snack (Eisenberg & Shell, 1986).

When, then, are children most likely to help? When they feel responsible to the person in need, have the skills that are needed, are happy, and do not think they have to give up a lot by helping. When are children least likely to help? When they feel neither responsible nor capable of helping, are in a bad mood, and believe that helping will entail a large personal sacrifice.

Using these guidelines, how do you explain why Antonio and Carla, the children in the vignette, watched idly as their older brother cried? Hint: The last two factors—mood and cost—are not likely to be involved. However, the first two factors may explain Antonio and Carla's failure to help their older brother. My explanation appears on page 384, just before "Check Your Learning."

So far, we've seen that altruistic behavior is determined by children's skills (such as perspective taking) and by characteristics of situations (such as whether children feel competent to help in a particular situation). Whether children are altruistic is also determined by socialization, the topic of the next section.

## Socializing Prosocial Behavior

Dr. Martin Luther King Jr. said that his pursuit of civil rights for African Americans was particularly influenced by three people: Henry David Thoreau (a 19th-century American philosopher), Mohandas Gandhi (the leader of the Indian movement for independence from England), and his father, Dr. Martin Luther King Sr. As is true of many humanitarians, Dr. King's prosocial behavior started in childhood, at home. But how do parents foster altruism in their children? Several factors contribute:

- *Modeling.* When children see adults helping and caring for others, they often imitate such prosocial behavior (Eisenberg et al., 2006). Of course, parents are the models to whom children are most continuously exposed, so they exert a powerful influence. Parents who report frequent feelings of warmth and concern for others tend to have children who experience stronger feelings of empathy When a mother is helpful and responsive, her children often imitate her by being cooperative, helpful, sharing, and less critical of others. In a particularly powerful demonstration of the impact of parental modeling, people who had risked their lives during World War II to protect Jews from the Nazis often reported their parents' emphasis on caring for all people (Oliner & Oliner, 1988).

- *Disciplinary practices.* Children behave prosocially more often when their parents are warm and supportive, set guidelines, and provide feedback; in contrast, prosocial behavior is less common when parenting is harsh, threatening, and includes frequent physical punishment (Asbury et al., 2003; Eisenberg & Fabes, 1998). Particularly important is parents' use of reasoning as a disciplinary tactic, with the goal of helping children see how their actions affect others. For example, after 4-year-old Annie grabbed some crayons from a playmate, her father told Annie, "You shouldn't just grab things away from people. It makes them angry and unhappy. Ask first, and if they say "no," then you mustn't take them."

- *Opportunities to behave prosocially.* You need to practice to improve motor skills and the same is true of prosocial behaviors—children and adolescents are more likely to act prosocially when they're routinely given the opportunity to help and cooperate with others. At home, children can help with household tasks, such as cleaning and setting the table. Adolescents can be encouraged to participate in community service, such as working at a food pantry or, like the teenager in the photo, helping older adults. Experiences like these help to sensitize children and adolescents to the needs of others and allows them to enjoy the satisfaction of helping (Grusec, Goodnow, & Cohen, 1996; McLellan & Youniss, 2003).

Thus, a host of factors, summarized in the table on page 384, contribute to children's prosocial behavior.

Paula worries that her son Elliot is too selfish and wishes that he was more caring and compassionate. As a parent, what could Paula do to encourage Elliot to be more concerned about others' welfare?

**12.3**

After children and adolescents have had the opportunity to help others, they often continue to be helpful because they better understand the needs of others.

## SUMMARY TABLE

### FACTORS CONTRIBUTING TO CHILDREN'S PROSOCIAL BEHAVIOR

| General Category | Types of Influence | Children are more likely to help when . . . |
|---|---|---|
| Skills | Perspective taking | they can take another person's point of view. |
| | Empathy | they feel another person's emotions. |
| | Moral reasoning | they base moral decisions on fairness. |
| Situational influences | Feelings of responsibility | they feel responsible to the person in need. |
| | Feelings of competence | they feel competent to help. |
| | Mood | they're in a good mood. |
| | Cost of altruism | the cost of prosocial behavior is small. |
| Parents' influence | Modeling | parents behave prosocially themselves. |
| | Discipline | parents reason with them. |
| | Opportunities | they practice helping at home and elsewhere. |

Combining all these ingredients, we can describe the development of children's altruistic behavior this way: As children get older, their perspective taking and empathic skills develop, which enables them to see and feel another's needs. Nonetheless, children are never invariably altruistic (or, fortunately, invariably non-altruistic) because properties of situations dictate altruistic behavior, too.

As parents and other adults try to encourage children's prosocial behavior, one of the biggest obstacles is aggressive behavior, which is common throughout childhood and adolescence. In the next module, we'll look at some of the forces that contribute to children's aggression.

*Answer to question on page 380 about why Antonio and Carla didn't help:* Here are two explanations: First, neither Antonio nor Carla may have felt sufficiently responsible to help because (a) with two children who could help, each child's feeling of individual responsibility is reduced, and (b) younger children are less likely to feel responsible for an older brother. Second, it's my guess that both children have been told not to use the VCR by themselves. Consequently, they don't feel competent to help because they don't know how it works or what they should do to help Juan remove his finger.

**12.3** First, Paula can be sure to model the same behavior that she'd like to encourage in her son—she needs to be compassionate herself. Second, when disciplining Elliot, Paula should try to reason with him, emphasizing how his behavior causes others to feel. Third, Paula can ask Elliot to help around the house and suggest that he do some volunteer activity in the community.

### CHECK YOUR LEARNING

**RECALL**   Describe developmental change in prosocial behavior.

What are the situations in which children are most likely to help others?

**INTERPRET**   Why must a full account of children's prosocial behavior include an emphasis on skills (e.g., empathy) as well as situations (e.g., whether a child feels responsible)?

**APPLY**   Helping with household chores and voluntary community service often increase children's prosocial behavior. Of the skills underlying prosocial behavior (page 381), which do you think are most affected by children's experiences helping at home and elsewhere?

# AGGRESSION

## 12.4

**LEARNING OBJECTIVES**

- When does aggressive behavior first emerge? How stable is aggression across childhood, adolescence, and adulthood?

- How do families, television, and the child's own thoughts contribute to aggression?

- Why are some children victims of aggression?

Change and Stability

Roots of Aggressive Behavior

Victims of Aggression

*Every day, 7-year-old Reza follows the same routine when he gets home from school: He watches one action-adventure cartoon on TV after another until it's time for dinner. Reza's mother is disturbed by her son's constant TV viewing, particularly because of the amount of violence in the shows that he likes. Her husband tells her to stop worrying: "Let him watch what he wants to. It won't hurt him and, besides, it keeps him out of your hair."*

If you think back to your years in elementary school, you can probably remember a class "bully"—a child who was always teasing classmates and picking fights. **Such acts typify *aggression*, behavior meant to harm others.** Aggressiveness is not the same as assertiveness, even though laypeople often use these words interchangeably. You've probably heard praise for an "aggressive businessperson" or a ballplayer who was "aggressive at running the bases." Psychologists and other behavioral scientists, however, would call these behaviors assertive. Assertive behaviors are goal-directed actions to further the legitimate interests of individuals or the groups they represent, while respecting the rights of other persons. In contrast, aggressive behavior, which may be physical or verbal, is intended to harm, damage, or injure and is carried out without regard for the rights of others.

In this module, we will examine aggressive behavior in children and see how it changes with age. Then we'll examine some causes of children's aggression and, in the process, learn more about the impact of Reza's TV watching on his behavior.

In instrumental aggression, children use force to achieve a goal, such as taking a toy from another child.

## Change and Stability

By the time youngsters are old enough to play with one another, they show aggression. When 1- and 2-year-olds play, conflicts frequently arise over contested playthings, and youngsters often use aggression to resolve their conflicts (Coie & Dodge, 1998). **In *instrumental aggression*, a child uses aggression to achieve an explicit goal.** Instrumental aggression would include shoving a child to get at the head of a lunch line or, as shown in the photo, grabbing a toy away from another child. By the start of the elementary-school years, another form of aggression emerges (Coie et al., 1991). *Hostile aggression* **is unprovoked and seems that its sole goal is to**

VIDEO 12.2

Bullying

VIDEO 12.3

Reactive
aggression

VIDEO 12.4

Relational
aggression

**intimidate, harass, or humiliate another child.** Hostile aggression is illustrated by a child who spontaneously says, "You're stupid!" and then kicks the other child. **Yet another common type of aggression is *reactive aggression*, in which one child's behavior leads to another child's aggression.** Reactive aggression would include a child who loses a game and then punches the child who won, or a child not chosen for the starring role in a play kicking the child who was selected.

Instrumental, hostile, and reactive aggression are most likely to be expressed physically in younger children. As children get older, they more often use language to express their aggression (Dodge, Coie, & Tremblay, 2006). **A particularly common form of verbal aggression is *relational aggression*, in which children try to hurt others by undermining their social relationships.** In relational aggression, which is more typical of girls than boys, children try to hurt others by telling friends to avoid a particular classmate, by spreading malicious gossip, or by making remarks meant to hurt others (Crick et al., 2004). Two true stories from my child-development students portray relational aggression. After a heated argument in second grade, one student's former friend had written "Erin is a big jerk" in block letters on the sidewalk where everyone walking to school would see the message. Another student, Beth, told me that after she'd beaten a classmate in the fifth-grade spelling bee, the classmate's friends formed the "I hate Beth" club.

**STABILITY OF AGGRESSION OVER TIME.**   Forms of aggression change with development, but individual children's tendencies to behave aggressively are stable over time, particularly among those children who are highly aggressive at a young age. Each of the following longitudinal studies shows that many aggressive young children grow up to be adolescents and adults who are aggressive, sometimes violent, and often commit crimes:

- In a study of about 500 boys growing up in Pittsburgh (Raine et al., 2005), among the 7-year-olds judged by their teachers to be highly aggressive, more than half had committed serious acts of delinquency (e.g., stealing a car, attacking others with the aim to hurt or kill) by age 17.
- In a study of more than 900 Canadian girls (Coté et al., 2001), 6-year-olds who had been rated by their teachers as frequently disrupting class (e.g., they were disobedient or they bullied classmates) were 4 to 5 times more likely to be diagnosed, as teenagers, with conduct disorder, a disorder in which individuals are chronically aggressive, destroy property, and lie or steal.
- In a study involving more than 1000 Swedish 10-year-olds (Stattin & Magnusson, 1989), nearly half of the boys rated as most aggressive by their teachers had, as adults, committed major offenses such as assault, theft, or robbery.

*Highly aggressive children often grow up to be adults who are aggressive, violent, and commit crimes.*

Violent behavior in adulthood is not the only long-term outcome of childhood aggression; poor adjustment to high school (e.g., dropping out, failing a grade) and unemployment are others (Ladd, 2003). In one study, aggressive 8-year-olds tended to do poorly in high school, leaving them few options for work as young adults and putting them at risk for problem drinking. By their early 30s, many highly aggressive 8-year-olds had been unemployed for more than 2 years (Kokko & Pulkkinen, 2000).

Findings from these and similar studies show that aggression is *not* simply a case of playful pushing and shoving that children always outgrow. To the contrary, a small minority of children who are highly aggressive develop into young adults who create havoc in society. What causes children to behave aggressively? Let's look at some of the roots of aggressive behavior.

## Roots of Aggressive Behavior

Psychologists once believed that aggression was caused by frustration. The idea was that when children or adults were blocked from achieving a goal, they became frustrated and they aggressed, often against the interfering person or object. Today, however, scientists look to many other causes, including biological factors, the family, the child's community and culture, and the child's own thoughts.

**BIOLOGICAL CONTRIBUTIONS.**   *Born to be Bad* is the title of at least two movies, two CDs (one by George Thorogood and one by Joan Jett), and three books. Implicit in this popular title is the idea that from birth some individuals follow a developmental track that leads to destructive, violent, or criminal behavior. In other words, the claim is that biology sets the stage for people to be aggressive long before experience can affect development.

Is there any truth to this idea? In fact, biology and heredity *do* contribute to aggressive and violent behavior, but not in the manner suggested by the epithet "born to be bad." Twin studies make it clear that heredity contributes: Identical twins are usually more alike in their levels of physical aggression than are fraternal twins (Dionne et al., 2002). But these studies do not tell us that aggression per se is inherited; instead they indicate that some children inherit factors that place them at risk for aggressive or violent behavior. Temperament seems to be one such factor: Youngsters who are temperamentally difficult, overly emotional, or inattentive are, for example, more likely to be aggressive (Campbell, 2000; Olson et al., 2000). And levels of hormones contribute: Boys with higher levels of the hormone testosterone are often more irritable and have greater body mass (Olweus et al., 1988; Tremblay et al., 1998).

Neither difficult temperament nor higher levels of testosterone *cause* a child to be aggressive. But they do make aggressive behavior more likely: For instance, children who are emotional and easily irritated may be disliked by their peers and be in frequent conflict with them, opening the door for aggressive responses. Thus, biological factors place children at risk for aggression; to understand which children actually become aggressive, we need to look elsewhere.

**IMPACT OF THE FAMILY.**   Although few parents deliberately teach their children to harm others, early family experiences are a prime training ground for learning patterns of aggression. Parents' approach to discipline is crucial. When parents use physical punishment or threats to discipline their children, the hidden message to children is that physical force "works" as a means of controlling others. A parent like the one in the photo is saying, in effect, "The best way to get people to do what you want is to hurt them" (Patterson, 2002). In one study (Dodge, Bates, & Pettit, 1990) children who had been punished so harshly that they were injured were rated twice as aggressive as children who had not experienced such harsh punishment. But strong or aggressive parental responses are not essential in making a child aggressive. When parents are coercive, unresponsive, and emotionally uninvested, their children are more likely to be aggressive (Hart et al., 1998; Rubin, Bukowski, & Parker, 1998).

In many families with aggressive children, a vicious circle seems to develop. Compared to families with nonaggressive children, both aggressive children and their parents are more likely to respond to neutral behavior with aggression. What's more, after an aggressive exchange has begun, both parents and children are likely to escalate the exchange, rather than break it off. And once a child has been labeled aggressive by parents and others, that child is more likely

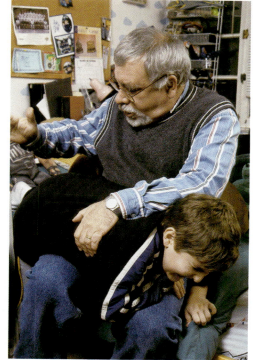

When parents often use physical punishment, their children are more likely to become aggressive.

to be accused of aggression and to be singled out for punishment, even when the child has been behaving entirely appropriately on the occasion in question (Patterson, 2002). The "aggressive child" will be accused of all things that go wrong—from missing cookies to broken appliances—and other children's misbehaviors will be ignored.

Parents contribute to children's aggressive behavior by using physical punishment and by failing to monitor their children's behavior.

Another aspect of parental behavior that's been linked to aggression is *monitoring*, which refers to parents' knowledge of where their children are, what they're doing, and who they're with. When parents don't monitor their children's behavior, this is associated with more frequent aggression (Pettit et al., 2001). Of course, monitoring requires children's cooperation to a certain extent and children who are chronically aggressive often do not cooperate (e.g., teenagers not answering their cell phones when they see that a parent is calling), in part because they see monitoring as intrusive (Laird et al., 2003).

So far we've seen that children's aggression is linked to parents' use of physical punishment and to their lack of monitoring. To this list we need to add another critical aspect of family life—the presence of conflict. When parents constantly argue and fight, their children are much more likely to be aggressive (Ingoldsby et al., 1999). Of course, children have ringside seats for many of these confrontations and thus they can see firsthand how parents use verbal and physical aggression against each other. And, sadly, children come to believe that these patterns of interacting represent "natural" ways of solving problems within a family (Graham-Bermann & Brescoll, 2000).

**INFLUENCE OF COMMUNITY AND CULTURE.** Parents are hardly alone in giving important lessons about aggression. Other influential voices within children's lives deliver powerful messages about aggressive behavior.

- *Television and media games.* Most TV programs targeted for children contain acts of physical aggression (Wilson et al., 2002). And the average American youngster will see several *thousand* murders on TV before reaching adolescence (Waters, 1993). (If you find these numbers hard to believe, try the activities described in "See for Yourself" at the end of the chapter.) What does research tell us about this steady diet of televised mayhem and violence? Will Reza, the avid cartoon watcher in the vignette at the beginning of the module, become more aggressive? Or, as his father believes, is his TV watching simply fun? In fact, longitudinal studies have consistently found that children exposed to much media violence often grow up to be aggressive and violent adults. This is true even when confounding variables such as parents' education and family income are controlled. What's more, playing violent video games seems to lead to aggressive violent behavior in much the same way that watching violent TV does (Anderson et al., 2003). In short, Reza's father is clearly wrong: Frequent exposure to media violence makes children more aggressive.

- *Peers.* Aggressive children often befriend other aggressive children. The outcome is hardly surprising: Aggressive friends support and encourage each other's aggressive behavior (Bagwell, 2004; Gifford-Smith et al., 2005). Just as friends drawn together by a mutual interest in music enjoy listening to CDs together, friends whose common bond is their aggressive behavior enjoy teaming up to attack their peers. Aggressive adolescents often join gangs, which has a catalytic effect on aggressive and violent behavior. That is, even though adolescents who join gangs are already aggressive, their membership in a gang leads to more frequent and more violent antisocial behavior (Thornberry et al., 2003).

- *Poverty.*   Aggressive and antisocial behavior is more common among children living in poverty than among children who are economically advantaged (Keiley et al., 2000). Some of the impact of poverty can be explained by factors that we've already considered. For example, living in poverty is extremely stressful for parents and often leads to the very parental behaviors that promote aggression—harsh discipline and lax monitoring (Tolan, Gorman-Smith, & Henry, 2003). But other links from poverty to violent behavior are new. For example, violent crime is far more common in poverty-stricken neighborhoods. Older children and adolescents exposed to such violence are, as they get older, more likely to be aggressive and violent themselves (Binghenheimer, Brennan, & Earls, 2005).

**COGNITIVE PROCESSES.**   The perceptual and cognitive skills described in Chapters 6 through 8 also play a role in aggression. Dodge, Bates, and Pettit (1990) were the first to explore the cognitive aspects of aggression. They discovered that aggressive boys often respond aggressively because they are not skilled at interpreting other people's intentions and, without a clear interpretation in mind, they respond aggressively by default. That is, aggressive boys far too often think, "I don't know what you're up to, and, when in doubt, attack." In the "Spotlight on Theories" feature, we'll learn more about a theory of cognitive processing that's helping to reveal how aggressive children think about other people.

## *Spotlight on Theories*
## Social Information Processing Theory and Children's Aggressive Behavior

### BACKGROUND
Genetics, parents, TV, peers, and poverty all contribute to make some children prone to aggression. What these influences have in common is that they lead some children to see the world as a hostile place in which they must be wary of other people. But precisely characterizing the aggressive child's hostile view has been a challenge.

### THE THEORY
To explain how children perceive, interpret, and respond to people, Nicki R. Crick and Kenneth Dodge (1994; Dodge & Crick, 1990; Dodge & Rabiner, 2004) formulated an information-processing model of children's thinking, which is shown in the diagram on page 390. According to the model, responding to a social stimulus involves several steps. First, children selectively attend to certain features of the social stimulus but do not attend to others. Second, children try to interpret the features that they have processed; that is, they try to give meaning to the social stimulus. Third, children evaluate their goals for the situation. Fourth, children retrieve from memory a behavioral response that is associated with the interpretation and goals of the situation. Fifth, children evaluate this response to determine if it is appropriate. Finally, the child proceeds with the behavior.

Applied to aggressive children, the theory says that aggressive children's processing is biased and restricted in many of the steps in the diagram and that this flawed information processing is part of what leads these children to be more aggressive: They systematically misperceive people's actions (Crick & Werner, 1998; Egan, Monson, & Perry, 1998).

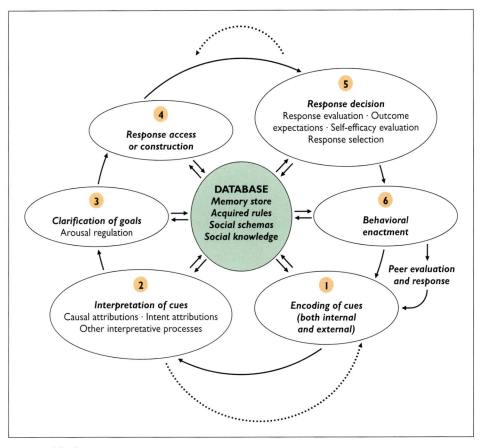

Figure 12-4

**HYPOTHESIS:** According to social-information-processing theory, aggressive children's processing of social information (e.g., people) is biased in each of the stages depicted in the diagram. In the second stage of processing—interpretation of cues—this bias leads to the hypothesis that aggressive children should interpret cues in hostile terms when this interpretation is not warranted. For example, when another child has broken a toy and has a surprised, chagrined look on her face, an aggressive child should be more likely than a nonaggressive child to believe that the child broke the toy on purpose.

**TEST:** Crick, Grotpeter, and Bigbee (2002) evaluated this hypothesis by presenting hypothetical scenarios to physically aggressive and nonaggressive elementary-school children. In each scenario, a child's action led to undesirable consequences but the child's intentions are not clearly specified. For example, in one scenario, the participating child was asked to imagine overhearing two children talking about a party to which the participating child had not been invited. Children in the study were asked why the children in the scenario had acted this way and whether they were being mean. Aggressive children were much more likely to believe that children in the scenario were being mean and that they had hostile intentions (e.g., "they're not inviting me so they can get back at me") but nonaggressive children usually believed that children in the scenario had benign intentions (e.g., "They're gonna invite me; they just haven't yet").

CONCLUSION: When confronted with situations in which a person's intentions aren't clear, aggressive children often believe that others are acting for hostile reasons. In other words, for aggressive children, seeing others as "out to get them" often seems to be a default interpretation of ambiguous social situations.

APPLICATION: If aggressive children are unskilled at interpreting and responding to others' actions, would training in these skills improve their social behavior? The answer seems to be "yes" (Dodge & Crick, 1990). One approach is to teach aggressive children that aggression is painful and does not solve problems, that intentions can be understood by attending to relevant cues, and that there are more effective, prosocial ways to solve interpersonal disputes. In a study by Guerra and Slaby (1990), adolescents incarcerated for committing violent acts received training designed to increase their understanding of social situations. For example, they were taught to pay attention to nonhostile cues in a social situation, to think of alternative ways of responding to social problems, and to evaluate responses in terms of their consequences. Supervisors at the correctional facility judged that the adolescents were better adjusted following training than before. They were less aggressive, less impulsive, and more flexible in their solutions. ■

> Aggressive children often interpret neutral behavior in hostile terms.

Improving social skills in aggressive adolescents is beneficial, but in the long run a more productive approach is to teach young children constructive ways to resolve conflicts without relying on aggression. An example of this approach is Fast Track (Conduct Problems Prevention Research Group, 2004), a program designed to teach first-grade children to understand and regulate their emotions and to help them learn effective social skills (e.g., how to make friends, how to share). This training reduced aggressive and disruptive behavior in classrooms; plus, the participating children had improved social skills and more successful peer interactions.

## Victims of Aggression

Every aggressive act is directed at someone. Most schoolchildren are the targets of an occasional aggressive act—a shove or kick to gain a desired toy, or a stinging insult by someone trying to save face. However, a small percentage of children are chronic targets of bullying. In both Europe and the United States, about 10% of elementary-school children and adolescents are chronic victims of aggression (Kochenderfer & Ladd, 1996; Olweus, 1994). Dorothy Allison provides a frightening glimpse of this victimization in her novel *Bastard Out of Carolina.* As Shannon got on the school bus, she walked

> past a dozen hooting boys and another dozen flushed and whispering girls. As she made her way up the aisle, I watched each boy slide to the end of his seat to block her sitting with him and every girl flinch away as if whatever Shannon had might be catching. In the seat ahead of us Danny Yarboro leaned far over into the aisle and began making retching noises. "Cootie train! Cootie train" somebody yelled as the bus lurched into motion and Shannon still hadn't found a seat (pp. 153–154).

In this episode, Shannon is the victim of verbal bullying. But victimization by physical force also occurs frequently: Think of a child who is beat up daily on the

**12.4**  Brandon is constantly picked on by other kids at his school: The girls tease him and the boys often start fights with him. What could he and his parents do to improve his peer relations?

playground. And other children are chronic targets of relational aggression: Think of children who are constantly the subject of rumors spread by their classmates (Crick, Casas, & Nelson, 2002).

As you can imagine, being tormented daily by their peers is hard on children. Research consistently shows that children who are chronic victims of aggression are often lonely, anxious, and depressed; they dislike school; and they have low self-esteem (Graham & Juvonen, 1998; Ladd & Ladd, 1998). And, although most children are happier when no longer victimized, the harmful effects linger for some children: They are still lonely and sad despite not having been victims for 1 or 2 years (Kochenderfer-Ladd & Wardrop, 2001).

Why do some children suffer the sad fate of being victims? Some victims are actually aggressive themselves (Olweus, 1978; Schwartz et al., 1997). These youngsters often overreact, are restless, and are easily irritated. Their aggressive peers

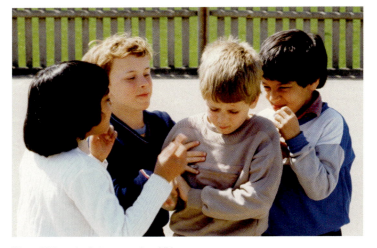

When children give in to aggressive children, they often become chronic victims of aggression.

soon learn that these children are easily baited. A group of children will, for example, insult or ridicule them, knowing that they will probably start a fight even though they are outnumbered. Other victims tend to be withdrawn and submissive. They are unwilling or unable to defend themselves from their peers' aggression, and so they are usually referred to as passive victims (Ladd & Ladd, 1998; Olweus, 1978). When attacked, like the child in the photo, they show obvious signs of distress and usually give in to their attackers, thereby rewarding the aggressive behavior. Thus, both aggressive and withdrawn–submissive children end up as victims; and this pattern holds for children in China as well as for children in North America (Schwartz, Chang, & Farver, 2001).

How do children end up as victims? Family history and parenting help decide. To understand these forces, we need to distinguish victims who overreact from those who respond passively, and within the latter group, distinguish boys from girls. Victims who overreact often come from hostile, punitive, or even abusive family environments (Schwartz et al., 1997). Among passive victims, boys tend to have mothers who are overprotective or emotionally overinvolved with them; in contrast, girls who are passive victims tend to have mothers who are controlling and unresponsive (Ladd & Ladd, 1998).

**Some children who are chronic victims of aggression overreact when provoked; others withdraw and submit to aggression.**

Some victims try to cope with the problem themselves, but this is complicated because different strategies seem to work best for boys and girls (Kochenderfer-Ladd & Skinner, 2002). One strategy for victimized children is to turn to peers for support, by telling them how it feels to be victimized or by asking them for help directly. This strategy works for girls but backfires for boys: Boys' classmates like them even less as a result, perhaps because boys are expected to cope with problems alone and peers shun boys who seek help. A strategy that has costs and benefits for boys is ignoring the victimization—pretending that it's not happening or saying that it doesn't matter. When victimized boys do this, they tend to be more anxious (the cost) but their peers like them more (the benefit).

Rather than letting children cope alone with victimization (using strategies that may or may not work), a better approach is to teach victimized children ways of dealing with aggression that are more effective than either overreacting or withdrawing passively (e.g., don't lash out when you're insulted; don't show that you're afraid when you're threatened). In addition, increasing self-esteem can help. When attacked, children with low self-esteem may think, "I'm a loser and have to put up with this because I have no choice." Increasing children's self-esteem makes them less tolerant of personal attacks (Egan & Perry, 1998). Finally, one of the easiest ways to help victims is to foster their friendships with peers. When children have friends, they're not as likely to be victimized (Bollmer et al., 2005).

Throughout this module, we've seen the harm caused by aggression: Victims are hurt and children who are chronically aggressive often lead problem-filled lives. Yet, the research described in this module has also identified many of the roots of aggressive behavior and suggested how children can learn other, more constructive ways to interact with peers.

## CHECK YOUR LEARNING

**RECALL** Describe the different forms of aggression and the ages when they typically appear.

Summarize the primary phases of decision making in Crick and Dodge's information-processing model and the biases that are found in aggressive children's decision making.

**INTERPRET** Compare the impact of nature and nurture on children's aggressive behavior.

**APPLY** Suppose that a group of elementary-school teachers wanted to know how to reduce the amount of aggressive behavior in their classrooms. What advice would you give them?

In the short term, Brandon should try to look and act as if the teasing and fighting doesn't bother him; in the longer term, one of the best things he can do is to make more friends in his class.

**12.4**

## ≋ UNIFYING THEMES: Continuity

This chapter has some nice illustrations of the theme that *early development is related to later development but not perfectly*. For example, we learned on page 367 that preschoolers who were best able to delay gratification were, as adolescents, less likely to yield to temptation and to be distractible. Yet the correlations were far from 1, which means that many preschoolers who quickly gave into temptation became adolescents who were not distractible. The same conclusion is evident in the results of longitudinal studies of aggressive children (page 386). Many of these children commit serious crimes as adults, but not all do. Behaving aggressively in childhood definitely increases the odds of adult criminal activity, but it does not guarantee it.

## SEE FOR YOURSELF

This assignment may seem like a dream come true—you are being required to watch TV. Pick an evening when you can watch network television programming from 8 until 10 P.M. (prime time). Your job is to count each instance of (a) physical force by one person against another and (b) threats of harm to compel another to act against his or her will. Select one network randomly and watch the program for 10 minutes. Then turn to another network and watch that program for 10 minutes. Continue changing the channels every 10 minutes until the 2 hours are over. Of course, it won't be easy to follow the plots of all these programs, but you will end up with a wider sample of programming this way. Repeat this procedure on a Saturday morning when you can watch 2 hours of children's cartoons (not *South Park!*).

Now simply divide the total number of aggressive acts by 4 to estimate the amount of aggression per hour. Then multiply this figure by 11,688 to estimate the number of aggressive acts seen by an average adolescent by age 19. (Why 11,688? Two hours of daily TV viewing—a very conservative number—multiplied by 365 days and 16 years.) Then ponder the possible results of that very large number. If your parents told you, nearly 12,000 times, that stealing was okay, would you be more likely to steal? Probably. Then what are the consequences of massive exposure to the televised message, "Solve conflicts with aggression"? See for yourself!

## RESOURCES

For more information about . . .

**people who have devoted their lives to helping others,** read Anne Colby and William Damon's *Some Who Do Care: Contemporary Lives of Moral Commitment* (The Free Press, 1992). The authors, developmental psychologists interested in moral development, use biographies of humanitarians to identify the forces that make some people commit their lives to helping others.

**children's aggression,** visit the Web site of the National Youth Violence Prevention Resource Center
http://www.safeyouth.org/scripts/teens.asp
which is sponsored by Centers for Disease Control and Prevention and other agencies of the United States government.

## KEY TERMS

aggression  385
altruism  380
conventional level  372
empathic orientation  377
empathy  381
hedonistic orientation  376
hostile aggression  385
immanent justice  370
instrumental aggression  385
Just Communities  379
monitoring  388
moral realism  370

moral relativism  370
needs-oriented orientation  376
personal domain  377
postconventional level  372
preconventional level  372
prosocial behavior  380
reactive aggression  386
relational aggression  386
self-control  364
social conventions  377
stereotyped, approval-focused orientation  377

# SUMMARY

## 12.1 SELF-CONTROL

### Beginnings of Self-Control

At 1 year, infants are first aware that others impose demands on them; by 3 years, youngsters can devise plans to regulate their behavior. During the school-age years, children become better able to control their behavior.

Children differ in their self-control, but individuals are fairly consistent over time: Preschoolers who have good self-control tend to become adolescents and adults with good self-control.

### Influences on Self-Control

Children who have the best self-control tend to have parents who are loving, set limits, and discuss discipline with them. When parents are overly strict, their children have less self-control, not more.

Temperament helps determine how parents influence their children's self-control. With temperamentally fearful children, gentle reminders are effective; with fearless children, parents should appeal to the attachment relationship.

### Improving Children's Self-Control

Children are better able to regulate their own behavior when they have plans to help them remember the importance of the goal and something to distract them from tempting objects.

## 12.2 REASONING ABOUT MORAL ISSUES

### Piaget's Views

Piaget theorized that 5- to 7-year-olds are in a stage of moral realism. They believe that rules are created by wise adults; therefore, rules must be followed and cannot be changed. At about 8 years, children enter a stage of moral relativism, believing that rules are created by people to help them get along.

### Kohlberg's Theory

Kohlberg proposed that moral reasoning includes preconventional, conventional, and postconventional levels. Moral reasoning is first based on rewards and punishments, and, later, on personal moral codes. As predicted by Kohlberg's theory, people progress through the stages in sequence and do not regress, and morally advanced reasoning is associated with more frequent moral behavior. However, few people attain the most advanced levels, and cultures differ in the bases for moral reasoning.

### Beyond Kohlberg's Theory

Gilligan proposed that females' moral reasoning is based on caring and responsibility for others, not justice. Research does not support consistent sex differences, but has found that males and females both consider caring as well as justice in their moral judgments, depending on the situation.

According to Eisenberg, children's reasoning about prosocial dilemmas shifts from a self-interested, hedonistic orientation to concern for others based on empathy.

During the preschool years, children differentiate moral rules, social conventions, and personal choices. They believe, for example, that social conventions can be changed but moral rules cannot. And they understand that breaking a moral rule produces a harsher punishment than breaking a social convention.

### Promoting Moral Reasoning

Many factors can promote more sophisticated moral reasoning, including observing others reason at more advanced levels, and discussing moral issues with peers, teachers, and parents.

## 12.3 HELPING OTHERS

### Development of Prosocial Behavior

Even toddlers know when others are upset, and they try to offer comfort. As children grow older, they more often see the need to act prosocially and are more likely to have the skills to do so.

### Skills Underlying Prosocial Behavior

Children are more likely to behave prosocially when they are able to take others' perspectives, are empathic, and have more advanced moral reasoning.

### Situational Influences

Children's prosocial behavior is often influenced by situational characteristics. Children more often behave prosocially when they feel that they should and can help, when they are in a good mood, and when they believe that they have little to lose by helping.

### Socializing Prosocial Behavior

Parenting approaches that promote prosocial behavior include modeling prosocial behavior, using reasoning in discipline, and giving children frequent opportunities inside and outside the home to use their prosocial skills.

## 12.4 AGGRESSION

### Change and Stability

Typical forms of aggression in young children include instrumental, hostile, and reactive aggression. As children grow older, physical aggression decreases and relational aggression becomes more common. Overall levels of aggression are fairly stable, which means that very aggressive young children often become involved in criminal activities as adolescents and adults.

### Roots of Aggressive Behavior

Children's aggressive behavior has many sources: genetics, harsh parenting, viewing violence on TV and in other media, aggressive peers, living in poverty, and biased interpretation of people's behavior.

### Victims of Aggression

Children who are chronic targets of aggression are often lonely and anxious. Some victims of aggression tend to overreact when provoked; others tend to withdraw and submit. Victimization can be overcome by increasing children's social skills, their self-esteem, and their number of friends.

**You barely have the phone to your ear before your brother-in-law shouts, "Camille had the baby!"**

"A boy or a girl?" you ask. Why are people so interested in a baby's sex? The answer is that being a boy or girl is not simply a biological distinction. **Instead, these terms are associated with distinct *social roles* which are cultural guidelines for people's behavior. Starting in infancy, children learn about *gender roles*—behaviors considered appropriate for males and females.** As youngsters learn these roles, they begin to identify with one of these groups. **Children forge a *gender identity*, the perception of oneself as either male or female.**

In this chapter, we will see how children acquire a gender role and a gender identity. We'll begin, in Module 13.1, by considering cultural stereotypes of males and females. In Module 13.2, we will examine actual psychological differences between boys and girls. In Module 13.3, we'll focus on how children come to identify with one sex. Finally, in Module 13.4, we'll discuss recent changes in gender roles. Throughout this chapter, I'll use *sex* to refer to aspects of males and females that are clearly biological (such as differences in anatomy) and the term *gender* to refer to all other characteristics that relate to maleness and femaleness.

**13.1**     **Gender Stereotypes**

**13.2**     **Differences Related to Gender**

**13.3**     **Gender Identity**

**13.4**     **Gender Roles in Transition**

1    The Science of Child Development

2    Genetic Bases of Child Development

3    Prenatal Development, Birth, and the Newborn

4    Growth and Health

5    Perceptual and Motor Development

6    Theories of Cognitive Development

7    Cognitive Processes and Academic Skills

8    Intelligence and Individual Differences in Cognition

9    Language and Communication

10    Emotional Development

11    Understanding Self and Others

12    Moral Understanding and Behavior

# Gender
# and Development

14    Family Relationships

15    Influences Beyond the Family

13

# 13.1 GENDER STEREOTYPES

**How Do We View Men and Women?**

**Learning Gender Stereotypes**

## LEARNING OBJECTIVES

- What are gender stereotypes, and how do they differ for males and females?
- How do gender stereotypes influence behavior?
- When do children learn their culture's stereotypes for males and females?

*When Nancy was 7 months pregnant, her 11-year-old son, Clark, announced that he really wanted a brother, not a sister. Clark explained, "A sister would drive me crazy. Girls never make up their minds about stuff, and they get all worked up over nothin'." "Where did Clark get these ideas?" Nancy wondered. "Is this typical for 11-year-olds?"*

**All cultures have *gender stereotypes*—beliefs about how males and females differ in personality traits, interests, and behaviors.** Of course, because stereotypes are beliefs, they may or may not be true. In this module, we'll look at the features associated with gender stereotypes and discover when children like Clark learn about gender stereotypes.

## How Do We View Men and Women?

"Terry is active, independent, competitive, and aggressive." As you were reading this sentence, you probably assumed that Terry was a male. Why? Although Terry is a common name for both males and females, the adjectives used to describe Terry are more commonly associated with men than with women. In fact, more than 30 years of research shows that most adults associate different traits with men and women (Best, 2001; Lueptow, Garovich-Szabo, & Lueptow, 2001; Lutz & Ruble, 1995). Men are said to be independent, competitive, aggressive, outgoing, ambitious, self-confident, and dominant. **These male-associated traits are called *instrumental* because they describe individuals who act on the world and influence it.** In contrast, women are said to be emotional, kind, creative, considerate, gentle, excitable, and aware of others' feelings. **Female-associated traits are called *expressive*, because they describe emotional functioning and individuals who value interpersonal relationships.**

In the "Cultural Influences" feature, we'll see whether these views are shared by adults worldwide.

### *Cultural Influences*
**Around the World With Four Gender Stereotypes**

Are men seen as aggressive and independent worldwide? And are women seen as emotional and gentle worldwide? Or are these stereotypes of men and women unique to the United States? John Williams and Deborah Best (1990) addressed these questions in an ambitious project involving 300 different traits and participants in 30 countries. The graphs on page 399 present the results for just 4 traits and 7 countries. You can see that each trait shows considerable cultural variation. For example, virtually all American participants consider men aggressive, but only a slight majority of Nigerian participants do. Thus, American views of men and

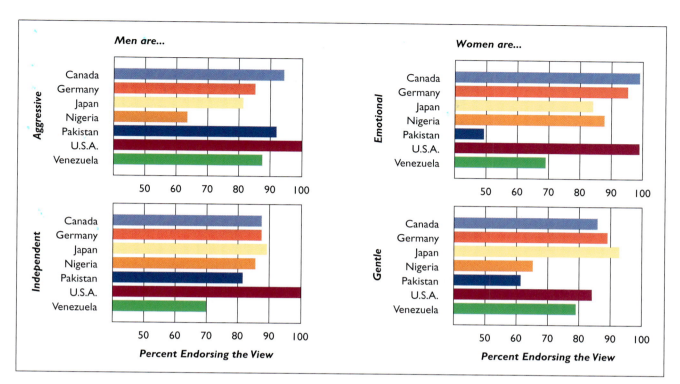

FIGURE 13-1

women are not shared worldwide. In fact, what's notable about the research results is that Americans' gender stereotypes are more extreme than are those in any other country listed. Keep this in mind as you think about what men and women can and cannot do and what they should and should not do. Your ideas about gender are shaped by your culture's beliefs, which are not held universally. ▪

Understanding our tendency to stereotype gender behavior is important because stereotypes are very limiting (Smith & Mackie, 2000). If we have stereotyped views, we expect males to act in particular ways and females to act in other ways, and we respond to males and females solely on the basis of gender, not as individuals. For example, do you assume the youngster in the photo is a girl based on her taste in toys? Assuming the child is a girl would, in turn, probably lead you to think she plays more quietly and is more easily frightened than if you assume the child is a boy (Stern & Karraker, 1989). Making stereotyped assumptions about gender leads to a whole host of inferences about behavior and personality that may not be true.

When do children begin to learn their culture's stereotypes for males and females? We'll answer this question in the next section.

## Learning Gender Stereotypes

Children don't live in a gender-neutral world for long. Although 12-month-old boys and girls look equally at gender-stereotyped toys, 18-month-olds do not: Girls look longer at pictures of dolls than pictures of trucks but boys look longer at pictures of trucks (Serbin et al., 2001). By 4 years, children's knowledge of gender-stereotyped activities is extensive: They believe that

Gender stereotypes lead us to assume that this child is a girl simply because the child is playing with a doll.

girls play hopscotch but that boys play football; girls help bake cookies but boys take out the trash; and women feed babies but men chop wood (Gelman, Taylor, & Nguyen, 2004). And they've begun to learn about behaviors and traits that are stereotypically masculine or feminine. Preschoolers believe that boys are more often aggressive physically but girls tend to be aggressive verbally (Giles & Heyman, 2005).

During the elementary school years, children expand their knowledge of gender-stereotyped traits and behaviors; by the time they enter middle school, their ideas of gender stereotypes are virtually as well formed as those of adults. Children's growing understanding of gender stereotypes was demonstrated in a study by Deborah Best and her colleagues (1977). Children were asked if 16 stereotypically masculine and 16 stereotypically feminine traits were more typical of boys or girls. At age 5, boys and girls judged one third of the traits the way adults would; by age 11, they judged about 90% of the traits according to adult stereotypes. The table shows the traits that children judged stereotypically at ages 5 and 11. A check means that boys and girls agreed with the listed stereotype.

**TABLE 13-1**

### CHILDREN'S STEREOTYPES OF BOYS AND GIRLS

| Boys are . . . | 5-year-olds | 11-year-olds | Girls are . . . | 5-year-olds | 11-year-olds |
|---|:---:|:---:|---|:---:|:---:|
| strong | ✓ | ✓ | emotional | ✓ | ✓ |
| aggressive | ✓ | ✓ | gentle | ✓ | ✓ |
| disorderly | ✓ | ✓ | soft-hearted | ✓ | ✓ |
| cruel | ✓ | ✓ | affectionate | ✓ | ✓ |
| coarse | ✓ | ✓ | weak | ✓ | ✓ |
| ambitious | ✓ | ✓ | appreciative | | ✓ |
| dominant | ✓ | ✓ | excitable | | ✓ |
| adventurous | | ✓ | sophisticated | | ✓ |
| independent | | ✓ | fickle | | ✓ |
| loud | | ✓ | meek | | ✓ |
| boastful | | ✓ | submissive | | ✓ |
| jolly | | ✓ | whiny | | ✓ |
| steady | | ✓ | talkative | | ✓ |
| confident | | ✓ | frivolous | | ✓ |

Source: Based on Best et al., 1977.

**13.1**   Abigail believes that girls are gentler than boys, that boys are stronger than girls, but that boys and girls are equally talkative and confident. With these stereotypes, how old is Abigail likely to be?

Obviously, by 11 years, children have adultlike knowledge of gender stereotypes; in this regard, Clark's view of girls in the opening vignette is quite typical for his age. Children understand gender stereotypes by the time they enter kindergarten, and their understanding grows throughout the elementary-school years (Etaugh & Liss, 1992).

During the elementary-school years, children also learn that the traits and occupations associated with males tend to have higher social status than those associated with females. They learn, for example, that lawyers and engineers have more social status than social workers and flight attendants. Children apparently learn a simple rule—something like "Jobs for men are more prestigious than jobs for women"—because children learning unfamiliar jobs (e.g., a chandler makes candles) rate these occupations as more prestigious if they're illustrated with men than with women (Liben, Bigler, & Krogh, 2001).

As children develop, they also begin to understand that gender stereotypes do not always apply; older children are more willing than younger children to ignore stereotypes when judging other children. For example, told about a boy who likes to play with girls and pretend to iron, preschoolers think he would still want to play with masculine toys. By the middle elementary-school years, however, children realize that this boy's interests are not stereotypic and he would rather play with stereotypically feminine toys (Martin, 1989).

Thus, although older children are more familiar with gender stereotypes, they see these stereotypes as general guidelines for behavior that are not necessarily binding for all boys and girls (Signorella, Bigler, & Liben, 1993; Taylor, 1996). In fact, older children consider gender stereotypes less binding than many social conventions and moral rules (Levy, Taylor, & Gelman, 1995; Serbin, Powlishta, & Gulko, 1993). This change is due to cognitive growth: As we saw in Module 11.3, in the context of views of different racial and ethnic groups, older children's cognitive development allows them to understand that stereotypes are generalizations that do not necessarily apply to all people (Bigler & Liben, 1992).

Increased age is not the only factor leading to more flexible views of stereotypes. Girls tend to be more flexible about stereotypes (Ruble & Martin, 1998), perhaps because they see that male-stereotyped traits are more attractive and have more status than female-stereotyped traits. Social class also contributes. Adolescents and young adults (but not children) from middle-class homes tend to have more flexible ideas about gender than individuals from lower class homes (e.g., Serbin et al., 1993). This difference may be due to education: Better-educated middle-class parents may impart less rigid views of gender to their children.

Ethnicity is another factor associated with flexible views of gender. Some studies find that African American youngsters have more flexible ideas about gender than their European American peers (e.g., Bardwell, Cochran, & Walker, 1986). Compared to European American mothers, African American mothers are more frequently employed outside the home and this may contribute to their children's more open attitudes.

At this point, perhaps you're wondering whether there's any truth to gender stereotypes. For example, are boys really more dominant than girls? Are girls really more excitable than boys? For answers to these questions, let's go to Module 13.2.

> By the end of elementary school, children know adults' stereotypes of males and females and understand that these stereotypes are not binding on individuals.

## CHECK YOUR LEARNING

RECALL  How do older children's gender stereotypes differ from those of younger children?

What groups of children tend to have more flexible views of gender stereotypes?

INTERPRET  Compare and contrast instrumental traits with expressive traits.

APPLY  Examine the traits listed in the table on page 400. How might Piaget have explained the differences between 5- and 11-year-olds' responses?

**13.1** She's probably about 5. (A more conservative estimate would be to say that she's in the early elementary school years.) The logic behind this estimate is that she has learned some of the typical stereotypes of boys and girls (e.g., that girls are gentler than boys) but has yet to learn others (e.g., that boys are more confident than girls).

## 13.2    DIFFERENCES RELATED TO GENDER

Differences in Physical Development and Behavior

Differences in Intellectual Abilities and Achievement

Differences in Personality and Social Behavior

Frank Talk about Gender Differences

**LEARNING OBJECTIVES**

- How do boys and girls differ in physical development, intellectual abilities, and social behavior?

- What factors are responsible for these gender differences?

- What are the implications of these gender differences for boys' and girls' development?

*All through elementary and middle school, Darlene was one of the best students. When she moved into high school, she was particularly proud that she always got the highest grades in her math classes. But she noticed that, as each year went by, even though she got the best grades in math, the boys got higher scores on the standardized tests given every spring.*

Is Darlene's experience typical? Do girls usually get higher grades than boys in math class but lower scores on standardized tests? Some of the first answers to these questions came in *The Psychology of Sex Differences*, a book by Eleanor Maccoby and Carol Jacklin published in 1974. Maccoby and Jacklin did no new research; instead, they summarized results from approximately 1,500 research studies that had been done over the years on gender differences. According to Maccoby and Jacklin,

physical differences between the sexes are obvious and universal. The psychological differences are not. The folklore that has grown up about them is often vague and inconsistent. We believe there is a great deal of myth in the popular view about sex differences. There is also some substance. . . . we hope to be able to identify the generalizations that may be relied upon with some confidence (p. 3).

*Maccoby and Jacklin concluded that girls have greater verbal ability but that boys have greater mathematical and spatial ability and are more aggressive.*

Maccoby and Jacklin's method was quite simple: First they searched psychological journals for studies on gender differences. Then they categorized the studies according to the behaviors that were studied and the ages of the children. Finally, they examined the results for gender differences. For example, girls are thought to be more sensitive to touch, but Maccoby and Jacklin found that, in 6 studies of touch sensitivity, infant boys and girls were equally sensitive. In 3 other studies, girls were more sensitive. In 11 studies of older children and adults, 9 found no differences and 2 found that females were more sensitive. Maccoby and Jacklin concluded that "if a sex difference exists in touch sensitivity . . . our survey has revealed only hints of it" (1974, p. 23).

Maccoby and Jacklin examined many studies of cognition and social behavior, concluding that gender differences had been established in only four areas: Girls have greater verbal ability whereas boys have greater mathematical and visual–spatial ability, and boys are more aggressive than girls. Just as important, Maccoby and Jacklin did not find evidence to support popular ideas that girls are more social and suggestible than boys, have lower self-esteem, are less analytic in thinking, and lack achievement motivation.

Some critics challenged Maccoby and Jacklin on the grounds that they had included some weak studies and defined behaviors in ways that other researchers might not (Block, 1976). Others questioned outright findings about some specific behaviors. The debate stimulated more research; some of this research applied new statistical techniques that allowed for finer analysis, such as meta-analysis. Many developmentalists now believe that gender differences are more extensive than Maccoby and Jacklin suggested, but their book remains a classic because its comprehensiveness provided an excellent starting point for further research.

In the remainder of this module, we'll see what we've discovered about gender differences since Maccoby and Jacklin's classic analysis. We'll focus on differences in physical development, cognitive processes, and social behavior.

## Differences in Physical Development and Behavior

Of course, differences in the reproductive system are what differentiate boys and girls, along with differences in secondary sex characteristics such as lower voices and facial hair in boys and breast development and wider hips in girls. Boys are usually larger and stronger than girls, which means that they often physically outperform girls. You can see the difference at high-school track meets: Boys usually run faster, jump higher, and throw objects farther and more accurately. And, as the diagram shows, long before high-school, boys throw and jump farther than girls. Outside of sports, on tasks that involve fine-motor coordination, such as tracing and drawing, girls do better than boys (Thomas & French, 1985).

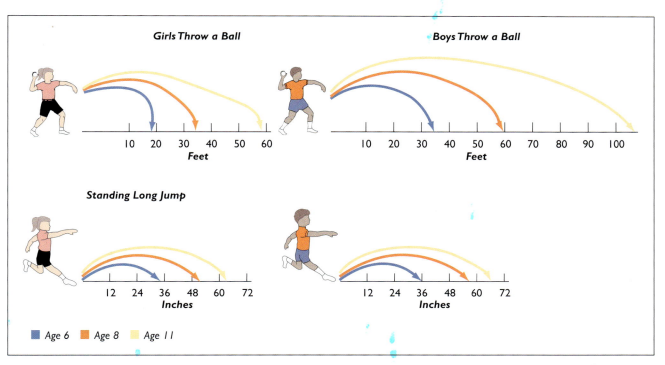

**Girls Throw a Ball**   **Boys Throw a Ball**

Feet   Feet

**Standing Long Jump**

Inches   Inches

■ Age 6   ■ Age 8   ■ Age 11

FIGURE 13-2

Some of the gender differences in gross-motor skills that require strength reflect the fact that as children approach and enter puberty, girls' bodies have proportionately more fat and less muscle than boys' bodies. This difference explains why, for example, boys can hang from a bar using their arms and hands much longer than girls can. However, for other gross-motor skills, such as running, throwing, and catching, body composition is much less important (Smoll & Schutz, 1990). In these cases, children's experience is crucial. During recess, elementary-school girls are

Boys are physically more active than girls, a difference that's evident when you watch children on a playground.

Girls tend to have better reading skills than boys, which may be due to reading often being stereotyped as an activity for girls.

more often found swinging, jumping rope, or perhaps talking quietly in a group; in contrast, boys are playing football or shooting baskets. Many girls and their parents believe that sports and physical fitness are less valuable for girls than boys (Eccles, Jacobs, & Harold, 1990). Consequently, girls spend less time in these sports and fitness-related activities than boys, depriving them of opportunities to practice, which is essential for developing motor skills (Eccles & Harold, 1991).

As infants, boys are more active than girls, and this difference increases during childhood (Eaton & Enns, 1986). For example, in a classroom, boys are more likely than girls to have a hard time sitting still. On playgrounds like those in the photos, boys more often play vigorously and girls, quietly. And, recall from Module 5.2 that boys are three times more likely than girls to be diagnosed with attention deficit hyperactivity disorder.

Girls tend to be healthier than boys. Female embryos are more likely than male embryos to survive prenatal development. This trend continues after birth. Infant boys are more prone to birth complications, and throughout life boys are more prone to many diseases and dysfunctions (Jacklin, 1989). Finally, adolescent boys and young men are more likely to engage in unhealthy, risk-taking behaviors, including drinking, reckless driving, and sexual activity (Byrnes, Miller, & Schafer, 1999).

To summarize, boys tend to be bigger, stronger, and more active; girls tend to have better fine-motor coordination and to be healthier. In the next section, which concerns intellectual skills, you'll again see that gender differences vary from one skill to the next.

## Differences in Intellectual Abilities and Achievement

Of the four gender-based differences discovered by Maccoby and Jacklin (1974), three concern intellectual skills: Girls tend to have greater verbal skill but boys tend to have greater mathematical and visual–spatial skill. Since Maccoby and Jacklin's work, we've learned much about the nature of gender differences in these areas.

**VERBAL ABILITY.**    Girls have larger vocabularies than boys and are more talkative (Feldman et al., 2000; Leaper & Smith, 2004). During elementary school and high school, girls read, write, and spell better than boys, and this difference is found in virtually all industrialized countries (Halpern, 2004). Finally, more boys are diagnosed with language-related problems such as reading disability or specific language impairment (Wicks-Nelson & Israel, 2006).

Why are girls more talented verbally than boys? Part of the explanation may lie in biological forces. The left hemisphere of the brain, which is central to language (see Module 4.3), may mature more rapidly in girls than in boys (Diamond et al., 1983). But experience also contributes. During the toddler years, mothers talk more to daughters than to sons (Leaper, Anderson, & Sanders, 1998). And, by the elementary-school years reading is often stereotyped as an activity for girls (Huston, 1983), which may make girls, such as the one in the photo, more willing than boys to invest time and effort in mastering verbal skills like reading.

**SPATIAL ABILITY.** In Module 8.1, you saw that spatial ability is a component of most models of intelligence. **One aspect of spatial ability is *mental rotation*, the ability to imagine how an object will look after it has been moved in space.** The items in the figure test mental rotation: The task is to determine which of the figures labeled A through E are rotated versions of the figure in the box on the left. From childhood on, boys tend to have better mental-rotation skill than girls (Govier & Salisbury, 2000; Voyer, Voyer, & Bryden, 1995). (The correct answers are C and D.)

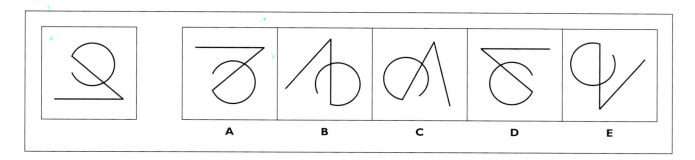

FIGURE 13-3

Spatial ability also involves determining relations between objects in space while ignoring distracting information. For example, which of the tilted bottles of water in the figure has the waterline drawn correctly? In an upright bottle, the waterline is at right angles to the sides of the bottle, but selecting the correct answer for the tilted bottle (A, in this case) requires that you ignore the conflicting perceptual information provided by the sides of the bottle. From adolescence on, boys are more accurate than girls on these kinds of spatial tasks (Voyer, Voyer, & Bryden, 1995).

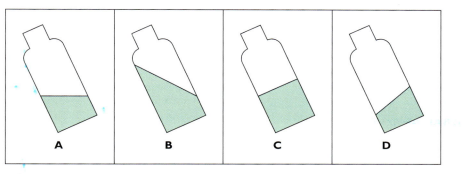

FIGURE 13-4

Explanations for gender differences in spatial ability abound:

• A recessive gene on the X chromosome may promote spatial ability (Thomas & Kail, 1991). In this type of inheritance, males only have to inherit a recessive gene from their mother to score high in spatial ability, but females must inherit the recessive gene from both parents.

• The right hemisphere of the brain may be more specialized for spatial processing in males than in females, perhaps because boys mature more slowly than girls (Rilea, Roskos-Ewoldsen, & Boles, 2004; Waber, 1977).

• Boys are more likely than girls to participate in activities that foster spatial skill, such as estimating the trajectory of an object moving through space

Playing video games can enhance a child's spatial skill; because boys play video games more often than girls, this may contribute to a gender difference in spatial skill.

(e.g., a baseball), using two-dimensional plans to assemble an object such as a scale model (Baenninger & Newcombe, 1995), or, like the boys in the photo, playing video games that involve visual-perceptual skills (Okagaki & Frensch, 1994).

Each of these possible explanations of gender differences in spatial ability is supported by some studies but not by others. And, of course, the explanations are not necessarily mutually exclusive. Biological and experiential forces may both contribute to gender differences in spatial ability, just as both contribute to gender differences in verbal ability. Thus, parents and others can foster verbal and spatial abilities in boys and girls because each is influenced considerably by experience.

**MATHEMATICS.** Gender differences in math skill are complex. Let's start with performance on standardized math achievement tests. Standardized tests emphasize computational skills during the elementary- and middle-school years, and girls usually score higher than boys. Solving problems and applying math concepts are emphasized in high school and college; here boys often score higher than girls. Thus, initially girls excel in math computation, but later boys excel in math problem solving (Hyde, Fennema, & Lamon, 1990). The gender difference remains even when boys and girls take an equal number of math courses (Kimball, 1989). Finally, the gender difference in performance on math achievement tests is not restricted to the United States but is found in most industrialized nations (Halpern, 2004).

Paradoxically, the results are different for grades in math courses. Often no differences are detected in boys' and girls' grades, but when a difference occurs, it invariably favors girls. This is even true for courses in high school and college—when males are getting higher scores on achievement tests (Kimball, 1989). Darlene's experience, described in the module-opening vignette, is common: Girls get better grades in math courses but lower scores on standardized tests of math achievement.

Why should females get lower scores on tests of math achievement but higher grades in math courses? One explanation is based on the concept of stereotype threat, which was introduced in Module 8.2. According to this view, when girls such as the ones in the photo take standardized achievement tests, they are anxious for fear of confirming the stereotype and they do poorly as a result (Nosek, Banaji, & Greenwald, 2002; Shih, Pittinsky, & Ambady, 1999).

Stereotype threat may cause girls to get lower scores on math achievement tests: Girls worry about doing poorly—confirming the stereotype—so they do poorly as a result.

Because of findings like these, educators have worked hard to reduce gender stereotypes associated with math (Secada, Fennema, & Adajian, 1995). Nevertheless, gender differences in math continue. Hedges and Nowell (1995) evaluated data from the National Assessment of Educational Progress (NAEP), which administers standardized tests in several areas to approximately 70,000 to 100,000 American students in grades 3, 7, and 11. The researchers found that the gender difference in math achievement has been remarkably constant since the NAEP test was first administered in 1978.

Why are gender differences in math so persistent? One possibility is that biological factors contribute. In particular, spatial ability, which we just discussed, may play a role. Some aspects of math are easier to understand if they can be visualized mentally. For example, being able to imagine a three-dimensional space where lines and planes intersect simplifies learning geometry. Boys may be more successful in some areas of math because they more often have the spatial skills that promote understanding (Casey et al., 1997).

Most likely, the gender difference in math is due to multiple factors. Some have roots in biology (e.g., spatial skill) but others have roots in experience (e.g., stereotypes concerning math). As you'll see in the next section, nature and nurture also contribute to gender differences in personality and social behavior.

## Differences in Personality and Social Behavior

Are there differences in personality and social behavior between boys and girls? In the 1970s, Maccoby and Jacklin (1974) found convincing evidence of only one gender difference in this realm: Boys were more aggressive than girls. In this section, we'll see what researchers have discovered in the ensuing 30 years.

**AGGRESSIVE BEHAVIOR.**   No one doubts Maccoby and Jacklin's conclusion that boys are more aggressive physically than girls. As mentioned in Module 12.4 and as you can see in the photos, the gender difference in physical aggression is readily observed. No matter how you slice it, boys are more aggressive than girls (Collaer & Hines, 1995; Martin & Ross, 2005). Of course, some qualifications apply. Boys are not always aggressive. They are, for example, more likely to be physically aggressive toward other boys than toward girls (Maccoby & Jacklin, 1980): Boys may try to beat up other boys, but, as a general rule, they don't try to beat up girls. And, when they're provoked, girls can be physically aggressive, too (Bettencourt & Miller, 1996).

Brianna is the mother of    **13.2**
fraternal twins, a boy and
a girl, who are just starting
elementary school. She's
determined that both of her
children will excel in reading and
math. Are Brianna's goals
realistic?

Worldwide, boys are more physically aggressive than girls.

Physical aggression is far more common among boys than among girls.

Because boys and men are more aggressive in virtually all cultures and because males in nonhuman species are also more aggressive, scientists are convinced that biology contributes heavily to this gender difference. **Aggressive behavior has been linked to *androgens*, hormones secreted by the testes.** Androgens do not lead to aggression directly. Instead, androgens make it more likely that boys will be aggressive by making them more excitable or easily angered and by making boys stronger (e.g., Marcus et al., 1985).

Just because hormones are involved, though, we can't ignore experience. The media are filled with aggressive male models—from Vin Diesel to Jedi Knights—who are rewarded for their behavior. What's more, parents are more likely to use physical punishment with sons than with daughters and are more tolerant of aggressive behavior in sons than in daughters (Block, 1978; Condry & Ross, 1985). As we saw in Module 12.4, these are just the sort of experiences that precipitate a vicious cycle of increasing aggression; and this cycle is much more common for boys than girls. Although androgens may make boys more prone to aggression, experience encourages boys rather than girls to express their aggression physically.

Although boys' aggression may be more obvious because of its physical nature, girls can be aggressive, too. In Module 12.4, we saw that girls rely upon relational aggression, in which they try to hurt others by damaging their relationships with peers (Crick & Grotpeter, 1995). They may call children names, make fun of them, spread rumors about them, or—just as bad—pointedly ignore them. Thus, when boys want to harm peers, they try to hurt them physically but girls try to damage their relationships with peers.

**EMOTIONAL SENSITIVITY.** According to the stereotypes listed on page 400, girls are better able to express their emotions and interpret others' emotions. In fact, this is a gender difference supported by research (Hall & Halberstadt, 1981; Weinberg et al., 1999). For example, throughout infancy, childhood, and adolescence, girls identify facial expressions (e.g., happy face versus a sad face) more accurately than boys do (McClure, 2000).

Most developmentalists believe that the gender difference in emotional sensitivity reflects both nature and nurture. On the nature side, regions of the brain's temporal lobe that play a leading role in processing emotional expression develop more rapidly in girls than in boys (McClure, 2000). On the nurture side, parents are more "feeling-oriented" with daughters than with sons. They are more likely to talk about emotions with daughters than with sons and to emphasize the importance of considering others' feelings (Kuebli, Butler, & Fivush, 1995; Zahn-Waxler, Cole, & Barrett, 1991).

**SOCIAL INFLUENCE.** Another gender stereotype is that females are more easily influenced by others—that is, they are, more persuadable. In fact, young girls are more likely than young boys to comply with an adult's request, and they are more likely to seek an adult's help (Jacklin & Maccoby, 1978). Girls and women are also influenced more than boys and men by persuasive messages and others'

Girls are more likely to agree to others' suggestions because they value group harmony more than boys do.

behavior, especially when they are under group pressure (Becker, 1986; Eagly, Karau, & Makhijani, 1995). However, these gender differences may stem from the fact that females value group harmony more than boys and thus seem to give in to others (Miller, Danaher, & Forbes, 1986; Strough & Berg, 2000). For instance, at a meeting like the one in the photo, girls are just as likely as boys to recognize the flaws in a bad idea, but girls are more willing to go along simply because they don't want the group to start arguing.

**DEPRESSION.** Depression, a disorder in which individuals are chronically sad and irritable and have low self-esteem, is rare in childhood but becomes much more common in adolescence, particularly among teenage girls like the one in the photo (Avenevoli & Steinberg, 2001). According to current theories (Hankin & Abramson, 2001), depression is often triggered when adolescents experience a negative life event (e.g., flunk a major exam) and interpret this event negatively (e.g., "I'm so stupid; my friends won't want to be with me if they know I'm this dumb").

Applied to the sex difference in depression during adolescence, this approach emphasizes that girls experience more frequent negative life events such as dissatisfaction with their appearance after pubertal change or conflict with close friends. Also, girls are more apt to interpret these negative

Adolescent girls are far more prone to depression than adolescent boys are, in part because girls often interpret negative life events as being very harmful.

life events in harmful terms, emphasizing social–emotional consequences to a far greater extent than boys do. For example, I knew a 15-year-old boy who, after 9 years of playing soccer, was the only player cut from the high-school team. Although upset briefly, within days he had decided to go out for cross-country and ended up having a successful and rewarding career running. In the same circumstances, a girl might well have spent more time focusing on the harmful consequences—"I won't be able to hang with my soccer friends," "I stink at sports"—the kind of thinking that would put her at risk for a bout of depression.

At this point, perhaps you're wondering about the role of hormones in depression. After all, adolescence is often portrayed as a time when hormones are running wild and causing huge mood swings. In fact, researchers have found few consistent connections between depression (and other mood disorders) and levels of hormones (Buchanan, Eccles, & Becker, 1992). That is, although levels of female hormones such as progesterone and estrogen definitely rise with the onset of puberty, these changes play no more than a small role in the onset of depression in teenage girls.

**Depression is more common among adolescent girls than adolescent boys.**

## Frank Talk About Gender Differences

The gender differences we've discussed in this module are summarized in the table on page 410.

What should we make of these differences? What do they tell us about the experience of growing up male versus growing up female?

**SUMMARY TABLE**

### SEX DIFFERENCES IN PHYSICAL AND BEHAVIORAL DEVELOPMENT

| General Area | Specific Domain | Nature of Difference |
|---|---|---|
| **Physical Development** | | |
| | Motor skills | Boys excel at tasks that require strength but girls do better on tasks that require fine-motor coordination. |
| | Activity | Beginning in infancy, boys are more active than girls. |
| | Health | From conception through adulthood, girls are healthier. |
| **Intellectual Abilities** | | |
| | Verbal ability | Girls have larger vocabularies; they also read, write, and spell better. |
| | Spatial ability | Boys are better on mental-rotation tasks and in determining relations between objects in space. |
| | Mathematics | Girls get better grades in math but boys get higher scores on standardized tests. |
| **Personality and Social Behavior** | | |
| | Aggression | Boys are more aggressive physically; girls rely more on relational aggression. |
| | Emotional sensitivity | Girls are better able to identify and express emotions. |
| | Social influence | Because girls value group harmony more than boys do, girls are more susceptible to others' influence. |
| | Depression | Beginning in adolescence, girls are more prone to depression than boys. |

**FIGURE 13-5**

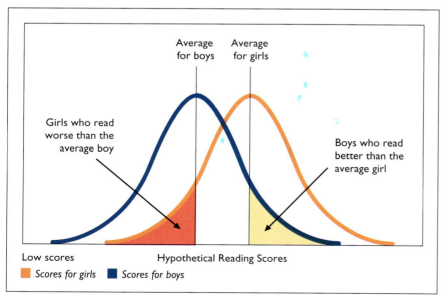

First, remember that the gender differences described in this module represent differences in the *average scores* for boys and girls, differences that are relatively small. For example, the diagram shows the distribution of scores on a hypothetical reading test. As we would expect, overall girls do better than boys. However, the distributions of girls' and boys' scores overlap substantially. The area shaded in yellow shows the large percentage of boys who have higher reading scores than the average girl and the area shaded in red shows the large percentage of girls who have lower reading scores than the average boy. The diagram makes it obvious that a difference in average scores does *not* mean that girls read well and boys read poorly. Consequently, a boy who wants to become a writer should not be deterred because of small differences in average scores for boys and girls. Of course, we could draw similar diagrams in the other domains in which boys and girls differ, with the same conclusion. Gender differences are small, which means that boys' and girls' scores overlap considerably.

Second, think about the huge number of abilities, behaviors, and traits that have not been considered in this module. Boys and girls do not differ in many, many aspects of cognition, personality, and social behavior, a point that is easily lost when focusing on gender differences. In reality, a list of ways that boys and girls are similar is much longer than a list of differences. In cognitive processing, memory, and understanding people—to name just a few areas—boys and girls are much more alike than different. If development is a journey, both boys and girls have many choices as they travel; few, if any, routes have signs that say "for girls only" or "for boys only."

In this module, we've focused on the behaviors and skills in which boys and girls differ; in the next, we'll see how children acquire a gender identity, a sense of "being a boy" or "being a girl."

## CHECK YOUR LEARNING

**RECALL** What were the primary gender differences that Maccoby and Jacklin described in their 1974 book?

Summarize features of personality and social behavior in which boys and girls differ.

**INTERPRET** How do nature and nurture contribute to gender differences in intellectual abilities and achievement?

**APPLY** Based on what you know about differences between boys and girls in intellectual abilities and social behavior, how might this module differ in the 40th edition of this book, published in 2106?

Yes, her son and daughter may both be excellent students. But if the typical pattern of gender differences holds, her daughter may be the better reader and her son the better mathematician.    **13.2**

# GENDER IDENTITY    13.3

## LEARNING OBJECTIVES

- How do parents, peers, and the media influence children's learning of gender roles?

- How do cognitive theories explain children's learning of gender roles?

- How does biology influence children's learning of gender roles?

The Socializing Influences of People and the Media

Cognitive Theories of Gender Identity

Biological Influences

*Taryn, who has just turned 4, knows that she's a girl but is convinced that she'll grow up to be a man. Taryn plays almost exclusively with boys and her favorite toys are trucks and cars. Taryn tells her parents that when she's bigger, she'll grow a beard and be a daddy. Taryn's father is confident that his daughter's ideas are a natural part of a preschooler's limited understanding of gender, but her mother wonders if they've neglected some important aspect of Taryn's upbringing.*

According to the old saying, "Boys will be boys and girls will be girls," but how, in fact, do boys become boys and girls become girls when it comes to gender roles? That is, how do children acquire their culture's roles for males and females? And how do children develop a sense of identity as a male or female? We'll answer these questions in this module and, as we do, learn whether Taryn's wish to grow up to be a man is typical for youngsters her age.

## The Socializing Influences of People and the Media

Folklore holds that parents and other adults—teachers and television characters, for example—directly shape children's behavior toward the roles associated with their sex. Boys are rewarded for boyish behavior and punished for girlish behavior.

The folklore even has a theoretical basis: According to social cognitive theorists like Albert Bandura (1977, 1986; Bandura & Bussey, 2004) and Walter Mischel (1970), children learn gender roles in much the same way they learn other social behaviors—by watching the world about them and learning the outcomes of actions. Thus, children learn what their culture considers appropriate behavior for males and females by simply watching how adults and peers act. How well does research support social cognitive theory? Let's look first at research done with parents.

**PARENTS.** An extensive meta-analysis of 172 studies involving 27,836 children (Lytton & Romney, 1991) found that parents often treat sons and daughters similarly: Parents interact equally with sons and daughters, are equally warm to both, and encourage both sons and daughters to achieve and be independent. However, in behavior related to gender roles, parents respond differently to sons and daughters (Lytton & Romney, 1991). Activities such as playing with dolls, dressing up, or helping an adult are encouraged more often in daughters than in sons; rough-and-tumble play and playing with blocks are encouraged more in sons than in daughters. And parents tolerate mild aggression more in sons than in daughters (Martin & Ross, 2005). And, as we'll see in the "Focus on Research" feature, when young children make stereotyped comments, their mothers usually go along with them.

> *Parents treat sons and daughters similarly, except for gender-related behavior.*

## *Focus on Research*

### How Mothers Talk to Children About Gender

*Who were the investigators, and what was the aim of the study?* Imagine a mother and her preschool son reading a picture book together. Seeing a picture of a girl catching a frog, he says, "Girls hate frogs!" Seeing a picture of a boy playing football, he exclaims, "Yes, Daniel and I like playing football!" When mothers hear the children make gender-stereotyped statements like these, what do they do? Susan Gelman, Marianne Taylor, and Simone Nguyen (2004) conducted a study to answer this question.

*How did the investigators measure the topic of interest?* Gelman and colleagues created books that included 16 pictures. Half of the pictures showed a child or adult in a gender stereotyped activity (e.g., a girl sewing, a man driving a truck); half showed a child or adult in an activity that was counter to gender stereotypes (e.g., a boy baking, a woman firefighter). Mothers were simply asked to go through the picture book with the children, as they might do at home. They were not told about the investigators' interest in gender. Mothers and children were videotaped as they looked at the books.

*Who were the participants in the study?* The study included 72 pairs of mothers and children: of the children, 24 were 2-year-olds, 24 were 4-year-olds, and 24 were 6-year-olds. At each age, half of the children were girls.

*What was the design of the study?* This study was correlational because Gelman and colleagues were interested in the relations that existed naturally between children's speech and a mother's reply to children's speech, the child's age, and the child's sex. The study was cross-sectional because it included 2-year-olds, 4-year-olds, and 6-year-olds, each tested once.

*Were there ethical concerns with the study?* No; most children enjoy reading picture books with their parents.

*What were the results?* First the investigators determine the number of stereotyped statements that children made, including those that endorsed a stereotype— "Jackie and Sherry love to play with dolls!"—as well as those that deny a counter stereotype—"Boys aren't ballet dancers!" The 2-year-olds averaged about 24 of the statements; the 4- and 6-year-olds averaged about 30. Then the mother's response to stereotyped comments was classified in 1 of 8 categories; I'll describe just three of them for simplicity.

- The mother *affirmed* her child's remark: "Yes, girls *do* like playing with dolls!"
- The mother *repeated* the child's remark as a question: "Are you sure boys aren't dancers?"
- The mother *negated* the child's remark: "Oh yes, boys *can* be dancers."

The percentage of times that mothers used each of these responses is shown in the graph. You can see that mothers agreed with their child's remarks about one third of the time. They almost never disagreed directly with their children: Fewer than 2% of mothers' comments fell in this category. But they did rephrase their children's statements as questions about 20% of the time, which is a subtle way for a mother to dispute her child. Overall, mothers' responses were very similar for sons and daughters; they were much the same for 2-, 4-, and 6-year-olds and so the data in the graphs are averaged across the three age groups.

*What did the investigators conclude?* Gelman and colleagues (2002) concluded that " . . . mothers are surprisingly accepting of children's stereotyping statements . . . Mothers rarely directly contradicted a child's gender stereotype statement, and in fact more often affirmed the child's stereotype than questioned it."

*What converging evidence would strengthen these conclusions?* The mothers in this sample were very well educated: Most were college graduates. It would be important to see whether mothers with less education respond in a similar fashion. In addition, it would be valuable to know the impact of a mother's reply on her child's gender stereotyping. When mothers question children's stereotyped statements, do children rethink their concepts? Or is this form of feedback too subtle to affect preschool children, particularly younger ones? ■

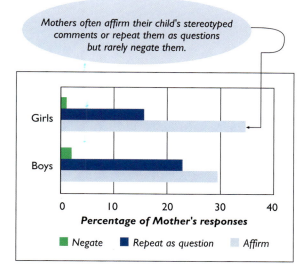

Mothers often affirm their child's stereotyped comments or repeat them as questions but rarely negate them.

■ Negate   ■ Repeat as question   ▢ Affirm

FIGURE 13-6

Fathers are more likely than mothers to treat their children in a stereotyped manner.

Fathers are more likely than mothers to treat sons and daughters differently. More than mothers, fathers such as the one in the photo often encourage gender-related play. Fathers also push their sons more but accept dependence in their daughters (Snow, Jacklin, & Maccoby, 1983). A father, for example, may urge his frightened young son to jump off the diving board ("Be a man!") but not be so insistent with his daughter ("That's okay, honey"). Apparently mothers are more likely to respond based on their knowledge of the individual child's needs, but fathers respond based on gender stereotypes. A mother responds to her son knowing that he's smart but unsure of himself; a father may respond because of what he thinks boys should be like.

Of course, adults differ in their views on the relative rights and roles of males and females. Some have very traditional views, believing, for example, that men should be hired preferentially for some jobs and that it's more important for sons than daughters to attend college; others have more gender-neutral views, believing, for example, that women should have the same business and professional opportunities as men and that daughters should have the same educational opportunities as sons. It would be surprising if parents did not convey these attitudes to their children, and indeed they do. A meta-analysis of 48 studies including more than 10,000 pairs of parents and children showed that children's gender-related interests, attitudes, and self-concepts are more traditional when their parents have traditional views and more gender-neutral when their parents have nontraditional views (Tenenbaum & Leaper, 2002).

**TEACHERS.** After parents, teachers may be the most influential adults in children's lives. Many teachers help to differentiate gender roles by making gender salient in the classroom. In elementary schools, students may be told to form separate lines for boys and girls like the ones shown in the photo. Or teachers may praise the girls as a group for being quiet during a video while criticizing the boys for laughing (Thorne, 1993). In addition, teachers spend more time interacting with boys than girls. Teachers call on boys more frequently, praise them more for their schoolwork, and spend more time scolding them for disruptive classroom behavior (Good & Brophy, 1996). By using sex as a basis for differentiating children and by giving boys more attention, teachers foster gender-role learning (Ruble, Martin, & Berenbaum, 2006).

Teachers often make gender salient in school by treating boys and girls differently when there's no reason to do so.

**PEERS.** By 3 years, most children's play shows the impact of gender stereotypes—boys prefer blocks and trucks, whereas girls prefer tea sets and dolls—and youngsters are critical of peers who engage in cross-gender play (Langlois & Downs, 1980). This is particularly true of boys who like feminine toys or who play at feminine activities. Boys who play with dolls and girls (like the one in the photo on page 415) who play with trucks will both be ignored, teased, or ridiculed by their peers, but a boy will receive harsher treatment than a girl (Levy, Taylor, & Gelman, 1995). Once children learn rules about gender-typical play, they often harshly punish peers who violate those rules.

Peers influence gender roles in another way, too. Between 2 and 3 years of age, children begin to prefer playing with same-sex peers (Martin & Fabes, 2001). Little boys play together with cars, and little girls play together with dolls. This preference increases during childhood, reaching a peak in preadolescence. By age 10 or 11, the vast majority of peer activity is with same-sex children and most of this involves sex-typed play: Boys are playing sports or playing with cars or action figures; girls are doing artwork or playing with pets or dolls (McHale et al., 2004). Then the tide begins to turn, but even in adulthood time spent at work and at leisure is quite commonly segregated by gender (Hartup, 1983). This tendency for boys to play with boys and girls with girls has several distinctive features (Maccoby, 1990, 1998):

Preschool children often tease their peers who engage in cross-gender play.

- In some cultures, adults select playmates for children. However, in cultures where children choose playmates, boys select boys as playmates and girls select girls.
- Children spontaneously select same-sex playmates. Adult pressure ("James, why don't you play with John, not Amy") is not necessary.
- Children resist parents' efforts to get them to play with members of the opposite sex. Girls are often unhappy when parents encourage them to play with boys, and boys complain when parents urge them to play with girls.
- Children's reluctance to play with members of the opposite sex is not restricted to gender-typed games, such as playing house or playing with cars. Boys and girls prefer same-sex playmates even in gender-neutral activities such as playing tag or doing puzzles.

Why do boys and girls seem so attracted to same-sex play partners? Eleanor Maccoby (1990, 1998) believes that two factors are critical. First, boys specifically prefer rough-and-tumble play and generally are more competitive and dominating in their interactions. Girls' play is not as rough and is less competitive, so Maccoby argues that boys' style of play may be aversive to girls.

Second, when girls and boys play together, girls do not readily influence boys. **Girls' interactions with one another are typically *enabling*—their actions and remarks tend to support others and sustain the interaction.** When drawing together, one girl might say to another, "Cool picture" or "What do you want to do now?" **In contrast, boy's interactions are often *constricting*—one partner tries to emerge as the victor by threatening or contradicting the other, by exaggerating, and so on.** In the same drawing task, one boy might say to another, "My picture's better" or "Drawing is stupid—let's watch TV." When these styles are brought together, girls find that their enabling style is ineffective with boys. The same subtle overtures that work with other girls have no impact on boys. Boys ignore girls' polite suggestions about what to do and ignore girls' efforts to resolve conflicts with discussion.

You can see these differences in a study by Leman, Ahmed, and Ozarow (2005), who watched 8-year-old boys and girls as they tried to solve problems together. Girls were far more likely to collaborate;

**Question**

| Rick has encouraged his 4-year-old son to play | **13.3** |

with the 5-year-old girl who lives next door, but his son will have none of it—he refuses every time. Rick thinks that his son is being unreasonable and stubborn. Do you agree?

Boys and girls don't play together because girls don't like boys' style of play and because girls find that their enabling interaction style is ineffective with boys.

they encouraged each other's solution strategies and helped the other pursue a strategy. In contrast, boys were far more likely to begin a strategy without consulting the other person and to overtly disagree with a partner's plan.

Some theorists believe that these contrasting styles may have an evolutionary basis (Geary et al., 2003). Boys' concerns about dominating others may stem from a concern with establishing one's rank among a group of males because those males at the upper ranks have better access to mates and better access to resources needed for offspring. Girls' concerns about affiliation may be a by-product of the fact that women traditionally left their own communities (and relatives) to live in a husband's community. Having no relatives nearby enhanced the value of a close friend, which placed a premium on the affiliative behaviors that lead to and maintain friendships.

Regardless of the exact cause, early segregation of playmates by style of play means that boys learn primarily from boys and girls from girls. Over time, such social segregation by sex reinforces gender differences in play. Martin and Fabes (2001), for example, conducted a longitudinal study of same-sex play in preschool and kindergarten children. When young boys spent most of their time playing with other boys at the beginning of the school year, by the end of the year their play was more active and more aggressive. In contrast, when young girls spent most of their time playing with other girls at the beginning of the school year, by the end of the year their play was less active and less aggressive. Boys and girls who spent more time playing with other-sex children didn't show these changes. Thus, young boys and girls teach each other gender-appropriate play. As they do, this helps solidify a youngster's emerging sense of membership in a particular gender group and sharpens the contrast between genders.

**TELEVISION.** Another source of influence on gender-role learning is television, which often portrays males and females in stereotyped ways. Women on television tend to be cast in romantic, marital, or family roles; they are depicted as emotional, passive, and weak. Men are more often cast in leadership or professional roles and are depicted as rational, active, and strong (Jacobson, 2005).

What is the impact of these stereotyped portrayals? As you can imagine, children who watch a lot of TV end up with more stereotyped views of males and females. For example, Kimball (1986) studied gender-role stereotypes in a small Canadian town that could not receive TV programs until a transmitter was installed in 1974. Children's views of personality traits, behaviors, occupations, and peer relations were measured before and after TV was introduced.

> TV often portrays males and females in stereotyped ways and children who watch TV frequently learn these stereotypes.

Boys' views became more stereotyped on all four dimensions. For example, in their more stereotyped views of occupations, boys now believed that girls could be teachers and cooks whereas boys could be physicians and judges. Girls' views became more stereotyped only for traits and peer relations. After TV was introduced, girls believed that boasting and swearing were characteristic of boys and that sharing and helping were characteristic of girls. Findings like these indicate that TV viewing causes children to adopt many of the stereotypes that dominate television programming (Signorielli & Lears, 1992).

Let's now return to our original question: How well does research support the social learning explanation of gender roles? Studies of parents, teachers, and peers show that children learn much about gender roles simply by observing males and females. But simple observation of real-life models or television characters cannot be the entire explanation. After all, young boys traditionally have far more opportunities to observe their mother's behavior than their father's, but are more likely to imitate their father (for example, by using hammer and saw) than their mother (for example, by cooking). Thus, an important element in learning about gender is identifying with one gender and then actively seeking out activities that are typical for that gender. This aspect of gender role learning is the focus of cognitive theories, which we'll examine in the next section.

## Cognitive Theories of Gender Identity

According to Lawrence Kohlberg (1966; Kohlberg & Ullian, 1974), full understanding of gender develops gradually and involves three elements.

- *Gender labeling*: **By age 2 or 3, children understand that they are either boys or girls and label themselves accordingly.**

- *Gender stability*: **During the preschool years, children begin to understand that gender is stable—Boys become men and girls become women.** However, children in this stage believe that a girl who wears her hair like a boy will become a boy and that a boy who plays with dolls will become a girl (Fagot, 1985).

- *Gender consistency*: **Between 4 and 7 years, most children understand that maleness and femaleness do not change over situations or according to personal wishes.** They understand that a child's sex is unaffected by the clothing that a child wears or the toys that a child likes.

Taryn, the 4-year-old in the opening vignette, is in the first stage—she knows that she's a girl. However, she has yet to develop a sense of gender stability or gender consistency. **When children understand labels, stability, and consistency, they have mastered *gender constancy*.**

Kohlberg's theory specifies *when* children begin learning about gender-appropriate behavior and activities (once they understand gender constancy) but not *how* such learning takes place. A theory that addresses the "how" of gender learning is the focus of the "Spotlight on Theories" feature.

VIDEO 13.1
Gender Consistency

## *Spotlight on Theories*
### Gender Schema Theory

*BACKGROUND*

Preschool children learn gender roles rapidly. The environment, of course, provides many clues about typical roles for males and females. But how do children use these clues to learn about the behaviors and characteristics typically associated with their sex?

*THE THEORY*

A theory proposed by Carol Martin (Martin & Ruble, 2004; Martin et al., 1999), illustrated in the diagram on page 418, addresses how children learn about gender. **In *gender-schema theory*, children first decide if an object, activity, or behavior is female or male, then use this information to decide whether or not they should learn more about the object, activity, or behavior.** That is, once children know their gender, they pay attention primarily to experiences and events that are gender

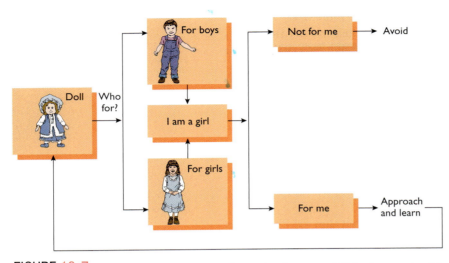

FIGURE 13-7

appropriate (Martin & Halverson, 1987). According to gender-schema theory, a preschool boy who is watching a group of girls playing in sand will decide that playing in sand is for girls and that, because he is a boy, playing in sand is not for him. Seeing a group of older boys playing football, he will decide that football is for boys, and because he is a boy, football is acceptable and he should learn more about it.

**HYPOTHESIS:** According to gender-schema theory, children first establish gender identity, then begin actively learning about gender roles. Consequently, children who have established a gender identity should know much about gender roles but children who have not established a gender identity should know little about gender roles.

**TEST:** Martin and Little (1990) measured preschool children's understanding of gender by asking them questions about gender labeling ("point to the picture of the boy"), gender stability ("what will you be when you grow up?"), and gender consistency ("Would you still be a boy if you wore girls' clothes and played with dolls?"). They also measured children's knowledge of gender-stereotyped activities (e.g., that girls play with dolls and that boys play with airplanes). The youngest children in heir study—$3\frac{1}{2}$- to 4-year-olds—did not understand gender constancy and knew little of gender-stereotyped activities. By age 4, children understood gender constancy but till knew little of gender-stereotyped activities. By $4\frac{1}{2}$ years, many children understood gender constancy and knew gender-typical and gender-atypical activities. Importantly, there were no children who lacked gender constancy but knew about gender-stereotyped activities, a combination that would be impossible according to gender-schema theory.

**CONCLUSION:** As predicted, gender constancy—the understanding that I am and always will be a boy (or girl)—is the catalyst for learning about gender roles. As Martin and Ruble (2004) put it, "Children are gender detectives who search for cues about gender—who should or should not engage in a particular activity, who can play with whom, and why girls and boys are different" (p. 67).

**APPLICATION:** After children understand gender, it's as if they see the world through special glasses that allow only gender-typical activities to be in focus (Liben & Bigler, 2002). For parents who don't want their children limited to traditional views of gender and to traditional gender roles, it may be tempting to encourage children to remove the gender-tinted glasses in favor of more neutral glasses. But, once a child has acquired gender identity, that's probably easier said than done. A better strategy may be to expose children to many counterstereotyped examples: By showing girls women who fly planes, work in construction, and manage companies and by showing boys men who are nurses, preschool teachers, or dental hygienists, children can learn a much broader definition of what it means to be male or female. ■

Gender schema theory shows that "male" and "female" become much more salient in children's world after they understand gender. Consistent with this theory, I remember vividly taking my 4-year-old daughter Laura to watch my son Ben play football. I wondered if she would become so bored and restless that we'd need to leave. Wrong. Laura immediately discovered the cheerleaders (all girls) and insisted we sit right in front of them. Throughout the game (and the rest of the season), Laura's eyes were riveted to the cheerleaders' every move, and when we'd get home, she'd imitate their routines. According to gender-schema theory, 4-year-old Laura knew that cheerleading was for girls and that because she was a girl, she needed to learn everything about it.*

After children have gender identity, their tastes in TV programs begin to shift along gender-specific lines (Luecke-Aleksa et al., 1995) and they begin to use gender labels to evaluate toys and activities. Shown an unfamiliar toy and told that children of a specific sex *really* like this toy, children like the toy much more if others of their sex do, too (Martin, Eisenbud, & Rose, 1995). This selective viewing of the world explains a great deal about children's learning of gender roles, but as we'll see in the next section, there is a final important element that needs to be considered.

## Biological Influences

Most child-development researchers agree that biology contributes to gender roles and gender identity. Evolutionary developmental psychology, for example, reminds us that men and women performed vastly different roles for much of human history: Women were more invested in child rearing and men were more invested in providing important resources (e.g., food, protection) for their offspring (Geary, 2002). In adapting to these roles, different traits and behaviors evolved for men and women. For example, men became more aggressive because that was adaptive in helping them ward off predators.

> According to evolutionary developmental psychology, different traits and behaviors have evolved in men and women.

Another way to consider biological influences on gender is in terms of sex hormones such as androgen and estrogen. In Module 13.2, we saw that hormones are a factor in gender differences in aggression but that research has produced inconsistent findings concerning the impact of hormones on spatial ability and depression. What about the impact of hormones on gender-stereotyped play? **Some fascinating insights come from studies of children with *congenital adrenal hyperplasia* (CAH), a genetic disorder in which, beginning in prenatal development, the adrenal glands secrete large amounts of androgen.** The extra androgen doesn't affect a baby boy's physical development; but in baby girls it can enlarge the clitoris so that it resembles a penis. Girls affected by CAH have surgery during infancy to correct their physical appearance and they receive hormone therapy to correct the imbalance of androgen. Nevertheless, during childhood and adolescence, girls with CAH prefer masculine activities (such as playing with cars instead of dolls) and male playmates to a much greater extent than girls not exposed to these amounts of androgen (Berenbaum & Snyder, 1995; Collaer & Hines, 1995). And these effects are largest for girls who have the greatest exposure to androgen during prenatal development (Berenbaum, Duck, & Bryk, 2000; Servin et al., 2003). Apparently the androgen not only masculinizes the genitals in baby girls, but also affects the prenatal development of brain regions critical for masculine and feminine gender-role behavior.

---

*But, during the elementary school years, she abandoned cheerleading for soccer and basketball.

Perhaps the most accurate conclusion to draw is that biology, the socializing influence of people and media, and the child's own efforts to understand gender-typical behavior all contribute to gender roles and differences. Recognizing the interactive nature of these influences on gender learning also enables us to better understand how gender roles are changing today, which is the focus of the last module.

**Q&Answer**

**13.3** No. Worldwide, boys rarely pick girls as play partners and they resist when urged to do so by others. Rick's son is simply acting as most boys his age would. (And as most girls would, if the tables were turned.)

## CHECK YOUR LEARNING

**RECALL** Describe the forces of socialization that contribute to a child's development of gender identity.

Describe cognitive theories of gender identity.

**INTERPRET** How does children's acquisition of gender identity compare with growth in self-concept, described in Module 11.1?

**APPLY** The popular view is that children learn gender roles from adults (and society at large). But children are active participants in gender-role learning. Describe how children influence learning of gender roles.

## 13.4    GENDER ROLES IN TRANSITION

**Emerging Gender Roles**

**Beyond Traditional Gender Roles**

### LEARNING OBJECTIVES

- What is androgyny, and how is it related to traditional conceptions of masculinity and femininity?

- Can parents rear gender-neutral children?

*Meda and Perry want their 6-year-old daughter, Hope, to pick activities, friends, and ultimately a career based on her interests and abilities, rather than on her gender. They have done their best to encourage gender-neutral values and behavior. Both are therefore astonished that Hope seems to be totally indistinguishable from other 6-year-olds reared by conventional parents. Hope's close friends are all girls. When Hope is with her friends, they play house or play with dolls. What seems to be going wrong with Meda and Perry's plans for a gender-neutral girl?*

Gender roles are not etched in stone; they change with the times. In the United States, the range of acceptable roles for girls and boys and women and men has never been greater than today. For example, fathers such as the man in the photo stay home to be the primary caregivers for children, and some women work full time as sole support for the family. What is the impact of these changes on children? In this module, we'll answer this question by looking at new gender roles and at efforts by parents like Meda and Perry to rear gender-neutral children.

Gender roles continue to evolve and the range of acceptable roles for men and women continues to expand.

### Emerging Gender Roles

Traditionally, masculinity and femininity were seen as ends of a continuum: Children possessing many traits associated with males were considered highly masculine, and youngsters possessing many traits associated with females were considered highly feminine. A newer view of gender roles is based on the independent dimensions of instrumentality and expressiveness that were described in Module 13.1. In this view, traditional males are rated high on instrumentality but low on expressiveness, whereas traditional females are low on instrumentality but high on expressiveness. In other words, this approach recognizes that other combinations of traits are possible. *Androgynous* **persons are rated high on both the instrumental and expressive dimensions.** (The term *androgyny* originated from the Greek words for male, *andro*, and female, *gyn*.) That is, androgynous individuals combine many of the traits listed in the table on page 400: They can be both independent and emotional, self-confident and considerate, ambitious and creative.

Many theorists (e.g., Bem, 1998) argue that the ability to react with both instrumental and expressive behaviors is psychologically healthier than reacting primarily with one or the other. In fact, androgynous children often are better adjusted than children whose gender roles are highly stereotyped (Norlander, Erixon, & Archer, 2000). But the benefits of androgyny are greater for girls than for boys. Androgynous girls have higher self-esteem than expressive girls and are more likely to express their thoughts and feelings publicly (Harter et al., 1998). For example, a girl like the one in the photo, who is independent and ambitious as well as considerate and creative, is more likely to feel positive about herself than a girl who embodies only the expressive traits traditionally associated with females.

Evidently, a balance of expressiveness and instrumentality may be especially adaptive across life's many tasks. Being independent and confident has benefits at home and work, but so does being kind and considerate. Teaching children to adopt nontraditional views of gender is no simple task, however, as we'll see in the next section.

Girls benefit from an androgynous gender role that combines the independence and self-confidence of the instrumental dimension with the emotional and considerate aspects of the expressive dimension.

## Beyond Traditional Gender Roles

Many researchers (e.g., Eagly, 1995) believe gender is overemphasized to children. They argue that adults often group children by gender unnecessarily. Consider, for example, a minister who rewards perfect church attendance with blue pencils for boys and pink pencils for girls. Children's gender is irrelevant to the reason for the reward, yet distinguishing boys and girls makes gender seem important and increases children's gender stereotypes (Bigler, 1995).

Many developmentalists believe that gender should be linked strictly to reproductive function instead of, as now, to traits, behaviors, and abilities. Is this possible? Children can certainly learn less stereotyped views of gender, at least in the short run. In one study (Bigler & Liben, 1990), some 6- to 11-year-olds were taught how to decide if a person can perform a particular job or occupation. They were told that the person's sex was not relevant; instead, they should decide if the person would like to do at least some of the activities that are part of the job and if the person has some of the skills necessary for the job. For example, to be a construction worker, a person should like to build things and should know how to drive heavy machinery.

When tested later on their attitudes toward household activities and occupations, these children had significantly fewer stereotyped responses than children who had not been taught to think of occupations in terms of interests and skills. That is,

**Q&A Question**

**13.4**

Mrs. Bower has her second grade class form two lines—one for boys and one for girls—before they walk to the cafeteria for lunch. What do you think of this practice?

children who have this type of training are more likely to think it perfectly natural for women to be construction workers or men to be nurses.

Short-term interventions like the one just described show that more balanced attitudes and behaviors are possible (Gash & Morgan, 1993). But accomplishing change over the long term in a natural setting may be more complicated, based on some results of the Family Lifestyles Project (Weisner & Wilson-Mitchell, 1990). This research examined families in which the parents were members of the 1960s and 1970s counterculture and deeply committed to rearing their children without traditional gender stereotypes. In these families, men and women shared the household, financial, and child-care tasks.

The Family Lifestyle Project indicates that parents like Meda and Perry in this module's opening vignette can influence some aspects of gender stereotyping more readily than others. The children studied in the Family Lifestyles Project had few stereotypes about occupations: They agreed that girls could be president of the United States and drive trucks and that boys could be nurses and secretaries. They also had fewer stereotyped attitudes about the use of objects: Boys and girls were equally likely to use an iron, a shovel, hammer and nails, and needle and thread. Nevertheless, children in these families tended to have same-sex friends, and they liked gender-stereotyped activities: The boys enjoyed physical play and the girls enjoyed drawing and reading.

> **Children can be taught to have fewer gender stereotypes, but changing children's style of play and their playmates is difficult.**

It should not surprise you that some features of gender roles and identities are influenced more readily by experience than others. For 250,000 years, *Homo sapiens* have existed in small groups of families, hunting animals and gathering vegetation. Because women have borne the children and cared for them, it has been adaptive for women to be caring and nurturing. As we saw in Module 10.3, a nurturing caregiver increases the odds of a secure attachment and, ultimately, the survival of the infant. Men's responsibilities included hunting and protecting the family unit from predators, roles for which physical strength and aggressiveness were crucial.

Circumstances of life in the 21st century are, of course, substantially different: Often, both men and women are employed outside the home and both men and women care for children. Nevertheless, the cultural changes of the past few decades cannot erase hundreds of thousands of years of evolutionary history (Geary, 2002). We should not be surprised that boys and girls play differently, that girls tend to be more supportive in their interactions with others, and that boys are usually more aggressive physically.

The "Improving Children's Lives" feature suggests ways children can be helped to go beyond traditional gender roles and learn the best from both roles.

### *Improving Children's Lives*

### Encouraging Valuable Traits, Not Gender Traits

Parents and other adults can encourage children to learn the best from both of the traditional gender roles. Being independent, confident, caring, and considerate are valuable traits for all people, not just for boys or girls. Here are some guidelines to help achieve these aims:

- Since children learn gender roles from those around them, parents should be sure that they themselves are not gender bound. Mothers and fathers can mow lawns, make repairs, and work outside the home. Mothers and fathers can prepare meals, do laundry, and care for the young. This *does* make a difference: I've always done most of the laundry in our house, and my daughter, at 5, was astonished when I told her that in most homes mothers do the wash.

- Parents should not base decisions about children's toys, activities, and chores on the child's sex. They should decide if a toy, activity, or chore is appropriate for the child as an individual (based on age, abilities, and interests), rather than because the child is a boy or girl.

- Forces outside the home, such as media and teachers, often work against parents who want their children to go beyond traditional gender roles. It's neither feasible nor wise to shelter children from these influences, but parents can encourage them to think critically about others' gender-based decisions. When band teachers insist that boys play trumpets and trombones while girls play clarinets and flutes, parents should ask children whether this makes sense. When a TV program shows a man coming to aid the stereotypic damsel in distress, parents should ask the child why the woman simply didn't get herself out of her predicament.

By following these guidelines, adults can help children to develop all their talents, not just those that fit traditional views associated with males and females. ▪

## CHECK YOUR LEARNING

RECALL  What characteristics make up androgyny?

What elements of gender stereotyping seem fairly easy to change? What elements seem more resistant to change?

INTERPRET  Why might girls benefit more than boys from an androgynous gender role?

APPLY  What advice would you give to a mother who wants her daughter to grow to be gender-free in her attitudes, beliefs, and aspirations?

Forming two lines may be a good idea, but there's no reason why one should be for boys and the other for girls. After all, boys and girls are going to the same place, for the same reason. Segregating boys and girls needlessly, as in this case, simply makes gender seem more important than it really is.

**13.4**

## ⚒ UNIFYING THEMES: Connections

Research on gender illustrates the theme that *development in different domains is connected*. Think about how children learn gender roles. According to conventional wisdom, children acquire masculine or feminine traits and behaviors through socialization by parents and other knowledgeable persons in the child's culture. This process is important, but we saw that learning gender roles is not simply a social phenomenon: Cognitive processes are essential. Kohlberg's theory shows that children don't really begin to learn about gender until they understand that they will remain a boy or girl for life. Once they understand gender constancy, gender-schema theory shows how children use this information to decide which experiences are relevant to them. Biology apparently contributes, too, although we still don't really understand how. Biology, cognition, and social forces all shape the unique gender role that individual boys or girls play.

## SEE FOR YOURSELF

To see that older children know more about gender stereotypes and understand that stereotypes are not binding, you'll need to create some simple stories that illustrate stereotyped traits. You could create stories for any of the traits listed in the table on page 400, but I suggest that you use "independent," "confident," "appreciative," and "gentle." Each story should include two to three sentences that describe a child. Be sure that your stories contain no other clues that would hint that the child in the story is a boy or a girl. For example, this story illustrates "independent":

> I know a child who likes to do things without help from adults. This child likes to do homework without help and enjoys traveling alone to visit cousins who live in another city.

Read your stories to some 11- and 12-year-olds. After you've read each story, ask, "Is this child a boy, a girl, or could it be either?" Record the reply, and then ask, "Would most people think that the child is a boy or would most think that the child is a girl?"

In the first question, you're measuring children's understanding that gender stereotypes are flexible. You should find that children answer with "either one" about half of the time, indicating that they believe in some, but not total, flexibility in gender stereotypes. In the second question, you're measuring children's awareness of gender stereotypes. You should find that most children always answer the second question stereotypically: that people would identify the independent and confident children as boys and the appreciative and gentle children as girls. See for yourself!

## RESOURCES

For more information about . . .

gender differences, try Matt Ridley's *The red queen: Sex and the evolution of human nature* (New York: Harper Perennial, 2003), in which the author, a well-known science writer, examines how the biological imperative to reproduce has influenced human behavior and contributed to differences between males and females.

how to increase the impact of women on technology, visit the Web site of the Anita Borg Institute for Women and Technology: **http://www.anitaborg.org**

## KEY TERMS

androgens  407
androgynous  421
congenital adrenal hyperplasia (CAH)  419
constricting  415
enabling  415
expressive traits  398
gender consistency  417
gender constancy  417
gender identity  396

gender labeling  417
gender role  396
gender-schema theory  417
gender stability  417
gender stereotypes  398
instrumental traits  398
mental rotation  405
social role  396

## SUMMARY

## 13.1 GENDER STEREOTYPES

### How Do We View Men and Women?

Instrumental traits describe individuals who are acting on the world and are usually associated with males. Expressive traits describe individuals who value interpersonal relationships and are usually associated with females.

### Learning Gender Stereotypes

By age 4, children have substantial knowledge of gender-stereotyped activities; during the elementary-school years, they come to know gender-stereotyped traits and behaviors. Older children also understand that traits and occupations associated with males have higher social status and that stereotypes are not necessarily binding.

## 13.2 DIFFERENCES RELATED TO GENDER

In *The Psychology of Sex Differences*, published in 1974, Eleanor Maccoby and Carol Jacklin concluded that males and females differed in only four areas—verbal ability, spatial ability, math achievement, and aggression. Subsequent investigators have used their work as the starting point for analyzing gender differences.

### Differences in Physical Development and Behavior

Boys tend to be bigger, stronger, and more active than girls, who tend to have better fine-motor coordination and to be healthier.

### Differences in Intellectual Abilities and Achievement

Girls excel in verbal skills whereas boys excel in spatial ability. Girls get better grades in math; boys get better scores on math achievement tests. This difference in math skill has remained the same over the past few decades. Differences in intellectual abilities reflect both hereditary and environmental factors.

### Differences in Personality and Social Behavior

Boys are more aggressive physically than girls, and biology probably contributes heavily to this difference. Girls usually express their aggression by trying to damage other children's relations with peers.

Girls are more sensitive to others' feelings and are more influenced by others; both differences are probably due to experience. Adolescent girls are more prone to depression.

### Frank Talk About Gender Differences

Most gender differences are fairly small, which means that abilities for boys and girls overlap considerably. Also, despite the emphasis on gender differences, boys and girls are quite similar in many aspects of cognition, personality, and social behavior.

## 13.3 GENDER IDENTITY

### The Socializing Influences of People and the Media

Parents treat sons and daughters similarly, except in gender-related behavior. Fathers may be particularly important in teaching about gender because they are more likely to treat sons and daughters differently. Teachers foster gender-role learning by making gender salient.

By the preschool years, peers discourage cross-gender play by ridiculing peers who do it. Peers also influence gender roles because children play almost exclusively with same-sex peers.

Television depicts men and women in a stereotyped fashion, and children who watch a lot of television are likely to have very stereotyped views of men and women.

### Cognitive Theories of Gender Identity

According to Kohlberg's theory, children gradually learn that gender is constant over time and cannot be changed according to personal wishes. After children understand gender constancy, they begin to learn gender-typical behavior. According to gender-schema theory, children learn about gender by paying attention to behaviors of members of their own sex and ignoring behaviors of members of the other sex.

### Biological Influences

The idea that biology influences some aspects of gender roles is supported by research on females exposed to male hormones during prenatal development.

## 13.4 GENDER ROLES IN TRANSITION

### Emerging Gender Roles

Androgynous persons embody both instrumental and expressive traits. Androgynous girls have higher self-esteem than traditional girls and are more likely to express themselves publicly; androgynous boys have about the same level of self-esteem as traditional boys.

### Beyond Traditional Gender Roles

Training studies show that children can learn less-stereotyped views of gender, but studies of parents trying to rear gender-neutral children suggest that many stereotyped behaviors are resistant to change.

*Family.* **The term is as sacred to most Americans as baseball, apple pie, and Chevrolet.** But what comes to mind when you think of family? Television gives us one answer—from *Leave It to Beaver* to *Family Ties* to *Everybody Loves Raymond*, the American family is portrayed as a mother, father, and their children. In reality, of course, American families are as diverse as the people in them. Some families consist of a single parent and an only child. Others include two parents, many children, and grandparents or other relatives.

All these family configurations, however, have a common goal: nurturing children and helping them become full-fledged adult members of their culture. To learn how families achieve these goals, we'll begin, in Module 14.1, by looking at relationships between parents and children. Next, in Module 14.2, we'll see how families are changing in the 21st century. Then, in Module 14.3, we'll look at relationships between siblings. Finally, in Module 14.4, we'll examine the forces that can cause parents to abuse their children.

**14.1** Parenting

**14.2** The Changing Family

**14.3** Brothers and Sisters

**14.4** Maltreatment: Parent–Child Relationships Gone Awry

1   The Science of Child Development

2   Genetic Bases of Child Development

3   Prenatal Development, Birth, and the Newborn

4   Growth and Health

5   Perceptual and Motor Development

6   Theories of Cognitive Development

7   Cognitive Processes and Academic Skills

8   Intelligence and Individual Differences in Cognition

9   Language and Communication

10  Emotional Development

11  Understanding Self and Others

12  Moral Understanding and Behavior

13  Gender and Development

# Family Relationships

15  Influences Beyond the Family

14

# 14.1 PARENTING

The Family as a System

Styles of Parenting

Parental Behavior

Influences of the Marital System

Children's Contributions

## LEARNING OBJECTIVES

- What is a systems view of family dynamics?

- What are the different styles of parenting?

- What parental behaviors affect children's development?

- How are children influenced by the quality of their parents' marital relationship?

- How do children help determine how parents rear them?

*Tanya and Sheila, both sixth graders, wanted to go to a Kelly Clarkson concert with two boys from their school. When Tanya asked if she could go, her mom said, "No way!" Tanya responded defiantly, "Why not?" In return, her mother exploded, "Because I say so. That's why. Stop pestering me." Sheila wasn't allowed to go either. When she asked why, her mom said, "I just think you're still too young to be dating. I don't mind your going to the concert. If you want to go just with Tanya, that would be fine. What do you think of that?"*

The vignette illustrates what we all know well from personal experience—parents go about child rearing in many different ways. In this module, you'll learn about different approaches that parents take to raising children. But let's begin by thinking about parents as an important element in the family system.

## The Family as a System

Families are rare in the animal kingdom. Only human beings and a handful of other species form family-like units. Why? Compared to the young in other species, children develop slowly. And because children are immature—unable to care for themselves for many years—the family structure evolved as a way to protect and nurture young children during their development (Bjorklund, Yunger, & Pellegrini, 2002). Of course, modern families serve many other functions as well—they're economic units and they provide emotional support—but child rearing remains the most salient and probably the most important family function.

> In the systems view of families, parents and children influence each other and parent-child relations are influenced by other individuals and institutions.

As we think about original and modern families, it's tempting to believe that parents' actions are all that really matter. That is, through their behavior, parents directly and indirectly determine their children's development. This view of parents as "all powerful" was part of early psychological theories (e.g., Watson, 1925) and is held even today by some first-time parents. But most theorists now view families from a contextual perspective (described in Module 1.2). That is, families form a system of interacting elements—parents and children influence one another (Cox & Paley, 2003) and families are part of a much larger system that includes extended family, friends, and teachers as well as institutions that influence development (e.g., schools).

This systems view of children and families is exmplified in a theory proposed by Bronfenbrenner (1995; Bronfenbrenner & Morris, 2006) in which the developing child is embedded in a series of complex and interactive systems. As the diagram on page 429 shows, the environment is divided into five components: the microsystem, the mesosystem, the exosystem, the macrosystem, and the chronosystem. **At any point in life, the *microsystem* consists of the people and objects in an individual's immediate environment.** These are the people closest to a child, such as parents or siblings. Some children have more than one microsystem; for example, a young child might have the microsystems of the family and of the day-care setting. As you can imagine, microsystems strongly influence development.

**Microsystems themselves are connected to create the *mesosystem*.** The mesosystem represents the fact that what happens in one microsystem is likely to influence others. Perhaps you've found that if you have a stressful day at work or school, you're grouchy at home. This indicates that your mesosystem is alive and well; your microsystems of home and work are interconnected emotionally for you.

**The *exosystem* refers to social settings that a person may not experience firsthand but that still influence development.** For example, a mother's work environment is part of her child's exosystem, because she may pay more attention to her child when her work is going well and less attention when she's under a great deal of work-related stress. Although the influence of the exosystem is at least secondhand, its effects on the developing child can be quite strong. Think about the woman in the photo, who doesn't look as if she's having a good day at work; do you think she'll do her best mothering when she gets home? Probably not, which means that the workplace has affected her child's development.

**The broadest environmental context is the *macrosystem*, the subcultures and cultures in which the microsystem, mesosystem, and exosystem are embedded.** A mother, her workplace, her child, and the child's school are part of a larger cultural setting, such as Asian Americans living in Southern California or Italian Americans living in large cities on the East Coast. Members of these cultural groups share a common identity, a common heritage, and common values. The macrosystem evolves over time; what is true about a particular culture today may or may not have been true in the past and may or may not be true in the future. Thus, each successive generation of children develops in a unique macrosystem.

**Finally, these systems all change over time, a dimension known as the *chronosystem*.** This dimension reminds us that microsystem, mesosystem, exosystem, and macrosystem are not static but are often in flux. For example, the child's microsystem changes when an older sister leaves home to attend college and the child's exosystem changes when a mother leaves an easy but low-paying job for a more challenging but higher paying job. And, of course, children themselves are changing over time, which often influences the way in which they are affected by the other elements in the system. For example, a family's move to a distant city may affect a school-age child more than a toddler because the older child must change schools and replace long-term friends (Adams, 2004).

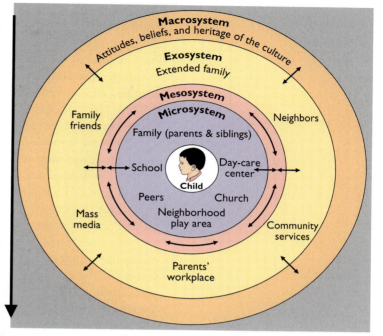

FIGURE 14-1

According to a systems approach to parenting, a parent who has a frustrating day at work may be a less effective parent when she gets home.

When viewed as part of an interactive system like the one shown in the diagram on page 429, parents still influence their children, both directly—for example, by encouraging them to study hard—and indirectly—for example, by being generous and kind to others. However, the influence is no longer exclusively from parent to children but is mutual: Children influence their parents, too. By their behaviors, attitudes, and interests, children affect how their parents behave toward them. When children resist discipline, for example, parents may become less willing to reason with them and more inclined to use force.

Even more subtle influences become apparent when families are viewed as systems of interacting elements. For example, fathers' behaviors can affect mother–child relationships. A demanding husband may leave his wife with little time, energy, or interest in helping her daughter with her homework. Or, when siblings argue constantly, parents may become preoccupied with avoiding problems rather than encouraging their children's development.

These examples show that narrowly focusing on parents' impact on children misses the complexities of family life. But there is even more to the systems view. The family itself is embedded in other social systems, such as neighborhoods and religious institutions (Parke & Buriel, 1998). These other institutions can affect family dynamics. Sometimes they simplify child rearing, as when neighbors are trusted friends and can help care for each other's children. Other times, however, they complicate child rearing. Grandparents who live nearby can create friction within the family. At times, the impact of the larger systems is indirect, as when work schedules cause a parent to be away from home or when schools must eliminate programs that benefit children.

In the remainder of this module, we'll describe parents' influences on children and then see how children affect their parents' behavior.

## Styles of Parenting

Parenting can be described in terms of general dimensions that are like personality traits in that they represent stable aspects of parental behavior—aspects that remain across different situations, creating a characteristic manner or style in which parents interact with their children (Holden & Miller, 1999). When parenting is viewed in this way, two general dimensions of parental behavior emerge. One is the degree of warmth and responsiveness that parents show their children. At one end of the spectrum are parents who are openly warm and affectionate with their children. They are involved with them, respond to their emotional needs, and spend considerable time with them. At the other end of the spectrum are parents who are relatively uninvolved with their children and sometimes even hostile toward them. These parents often seem more focused on their own needs and interests than those of their children. Warm parents enjoy hearing their children describe the day's activities; uninvolved or hostile parents aren't interested, considering it a waste of their time. Warm parents see when their children are upset and try to comfort them; uninvolved or hostile parents pay little attention to their children's emotional states and invest little effort comforting them when they're upset. As you might expect, children benefit from warm and responsive parenting (Pettit, Bates, & Dodge, 1997; Zhou et al., 2002).

A second general dimension of parental behavior involves control. Some parents are dictatorial: They try to regulate every facet of their children's lives, like a puppeteer controlling a marionette. At the other extreme are parents who exert little or no control over their children: These children do whatever they want without

asking parents first or worrying about their parents' response. What's best for children is an intermediate amount of control, when parents set reasonable standards for their children's behavior, expect their children to meet them, and monitor their children's behavior (i.e., they also usually know where their children are, what they're doing, and with whom). When parents have reasonable expectations for their children and keep tabs on their activity—for example, a mother knows that her 12-year-old is staying after school for choir practice, then going to the library—their children tend to be better adjusted (Kilgore, Snyder, & Lentz, 2000).

When the dimensions of warmth and control are combined, the result is four prototypic styles of parenting, as shown in the diagram (Baumrind, 1975, 1991).

- *Authoritarian parenting* combines high control with little warmth. These parents lay down the rules and expect them to be followed without discussion. Hard work, respect, and obedience are what authoritarian parents wish to cultivate in their children. There is little give-and-take between parent and child because authoritarian parents do not consider children's needs or wishes. This style is illustrated by Tanya's mother in the opening vignette, who feels no obligation whatsoever to explain her decisions.

- *Authoritative parenting* combines a fair degree of parental control with being warm and responsive to children. Authoritative parents explain rules and encourage discussion. This style is exemplified by Sheila's mother in the opening vignette. She explained why she did not want Sheila going to the concert and encouraged her daughter to discuss the issue with her.

- *Permissive parenting* offers warmth and caring but little parental control. These parents generally accept their children's behavior and punish them infrequently. A permissive parent would readily agree to Tanya or Sheila's request to go to the concert, simply because it is something the child wants to do.

- *Uninvolved parenting* provides neither warmth nor control. Uninvolved parents provide for their children's basic physical and emotional needs but little else. These parents try to minimize the amount of time spent with their children and avoid becoming emotionally involved with them. Returning to the vignette, if Tanya or Sheila had uninvolved parents, she might have simply gone to the concert without asking, knowing that her parents wouldn't care and would rather not be bothered.

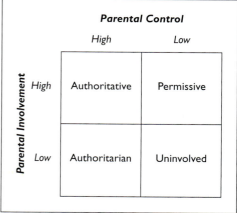

FIGURE 14-2

Research consistently shows that authoritative parenting is best for most children most of the time. Children with authoritative parents tend to be responsible, self-reliant, and friendly, and have higher grades (Amato & Fowler, 2002; Aunola, Stattin, & Nurmi, 2000). In contrast, children with authoritarian parents are often unhappy, have low self-esteem, and frequently are overly aggressive (e.g., Silk et al., 2003). Finally, children with permissive parents are often impulsive and have little self-control whereas children with uninvolved parents often do poorly in school and are aggressive (Aunola et al., 2000; Barber & Olsen, 1997). Thus, children typically thrive on a parental style that combines control, warmth, and affection.

**VARIATIONS ASSOCIATED WITH CULTURE AND SOCIOECONOMIC STATUS.** The general aim of child rearing—helping children become contributing members of their cultures—is much the same worldwide (Whiting & Child, 1953); and warmth

Authoritative parenting fosters achievement in school and self-reliance.

and control are universal aspects of parents' behavior. But views about the "proper" amount of warmth and the "proper" amount of control vary with particular cultures. European Americans want their children to be happy and self-reliant individuals; and they believe these goals are best achieved when parents are warm and exert moderate control (Goodnow, 1992). In many Asian and Latin American countries, however, individualism is less important than cooperation and collaboration (Okagaki & Sternberg, 1993). In China, for example, Confucian principles dictate that parents are always right and that emotional restraint is the key to family harmony (Chao, 2001). In fact, consistent with their cultural values, mothers and fathers in China are more likely to emphasize parental control and are less likely to express affection than are mothers and fathers in the United States (Lin & Fu, 1990). Thus, cultural values help specify appropriate ways for parents to interact with their offspring.

Not only do parental styles vary *across* cultures, they vary *within* cultures, depending on parents' socioeconomic status. Within the United States, parents with lower socioeconomic status tend to be more controlling and more punitive—characteristics associated with the authoritarian parenting style—than are parents with higher socioeconomic status (Hoff-Ginsberg & Tardif, 1995). This difference may reflect educational differences that help to define socioeconomic status. Parents with higher socioeconomic status are, by definition, more educated and, consequently often see development as a more complex process that requires the more nuanced and child-friendly approach that marks authoritative parenting (Skinner, 1985). Another contributing factor derives from another variable that defines socioeconomic status—income. Due to their limited financial resources, parents with lower socioeconomic status often lead more stressful lives (e.g., they wonder whether they'll have enough money at the end of the month for groceries) and are far more likely to live in neighborhoods where violence, drugs, and crime are commonplace. Thus, parents with lower socioeconomic status may be too stressed to invest the energy needed for authoritative parenting and the authoritarian approach—with its emphasis on the child's immediate compliance—may actually protect children growing up in dangerous neighborhoods (Parke & Buriel, 1998).

These different styles are critical for understanding parenting, but there's more to effective child rearing, as we'll see in the next section.

## Parental Behavior

A *style* is a broad characterization of how parents typically behave. If, for example, I describe a parent as using an authoritarian style, you immediately have a sense of that parent's typical ways of interacting with his or her children. Nevertheless, the price for such a general description is that it tells us little about how parents behave in specific situations and how these parental behaviors influence children's development. Put another way, what specific behaviors can parents use to influence their children? Researchers who study parents name three: direct instruction, modeling, and feedback.

**Parents influence children through direct instruction, by acting as models, and by providing feedback.**

**DIRECT INSTRUCTION.** Parents often tell their children what to do. But simply playing the role of drill sergeant in ordering children around—"Clean your room!" "Turn off the TV!"—is not very effective. **A better approach is *direct instruction*, telling a child what to do, when, and why.** Instead of just shouting "Share your candy with your brother!" a parent should explain when and why it's important to share with a sibling.

In addition, just as coaches help athletes master sports skills, parents can help their youngsters master social and emotional skills. Parents can explain links between emotions and behavior—"Catlin is sad because you broke her crayon" (Gottman, Katz, & Hooven, 1996). They can also teach how to deal with difficult social situations—"When you ask Lindsey if she can sleep over, do it privately so you won't hurt Kaycee's or Hannah's feelings" (Mize & Pettit, 1997). In general, children who get this sort of parental "coaching" tend to be more socially skilled and, not surprisingly, get along better with their peers. (I'll have more to say about this in Module 15.1.)

Direct instruction and coaching are particularly powerful when paired with modeling. Urging children to act in a particular way, such as sharing with others, is more compelling when children also see others sharing. In the next section, we'll see how children learn by observing others.

**LEARNING BY OBSERVING.**    Children learn a great deal from parents simply by watching them. For example, in Module 12.4 we saw that youngsters often learn how to interact with others by watching how their parents interact. The parents' modeling and the youngsters' observational learning thus lead to imitation, so children's behavior resembles the behavior they observe. *Observational learning* **can also produce** *counterimitation*, **learning what should not be done.** If an older brother like the one in the photo has been mean to a classmate and the father punishes him, the younger sister may learn to be friendly instead of mean.

**FEEDBACK.**    By giving feedback to their children, parents indicate whether a behavior is appropriate and should continue or is inappropriate and should stop. Feedback comes in two general forms. *Reinforcement* **is any action that increases the likelihood of the response that it follows.** Parents may use praise to reinforce a child's studying or give a reward for completing household chores. *Punishment* **is any action that discourages the reoccurrence of the response that it follows.** Parents may forbid children to watch television when they get poor grades in school or make children go to bed early for neglecting household chores.

Of course, parents have been rewarding and punishing their children for centuries, so what do psychologists know that parents don't know already? In fact, researchers have made some surprising discoveries concerning the nature of reward and punishment. **Parents often unwittingly reinforce the very behaviors they want to discourage, a situation called the** *negative reinforcement trap* (Patterson, 1980). The negative reinforcement trap occurs in three steps, most often between a mother and her son. In the first step, the mother tells her son to do something he doesn't want to do. She might tell him to clean up his room, to come inside while he's outdoors playing with friends, or to study instead of watching television. In the next step, the son responds with some behavior that most parents find intolerable: He argues, complains, or whines—not just briefly, but for an extended period. In the last step, the mother gives in—saying that the son needn't do as she told him initially—simply to get the son to stop the behavior that is so intolerable.

The feedback to the son is that arguing (or complaining or whining) works; the mother rewards that behavior by withdrawing the request that the son did not like. That is, although we usually think a behavior is strengthened when it is followed by the presentation of something that is valued, behavior is also strengthened when it is followed by removing something that is disliked.

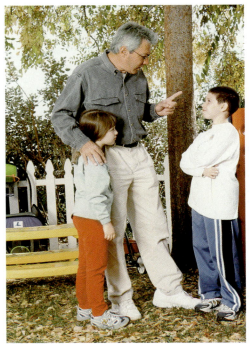

By watching others (observational learning), children can learn behaviors that are expected (and may be rewarded) as well as behaviors that are considered inappropriate (and may lead to punishment).

When 10-year-old Dylan's family got a puppy, he agreed to walk it every day after school. But when his mom asks him to do this, he gets angry because he'd rather watch TV. They argue for about 15 minutes, then Dylan's mom gives up and walks the dog herself. And Dylan goes back to watching TV. Analyze this situation. What could Dylan's mom do to prevent these regular arguments?

**14.1**

As for punishment, research (Parke, 1977) shows that punishment works best when

- administered directly after the undesired behavior occurs, rather than hours later;
- an undesired behavior always leads to punishment, rather than usually or occasionally;
- accompanied by an explanation of why the child was punished and how punishment can be avoided in the future; and
- the child has a warm, affectionate relationship with the person administering the punishment.

> **Punishment has limited value because it suppresses behaviors but does not eliminate them and it often has undesirable side effects.**

At the same time, research reveals some serious drawbacks to punishment. One is that punishment is primarily suppressive: Punished responses are stopped, but only temporarily if children do not learn new behaviors to replace those that were punished. For example, denying TV to brothers who are fighting stops the undesirable behavior, but fighting is likely to recur unless the boys learn new ways of solving their disputes.

A second drawback is that punishment can have undesirable side effects. Children become upset as they are being punished, which makes it unlikely that they will understand the feedback that punishment is meant to convey. A child denied TV for misbehaving may become angry over the punishment itself and ignore why he's being punished. What's more, as we saw in Module 12.4, when children are punished physically, they often imitate this behavior with peers and younger siblings (Whitehurst & Vasta, 1977). Children who are spanked often use aggression to resolve their disputes with others, and are more likely to have behavioral problems (Bradley et al., 2001).

Time out, in which children are isolated socially, is a particularly effective form of punishment.

One method combines the best features of punishment while avoiding its shortcomings. **In *time-out*, a child who misbehaves must briefly sit alone in a quiet, unstimulating location.** Some parents have children sit alone in a bathroom; others have children sit alone in a room, as shown in the photo. Time-out is punishing because it interrupts the child's ongoing activity and isolates the child from other family members, toys, books, and, generally, all forms of rewarding stimulation.

The period is sufficiently brief—usually just a few minutes—for a parent to use the method consistently. During time-out, both parent and child typically calm down. Then, when time-out is over, a parent can talk with the child and explain why the punished behavior is objectionable and what the child should do instead. "Reasoning" like this—even with preschool children—is effective because it emphasizes why a parent punished initially and how punishment can be avoided in the future.

Thus, parents can influence children by direct instruction, by modeling behavior that they value and not modeling what they don't want their children to learn, by giving feedback, and by adhering to the parenting styles that we examined in the first section of this module. In the next section, we'll explore a final, less direct way in which parents influence their children's development.

## Influences of the Marital System

When Derek returned from 7-Eleven with a six pack of beer and chips instead of diapers and baby food, Anita exploded in anger. "How could you! I used the last diaper an hour ago!" Huddled in the corner of the kitchen, their son Randy watched yet another episode in the daily soap opera that featured Derek and Anita.

Although Derek and Anita aren't arguing about Randy—in fact, they're so wrapped up in their conflict that they forget he's in the room—it's hard to conceive that a child would emerge unscathed from such constant parental conflict. And research shows that chronic parental conflict is harmful for children. Parental conflict affects children's development through three distinct mechanisms. First, seeing parents fight jeopardizes a child's feeling that the family is stable and secure, making a child feel anxious, frightened, and sad (Davies et al., 2004). Second, chronic conflict between parents often spills over into the parent–child relationship. A wife who finds herself frequently arguing with and confronting her husband may adopt a similarly ineffective style in interacting with her children (Cox, Paley, & Harter, 2001). Third, when parents invest time and energy fighting with each other, they're often too tired or too preoccupied to invest themselves in high-quality parenting (Katz & Woodlin, 2002).

Of course, all marriages experience conflict at some point. Does this mean that all children bear at least some scars? Not necessarily. Many parents resolve conflicts in a manner that's constructive instead of destructive. To see this, suppose that one parent believes their child should attend a summer camp but the other parent believes it's too expensive and not worth it because the child attended the previous summer. Instead of shouting and name-calling (e.g., "You're always such a cheapskate!") some parents seek mutually acceptable solutions: The child could attend the camp if she earns money to cover part of the cost or the child could attend a different, less expensive camp. When families like the one in the photo routinely resolve disagreements this way, children actually respond *positively* to conflict apparently because it shows that their family is cohesive and able to withstand life's problems (Goeke-Moray et al., 2003).

The extent and resolution of conflict is an obvious way in which the parental system affects children, but it's not the only way. Many mothers and fathers form an effective parental team, working together in a coordinated and complementary fashion toward goals that they share for their child's development. For example, Mom and Dad may agree that their daughter is smart and athletically skilled and that she should excel in both domains. Consequently, they're quite happy to help her achieve these goals. Mom gives her basketball tips and Dad edits her school essays.

But not all parents work together well. Sometimes they don't agree on goals: One parent values sports over schoolwork while the other reverses these priorities. Sometimes parents actively compete for their child's attention: Mom may want to take the child shopping but Dad wants to take her to a ball game. Finally, parents sometimes act as gatekeepers, limiting one another's participation in parenting. Mom may feel that infant care is solely her turf and not allow Dad to participate. Or Dad may claim all school-related tasks and discourage Mom from getting involved.

These many examples show that, just as a doubles tennis team won't win many matches when each player ignores his or her partner, parenting is far less effective when parents try to "go it alone" instead of working together, trying to achieve goals that they share, using methods that they both accept. Lack of teamwork, competition,

When parents resolve conflicts constructively, their children respond positively to conflict.

and gatekeeping can lead to problems, causing children, for example, to become withdrawn (McHale et al., 2002). Thus, in understanding parents' impact on children's development, we need to consider the nature of the marital relationship as well as parenting style and specific parenting behaviors (e.g., parents' use of feedback).

In the next section, we'll switch perspectives and see how children affect parenting behavior.

## Children's Contributions

I emphasized earlier that the family is a dynamic, interactive system with parents and children influencing each other. In fact, children begin at birth to influence the way their parents treat them. Let's look at two characteristics of children that influence how parents treat them.

*Age.* Parenting changes as children grow. The same parenting that is marvelously effective with infants and toddlers is inappropriate for adolescents. These age-related changes in parenting are evident in the two basic dimensions of parental behavior—warmth and control. Warmth is beneficial throughout development— toddlers and teens alike enjoy knowing that others care about them. But the manifestation of parental affection changes, becoming more reserved as children develop. The enthusiastic hugging and kissing that delights toddlers embarrasses adolescents. Parental control also changes as children develop (Maccoby, 1984; Vazsonyi, Hibbert, & Snider, 2003). As children develop cognitively and are better able to make their own decisions, parents gradually relinquish control and expect children to be responsible for themselves. For instance, parents of elementary-school children often keep track of their children's progress on school assignments, but parents of adolescents don't, expecting their children to do this themselves.

> Parental behavior often is affected by children's age and temperament.

*Temperament and behavior.* A child's temperament can have a powerful effect on parental behavior (Brody & Ge, 2001). To illustrate the reciprocal influence of parents and children, imagine two children with different temperaments as they respond to a parent's authoritative style. The first child has an "easy" temperament, complying readily with parental requests and responding well to family discussions about parental expectations. These parent–child relations are a textbook example of successful authoritative parenting. But suppose, like the child in the photo, the second child has a "difficult temperament" and complies reluctantly and sometimes not at all. Over time, the parent becomes more controlling and less affectionate. The child in turn complies even less in the future, leading the parent to adopt an authoritarian parenting style (Bates et al., 1998).

An example of the impact of children's behavior on parents is that, when children respond to parents defiantly, their parents often resort to harsher forms of punishment.

As this example illustrates, parenting behaviors and styles often evolve as a consequence of the child's behavior. With a moderately active young child who is eager to please adults, a parent may discover that a modest amount of control is adequate. But for a very active child who is not as eager to please, a parent may need to be more controlling and directive (Brody & Ge, 2001; Hastings & Rubin, 1999). Influence is reciprocal: Children's behavior helps determine how parents treat them and the resulting parental behavior influences children's behavior, which in turn causes parents to again change their behavior (Stoolmiller, 2001).

As time goes by, these reciprocal influences lead many families to adopt routine ways of interacting with each other. Some families end up functioning smoothly: Parents and children cooperate, anticipate each other's needs, and are generally happy. Unfortunately, other families end up troubled: Disagreements are common, parents spend much time trying unsuccessfully to control their defiant children, and everyone is often angry and upset (Belsky, Woodworth, & Crnic, 1996; Kochanska, 1997).

Over the long term, such troubled families do not fare well, so it's important that these negative reciprocal influences are nipped in the bud (Carrere & Gottman, 1999; Christensen & Heavey, 1999).

### CHECK YOUR LEARNING

**RECALL** Describe ways in which the marital system contributes to children's development.

What are some of the ways in which children influence their own development?

**INTERPRET** Compare the styles approach to parenting with the approach that focuses on parental behavior per se. What are the strengths of each?

**APPLY** Imagine a family in which Mom and Dad both work full time outside the home. Mom's employer wants her to take a new position in a distant small town. Mom is tempted because the position represents a promotion with much more responsibility and much higher pay. However, because the town is so small, Dad couldn't get a job comparable to the one he has now, which he loves. Based on what you know about Bronfenbrenner's family systems theory (pages 428–430), how might the move affect the couple's 10-year-old daughter and 4-year-old son?

This is a classic negative reinforcement trap: (1) Mom asks her son to do something, (2) he refuses and argues endlessly, and (3) Mom gives in to end the argument, thereby reinforcing the argumentative behavior. Dylan's mom has a couple of alternatives. She could remind Dylan of the original agreement and hold fast to the rule that he can't watch TV until he's walked the dog. But maybe this rule isn't a good one any longer, for reasons that neither Dylan nor his mom could anticipate when they got the puppy. Then she and Dylan should talk about the agreement and find another way in which he can shoulder part of the responsibility of puppy care.

**14.1**

# THE CHANGING FAMILY   **14.2**

**LEARNING OBJECTIVES**

- What are some of the effects of divorce on children?

- How do children adjust to a parent's remarriage?

- How effective as parents are grandparents and gay parents?

Impact of Divorce on Children

Blended Families

The Role of Grandparents

Children of Gay and Lesbian Parents

*Jack has lived with his dad for the 4 years since his parents' divorce; he visits his mother every other weekend. Although Jack was confused and depressed when his parents divorced, he has come to terms with the new situation. He's excelling in school, where he is well liked by peers and teachers. One of Jack's friends is Troy. Troy's parents are married but bicker constantly since his dad lost his job. His parents are unable to agree on anything; the pettiest event or remark triggers an argument. Troy's grades have fallen, and whereas he was once a leader among the boys in his class, now he prefers to be alone.*

The American family has been changing steadily since the middle of the 20th century. First, people are older when they marry—the age of first marriage is up nearly 5 years since the 1950s (U.S. Census Bureau, 1998). Second, families are smaller, having decreased from an average of more than 3 children in 1960 to fewer than

2 children today (U.S. Census Bureau, 2004). Finally, more children are growing up in single-parent families due to a doubling of the divorce rate since the 1960s and a doubling of the percentage of babies born to unwed mothers (Children's Defense Fund, 2004).

Because of these and other societal changes, today the family takes on many different forms in the United States and in other industrialized nations. In this module, we'll look at several of these forms and see how children develop within them. As we do, we'll look at the impact of divorce on Jack and the impact of marital conflict on Troy.

## Impact of Divorce on Children

Like Jack, many American youngsters' parents divorce. Nearly half of all first marriages end in divorce and every year approximately 1 million American children have parents who divorce (Amato, 2001). According to all theories of child development, divorce is distressing for children because it involves conflict between parents and usually separation from one of them. Do the disruptions, conflict, and stress associated with divorce affect children? Of course they do. Having answered this easy question, however, many more difficult questions remain: Are all aspects of children's lives affected equally by divorce? *How* does divorce influence development? Why is divorce more stressful for some children than others?

**WHAT ASPECTS OF CHILDREN'S LIVES ARE AFFECTED BY DIVORCE?**    By 2000, nearly 200 studies on divorce had been conducted, involving tens of thousands of preschool- through college-age children. Comprehensive meta-analyses of this research reveal that in school achievement, conduct, adjustment, self-concept, and parent–child relations, children whose parents had divorced fared poorly compared to children from intact families (Amato, 2001; Amato & Keith, 1991). However, the effects of divorce dropped from the 1970s to 1980s, perhaps because as divorce became more frequent in the 1980s, it became more familiar and less frightening. The effects of divorce increased again in the 1990s, perhaps reflecting a widening gap in income between single- and two-parent families (Amato, 2001).

When children of divorced parents become adults, the effects of divorce persist. As adults, children of divorce are more likely to experience conflict in their own marriages, to have negative attitudes toward marriage, and to become divorced themselves. Also, they report less satisfaction with life and are more likely to become depressed (Hetherington & Kelly, 2002; Segrin, Taylor, & Altman, 2005). These findings don't mean that children of divorce are destined to have unhappy, conflict-ridden marriages that inevitably lead to divorce, but children of divorce are at greater risk for such an outcome.

The 1st year following a divorce is often rocky for parents and children alike. But beginning in the 2nd year, most children begin to adjust to their new circumstances (Hetherington & Kelly, 2002). Children adjust to divorce more readily if their divorced parents cooperate with each other, especially on disciplinary matters (Buchanan & Heiges, 2001). **In *joint custody*, both parents retain legal custody of the children.** Children benefit from joint custody if their parents get along well (Bauserman, 2002).

Of course, many parents do not get along after a divorce, which eliminates joint custody as an option. Traditionally, mothers have been awarded custody; but in recent years fathers have increasingly often been given custody, especially of sons. This practice coincides with findings that children such as Jack, the other boy in the opening vignette, often adjust better when they live with same-sex parents: Boys often fare better with fathers and girls fare better with mothers (McLanahan, 1999). One reason boys are often better off with their fathers is that boys are likely to become involved in negative reinforcement traps (described in Module 14.1) with their mothers. Another explanation is that both boys and girls may forge stronger emotional relationships with same-sex parents than with other-sex parents (Zimiles & Lee, 1991).

**HOW DOES DIVORCE INFLUENCE DEVELOPMENT?**    Divorce usually results in several changes in family life that affect children (Amato & Keith, 1991). First, the absence of one parent means that children lose a role model, a source of parental help and emotional support, and a supervisor. For instance, a single parent may have to choose between helping one child complete an important paper or watching another child perform in a school play. Since she can't do both, one child will miss out.

Second, single-parent families experience economic hardship, which creates stress and often means that activities once taken for granted are no longer available (Goodman et al., 1998). A single parent may no longer be able to afford books for pleasure reading, music lessons, or other activities that promote child development. Moreover, when a single parent worries about having enough money for food and rent, she has less energy and effort to devote to parenting.

Third, as we saw in Module 14.1, conflict between parents is extremely distressing to children and adolescents (Leon, 2003), particularly for children who are emotionally insecure (Davies & Cummings, 1998). In fact, many of the problems ascribed to divorce are really caused by marital conflict occurring before the divorce (Erel & Burman, 1995; Shaw, Winslow, & Flanagan, 1999). Children like Troy, the boy in the opening vignette whose parents are married but fight constantly, often show many of the same effects associated with divorce (Katz & Woodin, 2002).

> Divorce affects children through the loss of a role model, economic hardship, and exposure to conflict.

**WHICH CHILDREN ARE MOST AFFECTED BY DIVORCE? WHY?**    Some children are more affected by divorce than others. Amato and Keith's (1991) analysis, for example, showed that although the overall impact of divorce is the same for boys and girls, divorce is more harmful when it occurs during childhood and adolescence than during the preschool or college years. Also, children who are temperamentally more emotional tend to be more affected by divorce (Lengua et al., 1999).

Some children suffer more from divorce because of their tendency to interpret events negatively. We know, from Module 12.4, that two children often have differing interpretations of exactly the same social event. Suppose, for example, that a father forgets to take a child on a promised outing. One child might believe that an emergency prevented the father from taking the child. A second child might believe that the father hadn't really wanted to spend time with the child in the first place and will never make similar plans again. Children who—like the second child—tend to interpret life events negatively are more likely to have behavioral problems following divorce (Mazur et al., 1999).

Finally, children's efforts to cope with divorce-related stress can influence the impact of divorce. When children actively cope with their parents' divorce—either by trying to solve a problem or by trying to make it feel less threatening—they gain confidence in their ability to control future events in their lives. This protects children from behavioral disorders such as anxiety or depression (Sandler et al., 2000).

Just as children can reduce the harm of divorce by being active problem solvers, parents can make divorce easier on their children. The "Improving Children's Lives" feature has some tips on ways parents can make divorce less stressful for their children.

*Improving Children's Lives*

**Helping Children Adjust After Divorce**

Divorce causes major changes in children's lives that are very stressful. Here are some ways parents can reduce stress and help children adjust to their new life circumstances. Parents should

- explain together to children why they are divorcing and what their children can expect to happen to them.
- reassure children that they will always love them and always be their parents; parents must back up these words with actions by remaining involved in their children's lives, despite the increased difficulty of doing so.
- expect that their children will sometimes be angry or sad about the divorce, and they should encourage children to discuss these feelings with them.

Parents should not

- compete with each other for their children's love and attention; children adjust to divorce best when they maintain good relationships with both parents.
- take out their anger with each other on their children.
- criticize their ex-spouse in front of the children.
- ask children to mediate disputes; parents should work out problems without putting the children in the middle.

Following all these rules all the time is not easy. After all, divorce is stressful and painful for adults, too. But parents owe it to their children to try to follow most of these rules most of the time to minimize the disruptive effects of their divorce on their children's development. ■

## Blended Families

Following divorce, most children live in a single-parent household for about 5 years. However, like the adults in the photo, more than two thirds of men and women eventually remarry (Glick, 1989; Glick & Lin, 1986). **The resulting unit, consisting of a biological parent, stepparent, and children, is known as a *blended family*.** (Other terms for this family configuration are "remarried family" and "reconstituted family.")

As divorce became more common in the 20th century, so did blended families, in which children live with a stepparent and sometimes with stepsiblings.

Because mothers are more often granted custody of children, the most common form of blended family is a mother, her children, and a stepfather. Most stepfathers do not participate actively in childrearing; they often seem reluctant to become involved (Clarke-Stewart & Bretano, 2005). Nevertheless, boys typically benefit from the presence of a stepfather, particularly when he is warm and involved. Preadolescent girls, however, do not adjust readily to their mother's remarriage, apparently because it disrupts the intimate relationship they have established with her (Bray, 1999; Visher, Visher, & Pasley, 2003).

These adjustments are more difficult when mothers of adolescents remarry. Adolescents do not adapt to the new family circumstances as easily as children do; they're more likely to challenge a stepfather's authority.

And adjustment is more difficult when a stepfather brings his own biological children. In such families, parents sometimes favor their biological children over their stepchildren—they're more involved with and warmer toward their biological children. Such preferential treatment almost always leads to conflict and unhappiness (Dunn & Davies, 2001; Hetherington, Bridges, & Insabella, 1998). And when the mother and stepfather argue, children usually side with their biological parents (Dunn, O'Connor, & Cheng, 2005).

The best strategy for stepfathers is to be interested in their new stepchildren but avoid encroaching on established relationships. Newly remarried mothers must be careful that their enthusiasm for their new spouse does not come at the expense of time and affection for their children. And both parents and children need to have realistic expectations. The blended family can be successful and beneficial for children and adolescents, but it takes effort because of the complicated relationships, conflicting loyalties, and jealousies that usually exist (Anderson et al., 1999; White & Gilbreth, 2001).

> Children in blended families often worry that remarriage will damage the close relationship they have with their biological parent.

Much less is known about blended families consisting of a father, his children, and a stepmother, though several factors make a father's remarriage difficult for his children. First, fathers are often awarded custody when judges believe that children are unruly and will profit from a father's "firm hand." Consequently, many children living with their fathers do not adjust well to many of life's challenges, which certainly includes a father's remarriage. Second, fathers are sometimes granted custody because they have a particularly close relationship with their children, especially their sons. When this is the case, children sometimes fear that their father's remarriage will disturb this relationship (Buchanan, Maccoby, & Dornbusch, 1996). Finally, noncustodial mothers are more likely than noncustodial fathers to maintain close and frequent contact with their children (Maccoby et al., 1993). The constant presence of the noncustodial mother may interfere with a stepmother's efforts to establish close relationships with her stepchildren, particularly with her stepdaughters.

Over time, children adjust to the blended family. If the marriage is happy, most children profit from the presence of two caring adults. Unfortunately, second marriages are slightly more likely than first marriages to end in divorce, so many children relive the trauma. As you can imagine, another divorce—and possibly another remarriage—severely disrupts children's development, accentuating the problems that followed the initial divorce (Dunn, 2002).

## The Role of Grandparents

With people living longer, three-generation families—with child, parents, and grandparents—are becoming the norm in many industrialized nations. Most American children see their grandparents at least once a month, more often if they live nearby. Grandmothers are usually more involved with grandchildren than grandfathers, and some scientists believe this is an evolutionary adaptation. That is, for most of human history, the onset of menopause has coincided, approximately, with the birth of grandchildren. Genetically speaking, middle-aged women may be more valuable caring for their grandchildren—making sure that they survive to bear further children— than in bearing additional children of their own (Smith & Drew, 2002).

What roles do grandparents play in children's lives? One recent analysis suggested five specific styles of grandparenting (Mueller & Elder, 2003):

**14.2** Ollie, a 4-year-old, sees his grandparents several times a week. They take him to preschool on Monday and Wednesday, and try to do something special, such as getting an ice cream cone, each week. And they don't hesitate to remind him to say "please" and "thank you" and to wait his turn. What grandparental role best describes Ollie's grandparents?

- *Influential grandparents* are very close to their grandchildren, are very involved in their lives, and frequently perform parental roles, including discipline.

- *Supportive grandparents* are similar to influential grandparents—close and involved with grandchildren—but do not take on parental roles.

- *Authority-oriented grandparents* provide discipline for their grandchildren but otherwise are not particularly active in their grandchildren's lives.

- *Passive grandparents* are caught up in their grandchildren's development but not with the intensity of influential or supportive grandparents; they do not assume parental roles.

- *Detached grandparents* are uninvolved with their grandchildren.

The first two grandparental roles—influential and supportive—are those in which grandparents are most involved with their grandchildren. Several factors determine whether grandparents assume these involved roles. Some factors are practical: Grandparents are more involved when they live near their grandchildren and when they have few rather than many grandchildren. Other factors concern grandparents' relationships with their children and their own grandparents: Grandparents are more concerned when their children (i.e., the grandchildren's parents) encourage such involvement and when they knew their own maternal grandparent. Finally, the influential and supportive roles are more often taken by maternal grandparents than by paternal grandparents (Mueller & Elder, 2003). Obviously, no single factor determines the extent to which a grandparent takes an active role in a grandchild's development.

## Cultural Influences

### Grandmothers in African American Families

Approximately 1 in 8 African American children lives with a grandmother, compared to only 1 in 15 European American children (Field, 2003). Why is this? A quarter of all African American children grow up in chronic poverty, and living with relatives is one way of sharing—and thereby reducing—the costs associated with housing and child care.

African American grandmothers who live with their daughters and their children frequently become involved in rearing their grandchildren, adopting the role of influential grandparent (Pearson et al., 1990). When the daughter is a teenage mother, the grandmother may be the child's primary caregiver, an arrangement that benefits both the adolescent mother and the child. Freed from the obligations of child rearing, the adolescent mother is able to improve her situation by, for example, finishing school. The child benefits because grandmothers are often more effective mothers than teenage mothers: Grandmothers are less punitive and, like the grandmother in the photo, are very responsive to their grandchildren (Chase-Lansdale, Brooks-Gunn, & Zamsky, 1994; Smith & Drew, 2002).

African American grandmothers often play an active role in rearing their grandchildren, which benefits the grandchildren.

Another benefit is that when grandmothers have positive relationships with the young mother and young father, they get along better with each other, and parent more effectively (Krishnakumar & Black, 2003).

This family arrangement works well for children. In terms of achievement and adjustment, children living with their mothers and grandmothers resemble children living in two-parent families, and they tend to be better off than children in single-parent families (Wilson, 1989). Even when grandmothers are not living in the house, children benefit when their mothers receive social and emotional support from grandmothers and other relatives: Children are more self-reliant and less likely to become involved in delinquent activities such as drug use and vandalism (Taylor & Roberts, 1995).

Thus, grandmothers and other relatives can ease the burden of child rearing in African American families living in poverty, and, not surprisingly, children benefit from the added warmth, support, and guidance of an extended family. ■

Grandparents are especially active in the lives of immigrant and minority children, often taking on parental roles (Hernandez, 2004; Minkler-Fuller & Thomson, 2005). The "Cultural Influences" feature describes the important role of grandmothers in African American family life.

By acting as surrogate parents, grandparents can affect their grandchildren's lives directly. However, grandparents also affect their grandchildren indirectly, through intergenerational transmission of parental attitudes and practices. For example, if parents are affectionate with their children, when these children become parents themselves, they will tend to be affectionate with their own children. In other words, the grandparents' affectionate behavior results in their grandchildren experiencing affectionate care. Thus, it is important to think about the indirect as well as the direct influences that grandparents have on their grandchildren (Smith & Drew, 2002).

## Children of Gay and Lesbian Parents

Several million youngsters in the United States have a gay or lesbian parent (Patterson, 2002). In most of these situations, children were born in a heterosexual marriage that ended in divorce when one parent revealed his or her homosexuality. Less frequent, but becoming more common, are children born to single lesbians or to lesbian couples who have children through artificial insemination or adoption.

Research on gay and lesbian parents and their children is scarce, and most has involved children who were born to a heterosexual marriage that ended in divorce when the mother came out as a lesbian. Most of these lesbian mothers are European American and well educated (Patterson, 2002).

As parents, gay and lesbian couples are more similar to heterosexual couples than they are different. There is no indication that gay and lesbian parents are less effective parents than heterosexual parents. In fact, some evidence suggests that gay men may be especially responsive to children's needs, perhaps because their self-concepts include emotional sensitivity that is traditionally associated with the female gender role (Patterson, 2004).

Children reared by gay and lesbian parents seem to develop much like children reared by heterosexual couples (Golombok et al., 2003; Patterson, 2002). Preschool boys and girls apparently identify with their own sex and acquire the usual accompaniment of gender-based preferences, interests, activities, and friends. As adolescents,

> In most respects—including gender roles, self-concept, and social skill—children of gay and lesbian parents resemble children of heterosexual parents.

they continue to thrive and the vast majority are heterosexual (Wainright, Russell, & Patterson, 2004). In other respects—such as self-concept, social skill, moral reasoning, and intelligence—children of lesbian mothers resemble children of heterosexual parents. For example, in one study of 80 families—55 headed by a lesbian and 25 headed by a heterosexual—the children were comparable in social competence and behavioral adjustment (Chan, Raboy, & Patterson, 1998).

Research on children reared by gay and lesbian couples, along with findings concerning African American grandmothers, reminds us that "good parenting" can assume many different forms. These research results also challenge the conventional wisdom that a two-parent family with mother and father both present *necessarily* provides the best circumstances for development. Multiple adults *are* important— that's evident from research on the impact of divorce on children—but *who* the adults are seems to matter less than what they do. Children benefit from good parenting skills, whether it's a mother and father or grandparents—or two women or two men—doing the parenting.

**14.2** Ollie's grandparents are best described as influential because they're very involved in his life and because they take on parental tasks, including discipline.

## CHECK YOUR LEARNING

**RECALL** Describe the different grandparental roles and the factors that influence which roles grandparents take on.

What is known about development in children of gay and lesbian parents?

**INTERPRET** From a child's perspective, what are the pros and cons of a blended (remarried) family?

**APPLY** Suppose that a couple argues constantly. They've tried to resolve their differences in counseling, but this was unsuccessful and now they're considering a divorce. They are the parents of two school-age children. What advice would you give them?

## 14.3 BROTHERS AND SISTERS

Firstborn, Laterborn, and Only Children

Qualities of Sibling Relationships

### LEARNING OBJECTIVES

- How do firstborn, laterborn, and only children differ?

- How do sibling relationships change as children grow? What determines how well siblings get along?

*Bob and Alice adored their 2-year-old son, Robbie, who was friendly, playful, and always eager to learn new things. In fact, Bob thought Robbie was nearly perfect and saw no reason to tempt fate by having another child. However, Alice had heard stories that only children were conceited, spoiled, and unfriendly. Alice was sure that Robbie would grow up like this unless she and Bob had another child. What to do?*

For most of a year, all firstborn children are only children like Robbie. Some children remain "onlies" forever, but most get brothers and sisters. Some firstborns are joined by many siblings in rapid succession; others are simply joined by a single brother or sister. As the family acquires these new members, parent–child relationships become more complex (Brody, 2004). Parents can no longer focus on a single child but must adjust to the needs of multiple children. Just as important, siblings influence each other's development, not just during childhood but, as the cartoon reminds us, throughout life. To understand sibling influence, let's look at differences between firstborns, laterborns, and only children.

## Firstborn, Laterborn, and Only Children

Firstborn children are often "guinea pigs" for most parents, who have lots of enthusiasm but little practical experience rearing children. Parents typically have high expectations for their firstborns and are both more affectionate and more punitive with them. As more children arrive, parents become more adept at their roles, having learned "the tricks of the parent trade" with earlier children. With laterborn children, parents have more realistic expectations and are more relaxed in their discipline (e.g., Baskett, 1985).

The different approaches that parents take with their firstborns and laterborns help explain differences that are commonly observed between these children. Firstborn children generally have higher scores on intelligence tests and are more likely to go to college. They are also more willing to conform to parents' and adults' requests. Laterborn children, perhaps because they are less concerned about pleasing parents and adults but need to get along with older siblings, are more popular with their peers and more innovative (Herrera et al., 2003; Sulloway, 2005).

And what about only children? Alice, the mother in the opening vignette, was well acquainted with the conventional wisdom, which says that parents like the ones in the photo dote on "onlies," with the result that the children are selfish and egotistical. Is the folklore correct? From a comprehensive analysis of more than 100 studies, the answer is "no." In fact, only children were found more likely to succeed in school than other children and to have higher levels of intelligence, leadership, autonomy, and maturity (Falbo & Polit, 1986).

This research has important implications for China, where only children are the norm due to government efforts to limit family size. The "Child Development and Family Policy" feature tells the story.

Contrary to the folklore, only children are not spoiled brats; instead, they tend to do well in school and often are leaders.

## *Child Development and Family Policy*
### Assessing the Consequences of China's One-Child Policy

With more than a billion citizens, the People's Republic of China has the largest population in the world. In the middle of the 20th century, Chinese leaders recognized that a large, rapidly growing population was a serious obstacle to economic growth and an improved standard of living. Consequently, the Chinese government implemented several programs to limit family size and since 1979 has had a policy of one child per family. The policy was promoted with billboards like the one in the photo that advertised the benefits of having only one child. Parents were encouraged to use contraceptives and, more importantly, one-child families received

Since 1979, the Chinese government has had a policy of encouraging parents to have only one child.

many economic benefits: cash bonuses, better health and child care, and more-desirable housing.

The policy has been effective in reducing the birth rate in China; and now social scientists are evaluating the impact of the one-child policy on children and their families. For example, traditionally the Chinese have valued well-behaved children who get along well with others. Would the only children in today's China be less cooperative and more self-centered than previous generations of Chinese youngsters? The answer seems to be "no." Many studies have compared only and non-only children in China; most comparisons find no differences; when differences are found, the advantage often goes to the only child (Hart et al., 1998; Jiao, Ji, & Jing, 1996; Wang et al., 2000).

As Chinese only children enter adulthood, a new concern will be care of the elderly. Traditionally, children have been responsible for their aging parents. This task becomes more demanding—financially and psychologically—when it cannot be shared with other siblings. Research will be needed to determine whether older people receive adequate care and to determine the impact on only children of providing such care. Through this sort of research, psychologists and other social scientists will play an important role in helping to determine the long-term consequences of China's decision to limit family size. ■

Beginning in the 1960s, interracial adoption became very common in the United States.

**ADOPTED CHILDREN.** The U.S. government doesn't keep official statistics on the number of adopted children, but the best estimate is that about 2 to 4% of U.S. children are adopted. The majority of adoptive parents are middle-class European Americans and, until the 1960s, so were adopted children. However, improved birth control and legalized abortion in the late 1960s meant that hardly any European American infants were relinquished for adoption. Consequently, beginning in the 1960s, parents began to adopt children of other races, as shown in the photo, and children from other countries. At the same time, parents began to adopt children with special needs, such as chronic medical problems or exposure to maltreatment (Brodzinsky & Pinderhughes, 2002; Gunnar, Bruce, & Grotevant, 2000).

As adoption became more common, the myth of the "adopted child syndrome" blossomed. According to this myth, adopted children are more prone to behavioral problems, substance use, and criminal activity, presumably because of the special challenges they face in establishing a unique identity, which we explored in Module 11.1 (Finley, 1999). Is there any truth to the myth? In fact, when compared to children living with biological parents, adopted children are quite similar in terms of temperament, mother–infant attachment, and cognitive development (Brodzinsky & Pinderhughes, 2002).

But some findings *are* consistent with the myth. Adopted children are more prone to problems adjusting to school and to conduct disorders, such as being overly aggressive (Miller et al., 2000). To a certain extent, this finding reflects the fact that adoptive parents are more likely to seek help for their adoptive children because they are more affluent and can afford it, and because they are used to dealing with agencies that provide mental health services. Also, the extent of these problems hinges on the age when the child was adopted and the quality of their care prior to adoption (Brodzinsky & Pinderhughes, 2002; Gunnar et al., 2000). Problems are much more common when children are adopted at an older age (and thus probably are separated from an attachment figure) and when their care before adoption was poor (e.g., they were institutionalized or lived in a series of foster homes).

Perhaps the best way to summarize this research is that adoption per se is not a fundamental developmental challenge for most children. But quality of life before adoption certainly places some adopted children at risk. And it's important to remember that most adopted children fare quite well.

In discussing firstborn, laterborn, only, and adopted children, we have not yet considered relationships that exist between siblings. These can be powerful forces on development, as we'll see in the next section.

> **Adopted children are more prone to problems, typically due to poor quality of life before their adoption.**

## Qualities of Sibling Relationships

From the very beginning, sibling relationships are complicated. On the one hand, most expectant parents are excited by the prospect of another child, and their enthusiasm is contagious: Their children, too, eagerly await the arrival of the newest family member. On the other hand, the birth of a sibling is often distressing for older children, who may become withdrawn or return to more childish behavior because of the changes that occur in their lives, particularly the need to share parental attention and affection (Gottlieb & Mendelson, 1990). However, distress can be avoided if parents remain responsive to their older children's needs (Howe & Ross, 1990). In fact, one of the benefits of a sibling's birth is that fathers become more involved with their older children (Stewart et al., 1987).

Many older siblings enjoy helping their parents take care of newborns. Older children play with the baby, console it, feed it, or change its diapers. In middle-class Western families, such caregiving often occurs in the context of play, with parents nearby. But in some cultures, children—particularly girls like the one in the photo—play an important role in providing care for their younger siblings (Zukow-Goldring, 2002).

As the infant grows, interactions between siblings become more frequent and more complicated. For example, toddlers tend to talk more to parents than to older siblings. But, by the time the younger sibling is 4 years old, the situation

In many developing countries, older siblings are actively involved in caring for their younger siblings.

Calvin, age 8, and his younger sister, Hope, argue over just about everything and constantly compete for their parents' attention. Teenage sisters Hilary and Elizabeth love doing everything together and enjoy sharing clothes and secrets about their teen romances. Why might Calvin and Hope get along so poorly but Elizabeth and Hillary get along so well?

**14.3**

Parents can foster good sibling relationships by treating children fairly and by getting along with each other.

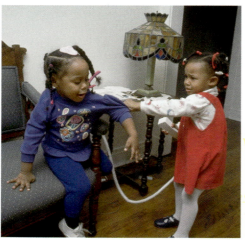

Preschool children often argue because they lack the social skills to settle disagreements in a mutually beneficial manner.

is reversed: Now young siblings talk more to older siblings than to their mother (Brown & Dunn, 1992). Older siblings become a source of care and comfort for younger siblings when they are distressed or upset (Garner, Jones, & Palmer, 1994) and older siblings serve as teachers for their younger siblings, teaching them to play games or how to cook simple foods (Maynard, 2002). Finally, when older children do well in school and are popular with peers, younger siblings often follow suit (Brody et al., 2003).

As time goes by, some siblings grow close, becoming best friends in ways that nonsiblings can never be. Other siblings constantly argue, compete, and simply do not get along with each other. The basic pattern of sibling interaction seems to be established early in development and remains fairly stable. Dunn, Slomkowski, and Beardsall (1994), for example, interviewed mothers twice about their children's interaction, first when the children were 3- and 5-year-olds and again 7 years later, when the children were 10- and 12-year-olds. Dunn and her colleagues found that siblings who got along as preschoolers often continued to get along as young adolescents, whereas siblings who quarreled as preschoolers often quarreled as young adolescents.

Why are some sibling relationships filled with love and respect, but others are dominated by jealousy and resentment? Put more simply, what factors contribute to the quality of sibling relationships? First, children's sex and temperament matter. Sibling relations are more likely to be warm and harmonious between siblings of the same sex than between siblings of the opposite sex (Dunn & Kendrick, 1981) and when neither sibling is temperamentally emotional (Brody, Stoneman, & McCoy, 1994). Age is also important: Sibling relationships generally improve as the younger child approaches adolescence because siblings begin to perceive one another as equals (Buhrmester & Furman, 1990).

Parents contribute to the quality of sibling relationships, both directly and indirectly (Brody, 1998). The direct influence stems from parents' treatment. Siblings more often get along when they believe that parents have no "favorites" but treat all siblings fairly (Kowal & Kramer, 1997). When parents lavishly praise one child's accomplishments while ignoring another's, children notice the difference and their sibling relationship suffers (Updegraff et al., 2005).

This doesn't mean that parents must treat all their children the same. Children understand that parents should treat their kids differently—based on their age or personal needs. Only when differential treatment is not justified do sibling relationships deteriorate (Kowal & Kramer, 1997). In fact, during adolescence, siblings get along better when each has a unique, well-defined relationship with parents (Feinberg et al., 2003).

The indirect influence of parents on sibling relationships stems from the quality of the parents' relationship with each other: A warm, harmonious relationship between parents fosters positive sibling relationships; conflict between parents is associated with conflict between siblings (Erel, Margolin, & John, 1998; Volling & Belsky, 1992). When parents don't get along, they no longer treat their children the same, leading to conflict among siblings (Brody et al., 1994).

One practical implication of these findings is that in their pursuit of family harmony (what many parents call "peace and quiet"), parents can influence some of the factors affecting sibling relationships but not others. Parents can help reduce friction between siblings by being equally affectionate, responsive, and caring with all of their children and by caring for one another. At the same time, some dissension is natural in families, especially those with young boys and girls: Children's different interests lead to arguments, like the one in the photo. Faced with common simple conflicts—Who decides which TV show to watch? Who gets to eat the last cookie? Who gets to hold the new puppy?—a 3-year-old brother and a 5-year-old sister *will* argue because they lack the social and cognitive skills that allow them to find mutually satisfying compromises.

When siblings do fight—particularly young children—parents should intervene. When parents explain one sibling's behavior to another (e.g., "He covered his eyes 'cause he was scared"), siblings have more positive interactions (Kojima, 2000). And, by helping their children settle differences, parents show children more sophisticated ways to negotiate; later, children often try to use these techniques themselves instead of fighting (Pearlman & Ross, 1997). Parents especially need to intervene when conflicts escalate to the point that siblings are acting aggressively, yelling or swearing, or making denigrating comments. Obviously, parents need to protect their children from each other. But, more importantly, if left unchecked, over time such conflicts can lead to behavior problems (Garcia et al., 2000).

## CHECK YOUR LEARNING

**RECALL** Summarize what's known about psychological development of adopted children.

How do sibling relationships change as children grow?

**INTERPRET** What research findings suggest continuity in the quality of sibling relationships? What findings suggest discontinuity?

**APPLY** Suppose your sister has a 2-year-old child. She and her husband are deciding whether to have another child. Describe to her the advantages and disadvantages of having two children versus having only one.

**Q&Answer**

**14.3** There are two obvious reasons why Elizabeth and Hilary get along better than Calvin and Hope. First, they're both girls and same-sex sibs tend to have better relationships. Second, they're both adolescents and sibling relationships tend to approve during these years.

# MALTREATMENT: PARENT–CHILD RELATIONSHIPS GONE AWRY

# 14.4

## LEARNING OBJECTIVES

- What are the consequences of child maltreatment?

- What factors cause parents to mistreat their children?

- How can maltreatment be prevented?

Consequences of Maltreatment

Causes of Maltreatment

Preventing Maltreatment

*The first time 7-year-old Max came to school with bruises on his face, he said he'd fallen down the basement steps. When Max had similar bruises a few weeks later, his teacher spoke with the school principal, who contacted local authorities. They discovered that Max's mother hit him with a paddle for even minor misconduct; for serious transgressions, she beat Max and made him sleep alone in an unheated, unlighted basement.*

Unfortunately, cases like Max's occur far too often in modern America. Maltreatment comes in many forms (Cicchetti & Toth, 2006). The two that often first come to mind are physical abuse involving assault that leads to injuries and sexual abuse involving fondling, intercourse, or other sexual behaviors. Another form of maltreatment is neglect, not giving children adequate food, clothing, or medical care. And, as the poster reminds us, children can also be harmed by psychological abuse—ridicule, rejection, and humiliation (Wicks-Nelson & Israel, 2006).

Maltreatment comes in many forms, including psychological or emotional abuse.

The frequency of these various forms of child maltreatment is difficult to estimate because so many cases go unreported. According to the U.S. Department of Health and Human Services (2005), approximately 1 million children annually suffer maltreatment or neglect. About 60% are neglected, about 20% are abused physically, about 10% are abused sexually, and 10% are maltreated psychologically.

We'll begin this module by looking at the consequences of maltreatment, then look at some causes, and, finally, examine ways to prevent maltreatment. As we do, we'll discover what led Max to suffer as he did.

## Consequences of Maltreatment

You probably aren't surprised to learn that the prognosis for youngsters like Max is not very good. Some, of course, suffer permanent physical damage. Even when there is no lasting physical damage, children's social and emotional development is often disrupted. They tend to have poor relationships with peers, often because they are too aggressive (Bolger & Patterson, 2001; Cicchetti & Toth, 2006). Their cognitive development and academic performance are also disturbed. Abused youngsters tend to get lower grades in school, score lower on standardized achievement tests, and be retained in a grade rather than promoted. Also, school-related behavior problems, such as being disruptive in class, are common, in part because maltreated children don't regulate their emotions well (Maughan & Cicchetti, 2002; Shonk & Cicchetti, 2001).

Adults who were abused as children often experience emotional problems such as depression or anxiety, are more prone to think about or attempt suicide, and are more likely to abuse spouses and their own children (Malinosky-Rummell & Hansen, 1993). In short, when children are maltreated, virtually all aspects of their development are affected and these effects do not vanish with time.

## Causes of Maltreatment

Why would a parent abuse a child? Maybe you think parents would have to be severely disturbed or deranged to harm their own flesh and blood. Not really. The vast majority of abusing parents cannot be distinguished from nonabusing parents in terms of standard psychiatric criteria (Wolfe, 1985). That is, adults who mistreat their children are not suffering from any specific mental or psychological disorder, and they have no distinctive personality profile.

Modern accounts of child abuse no longer look to a single or even a small number of causes. Instead, a host of factors put some children at risk for abuse and protect others; the number and combination of factors determine if the child is a likely target for abuse (Cicchetti & Toth, 2006). Let's look at three of the most important factors: cultural context and community, the parents, and the children themselves.

**CULTURE AND COMMUNITY.** The most general category of contributing factors has to do with cultural values and the social conditions of the community in which parents rear their children. For example, a culture's view of physical punishment may contribute to child maltreatment. Many countries in Europe and Asia have strong cultural prohibitions against physical punishment. It simply isn't done and would be viewed in much the same way we would view American parents who punished by not feeding their child for a few days. In Sweden, for example, spanking is against the law and children can report their parents to the police. But the scene in the photo, a father spanking his child, is common in the United States. Countries that do not condone physical punishment tend to have lower rates of child maltreatment than the United States (U.S. Department of State, 2002).

In addition to cultural values, the communities in which children live can put them at risk for maltreatment and abuse. Living in poverty is one important risk factor: Maltreatment is more common in families living in poverty, in part because lack of money increases the stress of daily life (Duncan & Brooks-Gunn, 2000). When parents are worrying about whether they can buy groceries or pay the rent, they are more likely to punish their children physically instead of making the extra effort to reason with them. A second risk factor is social isolation: Abuse is

| 14.4 |

Kevin has never physically abused his 10-year-old son, Alex, but he constantly torments him emotionally. For example, when Alex got an F on a spelling test, Kevin screamed, "I skipped *Monday Night Football* just to help you but you still flunked. You're such a dummy." When Alex began to cry, Kevin taunted, "Look at Alex, crying like a baby." These interactions occur nearly every day. What are the likely effects of such repeated episodes of emotional abuse?

Child abuse is more common in countries that condone use of physical punishment.

more likely when families are socially isolated from other relatives or neighbors, because isolation deprives children of adults who could protect them and deprives parents of social support that would help them cope with life stresses (Coulton, Korbin, & Su, 1999).

Cultural values and community factors clearly contribute to child abuse, but they are only part of the puzzle. After all, although maltreatment is more common among families living in poverty, it does not occur in a majority of these families and it does occur in middle-class families, too. Consequently, we need to look for additional factors to explain why abuse occurs in some families but not others.

**PARENTS.**    Faced with the same cultural values and living conditions, why do only a handful of parents abuse or mistreat their children? That is, which characteristics increase the odds that a parent will abuse his or her children? Child-development researchers have identified several important factors (Azar, 2002; Bugental & Happaney, 2004). First, parents who maltreat their children often were maltreated themselves, which may lead them to believe that abuse is simply a normal part of childhood. This does not mean that abused children inevitably become abusing parents—only about one-third do. But a history of child abuse clearly places adults at risk for mistreating their own children (Cicchetti & Toth, 2006; Serbin & Karp, 2003). Second, parents who mistreat their children often use ineffective parenting techniques (e.g., inconsistent discipline), have such unrealistic expectations that their children can never meet them, and often believe that they are powerless to control their children. For example, when abusive parents do not get along with their children, they often chalk this up to factors out of their control, such as children having a difficult temperament or being tired that day; they're less likely to think that their own behavior contributed to unpleasant interactions. Third, in families where abuse occurs, the couple's interactions are often unpredictable, unsupportive, and unsatisfying for both husbands and wives. In other words, mistreatment of children is simply one symptom of family dysfunction. This marital discord makes life more stressful and more difficult for parents to invest effort in child rearing.

> Children are most likely to be abused when their culture condones physical punishment, their parents lack effective child-rearing skills, and their own behavior is aversive.

**CHILDREN'S CONTRIBUTIONS.**    To place the last few pieces in the puzzle, we must look at the abused children themselves. Our discussion in Module 14.1 of reciprocal influence between parents and children should remind you that children may inadvertently, through their behavior, bring on their own abuse (Sidebotham et al., 2003). In fact, infants and preschoolers are abused more often than older children. Why? They are easier targets of abuse and they are less able to regulate aversive behaviors that elicit abuse. You've probably heard stories about a parent who shakes a baby to death because the baby won't stop crying. Because younger children are more likely to cry or whine excessively—behaviors that irritate all parents sooner or later—they are more likely to be the targets of abuse.

For much the same reason, children who are frequently ill are more often abused. When children are sick, they're more likely to cry and whine, annoying their parents. Also, when children are sick, they need medical care, which means additional expense. In addition, they can't go to school, which means that parents must arrange alternate child care. By increasing the level of stress in a family, sick children can inadvertently become the targets of abuse (Sherrod et al., 1984).

Stepchildren form another group at risk for abuse (Daly & Wilson, 1996). Just as Cinderella's stepmother doted on her biological children but abused Cinderella, so stepchildren are more prone to be victims of abuse and neglect than are biological children. Adults are less invested emotionally in their stepchildren, and this lack of emotional investment leaves stepchildren more vulnerable.

Obviously, in all of these instances children are *not* at fault and do not deserve the abuse. Nevertheless, normal infant or child behavior can provoke anger and maltreatment from some parents.

Thus, many factors, summarized in the table, all contribute to child maltreatment. Any single factor will usually not result in abuse; maltreatment is more likely when risk factors start to add up. For example, several factors placed Max, the boy in the vignette, at risk for abuse: His family had moved to the community recently because his stepfather thought he could find work in the local plant; but the plant wasn't hiring, so his stepfather was unemployed and the family had little money saved. And Max had asthma, which meant there was regular expense for medication and occasional visits to the emergency room when he had a severe attack. All these factors combined to put Max at risk for maltreatment. (How many risk factors? My answer appears just before Check Your Learning on page 454.)

## SUMMARY TABLE

### FACTORS THAT CONTRIBUTE TO CHILD ABUSE

| General Category | Specific Factor |
|---|---|
| Cultural and community contributions | Abuse is more common in cultures that tolerate physical punishment. |
| | Abuse is more common when families live in poverty because of the stress associated with inadequate income. |
| | Abuse is more common when families are socially isolated because parents lack social supports. |
| Parents' contributions | Parents who abuse their children were often maltreated themselves as children. |
| | Parents who abuse their children often have poor parenting skills (e.g., unrealistic expectations, inappropriate punishment). |
| Children's contributions | Young children are more likely to be abused because they cannot regulate their behavior. |
| | Ill children are more likely to be abused because their behavior while ill is often aversive. |
| | Stepchildren are more likely to be abused because stepparents are less invested in their stepchildren. |

## Preventing Maltreatment

The complexity of child abuse dashes any hopes for a simple solution. Because maltreatment is more apt to occur when several contributing factors are present, eradicating child maltreatment would entail a massive effort. American attitudes toward "acceptable" levels of punishment and poverty would have to change. American children will be abused as long as physical punishment is considered acceptable and as long as poverty-stricken families live in chronic stress from simply trying to provide food and shelter. Parents also need counseling and training in parenting skills. Abuse will continue as long as parents remain ignorant of effective methods of parenting and discipline.

> *The risk of child abuse can be reduced by providing social supports and by teaching effective parenting skills.*

It would be naïve to expect all of these changes to occur overnight. However, by focusing on some of the more manageable factors, the risk of maltreatment can be reduced. Social supports help. When parents know they can turn to other helpful adults for advice and reassurance, they better manage the stresses of child rearing that might otherwise lead to abuse. And families can be taught more effective ways of coping with situations that might otherwise trigger abuse (Wicks-Nelson & Israel, 2006). Through role-playing sessions, parents can learn the benefits of authoritative parenting and effective ways of using feedback and modeling (described in Module 14.1) to regulate children's behavior.

Providing social supports and teaching effective parenting are typically done when maltreatment and abuse have already occurred. Of course, preventing maltreatment in the first place is more desirable and more cost-effective. For prevention, one useful tool is familiar—early childhood intervention programs. That is, maltreatment and abuse can be cut in half when families participate for 2 or more years in intervention programs that include preschool education along with family support activities aimed at encouraging parents to become more involved in their children's education (Reynolds & Robertson, 2003). When parents participate in these programs, they become more committed to their children's education. This leads their children to be more successful in school, reducing a source of stress and enhancing parents' confidence in their child-rearing skills, reducing the risks of maltreatment in the process.

Finally, we need to remember that most parents who have mistreated their children deserve compassion, rather than censure. In most cases, parents and children are attached to each other; maltreatment is a consequence of ignorance and burden, not malice.

*Answer to question on page 453 about the number of risk factors:* **Four factors** put Max at risk: social isolation (just moved to the community), poverty (unemployed, no savings), he is a stepchild, and he has a chronic illness.

**14.4** If this emotional abuse continues, virtually every aspect of Alex's psychological development is likely to be harmed. That is, Alex will do poorly in school, his social and emotional development will be impaired, he won't get along well with peers, and he'll be at risk for psychological disorders such as depression.

## CHECK YOUR LEARNING

**RECALL** Describe the different factors that lead to child abuse.
How can we prevent child abuse?

**INTERPRET** How does child abuse demonstrate, in an unfortunate way, that children are sometimes active contributors to their own development?

**APPLY** Suppose that you read a letter to the editor of your local paper in which the author claims that parents who abuse their children are mentally ill. If you were to write a reply, what would you say?

## UNIFYING THEMES: Active Children

In this chapter, I want to emphasize the theme that *children influence their own development*. This may seem to be an unusual chapter to emphasize this theme because, after all, we usually think of how parents influence their children. But several times in this chapter we've seen that parenting is determined, in part, by children themselves. We saw that parents change their behavior as their children grow older. Parents also adjust their behavior depending on how their children respond to previous efforts to discipline. And, in discussing causes of child maltreatment, we discovered that younger and sick children often unwittingly place themselves at risk for abuse because of their behavior. Constant whining and crying is trying for all parents and prompts a small few to harm their children.

Of course, parents do influence their children's development in many important ways. But effective parenting recognizes that there is no all-purpose formula that works for all children or, for that matter, for all children in one family. Instead, parents must tailor their child-rearing behavior to each child, recognizing his or her unique needs, strengths, and weaknesses.

## SEE FOR YOURSELF

Many students find it hard to believe that parents actually use the different styles described in Module 14.1. To observe how parents differ in their warmth and control, visit a place where parents and children interact together. Shopping malls and fast-food restaurants are two good examples. Observe parents and children, then judge their warmth (responsive to the child's needs versus uninterested) and degree of control (relatively controlling versus uncontrolling). As you observe, decide whether parents are using feedback and modeling effectively. You should observe an astonishing variety of parental behavior, some effective and some not. See for yourself!

## RESOURCES

For more information about . . .

**divorce,** try Mavis Hetherington and John Kelly's *For Better or Worse: Divorce Reconsidered* (W. W. Norton, 2003), in which the authors—one the world's foremost authority on divorce and the other a professional writer—trace the findings from a 30-year study to explain how divorce affects families. They also provide many practical suggestions for dealing with problems associated with divorce.

**how to deal with all of the different problems large and small that come up in rearing children,** visit the Today's Parent Web site, **http://www.todaysparent.com**

## KEY TERMS

authoritarian parenting  431
authoritative parenting  431
authority-oriented grandparents  442
blended family  440
chronosystem  429
counterimitation  433
detached grandparents  442
direct instruction  432
exosystem  429
influential grandparents  442
joint custody  438
macrosystem  429

mesosystem  429
microsystem  429
negative reinforcement trap  433
observational learning  433
passive grandparents  442
permissive parenting  431
punishment  433
reinforcement  433
supportive grandparents  442
time-out  434
uninvolved parenting  431

# SUMMARY

## 14.1 PARENTING

### The Family as a System

According to the systems approach, the family is an evolutionary adaptation that consists of interacting elements—parents and children influence each other. The family itself is embedded in a context of interconnected systems that range from the microsystem (people and objects in the child's immediate environment) to the macrosystem (the cultures and subcultures in which all the other systems are embedded).

### Styles of Parenting

One dimension of parenting is the degree of parental warmth: Children clearly benefit from warm, caring parents. Another dimension is control. Effective parental control involves setting appropriate standards and enforcing them consistently. Combining warmth and control yields four parental styles: (a) authoritarian parents are controlling but uninvolved, (b) authoritative parents are controlling but responsive to their children, (c) indulgent–permissive parents are loving but exert little control, and (d) indifferent–uninvolved parents are neither warm nor controlling. Authoritative parenting is usually best for children.

Child rearing is influenced by culture and family configuration. Compared to American parents, Chinese parents are more controlling and less affectionate. And parents living in poverty often rely more heavily on authoritarian parenting.

### Parental Behavior

Parents influence development by direct instruction and coaching. In addition, parents serve as models for their children, who sometimes imitate parents' behavior directly and sometimes in ways that are the opposite of what they've seen (counterimitation).

Parents also use feedback to influence children's behavior. Sometimes parents fall into the negative reinforcement trap, inadvertently reinforcing behaviors that they want to discourage. Punishment is effective when it is prompt, consistent, accompanied by an explanation, and delivered by a person with whom the child has a warm relationship. Time-out is one useful form of punishment.

### Influences of the Marital System

Chronic conflict is harmful to children, but children can actually benefit when their parents solve problems constructively. Not all parents work well together, because they disagree in child-rearing goals or methods.

### Children's Contributions

Parenting is influenced by characteristics of children themselves, such as their age and temperament.

## 14.2 THE CHANGING FAMILY

### Impact of Divorce on Children

Divorce harms children in many ways, ranging from school achievement to adjustment. The impact of divorce stems from less supervision of children, economic hardship, and parental conflict.

### Blended Families

When a mother remarries, daughters sometimes have difficulty adjusting because the new stepfather encroaches on an intimate mother–daughter relationship. A father's remarriage can cause problems because children fear that the stepmother will disturb intimate father–child relationships and because of tension between the stepmother and the noncustodial mother.

### The Role of Grandparents

Grandparents play many different roles with their grandchildren; the influential and supportive roles are two in which grandparents are particularly active in rearing grandchildren. In African American families, grandmothers often live with their daughters, an arrangement that benefits children. Grandparents also influence their grandchildren indirectly, through the way they reared the child's parents.

### Children of Gay and Lesbian Parents

Research on gay and lesbian parents suggests that they are more similar to heterosexual parents than different and that their children develop much like children reared by heterosexual couples.

## 14.3 BROTHERS AND SISTERS

### Firstborn, Laterborn, and Only Children

Firstborn children often are more intelligent and more likely to go to college, but laterborn children are more popular and more innovative. Only children are comparable to children with siblings on most dimensions. In many respects, adopted children are similar to children living with their biological parents. Some adopted children have problems, primarily when they were adopted at an older age and when their quality of care before being adopted was poor.

### Qualities of Sibling Relationships

The birth of a sibling can be stressful for older children, particularly when parents ignore their older child's needs. Siblings get along better when they are of the same sex, believe that parents treat them fairly, enter adolescence, and have parents who get along well.

## 14.4 MALTREATMENT: PARENT–CHILD RELATIONSHIPS GONE AWRY

### Consequences of Maltreatment

Children who are maltreated sometimes suffer permanent physical damage. Their peer relationships are often poor, and they tend to lag in cognitive development and academic performance.

### Causes of Maltreatment

A culture's views on violence, poverty, and social isolation can foster child maltreatment. Parents who abuse their children are often unhappy, socially unskilled individuals. Younger, unhealthy children are more likely to be targets of maltreatment, as are stepchildren.

### Preventing Maltreatment

Prevention programs often focus on providing families with new ways of coping with problems and providing parents with resources to help them cope with stress.

If you stand outside a kindergarten classroom on the first day of school, you'll probably see some children crying, fearful of facing a novel environment on their own. What may surprise you is that many parents, too, are struggling to hold back their tears. Why? Parents realize that when their children begin school, they are taking an important step toward independence. Other forces now become influential in children's lives, sometimes challenging parents' influence. Among these forces are children's agemates (their peers), the media, and school itself. In this chapter, we'll look at peer influence in Module 15.1. Next, in Module 15.2, we'll see how electronic media—particularly television and computers—affect children's development. Finally, in Module 15.3, we'll examine the influences on children's development of other cultural institutions, including day care, the workplace, neighborhoods, and schools.

**15.1**    Peers

**15.2**    Electronic Media

**15.3**    Institutional Influences

15

1    The Science of Child Development

2    Genetic Bases of Child Development

3    Prenatal Development, Birth, and the Newborn

4    Growth and Health

5    Perceptual and Motor Development

6    Theories of Cognitive Development

7    Cognitive Processes and Academic Skills

8    Intelligence and Individual Differences in Cognition

9    Language and Communication

10   Emotional Development

11   Understanding Self and Others

12   Moral Understanding and Behavior

13   Gender and Development

14   Family Relationships

# Influences Beyond the Family

# 15.1    PEERS

Development of Peer
Interactions

Friendship

Romantic Relationships

Groups

Popularity and Rejection

## LEARNING OBJECTIVES

- When do youngsters first begin to interact with each other, and how do these interactions change during infancy, childhood, and adolescence?

- Why do children become friends, and what are the benefits of friendship?

- When do romantic relationships emerge in adolescence?

- What are the important features of groups in childhood and adolescence? How do groups influence individuals?

- Why are some children more popular than others? What are the causes and consequences of being rejected?

> *For 6 months, 17-year-old Gretchen has been dating Jeff, an 18-year-old. They have had sex several times, each time without contraception. Gretchen suggested to Jeff that he buy some condoms but he didn't want to because someone might see him at the drug store and that would be too embarrassing. And, although she never mentions it to Jeff, Gretchen sometimes thinks that getting pregnant would be cool: Then she and Jeff could move into their own apartment and begin a family.*

Many of the major developmental theorists—including Freud, Erikson, Piaget, and Vygotsky—believed that children's development is strongly shaped by their interactions and relationships with peers. Whether occurring with classmates, a small circle of friends, or in a romantic relationship like Gretchen's, children's and adolescents' interactions with peers are important developmental events.

In this module, we'll trace the development of peer interactions. Then we'll look at friendship and romantic relationships, where we'll better understand why Gretchen and Jeff are having unprotected sex. Finally, we'll consider children's membership in groups, including their social status within those groups.

## Development of Peer Interactions

Peer interactions begin surprisingly early in infancy. Two 6-month-olds together will look, smile, and point at one another. Over the next few months, infants laugh and babble when with other infants (Rubin, Bukowski, & Parker, 2006).

Beginning at about the first birthday and continuing through the preschool years, peer relations rapidly become more complex. **In a classic early study, Parten (1932) identified a developmental sequence that began with *nonsocial play*—children playing alone or watching others play but not playing themselves.** Later, children progressed to more elaborate forms of play with each child having a well-defined role. Today, researchers no longer share Parten's view that children move through each stage of play in a rigid sequence, but the different forms of play that she distinguished are useful nonetheless.

**The first type of social play to appear—soon after the first birthday—is *parallel play:* youngsters play alone but maintain a keen interest in what other**

VIDEO 15.1

Parten's Play Categories

**children are doing.** For example, each boy in the photo has his own toy but is watching the other play, too. During parallel play, exchanges between youngsters begin to occur. When one talks or smiles, the other usually responds (Howes, Unger, & Seidner, 1990).

Beginning at roughly 15 to 18 months, toddlers no longer just watch one another at play. **In *associative play*, youngsters engage in similar activities, talk or smile at one another, and offer each other toys.** Play is now truly interactive (Howes & Matheson, 1992). An example of simple social play would be two 20-month-olds pushing toy cars along the floor, making "car sounds," and periodically trading cars.

**Toward the second birthday, *cooperative play* begins: Now children organize their play around a distinct theme and take on special roles based on the theme.** For example, children may play "hide-and-seek" and alternate roles of hider and finder, or they may have a tea party and alternate being the host and guest. By the time children are $3\frac{1}{2}$ to 4 years old, parallel play is much less common and cooperative play is the norm. Cooperative play typically involves peers of the same sex, a preference that increases until, by age 6, youngsters choose same-sex playmates about two thirds of the time (LaFreniere, Strayer, & Gauthier, 1984).

In parallel play, children play alone but pay close attention to what other nearby children are doing as they play.

**MAKE-BELIEVE.** During the preschool years, cooperative play often takes the form of make-believe. Preschoolers have telephone conversations with imaginary partners or pretend to drink imaginary juice. In early phases of make-believe, children rely on realistic props to support their play. While pretending to drink, younger preschoolers use a real cup; while pretending to drive a car, they use a toy steering wheel. In later phases of make-believe, children no longer need realistic props; instead, they can imagine that a block is the cup, or, like the boys in the photo, that a paper plate is the steering wheel. Of course, this gradual movement toward more abstract make-believe is possible because of cognitive growth that occurs during the preschool years (Striano, Tomasello, & Rochat, 2001).

When preschool children engage in make-believe, they often use props to support their play; these props are usually very concrete in younger preschoolers but can be more abstract in older preschoolers.

When children pretend, are they confused? After all, people take on new roles (the child becomes a teacher) and objects take on new identities (the banana becomes a phone), changes that would seem ripe for children to mistake the real world from the pretend one. In fact, young children rarely mix up pretense with reality. Why? When playing, children usually tell play partners that they want to pretend ("Let's pretend"), then describe those aspects of reality that are being changed ("I'll be the pilot and this is my plane," referring to the couch). It's as if children mutually agree to enter a parallel universe where just a few properties are changed (Rakoczy, Tomasello, & Striano, 2004).

As you might suspect, make-believe reflects the values important in a child's culture (Bornstein et al., 1999). For example, Farver and Shin (1997) studied make-believe play of European American preschoolers and Korean American preschoolers. The Korean American children came from recently immigrated families, so they still held

VIDEO 15.2

Sociodramatic play (Social Pretend Play)

traditional Korean values, such as an emphasis on the family and on harmony over conflict. The two groups of children differed in the themes of their make-believe play. Adventure and fantasy were favorite themes for European American youngsters, but family roles and everyday activities were favorites of the Korean American children.

In addition, the groups differed in their style of play during make-believe. European American children were more assertive in their make-believe and more likely to disagree with their play partner's ideas about pretending ("*I* want to be the king; *you* be the mom!"). Korean American children were more polite and more likely to strive for harmony ("Could I *please* be king?"). Thus, cultural values influence both the content and the form of make-believe.

> Make-believe play promotes cognitive development and lets children explore emotional topics that frighten them.

Make-believe play is not only entertaining for children, but also promotes cognitive development. Children who spend much time in make-believe play tend to be more advanced in language, memory, and reasoning (Bergen & Mauer, 2000). They also tend to have a more sophisticated understanding of other people's thoughts, beliefs, and feelings (Lindsey & Colwell, 2003).

Yet another benefit of make-believe is that it allows children to explore topics that frighten them. Children who are afraid of the dark may reassure a doll who is also afraid of the dark. By explaining to the doll why she shouldn't be afraid, children come to understand and regulate their own fear of darkness. Or children may pretend that a doll has misbehaved and must be punished, which allows them to experience the parent's anger and the doll's guilt. Make-believe allows children to explore other emotions, too, including joy and affection (Gottman, 1986).

For many preschool children, make-believe play involves imaginary companions. Children can usually describe their imaginary playmates in some detail, mentioning sex and age as well as hair and eye color. Imaginary companions were once thought to be fairly rare and a sign of possible developmental problems. But recent research shows that many preschoolers, particularly firstborn and only children, report imaginary companions (Taylor et al., 2004).

What's more, an imaginary companion is associated with many *positive* social characteristics (Gleason, 2002): Preschoolers with imaginary friends tend to be more sociable and have more real friends than other preschoolers. Furthermore, vivid fantasy play with imaginary companions does not mean that the distinction between fantasy and reality is blurred: Children with imaginary companions can distinguish fantasy from reality just as accurately as youngsters without imaginary companions (Taylor et al., 1993).

**SOLITARY PLAY.** At times throughout the preschool years, many children prefer to play alone. Should parents be worried? Usually, no. Solitary play comes in many forms and most are normal—even healthy. Spending free playtime alone coloring, solving puzzles, or assembling Legos® is not a sign of maladjustment. Many youngsters enjoy solitary activities and, at other times, choose very social play.

However, some forms of solitary play *are* signs that children are uneasy interacting with others (Coplan et al., 2001; Harrist et al., 1997). One type of unhealthy solitary play is wandering aimlessly. Sometimes children go from one preschool activity center to the next, as if trying to decide what to do. But really they just keep wandering, never settling into play with others or into constructive solitary play. Another unhealthy type of solitary play is hovering: A child stands nearby peers who are playing, watching them play but not participating. Over time, these behaviors do not bode well for youngsters (as we'll see on pages 473–474), so it's best for these youngsters to see a professional who can help them overcome their reticence in social situations (Ladd, 1998).

**PARENTAL INFLUENCE.**   Parents get involved in their preschool children's play in several ways (Parke & O'Neill, 2000):

- *Playmate.* Many parents enjoy the role of playmate (and many parents deserve an Oscar for their performances). They use the opportunity to scaffold their children's play (see Module 6.2), often raising it to more sophisticated levels (Tamis-LeMonda & Bornstein, 1996). For example, if a toddler is stacking toy plates, a parent might help the child stack the plates (play at the same level) or might pretend to wash each plate (play at a more advanced level). When parents demonstrate more advanced forms of play, their children often play at the more advanced levels later (Lindsey & Mize, 2000).

- *Social director.* It takes two to interact and young children rely on parents to create opportunities for social interactions. Many parents of young children arrange visits with peers, enroll children in activities (e.g., preschool programs), and take children to settings that attract young children (e.g., parks, swimming pools). All this effort is worth it: Children whose parents provide them with frequent opportunities for peer interaction tend to get along better with their peers (Ladd & Pettit, 2002).

- *Coach.* Successful interactions are based on a host of skills, including how to initiate an interaction, make joint decisions, and resolve conflicts. When parents help their children acquire these skills, children tend to be more competent socially and to be more accepted by their peers (Parke et al., 2004). But there's a catch: The coaching needs to be constructive for children to benefit. Parent-coaches sometimes make suggestions that aren't very clear or are actually misguided. Bad coaching is worse than none at all, as it harms children's peer relations (Russell & Finnie, 1990).

- *Mediator.* When young children play, they often disagree, argue, and sometimes fight. As shown in the photo, children play more cooperatively and longer when parents are present to help iron out conflicts (Mize, Pettit, & Brown, 1995). When young children can't agree on what to play, a parent can negotiate a mutually acceptable activity. When both youngsters want to play with the same toy, a parent can arrange for them to share. Here, too, parents scaffold their preschoolers' play, smoothing the interaction by providing some of the social skills that preschoolers lack.

One way in which parents facilitate their children's play is by taking on the role of mediator—parents help to resolve the disputes that inevitably develop when young children play.

In addition to these direct influences on children's play, parents influence children's play indirectly, via the quality of the parent–child attachment relationship. Recall from Module 10.3 that children's relationships with peers are most successful when, as infants, they had a secure attachment relationship with their mother (Schneider, Atkinson, & Tardif, 2001; Wood, Emmerson, & Cowan, 2004). A child's relationship with his or her parents is the internal working model for all future social relationships. When the parent–child relationship is of high quality and emotionally satisfying, children are encouraged to form relationships with other people. Another possibility is that a secure attachment relationship with the mother makes an infant feel more confident about exploring the environment, which, in turn, provides more opportunities to interact with peers. These two views are not mutually exclusive; both may contribute to the relative ease with which securely attached children interact with their peers (Hartup, 1992b).

**PEER RELATIONS AFTER PRESCHOOL.** When children attend elementary school, the context of peer relations changes dramatically (Rubin et al., 2006). Not only does the sheer number of peers increase dramatically, but children are often exposed to a far more diverse set of peers than before. In addition, children find themselves interacting with peers in situations that range from reasonably structured with much adult supervision (e.g., a classroom) to largely unstructured with minimal adult supervision (e.g., a playground during recess).

An obvious change in children's peer relations during the elementary-school years is that, due to more experience with peers as well as cognitive and language development, children get along better than when they were younger. They become more skilled at initiating and maintaining interactions. And they use more sophisticated methods to resolve conflicts, such as negotiation (Laursen, Finkelstein, & Betts, 2001).

What do school-age children do when they're together? In one study (Zarbatany, Hartmann, & Rankin, 1990), investigators asked Canadian students in grades 5 and 6 how they spent their time with peers. The students in the study indicated how often they participated with peers in each of 29 different activities. The results, shown in the graph, are not too surprising, eh? The most common activities with peers are simple—just being together and talking (Larson, 2001).

The graph also highlights another important feature of peer relations during the elementary-school years. Children reported that they played physical games a few times each week, which reflects, in part, the emergence of a special type of play in school-age children. **In *rough-and-tumble play*, children playfully chase, punch, kick, shove, fight, and wrestle with peers.** Notice the word *play* in this

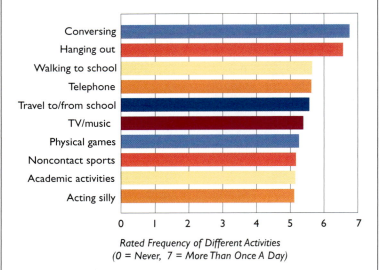

Conversing
Hanging out
Walking to school
Telephone
Travel to/from school
TV/music
Physical games
Noncontact sports
Academic activities
Acting silly

*Rated Frequency of Different Activities
(0 = Never, 7 = More Than Once A Day)*

**FIGURE 15-1**

definition: Unlike aggression, where the intention is to do harm, rough-and-tumble play is for fun. When children are involved in rough-and-tumble play, they are usually smiling and sometimes laughing (Pellegrini, 2004). When parents or teachers intervene, the youngsters usually explain that there's no problem, they're just playing. Rough-and-tumble play is more common among boys than girls, and girls' rough-and-tumble play tends to emphasize running and chasing over wrestling and fighting.

As children move into adolescence, three features of their peer relationships loom large: Friendships become more intimate, youth have their first romantic relationships, and groups take on greater significance. These changes are so important that we'll consider each one separately. Let's start with friendship.

VIDEO 15.3
Rough-and-
Tumble Play

## Friendship

Over time, even young children develop special relationships with certain peers. *Friendship* **is a voluntary relationship between two people involving mutual liking.** By age 4 or 5 years, most children claim to have a "best friend." If you ask them how they can tell a child is their best friend, their response will probably resemble 5-year-old Katelyn's:

INTERVIEWER:    Why is Heidi your best friend?

KATELYN:    Because she plays with me. And she's nice to me.

INTERVIEWER:    Are there any other reasons?

KATELYN:    Yeah, Heidi lets me play with her dolls.

Thus, the key elements of friendship for preschool and younger elementary-school children are that children like each other and enjoy playing together.

As children develop, their friendships become more complex. For older elementary-school children (8 to 11 years), mutual liking and shared activities are joined by features that are more psychological in nature—trust and assistance. At this age, children expect that they can depend on their friends—their friends will be nice to them, will keep their promises, and won't say mean things about them to others. And they expect friends to step forward in times of need: A friend should willingly help with homework or willingly share a snack.

Adolescence adds another layer of complexity to friendships. Mutual liking, common interests, and trust remain. In fact, trust becomes even more important in adolescent friendships. New to adolescence is intimacy—friends now confide in one another, sharing personal thoughts and feelings. Teenagers will reveal their excitement over a new romance or disappointment at not being cast in a school musical. Intimacy is more common in friendships among girls, who are more likely than boys to have one exclusive "best friend" (Markovits, Benenson, & Dolenszky, 2001). Because intimacy is at the core of their friendships, girls are also more likely to be concerned about the faithfulness of their friends and worry about being rejected (Benenson & Christakos, 2003).

The emergence of intimacy in adolescent friendships means that friends also come to be seen as sources of social and emotional support. Elementary school children generally rely on close family members—parents, siblings, and grandparents—as primary sources of support when they need help or are upset. But adolescents turn to close friends instead. Because adolescent friends share intimate thoughts and feelings, they can provide support during emotional or stressful periods (Levitt, Guacci-Franco, & Levitt, 1993).

Hand in hand with the emphasis on intimacy is loyalty. Having confided in friends, adolescents expect friends to stick with them through good and bad times. If a friend is disloyal, adolescents are afraid that they may be humiliated because their intimate thoughts and feelings will become known to a much broader circle of people (Berndt & Perry, 1990).

**WHO BECOME FRIENDS?**    In childhood and adolescence, most friends are like those shown in the photo—alike in age, sex, and race (Hamm, 2000; Hartup, 1992a). Because friends are supposed to treat each other as equals, friendships are rare between an older, more experienced child and a younger, less experienced child. Because children typically play with same-sex peers (see Module 13.3), boys and girls rarely become close friends.

Friendships are more common between children and adolescents from the same race or ethnic group than between those from different groups, reflecting racial segregation in American society. Friendships among children of different groups are more common in schools where classes are smaller (Hallinan & Teixeira, 1987) and when a child's school and neighborhood are ethnically diverse (Quillian & Campbell, 2003).

**Friendship is based on mutual liking and common interests in childhood and adolescence; intimacy becomes a part of friendships in adolescence, particularly for girls.**

If Heidi is still Katelyn's best friend in high school, how would Katelyn's description of their friendship differ from the description she gave as a 5-year-old?    **15.1**

Friends are typically alike in age, sex, race, and attitudes.

Of course, friends are usually alike not only in age, sex, and race, but also in attitudes toward school, recreation, using drugs, and plans for the future (Hamm, 2000; Newcomb & Bagwell, 1995). Tom, who enjoys school, likes to read, and plans to go to Harvard, will probably not befriend Barry, who thinks that school is stupid, listens to MP3s constantly, and plans to quit high school to become a rock star (Haselager et al., 1998). As time passes, friends become more similar in their attitudes and values (Berndt & Murphy, 2002). Nevertheless, friends are not photocopies of each other; friends are less similar, for example, than spouses or dizygotic twins (Rushton & Bons, 2005).

Although children's friendships are overwhelmingly with members of their own sex, a few children have friendships with opposite-sex children. Who are these children, and why do they have opposite-sex friendships? Boys and girls are equally likely to have opposite-sex friendships. The important factor in understanding these children is whether they have same- and opposite-sex friends or *only* opposite-sex friends. Children with same- and opposite-sex friendships tend to be very well adjusted, whereas children with only opposite-sex friendships tend to be unpopular and less competent academically and socially, and to have lower self-esteem. Apparently, children with both same- *and* opposite-sex friends are so socially skilled and popular that both boys and girls are eager to be their friends. In contrast, children with only opposite-sex friendships are socially unskilled, unpopular youngsters who are rejected by their same-sex peers and form friendships with opposite-sex children as a last resort (Bukowski, Sippola, & Hoza, 1999).

**QUALITY AND CONSEQUENCES OF FRIENDSHIP.** If you think back to your childhood friendships, you probably remember some that were long lasting and satisfying as well as others that rapidly wore thin and soon dissolved. What accounts for these differences in the quality and longevity of friendships? Sometimes friendships are brief because children have the skills to create friendships—they know funny stories, they kid around, they know good gossip—but lack the skills to sustain those friendships—they can't keep secrets, or they're too bossy (Jiao, 1999; Parker & Seal, 1996). Sometimes friendships end because, when conflicts arise, children are more concerned about their own interests and are unwilling to compromise or negotiate (Fonzi et al., 1997; Rose & Asher, 1999). And sometimes friendships dissolve when children discover that their needs and interests aren't as similar as they thought initially (Gavin & Furman, 1996; Poulin & Boivin, 2000).

> When children have good friends, they are more likely to behave prosocially and are better adjusted.

Considering that friendships disintegrate for many reasons, you're probably reminded that truly good friends are to be treasured. In fact, researchers consistently find that children benefit from having good friends. Compared to children who lack friends, children with good friends have higher self-esteem, are less likely to be lonely and depressed, and more often act prosocially—sharing and cooperating with others (Burk & Laursen, 2005; Hartup & Stevens, 1999). Children with good friends cope better with life stresses, such as the transition from elementary school to middle school or junior high (Berndt & Keefe, 1995), and they're less likely to be victimized by peers (Schwartz et al., 2000). The benefits of friendship are also long lasting: Children who have friends have greater self-worth as young adults (Bagwell, Newcomb, & Bukowski, 1998). Thus, for many adolescents friends are important resources. Children learn from their friends and turn to them for support in times of stress.

We need to recognize, however, that not all friendships are beneficial for children and adolescents (Bagwell, 2004). For example, when aggressive children are friends, they become more antisocial as time goes by (Dishion, Poulin, & Burraston, 2001). Similarly, when teens engage in risky behavior (e.g., they drink, smoke, or have sex), they often encourage each other's risky behavior (Bot et al., 2005; Curran, Stice, & Chassin, 1997). The "Focus on Research" feature describes a study that shows this impact of friends.

## Focus on Research
### Influence of Best Friends on Sexual Activity

*Who were the investigators, and what was the aim of the study?* James Jaccard, Hart Blanton, and Tonya Dodge (2005) set out to determine whether close friends influence adolescents' sexual behavior. That is, they wanted to know whether adolescents were more likely to be sexually active when their closest same-sex friend was sexually active.

*How did the investigators measure the topic of interest?* Jaccard and his colleagues used data from the *Add Health* database, which includes information obtained from more than 20,000 U.S. adolescents in grades 7–12. They completed questionnaires and were interviewed on a wide range of topics concerning adolescent health and development. Best friends were determined by asking adolescents to name five same-sex friends and then indicate the time spent with each in the past week. Sexual activity was determined by asking teens whether they had ever had sexual intercourse, and, if so, how recently.

*Who were the children in the study?* The investigators focused on a subsample of nearly 1700 adolescents—837 boys, 851 girls—who were interviewed twice and who were not married.

*What was the design of the study?* This study was correlational because Jaccard and colleagues were interested in the relation that existed naturally between two variables: whether an adolescent was sexually active and whether an adolescent's best friend was sexually active. The study was longitudinal because adolescents were interviewed twice, approximately a year apart.

*Were there ethical concerns with the study?* You bet. This is one of the few child-development studies that's been debated on the floor of the U.S. Congress! The initial version of the project, proposed in the late 1980s, was motivated by the growing AIDS epidemic and focused solely on adolescent sexual risk-taking. After the National Institutes of Health (NIH) decided to fund the project, many conservative groups protested, arguing that the project actually endorsed the adolescent sexual behaviors that it was designed to study. The NIH withdrew the funds but a compromise was reached in 1993: the U.S. Congress passed legislation calling for a much broader longitudinal study, one that would examine adolescent health and well-being, the factors that jeopardize adolescent health, and behaviors that promote health. The result was the National Longitudinal Study of Adolescent Health—*Add Health* for short.

Parents and adolescents both gave consent to participate. In addition, the *Add Health* project has gone to great lengths to ensure that no individual's name can be linked to his or her responses to any question. For example, for questions on sensitive topics, adolescents listened to questions played on a tape recorder and they entered their answers directly into a laptop computer.

*What were the results?* When adolescents were interviewed the first time, the correlation between an adolescent being sexually active and an adolescent's best friend being sexually active was .34 for boys and .40 for girls. This shows a tendency for best friends to be alike in their sexual experience. But are adolescents more likely to be sexually active when their best friends are? The investigators answered this question by examining adolescents' sexual activity over the year. They found that when best friends were sexually active over the year, 56% of adolescents were sexually active during the same period; in contrast, when best friends were sexually inactive, only 24% of adolescents were sexually active. Thus, over time, adolescents were more likely to be sexually active when their best friend was, too. This was true for adolescents who were sexually active at the initial interview as well as for those who had been inactive sexually.

*What did the investigators conclude?* Adolescent friendships are based on similarity and, once formed, like-minded friends can encourage and support each other's behavior. In this case, they can support each other's sexual activity or inactivity. However, friendships are not all-powerful in this regard. When adolescents' best friends were sexually active over the year, 56% of the adolescents followed their friends in becoming sexually active but 44% did not. As Jaccard et al. put it, ". . . adolescent peer and social networks exert considerable impact on a wide range of behaviors, such as musical interests, clothing preference, and extracurricular activities. . . . [However] . . . peer influence is just one of a number of factors that contribute to adolescent risk behavior" (p. 144).

*What converging evidence would strengthen these conclusions?* One useful step would be to continue the longitudinal study to examine the influence of friends over a longer term. Another important addition would be to examine the impact of an extended peer network, not simply an adolescent's best friend. ■

Thus, friendships are one important way peers influence development. Peers also influence development through romantic relationships, the topic of the next section.

## Romantic Relationships

The social landscape adds a distinctive landmark in adolescence—romantic relationships. These are uncommon during elementary school but in one study of U.S. children and adolescents, about 50% of 15-year-olds and 70% of 18-year-olds had had a romantic relationship within the previous $1\frac{1}{2}$ years. And most 18-year-olds had been involved in a romance lasting nearly a year (Carver, Joyner, & Udry, 2003).

Not only do romantic relationships become more common as children develop, their function changes: For younger adolescents, romantic relationships offer companionship like that provided by a best friend and an outlet for sexual exploration. For older adolescents like those in the photo, trust and support become important features of romantic relationships (Shulman & Kipnis, 2001).

Cultural factors influence romantic relationships. European American parents tend to encourage independence in their teenagers more than traditional Hispanic American and Asian American parents, who emphasize family ties and loyalty to parents. Romantic relationships are a sign of independence and usually result in less time spent with family, which explains why Hispanic American and Asian American adolescents often begin to date at an older age and date less frequently (Xiaohe & Whyte, 1990).

When older adolescents are romantically involved, they believe that trust and support are an important part of their relationship.

It's tempting to dismiss teen romances as nothing more than "puppy love" but they are often developmentally significant. On the one hand, adolescents involved in a romantic relationship are often more self-confident (Harter, 2006). On the other hand, they report more emotional upheaval and conflict (Joyner & Udry, 2000). In addition, early dating with many different partners is associated with a host of problems in adolescence (e.g., drug use, lower grades) and is associated with less satisfying romantic relationships in adulthood (Collins, 2003; Zimmer-Gembeck, Siebenbruner, & Collins, 2001).

**SEXUAL BEHAVIOR.**   Sexual exploration is an important feature of romantic relationships for younger adolescents. In fact, by the end of high school, roughly two thirds of American adolescents will have had intercourse at least once (U.S. Department of Health and Human Services, 2004). Why are some adolescents sexually active? Parents are influential: Adolescents are less likely to have sex when they feel close to their parents, when parents monitor their teenagers' activities, and when parents' values discourage sex (Miller, Benson, & Galbraith, 2001). Peers matter, too. Adolescents are more likely to have sex when their peers approve and when they believe their peers are also having sex (Brown & Theobald, 1999).

> Adolescents frequently fail to use contraception, which is why so many teens become pregnant.

Adolescents' sexual behavior is a cause for concern because approximately 1 in 11 American adolescent girls becomes pregnant; about half of them give birth. The result is that nearly a half million babies are born to American teenagers annually. African American, Native American, and Hispanic American adolescents are the most likely to become teenage moms; Asian American adolescents are the least likely (Martin et al., 2005).

As we saw in Module 4.2, teenage mothers and their children usually face bleak futures. If this is the case, why do so many teens become pregnant? The answer is simple: Sexually active teenagers often fail to use birth control. Adolescents' infrequent use of contraceptives can be traced to several factors (Gordon, 1996):

- *Ignorance:* Many adolescents are seriously misinformed about the facts of conception. For example, many do not know when conception is most likely to occur during the menstrual cycle.
- *Illusion of invulnerability:* Too many adolescents deny reality. They believe they are invincible—"It couldn't happen to me"—and that only others become pregnant.
- *Lack of motivation:* For some adolescent girls, like Gretchen from the module-opening vignette, becoming pregnant is appealing. They think having a child is a way to break away from parents, gain status as an independent-living adult, and have "someone to love them."
- *Lack of access:* Some teenagers do not know where to obtain contraceptives, and others, like Jeff in the vignette, are embarrassed to buy them. Still others don't know how to use contraceptives.

What's the best way to reduce adolescent sexual behavior and teen pregnancy? Programs that focus primarily on abstinence receive lots of headlines, but they are not consistently effective; some versions may work, but many do not (Kirby, 2002). In contrast, comprehensive sex education programs *are* effective (Kirby, 2001). These programs teach the biological aspects of sex and emphasize responsible sexual behavior or abstaining from premarital sex altogether. They also include discussions of the pressures to become involved sexually and ways to respond to this pressure. A key element is that in role-playing sessions students practice strategies for refusing to

About 5% of adolescents find themselves attracted to members of their own sex and identify themselves as gay or lesbian.

have sex. Youth who participate in programs like these are less likely to have intercourse; when they do have intercourse, they are more likely to use contraceptives (Kirby, 2001).

**SEXUAL ORIENTATION.** For most adolescents, sexual behavior involves members of the opposite sex. However, in early and mid-adolescence, roughly 15% of teens experience a period of sexual questioning, during which they sometimes report emotional and sexual attractions to members of their own sex (Carver, Egan, & Perry, 2004). For most adolescents, these experiences are simply a part of the larger process of role experimentation common to adolescence. However, like the teens in the photo, about 5% of teenage boys and girls identify their sexual orientation as gay (Rotherman-Borus & Langabeer, 2001).

The roots of sexual orientation are poorly understood. Scientists have, however, discredited several theories of sexual orientation. Research (Bell, Weinberg, & Hammersmith, 1981; Golombok & Tasker, 1996; Patterson, 1992) shows that each of the following is *false:*

- Sons become gay when raised by a domineering mother and a weak father.
- Girls become lesbians when their father is their primary role model.
- Children raised by gay or lesbian parents usually adopt their parents' sexual orientation.
- Gay and lesbian adults were, as children, seduced by an older person of their sex.

If all these ideas are false, what determines a person's sexual orientation? The exact factors probably differ from one person to the next, but many scientists today believe that biology plays an important role (Lalumière, Blanchard, & Zucker, 2000). Some evidence suggests that heredity and hormones influence sexual orientation (Bailey, Dunne, & Martin, 2000). Another idea is based on the finding that men are more often gay when they have older brothers and this effect gets stronger with each additional older brother; the explanation for this effect is that a pregnant woman's immune system responds to some biochemical feature of a male fetus. The response is weak at first but increases with each successive male, ultimately affecting brain development in laterborn sons (Bogaert, 2003).

**Biology probably contributes to sexual orientation, but the precise mechanism is unknown.**

Yet another intriguing idea—one that applies to males and females—is that genes and hormones don't produce sexual orientation per se but lead to temperaments that affect children's preference for same- and opposite-sex activities (Bem, 1996). Children who do not enjoy gender-typical activities come to see themselves as different and thus ultimately acquire a different gender identity.

Although the origins of sexual orientation are not yet well understood, it is clear that gay and lesbian individuals face many challenges. Their family and peer relationships are often disrupted, and they endure verbal and physical attacks. Given these problems, it's not surprising that gay and lesbian youth often experience mental health problems (D'Augelli, 2002). In recent years, social changes have helped gay and lesbian youth respond more effectively to these challenges. The "official" stigma associated with being gay or lesbian was removed in 1973 when the American Psychological Association and the American Psychiatric Association declared that homosexuality was not a psychological disorder. Other helpful changes include more (and more visible) role models and more centers for gay and lesbian youth. These resources are making it easier for gay and lesbian youth to understand their sexual orientation and to cope with the many other demands of adolescence.

In concluding this section, we need to recognize that sexual behavior and sexuality are enormously complicated and emotionally charged issues, even for adults. Adults who deal with adolescents need to recognize this complexity and help provide teenagers with skills for dealing with the issues involved in their emerging sexuality.

## Groups

During adolescence, groups become an important feature of social life. Two types of groups are particularly common during adolescence. **A *clique* consists of four to six individuals who are good friends and, consequently, tend to be similar in age, sex, race, and interests.** Members of a clique spend time together and often dress, talk, and act alike. Cliques are often part of a larger group, too. **A *crowd* is a larger mixed-sex group of older children or adolescents who have similar values and attitudes and are known by a common label.** Maybe you remember some of the different crowds from your own youth? *Jocks, preppies, burnouts, nerds,* and *brains*—adolescents use these or similar terms to refer to crowds of older children or adolescents (Brown et al., 1993; Cairns et al., 1995).

Some crowds have more status than others. For example, students in many junior and senior high schools claim that the jocks are the most prestigious crowd, whereas the burnouts are among the least prestigious. Self-esteem in older children and adolescents often reflects the status of their crowd. During the school years, youth from high-status crowds tend to have greater self-esteem than those from low-status crowds (Brown & Lohr, 1987).

Why do some students become nerds while others join the burnouts? Parenting style (discussed in Module 14.1) is part of the answer. A study by Brown and his colleagues (1993) examined the impact of three parental practices on students' membership in particular crowds. The investigators measured the extent to which parents emphasized academic achievement, monitored their children's out-of-school activities, and involved their children in joint decision making. When parents emphasized achievement, their children were more likely to be in the popular, jock, and normal crowds and less likely to be in the druggie crowd. When parents monitored out-of-school behavior, their children were more likely to be in the brain crowd and less likely to be in the druggie crowd. Finally, when parents included their children in joint decision making, their children were more likely to be in the brain and normal crowds and less likely to be in the druggie crowd. These findings were true for African American, Asian American, European American, and Hispanic American children and their parents.

What seems to happen is that when parents practice authoritative parenting—they are warm but controlling—their children become involved with crowds that endorse adult standards of behavior (for example, normals, jocks, brains). But, when parents' style is neglectful or permissive, their children are less likely to identify with adult standards of behavior and, instead, join crowds like druggies that disavow adult standards.

**GROUP STRUCTURE.** Groups—whether in school, at a summer camp, or anyplace else—typically have a well-defined structure. **Most groups have a *dominance hierarchy* consisting of a leader to whom all other members of the group defer.** Other members know their position in the hierarchy. They yield to members who are above them in the hierarchy and assert themselves over members who are below them. A dominance hierarchy is useful in reducing conflict and allocating resources within groups because every member knows his or her place.

What determines where members stand in the hierarchy? With children, especially boys, physical power is often the basis for the dominance hierarchy. The leader is usually the most physically intimidating child (Hawley, 1999). Among girls and older boys, hierarchies are often based on individual traits that relate to the group's main function. At a summer camp, for example, the leaders most often are the children with the greatest camping experience. Among Girl Scouts, girls chosen to be patrol leaders tend to be bright and goal oriented and to have new ideas (Edwards, 1994). These characteristics are appropriate because the primary function of patrols is to help plan activities for the entire troop of Girl Scouts. Thus, leadership based on key skills is effective because it gives the greatest influence to those with the skills most important to group functioning (Hartup, 1983).

**PEER PRESSURE.** Groups establish *norms*—standards of behavior that apply to all group members—and groups may pressure members to conform to these norms. Such "peer pressure" is often characterized as an irresistible, harmful force. The stereotype is that teenagers exert enormous pressure on each other to behave antisocially. In reality, peer pressure is neither all-powerful nor always evil. For example, most junior and senior high students resist peer pressure to behave in ways that are clearly antisocial, such as stealing (Brown, Lohr, & McClenahan, 1986). Peer pressure can be positive, too; peers often urge one another to participate in school activities, such as trying out for a play or working on the yearbook, or to become involved in community action projects, such as Habitat for Humanity.

Peers are most influential when standards for appropriate behavior are fuzzy, as in the case of clothing.

Peer pressure is most powerful when the standards for appropriate behavior are not clear-cut. Taste in music and clothing, for example, is completely subjective, so youths conform to peer group guidelines, as you can see in the all-too-familiar sight shown in the photo—teen-age girls all wearing "cool" clothing.

Similarly, standards on smoking, drinking, and using drugs are often fuzzy. Drinking is a good case in point. Parents and groups like SADD (Students Against Driving Drunk) may discourage teens from drinking, yet American culture is filled with youthful models who drink, seem to enjoy it, and suffer no apparent ill effects. To the contrary, they seem to enjoy life even more. With such contradictory messages, it is not surprising that youth look to their peers for answers (Urberg, Deirmenciolu, & Pilgrim, 1997). Consequently, some youth drink (or smoke, use drugs, or have sex) to conform to their group's norms, whereas others abstain, again reflecting their group's norms.

## Popularity and Rejection

Eileen is definitely the most popular child in her class. Other youngsters always want to play with her and sit near her at lunch or on the school bus. In contrast, Jay is the least popular child in the class. When he tries to join a game of foursquare, the others quit. Students in the class dislike Jay as much as they like Eileen.

Popular and rejected children like Eileen and Jay can be found in every classroom and neighborhood. In fact, studies of popularity (Hymel et al., 2004) reveal that most children can be placed in one of five categories:

- *Popular children* are liked by many classmates.
- *Rejected children* are disliked by many classmates.

- *Controversial children* are both liked and disliked by classmates.
- *Average children* are liked and disliked by some classmates but without the intensity found for popular, rejected, or controversial children.
- *Neglected children* are ignored by classmates.

VIDEO 15.4
Neglected child

Of these categories, we know most about popular and rejected children. Each of these categories actually includes two subtypes. Most popular children are skilled academically and socially. They are good students who are usually friendly, cooperative, and helpful. They are more skillful at communicating and better at integrating themselves into an ongoing conversation or play session—they "fit in" instead of "barging in" (Rubin et al., 2006). A smaller group of popular children includes physically aggressive boys who pick fights with peers and relationally aggressive girls who, like the "Plastics" in the film *Mean Girls*, thrive on manipulating social relationships. Although these youth are not particularly friendly, their antisocial behavior nevertheless apparently has a certain appeal to peers (Cillesen & Rose, 2005; Rose, Swenson, & Waller, 2004).

Are these avenues to popularity specific to American children, or do they apply more generally? The "Cultural Influences" feature has the answer.

> Most popular children are socially skilled—they're friendly, cooperative, and helpful—but some popular children are aggressive.

## Cultural Influences
### Keys to Popularity

In America, popular children seem to know how to get along with others. These results don't apply just to American children; they hold for children in many cultures around the world, including Canada, European countries, Israel, and China (e.g., Casiglia, Coco, & Zappulla, 1998). Sometimes, however, popular children have other characteristics that are unique to their cultural setting. In Israel, for example, popular children are more likely to be direct and assertive than in other countries (Krispin, Sternberg, & Lamb, 1992). In China, popular children are more likely to be shy than in other countries (Chen, Rubin, & Li, 1995). Evidently, good social skills are at the core of popularity in most countries, but other features may also be important, reflecting culturally specific values. ■

As for rejected children, many are overly aggressive, hyperactive, socially unskilled, and unable to regulate their emotions. These children are usually much more hostile than popular–aggressive children and seem to view aggression as an end—which peers dislike—instead of using aggression as a means toward other ends—which peers may not actually like but grudgingly respect (Prinstein & Cillesen, 2003). Other rejected children are shy, withdrawn, timid, and, not surprisingly, lonely (Asher & Paquette, 2003; Hart et al., 2000).

**CONSEQUENCES OF REJECTION.**   No one enjoys being rejected. Not surprisingly, peer rejection poses a major obstacle in children's development. Over the course of kindergarten, for example, rejected youngsters become less involved in classroom activities; they end the year feeling lonely and disliking school (Buhs & Ladd, 2001). Repeated peer rejection in childhood can also have serious long-term consequences (DeRosier, Kupersmidt, & Patterson, 1995; Downey et al., 1998; Ladd, 1998). Rejected youngsters are more likely than youngsters in the other categories to drop out of school, commit juvenile offenses, and suffer from psychopathology.

**CAUSES OF REJECTION.** Peer rejection can be traced, at least in part, to parental influence (Ladd, 1998). Children see how their parents respond to different social situations and often imitate these responses later. Parents who are friendly and cooperative with others demonstrate effective social skills. Parents who are belligerent and combative demonstrate much less effective social skills. In particular, when parents typically respond to interpersonal conflict like the couple in the photo—with intimidation or aggression—their children may imitate them; this hampers their development of social skills and makes them less popular in the long run (Keane, Brown, & Crenshaw, 1990).

Parents' disciplinary practices also affect their children's social skill and popularity. Inconsistent discipline—punishing a child for misbehaving one day and ignoring the same behavior the next—is associated with antisocial and aggressive behavior, paving the way to rejection (Dishion, 1990). Consistent punishment that is tied to parental love and affection is more likely to promote social skill and, in the process, popularity (Dekovic & Janssens, 1992).

In sum, parenting can lead to an aggressive interpersonal style in a child, which in turn leads to peer rejection. The implication, then, is that by teaching youngsters (and their parents) more effective ways of interacting with others, we can make rejection less likely. With improved social skills, rejected children would not need to resort to antisocial behaviors. Rejected children (and other types of unpopular children) can be taught how to initiate interaction, communicate clearly, and be friendly. They can also be discouraged from behaviors that peers dislike, such as whining and fighting. This training is very similar to the training given aggressive adolescents, who are typically unpopular (see Module 12.4). Training of this sort does work. Rejected children can learn skills that lead to peer acceptance and thereby avoid the long-term harm associated with being rejected (LaGreca, 1993; Mize & Ladd, 1990).

Throughout this module, we've seen that peers affect children's development in many ways—for example, through different forms of play, through friendships, and through participation in social groups. Beginning in the next module, we'll look at important *nonsocial* influences on children's development, starting with media such as television and computers.

Many rejected children are too aggressive and some learn this style of interaction from watching their parents in conflict.

> When children are rejected, they do less well in school, have lower self-esteem, and more often have behavioral problems.

**15.1** As a teenager, Katelyn's description of Heidi would focus more on intimacy. She might say, "I can tell Heidi stuff—special stuff, like secrets—that I wouldn't tell anyone else. And I know she'll keep my secrets." And Katelyn might mention that Heidi is loyal—willing to stand by her when other kids are teasing her.

## Check Your Learning

**RECALL** Describe the factors that seem to contribute to an adolescent's or young adult's sexual orientation.

How and when are teenagers most susceptible to peer pressure?

**INTERPRET** How might developmental change in peer interactions during infancy and the preschool years be explained by Piaget's stages of cognitive development, described in Module 6.1?

**APPLY** On page 472, you met Jay, who is the least popular child in his class. Jay's mom is worried about her son's lack of popularity and wants to know what she can do to help her son. Jay's dad thinks that Jay's mom is upset over nothing—he argues that, like fame, popularity is fleeting, and that Jay will turn out okay in the end. What advice would you give to Jay's parents?

# ELECTRONIC MEDIA                    15.2

## LEARNING OBJECTIVES

Television

Computers

- How does watching television affect children's attitudes and behavior?

- How does TV viewing influence children's cognitive development?

- How do children use computers at home and in school?

*Whenever Bill visits his granddaughter, Harmony, he is struck by the amount of time Harmony spends watching television. Many of the programs she watches are worthwhile. Nevertheless, Bill wonders if such a steady diet of TV watching might somehow be harmful. Images pop on and off the screen so rapidly that Bill wonders how Harmony will ever learn to pay attention. And he worries that she won't be as attentive in other settings that aren't as rich in video stimulation.*

In generations past, children learned their culture's values from parents, teachers, religious leaders, and print media. These sources of cultural knowledge are still with us, but they coexist with new technologies that do not always portray parents' values. Think about some of the technological developments that contemporary children take for granted that were completely foreign to youngsters growing up just a few decades ago. Your list would probably include cable TV, CD and DVD players, video game players, personal computers, cell phones that take pictures and play music, pagers, and the Internet. More forces than ever before can potentially influence children's development. Two of these technologies—television and computers—are the focus of this module. As we look at their influence, we'll see if Bill's concern for his granddaughter is well founded.

## Television

The cartoon exaggerates TV's impact on American children, but only somewhat. After all, think about how much time you spent in front of a TV while you were growing up. If you were a typical U.S. child and adolescent, you spent much more time watching TV than interacting with your parents or friends or in school. The numbers tell an incredible story. School-age children spend about 20 to 25 hours each week watching TV (Roberts, Foehr, & Rideout, 2005). Extrapolated through adolescence, the typical American high-school graduate has watched 15,000 hours of TV—nearly 2 full years of watching TV 24/7! No wonder social scientists and laypeople alike think TV plays an important role in socializing American children.

For most youngsters, viewing time increases gradually during the preschool and elementary-school years, reaching a peak just before adolescence. Boys watch more TV than girls. Also, children with lower IQs watch more than those with higher IQs; children from lower income families watch more TV than children from higher income families (Huston & Wright, 1998).

It is hard to imagine that all this TV viewing would not affect children's behavior. For this reason, scientists have been studying the impact of TV since the 1950s. Much of the research has addressed the impact of the medium per se; other research has examined the impact of the contents of TV programs (Huston & Wright, 1998). In this section, we'll look at the results of both types of research.

"MRS. HORTON, COULD YOU STOP BY SCHOOL TODAY?"

**THE MEDIUM IS THE MESSAGE OR IS IT?** When TV first became popular, critics argued that the medium itself—independent of the contents of programs— has several harmful effects on viewers, particularly children (Huston & Wright, 1998). Among the criticisms were these:

- Because TV programs consist of many brief segments presented in rapid succession, children who watch a lot of TV develop short attention spans and have difficulty concentrating in school.
- Because TV provides ready-made, simple-to-interpret images, children who watch a lot of TV become passive, lazy thinkers and become less creative.
- Children who spend a lot of time watching TV spend less time in more productive and valuable activities, such as reading, participating in sports, and playing with friends.

In fact, as stated, none of these criticisms is consistently supported by research. The first criticism—TV watching reduces attention span—is the easiest to dismiss. Research repeatedly shows that increased TV viewing does not lead to reduced attention, greater impulsivity, reduced task persistence, or increased activity levels (Huston & Wright, 1998). The *contents* of TV programs can influence these dimensions of children's behavior—children who watch impulsive models behave more impulsively themselves—but TV per se does not harm children's ability to pay attention. Bill, the grandfather in the opening vignette, need not worry that his granddaughter's TV viewing will limit her ability to pay attention later in life.

> **TV influences children through the contents of programs, not as a medium per se.**

As for the criticism that TV viewing fosters lazy thinking and stifles creativity, the evidence is mixed. Many studies find no link between the amount of TV viewing and creativity. For example, Anderson and colleagues (2001) found that the amount of time spent watching TV during the preschool years was unrelated to creativity during adolescence. Other studies, however, find a negative relation: As children watch more TV, they tend to be less creative on tests of divergent thinking like those described in Module 8.3 (Valkenburg & van der Voort, 1994; 1995). Child-development researchers don't know why the negative effects aren't found more consistently, although one idea is that the effects depend on which programs children watch, rather than simply the amount of TV watched.

Finally, according to the last criticism, TV viewing replaces other socially more desirable activities: The simple-minded view is that every hour of TV viewing replaces an hour of some more valuable activity, such as reading or doing homework. To illustrate the problems with this view, let's look at reading. The correlation between time spent watching TV and time spent reading *is* negative—heavy TV viewers read less (Huston & Wright, 1998). But we need to be cautious in interpreting this correlation (see Figure 1-2 on page 26). The easy interpretation is that watching much TV causes children to read less. However, other evidence suggests an alternate interpretation is more plausible: Children who are poor readers (and thus are unlikely to spend much time reading) end up watching a lot of TV. For youngsters who read poorly, an hour spent watching TV replaces some activity, but not an hour that would have been spent reading (Huston & Wright, 1998).

The research on each of these criticisms points to one conclusion: To understand the impact of TV on children, we need to move past the medium per se and consider other variables, including the contents of TV programs. In fact, scientists have discovered that TV does, indeed, substantially affect children's development, as you'll see in the next three sections.

**15.2** Brent is a 6-year-old boy who loves to read. His parents are thinking about limiting his TV viewing because they're afraid it will cut into the time he spends reading. Do research findings suggest that Brent's parents are on the right track?

**INFLUENCE ON ATTITUDES AND SOCIAL BEHAVIOR.**    Children are definitely influenced by what they see on TV (Browne & Hamilton-Giachritsis, 2005). In Module 12.4, for example, we saw how some children become more aggressive after viewing violence on television; and in Module 13.3 we saw how children adopt gender stereotypes from TV.

Television can definitely have negative effects, but can TV be put to prosocial goals? Can TV viewing help children learn to be more generous and cooperative and have greater self-control? Yes: Youngsters who watch TV shows that emphasize prosocial behavior, such as *Mister Rogers' Neighborhood*, are more likely to behave prosocially (Mares & Woodard, 2005). Nevertheless, two factors restrict the actual prosocial impact of TV viewing. First, prosocial behaviors are portrayed on TV far less frequently than aggressive behaviors, so opportunities to learn the former from television are limited. Second, the relatively small number of prosocial programs compete with other kinds of television programs and other non-TV activities for children's time, so children simply may not watch the few prosocial programs that are televised. Consequently, we are far from harnessing the power of television for prosocial uses.

**INFLUENCE ON CONSUMER BEHAVIOR.**    Sugary cereals, hamburgers and French fries, snack foods, toys, jeans, and athletic shoes. A phenomenal number of TV advertisements for these products are directed toward children and adolescents. A typical U.S. youth may see more than 100 commercials a day (Linn, 2004)! Children as young as 3 years can distinguish commercials from programs, though preschoolers believe commercials are simply a different form of entertainment—one designed to inform viewers. Not until age 8 or 9 do children begin to understand the persuasive intent of commercials; a few years later, children realize that commercials are not always truthful (Linn, 2005; Oates, Blades, & Gunter, 2002). They understand that a toy rocket will not really fly or that a doll will not really talk, contrary to how they're shown in commercials.

Like adults, children learn about products from TV commercials and they often urge parents to buy those products for them.

Even though children and adolescents come to understand the real intent of commercials, commercials are still effective sales tools (Smith & Atkin, 2003). Children grow to know many of the products advertised on TV (Valkenburg & Buijzen, 2005) and, like the youngster in the photograph, urge parents to buy products they've seen on television. And among adolescents, exposure to TV programs that contain commercials for alcohol (e.g., beer ads) is associated with more frequent drinking of alcohol (Stacy et al., 2004). This selling power of TV has long concerned advocates for children because so many commercials are for foods that have little nutritional value and can lead to obesity and tooth decay. The U.S. government once regulated the amount and type of advertising on children's TV programs (Huston, Watkins, & Kunkel, 1989), but today the responsibility falls largely to parents.

**INFLUENCE ON COGNITION.**    The year 1969 was a watershed in the history of children's television. That year marked the appearance of a program designed to use the power of video and animation to foster preschool skills, including recognizing letters and numbers, counting, and building vocabulary. The program achieved its goals. Preschoolers who watched the show regularly were more proficient at the targeted academic skills than preschoolers who watched infrequently. Regular viewers also adjusted to school more readily, according to teachers' ratings (Bogatz & Ball, 1972).

For more than 3 decades, *Sesame Street* has had tremendous success in helping preschool children acquire many of the skills needed for success in school, such as knowing the names of letters and knowing how to count.

By now, of course, you know that I'm talking about Big Bird, Bert, Ernie, and other members of the cast of *Sesame Street*, shown in the photo. For more than 30 years, *Sesame Street*, produced originally by Children's Television Workshop, has helped educate generations of preschoolers (Fisch, Truglio, & Cole, 1999). Today, mothers and fathers who watched *Sesame Street* as preschoolers are watching with their own youngsters. Remarkably, the time preschool children spend watching *Sesame Street* predicts their grades in high school and the amount of time they spend reading as adolescents (Anderson et al., 2001).

Building on the success of *Sesame Street*, Children's Television Workshop developed a number of other successful programs. *Electric Company* teaches reading skills, *3-2-1 Contact* focuses on science and technology, and *Square One TV* teaches mathematics (Fisch & McCann, 1993). Other public television programs include *Reading Rainbow*, which introduces children's books; *Where in Time Is Carmen Sandiego?*, which teaches history; and *Ghostwriter*, which focuses on writing. Although these programs are no longer in production (except for *Sesame Street*), they are still shown on cable networks and demonstrate that children can learn academic skills and useful social skills from TV. Thus, TV can be beneficial if parents monitor their youngsters' viewing and if they insist that the television industry improves the quality and variety of programs available for children and adolescents.

The "Improving Children's Lives" feature includes some guidelines for ensuring that TV's influence on children is positive.

## *Improving Children's Lives*
### Get the Kids Off the Couch!

If you know a child who sits glued to the TV screen from after school until bedtime, it's time to take action. Here are some suggestions:

- Children need absolute rules concerning the amount of TV and the types of programs that they can watch. These rules must be enforced consistently.

- Children shouldn't fall into the trap of "I'm bored, so I'll watch TV." Children should be encouraged to know what they want to watch before they turn on the TV.

- Adults should watch TV with children and discuss the programs. For example, parents can express their disapproval of a character's use of aggression and suggest other means of resolving conflicts. Parents can also point to the stereotypes that are depicted. The aim is for children to learn that TV's account of the world is often inaccurate and that TV should be watched critically.

- Parents need to be good TV viewers themselves. The first two tips listed here apply to viewers of all ages. When a child is present, parents shouldn't watch violent programs or others that are inappropriate for the young. And parents should watch TV deliberately and selectively, instead of mindlessly channel surfing. ■

## Computers

Some observers believe that computers are creating a "digital childhood"—an era in which new media are transforming the lives of American children (Cocking, 2001). In this section, we'll look at children's use of computers at home and in school.

**COMPUTERS IN THE HOME.**   More than 80% of American youth live in homes with a computer (Roberts et al., 2005). And they begin to use the computer at a remarkably young age. Many $2\frac{1}{2}$-year-olds play computer games while seated on a parent's lap; by $3\frac{1}{2}$, children play computer games independently, controlling a mouse themselves (Calvert et al., 2005).

How do children and adolescents use computers? Most children and adolescents use computers to access the Internet. When children are online, what are they doing? First, they do their schoolwork—children use the Internet to help them find information for school assignments. Second, they communicate—they use e-mail and instant messaging to "talk" with nearby and distant friends and relatives (Gross, 2004). Third, they provide their own entertainment—they play games online or search for information related to interests and hobbies (Roberts et al., 2005).

Another frequent use of computers, particularly for boys, is playing games. And, just as children and adolescents are influenced by the TV programs they watch, they're influenced by the contents of the computer games they play. On the one hand, many popular games including *Tetris* and *Star Fox* involve basic perceptual–spatial skills, such as estimating the trajectory of a moving object. When children play such games frequently, their spatial skills often improve (Subrahmanyam et al., 2001). On the other hand, many popular games, such *Counter-Strike* and *Grand Theft Auto* are violent, with players killing game characters in extraordinarily gruesome ways. Just as exposure to televised violence can make children behave more aggressively, playing violent video games can make children more aggressive (Anderson et al., 2003).

In many respects, home computers have changed the *how* of childhood and adolescence but not the *what*. As with previous generations, children and adolescents still play games, connect with peers, and do homework. The home computer simply provides a different means for accomplishing these tasks. As we'll see in the next section, much the same is true of computers in schools.

**COMPUTERS IN THE CLASSROOM.**   New technologies—whether TV, videotape, or pocket calculator—soon find themselves in the classroom. Personal computers are no exception; virtually all American public schools now use personal computers to aid instruction. Computers serve many functions in the classroom (Roschelle et al., 2000). One is that of tutor: Children use computers to learn reading, spelling, arithmetic, science, and social studies. Computers allow instruction to be individualized and interactive. Students proceed at their own pace, receiving feedback and help when necessary. Computers are also a valuable medium for experiential learning. Simulation programs allow students to explore the world in ways that would be impossible or dangerous otherwise. Students can change the law of gravity or see what happens to a city when no taxes are imposed. Finally, computers can help students achieve traditional academic goals (Steelman, 1994). A graphics program can allow artistically untalented students to produce beautiful illustrations. A word-processing program can relieve much of the drudgery associated with revising, thereby encouraging better writing.

> Computers are used in schools as tutors, for experiential learning, and to help children accomplish traditional academic goals more easily.

Overall, then, computers are like television in that the technology per se doesn't necessarily influence children's development. However, the way the technology is used—for example, watching violent TV programs or using word-processing software to revise a short story—can affect children, positively or negatively depending on the use. In the next module, we'll see whether institutions such as neighborhoods and schools also influence children in this manner.

**15.2** | Probably not. Children who read well and enjoy reading will find time to read. Research suggests that, for these youngsters, TV viewing will not replace time spent reading. Frankly, a better strategy would be to have limits on *what* he watches on TV, not on how much he watches.

---

### CHECK YOUR LEARNING

**RECALL**   Summarize research that has examined the impact on children of TV as a medium.
   What are the primary ways in which computers are used in schools?

**INTERPRET**   Compare and contrast the ways in which TV viewing and Web surfing might affect children's development.

**APPLY**   What if you had the authority to write new regulations for children's TV programs. What shows would you encourage? What shows would you want to limit?

---

## 15.3     INSTITUTIONAL INFLUENCES

**Day Care**

**Part-Time Employment**

**Neighborhoods**

**School**

### LEARNING OBJECTIVES

- How are children affected by nonparental child care?
- What is the impact of part-time employment on children's development?
- How are children influenced by their neighborhoods?
- What are the hallmarks of effective schools and effective teachers?

> *When 15-year-old Aaron announced that he wanted an after-school job at the local supermarket, his mother was delighted, believing that he would learn much from the experience. Five months later, she had her doubts. Aaron had lost interest in school, and they argued constantly about how he spent his money.*

So far in this chapter, we've seen the potent influences of peers and media on children's development. Yet there are other noteworthy influences on children and their development—cultural institutions where children spend much of their lives. In this module, we'll look at four such institutions: day care, the workplace, neighborhoods, and school. As we do, we'll see whether part-time jobs like Aaron's help or harm youth.

### Day Care

Each day, approximately 12 million U.S. children age 5 and under are cared for by someone other than their mother, a phenomenon linked to more dual-earner couples and to more single-parent households in the United States in the 21st century. Three forms of child care are most common: (1) children stay at home, where they receive care from a relative such as a father or grandparent, (2) children receive care in the home of a child-care provider, and (3) children attend day-care or nursery-school programs (Children's Defense Fund, 2005). The patterns are very similar for European American, African American, and Hispanic American youngsters (Singer et al., 1998).

Many parents, particularly mothers, have misgivings about their children spending so much time in the care of others. Should parents worry? Does nonmaternal care harm children? Before turning to research for answers to these questions, let's put them in historical and cross-cultural perspective. Although nonmaternal care of children is often portrayed as unnatural—and therefore potentially harmful—the truth is that for most of history and in most cultures, a majority of children have been cared for by someone other than the mother, at least some of the time (Lamb, 1999). When viewed from the larger perspective of history, there is nothing "natural" or "traditional" about mothers having nearly exclusive responsibility for child care.

Nevertheless, in the United States (and many other industrialized countries) since World War II, the cultural ideal has been that children are better off when cared for at home by their mothers. Does research support the cultural ideal? In answering this question, most researchers worried about the impact of child care on mother–infant attachment. But, as we saw in Module 10.3, the Early Child-Care study conducted by the National Institute of Child Health and Human Development showed that attachment security was affected by child care only when less sensitive mothers had their infants in low-quality child care.

Of course, the effects of day care need not be limited to attachment; other aspects of children's development might be affected, and these have been investigated in other reports from the Early Child Care study. Here, too, the general finding is that time spent in day care is not a critical factor. There are some exceptions—for example, when children spend many hours each week in day care, they more often have behavior problems. To illustrate, children in the Early Child Care study who had spent the most time in day care as infants and preschoolers were, as kindergartners, more likely to be aggressive with peers and to have conflicts with adults (Early Child Care Research Network, 2003).

**Parents can enroll their children in high-quality day care without fearing harmful consequences.**

However, the more important factor in understanding the impact of child care is the quality of care that children receive: Not surprisingly, better care is linked to better outcomes. High-quality child care means a relatively small number of children per caregiver (e.g., 3 infants or toddlers per caregiver, four 2-year-olds per caregiver) along with well-educated and well-trained caregivers. In addition, in high-quality child care, caregivers are warm and responsive, and they provide age-appropriate activities that are designed to promote cognitive and social development (Marshall, 2004). When children are enrolled in programs that meet these standards, they often grow cognitively and socioemotionally. What's more, these benefits are seen regardless of the child's socioeconomic status (Votruba-Drzal, Coley, & Chase-Lansdale, 2004). Thus, working parents can enroll their infants and preschoolers in high-quality day-care programs with no fear of harmful consequences.

When children enter elementary school, child care becomes easier for working parents. However, many children still need care after school. Historically, after-school programs have focused on recreation: children played games and sports, did arts and crafts, or participated in musical or dramatic productions. Recently, however, many after-school programs have focused more on academics. Children attending such programs often show modest improvements in school achievement, particularly when they attend higher quality programs (Vandell, Pierce, & Dadisman, 2005).

In addition, many children and adolescents participate in structured activities after school; familiar examples would include sports, school clubs, and music lessons. Although youth typically participate for pleasure, these activities also provide needed after-school care for some participants. As a general rule, children and adolescents benefit from participating: They often are better adjusted, have higher self-esteem, and are less likely to have behavioral problems. The main exception is participation in sports, where the findings are mixed. In some studies (e.g., Darling, Caldwell, & Smith, 2005), adolescents involved in sports are more likely to drink alcohol and to have lower grades. But not all studies report this outcome; the results may depend, for example, on attitudes toward sports in the school (Vandell et al., 2005).

Finally, many school-age children and adolescents—nearly 20% of all 5- to 13-year-olds in the United States—receive no formal care after school; they are left alone to care for themselves (Smith, 2000). **Children who care for themselves are sometimes called _latchkey children_, a term that originated more than 200 years ago to describe children who raised a door latch to enter their own homes.** Some latchkey children, like the child in the photo, stay at home alone (sometimes with parental supervision in absentia via the telephone). Others may stay at friends' homes where adults are sometimes present, or they may be unsupervised in public places such as shopping malls.

Many American children care for themselves after school, an arrangement that can be safe, depending on the child's age, maturity, the neighborhood, and the rules established for the child.

The popular perception is that latchkey children are a frightened, endangered lot. But research provides little support for this view. To the contrary, most older children and adolescents who care for themselves at home after school fare as well as children in the care of parents or other adults (Sarampote, Bassett, & Winsler, 2004). Research does reveal one group that is at risk—children and adolescents who spend their after-school hours away from home, unsupervised. These individuals are more prone to antisocial influences of peers and more prone to engage in problem behavior (Coley, Morris, & Hernandez, 2004).

**Children can care for themselves after school if they are mature, their neighborhood is safe, and they are supervised by an adult.**

This generally rosy picture does not mean that parents should begin self-care without careful planning. Many states provide specific guidelines to help parents decide whether a child is capable of self care (e.g., Connecticut Department of Children and Families, 2003). Parents are urged to consider their child's age—many experts would recommend that children are not capable of self-care until they're 12, but others would say that some 8-year-olds can care for themselves briefly (1 to $1\frac{1}{2}$ hours) during the day. More important than age is the child's maturity: Is the child responsible? Does the child make good decisions on his or her own? Parents should also consider the child's attitudes and feelings about being left alone: Is the child anxious about being alone in the house? Finally, it's important for parents to consider their neighborhood: Is it safe? Are there trusted neighbors that the child can turn to if necessary?

If questions like these can be answered "yes," then self-care will probably work. But it's important that children be prepared for self-care. They need to know after-school routines (for example, acceptable ways of getting home from school and how to check in with a parent), rules for their own behavior after school (for example, acceptable and unacceptable activities), guidelines on how to handle emergencies, and emergency phone numbers (American Academy of Child and Adolescent Psychiatry, 2000).

Fortunately, employers have begun to realize that convenient, high-quality child care makes for a better employee. Businesses are realizing that the availability of excellent child care helps attract and retain a skilled labor force. And cities help by modifying their zoning codes so that new shopping complexes and office buildings must include child-care facilities, like those in the photo. With effort, organization, and help from the community and business, high-quality child care can be available to all families.

## Part-Time Employment

The teen in the photo below is engaged in an American adolescent ritual—the part-time job. Today, about 25% of high school freshmen have a part-time job and about 75% of high school seniors do (Bureau of Labor Statistics, 2005). About two thirds of these youth work in retail and half of those are employed in the food and beverage industry (U.S. Department of Labor, 2000).

Most adults praise teens for working, believing that early exposure to the workplace teaches self-discipline, self-confidence, and important job skills (Snedeker, 1982). For most adolescents, however, the reality is very different. Part-time work can actually be harmful, for several reasons:

1. *School performance suffers.* When students work more than approximately 15 hours per week, they devote less time to homework and are more apt to cut classes. Not surprisingly, their grades are lower than those of their peers who work less or not at all (Steinberg, Fegley, & Dornbusch, 1993). Why should 15 hours of work be so detrimental to school performance? A 15-hour work

Because many employees—particularly mothers who work full-time outside of the home—want high-quality child care available, many companies now provide such care on site.

Many American adolescents hold part-time jobs; these can be beneficial but not when adolescents work more than 20 hours weekly.

When adolescents work long hours in a part-time job, they often have trouble juggling the demands of work, school, and sleep!

**When adolescents work many hours in part-time jobs, they do worse in school, often have behavioral problems, and experience misleading affluence.**

schedule usually means four 3-hour shifts after school and another 3-hour shift on the weekend. This would seem to leave ample opportunity to study, but only if students use their time effectively. In fact, many high-school students apparently do not have the foresight and discipline necessary to consistently meet the combined demands of work and school. Like the boy in the photo, many teens have great difficulty balancing work, study, and sleep.

2.  *There are mental health and behavioral problems.* Adolescents who work long hours—more than 15 or 20 hours a week—are more likely to experience anxiety and depression, and their self-esteem often suffers. Many adolescents find themselves in jobs that are repetitive and boring but stressful, and such conditions undermine self-esteem and breed anxiety. Extensive part-time work frequently leads to substance abuse, including cigarettes, alcohol, marijuana, and cocaine (Bachman & Schulenberg, 1993; Mortimer et al., 1996). Extensive work is also associated with more frequent problem behavior, including violence toward others, trouble with police, and arguments with parents (Staff & Uggen, 2003).

    Why employment is associated with all of these problems is not clear. Perhaps employed adolescents turn to drugs to help them cope with the anxiety and depression brought on by work. Arguments with parents may become more common because anxious, depressed adolescents are more prone to argue or because wage-earning adolescents may believe that their freedom should match their income. Whatever the exact mechanism, extensive part-time work is clearly detrimental to the mental health of most adolescents.

3.  *Affluence is misleading.* Adults sometimes argue that work is good for teenagers because it teaches them "the value of a dollar." Here, too, reality is at odds with the adage. The typical teenage pattern is to "earn and spend." Working adolescents spend most of their earnings on themselves—to buy clothing, snack food, or cosmetics, and to pay for entertainment. Few working teens set aside much of their income for future goals, such as a college education, or use it to contribute to their family's expenses (Shanahan et al., 1996a; 1996b). Because parents customarily pay for many of the essential expenses associated with truly independent living—rent, utilities, and groceries, for example—working adolescents often have a vastly higher percentage of their income available for discretionary spending than working adults. Thus, for many teens, the part-time work experience provides unrealistic expectations about how income can be allocated (Bachman, 1983).

The message that emerges repeatedly from research on part-time employment is hardly encouraging. Like Aaron, the teenage boy in the vignette, many adolescents who work long hours at part-time jobs do not benefit from the experience. To the contrary, they do worse in school, are more likely to have behavioral problems, and learn how to spend money rather than how to manage it. These effects are similar for adolescents from different ethnic groups (Steinberg & Dornbusch, 1991) and are comparable for boys and girls (Bachman & Schulenberg, 1993). Ironically, though, there is a long-term benefit: Young adults who had a stressful part-time job as an adolescent are better able to cope with stressful adult jobs (Mortimer & Staff, 2004). They're apparently better prepared to cope with the corresponding stresses of full-time employment.

Does this mean that teenagers who are still in school should never work part-time? Not necessarily. Part-time employment *can* be a good experience, depending on the circumstances. One key is the number of hours of work. Although the exact number of hours varies, of course, from one student to the next, most students could easily work 5 hours weekly without harm, and many could work 10 hours weekly. Another key is the type of job. When adolescents have jobs that allow them to use their skills (for example, bookkeeping, computing, or typing) and acquire new ones, self-esteem is enhanced, and they learn from their work experience (Mortimer, Harley, & Staff, 2002). Yet another factor is how teens spend their earnings. When they save their money or use it to pay for clothes and school expenses, relations with their parents often improve (Shanahan et al., 1996a, 1996b).

By these criteria, who is likely to show the harmful effects of part-time work? A teen who spends 30 hours a week bagging groceries and spends most of it on CDs or videos. And who is likely to benefit from part-time work? A teen who likes to tinker with cars, who spends Saturdays working in a repair shop, and who sets aside some of his earnings for college.

Finally, summer jobs typically do not involve conflict between work and school. Consequently, many of the harmful effects associated with part-time employment during the school year do not hold for summer employment. In fact, such employment sometimes enhances adolescents' self-esteem, especially when they save part of their income for future plans (Marsh, 1991).

## Neighborhoods

For years, Mr. Rogers greeted preschool children singing, "It's a beautiful day in my neighborhood" and telling young viewers, "I've always wanted a neighbor just like you." Mr. Roger's neighborhood is indeed safe and nurturing, but not all children are so fortunate; their neighborhoods are neither safe nor nurturing. Do these differences in neighborhoods affect children's lives? We'll answer this question in the next few pages.

Before we consider how neighborhoods affect children, we need to decide what constitutes a neighborhood. Sometimes researchers define neighborhoods in terms of school districts or other government boundaries, but the most commonly accepted approach in the U.S. is to define neighborhoods in terms of census tracts. These usually include 3,000 to 8,000 people living in an area that has, according to local authorities, some identity based on physical features (e.g., streets, a commercial district, proximity to a school) or social features (e.g., most residents are members of the same racial or ethnic group). Using census-tract information, researchers have identified two features of neighborhoods that are particularly useful when it comes to understanding children's development: *socioeconomic status*, reflecting the income and education of the residents, and *stability*, typically defined as the percentage of residents who have lived in the neighborhood for several years (Leventhal & Brooks-Gunn, 2003).

Of course, defining neighborhoods in terms of these features of census tracts is not perfect; this approach ignores some potentially important features of neighborhoods. For example, they don't consider safety per se and they don't measure the presence of institutions like a church, temple, or school that can provide focus and vitality to a neighborhood. But the advantage is that census tracts are defined in a standard way across the United States and mountains of data concerning census tracts are available to researchers.

Nick is a 16-year-old who would love to have a career in the entertainment industry—TV, movies, or maybe in music. For now, he works two nights a week (about 8 hours total) as an usher at a local movie theater. At his parents' request, one third of his take-home pay goes into a college fund. Will this part-time job be harmful to Nick?

Do neighborhoods matter? Yes; all other things being equal, children benefit from living in a neighborhood where most of the adults are well educated and economically advantaged. These benefits are seen for both school achievement and psychological adjustment. In other words, when children live in economically advantaged neighborhoods, they tend to do better in school and are somewhat less likely to have behavioral and emotional problems (Ackerman & Brown, 2006; Mistry et al., 2004).

Researchers agree that neighborhoods per se do not influence children's behavior. Instead, as we would expect from the contextual model of parenting (described in Module 14.1), the impact of neighborhoods is indirect, transmitted through people (parents and peers, primarily) and other social institutions. Several pathways of influence are possible (Leventhal & Brooks-Gunn, 2000). One concerns the availability of institutional resources: Economically advantaged neighborhoods more often have the kinds of resources that enhance children's development: libraries like the one in the

photo, museums, quality day care, and good schools to foster children's cognitive development; medical services to provide for children's physical and mental health; and opportunities for adolescents to find work. In economically advantaged neighborhoods that tend to have these resources, children are more likely to have experiences that lead to school success, to good health, and to the ability to find part-time jobs as teenagers. In contrast, in economically disadvantaged neighborhoods that frequently lack these resources, children are often prepared inadequately for school, receive little medical care, and are unable to find jobs as teenagers, so they turn to delinquent or criminal behavior.

More affluent neighborhoods are more likely to contain resources important for children's development, such as a library, excellent medical care, and high-quality child care.

This impact of neighborhood is illustrated in a novel field study by Leventhal and Brooks-Gunn (2004), who studied families living in New York City who were participating in a federally funded project known as the Moving to Opportunity for Fair Housing Demonstration. Some of the families enrolled in the project were randomly assigned to a condition in which they received vouchers that could be used to move from their current housing (where at least 40% of the residents were living in poverty) to neighborhoods where fewer than 10% of the residents lived in poverty. Other participating families were assigned to a condition in which they remained in their current housing, where poverty was common. Approximately 3 years later, adolescent boys in the first group had much higher achievement scores than boys in the second group, because they spent more time on homework and felt safer in their new school. In other words, when families moved to a new neighborhood that was relatively free of poverty and that had better schools—they were safer and had an atmosphere that encouraged academic success—adolescent boys experienced greater achievement in school.

A second way in which neighborhoods affect children and adolescents is based on the fact that, because economically advantaged neighborhoods are more likely to be stable, they are more cohesive and close-knit, which means residents take a greater interest in neighborhood goings-on, including those of children and adolescents (Leventhal & Brooks-Gunn, 2000). Suppose, for example, adults see the two boys in the photo on page 482 slugging it out in the park. In a cohesive neighborhood, adults are more likely to intervene (e.g., break up the fight and scold the children for fighting) because they are committed to its residents; in a less cohesive neighborhood, adults might ignore the children because they don't want the hassle of getting involved. Thus, in cohesive neighborhoods, residents are much more likely to monitor the activities of neighborhood children, making it less likely that children get in trouble.

Yet another link between poverty and children's development reflects the fact that when children live in poverty, their home life is often described as chaotic. Their residence is often crowded and noisy and their lives are often relatively unstructured and unpredictable. For example, children may not have a set time for doing homework. Living in such chaos often engenders a sense of helplessness: Children feel as if they have little control over their own lives. And children's feelings of helplessness are often associated with mental health problems and school failure (Bradley & Corwyn, 2002; Evans et al., 2005).

Finally, neighborhoods affect children through their impact on parenting behavior. One account of this link is the focus of the "Spotlight on Theories" feature.

People living in poorer neighborhoods are less likely to know their neighbors and, consequently, are less likely to get involved in their neighbors' lives; for example, when children are fighting, they may be reluctant to stop the fight because they don't know the children.

## Spotlight on Theories
### The Family Economic Stress Model

#### BACKGROUND

The harmful effects of poverty on children have been known for centuries; but only recently have researchers attempted to understand the many different ways in which poverty harms children. Among the most difficult to understand is the way in which poverty causes children to receive less effective parenting.

#### THE THEORY

Adults living in chronic poverty often experience much stress, from constantly worrying about whether they will have enough money to buy food or to pay rent. Rand Conger and Glen Elder (1994) proposed the family economic stress model (FESM) to explain how such poverty-induced stress could affect children's development. According to FESM, economic hardship results in a serious of consequences:

1. parents find that their income is not adequate to meet their needs;

2. this economic pressure affects parents' mental health, causing some to become depressed;

3. once depressed, the quality of the marital relationship should decline;

4. this results in less effective parenting (parents are not as warm with their children, praise them less frequently, and, instead, are often angry with them); and

5. because children receive less effective parenting, behavioral problems are common (e.g., children become anxious or angry).

Thus, in FESM, poverty harms children's development because parents struggling to make ends meet become depressed, and parent less effectively.

**HYPOTHESIS:** When parents' economic situation changes for the worse—for example, one or both parents lose a job and can't find a comparable new job—this should

> Children growing up in poverty have access to fewer resources, are monitored less often by neighbors, and experience less effective parenting.

start the cascade of consequences described in the FESM: Diminished income causes economic stress, which leads to depression, which leads to marital conflict and ineffective parenting, which finally disrupts children's development.

TEST: Solantaus, Leinonen, and Punamäki (2004) provided a novel evaluation of this hypothesis by looking at families in Finland in the early 1990s when that country experienced a deep economic decline that compared to the Great Depression in the United States in the 1930s. They took advantage of the fact that a large cross-section of Finnish families had been studied in the late 1980s, before the onset of the depression. Then, children and their families were studied again in 1994 when the economic recession was at its peak. Solantaus and colleagues obtained measures of all the key constructs in FESM: family economic hardship, parental mental health, quality of marital interaction, parenting quality, and children's mental health. All were measured with questionnaires, which were completed by parents, children, and the children's teachers. Each of the links in FESM were supported: (1) families who experienced more economic pressure reported more mental health problems, (2) parents who had more mental problems reported that their marriages were less satisfying, (3) a less-satisfying marriage was associated with lower quality parenting, and (4) lower quality parenting was associated with more frequent mental health problems in children.

CONCLUSION: Solantaus and colleagues found the outcomes predicted from FESM: Economic hardship triggered a sequence of events that ultimately harmed children's mental health. As they phrased it, "[The family] is a relationship unit, but it is also an economic unit. . . . This means that economic and relationship issues are intertwined, making the relationships vulnerable when the economy collapses" (p. 425).

APPLICATION: Based on these findings, we can add "improving children's mental health" to the long list of reasons to eliminate poverty. Until that happens, these findings and the FESM model remind us of the difficulties of parenting effectively while living in poverty. Families living in poverty often need immediate help (e.g., services for parents and children who have mental health problems) as they pursue their longer term goal of leaving poverty. ■

Chronic poverty is particularly hard for parents because they usually have few social supports to help them cope with stress. When adults living in economically advantaged neighborhoods find life so stressful that they need help, they can turn to neighbors or health-care professionals. In contrast, adults living in poverty are less likely to turn to either a neighbor (because they don't know anyone well enough due to instability in the neighborhood) or a health-care professional (because one is not available nearby or they can't afford it). Thus, adults living in chronic poverty experience a "double whammy"—more stress and fewer resources to cope with stress—which contributes to less effective parenting.

Thus, children growing up in economically disadvantaged neighborhoods typically have access to fewer institutional resources, are monitored less often by neighbors, often lead chaotic lives, and experience less effective parenting brought on by chronic stress. At the same time, the research suggests that an effective way to invest in poverty-ridden neighborhoods is by providing additional institutional resources (Leventhal & Brooks-Gunn, 2000). When neighborhoods have good child care and good schools, many opportunities for recreation, and effective health care, children benefit directly. They also benefit indirectly because when parents feel less stress they parent more effectively, and because residents are less likely to move, contributing to neighborhood cohesiveness.

Schools are such a salient resource for children that we need to know what makes them effective; that's our next topic.

## School

At age 5 or 6, most American children head off to kindergarten, starting an educational journey that lasts 13 years for most and more than 17 years for some. How do schools influence children's development? Answering this question is difficult because American education is a smorgasbord, reflecting local control by communities throughout the United States. Schools differ on many dimensions, including their emphasis on academic goals and parent involvement. Teachers, too, differ in many ways, such as how they run their classrooms and how they teach. These and other variables affect how much students learn, as you'll see in the next few pages. Let's begin with school-based influences.

**SCHOOL-BASED INFLUENCES ON STUDENT ACHIEVEMENT.** Roosevelt High School, in the center of Detroit, has an enrollment of 3,500 students in grades 9 to 12. Opened in 1936, the building shows its age. The rooms are drafty, the desks are decorated with generations of graffiti, and new technology means an overhead projector. Nevertheless, attendance at Roosevelt is good, most students graduate, and many continue their education at community colleges and state universities. Southport High School, in Boston, has about the same enrollment as Roosevelt High and the building is about the same age. Yet truancy is commonplace at Southport, where fewer than half the students graduate and almost none go to college.

These schools are hypothetical, but accurately portray American education. Some schools are much more successful than others, regardless of whether success is defined in terms of the percentage of students who are literate, graduate, or go to college. Why are some schools successful and not others? Researchers (Good & Brophy, 2002; Hill & Taylor, 2004; Stevenson & Stigler, 1992; Wentzel, 2002) have identified a number of factors linked with successful schools:

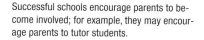

*Successful schools emphasize academics, provide a safe climate, involve parents, and monitor students' progress.*

- *Staff and students alike understand that academic excellence is the primary goal and standards are set accordingly.* The school day emphasizes instruction, and students are recognized publicly for their academic accomplishments.

- *The school climate is safe and nurturing.* Students know that they can devote their energy to learning (instead of worrying about being harmed in school), and they know the staff truly wants to see them succeed.

- *Parents are involved.* In some cases, this may be through formal arrangements, such as parent–teacher organizations. Or it may be informal. Parents may spend some time each week in school grading papers or, like the dad in the photo, tutoring a child. Such involvement signals both teachers and students that parents are committed to students' success.

Successful schools encourage parents to become involved; for example, they may encourage parents to tutor students.

- *Progress of students, teachers, and programs is monitored.* The only way to know if schools are succeeding is by measuring performance. Students, teachers, and programs need to be evaluated regularly, using objective measures that reflect academic goals. In schools that follow these guidelines, students usually succeed. In schools where the guidelines are ignored, students more often fail.

Of course, on a daily basis, individual teachers have the most potential for impact. Let's see how teachers can influence their students' achievement.

**TEACHER-BASED INFLUENCES.**    Take a moment to recall your teachers in elementary school, junior high, and high school. Some you probably remember fondly, because they were enthusiastic and innovative and they made learning fun. You may remember others with bitterness. They seemed to have lost their love of teaching and children, making class a living hell. Your experience tells you that some teachers are better than others, but what exactly makes a good teacher? Personality and enthusiasm are not the key elements. Although you may enjoy warm and eager teachers, research (Good & Brophy, 2002; Stevenson & Stigler, 1992; Walberg, 1995) shows several other factors are critical when it comes to students' achievement. Students tend to learn the most when teachers

Students learn less when their teachers spend time disciplining students instead of teaching them.

- *manage the classroom effectively so they can devote most of their time to instruction.* When teachers like the man in the photo spend a lot of time disciplining students, or when students do not move smoothly from one class activity to the next, instructional time is wasted, and students are apt to learn less.

- *believe they are responsible for their students' learning and that their students will learn when taught well.* When students don't understand a new topic, these teachers repeat the original instruction (in case the student missed something) or create new instruction (in case the student heard everything but just didn't "get it"). These teachers keep plugging away because they feel at fault if students don't learn.

- *pay careful attention to pacing.* They present material slowly enough that students can understand a new concept, but not so slowly that students get bored.

- *emphasize mastery of topics.* Teachers should introduce a topic, then give students many opportunities to understand, practice, and apply the topic. Just as you'd find it hard to go directly from driver's ed to driving a race car, students more often achieve when they grasp a new topic thoroughly, then gradually move on to other, more advanced topics.

- *teach actively.* They don't just talk or give students an endless stream of worksheets. Instead, they demonstrate topics concretely or have hands-on demonstrations for students. They also have students participate in class activities and encourage students to interact, generating ideas and solving problems together.

- *value tutoring.* They work with students individually or in small groups, so they can gear their instruction to each student's level and check each student's understanding. They also encourage peer tutoring, in which more capable students tutor less capable students. Children who are tutored by peers do learn, and so do the tutors, evidently because teaching helps tutors organize their knowledge.

- *teach children techniques for monitoring and managing their own learning.* Students are more likely to achieve when they are taught how to recognize the aims of school tasks and know effective strategies for achieving those aims (like those described on pages 201–203).

Thus, what makes for effective schools and teachers? No single element is crucial. Instead, many factors contribute to make some schools and teachers remarkably effective. Some of the essential ingredients include parents who are involved, teachers who care deeply about their students' learning and manage classrooms well, and a school that is safe, nurturing, and emphasizes achievement.

Of course, many schools are not very successful. However, as parents, teachers, and concerned citizens, we need to resist the idea that any single magic potion can cure a school's ills. As we have seen throughout this book, the outcome of development—in this case, academic achievement—is determined by many factors, including environmental forces (e.g., parents, teachers) as well as the contributions of children themselves. To foster academic success, we need to consider all these factors, not focus narrowly on only one or two.

On a more general note, understanding why and how children succeed in school (and in other domains of life) is indeed a challenging puzzle. But, scientists are making remarkable progress in solving the child-development puzzle; as we end the book, I hope you've enjoyed learning about their discoveries. Thanks for reading.

> *Effective teachers manage classrooms well, believe they are responsible for students' learning, pace their teaching, emphasize mastery, teach actively, value tutoring, and teach children to monitor their learning.*

## CHECK YOUR LEARNING

**RECALL** What is known about the impact of part-time employment on adolescents?

Summarize the ways in which poverty can influence children's development.

**INTERPRET** Compare and contrast the ways in which schools (as institutions) affect children's learning with the ways in which teachers affect children's learning.

**APPLY** Imagine that you've taken a new job, which means that your 10-year-old daughter would need to care for herself at home from after school until about 6 P.M. What would you do to decide whether she's capable of such self-care? If you decided that she is capable, what would you do to prepare her?

**15.3**

Probably not. He's not working enough for the job to interfere too much with school. Plus, he's interested in working in the entertainment industry, so there's some benefit to learning the business "from the ground up." Finally, he's saving a substantial amount of his pay, which means he's less likely to experience misleading affluence.

## 🌊 UNIFYING THEMES: Continuity

In this last chapter of the book, I want to remind you that *early development is related to later development but not perfectly.* Children who are rejected by their peers are, over time, more likely to do poorly in school, have lower self-esteem, and have behavioral problems. Of course, not all rejected children suffer this fate. Some do well in school, have high self-esteem, and avoid behavioral problems. Positive outcomes are more likely to occur when children learn effective skills for interacting with others. As we've seen many times in previous chapters, early experiences often point children toward a particular developmental path, but later experiences can cause them to change course.

## SEE FOR YOURSELF

The best way to understand the differences between good and bad teaching is to visit some actual school classrooms. Try to visit three or four classes in at least two different schools. (You can usually arrange this by speaking with the school's principal.) Take along the principles of good teaching that are listed on pages 490–491. Start by watching how the teachers and children interact. Then, decide how much the teacher relies on each of the principles. You'll probably see that most teachers use some but not all of these principles. And you'll also see that, in today's classroom, consistently following all the principles is very challenging. See for yourself!

## RESOURCES

For more information about . . .

**Why some children and families are able to overcome poverty,** read *Managing to Make it: Urban Families and Adolescent Success* (University of Chicago Press, 2000), by Frank F. Furstenberg, Thomas D. Cook, Jacquelynne Eccles, Glen H. Elder Jr., and Arnold Sameroff, which chronicles the way in which some parents living in poverty help to shield their children from dangers associated with living in poverty and, instead, direct them toward positive outcomes.

**the impact of child care on children's development,** visit the Web site of The NICHD Study of Early Child Care and Youth Development, **http://secc.rti.org/**

## KEY TERMS

associative play  461
clique  471
cooperative play  461
crowd  471
dominance hierarchy  471

friendship  464
latchkey children  482
nonsocial play  460
parallel play  460
rough-and-tumble play  464

# SUMMARY

## 15.1 PEERS

### Development of Peer Interactions

Children's first real social interactions, at about 12 to 15 months, take the form of parallel play, in which infants play alone while watching each other. At about 2 years, cooperative play organized around a theme becomes common.

Make-believe play is also common and, in addition to being fun, promotes cognitive development and lets children examine frightening topics. Most solitary play is harmless. Parents foster children's play by acting as skilled playmates, serving as social director for their children, coaching social skills, and mediating disputes.

Beyond preschool, peer relations improve and emphasize talking and being together, as well as rough-and-tumble play.

### Friendship

Friendships among preschoolers are based on common interests and getting along well. As children grow, loyalty, trust, and intimacy become more important features in their friendships. Friends are usually similar in age, sex, race, and attitudes. Children with friends are more skilled socially and better adjusted.

### Romantic Relationships

For younger adolescents, romantic relationships offer companionship and the possibility of sexual exploration; for older adolescents, they provide trust and support.

Some adolescents are attracted to same-sex peers. Pregnancy is common because many adolescents engage in unprotected sex. Comprehensive sex education is effective in reducing teenage sexual activity.

Adolescents often wonder about their sexual orientation but only a small percentage report having homosexual experiences. Research has discredited many explanations of the origins of homosexual orientations but suggests some sort of biological influences.

### Groups

Older children and adolescents often form cliques—small groups of like-minded individuals that become part of a crowd. Members of higher-status crowds often have higher self-esteem.

Most groups have a dominance hierarchy, a well-defined structure with a leader at the top. Physical power often determines the dominance hierarchy, particularly among younger boys. With older children and adolescents, dominance hierarchies are more often based on skills that are important to group functioning.

Peers are particularly influential when standards of behavior are unclear, such as for taste in music or clothing, or concerning drinking.

### Popularity and Rejection

Many popular children are socially skilled; they generally share, cooperate, and help others. Other popular children use aggression to achieve social goals. Some children are rejected by their peers because they are too aggressive; others are rejected for being shy. Both groups of rejected children are often unsuccessful in school and have behavioral problems.

## 15.2 ELECTRONIC MEDIA

### Television

Many popular criticisms about TV as a medium (e.g., it shortens children's attention span) are not supported by research. However, the content of TV programs can affect children. Youngsters who frequently watch prosocial TV become more skilled socially, and preschoolers who watch *Sesame Street* improve their academic skills and adjust more readily to school.

### Computers

At home, children use computers to play games (and are influenced by the contents of the games they play) and to access the Internet. Computers are used in school as tutors, to provide experiential learning, and as a multipurpose tool to achieve traditional academic goals.

## 15.3 INSTITUTIONAL INFLUENCES

### Day Care

Many U.S. children are cared for by a father or other relative, in a day-care provider's home or in a day-care center. When children attend high-quality child care, this fosters their cognitive and socioemotional development. After-school programs and structured activities are often beneficial, too. Children can care for themselves after school if they are mature enough, live in a safe neighborhood, and are supervised by an adult.

### Part-Time Employment

Adolescents who are employed more than 15 hours per week during the school year typically do poorly in school, often have lowered self-esteem and increased anxiety, and have problems interacting with others. Employed adolescents save relatively little of their income. Instead, they spend most of it on themselves, which can give misleading expectations about how to allocate income.

Part-time employment can be beneficial if adolescents work relatively few hours, if the work allows them to use existing skills or acquire new ones, and if teens save some of their earnings. Summer employment can also be beneficial.

### Neighborhoods

Children are more likely to thrive when they grow up in a neighborhood that is economically advantaged and stable. These neighborhoods are better for children because more institutional resources (e.g., schools) are available, because residents are more likely to monitor neighborhood children's behavior, because home life is predictable, and because parents are not living in chronic stress associated with poverty.

### School

Schools influence students' achievement in many ways. Students are most likely to achieve when their school emphasizes academic excellence, has a safe and nurturing environment, monitors pupils' and teachers' progress, and encourages parents to be involved.

Students achieve at higher levels when their teachers manage classrooms effectively, take responsibility for their students' learning, teach mastery of material, pace material well, value tutoring, and show children how to monitor their own learning.

# GLOSSARY

## A

**accommodation** According to Piaget, changing existing knowledge based on new knowledge.

**achievement status** The identity status in Marcia's theory in which adolescents have explored alternative identities and are now secure in their chosen identities.

**active–passive child issue** The issue of whether children are simply at the mercy of the environment (passive child) or actively influence their own development through their own unique individual characteristics (active child).

**adolescent egocentrism** The self-absorption that is characteristic of teenagers as they search for identity.

**African American English** A dialect of standard English spoken by some African Americans that has slightly different grammatical rules than standard English.

**age of viability** The age at which a fetus can survive because most of its bodily systems function adequately, typically at 7 months after conception.

**aggression** Behavior meant to harm others.

**allele** A variation of a specific gene.

**altruism** Prosocial behavior, such as helping and sharing, in which the individual does not benefit directly from his or her behavior.

**amniocentesis** A prenatal diagnostic technique that involves withdrawing a sample of amniotic fluid through the abdomen using a syringe.

**amniotic fluid** Fluid in the amnion that cushions the embryo and maintains a constant temperature.

**amniotic sac** An inner sac in which the developing child will rest.

**analytic ability** In Robert Sternberg's theory of intelligence, the ability to analyze problems and generate different solutions.

**androgens** Hormones secreted by the testes that influence aggressive behavior.

**androgynous** Having a combination of gender-role traits that includes both instrumental and expressive behaviors.

**anorexia nervosa** A persistent refusal to eat, accompanied by an irrational fear of being overweight.

**Apgar score** A measure to evaluate the newborn's condition, based on breathing, heart rate, muscle tone, presence of reflexes, and skin tone.

**applied developmental science** A scientific discipline that uses child-development research to promote healthy development, particularly for vulnerable children and families.

**assimilation** According to Piaget, taking in information that is compatible with what one already knows.

**associative play** A form of play in which toddlers engage in similar activities, talk or smile at one another, and offer each other toys.

**attachment** The affectionate, reciprocal relationship that is formed at about 6 or 7 months between an infant and his or her primary caregiver, usually the mother.

**attention** Processes that determine which information will be processed further by an individual.

**attributions** An individual's personal explanation for success or failure.

**auditory threshold** The quietest sound that a person can hear.

**authoritarian parenting** A style of parenting that combines high levels of control and low levels of warmth toward children.

**authoritative parenting** A style of parenting that combines a moderate degree of control with being warm and responsive toward children.

**authority-oriented grandparents** Grandparents who provide discipline for their grandchildren but otherwise are not particularly active in their grandchildren's lives.

**autobiographical memory** A person's memory of the significant events and experiences of his or her own life.

**automatic processes** Cognitive activities that require virtually no effort.

**autosomes** The first 22 pairs of chromosomes.

**avoidant attachment** A relationship in which infants turn away from their mothers when they are reunited following a brief separation.

**axon** A tubelike structure that emerges from the cell body and transmits information to other neurons.

## B

**babbling** Speechlike sounds that consist of vowel–consonant combinations.

**baby biographies** Detailed, systematic observations of individual children, often by famous scientists, that helped to pave the way for objective research on children.

**basal metabolic rate** The speed with which the body consumes calories.

**basic cry** A cry that starts softly and gradually becomes more intense; often heard when babies are hungry or tired.

**basic emotions** Emotions that are experienced by people worldwide and that consist of a subjective feeling, a physiological change, and an overt behavior; examples include happiness, anger, and fear.

**behavioral genetics** The branch of genetics that deals with inheritance of behavioral and psychological traits.

**blastocyst** The fertilized egg 4 days after conception; consists of about 100 cells and resembles a hollow ball.

**blended family** A family consisting of a biological parent, a stepparent, and children.

**body mass index (BMI)** An adjusted ratio of weight to height used to define overweight.

**breech presentation** A birth in which the feet or bottom are delivered first, before the head.

**bulimia nervosa** An eating disorder in which individuals alternate between bingeing (when they eat uncontrollably) and purging through self-induced vomiting or with laxatives.

## C

**cardinality principle** The counting principle that the last number name denotes the number of objects being counted.

**cell body** The center of the neuron that keeps the neuron alive.

**centration** Narrowly focused thinking characteristic of Piaget's preoperational stage.

**cerebral cortex** The wrinkled surface of the brain that regulates many functions that are distinctly human.

**cesarean section (C-section)** A surgical procedure in which an incision is made in the abdomen to remove the baby from the uterus.

**chorionic villus sampling (CVS)** A prenatal diagnostic technique that involves taking a sample of tissue from the chorion.

**chromosomes** Threadlike structures in the nucleus of the cell that contain genetic material.

**chronosystem** In Bronfenbrenner's systems view, the idea that the microsystem, mesosystem, exosystem, and macrosystem are not static but change over time.

**clique** Small groups of friends who are similar in age, sex, race, and interests.

**cognitive-developmental perspective** An approach to development that focuses on how children think and on how their thinking changes over time.

**cognitive self-regulation** Skill at identifying goals, selecting effective strategies, and accurate monitoring; a characteristic of successful students.

**components** Basic cognitive processes that, in Sternberg's componential subtheory, are the basis of intelligence.

**comprehension** The process of extracting meaning from a sequence of words.

**concrete operational stage** The third of Piaget's stages, from 7 to 11 years, in which children first use mental operations to solve problems and to reason.

**cones** Specialized neurons in the back of the eye that detect wavelength of light and, therefore, color.

**confounded** As applied to the design of experiments, an error in which variables are combined instead of evaluated independently, making the results of the experiment ambiguous.

**congenital adrenal hyperplasia (CAH)** A genetic disorder in which girls are masculinized because the adrenal glands secrete large amounts of androgen during prenatal development.

**constricting** An interaction style, common among boys, in which one child tries to emerge as the victor by threatening or contradicting the others, by exaggerating, and so on.

**constructivism** The view, associated with Piaget, that children are active participants in their own development who systematically construct ever more sophisticated understandings of their worlds.

**contextual subtheory** In Sternberg's triarchic theory, the idea that intelligent behavior involves adapting to an environment to achieve one's goals.

**continuity–discontinuity issue** An issue concerned with whether a developmental phenomenon follows a smooth progression throughout the life span or a series of abrupt shifts.

**conventional level** The second level of reasoning in Kohlberg's theory, where moral reasoning is based on society's norms.

**convergent thinking** Using information to arrive at one standard, correct answer.

**cooing** Early vowel-like sounds that babies produce.

**cooperative play** Play that is organized around a theme, with each child taking on a different role; begins at about 2 years of age.

**core knowledge theories** The view that infants are born with rudimentary knowledge of the world that is elaborated based on children's experiences.

**corpus callosum** A thick bundle of neurons that connects the two cerebral hemispheres.

**correlation coefficient** A statistic that reveals the strength and direction of the relation between two variables.

**correlational study** A research design in which investigators look at relations between

variables as they exist naturally in the world.

**cortex** The wrinkled outer surface of the brain that regulates many important human behaviors.

**counterimitation** A type of observational learning in which the child observes and learns what should not be done.

**creative ability** In Robert Sternberg's theory of intelligence, the ability to deal adaptively with novel situations and problems.

**critical period** A time in development when a specific type of learning can take place; before or after the critical period, the same learning is difficult or even impossible.

**cross-sectional study** A research design in which people of different ages are compared at the same point in time.

**crowd** A large group that includes many cliques with similar attitudes and values.

**crowning** The appearance of the top of the baby's head during labor.

**crystallization** The first phase in Super's theory of career development, in which adolescents use their emerging identities for ideas about careers.

**crystallized intelligence** A person's culturally influenced accumulated knowledge and skills, including understanding printed language, comprehending language, and knowing vocabulary.

**culture** The knowledge, attitudes, and behavior associated with a group of people.

**culture-fair intelligence tests** Tests designed to reduce the impact of different experiences by including items based on experiences common to many cultures.

# D

**decoding** The ability to identify individual words.

**deductive reasoning** Drawing conclusions from facts; characteristic of formal operational thought.

**dendrite** The end of the neuron that receives information; it looks like a tree with many branches.

**deoxyribonucleic acid (DNA)** A molecule composed of four nucleotide bases; the biochemical basis of heredity.

**dependent variable** The behavior that is observed after other variables are manipulated.

**depression** A disorder characterized by pervasive feelings of sadness, irritability, and low self-esteem.

**detached grandparents** Grandparents who are uninvolved with their grandchildren.

**differentiation** Distinguishing and mastering individual motions.

**diffusion status** The identity status in Marcia's theory in which adolescents do not have an identity and are doing nothing to achieve one.

**direct instruction** A parental behavior in which adults try to influence their children's behavior by telling them what to do, when, and why.

**dismissive adults (attachment representation)** A representation of parent–child relations in which adults describe childhood experiences in very general terms and often idealize their parents.

**disorganized (disoriented) attachment** A relationship in which infants don't seem to understand what's happening when they are separated and later reunited with their mothers.

**display rules** Culturally specific standards for appropriate expressions of emotion in a particular setting or with a particular person or persons.

**divergent thinking** Thinking in novel and unusual directions.

**dizygotic (fraternal) twins** Twins that are the result of the fertilization of two separate eggs by two sperm.

**dominance hierarchy** An ordering of individuals within a group in which group members with lower status defer to those with greater status.

**dominant** The form of an allele whose chemical instructions are followed.

**doula** A person familiar with childbirth who provides emotional and physical support throughout labor and delivery.

**Down syndrome** A disorder, caused by an extra chromosome, in which individuals are mentally retarded and have a distinctive appearance.

**dynamic systems theory** A theory that views development as involving many distinct skills that are organized and reorganized over time to meet demands of specific tasks.

**dynamic testing** An approach to intelligence testing that measures a child's learning potential by having the child learn something new in the presence of the examiner and with the examiner's help.

# E

**ectoderm** The outer layer of the embryo, which becomes the hair, outer layer of skin, and nervous system.

**ego** According to Freud, the rational component of the personality; develops during the first few years of life.

**egocentrism** Difficulty in seeing the world from another's point of view; typical of children in Piaget's preoperational stage.

**elaboration** A memory strategy in which information is embellished to make it more memorable.

**electroencephalogram (EEG)** A pattern of brain waves recorded from electrodes placed on the scalp.

**embryo** The name given to the developing baby once the zygote is completely embedded in the uterine wall.

**emotional intelligence** The ability to use one's own and others' emotions effectively for solving problems and living happily.

**empathic orientation** According to Eisenberg, a level of prosocial reasoning common in some children and many adolescents in which their thinking considers the injured child's perspective and how their own actions would make the child feel.

**empathy** Experiencing another person's feelings.

**enabling** An interaction style, common among girls, in which children's actions and remarks tend to support others and to sustain the interaction.

**encoding processes** The cognitive processes that transform the information in a problem into a mental representation.

**endoderm** The inner layer of the embryo, which becomes the lungs and the digestive system.

**epiphyses** Ends of bone tissue, which are formed first before the center is formed.

**equilibration** According to Piaget, the process by which children reorganize their schemes and, in the process, move to the next developmental stage.

**ethnic identity** The feeling that one is part of an ethnic group and the understanding of special customs and traditions of the group's culture and heritage.

**ethological theory** A theory in which development is seen from an evolutionary perspective and behaviors are examined for their survival value.

**evolutionary psychology** The theoretical view that many human behaviors represent successful adaptation to the environment.

**executive functioning** A mechanism of growth that includes inhibitory processes, planning, and cognitive flexibility.

**exosystem** According to Bronfenbrenner, social settings that influence one's development even though one does not experience them firsthand.

**experiment** A systematic way of manipulating factors that a researcher thinks cause a particular behavior.

**expressive style** A style of language learning that describes children whose vocabularies include many social phrases that are used like one word.

**expressive traits** Psychological characteristics that describe a person who is focused on emotions and interpersonal relationships.

## F

**familial mental retardation** A form of mental retardation that does not involve biological damage but represents the low end of the normal distribution of intelligence.

**fast mapping** The fact that children make connections between new words and referents so quickly that they can't be considering all possible meanings.

**fetal alcohol syndrome (FAS)** A disorder affecting babies whose mothers consumed large amounts of alcohol while they were pregnant.

**fetal medicine** The branch of medicine that deals with treating prenatal problems.

**field experiment** A type of experiment in which the researcher manipulates independent variables in a natural setting so that the results are more likely to be representative of behavior in real-world settings.

**fine-motor skills** Motor skills associated with grasping, holding, and manipulating objects.

**fluid intelligence** The ability to perceive relations among stimuli.

**foreclosure status** The identity status in Marcia's theory in which adolescents have an identity that was chosen based on advice from adults, rather than one that was a result of personal exploration of alternatives.

**formal operational stage** The fourth of Piaget's stages, from roughly age 11 into adulthood, in which children and adolescents can apply mental operations to abstract entities, allowing them to think hypothetically and reason deductively.

**friendship** A voluntary relationship between two people involving mutual liking.

**frontal cortex** A brain region that regulates personality and goal-directed behavior.

**functional magnetic resonance imaging (f-MRI)** A technique for measuring brain activity that uses magnetic fields to track the flow of blood in the brain.

**fuzzy trace theory** A theory proposed by Brainerd and Reyna in which experiences can be stored in memory verbatim or in terms of their basic meaning (gist).

## G

**gender consistency** The understanding, usually acquired between ages 4 and 7 years, that maleness and femaleness do not change over situations or according to personal wishes.

**gender constancy** A stage in which children have mastered gender labels, gender stability, and gender consistency.

**gender identity** The perception of oneself as either male or female.

**gender labeling** Children's understanding, by 2 or 3 years, that they are either boys or girls, and their use of these words to label themselves.

**gender role** Culturally prescribed behaviors considered appropriate for males and females.

**gender-schema theory** A theory that children learn gender roles by first deciding if an object, activity, or behavior is female or male, then using this information to decide whether they should learn more about the object, activity, or behavior.

**gender stability** Children's understanding, during the preschool years, that gender does not change: Boys become men and girls become women.

**gender stereotypes** Beliefs and images about males and females that are not necessarily true.

**gene** A group of nucleotide bases that provide a specific set of biochemical instructions.

**genetic engineering** A branch of fetal medicine in which defective genes are replaced with synthetic normal genes.

**genotype** A person's hereditary makeup.

**germ disc** A small cluster of cells near the center of the zygote that develops into the baby.

**gifted** Traditionally, individuals with intelligence test scores of at least 130.

**grammar** A language's rules for combining words to create sentences.

**grammatical morphemes** Words or endings of words that make a sentence grammatical.

**growth hormone** A hormone, secreted by the pituitary gland during sleep, that regulates growth by triggering the release of other hormones that cause muscles and bones to grow.

**guided participation** According to Vygotsky, structured interactions between a child and another more knowledgeable person; these are thought to promote cognitive growth.

## H

**habituation** Becoming unresponsive to a stimulus that is presented repeatedly.

**hedonistic orientation** According to Eisenberg, a level of prosocial reasoning common in preschool and elementary-school children in which they emphasize pursuing their own pleasure.

**hemispheres** The right and left halves of the cortex.

**heterozygous** When the genes for hereditary characteristics differ from each other.

**heuristics** Rules of thumb that are handy for solving problems but that do not guarantee a solution.

**homozygous** When the genes for hereditary characteristics are the same.

**Huntington's disease** A type of dementia caused by a dominant allele; characterized by degeneration of the nervous system.

**hypoxia** Lack of oxygen during delivery, typically because the umbilical cord becomes pinched or tangled during delivery.

## I

**id** According to Freud, the element of personality that wants immediate gratification of bodily wants and needs; present at birth.

**illusion of invulnerability** The belief, common among adolescents, that misfortune only happens to others.

**imaginary audience** Adolescents' feeling that their behavior is constantly being watched by their peers.

**imitation (observational learning)** Learning that takes place simply by observing others.

**immanent justice** A characteristic of the stage of moral realism in which children believe that breaking a rule always leads to punishment.

**implantation** The process in which the zygote burrows into the uterine wall and establishes connections with a woman's blood vessels.

**implementation** The third phase in Super's theory of career development, in which individuals enter the workforce.

**imprinting** Learning that occurs during a critical period soon after birth or hatching, as demonstrated by chicks creating an emotional bond with the first moving object they see.

**incomplete dominance** The situation in which one allele does not dominate another completely.

**independent variable** The factor that is manipulated by the researcher in an experiment.

**infant-directed speech** Speech that adults use with babies that is slow and loud and has exaggerated changes in pitch.

**infantile amnesia** The inability to remember events from early in one's life.

**infant mortality** The number of infants out of 1,000 births who die before their first birthday.

**influential grandparents** Grandparents who are very close to their grandchildren, are very involved in their lives, and frequently perform parental roles, including discipline.

**information-processing theory** A view that human cognition consists of mental hardware and mental software.

**informed consent** A person's decision to participate in research after having been told enough about the research to make an educated decision; children are not legally capable of giving informed consent.

**inhibitory processes** Processes that prevent task-irrelevant information from entering working memory.

**inner speech** Vygotsky's term for thought.

**instrumental aggression** Aggression used to achieve an explicit goal.

**instrumental traits** Psychological characteristics that describe a person who acts on and influences the world.

**integration** Linking individual motions into a coherent, coordinated whole.

**intelligence quotient (IQ)** A ratio of mental age to chronological age, multiplied by 100.

**internal working model** An infant's understanding of how responsive and dependable the mother is; thought to influence close relationships throughout the child's life.

**interposition** A perceptual cue to depth based on the fact that nearby objects partially obscure more distant objects.

**intersensory redundancy** Information that is presented simultaneously to different sensory modes, such as rhythm.

**intersubjectivity** According to Vygotsky, mutual, shared understanding among people who are participating in an activity together.

**intonation** A pattern of rising and falling pitch in speech or babbling that often indicates whether the utterance is a statement, question, or command.

**in vitro fertilization** The technique of fertilizing eggs with sperm in a petri dish and then transferring several of the fertilized eggs to the mother's uterus, where they might implant in the lining of the uterine wall.

## J

**joint custody** When both parents retain legal custody of their children following a divorce.

**Just Communities** Special groups of students and teachers within public high schools created by Kohlberg to foster discussion and expose students to more advanced moral thinking.

## K

**knowledge-telling strategy** A strategy for writing, often used by younger writers, in which information is written in sequence as it is retrieved from memory.

**knowledge-transforming strategy** A strategy for writing, often used by older writers, in which they decide what information to include and how best to organize it for the point they wish to convey to their reader.

## L

**language** Any rule-based system for expressing ideas.

**latchkey children** Children who care for themselves after school.

**learning disability** When a child with normal intelligence has difficulty mastering at least one academic subject.

**linear perspective** A cue to depth perception based on the fact that parallel lines come together at a single point in the distance.

**locomotion** The ability to move around in the world.

**longitudinal study** A research design in which a single cohort is studied over multiple times of measurement.

**long-term memory** A permanent storehouse for memories that has unlimited capacity.

## M

**macrosystem** According to Bronfenbrenner, the cultural and subcultural settings in which the microsystems, mesosystems, and exosystems are embedded.

**mad cry** A more intense version of a basic cry.

**malnutrition** Being small for one's age because of inadequate nutrition.

**maturational theory** The view that child development reflects a specific and prearranged scheme or plan within the body.

**means–ends analysis** A problem-solving heuristic in which people determine the difference between the current and desired situations, then do something to reduce the difference.

**memory strategies** Activities that improve remembering.

**menarche** The onset of menstruation.

**mental age (MA)** In intelligence testing, a measure of children's performance corresponding to the chronological age of those whose performance equals the child's.

**mental operations** Cognitive actions that can be performed on objects or ideas.

**mental retardation** A disorder in which, before 18 years of age, individuals have substantially below-average intelligence and problems adapting to an environment.

**mental rotation** One aspect of spatial ability involving the ability to imagine how an object will look after it has been moved in space.

**mesoderm** The middle layer of the embryo, which will become the muscles, bones, and circulatory system.

**mesosystem** According to Bronfenbrenner, the interrelations between different microsystems.

**meta-analysis** A tool that allows researchers to synthesize the results of many studies to estimate relations between variables.

**metacognitive knowledge** A person's knowledge and awareness of cognitive processes.

**metamemory** A person's informal understanding of memory; includes the ability to diagnose memory problems accurately and to monitor the effectiveness of memory strategies.

**microgenetic study** A special type of longitudinal study in which children are tested repeatedly over a span of days or weeks, with the aim of observing change directly as it occurs.

**microsystem** According to Bronfenbrenner, the people and objects that are present in one's immediate environment.

**monitoring** As applied to parent–child relations, parents' knowledge of where their children are, what they're doing, and with whom.

**monozygotic (identical) twins** Twins that result when a single fertilized egg splits to form two new individuals.

**moral realism** A stage described by Piaget that begins at about 5 years and continues through age 7, in which children believe that rules are created by wise adults and therefore must be followed and cannot be changed.

**moral relativism** A stage described by Piaget that begins at about age 8, in which children understand that rules are created by people to help them get along.

**moratorium status** The identity status in Marcia's theory in which adolescents are still examining different alternatives and have yet to find a satisfactory identity.

**motor skills** Coordinated movements of the muscles and limbs.

**myelin** A fatty sheath that surrounds neurons in the central nervous system and allows them to transmit information more rapidly.

# N

**naïve psychology** Our informal beliefs about other people and their behavior.

**naming explosion** A period, beginning at about age 18 months, in which children learn new words very rapidly.

**naturalistic observation** A method of observation in which children are observed as they behave spontaneously in a real-life situation.

**nature–nurture issue** An issue concerning the manner in which genetic and environmental factors influence development.

**needs-oriented orientation** According to Eisenberg, a level of prosocial reasoning common in some preschool and many elementary-school children in which they are concerned about others' needs and want to help.

**negative affect** A dimension of temperament that refers to the extent to which a child is angry, fearful, frustrated, shy, and not easily soothed.

**negative correlation** A relation between two variables in which larger values on one variable are associated with smaller values on a second variable.

**negative reinforcement trap** A situation in which parents often unwittingly reinforce the very behaviors they want to discourage; particularly likely between mothers and sons.

**neural plate** A flat group of cells present in prenatal development that becomes the brain and spinal cord.

**neuron** A cell that is the basic unit of the brain and nervous system; specializes in receiving and transmitting information.

**neurotransmitters** Chemicals released by terminal buttons that carry information to nearby neurons.

**niche picking** The process of deliberately seeking environments that are compatible with one's genetic makeup.

**non-REM (regular) sleep** Sleep in which heart rate, breathing, and brain activity are steady.

**nonshared environmental influences** Forces within a family that make children different from one another.

**nonsocial play** An early form of play, identified by Parten (1932), in which children play alone or watch others play but do not play themselves.

**norepinephrine** A neurotransmitter that helps regulate brain centers that allow people to experience pleasure; below-normal levels of norepinephrine may contribute to depression.

# O

**object permanence** The understanding, acquired in infancy, that objects exist independently of oneself.

**one-to-one principle** The counting principle that states that there must be one and only one number name for each object counted.

**operant conditioning** A view of learning, proposed by Skinner, that emphasizes reward and punishment.

**ordinality** The fact that numbers can differ in magnitude; some values are greater than others.

**organic mental retardation** Mental retardation that can be traced to a specific biological or physical problem.

**organization** A memory strategy in which information to be remembered is structured so that related information is placed together.

**orienting response** The response to an unfamiliar or unusual stimulus in which a person startles, fixates the eyes on the stimulus, and shows changes in heart rate and brainwave patterns.

**osteoporosis** A disease, common among women over age 50, in which a person's bones become thin and brittle, and, as a consequence, sometimes break.

**overextension** When children define words more broadly than adults do.

**overregularization** Children's application of rules to words that are exceptions to the rule; used as evidence that children master grammar by learning rules.

# P

**pain cry** A cry that begins with a sudden, long burst, followed by a long pause and gasping.

**parallel play** When children play alone but are aware of and interested in what another child is doing; occurs soon after the first birthday.

**passive grandparents** Grandparents who are caught up in their grandchildren's development but not with the intensity of influential or supportive grandparents; they do not assume parental roles.

**period of the fetus** The longest period of prenatal development, extending from the ninth week after conception until birth.

**permissive parenting** A style of parenting that offers warmth and caring but little parental control over children.

**personal domain** The domain of decisions concerning one's body (e.g., what to eat and wear) and choices of friends or activities.

**personal fable** The feeling of many adolescents that their feelings and experiences are unique and have never been experienced by anyone else before.

**phenotype** The physical, behavioral, and psychological features that are the result of the interaction between one's genes and the environment.

**phonemes** Unique speech sounds that can be used to create words.

**phonological awareness** The ability to hear the distinctive sounds associated with specific letters.

**phonology** The sounds of a language.

**placenta** The structure through which nutrients and wastes are exchanged between the mother and the developing child.

**plasticity** In the context of neural development, the extent to which brain organization is flexible.

**polygenic inheritance** When phenotypes are the result of the combined activity of many separate genes.

**population** A broad group of children that are the usual focus of research in child development.

**positive correlation** A relation between two variables in which larger values on one variable are associated with larger values on a second variable.

**postconventional level** The third level of reasoning in Kohlberg's theory, in which morality is based on a personal moral code.

**postpartum depression** A condition affecting 10 to 15 percent of new mothers in which irritability continues for months and is often accompanied by feelings of low self-worth, disturbed sleep, poor appetite, and apathy.

**practical ability** In Robert Sternberg's theory of intelligence, the ability to know which solutions to problems are likely to work.

**pragmatics** How people use language to communicate effectively.

**preconventional level** The first level of reasoning in Kohlberg's theory, where moral reasoning is based on external forces.

**prejudice** A view of other people, usually negative, that is based on their membership in a specific group.

**premature infant** A baby born before the 38th week after conception.

**prenatal development** The many changes that turn a fertilized egg into a newborn human.

**preoccupied adults (attachment representation)** A representation of parent–child relations in which adults describe childhood experiences emotionally and often express anger or confusion regarding relationships with their parents.

**preoperational stage** The second of Piaget's stages, from 2 to 7 years, in which children first use symbols to represent objects and events.

**primary sex characteristics** Changes in bodily organs directly involved in reproduction (i.e., the ovaries, uterus, and vagina in girls and the scrotum, testes, and penis in boys) that are signs of physical maturity.

**private speech** Comments that are not intended for others but that help children regulate their own behavior.

**propositions** Ideas created during reading by combining words.

**prosocial behavior** Any behavior that benefits another person.

**psychodynamic theory** A view first formulated by Sigmund Freud in which development is largely determined by how well people resolve conflicts they face at different ages.

**psychometricians** Psychologists who specialize in the measurement of psychological characteristics such as intelligence and personality.

**psychosocial theory** A theory proposed by Erik Erikson in which personality development is the result of the interaction of maturation and societal demands.

**puberty** A collection of physical changes that marks the onset of adolescence, such as the growth spurt and the growth of breasts or testes.

**punishment** Applying an aversive stimulus (e.g., a spanking) or removing an attractive stimulus (e.g., TV viewing); an action that discourages the reoccurrence of the response that it follows.

# R

**rapid-eye-movement (REM) sleep (irregular sleep)** Irregular sleep in which an infant's eyes dart rapidly beneath the eyelids, while the body is quite active.

**reaction range** The phenomenon that a particular genotype can interact with various environments to produce a range of phenotypes.

**reactive aggression** Aggression prompted by another child's behavior.

**recessive** An allele whose instructions are ignored when it is combined with a dominant allele.

**referential style** A style of language learning that describes children whose vocabularies are dominated by names of objects, persons, or actions.

**reflexes** Unlearned responses that are triggered by specific stimulation.

**rehearsal** A memory strategy that involves repetitively naming information that is to be remembered.

**reinforcement** A consequence that increases the likelihood that a behavior will be repeated in the future.

**relational aggression** A form of verbal aggression in which children try to hurt others by undermining their social relationships.

**relative size** A perceptual cue to depth based on the fact that nearby objects look substantially larger than objects in the distance.

**reliability** As applied to tests, how consistent test scores are from one testing time to another.

**research design** An overall conceptual plan for research; the two most common are correlational and experimental designs.

**resistant attachment** A relationship in which, after a brief separation, infants want to be held but are difficult to console.

**response bias** The tendency for research participants to respond in ways that are socially more acceptable.

**retinal disparity** A perceptual cue to depth based on the fact that, when a person views an object, the retinal images in the left and right eyes differ.

**rough-and-tumble play** A form of play common during the elementary-school years in which children playfully chase, punch, kick, shove, fight, and wrestle with peers.

# S

**sample** A group of children drawn from a population that participates in research.

**savants** Individuals with mental retardation who are quite talented in one domain.

**scaffolding** A teaching style in which adults adjust the amount of assistance that they offer, based on the learner's needs.

**school phobia** An overwhelming fear of going to school and active resistance to attending school.

**script** The means by which people remember common events consisting of sequences of activities.

**secondary sex characteristics** Physical signs of maturity in body parts not linked directly to the reproductive organs (e.g., growth of breasts in girls, the appearance of facial hair in boys, the appearance of body hair in both boys and girls).

**secular growth trends** Changes in physical development from one generation to the next; for example, the fact that people in industrialized societies are larger and are maturing earlier than in previous generations.

**secure adults (attachment representation)** A representation of parent–child relations in which adults describe childhood experiences objectively and mention both positive and negative aspects of their parents.

**secure attachment** A relationship in which infants have come to trust and depend on their mothers.

**self-concept** Attitudes, behaviors, and values that a person believes make him or her a unique individual.

**self-conscious emotions** Emotions, such as pride, guilt, or embarrassment, that involve feelings of success when one's standards or expectations are met and feelings of failure when they aren't; emerge between 18 to 24 months of age.

**self-control** The ability to rise above immediate pressures and not give in to impulse.

**self-efficacy** The belief that one is capable of performing a certain task.

**self-esteem** A person's judgment and feelings about his or her own worth.

**self reports** Children's answers to questions about specific topics.

**semantic bootstrapping hypothesis** A view that children rely on their knowledge of word meanings to discover grammatical rules.

**semantics** The study of words and their meaning.

**sensorimotor stage** The first of Piaget's four stages of cognitive development, which lasts from birth to approximately 2 years, in which infants progress from responding reflexively to using symbols.

**sensory and perceptual processes** The means by which the nervous system receives, selects, modifies, and organizes stimulation from the world.

**sensory memory** A type of memory in which information is held in raw, unanalyzed form very briefly (no longer than a few seconds).

**serotonin** A neurotransmitter that helps regulate brain centers that allow people to experience pleasure; below-normal levels of serotonin may contribute to depression.

**sex chromosomes** The 23rd pair of chromosomes; these determine the sex of the child.

**sickle-cell trait** A disorder in which individuals show signs of mild anemia only when they are seriously deprived of oxygen; occurs in individuals who have one dominant allele for normal blood cells and one recessive sickle-cell allele.

**size constancy** The realization that an object's actual size remains the same despite changes in the size of its retinal image.

**small-for-date infants** Newborns who are substantially smaller than would be expected based on the length of time since conception.

**social cognitive theory** A theory developed by Albert Bandura in which children use reward, punishment, and imitation to try to understand what goes on in their world.

**social conventions** Arbitrary standards of behavior agreed to by a cultural group to help coordinate interactions of individuals within the group.

**social influence** As applied to teen pregnancies, the view that when teenage girls give birth, this triggers a set of events that make it harder for them to provide a positive environment for their children's development.

**social referencing** A phenomenon in which infants in an unfamiliar or ambiguous environment look at their mother or father, as if searching for cues to help them interpret the situation.

**social role** A set of cultural guidelines about how one should behave, especially with other people.

**social selection** As applied to teen pregnancies, the view that some teenage girls are more likely than others to become pregnant and these same factors put their children at risk.

**social smiles** Smiles that first appear at about 2 months of age, when infants see another human face.

**specification** The second phase in Super's theory of career development, in which adolescents learn more about specific lines of work and begin training.

**spermarche** The first spontaneous ejaculation of sperm-laden fluid; typically occurs at age 13.

**spina bifida** A disorder in which the embryo's neural tube does not close properly during the first month of pregnancy.

**stable-order principle** The counting principle that states that number names must always be counted in the same order.

**stereotyped, approval-focused orientation** According to Eisenberg, a level of prosocial reasoning common in many elementary-school children and adolescents in which they behave as they think society would expect "good people" to behave.

**stereotype threat** The self-fulfilling prophecy in which knowledge of stereotypes leads to anxiety and reduced performance consistent with the original stereotype.

**stranger wariness** An infant's apparent concern or anxiety in the presence of an unfamiliar adult, typically observed at about 6 months of age.

**stress** A person's physical and psychological responses to threatening or challenging situations.

**structured observation** A method in which the researcher creates a setting to elicit the behavior of interest.

**sudden infant death syndrome (SIDS)** A disorder in which a healthy baby dies suddenly, for no apparent reason, typically occurring between 2 and 4 months of age.

**superego** According to Freud, the moral component of the personality that has incorporated adult standards of right and wrong.

**supportive grandparents** Grandparents who are very close to and involved with their grandchildren, but do not take on parental roles.

**surgency/extraversion** A dimension of temperament that refers to the extent to which a child is generally happy, active, vocal, and seeks interesting stimulation.

**surrogate-parent grandparents** Grandparents who assume many of the normal roles of parents.

**synapse** The gap between one neuron and the next.

**synaptic pruning** Gradual loss of unused synapses, beginning in infancy and continuing into early adolescence.

**syntax** Rules that specify how words are combined to form sentences.

**systematic desensitization** A therapeutic technique that associates deep relaxation with progressively more anxiety-provoking situations.

**systematic observation** A method of observation in which investigators watch children and carefully record what they do or say.

## T

**telegraphic speech** A style of speaking common in 1-year-olds that includes only words directly relevant to meaning.

**temperament** A consistent style or pattern of behavior.

**teratogen** An agent that causes abnormal prenatal development.

**terminal buttons** Small knobs at the end of an axon that release neurotransmitters.

**texture gradient** A perceptual cue to depth based on the fact that the texture of objects changes from coarse but distinct for nearby objects to finer and less distinct for distant objects.

**theory** An organized set of ideas that is designed to explain development.

**theory of mind** An intuitive understanding of the connections among thoughts, beliefs, intentions, and behavior; develops rapidly in the preschool years.

**time-out** Punishment that involves removing a child who is misbehaving to a quiet, unstimulating environment.

**toddlers** Young children who have just learned to walk.

## U

**ultrasound** A prenatal diagnostic technique that involves bouncing sound waves off the fetus to generate an image of the fetus.

**umbilical cord** A structure containing veins and arteries that connects the developing child to the placenta.

**underextension** When children define words more narrowly than adults do.

**uninvolved parenting** A style of parenting that provides neither warmth nor control and that minimizes the amount of time parents spend with children.

## V

**validity** As applied to tests, the extent to which the test measures what it is supposed to measure.

**variable** Any factor subject to change.

**vernix** A thick, greasy substance that covers the fetus and protects it during prenatal development.

**villi** Finger-like projections from the umbilical blood vessels that are close to the mother's blood vessels and thus allow nutrients, oxygen, vitamins, and waste products to be exchanged between mother and embryo.

**visual acuity** The smallest pattern that one can distinguish reliably.

**visual cliff** A glass-covered platform that appears to have a "shallow" side and "deep" side; used to study infants' depth perception.

## W

**word recognition** The process of identifying a unique pattern of letters.

**working memory** A type of memory in which a small number of items can be stored briefly.

## Z

**zone of proximal development** The difference between what children can do with assistance and what they can do alone.

**zygote** The fertilized egg.

Aboud, F. E. (1993). The developmental psychology of racial prejudice. *Transcultural Psychiatric Research Review, 30,* 229–242.

Aboud, F. E. (2003). The formation of in-group favoritism and out-group prejudice in young children: Are they distinct attitudes? *Developmental Psychology, 39,* 48–60.

Ackerman, B. P. (1993). Children's understanding of the speaker's meaning in referential communication. *Journal of Experimental Child Psychology, 55,* 56–86.

Ackerman, B. P., & Brown, E. D. (2006). Income poverty, poverty co-factors, and the adjustment of children in elementary school. In R. V. Kail (Ed.), *Advances in child development and behavior* (Vol. 34). Amsterdam: Elsevier Academic Press.

Adam, E. K. (2004). Beyond quality: Parental and residential stability and children's adjustment. *Current Directions in Psychological Science, 13,* 210–213.

Adams, J. (1999). On neurodevelopmental disorders: Perspectives from neurobehavioral teratology. In H. Tager-Flusberg (Ed.), *Neurodevelopmental disorders* (pp. 451–468). Cambridge, MA: MIT Press.

Adams, M. J., Treiman, R., & Pressley, M. (1998). Reading, writing, and literacy. In W. Damon (Ed.), *Handbook of child psychology* (Vol. 4, pp. 275–355). New York: Wiley.

Adams, R. J., & Courage, M. L. (1995). Development of chromatic discrimination in early infancy. *Behavioral Brain Research, 67,* 99–101.

Adolph, K. (2003). Learning to keep balance. In R. V. Kail (Ed.), *Advances in child development and behavior* (Vol. 30, pp. 1–40). Orlando. FL: Academic Press.

Adolph, K. E. (1997). Learning in the development of infant locomotion. *Monographs of the Society for Research in Child Development, 62,* Serial No: 251, pp. 1–140.

Adolph, K. E. (2000). Specificity of learning: Why infants fall over a veritable cliff. *Psychological Science, 11,* 290–295.

Adolph, K. E., Eppler, M. A., & Gibson, E. J. (1993). Crawling versus walking infants' perception of affordances for locomotion over sloping surfaces. *Child Development, 64,* 1158–1174.

Adolph, K. E., Vereijken, B., & Denny, M. A. (1998). Learning to crawl. *Child Development, 69,* 1299–1312.

Aglow, J. C., & Measelle, J. R. (1993). *Berkeley puppet interview: Administration and scoring system manuals.* Berkeley: University of California.

Aguiar, A., & Baillargeon, R. (2002). Developments in young infants' reasoning about occluded objects. *Cognitive Psychology, 45,* 267–336.

Ainsworth, M. D. S. (1978). The development of infant–mother attachment. In B. M. Caldwell & H. N. Ricciuti (Eds.), *Review of child development research* (Vol. 3, 1–94). Chicago: University of Chicago Press.

Ainsworth, M. S. (1993). Attachment as related to mother–infant interaction. *Advances in Infancy Research, 8,* 1–50.

Akhtar, N., Jipson, J., & Callanan, M. (2001). Learning words through overhearing. *Child Development, 72,* 416–430.

Alberts, A. E. (2005). Neonatal behavioral assessment scale. In C. B. Fisher & R. M. Lerner (Eds.), *Encyclopedia of applied developmental science* (Vol. 1, pp. 111–115). Thousand Oaks, CA: Sage.

Allen, L., Cipielewski, J., & Stanovich, K. E. (1992). Multiple indicators of children's reading habits and attitudes: Construct validity and cognitive correlates. *Journal of Educational Psychology, 84,* 489–503.

Aman, C. J., Roberts, R. J., & Pennington, B. F. (1998). A neuropsychological examination of the underlying deficit in attention deficit hyperactivity disorder: Frontal lobe versus right parietal lobe theories. *Developmental Psychology, 34,* 956–969.

Amato, P. R. (2001). Children of divorce in the 1990s: An update of the Amato and Keith (1991) meta-analysis. *Journal of Family Psychology, 15,* 355–370.

Amato, P. R., & Fowler, F. (2002). Parenting practices, child adjustment, and family diversity. *Journal of Marriage and the Family, 64,* 703–716.

Amato, P. R., & Keith, B. (1991). Parental divorce and the well-being of children: A meta-analysis. *Psychological Bulletin, 110,* 26–46.

American Academy of Child and Adolescent Psychiatry. (2000). Home alone children. Retrieved October 7, 2005, from http://www.aacap.org/publications/factsfam/homealon.htm

American Academy of Pediatrics (AAP) Committee on Sports Medicine and Committee on School Health. (1989). Organized athletics for preadolescent children. *Pediatrics, 84,* 583–584.

American Academy of Pediatrics (AAP). (1992, Spring). Bedtime doesn't have to be a struggle. *Healthy Kids,* pp. 4–10.

American Psychiatric Association. (1994). *Diagnostic and statistical manual of mental disorders* (4th ed.). Washington, DC: Author.

Anand, K. J., & Hickey, P. R. (1987). Pain and its effect in the human neonate and fetus. *New England Journal of Medicine, 31,* 1321–1329.

Anastasi, A. (1988). *Psychological testing* (6th ed.). New York: Macmillan.

Andersen, A. M. N., Wohlfahrt, J., Christens, P., Olsen, J., & Melbye, M. (2000). Maternal age and fetal loss: Population based register linkage study. *British Medical Journal, 320,* 1708–1712.

Anderson, C. A., Berkowitz, L., Donnerstein, E., Huessmann, R., Johnson, J. D., Linz, D., Malamuth, N. M., & Wartella, E. (2003). The influence of media violence on youth. *Psychological Science in the Public Interest, 4,* 81–106.

Anderson, D. R., Huston, A. C., Schmitt, K. L., Linebarger, D. L., & Wright, J. C. (2001). Early childhood television viewing and adolescent behavior. *Monographs of the Society for Research in Child Development, 66*(Serial No. 264).

Anderson, E. R., Greene, S. M., Hetherington, E. M., & Clingempeel, W. G. (1999). The dynamics of parental remarriage: Adolescent, parent, and sibling. In E. M. Hetherington (Ed.), *Coping with divorce, single parenting, and remarriage: A risk and resiliency perspective.* pp. 295–319. Mahwah, NJ: Erlbaum.

Anderson, S. W., Damasio, H., Tranel, D., & Damasio, A. R. (2001). Long-term sequelae of prefrontal cortex damage acquired in early childhood. *Developmental Neuropsychology, 18,* 281–296.

Anglin, J. M. (1993). Vocabulary development: A morphological analysis. *Monographs of the Society for Research in Child Development, 58*(10, Serial No. 238).

Annett, M. (2002). *Handedness and brain asymmetry: The right shift theory.* New York: Psychology Press.

Antonarakis, S. E., & the Down Syndrome Collaborative Group. (1991). Parental origin of the extra chromosome in trisomy 21 as indicated by analysis of DNA polymorphisms. *New England Journal of Medicine, 324,* 872–876.

Apgar, V. (1953). A proposal for a new method of evaluation of the newborn infant. *Current Researches in Anesthesia and Analgesia, 32,* 260–267.

Archer, N., & Bryant, P. (2001). Investigating the role of context in learning to read: A direct test of Goodman's model. *British Journal of Psychology, 92,* 579–591.

Arnold, L. E., Chuang, S., Davies, M., Abikoff, H. B., Conners, C. K., Elliott, G. R. et al. (2004). Nine months of multicomponent behavioral treatment for ADHD and effectiveness of MTA fading procedures. *Journal of Abnormal Child Psychology, 32,* 39–51.

Arseneault, L., Tremblay, R. E., Boulerice, B., & Saucier, J. F. (2002). Obstetrical complications and violent delinquency: Testing two developmental pathways. *Child Development, 73,* 496–508.

Asbury, K., Dunn, J. F., Pike, A., & Plomin, R. (2003). Nonshared environmental influences on individual differences in early behavioral development: A monozygotic twin differences study. *Child Development, 74,* 933–943.

Ashcraft, M. H. (1982). The development of mental arithmetic: A chronometric approach. *Developmental Review, 2,* 212–236.

Asher, S. R., & Paquette, J. A. (2003). Loneliness and peer relations in childhood. *Current Directions in Psychological Science, 12,* 75–78.

Aslin, R. N. (1987). Visual and auditory discrimination in infancy. In J. D. Osofsky (Ed.), *Handbook of infant development* (2nd ed.). New York: Wiley.

Aslin, R. N., Jusczyk, P. W., & Pisoni, D. B. (1998). Speech and auditory processing during infancy: Constraints on and precursors to language. In W. Damon (Ed.), *Handbook of child psychology* (Vol. 2). New York: Wiley.

Aslin, R. N., Saffran, J. R., & Newport, W. L. (1998). Computation of conditional probability statistics by 8-month-old infants. *Psychological Science, 9,* 321–324.

Au, T. K., & Glusman, M. (1990). The principle of mutual exclusivity in word learning: To honor or not to honor? *Child Development, 61,* 1474–1490.

Aunola, K., Stattin, H., & Nurmi, J.-E. (2000). Parenting styles and adolescents' achievement strategies. *Journal of Adolescence, 23,* 205–222.

Avenevoli, S., & Steinberg, L. (2001). The continuity of depression across the adolescent transition. *Advances in Child Development and Behavior, 28,* 139–173.

Averill, J. A. (1980). A constructivist view of emotion. In R. Plutchik & H. Kellerman (Eds.), *Emotion: Theory, research, and experience: Vol. 1 Theories of emotion.* New York: Academic Press.

Ayduk, O., Mendoza-Denton, R., Mischel, W., Downey, G., Peake, P. K., & Rodriguez, M. (2000). Regulating the interpersonal self: Strategic self-regulation for coping with rejection sensitivity. *Journal of Personality and Social Psychology, 79,* 776–792.

Azar, S. T. (2002). Parenting and child maltreatment. In M. Bornstein (Ed.), *Handbook of parenting* (Vol 4, pp. 361–388). Mahwah, NJ: Erlbaum.

Bachman, J. (1983, Summer). Premature affluence: Do high school students earn too much? *Economic Outlook USA,* 64–67.

Bachman, J. G., & Schulenberg, J. (1993). How part-time work intensity relates to drug use, problem behavior, time use, and satisfaction among high school seniors: Are these consequences or merely correlates? *Developmental Psychology, 29,* 229–230.

Backscheider, A. G., Shatz, M., & Gelman, S. A. (1993). Preschoolers' ability to distinguish living kinds as a function of regrowth. *Child Development, 64,* 1242–1257.

Baddeley, A. (1996). Exploring the central executive. *Quarterly Journal of Experimental Psychology: Human Experimental Psychology, 49,* 5–28.

Baenninger, M., & Newcombe, N. (1995). Environmental input to the development of sex-related differences in spatial and mathematical ability. *Learning & Individual Differences, 7*, 363–379.

Baer, D. M., & Wolf, M. M. (1968). The reinforcement contingency in preschool and remedial education. In R. D. Hess & R. M. Baer (Eds.), *Early education*. Chicago: Aldine.

Bagwell, C. L. (2004). Friendships, peer networks and antisocial behavior. In J. B. Kupersmidt & K. A. Dodge (Eds.), *Children's peer relations* (pp. 37–57). Washington DC: American Psychological Association.

Bagwell, C. L., Newcomb, A. F., & Bukowski, W. M. (1998). Preadolescent friendship and peer rejection as predictors of adult adjustment. *Child Development, 69*, 140–153.

Bahrick, L. E., & Lickliter, R. (2000). Intersensory redundancy guides attentional selectivity and perceptual learning in infancy. *Developmental Psychology, 36*, 190–201.

Bahrick, L. E., & Lickliter, R. (2002). Intersensory redundancy guides early perceptual and cognitive development. In R. V. Kail (Ed.), *Advances in child development and behavior* (Vol. 30, pp. 153–177). Orlando, FL: Academic Press.

Bahrick, L. E., Lickliter, R., & Flom, R. (2004). Intersensory redundancy guides the development of selective attention, perception, and cognition in infancy. *Current Directions in Psychological Science, 13*, 99–102.

Bailey, D. A., & Rasmussen, R. L. (1996). Sport and the child: Physiological and skeletal issues. In F. L. Smoll & R. E. Smith (Eds.), *Children and youth in sport: A biopsychological perspective* (pp. 187–199). Dubuque, IA: Brown & Benchmark.

Bailey, J. M., Dunne, M. P., & Martin, N. G. (2000). Genetic and environmental influences on sexual orientation and its correlates in an Austrian twin sample. *Journal of Personality and Social Psychology, 78*, 524–436.

Baillargeon, R. (1987). Object permanence in $3\frac{1}{2}$- and $4\frac{1}{2}$-month-old infants. *Developmental Psychology, 23*, 655–664.

Baillargeon, R. (1994). How do infants learn about the physical world? *Current Directions in Psychological Science, 3*, 133–140.

Baillargeon, R. (1998). Infants' understanding of the physical world. *Advances in Psychological Science, 2*, 503–529.

Baillargeon, R. (2004). Infants' reasoning about hidden objects: Evidence for event-general and event-specific expectations. *Developmental Science, 7*, 391–424.

Baker, C. (1993). *Foundations of bilingual education and bilingualism*. Clevedon, England: Multilingual Matters.

Baker, L. (1994). Fostering metacognitive development. In H. W. Reese (Ed.), *Advances in child development and behavior* (Vol. 25). San Diego: Academic Press.

Baker, L., & Brown, A. L. (1984). Metacognitive skills and reading. In P. D. Pearson (Ed.), *Handbook of reading research: Part 2*. New York: Longman.

Bakermans-Kranenburg, M., van IJzendoorn, M. H., & Juffer, F. (2003). Less is more: Meta-analyses of sensitivity and attachment interventions in early childhood. *Psychological Bulletin, 129*, 195–215.

Bancroft, J., Axworthy, D., & Ratcliffe, S. (1982). The personality and psycho-sexual development of boys with 47–XXY chromosome constitution. *Journal of Child Psychology and Psychiatry, 23*, 169–180.

Bandura, A. (1977). *Social learning theory*. Englewood Cliffs, NJ: Prentice-Hall.

Bandura, A. (1986). *Social foundations of thought and action: A social-cognitive theory*. Englewood Cliffs, NJ: Prentice-Hall.

Bandura, A. Social-cognitive theory. In A. E. Kazdin (Ed.), *Encyclopedia of psychology* (Vol. 7, pp. 329–332). Washington DC: American Psychological Association.

Bangert-Downs, R. L. (1993). The word processor as an instructional tool: A meta-analysis of word processing in writing instruction. *Review of Educational Research, 63*, 69–93.

Barber, B. K., & Olsen, J. A. (1997). Socialization in context: Connection, regulation, and autonomy in the family, school, and neighborhood, and with peers. *Journal of Adolescent Research, 12*, 287–315.

Bardwell, J. R., Cochran, S. W., & Walker, S. (1986). Relationship of parental education, race, and gender to sex role stereotyping in five-year-old kindergartners. *Sex Roles, 15*, 275–281.

Barenboim, C. (1981). The development of person perception in childhood and adolescence: From behavioral comparisons to psychological constructs to psychological comparisons. *Child Development, 52*, 129–144.

Barinaga, M. (1997). Researchers find signals that guide young brain neurons. *Science, 278*, 385–386.

Barkley, R. A. (1990). Attention deficit disorders: History, definition, and diagnosis. In M. Lewis & S. M. Miller (Eds.), *Handbook of developmental psychopathology*. New York: Plenum.

Barkley, R. A. (1994). Impaired delayed responding: A unified theory of attention-deficit hyperactivity disorder. In R. A. Barkley (Ed.), *Disruptive behavior disorders in childhood*. New York: Plenum.

Barton, M. E., & Tomasello, M. (1991). Joint attention and conversation in mother-infant-sibling triads. *Child Development, 62*, 517–529.

Bartsch, K., & Wellman, H. M. (1995). *Children talk about the mind*. New York: Oxford University Press.

Baskett, L. M. (1985). Sibling status effects: Adult expectations. *Developmental Psychology, 21*, 441–445.

Basso, K. H. (1970). *The Cibecue Apache*. New York: Holt, Rinehart, and Winston.

Bates, E. (1994). Modularity, domain specificity, and the development of language. *Discussions in Neuroscience, 10*, 136–149.

Bates, E., Benigni, L., Bretherton, I., Camaioni, L., & Volterra, V. (1979). *The emergence of symbols: Cognition and communication in infancy*. New York: Academic Press.

Bates, E., Bretherton, I., & Snyder, L. (1988). *From first words to grammar: Individual differences and dissociable mechanisms*. New York: Cambridge University Press.

Bates, J. E., Pettit, G. S., Dodge, K. A., & Ridge, B. (1998). Interaction of temperamental resistance to control and restrictive parenting in the development of externalizing behavior. *Developmental Psychology, 34*, 982–995.

Bates, J. E., Viken, R. J., Alexander, D. B., Beyers, J., & Stockton, L. (2002). Sleep and adjustment in preschool children: Sleep diary reports by mothers relate to behavioral reports by teachers. *Child Development, 73*, 62–74.

Bauer, P. J. (2004). Getting explicit memory off the ground: Steps toward construction of a neuro-developmental account of changes in the first two years of life. *Developmental Review, 24*, 347–373.

Bauer, P. J. (2006). Event memory. In W. Damon & R. M. Lerner (Eds.), *Handbook of child psychology* (6th ed., Vol. 2.). New York: Wiley.

Bauer, P. J., Burch, M. M., & Kleinknecht, E. F. (2002). Developments in early recall memory: Normative trends and individual differences. In R. V. Kail (Ed.), *Advances in child development and behavior* (Vol. 30, pp. 103–153). San Diego: Academic Press.

Baumeister, R. F., Campbell, J. D., Krueger, J. I., & Vohs, K. D. (2003). Does high self-esteem cause better performance, interpersonal success, happiness, or healthier lifestyles? *Psychological Science in the Public Interest, 4*, 1–44.

Baumrind, D. (1975). *Early socialization and the discipline controversy*. Morristown, NJ: General Learning Press.

Baumrind, D. (1991). Parenting styles and adolescent development. In R. M. Lerner, A. C. Petersen, & J. Brooks-Gunn (Eds.), *Encyclopedia of adolescence*. New York: Garland.

Bauserman, R. (2002). Child adjustment in joint-custody versus sole-custody arrangements: A meta-analytic review. *Journal of Family Psychology, 16*, 91–102.

Bayley, N. (1970). Development of mental abilities. In P. H. Mussen (Ed.), *Carmichael's manual of child psychology*. New York: Wiley.

Bayley, N. (1993). *Bayley scales of infant development: Birth to two years* (2nd ed.). San Antonio, TX: Psychological Corporation.

Beal, C. R. (1996). The role of comprehension monitoring in children's revision. *Educational Psychology Review, 8*, 219–238.

Beal, C. R., & Belgrad, S. L. (1990). The development of message evaluation skills in young children. *Child Development, 61*, 705–712.

Becker, B. J. (1986). Influence again: An examination of reviews and studies of gender differences in social influence. In J. S. Hyde & M. C. Linn (Eds.), *The psychology of gender differences. Advances through meta-analysis*. Baltimore, MD: Johns Hopkins University Press.

Behnke, M., & Eyler, F. D. (1993). The consequences of prenatal substance use for the developing fetus, newborn, and young child. *International Journal of the Addictions, 28*, 1341–1391.

Bell, A. P., Weinberg, M. S., & Hammersmith, S. K. (1981). *Sexual preference: Its development in men and women*. New York: Simon & Schuster.

Belsky, J., Fish, M., & Isabella, R. A. (1991). Continuity and discontinuity in infant negative and positive emotionality: Family antecedents and attachment consequences. *Developmental Psychology, 27*, 421–431.

Belsky, J., Jaffee, S. R., Sligo, J., Woodward, L., & Silva, P. A. (2005). Intergenerational transmission of warm-sensitive-stimulating parenting: A prospective study of mothers and fathers of 3-year-olds. *Child Development, 76*, 384–396.

Belsky, J., Steinberg, L., & Draper, P. (1991). Childhood experience, interpersonal development, and reproductive strategy: An evolutionary theory of socialization. *Child Development, 62*, 647–670.

Belsky, J., Woodworth, S., & Crnic, K. (1996). Trouble in the second year: Three questions about family interaction. *Child Development, 67*, 556–578.

Bem, D. J. (1996). Exotic becomes erotic: A developmental theory of sexual orientation. *Psychological Review, 103*, 320–335.

Benenson, J. F., & Christakos, A. (2003). The greater fragility of females' versus males' closest same-sex friendships. *Child Development, 74*, 1123–1129.

Benton, S. L., Corkill, A. J., Sharp, J. M., Downey, R. G., et al. (1995). Knowledge, interest, and narrative writing. *Journal of Educational Psychology, 87*, 66–79.

Bereiter, C., & Scardamalia, M. (1987). *The psychology of written composition*. Hillsdale, NJ: Erlbaum.

Berenbaum, S. A., Duck, S. C., & Bryk, K. (2000). Behavioral effects of prenatal vs. postnatal androgen excess in children with 21-hydroxylase-deficient congenital adrenal hyperplasia. *Journal of Clinical Endocrinology and Metabolism, 85*, 727–733.

Berenbaum, S. A., & Snyder, E. (1995). Early hormonal influences on childhood sex-typed activity and playmate preferences: Implications for the development of sexual orientation. *Developmental Psychology, 31*, 31–42.

Bergen, D., & Mauer, D. (2000). Symbolic play, phonological awareness, and literacy skills at three age levels. In K. A. Roskos & J. F. Christie (Eds.), *Play and literacy in early childhood: Research from multiple perspectives* (pp. 45–62). Mahwah, NJ: Erlbaum.

Berk, L. E. (1992). Children's private speech: An overview of theory and the status of research. In R. M. Diaz & L. E. Berk (Eds.), *Private speech: From social interaction to self-regulation*. Hillsdale, NJ: Erlbaum.

Berko, J. (1958). The child's learning of English morphology. *Word, 14*, 150–177.

Berkowitz, M. W., & Gibbs, J. C. (1985). The process of moral conflict resolution and moral development. In M. W. Berkowitz (Ed.), *Peer conflict and psychological growth* (pp. 71–84). San Francisco: Jossey-Bass.

Berndt, T. J., & Keefe, K. (1995). Friends' influence on adolescents' adjustment to school. *Child Development, 66,* 1312–1329.

Berndt, T. J., & Murphy, L. M. (2002). Influences of friends and friendships: Myths, truths, and research recommendations. *Advances in Child Development and Behavior, 30,* 275–310.

Berndt, T. J., & Perry, T. B. (1990). Distinctive features and effects of adolescent friendships. In R. Montemeyer, G. R. Adams, & T. P. Gullotta (Eds.), *From childhood to adolescence: A transition period?* London: Sage.

Bertenthal, B. H., & Clifton, R. K. (1998). Perception and action. In W. Damon (Ed.), *Handbook of child psychology* (Vol. 2). New York: Wiley.

Berthier, N. E. (1996). Learning to reach: A mathematical model. *Developmental Psychology, 32,* 811–823.

Best, C. T. (1995). Learning to perceive the sound pattern of English. In C. Rovee-Collier (Ed.), *Advances in infancy research.* Norwood, NJ: Ablex.

Best, D. L. (2001). Gender concepts: Convergence in cross-cultural research and methodologies. *Cross-Cultural Research: The Journal of Comparative Social Science, 35,* 23–43.

Best, D. L., Williams, J. E., Cloud, J. M., Davis, S. W., Robertson, L. S., Edwards, J. R., Giles, H., & Fowles, J. (1977). Development of sex-trait stereotypes among young children in the United States, England, and Ireland. *Child Development, 48,* 1375–1384.

Bettencourt, B. A., & Miller, N. (1996). Gender differences in aggression as a function of provocation: A meta-analysis. *Psychological Bulletin, 119,* 422–447.

Bhatt, R. S., Bertin, E., Hayden, A., & Reed, A. (2005). Face processing in infancy: Developmental changes in the use of different kinds of relational information. *Child Development, 76,* 169–181.

Bialystok, E. (1988). Levels of bilingualism and levels of linguistic awareness. *Developmental Psychology, 24,* 560–567.

Bialystok, E. (1997). Effects of bilingualism and biliteracy on children's emerging concepts of print. *Developmental Psychology, 33,* 429–440.

Bialystok, E., Shenfield, T., & Codd, J. (2000). Languages, scripts, and the environment: Factors in developing concepts of print. *Developmental Psychology, 36,* 66–76.

Bigler, R., Brown, C., & Markell, M. (2001). When groups are not created equal: Effects of group status on the formation of intergroup attitudes in children. *Child Development, 72,* 1151–1162.

Bigler, R. S. (1995). The role of classification skill in moderating environmental influences on children's gender stereotyping: A study of the functional use of gender in the classroom. *Child Development, 66,* 1072–1087.

Bigler, R. S., Jones, L. C., & Lobliner, D. B. (1997). Social categorization and the formation of intergroup attitudes in children. *Child Development, 68,* 530–543.

Bigler, R. S., & Liben L. S. (1990). The role of attitudes and interventions in gender-schematic processing. *Child Development, 61,* 1440–1452.

Bigler, R. S., & Liben, L. S. (1992). Cognitive mechanisms in children's gender stereotyping: Theoretical and educational implications of a cognitive-based intervention. *Child Development, 63,* 1351–1363.

Bingenheimer, J. B., Brennan, R. T., & Earls, F. J. (2005). Firearm violence exposure and serious violent behavior. *Science, 308,* 1323–1326.

Birch, L. L. (1991). Obesity and eating disorders: A developmental perspective. *Bulletin of the Psychonomic Society, 29,* 265–272.

Birch, L. L., & Fisher, J. A. (1995). Appetite and eating behavior in children. *Pediatric Clinics of North America, 42,* 931–953.

Birch, S. A. J., & Bloom, P. (2002). Preschoolers are sensitive to the speaker's knowledge when learning proper names. *Child Development, 73,* 434–444.

Birman, D., & Trickett, E. J. (2001). Cultural transitions in first-generation immigrants: Acculturation of Soviet Jewish refugee adolescents and parents. *Journal of Cross-Cultural Psychology, 32,* 456–477.

Bjorklund, D. F. (2005). *Children's thinking: Cognitive development and individual differences* (4th ed.). Belmont CA: Wadsworth.

Bjorklund, D. F., & Pellegrini, A. D. (2000). Child development and evolutionary psychology. *Child Development, 71,* 1687–1708.

Bjorklund, D. F., & Rosenblum, K. E. (2002). Context effects in children's selection and use of simple arithmetic strategies. *Journal of Cognition and Development, 3,* 225–242.

Bjorklund, D. F., Yunger, J. L., & Pellegrini, A. D. (2002). The evolution of parenting and evolutionary approaches to childrearing. In M. H. Bornstein (Ed.), *Handbook of parenting, Vol. 2: Biology and ecology of parenting* (pp. 3–30). Mahwah, NJ: Erlbaum.

Black-Gutman, D., & Hickson, F. (1996). The relationship between racial attitudes and social-cognitive development in children: An Australian study. *Developmental Psychology, 32,* 448–456.

Blake, J., O'Rourke, P., & Borzellino, G. (1994). Form and function in the development of pointing and reaching gestures. *Infant Behavior & Development, 17,* 195–203.

Blamey, P., Barry, J., Bow, C., Sarant, J., Paatsch, L., & Wales, R. (2001). The development of speech production following cochlear implantation. *Clinical Linguistics & Phonetics, 15,* 363–382.

Block, J. (1976). Debatable conclusions about sex differences. *Contemporary Psychology, 21,* 517–522.

Block, J. H. (1978). Another look at sex differentiation in the socialization behaviors of mothers and fathers. In J. Sherman & F. L. Denmark (Eds.), *Psychology of women: Future directions for research* (pp. 29–87). New York: Psychological Dimensions.

Bloom, L., Margulis, C., Tinker, E., & Fujita, N. (1996). Early conversations and word learning: Contributions from child and adult. *Child Development, 67,* 3154–3175.

Bloom, L., Rocissano, L., & Hood, L. (1976). Adult-child discourse: Developmental interaction between information processing and linguistic knowledge. *Cognitive Psychology, 8,* 521–552.

Bloom, L., & Tinker, E. (2001). The intentionality model and language acquisition. *Monographs of the Society for Research in Child Development, 66* (Serial No. 267).

Bogaert, A. F. (2003). Number of older brothers and sexual orientation: New tests and the attraction/behavior distinction in two national probability samples. *Journal of Personality and Social Psychology, 84,* 644–652.

Bogatz, G. A., & Ball, S. (1972). *The second year of "Sesame Street": A continuing evaluation.* Princeton, NJ: Educational Testing Service.

Bolger, K. E., & Patterson, C. J. (2001). Developmental pathways from child maltreatment to peer rejection. *Child Development, 72,* 549–568.

Bollmer, J. M., Milich, R. Harris, M. J., & Maras, M. A. (2005). A friend in need: The role of friendship quality as a protective factor in peer victimization and bullying. *Journal of Interpersonal Violence, 20,* 701–712.

Bornstein, M. H. (1981). Psychological studies of color perception in human infants: Habituation, discrimination and categorization, recognition, and conceptualization. *Advances in Infancy Research, 1,* 1–40.

Bornstein, M. H. (1997). Stability in mental development from early life: Methods, measures, models, meanings, and myths. In G. E. Butterworth & F. Simion (Eds.), *The development of sensory, motor, and cognitive capacities in early infancy: From sensation to perception.* Hove, England: Psychology Press.

Bornstein, M. H., & Arterberry, M. E. (2003). Recognition, discrimination, and categorization of smiling by 5-month-old infants. *Developmental Science, 6,* 585–599.

Bornstein, M. H., Haynes, O. M., Pascual, L., Painter, K. M., & Galperin, C. (1999). Play in two societies: Pervasiveness of process, specificity of structure. *Child Development, 70,* 317–331.

Bot, S. M., Engels, R. C. M. E., Knibbe, R. A., & Meeus, W. H. J. (2005). Friend's drinking behaviour and adolescent alcohol consumption: The moderating role of friendship characteristics. *Addictive Behaviors, 30,* 929–947.

Bouchard, T. J. (2004). Genetic influence on human psychological traits. *Current Directions in Psychological Science, 13,* 148–151.

Bowlby, J. (1953). *Child care and the growth of love.* London: Penguin.

Bowlby, J. (1969). *Attachment and loss* (Vol. 1). New York: Basic Books.

Bradley, L., & Bryant, P. E. (1983). Categorising sounds and learning to read—a causal connection. *Nature, 301,* 419–421.

Bradley, R. H., Caldwell, B. M., Rock, S. L., Ramey, C. T., Barnard, K. E., Gray, C., et al. (1989). Home environment and cognitive development in the first 3 years of life: A collaborative study involving six sites and three ethnic groups in North America. *Developmental Psychology, 25,* 217–235.

Bradley, R. H., & Corwyn, R. F. (2002). Socioeconomic status and child development. *Annual Review of Psychology, 53,* 371–399.

Bradley, R. H., Corwyn, R. F., Burchinal, M., McAdoo, H. P., & Coll, C. G. (2001). The home environments of children in the United States Part II: Relations with behavioral development through age thirteen. *Child Development, 72,* 1868–1886.

Braet, C., Mervielde, I., & Vandereycken, W. (1997). Psychological aspects of childhood obesity: A controlled study in a clinical and nonclinical sample. *Journal of Pediatric Psychology, 22,* 59–71.

Braine, M. D. S. (1992). What sort of innate structure is needed to "bootstrap" into syntax? *Cognition, 45,* 77–100.

Brainerd, C. J. (1996). Piaget: A centennial celebration. *Psychological Science, 7,* 191–203.

Brainerd, C. J., & Reyna, V. F. (2004). Fuzzy-trace theory and memory development. *Developmental Review, 24,* 396–439.

Brainerd, C. J., & Reyna, V. F. (2005). *The science of false memory.* New York: Oxford University Press.

Brainerd, C. J., Reyna, V. F., & Forrest, T. J. (2002). Are young children susceptible to the false-memory illusion? *Child Development, 73,* 1363–1377.

Bray, J. H. (1999). From marriage to remarriage and beyond: Findings from the Developmental Issues in Stepfamilies Research Project. In E. M. Hetherington (Ed.), *Coping with divorce, single parenting, and remarriage: A risk and resilience perspective* (pp. 295–319). Mahwah, NJ: Erlbaum.

Brazelton, T. B., & Nugent, J. K. (1995). *Neonatal behavioral assessment scale* (3rd ed.). London: MacKeith.

Brazelton, T. B., Nugent, J. K., & Lester, B. M. (1987). Neonatal behavioral assessment scale. In J. D. Osofsky (Ed.), *Handbook of infant development* (2nd ed.). New York: Wiley.

Brennan, P. A., Grekin, E. R., Mortensen, E. L., & Mednick, S. A. (2002). Relationship of maternal smoking during pregnancy with criminal arrest and hospitalization for substance abuse in male and female adult offspring. *American Journal of Psychiatry, 159,* 48–54.

Brockington, I. (1996). *Motherhood and mental health.* Oxford, England: Oxford University Press.

Brody, G. H. (1998). Sibling relationship quality: Its causes and consequences. *Annual Review of Psychology, 49,* 1–24.

Brody, G. H. (2004). Siblings' direct and indirect contributions to child development. *Current Directions in Psychological Science, 13,* 124–126.

Brody, G. H., & Ge, X. (2001). Linking parenting processes and self-regulation to psychological functioning and alcohol use during early adolescence. *Journal of Family Psychology, 15*, 82–94.

Brody, G. H., Kim, S., Murry, V. M., & Brown, A. C. (2003). Longitudinal direct and indirect pathways linking older sibling competence to the development of younger sibling competence. *Developmental Psychology, 39*, 618–628.

Brody, G. H., Stoneman, A., & McCoy, J. K. (1994). Forecasting sibling relationships in early adolescence from child temperaments and family processes in middle childhood. *Child Development, 65*, 771–784.

Brodzinsky, D. M., & Pinderhughes, E. (2002). Parenting and child development in adoptive families. In M. H. Bornstein (Ed.), *Handbook of parenting; Vol. 1. Children and parenting* (pp. 279–311). Mahwah, NJ: Erlbaum.

Bronfenbrenner, U. (1995). Developmental ecology through space and time: A future perspective. In P. Moen, G. H. Elder, Jr., & K. Luscher (Eds.), *Examining lives in context: Perspectives on the ecology of human development*. Washington, DC: American Psychological Association.

Bronfenbrenner, U., & Morris, P. (1998). The ecology of developmental processes. In R. M. Lerner (Ed.), *Handbook of child psychology* (5th ed., Vol. 1, pp. 993–1028). New York: J. Wiley.

Bronfenbrenner, U., & Morris, P. (2006). The ecology of developmental processes. In W. Damon & R. M. Lerner (Eds.), *Handbook of child psychology* (6th ed. Vol. 1). New York: Wiley.

Brooks-Gunn, J., Klebanov, P. K., & Duncan, G. J. (1996). Ethnic differences in children's intelligence test scores: Role of economic deprivation, home environment, and maternal characteristics. *Child Development, 67*, 396–408.

Brown, B. B., & Lohr, M. J. (1987). Peer-group affiliation and adolescent self-esteem: An integration of ego-identity and symbolic-interaction theories. *Journal of Personality and Social Psychology, 52*, 47–55.

Brown, B. B., Lohr, M. J., & McClenahan, E. L. (1986). Early adolescents' perceptions of peer pressure. *Journal of Early Adolescence, 6*, 139–154.

Brown, B. B., Mounts, N., Lamborn, S. D., & Steinberg, L. (1993). Parenting practices and peer group affiliation in adolescence. *Developmental Psychology, 64*, 467–482.

Brown, B. B., & Theobald, W. (1999). How peers matter: A research synthesis of peer influences on adolescent pregnancy. In P. Bearman, H. Bruckner, B. B. Brown, W. Theobald, & S. Philliber (Eds.), *Peer potential: Making the most of how teens influence each other*. Washington DC: National Campaign to Prevent Teen Pregnancy.

Brown, C. S., & Bigler, R. S. (2002). Effects of minority status in the classroom on children's intergroup attitudes. *Journal of Experimental Child Psychology, 83*, 77–110.

Brown, J. R., & Dunn, J. (1992). Talk with your mother or your sibling? Developmental changes in early family conversations about feelings. *Child Development, 63*, 336–349.

Brown, J. R., & Dunn, J. (1996). Continuities in emotion understanding from three to six years. *Child Development, 67*, 789–802.

Brown, J. V., Bakeman, R., Coles, C. D., Platzman, K. A., & Lynch, M. E. (2004). Prenatal cocaine exposure: A comparison of 2-year-old children in parental and nonparental care. *Child Development, 75*, 1282–1295.

Brown, R. (1973). *A first language: The early stages.* Cambridge, MA: Harvard University Press.

Brown, R., Pressley, M., Van Meter, P., & Schuder, T. (1996). A quasi-experimental validation of transactional strategies instruction with low-achieving second-grade readers. *Journal of Educational Psychology, 88*, 18–37.

Browne, K. D., & Hamilton-Giachritsis, C. (2005). The influence of violent media on children and adolescents: A public-health approach. *Lancet, 365*, 702–710.

Bruck, M., & Ceci, S. J. (1995). Amicus brief for the case of State of New Jersey vs Michaels presented by Committee of Concerned Social Scientists. *Psychology, Public Policy, and Law, 1*, 272–322.

Buchanan, C. M., & Heiges, K. L. (2001). When conflict continues after the marriage ends: Effects of postdivorce conflict on children. In J. Grych & F. D. Fincham (Eds.), *Interparental conflict and child development* (pp. 337–362). New York: Cambridge University Press.

Buchanan, C.M., Eccles, J.S., & Becker, J.B. (1992). Are adolescents the victims of raging hormones? Evidence for activational effects of hormones on moods and behavior at adolescence. *Psychological Bulletin, 111*, 62–107.

Buchanan, C. M., Maccoby, E. E., & Dornbusch, S. M. (1996). *Adolescents after divorce.* Cambridge MA: Harvard University Press.

Buchholz, M., Karl, H. W., Pomietto, M., & Lynn, A. (1998). Pain scores in infants: A modified infant pain scale versus visual analogue. *Journal of Pain & Symptom Management, 15*, 117–124.

Bugental, D. B., & Happaney, K. (2004). Predicting infant maltreatment in low-income families: The interactive effects of maternal attributions and child status at birth. *Developmental Psychology, 40*, 234–243.

Buhrmester, D., & Furman, W. (1990). Perceptions of sibling relationships during middle childhood and adolescence. *Child Development, 61*, 1387–1398.

Buhs, E. S., & Ladd, G. W. (2001). Peer rejection as antecedent of young children's school adjustment: An examination of mediating processes. *Developmental Psychology, 37*, 550–560.

Bukowski, W. M., Sippola, L. K., & Hoza, B. (1999). Same and other: Interdependency between participation in same- and other-sex friendships. *Journal of Youth and Adolescence, 28*, 439–459.

Bullock, M., & Lütkenhaus, P. (1990). Who am I? The development of self-understanding in toddlers. *Merrill-Palmer Quarterly, 36*, 217–238.

Bureau of Labor Statistics. (2005). Work activity of high school students: Data from the National Longitudinal Study of Youth. Retrieved September 29, 2005, from http://www.bls.gov/news.release/pdf/nlsyth.pdf

Burk, W. J., & Laursen, B. (2005). Adolescent perceptions of friendship and their associations with individual adjustment. *International Journal of Behavioral Development. 29*, 156–164.

Burnham, D., & Dodd, B. (2004). Auditory-visual speech integration by prelinguistic infants: Perception of an emergent consonant in the McGurk effect. *Developmental Psychobiology, 45*, 204–220.

Buss, K. A., & Goldsmith, H. H. (1998). Fear and anger regulation in infancy: Effects on the temporal dynamics of affective expression. *Child Development, 69*, 359–374.

Buss, K. A., & Kiel, E. J. (2004). Comparison of sadness, anger, and fear facial expressions when toddlers look at their mothers. *Child Development, 75*, 1761–1773.

Byrne, B. M., & Gavin, D. A. W. (1996). The Shavelson model revisited: Testing for the structure of academic self-concept across pre-, early, and late adolescents. *Journal of Educational Psychology, 88*, 215–228.

Byrnes, J. P., Miller, D. C., & Schafer, W. D. (1999). Gender differences in risk taking: A meta-analysis. *Psychological Bulletin, 125*, 367–383.

Cain, K. (1999). Ways of reading: How knowledge and use of strategies are related to reading comprehension. *British Journal of Developmental Psychology, 17*, 293–312.

Cairns, R. B., Leung, M. C., Buchannan, L., & Cairns, B. D. (1995). Friendships and social networks in childhood and adolescence: Fluidity, reliability, and interrelations. *Child Development, 66*, 1330–1345.

Caldwell, M.S., Rudolph, K. D., Troop-Gordon, W., & Kim, D-Y. (2004). Reciprocal influences among relational self-views, social disengagement, and peer stress during early adolescence. *Child Development, 75*, 1140–1154.

Callahan, C. M. (2000). Intelligence and giftedness. In R. J. Sternberg (Ed.), *Handbook of intelligence* (pp. 159–175). Cambridge, England: Cambridge University Press.

Callanan, M. A., & Sabbagh, M. A. (2004). Multiple labels for objects in conversations with young children: Parents' language and children's developing expectations about word meanings. *Developmental Psychology, 40*, 746–763.

Calvert, S. L., Rideout, V. J., Woolard, J. L., Barr, R. F., & Strouse, G. (2005). Age, ethnicity, and socioeconomic patterns in early computer use: A national survey. *American Behavioral Scientist, 48*, 590–607.

Cameron, C. A., Edmunds, G., Wigmore, B., Hunt, A. K., & Linton, M. J. (1997). Children's revision of textual flaws. *International Journal of Behavioral Development, 20*, 667–680.

Campbell, F. A., Pungello, E. P., Miller-Johnson, S., Burchinal, M., & Ramey, C. T. (2001). The development of cognitive and academic abilities: Growth curves from an early childhood educational experiment. *Developmental Psychology, 37*, 231–242.

Campbell, F. A., & Ramey, C. T. (1994). Effects of early intervention on intellectual and academic achievement: A follow-up study of children from low-income families. *Child Development, 65*, 684–698.

Campbell, R., & Sais, E. (1995). Accelerated metalinguistic (phonological) awareness in bilingual children. *British Journal of Developmental Psychology, 13*, 61–68.

Campbell, S. B. (2000). Developmental perspectives on attention deficit disorder. In A. Sameroff, M. Lewis, & S. Miller (Eds.), *Handbook of child psychopathology* (2nd ed., pp 383–401). New York: Plenum.

Campbell, S. B., Cohn, J. F., Flanagan, C., Popper, S., & Meyers, T. (1992). Course and correlates of postpartum depression during the transition to parenthood. *Development and Psychopathology, 4*, 29–47.

Campos, J. J., Hiatt, S., Ramsay, D., Henderson, C., & Svejda, M. (1978). The emergence of fear on the visual cliff. In M. Lewis & L. Rosenblum (Eds.), *The origins of affect*. New York: Plenum.

Camras, L. A., Oster, H., Campos, J., Campos, R., Ujiie, T., Miyake, K., et al. (1998). Production of emotional facial expressions in European, American, Japanese, and Chinese infants. *Developmental Psychology, 34*, 616–628.

Canfield, R. L., & Smith, E. G. (1996). Number-based expectations and sequential enumeration by 5-month-old infants. *Developmental Psychology, 32*, 269–279.

Cannon, T. D., Rosso, I. M., Hollister, J. M., Bearden, C. E., Sanchez, L. E., & Hadley, T. (2000). A prospective cohort study of genetic and perinatal influences in the etiology of schizophrenia. *Schizophrenia Bulletin, 26*, 351–366.

Capelli, C. A., Nakagawa, N., & Madden, C. M. (1990). How children understand sarcasm: The role of context and intonation. *Child Development, 61*, 1824–1841.

Carey, S. (1992). Becoming a face expert. In V. Bruce, A. Cowey, A. W. Ellis, & D. I. Perrett (Eds.), *Processing the facial image*. Oxford, England: Clarendon Press.

Carlo, G., Koller, S. H., Eisenberg, N., Da Silva, M. S., & Frohlich, C. B. (1996). A cross-national study on the relations among prosocial moral reasoning, gender role orientations, and prosocial behaviors. *Developmental Psychology, 32*, 231–240.

Carlson, E. A. (1998). A prospective longitudinal study of attachment disorganization/disorientation. *Child Development, 69*, 1107–1128.

Carlson Jones, D. (2004). Body image among adolescent girls and boys: A longitudinal study. *Developmental Psychology, 40*, 823–835.

Carlson, S. M., Mandell, D. J., & Williams, L. (2004). Executive function and theory of mind: Stability and prediction from ages 2 to 3. *Developmental Psychology, 40*, 1105–1122.

Carpenter, P. A., & Daneman, M. (1981). Lexical retrieval and error recovery in reading: A model based on eye fixations. *Journal of Verbal Learning and Verbal Behavior, 20*, 137–160.

Carrere, S., & Gottman, J. M. (1999). Predicting the future of marriages. In E. M. Hetherington (Ed.), *Coping with divorce, single parenting, and remarriage: A risk and resiliency perspective.* Mahwah, NJ: Erlbaum.

Carroll, J. B. (1993). *Human cognitive abilities: A survey of factor-analytic studies.* New York: Cambridge University Press.

Carroll, J. B. (1996). A three-stratum theory of intelligence: Spearman's contribution. In I. Dennis & P. Tapsfield (Eds.), *Human abilities: Their nature and measurement.* Mahwah, NJ: Erlbaum.

Carroll, J. L., & Loughlin, G. M. (1994). Sudden infant death syndrome. In F. A. Oski, C. D. DeAngelis, R. D. Feigin, J. A. McMillan, & J. B. Warshaw (Eds.), *Principles and practice of pediatrics.* Philadelphia: Lippincott.

Carskadon, M. A. (2002). Factors influencing sleep patterns of adolescents. In M. A. Carskadon (Ed.), *Adolescent sleep patterns: Biological, social, and psychological influences* (pp. 4–26). New York: Cambridge University Press.

Carver, K., Joyner, K., & Udry, J. R. (2003). National estimates of adolescent romantic relationships. In P. Florsheim (Ed.), *Adolescent romantic relations and sexual behavior: Theory, research, and practical implications* (pp. 23–56). Mahwah, NJ: Erlbaum.

Carver, P. R., Egan, S. K., & Perry, D. G. (2004). Children who question their heterosexuality. *Developmental Psychology, 40*, 43–53.

Casaer, P. (1993). Old and new facts about perinatal brain development. *Journal of Child Psychology and Psychiatry, 34*, 101–109.

Case, R. (1992). *The mind's staircase: Exploring the conceptual underpinnings of children's thought and knowledge.* Hillsdale, NJ: Erlbaum.

Casey, B. J., Tottenham, N., Liston, C., & Durston, S. (2005). Imaging the developing brain: What have we learned about cognitive development? *Trends in Cognitive Sciences, 9*, 104–110.

Casiglia, A. C., Coco, A. L., & Zappulla, C. (1998). Aspects of social reputation and peer relationships in Italian children: A cross-cultural perspective. *Developmental Psychology, 34*, 723–730.

Caspi, A., Roberts, B. W., & Shiner, R. L. (2005). Personality development: Stability and change. *Annual Review of Psychology, 56*, 453–484.

Cassidy, J. (1994). Emotion regulation: Influences of attachment relationships. *Monographs of the Society for Research in Child Development, 59*, Serial No. 240, 228–283.

Cattell, R. B. (1965). *The scientific analysis of personality.* Baltimore: Penguin.

Ceci, S. J., & Bruck, M. (1995). *Jeopardy in the courtroom: A scientific analysis of children's testimony.* Washington, DC: American Psychological Association.

Ceci, S. J., & Bruck, M. (1998). Children's testimony: Applied and basic issues. In W. Damon (Ed.), *Handbook of child psychology* (Vol. 4). New York: Wiley.

Centers for Disease Control and Prevention. (2000). *Childhood injury fact sheet.* http://www.cdc.gov/ncipc/factsheets/childh.htm

Cerella, J., & Hale, S. (1994). The rise and fall in information-processing rates over the life span. *Acta Psychologica, 86*, 109–197.

Cervantes, C. A., & Callanan, M. A. (1998). Labels and explanations in mother-child emotion talk: Age and gender differentiation. *Developmental Psychology, 34*, 88–98.

Chan, R. W., Raboy, B., & Patterson, C. J. (1998). Psychosocial adjustment among children conceived via donor insemination by lesbian and heterosexual mothers. *Child Development, 69*, 443–457.

Chandler, M., & Moran, T. (1990). Psychopathy and moral development: A comparative study of delinquent and nondelinquent youth. *Development and Psychopathology, 2*, 227–246.

Chanquoy, L. (2001). How to make it easier for children to revise their writing: A study of text revision from 3rd to 5th grades. *British Journal of Educational Psychology, 71*, 15–41.

Chao, R. K. (2001). Extending research on the consequences of parenting style for Chinese Americans and European Americans. *Child Development, 72*, 1832–1843.

Chapman, P. D. (1988). *Schools as sorters: Lewis M. Terman, applied psychology, and the intelligence testing movement, 1890–1930.* New York: New York University Press.

Chase-Lansdale, P. L., Brooks-Gunn, J., & Zamsky, E. S. (1994). Young African-American multigenerational families in poverty: Quality of mothering and grandmothering. *Child Development, 65*, 373–393.

Chavous, T. M., Bernat, D. H., Schmeelk-Cone, K., Caldwell, C. H., Kohn-Wood, L., & Zimmerman, M. A. (2003). Racial identity and academic attainment among African American adolescents. *Child Development, 74*, 1076–1090.

Chen, X., Rubin, K. H., & Li, Z. (1995). Social functioning and adjustment in Chinese children. *Developmental Psychology, 31*, 531–539.

Chen, Z., & Klahr, D. (1999). All other things being equal: Acquisition and transfer of the control of variable strategy. *Child Development, 70*, 1098–1120.

Chi, M. T. H. (1978). Knowledge structures and memory development. In R. Siegler (Ed.), *Children's thinking: What develops?* Hillsdale, NJ: Erlbaum.

Children's Defense Fund. (1996). *The state of America's children yearbook, 1996.* Washington, DC: Author.

Children's Defense Fund. (2004). *The state of America's children: 2004.* Washington DC: Author.

Children's Defense Fund. (2003). Child care basics. Retrieved October 7, 2003, from http://www.childrensdefense.org/earlychildhood/childcare

Chilman, C. S. (1983). *Adolescent sexuality in a changing American society* (2nd ed.). New York: Wiley.

Chomitz, V. R., Cheung, L. W. Y., & Lieberman, E. (1995). The role of lifestyle in preventing low birth weight. *The Future of Children, 5*, 121–138.

Chomsky, N. (1957). *Syntactic structures.* The Hague: Mouton.

Chomsky, N. (1995). *The minimalist program.* Cambridge: MIT Press.

Chorpita, B. F., & Barlow, D. H. (1998). The development of anxiety: The role of control in the early environment. *Psychological Bulletin, 124*, 3–21.

Christensen, A., & Heavey, C. L. (1999). Intervention for couples. *Annual Review of Psychology, 50*, 165–190.

Cicchetti, D., & Toth, S. L. (2006). Developmental psychopathology and preventive intervention. In W. Damon & R. M. Lerner (Eds.), *Handbook of child psychology* (Vol. 4). New York: Wiley.

Cillessen, A. H. N., & Rose, A. (2005). Understanding popularity in the peer system. *Current Directions in Psychological Science, 14*, 102–105.

Cipani, E. (1991). Educational classification and placement. In J. L. Matson & J. A. Mulick (Eds.), *Handbook of mental retardation* (2nd ed.). New York: Pergamon.

Clark, K. B. (1945). A brown girl in a speckled world. *The Journal of Social Issues, 1*, 10–15.

Clark, K. B. & Clark, M. K. (1940). Skin color as a factor in racial identification of Negro preschool children. *The Journal of Social Psychology, 11*, 159–169.

Clarke-Stewart, K. A., & Bretano, C. (2005). *Till divorce do us part.* New Haven CT: Yale University Press.

Clements, D. H. (1995). Teaching creativity with computers. *Educational Psychology Review, 7*, 141–161.

Clifton, R., Perris, E., & Bullinger, A. (1991). Infants' perception of auditory space. *Developmental Psychology, 27*, 187–197.

Cnattingius, S. (2004). The epidemiology of smoking during pregnancy: Smoking prevalence, maternal characteristics, and pregnancy outcomes. *Nicotine & Tobacco Research, 6*, S125–S140.

Cocking, R. R. (2001). Editor's introduction to the special issue: Children in the digital age. *Journal of Applied Developmental Psychology, 22*, 1–2.

Cohen, S., & Williamson, G. M. (1991). Stress and infectious disease in humans. *Psychological Bulletin, 109*, 5–24.

Coie, J. D., Dodge, K. A., Terry, R., & Wright, V. (1991). The role of aggression in peer relations: An analysis of aggression episodes in boys' play groups. *Child Development, 62*, 812–826.

Coie, J. D., & Dodge, K. A. (1998). Aggression and antisocial behavior. In W. Damon (Ed.), *Handbook of child psychology* (Vol. 3., pp. 779–862). New York: Wiley.

Colby, A., Kohlberg, L., Gibbs, J. C., & Lieberman, M. (1983). A longitudinal study of moral development. *Monographs of the Society for Research in Child Development, 48* (Serial No. 200).

Cole, D. A. (1991). Change in self-perceived competence as a function of peer and teacher evaluation. *Developmental Psychology, 27*, 682–688.

Cole, D. A., Maxwell, S. E., Martin, J. M., Peeke, L. G., Seroczynski, A. D., Tram, J. M., et al. (2001). The development of multiple domains of child and adolescent self-concept: A cohort sequential longitudinal design. *Child Development, 72*, 1723–1746.

Cole, M. (2006). Culture and cognitive development in phylogenetic, historical and ontogenetic perspective. In W. Damon & R. M. Lerner (Eds.), *Handbook of child psychology* (6th ed., Vol. 2). New York: Wiley.

Cole, P. M., Bruschi, C. J., & Tamang, B. L. (2002). Cultural differences in children's emotional reactions to difficult situations. *Child Development, 73*, 983–996.

Coley, R. L., Morris, J. E., & Hernandez, D. (2004). Out-of-school care and problem behavior trajectories among low-income adolescents: Individual, family, and neighborhood characteristics as added risks. *Child Development, 75*, 948–965.

Collaer, M. L., & Hines, M. (1995). Human behavioral sex differences: A role for gonadal hormones during early development? *Psychological Bulletin, 118*, 55–107.

Collins, W. A. (2003). More than myth: The developmental significance of romantic relationships during adolescence. *Journal of Research on Adolescence, 13*, 1–24.

Coltheart, M., Curtis, B., Atkins, P., & Haller, M. (1993). Models of reading aloud: Dual-route and parallel-distributed-processing approaches. *Psychological Review, 100*, 589–608.

Committee on Genetics. (1996). Newborn screening fact sheet. *Pediatrics, 98*, 473–501.

Condry, J. C., & Ross, D. F. (1985). Sex and aggression: The influence of gender label on the perception of aggression in children. *Child Development, 56*, 225–233.

Conduct Problems Prevention Research Group. (2004). The Fast Track experiment: Translating the developmental model into a prevention design. In J. B. Kupersmidt & K. A. Dodge (Eds.), *Children's peer relations: From development to intervention* (pp. 181–208). Washington DC: American Psychological Association.

Conger, R. D., & Elder, G. H. (1994). *Families in troubled times: Adapting to change in rural America.* New York: Aldine De Gruyter.

Connecticut Department of Children and Families. (2003). Leaving your child home alone. Retrieved October 7, 2005, from http://www.state.ct.us/dcf/

Connor, C. M., & Zwolan, T. A. (2004). Examining multiple sources of influence on the reading comprehension skills of children who use cochlear implants. *Journal of Speech, Language, and Hearing Research, 47*, 509–526.

Cooke, R. (2005, January 18). On the eve of medical history; Experts say gene therapy had learned its lessons and is poised for a breakthrough. *Newsday*, p. B10.

Coopersmith, S. (1967). *The antecedents of self-esteem*. San Francisco: W. H. Freeman.

Coplan, R. J., Gavinski-Molina, M. H., Lagace-Seguin, D. G., & Wichmann, C. (2001). When girls versus boys play alone: Nonsocial play and adjustment in kindergarten. *Developmental Psychology, 37*, 464–474.

Copper, R. L., Goldenberg, R. L., Das, A., Elder, N., et al. (1996). The preterm prediction study: Maternal stress is associated with spontaneous preterm birth at less than thirty-five weeks' gestation. *American Journal of Obstetrics & Gynecology, 175*, 1286–1292.

Corbin, C. B., & Pangrazi, R. P. (1992). Are American children and youth fit? *Research Quarterly for Exercise and Sport, 63*, 96–106.

Cornelius, M., Taylor, P., Geva, D., & Day, N. (1995). Prenatal tobacco exposure and marijuana use among adolescents: Effects on offspring gestational age, growth, and morphology. *Pediatrics, 95*, 738–743.

Cornwell, K. S., Harris, L. J., & Fitzgerald, H. E. (1991). Task effects in the development of hand preference in 9-, 13-, and 20-month-old infant girls. *Developmental Neuropsychology, 7*, 19–34.

Cosmides, L., & Tooby, J. (2000). Evolutionary psychology and the emotions. In M. Lewis & J. Haviland-Jones (Eds.), *Handbook of emotions* (2nd ed., pp. 91–115). New York: Guilford.

Costa, P. T., & McRae, R. R. (2001). A theoretical context for adult temperament. In T. D. Wachs & G. A. Kohnstamm (Eds.), *Temperament in context* (pp. 1–21). Mahwah, NJ: Erlbaum.

Costin, S. E., & Jones, D. C. (1992). Friendship as a facilitator of emotional responsiveness and prosocial interventions among young children. *Developmental Psychology, 28*, 941–947.

Coté, S., Zoccolillo, M., Tremblay, R. E., Nagin, D., & Vitaro, F. (2001). Predicting girls' conduct disorder in adolescence from childhood trajectories of disruptive behaviors. *Journal of the American Academy of Child and Adolescent Psychiatry, 40*, 678–684.

Coulton, C. J., Korbin, J. E., & Su, M. (1999). Neighborhoods and child maltreatment: A mutli-level study. *Child Abuse and Neglect, 23*, 1019–1040.

Courage, M. L., & Howe, M. L. (2004). Advances in early memory development research: Insights about the dark side of the moon. *Developmental Review, 24*, 6–32.

Cox, M. J., Owen, M. T., Henderson, V. K., & Margand, N. A. (1992). Prediction of infant-father and infant-mother attachment. *Developmental Psychology, 28*, 474–483.

Cox, M. J., & Paley, B. (2003). Understanding families as systems. *Current Directions in Psychological Science, 12*, 193–196.

Cox, M. J., Paley, B., & Harter, K. (2001). Interparental conflict and parent-child relationships. In J. H. Grych & F. D. Fincham (Eds.), *Interparental conflict and child development* (pp. 249–272). New York: Cambridge University Press.

Craig, K. D., Whitfield, M. F., Grunau, R. V. E., Linton, J., & Hadjistavropoulos, H. D. (1993). Pain in the preterm neonate: Behavioural and physiological indices. *Pain, 52*, 238–299.

Creusere, M. A. (1999). Theories of adults' understanding and use of irony and sarcasm: Applications to and evidence from research with children. *Developmental Review, 19*, 213–262.

Crick, N. R., & Dodge, K. A. (1994). A review and reformulation of social information-processing mechanisms in children's social adjustment. *Psychological Bulletin, 115*, 74–101.

Crick, N. R., Casas, J. F., & Nelson, D. A. (2002). Toward a more comprehensive understanding of peer maltreatment: Studies of relational victimization. *Current Directions in Psychological Science, 11*, 98–101.

Crick, N. R., & Grotpeter, J. K, (1995). Relational aggression, gender, and social-psychological adjustment. *Child Development, 66*, 710–722.

Crick, N. R., Ostrov, J. M., Appleyard, K., Jansen, E. A., & Casas, J. F. (2004). Relational aggression in early childhood: "You can't come to my birthday party unless." In M. Puttalaz & K. L. Bierman (Eds.), *Aggression, antisocial behavior, and violence among girls* (pp. 71–89). New York: Guilford.

Crick, N. R., Grotpeter, J. K., & Bigbee, M. A. (2002). Relationally and physically aggressive children's intent attributions and feelings of distress for relational and instrumental peer provocations. *Child Development, 73*, 1134–1142.

Crick, N. R., & Werner, N. E. (1998). Response decision processes in relational and overt aggression. *Child Development, 69*, 1630–1639.

Crockenberg, S. B., & Smith, P. (2002). Antecedents of mother-infant interaction and irritability in the first 3 months of life. *Infant Behavior and Development, 25*, 2–15.

Cuellar, I., Nyberg, B., Maldonado, R. E., & Roberts, R. E. (1997). Ethnic identity and acculturation in a young adult Mexican-origin population. *Journal of Community Psychology, 25*, 535–549.

Cunningham, A. E., Perry, K. E., Stanovich, K. E., & Share, D. L. (2002). Orthographic learning during reading: Examining the role of self-teaching. *Journal of Experimental Child Psychology, 82*, 185–199.

Curran, P. J., Stice, E., & Chassin, L. (1997). The relation between adolescent alcohol use and peer alcohol use: A longitudinal random coefficients model. *Journal of Consulting and Clinical Psychology, 65*, 130–140.

Curtain, S. C., & Park, M. M. (1999). Trends in the attendant, place, and timing of births and in the use of obstetric interventions: United States, 1989–1997. *National Vital Statistics Report, 47*, 1–12.

Curtiss, S. (1989). The independence and task-specificity of language. In M. H. Bornstein & J. S. Bruner (Eds.), *Interaction in human development* (pp. 105–137). Hillsdale, NJ: Erlbaum.

D'Augelli, A. (2002). Mental health problems among lesbian, gay, and bisexual youths ages 14 to 21. *Clinical Child Psychology and Psychiatry, 7*, 433–456.

Daley, T. C., Whaley, S. E., Sigman, M. D., Espinosa, M. P., & Neumann, C. (2003). IQ on the rise: The Flynn effect in rural Kenyan children. *Psychological Science, 14*, 215–219.

Daly, M., & Wilson, M. (1996). Violence against stepchildren. *Current Directions in Psychological Science, 5*, 77–81.

Damon, W., & Hart, D. (1988). *Self-understanding in childhood and adolescence*. New York: Cambridge University Press.

Dannemiller, J. L. (1998). Color constancy and color vision during infancy: Methodological and empirical issues. In V. Walsh & J. Kulikowski (Eds.), *Perceptual constancy: Why things look as they do*. New York: Cambridge University Press.

Darling, N., Caldwell, L. L., & Smith, R. (2005). Participation in school-based extracurricular activities and adolescent adjustment. *Journal of Leisure Research, 37*, 51–76.

Davidson, F. H., & Davidson, M. M. (1994). *Changing childhood prejudice: The caring work of the schools*. Westport, CT: Bergin & Garvey/Greenwood.

Davies, P. T., & Cummings, E. M. (1998). Exploring children's emotional security as a mediator of the link between marital relations and child adjustment. *Child Development, 69*, 124–139.

Davies, P. T., Cummings, E. M., & Winter, M. A. (2004). Pathways between profiles of family functioning,

child security in the interparental subsystem, and child psychological problems. *Development and Psychopathology, 16*, 525–550.

Davis, B. L., MacNeilage, P. F., Matyear, C. L., & Powell, J. K. (2000). Prosodic correlates of stress in babbling: An acoustical study. *Child Development, 71*, 1258–1270.

Davis, E. P., Bruce, J., Snyder, K., & Nelson, C. A. (2003). The X-trials: Neural correlates of an inhibitory control task in children and adults. *Journal of Cognitive Neuroscience, 15*, 432–443.

Dawson, G., Ashman, S. B., Panagiotides, H., Hessl, D. Self, J., Yamada, E., & Embry, L. (2003). Preschool outcomes of children of depressed mothers: Role of maternal behavior, contextual risk, and children' brain activity. *Child Development, 74*, 1158–1175.

Day, J. D., Engelhardt, S. E., Maxwell, S. E., & Bolig, E. E. (1997). Comparison of static and dynamic assessment procedures and their relation to independent performance. *Journal of Educational Psychology, 89*, 358–368.

De Beni, R., & Palladino, P. (2000). Intrusion errors in working memory tasks: Are they related to reading comprehension ability? *Learning & Individual Differences, 12*, 131–143.

de Castro, B. O., Veerman, J. W., Koops, W., Bosch, J. D., & Monshouwer, H. J. (2002). Hostile attribution of intent and aggressive behavior: A meta-analysis. *Child Development, 73*, 916–934.

de Jong, P. F., & Leseman, P. P. M. (2001). Lasting effects of home literacy on reading achievement in school. *Journal of School Psychology, 39*, 389–414.

DeCasper, A. J., & Spence, M. J. (1986). Prenatal maternal speech influences newborns' perception of speech sounds. *Infant Behavior and Development, 9*, 133–150.

Dekovic, M., & Janssens, J. M. (1992). Parents' child-rearing style and child's sociometric status. *Developmental Psychology, 28*, 925–932.

Delaney, C. (2000). Making babies in a Turkish village. In J. S. DeLoache & A. Gottlieb (Eds.), *A world of babies: Imagined child care guides for seven societies*. New York: Cambridge University Press.

Dellas, M., & Jernigan, L. P. (1990). Affective personality characteristics associated with undergraduate ego identity formation. *Journal of Adolescent Research, 5*, 306–324.

DeLoache, J. S. (1984). Oh where, oh where: Memory-based searching by very young children. In C. Sophian (Ed.), *Origins of cognitive skills*. Hillsdale, NJ: Erlbaum.

DeLoache, J. S. (1995). Early understanding and use of models: The modal model. *Current Directions in Psychological Science, 4*, 109–113.

DeLoache, J. S., Miller, K. F., & Pierroutsakos, S. L. (1998). Reasoning and problem solving. In W. Damon (Ed.), *Handbook of child psychology* (5th ed., Vol. 2, pp. 801–850). New York: Wiley.

DeLoache, J. S., Miller, K. F., & Rosengren, K. S. (1997). The credible shrinking room: Very young children's performance with symbolic and nonsymbolic relations. *Psychological Science, 8*, 308–313.

Dempster, F. N. (1995). Interference and inhibition in cognition: An historical perspective. In F. N. Dempster & C. J. Brainerd (Eds.), *Interference and inhibition in cognition*. San Diego, CA: Academic Press.

DeRosier, M. E., Kupersmidt, J. B., & Patterson, C. J. (1995). Children's academic and behavioral adjustment as a function of the chronicity and proximity of peer rejection. *Child Development, 65*, 1799–1813.

Detterman, D. K., Gabriel, L. T., & Ruthsatz, J. M. (2000). Intelligence and giftedness. In R. J. Sternberg (Ed.), *Handbook of intelligence* (pp. 141–158). Cambridge, England: Cambridge University Press.

deVilliers, J. G., & deVilliers, P. A. (1985). The acquisition of English. In D. I. Slobin (Ed.), *The cross-linguistic study of language acquisition*. Hillsdale, NJ: Erlbaum.

Dewey, K. G. (2001). Nutrition, growth, and complementary feeding of the breastfed infant. *Pediatric Clinics of North America, 48,* 87–104.

DeWolff, M. S., & van IJzendoorn, M. H. (1997). Sensitivity and attachment: A meta-analysis on parental antecedents of infant attachment. *Child Development, 68,* 571–591.

Dews, S., Winner, E., Kaplan, J., Rosenblatt, E., Hunt, M., Lim, K., et al. (1996). Children's understanding of the meaning and functions of verbal irony. *Child Development, 67,* 3071–3085.

Diamond, M., Johnson, R., Young, D., & Singh, S. (1983). Age-related morphologic differences in the rat cerebral cortex and hippocampus: Male-female; right-left. *Experimental Neurology, 81,* 1–13.

Dick, D. M., & Rose, R. J. (2002). Behavior genetics: What's new? What's next? *Current Directions in Psychological Science, 11,* 70–74.

Dick, D. M., Rose, R. J., Viken, R. J., & Kaprio, J. (2000). Pubertal timing and substance abuse: Associations between and within families across late adolescence. *Developmental Psychology, 36,* 180–189.

Dickens, W. T., & Flynn, J. R. (2001). Heritability estimates versus large environmental effects: The IQ paradox resolved. *Psychological Review, 108,* 346–369.

Dick-Read, G. (1959). *Childbirth without fear.* New York: Harper and Brothers.

Diesendruck, G., Markson, L., Akhtar, N., & Reudor, A. (2004). Two-year-olds' sensitivity to speakers' intent: An alternative account of Samuelson and Smith. *Developmental Science, 7,* 33–41.

Dionne, G., Dale, P. S., Boivin, M., & Plomin, R. (2003). Genetic evidence for bidirectional effects of early lexical and grammatical development. *Child Development, 74,* 394–412.

Dionne, G., Tremblay, R., Boivin, M., Laplante, D., & Perusse, D. (2003). Physical aggression and expressive vocabulary in 19-month-old twins. *Developmental Psychology, 39,* 261–273.

DiPietro, J. A. (2004). The role of prenatal maternal stress in child development. *Current Directions in Child Development, 13,* 71–74.

DiPietro, J. A., Caulfield, L., Costigan, K. A., Merialdi, M., Nguyen, R. H. N., Zavaleta, N., et al. (2004). Fetal neurobehavioral development: A tale of two cities. *Developmental Psychology, 40,* 445–456.

DiPietro, J. A., Hodgson, D. M., Costigan, K. A., & Hilton, S. C. (1996). Fetal neurobehavioral development. *Child Development, 67,* 2553–2567.

DiPietro, J. A., Hodgson, D. M., Costigan, K. A., & Johnson, T. R. B. (1996). Fetal antecedents of infant temperament. *Child Development, 67,* 2568–2583.

Dishion, T. J. (1990). The family ecology of boys' peer relations in middle childhood. *Child Development, 61,* 874–892.

Dishion, T. J., Poulin, F., & Burraston, B. (2001). Peer group dynamics associated with iatrogenic effects in group interventions with high-risk young adolescents. In D. W. Nangle & C. A. Erdley (Eds.), *The role of friendship in psychological adjustment* (pp. 79–92). San Francisco: Jossey-Bass.

Dockrell, J., & McShane, J. (1993). *Children's learning difficulties: A cognitive approach.* Cambridge, England: Blackwell Publishers.

Dodge, K. Coie, J., & Tremblay, R. E. (2006). Aggression. In W. Damon & R. M. Lerner (Eds.), *Handbook of child psychology,* Vol. 3 (6th ed.). New York: Wiley.

Dodge, K. A., Bates, J. E., & Pettit, G. S. (1990). Mechanisms in the cycle of violence. *Science, 250,* 1678–1683.

Dodge, K. A., & Crick, N. R. (1990). Social information-processing bases of aggressive behavior in children. *Personality and Social Psychology Bulletin, 16,* 8–22.

Dodge, K. A., & Rabiner, D. (2004). Returning to roots: On social information processing and moral development. *Child Development, 75,* 1003–1008.

Donnellan, M. B., Trzesniewski, K. H., Robins, R. W., Moffitt, T. E., & Caspi, A. (2005). Low self-esteem is related to aggression, antisocial behavior, and delinquency. *Psychological Science, 16,* 328–335.

Donovan, W. L., Leavitt, L. A., & Walsh, R. O. (2000). Maternal illusory control predicts socialization strategies and toddler compliance. *Developmental Psychology, 36,* 402–411.

Downey, G., Lebolt, A., Rincon, C., & Freitas, A. L. (1998). Rejection sensitivity and children's interpersonal difficulties. *Child Development, 69,* 1074–1091.

Downey, J., Elkin, E. J., Ehrhardt, A. A., Meyer-Bahlburg, H. F. L., Bell, J. J., & Morishima, A. (1991). Cognitive ability and everyday functioning in women with Turner syndrome. *Journal of Learning Disabilities, 24,* 32–39.

Draghi-Lorenz, R., Reddy, V., & Costall, A. (2001). Rethinking the development of "nonbasic" emotions: A critical review of existing theories. *Developmental Review, 21,* 263–304.

Duncan, G. J., & Brooks-Gunn, J. (2000). Family poverty, welfare reform, and child development. *Child Development, 71,* 188–196.

Dunham, P. J., Dunham, F., & Curwin, A. (1993). Joint-attentional states and lexical acquisition at 18 months. *Developmental Psychology, 29,* 827–831.

Dunn, J. (1996). Family conversations and the development of social understanding. In B. Bernstein & J. Brannen (Eds.), *Children, research, and policy: Essays for Barbara Tizard* (pp. 81–95). Philadelphia: Taylor & Francis.

Dunn, J. (2002). Mindreading, emotion understanding, and relationships. In W. Hartup & R. K. Silbereisen (Eds.), *Growing points in developmental science: An introduction* (pp. 167–176). New York: Psychology Press.

Dunn, J. (2002). Sibling relationships. In P. K. Smith & C. H. Hart (Eds.), *Handbook of childhood social development* (pp. 223–237). Malden, MA: Blackwell.

Dunn, J., & Davies, L. (2001). Sibling relationships and interpersonal conflict. In J. Grych & F. D. Fincham (Eds.), *Interparental conflict and child development* (pp. 273–290). New York: Cambridge University Press.

Dunn, J., & Kendrick, C. (1981). Social behavior of young siblings in the family context: Differences between same-sex and different-sex dyads. *Child Development, 52,* 1265–1273.

Dunn, J., O'Connor, T. G., & Cheng, H. (2005). Children's responses to conflict between their different parents: Mothers, stepfathers, nonresident fathers, and nonresident stepmothers. *Journal of Clinical Child and Adolescent Psychology, 34,* 223–234.

Dunn, J., Slomkowski, C., & Beardsall, L. (1994). Sibling relationships from the preschool period through middle childhood and early adolescence. *Developmental Psychology, 30,* 315–324.

Dunson, D. B., Colombo, B., & Baird, D. D. (2002). Changes in age in the level and duration of fertility in the menstrual cycle. *Human Reproduction, 17,* 1399–1403.

Durik, A. M., Hyde, J. S., & Clark, R. (2000). Sequelae of cesarean and vaginal deliveries: Psychosocial outcomes for mothers and infants. *Developmental Psychology, 36,* 251–260.

Eacott, M. J. (1999). Memory for the events of early childhood. *Current Directions in Psychological Science, 8,* 46–49.

Eagly, A. H. (1995). The science and politics of comparing women and men. *American Psychologist, 50,* 145–158.

Eagly, A. H., Karau, S. J., & Makhijani, M. G. (1995). Gender and the effectiveness of leaders: A meta-analysis. *Psychological Bulletin, 117,* 125–145.

Early Child Care Research Network. (2003). Does amount of time spent in child care predict socioemotional adjustment during the transition to kindergarten? *Child Development, 74,* 976–1005.

Easterbrook, M. A., Kisilevsky, B. S., Hains, S. M. J., & Muir, D. W. (1999). Faceness or complexity: Evidence from newborn visual tracking of facelike stimuli. *Infant Behavior & Development, 22,* 17–35.

Eaton, W. O., & Enns, L. R. (1986). Sex differences in human motor activity level. *Psychological Bulletin, 100,* 19–28.

Eccles, J. S., & Harold, R. D. (1991). Gender differences in sport involvement: Applying the Eccles' expectancy-value model. *Journal of Applied Sports Psychology, 3,* 7–35.

Eccles, J. S., Jacobs, J. E., & Harold, R. D. (1990). Gender role stereotypes, expectancy effects, and parents' socialization of gender differences. *Journal of Social Issues, 46,* 183–201.

Edwards, C. A. (1994). Leadership in groups of school-age girls. *Developmental Psychology, 30,* 920–927.

Egan, S. K., Monson, T. C., & Perry, D. G. (1998). Social-cognitive influences on change in aggression over time. *Developmental Psychology, 34,* 996–1006.

Ehri, L. C., Nunes, S. R., Willows, D. M., Schuster, B. V., Yaghoub Zadeh, Z., & Shanahan, T. (2001). Phonemic awareness instruction helps children learn to read: Evidence from the National Reading Panel's meta-analysis. *Reading Research Quarterly, 36,* 250–287.

Eisenberg, N. (1982). The development of reasoning regarding prosocial behavior. In N. Eisenberg (Ed.), *The development of prosocial behavior.* New York: Academic Press.

Eisenberg, N. (1986). *Altruistic emotion, cognition, and behavior.* Hillsdale, NJ: Erlbaum.

Eisenberg, N. (2000). Emotion, regulation, and moral development. *Annual Review of Psychology, 51,* 665–697.

Eisenberg, N., Carlo, G., Murphy, B., & Van Court, P. (1995). Prosocial development in late adolescence: A longitudinal study. *Child Development, 66,* 1179–1197.

Eisenberg, N., Cumberland, A., Spinrad, T. L., Fabes, R. A., Shepard, S. A., Reiser, M., et al. (2001). The relations of regulation and emotionality to children's externalizing and internalizing problem behavior. *Child Development, 72,* 1112–1134.

Eisenberg, N., & Fabes, R. A. (1998). Prosocial development. In W. Damon (Ed.), *Handbook of child psychology* (Vol. 3, pp. 701–778). New York: Wiley.

Eisenberg, N., Fabes, R. A., & Spinrad, T. (2006). Prosocial development. In W. Damon & R. M. Lerner (Eds.), *Handbook of child psychology* Vol. 3 (6th ed). New York: Wiley.

Eisenberg, N., & Morris, A. S. (2002). Children's emotion-related regulation. *Advances in Child Development and Behavior, 30,* 189–229.

Eisenberg, N., Sadovsky, A., Spinrad, T. L., Fabes, R. A., Losoya, S. H., Valienta, C. et al. (2005). The relations of problem behavior status to children's negative emotionality, effortful control, and impulsivity: Concurrent relations and prediction of change. *Developmental Psychology, 41,* 193–211.

Eisenberg, N., & Shell, R. (1986). Prosocial moral judgment and behavior in children: The mediating role of cost. *Personality and Social Psychology Bulletin, 12,* 426–433.

Eisenberg, N., Shepard, S. A., Fabes, R. A., Murphy, B. C., & Guthrie, I. K. (1998). Shyness and children's emotionality, regulation, and coping: Contemporaneous, longitudinal, and across-context relations. *Child Development, 69,* 767–790.

Eisenberg, N., Zhou, Q., & Koller, S. (2001). Brazilian adolescents' prosocial moral judgment and behavior: Relations to sympathy, perspective taking, gender-role orientation, and demographic characteristics. *Child Development, 72,* 518–534.

Eizenman, D. R., & Bertenthal, B. I. (1998). Infants' perception of object unity in translating and rotating displays. *Developmental Psychology, 34,* 426–434.

Elkind, D. (1978). *The child's reality: Three developmental themes.* Hillsdale, NJ: Erlbaum.

Elkind, D., & Bowen, R. (1979). Imaginary audience behavior in children and adolescents. *Developmental Psychology, 15,* 38–44.

Ellis, B. J. (2004). Timing of pubertal maturation in girls: An integrated life history approach. *Psychological Bulletin, 130,* 920–958.

Ellis, B. J., Bates, J. E., Dodge, K. A., Fergusson, D. M., Horwood, L. J., Pettit, G. S., et al. (2003). Does father absence place daughters at special risk for early sexual activity and teenage pregnancy? *Child Development, 74,* 801–821.

Ellis, B. J., & Garber, J. (2000). Psychosocial antecedents of variation in girls' pubertal timing: Maternal depression, stepfather presence, and marital and family stress. *Child Development, 71,* 485–501.

Ellis, B. J., McFadyen-Ketchum, S., Dodge, K. A., Pettit, G. S., & Bates, J. E. (1999). Quality of early family relationships and individual differences in the timing of pubertal maturation in girls: A longitudinal test of an evolutionary model. *Journal of Personality and Social Psychology, 77,* 387–401.

Ellis, S., & Siegler, R. S. (1997). Planning and strategy choice, or why don't children plan when they should? In S. L. Friedman & E. K. Scholnick (Eds.), *The developmental psychology of planning: Why, how, and when do we plan?* (pp. 183–208). Hillsdale, NJ: Erlbaum.

Ellis, W. K., & Rusch, F. R. (1991). Supported employment: Current practices and future directions. In J. L. Matson & J. A. Mulick (Eds.), *Handbook of mental retardation* (2nd ed.). New York: Pergamon.

Enns, J. T. (1990). Relations between components of visual attention. In J. T. Enns (Ed.), *The development of attention.* Amsterdam: North Holland.

Epstein, L. H., & Cluss, P. A. (1986). Behavioral genetics of childhood obesity. *Behavior Therapy, 17,* 324–334.

Epstein, L. H., Valoski, A. M., Vara, L. S., McCurley, J., et al. (1995). Effects of decreasing sedentary behavior and increasing activity on weight change in obese children. *Health Psychology, 14,* 109–115.

Erel, O., & Burman, B. (1995). Interrelatedness of marital relations and parent-child relations: A meta-analytic review. *Psychological Bulletin, 118,* 108–132.

Erel, O., Margolin, G., & John, R. S. (1998). Observed sibling interaction: Links with the marital and the mother-child relationship. *Developmental Psychology, 34,* 288–298.

Erikson, E. H. (1968). *Identity: Youth and crisis.* New York: Norton.

Ernst, M., Moolchan, E. T., & Robinson, M. L. (2001). Behavioral and neural consequences of prenatal exposure to nicotine. *Journal of the American Academy of Child & Adolescent Psychiatry, 40,* 630–641.

Eskritt, M., & Lee, K. (2002). Remember when you last saw that card?: Children's production of external symbols as a memory aid. *Developmental Psychology, 38,* 254–266.

Etaugh, C., & Liss, M. B. (1992). Home, school, and playroom: Training grounds for adult gender roles. *Sex Roles, 26,* 129–147.

Evans, G. W., Gonnella, C., Marcynyszyn, L. A., Gentile, L., & Salpekar, N. (2005). The role of chaos in poverty and children's socioemotional adjustment. *Psychological Science, 16,* 560–565.

Evans, M., Platt, L., & De La Cruz, F. (Eds.). (2001). *Fetal therapy.* New York: Parthenon.

Evans, M. I., Hulme, R. F., Lewis, P., Feldman, B., & Yaron, Y. (2001). Pharmacologic fetal therapy. In M. Evans, L. Platt, & F. De La Cruz (Eds.). *Fetal therapy* (pp. 67–76). New York: Parthenon.

Eyer, D. E. (1992). *Mother-infant bonding: A scientific fiction.* New Haven, CT: Yale University Press.

Fabes, R. A., Eisenberg, N., Jones, S., Smith, M., Guthrie, I., Poulin, R., et al. (1999). Regulation, emotionality, and preschoolers' socially competent peer interactions. *Child Development, 70,* 432–442.

Fabes, R. A., Eisenberg, N., Smith, M. C., & Murphy, B. C. (1996). Getting angry at peers: Associations with liking of the provocateur. *Child Development, 67,* 942–956.

Fagot, B. I. (1985). Changes in thinking about early sex role development. *Developmental Review, 5,* 83–98.

Falbo, T., & Polit, E. F. (1986). Quantitative review of the only child literature: Research evidence and theory development. *Psychological Bulletin, 100,* 176–186.

Falk, D., & Bornstein, M. H. (2005). Infant reflexes. In C. B. Fisher & R. M. Lerner (Eds.), *Encyclopedia of applied developmental science* (Vol. 1, pp. 581–582). Thousand Oaks, CA: Sage.

Farrar, M. J., & Boyer-Pennington, M. (1999). Remembering specific episodes of a scripted event. *Journal of Experimental Child Psychology, 73,* 266–288.

Farver, J. M., & Shin, Y. L. (1997). Social pretend play in Korean- and Anglo-American preschoolers. *Child Development, 68,* 544–556.

Fasig, L. (2002). Calling all researchers . . . *SRCD Developments, 45,* 3–5.

Fasig, L. G. (2000). Toddlers' understanding of ownership: Implications for self-concept development. *Social Development, 9,* 370–382.

Federal Interagency Forum on Child and Family Statistics. (2000). *America's children: Key national indicators of well-being, 2000.* Washington, DC: U.S. Government Printing Office.

Feigenson, L., Carey, S., & Hauser, M. (2002). The representations underlying infants' choice of more: Object files versus analog magnitudes. *Psychological Science, 13,* 150–156.

Feinberg, M. E., McHale, S. M., Crouter, A. C., & Cumsille, P. (2003). Sibling differentiation: Sibling and parent relationships trajectories in adolescence. *Child Development, 74,* 1261–1274.

Feldhusen, J. F. (1996). Motivating academically able youth with enriched and accelerated learning experiences. In C. P. Benbow & D. J. Lubinski (Eds.), *Intellectual talent: Psychometric and social issues.* Baltimore: Johns Hopkins Press.

Feldman, H. M., Dollaghan, C. A., Campbell, T. F., Kurs-Lasky, M., Janosky, J. E., & Paradise, J. L. (2000). Measurement properties of the MacArthur Communicative Development Inventories at ages one and two years. *Child Development, 71,* 310–322.

Feldman, S. S., & Wentzel, K. R. (1990). The relationship between parental styles, sons' self-restraint, and peer relations in early adolescence. *Journal of Early Adolescence, 10,* 439–454.

Feldman, R., & Klein, P. S. (2003). Toddler's self-regulated compliance to mothers, caregivers, and fathers: Implications for theories of socialization. *Developmental Psychology, 39,* 680–692.

Fenson, L., Dale, P. S., Reznick, J. S., Bates, E., et al. (1994). Variability in early communicative development. *Monographs of the Society for Research in Child Development, 59* (Whole No. 173).

Fergusson, D. M., Horwood, L. J., & Shannon, F. T. (1987). Breastfeeding and subsequent social adjustment in six- to eight-year-old children. *Journal of Child Psychology and Psychiatry and Allied Disciplines, 28,* 379–386.

Fergusson, D. M., & Woodward, L. J. (2000). Teenage pregnancy and female educational underachievement: A prospective study of a New Zealand birth cohort. *Journal of Marriage & the Family, 62,* 147–161.

Ferreol-Barbey, M., Piolat, A., & Roussey, J. (2000). Text recomposition by eleven-year-old children: Effects of text length, level of reading comprehension, and mastery of prototypical schema. *Archives de Psychologie, 68,* 213–232.

Field, T., Hernandez-Reif, M., & Freedman, J. (2004). Stimulation programs for preterm infants. *SRCD Social Policy Report, 18,* No. 1.

Field, T. M. (1990). *Infancy.* Cambridge, MA: Harvard University Press.

Field, T. M., & Widmayer, S. M. (1982). Motherhood. In B. J. Wolman (Ed.), *Handbook of developmental psychology.* Englewood Cliffs, NJ: Prentice Hall.

Fields, J. (2003). *Children's living arrangements and characteristics:* March 2002. (Current Population Reports, P20-547). Washington DC: U.S. Census Bureau.

Finley, G. E. (1999). Children of adoptive families. In W. K. Silverman & T. H. Ollendick (Eds.), *Developmental issues in the clinical treatment of children* (pp. 358–370). Boston: Allyn and Bacon.

Fisch, S., & McCann, S. K. (1993). Making broadcast television participative: Eliciting mathematical behavior through Square One TV. *Educational Technology Research and Development, 41,* 103–109.

Fisch, S., Truglio, R. T., & Cole, C. F. (1999). The impact of *Sesame Street* on preschool children: A review and synthesis of 30 years' research. *Media Psychology, 1,* 165–190.

Fischer, M., Barkley, R. A., Fletcher, K. E., & Smallish, L. (1993). The adolescent outcome of hyperactive children: Predictors of psychiatric, academic, social, and emotional adjustment. *Journal of the American Academy of Child and Adolescent Psychiatry, 32,* 324–332.

Fisher, C. (1996). Structural limits on verb mapping: The role of analogy in children's interpretations of sentences. *Cognitive Psychology, 31,* 41–81.

Fisher, C. B., & Lerner, R. M. (2005). Introduction. In C. B. Fisher & R. M. Lerner (Eds.), *Encyclopedia of applied developmental science* (Vol. 1., pp. xli–li). Thousand Oaks, CA: Sage.

Fitzgerald, J. (1987). Research on revision in writing. *Review of Educational Research, 57,* 481–506.

Flavell, J. H. (1985). *Cognitive development* (2nd ed.). Englewood Cliffs, NJ: Prentice-Hall.

Flavell, J. H. (1996). Piaget's legacy. *Psychological Science, 7,* 200–203.

Flavell, J. H. (1999). Cognitive development: Children's knowledge about the mind. *Annual Review of Psychology, 50,* 21–45.

Flavell, J. H. (2000). Development of children's knowledge about the mental world. *International Journal of Behavioral Development, 24,* 15–23.

Flavell, J. H., Flavell, E. R., & Green, F. L. (2001). Development of children's understanding of connections between thinking and feeling. *Psychological Science, 12,* 430–432.

Flynn, J. R. (1998). IQ gains over time: Toward finding the causes. In U. Neisser (Ed.), *The rising curve: Long-term gains in IQ and related measures* (pp. 25–66). Washington, DC: American Psychological Association.

Flynn, J. R. (1999). Searching for justice: The discovery of IQ gains over time. *American Psychologist, 54,* 5–20.

Fonzi, A., Schneider, B. H., Tani, F., & Tomada, G. (1997). Predicting children's friendship status from their dynamic interaction in structured situations of potential conflict. *Child Development, 68,* 496–506.

Foreyt, J. P., & Goodrick, G. K. (1995). Obesity. In R. T. Ammerman & M. Hersen (Eds.), *Handbook of child behavior therapy in the psychiatric setting.* New York: Wiley.

Foster, S. H. (1986). Learning discourse topic management in the preschool years. *Journal of Child Language, 13,* 231–250.

Fox, N. A., Kimmerly, N. L., & Schafer, W. D. (1991). Attachment to mother/attachment to father: A meta-analysis. *Child Development, 62,* 210–225.

Frank, D. A., Augustyn, M., Knight, W. G., Pell, T., & Zuckerman, B. (2001). Growth, development, and behavior in early childhood following prenatal cocaine exposure: A systematic review. *Journal of the American Medical Association, 285,* 1613–1625.

Franklin, A., Pilling, M., & Davies, I. (2005). The nature of infant color categorization: Evidence from eye movements on a target detection task. *Journal of Experimental Child Psychology, 91,* 227–248.

Franquart-Declercq, C., & Gineste, M. (2001). Metaphor comprehension in children. *Annee Psychologique, 101,* 723–752.

Fredriksen, K., Rhodes, J., Reddy, R., & Way, N. (2004). Sleepless in Chicago: Tracking the effects of adolescent sleep loss during the middle school years. *Child Development, 75,* 84–95.

Fried, A. (2005). Depression in adolescence. In C. B. Fisher & R. M. Lerner (Eds.), *Encyclopedia of applied developmental science* (Vol. 1, pp. 332–334). Thousand Oaks, CA: Sage.

Fried, P. A., O'Connell, C. M., & Watkinson, B. (1992). 60- and 72-month follow-up of children prenatally exposed to marijuana, cigarettes, and alcohol: Cognitive and language assessment. *Journal of Developmental & Behavioral Pediatrics, 13,* 383–391.

Friedman, J. M., & Polifka, J. E. (1996). *The effects of drugs on the fetus and nursing infant: A handbook for health care professionals.* Baltimore: Johns Hopkins University Press.

Frye, D. (1993). Causes and precursors of children's theories of mind. In D. F. Hay & A. Angold (Eds.), *Precursors and causes in development and psychopathology.* Chichester, England: Wiley.

Gagliardi, A. (2005). Postpartum depression. In C. B. Fisher & R. M. Lerner (Eds.), *Encyclopedia of applied developmental science* (Vol. 2, pp. 867–870). Thousand Oaks, CA: Sage.

Galler, J. R., & Ramsey, F. (1989). A follow-up study of the influence of early malnutrition on development: Behavior at home and at school. *Journal of the American Academy of Child and Adolescent Psychiatry, 28,* 254–261.

Galler, J. R., Ramsey, F., & Forde, V. (1986). A follow-up study of the influence of early malnutrition on subsequent development: 4. Intellectual performance during adolescence. *Nutrition and Behavior, 3,* 211–222.

Gangestad, S. W., & Thornhill, R. (1997). Human sexual selection and developmental stability. In J. A. Simpson & D. T. Kenrick (Eds.), *Evolutionary social psychology* (pp. 169–196). Mahwah, NJ: Erlbaum.

Garber, J., Robinson, N. S., & Valentiner, D. (1997). The relation between parenting and adolescent depression: Self-worth as a mediator. *Journal of Adolescent Research, 12,* 12–33.

Garcia, M. M., Shaw, D. S., Winslow, E. B., & Yaggi, K. E. (2000). Destructive sibling conflict and the development of conduct problems in young boys. *Developmental Psychology, 36,* 44–53.

Gardner, H. (1983). *Frames of mind: The theory of multiple intelligences.* New York: Basic Books.

Gardner, H. (1993). *Multiple intelligences: The theory in practice.* New York: Basic Books.

Gardner, H. (1995). Reflections on multiple intelligences: Myths and messages. *Phi Delta Kappan, 77,* 200–203, 206–209.

Gardner, H. (1999). *Intelligence reframed: Multiple intelligences for the 21st century.* New York: Basic Books.

Gardner, H. (2002). *MI millennium: Multiple intelligences for the new millennium* [video recording]. Los Angeles: Into the Classroom Media.

Gardner, W., & Rogoff, B. (1990). Children's deliberateness of planning according to task circumstances. *Developmental Psychology, 26,* 480–487.

Garner, P. W., Jones, D. C., & Palmer, D. J. (1994). Social cognitive correlates of preschool children's sibling caregiving behavior. *Developmental Psychology, 30,* 905–911.

Gartstein, M. A., Knyazev, G. G., & Slobodskaya, H. R. (2005). Cross-cultural differences in the structure of infant temperament: United States of America and Russia. *Infant Behavior and Development, 28,* 54–61.

Garvey, C., & Berninger, G. (1981). Timing and turn taking in children's conversations. *Discourse Processes, 4,* 27–59.

Gash, H., & Morgan, M. (1993). School-based modifications of children's gender-related beliefs. *Journal of Applied Developmental Psychology, 14,* 277–287.

Gathercole, S. E., Willis, C. S., Emslie, H., & Baddeley, A. D. (1992). Phonological memory and vocabulary development during the early school years: A longitudinal study. *Developmental Psychology, 28,* 887–898.

Gaulin, S. J. C., & McBurney, D. H. (2001). *Psychology: An evolutionary approach.* Upper Saddle River, NJ: Prentice-Hall.

Gauvain, M. (1998). Cognitive development in social and cultural context. *Current Directions in Psychological Science, 7,* 188–192.

Gavin, L. A., & Furman, W. (1996). Adolescent girls' relationships with mothers and best friends. *Child Development, 67,* 375–386.

Ge, X., Brody, G. H., Conger, R. D., Simons, R. L., & Murry, V. M. (2002). Contextual amplification of pubertal transition effects on deviant peer affiliation and externalizing behavior among African American children. *Developmental Psychology, 38,* 45–54.

Ge, X., Conger, R. D., & Elder, G. H. (2001). Pubertal transition, stressful life events, and the emergence of gender differences in adolescent depressive symptoms. *Developmental Psychology, 37,* 404–417.

Ge, X., Kim, I. J., Brody, G. H., Conger, R. D., Simons, R. L., Gibbons, F. X., et al. (2003). It's about timing and change: Pubertal transition effects on symptoms of major depression among African American youths. *Developmental Psychology, 39,* 430–439.

Geary, D. C. (2002). Sexual selection and human life history. In R. V. Kail (Ed.), *Advances in child development and behavior* (Vol. 30, pp. 41–102). San Diego, CA: Academic Press.

Geisel, T. (1960). *Green eggs and ham, by Dr. Seuss.* New York: Beginner.

Gelman, R., & Meck, E. (1986). The notion of principle: The case of counting. In J. Hiebert (Ed.), *Conceptual and procedural knowledge: The case of mathematics.* Hillsdale, NJ: Erlbaum.

Gelman, S. A., Coley, J. D., Rosengren, K. S., Hartman, E., & Pappas, A. (1998). Beyond labeling: The role of maternal input in the acquisition of richly structured categories. *Monographs of the Society for Research in Child Development, 63* (Serial No. 253).

Gelman, S A., Taylor, M. G., & Nguyen, S. P. (2004). Mother-child conversations about gender. *Monographs of the Society for Research in Child Development, 69* (Serial No. 275).

Gelman, S. A., & Gottfried, G. M. (1996). Children's casual explanations of animate and inanimate motion. *Child Development, 67,* 1970–1987.

George, C., Kaplan, N., & Main, M. (1985). *The adult attachment interview.* Unpublished manuscript, University of California, Department of Psychology, Berkeley.

Gerken, L. (2005). What develops in language development? In R. V. Kail (Ed.), *Advances in child development and behavior* (Vol. 33, pp. 153–192). San Diego, CA: Elsevier.

Gershkoff-Stowe, L., & Smith, L. B. (2004). Shape and the first hundred nouns. *Child Development, 75,* 1098–1114.

Gibbs, J. C., Clark, P. M., Joseph, J. A., Green, J. L., Goodrick, T. S., & Makowski, D. (1986). Relations between moral judgment, moral courage, and field independence. *Child Development, 57,* 185–193.

Gibson, E. J., Riccio, G., Schmuckler, M. A., Stoffregen, T. A., Rosenberg, D., & Taormina, J. (1987). Detection of the traversability of surfaces by crawling and walking infants. *Journal of Experimental Psychology: Human Perception & Performance, 13,* 533–544.

Gibson, E. J., & Walk, R. D. (1960). The "visual cliff." *Scientific American, 202,* 64–71.

Gifford-Smith, M., Dodge, K. A., Dishion, T. J. & McCord, J. (2005). Peer influence in children and adolescents: Crossing the bridge from developmental to intervention science. *Journal of Abnormal Child Psychology, 33,* 255–265.

Gilligan, C. (1982). *In a different voice: Psychological theory and women's development.* Cambridge, MA: Harvard University Press.

Gilligan, C., & Attanucci, J. (1988). Two moral orientations: Gender differences and similarities. *Merrill-Palmer Quarterly, 34,* 223–237.

Gleason, T. R. (2002). Social provisions of real and imaginary relationships in early childhood. *Developmental Psychology, 38,* 979–992.

Glick, P. C. (1989). The family life cycle and social change. *Family Relations, 38,* 123–129.

Glick, P. C., & Lin, S. (1986). Recent changes in divorce and remarriage. *Journal of Marriage and the Family, 48,* 737–747.

Goeke-Morey, M. C., Cummings, E. M., Harold, G. T., & Shelton, K. H. (2003). Categories and continua of destructive and constructive conflict tactics from the perspective of U.S. and Welsh children. *Journal of Family Psychology, 17,* 327–338.

Goldenberg, R. L., & Klerman, L. V. (1995). Adolescent pregnancy—Another look. *New England Journal of Medicine, 332,* 1161–1162.

Goldfield, B. A., & Reznick, J. S. (1990). Early lexical acquisition: Rate, content, and the vocabulary spurt. *Journal of Child Language, 17,* 171–184.

Goldman, L. S., Genel, M., Bezman, R. J., & Slanetz, P. J. (1998). Diagnosis and treatment of attention-deficit/hyperactivity disorder in children and adolescents. *Journal of the American Medical Association, 279,* 1100–1107.

Goldsmith, H. H., Buss, K. A., & Lemery, K. S. (1997). Toddler and childhood temperament: Expanded content, stronger genetic evidence, new evidence for the importance of environment. *Developmental Psychology, 33,* 891–905.

Goldsmith, H. H., & Harman, C. (1994). Temperament and attachment: Individuals and relationships. *Current Directions in Psychological Science, 3,* 53–57.

Goleman, D. (1995). *Emotional intelligence: Why it can matter more than IQ.* New York: Bantam.

Goleman, D. (1998). *Working with emotional intelligence.* New York: Bantam.

Goleman, D., Bayatzis, R., & McKee, A. (2002). *Primal leadership: Realizing the power of emotional intelligence.* Boston: Harvard Business Press.

Golinkoff, R. M. (1993). When is communication a "meeting of minds"? *Journal of Child Language, 20,* 199–207.

Golombok, S., MacCallum, F., & Goodman, E. (2001). The "test-tube" generation: Parent-child relationships and the psychological well-being of in vitro fertilization children at adolescence. *Child Development, 72,* 599–608.

Golombok, S., Murray, C., Jadva, V., MacCallum, F., & Lycett, E. (2004). Families created through surrogacy arrangements: Parent-child relationships in the first year of life. *Developmental Psychology, 40,* 400–411.

Golombok, S., Perry, B., Burston, A., Murray, C., Mooney-Somers, J., Stevens, M., & Golding, J. (2003). Children with lesbian parents: A community study. *Developmental Psychology, 39,* 20–33.

Golombok, S., & Tasker, F. (1996). Do parents influence the sexual orientation of their children? Findings from a longitudinal study of lesbian families. *Developmental Psychology, 32,* 3–11.

Gonzales, P., Guzmán, J. C., Partelow, L., Pahlke, E., Jocelyn, L., Kastberg, D., et al. (2004). *Highlights from the Trends in International Mathematics and Science Study (TIMSS) 2003.* U.S. Department of Education, National Center for Education Statistics. Washington, DC: U.S. Government Printing Office.

Good, T. L., & Brophy, J. E. (1996). *Looking in classrooms* (7th ed.). New York: Addison-Wesley.

Good, T. L., & Brophy, J. E. (2002). *Looking in classrooms* (9th ed.). Boston: Allyn & Bacon.

Goodman, G. S., Emery, R. E., & Haugaard, J. J. (1998). Developmental psychology and law: Divorce, child maltreatment, foster care, and adoption. In W. Damon (Ed.), *Handbook of child psychology* (Vol. 4). New York: Wiley.

Goodnow, J. J. (1992). *Parental belief systems: The psychological consequences for children.* Hillsdale, NJ: Erlbaum.

Goodwyn, S. W., & Acredolo, L. P. (1993). Symbolic gesture versus word: Is there a modality advantage for onset of symbol use? *Child Development, 64,* 688–701.

Gordon, B. N., Baker-Ward, L., & Ornstein, P. A. (2001). Children's testimony: A review of research on memory for past experiences. *Clinical Child & Family Psychology Review, 4,* 157–181.

Gordon, C. P. (1996). Adolescent decision making: A broadly based theory and its application to the prevention of early pregnancy. *Adolescence, 31,* 561–584.

Gordon, R. A., Chase-Lansale, P. L., & Brooks-Gunn, J. (2004). Extended households and the life course of young mothers: Understanding the associations using a sample of mothers with premature, low birth weight babies. *Child Development, 75,* 1013–1038.

Gottesman, I. R., & Hanson, D. R. (2005). Human development: Biological and genetic processes. *Annual Review of Psychology, 56,* 263–286.

Gottfredson, L. S. (1997). Why g matters: The complexity of everyday life. *Intelligence, 24,* 79–132.

Gottlieb. G. (2000). Environmental and behavioral influences on gene activity. *Current Directions in Psychological Science, 9,* 93–97.

Gottlieb, L. N., & Mendelson, M. J. (1990). Parental support and firstborn girls' adaptation to the birth of a sibling. *Journal of Applied Developmental Psychology, 11,* 29–48.

Gottman, J. M. (1986). The world of coordinated play: Same- and cross-sex friendships in children. In J. M. Gottman & J. G. Parker (Eds.), *Conversations of friends.* New York: Cambridge University Press.

Gottman, J. M., Katz, L. F., & Hooven, C. (1996). Parental meta-emotion philosophy and the emotional life of families: Theoretical models and preliminary data. *Journal of Family Psychology, 10,* 243–268.

Goubet, N., Clifton, R. K., & Shah, B. (2001). Learning about pain in preterm newborns. *Journal of Developmental and Behavioral Pediatrics, 22,* 418–424.

Governor's Task Force on Children's Justice. (1998). *Forensic interviewing protocol.* Lansing, MI: Author.

Govier, E., & Salisbury, G. (2000). Age-related sex differences in performance on a side-naming spatial task. *Psychology, Evolution, & Gender, 2,* 209–222.

Graesser, A. C., Singer, M., & Trabasso, T. (1994). Constructing inferences during narrative text comprehension. *Psychological Review, 101,* 371–395.

Graham, S., Berninger, V. W., Abbott, R. D., Abbott, S. P., & Whitaker, D. (1997). Role of mechanics in composing of elementary school students: A new methodological approach. *Journal of Educational Psychology, 89,* 170–182.

Graham, S., Harris, K. R., & Fink, B. (2000). Is handwriting causally related to learning to write? Treatment of handwriting problems in beginning writers. *Journal of Educational Psychology, 92,* 620–633.

Graham-Bermann, S. A., & Brescoll, V. (2000). Gender, power, and violence: Assessing the family stereotypes of the children of batterers. *Journal of Family Psychology, 14,* 600–612.

Graham, S., & Juvonen, J. (1998). Self-blame and peer victimization in middle school: An attributional analysis. *Developmental Psychology, 34,* 587–599.

Granrud, C. E. (1986). Binocular vision and spatial perception in 4- and 5-month-old infants. *Journal of Experimental Psychology: Human Perception and Performance, 12,* 36–49.

Grantham-McGregor, S., Ani, C., & Fernald, L. (2001). The role of nutrition in intellectual development. In R. J. Sternberg & E. L. Grigorenko (Eds.), *Environmental effects on cognitive abilities* (pp. 119–155). Mahwah, NJ: Erlbaum.

Graves, R., & Landis, T. (1990). Asymmetry in mouth opening during different speech tasks. *International Journal of Psychology, 25,* 179–189.

Gray, S. W., & Klaus, R. A. (1965). An experimental preschool program for culturally deprived children. *Child Development, 36,* 887–898.

Greenberg, M. T., & Crnic, K. A. (1988). Longitudinal predictors of developmental status and social interaction in premature and full-term infants at age two. *Child Development, 59,* 554–570.

Greenfield, P. M. (1998). The cultural evolution of IQ. In U. Neisser (Ed.), *The rising curve: Long-term gains in IQ and related measures* (pp. 81–123). Washington DC: American Psychological Association.

Grigorenko, E. L., Jarvin, L., & Sternberg, R. J. (2002). School-based tests of the triarchic theory of intelligence: Three settings, three samples, three syllabi. *Contemporary Educational Psychology, 27,* 167–208.

Grigorenko, E. L., & Sternberg, R. J. (1998). Dynamic testing. *Psychological Bulletin, 124,* 75–111.

Groen, G. J., & Resnick, L. B. (1977). Can preschool children invent addition algorithms? *Journal of Educational Psychology, 69,* 645–652.

Gross, E. F. (2004). Adolescent internet use: What we expect, what teens report. *Journal of Applied Developmental Psychology, 25,* 633–649.

Grusec, J. E., Goodnow, J. J., & Cohen, L. (1996). Household work and the development of concern for others. *Developmental Psychology, 32,* 999–1007.

Guerra, N. G., & Slaby, R. G. (1990). Cognitive mediators of aggression in adolescent offenders: 2. Intervention. *Developmental Psychology, 26,* 269–277.

Guillemin, J. (1993). Cesarean birth: Social and political aspects. In B. K. Rothman (Ed.), *Encyclopedia of childbearing.* Phoenix, AZ: Oryx Press.

Gunnar, M. R., Bruce, J., & Grotevant, H. D. (2000). International adoption of institutionally reared children: Research and policy. *Development and Psychopathology, 12,* 677–693.

Gurucharri, C., & Selman, F. L. (1982). The development of interpersonal understanding during childhood, preadolescence, and adolescence: A longitudinal follow-up study. *Child Development, 53,* 924–927.

Guttentag, R., & Ferrell, J. (2004). Reality compared with its alternatives: Age differences in judgments of regret and relief. *Developmental Psychology, 40,* 765–775.

Guttmacher, A. F., & Kaiser, I. H. (1986). *Pregnancy, birth, and family planning.* New York: New American Library.

Halford, G. S. (1993). *Children's understanding: The development of mental models.* Hillsdale, NJ: Erlbaum.

Hall, D. G., Lee, S. C., & Belanger, J. (2001). Young children's use of syntactic cues to learn proper names and count nouns. *Developmental Psychology, 37,* 298–307.

Hall, G. S. (1904). *Adolescence, 1.* New York: Appleton.

Hall, J. A., & Halberstadt, A. G. (1981). Sex roles and nonverbal communication skills. *Sex Roles, 7,* 273–287.

Hallinan, M. T., & Teixeira, R. A. (1987). Opportunities and constraints: Black-white differences in the formation of interracial friendships. *Child Development, 58,* 1358–1371.

Halpern, L. F., MacLean, W. E., & Baumeister, A. A. (1995). Infant sleep-wake characteristics: Relation to neurological status and the prediction of developmental outcome. *Developmental Review, 15,* 255– 291.

Hamilton, C. E. (2000). Continuity and discontinuity of attachment from infancy through adolescence. *Child Development, 71,* 690–694.

Hamm, J. V. (2000). Do birds of a feather flock together? The variable bases for African American, Asian American, and European American adolescents' selection of similar friends. *Developmental Psychology, 36,* 209–219.

Hammill, D. D. (1990). On defining learning disabilities: An emerging consensus. *Journal of Learning Disabilities, 23,* 74–84.

Hankin, B. L., & Abramson, L. Y. (2001). Development of gender differences in depression: An elaborated cognitive vulnerability-transactional stress theory. *Psychological Bulletin, 127,* 773–796.

Hannon, E. E., & Trehub, S. E. (2005). Metrical categories in infancy and adulthood. *Psychological Science, 16,* 48–55.

Harley, K., & Reese, E. (1999). Origins of autobiographical memory. *Developmental Psychology, 35,* 1338–1348.

Harlow, H. F., & Harlow, M. K. (1965). The affectional systems. In A. M. Schrier, H. F. Harlow, & F. Stollnitz (Eds.), *Behavior of nonhuman primates* (Vol. 2.) New York: Academic Press.

Harris, B., Lovett, L., Newcombe, R. G., Read, G. F., Walker, R., & Riad-Fahmy, D. (1994). Maternity blues and major endocrine changes: Cardiff puerperal mood and hormone study II. *British Medical Journal, 308,* 949–953.

Harris, P. L., Brown, E., Marriot, C., Whithall, S., & Harmer, S. (1991). Monsters, ghosts, and witches: Testing the limits of the fantasy-reality distinction in young children. *British Journal of Developmental Psychology, 9,* 105–123.

Harris, P. L., de Rosnay, M., & Pons, F. (2005). Language and children's understanding of mental states. *Current Directions in Psychological Science, 14,* 69–73.

Harrist, A. W., Zaia, A. F., Bates, J. E., Dodge, K. A., & Pettit, G. S. (1997). Subtypes of social withdrawal in early childhood: Sociometric status and social-cognitive differences across four years. *Child Development, 68,* 278–294.

Hart, C. H., Nelson, D. A., Robinson, C. C., Olsen, S. F., & McNeilly-Choque, M. K. (1998). Overt and relational aggression in Russian nursery-school-age children: Parenting style and marital linkages. *Developmental Psychology, 34,* 687–697.

Hart, C. H., Yang, C., Nelson, L. J., Robinson, C. C., Olsen, J. A. & Nelson, D. A. (2000). Peer acceptance in early childhood and subtypes of socially withdrawn behavior in China, Russia, and the United States. *International Journal of Behavioral Development, 24,* 73–81.

Harter, S. (1985). *Manual for the self-perception profile for children.* Denver, CO: University of Denver.

Harter, S. (1990). Self and identity development. In S. S. Feldman & G. R. Elliott (Eds.), *At the threshold: The developing adolescent.* Cambridge, MA: Harvard University Press.

Harter, S. (1994). Developmental changes in self-understanding across the 5 to 7 shift. In A. Sameroff & M. M. Haith (Eds.), *Reason and responsibility: The passage through childhood.* Chicago: University of Chicago Press.

Harter, S. (1999). *The construction of the self: A developmental perspective.* New York: Guilford.

Harter, S. (2005). Self-concepts and self-esteem, children and adolescents. In C. B. Fisher & R. M. Lerner (Eds.), *Encyclopedia of applied developmental science* (Vol. 2, pp. 972–977). Thousand Oaks, CA: Sage.

Harter, S. (2006). The self. In W. Damon & R. M. Lerner (Eds.), *Handbook of child psychology* (6th ed., Vol. 3). New York: Wiley.

Harter, S., & Monsour, A. (1992). Developmental analysis of conflict caused by opposing attributes in the adolescent self-portrait. *Developmental Psychology, 28,* 251–260.

Harter, S., & Pike, R. (1984). The pictorial scale of perceived competence and social acceptance for young children. *Child Development, 55,* 1969–1982.

Harter, S., Waters, P., & Whitesell, N. R. (1998). Relational self-worth: Differences in perceived worth as a person across interpersonal contexts among adolescents. *Child Development, 69,* 756–766.

Harter, S., Waters, P. L., Whitesell, N. R., & Kastelic, D. (1998). Level of voice among female and male high school students: Relational context, support, and gender orientation. *Developmental Psychology, 34,* 892–901.

Hartup, W. W. (1983). Peer relations. In P. H. Mussen (Ed.), *Handbook of child psychology* (Vol. 4). New York: Wiley.

Hartup, W. W. (1992a). Peer relations in early and middle childhood. In V. B. Van Hasselt & M. Hersen (Eds.), *Handbook of social development: A lifespan perspective.* New York: Plenum.

Hartup, W. W. (1992b). Friendships and their developmental significance. In H. McGurk (Ed.), *Contemporary issues in childhood social development.* London: Routledge.

Hartup, W. W., & Stevens, N. (1999). Friendships and adaptation across the life span. *Current Directions in Psychological Science, 8,* 76–79.

Haselager, G. J. T., Hartup, W. W., van Lieshout, C. F. M., & Riksen-Walraven, J. M. A. (1998). Similarities between friends and nonfriends in middle childhood. *Child Development, 69,* 1198–1208.

Haslam, C., & Lawrence, W. (2004). Health-related behavior and beliefs of pregnant smokers. *Health Psychology, 23,* 486–491.

Hastings, P. D., & Rubin, K. H. (1999). Predicting mothers' beliefs about preschool-aged children's social behavior: Evidence for maternal attitudes moderating child effects. *Child Development, 70,* 722–741.

Haviland, J. M., & Lelwica, M. (1987). The induced affect response: 10-week-old infants' responses to three emotion expressions. *Developmental Psychology, 23,* 97–104.

Hawley, P. H. (1999). The ontogenesis of social dominance: A strategy-based evolutionary perspective. *Developmental Review, 19,* 7–132.

Hay, D. F., Pawlby, S., Angold, A., Harold, G. T., & Sharp, D. (2003). Pathways to violence in the children of mothers who were depressed postpartum. *Developmental Psychology, 39,* 1083–1094.

Hayes, D. P. (1988). Speaking and writing: Distinct patterns of word choice. *Journal of Memory and Language, 27,* 572–585.

Hedges, L. V., & Nowell, A. (1995). Sex differences in mental test scores, variability, and numbers of high-scoring individuals. *Science, 269,* 41–45.

Herman, M. (2004). Forced to choose: Some determinants of racial identification in multiracial adolescents. *Child Development, 75,* 730–748.

Hernandez, D. J. (2004). Demographic change and the life circumstances of immigrant families. *Future of Children, 14,* 17–47.

Herrera, N. C., Zajonc, R. B., Wieczorkowska, G., & Cichomski, B. (2003). Beliefs about birth rank and their reflection in reality. *Journal of Personality and Social Psychology, 85,* 142–150.

Herrnstein, R. J., & Murray, C. (1994). *The bell curve: Intelligence and class structure in American life.* New York: Free Press.

Hertenstein, M. J., & Campos, J. J. (2004). The retention effects of an adult's emotional displays on infant behavior. *Child Development, 75,* 595–613.

Hespos, S. J., & Baillargeon, R. (2001). Reasoning about containment event in very young infants. *Cognition, 78,* 207–245.

Hess, U., & Kirouac, G. (2000). Emotion expression in groups. In M. Lewis & J. Haviland-Jones (Eds.), *Handbook of emotions* (2nd ed., pp. 368–381). New York: Guilford.

Hetherington, E. M., Bridges, M., & Insabella, G. M. (1998). Five perspectives on the association between divorce and remarriage and children's adjustment. *American Psychologist, 53,* 167–184.

Hetherington, E. M., & Kelly, J. (2002). *For better or for worse: Divorce reconsidered.* New York: W. W. Norton.

Hetherington, S. E. (1990). A controlled study of the effect of prepared childbirth classes on obstetric outcomes. *Birth, 17,* 86–90.

Heyman, G. D., & Gelman, S. A. (1999). The use of trait labels in making psychological inferences. *Child Development, 70,* 604–619.

Higgins, A. (1991). The Just Community approach to moral education: Evolution of the idea and recent findings. In W. M. Kurtines & J. L. Gewirtz (Eds.), *Handbook of moral behavior and development* (Vol. 3). Hillsdale, NJ: Erlbaum.

Hill, J. L., Brooks-Gunn, J., & Waldfogel, J. (2003). Sustained effects of high participation in an early intervention for low-birth-weight premature infants. *Developmental Psychology, 39,* 730–744.

Hill, N. E., & Taylor, L. E. (2004). Parental school involvement and children's academic achievement: Pragmatics and issues. *Current Directions in Psychological Science, 13,* 161–164.

Ho, C. S., & Fuson, K. C. (1998). Children's knowledge of teen quantities as tens and ones: Comparisons of Chinese, British, and American kindergartners. *Journal of Educational Psychology, 90,* 536–544.

Hoff, E. (2003). The specificity of environmental influence: Socioeconomic status affects early vocabulary developmental via maternal speech. *Child Development, 74,* 1368–1378.

Hoff, E. (2005). *Language development* (3rd ed.). Belmont, CA: Thomson Wadsworth.

Hoff, E., & Naigles, L. (2002). How children use input to acquire a lexicon. *Child Development, 73,* 418–433.

Hoff-Ginsberg, E., & Tardif, T. (1995). Socioeconomic status and parenting. In M. H. Bornstein (Ed.), *Handbook of parenting* (Vol 2, pp. 161–188). Mahwah, NJ: Erlbaum.

Hoffman, M. L. (1988). Moral development. In M. H. Bornstein & M. E. Lamb (Eds.), *Developmental psychology: An advanced textbook* (2nd ed.). Hillsdale, NJ: Erlbaum.

Hoffman, M. L. (1994). Discipline and internalization. *Developmental Psychology, 30,* 26–28.

Hoffman, M. L. (2000). *Empathy and moral development: Implications for caring and justice.* Cambridge, UK: Cambridge University Press.

Hogge, W. A. (1990). Teratology. In I. R. Merkatz & J. E. Thompson (Eds.), *New perspectives on prenatal care.* New York: Elsevier.

Hoier, S. (2003). Father absence and age at menarche: A test of four evolutionary models. *Human Nature, 14,* 209–233.

Holden, G. W., & Miller, P. C. (1999). Enduring and different: A meta-analysis of the similarity in parents' child rearing. *Psychological Bulletin, 125,* 223–254.

Hollich, G. J., Hirsh-Pasek, K., & Golinkoff, R. M. (2000). Breaking the language barrier: An emergentist coalition model for the origins of word learning. *Monographs of the Society for Research in Child Development, 65* (Serial No. 262).

Hollon, S. D., Haman, K. I., & Brown, L. L. (2002). Cognitive-behavioral treatment of depression. In I. H. Gotlib & C. L. Hammen (Eds.), *Handbook of depression* (pp. 383–403). New York: Guilford.

Holowka, S., & Petitto, L. A. (2002). Left hemisphere cerebral specialization for babies while babbling. *Science, 297,* 1515.

Hood, B., Carey, S., & Prasada, S. (2000). Predicting the outcomes of physical events: Two-year-olds fail to reveal knowledge of solidity and support. *Child Development, 71,* 1540–1554.

Horowitz, F. D., & O'Brien, M. (1986). Gifted and talented children: State of knowledge and directions for research. *American Psychologist, 41,* 1147–1152.

Houston, D. M., & Jusczyk, P. W. (2003). Infants' long-term memory for the sound patterns of words and voices. *Journal of Experimental Psychology: Human Perception and Performance, 29,* 1143–1154.

Howe, M. L., & Courage, M. L. (1997). The emergence and early development of autobiographical memory. *Psychological Review, 104,* 499–523.

Howe, N., & Ross, H. S. (1990). Socialization perspective taking and the sibling relationship. *Developmental Psychology, 26,* 160–165.

Howes, C., & Matheson, C. C. (1992). Sequences in the development of competent play with peers: Social and social pretend play. *Developmental Psychology, 28,* 961–974.

Howes, C., Unger, O., & Seidner, L. B. (1990). Social pretend play in toddlers: Parallels with social play and with solitary pretend. *Child Development, 60,* 77–84.

Hubbard, F. O. A., & van IJzendoorn, M. H. (1991). Maternal unresponsiveness and infant crying across the first 9 months: A naturalistic longitudinal study. *Infant Behavior and Development, 14,* 299–312.

Hudson, J. A., Shapiro, L. R., & Sosa, B. B. (1995). Planning in the real world: Preschool children's scripts and plans for familiar events. *Child Development, 66,* 984–998.

Huizink, A., Robles de Medina, P., Mulder, E., Visser, G., & Buitelaar, J. (2002). Psychological measures of prenatal stress as predictors of infant temperament. *Journal of the American Academy of Child and Adolescent Psychiatry, 41,* 1078–1085.

Hulit, L. M., & Howard, M. R. (2002). *Born to talk: An introduction to speech and language development* (3rd ed.). Boston: Allyn and Bacon.

Huston, A. C. (1983). Sex typing. In P. H. Mussen (Ed.), *Handbook of child psychology* (Vol. 4). New York: Wiley.

Huston, A. C., Watkins, B. A., & Kunkel, D. (1989). Public policy and children's television. *American Psychologist, 44,* 424–433.

Huston, A. C., & Wright, J. C. (1998). Mass media and children's development. In W. Damon (Ed.), *Handbook of child psychology* (Vol. 4). New York: Wiley.

Hutchins, E. (1983). Understanding Micronesian navigation. In D. A. Gentner & A. Stevens (Eds.), *Mental models.* Hillsdale, NJ: Erlbaum.

Huth-Bocks, A. C., Levendosky, A. A., Bogat, G. A., & von Eye, A. (2004). The impact of maternal characteristics and contextual variables on infant-mother attachment. *Child Development, 75,* 480–496.

Huttenlocher, J., Haight, W., Bryk, A., Seltzer, M., & Lyons, T. (1991). Early vocabulary growth: Relation to language input and gender. *Developmental Psychology, 27,* 236–248.

Hyde, J. S., Fennema, E., & Lamon, S. J. (1990). Gender differences in mathematics performance: A meta-analysis. *Psychological Bulletin, 107,* 139–155.

Hymel, S., Vaillancourt, T., McDougall, P., & Renshaw, P. D. (2004). Peer acceptance and rejection in childhood. In P. K. Smith & C. H. Hart (Eds.), *Blackwell handbook of childhood social development* (pp. 265–284). Malden, MA: Blackwell.

Ingoldsby, E. M., Shaw, D. S., Owens, E. B., & Winslow, E. B. (1999). A longitudinal study of interparental conflict, emotional and behavioral reactivity, and preschoolers' adjustment problems among low-income families. *Journal of Abnormal Child Psychology, 27,* 343–356.

Inhelder, B., & Piaget, J. (1958). *The growth of logical thinking from childhood to adolescence.* New York: Basic Books.

Institute of Medicine. (1990). *Nutrition during pregnancy.* Washington, DC: National Academy Press.

International Food Information Council Foundation. (2000). *Starting solids: A guide for parents and child care providers.* Washington, DC: Author.

Israel, A. C., Guile, C. A., Baker, J. E., & Silverman, W. K. (1994). An evaluation of enhanced self-regulation training in the treatment of childhood obesity. *Journal of Pediatric Psychology, 19,* 737–749.

Iverson, J. M., & Goldin-Meadow, S. (2005). Gesture paves the way for language development . *Psychological Science, 16*, 367–371.

Izard, C. E. (1991). *The psychology of emotions.* New York: Plenum.

Izard, C. E., & Ackerman, B. P. (2000). Motivational, organizational, and regulatory functions of discrete emotions. In M. Lewis & J. Haviland-Jones (Eds.), *Handbook of emotions* (2nd ed., pp. 253–264). New York: Guilford.

Izard, C. E., Fantauzzo, C. A., Castle, J. M., Haynes, O. M., Rayias, M. F., & Putnam, P. H. (1995). The ontogeny and significance of infants' facial expressions in the first 9 months of life. *Developmental Psychology, 31*, 997–1013.

Jaccard, J., Blanton, H., & Dodge, T. (2005). Peer influences on risk behavior: An analysis of the effects of a close friend. *Developmental Psychology, 41*, 135–147.

Jacklin, C. N. (1989). Female and male: Issues of gender. *American Psychologist, 44*, 127–133.

Jacklin, C. N., & Maccoby, E. E. (1978). Social behavior at thirty-three months in same-sex and mixed-sex dyads. *Child Development, 49*, 557–569.

Jacobi, C., Hayward, C., de Zwaan, M., Kraemer, H. C., & Agras, W. S. (2004). Coming to terms with risk factors for eating disorders: Application of risk terminology and suggestions for a general taxonomy . *Psychological Bulletin, 130*, 19–65.

Jacobs, J. E., & Klaczynski, P. A. (2002). The development of judgment and decision making during childhood and adolescence. *Current Directions in Psychological Science, 11*, 145–149.

Jacobson, J. L., & Jacobson, S. W. (1996). Intellectual impairment in children exposed to polychlorinated biphenyls in utero. *The New England Journal of Medicine, 335*, 783–789.

Jacobson, J. L., Jacobson, S. W., Sokol, R. J., & Ager, J. W. (1998). Relation of maternal age and pattern of pregnancy drinking to functionally significant cognitive deficit in infancy. *Alcoholism: Clinical and Experimental Research, 22*, 345–351.

Jacobson, S. W., & Jacobson, J. L. (2000). Teratogenic insult and neurobehavioral function in infancy and childhood. In C. A. Nelson (Ed.), *The Minnesota Symposium on Child Psychology; Vol. 31. The effects of early adversity on neurobehavioral development* (pp. 61–112). Mahwah, NJ: Erlbaum.

Jaffe, J., Beatrice, B., Stanley, F., Crown, C. L., & Jasnow, M. D. (2001). Rhythms of dialogue in infancy: Coordinated timing in development. *Monographs of the Society for Research in Child Development, 66*(Serial No. 265).

Jaffee, S., & Hyde, J. S. (2000). Gender differences in moral orientation: A meta-analysis. *Psychological Bulletin, 126*, 703–726.

Jaswal, V. K. (2004). Don't believe everything you hear: Preschoolers' sensitivity to speaker intent in category induction. *Child Development, 76*, 1871–1885.

Jensen, P. S., Hinshaw, S. P., Swanson, J. M., Greenhill, L. L., Conners, C. K., Arnold, L. E., et al. (2001). Findings from the NIMH Multimodal Treatment Study of ADHD (MTA): Implications and applications for primary care providers. *Journal of Developmental and Behavioral Pediatrics, 22*, 60–73.

Jiao, S., Ji, G., & Jing, Q. (1996). Cognitive development of Chinese urban only children and children with siblings. *Child Development, 67*, 387–395.

Jiao, Z. (1999, April). *Which students keep old friends and which become new friends across a school transition?* Paper presented at the 1999 meeting of the Society for Research in Child Development, Albuquerque, New Mexico.

Johanson, R. B., Rice, C., Coyle, M., Arthur, J., Anyanwu, L., Ibrahim, J., et al. (1993). A randomized prospective study comparing the new vacuum extractor policy with forceps delivery. *British Journal of Obstetrics and Gynecology, 100*, 524–530.

Johnson, M. H. (2000). Functional brain development in infants: Elements of an interactive specialization framework. *Child Development, 71*, 75–81.

Johnson, S. P. (2001). Visual development in human infants: Binding features, surfaces, and objects. *Visual Cognition, 8*, 565–578.

Johnson, S. P., & Aslin, R. N. (1995). Perception of object unity in 2-month-old infants. *Developmental Psychology, 31*, 739–745.

Jones, D., & Christensen, C. A. (1999). Relationship between automaticity in handwriting and students' ability to generate written text. *Journal of Educational Psychology, 91*, 44–49.

Joseph, R. (2000). Fetal brain behavior and cognitive development. *Developmental Review, 20*, 81–98.

Joyner, K., & Udry, J. R. (2000). You don't bring me anything but down: Adolescent romance and depression. *Journal of Health and Social Behavior, 41*, 369–391.

Jusczyk, P. W. (1995). Language acquisition: Speech sounds and phonological development. In J. L. Miller & P. D. Eimas (Eds.), *Handbook of perception and cognition: Vol. 11. Speech, language, and communication.* Orlando, FL: Academic Press.

Jusczyk, P. W. (2002). How infants adapt speech-processing capacities to native-language structure. *Current Directions in Psychological Science, 11*, 15–18.

Kagan, J. (1989). Temperamental contributions to social behavior. *American Psychologist, 44*, 668–674.

Kagan, J., Arcus, D., Snidman, N., Feng, W. Y., Hendler, J., & Greene, S. (1994). Reactivity in infants: A cross-national comparison. *Developmental Psychology, 30*, 342–345.

Kagan, J., & Moss, H. A. (1962). *Birth to maturity: A study in psychological development.* New York: Wiley.

Kaijura, H., Cowart B. J., & Beauchamp, G. K. (1992). Early developmental change in bitter taste responses in human infants. *Developmental Psychobiology, 25*, 375–386.

Kail, R. (1990). *The development of memory in children* (3rd ed.). New York: W. H. Freeman.

Kail, R. (2002). Developmental change in proactive interference. *Child Development, 73*, 1703–1714.

Kail, R. (2004). Cognitive development includes global and domain-specific processes. *Merrill-Palmer Quarterly, 50*, 445–455.

Kail, R. V. (2005). Speed of processing in childhood and adolescence: Nature, consequences, and implications for understanding atypical development. In J. DeLuca & J. H. Kalmar (Eds.), *Information processing speed in clinical populations.* New York: Psychology Press.

Kail, R., & Hall, L. K. (1999). Sources of developmental change in children's word-problem performance. *Journal of Educational Psychology, 91*, 660–668.

Kako, E. (1999). Elements of syntax in the systems of three language-trained animals. *Animal Learning and Behavior, 27*, 1–14.

Kamerman, S. B. (1993). International perspectives on child care policies and programs. *Pediatrics, 91*, 248–252.

Kandel, E., & Mednick, S. A. (1991). Perinatal complications predict violent offending. *Criminology, 29*, 519–529.

Kaplan, P. S., Goldstein, M. H., Huckeby, E. R., & Cooper, R. P. (1995). Habituation, sensitization, and infants' responses to motherese speech. *Developmental Psychobiology, 28*, 45–57.

Karniol, R. (1989). The role of manual manipulative states in the infant's acquisition of perceived control over objects. *Developmental Review, 9*, 205–233.

Katz, L. F., & Woodin, E. M. (2002). Hostility, hostile detachment, and conflict engagement in marriages: Effects on child and family functioning. *Child Development, 73*, 636–652.

Katz, P., Nachtigall, R., & Showstack, J. (2002). The economic impact of the assisted reproductive technologies. *Nature Medicine, 8*, S29–S32.

Keane, S. P., Brown, K. P., & Crenshaw, T. M. (1990). Children's intention-cue detection as a function of maternal social behavior: Pathways to social rejection. *Developmental Psychology, 26*, 1004–1009.

Kearney, C. A., & Silverman, W. K. (1995). Family environment of youngsters with school refusal behavior: A synopsis with implications for assessment and treatment. *American Journal of Family Therapy, 23*, 59–72.

Keiley, M. K., Bates, J. F., Dodge, K. A., & Pettit, G. (2000). A cross-domain growth analysis: Externalizing and internalizing behaviors during 8 years of childhood. *Journal of Abnormal Child Psychology, 28*, 161–179.

Keller, H., Yovsi, R., Borke, J., Kartner, J., Jensen, H., & Papaligoura, Z. (2004). Developmental consequences of early parenting experiences: Self-recognition and self-regulation in three cultural communities. *Child Development, 75*, 1745–1760.

Keller, M., Edelstein, W., Schmid, S., Fang, F., & Fang, G. (1998). Reasoning about responsibilities and obligations in close relationships: A comparison across two cultures. *Developmental Psychology, 34*, 731–741.

Kellman, P. J., & Banks, M. S. (1998). Infant visual perception. In W. Damon (Ed.), *Handbook of child psychology* (Vol. 2). New York: Wiley.

Kertes, D. A., & Gunnar, M. R. (2004). Evening activities as a potential confound in research on the adrenocortical system in children. *Child Development, 75*, 193–204.

Kilgore, K., Snyder, J., & Lentz, C. (2000). The contribution of parental discipline, parental monitoring, and school risk to early-onset conduct problems in African American boys and girls. *Developmental Psychology, 36*, 835–845.

Killen, M., & McGlothlin, H. (2005). Prejudice in childhood. In C. B. Fisher & R. M. Lerner (Eds.), *Encyclopedia of applied developmental science* (Vol. 2, pp. 870–872). Thousand Oaks, CA: Sage.

Kim, Y. H., & Goetz, E. T. (1994). Context effects on word recognition and reading comprehension of good and poor readers: A test of the interactive compensatory hypothesis. *Reading Research Quarterly, 29*, 178–188.

Kimball, M. M. (1986). Television and sex-role attitudes. In T. M. Williams (Ed.), *The impact of television* (pp. 265–301). New York: Academic Press.

Kimball, M. M. (1989). A new perspective on women's math achievement. *Psychological Bulletin, 105*, 198–214.

King, V., Elder, G. H., & Whitbeck, L. B. (1997). Religious involvement among rural youth: An ecological and life-course perspective. *Journal of Research on Adolescence, 7*, 431–456.

Kirby, D. (2001). *Emerging answers: Research findings on programs to reduce teen pregnancy (summary).* Washington, DC: National Campaign to Prevent Teen Pregnancy.

Kirby, D. (2002). *Do abstinence-only programs delay the initiation of sex among young people and reduce teen pregnancy?* Washington, DC: National Campaign to Prevent Teen Pregnancy.

Klaczynski, P. A. (2000). Motivated scientific reasoning biases, epistemological beliefs, and theory polarization. *Child Development, 71*, 1347–1366.

Klaczynski, P. A. (2004). A dual-process model of adolescent development: Implications for decision making, reasoning, and identity. In R. Kail (Ed.), *Advances in Child Development and Behavior* (Vol. 32, pp. 73–123). San Diego, CA: Elsevier.

Klahr, D. (1985). Solving problems with ambiguous subgoal ordering: Preschoolers' performance. *Child Development, 56*, 940–952.

Klaus, M., & Kennell, H. H. (1976). *Mother-infant bonding.* St. Louis: Mosby.

Kochanska, G. (1991). Socialization and temperament in the development of guilt and conscience. *Child Development, 62*, 1379–1392.

Kochanska, G. (1993). Toward a synthesis of parental socialization and child temperament in early development of conscience. *Child Development, 64,* 325–347.

Kochanska, G. (1995). Children's temperament, mothers' discipline, and security of attachment: Multiple pathways to emerging internalization. *Child Development, 66,* 597–615.

Kochanska, G. (1997). Mutually responsive orientation between mothers and their young children: Implications for early socialization. *Child Development, 68,* 94–112.

Kochanska, G. (1997a). Multiple pathways to conscience for children with different temperaments: From toddlerhood to age 5. *Developmental Psychology, 33,* 228–240.

Kochanska, G., DeVet, K., Goldman, M., Murray, K., et al. (1994). Maternal reports of conscience development and temperament in young children. *Child Development, 65,* 852–868.

Kochanska, G., Coy, K. C., & Murray, K. T. (2001). The development of self-regulation in the first four years of life. *Child Development, 72,* 1091–1111.

Kochanska, G., Gross, J. N., Lin, M., & Nichols, K. E. (2002). Guilt in young children: Development, determinants, and relations with a broader system of standards. *Child Development, 73,* 461–482.

Kochanska, G., Murray, K. T., & Harlan, E. T. (2000). Effortful control in early childhood: Continuity and change, antecedents, and implications for social development. *Developmental Psychology, 36,* 220–232.

Kochanska, G., & Radke-Yarrow, M. (1992). Inhibition in toddlerhood and the dynamics of the child's interaction with an unfamiliar peer at age five. *Child Development, 63,* 325–335.

Kochenderfer, B. J., & Ladd, G. W. (1996). Peer victimization: Cause or consequence of school maladjustment? *Child Development, 67,* 1305–1317.

Kochenderfer-Ladd, B., & Skinner, K. (2002). Children's coping strategies: Moderators of the effects of peer victimization? *Developmental Psychology, 38,* 267–278.

Kochenderfer-Ladd, B., & Wardrop, J. L. (2001). Chronicity and instability of children's peer victimization experiences as predictors of loneliness and social satisfaction trajectories. *Child Development, 72,* 134–151.

Kogan, N. (1983). Stylistic variation in childhood and adolescence: Creativity, metaphor, and cognitive style. In P. H. Mussen (Ed.), *Handbook of child psychology* (Vol. 3). New York: Wiley.

Kohlberg, L. (1966). A cognitive-developmental analysis of children's sex-role concepts and attitudes. In E. E. Maccoby (Ed.), *The development of sex differences.* Stanford: Stanford University Press.

Kohlberg, L. (1969). Stage and sequence: The cognitive-developmental approach to socialization. In D. Goslin (Ed.), *Handbook of socialization theory and research* (pp. 347–480). Chicago: Rand McNally.

Kohlberg, L., & Ullian, D. Z. (1974). Stages in the development of psychosexual concepts and attitudes. In R. C. Friedman, R. M. Richart, & R. L. Van Wiele (Eds.), *Sex differences in behavior.* New York: Wiley.

Kojima, Y. (2000). Maternal regulation of sibling interactions in the preschool years: Observational study in Japanese families. *Child Development, 71,* 1640–1647.

Kokis, J. V., Macpherson, R., Toplak, M. E., West, R. F., & Stanovich, K. E. (2002). Heuristic and analytic processing: Age trends and associations with cognitive ability and cognitive styles. *Journal of Experimental Child Psychology, 83,* 26–52.

Kokko, K., & Pulkkinen, L. (2000). Aggression in childhood and long-term unemployment in adulthood: A cycle of maladaptation and some protective factors. *Developmental Psychology, 36,* 463–472.

Kolb, B. (1989). Brain development, plasticity, and behavior. *American Psychologist, 44,* 1203–1212.

Kolberg, K. J. S. (1999). Environmental influences on prenatal development and health. In T. L. Whitman & T. V. Merluzzi (Eds.), *Life-span perspectives on health and illness* (pp. 87–103). Mahwah, NJ: Erlbaum.

Kopp, C. B. (1987). The growth of self-regulation: Caregivers and children. In N. Eisenberg (Ed.), *Contemporary topics in developmental psychology.* New York: Wiley.

Kopp, C. B. (1997). Young children: Emotion management, instrumental control, and plans. In S. L. Friedman & E. K. Scholnick (Eds.), *The developmental psychology of planning: Why, how, and when do we plan?* (pp. 103–124). Mahwah, NJ: Erlbaum.

Kopp, C. B., & McCall, R. B. (1982). Predicting later mental performance for normal, at-risk, and handicapped infants. In P. B. Baltes & O. G. Brim (Eds.), *Life-span development and behavior* (Vol. 4). New York: Academic Press.

Kopp, C. B., & Neufeld, S. J. (2003). Emotional development during infancy. In R. Davidson, K. Scherer, & H. H. Goldsmith (Eds.), *Handbook of affective sciences* (pp. 347–374). Oxford UK: Oxford University Press.

Kotovsky, L., & Baillargeon, R. (1998). The development of calibration-based reasoning about collision events in young infants. *Cognition, 67,* 311–351.

Kowal, A., & Kramer, L. (1997). Children's understanding of parental differential treatment. *Child Development, 68,* 113–126.

Krebs, D., & Gillmore, J. (1982). The relationship among the first stages of cognitive development, role-taking abilities, and moral development. *Child Development, 53,* 877–886.

Krishnakumar, A., & Black, M. M. (2003). Family processes within three-generation households and adolescents mothers' satisfaction with father involvement. *Journal of Family Psychology, 17,* 488–498.

Krispin, O., Sternberg, K. J., & Lamb, M. E. (1992). The dimensions of peer evaluation in Israel: A cross-cultural perspective. *International Journal of Behavioral Development, 15,* 299–314.

Kroger, J. (2005). Identity statuses. In C. B. Fisher & R. M. Lerner (Eds.), *Encyclopedia of applied developmental science* (Vol. 1, pp. 567–568). Thousand Oaks, CA: Sage.

Kroger, J., & Green, K. E. (1996). Events associated with identity status change. *Journal of Adolescence, 19,* 477–490.

Kuebli, J., Butler, S., & Fivush, R. (1995). Mother-child talk about past emotions: Relations of maternal language and child gender over time. *Cognition & Emotion, 9,* 265–283.

Kuhl, P. K., Andruski, J. E., Chistovich, I. A., Chistovich, L. A., Kozhevnikova, E. V., Ryskina, V. L., et al. (1997). Cross-language analysis of phonetic units in language addressed to infants. *Science, 277,* 684–686.

Kuhn, D. (2000). Metacognitive development. *Current Directions in Psychological Science, 9,* 178–181.

Kuhn, D., Garcia-Mila, M., Zohar, A., & Andersen, C. (1995). Strategies of knowledge acquisition. *Monographs of the Society for Research in Child Development, 60* (Serial No. 245).

Kunzig, R. (1998). Climbing through the brain. *Discover, 19,* 60–69.

Ladd, G. W. (1998). Peer relationships and social competence during early and middle childhood. *Annual Review of Psychology, 50,* 333–359.

Ladd, G. W. (2003). Probing the adaptive significance of children's behavior and relationships in the school context: A child by environment perspective. In R. V. Kail (Ed.), *Advances in child development and behavior* (Vol. 31). San Diego, CA: Academic Press.

Ladd, G. W., & Ladd, B. K. (1998). Parenting behaviors and parent-child relationships: Correlates of peer victimization in kindergarten? *Developmental Psychology, 34,* 1450–1458.

Ladd, G. W., & Pettit, G. S. (2002). Parents and children's peer relationships. In M. Bornstein (Ed.), *Handbook of parenting: Vol. 4* (2nd ed., pp. 377–409). Hillsdale, NJ: Erlbaum.

LaFreniere, P., Strayer, F. F., & Gauthier, R. (1984). The emergence of same-sex affiliative preferences among preschool peers: A developmental/ethnological perspective. *Child Development, 55,* 1958–1965.

Lagattuta, K. H., & Wellman, H. M. (2002). Differences in early parent-child conversations about negative versus positive emotions: Implications for the development of psychological understanding. *Developmental Psychology, 38,* 564–580.

Lagattuta, K. H., Wellman, H. M., & Flavell, J. H. (1997). Preschoolers' understanding of the link between thinking and feeling: Cognitive cuing and emotional change. *Child Development, 68,* 1081–1104.

LaGreca, A. M. (1993). Social skills training with children: Where do we go from here? *Journal of Clinical Child Psychology, 22,* 288–298.

Laird, R. D., Pettit, G. S., Dodge, K. A., & Bates, J. E. (2003). Changes in parents' monitoring knowledge: Links with parenting, relationships quality, adolescent beliefs and antisocial behavior. *Social Development, 12,* 401–419.

Lalumière, M. L., Blanchard, R., & Zucker, K. J. (2000). Sexual orientation and handedness in men and women: A meta-analysis. *Psychological Bulletin, 126,* 575–592.

Lamaze, F. (1958). *Painless childbirth.* London: Burke.

Lamb, M. E. (1999). Nonparental child care. In M. E. Lamb (Ed.), *Parenting and child development in "nontraditional" families.* Mahwah, NJ: Erlbaum.

Lamb, M. E., Sternberg, K. J., & Esplin, P. W. (2000). Effects of age and delay on the amount of information provided by alleged sex abuse victims in investigative interviews. *Child Development, 71,* 1586–1596.

Lampinen, J. M., & Smith, V. L. (1995). The incredible (and sometimes incredulous) child witness: Child eyewitnesses' sensitivity to source credibility cues. *Journal of Applied Psychology, 80,* 621–627.

Lane H., & Bahan, B. (1998). Ethics of cochlear implantation in young children: A review and reply from a DEAF-WORLD perspective. *Otolaryngology—Head and Neck Surgery, 119,* 293–313.

Lane, H. L. (1992). *The mask of benevolence: Disabling the deaf community.* New York: Knopf.

Langlois, J. H., & Downs, A. C. (1980). Mothers, fathers, and peers as socialization agents of sex-typed play behaviors in young children. *Child Development, 51,* 1237–1247.

Langlois, J. H., Ritter, J. M., Roggman, L. A., & Vaughn, L. S. (1991). Facial diversity and infant preferences for attractive faces. *Developmental Psychology, 27,* 79–84.

Lanza, E. (1992). Can bilingual two-year-olds code-switch? *Journal of Child Language, 19,* 633–658.

Larson, R. W. (1997). The emergence of solitude as a constructive domain of experience in early adolescence. *Child Development, 68,* 80–93.

Larson, R. W. (2000). Toward a psychology of positive youth development. *American Psychologist, 55,* 170–183.

Larson, R. W. (2001). How U.S. children and adolescents spend time: What it does (and doesn't) tell us about their development. *Current Directions in Psychological Science, 10,* 160–164.

Laursen, B., & Collins, W. A. (1994). Interpersonal conflict during adolescence. *Psychological Bulletin, 115,* 197–209.

Laursen, B., Finkelstein, B. D., & Betts, N. T. (2001). A developmental meta-analysis of peer conflict resolution. *Developmental Review, 21,* 423–449.

Lazar, I., & Darlington, R. (1982). Lasting effects of early education: A report from the Consortium for Longitudinal Studies. *Monographs of the Society for Research in Child Development, 47,* (2–3, Serial No. 195).

Leach, P. (1991). *Your baby and child: From birth to age five* (2nd ed.). New York: Knopf.

Leaper, C., Anderson, K. J., & Sanders, P. (1998). Moderators of gender effects on parents' talk to their children: A meta-analysis. *Developmental Psychology, 34,* 3–27.

Leaper, C., & Smith, T. E. (2004). A meta-analytic review of gender variations in children's language use: Talkativeness, affiliative speech, and assertive speech. *Developmental Psychology, 40,* 993–1027.

Lecanuet, J. P., Granier-Deferre, C., & Busnel, M. C. (1995). Human fetal auditory perception. In J. P. Lecanuet, W. P. Fifer, N. A. Krasnegor, & W. P. Smotherman (Eds.), *Fetal development: A psychobiological perspective.* Hillsdale, NJ: Erlbaum.

Ledebt, A. (2000). Changes in arm posture during the early acquisition of walking. *Infant Behavior and Development, 23,* 79–89.

Ledebt, A., van Wieringen, P. C. W., & Saveslsbergh, G. J. P. (2004). Functional significance of foot rotation in early walking. *Infant Behavior and Development, 27,* 163–172.

Lee, K. T., Mattson, S. N., & Riley, E. P. (2004). Classifying children with heavy prenatal alcohol exposure using measures of attention. *Journal of the International Neuropsychological Society, 10,* 271–277.

Leichtman, M. D., & Ceci, S. L. (1995). The effects of stereotypes and suggestions on preschoolers' reports. *Developmental Psychology, 31,* 568–578.

LeMare, L. J., & Rubin, K. H. (1987). Perspective taking and peer interaction: Structural and developmental analyses. *Child Development, 58,* 306–315.

Lengua, L. J., Sandler, I. N., West, S. G., Wolchik, S. A., & Curran, P. J. (1999). Emotionality and self-regulation, threat appraisal, and coping in children of divorce. *Development & Psychopathology, 11,* 15–37.

Lengua, L. J., West, S. G., & Sandler, I. N. (1998). Temperament as a predictor of symptomatology in children: Addressing contamination of measures. *Child Development, 69,* 164–181.

Leon, K. (2003). Risk and protective factors in young children's adjustment to parental divorce: A review of the research. *Family Relations, 52,* 258–270.

Leventhal, T., & Brooks-Gunn, J. (2000). The neighborhoods they live in: The effects of neighborhood residence on child and adolescent outcomes. *Psychological Bulletin, 126,* 309–337.

Leventhal, T., & Brooks-Gunn, J. (2003). Children and youth in neighborhood contexts. *Current Directions in Psychological Science, 12,* 27–31.

Leventhal, T., & Brooks-Gunn, J. (2004). A randomized study of neighborhood effects on low-income children's educational outcomes. *Developmental Psychology, 40,* 488–507.

Levine, L. E. (1983). Mine: Self-definition in 2-year-old boys. *Developmental Psychology, 19,* 544–549.

Levine, L. E., & Waite, B. M. (2000). Television viewing and attentional abilities in fourth and fifth grade children. *Journal of Applied Developmental Psychology, 21,* 667–679.

Levine, L. J. (1995). Young children's understanding of the causes of anger and sadness. *Child Development, 66,* 697–709.

Levitt, A. G., & Utman, J. A. (1992). From babbling towards the sound systems of English and French: A longitudinal two-case study. *Journal of Child Language, 19,* 19–49.

Levitt, M. J., Guacci-Franco, N., & Levitt, J. L. (1993). Convoys of social support in childhood and early adolescence: Structure and function. *Developmental Psychology, 29,* 811–818.

Levy, B. A., Gong, Z., Hessels, S., Evans, M. A., & Jared, D. (2006). Understanding print: Early reading development and the contributions of home literacy experiences. *Journal of Experimental Child Psychology, 93,* 63–93.

Levy, G. D., & Boston, M. B. (1994). Preschoolers' recall of own-sex and other-sex gender scripts. *Journal of Genetic Psychology, 155,* 367–371.

Levy, G. D., Taylor, M. G., & Gelman, S. A. (1995). Traditional and evaluative aspects of flexibility in gender roles, social conventions, moral rules, and physical laws. *Child Development, 66,* 515–531.

Levy, J. (1976). A review of evidence for a genetic component in the determination of handedness. *Behavior Genetics, 6,* 429–453.

Lewis, M. (1997). The self in self-conscious emotions. In J. G. Snodgrass & R. L. Thompson (Eds.), *The self across psychology: Self-awareness, self-recognition, and the self-concept* (pp. 119–142). New York: New York Academy of Sciences.

Lewis, M. (2000). The emergence of human emotions. In M. Lewis & J. Haviland-Jones (Eds.), *Handbook of emotions* (2nd ed., pp. 265–280). New York: Guilford.

Lewis, M. D., Koroshegyi, C., Douglas, L., & Kampe, K. (1997). Age-specific associations between emotional responses to separation and cognitive performance in infancy. *Developmental Psychology, 33,* 32–42.

Lewis, M., & Ramsay, D. (2004). Development of self-recognition, personal pronoun use, and pretend play during the second year. *Child Development, 75,* 1821–1831.

Lewis, M., Ramsay, D. S., & Kawakami, K. (1993). Differences between Japanese infants and Caucasian American infants in behavioral and cortisol response to inoculation. *Child Development, 64,* 1722–1731.

Lewkowicz, D. J. (2000a). Infants' perception of the audible, visible, and bimodal attributes of multimodal syllables. *Child Development, 71,* 1241–1257.

Lewkowicz, D. J. (2000b). The development of intersensory perception: An epigenetic systems/limitations view. *Psychological Bulletin, 126,* 281–308.

Lewontin, R. C. (1976). Race and intelligence. In N. J. Block & G. Dworkin (Eds.), *The IQ controversy* (pp. 78–92). New York: Pantheon Books.

Liben, L. S., & Bigler, R. S. (2002). The developmental course of gender differentiation. *Monographs of the Society for Research in Child Development, 67* (Serial No. 269).

Liben, L. S., Bigler, R. S., & Krogh, H. R. (2001). Pink and blue collar jobs: Children's judgments of job status and job aspirations in relation to sex of worker. *Journal of Experimental Child Psychology, 79,* 346–363.

Lieberman, M., Doyle, A., & Markiewicz, D. (1999). Developmental patterns in security of attachment to mother and father in late childhood and early adolescence: Associations with peer relations. *Child Development, 70,* 202–213.

Lillard, A. (1999). Developing a cultural theory of mind: The CIAO approach. *Current Directions in Psychological Science, 8,* 57–61.

Lin, C. C., & Fu, V. R. (1990). A comparison of childrearing practices among Chinese, immigrant Chinese, and Caucasian-American parents. *Child Development, 61,* 429–433.

Linden, M. G., Bender, B. G., Harmon, R. J., Mrazek, D. A., & Robinson, A. (1988). 47–XXX: What is the prognosis? *Pediatrics, 82,* 619–630.

Lindsey, E. W., & Colwell, M. J. (2003). Preschoolers' emotional competence: Links to pretend and physical play. *Child Study Journal, 33,* 39–52.

Lindsey, E. W., & Mize, J. (2000). Parent-child physical and pretense play: Links to children's social competence. *Merrill-Palmer Quarterly, 46,* 565–591.

Linn, S. (2004). *Consuming kids: The hostile takeover of childhood.* New York: New Press.

Linn, S. (2005). The commercialization of childhood. In S. Oldman (Ed.), *Childhood lost: How American culture is failing our kids* (pp. 107–122). Westport CT: Praeger.

Liu, H.-M., Kuhl, P. K., & Tsao, F.-M. (2003). An association between mothers' speech clarity and infants' speech discrimination skills. *Developmental Science, 6,* F1–F10.

Livesley, W. J., & Bromley, D. B. (1973). *Person perception in childhood and adolescence.* New York: Wiley.

Loehlin, J. C. (2000). Group differences in intelligence. In R. J. Sternberg (Ed.), *Handbook of intelligence* (pp. 176–193). New York: Cambridge University Press.

Looney, M. A., & Plowman, S. A. (1990). Passing rates of American children and youth on the FITNESSGRAM criterion-referenced physical fitness standards. *Research Quarterly of Exercise and Sport, 61,* 215–223.

Lord, S. E., Eccles, J. S., & McCarthy, K. A. (1994). Surviving the junior high transition: Family processes and self-perception as protective and risk factors. *Journal of Early Adolescence, 14,* 162–199.

Lowry, R., Wechsler, H., Kann, L., & Collins, J. L. (2001). Recent trends in participation in physical education among U.S. high school students. *Journal of School Health, 71,* 145–152.

Luecke-Aleksa, D., Anderson, D. R., Collins, P. A., & Schmitt, K. L. (1995). Gender constancy and television viewing. *Developmental Psychology, 31,* 773–780.

Lueptow, L. B., Garovich-Szabo, L., & Lueptow, M. B. (2001). Social change and the persistence of sex typing: 1974–1997. *Social Forces, 80,* 1–36.

Luthar, S. S., Zigler, E., & Goldstein, D. (1992). Psychosocial adjustment among intellectually gifted adolescents: The role of cognitive-developmental and experiential factors. *Journal of Child Psychology and Psychiatry and Allied Disciplines, 33,* 361–373.

Lutz, S. E., & Ruble, D. N. (1995). Children and gender prejudice: Context, motivation, and the development of gender conception. In R. Vasta (Ed.), *Annals of child development* (Vol. 10, pp. 131–166). London: Jessica Kingsley.

Lyon, G. R. (1996). Learning disabilities. In E. J. Mash & R. A. Barkley (Eds.), *Child psychopathology.* New York: Guilford.

Lytton, H., & Romney, D. M. (1991). Parents' differential socialization of boys and girls: A meta-analysis. *Psychological Bulletin, 109,* 267–296.

Maccoby, E. E. (1984). Socialization and developmental change. *Child Development, 55,* 317–328.

Maccoby, E. E. (1990). Gender and relationships: A developmental account. *American Psychologist, 45,* 513–520.

Maccoby, E. E. (1998). *The two sexes: Growing up apart, coming together.* Cambridge, MA: Belknap Press.

Maccoby, E. E., Buchanon, C. M., Mnookin, R. H., & Dornbusch, S. M. (1993). Postdivorce roles of mothers and fathers in the lives of their children. *Journal of Family Psychology, 7,* 24–38.

Maccoby, E. E., & Jacklin, C. N. (1974). *The psychology of sex differences.* Stanford, CA: Stanford University Press.

Maccoby, E. E., & Jacklin, C. N. (1980). Sex differences in aggression: A rejoinder and reprise. *Child Development, 51,* 964–980.

MacWhinney, B. (1998). Models of the emergence of language. *Annual Review of Psychology, 49,* 199–227.

Main, M., & Cassidy, J. (1988). Categories of response to reunion with the parent at age 6: Predictable from infant attachment classifications and stable over a 1-month period. *Developmental Psychology, 24,* 415–426.

Malinosky-Rummell, R., & Hansen, D. J. (1993). Long-term consequences of childhood physical abuse. *Psychological Bulletin, 114,* 68–79.

Mandel, D. R., Jusczyk, P. W., & Pisoni, D. B. (1995). Infants' recognition of the sound patterns of their own names. *Psychological Science, 6,* 314–317.

Mangelsdorf, S., Gunnar, M., Kestenbaum, R., Lang, S., & Andreas, D. (1990). Infant proneness-to-distress temperament, maternal personality, and mother-infant attachment: Associations and goodness of fit. *Child Development, 61,* 820–831.

Mangelsdorf, S. C. (1992). Developmental changes in infant-stranger interaction. *Infant Behavior and Development, 15,* 191–208.

Mangelsdorf, S. C., Shapiro, J. R., & Marzolf, D. (1995). Developmental and temperamental differences in emotional regulation in infancy. *Child Development, 66,* 1817–1828.

Maratsos, M. (1998). The acquisition of grammar. In W. Damon (Ed.), *Handbook of child psychology* (Vol. 2). New York: Wiley.

Marcia, J. E. (1980). Identity in adolescence. In J. Adelson (Ed.), *Handbook of adolescent psychology.* New York: Wiley.

Marcia, J. E. (1991). Identity and self-development. In R. M. Lerner, A. C. Petersen, & J. Brooks-Gunn (Eds.), *Encyclopedia of adolescence* (Vol. 1). New York: Garland.

Marcus, G. F., Pinker, S., Ullman, M., Hollander, M., Rosen, T. J., & Xu, F. (1992). Overregularization in language acquisition. *Monographs of the Society for Research in Child Development, 58*(4, Serial No. 228).

Marcus, J., Maccoby, E. E., Jacklin, C. N., & Doering, C. H. (1985). Individual differences in mood in early childhood: Their relation to gender and neonatal sex steroids. *Developmental Psychobiology, 18,* 327–340.

Mares, M.-L., & Woodard, E. (2005). Positive effects of television on children's social interactions: A meta-analysis. *Media Psychology, 7,* 301–322.

Markovits, H., Benenson, J., & Dolensky, E. (2001). Evidence that children and adolescents have internal models of peer interactions that are gender differentiated. *Child Development, 72,* 879–886.

Markovits, H., & Vachon, R. (1989). Reasoning with contrary-to-fact propositions. *Journal of Experimental Child Psychology, 47,* 398–412.

Marsh, H. W. (1991). Employment during high school: Character building or a subversion of academic goals? *Sociology of Education, 64,* 172–189.

Marsh, H. W., Chessor, D., Craven, R., & Roche, L. (1995). The effects of gifted and talented programs on academic self-concept: The big fish strikes again. *American Educational Research Journal, 32,* 285–319.

Marsh, H. W., Ellis, L. A., & Craven, R. G. (2002). How do preschool children feel about themselves? Unraveling measurement and multidimensional self-concept structure. *Developmental Psychology, 38,* 376–393.

Marsh, H. W., & Yeung, A. S. (1997). Causal effects of academic self-concept on academic achievement: Structural equation models of longitudinal data. *Journal of Educational Psychology, 89,* 41–54.

Marshall, N. L. (2004). The quality of early child care and children's development. *Current Directions in Psychological Science, 13,* 165–168.

Martin, C. L. (1989). Children's use of gender-related information in making social judgments. *Developmental Psychology, 25,* 80–88.

Martin, C. L., Eisenbud, L., & Rose, H. (1995). Children's gender-based reasoning about toys. *Child Development, 66,* 1453–1471.

Martin, C. L., & Fabes, R. A. (2001). The stability and consequences of young children's same-sex peer interactions. *Developmental Psychology, 37,* 431–446.

Martin, C. L., Fabes, R. A., Evans, S. M., & Wyman, H. (1999). Social cognition on the playground: Children's beliefs about playing with girls versus boys and their relations to sex segregated play. *Journal of Social and Personal Relationships, 16,* 751–772.

Martin, C. L., & Little, J. K. (1990). The relation of gender understandings to children's sex-typed preferences and gender stereotypes. *Child Development, 61,* 1427–1439.

Martin J. A., Hamilton, B. E., Sutton, P. D., et al. (2005). *Births: Final data for 2003.* (*National vital statistics reports* Vol. 54, No. 2). Hyattsville, MD: National Center for Health Statistics.

Martin, J. A., Hamilton, B. E., Ventura, S. J., Menacker, F., & Park, M. M. (2002). Births: Final data for 2000. *National Vital Statistics Reports, 50,* 1–5.

Martin, R. P., Olejnik, S., & Gaddis, L. (1994). Is temperament an important contributor to schooling outcomes in elementary school? Modeling effects of temperament and scholastic ability on academic achievement. In W. B. Casey & S. C. McDevitt (Eds.), *Prevention and early intervention.* New York: Brunner/Mazel.

Masur, E. F. (1995). Infants' early verbal imitation and their later lexical development. *Merrill-Palmer Quarterly, 41,* 286–306.

Mattys, S. L., & Jusczyk, P. W. (2001). Phonotactic cues for segmentation of fluent speech by infants. *Cognition, 78,* 91–121.

Mattys, S. L., Jusczyk, P. W., Luce, P. A., & Morgan, J. L. (1999). Phonotactic and prosodic effects on word segmentation in infants. *Cognitive Psychology, 38,* 465–494.

Matusov, E., Bell, N., & Rogoff, B. (2002). Schooling as cultural process: Working together and guidance by children from schools differing in collaborative practices. In R. V. Kail & H. W. Reese (Eds.), *Advances in child development and behavior* (Vol. 29, pp. 129–160). San Diego, CA: Academic Press.

Maughan, A., & Cicchetti, D. (2002). Impact of child maltreatment and interadult violence on children's emotion regulation abilities and socioemotional adjustment. *Child Development, 73,* 1525–1542.

Mayer, J. D., Caruso, D. R., & Salovey, P. (1999). Emotional intelligence meets traditional standards for an intelligence. *Intelligence, 27,* 267–298.

Mayer, J. D., Salovey, P., & Caruso, D. R. (2000). Selecting a measure of emotional intelligence: The case for ability scales. In R. Bar-On & J. D. A. Parker (Eds.), *Handbook of emotional intelligence* (pp. 320–342). San Francisco: Jossey-Bass.

Maynard, A. E. (2002). Cultural teaching: The development of teaching skills in Maya sibling interactions. *Child Development, 73,* 969–982.

Mazur, E., Wolchik, S. A., Virdin, L., Sandler, I. N., & West, S. G. (1999). Cognitive moderators of children's adjustment to stressful divorce events: The role of negative cognitive errors and positive illusions. *Child Development, 70,* 231–245.

McCall, R. B. (1989). Commentary. *Human Development, 32,* 177–186.

McCall, R. B., Applebaum, M. I., & Hogarty, P. S. (1973). Developmental changes in mental performance. *Monographs of the Society for Research in Child Development, 38*(Whole No. 150).

McCarty, M. E., & Ashmead, D. H. (1999). Visual control of reaching and grasping in infants. *Developmental Psychology, 35,* 620–631.

McCarty, M. E., Clifton, R. K., Ashmead, D. H., Lee, P., & Goubet, N. (2001). How infants use vision for grasping objects. *Child Development, 72,* 973–987.

McClure, E. B. (2000). A meta-analytic review of sex differences in facial expression processing and their development in infants, children, and adolescents. *Psychological Bulletin, 126,* 424–453.

McCormick, C. (2000). Twin miracles: Mashpee mother has groundbreaking surgery to save her two fetuses. *Cape Cod Times,* August 26, 2000. Retrieved May 10, 2002 from http://www.capecodonline.com/cctimes/archives/2000/aug/26/twinmiracles26.htm

McCormick, C. B., & Pressley, M. (1997). *Educational psychology.* New York: Longman.

McCutchen, D., Covill, A., Hoyne, S. H, & Mildes, K. (1994). Individual differences in writing: Implications of translating fluency. *Journal of Educational Psychology, 86,* 256–266.

McCutchen, D., Francis, M., & Kerr, S. (1997). Revising for meaning: Effects of knowledge and strategy. *Journal of Educational Psychology, 89,* 667–676.

McDonald, E. J., McCabe, K., Yeh, M., Lau, A., Garland, A., & Hough, R. L. (2005). Cultural affiliation and self-esteem as predictors of internalizing problems among Mexican American adolescents. *Journal of Clinical Child and Adolescent Psychology, 34,* 163–171.

McGee, L. M., & Richgels, D. J. (2004). *Literacy's beginnings* (4th ed). Boston: Allyn and Bacon.

McGee, R., Williams, S., & Feehan, M. (1992). Attention deficit disorder and age of onset of problem behaviors. *Journal of Abnormal Child Psychology, 20,* 487–502.

McGraw, M. B. (1935). *Growth: A study of Johnny and Jimmy.* East Norwalk, CT: Appleton-Century-Crofts.

McHale, J. P., Laurette, A., Talbot, J., & Pourquette, C. (2002). Retrospect and prospect in the psychological study of coparenting and family group process. In J. P. McHale & W. Grolnick (Eds.), *Retrospect and prospect in the psychological study of families* (pp. 127–165). Mahwah, NJ: Erlbaum.

McKown, C., & Weinstein, R. S. (2003). The development and consequences of stereotype consciousness in middle childhood. *Child Development, 74,* 498–515.

McKusick, V. A. (1995). *Mendelian inheritance in man: Catalogs of autosomal dominant, autosomal recessive, and X-linked phenotypes* (10th ed.). Baltimore: Johns Hopkins University Press.

McLanahan, S. (1999). Father absence and the welfare of children. In E. M. Hetherington (Ed.), *Coping with divorce, single parenting, and remarriage: A risk and resilience perspective* (pp. 117–145). Mahwah, NJ: Erlbaum.

McLellan, J. A., & Youniss, J. (2003). Two systems of youth service: Determinants of voluntary and required youth community service. *Journal of Youth and Adolescence, 32,* 47–58.

McManus, I. C., Sik, G., Cole, D. R., Kloss, J., Mellon, A. F., & Wong, J. (1988). The development of handedness in children. *British Journal of Developmental Psychology, 6,* 257–273.

Measelle, J. R., Aglow, J. C., Cowan, P. A., & Cowan, C. P. (1998). Assessing young children's views of their academic, social, and emotional lives: An evaluation of the self-perception scales of the Berkeley puppet interview. *Child Development, 69,* 1556–1576.

Meltzoff, A. N. (1995). Understanding the intentions of others: Re-enactment of intended acts by 18-month-old children. *Developmental Psychology, 31,* 838–850.

Mennella, J. A., & Beauchamp, G. K. (1996). The human infant's response to vanilla flavors in mother's milk and formula. *Infant Behavior and Development, 19,* 13–19.

Mennella, J., & Beauchamp, G. K. (1997). The ontogeny of human flavor perception. In G. K. Beauchamp & L. Bartoshuk (Eds.), *Tasting and smelling. Handbook of perception and cognition.* San Diego, CA: Academic Press.

Mennella, J. A., Jagnow, C. P., & Beauchamp, G. K. (2001). Prenatal and postnatal flavor learning by human infants. *Pediatrics, 107,* e88.

Messinger, D. S. (2002). Positive and negative: Infant facial expressions and emotions. *Current Directions in Psychological Science, 11,* 1–6.

Miceli, P. J., Whitman, T. L., Borkowsky, J. G., Braungart-Riekder, J., & Mitchell, D. W. (1998). Individual differences in infant information processing: The role of temperamental and maternal factors. *Infant Behavior and Development, 21,* 119–136.

Milberger, S., Biederman, J., Faraone, S. V., Guite, J., & Tsuang, M. T. (1997). Pregnancy, delivery and infancy complication, and attention deficit hyperactivity disorder: Issues of gene-environment interaction. *Biological Psychiatry, 41,* 65–75.

Miller, B. C., Benson, B., & Galbraith, K. A. (2001). Family relationships and adolescent pregnancy risk: A research synthesis. *Developmental Review, 21,* 1–38.

Miller, B. C., Fan, X., Christensen, M., Grotevant, H. D., & van Dulmen, M. (2000). Comparisons of adopted and nonadopted adolescents in a large, nationally representative sample. *Child Development, 71,* 1458–1473.

Miller, J. G., & Bersoff, D. M. (1992). Culture and moral judgment: How are conflicts between justice and interpersonal responsibilities resolved? *Journal of Personality and Social Psychology, 62,* 541–554.

Miller, K. F., Smith, C. M., Zhu, J., & Zhang, H. (1995). Preschool origins of cross-national differences in mathematical competence: The role of number-naming systems. *Psychological Science, 6,* 56–60.

Miller, P. A., Eisenberg, N., Fabes, R. A., & Shell, R. (1996). Relations of moral reasoning and vicarious emotion to young children's prosocial behavior toward peers and adults. *Developmental Psychology, 32,* 210–219.

Miller, P. M., Danaher, D. L., & Forbes, D. (1986). Sex-related strategies of coping with interpersonal conflict in children aged five to seven. *Developmental Psychology, 22,* 543–548.

Mills, C. M., & Keil, F. C. (2005). The development of cynicism. *Psychological Science, 16,* 385–390.

Minkler, M., & Fuller-Thomson, E. (2005). African American grandparents raising grandchildren: A national study using the Census 2000 American Community Survey. *Journals of Gerontology: Psychological Sciences and Social Sciences, 60B,* S82–S92.

Mischel, W. (1970). Sex-typing and socialization. In P. H. Mussen (Ed.), *Carmichaels' manual of child psychology* (Vol. 2). New York: Wiley.

Mischel, W., & Ebbesen, E. (1970). Attention in delay of gratification. *Journal of Personality and Social Psychology, 16,* 329–337.

Mischel, W., Cantor, N., & Feldman, S. (1996). Principles of self-regulation: The nature of willpower and self-control. In E. T. Higgins & A. W. Kruglanski (Eds.), *Social psychology: Handbook of basic principles* (pp. 329–360). New York: Guilford Press.

Mistry, R. S., Biesanz, J. C., Taylor, L. C., Burchinal, M., & Cox, M. J. (2004). Family income and its relation to preschool children's adjustment for families in the NICHD Study of Early Child Care. *Developmental Psychology, 40,* 727–745.

Mix, K. S., Huttenlocher, J., & Levine, S. C. (2002). Multiple cues for quantification in infancy: Is number one of them? *Psychological Bulletin, 128,* 278–294.

Mize, J., & Ladd, G. W. (1990). A cognitive social-learning approach to social skill training with low-status preschool children. *Developmental Psychology, 26,* 388–397.

Mize, J., & Pettit, G. S. (1997). Mothers' social coaching, mother-child relationship style, and children's peer competence: Is the medium the message? *Child Development, 68,* 312–332.

Mize, J., Pettit, G. S., & Brown, E. G. (1995). Mothers' supervision of their children's peer play: Relations with beliefs, perceptions, and knowledge. *Developmental Psychology, 31,* 311–321.

Mizes, J., Scott, P., & Tonya, M. (1995). Eating disorders. In M. Hersen & R. T. Ammerman (Eds.), *Handbook of prevention and treatment with children and adolescents: Intervention in the real world context.* New York: Wiley.

Moats, L. C., & Lyon, G. R. (1993). Learning disabilities in the United States: Advocacy, science, and the future of the field. *Journal of Learning Disabilities, 26,* 282–294.

Moffitt, T. E., Caspi, A., Belsky, J., & Silva, P. A. (1992). Childhood experience and the onset of menarche: A test of a sociobiological model. *Child Development, 63,* 47–58.

Molfese, D. L., & Burger-Judisch, L. M. (1991). Dynamic temporal-spatial allocation of resources in the human brain: An alternative to the static view of hemisphere differences. In F. L. Ketterle (Ed.), *Cerebral laterality: Theory and research. The Toledo symposium.* Hillsdale, NJ: Erlbaum.

Mondloch, C. J., Lewis, T. L., Budreau, D. R., Maurer, D., Dannemiller, J. L., et al. (1999). Face perception during infancy. *Psychological Science, 10,* 419–422.

Monk, C., Fifer, W. P., Myers, M. M., Sloan, R. P., Trien, L., & Hurtado, A. (2000). Maternal stress responses and anxiety during pregnancy: Effects on fetal heart rate. *Developmental Psychobiology, 36,* 67–77.

Montague, D. P., & Walker-Andrews, A. S. (2001). Peekaboo: A new look at infants' perception of emotion expressions. *Developmental Psychology, 37,* 826–838.

Moore, K. L., & Persaud, T. V. N. (1993). *Before we are born* (4th ed.). Philadelphia: W. B. Saunders.

Moore, M. R., & Brooks-Gunn, J. (2002). Adolescent parenthood. In M. H. Bornstein (Ed.), *Handbook of parenting: Vol. 3: Being and becoming a parent* (2nd ed., pp. 173–214). Mahwah, NJ: Erlbaum.

Morgan, B., & Gibson, K. R. (1991). Nutritional and environmental interactions in brain development. In K. R. Gibson & A. C. Peterson (Eds.), *Brain maturation and cognitive development: Comparative and cross-cultural perspectives.* New York: Aldine De Gruyter.

Morgane, P. J., Austin-LaFrance, R., Bronzino, J. D., Tonkiss, J., Diaz-Cintra, S., et al. (1993). Prenatal malnutrition and development of the brain. *Neuroscience and Biobehavioral Reviews, 17,* 91–128.

Morris, S. C., Taplin, J. E., & Gelman, S. A. (2000). Vitalism in naïve biological thinking. *Developmental Psychology, 36,* 582–595.

Mortimer, J. T., Finch, M. D., Rye, S., Shanahan, M. J., & Call, K. T. (1996). The effects of work intensity on adolescent mental health, achievement, and behavioral adjustment: New evidence from a prospective study. *Child Development, 67,* 1243–1261.

Mortimer, J. T., Harley, C., & Staff, J. (2002). The quality of work and youth mental health. *Work & Occupations, 29,* 166–197.

Mortimer, J. T., & Staff, J. (2004). Early work as a source of developmental discontinuity during the transition to adulthood. *Development and Psychopathology, 16,* 1047–1070.

Morton, J., & Johnson, M. H. (1991). CONSPEC and CONLERN: A two-process theory of infant face recognition. *Psychological Review, 98,* 164–181.

Moses, L. J., Baldwin, D. A., Rosicky, J. G., & Tidball, G. (2001). Evidence for referential understanding in the emotions domain at twelve and eighteen months. *Child Development, 72,* 718–735.

Moss, E., Rousseau, D., Parent, S., St-Laurent, D., & Saintonge, J. (1998). Correlates of attachment at school age: Maternal reported stress, mother-child interaction, and behavior problems. *Child Development, 69,* 1390–1405.

Mueller, M. M., & Elder, G. H. (2003). Family contingencies across the generations: Grandparent-grandchild relationships in holistic perspective. *Journal of Marriage and the Family, 65,* 404–417.

Mumme, D. L., Fernald, A., & Herrera, C. (1996). Infants' responses to facial and vocal emotional signals in a social referencing paradigm. *Child Development, 67,* 3219–3237.

Murphy, N., & Messer, D. (2000). Differential benefits from scaffolding and children working alone. *Educational Psychology, 20,* 17–31.

Mustanski, B. S., Viken, R. J., Kaprio, J., Pulkkinen, L., & Rose, R. J. (2004). Genetic and environmental influences on pubertal development: Longitudinal data from Finnish twins at ages 11 and 14. *Developmental Psychology, 40,* 1188–1198.

Muter, V., Hulme, C., Snowling, M. J., & Stevenson, J. (2004). Phonemes, rimes, vocabulary, and grammatical skills as foundations of early reading development: Evidence from a longitudinal study. *Developmental Psychology, 40,* 665–681.

Nadig, A. S., & Sedivy, J. C. (2002). Evidence of perspective-taking constraints in children's on-line reference resolution. *Psychological Science, 13,* 329–336.

Naigles, L. G., & Gelman, S. A. (1995). Overextensions in comprehension and production revisited: Preferential-looking in a study of dog, cat, and cow. *Journal of Child Language, 22,* 19–46.

Nation, K., Adams, J. W., Bowyer-Crane, C. A., & Snowling, M. J. (1999). Working memory deficits in poor comprehenders reflect underlying language impairments. *Journal of Experimental Child Psychology, 73,* 139–158.

National Center for Health Statistics. (1999). *Vital statistics of the United States, 1993: Vol. 1. Natality* (Centers for Disease Control Publication No. PHS 99–1100). Hyattsville, MD: Centers for Disease Control.

National High Blood Pressure Education Program Working Group on Hypertension Control in Children and Adolescents. (1996). Update on the 1987 task force report on high blood pressure in children and adolescents: A working group report from the National High Blood Pressure Education Program. *Pediatrics, 98,* 649–658.

National Institutes of Health. (2000). *To reduce SIDS risk, doctor's advice most important in choice of placing infants to sleep on their backs.* Washington, DC: Author.

Neisser, U., Boodoo, G., Bouchard, T. J., Boykin, A. W., Brody, N., Ceci, S. J., et al. (1996). Intelligence: Knowns and unknowns. *American Psychologist, 51,* 77–101.

Nelson, K. (1973). Structure and strategy in learning to talk. *Monographs of the Society for Research in Child Development, 38*(Serial No. 149).

Nelson, K. (1993). Explaining the emergence of autobiographical memory in early childhood. In A. F. Collins & S. E. Gathercole (Eds.), *Theories of memory.* Hove, England: Erlbaum.

Nelson, K. (2001). Language and the self: From the "Experiencing I" to the "Continuing Me." In C. Moore & K. Lemmon (Eds.), *The self in time: Developmental perspectives* (pp. 15–33). Mahwah, NJ: Erlbaum.

Nelson, K., & Fivush, R. (2004). The emergence of autobiographical memory: A social cultural developmental theory. *Psychological Review, 111,* 486–511.

Nesdale, D., & Flesser, D. (2001). Social identity and the development of children's group attitudes. *Child Development, 72,* 506–517.

Nesdale, D., Maass, A., Durkin, K., & Griffiths, J. (2005). Group norms, threat, and children's ethnic racial prejudice. *Child Development, 76,* 652–663.

Nevid, J. S., Rathus, S. A., & Greene, B. (2003). *Abnormal psychology in a changing world* (5th ed.). Upper Saddle River, NJ: Prentice-Hall.

Newcomb, A. F., & Bagwell, C. L. (1995). Children's friendship relations: A meta-analytic review. *Psychological Bulletin, 117,* 306–347.

Newport, E. L. (1991). Contrasting conceptions of the critical period for language. In S. Carey & R. Gelman (Eds.), *The epigenesis of mind: Essays on biology and cognition* (pp. 111–130). Hillsdale, NJ: Erlbaum.

NICHD Early Child Care Research Network. (1997). The effects of infant child care on infant-mother attachment security: Results of the NICHD Study of Early Child Care. *Child Development, 68,* 860–879.

NICHD Early Child Care Research Network. (2001). Child-care and family predictors of preschool attachment and stability from infancy. *Developmental Psychology, 37,* 847–862.

NICHD. (2004). *The NICHD Community Connection.* Author.

Nisbett, R. E. (2005). Heredity, environment, and race differences in IQ: A commentary on Rushton and Jensen (2005). *Psychology, Public Policy, and Law, 1,* 302–310.

Nolen-Hoeksema, S., & Girgus, J. S. (1994). The emergence of gender differences in depression during adolescence. *Psychological Bulletin, 115,* 424–443.

Nosek, B. A., Banaji, M. R., & Greenwald, A. G. (2002). Math = male, me = female, therefore math not = me. *Journal of Personality and Social Psychology, 83*, 44–59.

Notaro, P. C., Gelman, S. A., & Zimmerman, M. A. (2001). Children's understanding of psychogenic bodily reactions. *Child Development, 72*, 444–459.

Nucci, L., & Weber, E. (1995). Social interactions in the home and the development of young children's conception of the personal. *Child Development, 66*, 1438–1452.

Nuñez, J., Sr., & Yonas, A. (1994). Effects of luminance and texture motion on infant defensive reactions to optical collision. *Infant Behavior and Development, 17*, 165–174.

Nurmi, J., Poole, M. E., & Kalakoski, V. (1996). Age differences in adolescent identity exploration and commitment in urban and rural environments. *Journal of Adolescence, 19*, 443–452.

Oakhill, J. V., & Cain, K. E. (2004). The development of comprehension skills. In T. Nunes & P. E. Bryant (Eds.), *Handbook of children's literacy* (pp. 155–180). Dordrecht: Kluwer Academic Publishers.

Oates, C., Blades, M., & Gunter, B. (2002). Children and television advertising: When do they understand persuasive intent? *Journal of Consumer Behaviour, 1*, 238–245.

Ochs, E. (1988). *Culture and language development.* Cambridge: Cambridge University Press.

O'Conner, T., Heron, J., Golding, J., Beveridge, M., & Glover, V. (2002). Maternal antenatal anxiety and children's behavioural/emotional problems at 4 years. *British Journal of Psychiatry, 180*, 502–508.

O'Donnell Eisbach, A. (2004). Children's developing awareness of diversity in people's trains of thought. *Child Development, 75*, 1694–1707.

Offer, D., Ostrov, E., Howard, K. I., & Atkinson, R. (1988). *The teenage world: Adolescents' self-image in ten countries.* New York: Plenum.

Okagaki, L., & Frensch, P. A. (1994). Effects of video game playing on measures of spatial performance: Gender effects in late adolescence. *Journal of Applied Developmental Psychology, 15*, 33–58.

Okagaki, L., & Sternberg, R. J. (1993). Parental beliefs and children's school performance. *Child Development, 64*, 36–56.

Okie, S. (2000, April 12). Over the tiniest patients, big ethical questions: Fetal surgery's growing reach raises issues of need and risks. *Washington Post*, pp. A1, A16.

Oliner, S. P., & Oliner, P. M. (1988). *The altruistic personality: Rescuers of Jews in Nazi Europe.* New York: Free Press.

Olsen, O. (1997). Meta-analysis of the safety of home birth. *Birth—Issues in Perinatal Care, 24*, 4–13.

Olson, S. L., Bates, J. E., Sandy, J. M., & Lanthier, R. (2000). Early developmental precursors of externalizing behavior in middle childhood and adolescence. *Journal of Abnormal Child Psychology, 28*, 119–133.

Olson, S. L., Sameroff, A. J., Kerr, D. C. R., Lopez, N. L., & Wellman, H. M. (2005). Developmental foundations of externalizing problems in young children: The role of effortful control. *Development and Psychopathology, 17*, 25–45.

Olweus, D. (1978). *Aggression in the schools: Bullies and whipping boys.* Washington, DC: Hemisphere.

Olweus, D. (1994). Bullying at school: Basic facts and effects of school based intervention program. *Journal of Child Psychology and Psychiatry, 35*, 1171–1190.

Olweus, D., Mattson, A., Schalling, D., & Low, H. (1988). Circulating testosterone levels and aggression in adolescent males: A causal analysis. *Psychosomatic Medicine, 50*, 261–272.

O'Moore, M., & Kirkham, C. (2001). Self-esteem and its relationship to bullying behavior. *Aggressive Behavior, 27*, 269–283.

O'Neill, D. K. (1996). Two-year-old children's sensitivity to a parent's knowledge state when making requests. *Child Development, 67*, 659–677.

Opfer, J. E., & Siegler, R. S. (2004). Revisiting preschoolers' living things concept: A microgenetic analysis of conceptual change in basic biology. *Cognitive Psychology, 49*, 301–332.

Paarlberg, K. M., Vingerhoets, A. J. J. M., Passchier, J., Dekker, G. A., et al. (1995). Psychosocial factors and pregnancy outcome: A review with emphasis on methodological issues. *Journal of Psychosomatic Research, 39*, 563–595.

Padilla, A. M., Lindholm, K. J., Chen, A., Duran, R., Hakuta, K., Lambert, W., et al. (1991). The English-only movement. Myths, reality, and implications for psychology. *American Psychologist, 46*, 120–130.

Parault, S. J., & Schwanenflugel, P. J. (2000). The development of conceptual categories of attention during the elementary school years. *Journal of Experimental Child Psychology, 75*, 245–262.

Parazzini, F., Luchini, L., La Vecchia, C., & Crosignani, P. G. (1993). Video display terminal use during pregnancy and reproductive outcome—A meta-analysis. *Journal of Epidemiology and Community Health, 47*, 265–268.

Parcel, G. S., Simons-Morton, B. G., O'Hara, N. M., Baranowski, T., Kolbe, L. J., & Bee, D. E. (1989). School promotion of healthful diet and exercise behavior: An integration of organizational change and social learning theory interventions. *Journal of School Health, 57*, 150–156.

Parke, R. D. (1977). Punishment in children: Effects, side effects and alternative strategies. In H. L. Hom, Jr. & A. Robinson (Eds.), *Psychological processes in early education.* New York: Academic.

Parke, R. D. (2002). Fathers and families. In M. H. Bornstein (Ed.), *Handbook of parenting; Vol. 3. Being and becoming a parent* (pp. 27–73). Mahwah, NJ: Erlbaum.

Parke, R. D. (2004). The Society for Research in Child Development at 70: Progress and Promise. *Child Development, 75*, 1–24.

Parke, R. D., & Buriel, R. (1998). Socialization in the family: Ethnic and ecological perspectives. In W. Damon (Ed.), *Handbook of child psychology* (Vol. 3). New York: Wiley.

Parke, R. D., Coltrane, S., Duffy, S., Buriel, R., Dennis, J., Powers, J., et al. (2004). Economic stress, parenting, and child adjustment in Mexican American and European American families. *Child Development, 75*, 1632–1656.

Parke, R. D., & O'Neil, R. (2000). The influence of significant others on learning about relationships: From family to friends. In R. S. L. Mills & S. Duck (Eds.), *The developmental psychology of personal relationships* (pp. 15–47). New York: Wiley.

Parker, J. G., & Seal, J. (1996). Forming, losing, renewing, and replacing friendships: Applying temporal parameters to the assessment of children's friendship experiences. *Child Development, 67*, 2248–2268.

Parritz, R. H. (1996). A descriptive analysis of toddler coping in challenging circumstances. *Infant Behavior and Development, 19*, 171–180.

Parten, M. (1932). Social participation among preschool children. *Journal of Abnormal and Social Psychology, 27*, 243–269.

Pascalis, O., de Hann, M., & Nelson, C. A. (2002). Is face processing species-specific during the first year of life? *Science, 296*, 1321–1323.

Passarotti, A. M., Paul, B. M., Bussiere, J. R., Buxton, R. B., Wong, E. C., & Stiles, J. (2003). The development of face and location processing: an fMRI study. *Developmental Science, 6*, 100–117.

Patterson, C. J. (1992). Children of lesbian and gay parents. *Child Development, 63*, 1025–1042.

Patterson, C. J. (2002). Lesbian and gay parenthood. In M. H. Bornstein (Ed.), *Handbook of parenting: Vol. 3. Status and social conditions of parenting* (2nd ed., pp. 317–338). Mahwah, NJ: Erlbaum.

Patterson, C. J. (2004). Gay fathers. In M. E. Lamb (Ed.), *The role of the father in child development* (pp. 397–416). New York: Wiley.

Patterson, G. R. (1980). Mothers: The unacknowledged victims. *Monographs of the Society for Research in Child Development, 45*(5, Serial No. 186).

Patterson, G. R. (2002). The early development of coercive family processes. In J. B. Reid, G. R. Patterson, & J. Snyder (Eds.), *Systems and development: The Minnesota symposium on child psychology,* (Vol. 22, pp. 167–209). Hillsdale NJ: Erlbaum.

Patterson, M., & Werker, J. F. (2003). Two-month-old infants match phonetic information in lips and voice. *Developmental Science, 6*, 191–196.

Peake, P. K., Hebl, M., & Mischel, W. (2002). Strategic attention deployment for delay of gratification in working and waiting situations. *Developmental Psychology, 38*, 313–326.

Pearlman, M., & Ross, H. S. (1997). The benefits of parent intervention in children's disputes: An examination of concurrent changes in children's fighting styles. *Child Development, 68*, 690–700.

Pearson, J. L., Hunter, A. G., Ensminger, M. E., & Kellam, S. G. (1990). Black grandmothers in multigenerational households: Diversity in family structure and parenting involvement in the Woodlawn community. *Child Development, 61*, 434–442.

Pederson, D. R., Gleason, K. E., Moran, G., & Bento, S. (1998). Maternal attachment representations, maternal sensitivity, and the infant-mother attachment relationship. *Developmental Psychology, 34*, 925–933.

Pellegrini, A. D. (2004). Rough-and-tumble play from childhood through adolescence: Development and possible functions. In P. K. Smith & C. H. Hart (Eds.), *Blackwell handbook of childhood social development* (pp. 438–453). Malden, MA: Blackwell.

Pelphrey, K. A., Reznick, J. S., Davis Goldman, B., Sasson, N., Morrow, J., Donahoe, A., et al. (2004). Development of visuospatial memory in the second half of the first year. *Developmental Psychology, 40*, 836–851.

Pennington, B. F., Groisser, D., & Welsh, M. C. (1993). Contrasting cognitive deficits in attention deficit hyperactivity disorder versus reading disability. *Developmental Psychology, 29*, 511–523.

Pennington, B. F., Willcutt, E., & Rhee, S. H. (2005). Analyzing comorbidity. In R. V. Kail (Ed.), *Advances in child development and behavior* (Vol. 33, pp. 263–304). San Diego, CA: Elsevier.

Pennisi, E. (2005). Why do humans have so few genes? *Science, 309*, 80.

Pepler, D. J., Craig, W., & Roberts, W. L. (1998). Observations of aggressive and nonaggressive children on the school playground. *Merrill-Palmer Quarterly, 44*, 55–76.

Perfetti, C. A., & Curtis, M. E. (1986). Reading. In R. F. Dillon & R. J. Sternberg (Eds.), *Cognition and instruction.* Orlando, FL: Academic Press.

Perry, M. (2000). Explanations of mathematical concepts in Japanese, Chinese, and U.S. first- and fifth-grade classrooms. *Cognition & Instruction, 18*, 181–207.

Peterson, C. (1996). *The psychology of abnormality.* Fort Worth TX: Harcourt Brace.

Peterson, C., & Rideout, R. (1998). Memory for medical emergencies experienced by 1- and 2-year-olds. *Developmental Psychology, 34*, 1059–1072.

Peterson, C., & Slaughter, V. (2003). Opening windows into the mind: Mothers' preferences for mental state explanations and children's theory of mind. *Cognitive Development, 18*, 399–429.

Peterson, L. (1983). Role of donor competence, donor age, and peer presence on helping in an emergency. *Developmental Psychology, 19*, 873–880.

Petrie, R. H. (1991). Intrapartum fetal evaluation. In S. G. Gabbe, J. R. Niebyl, & J. L. Simpson (Eds.), *Obstetrics: Normal & problem pregnancies* (2nd ed.). New York: Churchill Livingstone.

Pettit, G. S., Bates, J. E., & Dodge, K. A. (1997). Supportive parenting, ecological context, and children's adjustment: A seven-year longitudinal study. *Child Development, 68*, 908–923.

Pettit, G. S., Laird, R. D., Dodge, K. A., Bates, J. E., & Criss, M. N. (2001). Antecedents and behavior problem outcomes of parental monitoring and psychological control in early adolescence. *Child Development, 72*, 283–598.

Phillips-Silver, J., & Trainor, L. J. (2005). Feeling the beat: Movement influences infant rhythm perception. *Science, 308*, 1430.

Phinney, J. (1989). Stage of ethnic identity in minority group adolescents. *Journal of Early Adolescence, 9*, 34–49.

Phinney, J. (1990). Ethnic identity in adolescents and adults. *Psychological Bulletin, 108*, 499–514.

Phinney, J. S. (2005). Ethnic identity development in minority adolescents. In C. B. Fisher & R. M. Lerner (Eds.), *Encyclopedia of applied developmental science* (Vol. 1, pp. 420–423). Thousand Oaks, CA: Sage.

Phinney, J. S., & Chavira, V. (1992). Ethnic identity and self-esteem: An exploratory longitudinal study. *Journal of Adolescence, 15*, 271–281.

Phinney, J. S., Ong, A., & Madden, T. (2000). Cultural values and intergenerational value discrepancies in immigrant and non-immigrant families. *Child Development, 71*, 528–539.

Piaget, J., & Inhelder, B. (1956). *The child's conception of space*. Boston: Routledge & Kegan Paul.

Pierce, S. H., & Lange, G. (2000). Relationships among metamemory, motivation, and memory performance in young school-age children. *British Journal of Developmental Psychology, 18*, 121–135.

Pinker, S. (1989). *Learnability and cognition: The acquisition of argument structure*. Cambridge, MA: MIT Press.

Pinquart, M. (2005). Self-concept. In C. B. Fisher & R. M. Lerner (Eds.), *Encyclopedia of applied developmental science* (Vol. 2, pp. 971–972). Thousand Oaks, CA: Sage.

Plomin, R., & Crabbe, J. (2000). DNA. *Psychological Bulletin, 126*, 806–828.

Plomin, R., DeFries, J. C., & McClearn, G. E. (1990). *Behavioral genetics: A primer* (2nd ed.). New York: Freeman.

Plomin, R., DeFries, J. C., McClearn, G. E., & McGuffin, P. (2001). *Behavioral genetics* (4th ed.). New York: Freeman.

Plomin, R., & Petrill, S. A. (1997). Genetics and intelligence: What's new? *Intelligence, 24*, 53–77.

Plomin, R., & Spinath, F. (2004). Intelligence: Genes, genetics, and genomics. *Journal of Personality and Social Psychology, 86*, 112–129.

Pollitt, E. (1994). Poverty and child development: Relevance of research in developing countries to the United States. *Child Development, 65*, 283–295.

Poole, D. A., & Lamb, M. E. (1998). *Investigative interviews of children: A guide for helping professionals*. Washington, DC: American Psychological Association.

Poole, D. A., & Lindsay, D. S. (1995). Interviewing preschoolers: Effects of nonsuggestive techniques, parental coaching, and leading questions on reports of nonexperienced events. *Journal of Experimental Child Psychology, 60*, 129–154.

Porter, R. H., & Winberg, J. (1999). Unique salience of maternal breast odors for newborn infants. *Neuroscience & Biobehavioral Reviews, 23*, 439–449.

Poulin, F., & Boivin, M. (2000). The role of proactive and reactive aggression in the formation and development of boys' friendships. *Developmental Psychology, 36*, 233–240.

Poulin-Dubois, D., & Forbes, J. N. (2002). Toddlers' attention to intentions-in-action in learning novel action words. *Developmental Psychology, 38*, 104–114.

Poulson, C. L., Kymissis, E., Reeve, K. F., Andreatos, M., & Reeve, L. (1991). Generalized vocal imitation in infants. *Journal of Experimental Child Psychology, 51*, 267–279.

Power, F. C., Higgins, A., & Kohlberg, L. (1989). *Lawrence Kohlberg's approach to moral education*. New York: Columbia University Press.

Powlishta, K., Serbin, L. A., Doyle, A., & White, D. R. (1994). Gender, ethnic, and body type biases: The generality of prejudice in childhood. *Developmental Psychology, 30*, 526–536.

Priel, B., & deSchonen, S. (1986). Self-recognition: A study of a population without mirrors. *Journal of Experimental Child Psychology, 41*, 237–250.

Principe, G. F., & Ceci, S. J. (2002). I saw it with my own ears: The effects of peer conversations on preschoolers' reports of nonexperienced events. *Journal of Experimental Child Psychology, 83*, 1–25.

Prinstein, M. J., & Cillessen, A. H. N. (2003). Forms and functions of adolescent peer aggression associated with high levels of peer status. *Merrill Palmer Quarterly, 49*, 310–342.

Project Zero. (1999). *Project SUMIT: Schools Using Multiple Intelligence Theory*. Retrieved from the World Wide Web: http://pzweb.harvard.edu/SUMIT/OUTCOMES.HTM

Puhl, R. M., & Brownell, K. D. (2005). Bulimia nervosa. In C. B. Fisher & R. M. Lerner (Eds.), *Encyclopedia of applied developmental science* (Vol. 1, pp. 192–195). Thousand Oaks, CA: Sage

Quas, J. A., Goodman, G. S., Bidrose, S., Pipe, M., Craw, S., & Ablin, D. S. (1999). Emotion and memory: Children's long-term remembering, forgetting, and suggestibility. *Journal of Experimental Child Psychology, 72*, 235–270.

Quillian, L., & Campbell, M. E. (2003). Beyond black and white: The present and future of multiracial friendship segregation. *American Sociological Review, 68*, 540–566.

Quinn, P. H. (2004). Development of subordinate-level categorization in 3- to 7-month-old infants. *Child Development, 75*, 886–899.

Raine, A., Moffitt, T. E., Caspi, A., Loeber, R., Stouthamer-Loeber, M., & Lynam, D. (2005). Neurocognitive impairments in boys on the life-course persistent antisocial path. *Journal of Abnormal Psychology, 114*, 38–49.

Rakic, P. (1995). Corticogenesis in human and nonhuman primates. In M. S. Gazzaniga (Ed.), *The cognitive neurosciences*. Cambridge, MA: MIT Press.

Rakison, D. H., & Hahn, E. R. (2004). The mechanisms of early categorization and induction: Smart or dumb infants? *Advances in Child Development and Behavior, 32*, 281–322.

Rakison, D. H., & Poulin-Dubois, D. (2001). Developmental origin of the animate-inanimate distinction. *Psychological Bulletin, 127*, 209–228.

Rakoczy, H., Tomasello, M., & Striano, T. (2004). Young children know that trying is not pretending: A test of the "behaving-as-if" construal of children's early concept of pretense. *Developmental Psychology, 40*, 388–399.

Raman, L., & Gelman, S. A. (2005). Children's understanding of the transmission of genetic disorders and contagious illnesses. *Developmental Psychology, 41*, 171–182.

Ramey, C. T., & Campbell, F. A. (1991). Poverty, early childhood education, and academic competence: The Abecedarian experiment. In A. Huston (Ed.), *Children reared in poverty*. New York: Cambridge University Press.

Ransjoe-Arvidson, A. B., Matthiesen, A. S., Lilja, G., Nissen, E., Widstroem, A. M., & Uvnaes-Moberg, K. (2001). Maternal analgesia during labor disturbs newborn behavior: Effects on breastfeeding, temperature, and crying. *Birth-Issues in Perinatal Care, 28*, 5–12.

Rapport, M. D. (1995). Attention-deficit hyperactivity disorder. In M. Hersen & R. T. Ammerman (Eds.), *Advanced abnormal child psychology*. Hillsdale, NJ: Erlbaum.

Rathunde, K. R., & Csikszentmihalyi, M. (1993). Undivided interest and the growth of talent: A longitudinal study of adolescents. *Journal of Youth and Adolescence, 22*, 385–405.

Rayner, K., Foorman, B. R., Perfetti, C. A. Pesetsky, D., & Seidenberg, M. S. (2001). How psychological science informs the teaching of reading. *Psychological Science in the Public Interest, 2*, 31–75.

Rayner, K., Foorman, B. R., Perfetti, C. A., Pesetsky, D., & Seidenberg, M. S. (2002). How should reading be taught? *Scientific American, 286*, 85–91.

Reese, E., & Cox, A. (1999). Quality of adult book reading affects children's emergent literacy. *Developmental Psychology, 35*, 20–28.

Reich, P. A. (1986). *Language development*. Englewood Cliffs, NJ: Prentice-Hall.

Reid, D. H., Wilson, P. G., & Faw, G. D. (1991). Teaching self-help skills. In J. L. Matson & J. A. Mulick (Eds.), *Handbook of mental retardation* (2nd ed.). New York: Pergamon.

Reimer, M. S. (1996). "Sinking into the ground": The development and consequences of shame in adolescence. *Developmental Review, 16*, 321–363.

Repacholi, B. M. (1998). Infants' use of attentional cues to identify the referent of another person's emotional expression. *Developmental Psychology, 34*, 1017–1025.

Reynolds, A. J., & Robertson, D. L. (2003). School-based early intervention and later child maltreatment in the Chicago Longitudinal Study. *Child Development, 74*, 3–26.

Ricciardelli, L. A., & McCabe, M. P. (2004). A biopsychosocial model of disordered eating and the pursuit of muscularity in adolescent boys. *Psychological Bulletin, 130*, 179–205.

Rice, M. L., Huston, A. C., Truglio, R., & Wright, J. (1990). Words from "Sesame Street": Learning vocabulary while viewing. *Developmental Psychology, 26*, 421–428.

Richards, J. E., & Anderson, D. R. (2004). Attentional intertia in children's extended looking at television. In R. V. Kail (Ed.), *Advances in child development and behavior* (Vol. 32, pp. 65–212). San Diego, CA: Elsevier.

Richters, J. E., Arnold, L. E., Jensen, P. S., Abikoff, H., Conners, C. K., & Greenhill, L. L., et al. (1995). NIMH collaborative multisite multimodal treatment study of children with ADHD: I. Background and rationale. *Journal of the American Academy of Child and Adolescent Psychiatry, 34*, 987–1000.

Roberts, D. F., Foehr, U. G., & Rideout, V. (2005). *Generation M: Media in the lives of 8–18 year olds*. Menlo Park, CA: Henry J. Kaiser Family Foundation.

Roberts, J. E., Burchinal, M., & Durham, M. (1999). Parents' report of vocabulary and grammatical development of African American preschoolers: Child and environmental associations. *Child Development, 70*, 92–106.

Roberts, R. E., Phinney, J. S., Masse, L. C., Chen, Y. R., Roberts, C. R., & Romero, A. (1999). The structure of ethnic identity of young adolescents from diverse ethnocultural groups. *Journal of Early Adolescence, 19*, 301–322.

Robinson, A., & Clinkenbeard, P. R. (1998). Giftedness: An exceptionality examined. *Annual Review of Psychology, 49*, 117–139.

Robinson, E. J., Champion, H., & Mitchell, P. (1999). Children's ability to infer utterance veracity from speaker informedness. *Developmental Psychology, 35*, 535–546.

Rochat, P. (2001). Origins of self-concept. In G. Bremmer & A. Fogel (Eds.), *Blackwell handbook of infant development* (pp. 191–212). Malden, MA: Blackwell.

Roebers, C. M., & Schneider, W. (2005). The strategic regulation of children's memory performance and suggestibility. *Journal of Experimental Child Psychology, 91*, 24–44.

Roffwarg, H. P., Muzio, J. N., & Dement, W. C. (1966). Ontogenetic development of the human sleep-dream cycle. *Science, 152*, 604–619.

Rogoff, B. (1998). Cognition as a collaborative process. In W. Damon (Ed.), *Handbook of child psychology* (5th ed., Vol. 2, pp. 679–744). New York: Wiley.

Rogoff, B. (2003). The *cultural nature of human development.* New York: Oxford University Press.

Rogoff, B., Mistry, J., Goncu, A., & Mosier, C. (1993). Guided participation in cultural activity by toddlers and caregivers. *Monographs of the Society for Research in Child Development, 58*(Serial No. 236).

Roschelle, J. M., Pea, R. D., Hoadley, C. M., Gordin, D. N., & Means, B. M. (2000). Changing how and what children learn in school with computer-based technologies. *Future of Children, 10,* 76–101.

Rose, A. J., & Asher, S. R. (1999). Children's goals and strategies in response to conflicts within a friendship. *Developmental Psychology, 35,* 69–79.

Rose, A. J., Swenson, L. P., & Waller, E. M. (2004). Overt and relational aggression and perceived popularity: Developmental differences in concurrent and prospective relations. *Developmental Psychology, 40,* 378–387.

Rose, S. A., Feldman, J. F., Futterweit, L. R., & Jankowski, J. J. (1997). Continuity in visual recognition memory: Infancy to 11 years. *Intelligence, 24,* 381–392.

Rosengren, K. S., Gelman, S. A., Kalish, C., & McCormick, M. (1991). As time goes by: Children's early understanding of growth in animals. *Child Development, 62,* 1302–1320.

Rosenthal, D. A., & Feldman, S. S. (1992). The relationship between parenting behaviour and ethnic identity in Chinese-American and Chinese-Australian adolescents. *International Journal of Psychology, 27,* 19–31.

Rosenthal, R., Rosnow, R. L., & Rubin, D. B. (2000). *Contrasts and effect sizes in behavioral research: A correlational approach.* Cambridge, U.K.: Cambridge University Press.

Rostenstein, D., & Oster, H. (1997). Differential facial responses to four basic tastes in newborns. In P. Ekman & E. L. Rosenberg (Eds.), *What the face reveals: Basic and applied studies of spontaneous expression using the Facial Action Coding System (FACS).* New York: Oxford University Press.

Rotenberg, K. J., & Mayer, E. V. (1990). Delay of gratification in native and white children: A cross-cultural comparison. *International Journal of Behavioral Development, 13,* 23–30.

Rothbart, M. K. (2004).Temperament and the pursuit of an integrated developmental psychology. *Merrill-Palmer Quarterly, 50,* 492–505.

Rothbart, M. K., & Hwang, J. (2005). Temperament and the development of competence and motivation. In A. J. Elliot & C. S. Dweck (Eds.), *Handbook of competence and motivation* (pp. 167–184). New York: Guilford.

Rothbart, M. K., & Rueda, M. R. (2005). The development of effortful control. In U. Mayr, E. Awh, & S. W. Keele (Eds.), *Developing individuality in the human brain: A tribute to Michael I. Posner* (pp. 167–188). Washington DC: American Psychological Association.

Rothbaum, F., Weisz, J., Pott, M., Miyake, K., & Morelli, G. (2000). Attachment and culture: Security in the United States and Japan. *American Psychologist, 55,* 1093–1104.

Rotherman-Borus, M. J., & Langabeer, K. A. (2001). Developmental trajectories of gay, lesbian, and bisexual youths. In A. R. D'Augelli & C. Patterson (Eds.), *Lesbian, gay, and bisexual identities among youth: Psychological perspectives* (pp. 97–128). New York: Oxford University Press.

Rovee-Collier, C. (1987). Learning and memory in infancy. In J. D. Osofsky (Ed.), *Handbook of infant development* (2nd ed.). New York: Wiley.

Rovee-Collier, C. (1997). Dissociations in infant memory: Rethinking the development of implicit and explicit memory. *Psychological Review, 104,* 467–498.

Rovee-Collier, C. (1999). The development of infant memory. *Current Directions in Psychological Science, 8,* 80–85.

Rovee-Collier, C. (2000). Memory in infancy and early childhood. In E. Tulving & F. I. M. Craik (Eds.), *The Oxford handbook of memory.* New York: Oxford University Press.

Rubin, K., Bukowski, W., & Parker, J. (2006). Peer interaction and social competence. In W. Damon & R. M. Lerner (Eds.), *Handbook of child psychology* (6th ed, Vol. 3.). New York: Wiley.

Rubinsten, O., Henik, A., Berger, A., & Shahar-Shalev, S. (2002). The development of internal representations of magnitude and their association with Arabic numerals. *Journal of Experimental Child Psychology, 81,* 74–92.

Ruble, D. N., Boggiano, A. D., Feldman, N. S., & Loebl, N. H. (1980). Developmental analysis of the role of social comparison in self-evaluation. *Developmental Psychology, 16,* 105–115.

Ruble, D. N., & Martin, C. L. (1998). Gender development. In W. Damon (Ed.), *Handbook of child psychology: Vol. 3. Social, emotional, and personality development* (5th ed., pp. 933–1016). New York: Wiley.

Rudolph, K. D., Caldwell, M. S., & Conley, C. S. (2005). Need for approval and children's well-being. *Child Development, 76,* 309–323.

Ruff, H. A., & Capozzoli, M. C. (2003). Development of attention and distractibility in the first 4 years of life. *Developmental Psychology, 39,* 877–890.

Ruffman, T., Perner, J., & Parkin, L. (1999). How parenting style affects false belief understanding. *Social Development, 8,* 395–411.

Ruffman, T., Slade, L., & Crowe, E. (2002). The relation between children's and mothers' mental state language and theory-of-mind understanding. *Child Development, 73,* 734–751.

Rushton, J. P., & Bonds, T. A. (2005). Mate choice and friendship in twins. *Psychological Science, 16,* 555–559.

Russell, A., & Finnie, V. (1990). Preschool children's social status and maternal instructions to assist group entry. *Developmental Psychology, 26,* 603–611.

Rutland, A., Cameron, L., Milne, A., & McGregor, P. (2005). Social norms and self-presentation. Children's implicit and explicit intergroup attitudes. *Child Development, 76,* 451–466.

Rymer, R. (1993). *Genie.* New York: HarperCollins.

Sadeh, A., Gruber, R., & Raviv, A. (2002). Sleep, neurobehavioral functioning, and behavior problems in school-age children. *Child Development, 73,* 405–417.

Sadeh, A., Raviv, A., & Gruber, R. (2000). Sleep patterns and sleep disruptions in school-age children. *Developmental Psychology, 36,* 291–301.

Saffran, J. R., Aslin, R. N., & Newport, E. L. (1996). Statistical learning by 8-month-old infants. *Science, 274,* 1926–1928.

Sagi, A., Koren-Karie, N., Gini, M., Ziv, Y., & Joels, T. (2002). Shedding further light on the effects of various types and quality of early child care on infant-mother attachment relationship: The Haifa study of early child care. *Child Development, 73,* 1166–1186.

Sagi, A., van IJzendoorn, M. H., Aviezer, O., Donnell, F., & Mayseless, O. (1994). Sleeping out of home in a kibbutz communal arrangement: It makes a difference for infant-mother attachment. *Child Development, 65,* 992–1004.

Sandler, I. N., Tein, J.-Y., Mehta, P., Wolchik, S., & Ayers, T. (2000). Coping efficacy and psychological problems of children of divorce. *Child Development, 71,* 1099–1118.

Sarampote, N. C., Bassett, H. H., & Winsler, A. (2004). After-school care: Child outcomes and recommendations for research and policy. *Child & Youth Care Forum, 33,* 329–348.

Savage-Rumbaugh, E. S., Murphy, J., Sevcik, R. A., Brakke, K. E., Williams, S. L., & Rumbaugh, D. M. (1993). Language comprehension in ape and child. *Monographs of the Society for Research in Child Development, 58*(34, Serial No. 233).

Saxe, G. B. (1988). Candy selling and math learning. *Educational Researcher, 17,* 14–21.

Scarr, S. (1992). Developmental theories for the 1990s: Development and individual differences. *Child Development, 63,* 1–19.

Scarr, S., & McCartney, K. (1983). How people make their own environments: A theory of genotype-environment effects. *Child Development, 54,* 424–435.

Schaal, B. Soussignan, R., & Marlier, L. (2002). Olfactory cognition at the start of life: The perinatal shaping of selective odor responsiveness. In C. Rouby et al., (Eds.), *Olfaction, taste, and cognition* (pp. 421–440). Cambridge, UK: Cambridge University Press.

Schauble, L. (1996). The development of scientific reasoning in knowledge-rich contexts. *Developmental Psychology, 32,* 102–119.

Schmidt, F. L., & Hunter, J. E. (1998). The validity and utility of selection methods in personnel psychology: Practical and theoretical implications of 85 years of research findings. *Psychological Bulletin, 124,* 262–274.

Schneider, B. H., Atkinson, L., & Tardif, C. (2001). Child-parent attachment and children's peer relations: A quantitative review. *Developmental Psychology, 37,* 86–100.

Schneider, W., & Bjorklund, D. F. (1998). Memory. In W. Damon (Ed.), *Handbook of child psychology* (Vol. 2). New York: Wiley.

Schnorr, T. M., Grajewski, B. A., Hornung, R. W., Thun, M. J., Egeland, G. M., Murray, W. E., et al. (1991). Video display terminals and the risk of spontaneous abortion. *New England Journal of Medicine, 324,* 727–733.

Schwartz, C. E., Wright, C. I., Shin, L. M., Kagan, J., & Rauch, S. L. (2003). Inhibited and uninhibited infants "grown up": Adult amygdalar response to novelty. *Science, 300,* 1952–1953.

Schwartz, D., Dodge, K. A., Pettit, G. S., & Bates, J. E. (1997). The early socialization of aggressive victims of bullying. *Child Development, 68,* 665–675.

Schwartz, D., Chang, L., & Farver, J. M. (2001). Correlates of victimization in Chinese children's peer groups. *Developmental Psychology, 37,* 520–532.

Schwartz, D., Dodge, K. A., Pettit, G. S., Bates, J. E., & The Conduct Problems Prevention Research Group. (2000). Friendship as a moderating factor in the pathway between early harsh home environment and later victimization in the peer group. *Developmental Psychology, 36,* 646–662.

Scott, W. A., Scott, R., & McCabe, M. (1991). Family relationships and children's personality: A cross-cultural, cross-source comparison. *British Journal of Social Psychology, 30,* 1–20.

Sears, R. R. (1975). Your ancients revisited: A history of child development. In E. M. Hetherington (Ed.), *Review of child development research* (Vol. 5, pp. 1–73). Chicago: University of Chicago Press.

Secada, W. G., Fennema, E., & Adajian, L. B. (Eds.). (1995). *New directions for equity in mathematics education.* New York: Cambridge University Press.

Segrin, C., Taylor, M. E., & Altman, J. (2005). Social cognitive mediators and relational outcomes associated with parental divorce. *Journal of Social and Personal Relationships, 22,* 361–377.

Seifer, R., Schiller, M., Sameroff, A. J., Resnick, S., & Riordan, K. (1996). Attachment, maternal sensitivity, and infant temperament during the first year of life. *Developmental Psychology, 32,* 12–25.

Selman, R. L. (1980). *The growth of interpersonal understanding: Developmental and clinical analyses.* New York: Academic Press.

Selman, R. L. (1981). The child as a friendship philosopher: A case study in the growth of interpersonal understanding. In S. R. Asher & J. M. Gottman (Eds.), *The development of children's friendships.* Cambridge, England: Cambridge University Press.

Selman, R. L., & Byrne, D F. (1974). A structural-developmental analysis of levels of role-taking in middle childhood. *Child Development, 45,* 803–806.

Sénéchal, M., & LeFevre, J. (2002). Parental involvement in the development of children's reading skill: A five-year longitudinal study. *Child Development, 73,* 445–460.

Sénéchal, M., Thomas, E., & Monker, J. (1995). Individual differences in 4-year-old children's acquisition of vocabulary during storybook reading. *Journal of Educational Psychology, 87,* 218–229.

Serbin, L., & Karp, J. (2003). Intergenerational studies of parenting and the transfer of risk from parent to child. *Current Directions in Psychological Science, 12,* 138–142.

Serbin, L. A., Poulin-Dubois, D., Colburne, K. A., Sen, M. G., & Eichstedt, J. A. (2001). Gender stereotyping in infancy: Visual preferences for and knowledge of gender-stereotyped toys in the second year. *International Journal of Behavioral Development, 25,* 7–15.

Serbin, L. A., Powlishta, K. K., & Gulko, J. (1993). The development of sex typing in middle childhood. *Monographs of the Society for Research in Child Development, 58*(Serial No. 232).

Serdula, M. K., Ivery, D., Coates, R. J., Freedman, D. S., Williamson, D. F., & Byers, T. (1993). Do obese children become obese adults? A review of the literature. *Preventive Medicine, 22,* 167–177.

Seyfarth, R., & Cheney, D. (1996). Inside the mind of a monkey. In M. Bekoff & D. Jamieson (Eds.), *Readings in animal cognition.* Cambridge, MA: MIT Press.

Shanahan, M. J., Elder, G. H., Burchinal, M., & Conger, R. D. (1996a). Adolescent earnings and relationships with parents: The work-family nexus in urban and rural ecologies. In J. T. Mortimer & M. D. Finch (Eds.), *Adolescents, work, and family: An intergenerational developmental analysis.* Thousand Oaks, CA: Sage.

Shanahan, M. J., Elder, G. H., Burchinal, M., & Conger, R. D. (1996b). Adolescent paid labor and relationships with parents: Early work-family linkages. *Child Development, 67,* 2183–2200.

Share, D. L. (1999). Phonological recoding and orthographic learning: A direct test of the self-teaching hypothesis. *Journal of Experimental Child Psychology, 72,* 95–129.

Sharpe, R. M., & Skakkebaek, N. E. (1993). Are oestrogens involved in falling sperm counts and disorders of the male reproductive tract? *Lancet, 341,* 1392–1395.

Shatz, M. (1983). Communication. In P. H. Mussen (Ed.), *Handbook of child psychology* (Vol. 3). New York: Wiley.

Shatz, M., & Gelman, R. (1973). The development of communication skills: Modifications in the speech of young children as a function of listener. *Monographs of the Society for Research in Child Development, 38*(5, Serial No. 152).

Shaw, D. S., Winslow, E. B., & Flanagan, C. (1999). A prospective study of the effects of marital status and family relations on young children's adjustment among African American and European American families. *Child Development, 70,* 742–755.

Shaw, G. M. (2001). Adverse human reproductive outcomes and electromagnetic fields: A brief summary of the epidemiologic literature. *Bioelectromagnetics, 5,* S5–18.

Shaw, G. M., Schaffer, D., Velie, E. M., Morland, K., & Harris, J. A. (1995). Periconceptional vitamin use, dietary folate, and the occurrence of neural tube defects. *Epidemiology, 6,* 219–226.

Sherman, D. K., Iacono, W. G., & McGue, M. K. (1997). Attention-deficit hyperactivity disorder dimensions: A twin study of inattention and impulsivity-hyperactivity. *Journal of the American Academy of Child and Adolescent Psychiatry, 36,* 745–753.

Sherrod, K. B., O'Connor, S., Vietze, P. M., & Altemeier, W. A., III (1984). Child health and maltreatment. *Child Development, 55,* 1174–1183.

Shi, R., & Werker, J. F. (2001). Six-month old infants' preference for lexical words. *Psychological Science, 12,* 70–75.

Shih, M., Pittinsky, T. L., & Ambady, N. (1999). Stereotype susceptibility: Identity salience and shifts in quantitative performance. *Psychological Science, 10,* 80–83.

Shoda, Y., Mischel, W., & Peake, P. K. (1990). Predicting adolescent cognitive and self-regulatory competencies from preschool delay of gratification: Identifying diagnostic conditions. *Developmental Psychology, 26,* 978–986.

Shonk, S. M., & Cicchetti, D. (2001). Maltreatment, competency deficits, and risk for academic and behavioral maladjustment. *Developmental Psychology, 37,* 3–17.

Shulman, S., & Kipnis, O. (2001). Adolescent romantic relationships: A look from the future. *Journal of Adolescence, 24,* 337–351.

Shuter-Dyson, R. (1982). Musical ability. In D. Deutsch (Ed.), *The psychology of music.* New York: Academic Press.

Shwe, H. I., & Markman, E. M. (1997). Young children's appreciation of the mental impact of their communicative signals. *Developmental Psychology, 33,* 630–636.

Sicotte, N. L., Woods, R. P., & Mazziotta, J. C. (1999). Handedness in twins: A meta-analysis. *Laterality: Asymmetries of Body, Brain, and Cognition, 4,* 265–286.

Siddiqui, A. (1995). Object size as a determinant of grasping in infancy. *Journal of Genetic Psychology, 156,* 345–358.

Sidebotham, P., Heron, J., & the ALSPAC Study Team. (2003). Child maltreatment in the "children of the nineties:" the role of the child. *Child Abuse and Neglect, 27,* 337–352.

Siegler, R. S. (1976). Three aspects of cognitive development. *Cognitive Psychology, 8,* 481–520.

Siegler, R. S. (1981). Developmental sequences within and between concepts. *Monographs of the Society for Research in Child Development, 46*(Serial No. 189).

Siegler, R. S. (1986). Unities in strategy choices across domains. In M. Perlmutter (Ed.), *Minnesota symposia on child development* (Vol. 19). Hillsdale, NJ: Erlbaum.

Siegler, R. S. (1996). *Emerging minds: The process of change in children's thinking.* New York: Oxford University Press.

Siegler, R. S. (2000). The rebirth of children's learning. *Child Development, 71,* 26–35.

Siegler, R. S., & Alibali, M. W. (2005). *Children's thinking* (4th ed). Upper Saddle River, NJ: Prentice Hall.

Siegler, R. S., & Ellis, S. (1996). Piaget on childhood. *Psychological Science, 7,* 211–215.

Siegler, R. S., & Jenkins, E. (1989). *How children discover new strategies.* Hillsdale, NJ: Erlbaum.

Siegler, R. S., & Robinson, M. (1982). The development of numerical understandings. In H. W. Reese & L. P. Lipsitt (Eds.), *Advances in child development and behavior* (Vol. 16). New York: Academic Press.

Siegler, R. S., & Shrager, J. (1984). Strategy choices in addition and subtraction: How do children know what to do? In C. Sophian (Ed.), *Origins of cognitive skills.* Hillsdale, NJ: Erlbaum.

Signorella, M. L., Bigler, R. S., & Liben, L. S. (1993). Developmental differences in children's gender schemata about others: A meta-analytic review. *Early gender-role development. Developmental Review, 13,* 147–183.

Signoriello, N., & Lears, M. (1992). Children, television, and conceptions about chores: Attitudes and behaviors. *Sex Roles, 27,* 157–170.

Silk, J. S., Morris, A. S., Kanaya, T., & Steinberg, L. D. (2003). Psychological control and autonomy granting: Opposite ends of a continuum or distinct constructs? *Journal of Research on Adolescence, 13,* 113–128.

Silverman, W. K., La Greca, A. M., & Wasserstein, S. (1995). What do children worry about? Worries and their relations to anxiety. *Child Development, 66,* 671–686.

Simcock, G. & Hayne, H. (2002). Breaking the barrier? Children fail to translate their preverbal memories into language. *Psychological Science, 13,* 225–231.

Simmons, R., & Blyth, D. (1987). *Moving into adolescence.* New York: Aldine de Gruyter.

Simons, D. J., & Keil, F. C. (1995). An abstract to concrete shift in the development of biological thought: The insides story. *Cognition, 56,* 129–163.

Simons-Morton, B. G., McKenzie, T. J., Stone, E., Mitchell, P., Osganian, V., Strikmiller, P. K., et al. (1997). Physical activity in the multiethnic population of third graders in four states. *American Journal of Public Health, 87,* 45–50.

Simpson, E. L. (1974). Moral development research: A case study of scientific cultural bias. *Human Development, 17,* 81–106.

Simpson, J. M. (2001). Infant stress and sleep deprivation as an aetiological basis for the sudden infant death syndrome. *Early Human Development, 61,* 1–43.

Singer, J. D., Fuller, B., Keiley, M. K., & Wolf, A. (1998). Early child-care selection: Variation by geographic location, maternal characteristics, and family structure. *Developmental Psychology, 34,* 1129–1144.

Singer, L. T., Arendt, R., Minnes, S., Farkas, K., Salvator, A., Kirchner, H. L., et al. (2002). Cognitive and motor outcomes of cocaine-exposed infants. *Journal of the American Medical Association, 287,* 1952–1960.

Skinner, B. F. (1957). *Verbal behavior.* New York: Appleton-Century-Crofts.

Skinner, E. A. (1985). Determinants of mother-sensitive and contingent-responsive behavior: The role of childbearing beliefs and socioeconomic status. In I. E. Sigel (Ed.), *Parental belief systems: The psychological consequences for children* (pp. 51–82). Hillsdale, NJ: Erlbaum.

Slater, A. M., Quinn, P. C., Hayes, R., & Brown, E. (2000). The role of facial orientation in newborn infants' preference for attractive faces. *Developmental Science, 3,* 181–185.

Slobin, D. I. (1985). Cross-linguistic evidence for the language-making capacity. In D. I. Slobin (Ed.), *The cross-linguistic study of language acquisition: Vol. 2. Theoretical issues.* Hillsdale, NJ: Erlbaum.

Smetana, J. G. (2002). Culture, autonomy, and personal jurisdiction in adolescent-parent relationships. *Advances in Child Development and Behavior, 29,* 52–87.

Smith, E. R., & Mackie, D. M. (2000). *Social psychology* (2nd ed.). Philadelphia: Psychology Press.

Smith, K. (2000). Who's minding the kids? Child care arrangements: Fall 1995. *Current Population Reports,* P70–70. Washington DC: U. S. Census Bureau.

Smith, L. B. (2000). How to learn words: An associative crane. In R. Golinkoff & K. Hirsch-Pasek (Eds.), *Breaking the word learning barrier* (pp. 51–80). Oxford, England: Oxford University Press.

Smith, L. B., Jones, S. S., Landau, B., Gershkoff-Stowe, L., & Samuelson, L. (2002). Object name learning provides on-the-job training for attention. *Psychological Science, 13,* 13–19.

Smith, L. B., Quittner, A. L, Osberger, M. J., & Miyamoto, R. (1998). Audition and visual attention: The developmental trajectory in deaf and hearing populations. *Developmental Psychology, 34,* 840–850.

Smith, P. K., & Drew, L. M. (2002). Grandparenthood. In M. H. Bornstein (Ed.), *Handbook of parenting: Vol. 3. Status and social conditions of parenting* (2nd ed., pp. 141–172). Mahwah, NJ: Erlbaum.

Smith, R. (1999, March). The timing of birth. *Scientific American,* 68–75.

Smith, R. E., & Smoll, F. L. (1996). The coach as the focus of research and intervention in youth sports. In F. L. Smoll & R. E. Smith (Eds.), *Children and youth in sport: A biopsychological perspective* (pp. 125–141). Dubuque, IA: Brown & Benchmark.

Smith, R. E., & Smoll, F. L. (1997). Coaching the coaches: Youth sports as a scientific and applied behavioral setting. *Current Directions in Psychological Science, 6,* 16–21.

Smith, S. L., & Atkin, C. (2003). Television advertising and children: Examining the intended and unintended effects. In E. L. Palmer & B. M. Young (Eds.), *The faces of televisual media: Teaching, violence, selling to children* (pp. 301–326). Mahwah, NJ: Erlbaum.

Smock, T. K. (1999). *Physiological psychology: A neuroscience approach.* Upper Saddle River, NJ: Prentice-Hall.

Smoll, F. L., & Schutz, R.W. (1990). Quantifying gender differences in physical performance: A developmental perspective. *Developmental Psychology, 26,* 360–369.

Smoll, F. L., Smith, R. E., Barnett, N. P., & Everett, J. J. (1993). Enhancement of children's self-esteem through social support training for youth sport coaches. *Journal of Applied Psychology, 78,* 602–610.

Snedeker, B. (1982). *Hard knocks: Preparing youth for work.* Baltimore, MD: Johns Hopkins University Press.

Snow, C. W. (1998). *Infant development* (2nd ed.). Upper Saddle River, NJ: Prentice-Hall.

Snow, M. E., Jacklin, C. N., & Maccoby, E. E. (1983). Sex-of-child differences in father-child interaction at one year of age. *Child Development, 54,* 227–232.

Sodian, B., Zaitchik, D., & Carey, S. (1991). Young children's differentiation of hypothetical beliefs from evidence. *Child Development, 62,* 753–766.

Solantaus, T., Leinonen, J., & Punamäka, R.-L. (2004). Children's mental health in times of economic recession: Replication and extension of the family economic stress model in Finland. *Developmental Psychology, 40,* 412–429.

Sommerville, J. A., & Woodward, A. L. (2005). Pulling out the intentional structure of action: The relation between action processing and action production in infancy. *Cognition, 95,* 1–30.

Sousa, P., Altran, S., & Medin, D. (2002). Essentialism and folkbiology: Further evidence from Brazil. *Journal of Cognition and Culture, 2,* 195–223.

Spearman, C. (1904). "General intelligence" objectively determined and measured. *American Journal of Psychology, 15,* 201–293.

Spelke, E. S. (1994). Initial knowledge: Six suggestions. *Cognition, 50,* 431–445.

Spitz, R. A. (1965). *The first year of life.* New York: International Universities Press.

Springer, K., & Keil, F. C. (1991). Early differentiation of causal mechanisms appropriate to biological and nonbiological kinds. *Child Development, 62,* 767–781.

Sroufe, L. A., & Waters, E. (1976). The ontogenesis of smiling and laughter: A perspective on the organization of development in infancy. *Psychological Review, 83,* 173–189.

St. George, I. M., Williams, S., & Silva, P. A. (1994). Body size and the menarche: The Dunedin study. *Journal of Adolescent Health, 15,* 573–576.

St. James-Roberts, I., & Plewis, I. (1996). Individual differences, daily fluctuations, and developmental changes in amounts of infant waking, fussing, crying, feeding, and sleeping. *Child Development, 67,* 2527–2540.

Stacy, A. W., Zoog, J. B., Undger, J. B., & Dent, C. W. (2004). Exposure to televised alcohol ads and subsequent alcohol use. *American Journal of Health Behavior, 28,* 498–509.

Staff, J., & Uggen, C. (2003). The fruits of good work: Early work experiences and adolescent deviance. *Journal of Research in Crime and Delinquency, 40,* 263–290.

Stattin, H., & Magnusson, D. (1989). The role of early aggressive behavior in the frequency, seriousness, and types of later crime. *Journal of Consulting and Clinical Psychology, 57,* 710–718.

Steele, C. M. (1997). A threat in the air: How stereotypes shape intellectual identity and performance. *American Psychologist, 52,* 613–629.

Steele, C. M., & Aronson, J. (1995). Stereotype threat and the intellectual test performance of African Americans. *Journal of Personality and Social Psychology, 69,* 797–811.

Steelman, J. D. (1994). Revision strategies employed by middle level students using computers. *Journal of Educational Computing Research, 11,* 141–152.

Steinberg, L. (1990). Autonomy, conflict, and harmony in the family relationship. In S. S. Feldman & G. R. Elliott (Eds.), *At the threshold: The developing adolescent.* Cambridge, MA: Harvard University Press.

Steinberg, L. D. (1999). *Adolescence* (5th ed.). Boston, MA: McGraw-Hill.

Steinberg, L., & Dornbusch, S. M. (1991). Negative correlates of part-time employment during adolescence: Replication and elaboration. *Developmental Psychology, 27,* 304–313.

Steinberg, L., Fegley, S., & Dornbusch, S. M. (1993). Negative impact of part-time work on adolescent adjustment: Evidence from a longitudinal study. *Developmental Psychology, 29,* 171–180.

Steiner, J. E., Glaser, D., Hawilo, M. E., & Berridge, K. C. (2001). Comparative expression of hedonic impact: Affective reactions to taste by human infants and other primates. *Neuroscience & Biobehavioral Reviews, 25,* 53–74.

Stern, M., & Karraker, K. H. (1989). Sex stereotyping of infants: A review of gender labeling studies. *Sex Roles, 20,* 501–522.

Sternberg, C. R., & Campos, J. (1990). The development of anger expressions in infancy. In N. Stein, B. Leventhal, & T. Trabasso (Eds.), *Psychological and biological approaches to emotion.* Hillsdale, NJ: Erlbaum.

Sternberg, R. J. (1999). The theory of successful intelligence. *Review of General Psychology, 3,* 292–316.

Sternberg, R. J., Castejon, J. L., Prieto, M. D. Hautamaki, J., & Grigorenko, E. L. (2001). Confirmatory factor analysis of the Sternberg Triarchic Abilities Test in three international samples: An empirical test of the triarchic theory of intelligence. *European Journal of Psychological Assessment, 17,* 1–16.

Sternberg, R. J., & Grigorenko, E. L. (2002). *Dynamic testing: The nature and measurement of learning potential.* New York: Cambridge University Press.

Sternberg, R. J., Grigorenko, E. L., & Kidd, K. K. (2005). Intelligence, race, and genetics. *American Psychologist, 60,* 46–59.

Sternberg, R. J., & Kaufman J. C. (1998). Human abilities. *Annual Review of Psychology, 49,* 479–502.

Stevenson, H. W., & Lee, S. (1990). Contexts of achievement. *Monographs of the Society for Research in Child Development, 55*(Serial No. 221).

Stevenson, H. W., & Stigler, J. W. (1992). *The learning gap.* New York: Summit Books.

Stewart, L., & Pascual-Leone, J. (1992). Mental capacity constraints and the development of moral reasoning. *Journal of Experimental Child Psychology, 54,* 251–287.

Stewart, P., Reihman, J., Lonky, E., Darvill, T., & Pagano, J. (2000). Prenatal PCB exposure and neonatal behavioral assessment scale (NBAS) performance. *Neurotoxicology and Teratology, 22,* 21–29.

Stewart, R. B., Mobley, L. A., Van Tuyl, S. S., & Salvador, W. A. (1987). The firstborns' adjustment to the birth of a sibling: A longitudinal assessment. *Child Development, 58,* 341–355.

Stice, E., Presnell, K., & Bearman, S. K. (2001). Relation of early menarche to depression, eating disorders, substance abuse, and comorbid psychopathology among adolescent girls. *Developmental Psychology, 37,* 608–619.

Stice, E., & Shaw, H. (2004). Eating disorder prevention programs: A meta-analytic review. *Psychological Bulletin, 130,* 206–227.

Stifter, C. A., & Fox, N. A. (1990). Infant reactivity: Physiological correlates of newborn and 5-month temperament. *Developmental Psychology, 26,* 582–588.

Stifter, C. A., Spinrad, T. L., & Braungart-Rieker, J. M. (1999). Toward a developmental model of child compliance: The role of emotion regulation in infancy. *Child Development, 70,* 21–32.

Stigler, J. W., Gallimore, R., & Hiebert, J. (2000). Using video surveys to compare classrooms and teaching across cultures: Examples and lessons from the TIMSS video studies. *Educational Psychologist, 35,* 87–100.

Stiles, J. (2001). Neural plasticity and cognitive development. *Developmental Neuropsychology, 18,* 237–272.

Stiles, J., Reilly, J., Paul, B., & Moses, P. (2005). Cognitive development following early brain injury: Evidence for neural adaptation. *Trends in Cognitive Sciences, 9,* 136–143.

Stoolmiller, M. (2001). Synergistic interaction of child manageability problems and parent-discipline tactics in predicting future growth in externalizing behavior for boys. *Developmental Psychology, 37,* 814–825.

Strauss, M. S., & Curtis, L. E. (1984). Development of numerical concepts in infancy. In C. Sophian (Ed.), *Origins of cognitive skills.* Hillsdale, NJ: Erlbaum.

Strayer, J., & Roberts, W. (2004). Children's anger, emotional expressiveness, and empathy: Relations with parents' empathy, emotional expressiveness, and parenting practices. *Social Development, 13,* 229–254.

Striano, T., Tomasello, M., & Rochat, P. (2001). Social and object support for early symbolic play. *Developmental Science, 4,* 442–455.

Strough, J., & Berg, C. A. (2000). Goals as a mediator of gender differences in high-affiliation dyadic conversations. *Developmental Psychology, 36,* 117–125.

Stunkard, A. J., Sorensen, T. I. A., Hanis, C., Teasdale, T. W., Chakraborty, R., Schull, W. J., et al. (1986). An adoption study of human obesity. *New England Journal of Medicine, 314,* 193–198.

Subrahmanyam, K., Greenfield, P., Kraut, R., & Gross, E. (2001). The impact of computer use on children's and adolescents' development. *Journal of Applied Developmental Psychology, 22,* 7–30.

Sullivan, L. W. (1987). The risks of the sickle-cell trait: Caution and common sense. *New England Journal of Medicine, 317,* 830–831.

Sulloway, F. J. (1995). Birth order and evolutionary psychology: A meta-analytic overview. *Psychological Inquiry, 6,* 75–80.

Sundet, J. M., Barlaugh, D. G., & Torjussen, T. M. (2004). The end of the Flynn effect? A study of secular trends in mean intelligence scores of Norwegian conscripts during half a century. *Intelligence, 32,* 349–362.

Super, C. M. (1981). Cross-cultural research on infancy. In H. C. Triandis & A. Heron (Eds.), *Handbook of cross-cultural psychology: Vol. 4. Developmental psychology.* Boston: Allyn & Bacon.

Super, C. M., Herrera, M. G., & Mora, J. O. (1990). Long-term effects of food supplementation and psychosocial intervention on the physical growth of Colombian infants at risk of malnutrition. *Child Development, 61,* 29–49.

Super, D. E. (1976). *Career education and the meanings of work.* Washington, DC: U.S. Offices of Education.

Super, D. E. (1990). A life-span, life-space approach to career development. In D. Brown & L. Brooks (Eds.), *Career choice and development: Applying theories to practice* (pp. 197–261). San Francisco: Jossey Bass.

Suzuki, L., & Aronson, J. (2005). The cultural malleability of intelligence and its impact on the racial/ethnic hierarchy. *Psychology, Public Policy, and Law, 11,* 320–327.

Svirsky, M. A., Robbins, A. M., Kirk, K. I., Pisoni, D. B., & Miyamoto, R. T. (2000). Language development in profoundly deaf children with cochlear implants. *Psychological Science, 11,* 153–158.

Tager-Flusberg, H. (1993). Putting words together: Morphology and syntax in the preschool years. In J. Berko Gleason (Ed.), *The development of language* (3rd ed.). New York: Macmillan.

Tamis-LeMonda, C. S., & Bornstein, M. H. (1996). Variation in children's exploratory, nonsymbolic, and symbolic play: An explanatory multidimensional framework. In C. Rovee-Collier & L. P. Lipsitt (Eds.), *Advances in infancy research* (Vol. 10). Norwood, NJ: Ablex.

Tamis-LeMonda, C. S., & Bornstein, M. H. (2002). Maternal responsiveness and early language acquisition. In R. V. Kail & H. W. Reese (Eds.), *Advances in child development* (Vol. 29, pp. 90–127). San Diego, CA: Academic Press.

Tanner, J. M. (1970). Physical growth. In P. H. Mussen (Ed.), *Carmichael's manual of child psychology* (3rd ed.). New York: Wiley.

Tanner, J. M. (1990). *Fetus into man: Physical growth from conception to maturity* (2nd ed.) Cambridge, MA: Harvard University Press.

Taylor, H. G., Klein, N., Minich, N. M., & Hack, M. (2000). Middle-school-age outcomes in children with very low birthweight. *Child Development, 71*, 1495–1511.

Taylor, M., Carlson, S. M., Maring, B. L., Gerow, L., & Charley, C. M. (2004). The characteristics and correlates of fantasy in school-age children: Imaginary companions, impersonation, and social understanding. *Developmental Psychology, 40*, 1173–1187.

Taylor, M., Cartwright, B. S., & Carlson, S. M. (1993). A developmental investigation of children's imaginary companions. *Developmental Psychology, 29*, 276–285.

Taylor, M. G. (1996). The development of children's beliefs about social and biological aspects of gender differences. *Child Development, 67*, 1555–1571.

Taylor, R. D., & Roberts, D. (1995). Kinship support and maternal and adolescent well-being in economically disadvantaged African-American families. *Child Development, 66*, 1585–1597.

Teichman, Y. (2001). The development of Israeli children's images of Jews and Arabs and their expression in human figure drawings. *Developmental Psychology, 37*, 749–761.

Teti, D. M. (2005). Intervention for premature infants. In C. B. Fisher & R. M. Lerner (Eds.), *Encyclopedia of applied developmental science* (Vol. 1, pp. 582–586). Thousand Oaks, CA: Sage.

Thelen, E., & Smith, L. B. (1998). Dynamic systems theories. In W. Damon (Ed.), *Handbook of child psychology* (Vol. 1). New York: Wiley.

Thelen, E., & Ulrich, B. D. (1991). Hidden skills. *Monographs of the Society for Research in Child Development, 56*(Serial No. 223).

Thelen, E., Ulrich, B. D., & Jensen, J. L. (1989). The developmental origins of locomotion. In M. H. Woollacott & A. Shumway-Cook (Eds.), *Development of posture and gait across the life span*. Columbia: University of South Carolina Press.

Thiessen, E. D., & Saffran, J. R. (2003). When cues collide: Use of stress and statistical cues to word boundaries by 7- to 9-month-old infants. *Developmental Psychology, 39*, 706–716.

Thomas, A., & Chess, S. (1977). *Temperament and development*. New York: Brunner/Mazel.

Thomas, A., Chess, S., & Birch, H. G. (1968). *Temperament and behavior disorders in children*. New York: New York University Press.

Thomas, H., & Kail, R. (1991). Sex differences in the speed of mental rotation and the X-linked genetic hypothesis. *Intelligence, 15*, 17–32.

Thomas, J. R., & French, K. E. (1985). Gender differences across age in motor performance: A meta-analysis. *Psychological Bulletin, 98*, 260–282.

Thompson, G. G. (1952). *Child psychology*. Boston: Houghton Mifflin.

Thompson, R. A. (1998). Early socio-personality development. In N. Eisenberg (Ed.), *Handbook of child psychology: Vol. 3. Social, emotional, and personality development* (5th ed., pp. 25–104). New York: Wiley.

Thompson, R. A. (2000). The legacy of early attachments. *Child Development, 71*, 145–152.

Thompson, R. A., Laible, D. J., & Ontai, L. L. (2003). Early understandings of emotion, morality, and self: Developing a working model. *Advances in Child Development and Behavior, 31*, 137–172.

Thompson, R. A., & Limber, S. (1991). "Social anxiety" in infancy: Stranger wariness and separation distress. In H. Leitenberg (Ed.), *Handbook of social and evaluation anxiety*. New York: Plenum.

Thornberry, T. P., Krohn, M. D., Lizotte, A. J., Smith, C. A., & Tobin, K. (2003). *Gangs and delinquency in developmental perspective*. New York: Cambridge University Press.

Thorne, B. (1993). *Gender play: Girls and boys in school*. New Brunswick, NJ: Rutgers University Press.

Thurstone, L. L., & Thurstone, T. G. (1941). Factorial studies in intelligence. *Psychometric Monograph*, No. 2.

Tincoff, R., & Jusczyk, P. W. (1999). Some beginnings of word comprehension in 6-month-olds. *Psychological Science, 10*, 172–175.

Tisak, M. (1993). Preschool children's judgements of moral and personal events involving physical harm and property damage. *Merrill-Palmer Quarterly, 39*, 375–390.

Tolan, P. H., Gorman-Smith, D., & Henry, D. B. (2003). The developmental ecology of urban males' youth violence. *Developmental Psychology, 39*, 274–291.

Torgesen, J. K. (2004). Learning disabilities: An historical and conceptual overview. In B. Y. L. Wong (Ed.), *Learning about learning disabilities* (3rd ed., pp. 3–40). San Diego: Elsevier.

Trainor, L. J., Austin, C. M., & Desjardins, R. N. (2000). Is infant-directed speech prosody a result of the vocal expression of emotion? *Psychological Science, 11*, 188–195.

Trainor, L. J., & Heinmiller, B. M. (1998). The development of evaluative responses to music: Infants prefer to listen to consonance over dissonance. *Infant Behavior and Development, 21*, 77–88.

Treiman, R., & Kessler, B. (2003). The role of letter names in the acquisition of literacy. *Advances in Child Development and Behavior, 31*, 105–135.

Tremblay, R. E., Schall, B., Boulerice, B., Arsonault, L., Soussignan, R. G., & Paquette, D. (1998). Testosterone, physical aggression, and dominance and physical development in adolescence. *International Journal of Behavioral Development, 22*, 753–777.

Troseth, G. L., Pierroutsakos, S. L., & DeLoache, J. S.. (2004). From the innocent to the intelligent eye: The early development of pictorial competence. In R. V. Kail (Ed.), *Advances in child development and behavior* (Vol. 32, pp. 1–35). San Diego, CA: Elsevier.

Tsao, F.-M., Liu, H.-M., & Kuhl, P. K. (2004). Perception in infancy predicts language development in the second year of life: A longitudinal study. *Child Development, 75*, 1067–1084.

Tudge, J. R. H., Winterhoff, P. A., & Hogan, D. M. (1996). The cognitive consequences of collaborative problem solving with and without feedback. *Child Development, 67*, 2892–2909.

Turati, C. (2004). Why faces are not special to newborns: An alternative account of the face preference. *Current Directions in Psychological Science, 13*, 5–8.

Turiel, E. (1998). The development of morality. In W. Damon (Ed.), *Handbook of child psychology, Vol. 3: Social, emotional, and personality development* (pp. 863–932). New York: Wiley.

Turiel, E. (2006). The development of morality. In W. Damon & R. M. Lerner (Eds.), *Handbook of child psychology*, Vol. 3 (6th ed.) New York: Wiley.

Turiel, E., & Neff, K. (2000). Religion, culture, and beliefs about reality in moral reasoning. In K. S. Rosengren, C. N. Johnson, & P. L. Harris (Eds.), *Imagining the impossible: Magical, scientific, and religious thinking in children* (pp. 269–304). New York: Cambridge University Press.

Turkheimer, E., & Waldron, M. (2000). Nonshared environment: A theoretical, methodological, and quantitative review. *Psychological Bulletin, 126*, 78–108.

Turley, R. N. L. (2003). Are children of young mothers disadvantaged because of their mother's age or family background? *Child Development, 74*, 465–474.

Twenge, J. M., & Campbell, W. K. (2001). Age and birth cohort differences in self-esteem: A cross-temporal meta-analysis. *Personality & Social Psychology Review, 5*, 321–344.

Umbel, V. M., Pearson, B. Z., Fernandez, M. C., & Oller, D. K. (1992). Measuring bilingual children's receptive vocabularies. *Child Development, 63*, 1012–1020.

United Nations Children's Fund. (2004). *The state of the world's children 2005*. New York: Author.

United States Bureau of the Census. (1995). *Statistical abstract of the United States* (115th ed.). Washington, DC: U.S. Government Printing Office.

United States Census Bureau. (1998). *Marital status and living arrangements, March 1998. Current population reports*. Washington DC: U.S. Government Printing Office.

United States Census Bureau. (2004). *Statistical abstract of the United States* (124th ed.). Washington DC: U.S. Government Printing Office.

United States Department of Agriculture. (2000). Dietary guidelines for Americans, 2000 (5th ed.). *Home and garden bulletin*, No. 32.

United States Department of Health and Human Services. (2001). *The Surgeon General's call to action to prevent and decrease overweight and obesity*. Rockville, MD: Author.

United States Department of Health and Human Services. (2004). *2002 Assisted reproductive technology success rates*. Author.

United States Department of Health and Human Services. (2004). Youth risk behavior surveillance. *Morbidity and Mortality Weekly Report, 53*(No. SS-2). Atlanta, GA: Centers for Disease Control and Prevention.

United States Department of Health and Human Services. (2005). *Child maltreatment 2004: Summary of key findings*. Washington DC: National Clearinghouse on Child Abuse and Neglect Information.

United States Department of Labor. (2000). *Report on the Youth Labor Force*. Washington DC: Author.

United States Department of State. (2002). *Country reports on human rights practices, 2001*. Retrieved from the World Wide Web November 15, 2002, http://www.state.gov/g/drl/rls/hrrpt/2001/

Updegraff, K. A., Thayer, S. M., Whiteman, S. D., Denning D. J., & McHale, S. M. (2005). Aggression in adolescents' sibling relationships: Links to sibling and parent-adolescent relationship quality. *Family Relations: Interdisciplinary Journal of Applied Family Studies, 54*, 373–385.

Urberg, K. A., Deirmenciolu, S. M., & Pilgrim, C. (1997). Close friend and group influence on adolescent cigarette smoking and alcohol use. *Developmental Psychology, 33*, 834–844.

Valkenburg, P. M., & Buijzen, M. (2005). Identifying determinants of young children's brand awareness: Television, parents, and peers. *Journal of Applied Developmental Psychology, 26*, 456–468.

Valkenburg, P. M., & van der Voort, T. H. A. (1994). Influence of TV on daydreaming and creative imagination: A review of research. *Psychological Bulletin, 116*, 316–339.

Valkenburg, P. M., & van der Voort, T. H. A. (1995). The influence of television on children's daydreaming styles: A 1-year-panel study. *Communication Research, 22*, 267–287.

van den Boom, D. C. (1994). The influence of temperament and mothering on attachment and exploration: An experimental manipulation of sensitive responsiveness among lower-class mothers with irritable infants. *Child Development, 65*, 1457–1477.

van den Boom, D. C. (1995). Do first-year intervention effects endure? Follow-up during toddlerhood of a sample of Dutch irritable infants. *Child Development, 66,* 1798–1816.

Van Hof, P., van der Kamp, J., & Savelsbergh, G. J. P. (2002). The relation of unimanual and bimanual reaching to crossing the midline. *Child Development, 73,* 1352–1362.

van IJzendoorn, M. (1995). Adult attachment representations, parental responsiveness, and infant attachment: A meta-analysis on the predictive validity of the Adult Attachment Interview. *Psychological Bulletin, 117,* 387–403.

van IJzendoorn, M. H., Vereijken, C. M. J. L., Bakermans-Kranenburg, M. J., & Riksen-Walraven, J. (2004). Assessing attachment security with the Attachment Q Sort: Meta-analytic evidence for the validity of the observer AQS. *Child Development, 75,* 1188–1213.

Vandell, D. L., Pierce, K. M., & Dadisman, K. (2005). Out-of-school settings as a developmental context for children and youth. In R. V. Kail (Ed.), *Advances in child development and behavior* (Vol. 33, pp. 43–77). Amsterdam: Elsevier Academic Press.

van der Mark, I. L., van IJzendoorn, M. H., & Bakermans-Kranenburg, M. J. (2002). Development of empathy in girls during the second year of life: Associations with parenting, attachment, and temperament. *Social Development, 11,* 451–468.

Vander Wal, J. S., & Thelen, M. H. (2000). Eating and body image concerns among obese and average-weight children. *Addictive Behaviors, 25,* 775–778.

Vazsonyi, A. T., Hibbert, J. R., & Snider, J. B. (2003). Exotic enterprise no more? Adolescent reports of family and parenting practices from youth in four countries. *Journal of Research on Adolescence, 13,* 129–160.

Verma, I. M. (1990). Gene therapy. *Scientific American, 263,* 68–84.

Verschueren, K., Buyck, P., & Marcoen, A. (2001). Self-representations and socioemotional competence in young children: A 3-year longitudinal study. *Developmental Psychology, 37,* 126–134.

Visher, E. B., Visher, J. S., & Pasley, K. (2003). Remarriage families and stepparenting. In F. Walsh (Ed.), *Normal family processes* (pp. 153–175). New York: Guilford.

Volling, B. L., & Belsky, J. (1992). The contribution of mother-child and father-child relationships to the quality of sibling interaction: A longitudinal study. *Child Development, 63,* 1209–1222.

Vorhees, C. V., & Mollnow, E. (1987). Behavior teratogenesis: Long-term influences on behavior. In J. D. Osofsky (Ed.), *Handbook of infant development* (2nd ed.). New York: Wiley.

Votruba-Drzal, E., Coley, R. L., & Chase-Lansdale, P. L. (2004). Child care and low-income children's development: Directed and moderated effects. *Child Development, 75,* 296–312.

Voyer, D., Voyer, S., & Bryden, M. P. (1995). Magnitude of sex differences in spatial abilities: A meta-analysis and consideration of critical variables. *Psychological Bulletin, 117,* 250–270.

Vygotsky, L. S. (1934/1986). *Thought and language* (A. Kozulin, Trans.). Cambridge, MA: MIT Press. [Original work published in 1934.]

Vygotsky, L. S. (1978). *Mind in society: The development of higher psychological processes* (M. Cole, V. John-Steiner, S. Scribner, & E. Soubermen, Eds.). Cambridge, MA: Harvard University Press.

Waber, D. P. (1977). Sex differences in mental abilities, hemispheric lateralization, and rate of physical growth at adolescence. *Developmental Psychology, 13,* 29–38.

Wachs, T. D. (1983). The use and abuse of environment in behavior-genetic research. *Child Development, 54,* 396–407.

Wachs, T. D., & Bates, J. E. (2001). Temperament. In G. Bremner & A. Fogel (Eds.), *Blackwell handbook of infant development* (pp. 465–501). Malden, MA: Blackwell.

Wainwright, J. L., Russell, S. T., & Patterson, C. J. (2004). Psychosocial adjustment, school outcomes, and romantic relationships of adolescents with same-sex parents. *Child Development, 75,* 1886–1898.

Walberg, H. J. (1995). General practices. In G. Cawelti (Ed.), *Handbook of research on improving student achievement.* Arlington, VA: Educational Research Service.

Walker, L. J. (1980). Cognitive and perspective-taking prerequisites for moral development. *Child Development, 51,* 131–139.

Walker, L. J., & Taylor, J. H. (1991). Family interactions and the development of moral reasoning. *Child Development, 62,* 264–283.

Walker, L. J., Hennig, K. H., & Krettenauer, T. (2000). Parent and peer contexts for children's moral reasoning development. *Child Development, 71,* 1033–1048.

Wang, D., et al. (2000). Physical and personality traits of preschool children in Fuzhou, China: Only child vs. sibling. *Child: Care, Health, and Development, 26,* 49–60.

Wang, S., & Baillargeon, R. (2005). Inducing infants to detect a physical violation in a single trial. *Psychological Science, 16,* 542–549.

Wang, S. S., & Brownell, K. D. (2005). Anorexia nervosa. In C. B. Fisher & R. M. Lerner (Eds.), *Encyclopedia of applied developmental science* (Vol. 1, pp. 83–85). Thousand Oaks, CA: Sage.

Warren, A. R., & McCloskey, L. A. (1993). Pragmatics: Language in social contexts. In J. Berko Gleason (Ed.), *The development of language* (3rd. ed., pp. 195–238). New York: Macmillan.

Warren-Leubecker, A., & Bohannon, J. N. (1989). Pragmatics: Language in social contexts. In J. Berko Gleason (Ed.), *The development of language* (2nd ed., pp. 327–368). Columbus, OH: Merrill.

Waters, E., & Cummings, E. M. (2000). A secure base from which to explore close relationships. *Child Development, 71,* 164–172.

Waters, E., Merrick, S., Treboux, D., Crowell, J., & Albersheim, L. (2000). Attachment security in infancy and early adulthood: A twenty-year longitudinal study. *Child Development, 71,* 684–689.

Waters, H. F. (1993, July 12). Networks under the gun. *Newsweek,* 64–66.

Waters, H. S. (1980). "Class news": A single-subject longitudinal study of prose production and schema formation during childhood. *Journal of Verbal Learning and Verbal Behavior, 19,* 152–167.

Watson, J. B. (1925). *Behaviorism.* New York: Norton.

Webb, S. J., Monk, C. S., & Nelson, C. A. (2001). Mechanisms of postnatal neurobiological development: Implications for human development. *Developmental Neuropsychology, 19,* 147–171.

Wechsler, D. (1991). *Manual for the Wechsler Intelligence Test for Children—III.* New York: The Psychological Corporation.

Weichold, K., & Silbereisen, R. K. (2005). Puberty. In C. B. Fisher & R. M. Lerner (Eds.), *Encyclopedia of applied developmental science* (Vol. 2, pp. 893–898). Thousand Oaks, CA: Sage.

Weinberg, M. K., & Tronick, E. Z. (1994). Beyond the face: An empirical study of infant affective configurations of facial, vocal, gestural, and regulatory behaviors. *Child Development, 65,* 1503–1515.

Weinberg, M. K., Tronick, E. Z., Cohn, J. F., & Olson, K. L. (1999). Gender differences in emotional expressivity and self-regulation during early infancy. *Developmental Psychology, 35,* 175–188.

Weisner, T. S., & Wilson-Mitchell, J. E. (1990). Nonconventional family lifestyles and sex typing in six-year-olds. *Child Development, 61,* 1915–1933.

Weissman, M. D., & Kalish, C. W. (1999). The inheritance of desired characteristics: Children's view of the role of intention in parent-offspring resemblance. *Journal of Experimental Child Psychology, 73,* 245–265.

Weizman, Z. O., & Snow, C. E. (2001). Lexical output as related to children's vocabulary acquisition: Effects of sophisticated exposure and support for meaning. *Developmental Psychology, 37,* 265–279.

Wellman, H. M. (1992). *The child's theory of mind.* Cambridge, MA: MIT Press.

Wellman, H. M. (1993). Early understanding of mind: The normal case. In S. Baron-Cohen, H. Tager-Flusberg, & D. J. Cohen (Eds.), *Understanding other minds: Perspectives from autism.* Oxford, England: Oxford University Press.

Wellman, H. M. (2002). Understanding the psychological world: Developing a theory of mind. In U. Goswami (Ed.), *Blackwell handbook of childhood cognitive development* (pp. 167–187). Malden, MA: Blackwell.

Wellman, H. M., Cross, D., & Watson, J. (2001). Meta-analysis of theory-of-mind development: The truth about false belief. *Child Development, 72,* 655–684.

Wellman, H. M., & Gelman, S. A. (1998). Knowledge acquisition in foundational domains. In W. Damon (Ed.), *Handbook of child psychology* (Vol. 2). New York: Wiley.

Wentworth, N., Benson, J. B., & Haith, M. M. (2000). The development of infants' reaches for stationary and moving targets. *Child Development, 71,* 576–601.

Wentzel, K. R. (2002). Are effective teachers like good parents? Teaching styles and student adjustment in early adolescence. *Child Development, 73,* 287–301.

Werker, J. F., & Tees, R. C. (1999). Influences on infant speech processing: Toward a new synthesis. *Annual Review of Psychology, 50,* 509–535.

Werner, E. E. (1995). Resilience in development. *Current Directions in Psychological Science, 4,* 81–85.

Werner, H. (1948). *Comparative psychology of mental development.* Chicago: Follet.

Wertsch, J. V., & Tulviste, P. (1992). L. S. Vygotsky and contemporary developmental psychology. *Developmental Psychology, 28,* 548–557.

Whitaker, R. C., Wright, J. A., Pepe, M. S., Seidel, K. D., & Dietz, W. H. (1997). Predicting obesity in young adulthood from childhood and parental obesity. *New England Journal of Medicine, 337,* 869–873.

White, L., & Gilbreth, J. G. (2001). When children have two fathers: Effects of relationships with stepfathers and noncustodial fathers on adolescent outcomes. *Journal of Marriage and the Family, 63,* 155–167.

White, S. H. (1996). The relationships of developmental psychology to social policy. In E. F. Zigler, S. L. Kagan, & N. W. Hall (Eds.), *Children, families, and government: Preparing for the twenty-first cetury.* New York: Cambridge University Press.

Whitehead, J. R., & Corbin, C. B. (1997). Self-esteem in children and youth: The role of sport and physical education. In K. R. Fox, et al. (Eds.), *The physical self: From motivation to well-being.* Champaign, IL: Human Kinetics.

Whitehurst, G. J., & Vasta, R. (1975). Is language acquired through imitation? *Journal of Psycholinguistic Research, 4,* 37–59.

Whitehurst, G. J., & Vasta, R. (1977). *Child behavior.* Boston: Houghton Mifflin.

Whiting, J. W. M., & Child, I. L. (1953). *Child training and personality: A cross-cultural study.* New Haven: Yale University Press.

Whitney, E. N., & Hamilton, E. M. N. (1987). *Understanding nutrition* (4th ed.). St. Paul: West.

Wicks-Nelson, R., & Israel, A. C. (2006). *Behavior disorders of childhood* (6th ed.). Upper Saddle River, NJ: Pearson Education.

Wiegers, T. A., van der Zee, J., & Keirse, M. J. (1998). Maternity care in the Netherlands: The changing home birth rate. *Birth, 25,* 190–197.

Willatts, P. (1999). Development of means-end behavior in young infants: Pulling a support to retrieve a distant object? *Developmental Psychology, 35,* 651–667.

Williams, J. E., & Best, D. L. (1990). *Measuring sex stereotypes: A thirty-nation study* (rev. ed.). Newbury Park, CA: Sage.

Williams, J. M. (1997). *Style: Ten lessons in clarity and grace* (5th ed.). New York: Longman.

Willinger, M. (1995). Sleep position and sudden infant death syndrome. *Journal of the American Medical Association, 273,* 818–819.

Wills, T. A., Sandy, J. M., Yaeger, A., & Shinar, O. (2001). Family risk factors and adolescent substance use: Moderation effects for temperament dimensions. *Developmental Psychology, 37,* 283–297.

Wilson, B. J., Smith, S. L., Potter, W. J., Kunkel, D., Linz, D., Colvin, C. M., & Donnerstein, E. (2002). Violence in children's television programming: Assessing the risks. *Journal of Communication, 52,* 5–35.

Wilson, E. O. (1975). *Sociobiology: The new synthesis.* Cambridge MA: Harvard University Press.

Wilson, G. T., Heffernan, K., & Black, C. M. D. (1996). Eating disorders. In E. J. Marsh & R. A. Barkley (Eds.), *Child psychopathology.* New York: Guilford.

Wilson, M. (1989). Child development in the context of the black extended family. *American Psychologist, 44,* 380–383.

Wilson, R. D. (2000). Amniocentesis and chorionic villus sampling. *Current Opinion in Obstetrics & Gynecology, 12,* 81–86.

Wilson, R. S. (1983). The Louisville Twin Study: Developmental synchronies in behavior. *Child Development, 54,* 298–316.

Winner, E. (2000). Giftedness: Current theory and research. *Current Directions in Psychological Science, 9,* 153–156.

Wintre, M. G., & Vallance, D. D. (1994). A developmental sequence in the comprehension of emotions: Intensity, multiple emotions, and valence. *Developmental Psychology, 30,* 509–514.

Wise, B. W., Ring, J., & Olson, R. K. (1999). Training phonological awareness with and without explicit attention to articulation. *Journal of Experimental Child Psychology, 72,* 271–304.

Wolfe, D. A. (1985). Child-abusive parents: An empirical review and analysis. *Psychological Bulletin, 97,* 462–482.

Wolff, P. H. (1987). *The development of behavioral states and the expression of emotions in early infancy.* Chicago: University of Chicago Press.

Wolfson, A. R., & Carskadon, M. A. (1998). Sleep schedules and daytime functioning in adolescents. *Child Development, 69,* 875–887.

Wolraich, M. L., Lindgren, S. D., Stumbo, P. J., Stegink, L. D., Appelbaum, M. I., & Kiritsy, M. C. (1994). Effects of diets high in sucrose or aspartame on the behavior and cognitive performance of children. *New England Journal of Medicine, 330,* 301–307.

Wong-Fillmore, L., Ammon, P., McLaughlin, B., & Ammon, M. S. (1985). *Learning English through bilingual instruction.* Rosslyn, VA: National Clearinghouse for Bilingual Education.

Wood, J. J., Emmerson, N. A., & Cowan, P. A. (2004). Is early attachment security carried forward into relationships with preschool peers? *British Journal of Developmental Psychology, 22,* 245–253.

Woodward, A. L., & Markman, E. M. (1998). Early word learning. In W. Damon (Ed.), *Handbook of child psychology* (Vol. 2). New York: Wiley.

Woollacott, M. H., Shumway-Cook, A., & Williams, H. (1989). The development of balance and locomotion in children. In M. H. Woollacott & A. Shumway-Cook (Eds.), *Development of posture and gait across the life span.* Columbia: University of South Carolina Press.

World Health Organization. (1997). Integrated management of childhood lllness: A WHO/UNICEF initiative. *Bulletin of the World Health Organization, 75,* Supplement 1.

World Health Organization. (1999). *Removing obstacles to healthy development.* World Health Organization.

Worobey, J. (2005). Effects of malnutrition. In C. B. Fisher & R. M. Lerner (Eds.), *Encyclopedia of applied developmental science* (Vol. 2, pp. 673–676). Thousand Oaks, CA: Sage.

Wright, I., Waterman, M., Prescott, H., & Murdoch-Eaton, D. (2003). A new Stroop-like measure of inhibitory function development: Typical developmental trends. *Journal of Child Psychology and Psychiatry, 44,* 561–575.

Wynn, K. (1992). Addition and subtraction by human infants. *Nature, 358,* 749–750.

Wynn, K. (1996). Infants' individuation and enumeration of actions. *Psychological Science, 7,* 164–169.

Xiaohe, X., & Whyte, M. K. (1990). Love matches and arranged marriages. *Journal of Marriage and the Family, 52,* 709–722.

Yang, Q., Rasmussen, S. A., & Friedman, J. M. (2002). Mortality associated with Down's syndrome in the USA from 1983 to 1997: A population-based study. *The Lancet, 359,* 1019–1025.

Yates, M., & Youniss, J. (1996). Community service and political-moral identity in adolescents. *Journal of Research on Adolescence, 6,* 271–284.

Yau, J., & Smetana, J. G. (2003). Conceptions of moral, social-conventional, and personal events among Chinese preschoolers in Hong Kong. *Child Development, 74,* 647–758.

Yeung, W. J., Sandberg, J. F., Davis-Kean, P. E., & Hofferth, S. L. (2001). Children's time with fathers in intact families. *Journal of Marriage and Family, 63,* 136–154.

Yonas, A., & Owsley, C. (1987). Development of visual space perception. In P. Salapatek & L. Cohen (Eds.), *Handbook of infant perception* (Vol. 2). Orlando, FL: Academic Press.

Young, S. K., Fox, N. A., & Zahn-Waxler, C. (1999). The relations between temperament and empathy in 2-year-olds. *Developmental Psychology, 35,* 1189–1197.

Yuill, N., & Pearson, A. (1998). The development of bases for trait attribution: Children's understanding of traits as causal mechanisms based on desire. *Developmental Psychology, 34,* 574–586.

Zahn-Waxler, C., Friedman, R. J., Cole, P. M., Mizuta, I., & Hiruma, N. (1996). Japanese and United States preschool children's responses to conflict and distress. *Child Development, 67,* 2462–2477.

Zahn-Waxler, C., Cole, P. M., & Barrett, K. C. (1991). Guilt and empathy: Sex differences and implications for the development of depression. In J. Garber & K. Dodge (Eds.), *The development of emotion regulation and dys-*

regulation (pp. 243–272). Cambridge, England: Cambridge University Press.

Zahn-Waxler, C., Radke-Yarrow, M., Wagner, E., & Chapman, M. (1992). Development of concern for others. *Developmental Psychology, 28,* 126–136.

Zarbatany, L., Hartmann, D. P., & Rankin, D. B. (1990). The psychological functions of preadolescent peer activities. *Child Development, 61,* 1067–1080.

Zelazo, N. A., Zelazo, P. R., Cohen, K. M., & Zelazo, P. D. (1993). Specificity of practice effects on elementary neuromotor patterns. *Developmental Psychology, 29,* 686–691.

Zelazo, P. R., Weiss, M. J., Papageorgiou, A. N., & Laplante, D. P. (1989). Recovery and dishabituation of sound localization among normal-, moderate-, and high-risk newborns: Discriminant validity. *Infant Behavior and Development, 12,* 321–340.

Zeman, J., & Garber, J. (1996). Display rules for anger, sadness, and pain: It depends on who is watching. *Child Development, 67,* 957–973.

Zeman, J., & Shipman, K. (1997). Social-contextual influences on expectancies for managing anger and sadness: The transition from middle childhood to adolescence. *Developmental Psychology, 33,* 917–924.

Zhou, Q., Eisenberg, N., Losoya, S. H., Fabes, R. A., Reiser, M., Guthrie, I. K., et al. (2002). The relations of parental warmth and positive expressiveness to children's empathy-related responding and social functioning: A longitudinal study. *Child Development, 73,* 893–915.

Zigler, E., & Finn-Stevenson, M. (1992). Applied developmental psychology. In M. H. Bornstein & M. E. Lamb (Eds.), *Developmental psychology: An advanced textbook.* Hillsdale, NJ: Erlbaum.

Zigler, E., & Styfco, S. J. (1994). Head Start: Criticisms in a constructive context. *American Psychologist, 49,* 127–132.

Zigler, E. F., & Muenchow, S. (1992). *Head Start: Inside story of America's most successful educational experiment.* New York: Basic Books.

Zimiles, H., & Lee, V. E. (1991). Adolescent family structure and educational progress. *Developmental Psychology, 27,* 314–320.

Zimmer-Gembeck, M. J., Seibenbruner, J., & Collins, W. A. (2001). Diverse aspects of dating: Associations with psychosocial functioning from early to middle adolescence. *Journal of Adolescence, 24,* 313–336.

Zimmerman, B. J. (2001). Theories of self-regulated learning and academic achievement: An overview and analysis. In B. J. Zimmerman & D. H. Schunk (Eds.), *Self-regulated learning and academic achievement: Theoretical perspectives* (2nd ed., pp. 1–37). Mahwah, NJ: Erlbaum.

Zinar, S. (2000). The relative contributions of word identification skill and comprehension-monitoring behavior to reading comprehension ability. *Contemporary Educational Psychology, 25,* 363–377.

Zins, J. E., Garcia, V. F., Tuchfarber, B. S., Clark, K. M., & Laurence, S. C. (1994). Preventing injury in children and adolescents. In R. J. Simeonsson et al. (Ed.), *Risk, resilience, and prevention: Promoting the well-being of all children* (pp. 183–202). Baltimore: Paul H. Brookes.

Zukow-Goldring, P. (2002). Sibling caregiving. In M. H. Bornstein (Ed.), *Handbook of parenting: Vol. 3. Status and social conditions of parenting* (2nd ed., pp. 253–286). Mahwah, NJ: Erlbaum.

# ACKNOWLEDGMENTS

## Photographs

**About the Author** Page xxxi Courtesy of Prof. Robert V. Kail Ph D.

**Chapter 1** Page 2 Photostock.com Page 9 Nina Leen/Time Life Pictures/Getty Images. Page 10 Alan Carey/The Image Works. Page 12 Getty Images Inc. - Stone Allstock. Page 13 (top) AP Wide World Photos. Page 13 (bottom) Laura Dwight/PhotoEdit Inc. Page 15 © Nicole Duplaix/Peter Arnold, Inc./Alamy. Page 19 David Young-Wolff/PhotoEdit Inc. Page 21 © Charles Gupton/CORBIS. All Rights Reserved. Page 22 Richard Hutchings/PhotoEdit Inc. Page 24 Tony Freeman/PhotoEdit Inc. Page 25 Pamela Johnson Meyer/Photo Researchers, Inc. Page 31 (top left) Dennis MacDonald, PhotoEdit. Page 31 (bottom left) Myrleen F. Cate, PhotoEdit. Page 31 (top middle) Michael Newman, PhotoEdit. Page 31 (bottom middle) Jan Mueller Photography. Page 31 (top right) Michael Newman, PhotoEdit. Page 31 (bottom right) David Young-Wolff/PhotoEdit Inc. Page 33 David Young-Wolff/PhotoEdit Inc.

**Chapter 2** Page 38 Photostock.com Page 40 (top) Dr. Gopal Murti/Science Photo Library/Custom Medical Stock Photo, Inc. Page 40 (bottom) Francis Leroy/Biocosmos/Science Photo Library/Photo Researchers, Inc. Page 41 (top) David Phillips/Photo Researchers, Inc. Page 41 (bottom) Alexander Tsiaras/Science Source/Photo Researchers, Inc. Page 42 Biophoto Associates/Photo Researchers, Inc. Page 47 Lauren Shear/Photo Researchers, Inc. Page 50 Laura Dwight/The Stock Connection. Page 56 Michael Newman/PhotoEdit Inc.

**Chapter 3** Page 60 Photostock.com Page 63 Photo Lennart Nilsson/Albert Bonniers Forlag. Page 64 (left) Photo Lennart Nilsson/Albert Bonniers Forlag. Page 64 (right) Petit Format/Nestle/Science Source/Photo Researchers, Inc. Page 66 Photo Lennart Nilsson/Albert Bonniers Forlag AB. Page 70 Amy C. Etra/PhotoEdit Inc. Page 72 David Young-Wolff/PhotoEdit Inc. Page 74 From "The Broken Cord" by Michael Dorris, New York: Harper & Row, 1989. Photo courtesy of Ann Streissguth/Fetal Alcohol & Drug Unit. Page 80 (top) Brownie Harris/Corbis/Stock Market. Page 80 (bottom) Science Source/Photo Researchers, Inc. Page 85 (top) Lawrence Migdale/Photo Researchers, Inc. Page 85 (bottom) Margaret Miller/Photo Researchers, Inc. Page 89 Tom Stewart/Corbis/Stock Market. Page 91 Prof. Robert V. Kail Ph D. Page 94 © Jennie Woodcock/Relections Photolibrary/CORBIS All Rights Reserved. Page 95 Stephen R. Swinburne/Stock Boston.

**Chapter 4** Page 100 © Royalty-Free/CORBIS. All Rights Reserved. Page 107 Francis Dean/The Image Works. Page 108 Bob Daemmrich/Stock Boston. Page 109 Andy Reynolds/Taxi/Getty Images. Page 112 Bill Gillette/Stock Boston. Page 115 David Young-Wolff/PhotoEdit Inc. Page 116 Prof. Robert V. Kail Ph D. Page 117 Kilkullen/Trocaire/Corbis/Sygma. Page 118 David Young-Wolff/PhotoEdit Inc. Page 119 Philip Gould/ Corbis/Bettmann. Page 121 (top) © Nazima Kowall/CORBIS. Page 212 (bottom) Rhoda Sidney/Stock Boston. Page 122 Lawrence Migdale/Stock Boston. Page 123 (top) Don W. Fawcett/Komuro/Science Source/Photo Researchers, Inc. Page 123 (middle) Getty Images, Inc. - PhotoDisc. Page 123 (bottom) Ed Reschke/Ed Reschke. Page 126 (top) Alexander Tsiaras/Stock Boston. Page 126 (bottom) Richard T. Nowitz/Corbis/Bettmann.

**Chapter 5** Page 132 Photostock.com Page 135 (top) Dion Ogust/The Image Works. Page 135 (bottom) AP Wide World Photos. Page 137 AP Wide World Photos. Page 139 Jose Luis Pelaez/Corbis/Bettmann. Page 141 (top) Michael Agliolo Productions/ImageState/International Stock Photography Ltd. Page 141 (bottom) Jan Mueller/Jan Mueller Photography. Page 143 Innervisions. Page 144 (top left) Joe Sohm/Chromosohm/The Image Works. Page 144 (top right) Tadao Kimura/Tadao Kimura. Page 144 (bottom left) Bob Daemmrich/Stock Boston. Page 144 (bottom right) John William Banagan/ Getty Images Inc. - Image Bank. Page 146 Pascalis, O., de Hann, M., & Nelson, C. A. (2002). Is face processing species-specific during the first year of life? *Science*, 296, 1321-3. Page 148 Laima Druskis/Pearson Education/PH College. Page 149 Coco McCoy/Rainbow. Page 151 (top) © Kevin R. Morris/

CORBIS. Page 151 (bottom) © Greg Flume/CORBIS. Page 153 Dexter Gormley. Page 154 Mitch Reardon/Photo Researchers, Inc. Page 155 Alan Carey/The Image Works. Page 156 (top) Felicia Martinez/PhotoEdit Inc. Page 156 (bottom) Michael Newman/PhotoEdit Inc. Page 157 Elizabeth Crews/The Image Works. Page 158 (top) Bill Bachmann/The Image Works. Page 158 (bottom) Prof. Robert V. Kail Ph D. Page 159 Barry Elz/ImageState/International Stock Photography Ltd.

**Chapter 6** Page 162 Photostock.com Page 165 © Lynne Siler/Focus Group/Alamy. Page 166 Laura Dwight/Laura Dwight Photography. Page 167 (top) Jan Mueller/Jan Mueller Photography. Page 167 (bottom) Julian Hirshowitz/Corbis/Bettmann. Page 165 (left, middle and right) Copyright © Laura Dwight Photography. Page 170 Richard Hutchings/Photo Researchers, Inc. Page 175 Tom & Dee Ann McCarthy/Corbis/Bettmann. Page 176 Ellen B. Senisi/The Image Works. Page 177 © LWA-JDC/CORBIS All Rights Reserved. Page 181 Michael Newman/PhotoEdit Inc.

**Chapter 7** Page 198 Photostock.com Page 200 Courtesy of Carolyn Rovee-Collier. Page 202 Prof. Robert V. Kail Ph D. Page 204 Gale Zucker/Stock Boston. Page 207 Prof. Robert V. Kail Ph D. Page 208 L. O'Shaughnessy/Visuals Unlimited. Page 213 Steve Shott © Dorling Kindersley. Page 214 David Mager/Pearson Learning Photo Studio. Page 217 Elizabeth Crews/The Image Works. Page 221 Ellen Senisi/The Image Works. Page 222 Laura Dwight/Laura Dwight Photography. Page 226 Jennie Woodcock; Reflections Photolibrary/Corbis/Bettmann. Page 230 Alan Oddie/PhotoEdit Inc. Page 232 Audrey Gottlieb/Audrey Gottlieb.

**Chapter 8** Page 236 Photostock.com Page 241 Edy Bonafe/Edy Bonafe. Page 244 (top) Macduff Everton/Macduff Everton Studio. Page 244 (bottom) Anna E. Zuckerman/PhotoEdit Inc. Page 248 Bob Daemmrich/The Image Works. Page 252 Bill Aron/PhotoEdit Inc. Page 253 Paul Conklin/PhotoEdit Inc. Page 257 Okoniewski/Getty Images, Inc. - Liaison. Page 260 (top) Lawrence Migdale/Stock Boston. Page 260 (bottom) SuperStock, Inc.

**Chapter 9** Page 366 © Royalty-Free/CORBIS. All Rights Reserved Page 271 Bob Daemmrich/Bob Daemmrich Photography, Inc. Page 275 (top) Spencer Grant/PhotoEdit Inc. Page 275 (bottom) David Young-Wolff/PhotoEdit Inc. Page 277 Topham/The Image Works. Page 281 Tom Prettyman/PhotoEdit Inc. Page 282 A. Ramey/PhotoEdit Inc. Page 283 Courtesy of Judy DeLoache. Page 288 Susan Kuklin/Science Source/Photo Researchers, Inc. Page 290 Jan Mueller/Jan Mueller Photography. Page 292 Amy Etra/PhotoEdit Inc. Page 293 Beaura Kathy Ringrose/Michael Tobin.

**Chapter 10** Page 300 Photostock.com Page 303 (left) Laura Dwight/Laura Dwight Photography. Page 303 (middle) Michael Newman/PhotoEdit Inc. Page 303 (right) Corbis - Comstock Images Royalty Free. Page 304 (top) © Elizabeth Hathon/CORBIS Stock Market. Page 304 (bottom) Prof. Robert V. Kail Ph D. Page 305 Myrleen Ferguson Cate/ PhotoEdit Inc. Page 307 © Ellen Senisi/The Image Works. Page 309 © Fat Chance Productions/Getty Images Inc. Page 313 Spencer Grant/PhotoEdit Inc. Page 315 Innervisions. Page 320 Mary Kate Denny/PhotoEdit Inc. Page 321 Don Boroughs/The Image Works. Page 322 Laura Dwight/Laura Dwight Photography. Page 324 Walter Gans/The Image Works.

**Chapter 11** Page 330 Photostock.com Page 332 Getty Images, Inc. Page 334 Comstock Images. Page 336 (top) Michael Newman/PhotoEdit Inc. Page 336 (bottom) Beaura Kathy Ringrose/Michael Tobin. Page 338 Bob Daemmrich/Stock Boston. Page 339 Bill Aron/PhotoEdit Inc. Page 346 David Young Wolff/PhotoEdit Inc. Page 355 Prof. Robert V. Kail Ph D. Page 357 Bob Daemmrich/Stock Boston. Page 358 © Robert Maass/CORBIS.

**Chapter 12** Page 362 Photostock.com Page 365 Elizabeth Hathon/Corbis/Stock Market. Page 368 Laura Dwight/Laura Dwight Photography. Page 370 Tony Freeman/PhotoEdit Inc. Page 374 © David Bacon/The Image Works. Page 376 Skjold/The Image Works. Page 377 Myrleen Ferguson

Cate/PhotoEdit Inc. Page 378 © Bob Daemmrich/Stock Boston. Page 380 © LAWRENCE MIGDALE/www.migdale.com. Page 381 AP Wide World Photos. Page 383 Tony Freeman/PhotoEdit Inc. Page 385 © Laura Dwight Photography. Page 387 Bill Aron/PhotoEdit Inc. Page 392 © Jennie Woodcock/CORBIS.

**Chapter 13** Page 396 Photostock.com Page 399 D. Young-Wolff/PhotoEdit Inc. Page 404 (top) Mark Downey/Mark Downey/Lucid Images. Page 404 (middle) Bernard Wolf/Bernard Wolf Photography. Page 404 (bottom) Myrleen Cate/Index Stock Imagery, Inc. Page 406 (top) David Young-Wolff/PhotoEdit Inc. Page 406 (bottom) Bob Daemmrich/Stock Boston. Page 407 (left) Bob Daemmrich/Stock Boston. Page 407 (right) © Bob Daemmrich/Stock Boston. Page 408 C.W. McKeen/The Image Works. Page 409 Nancy Sheehan/PhotoEdit Inc. Page 414 (top) Laura Dwight/Laura Dwight Photography. Page 414 (bottom) Tony Freeman/PhotoEdit Inc. Page 415 George Goodwin/George Goodwin Photography. Page 420 John Burke/Index Stock Imagery, Inc. Page 421 © Bob Daemmrich/The Image Works.

**Chapter 14** Page 426 Photostock.com Page 429 Ablestock/Hemera Technologies/Alamy Images. Page 433 Michael Newman/PhotoEdit Inc. Page 434 James Shaffer/PhotoEdit Inc. Page 435 Photolibrary.Com. Page 436 Mark Richards/PhotoEdit Inc. Page 440 Michael Newman/PhotoEdit Inc. Page 442 Pam Francis/Pam Francis Photography. Page 445 Bachmann/PhotoEdit Inc. Page 446 (top) A. Ramey/Woodfin Camp & Associates. Page 446 (bottom) Getty Images, Inc. Page 447 Cindy Charles/PhotoEdit Inc. Page 448 Cathlyn Melloan/Getty Images Inc. - Stone Allstock. Page 450 Copyright by the San Francisco Child Abuse Council. Reprinted with permission. Page 451 Stephen Agricola/The Image Works.

**Chapter 15** Page 458 Photostock.com Page 461 (top) David M. Grossman/David M. Grossman. Page 461 (bottom) Laura Dwight/Laura Dwight Photography. Page 463 Myrleen Ferguson Cate/PhotoEdit Inc. Page 465 D. Young-Wolff/PhotoEdit Inc. Page 468 Mary Kate Denny/PhotoEdit Inc. Page 470 Getty Images, Inc. Page 472 Rolf Bruderer/Corbis/Bettmann. Page 474 © David Young-Wolff/PhotoEdit, Inc. Page 477 Tony Freeman/PhotoEdit Inc. Page 478 R. Termine/CTW/Everett Collection. Page 482 © Jeff Dunn/Stock Boston/PNI. Page 483 (top) © Boulton-Wilson/Jeroboam. Page 483 (bottom) David Young-Wolff/PhotoEdit Inc. Page 484 © David Woolley/Getty Images, Inc. Page 486 Tony Freeman/PhotoEdit Inc. Page 487 Ellen Senisi/The Image Works. Page 489 Jose L. Pelaez/Corbis/Stock Market. Page 490 Blair Seitz/Photo Researchers, Inc.

## Cartoons, Figures, and Tables

**Chapter 1** Page 18 *Hi and Lois* © 1993. Reprinted with special permission of King Features Syndicate.

**Chapter 2** Fig. 2-5 Reprinted figure 1 in Plomin, R. et al. Nature, nurture, and cognitive development from 1 to 15 years: A parent-offspring adoption study. *Psychological Science, 8*, 442-447. Reprinted with permission from Blackwell Publishers.

**Chapter 3** Figs. 3-4 and 3-6 Reprinted figures 7-1 and 9-12 from Moore and Persaud: *Before We Are Born* (1993) Reprinted with permission from Elsevier Science.

**Chapter 4** Fig. 4-6 From J.M. Tanner (1989). *Fetus into Man.* Cambridge, MA: Harvard University Press. Reprinted by permission of the publishers. © 1978, 1989 by J. M. Tanner. Fig. 4-11 Reprinted figure 2 in A. Passarotti, the development of face and location processing an fMRI. *Developmental Science, 6,* pp. 108. Reprinted with permission from Blackwell Publishers.

**Chapter 6** Fig. 6-9 Reprinted figure 1 in Sommerville and Woodward (2005) *Cognition.* Reprinted with permission from Elsevier Science.Fig. 6-11 From U. Frith (1989). *Autism: Explaining the Enigma.* Oxford, UK: Blackwell Publishers. © Axel Scheffler, Illustrator. Reprinted with permission.

**Chapter 7** Fig. 7-1Reprinted figure 4, the development of infant memory, *Current Directions in Psychological Science, 8,* 80-85. Reprinted with permission from Blackwell Publishers. Fig. 7-4 From R. Kail (1990). *The Development of Memory in Children, 3rd ed.* New York: Freeman. © by W.H Freeman. Reprinted with permission. Fig. 7-8 With permission from Blackwell Publishing, Ltd. Fig. 7-9 From Siegler, Robert S.; Alibali, Martha W., *Children's Thinking, 4th Edition,* © 2005. Fig. 7-11 Adapted by permission from Macmillan Publishers Ltd: Karen Wynn, Addition and subtraction by human infants. Nature, Vol. 358, Issue 6389, pp. 749–750 © 1992.

**Chapter 8** Fig 8-1 From John B. Carroll (1993). *Human Cognitive Abilities.* New York: Cambridge University Press. Reprinted with the permission of Cambridge University Press. Fig. 8-3 Simulated items similar to those in the *Wechsler Intelligence Scales for Children, 4th ed.* © 2003 by The Harcourt Assessment, Inc. Reproduced by permission. All Rights Reserved. Fig. 8-4 From B. Bloom (1974). *Stability and Change in Human Characteristics.* New York: John Wiley & Sons. Copyright by Benjamin Bloom. Reprinted with permission. Fig. 8-6 Figure 1, page 236 from *Developmental Psychology, 37.* © 2001 by the American Psychological Association. Reprinted with permission. Fig. 8-8 © by Scholastic Testing Service, Inc., Bensonville, IL. Reprinted with permission.

**Chapter 9** Photo 9-2 Reprinted by permission of John L. Hart, FLP and Creators Syndicate, Inc.

**Chapter 11** Photo 11-1 Copyright by William Hoest Enterprises, Inc. Reprinted with permission. Fig. 11-2 Adapted from Fig. 1 in S. Hunter & R. Pike, (1984). The pictorial scale of perceived competence and social acceptance for young children. *Child Development, 55,* 1973. © Society for Research in Child Development, Inc. Reprinted with permission.

**Chapter 12** Photo 12-1 Calvin and Hobbs © 1993 Watterson. Distributed by Universal Press Syndicate. Reprinted with permission. All Rights Reserved. Fig. 12-3 Fig. 1 in A. Colby, L. Kohlberg, J. C. Gibbs, & M. Lieberman (1983). A longitudinal study of moral development. *Monographs of the Society for Research in Child Development, 48.* © Society for Research in Child Development, Inc. Reprinted with permission. Fig. 12-6 From N.R. Crick & K. A. Dodge (1994). A review and reformulation of social information-processing mechanisms in children's social adjustment. *Psychological Bulletin, 115,* 74–101. © 1994 by the American Psychological Association.

**Chapter 13** Fig. 13-3 From J. W. Pellegrino & R. Kail (1982). Process analysis of spatial aptitude, In R. Sternberg (Ed.), *Advances in the Psychology of Human Intelligence, Vol. 1.* Hillsdale, NJ: Lawrence Erlbaum Associates Reprinted with permission. Fig. 13-7 Adapted from C.L. Martin & C.F. Halvorsen, Jr. (1981). A schematic processing model of sex typing and stereotyping in children, *Child Development, 52,* 1121. © Society for Research in Child Development, Inc. Reprinted with permission.

**Chapter 14** Photo 14-8 PEANUTS © 1993 United Features Syndicate. Reprinted by permission. Photo 14-4 © by the San Francisco Child Abuse Council. Reprinted with permission.

**Chapter 15** Photo 15-9 © by Martha F. Campbell. Reprinted with permission.

# NAME INDEX

Abbott, R.D., 226
Abbott, S.P., 226
Abikoff, H.B., 150
Ablin, D.S., 207
Aboud, F.E., 355
Abramson, L.Y., 409
Ackerman, B.P., 296, 302, 486
Acredolo, L.P., 275
Adajian, L.B., 406
Adam, E.K., 429
Adams, J., 78, 224
Adams, M.J., 225
Adams, R.J., 138
Adolph, K.E., 153, 154
Ager, J.W., 74
Aglow, J.C., 343
Agras, W.S., 119
Aguiar, A., 188
Ahmed, S., 415
Ainsworth, M.D.S., 321, 322
Akhtar, N., 276
Albersheim, L., 323
Alberts, A.E., 92
Alexander, D.B., 105
Alibali, M.W., 173, 179, 217, 224, 225
Allen, L., 281
Allison, Dorothy, 391
Altemeier, W.A., III, 452
Altman, J., 438
Altran, S., 189
Aman, C.J., 149
Amato, P.R., 431, 438, 439
Ambady, N., 406
American Academy of Child and
   Adolescent Psychiatry, 483
American Academy of Pediatrics, 96,
   108
American Academy of Pediatrics
   Committee on Sports Medicine
   and Committee on School
   Health, 158
American Psychiatric Association,
   148
Ammon, M.S., 282
Ammon, P., 282
Anand, K.J., 135
Anastasi, A., 255
Andersen, A.M.N., 72–73
Andersen, C., 218
Anderson, C.A., 388, 479
Anderson, D.R., 126, 148, 419, 476,
   478
Anderson, E.R., 441
Anderson, K.J., 404
Anderson, S.W., 126
Andreas, D., 325
Andreatos, M., 273
Andruski, J.E., 271
Anglin, J.M., 274
Ani, C., 117, 118
Annett, M., 157
Antonarakis, S.E., 46
Anyanwu, L., 85
Apgar, V., 92
Applebaum, M.I., 149, 249
Archer, N., 222

Archer, T., 421
Arcus, D., 314
Arendt, R., 79
Arnold, L.E., 150
Aronson, J., 255
Arseneault, L., 88
Arterberry, M.E., 307
Arthur, J., 85
Asbury, K., 383
Ashcraft, M.H., 230
Asher, S.R., 466, 473
Ashman, S.B., 87
Ashmead, D.H., 155
Aslin, R.N., 96, 136, 142, 269, 270
Atkin, C., 477
Atkins, P., 221
Atkinson, L., 323, 463
Atkinson, R., 340
Attanucci, J., 375
Au, T.K., 276
Augustyn, M., 79
Aunola, K., 431
Austin, C.M., 271
Austin-LaFrance, R., 118
Avenevoli, S., 341, 409
Averill, J.A., 300
Aviezer, O., 324
Axworthy, D., 47
Ayduk, O., 367
Ayers, T., 439
Azar, S.T., 452
Bachman, J., 484
Backscheider, A.G., 189
Baddeley, A., 179, 279
Baenninger, M., 406
Baer, D.M., 12
Bagwell, C.L., 388, 466
Bahan, B., 272
Bahrick, L.E., 139, 140
Bailey, D.A., 158
Bailey, J.M., 470
Baillargeon, R., 186, 187, 188
Baird, D.D., 72
Bakeman, R., 79
Baker, C., 282
Baker, J.E., 120
Baker, L., 224, 226
Bakermans-Kranenburg, M., 322,
   325, 380
Baker-Ward, L., 210, 211
Baldwin, D.A., 308
Ball, S., 477
Banaji, M.R., 406
Bancroft, J., 47
Bandura, A., 12–13, 412
Bangert-Downs, R.L., 227
Banks, M.S., 138, 141, 144
Baranowski, T., 157
Barber, B.K., 431
Bardwell, J.R., 401
Barenboim, C., 352
Barinaga, M., 128
Barkley, R.A., 149, 150
Barlaugh, D.G., 252
Barlow, D.H., 306
Barnard, K.E., 252

Barnett, N.P., 158
Barr, R.F., 479
Barrett, K.C., 408
Barry, J., 272
Barton, M.E., 292
Bartsch, K., 192, 193
Baskett, L.M., 445
Bassett, H.H., 482
Basso, K.H., 112
Bates, E., 275, 279, 280, 289, 293
Bates, J.E., 105, 114, 313, 315, 317,
   387, 389, 392, 430, 436, 462, 466
Bauer, P.J., 200, 201, 206
Baumeister, A.A., 95
Baumeister, R.F., 350
Baumrind, D., 431
Bauserman, R., 438
Bayatzis, R., 241
Bayley, N., 248
Beal, C.R., 226, 296
Bearden, C.E., 88
Beardsall, L., 448
Bearman, S.K., 116
Beatrice, B., 71, 72
Beauchamp, G.K., 66, 135
Becker, B.J., 408
Becker, J.B., 409
Bee, D.E., 157
Behnke, M., 74
Belanger, J., 277
Belgrad, S.L., 296
Bell, A.P., 470
Bell, J.J., 47
Bell, N., 175
Belsky, J., 22, 29, 113, 314, 437, 448
Bem, D.J., 470
Bem, S.L., 421
Bender, B.G., 47
Benenson, J., 465
Benigni, L., 293
Benson, B., 469
Benson, J.B., 155
Bento, S., 325
Benton, S.L., 225
Bereiter, C., 225
Berenbaum, S., 414, 419
Berg, C.A., 408
Bergen, D., 462
Berger, A., 181
Berk, L.E., 177
Berko, J., 286
Berkowitz, L., 388, 479
Berkowitz, M.W., 378
Bernat, D.H., 339
Berndt, T.J., 465, 466
Berninger, G., 293
Berninger, V.W., 226
Berridge, K.C., 135
Bersoff, D.M., 375
Bertenthal, B.H., 153, 155
Bertenthal, B.I., 142
Berthier, N.E., 155
Bertin, E., 145
Best, C.T., 270
Best, D.L., 398, 400
Bettencourt, B.A., 407

Betts, N.T., 464
Beveridge, M., 70
Beyers, J., 105
Bezman, R.J., 149
Bhatt, R.S., 145
Bialystok, E., 282
Bidrose, S., 207
Biederman, J., 149
Biesanz, J.C., 486
Bigbee, M.A., 390
Bigler, R.S., 355, 356–57, 401,
   418, 421
Binet, Alfred, 6, 246
Binghenheimer, J.B., 389
Birch, H.G., 311, 316
Birch, L.L., 108, 120
Birch, S.A.J., 276
Birman, D., 339
Bjorklund, D.F., 179, 201, 203, 204,
   207, 216, 319, 428
Black, C.M.D., 118
Black, M.M., 443
Black-Gutman, D., 355, 356
Blades, M., 477
Blake, J., 293
Blamey, P., 272
Blanchard, R., 470
Blanton, H., 467
Block, J., 403
Block, J.H., 408
Bloom, L., 277, 290, 293, 296
Bloom, P., 276
Blyth, D., 116
Bogaert, A.F., 470
Bogat, G.A., 324, 477
Boggiano, A.D., 346
Bohannon, J.N., 294
Bohlin, G., 419
Boivin, M., 387, 466
Boles, D., 405
Bolger, K.E., 451
Bolig, E.E., 250
Bollmer, J.M., 393
Bolvin, M., 279, 387
Bonds, T.A., 466
Boodoo, G., 250, 254
Borke, J., 333
Borkowsky, J.G., 313
Bornstein, M.H., 93, 227, 248, 280,
   307, 461, 463
Borzellino, G., 293
Boston, M.B., 204
Bot, S.M., 467
Bouchard, T.J., 52, 250, 254
Boulerice, B., 88
Bow, C., 272
Bowen, R., 336
Bowlby, J., 319
Bowyer-Crane, C.A., 224
Boykin, A.W., 250, 254
Bradley, L., 221
Bradley, R.H., 252, 434, 487
Braet, C., 119
Braine, M.D.S., 289
Brainerd, C.J., 171, 205

Brakke, K.E., 288
Braungart-Rieker, J.M., 313, 367
Bray, J.H., 440
Brazelton, T.B., 85, 92
Brennan, P.A., 74, 389
Brescoll, V., 388
Bretano, C., 440
Bretherton, I., 280, 293
Bridges, M., 441
Brockington, I., 86, 87
Brody, G.H., 116, 436, 445, 448
Brody, N., 250, 254
Brodzinsky, D.M., 446, 447
Bromley, D.B., 352
Bronfenbrenner, U., 254, 428
Bronzino, J.D., 118
Brooks-Gunn, J., 71, 72, 89, 254, 442, 451, 485, 486, 488
Brophy, J.E., 414, 489, 490
Brown, A.C., 448
Brown, A.L., 226
Brown, B.B., 469, 471, 472
Brown, C., 356–57
Brown, C.S., 356–57
Brown, E., 145, 192
Brown, E.D., 486
Brown, E.G., 463
Brown, J.R., 308, 309, 448
Brown, J.V., 79
Brown, K.P., 474
Brown, L.L., 341
Brown, Louise, 40
Brown, Oliver, 357–58
Brown, R., 224, 285
Browne, K.D., 477
Brownell, K.D., 118, 119
Bruce, J., 180, 446, 447
Bruck, M., 208, 210, 211
Bruschi, C.J., 307
Bryant, P., 221, 222
Bryden, M.P., 405
Bryk, A., 280
Bryk, K., 419
Buchanan, C.M., 409, 438, 441
Buchannan, L., 471
Buchanon, C.M., 441
Buchholz, M., 135
Budreau, D.R., 145
Bugental, D.B., 452
Buhrmester, D., 448
Buhs, E.S., 473
Buijzen, M., 477
Buitelaar, J., 70
Bukowski, W., 387, 460, 464, 466, 473
Bullinger, A., 136
Bullock, M., 333
Burch, M.M., 200
Burchinal, M., 253, 280, 434, 484, 485, 486
Bureau of Labor Statistics, 483
Burger-Judisch, L.M., 126
Buriel, R., 430, 432, 463
Burk, W.J., 466
Burman, B., 439
Burnham, D., 140
Burraston, B., 466
Burston, A., 443
Busnel, M.C., 66
Buss, K.A., 309, 310, 313, 314
Bussey, K., 412
Bussiere, J., 126–27

Butler, S., 408
Buxton, R., 126–27
Buyck, P., 350
Byers, T., 120
Byrd-Craven, J., 416
Byrne, B.M., 345
Byrne, D.F., 354
Byrnes, J.P., 404
Cain, K., 223, 224
Cairns, B.D., 471
Cairns, R.B., 471
Caldwell, B.M., 252
Caldwell, C.H., 339
Caldwell, L.L., 482
Caldwell, M.S., 23, 350
Call, K.T., 484
Callahan, C.M., 257
Callanan, M.A., 276, 308
Calvert, S.L., 479
Camaioni, L., 293
Cameron, C.A., 226
Cameron, J., 356
Campbell, 387
Campbell, F.A., 253
Campbell, J.D., 350
Campbell, M.E., 465
Campbell, R., 282
Campbell, S.B., 87
Campbell, T.F., 404
Campbell, W.K., 346
Campos, J.J., 143, 304, 307, 308
Campos, R., 307
Camras, L.A., 307
Canfield, R.L., 227
Cannon, T.D., 88
Cantor, N., 368
Capelli, C.A., 297
Capozzoli, M.C., 148
Carey, S., 145, 188, 219, 228
Carlo, G., 374, 376, 377
Carlson, E.A., 323
Carlson, S.M., 193, 462
Carpenter, P.A., 224
Carrere, S., 437
Carroll, J.B., 239
Carroll, J.L., 95
Carskadon, M.A., 106, 340
Cartwright, B.S., 462
Caruso, D.R., 241
Carver, K., 468
Carver, P.R., 470
Casaer, P., 125
Casas, J.F., 392
Case, R., 180
Casey, B.J., 125, 126, 407
Casiglia, A.C., 473
Caspi, A., 113, 313, 315, 350
Cassidy, J., 322, 325
Castejon, J.L., 243
Castellanos, F.X., 407
Castle, J.M., 304
Cattell, R.B., 238
Caulfield, L., 66, 70
Ceci, S.J., 208, 209, 210, 211, 250, 254
Center for Disease Control and Prevention, 121
Cerella, J., 181
Cervantes, C.A., 308
Chakraborty, R., 120
Champion, H., 296
Chan, R.W., 444
Chandler, M., 374

Chang, L., 392
Chanquoy, L., 226
Chao, R.K., 432
Chapman, M., 380
Chapman, P.D., 245, 246
Charley, C.M., 462
Chase-Lansdale, P.L., 72, 442, 481
Chassin, L., 467
Chavira, V., 339
Chavous, T.M., 339
Chen, A., 282
Chen, X., 473
Chen, Y.R., 339
Chen, Z., 219
Cheney, D., 288
Cheng, H., 441
Chess, S., 311, 313, 316
Chessor, D., 349
Cheung, L.W.Y., 89
Chi, M.T.H., 203
Child, I.L., 431
Children's Defense Fund, 117, 438, 481
Chilman, C.S., 112
Chistovich, I.A., 271
Chistovich, L.A., 271
Chomitz, V.R., 89
Chomsky, N., 287, 288
Chorpita, B.F., 306
Christakos, A., 465
Christens, P., 72–73
Christensen, A., 437
Christensen, C.A., 226
Christensen, M., 447
Chuang, S., 150
Cicchetti, D., 449, 451, 452
Cichomski, B., 445
Cillessen, A.H.N., 473
Cintra, L., 118
Cipani, E., 259
Cipielewski, J., 281
Clark, K.B., 358–59
Clark, K.M., 122
Clark, M.K., 358
Clark, P.M., 374
Clark, R., 88
Clarke-Stewart, K.A., 440
Clements, D.H., 227
Clifton, R.K., 135, 136, 153, 155
Clingempeel, W.G., 441
Clinkenbeard, P.R., 257
Cloud, J.M., 400
Cluss, P.A., 120
Cnattingius, S., 74
Coates, R.J., 120
Cochran, S.W., 401
Cocking, R.R., 479
Coco, A.L., 473
Codd, J., 282
Cohen, J.D., 407
Cohen, K.M., 154
Cohen, L., 383
Cohen, S., 70
Cohn, J.F., 87, 408
Coie, J.D., 385, 386
Colburne, K.A., 399
Colby, A., 373
Cole, C.F., 478
Cole, D.A., 347, 348
Cole, D.R., 157
Cole, M., 177
Cole, P.M., 307, 408

Coles, C.D., 79
Coley, J.D., 189
Coley, R.L., 481, 482
Coll, C.G., 434
Collaer, M.L., 407, 419
Collins, J.L., 157
Collins, P.A., 419
Collins, W.A., 340, 469
Colombo, B., 72
Coltheart, M., 221
Coltrane, S., 463
Colvin, C.M., 388
Colwell, M.J., 462
Committee on Genetics, 45
Condry, J.C., 408
Conduct Problems Prevention Research Group, 391
Conger, R.D., 116, 484, 485, 487
Conley, C.S., 23
Connecticut Department of Children and Families, 482
Conners, C.K., 150
Connor, C.M., 272
Conover, D.L., 75
Cooke, R., 82
Cooper, R.P., 271
Coopersmith, S., 350
Copernicus, 165
Coplan, R.J., 462
Copper, R.L., 70
Corbin, C.B., 157, 158
Corkill, A.J., 225
Cornelius, M., 74
Cornwell, K.S., 156
Corwyn, R.F., 434, 487
Cosmides, L., 302
Costa, P.T., 315
Costall, A., 303
Costigan, K.A., 66, 70
Costin, S.E., 382
Coté, S., 386
Coulton, C.J., 452
Courage, M.L., 138, 200, 207
Covill, A., 226
Cowan, C.P., 343
Cowan, P.A., 343, 463
Cowart, B.J., 135
Cox, A., 281
Cox, M.J., 324, 428, 435, 486
Coy, K.C., 367
Coyle, M., 85
Crabbe, J., 52
Craig, K.D., 135
Craig, W., 21
Craven, R., 345, 349
Craw, S., 207
Crenshaw, T.M., 474
Creusere, M.A., 297
Cribb, P., 157
Crick, N.R., 386, 389, 390, 391, 392, 408
Crnic, K., 88, 437
Crockenberg, S.B., 93
Crosignani, P.G., 75
Cross, D., 193
Crouter, A.C., 415, 448
Crowe, E., 194
Crowell, J., 323
Crown, C.L., 71, 72
Csikszentmihalyi, M., 257
Cuellar, I., 340
Cumberland, A., 310, 430

Cummings, E.M., 323, 435, 439
Cumsille, P., 448
Cunningham, A.E., 223
Curran, P.J., 439, 467
Curtain, S.C., 85
Curtis, B., 221
Curtis, L.E., 227
Curtis, M.E., 224
Curtiss, S., 289
Curwin, A., 280
Cutrona, C.E., 116
Dadisman, K., 482
Dahl, R.E., 407
Dale, P.S., 275, 279, 387
Daley, T.C., 252
Daly, M., 452
Damasio, A.R., 126
Damasio, H., 126
Damon, W., 334
Danaher, D.L., 408
Daneman, M., 224
Dannemiller, J.L., 138, 142, 145
Darling, N., 482
Darlington, R., 253
Darvill, T., 92
Darwin, Charles, 6
Das, A., 70
Da Silva, M.S., 374
D'Augelli, A., 470
Davidson, F.H., 357
Davidson, M.M., 357
Davies, I., 138
Davies, L., 441
Davies, M., 150
Davies, P.T., 435, 439
Davis, B.L., 273
Davis, E.P., 180
Davis, S.W., 400
Davis Goldman, B., 200
Davis-Kean, P.E., 321
Dawson, G., 87
Day, J.D., 250
Day, N., 74
De Beni, R., 224
DeCasper, A.J., 66
DeFries, J.C., 47, 50
de Hann, M., 146–47
Deirmenciolu, S.M., 472
de Jong, P.F., 221
Dekker, G.A., 70
Dekovic, M., 474
De La Cruz, F., 81
Delaney, C., 94
Dellas, M., 337
DeLoache, J.S., 202, 216, 219, 283
Dement, W.C., 95
Dempster, F.N., 180
Denning, D.J., 448
Dennis, J., 463
Denny, M.A., 154
Dent, C.W., 477
DeRosier, M.E., 473
de Rosnay, M., 193
deSchonen, S., 333
Desjardins, R.N., 271
Detterman, D.K., 259
Devet, K., 367
deVilliers, J.G., 287
deVilliers, P.A., 287
Dewey, K.G., 106
De Wolff, M.S., 323
Dews, S., 296

de Zwaan, M., 119
Diamond, M., 404
Diaz-Cintra, S., 118
Dick, D.M., 52, 116
Dickens, W.T., 252
Dick-Read, G., 84
Diesendruck, G., 276
Dietz, W.H., 107
Dionne, G., 279, 387
DiPietro, J.A., 66, 70
Dishion, T.J., 388, 466, 474
Dockrell, J., 260
Dodd, B., 140
Dodge, K.A., 114, 317, 385, 386, 387,
    388, 389, 391, 392, 430, 436, 462,
    466
Dodge, T., 467
Doering, C.H., 407
Dolensky, E., 465
Dollaghan, C.A., 404
Donahoe, A., 200
Donnell, F., 324
Donnellan, M.B., 350
Donnerstein, E., 388, 479
Donovan, W.L., 367
Dornbusch, S.M., 441, 483, 484
Douglas, L., 320
Down, John Langdon, 46*n*
Downey, G., 367, 473
Downey, J., 47
Downey, R.G., 225
Downs, A.C., 414
Doyle, A., 323, 356
Draghi-Lorenz, R., 303
Draper, P., 113
Drew, L.M., 441, 442, 443
Duck, S.C., 419
Duffy, S., 463
Duncan, G.J., 254, 451
Dunham, F., 280
Dunham, P.J., 280
Dunn, J., 194, 308, 309, 441, 448
Dunne, M.P., 470
Dunson, D.B., 72
Duran, R., 282
Durham, M., 280
Durik, A.M., 88
Durkin, K., 356
Durston, S., 125, 126
Eacott, M.J., 207
Eagly, A.H., 408, 421
Earls, F.J., 389
Early Child Care Research Network,
    481
Easterbrook, M.A., 145
Eaton, W.O., 404
Ebbesen, E., 368
Eccles, J.S., 349, 404, 409
Edelstein, W., 374
Edmunds, G., 226
Edwards, C.A., 472
Edwards, J.R., 400
Egan, S.K., 389, 393, 470
Egeland, G.M., 75
Ehlinger, S., 157
Ehrhardt, A.A., 47
Ehri, L.C., 221
Eichstedt, J.A., 399
Eisenberg, N., 308, 310, 316, 374,
    376, 377, 381, 382, 383, 430
Eisenbud, L., 419
Eizenman, D.R., 142

Elder, G.H., 116, 336, 441, 484, 485,
    487
Elder, N., 70
Elkin, E.J., 47
Elkind, D., 336
Elliott, G.R., 150
Ellis, B.J., 55, 113, 114
Ellis, L.A., 345
Ellis, S., 171, 215
Ellis, W.K., 260
Embry, L., 87
Emerson, N.A., 463
Emery, R.E., 439
Emmerson, N.A., 463
Emslie, H., 279
Engelhardt, S.E., 250
Engels, R.C.M.E., 467
Enns, J.T., 148
Enns, L.R., 404
Ensminger, M.E., 442
Eppler, M.A., 153
Epstein, L.H., 120
Erel, O., 439, 448
Erikson, E.H., 335
Erixon, A., 421
Ernst, M., 74
Eskritt, M., 202
Espinosa, M.P., 252
Esplin, P.W., 210
Etaugh, C., 400
Evans, G.W., 487
Evans, M., 81
Evans, M.A., 220
Evans, S.M., 417
Everett, J.J., 158
Eyer, D.E., 86
Eyler, F.D., 74
Fabes, R.A., 308, 310, 316, 377, 381,
    383, 415, 416, 417, 430
Fagot, B.I., 417
Falbo, T., 445
Falk, D., 93
Fan, X., 447
Fang, F., 374
Fang, G., 374
Fantauzzo, C.A., 304
Faraone, S.V., 149
Farkas, K., 79
Farrar, M.J., 204
Farver, J.M., 392, 461
Fasig, L., 7, 333
Faw, G.D., 259
Federal Interagency Forum on Child
    and Family Statistics, 122
Feehan, M., 149
Fegley, S., 483
Feigenson, L., 228
Feinberg, M.E., 448
Feldhusen, J.F., 257
Feldman, H.M., 404
Feldman, J.F., 148
Feldman, N.S., 346
Feldman, R., 367, 368
Feldman, S.S., 339, 367
Feng, W.Y., 314
Fennema, E., 406
Fenson, L., 275, 279
Ferguson, D.M., 71, 106, 114
Fernald, A., 308
Fernald, L., 117, 118
Fernandez, M.C., 282
Ferrell, J., 306
Ferreol-Barbey, M., 224

Field, T.M., 89, 292, 321
Fields, J., 442
Fifer, W.P., 70
Finch, M.D., 484
Fink, B., 226
Finkelstein, B.D., 464
Finley, G.E., 447
Finnie, V., 463
Finn-Stevenson, M., 255
Fisch, S., 478
Fischer, M., 149
Fish, M., 314
Fisher, C., 277
Fisher, C.B., 7
Fisher, J.A., 108
Fitzgerald, H.E., 156
Fitzgerald, J., 226
Fivush, R., 206, 408
Fjølling, Asbjørn, 55
Flanagan, C., 87, 439
Flavell, E.R., 195
Flavell, J.H., 169, 171, 172, 195, 203,
    308
Flesser, D., 357
Fletcher, K.E., 149
Flynn, J.R., 252
Foehr, U.G., 475, 479
Fonzi, A., 466
Foorman, B.R., 222, 223
Forbes, D., 408
Forbes, J.N., 276
Forde, V., 117
Foreyt, J.P., 120
Forman, S.D., 407
Forrest, T.J., 205
Foster, S.H., 293
Fowler, F., 431
Fowles, J., 400
Fox, N.A., 303, 315, 316
Francis, M., 226
Frank, D.A., 79
Franklin, A., 138
Franquart-Declercq, C., 297
Fredriksen, K., 106
Freedman, D.S., 120
Freedman, J., 89
Freitas, A.L., 473
French, K.E., 403
French, S., 463
Frensch, P.A., 406
Freud, Sigmund, 6, 10
Fried, A., 341
Fried, P.A., 74
Friedman, J., 310
Friedman, J.M., 46, 74, 79
Friedman, R.J., 307
Frohlich, C.B., 374
Frye, D., 193
Fu, V.R., 432
Fujita, N., 293
Fuller, B., 481
Fuller-Thomson, E., 442
Furman, W., 448, 466
Fuson, K.C., 229
Futterweit, L.R., 148
Gabriel, L.T., 259
Gaddis, L., 316
Gagliardi, A., 87
Galbraith, K.A., 469
Galler, J.R., 117, 118
Gallimore, R., 232
Galperin, C., 461

Gandhi, Mohandas K., 383
Gangestad, S.W., 145
Garber, J., 113, 114, 308, 350
Garcia, M.M., 449
Garcia, V.F., 122
Garcia-Mila, M., 218
Gardner, H., 240, 242
Gardner, W., 215
Garland, A., 350
Garner, P.W., 448
Garovich-Szabo, L., 398
Gartstein, M.A., 312–13
Garvey, C., 293
Gash, H., 422
Gathercole, S.E., 279
Gaulin, S.J.C., 302, 319
Gauthier, R., 461
Gauvain, M., 175, 176
Gavin, D.A.W., 345
Gavin, L.A., 466
Gavinski-Molina, M.H., 462
Ge, X., 116, 436
Geary, D.C., 319, 416, 419, 422
Geisel, T., 221
Gelman, R., 228, 293, 294
Gelman, S.A., 188, 189, 195, 279,
    353, 400, 401, 412, 413, 414
Genel, M., 149
Gentile, L., 487
George, C., 325
Gerken, L., 289
Gerow, L., 462
Gershkoff-Stowe, L., 278
Gesell, Arnold, 9
Geva, D., 74
Gibbons, F.X., 116
Gibbs, J.C., 373, 374, 378
Gibson, E.J., 143, 153
Gibson, K.R., 123
Giedd, J.N., 407
Gifford-Smith, M., 388
Gilbreth, J.G., 441
Giles, H., 400
Gilligan, C., 375–76
Gillmore, J., 355
Gineste, M., 297
Gini, M., 326
Girgus, J.S., 341
Glaser, D., 135
Gleason, K.E., 325
Gleason, T.R., 462
Glick, P.C., 440
Glover, V., 70
Glusman, M., 276
Goeke-Morey, M.C., 435
Goetz, E.T., 222
Goldenberg, R.L., 70, 71
Goldfield, B.A., 279
Golding, J., 70, 443
Goldin-Meadow, S., 275
Goldman, L.S., 149
Goldman, M., 367
Goldsmith, H.H., 309, 313, 314, 325
Goldstein, D., 257
Goldstein, M.H., 271
Goleman, D., 241
Golinkoff, R.M., 276, 293
Golombok, S., 41, 443, 470
Goncu, A., 176
Gong, Z., 220
Gonnella, C., 487
Gonzales, P., 230

Good, T.L., 414, 489, 490
Goodman, E., 41
Goodman, G.S., 207, 439
Goodnow, J.J., 383, 432
Goodrick, G.K., 120
Goodrick, T.S., 374
Goodwyn, S.W., 275
Gordin, D.N., 479
Gordon, B.N., 210, 211
Gordon, C.P., 469
Gordon, R.A., 72
Gorman-Smith, D., 389
Gottesman, I.R., 54, 55
Gottfredson, L.S., 250
Gottfried, A.W., 252
Gottfried, G.M., 188
Gottlieb, G., 55
Gottlieb, L.N., 447
Gottman, J.M., 433, 437, 462
Goubet, N., 135, 155
Governor's Task Force, 211
Govier, E., 405
Graesser, A.C., 224
Graham, S., 226, 392
Graham-Bermann, 388
Grajewski, B.A., 75
Granier-Deferre, C., 66
Granrud, C.E., 142
Grantham-McGregor, S., 117, 118
Graves, R., 273
Gray, C., 252
Gray, S.W., 252
Green, F.L., 195
Green, J.L., 374
Green, K.E., 337
Greenberg, M.T., 88
Greene, B., 341
Greene, S., 314
Greene, S.M., 441
Greenfield, P., 479
Greenfield, P.M., 252
Greenhill, L.L., 150
Greenwald, A.G., 406
Grekin, E.R., 74
Griffiths, J., 356
Grigorenko, E.L., 243, 250, 256
Groen, G.J., 230
Groisser, D., 149
Gross, E.F., 479
Gross, J.N., 305
Grotevant, H.D., 446, 447
Grotpeter, J.K., 390, 408
Gruber, R., 105
Grunau, R.V.E., 135
Grusec, J.E., 383
Guacci-Franco, N., 465
Guerra, N.G., 391
Guile, C.A., 120
Guillemin, J., 88
Guite, J., 149
Gulko, J., 401
Gunnar, M.R., 23, 325, 446, 447
Gunter, B., 477
Gurewitsch, E.D., 66, 70
Gurucharri, C., 355
Guthrie, I.K., 310, 316, 383, 430
Guthrie, Robert, 55
Guttentag, R., 306
Guttmacher, A.F., 69
Guzmán, J.C., 230
Hack, M., 89
Hadjistavropoulos, H.D., 135

Hadley, T., 88
Hahn, E.R., 186, 188
Haight, W., 280
Hains, S.M.J., 145
Haith, M.M., 155
Hakuta, K., 282
Halberstadt, A.G., 408
Hale, S., 181
Halford, G.S., 214
Hall, D.G., 277
Hall, G.S., 6, 330
Hall, J.A., 408
Hall, L.K., 26, 215
Haller, M., 221
Hallinan, M.T., 465
Halpern, W.E., 75
Halpern, D.F., 250, 254, 404, 406
Halpern, L.F., 95
Halverson, C.F., 418
Haman, K.I., 341
Hamilton, B.E., 72, 469
Hamilton, C.E., 323
Hamilton, E.M.N., 69
Hamilton-Giachritsis, C., 477
Hamm, J.V., 465, 466
Hammersmith, S.K., 470
Hammill, D.D., 260
Hammond, M.A., 252
Hanis, C., 120
Hankin, B.L., 409
Hannon, E.E., 136
Hansen, D.J., 451
Hanson, D.R., 54, 55
Happaney, K., 452
Harlan, E., 365–66
Harley, C., 485
Harley, K., 207, 333
Harlow, H.F., 319
Harlow, S.M., 319
Harman, C., 325
Harmer, S., 192
Harmon, R.J., 47
Harold, G.T., 435
Harold, R.D., 404
Harris, B., 86
Harris, J.A., 69
Harris, K.R., 226
Harris, L.J., 156
Harris, M.J., 393
Harris, P.L., 192, 193
Harrist, A.W., 462
Hart, C.H., 387, 446, 473
Hart, D., 334
Harter, K., 435
Harter, S., 332, 334, 338, 343, 344,
    345, 346, 349, 350, 421, 469
Hartman, E., 189
Hartmann, D.P., 464
Hartup, W.W., 415, 464, 465, 466, 472
Haselager, G.J.T., 466
Haslam, C., 79
Hastings, P.D., 436
Haugaard, J.J., 439
Hauser, M., 228
Hautamaki, J., 243
Haviland, J.M., 307
Hawilo, M.E., 135
Hawley, P.H., 472
Haxby, J.V., 407
Hay, D., 87
Hayden, A., 145
Hayes, D.P., 281

Hayes, R., 145
Hayne, H., 207
Haynes, O.M., 304, 461
Hayward, C., 119
Heavey, C.L., 437
Hebl, M., 368
Hedges, L.V., 406
Heffernan, K., 118
Heiges, K.L., 438
Heinmiller, B.M., 136
Henderson, C., 143
Henderson, V.K., 324
Hendler, J., 314
Henik, A., 181
Hennig, K.H., 379
Henry, D.B., 389
Herman, M., 340
Hernandez, D.J., 442, 482
Hernandez-Reif, M., 89
Heron, J., 70, 452
Herrera, C., 308
Herrera, M.G., 118
Herrera, N.C., 445
Herrnstein, R.J., 255
Hertenstein, M.J., 308
Hespos, S.J., 187
Hess, U., 307
Hessels, S., 220
Hessl, D., 87
Hetherington, E.M., 438, 441
Hetherington, S.E., 85
Heyman, G.D., 353, 400
Hiatt, S., 143
Hibbert, J.R., 436
Hickey, P.R., 135
Hickson, F., 355, 356
Hiebert, J., 232
Higgins, A., 379
Hill, J.L., 89
Hill, N.E., 489
Hilton, S.C., 66
Hines, M., 407, 419
Hinshaw, S.P., 150
Hirsh-Pasek, K., 276
Hiruma, N., 307
Ho, C.S., 229
Hoadley, C.M., 479
Hoard, M.K., 416
Hodgson, D.M., 66
Hodgson, K., 200
Hoff, E., 271, 273, 277, 279, 280, 287
Hofferth, S.L., 321
Hoff-Ginsberg, E., 432
Hoffman, K.B., 347
Hoffman, M.L., 379, 380
Hogan, D.M., 180
Hogarty, P.S., 249
Hogge, W.A., 77
Hoier, S., 113
Holden, G.W., 430
Hollander, M., 286
Hollich, G.J., 276
Hollister, J.M., 88
Hollon, S.D., 341
Holowka, S., 273
Hood, B., 188
Hood, L., 296
Hooven, C., 433
Hornung, R.W., 75
Horowitz, F.D., 257
Horwood, L.J., 106, 114
Hough, R.L., 350

Houston, D.M., 270
Howard, K.I., 340
Howard, M.R., 290
Howe, M.L., 200, 207
Howe, N., 447
Howes, C., 461
Hoyne, S.H., 226
Hoza, B., 466
Hubbard, F.O.A., 94
Huckeby, E.R., 271
Hudson, J.A., 213
Huessman, R., 388, 479
Huizink, A., 70
Hulit, L.M., 290
Hulme, C., 221
Human Services, 119, 120, 122, 157
Hunt, A.K., 226
Hunt, J.M., 252
Hunt, M., 296
Hunter, A.G., 442
Hunter, J.E., 250
Hurtado, A., 70
Huston, A.C., 126, 281, 404, 475, 476, 477, 478
Hutchins, E., 244
Huth-Bocks, A.C., 324
Huttenlocher, J., 228, 280
Hwang, J., 312
Hyde, J.S., 88, 376, 406
Hymel, S., 472
Iacono, W.G., 149
Ibrahim, J., 85
IFICF, 106
Ingoldsby, E.M., 388
Inhelder, B., 168, 170
Insabella, G.M., 441
Institute of Medicine, 69
Isabella, R.A., 314
Israel, A.C., 120, 148, 404, 450, 454
Iverson, J.M., 275
Ivery, D., 120
Izard, C.E., 302, 303, 304
Jaccard, J., 467
Jacklin, C.N., 402, 404, 407, 408, 414
Jacobi, C., 119
Jacobs, J.E., 218, 404
Jacobson, J.L., 74, 76, 77
Jacobson, S.W., 74, 76, 77
Jacquez, F., 347
Jadva, V., 41
Jaffee, J., 71, 72
Jaffee, S., 376
Jaffee, S.R., 22, 29
Jagnow, C.P., 66
James, W., 332
Jankowski, J.J., 148
Janosky, J.E., 404
Janssens, J.M., 474
Jared, D., 220
Jarvin, L., 243
Jasnow, M.D., 71, 72
Jaswal, V.K., 276
Jenkins, E., 230
Jensen, H., 333
Jensen, J.L., 152
Jensen, P.S., 150
Jernigan, L.P., 337
Ji, G., 446
Jiao, S., 446
Jiao, Z., 466
Jing, Q., 446
Jipson, J., 276

Jocelyn, L., 230
Joels, T., 326
Johanson, R.B., 85
John, R.S., 448
Johnson, D.L., 252
Johnson, J.D., 388, 479
Johnson, L.B., 253
Johnson, M.H., 129, 145
Johnson, R., 404
Johnson, S.P., 141, 142
Johnson, T.R.B., 66
Jones, D., 226
Jones, D.C., 382, 448
Jones, L.C., 355
Jones, S., 310
Jones, S.S., 278, 340
Joseph, J.A., 374
Joseph, R., 66
Joyner, K., 468, 469
Juffer, F., 325
Jusczyk, P.W., 136, 269, 270
Juvonen, J., 392
Kagan, J., 314, 315
Kaijura, H., 135
Kail, R., 26, 179, 180, 181, 201, 207, 215, 405
Kaiser, I.H., 69
Kako, E., 288
Kalakoski, V., 335
Kalish, C.W., 188, 189
Kamerman, S.B., 90
Kampe, K., 320
Kanaya, T., 431
Kandel, E., 88
Kann, L., 157
Kaplan, J., 296
Kaplan, N., 325
Kaplan, P.S., 271
Kaprio, J., 113, 116
Karau, S.J., 408
Karl, H.W., 135
Karniol, R., 155
Karp, J., 452
Karraker, K.H., 399
Kartner, J., 333
Kastberg, D., 230
Kastelic, D., 421
Katz, L.F., 433, 435, 439
Katz, P., 41
Kaufman, J.C., 238, 244
Kawakami, K., 314
Keane, S.P., 474
Kearney, C.A., 306
Keefe, K., 466
Keil, F.C., 188, 189, 296
Keiley, M.K., 389, 481
Keirse, M.J., 85
Keith, B., 438, 439
Kellam, S.G., 442
Keller, H., 333
Keller, M., 374
Kellman, P.J., 138, 141, 144
Kelly, J., 438
Kemper, T., 118
Kendrick, C., 448
Kennell, H.H., 86
Kerr, D.C.R., 310
Kerr, S., 226
Kertes, D.A., 23
Kessler, B., 220
Kestenbaum, R., 325
Kidd, K.K., 256

Kiel, E.J., 310
Kilgore, K., 431
Killen, M., 357
Kim, D-Y., 350
Kim, I.J., 116
Kim, J.-Y., 415
Kim, S., 448
Kim, Y.H., 222
Kimball, M.M., 406, 416
Kimmerly, N.L., 303
King, M.L., Jr., 383
King, V., 336
Kipnis, O., 468
Kirby, D., 469, 470
Kirchner, H.L., 79
Kiritsy, M.C., 149
Kirk, K.I., 272
Kirkham, C., 350
Kirouac, G., 307
Kisilevsky, B.S., 145
Klaczynski, P.A., 218
Klahr, D., 216, 219
Klaus, M., 86
Klaus, R.A., 252
Klebanov, P.K., 254
Klein, N., 89, 367
Kleiner-Gathercoal, K.A., 145
Kleinknecht, E.F., 200
Klerman, L.V., 71
Kliegman, R., 79
Kloss, J., 157
Knibbe, R.A., 467
Knight, W.G., 79
Knyazev, G.G., 312–13
Kochanska, G., 305, 316, 365–66, 367, 368, 437
Kochenderfer, B.J., 391
Kochenderfer-Ladd, B., 392
Kogan, N., 257
Kohlberg, L., 371–75, 379, 417
Kohn-Wood, L., 339
Kojima, Y., 449
Kokis, J.V., 213
Kokko, K., 386
Kolb, B., 124
Kolbe, L.J., 157
Kolberg, K.J.S., 73
Koller, S.H., 374, 381
Kopp, C.B., 248, 364, 365
Korbin, J.E., 452
Koren-Karie, N., 326
Koroshegyi, C., 320
Kotovsky, L., 187
Kowal, A., 448
Kowalski, P.S., 346
Kozhevnikova, E.V., 271
Kraemer, H.C., 119
Kramer, L., 448
Kraut, R., 479
Krebs, D., 355
Krettenauer, T., 379
Krishnakumar, A., 443
Krispin, O., 473
Kroger, J., 337
Krogh, H.R., 401
Krueger, J.I., 350
Kuebli, J., 408
Kuhl, P.K., 271
Kuhn, D., 202, 218
Kunkel, D., 388, 477
Kunzig, R., 128
Kupersmidt, J.B., 473

Kurs-Lasky, M., 404
Kymissis, E., 273
Lacerda, F., 271
Ladd, B.K., 392
Ladd, G.W., 386, 391, 392, 462, 463, 473, 474
LaFreniere, P., 461
Lagace-Seguin, D.G., 462
Lagattuta, K.H., 308
La Greca, A.M., 306, 474
Laible, D.J., 309
Laird, R.D., 388
Lalumière, M.L., 470
Lamaze, F., 84
Lamb, M.E., 210, 211, 473, 481
Lambert, W., 282
Lamborn, S.D., 471
Lamon, S.J., 406
Lampinen, J.M., 208
Landau, B., 278
Landis, T., 273
Lane, H., 272
Lang, S., 325
Langabeer, K.A., 470
Lange, G., 202
Langlois, J.H., 145, 414
Lanza, E., 282
Laplante, D., 147, 279, 387
Larson, R.W., 158, 340, 464
Larsson, A., 419
Lau, A., 350
Laurence, S.C., 122
Laurette, A., 436
Laursen, B., 340, 464, 466
La Vecchia, C., 75
Lawrence, W., 79
Lazar, I., 253
Leach, P., 108
Leaper, C., 404, 414
Lears, M., 416
Lebolt, A., 473
Lecanuet, J.P., 66
Ledebt, A., 154
Lee, K., 202
Lee, K.T., 74
Lee, P., 155
Lee, S., 231, 232
Lee, S.C., 277
Lee, V.E., 439
LeFevre, J., 221
Leichtman, M.D., 208, 209
Leinonen, J., 488
Lelwica, M., 307
Leman, P.J., 415
LeMare, L.J., 355
Lemery, K.S., 313, 314
Lengua, L.J., 316, 439
Lentz, C., 431
Leon, K., 439
Lerner, R.M., 7
Leseman, P.P.M., 221
Lester, B.M., 85
Leung, M.C., 471
Levendosky, A.A., 324
Leventhal, T., 485, 486, 488
Levine, L.E., 334
Levine, L.J., 308
Levine, S.C., 228
Levitt, A.G., 273
Levitt, J.L., 465
Levitt, M.J., 465

Levy, B.A., 220
Levy, G.D., 204, 401, 414
Levy, J., 157
Lewis, M., 304, 305, 314, 333
Lewis, M.D., 320
Lewis, T.L., 145
Lewkowicz, D.J., 139, 271
Lewontin, R.C., 254
Li, Z., 473
Liben, L.S., 401, 418, 421
Lickliter, R., 139, 140
Lieberman, E., 89
Lieberman, M., 323, 373
Lilja, G., 85
Lillard, A., 190
Lim, K., 296
Limber, S., 304
Lin, C.C., 432
Lin, M., 305
Lin, S., 440
Linden, M.G., 47
Lindgren, S.D., 149
Lindholm, K.J., 282
Lindsay, D.S., 210
Lindsey, E.W., 462, 463
Linebarger, D.L., 126, 476, 478
Linn, S., 477
Linton, J., 135
Linton, M.J., 226
Linz, D., 388, 479
Liss, M.B., 400
Liston, C., 125, 126
Little, J.K., 418
Liu, H.-M., 271
Livesley, W.J., 352
Lobliner, D.B., 355
Locke, John, 5, 11, 19
Loebl, N.H., 346
Loehlin, J.C., 250, 254
Lohr, M.J., 471, 472
Lonky, E., 92
Looney, M.A., 157
Lopez, N.L., 310
Lord, S.E., 349
Lorenz, Konrad, 9–10
Losoya, S.H., 310, 430
Loughlin, G.M., 95
Lovett, L., 86
Lowry, R., 157
Luce, P.A., 270
Luchini, L., 75
Luecke-Aleksa, D., 419
Lueptow, L.B., 398
Lueptow, M.B., 398
Luthar, S.S., 257
Lütkenhaus, P., 333
Lutz, S.E., 398
Lycett, E., 41
Lynch, M.E., 79
Lynn, A., 135
Lyon, G.R., 260, 262
Lyons, T., 280
Lytton, H., 412
Maass, A., 356
McAdoo, H.P., 434
McBurney, D.H., 302, 319
McCabe, K., 350
McCabe, M., 349
McCabe, M.P., 119
McCall, R.B., 248, 249
MacCallum, F., 41
McCann, S.K., 478

McCarthy, K.A., 349
McCartney, K., 56
McCarty, M.E., 155
McClearn, G.E., 47, 50
McClenahan, E.L., 472
McCloskey, L.A., 294
McClure, E.B., 33, 408
Maccoby, E.E., 402, 404, 407, 408, 414, 415, 436, 441
McCord, J., 388
McCormick, C., 81
McCormick, C.B., 203
McCormick, M., 188
McCoy, J.K., 448
McCrae, R.R., 315
McCurley, J., 120
McCutchen, D., 226
McDonald, E.J., 350
McDougall, P., 472
McFadyen-Ketchum, S., 114
McGee, L.M., 225
McGee, R., 149
McGlothlin, H., 357
McGovern, A., 296
McGraw, M.B., 152
McGregor, P., 356
McGue, M.K., 149
McGuffin, P., 50
McHale, J.P., 436
McHale, S.M., 415, 448
McKee, A., 241
McKenzie, T.J., 157
Mackie, D.M., 399
McKown, C., 356
McKusick, V.A., 45
McLanahan, S., 439
McLaughlin, B., 282
MacLean, W.E., 95
McLellan, 383
McManus, I.C., 157
MacNeilage, P.F., 273
McNeilly-Choque, M.K., 387, 446
Macpherson, R., 213
McShane, J., 260
MacWhinney, B., 290
Madden, C.M., 297
Madden, T., 340
Magnusson, D., 386
Main, M., 322, 325
Makhijani, M.G., 408
Makowski, D., 374
Malamuth, N.M., 388, 479
Maldonado, R.E., 340
Malinosky-Rummell, R., 451
Mandel, D.R., 136
Mandell, D.J., 193
Mangelsdorf, S.C., 304, 305, 325
Maras, M.A., 393
Maratsos, M., 289
Marcia, J.E., 335, 337, 338
Marcoen, A., 350
Marcus, G.F., 286
Marcus, J., 407
Marcynyszyn, L.A., 487
Mares, M-L., 477
Margand, N.A., 324
Margolin, G., 448
Margulis, C., 293
Maring, B.L., 462
Markell, M., 356–57
Markiewicz, D., 323
Markman, E.M., 277, 294–95

Markovits, H., 170, 465
Markson, L., 276
Marlier, L., 135
Marriot, C., 192
Marsh, H.W., 345, 349, 350, 485
Marshall, N.L., 481
Martin, C.L., 401, 414, 415, 416, 417, 418, 419
Martin, J.A., 72, 469
Martin, J.L., 407, 412
Martin, J.M., 347
Martin, N.G., 470
Martin, R.P., 316
Marzolf, D., 304
Maschman, T., 347
Masse, L.C., 339
Masur, E.F., 280
Matheson, C.C., 461
Matthiesen, A.S., 85
Mattson, S.N., 74
Mattys, S.L., 270
Matusov, E., 175
Matyear, C.L., 273
Mauer, D., 462
Maughan, A., 451
Maurer, D., 145
Maxwell, S.E., 250, 347
Mayer, J.D., 241
Maynard, A.E., 448
Mayseless, O., 324
Mazur, E., 439
Mazziotta, J.C., 157
Means, B.M., 479
Measelle, J.R., 343
Meck, E., 228
Medin, D., 189
Mednick, S.A., 74, 88
Meeus, W.H.J., 467
Mehta, P., 439
Melbye, M., 72–73
Mellon, A.F., 157
Meltzoff, A.N., 192
Menacker, F., 72
Mendelson, M.J., 447
Mendoza-Denton, R., 367
Menella, J.A., 66
Meng, Z., 307
Mennella, J.A., 135
Merialdi, M., 66, 70
Merrick, S., 323
Mervielde, I., 119
Messer, D., 177
Messinger, D.S., 304
Meyer-Bahlburg, H.F.L., 47
Meyers, T., 87
Miceli, P.J., 313
Milberger, S., 149
Mildes, K., 226
Milich, R., 393
Miller, B.C., 447, 469
Miller, D.C., 404
Miller, J.G., 375
Miller, K.F., 216, 219, 229, 283
Miller, N., 407
Miller, P.A., 377
Miller, P.C., 430
Miller, P.M., 408
Miller-Johnson, S., 253
Mills, C.M., 296
Milne, A., 356
Minich, N.M., 89
Minkler, M., 442

Minnes, S., 79
Mischel, W., 367, 368, 412
Mistry, J., 176
Mistry, R.S., 486
Mitchell, D.W., 313
Mitchell, P., 157, 296
Mitchell, S., 252
Mix, K.S., 228
Miyake, K., 307, 322
Miyamoto, R.T., 137, 272
Mize, J., 433, 463, 474
Mizes, J., 118
Mizuta, I., 307
Mnookin, R.H., 441
Moats, L.C., 262
Mobley, L.A., 447
Moffitt, T.E., 113, 350
Molfese, D.L., 126
Mollnow, E., 77
Mondloch, C.J., 145
Monk, C.S., 70, 125, 129
Monker, J., 281
Monson, T.C., 389
Monsour, A., 334
Montague, D.P., 307
Moolchan, E.T., 74
Mooney-Somers, J., 443
Moore, K.L., 47
Moore, M.R., 71
Mora, J.O., 118
Moran, G., 325
Moran, T., 374
Morelli, G., 322
Morgan, B., 123
Morgan, J.L., 270
Morgan, M., 422
Morgane, P.J., 118
Morishima, A., 47
Morland, K., 69
Morris, A.S., 310, 431
Morris, J.E., 482
Morris, P., 254, 428
Morris, S.C., 189
Morrison, T., 266
Morrow, J., 200
Mortensen, E.L., 74
Mortimer, J.T., 484, 485
Morton, J., 145
Moses, L.J., 308
Moses, P., 126, 128
Mosier, C., 176
Moss, E., 323
Moss, H.A., 314
Mounts, N., 471
Mozart, W.A., 257
Mrazek, D.A., 47
Mueller, M.M., 441
Muenchow, S., 253
Muir, D.W., 145
Mulder, E., 70
Mumme, D.L., 308
Murdoch-Eaton, D., 180
Murphy, B., 376, 377
Murphy, B.C., 308, 310, 316, 383, 430
Murphy, J., 288
Murphy, L.M., 466
Murphy, N., 177
Murray, C., 41, 255, 443
Murray, K., 365–66, 367
Murray, K.T., 367
Murray, W.E., 75
Murry, V.M., 116, 448

Mustanski, B.S., 113
Muter, V., 221
Muzio, J.N., 95
Myers, M.M., 70
Nachtigall, R., 41
Nader, P.R., 157
Nadig, A.S., 294
Naigles, L., 279, 280
Nakagawa, N., 297
Nánez, J., Sr., 143
Nation, K., 224
National High Blood Pressure Education Program Working Group, 157
National Institutes of Health, 96
Neff, K., 374, 378
Neisser, U., 250, 254
Nelson, C.A., 125, 129, 146–47, 180
Nelson, D.A., 387, 392, 446, 473
Nelson, K., 128, 206, 207, 274, 280, 333
Nelson, L.J., 473
Nesdale, D., 356, 357
Neufeld, S.J., 364
Neumann, C., 252
Nevid, J.S., 341
Newcomb, A.F., 466
Newcombe, N., 406
Newcombe, R.G., 86
Newport, E.L., 270, 289
Newport, W.L., 136, 270
Nguyen, R.H.N., 66, 70
Nguyen, S.P., 400, 412
NICHD Early Child Care Research Network, 96, 326
Nichols, K.E., 305
Nisbett, R.E., 255
Nissen, E., 85
Nolen-Hoeksema, S., 341
Noll, Douglas C., 407
Nordenstroem, A., 419
Norlander, T., 421
Nosek, B.A., 406
Notaro, P.C., 195
Nowell, A., 406
Nucci, L., 378
Nugent, J.K., 85, 92
Numtee, C., 416
Nunes, S.R., 221
Nurmi, J., 335
Nurmi, J.-E., 431
Nyberg, B., 340
Nystrom, L.E., 407
Oakhill, J.V., 223
Oates, C., 477
O'Brien, M., 257
O'Brien, P.M.S., 85
Ochs, E., 292
O'Connell, C.M., 74
O'Conner, T., 70
O'Connor, S., 452
O'Connor, T.G., 441
O'Donnell Eisbach, A., 195
Offer, D., 340
O'Hara, N.M., 157
Okagaki, L., 406, 432
Okie, S., 81
Olejnik, S., 316
Oliner, 383
Oller, D.K., 282
Olsen, J., 72–73
Olsen, J.A., 431, 473
Olsen, O., 86

Olsen, S.F., 387, 446
Olson, K.L., 408
Olson, R.K., 261
Olson, S.L., 310
Olweus, D., 387, 391, 392
O'Moore, M., 350
O'Neil, R., 463
O'Neill, D.K., 294
Ong, A., 340
Ontai, L.L., 309
Opfer, J.E., 30, 190
Orendi, J.L., 407
Ornstein, P.A., 210, 211
O'Rourke, P., 293
Osberger, M.J., 137
Osganian, V., 157
Oster, H., 135, 307
Ostrov, E., 340
Owen, M.T., 324
Owsley, C., 144
Ozarow, L., 415
Paarlberg, K.M., 70
Paatsch, L., 272
Padilla, A.M., 282
Pagano, J., 92
Pahlke, E., 230
Painter, K.M., 461
Paley, B., 428, 435
Palladino, P., 224
Palmer, D.J., 448
Panagiotides, H., 87
Pangrazi, R.P., 157
Papageorgiou, A.N., 147
Papaligoura, Z., 333
Pappas, A., 189
Paquette, J.A., 473
Paradise, J.L., 404
Parault, S.J., 203
Parazzini, F., 75
Parcel, G.S., 157
Parent, S., 323
Park, M.M., 72, 85
Parke, R.D., 6, 321, 430, 432, 434, 463
Parker, J., 460, 464, 473
Parker, J.G., 350, 387, 466
Parkin, L., 194
Parritz, R.H., 310
Partelow, L., 230
Parten, M., 460
Pascalis, O., 146–47
Pascual, L., 461
Pascual-Leone, J., 373
Pasley, K., 440
Passarotti, A., 126–27
Passchier, J., 70
Patterson, C.J., 387, 388, 443, 444, 451, 470, 473
Patterson, G.R., 433
Patterson, M., 269
Paul, B., 126–27, 128
Pea, R.D., 479
Peake, P.K., 367, 368
Pearlman, M., 449
Pearson, A., 353
Pearson, B.Z., 282
Pearson, J.L., 442
Pederson, D.R., 325
Peeke, L.G., 347
Pell, T., 79
Pellegrini, A.D., 319, 428, 464
Pelphrey, K.A., 200
Pennington, B.F., 149

Pennisi, E., 42
Pepe, M.S., 107
Pepler, D.J., 21
Perfetti, C.A., 222, 223, 224
Perloff, R., 250, 254
Perner, J., 194
Perris, E., 136
Perry, B., 443
Perry, D.G., 389, 393, 470
Perry, K.E., 223
Perry, M., 232
Perry, T.B., 465
Persaud, T.V.N., 47
Perusse, D., 279, 387
Pesetsky, D., 222, 223
Peterson, C., 194, 207, 341
Peterson, L., 382
Petitto, L.A., 273
Petrie, R.H., 88
Petrill, S.A., 53, 54, 251
Pettit, G.S., 114, 317, 387, 388, 389, 392, 430, 433, 436, 462, 463, 466
Phillips-Silver, J., 139
Phinney, J., 338, 339, 340
Piaget, J., 13–14, 16, 164–74, 370–71
Pierce, K.M., 482
Pierce, S.H., 202
Pierroutsakos, S.L., 216, 219, 283
Pike, R., 343, 346
Pilgrim, C., 472
Pilling, M., 138
Pinderhughes, E., 446, 447
Pinker, S., 286, 288
Pinquart, M., 333
Piolat, A., 224
Pipe, M., 207
Pisoni, D.B., 136, 269, 272
Pittinsky, T.L., 406
Platt, L., 81
Platzman, K.A., 79
Plewis, I., 94, 95
Plomin, R., 47, 50, 52, 53, 54, 56, 251, 279, 387
Plowman, S.A., 157
Polifka, J.E., 74, 79
Polit, E.F., 445
Pollitt, E., 117, 118
Pomietto, M., 135
Pons, F., 193
Poole, D.A., 210, 211
Poole, M.E., 335
Popper, S., 87
Porter, R.H., 135
Pott, M., 322
Potter, W.J., 388
Poulin, F., 466
Poulin, R., 310
Poulin-Dubois, D., 188, 276, 399
Poulson, C.L., 273
Pourquette, C., 436
Powell, J.K., 273
Power, F.C., 379
Powers, J., 463
Powlishta, K.K., 356, 401
Prasada, S., 188
Prescott, P.A., 180
Presnell, K., 116
Pressley, M., 203, 224, 225
Priel, B., 333
Prieto, M.D., 243
Principe, G.F., 210
Prinstein, M.J., 473

Project Zero, 242
Puhl, R.M., 119
Pulkkinen, L., 113, 386
Punamäka, R-L., 488
Pungello, E.P., 253
Putnam, P.H., 304
Qualter, A., 296
Quas, J.A., 207
Quillian, L., 465
Quinn, P.C., 145
Quinn, P.H., 186
Quittner, A.L., 137
Rabiner, D., 389
Raboy, B., 444
Radke-Yarrow, M., 316, 380
Raine, A., 386
Rakic, P., 124
Rakison, D.H., 186, 188
Rakoczy, H., 461
Raman, L., 189
Ramey, C.T., 252, 253
Ramsay, D., 143, 333
Ramsay, D.S., 314
Ramsey, F., 117
Rankin, D.B., 464
Ransjoe-Arvidson, A.B., 85
Rapoport, J.L., 407
Rapport, M.D., 149
Rasmussen, R.L., 158
Rasmussen, S.A., 46
Ratcliffe, S., 47
Rathunde, K.R., 257
Rathus, S.A., 341
Rauch, S.L., 315
Raviv, A., 105
Rayias, M.F., 304
Rayner, K., 222, 223
Read, G.F., 86
Reddy, R., 106
Reddy, V., 303
Redman, C.W.E., 85
Reed, A., 145
Reese, E., 207, 281, 333
Reeve, K.F., 273
Reeve, L., 273
Reich, P.A., 275
Reid, D.H., 259
Reihman, J., 92
Reilly, J., 126, 128
Reimer, M.S., 306
Reiser, M., 310, 430
Renshaw, P.D., 472
Repacholi, B.M., 308
Resnick, L.B., 230
Resnick, S., 325
Reudor, A., 276
Reyna, V.F., 205
Reynolds, A.J., 454
Reznick, J.S., 200, 275, 279
Rhee, S.H., 149
Rhodes, J., 106
Riad-Fahmy, D., 86
Ricciardelli, L.A., 119
Riccio, G., 153
Rice, C., 85
Rice, M.L., 281
Richards, J.E., 148
Richgels, D.J., 225
Richters, J.E., 150
Rideout, R., 207
Rideout, V., 475, 479
Ridge, B., 317, 436

Riksen-Walraven, J., 322, 466
Rilea, S.L., 405
Riley, E.P., 74
Rincon, C., 473
Ring, J., 261
Riordan, K., 325
Ritter, J.M., 145
Robbins, A.M., 272
Roberts, B.W., 313, 315
Roberts, C.R., 339
Roberts, D., 443
Roberts, D.F., 475, 479
Roberts, J.E., 280
Roberts, R.E., 339, 340
Roberts, R.J., 149
Roberts, W., 381
Roberts, W.L., 21
Robertson, D.L., 454
Robertson, L.S., 400
Robins, R.W., 350
Robinson, A., 47, 257
Robinson, C.C., 387, 446, 473
Robinson, E.J., 296
Robinson, M., 229
Robinson, M.L., 74
Robinson, N.S., 350
Robles de Medina, P., 70
Rochat, P., 333, 461
Rocissano, L., 296
Rock, S.L., 252
Rodriguez, M., 367
Roebers, C.M., 27, 28
Roffwarg, H.P., 95
Roggman, L.A., 145
Rogoff, B., 175, 176, 215, 217
Romero, A., 339
Romney, D.M., 412
Roschelle, J.M., 479
Rose, A.J., 466, 473
Rose, H., 419
Rose, R.J., 52, 113, 116
Rose, S.A., 148
Rosen, T.J., 286
Rosenberg, D., 153
Rosenblatt, E., 296
Rosenblum, K.E., 216
Rosengren, K.S., 188, 189, 283
Rosenthal, D.A., 339
Rosenthal, R., 33
Rosicky, J.G., 308
Roskos-Ewoldsen, B., 405
Rosnow, R.L., 33
Ross, D.F., 408
Ross, H.S., 407, 412, 447, 449
Rosso, I.M., 88
Rostenstein, D., 135
Rothbart, M.K., 309, 312
Rothbaum, F., 322
Rotherman-Borus, M.J., 470
Rousseau, D., 323
Rousseau, Jean Jacques, 5, 9, 19
Roussey, J., 224
Rovee-Collier, C., 96, 148, 200, 201
Rubin, D.B., 33
Rubin, K.H., 355, 387, 436, 460, 464, 473
Rubinstein, O., 181
Ruble, D.N., 346, 398, 401, 414, 417, 418
Rudolph, K.D., 23, 350
Rueda, M.R., 309

Ruff, H.A., 148
Ruffman, T., 194
Ruiz, M.D., 347
Rumbaugh, D.M., 288
Rusch, F.R., 260
Rushton, J.P., 466
Russell, A., 463
Russell, S.T., 444
Ruthsatz, J.M., 259
Rutland, A., 356
Rye, S., 484
Rymer, R., 289
Ryskina, V.L., 271
Sabbagh, M.A., 276
Sadeh, A., 105
Sadovsky, A., 310
Saffran, J.R., 136, 270
Sagi, A., 324, 326
St. George, I.M., 113
St. James-Roberts, I., 94, 95
Saintonge, J., 323
Sais, E., 282
Salieri, A., 257
Salisbury, G., 405
Salovey, P., 241
Salpekar, N., 487
Salvador, W.A., 447
Salvator, A., 79
Sameroff, A.J., 310, 325
Samuelson, L., 278
Sanchez, L.E., 88
Sandberg, J.F., 321
Sanders, P., 404
Sandler, I.N., 316, 439
Sandy, J.M., 318
Sarampote, N.C., 482
Sarant, J., 272
Sasson, N., 200
Saucier, J.F., 88
Savage-Rumbaugh, E.S., 288
Savelsbergh, G.J.P., 154, 155
Saxe, G.B., 244
Scardamalia, M., 225
Scarr, S., 56
Schaal, B., 135
Schafer, W.D., 303, 404
Schaffer, D., 69
Schauble, L., 218
Schiller, M., 325
Schmeelk-Cone, K., 339
Schmid, S., 374
Schmidt, F.L., 250
Schmitt, K.L., 126, 419, 476, 478
Schmuckler, M.A., 153
Schneider, B.H., 323, 463, 466
Schneider, W., 27, 28, 201, 204, 207
Schnorr, T.M., 75
Schubert, A.B., 407
Schuder, T., 224
Schulenberg, J., 484
Schull, W.J., 120
Schulsinger, F., 120
Schuster, B.V., 221
Schutz, R.W., 109, 403
Schwanenflugel, P.J., 203
Schwartz, C.E., 315
Schwartz, D., 392, 466
Scott, P., 118
Scott, R., 349
Scott, W.A., 349
Seal, J., 466
Sears, R.R., 7

Secada, W.G., 406
Sedivy, J.C., 294
Segrin, C., 438
Seibenbruner, J., 469
Seidel, K.D., 107
Seidenberg, M.S., 222, 223
Seidner, L.B., 461
Seifer, R., 325
Self, J., 87
Selman, F.L., 355
Selman, R.L., 353, 354
Seltzer, M., 280
Sen, M.G., 399
Sénéchal, M., 221, 281
Serbin, L., 452
Serbin, L.A., 356, 399, 401
Serdula, M.K., 120
Seroczynski, A.D., 347
Servin, A., 419
Sevcik, R.A., 288
Seyfarth, R., 288
Shah, B., 135
Shahar-Shalev, S., 181
Shanahan, M.J., 484, 485
Shanahan, T., 221
Shannon, F.T., 106
Shapiro, J.R., 304
Shapiro, L.R., 213
Share, D.L., 223
Sharp, J.M., 225
Sharpe, R.M., 79
Shatz, M., 189, 292, 293, 294
Shaw, D.S., 439, 449
Shaw, G.M., 69, 75
Shaw, H., 119
Shell, R., 377, 382
Shelton, K.H., 435
Shenfield, T., 282
Shepard, S., 310
Shepard, S.A., 310, 316, 383, 430
Sherman, D.K., 149
Sherrod, K.B., 452
Shi, R., 270
Shih, M., 406
Shin, L.M., 315
Shin, Y.L., 461
Shinar, O., 318
Shiner, R.L., 313, 315
Shipman, K., 308
Shonk, S.M., 451
Showstack, J., 41
Shrager, J., 230
Shriver, S., 253
Shulman, S., 468
Shumway-Cook, A., 153
Shuter-Dyson, R., 241
Shwe, H.I., 294–95
Sicotte, N.L., 157
Siddiqui, A., 155
Sidebotham, P., 452
Siegel, L., 252
Siegler, R.S., 30, 171, 173, 179, 180, 190, 213, 214, 215, 217, 222, 224, 225, 229, 230
Sigman, M.D., 252
Signorella, M.L., 401
Signorielli, N., 416
Sik, G., 157
Silbereisen, R.K., 113, 116
Silk, J.S., 431
Silva, P.A., 22, 29, 113
Silverman, W.K., 120, 306

Simcock, G., 207
Simmons, R., 116
Simon, Theophile, 246
Simons, D.J., 188
Simons, R.L., 116
Simons-Morton, B.G., 157
Simpson, E.L., 374
Simpson, J.M., 95
Singer, J.D., 481
Singer, L.T., 79
Singer, M., 224
Singh, S., 404
Sippola, L.K., 466
Skakkebaek, N.E., 79
Skinner, B.F., 11–12, 13, 287
Skinner, E.A., 432
Skinner, K., 392
Slaby, R.G., 391
Slade, L., 194
Slanetz, P.J., 149
Slater, A.M., 145
Slaughter, V., 194
Sligo, J., 22, 29
Sloan, R.P., 70
Slobin, D.I., 288
Slobodskaya, H.R., 312–13
Slomkowski, C., 448
Smallish, L., 149
Smarsh, B., 296
Smetana, J.G., 377, 378
Smith, C.M., 229
Smith, E.G., 227
Smith, E.R., 399
Smith, L.B., 137, 152, 278, 340
Smith, M., 310
Smith, M.C., 308
Smith, P., 93
Smith, P.K., 441, 442, 443
Smith, R., 83, 482
Smith, R.E., 158
Smith, S.L., 388, 477
Smith, T.E., 404
Smith, V.L., 208
Smock, T.K., 105
Smoll, F.L., 109, 158, 403
Snedeker, B., 483
Snider, J.B., 436
Snidman, N., 314
Snow, C.E., 281
Snow, C.W., 94
Snow, M.E., 414
Snowling, M.J., 221, 224
Snyder, E., 419
Snyder, J., 431
Snyder, K., 180
Snyder, L., 280
Sodian, B., 219
Sokol, R.J., 74
Solantaus, T., 488
Sommerville, J.A., 190
Sorensen, T.I.A., 120
Sosa, B.B., 213
Sousa, P., 189
Soussignan, R., 135
Spearman, C., 239
Spelke, E.S., 183, 187
Spence, M.J., 66
Spinath, F., 56
Spinrad, T.L., 310, 367, 381
Spitz, R.A., 319
Springer, K., 188, 189
Sroufe, L.A., 304

Stacy, A.W., 477
Staff, J., 484, 485
Stanley, F., 71, 72
Stanovich, K.E., 213, 223, 281
Stattin, H., 386, 431
Steele, C.M., 255
Steelman, J.D., 479
Steginck, L.D., 149
Steinberg, L., 113, 340, 341, 409, 431, 471, 483, 484
Steiner, J.E., 135
Stephens, B.R., 145
Stern, M., 399
Sternberg, C.R., 304
Sternberg, K.J., 210, 473
Sternberg, R.J., 238, 242, 243, 244, 250, 254, 256, 432
Stevens, M., 443
Stevens, N., 466
Stevenson, H.W., 231, 232, 233, 307, 489, 490
Stevenson, J., 221
Stewart, L., 373
Stewart, P., 92
Stewart, R.B., 447
Stice, E., 116, 119, 467
Stifter, C.A., 315, 367
Stigler, J.W., 232, 233, 307, 489, 490
Stiles, J., 126–27, 128
St-Laurent, D., 323
Stockton, L., 105
Stoffregen, T.A., 153
Stolyarova, E.I., 271
Stone, E., 157
Stoneman, A., 448
Stoolmiller, M., 436
Strauss, M.S., 227
Strayer, F.F., 461
Strayer, J., 381
Striano, T., 461
Strikmiller, P.K., 157
Strough, J., 408
Strouse, G., 479
Stumbo, P.J., 149
Stunkard, A.J., 120
Styfco, S.J., 253
Su, M., 452
Subrahmanyam, K., 479
Sullivan, L.W., 44
Sulloway, F.J., 445
Sundberg, U., 271
Sundet, J.M., 252
Super, C.M., 118, 154
Super, D.E., 337
Sutton, P.D., 469
Suzuki, L., 255
Svejda, M., 143
Svirsky, M.A., 272
Swanson, J.M., 150
Swenson, L.P., 473
Tager-Flusberg, H., 285
Talbot, J., 436
Tamang, B.L., 307
Tamis-LeMonda, C.S., 280, 463
Tani, F., 466
Tanner, J.M., 105, 109
Taormina, J., 153
Taplin, J.E., 189
Tardif, C., 323, 463
Tardif, T., 432
Tasker, F., 470
Taylor, H.G., 89

Taylor, J.H., 373, 379
Taylor, L.C., 486
Taylor, L.E., 489
Taylor, M., 462
Taylor, M.E., 438
Taylor, M.G., 400, 401, 412, 414
Taylor, P., 74
Taylor, R.D., 443
Teasdale, T.W., 120
Tees, R.C., 269
Teichman, Y., 356
Tein, J.-Y., 439
Teixeira, R.A., 465
Tennenbaum, H.R., 414
Terman, Lewis, 246
Terry, R., 385
Teti, D.M., 89
Thayer, S.M., 448
Thelen, E., 152, 153
Thelen, M.H., 115
Theobald, W., 469
Thiessen, E.D., 270
Thomas, A., 311, 313, 316
Thomas, E., 281
Thomas, H., 405
Thomas, J.R., 403
Thompson, G.G., 282
Thompson, R.A., 304, 309, 323, 324
Thoreau, H.D., 383
Thornberry, T.P., 388
Thorne, B., 414
Thornhill, R., 145
Thun, M.J., 75
Thurstone, L.L., 239
Thurstone, T.G., 239
Tidball, G., 308
Tincoff, R., 270
Tinker, E., 277, 290, 293
Tisak, M., 371
Tolan, P.H., 389
Tomada, G., 466
Tomasello, M., 292, 461
Tonkiss, J., 118
Tonya, M., 118
Tooby, J., 302
Toplak, M.E., 213
Torgesen, J.K., 260
Torjussen, T.M., 252
Toth, S.L., 449, 451, 452
Tottenham, N., 125, 126
Trabasso, T., 224
Trainor, L.J., 136, 139, 271
Trainor, R.J., 407
Tram, J.M., 347
Tranel, D., 126
Treboux, D., 323
Trehub, S.E., 136
Treiman, R., 220, 225
Tremblay, R., 88, 279, 386, 387
Trickett, E.J., 339
Trien, L., 70
Tronick, E.Z., 304, 408
Troop-Gordon, W., 350
Troseth, G.L., 283
Truglio, R., 281, 478
Trzesniewski, K.H., 350
Tsao, F.-M., 271
Tsuang, M.T., 149
Tuchfarber, B.S., 122
Tucker, G.R., 282
Tudge, J.R.H., 180
Tulviste, P., 176

Turati, C., 145
Turiel, E., 374, 376, 377, 378
Turkheimer, E., 57
Turley, R.N.L., 70
Twenge, J.M., 346
Udry, J.R., 468, 469
Uggen, C., 484
Ujiie, T., 307
Ullian, D.Z., 417
Ullman, M., 286
Ulrich, B.D., 152, 153
Umbel, V.M., 282
Undger, J.B., 477
Unger, O., 461
UNICEF, 90
U.S. Census Bureau, 282, 437, 438
U.S. Department of Health and Human Services, 40, 119, 120, 122, 157, 450, 469
U.S. Department of Labor, 483
U.S. Department of State, 451
Updegraff, K.A., 448
Urberg, K.A., 472
Urbina, S., 250, 254
USDA, 107
Utman, J.A., 273
Uvnaes-Moberg, K., 85
Vachon, R., 408
Vaillancourt, T., 472
Valentiner, D., 350
Valienta, C., 310
Valkenburg, P.M., 476, 477
Vallance, D.D., 308
Valoski, A.M., 120
Van Court, P., 376, 377
Vandell, D.L., 482
van den Boom, D.C., 324
Vandereycken, W., 119
van der Kamp, J., 155
van der Mark, I.L., 380
van der Voort, T.H.A., 476
Vander Wal, J.S., 115
van der Zee, J., 85
van Dulmen, M., 447
Van Hof, P., 155
van IJzendoorn, M.H., 94, 322, 323, 325, 380
van Lieshout, C.F.M., 466
Van Meter, P., 224
Van Tuyl, S.S., 447
van Wieringen, P.C.W., 154
Vara, L.S., 120
Vasta, R., 287, 434
Vaughn, L.S., 145
Vazsonyi, A.T., 436
Velie, E.M., 69
Ventura, S.J., 72
Vereijken, B., 154
Vereijken, C.M.J.L., 322
Verma, I.M., 82
Verschueren, K., 350
Vietze, P.M., 452
Vigil, J., 416
Viken, R.J., 105, 113, 116
Vingerhoets, A.J.J.M., 70
Virdin, L., 439
Visher, E.B., 440
Visher, J.S., 440
Visser, G., 70
Vohs, K.D., 350
Volling, B.L., 448
Volterra, V., 293

von Eye, A., 324
Vorhees, C.V., 77
Votruba-Drzal, E., 481
Voyer, D., 405
Voyer, S., 405
Vygotsky, L.S., 14–15, 175, 177, 250, 368
Waber, D.P., 405
Wachs, T.D., 54, 313, 315
Wagner, E., 380
Wainwright, J.L., 444
Walberg, H.J., 490
Waldfogel, J., 89
Waldron, M., 57
Wales, R., 272
Walk, R.D., 143
Walker, L.J., 373, 378, 379
Walker, R., 86
Walker, S., 401
Walker-Andrews, A.S., 307
Waller, E.M., 473
Walsh, R.O., 367
Wang, D., 446
Wang, L., 307
Wang, S., 188
Wang, S.S., 118, 119
Wardrop, J.L., 392
Warren, A.R., 294
Warren, Earl, 358
Warren-Leubecker, A., 294
Wartella, E., 388, 479
Warwick, A., 85
Wasserstein, S., 306
Waters, E., 304, 323
Waters, H.F., 388
Waters, H.S., 225
Waters, P., 345
Waters, P.L., 421
Watkins, B.A., 477
Watkinson, B., 74
Watson, J.B., 6, 11, 193, 428
Way, N., 106
Webb, S.J., 125, 129
Weber, E., 378
Wechsler, D., 248, 250
Wechsler, H., 157
Weichold, K., 113, 116
Weinberg, M.K., 304, 408
Weinberg, M.S., 470
Weinstein, R.S., 356
Weisner, T.S., 422
Weiss, M.J., 147
Weissman, M.D., 189
Weisz, J., 322
Weizman, Z.O., 281
Wellman, H.M., 188, 192, 193, 308, 310
Welsh, M.C., 149
Wentworth, N., 155
Wentzel, K.R., 367, 489
Werker, J.F., 269, 270
Werner, E.E., 89
Werner, H., 153
Werner, N.E., 389
Wertsch, J.V., 176
West, R.F., 213
West, S.G., 316, 439
Whaley, S.E., 252
Whitaker, D., 226
Whitaker, R.C., 107
Whitbeck, L.B., 336
White, D.R., 356

White, L., 441
White, S.H., 7
Whitehead, J.R., 158
Whitehurst, G.J., 287, 434
Whiteman, S., 415
Whiteman, S.D., 448
Whitesell, N.R., 345, 346, 421
Whitfield, M.F., 135
Whithall, S., 192
Whiting, J.W.M., 431
Whitman, T.L., 313
Whitney, E.N., 69
Whyte, M.K., 468
Wichmann, C., 462
Wicks-Nelson, R., 148, 404, 450, 454
Widaman, K.F., 463
Widmayer, S.M., 292
Widstroem, A.M., 85
Wieczorkowska, G., 445
Wiegers, T.A., 85
Wigmore, B., 226
Willatts, P., 213
Willcutt, E., 149
Williams, H., 153
Williams, J.E., 398, 400
Williams, J.M., 226
Williams, L., 193
Williams, S., 113, 149
Williams, S.L., 288
Williams, T., 230
Williamson, D.F., 120
Williamson, G.M., 70
Willinger, M., 96

Willis, C.S., 279
Willows, D.M., 221
Wills, T.A., 318
Wilson, B.J., 380, 388
Wilson, G.T., 118
Wilson, M., 443, 452
Wilson, P.G., 259
Wilson, R.D., 81
Wilson, R.S., 251
Wilson-Mitchell, J.E., 422
Winberg, J., 135
Winner, E., 257, 296
Winsler, A., 482
Winslow, E.B., 439, 449
Winter, M.A., 435
Winterhoff, P.A., 180
Wintre, M.G., 308
Wise, B.W., 261
Wohlfahrt, J., 72–73
Wolchik, S., 439
Wolf, A., 481
Wolf, M.M., 12
Wolfe, D.A., 451
Wolff, P.H., 94
Wolfson, A.R., 340
Wolraich, M.L., 149
Wong, E., 126–27
Wong, J., 157
Wong-Fillmore, L., 282
Wood, J.J., 463
Woodard, E., 477
Woodin, E.M., 435, 439
Woods, R.P., 157

Woods, Tiger, 12–13
Woodward, A.L., 190, 277
Woodward, L., 22, 29, 114
Woodward, L.J., 71
Woodworth, S., 437
Woolard, J.L., 479
Woollacott, M.H., 153
World Health Organization, 120, 121
Worobey, J., 118
Wright, C.I., 315
Wright, I., 180
Wright, J., 281
Wright, J.A., 107
Wright, J.C., 126, 475, 476, 478
Wright, V., 385
Wyman, H., 417
Wynn, K., 227, 228
Xiaohe, X., 468
Xu, F., 286
Yaeger, A., 318
Yaggi, K.E., 449
Yaghoub Zadeh, Z., 221
Yamada, E., 87
Yang, C., 473
Yang, Q., 46
Yates, M., 336
Yau, 378
Yeh, M., 350
Yeung, A.S., 345, 350
Yeung, W.J., 321
Yonas, A., 143, 144
Young, D., 404
Young, S.K., 316

Youniss, J., 336, 383
Yovsi, R., 333
Yuill, N., 353
Yunger, J.L., 428
Zahn-Waxler, C., 307, 316, 380, 408
Zaia, A.F., 462
Zaitchik, D., 219
Zajonc, R.B., 445
Zamsky, E.S., 442
Zappulla, C., 473
Zarbatany, L., 464
Zavaleta, N., 66, 70
Zelazo, N.A., 154
Zelazo, P.D., 154
Zelazo, P.R., 147, 154
Zeman, J., 308
Zhang, H., 229
Zhou, Q., 381, 430
Zhu, J., 229
Zigler, E., 253, 255, 257
Zimiles, H., 439
Zimmer-Gembeck, M.J., 469
Zimmerman, B.J., 203
Zimmerman, M.A., 195, 339
Zinar, S., 224
Zins, J.E., 122
Ziv, Y., 326
Zohar, A., 218
Zoog, J.B., 477
Zucker, K.J., 470
Zuckerman, B., 79
Zukow-Goldring, P., 447
Zwolan, T.A., 272

Abstinence programs, 469
Abstract thinking, 169–71
Abuse. *See also* Maltreatment of children
  physical, 449–50
  psychological, 450
  sexual, 449–50
Academic achievement, cross-cultural
  findings on, 233
Academic competence, 343, 344, 348
Academic self-concept, 345
Academic self-esteem, 349, 350–51
Academic skills, 219
  number skills, 227–33
    adding and subtracting, 228, 230
    cultural differences in, 230–33
    learning to count, 228–29, 230
  reading, 220–24
    comprehension, 220, 223–24
    foundations of, 220–21
    recognizing words, 220, 221–23
  test-taking, 255
  writing, 225–27
Accidents, childhood deaths due to,
  121–22
Accommodation, 165
Achievement status, 337
Active children, theme of, 159, 195, 234
Active-passive child issue, 18–19
Activity(ies)
  gender differences in, 410
  after school, 482
Adaptation, girls' pubertal timing and,
  114–15
Adaptive behavior, 259, 467–68
  child rearing as, 319–20
*Add Health* database, 467–68
Addition, 228, 230
Adenine, 41–42
ADHD. *See* Attention deficit hyperactivity
  disorder (ADHD)
Adolescents/adolescence, 5
  accidental deaths in, 122
  aggression against, 391
  attributions by, 341
  in blended families, 440–41
  depression in, 341, 409
  egocentrism in, 336
  emotion regulation in, 310
  ethnic identity, 338–40
  expressions of emotion in, 308
  formal operational thinking in, 169–71
  growth spurt and puberty in, 102, 104,
    109–16
    bone growth, 104, 109–11
    mechanisms of, 112–15
    psychological impact of, 115–16
    sexual maturation, 111–12
  identity search in, 335–36
  immigrants, 339
  memory in, 305–6
  memory strategies in, 202
  nutritional needs of, 108
  parent-child relations, 340
  peer relations in, 465
  prejudice during, 356
  problem solving in, 213, 214–17
  prosocial reasoning in, 377
  self-concepts in, 334–35
  self-esteem in, 343, 345–46
  sexual activity in, best friends and,
    467–68
  sleep loss in, 106
  storm and stress in, 340
  writing strategies in, 225

Adopted children, 446–47
  behavioral genetic studies of, 51
Adopted child syndrome, myth of, 447
Adoption studies, 52
  of ADHD, 149
  of cognitive development, 53–54
  of intelligence, 251
  of weight, 120
Adrenal hyperplasia, congenital, 81
Adult Attachment Interview, 325
Advertisements, TV, 477
Affect, negative, 312, 313
African American English, 294
African Americans, 254, 255
  desegregation of schools, 357–59
  grandmothers in families, 442–43
  stereotype threat in, 255
  sudden infant death syndrome (SIDS)
    and, 96
African cultures, practices promoting
  motor development, 154
Afterbirth, 83–84
After-school programs, 481–82
Age
  of child, parenting changes and, 436
  of mother, prenatal development and,
    70–73
  of viability, 66
Aggression, 385–93
  birth complications and, 88
  change and stability in, 385–86
  friendship between aggressive children,
    466–67
  gender differences in, 402, 407–8, 410
  hostile, 385–86
  in children of mothers with
    postpartum depression, 87
  instrumental, 385
  parenting and, 474
  reactive, 386
  relational, 386, 408
  roots of, 387–91
    biological contributions, 387
    cognitive processes, 389
    community and cultural influence,
      388–89
    family impact, 387–88
    social information processing theory
      and, 389–91
  victims of, 391–93
AIDS, teratogenic effects of, 73
Albinism, 45
Alcohol
  ADHD and prenatal exposure to, 149
  fetal alcohol syndrome (FAS), 74
  as teratogen, 74–75
Alcohol-related neurodevelopmental dis-
  order (ARND), 74
Alert inactivity, newborn state of, 94
Alleles, 42
Allergies to food, 106, 107
Altruism, 380, 382
  cost of, 382, 384
  fostering, 383
American Academy of Pediatrics (AAP),
  96
American Association on Mental Retarda-
  tion (AAMR), 259
American Psychological Association and
  the American Psychiatric Associa-
  tion, 470
American Youth Soccer Organization, 158
Amnesia, infantile, 207
Amniocentesis, 80, 81

Amniotic fluid, 80, 83
Amniotic sac, 64
Amodal information, perception of,
  139–40
Amygdala, 201, 315
Analytic ability, 242
Androgens, 112, 407–8, 419
Androgyny, 421
Anger, 304, 307, 309
Anonymity in research, 34
Anorexia nervosa, 118, 119
Antidepressant drugs, 341
Antisocial behavior, 21, 389
Anxiety, self-control and, 367–68
Apache, celebration of menarche
  among, 112
Apgar score, 91–92
Applied developmental science, 7
Apprenticeship, development as, 175–78
Aristotle, 4–5
Arithmetic skills, 230
Asian Americans, 254
Asian cultures, emotional expression in,
  307, 314
Assertiveness, 385
Assimilation, 164, 165
Assisted reproductive technology, 40–41
Associative play, 461
Athletic competence, 343
Athletic self-esteem, 346
Attachment, 318–27
  avoidant, 322
  cultures and, 322
  disorganized (disoriented), 322
  growth of, 319–21
  in the making, 320
  mother-infant, 34, 321–22, 326, 481
  quality of, 321–22
    factors determining, 323–25
    stability, 322–23
    work, child care, and, 326
  resistant, 322
  role of fathers in, 320–21
  secure, 322
Attachment Q-Set, 322
Attention, 147–50
  ADHD and, 148–50
  defined, 147
  joint, 276
Attention-deficit disorder, 149
Attention deficit hyperactivity disorder
  (ADHD), 148–50, 404
  myths surrounding, 149
  symptoms of, 148–49
  treatment for, 149–50
Attention span, TV watching and, 476
Attitudes, TV's influence on, 477
Attributions, 341
Attrition, selective, 30
Audience, imaginary, 336
Auditory threshold, 136
Authoritarian parenting, 431, 432, 436
Authoritative parenting, 431, 436, 471
Authority, memory of event and, 207–10
Authority-oriented grandparents, 442
Autobiographical memory, 206–7, 333
Automatic processing, 180–81, 182
Autonomic system, NBAS evaluation of
  newborn's, 92
Autonomy versus shame and doubt, 11
Autosomes, 41
  abnormal, 47
Average children, 473

"Average" vs. "normal," 105
Avoidant attachment, 322
Axons, 123, 125
Babbling, 272–73
Babies. *See also* Infants; Newborns
  low birth weight, 89, 90, 95
  nutrition for, 106–7
  test-tube, 40
Babinski reflex, 93
Baby biographies, 6
Baby fat, 104
"Back to Sleep" campaign, 96
Balance, posture and, 152–53
Balance-scale problems, 213, 214, 215
Basal metabolic rate, 120
Bases, nucleotide, 42
Basic cry, 94
Basic emotions, 303–4, 305
*Bastard Out of Carolina* (Allison), 391
Bayley Scales of Infant Development,
  248, 249
Behavior(s)
  adaptive, 9–10
  antisocial, 21, 389
  continuity of, 29
  gender differences in, 403–5, 410
  naïve psychology about, 190–95
  prosocial, 21
  sampling, with tasks, 22–23
Behavioral conduct, 344
Behavioral genetics, 48–54
  defined, 48
  methods of, 50–52
  psychological characteristics affected by
    heredity, 52–54
Behavioral problems
  part-time work and, 484
  temperament and, 317–18
Behaviorism, 6
  on grammar acquisition, 287, 290
Bias
  in intelligence tests, 255
  response, 23
Biking accidents, 122
Bilingualism, 282
Binge eating and purging, 118
Biographies, baby, 6
Biological factors
  in aggression, 387
  in depression, 341
  in gender differences in verbal ability,
    404
  in gender identity, 419–20
  in mathematics ability, 407
  in sexual orientation, 470
  in temperament, 312–13
Biological perspective, 9–10, 15
Biology, naïve theories of, 188–90
Birth, 82–91
  adjusting to parenthood, 86–87
  approaches to childbirth, 84–86
  complications of, 87–91
  labor and delivery, 83–84
Birthing centers, 86
Blank slate, child as, 5, 11, 19
Blastocyst, 63
Blended families, 440–41
Blink reflex, 93
Bodily-kinesthetic intelligence, 240
Body fat
  in adolescence, 104, 109
  physical growth and, 104
Body hair, 111, 112
Body mass index (BMI), 119

Bone growth
in adolescence, 104, 109–11
osteoporosis and, 110–11
Bottle-feeding, 106
Boys. *See* Gender differences
Brain, 123–29
damage to
recovery of function after, 128
studies of children with, 125, 126
development of, 124–29
emerging structures, 124–25
malnutrition and, 118
memory and, 201
plasticity and, 128–29
structure and function, 125–28
in fetal period, 65
language processing regions of, 288
organization of mature, 123–24
prenatal development of, 69
right-hemisphere specialization for face
processing, 126–27
spatial ability and, 405
Brain activity, 24
Brain waves, 126
Brazilian culture, 244
Breast-feeding
advantages of, 106
reducing postpartum depression with,
87
Breast milk, infants' sensitivity to taste of,
135
Breasts, growth of, 111, 112
Breech presentation, 83, 87
Brightness constancy, 142
Broca's area, 288
*Brown* v. *Board of Education*, 358
Bulimia nervosa, 118–19
Bullying, 391–92
Burnouts, 471
Calcium, 108
bone growth and, 110
Calories
empty, 108
physical growth and, 106, 107, 108
Camp, summer, 472
Cardinality principle, 229
Care-based moral reasoning, 375–76
Career choice, identity and, 337–38
Career development, 337–38
Caring, ethic of, 375–76
Carolina Abecedarian Project, 253–54
Cartilage, 104
Cell body, 123
Census-tract information, 485
Centration, 168–69
Cephalopelvic disproportion, 87
Cerebral cortex, 65, 124, 126–27
Cervix, 83, 84
Cesarean section (C-section), 88
Child abuse, 200. *See also* Maltreatment of
children
interviewing children effectively about,
211
Childbirth. *See* Birth
Child care, attachment quality and, 326
*Child Development*, 34
Child development, 3–36. *See also* Birth;
Prenatal development
foundational theories of, 8–16
biological perspective, 9–10, 15
cognitive-developmental perspective,
13–14, 15, 16
contextual perspective, 14–15, 16
learning perspective, 11–13, 15, 16,
20
psychodynamic perspective, 10–11,
15
origins as science, 4–7
historical views of children and
childhood, 4–5
research in, 20–35

communicating results of, 34–35
ethical responsibilities in, 33–34
general designs for, 25–33
measurement, 21–25
research themes, 17–20
active-passive child issue, 18–19
connectedness of different developmental domains, 19–20
continuity-versus-discontinuity
issue, 17–18, 19
nature-nurture issue, 18, 19
Child Development and Family Policy
(China), 445–46
Childhood, 5
Child labor, 5–6
Child rearing, as adaptive behavior,
319–20
Children's Television Workshop, 478
China, one-child policy in, 445–46
Chinese Americans, 339
Chinese culture, parenting styles and, 432
Chorionic villus sampling (CVS), 80–81
Chromosomes, 40, 41–42
abnormal number of, 46–47
sex, 41
Chronological age (CA), 246
Chronosystem, 429
Clark University, 6
Classrooms, computers in, 479
Clique, 471
Coaches
in childbirth, 85
parents as, 463
sports, 158–59
Coaching, 433
Cocaine, 79
Cochlear implants, 137, 271–72
Coefficient of correlation (*r*), 25–26
Cognitive development, 163–97. *See also*
Academic skills
core-knowledge theories of, 183–96
gender stereotyping and, 401
hereditary and environmental bases of,
53–54
information-processing theory of,
178–82, 184
language development and, 289
make-believe play and, 462
moral reasoning and, 373
Piaget's theory of, 164–74, 212
basic principles of, 164–66, 173
concrete operational stage, 14, 165,
169, 170, 171
contributions to child development,
171–72
educational applications of, 172
formal operational stage, 14, 165,
169–71
preoperational stage, 14, 165,
167–69, 171
sensorimotor stage, 13–14, 165,
166–67, 171
weaknesses of, 173
prejudice and, 355–56
sociocultural perspective on, 173,
174–78, 184
TV's influence on, 477–78
understanding in core domains, 185–95
living things, 184, 188–90
objects and their properties, 167,
184, 186–88
people, 184, 190–95
Cognitive-developmental perspective,
13–14, 15, 16
Cognitive flexibility, 180
Cognitive functioning, prenatal exposure
to PCBs and, 75–76, 78
Cognitive processes, 200–219
in aggression, 389
in fast mapping, 277
memory, 200–211

autobiographical, 333
brain development and, 201
incentives and, 27–28
knowledge and, 203–11
long-term, 179
origins of, 200–201
phonological, 279
sensory, 179
strategies for remembering, 201–3
working, 179, 180, 181, 182, 224
problem solving, 212–19
developmental trends in, 212–14
features of children's and adolescents', 214–17
formal vs. concrete operational
thinking and, 170
planning and cognitive flexibility in,
180
scientific, 218–19
sleep and, 105
Cognitive self-regulation, 203
Cognitive theories
of gender identity, 417–19
gender schema theory, 417–19
of grammar acquisition, 289, 290
Cohort effects, 30, 32
Collaboration
cognitive development through, 175–78
problem solving through, 217
Color constancy, 142
Color perception, 138
Commercials, 477
Communication, 291–97. *See also*
Language
effective, 292
listening well, 296–97
speaking effectively, 293–96
turn taking in, 292–93
Community
aggressive behavior and, 388–89
child maltreatment and, 451–52, 453
Competence
academic, 343, 344, 348
athletic, 343
feelings of, 382, 384
mathematical, 230–31
Comprehension, 220, 223–24
Computer monitors, prenatal exposure to,
75
Computers, 479–80
Conclusions, premature, 218
Concrete operational stage, 14, 165, 169,
170, 171
Conditioning, operant, 11–12, 13
Conduct disorder, 386
teenage motherhood risk and, 71
Cones, 138
Confidentiality in research, 34
Conflict
in family, 388
between parents, 345
psychodynamic perspective on, 10–11
Confounded variables, 218, 219
Confucian principles, 432
Congenital adrenal hyperplasia (CAH),
81, 419
Connections, theme of, 19–20, 129
Consent, informed, 33
Conservation, 168–69
of liquids, 168
Constancies, perceptual, 142, 143
Constricting interactions, 415
Constructivism, 172
Consumer behavior, TV's
influence on, 477
Contextual perspective, 14–15, 16
Continuity, theme of, 29, 97, 393
Continuity-versus-discontinuity issue,
17–18, 19
Contraceptives, adolescents' infrequent
use of, 469

Contractions in labor and delivery, 83, 84
Control, parental, 436
Controversial children, 473
Conventional level of moral reasoning,
372, 373, 374
Conventions, social, 377
Convergent thinking, 257
Cooing, 272, 304
Cooperative play, 461
Coordinating skills for walking, 153–54
Core-knowledge theories of cognitive de-
velopment, 183–96
understanding in core domains, 185–96
living things, 184, 188–90
objects and their properties, 167,
184, 186–88
people, 184, 190–95
Corpus callosum, 124
Correlational studies, 25–26, 28, 32
Correlation coefficient (*r*), 25–26
Cost of altruism, 382, 384
Counseling, genetic, 46, 79
Counterimitation, 433
Counting
learning, 228–29, 230
principles of, 229
Creativity, 242, 257–59
fostering, 258
Crime, violent, 389
Critical periods, 9, 289
Cross-cultural studies of temperament,
312–13. *See also* Cultural
influences
Cross-sectional design, 30–31, 32
Crowd, 471
Crowning, 83
Crying, 315
cultural differences in, 314
of newborns, 94
Crystallization phase of career development, 337
Crystallized intelligence, 239
Cues
perception of objects and, 141–42,
143–45
sentence, 277
Cultural differences
in celebration of sexual maturity, 112
in emotional expression, 307
crying, 314
in mathematical competence, 230–31
Cultural influences
on aggressive behavior, 388–89
Asian number systems and learning
counting, 229
bilingualism, 282
on gender stereotypes, 398–99
of grandmothers in African American
families, 442–43
on identity, 338–39
on infant mortality, 90
on intelligence, 244
on moral reasoning, 374–75
motor development and, 154
parental scaffolding of children's learning and, 176–77
on play, 461–62
on popularity, 473
on school standards, 231–32
sickle-cell disease and, 44
sociocultural perspective and, 173,
174–78, 184
on temperament, 314
Cultural knowledge, sources of, 475
Culture, 14, 429
attachment and, 322
child maltreatment and, 451–52, 453
as developmental context, 14–15
parenting styles and, 431–32
play in, 415
Culture-fair intelligence tests, 255

Custody, joint, 438
Cystic fibrosis, 45
Cytomegalovirus, 73
Cytosine, 42
Day care, 480–83
    after-school programs, 481–82
    mother-infant attachment and, 481
Deafness, cochlear implants for, 271–72
Death
    childhood, causes of, 120–22
    sudden infant death syndrome (SIDS),
        95–96, 97
Deception in research, 34
Decoding words, 221–23
Deductive reasoning, 170–71
Deep relaxation, 306
Delivery, labor and, 83–84
Dendrites, 123, 125
Deoxyribonucleic acid (DNA), 41–42
    behavioral genetic studies using, 52
Dependent variable, 27
Depression, 341
    in adolescence, 341, 409
    gender differences in, 408–9, 410
    heredity and, 52–53
    hormones and, 409
    postpartum, 86–87
    puberty onset and, 113
Depth perception, 143–45
Desegregation of schools, 357–59
Desensitization, systematic, 306
Despair, integrity versus, 11
Detached grandparents, 442
*Developmental Psychology*, 34
Developmental research designs, 28–33
    cross-sectional design, 30–31, 32
    longitudinal design, 29–30, 32
    longitudinal-sequential studies, 31–32
    meta-analysis, 33
Diarrhea, deaths caused by, 120, 121
Diet
    balanced, 107, 108
    malnutrition and inadequate, 117–18
Diethylstilbestrol (DES), 79
Differentiation, 153
    of cells of blastocyst, 63
"Difficult" babies, 311
Diffusion status, 337
Dilemmas, moral, 371
Direct instruction, 432–33
Disciplinary practices
    aggressive behavior and, 387
    fostering altruism through, 383, 384
    peer rejection and, 474
Discontinuity-versus-continuity issue,
    17–18, 19
Disease(s)
    childhood deaths and, 120–21
    Huntington's, 45
    sickle-cell, 40, 42–44
    Tay-Sachs, 45
    as teratogens, 73
Disgust, 302–3
Dismissive adults, 325
Disorganized (disoriented) attachment,
    322
Display rules, 308, 309
Distance, using sound to estimate, 136
Distortions, memory, 204–6
Distress, 304
Divergent thinking, 257–58
Divorce, 438–40
    aspects of children's lives affected by,
        438–39
    children most affected by, 439
    helping children adjust after, 440
    influence on development, 439
Dizygotic (fraternal) twins, 50, 63, 157
DNA, 41–42
    behavioral genetic studies using, 52
Dog-cat-mouse problem, 216

Domains of development, connectedness
    of, 423
Domains of knowledge, 183–84
Dominance, incomplete genetic, 43–44
Dominance hierarchy, 471–72
Dominant allele, 42
    disorders associated with, 45
Doula, 85
Down syndrome, 46–47, 73, 259
    prenatal testing for, 81
Drinking, 472
Drives, 10
Drowning, childhood deaths by, 121
Drug(s)
    for ADHD, 149, 150
    antidepressant, 341
    reducing birth pain without, 85
    as teratogens, 73, 74–75
Dynamic systems theory, 152
    on fine-motor skills, 156
    on learning to walk, 153–54
Dynamic testing, 250
Early Child Care study, 326
Early childhood intervention programs,
    454
"Easy" babies, 311, 312
Eating
    internal vs. external cues to, 120
    learning to feed self, 155–56
    weight loss and, 120
Eating disorders, 118–19
Ectoderm, 63
Educably (mildly) mentally retarded, 260
Education, multiple intelligence theory
    and, 241–42
EEG, 126
Efe, 15
Effort, parents' beliefs about, 232
Effortful control, 312, 313
Eggs, 47
    fertilization of, 40
Ego, 10
Egocentrism, 168, 169, 381
    of adolescents, 336
    of preschool children, 353
Ejaculation, 111–12
Elaboration, 202
*Electric Company*, 478
Electroencephalogram (EEG), 126
Electronic media, 475–80
    computers, 479–80
    games, aggressive behavior and, 388
    gender identity and, 423
    television, 475–78
        aggressive behavior and, 388
        attitudes and social behavior and,
            477
        cognition and, 477–78
        consumer behavior and, 477
        criticism of, 476
        gender identity and, 416
        guidelines for watching, 478
        time spent watching, 157
        word learning from, 281
Elementary-school children
    aggression against, 391–92
    in concrete operational stage, 169, 171
    emotion recognition by, 308
    emotions in, 306
    gender stereotype learning in, 400
    gross-motor skills in, 403–4
    memory strategies, 202
    peer relations in, 464–65
    prejudice in, 355–56
    problem solving by, 215
    prosocial reasoning in, 376–77
    in Taiwan, 231–32
    writing strategies of, 225
Embryo, 63
    exposure to teratogens, 77, 78
    period of, 63–65, 67

Emotion(s), 301–11. *See also* Attachment;
    Temperament
    as adaptive, 302–3, 305
    basic, 303–4, 305
    complex, 305, 306, 307
    cultural differences in expressing, 307
    experiencing and expressing, 303–7
    facial expressions of, 33, 303–4
    function of, 302–3
    gender differences in sensitivity to, 408,
        410
    measuring, 303
    recognizing and using others', 307–9
    regulating, 309–10
    self-conscious, 305
    self-descriptions using, 334
Emotional bond, parent-infant, 86
Emotional intelligence, 241
*Emotional Intelligence* (Goleman), 241
Empathic orientation, 377
Empathy, 309, 381, 384
Employment, part-time, 483–85
Enabling interactions, 415
Encoding processes, 214
Endoderm, 63
England, 5–6
English, African American, 294
Enlightenment, Age of, 5
Environment, 14, 18
    brain development and role of, 128–29
    cognitive development and, 53–54
    family, 56
    genes' influence on, 56
    handedness and, 157
    heredity and, 48–58
        behavioral genetics, 48–54
        dynamic interaction of, 55–56
        paths from genes to behavior, 54–57
    intelligence testing and, 251–54
    nonshared influences of, 56–57
    obesity and, 120
    phenotypes and, 54
    puberty onset and, 113
    temperament and, 313–14, 317
    vocabulary growth and, 280
Environmental teratogens, 75–77
Epiphyses, 104
Equilibration, 165
Erikson, Erik, 10–11, 16
Errors, naming, 279
Estrogen, 112, 419
Ethical responsibilities in research, 33–34
Ethnic identity, 338–40
Ethnicity
    gender stereotyping and, 401
    intelligence tests and, 255–56
Ethological theory, 9–10
European Americans, 254
Evolution, theory of, 6
Evolutionary perspective, 9
    on resources and timing of puberty,
        114
    on social relationships, 319–20
Executive functioning, 180, 182
    theory of mind and, 193
Exercise(s)
    bone growth and, 110
    physical fitness and, 157–59
    weight-bearing, 110
    weight loss and, 120
Existential intelligence, 240
Exosystem, 429
Experience(s)
    active-passive child issue and, 19
    biological perspective on, 9
    learning perspective on, 11–12
    Locke on, 5
    Plato on, 5
    psychodynamic perspective on, 6, 10
Experimental studies, 27–28, 32
    scientific problem solving, 218–19

Exploration, teaching through, 172
Expressiveness, 421
Expressive style of learning language, 280
Expressive traits, 398
Extroversion, 48, 315
Eye-hand coordination, 155–56
Eyewitness testimony, 207–11
Fable, personal, 336
Faces
    perception of, 145–47
    right-hemisphere specialization for
        processing, 126–27
Facial expressions, 33, 303–4, 408
Facial hair, 111
False-belief tasks, 193
False memories, fuzzy trace theory and,
    205–6
Familial mental retardation, 259
Family(ies), 56, 426–57. *See also* Parents;
    Parenting
    aggressive behavior and, 387–88
    blended, 440–41
    child care guidelines for, 326
    children of gay and lesbian parents,
        443–44
    China's one-child policy, 446
    conflict in, 388
    development of small-for-date babies
        and, 89
    divorce in, 438–40
    grandparents' role in, 441–43
    intelligence and, 251–52
    maltreatment in, 449–55
        causes of, 451–53
        consequences of, 450–51
        preventing, 453–54
    sibling relationships, 444–49
        adopted children, 446–47
        firstborn, laterborn, and only chil-
            dren, 445–46
        qualities of, 447–49
    single-parent, 439
    as a system, 428–30
Family economic stress model, 487–88
Family history, 46
    of victims of aggression, 393
Family Lifestyles Project, 422
Family planning, 46
Fast mapping in word learning, 275–79
    cognitive factors in, 277
    constraints on word names and, 276–77
    joint attention and, 276
    naming errors and, 279
    sentence cues and, 277
Fast Track, 391
Fat
    body, 104, 109
    in diet, 107
Fathers. *See also* Parents; Parenting
    gender identity and, 414
    paternal investment theory of girls' pu-
        bertal timing, 114–15
    role in attachment, 320–21
Fear, 302, 304, 306
    self-control and, 367–68
Feedback, 433–34
Feelings, subjective, 303. *See also* Emo-
    tion(s)
Fels longitudinal project, 314
Fertility, age and, 72
Fertilization, 62
    in vitro, 41
Fetal alcohol syndrome (FAS), 74
Fetal heart rate, monitoring, 88
Fetal hypothyroidism, 81
Fetal medicine, 81–82
Fetal surgery, 81
Fetus
    behavior, 66–67
    exposure to teratogens, 77, 78
    period of, 65–68

Field experiment, 28
Fine-motor skills, 151, 155–57
Firearms, accidental deaths by, 122
Firstborn children, 445–46
Fitness, physical, 157–59
Flexibility, cognitive, 180
Fluid intelligence, 239
f-MRI, 126
Folic acid, 69
Foreclosure status, 337
Formal operational stage, 14, 165, 169–71
Formula, bottle-feeding with, 106
Fraternal (dizygotic) twins, 50, 63, 157
Friendships, 464–68
    defined, 464
    formation of, 465–66
    opposite-sex, 466
    quality and consequences of, 466–67
    sexual activity and, 467–68
Frontal cortex, 124, 126, 180
    memory and development of, 201
Frustration, 387
Functional approach to emotions, 302–3
Functional magnetic resonance imaging
    (f-MRI), 126
Fuzzy trace theory, 205–6
Gay and lesbian parents, children of,
    443–44
Gender differences, 402–11
    in ADHD, 148
    in eating disorders, 119
    in growth spurts, 109
    in intellectual abilities and achieve-
        ment, 404–7, 410
        mathematics, 402, 406–7, 410
        spatial ability, 402, 405–6, 410
        verbal ability, 402, 404, 410
    in moral reasoning, 376
    in personality and social behavior,
        407–9, 410
        aggressive behavior, 402, 407–8, 410
        depression, 408–9, 410
        emotional sensitivity, 408, 410
        social influence, 408, 410
    in physical development and behavior,
        404–5, 410
    pubertal changes and, 111–16
    in recognizing emotions in facial ex-
        pressions, 33
Gender identity, 396, 411–20
    biological influences on, 419–20
    cognitive theories of, 417–19
        gender schema theory, 417–19
    socializing influences on, 412–17
        fathers, 414
        mothers, 412–13
        peers, 414–16
        teachers, 414, 423
        television, 416
Gender roles, 396, 420–23
    emerging, 420–21
    peer influence on, 414–15
    beyond traditional, 421–22
Gender schema theory, 417–19
Gender stereotypes, 398–401
    cultural influences on, 398–99
    defined, 398
    learning, 399–401
General intelligence (g), 238–39, 345
Generativity versus stagnation, 11
Genes, 42
    expression of, 55
    influence on environment, 56
Genetic disorders, 44–48
    abnormal number of chromosomes,
        46–47
    genetic counseling and, 46, 79
    inherited, 44–46
Genetic engineering, 82
Genetics. See also Biological factors;
    Heredity

behavioral, 48–54
    defined, 48
    methods of, 50–52
    psychological characteristics affected
        by heredity, 52–54
ethnic differences in intelligence and,
    254–55
handedness and, 157
prenatal development and, 69–73
spatial ability and, 405
timing of pubertal events and, 113
Genital herpes, 73
Genitals, maturation of, 113
Genotype, 42, 54
    teratogen impact and, 77
Germ disc, 63
Gestures, 275
*Ghostwriter*, 478
Gifted children, 257–59
Gifted classes, self-esteem in, 349
Girls. See Gender differences
Girl Scouts, 472
Gist memory traces, 205–6
Global self-worth, 347–48
Government policies, impact of, 7
Governor's Task Force on Children's Jus-
    tice (Michigan), 211
Grade point average, WISC-III and, 250
Grammar, 268
    perspectives on acquisition of, 287–90
        behaviorist, 287, 290
        cognitive, 289, 290
        linguistic, 288–89, 290
        social-interaction, 289–90
Grammatical morphemes, 286–87
Grandparents, 441–43
Grasping, 155–56
Gross-motor skills, gender differences in,
    403–4
Groups, 471–74
    clique, 471
    crowd, 471
    pressure from, 472
    structure of, 471–72
Growth. See Physical growth
Growth charts, 102, 103
Growth hormone, 105, 112
Growth spurt, 102, 104, 109–16
    bone growth, 104, 109–11
    mechanisms of, 112–15
    psychological impact of, 115–16
    sexual maturation, 111–12
Guanine, 41–42
Guatemala, parental scaffolding in,
    176–77
Guided participation, 175
Guilt, initiative versus, 11
Habituation, 134, 147
    IQ and, 248
    to sound, 269
Hair, 111, 112
Handedness, 156–57
Hands, reaching and grasping, 155–56
Happiness, 302
Hardware, mental, 178–79
Head Start, 252–53
Healing, understanding living vs. nonliv-
    ing things and, 189
Health
    gender differences in, 404, 410
    physical fitness and, 157–59
    puberty onset and, 113
Hearing, 136–37
Hearing impairment in infancy, 137, 272
Heart rate, 23
Hedonistic orientation, 376
Height
    body mass index and, 119
    physical growth and, 102, 103
Helping behavior, temperament and,
    316–17. See also Prosocial behavior

Hemispheres of cerebral cortex, 124, 126
    right-hemisphere specialization for face
        processing, 126–27
Hemoglobin, 108
Heredity, 18, 40–59. See also Genetics
    aggressive behavior and, 387
    biology of, 40–42
    cognitive development and, 53–54
    depression and, 52–53
    environment and, 48–58
        behavioral genetics, 48–54
        dynamic interaction of, 55–56
        paths from genes to behavior,
            54–57
    genetic disorders, 44–48
        abnormal number of chromosomes,
            46–47
        genetic counseling and, 46, 79
        inherited, 44–46
    intelligence testing and, 251–54
    juvenile obesity and, 120
    sexual orientation and, 470
    single gene inheritance, 42–44
    temperament and, 313–14
Herpes, genital, 73
Heterozygous alleles, 42
Heuristics, 215
Hierarchy, dominance, 471–72
Hindu religion, 374–75
Hippocampus, 201
Hispanic Americans, 254, 339
    sickle-cell disease in, 44
Historical views of children and child-
    hood, 4–5
Home, computers in, 479
Home birth, 85–86
Home environments, intelligence and, 252
Homework, 232
*Homo sapiens*, 422
Homozygous alleles, 42
Hopping, learning, 154–55
Hormones
    aggressive behavior and, 407–8
    depression and, 409
    for fetal disorders, 81
    gender identity and, 419
    growth, 105, 112
    labor and delivery and, 83
    sexual orientation and, 470
    stress, menarche and, 113
Hospital birth, 84–85
Hostile aggression, 385–86
Hovering, 462
Hunger
    internal vs. external signals of, 120
    malnutrition and, 117–18
Huntington's disease, 45
Hyperactivity, ADHD and, 148, 149
Hypotheses, 8
Hypothetical reasoning, 170–71, 335
Hypothyroidism, fetal, 81
Hypoxia, 88
Id, 10
Identical (monozygotic) twins, 50, 63
    fetal surgery on, 81
    handedness in, 157
Identity, 335–42. See also Gender identity
    career choice and, 337–38
    cultural influences on, 338–39
    depression and, 341
    ethnic, 338–40
    storm and stress in, 340
    versus identity confusion, 11
Illness, understanding living vs. nonliving
    things and, 189
Illusion of invulnerability, 336, 469
Imaginary audience, 336
Imaginary companions, 462
Imitation (observational learning),
    12, 433
Immanent justice, 370

Immigrant adolescents, 339
Immigration, intelligence tests and,
    245–46
Implantation, 63
Implementation phase of career develop-
    ment, 338
Imprinting, 9
Impulsivity, ADHD and, 149
Inattention, ADHD and, 148
Incentives, memory and, 27–28
Incomplete dominance, 43–44
Independent variable, 27
India
    moral reasoning in, 374–75
    parental scaffolding in, 176–77
Indians, 339
Individual rights and justice, moral rea-
    soning based on, 374–75, 376
Industrial Revolution, 5–6
Industry versus inferiority, 11
Infant Behavior Questionnaire (IBQ-R),
    312–13
Infant-directed speech (motherese), 271
Infantile amnesia, 207
Infant intelligence tests, 248–49
Infant mortality, 90
Infants, 5. See also Mother-infant attach-
    ment; Parents
    abuse of, 452
    "conversations" with, 292–93
    emotions in, 303–5
        regulation of, 309–10
    face perception of, 145–47
    fine-motor skills in, 155–56
    gender differences in activity, 404
    gesturing in, 275
    guidelines for care of, 326
    handedness and, 156–57
    hearing impaired, 137, 272
    language learning in, 269–73, 276, 278
    malnutrition in, 117–18
    memory in, 200, 201
    motor development in, 152–53
    number skills of, 227–28
    orienting response and habituation in,
        147–48
    peer interactions between, 460–61
    perception of objects by, 141–42
    phoneme discrimination in, 269–70
    premature, 88, 95
    problem solving by, 213
    recognition of emotion in others,
        307–8
    self-control in, 365–66
    senses of, 135–38
    in sensorimotor stage, 165, 166–67, 171
    small-for-date, 88, 89
    sounds produced by, 268
    structure of temperament in, 312–13
    understanding of intentionality, 190–92
    word identification by, 270–71
Inferiority, industry versus, 11
Influential grandparents, 442
Information-processing theory of cogni-
    tive development, 178–82, 184
Informed consent, 33
Inheritance. See also Heredity
    polygenic, 49
    single gene, 42–44
        understanding living vs. nonliving
            things and, 188–89
Inherited genetic disorders, 44–46
Inhibition, 316
Inhibitory processes, 180, 182
Initiative versus guilt, 11
Innate knowledge, 5
Inner speech, 177
Instincts, 10
Institutional influences, 480–91
    day care, 480–83
        after-school programs, 481–82

mother-infant attachment and, 481
neighborhoods, 485–89
  defined, 485
  socioeconomic status of, 485, 486,
    487–88
  stability of, 485, 486–87
part-time employment, 483–85
school, 489–91
  factors influencing success of,
    489–90
  student achievement and, 489–90
  teacher-based influences, 490–91
Instruction, direct, 432–33
Instrumental aggression, 385
Instrumentality, 421
Instrumental orientation, 372
Instrumental traits, 398
Integrated Management of Childhood
    Illness (IMCI), 121
Integrity versus despair, 11
Intellectual abilities and achievement,
    gender differences in, 404–7, 410
  mathematics, 402, 406–7, 410
  spatial ability, 402, 405–6, 410
  verbal ability, 402, 404, 410
Intellectual development, 9. See also Cog-
    nitive development
Intelligence, 236–65
  below-average, 259
  crystallized, 239
  cultural influences on, 244
  emotional, 241
  fluid, 239
  Gardner's theory of multiple intelli-
    gences, 239–42, 245
    implications for education, 241–42
  general (g), 238–39, 345
  hierarchical theories of, 239, 345
  nature and nurture in, 263
  psychometric theories of, 238–39, 245
  of special children, 256–63
    gifted and creative children, 257–59
    with learning disabilities, 260–63
    with mental retardation, 259–60
  Sternberg's theory of successful intelli-
    gence, 242–45
    abilities comprising, 242–43
    testing, 243
  tests of, 236, 245–56
    bias in, 255
    culture-fair, 255
    hereditary and environmental factors
      in, 251–54
    impact of ethnicity and socioeco-
      nomic status on, 254–56
    individualized vs. group, 248
    infant tests, 248–49
    interpreting scores on, 256
    reliability of, 248–49
    Stanford-Binet test, 246–48, 250
    validity, 249–50
*Intelligence and Experience* (Hunt), 252
Intelligence quotient. *See* IQ
Intention, language learning and, 277
Intentional behavior, 166
Intentionality, understanding of, 190–92
Internal parts, understanding living vs.
    nonliving things and, 188
Internal working model, 324, 325
Internet, 479
Interpersonal intelligence, 240
Interpersonal norms, 372
Interposition, 144
Intersensory redundancy theory, 139–40
Intersubjectivity, 175
Interviewing children, guidelines for, 211
Interviews, 23, 24
Intimacy in adolescent friendships, 465
Intimacy versus isolation, 11
Intonation, 273, 287
Intrapersonal intelligence, 240

Introversion, 315
*Investigative Interviews of Children: A
    Guide for Helping Professionals*
    (Poole and Lamb), 211
In vitro fertilization, 41
Invulnerability, illusion of, 336, 469
IQ, 246–47
  associated with mental retardation, 259
  developmental profiles for, 251
  historical change in, 252
  infant tests and, 248–49
  stability of, 249
Iron, 108
Isolation
  child maltreatment and, 451–52
  intimacy versus, 11
Jocks, 471
Joint attention, 276
Joint custody, 438
*Journal of Experimental Child Psychology*,
    34
Journals, scientific, 34–35
Joy, 304
Judgment, social, 37–38
Just Communities, 379
Justice
  immanent, 370
  moral reasoning based on, 374–75, 376
Kindergarten children, prejudice in,
    355–56. *See also* Elementary-
    school children
Kinetic cues, 143
Klinefelter's syndrome, 47
Knowledge. *See also* Cognitive develop-
    ment; Learning
  comprehension with increased, 224
  domains of, 183–84
  innate, 5
  memory and, 203–11
    autobiographical memory, 206–7
    distortions and, 204–6
    eyewitness testimony and, 207–11
    scripts and, 204
  metacognitive, 203
  problem solving requiring specific,
    215–16
  writing and, 225
Korean values, 462
Labor, child, 5–6
Labor and delivery, 83–84
Language, 266–99
  autobiographical memory and, 206
  brain specialization for, 126
  capacity to use symbols, 167
  to communicate, 291–97
    listening well, 296–97
    speaking effectively, 293–96
    taking turns, 292–93
  connections to other developmental
    domains, 297
  as core domain, 183–84
  defined, 268
  elements of, 268–69
  grammar acquisition, 287–90
    behaviorist answer to, 287, 290
    cognitive answer to, 289, 290
    linguistic answer to, 288–89, 290
    social-interaction answer to, 289–90
  hearing sounds of, 136
  infantile amnesia and inadequate, 207
  in infants, 269–73, 276, 278
  learning, 183
    critical period for, 9, 289
    intersensory redundancy and, 140
  other symbols in, 283–84
  promoting development of, 291
  reading skills, 220–24
  sentences, 284–91
    complex, 286–87
    telegraphic speech, 285
  sign, 271

sounds, sensitivity to, 220–21
speech, 269–74
  first steps to, 272–74
  infant-directed (motherese), 271
  inner, 177
  about mental states, 194
  perceiving, 269–72
  private, 177
  telegraphic, 285
words, 274–84
  encouraging learning of, 280–82
  fast mapping meanings to, 275–79
  identifying, 270–72
  individual differences in learning,
    279–80
  as symbols, 274–75
Latchkey children, 482
Laterborn children, 445–46
Lead, as teratogen, 75
Leading questions, influence of, 210
Learning. *See also* Cognitive development;
    Knowledge
  to count, 228–29, 230
  critical period for, 9
  facilitating vs. directing, 172
  gender stereotypes, 399–401
  intersensory redundancy and, 140
  of language, 183
    critical period for, 9, 289
    intersensory redundancy and, 140
  in newborn, 96–97
  observational (imitation), 12, 433
  operant conditioning and, 12
  to read, 220–24
  readiness, 172
  to run and hop, 154–55
  scaffolding of, 176–77
  to walk, 152–54
  of words, 279–82
  to write, 225–27
Learning disabilities, 260–63
  diagnosing, 262
Learning perspective, 11–13, 15, 16, 20
Left-handedness, 157
Lesbian parents, 443–44, 470
Letters, learning names and sounds of,
    220, 221–22, 223
Light, wavelength of, 138
Linear perspective, 144
Linguistic intelligence, 240
Linguistic theory of grammar acquisition,
    288, 290
Listening well, 296–97
Living things, understanding of, 184,
    188–90
Locomotion, 151, 152–55
  coordinating skills, 153–54
  perceptual factors in, 153
  posture and balance, 152–53
  stepping, 153
  beyond walking, 154–55
Logical-mathematical intelligence, 240
Longitudinal design, 29–30, 32
Longitudinal-sequential studies, 31–32
Long-term memory, 179
  word retrieval from, 222–23
Low birth weight babies, 89
  infant mortality and, 90
  sudden infant death syndrome (SIDS)
    and, 95
Loyalty in adolescent friendships, 465
Macrosystem, 429
Mad cry, 94
Make-believe, 461–62
Malaria, 44
Malnutrition, 117–18
Maltreatment of children, 449–55
  causes of, 451–53
  consequences of, 450–51
  preventing, 453–54
Marital system, parenting and, 435–36

Mathematics
  cultural differences in competence in,
    230–31
  gender differences in, 402, 406–7, 410
  number skills, 227–33
Maturation. *See* Physical growth
Maturational theory, 9, 10
Mealtimes, guidelines for picky eaters, 108
Means-ends analysis, 215–16
Measurement, 21–25
  evaluating, 24
  physiological, 23–24
  representative sampling, 25
  sampling behavior with tasks, 22–23, 24
  self reports, 23, 24
  systematic observation, 21–22, 24
Media. *See* Electronic media
Mediator, parents as, 463
Memory, 200–211
  autobiographical, 333
  brain development and, 201
  incentives and, 27–28
  knowledge and, 203–11
  long-term, 179
  origins of, 200–201
  phonological, 279
  sensory, 179
  strategies for remembering, 201–3
  working, 179, 180, 181, 182, 224
Menarche, 111
  age at, 113
Meningitis, 137
Menopause, osteoporosis after, 110
Menstruation, 55, 111
Mental age (MA), 246
Mental development. *See* Cognitive devel-
    opment
Mental hardware, 178–79
Mental health, part-time work and, 484
Mental operations, 169
  applied to abstract entities, 169–71
Mental representation of problem, encod-
    ing, 214
Mental retardation, 46, 259–60
  defined, 259
  savants and, 240–41
  types of, 259
Mental rotation, 405
Mental software, 178
Mental states, understanding behavior in
    terms of, 193–94, 195
Mental structures for learning domains of
    knowledge, 183–84
Mental tests, 6
Mental verbs, use of, 192
Mercury, as teratogen, 75
Mesoderm, 63
Mesosystem, 429
Messages, nonliteral meanings of, 296–97
Meta-analysis, 33
Metabolic rate, basal, 120
Metacognition, 202–3
Metamemory, 203
Metaphors, 296–97
Microgenetic study, 29
Microsystem, 429
Mildly (educably) mentally retarded, 260
Milestones
  motor development, 152
  prenatal, 67
Mind, theory of, 192–94, 195
Mirror task, 332–33
Miscarriage, 72, 74
*Mister Rogers' Neighborhood*, 477
Mistrust, trust versus, 11
Modeling, fostering altruism through,
    383, 384
Models, scale, 283
Moderate mental retardation, 259–60
Modules for learning domains of knowl-
    edge, 183–84

Monitoring, 388
Monozygotic (identical) twins, 50, 63
    fetal surgery on, 81
    handedness in, 157
Mood, 384
    altruism an, 382
Moral dilemmas, 371
Moral realism, 370
Moral reasoning, 369–79, 384
    cultural influences on, 374–75
    domains of social judgment, 377–78
    Eisenberg's levels of prosocial reason-
        ing, 376–77
    Gilligan's ethic of caring, 375–76
    Kohlberg's theory of, 371–75
        levels of moral reasoning, 371–73
        support for, 373–75
    Piaget's views on, 370–71
    promoting, 378–79
    prosocial behavior and, 381
Moral relativism, 370
Moratorium status, 337
Moro reflex, 93
Morphemes, grammatical, 286–87
Motherese, 271
Mother-infant attachment, 34, 321–22
    day care and, 481
    early child care and, 326
Mothers
    age of, prenatal development and, 70–73
    gender identity and, 412–13
    physical changes after birth, 86
    teenage, 70–71, 469
    risks associated with, 71–73
Motion
    perception of objects and, 141–42
    understanding living vs. nonliving
        things and, 188
Motion parallax, 143
Motor activity, NBAS evaluation of new-
    born's, 92
Motor cortex, 128
Motor development, 9, 151–59
    cultural practices promoting, 154
    fine-motor skills, 151, 155–57
    gender differences in, 410
    locomotion, 151, 152–55
    milestones, 152
    physical fitness, 157–59
Motor vehicle accidents, 121, 122
Moving to Opportunity for Fair Housing
    Demonstration, 486
Multimodal Treatment Study of Children
    with ADHD (MTA), 150
Multiple intelligences, Gardner's theory
    of, 239–42, 245
    implications for education, 241–42
Muscle development, 104
    in adolescence, 104, 109
Musical intelligence, 240–41
Musical sounds, hearing, 136
Myelin, 123, 125
Naïve theories, 184
    of biology, 188–90
    of physics, 187–88
    of psychology, 190–95
        theory of mind, 192–94, 195
        understanding of intentionality,
            190–92
Naming errors, 279
Naming explosion, 275, 277
    shape bias and, 278
    timing of, 279
National Assessment of Educational
    Progress (NAEP), 406
National Association for Advancement of
    Colored People (NAACP), 357–58
National Association for Retarded Chil-
    dren, 55
National Bone Health Campaign
    (NBHC), 110–11

National Council of 100 Black Women, 96
National Institute of Mental Health, 150
National Institutes of Health (NIH), 96,
    467
National Longitudinal Study of Adoles-
    cent Health, 467–68
National Osteoporosis Foundation, 110
Natural childbirth, 84–86
Naturalistic intelligence, 240
Naturalistic observation, 21, 24
Nature and nurture, 18–19. See also Envi-
    ronment; Heredity
    in emergence of self-awareness, 359
    in emotional sensitivity, 408
    in intelligence, 263
Needs-oriented orientation, 376–77
Negation, 287
Negative affect, 312, 313
Negative correlation, 26
Negative reinforcement, 12
Negative reinforcement trap, 433, 439
Neglect, 450
Neglected children, 473
Neighborhoods, 485–89
    defined, 485
    socioeconomic status of, 485, 486,
        487–88
    stability of, 485, 486–87
Neonatal Behavioral Assessment Scale
    (NBAS), 92–93
Nerds, 471
Nervous system. See Brain; Reflexes
Neural plate, 124
Neural tube, 69
Neurons, 123
    migration to final positions in brain,
        124
    production of, in neural tube, 124
Neurotransmitters, 123, 341
Newborns, 91–97
    assessing, 91–93
    basic emotions in, 304
    face perception of, 145
    orienting response and habituation in,
        147
    perception and learning in, 96–97, 141
    reflexes, 93, 166
    senses of, 135, 137, 138
    states of, 94–96
New York Longitudinal Study, 311–12,
    315–16
New Zealand, 29, 30
Niche-picking, 56
Nicotine, as teratogen, 74
Nim Chimpsky, 288
Non-REM sleep, 95
Nonshared environmental influences,
    56–57
Nonsocial play, 460
Norepinephrine, 341
Norms
    group, 472
    interpersonal, 372
Nucleotide bases, 42
Number names, learning, 229
Number skills, 227–33
    adding and subtracting, 228, 230
    cultural differences in, 230–33
    learning to count, 228–29, 230
Nurse-midwife, 85, 86
Nurture-nature issue. See Nature and nur-
    ture
Nutrition
    physical growth and, 106–8
    prenatal development and, 69
    puberty onset and, 113
Obedience orientation, 372
Obesity
    childhood, 119–20
    low physical fitness and, 157
Object permanence, 167, 186

Objects
    perception of, 141–47
    understanding, 167, 184, 186–88
Object unity, 142
Observation
    naturalistic, 21, 24
    structured, 22, 24
    systematic, 21–22, 24
Observational learning (imitation), 12,
    433
Office of Economic Opportunity (OEO),
    253
"Off-time hypothesis" for boys, 116
Older children, self-esteem in, 343
Older women, pregnancy in, 72–73
One-to-one principle, 229
Only children, 445–46
Operant conditioning, 11–12, 13
Operational stage
    concrete, 165, 169, 170, 171
    formal, 165, 169–71
Opposable thumb, 151
Opposite-sex friendships, 466
Ordinality, 228
Organic mental retardation, 259
Organization (memory strategy), 202
Organization of writing, 225
Organs, embryonic development of, 64
Orienting response, 147
Osteoporosis, 110–11
Others, 351–59
    describing, 352–53
    prejudice against, 355–59
    understanding thought of, 353–55
Ovaries, development of, 66
Overextension error, 279
Overlapping waves model, 217, 230
Overregularization, 286
Ownership, understanding of, 333–34
Pacific cultures, 244
Pain
    of childbirth, reducing, 85
    infants' experience of, 135
Pain cry, 94
Palmar reflex, 93
Parallax, motion, 143
Parallel play, 460–61
Parenthood, adjusting to, 86–87
Parenting, 56, 428–37
    aggressive children and, 474
    children's influence on, 430, 436–37,
        454–55
    influences of marital system on, 435–36
    parental behavior, 432–34
    strategies for, 22
    styles of, 430–32
        authoritarian, 431, 432, 436
        authoritative, 431, 436, 471
        culture and, 431–32
        permissive, 431
        socioeconomic status and, 431–32
        uninvolved, 431
    of victims of aggression, 392
Parents. See also Family(ies); Fathers;
    Mothers
    abusive, 451, 452, 453. See also Mal-
        treatment of children
    of adolescents, 340, 469
        career development and, 338
    of aggressive children, 387–88
    altruism modeled from, 383, 384
    attachment relation with, 463
        during infancy, 318, 322–25
    attitudes toward academics, 232
    in chronic poverty, 488
    conflicts between, 435
    control by, 436
    crowd membership and, 471
    cues from, 308
    discipline from, 349–50
    gay or lesbian, 443–44, 470

gender identity and, 412–14
peer relations and, 463–64, 474
scaffolding by, 217
school involvement of, 489
self-control in children and, 367
self-worth of children and, 349–50
sibling relationships and, 448
of small-for-date babies, training pro-
    grams for, 89
social-emotional development and,
    318–19
storybook reading with, 221
warmth of, 436
word learning in children and, 276,
    280–81
Part-time employment, 483–85
Passive-active child issue, 18–19
Passive grandparents, 442
Passive voice, 287
Paternal investment theory of girls' pu-
    bertal timing, 114–15
PCBs, prenatal exposure to, 75–76, 78
Peers, 460–74
    aggressive behavior and, 388
    collaboration with, 217
    development of interactions with,
        460–64
        make-believe, 461–62
        parental influence on, 463–64
        after preschool, 464–65
        solitary play, 462
    friendships, 464–68
        formation of, 465–66
        opposite-sex, 466
        quality and consequences of, 466–67
        sexual activity and, 467–68
    gender identity and, 414–16
    groups, 471–74
        clique, 471
        crowd, 471
        structure of, 471–72
    influence on memory of event, 210
    parent-child attachment and, 323
    popularity with, 472–73
    pressure from, 472
    rejection by, 472–74
        causes of, 474
        consequences of, 473
    romantic relationships, 468–71
        cultural factors influencing, 468–69
        sexual behavior in, 469–70
        sexual orientation and, 470–71
    self-esteem and, 346, 350
Penis, 111
People, understanding, 184, 190–95
Perceptual development
    attention and, 147–50
    in newborn, 96–97
    perceiving objects, 141–47
        depth, 143–45
        faces, 145–47
        perceptual constancies, 142, 143
    perceptual cues for walking, 153
    senses and, 134–40
        hearing, 136–37
        integrating sensory information,
            138–40
        seeing, 137–38
        smell, 135
        taste, 135
        touch, 135
    sensitivity to quantity, 227
Perceptual experience, 5
Permissive parenting, 431
Personal domain, 377
Personal fable, 336
Personality
    development of, 9
    gender differences in, 407–9, 410
        depression, 408–9, 410
        emotional sensitivity, 408, 410

psychodynamic perspective on, 10–11
temperament and, 315
Perspective, linear, 144
Perspective taking, 353–55, 384
prosocial behavior and, 355, 381
Phenotypes, 42
associated with single gene pairs, 45
environment and, 54
Phenylalanine, 55
Phenylketonuria (PKU), 45, 55
genetic engineering to prevent, 82
Phobia, school, 306
Phonemes, 269–70
Phonics, teaching, 223
Phonological awareness, 220–21
Phonological memory, 279
Phonology, 268
Photographs, 283
Physical abuse, 449
Physical appearance, 344
Physical development, 9
gender differences in, 403–5, 410
Physical education classes, 157, 158
Physical fitness, 157–59
Physical growth, 100–131
adolescent growth spurt and puberty,
102, 104, 109–16
bone growth, 104, 109–11
mechanisms of, 112–15
psychological impact of, 115–16
sexual maturation, 111–12
challenges to, 117–22
accidents, 121–22
disease, 120–21
eating disorders, 118–19
malnutrition, 117–18
obesity, 119–20
features of, 102–4
mechanisms of, 105–8
nutrition, 106–8
sleep, 105–6
nervous system, 123–29
variations on average profile, 104–5
Physics, naïve theories of, 187–88
Physiological measures, 23–24
Physiological responses of emotion, 303
Pica, 119
Pictorial cues, 144
Pictures, 283
Pituitary gland, puberty and, 112–13
Placenta, 63, 64
as afterbirth, 83–84
Planning, problem solving and,
180, 215
Plasticity, brain, 128–29
Plato, 4–5
Play
associative, 461
cooperative, 461
gender-stereotyped, 419
make-believe, 461–62
nonsocial, 460
parallel, 460–61
pretend, 167
sex-typed, 415
solitary, 462
Playmate, parents as, 463
Pleasure, 304
Policy issues, 7
Polychlorinated biphenyls (PCBs), prena-
tal exposure to, 75–76, 78
Polygenic inheritance, 49
Popular children, 472, 473
Popularity, 472–73
Populations, sampling, 25
Positive correlation, 26
Positive reinforcement, 12
Postconventional level of moral reason-
ing, 372, 373, 374
Postpartum depression, 86–87
Posture, 152–53

Poverty
aggressive behavior and, 389
child maltreatment and, 451
children's development and, 486–87
chronic, 488
family economic stress model of,
487–88
malnutrition and, 117
Practical ability, 243
Practice effects, 30, 32
Pragmatics, 268
Preattachment, 320
Preconventional level of moral reasoning,
372, 373, 374
Preeclampsia, 87, 88
Pregnancy. *See also* Prenatal development
childbirth, 82–91
adjusting to parenthood, 86–87
approaches to, 84–86
complications of, 87–91
labor and delivery, 83–84
impact of stress on, 70
mother's age during, 70–73
nutrition during, 69
teen, 115, 469
Prejudice, 355–59
defined, 355
Premature infant, 88, 95
Prenatal care, 79–82
infant mortality and, 90
Prenatal development, 62–82
brain development in, 124–25
defined, 62
five steps toward healthy baby, 68
influences on, 68–79
general risk factors, 69–73
teratogens, 73–79
milestones, 67
period of embryo, 63–65, 67
period of fetus, 65–68
period of zygote, 62–63, 67
prenatal diagnosis and treatment,
79–82
Preoccupied adults, 325
Preoperational stage, 14, 165, 167–69, 171
Prepared childbirth, 84–86
Prereading skills, 221
Preschool children
abuse of, 452
attentional processes in, 148
autobiographical memory of, 206–7
bilingual, 282
communication by, 293–96
egocentrism of, 353
emotions in, 306
eyewitness testimony of, 208–11
fine-motor skills in, 156
gender identity formation and, 418
gender stereotype learning in, 399–400
with imaginary friends, 462
language learning in, 276, 277, 281, 283,
286–87, 293–94
means-ends analyses by, 216
memory strategies, 201–2
moral reasoning in, 371
naïve theories of biology, 188–90
number skills of, 229
nutritional needs of, 107–8
play in, 461–63
prejudice in, 355–56
in preoperational stage, 168, 171
problem solving by, 213
prosocial behavior in, 376–77, 380–81
self-concepts in, 335
self-control in, 365–66, 369
*Sesame Street* viewing by, 478
social judgment in, 378
theory of mind developed by, 192–94,
195
Preschool intervention programs, 252–54
Pretend play, 167

Primary sex characteristics, 111
Private speech, 177
Problem solving, 212–19
developmental trends in, 212–14
features of children's and adolescents',
214–17
formal vs. concrete operational thinking and, 170
planning and cognitive flexibility in,
180
scientific, 218–19
strategies for, 179–80, 182
Processing speed, age differences in, 181,
182
Profound mental retardation, 259
Prolapsed umbilical cord, 87, 88
Propositions, 223–24
Prosocial behavior, 21, 380–84
altruism, 380, 382, 383, 384
defined, 380
development of, 380–81
situational influences on, 382
skills underlying, 381–82
socializing, 383–84
television and, 477
Prosocial reasoning, 376–77
Prosopagnosia, 126
Proximal development, zone of, 175–76,
250
Prozac, 341
Psychodynamic theory, 10–11, 15
Psychological abuse, 450
Psychological development in adolescents,
115–16
*Psychology of Sex Differences, The* (Macco-
by & Jacklin), 402
Psychometricians, 238
Psychometric theories of intelligence,
238–39, 245
Psychosocial theory, 10–11
Psychosocial treatments for ADHD, 150
Psychotherapy, 341
Puberty, 102, 104, 109–16
bone growth, 109–11
early vs. late, impact of, 116
mechanisms of, 112–15
psychological impact of, 116
sexual maturation, changes with,
111–12
Pubic hair, 111
Punishment, 12, 433–34
Quantity, perception of, 227. *See also*
Number skills
Questionnaires, 23, 24
Questions, leading, 210
Racial segregation, 465
Racial stereotypes, 356
Rapid-eye-movement (REM) sleep, 95
Raven's Progressive Matrices, 255
Reaching, 155–56
Reaction range, 54
Reactive aggression, 386
Readiness to learn, 172
Reading, 220–24
comprehension, 220, 223–24
foundations of, 220–21
recognizing words, 220, 221–23
TV watching and, 476
word learning from, 281
Reading disability, 260–62
*Reading Rainbow*, 478
Reading skills, 220–24
comprehension, 220, 223–24
foundations of, 220–21
recognizing words, 220, 221–23
Realism, moral, 370
Reasoning, deductive, 170–71
Recessive alleles, 42, 45
Reciprocal relationships, 320
Red blood cells, 40, 42
Referential style of learning language, 280

Reflexes
defined, 93
of newborn, 93, 166
Regret, 305–6
Rehearsal (strategy), 202
Reinforcement, 12, 433
Rejection, 472–74
causes of, 474
consequences of, 473
Relatedness of development, 17–18
Relational aggression, 386, 408
Relative size, 144
Relativism, moral, 370
Relaxation, deep, 306
Reliability
of child witnesses, guidelines for im-
proving, 211
of intelligence tests, 248–49
of measure, 24
Relief, 305–6
Remembering, strategies for, 201–3. *See
also* Memory
REM sleep, 95
Report, research, 34–35
Representative sampling, 25
Reproductive organs, 111
Reproductive system, 403
Reproductive technology, assisted, 40–41
Research, 20–35
communicating results of, 34–35
on effortful control in toddlers and
preschoolers, 365–66
ethical responsibilities in, 33–34
general designs for, 25–33
measurement in, 21–25
on preschoolers' communication,
294–96
on reading disability, 261–62
on self-esteem in different domains,
347–48
on temperament, 316–17
themes in, 17–20
active-passive child issue, 18–19
connectedness of different developmental domains, 19–20
continuity-versus-discontinuity
issue, 17–18, 19
nature-nurture issue, 18, 19
Research designs, 25–33
correlational studies, 25–26, 28, 32
defined, 25
experimental studies, 27–28, 32
for studying age-related change (developmental designs), 28–33
cross-sectional design, 30–31, 32
longitudinal design, 29–30, 32
longitudinal-sequential studies,
31–32
meta-analysis, 33
Resistant attachment, 322
Resources, timing of puberty and, 114
Response, orienting, 147
Response bias, 23
Responsibility, feelings of, 382, 384
Retinal disparity, 143–44
Reversible mental operations, 169
Review boards, 34
Revising writing, skill at, 226–27
Rhymes, phonological awareness and, 221
Right-handedness, 157
Rights, moral reasoning based on, 374–75
Risk factors for eating disorders, 119
Ritalin, 149
Role playing, prejudice reduction
through, 356–57
Roles
gender, 396, 420–23
emerging, 420–21
peer influence on, 414–15
beyond traditional, 421–22
social, 396

Romantic relationships, 468–71
  cultural factors influencing, 468–69
  sexual behavior in, 469–70
  sexual orientation and, 470–71
Rooting reflex, 93
Rotation, mental, 405
Rubella, 73, 77, 78
Running, learning, 154
Sadness, 304
Safety programs, school-based, 122
Samples, 25
Sampling, representative, 25
Sampling behavior with tasks, 22–23, 24
Sarcasm, 297
SAT scores, self-control and, 367
Savants, 240–41
Scaffolding, 176–77, 217, 250, 463
  in teaching communication, 292
Scale models, 283
Schizophrenia, birth complications and
  later, 88
Scholastic competence, 343, 344
School(s), 489–91
  cultural differences in, 231–32
  desegregation of, 357–59
  factors influencing success of, 489–90
  free and reduced-price meals at, 118
  improving American, 233
  part-time work and, 483–84
  physical education classes in, 157, 158
  student achievement and, 489–90
  teacher-based influences, 490–91
School-age children
  ADHD in, 148
  emotions in, 306, 308
  nutritional needs during, 108
  self-concepts in, 335
School-based safety programs, 122
School phobia, 306
Scientific problem solving, 218–19
Scientist, child as, 165, 173, 218
Scripts, 204
Scrotum, 111
Seat belt, 121, 122
Secondary sex characteristics, 111, 403
Secular growth trends, 104
Secure adults, 325
Secure attachment, 322
Segregation, racial, 465
Selection, social, 71–72
Selective attrition, 30
Self-absorption, 336
Self-awareness
  nature and nurture in, 359
  origins of, 332–34
Self-care, 482
Self-concept, 332–42
  autobiographical memory and, 207
  defined, 332
  evolving, 334–35
  infantile amnesia and, 207
  search for identity, 335–42
    career choice and, 337–38
    cultural influences, 338–39
    depression and, 341
    ethnic, 338–40
    storm and stress in, 340
Self-conscious emotions, 305
Self-control, 364–69
  beginnings of, 364–67
  defined, 364
  improving, 368–69
  influences on, 367–68
  long-term consistency of, 367
Self-efficacy, 12–13
Self-esteem, 342–51
  academic, 349, 350–51
  androgyny and, 421
  changes in level of, 346–47
  crowd membership and, 471
  developmental change in, 345–48

in different domains, 347–48
  in gifted classes, 349
  low, 350–51
  measuring, 342–45
  peers and, 346, 350
  sources of, 348–50
  structure of, 345–46
  of victims of aggression, 392–93
Self-fulfilling prophecy, 255
Self-Perception Profile for Children
  (SPPC), 343–45
Self-reflection, 335
Self-reflective perspective taking, 354
Self-regulation, cognitive, 203
Self reports, 23, 24
Semantic bootstrapping theory, 288
Semantics, 268
Semen, 40
Sense organs, 134
Senses, 134–40
  fetal development and, 66
  hearing, 136–37
  integrating sensory information,
    138–40
  seeing, 137–38
  smell, 135
  taste, 135
  touch, 135
Sensorimotor stage, 13–14, 165, 166–67,
  171
Sensory cortex, 128
Sensory memory, 179
Sentence cues, 277
Sentences, 284–91
  complex, 286–87
  telegraphic speech, 285
Serotonin, 341
Sesame Street (TV show), 281, 478
Severe mental retardation, 259
Sex
  of siblings, quality of relationship and,
    448
  use of term, 396
Sex characteristics, secondary, 111, 403
Sex chromosomes, 41
  abnormal, 47
Sex difference(s). See Gender differences
Sex education programs, 469–70
Sex organs, fetal development of, 66
Sexual abuse, 449
  leading questions asked in case of, 210
Sexual behavior
  influence of best friends on, 467–68
  in romantic relationships, 469–70
Sexual maturation, 111–12
Sexual orientation, 470–71
Shame and doubt, autonomy versus, 11
Shape-bias theory of word learning,
  278–79
Shape constancy, 142, 143
Short-term hunger, 118
Shoulder presentation, 87
Shouting, 309
Sibling relationships, 444–49
  adopted children, 446–47
  firstborn, laterborn, and only children,
    445–46
  qualities of, 447–49
Siblings, developmental differences be-
  tween, 56
Sickle-cell disease, 40, 42–44
  cultural influences and, 44
Sickle-cell trait, 43–44
SIDS, 95–96, 97
Sight, 137–38
Sign language, 271
Simulation programs, 479
Single gene inheritance, 42–44
Single-parent households, 326, 439
Size, relative, 144
Size constancy, 142

Skeletal growth, 104
Skills. See Academic skills; Social skills
Sleep
  newborn state of, 94, 95–96
  non-REM, 95
  physical growth and, 105–6
  REM, 95
"Slow to warm up" babies, 311, 312
Small-for-date infants, 88, 89
Smell, sense of, 135
Smiles, social, 304
Smoking
  prenatal development and, 74
  sudden infant death syndrome (SIDS)
    and, 95
Social acceptance, 344, 348
Social behavior
  gender differences in, 407–9, 410
    aggressive behavior, 402, 407–8, 410
    social influence, 408, 410
  NBAS evaluation of newborn's, 92
  perspective taking and, 355
  television's influence on, 477
Social class, gender stereotyping and, 401
Social cognitive theory, 12
Social contract orientation, 372
Social conventions, 377
Social director, parents as, 463
Social-emotional relationship, 318–19. See
  also Attachment
Social environment, puberty onset and,
  113
Social groups, 355–56
Social influence
  gender differences in, 408, 410
  teenage motherhood risk and, 71–72
Social-informational perspective taking,
  354
Social information processing theory,
  389–91
Social interaction, 309
  grammar acquisition and, 289–90
Social isolation, child maltreatment and,
  451–52
Social judgment, domains of, 37–38
Social referencing, 308
Social relationships, evolutionary perspec-
  tive on, 319–20. See also Friendships
Social roles, 396
Social selection, teenage motherhood risk
  and, 71–72
Social skills
  aggressive behavior and, 391
  playing sports and learning, 158
Social smiles, 304
Social system morality, 372
Societal perspective taking, 354, 355
Society for Research in Child Develop-
  ment (SRCD), 6
Sociocultural perspective on cognitive de-
  velopment, 173, 174–78, 184
Socioeconomic status
  intelligence tests and, 254–56
  of neighborhood, 485, 486, 487–88
  parenting styles and, 431–32
  prejudice and, 356–57
Software, mental, 178
Solitary play, 462
Somatomedin, 105
Sounding out words, 222, 223
Source-monitoring skills, 210
Spatial ability, gender differences in, 402,
  405–6, 410
Spatial intelligence, 240–41
Speaking, effective, 293–96
Special children, intelligence of, 256–63
  gifted and creative children, 257–59
  with learning disabilities, 260–63
  with mental retardation, 259–60
Specification phase of career develop-
  ment, 337–38

Speech, 269–74. See also Language
  first steps to, 272–74
  infant-directed (motherese), 271
  inner, 177
  about mental states, children's theory of
    mind and, 194
  perceiving, 269–72
    language exposure and, 269–70
    word identification and, 270–72
  private, 177
  telegraphic, 285
Sperm, 40, 111–12
Spermarche, 111
Spina bifida, 69, 81
Spinal cord, prenatal development of, 69
Sports, participating in, 158–59
Square One TV, 478
SRCD, 6
Stability
  of attachment, 322–23
  of temperament, 314–15
Stable-order principle, 229
Stagnation, generativity versus, 11
Standardized tests, 236
  in mathematics, 406
Standards, setting higher, 233
Stanford-Binet test, 246–48, 250
Status, social. See Socioeconomic status
Stepparents, 440–41
Stepping motion, learning, 153
Stepping reflex, 93
Stereotypes
  approval-focused orientation, 377
  gender, 398–401
    cultural influences on, 398–99
    defined, 398
    learning, 399–401
  influence on preschoolers' memory,
    208–10
  racial, 356
Stereotype threat, 255, 406
Stillbirth, 72
Stimulant drugs, as ADHD treatment,
  149
Storm and stress in adolescence, 340
Stranger wariness, 304–5
Strange Situation, 321–22
Strategies
  counting, 230
  memory, 201–3
  problem solving, 179–80, 182,
    216–17
  reading, 224
Strength of correlation, 26
Stress
  attachment and, 323
  defined, 70
  prenatal development and, 70
  puberty onset and, 113
Structured observation, 22, 24
Subcultures, 429
Subjective feeling, 303
Subject-verb-object construction, 287
Subtraction, 228, 230
Successful intelligence, Sternberg's theory
  of, 242–45
  abilities comprising, 242–43
  testing, 243
Sucking reflex, 93, 166
Sudden infant death syndrome (SIDS),
  95–96, 97
Suggestions, influence on preschoolers'
  memory, 208–10
Summer camp, 472
Superego, 10
Supportive grandparents, 442
Surgency/extraversion, 312, 313
Surgery, fetal, 81
Swaddling, 94
Sweden, 451
Syllables, stressed, 270

Symbols
children's use of, 275
using, 167
words as, 274–75
Synapse, 123
Synaptic pruning, 125
Syntax, 268, 284–85
Syphilis, 73
Systematic desensitization, 306
Systematic observation, 21–22, 24
*Tabula rasa*, 5
Taiwan, schools in, 231–32
Tasks, sampling behavior with, 22–23, 24
Taste, sense of, 135
Tay-Sachs disease, 45
Teachers, gender identity and, 414, 423
Teaching
to foster cognitive growth, 172
reading, 223
scaffolding and, 176–77
Teenage motherhood, 70–71, 469
prenatal development and, 70–71
risks associated with, 71–73
Teenagers. *See also* Adolescents/adolescence
pregnancy in, 115, 469
resistance to monitoring, 388
Telegraphic speech, 285
Television, 475–78
aggressive behavior and, 388
attitudes and social behavior and, 477
cognition and, 477–78
consumer behavior and, 477
criticism of, 476
gender identity and, 416
guidelines for watching, 478
time spent watching, 157
word learning from, 281
Temperament, 311–18
aggressive behavior and, 387
behavior problems and, 317–18
biology of, 312–13
cross-cultural studies of, 312–13
cultural influences on, 314
defined, 311
environment and, 317
helping others and, 316–17
hereditary and environmental contributions to, 313–14
influence on child's own development, 327
other aspects of development and, 315–18
parental behavior and, 436
patterns of, 311–12
personality and, 315
research on, 316–17
self-control and, 367–68
sibling relations and, 448
stability of, 314–15
structure of, in infancy, 312–13
Teratogens, 73–79
diseases, 73
dose of, 78

drugs, 73, 74–75
environmental hazards, 75–77
prenatal development and, 77–79
timing of exposure to, 77, 78
Terminal buttons, 123
Testes, 66, 111
Testimony, eyewitness, 207–11
Testing, dynamic, 250
Testosterone, 113, 387
Tests
of intelligence, 236, 245–56
bias in, 255
culture-fair, 255
hereditary and environmental factors in, 251–54
impact of ethnicity and socioeconomic status on, 254–56
individualized vs. group, 248
infant tests, 248–49
interpreting scores on, 256
reliability of, 248–49
Stanford-Binet test, 246–48, 250
validity, 249–50
mental, 6
standardized, 236
Test-taking skills, 255
Test-tube baby, 40
Texture gradient, 144
Thalidomide, 73, 74, 77
Theory(ies)
defined, 8
foundational, 8–16
biological perspective, 9–10, 15
cognitive-developmental perspective, 13–14, 15, 16
contextual perspective, 14–15, 16
learning perspective, 11–13, 15, 16, 20
psychodynamic perspective, 10–11, 15
by infants, 13
of mind, 192–94, 195
Thinking. *See also* Cognitive development
convergent, 257
divergent, 257–58
Third-person perspective taking, 354–55
*3-2-1 Contact*, 478
Thumb, opposable, 151
Thymine, 41–42
Time-out, 434
Toddlers. *See also* Preschool children
defined, 152
guidelines for child care for, 326
handedness in, 156
memory in, 200–201
prosocial behavior in, 380–81
self-awareness in, 332–33
self-control in, 365–66
Topeka Board of Education, 358
Touch, sense of, 135
Touch sensitivity, 402
Transitive inference problems, 214
Trimester, prenatal development by, 67
Trisomy 21, 46*n*

True attachment, 320
Trust versus mistrust, 11
Turkey, parental scaffolding in, 176–77
Turner's syndrome, 47
Turn taking, 292–93
Tutoring, 490
computerized, 479
Twins, 50
dizygotic (fraternal), 50, 63, 157
monozygotic (identical), 50, 63
fetal surgery on, 81
handedness in, 157
Twin studies, 51–52
of ADHD, 149
of aggressive behavior, 387
of depression, 52–53
of intelligence, 251
of temperament, 313–14
Ultrasound, 80, 81
Umbilical cord, 64
prolapsed, 87, 88
Underextension error, 279
Understanding in core domains, 185–95
living things, 184, 188–90
objects and their properties, 167, 184, 186–88
people, 184, 190–95
Undifferentiated perspective taking, 354
Uninvolved parenting, 431
United Nations Children's Fund (UNICEF), 121
U.S. Centers for Disease Control and Prevention, 110
U.S. Congress, 467
U.S. Department of Health and Human Services' Office of Women's Health, 110
U.S. National Institute of Child Health and Human Development, 326
U.S. Public Health Service, 96
U.S. Surgeon General, 119, 157
Unity, object, 142
Universal ethical principles, 372
Uterus, implantation of blastocyst in, 63
Vaccinations, 121
Validity
of intelligence tests, 249–50
of measure, 24
Values, make-believe play and, 461–62
Variable(s), 21
confounded, 218, 219
correlation of, 26
dependent, 27
independent, 27
Verbal ability, gender differences in, 402, 404, 410
Verbatim memory traces, 205–6
Verbs, mental, 192
Vernix, 66, 91
Viability, age of, 66
Victims of aggression, 391–93
Video display terminals (VDTs), prenatal exposure to, 75

Villi from umbilical blood vessels, 64–65
Violent crime, 389
Visual acuity, 137–38
Visual cliff, 143
Visual cortex, 128
Visual cues for balance, 152–53
Visual expansion, 143
Vocabulary, growth of, 279–80
Waking activity, newborn state of, 94
Walking, learning, 152–54
Wandering aimlessly, 462
Wariness, stranger, 304–5
War on Poverty, 253
Wavelength of light, 138
*Webster's Third New International Dictionary*, 268
Wechsler Intelligence Scale for Children-III (WISC-III), 247–48, 250
Weight
body mass index and, 119
childhood obesity, 118–19
physical growth and, 102, 103
during pregnancy, 69
Weight-bearing exercises, 110
Weight-loss programs, 120
*Where in Time Is Carmen Sandiego?*, 478
Whole-language method, 223
Whole-word method, 223
*Wh* words, 287
Withdrawal reflex, 93
Witnesses, child, 207–11
Women. *See also* Mothers; Parenting; Parents
in the NAACP, 96
older, pregnancy in, 72–73
in workforce, 326
Word processing, 226
Words, 274–84
fast mapping meanings to, 275–79
identifying, 270–72
learning of
encouraging, 280–82
individual differences in, 279–80
shape-bias theory, 278–79
styles of, 280
recognition of, 220, 221–23
as symbols, 274–75
Work, attachment and, 326
Working memory, 179, 180, 181, 182, 224
World Health Organization (WHO), 121
Writing, 225–27
mechanical requirements of, 226
X chromosome, 41
X rays, as teratogen, 75
XXX syndrome, 47
XYY complement, 47
Y chromosome, 41
Zone of proximal development, 175–76, 250
Zygote, 63
exposure to teratogens, 77, 78
neural plate in, 124
period of, 62–63, 67

SINGLE PC LICENSE AGREEMENT AND LIMITED WARRANTY

READ THIS LICENSE CAREFULLY BEFORE OPENING THIS PACKAGE. BY OPENING THIS PACKAGE, YOU ARE AGREEING TO THE TERMS AND CONDITIONS OF THIS LICENSE. IF YOU DO NOT AGREE, DO NOT OPEN THE PACKAGE. PROMPTLY RETURN THE UNOPENED PACKAGE AND ALL ACCOMPANYING ITEMS TO THE PLACE YOU OBTAINED THEM [[FOR A FULL REFUND OF ANY SUMS YOU HAVE PAID FOR THE SOFTWARE]]. THESE TERMS APPLY TO ALL LICENSED SOFTWARE ON THE DISK EXCEPT THAT THE TERMS FOR USE OF ANY SHAREWARE OR FREEWARE ON THE DISKETTES ARE AS SET FORTH IN THE ELECTRONIC LICENSE LOCATED ON THE DISK:

1.  GRANT OF LICENSE and OWNERSHIP: The enclosed computer programs and data ("Software") are licensed, not sold, to you by Prentice-Hall, Inc. ("We" or the "Company") and in consideration of your purchase or adoption of the accompanying Company textbooks and/or other materials, and your agreement to these terms. We reserve any rights not granted to you. You own only the disk(s) but we and/or our licensors own the Software itself. This license allows you to use and display your copy of the Software on a single computer (i.e., with a single CPU) at a single location for academic use only, so long as you comply with the terms of this Agreement. You may make one copy for back up, or transfer your copy to another CPU, provided that the Software is usable on only one computer.

2.  RESTRICTIONS: You may not transfer or distribute the Software or documentation to anyone else. Except for backup, you may not copy the documentation or the Software. You may not network the Software or otherwise use it on more than one computer or computer terminal at the same time. You may not reverse engineer, disassemble, decompile, modify, adapt, translate, or create derivative works based on the Software or the Documentation. You may be held legally responsible for any copying or copyright infringement which is caused by your failure to abide by the terms of these restrictions.

3.  TERMINATION: This license is effective until terminated. This license will terminate automatically without notice from the Company if you fail to comply with any provisions or limitations of this license. Upon termination, you shall destroy the Documentation and all copies of the Software. All provisions of this Agreement as to limitation and disclaimer of warranties, limitation of liability, remedies or damages, and our ownership rights shall survive termination.

4.  LIMITED WARRANTY AND DISCLAIMER OF WARRANTY: Company warrants that for a period of 60 days from the date you purchase or adopt the accompanying textbook, the Software, when properly installed and used in accordance with the Documentation, will operate in substantial conformity with the description of the Software set forth in the Documentation, and that for a period of 30 days the disk(s) on which the Software is delivered shall be free from defects in materials and workmanship under normal use. The Company does not warrant that the Software will meet your requirements or that the operation of the Software will be uninterrupted or error-free. Your only remedy and the Company's only obligation under these limited warranties is, at the Company's option, return of the disk for a refund of any amounts paid for it by you or replacement of the disk. THIS LIMITED WARRANTY IS THE ONLY WARRANTY PROVIDED BY THE COMPANY AND ITS LICENSORS, AND THE COMPANY AND ITS LICENSORS DISCLAIM ALL OTHER WARRANTIES, EXPRESS OR IMPLIED, INCLUDING WITHOUT LIMITATION, THE IMPLIED WARRANTIES OF MERCHANTABILITY AND FITNESS FOR A PARTICULAR PURPOSE. THE COMPANY DOES NOT WARRANT, GUARANTEE OR MAKE ANY REPRESENTATION REGARDING THE ACCURACY, RELIABILITY, CURRENTNESS, USE, OR RESULTS OF USE, OF THE SOFTWARE.

5.  LIMITATION OF REMEDIES AND DAMAGES: IN NO EVENT, SHALL THE COMPANY OR ITS EMPLOYEES, AGENTS, LICENSORS, OR CONTRACTORS BE LIABLE FOR ANY INCIDENTAL, INDIRECT, SPECIAL, OR CONSEQUENTIAL DAMAGES ARISING OUT OF OR IN CONNECTION WITH THIS LICENSE OR THE SOFTWARE, INCLUDING FOR LOSS OF USE, LOSS OF DATA, LOSS OF INCOME OR PROFIT, OR OTHER LOSSES, SUSTAINED AS A RESULT OF INJURY TO ANY PERSON, OR LOSS OF OR DAMAGE TO PROPERTY, OR CLAIMS OF THIRD PARTIES, EVEN IF THE COMPANY OR AN AUTHORIZED REPRESENTATIVE OF THE COMPANY HAS BEEN ADVISED OF THE POSSIBILITY OF SUCH DAMAGES. IN NO EVENT SHALL THE LIABILITY OF THE COMPANY FOR DAMAGES WITH RESPECT TO THE SOFTWARE EXCEED THE AMOUNTS ACTUALLY PAID BY YOU, IF ANY, FOR THE SOFTWARE OR THE ACCOMPANYING TEXTBOOK. BECAUSE SOME JURISDICTIONS DO NOT ALLOW THE LIMITATION OF LIABILITY IN CERTAIN CIRCUMSTANCES, THE ABOVE LIMITATIONS MAY NOT ALWAYS APPLY TO YOU.

6.  GENERAL: THIS AGREEMENT SHALL BE CONSTRUED IN ACCORDANCE WITH THE LAWS OF THE UNITED STATES OF AMERICA AND THE STATE OF NEW YORK, APPLICABLE TO CONTRACTS MADE IN NEW YORK, AND SHALL BENEFIT THE COMPANY, ITS AFFILIATES AND ASSIGNEES. HIS AGREEMENT IS THE COMPLETE AND EXCLUSIVE STATEMENT OF THE AGREEMENT BETWEEN YOU AND THE COMPANY AND SUPERSEDES ALL PROPOSALS OR PRIOR AGREEMENTS, ORAL, OR WRITTEN, AND ANY OTHER COMMUNICATIONS BETWEEN YOU AND THE COMPANY OR ANY REPRESENTATIVE OF THE COMPANY RELATING TO THE SUBJECT MATTER OF THIS AGREEMENT. If you are a U.S. Government user, this Software is licensed with "restricted rights" as set forth in subparagraphs (a)-(d) of the Commercial Computer-Restricted Rights clause at FAR 52.227-19 or in subparagraphs (c)(1)(ii) of the Rights in Technical Data and Computer Software clause at DFARS 252.227-7013, and similar clauses, as applicable.

Should you have any questions concerning this agreement or if you wish to contact the Company for any reason, please contact in writing: Legal Department, Prentice Hall, One Lake Street, Upper Saddle River, NJ 07458. If you need assistance with technical difficulties, call: 1-800-677-6337.